PSYCHOLOGICAL EXPERTS IN DIVORCE ACTIONS

FOURTH EDITION

PSYCHOLOGICAL EXPERTS IN DIVORCE ACTIONS
FOURTH EDITION

Marc J. Ackerman

Andrew W. Kane

111 Eighth Avenue, New York, NY 10011
www.aspenpublishers.com

This publication is designed to provide accurate and authoritative information in regard to the subject matter covered. It is sold with the understanding that the publisher is not engaged in rendering legal, accounting, or other professional services. If legal advice or other professional assistance is required, the services of a competent professional should be sought.

© 2005 Aspen Publishers, Inc.
A Wolters Kluwer Company
www.aspenpublishers.com

Printed in the United States of America

1 2 3 4 5 6 7 8 9 0

Library of Congress Cataloging-in-Publication Data

Ackerman, Marc J.
    Psychological experts in divorce actions / Marc J. Ackerman, Andrew W.
Kane.—4th ed.
        p. cm.
    Includes bibliographical references and index.
    ISBN 0-7355-4926-5 (hardcover)
    1. Forensic psychology—United States. 2. Divorce suits—United
    States—Psychological aspects. 3. Evidence, Expert—United States. I.
    Kane, Andrew W. II. Title.

    KF8965.A93 2005
    347.73'67—dc22   2004026952

About Aspen Publishers

Aspen Publishers, headquartered in New York City, is a leading information provider for attorneys, business professionals, and law students. Written by preeminent authorities, our products consist of analytical and practical information covering both U.S. and international topics. We publish in the full range of formats, including updated manuals, books, periodicals, CDs, and online products.

Our proprietary content is complemented by 2,500 legal databases, containing over 11 million documents, available through our Loislaw division. Aspen Publishers also offers a wide range of topical legal and business databases linked to Loislaw's primary material. Our mission is to provide accurate, timely, and authoritative content in easily accessible formats, supported by unmatched customer care.

To order any Aspen Publishers title, go to *www.aspenpublishers.com* or call 1-800-638-8437.

To reinstate your manual update service, call 1-800-638-8437.

For more information on Loislaw products, go to *www.loislaw.com* or call 1-800-364-2512.

For Customer Care issues, e-mail *CustomerCare @aspenpublishers.com;* call 1-800-234-1660; or fax 1-800-901-9075.

Aspen Publishers
A Wolters Kluwer Company

SUBSCRIPTION NOTICE

This Aspen Publishers product is updated on a periodic basis with supplements to reflect important changes in the subject matter. If you purchased this product directly from Aspen Publishers, we have already recorded your subscription for the update service.

If, however, you purchased this product from a bookstore and wish to receive future updates and revised or related volumes billed separately with a 30-day examination review, please contact our Customer Service Department at 1-800-234-1660, or send your name, company name (if applicable), address, and the title of the product to:

ASPEN PUBLISHERS
7201 McKinney Circle
Frederick, MD 21704

As psychologists, we are aware of the fact that one's psychological makeup is a function of a combination of genetic predisposition and environmental influences. Our parents were obviously a strong influence on our development, resulting eventually in our professional choices and the characteristics necessary to be effective clinicians. For that reason, we dedicate this book to our parents, Bette and Donald Ackerman, and Mary and Harry Kane.

PREFACE

This book was written for the purpose of aiding attorneys in the difficult task of examining and cross-examining psychological experts in court actions. Attorneys entering into the areas of psychological expertise often find themselves confused and easily led astray. Unfortunately, as a result, much useful testimony is lost because the attorney does not know which questions to ask and how or when to ask them.

The book is not written from the point of view of "how to get the expert." Instead, it is written to provide "the information that you need" to do an intelligent examination and cross-examination of psychological experts and to address client-related psychological factors.

It is important to note that each chapter of this book is a summary of information used to teach an entire course in the training of psychologists. As a result, the authors selected the information that they felt attorneys were most likely to need in dealing with these matters, rather than including all of the available information. Most chapters are followed by a list of suggested questions for examination and cross-examination. The attorney is cautioned not to assume that every question will apply to every case. The questions are followed by references to the chapters within the book that will help the attorney understand the basis for the question. It is essential to read the chapter and understand the basis for each question, not merely list off the questions in court.

This is the fourth edition of this text. As much time has transpired between the third and fourth edition as occurred between the first and third editions. As a result, significant and profound changes have taken place within the field of child custody evaluations. Most of the chapters have been completely rewritten since the third edition was published and literally hundreds of new references have been added. Many of the issue areas that were prominent during the tenure of the first and second editions are no longer considered to be valuable components of custody work and have been eliminated from the current text.

Chapter 1 Since the writing of the last edition, the *Daubert Standard* has gained a foothold in the area of forensic psychology and has changed the direction and focus of work that is performed in this area. **Chapter 1** provides a lengthy explanation of how *Daubert* is relevant to custody cases.

Chapter 2 discusses the new 2002 American Psychological Association Code of Ethics. In particular, it emphasizes the changes that have taken place between the 1992 and 2002 Code and how they affect the interaction between psychologists and attorneys.

Chapter 3 covers psychological evaluations, test administration and standards, and the most recent research that has been published, since the third edition regarding psychologists' practices and family lawyers' and family judges' expectations in child custody evaluations.

Chapter 4 was almost completely rewritten to identify the variables that need to be considered when addressing how divorce affects families. Developmental milestones, recent research, and gender differences are discussed.

Chapter 5 provides a list of do's and don't's for attorneys and their clients involved in divorce actions. The attorney can evaluate how many of the do's the client is doing and how many don't's the client is doing, and make a subjective determination as to how the client is likely to fare in a custody case.

Chapter 6 Children are being asked to serve as witnesses more and more frequently. **Chapter 6** discusses how to prepare a child for court testimony, addresses a child's ability to remember events, and discusses what a child needs to anticipate in a court setting. Major new works have addressed the issue of suggestibility in young children's memory.

Chapter 7 deals with statistical concepts that will help the attorney interpret data from tests used in custody evaluations.

Chapter 8 discusses the major intelligence tests in use today. Since the publication of the last edition, almost all of the intelligence tests have gone through major revisions. The Kaufman Assessment Battery for Children, Wechsler Intelligence Scale for Children-Fourth Edition, the Wechsler Pre-School and Primary Scale of Intelligence-Third Edition, the Stanford Binet-Fifth Edition, and the Brief Intelligence Test all have new editions since the third edition of this book was published.

Chapter 9 The primary emphasis of **Chapter 9** is the utilization of the Minnesota Multiphasic Personality Inventory-2nd Edition (MMPI-2). Over 18,000 articles and books have been written about the MMPI/MMPI-2. A summary of these works, in addition to discussion of the Minnesota Multiphasic Personality Inventory-Adolescents (MMPI-A), the Millon Clinical Multiaxial Inventory-Second and Third Editions (MCMI-II and MCMI-III), and other similar tests is presented. Specific discussion centers around the use of the MMPI-2 in custody cases. The controversy about the use of the MCMI instruments in custody evaluations is addressed.

Chapter 10 covers the projective personality tests, including the Rorschach Psychodiagnostic Series, Thematic Apperception Test (TAT), and the Children's Apperception Test (CAT). In recent years there has been controversy over the use of the comprehensive system for scoring Rorschach. That controversy is discussed in detail in this chapter.

Chapter 11 has been virtually rewritten since the third edition. The emphasis of **Chapter 11** focuses on the utility of custody-related instruments as they apply to the *Daubert* Standard.

Chapters 12 and **13** cover physical and sexual abuse in detail. Hundreds of articles are written on these subjects each year. These chapters synthesize that research and quote the most recent findings as they apply to abuse and custody cases.

Chapters 14, 15, and **16** present special considerations involving mental disorders, alcohol and other drug abuse, and criminal history.

Chapter 17 discusses the fourth edition of the *Diagnostic and Statistical Manual* (DSM-IV), prepared by the American Psychiatric Association. It also compares the DSM-IV with the *International Classification of Diseases, 10th Edition* (ICD-10) and describes the advantages and shortcomings of each work. Some discussion about the preliminary work of DSM-V is included in this chapter.

Most chapters contain case digests that are presented to serve as a guide to relevant cases. The reader is encouraged to go to the original source for a full description of these cases.

Milwaukee, Wisconsin   MARC J. ACKERMAN
September 2004   ANDREW W. KANE

ACKNOWLEDGMENTS

Because this is the fourth edition of this book, there have been scores of people who have provided support and help over the years in bringing it to this level. They have been previously acknowledged in their continued support is greatly appreciated.

We discovered that writing this fourth edition was a much more arduous task than had been anticipated originally because we were updating three previous editions. Christine Vincent has been enormously helpful and supportive during this process, and has helped maintain our focus on what is important and what direction we should take in various areas. Without her help and support, the fourth edition would not be what it is today.

As noted in previous editions our wives, Stephanie Ackerman and Carole Kane, know better than anybody else the difficulty in preparing a text of this nature and the sacrifices that go along with doing so. In this particular case, producing this volume affected our personal lives, our vacation time, and our professional practices. Our wives' support and encouragement in completing this task has often gone above and beyond what would be expected of any spouse. Lynn Spencer, Marc Ackerman's former office manager, had been involved in all previous editions. She helped kick-off this edition, and her efforts are greatly appreciated. Lynn passed the ball to Roseanne Rech, who has done a yeomen's job of dealing with the pressures of timelines, the mountains of clerical work, and serving as a liaison between the authors and the publishers. While learning in trial by fire, her work is also greatly appreciated.

ABOUT THE AUTHORS

Marc J. Ackerman, Ph.D., is a licensed psychologist in the state of Wisconsin and has been involved in over 2,000 divorce-related cases in Wisconsin and throughout the United States. He has testified in hundreds of family law cases in more than 25 states during his career. Dr. Ackerman co-developed the Ackerman-Schoendorf Scales for Parent Evaluation of Custody (ASPECT), published in 1992 by Western Psychological Services and the Ackerman-Schoendorf Scales for Parent Evaluation of Custody-Short Form (ASPECT-SF) in 2000. In addition, he has authored the *Clinician's Guide to Child Custody Evaluations, Second Edition* (John Wiley & Sons, 2001), *The Essentials of Forensic Psychological Assessment* (John Wiley & Sons, 1999), *Does Wednesday Mean Mom's House or Dad's* (John Wiley & Sons, 1997), and the recently completed *Forensic Psychology Textbook* with Randy Otto, Ph.D. (John Wiley & Sons, 2005).

He served as a founding faculty member and dean of the Wisconsin School of Professional Psychology from 1981 to 1987 and the director of Clinical Training from 1981 to 1990. He is currently a full professor at the school. Dr. Ackerman also served as the president of both the Wisconsin Psychological Association and Milwaukee Area Psychological Association and is the current president of the Wisconsin Psychology Foundation. In addition, he served on the Wisconsin Psychological Association Ethics Committee for seven years, chairing its parent group for one year. A co-director of North Shore Psychotherapy Associates, Dr. Ackerman is also listed in the National Register of Health service Providers in Psychology, and a member of the American Psychological Association, the Wisconsin Psychological Association, the Milwaukee Area Psychological Association, and the Academy of Family Mediators.

He has written dozens of professional publications and given dozens of professional seminars throughout the United States to various bar and psychological associations. In April 1997 he gave two presentations at the joint American Bar Association and American Psychological Association Conference in Los Angeles. He has received two awards from the Wisconsin Psychological Association, one for outstanding contributions to the advancement of psychology as an applied profession, and the other for outstanding contributions to the profession of psychology through leadership.

Andrew W. Kane, Ph.D., is a licensed psychologist in private practice in Milwaukee, Wisconsin. He is a diplomate of the American Board of Assessment Psychologists. He is listed in the National Register of Health Service Providers in Psychology, and is a recipient of the Certificate of Professional Qualification in Psychology of the Association of State and Provincial Psychology Boards. Dr. Kane has been designated as an expert in more than 2,800 cases involving involuntary civil commitment, guardianship, family law, personal injury, children's court, criminal court, and other cases.

Dr. Kane was a founding faculty member of the Wisconsin School of Professional Psychology and is currently a professor at the school. He is also a clinical professor in the Department of Psychology at the University of Wisconsin–Milwaukee, and an associate clinical professor in the Department of Psychiatry and Behavioral Medicine at the Medical College of Wisconsin. He is the author or co-author of seven books and some four dozen professional papers and chapters.

Dr. Kane was a member of the Expert Panel on Psychiatric and Psychological Evidence of the American Bar Association's Commission on Mental and Physical Disability Law. Dr. Kane is a former president of the Wisconsin Psychological Association and of its Division of Forensic and Correctional Psychologists. He is also a former president of the Milwaukee Area Psychological Association. Dr. Kane served as a member of the board of the Wisconsin Psychological Association's forensic division, and of the Board of Governors of the Wisconsin Society of Clinical and Consulting Psychologists as well. Dr. Kane served as the chair of the Professional Issues Committee, and for ten years as a member of the Ethics Committee, of the Wisconsin Psychological Association.

Dr. Kane founded the Wisconsin Coalition on Sexual Misconduct by Psychotherapists and Counselors, a national model program in this problem area.

SUMMARY OF CONTENTS

TABLE OF CONTENTS

CHAPTER 1

THE EXPERT WITNESS

§ 1.1 Overview

One of the most significant trends in litigation has been the increased reliance on testimony by expert witnesses, and cases involving child custody issues and termination of parental rights are no exceptions. Thus, the selection, preparation, and presentation of an expert witness is frequently crucial to the outcome of a case.

While the Federal Rules of Evidence apply only in federal courts, most states have adopted either identical or similar rules of evidence, either through a ruling of the state's highest court or through legislation.[1] We will therefore use the Federal Rules of Evidence as a template for consideration of expert testimony.[2]

According to Federal Rule of Evidence 702,

> [i]f scientific, technical, or other specialized knowledge will assist the trier of fact to understand the evidence or to determine a fact in issue, a witness qualified as an expert by knowledge, skill, experience, training, or education, may testify thereto in the form of an opinion or otherwise, if (1) the testimony is based upon sufficient facts or data, (2) the testimony is the product of reliable principles and methods, and (3) the witness has applied the principles and methods reliably to the facts of the case. [Underlined portion was added to the old Rule 702, December 1, 2000.]

As a general rule, a witness who qualifies as an expert is permitted to testify to opinions and, in some states, to hearsay; in contrast, testimony of a lay witness is generally restricted to observed facts. A therapist may be called as a fact witness in any jurisdiction, subject to consideration of privilege under law, and in some jurisdictions may also be permitted to give expert testimony. As discussed in **Chapter 2,** however, a therapist should not be retained as an expert in a case.

Relevance

"Relevance" is defined by Federal Rule of Evidence 401 as "having any tendency to make the existence of any fact that is of consequence to the determination of the action more probable or less probable than it would be without the evidence." But under Federal Rule of Evidence 403 relevant evidence may be excluded "if its probative value is substantially outweighed by the danger of unfair prejudice, confusion of the issues, or misleading the jury, or by considerations of undue delay, waste of time, or needless presentation of cumulative evidence." A report of an evaluation that does not address the legal issues is not relevant and will not be admitted. A report that does not go beyond the level of understanding of the ordinary person, or that indicates the scientific merit of the expert's methodology, will also not be admitted—or, if admitted, will have less weight accorded it.[3]

---

[1] David A. Martindale & Jonathan W. Gould, *The Forensic Model: Ethics and Scientific Methodology Applied to Custody Evaluations*, 1 J. Child Custody: Res., Issues, & Practices 1–22 (2004) [hereinafter Martindale & Gould].

[2] The revised Federal Rules of Evidence may be downloaded from www.house.gov/judiciary/evid00.pdf.

[3] Kirk Heilbrun, Geoffrey R. Marczyk, & David DeMatteo, Forensic Mental Health Assessment: A Casebook 334 (Oxford Univ. Press 2002) [hereinafter Heilbrun et al., 2002].

Basis for Expert Testimony

Federal Rule of Evidence 703 provides the standard regarding bases for expert testimony:

> The facts or data in the particular case upon which an expert bases an opinion or inference may be those perceived by or made known to the expert at or before the hearing. If of a type reasonably relied upon by experts in the particular field in forming opinions or inferences upon the subject, the facts or data need not be admissible in evidence in order for the opinion or inference to be admitted. . . . [Underlined portion added December 1, 2000.]

Testimony Regarding Ultimate Issue

There is controversy regarding whether an expert should be permitted to testify regarding the ultimate issue in a case. Federal Rule of Evidence 704(a) indicates that "testimony in the form of an opinion or inference otherwise admissible is not objectionable because it embraces an ultimate issue to be decided by the trier of fact." Most states permit the expert to testify regarding the ultimate issue in civil matters if that testimony may be helpful to the trier of fact.[4]

Forensic psychologist Thomas Grisso sides with those who would not have the expert give an opinion on the ultimate legal issue, because "the final question has no answer that can be supported by scientific and clinical evidence alone. It requires applying legal and social values to make a choice," which is the domain of the judge or jury, not of the expert. However, Grisso acknowledges, "many perhaps most mental health professionals who perform divorce custody evaluations for courts" would disagree:

> They argue, and many judges agree, that the judge is in no better position than the clinician to decide what is best for the child. . . . Moreover, one, can argue that the judge is not at all required to conclude the case in the way that the clinician recommends. . . . From this perspective, asking the clinician to make a specific recommendation does no harm.[5]

The problem, according to Tillbrook, Mumley, and Grisso, is that both statutes and case law lack operational definitions, that is, "how much is enough" to meet the statutory or legal standard. Psychologists "have a mandate to avoid drawing conclusions not supported by clinical and/or empirical evidence. We argue that when clinicians testify to the ultimate legal issue, they are making inferences that exceed the data. . . . [T]here is no external criterion against which to measure the validity of this inference."[6]

On the other side, "attorneys and trial court judges regard ultimate-issue opinions as very important. . . . In some jurisdictions, [that] has led to legal statutes and rules of evidence that permit or require the examining clinician to reach a conclusion on the ultimate legal issue."[7]

---

[4] Daniel Shuman, Psychiatric and Psychological Evidence 9–12 (2d ed. 1996 Supp.) [hereinafter Psychiatric and Psychological Evidence, 2d ed.].

[5] Thomas Grisso, *Evolving Guidelines for Divorce/Custody Evaluations*, 28 Fam. & Conciliation Cts. Rev. 35, 40 (1990) [hereinafter Grisso].

[6] Chad, Tillbrook, Denise Mumley, & Thomas Grisso, *Avoiding Expert Opinions on the Ultimate Legal Question: The Case for Integrity*, 3 J. Forensic Psychol. Prac. 77–87, at 85 (2003).

[7] Gary B. Melton et al., Psychological Evaluation for the Courts 4 (2d ed. 1997) [hereinafter Melton et al.].

A survey of family court judges and family law attorneys found that 84 percent of the judges and 86 percent of the attorneys indicated that they wanted recommendations for custody, and 91 percent of the judges and 90 percent of the attorneys wanted recommendations for visitation as well.[8]

Opposition to "ultimate opinion" testimony is often more semantic than real, according to Rogers and Ewing. Those who oppose ultimate opinion testimony will often simply stop one step short of that opinion, while making it obvious what they would say if they were to testify about the ultimate opinion. Further, the need for avoiding what some think is the province of the factfinder is less since *Daubert*, since the judge, as gatekeeper, will exclude any proposed testimony that goes too far into the province of the factfinder. Thus, the expert witness need concern him- or herself with the quality of the data supporting all testimony, as required by *Daubert*, not with whether that testimony passes some arbitrary boundary.[9] Psychologist David Martindale and his colleagues note that "none of the major mental health professions has taken a position with regard to the appropriateness of recommendations offered by evaluators."[10]

Court-Appointed Experts

Federal Rule of Evidence 706 permits the court to "appoint any expert witnesses agreed upon by the parties, and may appoint expert witnesses of its own selection. . . . A witness so appointed shall advise the parties of the witness' findings, if any; the witness' deposition may be taken by any party; and the witness may be called to testify by the court or any party. The witness shall be subject to cross-examination by each party, including a party calling the witness. . . . Nothing in this rule limits the parties in calling expert witnesses of their own selection."

When Testimony May and Must Be Presented

The rules of evidence governing expert testimony are based on the assumption that there is a distinction between facts and opinions. Because the judge and jury are usually not chosen for their expertise in any particular area, they require assistance in some areas to understand the facts presented to them. Thus, people with expertise in areas such as the psychological assessment of adults and children, developmental psychology, family psychology, adult and child psychopathology, the effect of divorce and custody arrangements on adults and children, and forensic psychology are called on to go beyond the facts and to state opinions that may be helpful to the judge and/or jury in drawing conclusions.[11]

---

[8] James N. Bow & Francella A. Quinnell, *Critique of Child Custody Evaluations by the Legal Profession*, 42 Fam. C. Rev. 115–27 (2004).

[9] Richard Rogers & Charles Patrick Ewing, *The Prohibition of Ultimate Opinions: A Misguided Enterprise*, 3 J. Forensic Psychol. Prac. 65–75 (2003).

[10] David Martindale et al., *Providing Expert Testimony in Child Custody Litigation, in* P. Keller & S. Heyman, 10 Innovations in Clinical Practice: A Source Book 481, 485 (1991) [hereinafter Martindale].

[11] Psychiatric and Psychological Evidence, 2d ed. (2003 Supp.) at 7–3 to 7–4.2; M. Gindes, *Guidelines for Child Custody Evaluations for Psychologists: An Overview and Commentary*, 29 Fam. L. Q. 39–50 (1995).

Experts are not used when the doctrine of *res ipsa loquitur* ("the thing speaks for itself") applies or when problems are so blatant that any reasonable person could identify them as wrongful.[12]

> The ultimate goal of forensic assessment is the collection, organization and communication of information in a manner that makes the information and conclusions useful to lawyers, judges and jurors. Therefore, a forensic practitioner must develop skills in consultation, report writing and oral testimony.[13]

Further,

> [b]ecause of [the] premium on the accuracy of information provided to the factfinder, the results of psychological tests should not be used in isolation from history, medical findings, and observations of behavior made by others. . . . Impressions from psychological testing in the forensic context should most appropriately be treated as hypotheses subject to verification through history, medical tests, and third-party observations. This "verification step" is crucial in forensic assessment for two reasons. First, psychological testing typically does not provide data that are directly relevant to the immediate legal issue. . . . Second, data obtained through psychological testing may, for a variety of reasons, provide an inaccurate representation of the individual.[14]

In some circumstances, expert testimony *must* be presented; in others, it *may* be presented. Expert testimony *must* be presented when "psychiatric or psychological issues are material in a case and lay people are incapable of reaching rationally based conclusions on these issues without specialized assistance. Under these circumstances, if the party bearing the burden of production has not produced expert psychiatric or psychological testimony, a directed verdict is appropriate."[15]

Expert testimony *may* be presented when the judge determines that it would be helpful. So long as expert testimony contributes to the incremental validity of one side of a question before the court, it has a legitimate place in court.[16]

As indicated above, Federal Rule of Evidence 702 permits the introduction of expert testimony when "scientific, technical, or other specialized knowledge will assist the trier of fact to understand the evidence or to determine a fact in issue." Judges and juries expect expert witnesses to be unbiased educators, helping them to understand technical information necessary for their deliberations. Unfortunately, most judges do not appoint their own experts, most often because of a lack of funds to compensate the expert.[17]

---

[12] Donald T. Dickson, Law in the Health and Human Services 618 (1995) [hereinafter Dickson].

[13] J. Ondrovik & D. Hamilton, *Forensic Challenge: Expert Testimony*, 10 Am. J. Forensic Psychol. 15, 17 (1992) [hereinafter Ondrovik & Hamilton].

[14] Kirk Heilbrun, *The Role of Psychological Testing in Forensic Assessment*, 16 L. & Hum. Behav. 257, 263 (1992).

[15] Psychiatric and Psychological Evidence, 2d ed. (2003 Suppl.) at 7–3.

[16] Melton et al. at 4.

[17] Joe S. Cecil & Thomas E. Willging, Court-Appointed Experts: Defining the Role of Experts Appointed under Federal Rule of Evidence 706 (Federal Judicial Ct. 1993).

§ 1.2   *Daubert, Joiner*, and *Kumho*

Daubert

Prior to 1993, there was conflict among U.S. federal and appellate courts regarding whether general acceptance of a scientific method or technique within the professional community was required in order for expert testimony based on that method or technique to be considered adequately reliable and, therefore, admissible. In 1993, in *Daubert v. Merrell Dow Pharmaceuticals, Inc.*,[18] the U.S. Supreme Court held that the general acceptance test[19] was superseded by the Federal Rules of Evidence, enacted in 1975, and that general acceptance was not a necessary prerequisite for admissibility of expert testimony under Federal Rule of Evidence 702:

> We interpret the legislatively-enacted Federal Rules of Evidence as we would any statute. . . . Rule 402 provides the baseline: "All relevant evidence is admissible. . . . Evidence which is not relevant is not admissible. . . ." "Relevant evidence" is defined as that which has "any tendency to make the existence of any fact that is of consequence to the determination of the action more probable or less probable than it would be without the evidence." Rule 401.[20]
>
> Here there is a specific Rule that speaks to the contested issue. Rule 702. . . .[21]
>
> Nothing in the text of this Rule establishes "general acceptance" as an absolute prerequisite to admissibility. . . . [A] rigid "general acceptance" requirement would be at odds with the "liberal thrust" of the Federal Rules and their "general approach of relaxing the traditional barriers to 'opinion' testimony. . . ." That the *Frye* test was displaced by the Rules of Evidence does not mean, however, that the Rules themselves place no limits on the admissibility of purportedly scientific evidence. Nor is the trial judge disabled from screening such evidence. To the contrary, under the Rules the trial judge must ensure that any and all scientific testimony or evidence admitted is not only relevant, but reliable. . . .[22]
>
> The subject of an expert's testimony must be "scientific . . . knowledge." The adjective "scientific" implies a grounding in the methods and procedures of science. Similarly, the word "knowledge" connotes more than subjective belief or unsupported speculation. The term "applies to any body of known facts or to any body of ideas inferred from such facts or accepted as truths on good grounds." Webster's Third New International Dictionary 1252 (1986). . . . [I]n order to qualify as "scientific knowledge," an inference or assertion must be derived by the scientific method. Proposed testimony must be supported by appropriate validation—i.e., "good grounds," based on what is known. In short the requirement that an expert's testimony pertain to "scientific knowledge" establishes a standard of evidentiary reliability. . . .[23]
>
> Rule 702 further requires that the evidence or testimony "assist the trier of fact to understand the evidence or to determine a fact in issue." This condition goes primarily to relevance . . . , [including] "whether expert testimony proffered in the case is sufficiently tied to the facts of the case that it will aid the jury in resolving a factual dispute."[24]

---

[18] 509 U.S. 579, 113 S. Ct. 2786, 125 L. Ed. 2d 469 (1993).

[19] *Frye v. United States*, 54 App. D.C. 46, 293 F. 1013, 34 ALR 145 (1923).

[20] 509 U.S. at 579.

[21] *Id.* at 588.

[22] *Id.* at 589.

[23] *Id.* at 589–90.

[24] *Id.* at 591.

Unlike an ordinary witness . . . , an expert is permitted wide latitude to offer opinions, including those that are not based on first-hand knowledge or observation. . . . Presumably, this relaxation of the usual requirement of first-hand knowledge . . . is premised on an assumption that the expert's opinion will have a reliable basis in the knowledge and experience of his discipline.[25]

Faced with a proffer of expert scientific testimony, then, the trial judge must determine at the outset . . . whether the expert is proposing to testify to (1) scientific knowledge that (2) will assist the trier of fact to understand or determine a fact in issue. This entails a preliminary assessment of whether the reasoning or methodology underlying the testimony is scientifically valid and of whether that reasoning or methodology properly can be applied to the facts in issue. . . .[26]

Ordinarily, **a key question to be answered in determining whether a theory or technique is scientific knowledge that will assist the trier of fact will be whether it can be (and has been) tested.** . . . Another pertinent consideration is **whether the theory or technique has been subjected to peer review and publication.** Publication (which is but one element of peer review) is not a *sine qua non* of admissibility; it does not necessarily correlate with reliability . . . and in some instances well-grounded but innovative theories will not have been published. . . . But submission to the scrutiny of the scientific community is a component of "good science" in part because it increases the likelihood that substantive flaws in methodology will be detected. . . . Additionally, in the case of a particular scientific technique, the court ordinarily should consider **the known or potential rate of error.** . . . Finally, **"general acceptance"** can yet have a bearing on the inquiry. A "reliability assessment does not require, although it does permit, explicit identification of a relevant scientific community and an express determination of a particular degree of acceptance within that community. . . .[27]

The inquiry envisioned by Rule 702 is, we emphasize, a flexible one. Its overarching subject is the scientific validity—and thus the evidentiary relevance and reliability—of the principles that underlie a proposed submission. The focus, of course, must be solely on principles and methodology, not on the conclusions that they generate. . . .[28]

Vigorous cross-examination, presentation of contrary evidence, and careful instruction on the burden of proof are the traditional and appropriate means of attacking shaky but admissible evidence.[29]

[T]here are important differences between the quest for truth in the courtroom and the quest for truth in the laboratory. Scientific conclusions are subject to perpetual revision. Law, on the other hand, must resolve disputes finally and quickly. . . . We recognize that in practice, a gatekeeping role for the judge, no matter how flexible, inevitably on occasion will prevent the jury from learning of authentic insights and innovations. That, nevertheless, is the balance that is struck by the Rules of Evidence designed not for the exhaustive search for cosmic understanding but for the particularized resolution of legal disputes.[30]

In summary, the *Daubert* decision instructed federal trial courts to act as gatekeepers for expert evidence, and to apply the appropriate *Daubert* criteria to the case at bar. According to the Supreme Court in *Kumho Tire Co. v. Carmichael,*[31] the four "*Daubert* factors" are

---

[25] *Id.* at 592.

[26] *Id.* at 592–93.

[27] *Id.* at 593–94 (emphasis added).

[28] *Id.* at 594–95.

[29] *Id.* at 596.

[30] *Id.* at 596–97.

[31] 526 U.S. 137, 119 S. Ct. 1167, 143 L. Ed. 2d 238 (1999).

(1) "whether it can be and has been tested . . . [and] can be falsified"; (2) whether the "theory or technique has been subjected to peer review and publication"; (3) that consideration be given to the "known or potential rate of error"; and (4) that there is "general acceptance" of the particular technique within the scientific community.[32]

In addition, the Supreme Court in *Daubert* identified other relevant factors that may be applied by the trial court as part of its gatekeeping function: (1) that there be "evidentiary reliability,"[33] (2) that the expert's testimony "pertain to scientific knowledge," (3) that the "evidence or testimony assist the trier of fact to understand the evidence or to determine a fact in issue" (relevance), (4) "whether that reasoning or methodology properly can be applied to the facts in issue," and (5) the existence and maintenance of standards controlling the technique's operation."[34]

In footnote 9, the Supreme Court indicates that, while scientists "distinguish between 'validity' . . . and 'reliability' . . . our reference here is to evidentiary reliability—that is, trustworthiness."[35] It should be noted that some legal scholars list the *Daubert* factors slightly differently, for example, separating the testability requirement into "whether it is testable" and "whether it has been," and adding "whether there are standards controlling the technique's operation" as an additional *Daubert* factor.[36]

The Supreme Court explicitly indicated that this list is flexible, and these and/or other criteria are to be used by the trial courts to address the scientific validity of the evidence or testimony, emphasizing that it is the "principles and methodology, not . . . the conclusions that they generate" that must be addressed by the trial court. According to law professor David Faigman, "*Daubert's* ultimate legacy for the law is its insistence that legal policy and legal outcomes be crafted in light of a sophisticated appreciation for the complexity and subtlety of the state of the art of the science."[37]

Daubert also explicitly indicated that the goal of a court is to make a definitive decision, not to reach a consensus on an issue as the scientific community may do. As a result, the attorneys on the respective sides of an issue generally seek out experts from the opposing ends of the bell curve who will strengthen the arguments of one side or the other. In spite of this tendency, some experts feel a responsibility to be available for testimony in court, believing that the most qualified experts must be available if scientifically valid evidence is to be presented in court.[38]

---

[32] 526 U.S. at 137.

[33] 509 U.S. at 590.

[34] *Id.* at 593–94.

[35] Miryam R. Mitchell, *Daubert*, Its Progeny, and Their Effect on Family Law Litigation in State Courts, Paper presented to the American Academy of Matrimonial Lawyers, Kohala Coast, Haw. Mar. 3, 2000 [hereinafter Mitchell].

[36] E.J. Imwinkelried, *Evaluating the Reliability of Nonscientific Expert Testimony: A Partial Answer to the Questions Left Unresolved by* Kumho Tire Co. v. Carmichael, 52 M.L. Rev. 20–41, at 21 (2000) [hereinafter Imwinkelried].

[37] David L. Faigman, *The Gatekeepers: Scientific Expert Testimony in the Trial Process*, 23 Trial Law. 335–46 (1999).

[38] National Academy of Sciences, *The Age of Expert Testimony: Science in the Courtroom, Report of a Workshop* (Wash., D.C., Feb. 22, 2004). [hereinafter National Academy of Sciences], *available at* www.nap.edu/openbook/0309083109/html/.

In 1983, the Supreme Court ruled, in *Barefoot v. Estelle*,[39] that the testimony of a psychiatrist, testifying on the basis of his clinical experience, was admissible because "the rules of evidence generally extant at the federal and state levels anticipate that relevant, unprivileged evidence should be admitted and its weight left to the fact finder, who would have the benefit of cross-examination and contrary evidence by the opposing party."[40] This standard is very different from the one dictated by *Daubert*, suggesting that testimony based on clinical experience should be treated differently from testimony based on scientific research. When clinical testimony is based even in part on research, for example, on a psychological test or a diagnostic syndrome, courts have, however, been more willing to subject the testimony to a rigorous degree of scrutiny.[41]

Daubert II

The Supreme Court remanded *Daubert* to the U.S. Court of Appeals for the Ninth Circuit,[42] which indicated, in a ruling often referred to as "*Daubert II*," that

> [u]nder *Daubert*, we must engage in a difficult, two-part analysis. First, we must determine nothing less than whether the expert's testimony reflects "scientific knowledge," whether their findings are "derived by the scientific method," and whether their work product amounts to "good science. . . ." Second, we must ensure that the proposed expert testimony is "relevant to the task at hand . . . ," i.e., that it logically advances a material aspect of the proposing party's case. . . . The Supreme Court referred to this second prong of the analysis as the "fit" requirement. . . .[43]
>
> The first prong of *Daubert* puts federal judges in an uncomfortable position. The question of admissibility only arises if it is first established that the individuals whose testimony is being proffered are experts in a particular scientific field. . . . Yet something doesn't become "scientific knowledge" just because it's uttered by a scientist; nor can an expert's self serving assertion that his conclusions are "derived by the scientific method" be deemed conclusive. . . . [T]herefore, though we are largely untrained in science and certainly no match for any of the witnesses whose testimony we are reviewing, it is our responsibility to determine whether these experts' proposed testimony amounts to "scientific knowledge," constitutes "good science," and was "derived by the scientific method. . . ."[44]
>
> The [Supreme] Court recognized, however, that knowledge in this context does not mean absolute certainty. . . . Rather, the Court said, "in order to qualify as 'scientific knowledge,' an inference or assertion must be derived by the scientific method. . . ." Our task, then, is to analyze not what the experts say, but what basis they have for saying it. Which raises the question: How do we figure out whether scientists have derived their finding through the scientific method or whether their testimony is based on scientifically valid principles . . . ? . . . [T]he party presenting the expert must show that the expert's findings are based on sound science, and this will require some objective, independent validation of the expert's

---

[39] 463 U.S. 880 (1983).

[40] *Id.* at 898.

[41] Daniel W. Shuman, *When Time Does Not Heal: Understanding the Importance of Avoiding Unnecessary Delay in the Resolution of Tort Cases*, 6 Psychol. Pub. Pol'y & L. 880–97 (2002) [hereinafter Shuman 2002].

[42] Daubert v. Merrell Dow Pharms., Inc., 43 F.3d 1311 (9th Cir. 1995).

[43] *Id.* at 1315.

[44] *Id.* at 1315–16.

methodology. . . . We read the Supreme Court as instructing us to determine whether the analysis undergirding experts' testimony falls within the range of accepted standards governing how scientists conduct their research and reach their conclusions.[45]

One very significant fact to be considered is whether the experts are proposing to testify about matters growing naturally and directly out of research they have conducted independent of the litigation, or whether they have developed their opinions expressly for purposes of testifying. . . . That an expert testifies based on research he has conducted independent of the litigation provides important, objective proof that the research comports with the dictates of good science. . . . [This] provides the most persuasive basis for concluding that the opinions he expresses were "derived by the scientific method. . . ." If the proffered expert testimony is not based on independent research, the party proffering it must come forward with other objective, verifiable evidence that the testimony is based on "scientifically valid principles."

One means of showing this is by proof that the research and analysis supporting the proffered conclusions have been subjected to normal scientific scrutiny through peer review and publication. . . . Peer review and publication do not, of course, guarantee that the conclusions reached are correct; much published scientific research is greeted with intense skepticism and is not borne out by further research. But the test under *Daubert* is not the correctness of the expert's conclusions but the soundness of his methodology. . . . That the research is accepted for publication in a reputable scientific journal after being subjected to the usual rigors of peer review is a significant indication that it is taken seriously by other scientists, i.e., that it meets at least the criteria of good science. . . .[46]

Establishing that an expert's preferred testimony grows out of pre-litigation research or that the expert's research has been subjected to peer review are the two principal ways the proponent of expert testimony can show that the evidence satisfies the first prong of Rule 702. . . . Where such evidence is unavailable, the proponent of expert scientific testimony may attempt to satisfy its burden through the testimony of its own experts. For such a showing to be sufficient, the experts must explain precisely how they went about reaching their conclusions and point to some objective source—a learned treatise, the policy statement of a professional association, a published article in a reputable scientific journal or the like—to show that they have followed the scientific method, as it is practiced by (at least) a recognized minority of scientists in their field. . . .[47]

We [next] consider whether the testimony satisfies the second prong of Rule 702: Would plaintiffs' proferred scientific evidence "assist the trier of fact to . . . determine a fact in issue"? . . . In elucidating the second requirement of Rule 702, *Daubert* stressed the importance of the "fit" between the testimony and an issue in the case: "Rule 702's 'helpfulness' standard requires a valid scientific connection to the pertinent inquiry as a precondition to admissibility." . . .[48]

One criterion for trustworthiness (reliability, validity) of testimony, then, is whether the expert has personally done research in the area of testimony independent of the instant case, or whether he or she is utilizing information published in peer-reviewed journals to support his or her conclusions.[49] It is very strong evidence that the expert is expressing

---

[45] *Id.* at 1316–17.

[46] *Id.* at 1317–18.

[47] *Id.* at 1318–19.

[48] *Id.* at 1320.

[49] Bernalyn D. McGaughey & John D. Walker, *The Scientific Expert's Approaches to Litigation Testimony, in* James J. Brown, Scientific Evidence and Experts Handbook 43–67, at 44 (Aspen Law & Business 1999, 2002 Cum. Supp.).

opinions derived from scientific methodology if there is research that preceded, and is unrelated to, the litigation, upon which he or she bases testimony.[50]

Joiner

The U.S. Supreme Court reaffirmed its conclusions in *Daubert* in *General Electric Co. v. Joiner*,[51] and specified that the standard for reviewing the admission or exclusion of scientific evidence by federal district courts was abuse of discretion. "Nothing in either *Daubert* or the Federal Rules of Evidence requires a district court to admit opinion evidence which is connected to existing data only by the *ipse dixit* ["he said it himself"] of the expert."[52] By properly administering the Federal Rules of Evidence, the trial court may ensure that the proceedings are "justly determined" as well as "that the truth be ascertained."[53]

Kumho

In *Kumho Tire Co. v. Carmichael*,[54] the U.S. Supreme Court ruled that an individual may be considered an expert if he or she has any type of specialized knowledge or experience that may contribute to the factfinder's understanding of a case, even if the individual is not a scientist. Courts are admonished to make formal determinations regarding the relevance and reliability of all expert testimony, using criteria like those in *Daubert* for that purpose. As indicated in *Daubert*, it is up to the judge to choose the exact criteria utilized in a given case. Further,

> [e]xperts of all kinds tie observations to conclusions through the use of what Judge Learned Hand called "general truths derived from specialized experience." [Citation omitted.] And whether the specific expert testimony focuses upon specialized observations, the specialized translation of those observations into theory, a specialized theory itself, or the application of such a theory in a particular case, the expert's testimony often will rest "upon an experience confessedly foreign in kind to [the jury's] own." . . . And where such testimony's factual basis, data, principles, methods, or their application are called sufficiently into question . . . the trial judge must determine whether the testimony has "a reliable basis in the knowledge and experience of [the relevant] discipline."[55]
>
> The objective . . . is to make certain that an expert, whether basing testimony upon professional studies or personal experience, employs in the courtroom the same level of intellectual rigor that characterizes the practice of an expert in the relevant field. . . .[56]

Law professor Edward Imwinkelried indicates that, while little specific guidance was provided to trial courts, "the opinion did seem to underscore . . . [t]he factor of whether the expert had employed 'the same level of intellectual rigor' customary in practice. . . ."[57]

---

[50] Mitchell.

[51] 522 U.S. 136, 118 S. Ct. 512, 139 L. Ed. 2d 508 (1997).

[52] 139 L. Ed. 2d at 520.

[53] J. Breyer, concurring (citing Fed. R. Evid. 102).

[54] 526 U.S. 137, 119 S. Ct. 1167, 143 L. Ed. 2d 238 (1999).

[55] *Kumho*, 526 U.S. at 149 (citing *Daubert*, 509 U.S. at 592).

[56] *Id.* at 152.

[57] Imwinkelried at 28.

Taken together, *Daubert*, *Joiner*, and *Kumho* make it clear that judges have an obliga-tion to exercise their gatekeeping function in all cases involving expert testimony, and that appellate courts are to limit their reviews of admissibility questions regarding whether the trial judge abused his or her discretion.[58] Further, "[a]n expert's qualifications are a neces-sary but not sufficient condition of the admissibility of the expert's testimony. In the face of appropriate objection, the trial court must assess, as a threshold question, the validity and reliability of the methods and procedures relied on by the expert to reach any proffered opinions."[59]

In addition, "[c]onclusions cannot stand unless they are rationally supported by the data. And the data cannot stand unless they are generated by sound methodology."[60]

Forensic experts are advised to base their testimony or practice not only on the prevail-ing clinical standards of their communities but also on other, broader, bases of reliability such as research reported in peer-reviewed journals.[61] It would also be wise for experts to address the requirements of *Daubert*, whether or not the expert is from a "*Daubert* state." If the expert cannot defend the reliability of his or her testimony, the trial court could choose to exclude the testimony.[62]

The critical issue with regard to questions of "error rates" is the legal mandate to avoid false-positives. To the degree possible, psychological testimony should address the likeli-hood that a given result may be a false indictment of an individual.[63]

It should be noted, however, that trial judges are not obligated to question expert testi-mony; rather, it is up to the attorneys to identify admissibility issues and either bring motions before the court, address the issues during testimony before the jury, or choose to disregard them. The last option is most likely if, for example, experts on both sides face the same criticisms, if the *Daubert* challenge is seen as too costly, or if it is seen as a tac-tical advantage to present the criticisms to the jury.[64]

According to Attorney Miryam R. Mitchell, as of early 2000 there were no known cases of state-equivalent *Daubert* criteria being applied to expert testimony in family law litiga-tion. Given the spread of the *Daubert* criteria throughout the judiciary, however, it is only a matter of time before states that have adopted *Daubert* or FRE 702 in whole or in part subject expert testimony to the *Daubert* requirements.[65]

---

[58] John W. Parry, *Admissibility of Expert Evidence*, 24 Mental & Physical Disability L. Rep. 10 (2000).

[59] Shuman 2002.

[60] M.J. Saks, *The Aftermath of* Daubert: *An Evolving Jurisprudence of Expert Evidence*, 40 Jurimetrics 229–41, at 236 (2000).

[61] Eric A. Youngstrom & Christine P. Busch, *Expert Testimony in Psychology: Ramifications of Supreme Court Decision in* Kumho Tire Co., Ltd. v. Carmichael, 10 Ethics & Behav. 185–93, at 189 (2000) [hereinafter Youngstrom & Busch].

[62] Richard Wiener, Extending Daubert *beyond Scientific Expert Testimony*, 30 APA Monitor 47 (1999).

[63] Youngstrom & Busch at 189.

[64] D.W. Shuman & B.D. Sales, *Daubert's Wager*, J. Forensic Psychol. Prac. 1, 69–77 (2001); Mitchell.

[65] Mitchell.

Types of Expertise Required

The expert must have both an ability to do a high-quality assessment and the ability to understand what the assessment means in the context of the legal questions.[66]

> The former involves technical expertise [that] consists of the expert's having specialized skills in the areas of eliciting and clarifying the communications of persons who either have something to conceal . . . (e.g., sexually abusive parents), or who are impaired or otherwise limited . . . in their capacity to provide information about themselves and the significant events of their development and current circumstances. The principal tools of technical expertise are an array of psychological and other specialized "tests."[67]
>
> The latter form of expertise "consists of an expert's putative knowledge of the various content domains affecting [relevant questions], as well as that expert's putative specialized skill in interpreting the manifest content of the subjects' behaviors and communications." This means that the expert must possess substantial knowledge in each area the expert will investigate and communicate about. "It also means that the expert possesses recognized abilities to draw correct inferences from information yielded by her or his evaluations and review of documents. . . . These principal tools of cognate expertise comprise the ability to see or understand what the ordinary mind fails to see or understand."[68]

According to psychologist Howard Garb,

> there is general agreement that, depending on the type of judgment that is to be made by a judge or jury, expert witnesses should be allowed to (a) describe a person's history and mental status, (b) make diagnoses, (c) evaluate whether a person is malingering, (d) make predictions of behavior (or at least describe difficulties in predicting behavior), and (e) evaluate psychological processes related to competence. . . . Mental health professionals can assist judges and juries by describing a person's history . . . and mental status. Clinicians are consistent and focused in their gathering information . . . and they are able to make reliable ratings of mental status. . . . Mental health professionals are more consistent than laypersons in collecting information.
>
>   With regard to the diagnosis of mental disorders . . . , research on the reliability of psychodiagnoses made in everyday clinical practice indicates that acceptable levels of reliability have been obtained for many diagnostic categories but not for all categories. . . . Reliability has been low for personality disorders, and serious questions have been raised about the reliability of psychodiagnoses made for children. . . . A reason why reliability may be low for some diagnostic categories is that clinicians may not be adhering to the diagnostic criteria. . . .[69]

It should be noted that there is no diagnosis that automatically means that an individual cannot be an appropriate custodial and placement parent for his or her child, though a few diagnoses make it extraordinarily unlikely (for example, a paraphilia focused on sexual contact with children for which the individual has not received treatment). People with psychoses or developmental disabilities may need special services to be able to parent, but

---

[66] Grisso at 36.

[67] T. Horner et al., *Prediction, Prevention, and Clinical Expertise in Child Custody Cases in Which Allegations of Child Sexual Abuse Have Been Made*, 26 Fam. L.Q. 141, 143 (1992).

[68] *Id.* at 143–44.

[69] Howard Garb, *The Trained Psychologist as Expert Witness*, 12 Clinical Psychol. Rev. 451, 453–56 (1992) [hereinafter Garb].

with those services may be able to do well. Every case must be considered on its own merits. The expert's task is to identify whether, and to what degree, any disability interferes or is likely to interfere with adequate parenting.[70] Garb concludes that

> empirical research indicates that (a) judgments made by mental health professionals are frequently more valid than judgments made by laypersons and (b) forensically trained mental health professionals possess a body of specialized knowledge, not shared by other mental health professionals, that can be used to assist judges and juries. . . . As long as clinicians are aware of the limitations of their expertise, they can provide valuable expert testimony.[71]

§ 1.3   Need for a Model for Conducting an Evaluation

Child custody evaluations are among the most difficult forensic evaluations, involving at minimum the evaluation of two adults and one child, review of legal documents, contact with collaterals, review of medical documents, review of school records, and so forth. With the massive amount of information that must be considered, one must have a model that will foster the gathering and interpretation of information and communication regarding its relevance to and impact upon the ultimate decision that must be made by the court.[72]

A number of models might be considered in a child custody evaluation. One would be to follow the American Psychological Association's *Guidelines for Child Custody Evaluations in Divorce Proceedings.*[73] The Guidelines address the purpose of the evaluation. They focus on "parenting capacity, the psychological and developmental needs of the child, and the resulting fit";[74] the need for objectivity and impartiality; the scope of the evaluation, based on the referral question; the need to use "multiple methods of data gathering";[75] the need for accurate interpretation of the data; and the need to base recommendations on the "best psychological interests of the child."[76] (See **Chapter 3** for detailed discussion of the Guidelines.)

A second model would be to follow the AFCC Model Standards of Practice for Child Custody Evaluations.[77] The Model Standards address the appointment or choosing of an evaluator, the arrangements made with the parties, standards for the evaluator, evaluation

---

[70] Thomas Grisso, *Advances in Assessments for Legal Competencies, in* Thomas Grisso ed., Evaluating Competencies 1–20, at 12 (Kluwer/Plenum, 2d ed. 2003) [hereinafter Grisso 2003].

[71] Garb at 462.

[72] Kirk Heilbrun, Principles of Forensic Mental Health Assessment 83–96 (Kluwer/Plenum 2001) [hereinafter Heilbrun 2001]; Randy K. Otto, Jacqueline K. Buffington-Vollum, & John F. Edens, *Child Custody Evaluation, in* Alan M. Goldstein & Irving B. Weiner, "Handbook of Psychology" (John Wiley & Sons: 2003) [hereinafter Otto et al.].

[73] 49 Am. Psychol. 677–80 (1994).

[74] *Id.* at 678.

[75] *Id.* at 679.

[76] *Id.*

[77] 32 J. Fam. & Conciliation Ct. Rev. (1994).

procedures, areas to be evaluated, the report of the evaluation, and such ethical issues as the evaluator's responsibility to adhere to the requirements of his or her profession's ethical code, to function solely within his or her areas of expertise, and to appropriately limit conclusions based on the nature and extent of the evaluation conducted and the data gathered. (See **Chapter 3** for further discussion of the Model Standards.)

A third model would be to follow the structure of an instrument like the Ackerman-Schoendorf Scales for Parent Evaluation of Custody (ASPECT) for much of the content of the evaluation. The ASPECT addresses parental factors to be considered, the psychological instruments that might be utilized, the observation of each parent with each child, and various attributes of the evaluation of the child. (See **Chapter 11** for a detailed discussion of the ASPECT.)

A fourth model is termed by its authors "The Forensic Model."[78] Among other requirements, psychologists David Martindale and Jon Gould indicate that the evaluator must

1. Be familiar with relevant forensic interviewing techniques and requirements, and forensic use of psychological tests and other instruments.[79]

2. Be familiar with the laws relevant to child custody evaluations in the relevant jurisdiction, including any statutory or case law definitions of "the best interests of the child."

3. Conceptualize him- or herself as an extension of the court, contributing to a mind-set centered on objectivity and impartiality.[80]

4. Use tests and other instruments that validly and reliably assess functional abilities relevant to the questions before the court.[81]

5. While either structured or unstructured interviews may be utilized, make provision for questions that address information or issues that arise during the evaluation.[82]

6. Actively seek corroborating information, including documents, from collateral sources (for example, teachers, physicians).[83]

7. Include in reports both information that supports the evaluator's conclusions and information that is not supportive, and specify why he or she came to these conclusions in spite of the nonsupportive information.[84]

Regardless of the model used, the key element is that the expert accumulate enough evidence to be able to support his or her conclusions, including a strong empirical database that includes information about each parent and all children, as well as the scientific literature to support any conclusions made.[85]

---

[78] Martindale & Gould.

[79] *See also* Heilbrun 2001, at 26–36 and 121–36.

[80] *See also* Heilbrun 2001 at 36–46.

[81] *See also* Heilbrun 2001 at 107–15.

[82] *See also* Jonathan W. Gould, *Evaluating the Probative Value of Child Custody Evaluations: A Guide for Forensic Mental Health Professionals*, 1 J. Child Custody 77–96 (2004) [hereinafter Gould].

[83] *See also* Heilbrun 2001, at 167–76.

[84] *See also* Heilbrun 2001, at 48.

[85] Grisso 2003, at 17.

§ 1.4 Factors Affecting the Quality of Expert Testimony

The quality of expert testimony is dependent on a number of factors. First, psychology and psychiatry are not exact sciences. "Facts" in both fields are those data that the present state of knowledge indicates are accurate, but they are always subject to displacement by information that becomes available at a later time. Many conclusions are based on the data a given expert accepts as factual, although another expert may draw conclusions from a different database. The weight of scientific opinion may fall on one side or the other, but on a given issue there may be two or more legitimate opinions, each based on a significant foundation of data. Each position may be widely enough held to be considered as having gained general acceptance in the field.[86] The expert must know both sides of the argument and present data that supports his or her position. The expert should also identify for the court whether the position taken represents the majority or a minority point of view among experts in this forensic area.

Second, research has shown that psychologists and psychiatrists are far from perfect at predicting the future (except for making short-range predictions). In spite of this, they are frequently called upon to make long-range predictions—for example, which parent in a custody dispute would be the better parent to be awarded custody of the children until they reach legal age.[87]

Third, the quality of the expert's opinions depends on a number of factors. Different experts display different levels of familiarity with the professional literature, and the amount of personal experience in the area being testified about varies among experts. Some experts work much harder than others to gather data on which to base an opinion in a particular case. Up to a point, the more data the expert collects, and the more diverse the sources of information (for example, the divorcing couple, the children, teachers, and other professionals), the better.[88]

"Corroboration of information gathered in a forensic assessment is often vitally important. Thus, the practitioner should consider requests that certain information be subpoenaed or discovered. . . . The practitioner should document all efforts of collecting information, that is, who provides which information and refusals to provide information. . . . If the assessment is for the benefit of the attorney or the party, and thus protected by the attorney/client privilege, then the gathering of information may put the opposing counsel, or the court, on notice. Should this be the case, the attorney and the practitioner should have this understanding, and the attorney should certainly be informed that forensic assessments based upon self-report are often subject to extreme criticism in court."[89] Because

---

[86] Psychiatric and Psychological Evidence, 2d ed., at 7–9 to 7–10; Clements & Ciccone, *Ethics and Expert Witnesses: The Troubled Role of Psychiatrists in Court*, 12 Bull. Am. Acad. Psychiatry & L. 135–36 (1984).

[87] Psychiatric and Psychological Evidence, 2d ed., at 7–12 to 7–15; J. Ziskin, Coping with Psychiatric and Psychological Testimony, at 13, 14, 15–21, 260 (1981).

[88] Psychiatric and Psychological Evidence, 2d ed., at 7–15.

[89] Ondrovik & Hamilton at 19.

psychiatrists primarily rely upon interviews, their testimony is open to criticism on this basis. It is usually very advantageous to either have a psychologist do the evaluation or at least have a psychologist supplement the psychiatrist's interviews with psychological testing as well as evaluation and interpretation of any previous psychological testing that may be available. Both the psychiatrist and the psychologist need to consult collateral sources to supplement and amplify interview and testing data.[90] While utilizing the interview as the *sole* means of gathering data is not acceptable, it should be noted that an interview is, under nearly all circumstances, a requirement for any forensic evaluator.

> Standard psychiatric and psychological diagnostic techniques include an examination of the patient, in part because the clinical impressions of an experienced diagnostician are thought to play a major role in diagnostic decisions. . . . [A]n in-court opinion not based on a personal examination of the patient, when it is possible to do so, violates accepted practice. This failure should bear on the weight given the resulting opinions."[91]

(See also the discussion about the need for a personal interview in **Chapter 2.**)

Differences Between Science and Law

A judge at a workshop on science and law identified a number of differences between the two:

> (1) Law is backward-looking and its findings are based on precedent. . . . Science is forward-looking in assuming that the truth is not yet fully known; (2) propositions to be tested in science are predictive; experiments are designed to be repeatable. Theories to be proved in court arise out of situations that occurred in the past and cannot be repeated; (3) scientists recognize that "truth" is mutable and may evolve over a long period of time. In adjudication, "truth," at least for the limited purpose of resolving disputes, must become final in a relatively short time; (4) scientists are often uncomfortable in the courtroom, especially during cross-examination. The dialogue is controlled by the lawyers and the judge, not by the expert witness; (5) disputes in science are resolved over time by peer review and the scrutiny of the scientific community at large. Legal disputes are resolved by cross-examination. Courts are not designed to determine whether scientific conclusions are correct.[92]

A number of factors make the interface of psychology and the law a difficult one for the mental health professional. First, legal decisionmaking in law seems to require testimony that is either artificially certain or is made to appear unreliable. As scientists, psychologists are accustomed to regarding truth as established through an objective, impersonal study, yielding fully disclosed results, rather than the partisanship of the court. Second, scientific truth is based on high-level probabilities, generally a 5 percent or 1 percent probability that a given result is in error, rather than the lower probabilities in civil cases. Third, answers in psychology are always subject to change based on new information. Fourth, in the

---

[90] Gould; Steven B. Bisbing et al., Sexual Abuse by Professionals: A Legal Guide 519–21 (1995) [hereinafter Bisbing et al.].

[91] Psychiatric and Psychological Evidence, 2d ed. (1994, Supp. 2003) at 9–7.

[92] National Academy of Sciences at 22–23.

courtroom, each participant's role dictates what he or she says and does to a large degree. Fifth, psychologists generally see their roles as teaching or enlightening, rather than having to potentially defend every conclusion they draw.

However, the fact that there are difficulties in translating psychological answers into legal answers does not mean that the attempt should not be made. These difficulties are "inherent in the adversarial process and can be found any time a legal question requires non-legal information from experts."[93] "Clinicians have tended to be the ones who have pointed out the limitations on predicting behavior. But in *Barefoot v. Estelle*,[94] the U.S. Supreme Court reasoned that the fact-finding and adversary system would make up for the shortcomings of the predictions."[95]

Additional Benefits of Expert Testimony

The expert can also benefit the attorney by developing both general and specific questions for lay and expert witnesses, and helping to anticipate the arguments and theories of the opposition. It is also part of the expert's responsibilities to apprise the attorney of research, testing, and trends in professional areas that may affect the attorney's theories and plan of action.

§ 1.5   Choosing and Qualifying Expert Witnesses

Attorneys must have some understanding of the nature and meaning of the qualifications of a potential expert so they can retain the best-qualified expert for the given purpose. Courts have long favored physicians and the medical model. The medical model assumes that there is a "normal" mental status that is characterized by the absence of disease or pathology. When an individual's behavior deviates from this norm, it is assumed that there is a physical cause that can be addressed through active treatment, with a goal of returning the individual to a normal state of functioning. "The medical model of mental disorder views everything from anxiety to hallucination as a symptom, not as the problem."[96]

However, in child custody cases it is psychologists who have most of the relevant training and experience:

> Most expert testimony about relevant disordered behavior in a legal setting does not turn on organic or biological explanations for behavior, for which a medical school education may be important. Instead, psychological and behavioral theories tend to underlie most testimony by psychologists and psychiatrists, subjects on which psychologists have education and training at least equal to and perhaps superior to that of many psychiatrists.[97]

---

[93] Bales, *APA Rebuts Criticism of Clinician Witnesses*, 19 APA Monitor 17 (Sept. 19, 1988) (quoting letter from R. Fowler and J. Matarazzo).

[94] 463 U.S. 880 (1983).

[95] Bales, *APA Rebuts Criticism of Clinician Witnesses*, 19 APA Monitor 17 (Sept. 19, 1988).

[96] Psychiatric and Psychological Evidence, 2d ed. (1994, Supp. 2003).

[97] Psychiatric and Psychological Evidence, 2d ed. (1994, Supp. 2002) at 8–4.

Psychiatrists are licensed as physicians by the state in which they practice. Beyond this general licensing, no special training or education is necessary to represent oneself as a psychiatrist. One does not have to completed a psychiatric residency program to practice psychiatry. It is not necessary to be board certified. . . . [A]pproximately two-thirds of practicing psychiatrists are not board certified.[98]

Since medical school provides most physicians with only an introductory course in psychiatry and a psychiatric clinical rotation, a psychiatrist may have negligible education in psychological theories as compared with a Ph.D. or Psy.D. clinical psychologist who has received extensive education and training in these fields. Moreover, the field of academic psychiatry has itself gradually begun to utilize its medical expertise to explore the organic and biological facets of mental disorder, leaving the psychological arena to psychologists.[99]

It is also relevant that "some psychiatric examiners do not utilize psychological testing, relying completely on their clinical skills to determine whether an individual has sustained and is still suffering from a mental condition, a disability or impairment caused by an alleged trauma. . . . There has been ample research to the effect that psychiatric opinions are woefully inconsistent in assessing mental pathology."[100] Consequently, unless the testimony one seeks is primarily biological in nature, the expert retained should usually be a psychologist.

A desirable quality in an expert is that he or she be a member of the teaching faculty of a graduate or medical school, as these experts are relatively likely to keep up with professional developments and research and to have significant experience communicating ideas to other people. The same is true of experts who lecture before professional and lay groups. Because the task of the expert is to educate the judge and/or jury, experience as a teacher in any context may be very important.

The coeditors of *Trial Diplomacy Journal* quote rules authored by Harry Philo regarding selection of expert witnesses:

1. Hire the best person you can find.

2. Do not allow your expert to go one inch beyond his or her area or areas of expertise.

3. Insist that your expert tend slightly against you in any testimony so that each juror will be convinced that the expert is fair, reasonable, and competent.

4. Get a clear understanding of fees and costs.

5. Ask if your expert needs to do testing or have testing done.

6. Ask if your expert can prepare, or have prepared, demonstrative evidence.

7. Make certain that your expert has all the facts, both good and bad.

8. Make certain that your expert knows your theories of [the case].

9. You, rather than your expert, are responsible for adequate literature searches and thorough discovery unless it is clear that your expert is hired for that purpose.[101]

The authors of this text would particularly emphasize points 1, 7, 8, and 9. We have too often been confronted with new facts at a deposition or trial despite our requests to

---

[98] *Id.* at 4–7 to 4–8.

[99] *Id.* at 8–4.

[100] F. Melendez & E. Marcus, *Mental Distress Claims: Testing the Psychological Tests*, 11 Am. J. Forensic Psychiatry 19, 19 (1990).

[101] John Romano & Rodney Romano, *How to Avoid the Traps of Expert Witnesses: The Seven Deadly Sins*, 16 Trial Dipl. J. at iv–viii (1993) (quoting from Harry Philo, Lawyers' Desk Reference).

attorneys to give us all relevant information. Also, although the psychological expert may be expected to do literature searches in the area of his or her expertise, information the attorney can furnish from legal journals and the discovery process can markedly improve the quality of the expert's work. The attorney who is diligent in these areas will maximize the ability of the expert to do the job for which he or she was retained.

The expert should also be asked about any actual or potential conflicts of interest and about any "skeletons" in the expert's closet. See **Chapter 2.** The attorney needs to make a judgment regarding whether the conflicts of interest and/or skeletons are significant enough to either preclude utilizing the particular expert at all or limit use of the particular expert to consultation, utilizing a different expert as a witness.[102] For example, with complaints about child custody evaluators being the most common complaint made to the Ethics Committee of the American Psychological Association, it would not be unusual for a given expert to have had an ethics complaint filed against him or her. If the complaint was resolved without an adjudication of guilt, there should be no significant problem utilizing that expert in a case. If a complaint is only in process, though, the attorney must decide whether that is a liability that may prevent a given psychologist from doing an evaluation and offering testimony in a specific case.

Finally, as is discussed at length in § **2.8,** it should be noted that the attorney should not look to the client's psychotherapist as an expert witness. There are many problems associated with the therapist's trying to maintain two significantly different roles with the client, "therapist" and "expert." Although the attorney should certainly talk with the therapist and take advantage of the therapist's knowledge and expertise, it is very important that the attorney's expert be a different person.

§ 1.6   Definition of Psychologist

According to law professor Daniel Shuman, "[a] psychologist is a person who is trained to study and measure mental processes, and to diagnose and treat mental disorders."[103] Psychologists are licensed or certified in all 50 states and all Canadian provinces. The American Psychological Association indicates that it has about 148,000 psychologist members, fellows, and associates.[104] The Canadian Psychological Association has more than 13,000 members.[105]

Educational Requirements

In most jurisdictions, "psychologist" means an individual who possesses a doctoral degree in psychology, either a Ph.D. or a Psy.D. (doctor of psychology). Some states licensed individuals with master's degrees by grandfathering when the law was instituted, by following current statutes or administrative codes, or both (though most licensing laws are old enough that most master's-level psychologists have retired or will soon do so).

---

[102] Michael J. McHale et al., Expert Witnesses: Direct and Cross-Examination 97 (Supp. 1997) [hereinafter McHale 1997].

[103] Psychiatric and Psychological Evidence, 2d ed. (1994, Supp. 1997) at 4–13.

[104] APA member web site, accessed July 1, 2004.

[105] CPA press release, Feb. 3, 2003.

The typical Ph.D. or Psy.D. clinician majored in psychology as an undergraduate and took 10 or more courses in psychology and often others in related disciplines. The individual then went to graduate school, took 90 or more semester hours (or the equivalent) in the specialty area, and completed a full-time predoctoral internship for a full year, usually involving both inpatient and outpatient treatment.[106]

The individual with a Ph.D. completed graduate training that included supervised experience in the process of research and then conducted a research project as part of the doctoral degree requirements. The Psy.D. also received advanced training in statistics and research methods but may have no personal research experience. If the attorney needs an expert with research experience, the Ph.D. is usually the better candidate. If the amount of predoctoral clinical experience is more important, the Psy.D. may have more than a Ph.D. with the same number of years of training,[107] though many states require both a predoctoral internship year and a postdoctoral year of supervision prior to licensure. In most cases, it does not matter whether the psychologist has a Ph.D. or a Psy.D.

Areas of Specialization

There are six major areas of graduate study recognized by the American Psychological Association: clinical, counseling, school, industrial/organizational, neuropsychological, and experimental. In addition, there are a number of degree programs in forensic psychology throughout the United States, generally involving collaboration between a clinical program and a law school. **Table 1–1** lists the forensic psychology graduate programs identified by the Division of Psychology and Law of the American Psychological Association.[108] There are also many graduate programs that offer at least some forensic training.

In virtually all states, psychologists are licensed generally, not as specialists, even though psychologists are nearly all trained as specialists in one of the areas of psychological practice. Licensing laws for psychologists, state administrative codes, and professional ethical codes all require the psychologist to practice solely within his or her areas of training and competence. The attorney must be careful to retain whichever type of psychologist has the training and demonstrated competence to be able to testify as an expert in a particular lawsuit. If the attorney errs in doing so, there is a real possibility that opposing counsel could impeach the so-called expert for testifying about matters for which the expert neither was trained nor had experience. Consequently, it is important for the attorney to learn about the different areas of specialization within psychology and how each could potentially play a part in the litigation.

Finding the psychologist or other expert with the requisite knowledge and experience may be more difficult than it was even a decade ago. As knowledge about areas of forensic practice has increased, so has specialization in relatively narrow areas, for example, child custody. Many psychologists who do evaluations are not able to keep abreast of the research and increased knowledge base in both a primary area and other important areas of expert practice.[109] Furthermore, not all psychologists are trained, let alone equally trained and proficient, in the use of particular psychological tests.

---

[106] Psychiatric and Psychological Evidence, 2d ed. (1994) at 4–16.

[107] *Id.* (Supp. 2003) at 4–15.

[108] http://www.ap-ls.org/students/graduateIndex.html, accessed Dec. 6, 2004.

[109] Grisso at 36–37.

Table 1–1

Graduate-Level Forensic Psychology Programs

Clinical Ph.D./Psy.D. Programs
University of Alabama (clinical Ph.D. with a psychology-law concentration)
University of Arizona (Ph.D. and/or J.D.)
Alliant International University (Ph.D. in Forensic Psychology or Psy.D. in Forensic Psychology)
Carlos Albizo University in Miami (Psy.D. in Clinical Psychology with a concentration in Forensic Psychology)
Drexel University (J.D./Ph.D.)
University of Florida (Counseling Ph.D. with psychology-law concentration or J.D.)
Fordham University (Clinical Ph.D. with concentration in Forensic Psychology)
John Jay College of Criminal Justice-CUNY (M.A. or Ph.D.)
University of Nevada–Las Vegas (Clinical Ph.D. with concentration in Psychology and Law)
University of Nebraska (joint J.D. and Ph.D. or joint J.D. and M.A. in Psychology)
Nova Southeastern University (Psy.D. with a concentration in Clinical Forensic Psychology)
Sam Houston State University (Ph.D. in Forensic-Clinical Psychology)
Simon Fraser University (Ph.D. in Clinical-Forensic Psychology)
West Virginia University (Ph.D. in Clinical Psychology with emphasis in forensics)
Widener University (J.D./Psy.D. joint degree)

Non-Clinical Ph.D. Programs
University of Arizona (Ph.D. and/or J.D.)
Alliant International University (Ph.D. in Forensic Psychology or Psy.D. in Forensic Psychology)
Florida International University (Ph.D. in Psychology with an emphasis in Legal Psychology)
Georgetown University (Ph.D. in Psychology with concentration in Human Development and Public Policy and a Ph.D. in a joint program with a Master's in Public Policy)
John Jay College of Criminal Justice–CUNY (M.A. or Ph.D.)
University of Nevada–Reno (Ph.D. in Social Psychology with a concentration in psychology and law)
Pacific Graduate School of Psychology (joint Ph.D./J.D.)
Simon Fraser University (Ph.D. in Psychology in the psychology and law program)
University of Florida (Developmental Ph.D. with psychology-law concentration or J.D.)
University of Illinois at Chicago (Ph.D. with concentration in Psychology and Law)
University of Minnesota (Ph.D. in Social Psychology with a research concentration in social psychology and law)
University of Nebraska (joint J.D. and Ph.D. or joint J.D. and M.A. in Psychology)
University of Texas at El Paso (Ph.D. in Applied Psychology with the Legal Psychology Group)
University of Wyoming (Ph.D. with concentration in Psychology and Law)

Master's Programs
Castleton College (Master's in Forensic Psychology)
The Chicago School of Professional Psychology (M.A. in Forensic Psychology)
University of Denver (M.A. in Forensic Psychology)
John Jay College of Criminal Justice–CUNY (M.A. or Ph.D.)
Marymount University (M.A. in Forensic Psychology)
University of Nebraska (joint J.D. and Ph.D. or joint J.D. and M.A. in Psychology)
The Sage Colleges (M.A. in Forensic Psychology)
Tiffin University (M.A. in Criminal Justice in Forensic Psychology)

Clinical Psychologists

Most of the experts an attorney may wish to consult are clinical psychologists who have specialized in forensic psychology, either through a formal program or by working with an experienced colleague and thoroughly reviewing the relevant literature. Their training "prepares the future practitioner to evaluate and treat patients with severe psychological difficulties."[110] Most Ph.D.s and virtually all Psy.D.s are clinical psychologists, and nearly all are licensed or eligible for licensure for independent practice.

Counseling Psychologists

"Counseling psychology training is oriented toward preparing psychologists who intend to work with less severely disturbed individuals, usually in outpatient and higher education settings."[111] "Counseling psychology is unique in its attention both to normal developmental issues and to problems associated with physical, emotional, and mental disorders."[112] "Counseling psychologists are employed in a wide range of settings including college and university counseling centers, university research and teaching positions, independent practice, health care settings, hospitals, organizational consulting groups, and many others."[113]

Counseling psychologists complete a predoctoral internship lasting one year.[114] Counseling psychologists generally do well at dealing with ongoing problems in living, but less well than clinical psychologists, on the average, in assessing and treating serious psychopathology. A counseling psychologist may have an Ed.D., a Ph.D., or a Psy.D.

School Psychologists

"School psychologists are trained to evaluate, treat, and consult in areas directly related to educational problems of children and adolescents. The training emphasis is less on severe

---

[110] Psychiatric and Psychological Evidence, 2d ed. (1994) at 4–14.

[111] *Id.* at 4–15.

[112] APA Division of Counseling Psychology, "What Is a Counseling Psychologist." (Aug. 1999) (on file with author).

[113] Division of Counseling Psychology web site, www.div17.org/Students/difference.htm., accessed Aug. 27, 2004.

[114] Psychologist's Legal Handbook at 44.

emotional problems and more on evaluation and remediation of learning problems."[115] The internships for school psychologists last one academic year.[116] Thus, one would look to a school psychologist when educational problems figure prominently and diagnosis and treatment of psychopathology are less a factor.

Other

The specialty programs just described are evaluated by the American Psychological Association. Those individuals completing an APA-approved training program and internship are likely to have received a quality education. Two of the specialty programs, experimental and industrial/organizational, "do not require internships and are not granted APA approval."[117] The former primarily prepares psychologists for careers in teaching and research. Experimental psychologists are sometimes called upon as experts on memory or other areas of cognitive psychology, to testify about research but not about a specific individual. Industrial/organizational psychologists are trained to apply principles of psychology to business settings.

Postdoctoral Fellowships

There are postdoctoral fellowships in psychology for people who wish further specialized training, but relatively few people take advantage of them.[118] Neuropsychology, however, is an area in which postdoctoral fellowships are generally required.

Licensure Requirements

Licensing or certification is required by all 50 states and the 10 Canadian provinces, as well as the Virgin Islands, in order for an individual to work as a psychologist. Certification is generally under a "title act" that indicates that no one but a certified psychologist may use the term "psychologist" or any similar term to describe him- or herself or what he or she does. Licensing, in contrast, generally identifies a specific set of functions in a statute. Licensing and certification both normally indicate that the individual is permitted to practice independently, rather than under the supervision of another professional. Licensing of psychologists is generic—that is, like physicians, possession of the license permits a psychologist to practice in any area for which he or she has sufficient knowledge, experience, and training. The Model Act for Licensure from the Association of State and Provincial Psychology Boards (ASPPB), a voluntary organization of state and provincial licensing boards, defines the practice of psychology as

> [t]he observation, description, evaluation, interpretation and/or modification of human behavior by the application of psychological principles, methods, or procedures, for the

---

[115] Psychiatric and Psychological Evidence, 2d ed. (1994) at 4–15.

[116] Psychologist's Legal Handbook at 44.

[117] Psychiatric and Psychological Evidence, 2d ed. (1994) at 4–16.

[118] *Id.* at 4–15.

purpose of preventing or eliminating symptomatic, maladaptive, or undesired behavior and of enhancing interpersonal relationships, work and life adjustment, personal effectiveness, behavioral health and mental health. The practice of psychology includes, but is not limited to, psychological testing and the evaluation or assessment of personal characteristics, such as intelligence, personality, abilities, interests, aptitudes, and neuropsychological functioning; counseling, psychoanalysis, psychotherapy, hypnosis, biofeedback, and behavior analysis and therapy; diagnosis and treatment of mental and emotional disorder or disability, alcoholism and substance abuse, disorders of habit or conduct, as well as of the psychological aspects of physical illness, accident, injury, or disability; and psychoeducational evaluation, therapy, remediation, and consultation. Psychological services may be rendered to individuals, families, groups, organizations, institutions and the public. The practice of psychology shall be construed within the meaning of this definition without regard to whether payment is received for services rendered. The provision of any of the above-mentioned services or activities by any means, including electronic or telephonic, constitutes the practice of psychology.[119]

Psychologists are ethically and legally required to practice only within their areas of competence, so that an individual who wishes to specialize in one or more areas needs to get appropriate training and experience in order to ethically do so.

The difficulty of becoming licensed as a psychologist varies significantly among the states and provinces. Nearly all use a national examination—the Examination for Professional Practice in Psychology (EPPP)[120]—but each sets its own cutoff point on that examination. According to information accessed on the ASPPB web site, the most common cutoff is at the 70th percentile of those who took the examination on the same date. This corresponds to a raw score of 140 and a scaled score of 500, and is the ASPPB recommended cutoff. Exceptions include British Columbia (which is developing new bylaws), the District of Columbia (one-half standard deviation below the mean), New Brunswick (65th percentile), New York (equivalency score based on equating table and board review), Prince Edward Island (in the process of adopting the EPPP), Quebec (60th percentile), and the Virgin Islands (EPPP is required but passing score is not available).

The EPPP tests the biological bases of behavior (11 percent of the test items), the cognitive-affective bases of behavior (13 percent), social and multicultural bases of behavior (12 percent), growth and life span development (13 percent), assessment and diagnosis (14 percent), treatment/intervention (16 percent), research methods (6 percent), and ethical/legal/professional issues (15 percent). Detailed information regarding each of these categories may be accessed at *www.asppb.org/exam/epppsummary.htm*.

This national examination is used both for initial licensure and to help establish reciprocity from one state to the next. A psychologist submits the score to the state to which he or she is moving, and if the score exceeds the state's cutoff, the new state may grant a license without additional content examinations. However, most states add additional examinations—for example, in ethics or law. Most require at least one year of postdoctoral supervised experience prior to receipt of a license for independent practice.[121] Most states accept the recommendations of the ASPPB regarding requirements for licensing. A copy of the *ASPPB Code of Conduct* can be found in **Appendix I.**

---

[119] www.asppb.org, accessed June 30, 2004.

[120] Psychiatric and Psychological Evidence, 2d ed. (1994) at 4–16; Larry Bass et al., Professional Conduct and Discipline in Psychology 43 (1996) [hereinafter Bass].

[121] Psychiatric and Psychological Evidence, 2d ed. (1994) at 4–16.

Karl and Kristen Kirkland surveyed the 61 member boards of the ASPPB with regard to complaints received related to child custody evaluations.[122] Thirty-four of the 61 licensing boards (56 percent) responded to the survey. They identified 2,413 complaints related to child custody evaluations between 1990 and 1999, but only 27 of those (1 percent) were adjudicated with a finding of fault. Disciplinary actions ranged from continuing education to five years' probation. An unknown, but likely substantial, number of confidential letters admonishing psychologists about their practices had also been issued, but data are not available from most boards or the ASPPB Disciplinary Data Bank. Most boards reported a substantial increase in the number of complaints in recent years. The numbers suggest that psychologists who do child custody evaluations should expect a licensing complaint to be filed against them at some point. They also found that 11 percent of the ethics adjudications of the American Psychological Association relate to child custody matters.

The authors also found that, in the early 1980s, it was not unusual to find a psychologist allied with a legal team in an adversarial child custody contest. By the 1990s, however, ethics committees and licensing boards increasingly found that the "best interests of the child" standard required that psychologists be objective, independent, and child-oriented.

One state, Colorado, has responded to the marked increase of complaints by passing a law that prohibits its licensure board from disciplining psychologists on the basis of a child custody evaluation. The statute[123] indicates that "[t]he provisions of this article shall not apply to custodial evaluations undertaken in domestic relations cases in the courts of this state or domestic and child abuse evaluations undertaken for purposes of legal proceedings in the courts of this state."

Most licensing of psychologists is generic (no specialty designation as "clinical," "counseling," and so on), but some states recognize that some psychologists meet the requirements for listing in the National Register of Health Service Providers in Psychology. Those requirements are

1. A doctoral degree in psychology from an ASPPB/National Register Designated Doctoral Program in Psychology or an APA/CPA Accredited Program.
2. At least two years (3,000 hours) of supervised experience in health services, including
   a. One-year (1,500 hours) internship or training program meeting the National Register's Guidelines.
   b. One-year (1,500 hours) of supervised postdoctoral experience meeting the National Register's Guidelines.
3. An active, unrestricted license at the independent practice level.
4. No disciplinary action.[124]

According to the National Register web site, all Canadian provinces and 13 states accept National Register documentation of the earning of a doctoral degree, completion of an internship and postdoctoral year, and the EPPP score earned as a means of speeding the

---

[122] Karl Kirkland & Kristen L. Kirkland, *Frequency of Child Custody Evaluation Complaints and Related Disciplinary Action: A Survey of the Association of State and Provincial Psychology Boards*, 32 Prof. Psychol.: Res. & Prac. 171–74 (2001).

[123] Colo. Mental Health Stat. § 12-43-215(7) (1998).

[124] NRHSPP web site, accessed June 30, 2004.

process of licensing for a registrant. Five additional states accept documentation of all but the EPPP score. The National Register web site lists approximately 13,000 psychologists as of June 2004. Wherever clinical or health expertise is relevant, an attorney would do well to retain a psychologist who is listed there. The Canadian Register of Health Service Providers in Psychology has similar criteria.[125]

§ 1.7   Definition of Psychiatrist

The following definition of psychiatrist was drafted in conjunction with the Joint Commission on Interprofessional Affairs, consisting of representatives of the American Psychiatric Association, the American Nurses' Association, the American Psychological Association, and the National Association of Social Workers:

> A psychiatrist is a physician whose specialty is the diagnosis and treatment of people suffering from mental disorders. The properly trained psychiatrist can provide a comprehensive evaluation from a psychiatric point of view, a medical differential diagnosis, treatment planning, and multiple therapeutic and health-enhancing interventions. . . . The properly trained psychiatrist can then integrate . . . historical and examination materials with the physical examination and laboratory findings relevant to the symptoms presentation of this particular patient to evolve a diagnostic system (medical differential diagnosis). . . . It is this capacity to integrate all of these medical findings, and to use whatever treatment interventions are necessary and appropriate to influence them positively, that makes the psychiatrist unique.[126]

After medical school and an internship, most go into a residency program involving three years of seminars and colloquia and the provision of clinical services under supervision in both inpatient and outpatient settings. However, the residency is not necessary in order for a physician to call him- or herself a psychiatrist.[127] There are more than 35,000 practicing psychiatrists and psychiatric residents in the United States.[128]

§ 1.8   Difference between Psychologist and Psychiatrist

A common question is, "What is the difference between psychiatry and clinical psychology?" There is probably an 80 to 90 percent overlap between what the psychiatrist and clinical psychologist are able to do with their professional expertise. The major distinction between psychology and psychiatry is that psychiatrists can prescribe medication, while only psychologists can administer, score, and interpret psychological tests. As already stated, psychiatry has moved more toward the biological or organic aspects of mental

---

[125] Criteria for Listing in the Canadian Register of Health Service Providers in Psychology (2004); Canadian Register of Health Service Providers in Psychology, Ottawa, Ontario (1994).

[126] W. Frosch, *Toward a Definition of Psychiatry*, 26 Psychiatric News 38 (Apr. 19, 1991).

[127] Psychiatric and Psychological Evidence, 2d ed. (1994) at 4–7.

[128] American Psychiatric Association web site, www.psych.org/, accessed June 30, 2004.

health. Consequently, their expertise in prescribing medications has become a more central part of their work. There is a preliminary movement in some states to train psychologists to prescribe medications, with New Mexico and Louisiana having now passed legislation that will permit psychologists, once specialized training is completed, to prescribe certain medications. In addition, there are some psychologists working for the Department of Defense who have been prescribing medications for several years now.

In recent years psychologists have increasingly been allowed hospital co-admitting privileges with psychiatrists, or total admitting privileges independent of any other practitioners, depending upon the state in which they practice and the hospital with which they are affiliated. The national trend indicates that more and more states and hospitals are allowing psychologists to admit independently. These psychologists are allowed to admit patients, determine the necessary treatment, write orders, and perform all tasks that do not require a medical degree.

§ 1.9   Social Workers

Social workers, who have either a bachelor's or a master's degree (M.S.W., M.S.S.W.), are trained to help individuals in the context of the social and economic milieu—for example, to find a living setting that meets the individual's social, psychological, and physical needs.[129] Many social workers are also competent to evaluate children's developmental needs, each parent's emotional and economic stability, and each parent's ability to address the child's emotional, social, and economic needs. If the court orders a home study, it will typically be done by a trained social worker. All 50 states, the District of Columbia, Puerto Rico, and the Virgin Islands license or certify social workers at the master's level, and some states also license or certify at the bachelor's level. The national licensing organization for social workers is the American Association of State Social Work Boards, *www.aasswb.org/.*

It should be noted that because many people who have no educational background in social work are hired to do social work tasks, it becomes necessary to determine what training the "social worker" has. There are a few programs that grant Ph.D.s or Doctor of Social Work (DSW) degrees.

Social workers may receive certification through the Academy of Certified Social Workers (ACSW), within the National Association of Social Workers (NASW), and may use "ACSW" after their names when so certified. Certification information is available at the NASW web site, *www.socialworkers.org/credentials/credentials/acsw.asp.* Social workers who meet the requirements for ACSW certification are eligible for listing in the *NASW Register of Clinical Social Workers.* The NASW recognizes, and lists in the NASW Register, two levels of clinical social workers: the qualified clinical social worker and the diplomate in clinical social work. Information is available at the NASW web site, *www.socialworkers.org/credentials/credentials/qcsw.asp.* For requirements for the diplomate in clinical social work, see the "Social Workers" subheading in **§ 1.10,** discussing board certification.

Social workers are not utilized as expert witnesses as often as psychologists and psychiatrists are, but their expertise is sought in some cases, and social workers have been

---

[129] Randy Frances Kandel, Family Law: Essential Terms and Concepts (Aspen Publishers 2000); www.naswdc.org, accessed July 1, 2004.

accepted as experts by many trial courts, generally on the basis of their having relevant experience. Courts are also usually willing to allow hearsay testimony from a social worker if it meets the reliability test.[130]

§ 1.10   Board Certification/Other Professional Organizations

Board Certification

Psychologists

The **American Board of Professional Psychology** (ABPP), an organization founded in 1947, confers diplomate status upon psychologists on the basis of at least four years of postdoctoral experience and an examination conducted by a panel of diplomates involving all areas of practice. According to ABPP newsletters, between 1,000 and 1,500 diplomates were initially grandfathered, but since approximately 1950 all candidates have had to pass a formal examination.[131] As of January 2002, there were 180 diplomates in forensic psychology, 1,775 in clinical psychology, and 410 in clinical neuropsychology, out of a total of 3,205 diplomates.[132]

Diplomate status in forensic psychology is also conferred by the **American Board of Forensic Psychology** (ABFP), which was founded in 1978 but which has worked in conjunction with the ABPP since 1985.[133] The ABFP currently has 205 diplomates.[134]

The **American Board of Professional Neuropsychology** (ABPN) was incorporated in 1982 as an attempt to provide peer regulation for the field of neuropsychology. The Board requires, at a minimum, a doctoral degree in psychology, a minimum of three years of professional experience in neuropsychology, current licensure or certification, a minimum of 500 hours per year of providing neuropsychological services for five years preceding application, a written examination, a requirement that two work samples be submitted, and an oral examination. As of 2004, there were 192 ABPN-certified diplomates in neuropsychology.[135]

The **American Board of Assessment Psychology** (ABAP) was incorporated in 1993 as "the only international certification board for doctoral level psychologists with specialized expertise in psychological testing, test development and test battery administration." Several dozen diplomates were granted on the basis of the candidate's documented professional accomplishments when ABAP began. Since about 1998, applicants were required to submit vitae, recommendations, and work samples, and to go through an oral

---

[130] *See* Idaho v. Wright, 100 S. Ct. 3139 (1990) (reliability test).

[131] Russell Bent, Robert Goldberg, & Ralph Packard, *A Very Brief History of ABPP: 1947–1997*, 21 ABPP Specialist 4 & 19–20; Noble H. Kelley, *ABPP: The Early Years*, 22 ABPP Specialist 11.

[132] American Psychological Association web site, www.apa.org., accessed June 30, 2004.

[133] Steve Bank, An Open Letter to Division 41 Members Interested in the American Board of Forensic Psychology, 14 Am. Psychol.-L. Soc'y News 3 (1994).

[134] www.abfp.com/diplomate_search_results.asp, accessed July 1, 2004.

[135] http://abpn.net/member.php?search=1, accessed July 4, 2004.

examination. The ABAP had 168 diplomates as of July 2004.[136] While ABAP continues to exist as an independent body, it has also been made the Assessment Psychology Section of the Division of Clinical Psychology of the American Psychological Association. A similar arrangement has been in effect for a number of years between the American Psychology-Law Society and the Division of Forensic Psychology of the American Psychological Association. Members of the APA division are automatically members of the Society, but one may be a member of the Society without becoming a member of the APA division.

Psychiatrists

Some psychiatrists seek certification from the American Board of Psychiatry and Neurology (ABPN) through oral and written examinations after at least three years of practice. Specialty certification is available in neurology, in child psychiatry, and, as of 1992, in forensic psychiatry. ABPN psychiatrists who were not grandfathered in when the certification was initiated must have at least one year of accredited fellowship training in forensic psychiatry. Applicants must pass a 200-item, multiple-choice examination to be certified.[137]

Only one-third of practicing psychiatrists are board certified, and many who attempt to become board certified fail the examination.[138] In 1994, certification was limited to 10 years, requiring diplomates certified in that year and since to recertify. The recertification rate has exceeded 95 percent.[139] At present, there are approximately 200 board-certified forensic psychiatrists in the United States.

Social Workers

The Diplomate in Clinical Social Work was established in 1986 for social workers who meet criteria for advanced experience and training who pass an advanced clinical social work examination. Further information is available at *www.socialworkers.org/credentials/credentials/dcsw.asp*.

American Board of Examiners in Clinical Social Work   Founded in 1987, the ABECSW has credentialed more than 11,000 clinical social workers with the Board Certified Diplomate in Clinical Social Work (BCD). The Board has a code of ethics, available at *www.abecsw.org/info/org/i_abes_code.shtml*.

National Organization of Forensic Social Work   An organization founded in 1982, the National Organization of Forensic Social Work (NOFSW) certifies as diplomates those

---

[136] www.assessmentpsychologyboard.org/, accessed July 1, 2004; Communication with ABAP office, July 1, 2004.

[137] www.abpn.com/Downloads/2005subspec_cert_ifa.pdf, accessed July 5, 2004.

[138] Psychiatric and Psychological Evidence, 2d ed. (1994, Supp. 2003) at 8–9.

[139] 9 ABPN Update 4 (Winter 2004).

social workers who are heavily involved in providing social work consultation in the legal process. The NOFSW's web site is at *www.nofsw.org/*.

Other Certification Organizations

The **American Board of Medical Psychotherapists and Psychodiagnosticians** (ABMPP) originated in 1982. It is interdisciplinary, permitting psychologists, psychiatrists, social workers, and other mental health professionals to apply. More than 6,500 people had been certified as diplomates and fellows of this board as of July 2004.[140]

The **American College of Forensic Examiners International** (ACFEI), founded in 1992, claims to be the largest forensic organization in the world with more than 19,000 members, including some in every state and 23 foreign countries. It accepts applications from numerous disciplines, though it is "a participating member in the Specialty and Service Society of the American Medical Association." Applicants must meet the requirements of Rule 702 of the Federal Rules of Evidence, and pass a 50-question ethics examination prior to certification as a Diplomate of the American Board of Forensic Examiners. Information is available at *www.acfei.com/main.php*.

Other Professional Organizations

An essential part of an expert's qualifications is the list of organizations to which he or she belongs, particularly if membership is based in part or entirely on a formal process of peer review, rather than simply on the payment of dues to the organization. "Fellow" status in most organizations is predicated on such a peer review.

Psychologists

American Psychological Association   Full membership in the American Psychological Association (APA) is limited to psychologists with doctoral degrees (or master's degree associates for five years) who pay the membership fee. Specialty areas are represented by separate divisions—for example, Division 12 (Clinical Psychology) and Division 41 (Law and Psychology). The APA had more than 148,000 members and affiliates in 2004.[141] A copy of the APA Code of Ethics can be found in **Appendix B.**

American Psychology-Law Society   Founded in 1968, the American Psychology-Law Society overlaps with Division 41 of the American Psychological Association. Membership is open to APA members who pay the membership fee and to non-APA members who are interested in the topic. There were 1,951 members as of 2002.[142]

---

[140] Personal communication, ABMPP office (July 7, 2004).

[141] APA web site, www.apa.org., accessed July 1, 2004.

[142] *Id.*

National Register of Health Service Providers in Psychology   The National Register of Health Service Providers in Psychology (see **§ 1.6**) provides certification that the individual listed in their directory has met a high standard for training and experience. There were about 13,000 psychologists listed as of June 2004.[143]

Canadian Psychological Association   Founded in 1939, the Canadian Psychological Association has about 5,228 members out of an estimated 12,000 psychologists in Canada. It includes 23 Sections and two Interest Groups.[144] A copy of the Canadian Code of Ethics for Psychologists can be found in **Appendix H.**

Psychiatrists

American Psychiatric Association   Founded in 1844, the American Psychiatric Association had about 35,000 members in 2004,[145] representing about 70 percent of the psychiatrists in the United States. Members must be physicians with some training and experience in psychiatry. A copy of the American Psychiatric Association's *Principles of Medical Ethics With Annotations Especially Applicable to Psychiatry, 2001 Edition* (including amendments made in November 2003 that are expected to be approved in 2004) may be found at *www.psych.org/psych_pract/ethics/ethics.cfm.*

Canadian Psychiatric Association   Founded in 1951, the Canadian Psychiatric Association is similar to the American Psychiatric Association. The Canadian Psychiatric Association has about 2,750 paid members and residents.[146]

Canadian Academy of Psychiatry and Law   The Canadian Academy of Psychiatry and Law is for those Canadian psychiatrists who also practice in the forensic realm. Membership is open to psychiatrists who pay the membership fee.[147]

American Academy of Psychiatry and Law   Founded in 1969, the American Academy of Psychiatry and Law (AAPL) is an organization of psychiatrists interested in the practice of, and training in, legal psychiatry. It does not certify—any member of the American Psychiatric Association who is willing to pay the membership fee may join.[148] There were "more than 1,500 members" in 2004. A copy of the AAPL Ethics Guidelines for the Practice of Forensic Psychiatry, last revised in 1995, can be found at the APPL web site.[149]

---

[143] National Register web site, www.nationalregister.com/, accessed June 30, 2004.

[144] Personal communication, CPA, July 7, 2004; CPA web site, accessed July 1, 2004, www.cpa.ca/.

[145] APA web site, accessed July 1, 2004.

[146] CPA web site, www.cpa-apc.org/, accessed July 3, 2004.

[147] CAPL web site, www.caplnet.org/, accessed July 3, 2004.

[148] Psychiatric and Psychological Evidence, 2d ed. (1994) at 4–20.1.

[149] AAPL web site, www.aapl.org/index.html, accessed July 3, 2004.

Social Workers

National Association of Social Workers   Founded in 1955, the National Association of Social Workers is the primary membership organization for social workers. Membership is open to "professional social workers" who pay the membership dues. There were about 153,000 members in the NASW as of 2004.[150] The NASW estimates this to be about half of the "qualified professional social workers" in the United States. A copy of the NASW's Code of Ethics may be found at *www.socialworkers.org/pubs/code/code.asp.*

Multidisciplinary

American Orthopsychiatric Association   Founded in 1951, the American Orthopsychiatric Association is an interdisciplinary association for psychologists, psychiatrists, and social workers. The organization is concerned with clinical issues and issues of social justice, among people "engaged in preventive, treatment, and advocacy approaches to mental health."[151]

American Academy of Forensic Sciences   Founded in 1948, the American Academy of Forensic Sciences (AAFS) promotes education and research in the forensic sciences. It has more than 5,000 members from numerous disciplines in the United States, Canada, and 50 other nations. Most mental health experts are in the section on psychiatry and behavioral science. That section had about 168 members and affiliates as of July 2004.[152]

§ 1.11   Skills Needed by the Expert

According to forensic psychologist Charles Clark,

> [a]lthough there are attorneys who want and expect an expert witness to be an advocate for one side in a dispute, many more actually want what they ostensibly request, an objective opinion. They will wish to avoid being misguided by an overly favorable opinion in making their own decisions about a case, and they will be concerned that the appearance of advocacy will sink the expert witness' credibility.[153]

The psychologist is ethically required to be an advocate for his or her data, but not for either side. Rather, the ethical requirement is that the psychologist be both scientific and objective in his or her work on a case. While a psychologist who fails to honor this requirement may

---

[150] NASW web site, http://naswdc.org/, accessed July 3, 2004.

[151] Ortho web site, www.amerortho.org/, accessed July 4, 2004.

[152] AAFS web site, www.aafs.org/, accessed July 4, 2004.

[153] C. Clark, *Agreeing to Be an Expert Witness: Considerations of Competence and Role Integrity*, 16 Reg. Rep. 4, 5 (1990).

have quasi-judicial and witness immunity in court, he or she is not immune from an ethical or licensing adjudication for failure to follow the requirements of the ethical code and/or the state statute and administrative code for his or her profession.[154]

Given the distinctions among psychiatrists, psychologists, and social workers, and within the field of psychology itself, the attorney must define the skills needed by the expert and choose accordingly. For example, *if there are young children involved (10 years old or younger)*, the best expert would likely be a psychologist with graduate training in child clinical psychology and substantial experience in the provision of services to this age group. A number of child psychologists are also certified or licensed as school psychologists, adding to their qualifications and usefulness. *If there are children ages 11 to 12*, they may be appropriately evaluated by either a clinical child psychologist or a clinical psychologist who has done substantial work with adolescents, the choice depending in part on the level of maturity of the child. *Minor children 13 years or older* would appropriately be evaluated by a clinical psychologist having substantial experience with adolescents.

New Requirements in California

California has chosen to define with great specificity the knowledge, skills, and experience needed by a child custody evaluator in that state under Chapter 2.6 of the Special Rules for Trial Courts, accessible at *www.courtinfo.ca.gov/rules/titlefive/title5-1-285.htm#TopOfPage*. These demanding statutory requirements have made it more difficult for an individual to qualify as a child custody evaluator in California.

Limitations of Evaluators

Although a mental health professional can do a lot to educate attorneys and the court about psychological concepts and insights that may be relevant to a case, there are a number of limitations to the professional's abilities:

1. Mental health professionals are not lie detectors. Some psychological tests can address malingering, but nothing guarantees that an individual could not fool any professional.
2. Although professionals can often obtain a variety of information from an individual, they cannot always do any better at getting information from a reluctant individual than the attorney can.
3. Professionals can identify current factors fairly well, but they have substantial limitations in identifying relevant past or future factors.
4. Because people's motivations are very often ambiguous, accurate presentation of these motivations by the professional may also be ambiguous.

---

[154] Theodore Blau, The Psychologist as Expert Witness (John Wiley & Sons 1998) [hereinafter Blau 1998].

5. Because diagnoses and many behavioral descriptions and conclusions are relative and not absolute, the professional may also have to be equivocal to some degree to be accurate.[155]

§ 1.12 Sources of Experts

The following resources can provide attorneys with information about expert witnesses:

1. Professional organizations, particularly those that certify the expertise of members (see **§ 1.10** and **1.11**).

2. The grapevine: attorneys, judges, and others in the legal system with experience with particular experts.

3. Professional literature: authors of research or reports in the desired area of testimony. Because research quality and writing ability do not guarantee an ability to verbalize one's knowledge in a courtroom setting, the expertise of some authors should be utilized in trial preparation only.

4. Academic institutions: faculty members at colleges, universities, psychology professional schools, and medical schools. An individual who does research and/or teaching does not necessarily communicate knowledge well, so it may be necessary to utilize them in trial preparation only.

5. Professional witnesses and expert witness services. The former work more or less full-time providing expert testimony, perhaps as county or state hospital psychiatrists or as independent experts. The latter advertise in legal journals and magazines and are sources of the former. The advantage of professional witnesses is that they are experienced and tested. The disadvantage is that they may be identified with one side, and their testimony in previous trials may give opposing counsel substantial information about them and their probable testimony prior to a trial. Use of these kinds of experts is uncommon, however, comprising less than 5 percent of expert witnesses. Nearly all experts spend most of their time in their fields of expertise, not as witnesses.[156]

6. A psychologist or psychiatrist retained to assist with preparation of a case may, for a variety of reasons, be inappropriate as a testifying witness—but nevertheless an excellent source of recommendations for an expert who is skilled at doing evaluations and offering testimony.[157]

7. Court records in similar cases.

8. The Yellow Pages. Do any psychologists or psychiatrists indicate in their listings that they do forensic work?[158]

---

[155] Psychologist's Legal Handbook at 611.

[156] Psychiatric and Psychological Evidence, 2d ed. (1994, Supp. 2002) at 6–7 to 6–9.

[157] *Id.* at 18–2.

[158] McHale at 8.

§ 1.13   Utilization of Psychologists Licensed in Jurisdictions Outside the State in Which the Custody Contest Is Being Waged ("Foreign" Jurisdictions)

Although every state restricts the practice of psychology to those individually licensed in that state, it is possible in many jurisdictions for a psychologist to temporarily practice for a specific purpose, such as doing an evaluation for a court proceeding and testifying in court about that evaluation.

According to psychiatrist Robert Simon and law professor Daniel Shuman,[159] many states preclude psychologists and psychiatrists from practicing without a license from that specific state. If a forensic expert were to conduct an evaluation and/or testify in a state in which he or she is not licensed, the expert "may not be permitted to testify, may incur civil and criminal liability, or may face professional disciplinary action."[160] Experts may also find that their professional liability insurance does not cover actions brought while practicing without a license. Although there are only a small number of reports of problems for experts practicing across state lines, experts need to be aware of the potential for very serious problems when they practice outside the state(s) in which they are licensed. Violations are reported to the National Practitioner Data Bank, and a disciplinary action could be brought against an expert in his or her home state. It is also possible that a malpractice suit could be filed against a psychologist, psychiatrist, or social worker who is found to be practicing without a license in the jurisdiction in which a case is being tried.

Every state considers diagnosis and treatment to be components of the practice of medicine and psychology. A non-state-licensed forensic psychiatrist or psychologist is very likely to be required to diagnose, placing him or her in violation of state law.

Many states have exceptions for physicians or psychologists from contiguous states, generally based on reciprocity. Some laws require that the guest physician or psychologist be in consultation with or be supervised by a resident physician or psychologist.

There are, generally, two lines of case law. One indicates that state licensure is a minimum requirement for expert testimony in that state. A lack of the required license means a lack of competency or qualification to testify. The other line of case law treats licensure as only one of several factors relevant to whether the individual is qualified as an expert, and considers local licensure to relate to the weight given the testimony rather than to its admissibility. The authors cite Maryland and Illinois as states that, by statute, limit or exclude testimony by psychologists not licensed in those states. In contrast, Wisconsin permits out-of-state psychologists to practice in the state for up to 60 "working days" per year, though the psychologist must report the nature and extent of his or her practice in the state if the practice exceeds 20 working days in a single year.[161]

Experts who limit their activities to jury consultation or consultation with an attorney generally do not have to worry about licensing, because they are not diagnosing or treating anyone. If an expert is reviewing medical, psychological, or other health-related

---

[159] Robert I. Simon & Daniel W. Shuman, *Conducting Forensic Examinations on the Road: Are You Practicing Your Profession without a License?* 27 J. Am. Acad. Psychiatry & L. 75–82 (1999).

[160] *Id.* at 75.

[161] Wis. Stat. § 455.03.

records, it is not clear whether the expert needs a license, because such review generally includes drawing conclusions regarding diagnoses.

A psychologist or psychiatrist who considers accepting a case in another state must ascertain whether he or she needs a license from that state in order to avoid a possible licensing, civil, or criminal action against him or her. The psychologist or psychiatrist should ask the attorney requesting the consultation to identify the relevant statute(s) and administrative code, and to send a copy of all relevant sections to the psychologist or psychiatrist. The expert should not take the chance that the attorney will not accurately interpret the provisions, and a claim to that effect will not mitigate a licensing complaint. Given the relative ease with which the state statute(s) and administrative code can be accessed via the Internet, the expert is also advised to do his or her own search for relevant sections.[162] The authors also advise that it is not sufficient to have the out-of-state client consent to an evaluation and sign a statement that a doctor-patient relationship is not being created, because that will not protect an expert from laws designed to protect citizens from unqualified or incompetent professionals.

If the request for consultation comes from a court, the authors recommend that the expert inform the court of the licensing question and get a ruling regarding the relevance of licensing. The expert should still obtain a copy of the relevant statutes and administrative code and do a review him- or herself. The potential danger is too great to take a chance on making an error.

To obtain a temporary license from a state that allows temporary practice, the psychologist or physician should contact the licensing board in the state in which he or she wishes to consult. Current addresses for most state and provincial psychology licensing boards are available at *www.asppb.org.*

Psychologists may be able to facilitate the temporary licensing/certification process with the Certificate of Professional Qualification in Psychology (CPQ). It is a relatively new certification. Initiated in August of 1998 by the ASPPB, the CPQ is designed to facilitate psychologists' ability to practice in more than the jurisdiction of original licensure, whether on a temporary or permanent basis. As of July 2004, 30 jurisdictions in North America accept the CPQ. A number of other jurisdictions have voted to accept the CPQ and are in the process of making administrative and/or legislative changes necessary to implement the CPQ. A psychology licensing board that accepts the CPQ has agreed to accept the psychologist's educational training, supervised experience, and performance on the national examination or equivalent. CPQ holders may also be required to pass special requirements of a given board, such as a test on mental health laws or on ethics, or to be personally interviewed by the board.[163]

According to an article by Jill Tucillo, Nick DeFilippis, Robert Denney, and John Dsurney,[164] practicing one's profession in a state in which one is not licensed may have very serious consequences, including being unable to testify, civil (fines from $100 to $50,000 per day) or criminal liability (a felony in five states), and/or a disciplinary action

---

[162] A frequently-used web site is www.findlaw.com. Most states' web sites are also accessible at www.[enter name of state].gov.

[163] Report from the Association of State and Provincial Psychology Boards (Aug. 2002).

[164] Jill A. Tucillo, Nick A. DeFilippis, Robert L. Denney, & John Dsurney, *Licensure Requirements for Interjurisdictional Forensic Evaluations*, 33 Prof. Psychol.: Res. & Prac. 377–83 (2002).

by the licensing board (with report to the National Practitioner Data Bank). Failing to comply may also be an ethics violation, as psychologists are required to comply with laws related to the practice of psychology. Licensing boards also require widely varying amounts of information about the visiting psychologist, ranging from a statement of intended practice to graduate school transcripts plus letters of reference plus a curriculum vitae and more. Some boards also charge a "processing fee."

Table 1–2 indicates the requirements of each state regarding the performance of forensic evaluations by psychologists not licensed in that state. Many states grant temporary licensure for purposes such as conducting a forensic evaluation. Some will also provide formal licensure without requiring that a national or local examination be passed. Certification by the American Board of Professional Psychology (ABPP, see **§ 1.10**) eases the process in many jurisdictions. **Statutes and administrative codes change frequently. This table should serve as a guide, not a definitive statement of a state's law or administrative code. Check with the licensing board in any state in which you wish to temporarily practice.**

Table 1–2

Temporary Psychological Practice in the United States and Canada[©]

State or Province	Reciprocity?	CPQ Accepted?	Temporary Practice[1]
Alabama	No	No	No[2]
Alaska	No	No	No[3]
Alberta	CMRA[4]	Yes	Yes; maximum of one year
Arizona	No	In process of changing rules and statutes to permit acceptance	Yes; may testify as an expert witness or consult for up to 20 days/year
Arkansas	Yes	No	Permits forensic consultation on one case, including evaluation and testimony, with *prior* Board approval. Include license number, state, and approximate dates of evaluation and testimony, and location. No time limit.[5]
British Columbia	CMRA	Yes	Yes, if person meets endorsement criteria; may practice for up to 15 consecutive days per calendar year, and may apply for temporary registration twice in any calendar year.[6] Applies to expert witnesses.

Table 1–2

(*continued*)

State or Province	Reciprocity?	CPQ Accepted?	Temporary Practice[1]
California	No	Yes; must take California jurisprudence and ethics exam and provide evidence of course work in human sexuality, child abuse assessment, and, if licensed after 9/1/85, in AODA.	Yes; may practice in California for up to 30 days per calendar year.
Colorado	No	No	Yes; may practice for up to 20 days/calendar year. Must inform any client in Colorado that he/she is licensed in another state, not Colorado.[7]
Connecticut	No	Yes; requires passing state jurisprudence exam	Yes.
Delaware	No	No	Yes; if doctoral level, may practice up to 6 days per calendar year
District of Columbia	No	Yes; requires passing jurisprudence exam	Yes; may practice as an expert witness for up to 30 days
Florida	No	No	Yes; may practice psychology up to 5 days in any month or 15 days in any calendar year.[8]
Georgia	No	No	Yes; may practice psychology for up to 30 days/calendar year.[9]
Hawaii	No	No	Yes; if testifying as an expert witness or doing limited consulting, but does not include providing therapy.
Idaho	No	Yes	Yes, to testify as an expert witness.
Illinois	No	No	No[10]

Table 1–2

(*continued*)

State or Province	Reciprocity?	CPQ Accepted?	Temporary Practice[1]
Indiana	No	No	No. Psychologist must obtain an Indiana license to testify as an expert witness or do limited consultation.[11]
Iowa	Yes	No	Requires written summary of intent and verification of licensure in another jurisdiction; valid 10 consecutive business days or 15 days in any 90 day period.[12]
Kansas	No	No	Yes; up to 10 calendar days per year.
Kentucky	Yes	Yes	Yes, to testify as an expert witness; for maximum of 30 days in a period of 2 years. If practicing by electronic means or telephone into Kentucky, must register with the board and get board approval.
Louisiana	Only with Texas	Yes	Yes.[13]
Maine	No	No	Under discussion.
Manitoba	Yes; must pass jurisprudence exam	CMRA	Yes; if testifying as an expert witness.
Maryland	No	Yes; must also take state exam	Yes. Psychologist must send the Board a letter indicating what he/she will be doing, when, and for how long; a copy of his/her CV, and a copy of his/her homestate license, to be reviewed by the Board prior to the temporary practice.[14]
Massachusetts	No	No	May practice or consult an average of 1 day per month (12 days/year) without getting a Massachusetts license.[15]

Table 1–2

(*continued*)

State or Province	Reciprocity?	CPQ Accepted?	Temporary Practice[1]
Michigan	No	Yes	No, unless the psychologist is licensed in a contiguous state.[16]
Minnesota	No	No	Yes; if licensed at the doctoral level in another jurisdiction; up to 7 calendar days if serving as an expert witness.
Mississippi	Yes; must pass jurisprudence/ ethics oral exam	Yes; must pass jurisprudence/ ethics oral exam	Yes; may practice for up to 10 days during any 12-month period; must report the nature of intended practice and send copy of license to the Board *prior to* working in the state.[17]
Missouri	Yes; must pass jurisprudence exam	Yes	Yes, for testimony as an expert witness or for a limited consultation.
Montana	No	No	A limited consultation, (up to 60 days), is permitted.
Nebraska	No	Board has approved; statutes and rules in process of change to permit	Yes, up to 30 days/year of practice or consultation. Must register and pay fee.
Nevada	Yes	Yes	Yes, if testifying as an expert witness or doing a limited consultation; up to 30 days/year; requires invitation by Nevada-licensed psychologist.
New Brunswick	CMRA	Yes	Yes, if under supervision of a N.B licensed psychologist.[18]
New Hampshire	No	Yes	Testimony is permitted but treatment is not.[19]

Table 1–2

(*continued*)

State or Province	Reciprocity?	CPQ Accepted?	Temporary Practice[1]
New Jersey	No	Board has approved, but program is not yet effective	No
New Mexico	No	Yes	Yes, but only if court-ordered to do the evaluation.[20]
New York	No	No	Yes, may testify as an expert witness or consult up to 10 consecutive days or 15 intermittent days in any 90-day period.
Newfoundland/ Labrador	CMRA	Yes	No[21]
North Carolina	No	No	Yes, for up to 5 days per calendar year.[22]
North Dakota	No	No	No
Nova Scotia	Yes, CMRA	Yes; must also take oral exam	Yes, as expert witness or limited consultation.
Ohio	No	Yes; must also take oral exam	Yes, as expert witness or limited consultation or practice, up to 30 days/year; should get approval of board.
Oklahoma	Yes	Yes	Yes, as expert witness or for limited consultation; must inform board prior to providing services; limited to 5 days/calendar year.
Ontario	Both ASPPB and CMRA	Yes	Yes, as expert witness or for limited consultation; must register with the Board.
Oregon	No	Yes, but limited	Yes; may practice for up to 120 days.[23]
Pennsylvania	No	Yes; must take jurisprudence exam	Yes; may give notice of practice to board and practice up to 6 months; 16-month extension possible; if "on assignment" in PA 14 days or less, notice is not necessary.

Table 1–2

(*continued*)

State or Province	Reciprocity?	CPQ Accepted?	Temporary Practice[1]
Prince Edward Island	CMRA	In process	Yes, special certificate available if registered in other jurisdictions and briefly visiting Prince Edward Island.
Quebec	CMRA	Yes	Yes, as expert witness or to consult for up to 1 year.
Saskatchewan	Yes, CMRA	No	Only as expert witness, no practice of psychology permitted.[24]
South Carolina	No	No	Temporary license available for up to 60 days/year, cannot be renewed.
South Dakota	No	No	Yes, as expert witness or for limited consultation.
Tennessee	No	Yes [Rule 1180-2-.03]	Yes; up to 12 days in one year; requires written request for authorization, must include reason for request, dates of activities, and name of supervising Tennessee psychologist; letter from supervising psychologist and proof of valid license of out-of-state psychologist also required; Board must approve application.[25]
Texas	Yes; must pass jurisprudence exam	No	Yes, for up to 30 days in a calendar year. Must submit a request in writing to the board at least 30 days prior to working in Texas.
Utah	No	No	Yes, as expert witness or to consult on a limited basis with a Utah professional.
Vermont	No	Yes	Yes, for up to 10 days or 80 hours in any 12-month period; must obtain a temporary Vermont license.

Table 1–2

(*continued*)

State or Province	Reciprocity?	CPQ Accepted?	Temporary Practice[1]
Virgin Islands	No	No	Yes, temporary license available for up to 30 days/year.
Virginia	No	Yes	No
Washington	No	No	Yes, but must obtain a temporary permit to testify as an expert witness or to consult on a limited basis; maximum of 90 days per year.
West Virginia	No	No	Yes, up to 10 days per calendar year.[26]
Wisconsin	Board has approved, awaiting legislative approval. Must pass oral interview and jurisprudence exam	Yes; must pass jurisprudence exam and interview	Yes, may practice up to 20 working days without notifying the board; may practice up to 40 additional working days with board notification.
Wyoming	No	Yes	No[27]

All information obtained from the Association of State and Provincial Psychology Boards (*www.asppb.org*) unless otherwise indicated.

[1] Virtually all jurisdictions specify that the psychologist must have a valid license from a state or province that has requirements for licensing that are at least as stringent as are those of the jurisdiction in which the psychologist wishes to temporarily practice.

[2] Confirmed by personal communication with the Alabama Board, July 21, 2004. A psychologist may testify without an Alabama license, but may not conduct an evaluation within the state without an Alabama license.

[3] Confirmed by personal communication with the Alaska Board, July 21, 2004. A psychologist may testify without an Alaska license, but "[a]ny evaluations must be conducted outside of Alaska."

[4] CMRA: Canadian Mutual Recognition Agreement.

[5] Personal communication with the Arkansas Board, July 21, 2004. See Board Rules § 510-9-.03.

[6] Bylaws, British Columbia Board.

[7] Personal communication from the Colorado Board, July 21, 2004.

[8] Personal communication with the Florida Board, July 21, 2004. See § 490.014(2)(e) Florida statutes.

[9] Georgia Code Chapter 43-39.7.

[10] Confirmed by personal communication from the Illinois Board, July 27, 2004.

[11] Personal communication with Indiana Board, July 27, 2004.

[12] Iowa Chapter 240.8 (154(b). "Exemption to licensure. Psychologists residing outside the state of Iowa and intending to practice in Iowa under the provisions of Iowa Code section 154B.3(5) shall file a summary of intent to practice and provide verification of the license from the other jurisdiction. The summary shall be submitted to and approved by the board prior to practice in Iowa. The exemption shall be valid for 10 consecutive business days or not to exceed 15 business days in any 90-day period. The summary and supporting documentation shall be accompanied by a check or money order. . . ."

[13] R.S. 37-2365.D. "Any nonresident duly licensed or certified for independent practice as a psychologist in the state of his residence, and which state will permit residents of this State a like and similar privilege as provided herein may, **if associated with a psychologist who is a resident of the State of Louisiana and licensed under this Chapter,** practice as a psychologist or a period not to exceed thirty days in any calendar year to the same extent and manner as if licensed in this state." [emphasis added]

[14] Personal communication with the Maryland Board, July 21, 2004.

[15] Personal communication with the Massachusetts Board, Oct. 6, 2004.

[16] § 333.16171(h) of the Michigan Public Health Code.

[17] Personal communication with Mississippi Board, July 19, 2004.

[18] The Board is working on a mechanism to permit non-province-licensed psychologists to do evaluations. Until enacted, a psychologist could work under the supervision of a N.B. licensed psychologist. The psychologist must also tell the client, the court, and any other relevant individual or body that he/she is licensed in [jurisdiction] but is not licensed in New Brunswick, and the specific purpose for being in the Province. Prior notification of the Board of the purpose, dates, and location of the evaluation and testimony is requested. (Personal communications with New Brunswick Board, Nov. 1 and 4, 2004).

[19] "The Board considers expert testimony permissible as long as you are not doing treatment, your opinion is based on your knowledge and your role as an expert is for litigation purposes only. The Board would consider expressing to the Court any expert opinions about recommendations for treatment options to be conducted by someone else as practicing without a license." This policy became effective July 16, 2004. It appears that doing a child custody evaluation would exceed the level of permission granted, which is for testimony only.

[20] The psychologist must include a copy of the court order and other materials with a request sent to the New Mexico Board at least 30 days prior to the evaluation. There are also other conditions that must be met. See the New Mexico Administrative Code Section 16.22.3.8(G) at http://www.nmcpr.state.nm.us/nmac/cgi-bin/hse/homepagesearchengine.exe?url=http://www.nmcpr.state.nm.us/nmac/parts/title16/16.022.0003.htm; geturl;terms=psychology.

[21] Personal communication with the Newfoundland Board of Examiners in Psychology, Oct. 7, 2004.

[22] North Carolina Practice Act: § 90-270.4(a). "Nothing in this Article shall prevent the provision of expert testimony by psychologists who are otherwise exempted by this act." § 90-270.4(f). "Nothing in this Article is to be construed as prohibiting a psychologist who is not a resident of North Carolina who holds an earned doctoral, master's or specialist degree in psychology . . . and who is licensed or certified only in another jurisdiction, from engaging in the practice of psychology, including the provision of health services, in this State for up to five days in any calendar year. All such psychologists shall comply with supervision requirements established by the Board and shall notify the Board in writing of their intent to practice in North Carolina, prior to athe provision of any services in this state. . . ." § 970-270.5(f). A nonresident psychologist who is either licensed or certified by a similar Board in another jurisdiction . . . may be issued a temporary license by the Board for the practice of psychology in this State for a period not to exceed the aggregate of 30 days in any calendar year. . . ."

[23] "The Oregon Board of Psychologist Examiners may grant permits for up to 120 calendar days which expire no later than 6 months after issuance. OAR 858-010-0055 is the administrative rule regarding Limited Permits. . . . The visitors permit is for out-of-state psychologists that do not intend on seeking full licensure in Oregon, but are rather providing a service in Oregon for a time-specific period, then will return to their home state once services are completed. . . . The Board cautions out of state practitioners requesting a limited permit to

carefully revise abuse reporting laws in Oregon, [which] are different from most other jurisdictions." Requires completion of an "application for a limited permit to practice psychology in the state of Oregon," proof of licensure and good standing in one's home state, a specific description of the proposed work, payment of $100, and a notarized statement that one has read and understands Oregon laws related to the practice of psychology, and that one will abide by those laws while in Oregon.

[24] Personal communication with the Saskatchewan College of Psychologists, October 20, 2004.

[25] Tennessee rule 1180-2-.05(f).

[26] § 30-21-3, W. Virginia Statutes.

[27] Confirmed by personal correspondence with Wyoming Board, July 19, 2004.

© 2004 by Andrew W. Kane, Ph.D. Used with permission.

Virtually all jurisdictions permit a doctoral-level psychologist to testify in court. Many do not, however, permit that same psychologist to do an evaluation in that state without possessing a state license to practice psychology. Given the wide variation in rules and requirements, it is strongly recommended that a psychologist considering doing a child custody evaluation and/or testifying in any state in which he or she is not licensed check with the relevant licensing board and get the official word in writing.

§ 1.14   Expert's Attitude and Personality

Not every professional is capable of being an expert witness. The attorney needs to evaluate the following qualities in order to determine whether a potential expert would be appropriate for the attorney's case:

1.   Whether the expert has sufficient experience with child custody evaluations to clearly understand the process and the requirements of the law.

2.   If so, whether the expert is able to remain objective, thereby being able to convince a judge that he or she is testifying in the context of the best interests of the child, not as an advocate for either parent.

3.   Whether the expert is adequately comfortable with the court process. This includes a willingness to testify, a lack of defensiveness in general and especially during cross-examination, an ability to accept the fact that delays often occur during trials, and the ability to communicate clearly in his or her report and during testimony.

In this context, the attorney should assess whether the expert with whom he or she is consulting really wants to be involved with the case. The case may have sounded interesting to the expert initially, but the expert may have lost interest for a variety of reasons. The expert may also have relished the investigatory and consultation phases but be uncomfortable with or even fearful of the deposition and/or courtroom phase that follows. If this is the attorney's first consultation with the expert, the expert may not feel comfortable working with the attorney for some reason.[165]

---

[165] J. Cohn, *On the Practicalities of Being an Expert Witness*, 11 Am. J. Forensic Psychiatry 11 (1990) [hereinafter Cohn].

Regardless of the reason, if these or related problems exist, the expert will be far less helpful to a case than would be a neutral or positive expert. Attorneys who have reason to believe that any of these factors exist must discuss their concerns with the expert as soon as possible. When the expert's thoughts, feelings, or concerns cannot be adequately addressed, it is important to find a new expert if at all possible.

The editors of *Trial Diplomacy Journal* offer a number of suggestions regarding important attributes for an expert witness:

> The "character" and "demeanor" of the expert witness is absolutely vital and critical to your case. It is your duty and responsibility to choose the right expert for any given case. If you look for shortcuts, you will hurt your client's case. If you try to find an expert who will simply "hold your hand" as you proceed through the case, you will hurt the client's case. The following attributes are of critical importance in determining who your experts should be in any given case:

1. *Articulate*: Your expert must be able to articulate his or her points or opinions with clarity and in an easily understandable manner.

2. *Credible*: The expert must not only be truthful, but must be an individual perceived as truthful and honest by the trier of fact.

3. *Sincere*: A good expert is a sincere person.

4. *Authoritative:* Search for and utilize the services of an expert who is truly an authority in his or her given field. Watch out for someone who is a jack-of-all-trades. Also, beware of the expert who is more of a promoter and a "public relations expert" as opposed to a true expert.

5. *Correct:* Your expert must be correct in his or her opinions. . . .

6. *Uses Common Sense:* The expert's opinions and theories must make common sense to the judge and jury.

7. *A Solver*: When your expert is critical of the actions of the defendant, then your expert must have a reasonable and viable solution to the problem.

8. *Wise*: A good expert is a wise person.

9. *Strong on Cross-Examination:* A good expert is virtually invulnerable to problematic cross-examination.

10. *Teacher/Professor*: A good expert is a teacher or a classroom professor.[166]

§ 1.15   Work Product and Discovery

As was indicated with regard to the Federal Rules of Evidence, many states have adopted rules of civil procedure that mirror the Federal Rules of Civil Procedure. Federal Rule of Civil Procedure 26(b)(3) states that "in ordering discovery . . . the court shall protect against disclosure of the mental impressions, conclusions, opinions, or legal theories of an attorney or other representative of a party concerning the litigation." This does not, however, apply to expert witnesses. Attorneys are required by the Federal Rules

---

[166] John Romano & Rodney Romano, *How to Avoid the Traps of Expert Witnesses: The Seven Deadly Sins*, 16 Trial Dipl. J. at iv–viii (1993).

with respect to a witness who is retained or specially employed to provide expert testimony in the case . . . , [to provide] a written report prepared and signed by the witness. The report shall contain a complete statement of all opinions to be expressed and the basis and reasons therefor; the data or other information considered by the witness in forming the opinions; any exhibits to be used as a summary of or support for the opinions; the qualifications of the witness, including a list of all publications authored by the witness within the preceding ten years; the compensation to be paid for the study and testimony; and a listing of any other cases in which the witness has testified as an expert at trial or by deposition within the preceding four years.[167]

Expert witnesses, therefore, are primarily witnesses, and their knowledge is not given the protection afforded attorneys.[168] The only exception *may* be those notes produced by the expert who is generating hypotheses to be followed up through interviews, testing, or other procedures which *may* be considered to be "expert's work product" and accorded protection from discovery by some courts. It may also be possible for the retaining attorney to remove from the expert's file any documents that relate to the attorney's trial strategy or plan.[169] It is essential that the expert be aware of the requirements of the procedural rules in his or her jurisdiction, and adhere to them. It is also crucial that the expert draw conclusions regarding only those hypotheses that are supported by the accumulated data. Without an empirical basis supporting them, conclusions do not belong in a report or in testimony.[170]

> Almost the entire substantive basis for expert testimony should be documented in the evaluation, allowing the presenting attorney to use the expert's findings more clearly and effectively, the opposing attorney to prepare to challenge them, the judge to understand them, and the expert to communicate them.[171]

As indicated in **Chapter 2**'s discussion of "test integrity" (see **§ 2.25**), professional guidelines, ethical codes, and contracts with publishers all require psychologists to protect the contents of psychological tests they administer. It has been the experience of the authors of this text that courts have generally treated the test contents as "psychologist work product."

Federal Rule of Civil Procedure 26(b)(4)(B) allows another exception: the expert retained solely as a consultant to an attorney, not as a witness, *is not subject to discovery* unless there is "a showing of exceptional circumstances under which it is impracticable for the party seeking discovery to obtain facts or opinions on the same subject by other means." It should be noted, however, that an expert whose knowledge was not acquired in expectation of litigation or preparation for a trial does not have protection from discovery.[172] In general, if the expert's consultation addresses the "attorney's impressions,

---

[167] Fed. R. Civ. P. 26(a)(2)(B).

[168] Saks at 304–05.

[169] Blau 1998.

[170] Grisso 2003, at 18; Heilbrun 2001, at 241–44.

[171] Heilbrun et al. 2002, at 13.

[172] Psychiatric and Psychological Evidence, 2d ed. (1994, Supp. 2003) at 6–22.2.

conclusions, opinions, or legal research or theories, known as derivative matters," the consultant's work is considered part of the attorney's work product. Other matters have only qualified immunity from disclosure.[173]

Among the reasons for retaining an expert as a non-testifying consultant are that

1. Counsel is unclear regarding the merits of the case . . .
2. The case is of sufficient significance . . . that every available resource is considered
3. The case facts are complicated and the amount of evidence is considerable
4. Assistance is needed with trial preparation matters . . . and the pool of available experts with the requisite expertise . . . is limited
5. Assistance is needed with trial preparation matters but counsel does not wish to risk biasing his or her examining expert by engaging him in trial preparation related work.[174]

In addition, an attorney who needs to be educated regarding the technical aspects of a case may retain an expert for that limited purpose. The attorney can discuss the case fully with this expert, knowing that the attorney's work product is not discoverable from this individual. There is also an advantage when experts are sequestered during a trial. The expert who is to give testimony will be excluded from the courtroom, but the expert who is solely a consultant to the attorney will not be excluded and can therefore continue to advise the attorney regarding relevant matters.

An attorney may also retain an expert for the limited purpose of doing a partial evaluation, to ascertain the psychological status of the potential client. Such an evaluation might include an MMPI-2 and an interview at a minimum. It should not include any test that has a practice effect, especially an intelligence test that may be used in a child custody evaluation. On the basis of the partial evaluation, the attorney can decide whether he or she wishes to represent the client and/or whether to pursue sole or joint custody and/or primary or shared placement, and/or whether to have a complete custody evaluation. The inclusion of the MMPI-2 is particularly important, since its validity scales address the response style of the individual, including defensiveness, any attempt to make oneself look especially virtuous, and so forth. The psychologist who does a partial evaluation of only one party may not ethically recommend for or against that party's receiving custody of his or her child(ren). The evaluator may, however, indicate whether the results of the partial evaluation suggest that the party would or would not make an appropriate custodian, with the understanding that a complete child custody evaluation of both parents is necessary for a specific custody recommendation to be made.

Although the authors of this text do not recommend it, some attorneys will then choose to retain another, "clean," expert, and may discuss with this expert only those aspects of the case the attorney is willing to have shared through discovery—in other words, the most favorable aspects of the case. With this selective utilization of separate experts for separate tasks, the attorney maximizes the confidentiality of his or her work product while gaining maximum input on the technical aspects of the case. It must be noted, of course, that some jurisdictions may differ in their application of criteria regarding whether an expert's identity must be disclosed, whether an expert's work product is open to discovery, differences

---

[173] McHale at 3.

[174] Bisbing et al. at 526.

between consulting and testifying experts, and so forth. The attorney must be aware of any such differences and advise the expert of those differences as well.[175]

The attorney is also cautioned to ensure that the testifying expert is aware of any information that may come out in a deposition or trial, particularly on cross-examination, so that the expert is not taken by surprise. "If an issue is worth retaining an expert, allow and perhaps insist that all relevant procedures be performed in order to minimize efforts to discredit the expert."[176] And, finally, inform the expert about any viable arguments, so the expert can address them in his or her report and be prepared to address them in a deposition and in court.[177]

§ 1.16   Fees

Experts generally charge more for forensic evaluations than for regular evaluations because the former typically involve substantial numbers of telephone calls, significant stress, and a major disruption of the expert's professional practice.[178] This is particularly true when it comes to depositions and trials. The expert should be prepared to defend the higher fee for forensic matters, since many attorneys will, on cross-examination, attempt "to impugn the expert's impartiality."[179]

Experts customarily charge for time spent reviewing records, meeting with attorneys, traveling, and preparing reports. It is standard practice for the expert to bill in advance for time reserved for depositions, trials, and meetings, and to charge for the time reserved unless there is substantial notice of a cancellation or postponement.[180]

Retainers are generally expected, particularly by the more experienced experts. The retainer is normally based on an estimate of the amount of time required to complete the task requested by the attorney. In addition to ensuring payment, the retainer offers the advantage to both the expert and the attorney that it is clear the expert is being paid for his or her time and not for the content of the opinion rendered.[181]

Contingency fees are unethical. See § **2.29.** Contingency fees for experts who testify have also been found in some jurisdictions to violate public policy, and are "tactically foolish."[182] Further, Rule DR 7-109(c) of the American Bar Association Code of Professional Responsibility indicates that an attorney may not offer to compensate a witness "contingent upon the content of his testimony or the outcome of the case. . . ." Thus "ethical rules . . . do not allow arrangements for payment contingent on outcome."[183]

---

[175] Saks at 307.

[176] McHale at 62.

[177] *Id.* at 96.

[178] D. Schetky, *Ethical Issues in Forensic Child and Adolescent Psychiatry*, 31 J. Am. Acad. Child & Adolescent Psychiatry 403, 404 (1992) [hereinafter Schetky]; Heilbrun 2001, at 55.

[179] Heilbrun 2001, at 51.

[180] Schetsky at 404.

[181] *Id.*

[182] Psychiatric and Psychological Experts, 2d ed. (1994, Supp. 2002) at 6–12.1.

[183] Laird C. Kirkpatrick & Christopher B. Mueller, Evidence: Practice under the Rules 6.20 (Aspen Publishers 2003).

According to Elizabeth J. Cohen, an attorney in the ABA Center for Professional Responsibility, ethical rules in most states prohibit compensation of an expert witness on the basis of a contingency fee.[184] A sampling of rules or rulings by state bar associations supports the above statements. Rule 9.5 of the Colorado Bar Association indicates that "[c]ompensation of an expert witness may never be contingent upon the outcome or the content of the expert's testimony, or the court's acceptance of the witness as an expert witness." The commentary on the rule by the Interprofessional Committee of the CBA indicates that "[a]ny contingent witness fee naturally compromises the integrity of the testimony of that witness."[185] Eric T. Cooperstein of the Minnesota Office of Lawyers Professional Responsibility wrote that "[m]ost state ethics authorities . . . have come out strongly opposed to contingent payments to expert witnesses under both the Code and the Rules. In Pennsylvania, authorities noted that 'the purpose of [Rule 3.4(b)] is to assure that a court and jury will hear the honest conclusions of the expert unvarnished by the temptation to share in the recovery. [Citation omitted.] Other states, in rejecting contingent fee payments to expert witnesses, note additional problems with improper fee splitting, excessive fees, and loss of attorney control over negotiation and litigation strategy. . . .'"[186] Richard H. Underwood, Ethics Committee Chair, Kentucky Bar Association, wrote in an opinion dated November 1996, that "[a]ccording to a survey of state bar opinions, contingent fee agreements with consultants, consulting services, or litigation support services are improper if (1) the fee for the consultant comes out of the lawyer's contingent fee, or otherwise involves fee-splitting [Rule 5.4(a)] or if (2) they involve the payment of contingent fees for expert testimony. Expert witnesses may only be paid on an hourly or flat fee basis [Rule 3.4(b)]."[187] Thus, even if it were ethical for psychological experts to accept contingency fees, it would not be ethical for attorneys to pay such fees.

§ 1.17   Preparing the Expert

As a first order of business, the expert should be asked to make the attorney aware of everything the expert has published on the subject at issue, to ensure that there are no inconsistencies with the planned testimony. If any inconsistencies are found, they should be addressed during the direct examination, to prevent them from being used to discredit the expert during cross-examination.[188] If the expert is to be effective, he or she must be well prepared by the attorney:

1.   The expert should have access to all of the attorney's files, thus lessening the possibility that the expert might learn about some problem or data for the first time while

---

[184] Elizabeth J. Cohen, *Don't Take Experts from Strangers.* Originally published in the ABA Journal (2000), retrieved from http://expertpages.com/news/don't_take_experts.htm on July 8, 2004.

[185] Interprofessional Comm. Colo. Bar Ass'n, Expert Compensation and Expert Witness Fees, retrieved from www.cobar.org/group/display.cfm?GenID=1354 on July 9, 2004.

[186] Eric T. Cooperstein, Using Trial Consultants on a Contingent-Fee Basis, retrieved from www.courts.state.mn.us/lprb/fc00/fc032700.html on July 9, 2004.

[187] Richard H. Underwood, KBA E-394, retrieved from www.uky.edu/Law/Library/kba/kba394.htm on July 9, 2004.

[188] Dickson at 579.

on the stand. The expert's conclusions will also be more valid and reliable if based upon a full disclosure of all potentially relevant data. An expert who is denied full access to the attorney's file should consider refusing to be involved in a case, since the expert's credibility may suffer as a result.[189]

2. The attorney should advise the expert to be candid about the expert's findings, both positive and negative. This increases the expert's credibility and appearance of objectivity.

3. Experts should be aware that they must make all of their files accessible to the attorney(s) and that their statements in court must be consistent with the information in the files.

4. The attorney and the expert should review the expert's credentials and determine how to present them in court.

5. The attorney and the expert should discuss the data to be presented by the expert, concentrating on how to cover all the important points without overwhelming the listener.

6. The attorney should make certain that the expert understands that everything should be assumed to be discoverable, including any "personal notes" the expert may write. See §§ 1.15 and 2.26.

   The attorney should advise the expert whether to volunteer information that goes beyond the direct questions posed in a deposition or in court. Although the expert must give a full response to any questions asked, it is a judgment call as to whether to present information that exceeds the precise question asked. Do you want adverse counsel to know at the deposition how strong a case you have, so that settlement is more likely? Or do you want to save your strongest arguments for the courtroom?

   In considering litigation strategy, the attorney may want to select an expert who comes across as a strong advocate, or as a very gentle person with whom the jury can identify, or as a professorial type who is carefully teaching the judge and/or jury about the technical aspects of the case.[190]

   Make sure the expert understands exactly which aspects of the trial he or she is to particularly address—that is, areas the attorney plans to emphasize in his or her direct examination or areas that the opposing attorney is likely to address in cross-examination. In all cases, of course, the expert is ethically required to tell the truth and to present all the important data he or she possesses.[191]

7. The attorney should caution the expert to answer the questions succinctly, not exceeding the scope of the question in the expert's response. The expert should also be sure not to lose listeners through excessive use of technical terminology.

8. Experts should be prepared to discuss their fees and, if asked, to emphasize that they are being paid for professional services rather than for testimony. It should be noted that the expert is not asking to be paid fees in advance solely for fiscal reasons. Attorneys often attempt to imply under cross-examination that mental health experts are "bought" by the individual paying the fee. As a result, attorneys are at times reluctant to pay experts in advance for fear that it will appear the witness has been

---

[189] Bisbing et al. at 517; Joseph A. Davis, *Establishing a Successful Litigation Consulting Practice: What You Need to Know to Be a Credible Expert Witness, Part Two*, 6 Forensic Examiner 36, 37 (1997).

[190] Cohn at 12.

[191] *Id.* at 13.

bought. However, just the opposite is true: it is less likely that the witness will appear as a bought witness or hired gun if the fee is paid in advance, leaving the expert unencumbered in his or her testimony. In this way, the expert feels minimal pressure to provide testimony that will please the retaining attorney and minimal fear about receiving no fee. It is unethical for experts to work on a contingency basis because they must be accepted by the court as largely (if not entirely) objective and unbiased. Even if there is no contingency payment agreement, not paying the expert in advance for the work gives the appearance of a contingency arrangement, thereby reducing the impact of the expert's conclusions on the judge and/or jury.

At least one author suggests that experts charge a high enough flat fee for their "diagnostic and evaluative procedures" to permit them to make no additional charge for court time, on the basis that "charging by the hour for court testimony makes an almost disastrously negative impression on jurors."[192] The authors of this text, however, have never found that charging hourly fees for court time has been detrimental, particularly since the pretrial flat fee would have to be exceptionally high if it was intended to cover both preparation and a day or more of availability for court.

9. The attorney should prepare the expert regarding what to expect on cross-examination and in deposition. The cross-examination of an expert generally addresses five areas of testimony: lack of qualifications, bias, error in the observed or assumed facts, error in conclusion or opinion, and specific impeachments—that is, previous contradictory or inconsistent statements, writings, or general lack of credibility.[193] It is the cross-examining attorney's goal, in increasing order of difficulty, to "(1) obtain testimony favorable to your case; (2) damage the witness's credibility; (3) cause the witness to change his or her opinion; or (4) discredit the witness altogether."[194]

The attorney should remind the expert that the shortcomings of the mental health field may be used as a means of discrediting expert testimony. The expert should also be aware that because "well-recognized publications" or "learned treatises" may be used to discredit testimony, the expert should avoid lending credibility to them by accepting them as authoritative. Instead, the expert should state, "I accept that book as authoritative in the field with certain reservations," thereby permitting disagreement when necessary.[195] The expert may also ask the court to recess so that he or she can review the full context of a brief segment bracketed by opposing counsel. If confronted with an inconsistent excerpt from something the expert wrote in some publication, the expert may often be able to respond honestly that, in addition to its being an out-of-context segment, it is an out-of-date opinion—and the present testimony is based upon what the expert has learned since that publication.[196]

The expert should be reminded that opposing counsel may ask leading questions, use intimidating facial expressions and/or a hostile tone, sarcasm, or ridicule, attempt

---

[192] James L. Nicholson, *Expert Testimony for the Defense: Learning from Practical Experience*, 6 Forensic Examiner 20, 22 (1997).

[193] Medical Malpractice: Psychiatric Care at 452.

[194] Michael J. McHale et al., Expert Witnesses: Direct and Cross-Examination 3 (Supp. No. 2 1997).

[195] Medical Malpractice: Psychiatric Care at 455–56.

[196] Stanley Brodsky, Testifying in Court: Guidelines and Maxims for the Expert Witness 121 (1991) [hereinafter Brodsky].

to make the expert feel guilty of wrongdoing or incompetence, and/or phrase questions so that straightforward answers cannot be given. If any of these practices make the expert seem evasive, contrite, upset, or angry, the attorney may have succeeded in eroding the expert's credibility.[197] If the expert finds him- or herself under an *ad hominem* attack, it is recommended that the expert remember: "the *ad hominem* attack is typically not personal, remain calm and in control . . .; always remain consistent to your opinion, particularly when . . . books and respected treatises . . . have been quoted out of context . . .; [and that] the advantage is yours when an *ad hominem* attack is launched by the attorney."[198]

Finally, if the expert is subjected to an abusive deposition, the expert may be able to terminate the deposition on that basis, with a statement on the record as to the cause of the termination. The threat to have the expert cited for contempt can be addressed by the expert's willingness to tell the judge exactly why the deposition was abruptly ended. Experts are entitled to protect their private lives and to be treated with respect.

10. In his book *Medical Malpractice: Psychiatric Care*, Joseph Smith offers several specific suggestions regarding testimony-related behavior that an attorney should convey to the expert:

    a. Answer truthfully to the best of your knowledge ("I don't know" is perfectly acceptable)

    b. Keep responses simple, comprehensible to a lay jury

    c. Keep responses on point regarding the questions asked

    d. Reflect objectivity rather than mere subjective opinion in all responses

    e. Respond accordingly to questions requiring description; reserve interpretations and conclusions for later

    f. Do not respond immediately, but gather thoughts and weigh the answer

    g. Maintain awareness of the flow and implications of the questions

    h. Remain calm and answer directly and confidently.[199]

Practical and Procedural Tips

Attorneys should suggest that experts organize their notes in one or more tabulated binders, with an index to facilitate finding particular sections. This thorough preparation for court will suggest to the trier of fact that the expert prepared equally well for the evaluation. It will also suggest that the expert is interested in helping the court with its difficult job.[200] Attorneys should request experts to bring a good photocopy of their notes and anything they anticipate introducing into evidence or expect the other attorney(s) to introduce. Most courts will allow the introduction of a good photocopy rather than the original, thus allowing experts to keep their originals.[201]

---

[197] Dickson at 619.

[198] Joseph A. Davis, *Establishing a Successful Litigation Consulting Practice: What You Need to Know to Be a Credible Expert Witness, Part Two*, 6 Forensic Examiner 36, 37–38 (1997).

[199] Medical Malpractice: Psychiatric Care at 454.

[200] Martindale at 487–88.

[201] *Id.* at 487.

Experts should be reminded that they need to address the judge and/or jury when answering questions, particularly when long answers are given. It is easy for experts to forget this, and to face and address all their answers to the attorney asking the question.

Furthermore, experts should pay attention to what the judge and/or jury are doing. If it appears that the trier of fact is losing attention, the expert needs to stop talking, shorten the presentation, or make the presentation more interesting. If the judge is writing down the expert's salient points, it is important to notice when the judge stops writing and then stop talking, shorten the presentation, or find a way to make the presentation more interesting.[202]

Preparing the Expert for the Other Side

When preparing to depose the expert for the other side, the attorney needs to decide whether to (1) ask questions regarding all possibly relevant areas of inquiry, thereby educating the expert about the attorney's theory of the case and providing the expert an opportunity to prepare detailed responses for trial testimony, or (2) ask only those questions necessary to determine the conclusions already reached by the expert and the basis for those conclusions. Each approach has advantages and disadvantages, and the attorney should carefully consider his or her approach, in part in the context of "how much do I want the other side's expert (and the other attorney) to know about the issues I'll be presenting at trial?"

Familiarity with Legal Decisions and Terminology

In addition, the attorney should make certain that the expert is familiar with applicable case law and should, if necessary, provide the expert with copies of court decisions with which the expert must be familiar.[203]

Attorney Robert Strodel emphasizes the importance of ensuring that professionals have an adequate understanding of the legal meaning of words that have a different professional meaning. A specific example in which this is particularly important is with regard to causation. This term, he indicates, needs to be explained as being far less than the "scientific certainty" the professional normally utilizes—for example, the commonly accepted probability that a research result is due to chance of "less than 5 percent" or "less than 1 percent." Rather, the attorney wants to know about "reasonable medical certainty . . ., whether something 'could' or 'might' be caused by or result from a particular medical event." By discussing these concepts with the professional—whether the treating physician or psychologist, the expert retained by the attorney, or the other side's expert being deposed by the attorney—the result is very often much better than if the attorney simply assumes the professional understands the meaning of these terms.[204]

Furthermore, the attorney should be clear regarding the meaning of "reasonable degree of medical/professional/psychological/scientific" certainty in the relevant jurisdiction. There is no universally accepted standard for the degree of likelihood this entails.[205] Many,

---

[202] Cohn at 12.

[203] T. Blau, The Psychologist as Expert Witness 335 (1984).

[204] Robert C. Strodel, *Basics in Handling Treating and Expert Medical Witnesses*, 20 Trial Dipl. J. 157, 157–58 (1997) [hereinafter Strodel].

[205] Psychiatric and Psychological Evidence, 2d ed. (1994, Supp. 2003) at 9–9.1 to 9–10.

perhaps most, attorneys and courts consider it to be "more probably so than not so"—in other words, the 51st percentile. Many professionals consider it to be a higher level of certainty—for example, the 75th percentile, roughly corresponding with the usual meaning of "clear and convincing evidence." It is essential that the expert understands the meaning of the term in the relevant jurisdiction.[206]

An additional problem is that a phrase like "reasonable medical certainty" requires that the expert respond in good faith, rather than stating that a questionable statement is made to a reasonable degree of medical certainty because he or she wants the statement to be admitted. At the other end of the continuum, the expert who is excessively candid about the limits of a statement he or she has made may cause probative evidence to be excluded.[207]

Daubert Requirements

It is particularly important that the expert be aware of the requirements set down by the Supreme Court in *Daubert v. Merrell Dow Pharmaceuticals, Inc.*[208] Even if the state in which the case is being heard does not accept *Daubert, Joiner,* and/or *Kumho*, the principles in those cases are sound ones, and are effectively an outline for preparation for cross-examination. See § **1.2** for discussion of the relevant elements of those cases and of both the drafting committee and of the evidence law scholars who have commented on *Daubert* and its progeny.

It has been suggested that the expert who wishes to meet the *Daubert* requirements must (1) "use theoretically and psychometrically adequate data-gathering instruments"; (2) "draw conclusions using scientifically validated theoretical positions"; (3) "weigh and qualify testimony on the basis of the adequacy of theory and empirical research on the question being addressed"; and (4) "be prepared to defend the scientific status of your data-gathering methods during the process of qualification as an expert witness."[209]

The Standard of Practice

While some of the following may not apply in a given jurisdiction, psychologist H.D. Kirkpatrick indicates that there are 26 "minimum practice standards" that are now widely accepted in the field of child custody and visitation evaluations.[210] While Kirkpatrick's

---

[206] Strodel at 161; Jonas R. Rappeport, *Reasonable Medical Certainty*, 13 Bull. Am. Acad. Psychiatry & L. 5-15 (1985) ("[I]t is clear that reasonable medical certainty does not mean clear or positive certainty. It means whatever the court, lawyers, or [a] witness seems to want it to mean."); Bisbing et al. at 516 ("This is greater than a mere possibility and generally is viewed as 'more probable than not.'").

[207] Psychiatric and Psychological Evidence, 2d ed. (1994, Supp. 2003), at 9–11.

[208] 509 U.S. 579, 113 S. Ct. 2786 (1993).

[209] Frederick Rotgers & Deirdre Barrett, Daubert v. Merrell Dow *and Expert Testimony by Clinical Psychologists: Implications and Recommendations for Practice*, 27 Prof. Psychol.: Res. & Prac. 467, 471–72 (1996).

[210] H.D. Kirkpatrick, *A Floor, Not a Ceiling: Beyond Guidelines—An Argument for Minimum Standards of Practice in Conducting Child Custody and Visitations Evaluations*, 1 J. Child Custody 61–75, at 65–66 (2004).

complete list, together with the sources supporting his conclusions, is in **Chapter 3,** some comments are appropriate in the context of the present chapter:

3. The court is the evaluator's primary client.
    Comment: See **§ 1.3,** item 3, of "The Forensic Model," regarding the evaluator's being seen as an extension of the court, rather than having the court as the client.

4. The evaluator is either court-appointed or assigned by consent order.
    Comment: While this is desirable, litigants have a right to retain their own experts, and there is no ethical or legal prohibition on an expert's being retained by one of the litigants.[211]

5. The scope of the evaluation is anchored to specific referral questions.
    Comment: Ideally, the court will specify the questions to be addressed. In practice, many courts will issue only a general order indicating that the parents and children are to be evaluated. The evaluator must then use documents filed with the court, state law and case law, and an acceptable model for conducting the evaluation to determine what is to be done.

6. The evaluator obtains informed consent from all parties.
    Comment: Individuals who are ordered by the court to participate cannot strictly give "informed consent," since they are not free to refuse to participate. In this situation, one seeks assent rather than consent.[212]

12. The evaluator avoids multiple relationships, which can create role conflicts.
    Comment: Ideally, this can be strictly followed. In rural areas, however, it may be unavoidable.

13. The evaluator acknowledges any implicit or explicit limitations of psychological knowledge and techniques used in the evaluation.
    Comment: "Significant" belongs in front of "implicit or explicit," since potential limitations are substantial.

14. The evaluator avoids *ex parte* communication with counsel or the judge.
    Comment: Exception: mandatory reporting of child abuse, required in every state.

State Expert Testimony Standards

Identifying the standard(s) for expert testimony in various states is often difficult, because any list may become outdated the day it is published if a state legislature or the highest court in a state indicates that a different policy will henceforth be followed. According to Bernstein and Jackson,[213] while a number of states have adopted a standard other than "general acceptance," by the middle of 2003 only 27 states had adopted standards highly

---

[211] Otto et al.

[212] *See also* Heilbrun et al.: informed consent is not necessary if the evaluation is court-ordered (at 302), and it can be confusing if people are asked to give their informed consent and are later told that the report will go to the court regardless of the individual's consent or lack of consent (at 307).

[213] D.E. Bernstein & J.D. Jackson, The *Daubert* trilogy in the States, 44 Jurimetrics (2004, in press), accessed Apr. 6, 2004, Social Science Research Network Electronic Paper collection, http://ssrn.com/abstract=498786.

consistent with *Daubert*, and only nine states had adopted standards consistent with all three cases, *Daubert, Joiner,* and *Kumho:* Arkansas, Delaware, Louisiana, Massachusetts, Mississippi, Nebraska, Oklahoma, Texas, and Wyoming. For Louisiana, this is based upon two appellate court rulings; the Louisiana Supreme Court has not yet ruled on whether *Joiner* applies in that state. Six states have adopted *Daubert* and *Kumho* but not *Joiner:* Kentucky, Ohio, New Hampshire, North Carolina, Rhode Island, and South Dakota. Seven states have adopted *Daubert* but not all parts of *Joiner* or *Kumho:* Alaska, Connecticut, Montana, New Mexico, Oregon, Vermont, and West Virginia. Alabama has adopted *Daubert* solely for cases involving DNA evidence. Five other states (Colorado, Hawaii, Tennessee, Indiana, and Iowa) have adopted selected portions of *Daubert, Joiner,* and/or *Kumho,* but not the entirety of any of them. Maine has not adopted *Daubert* or its progeny, but its pre-revision version of Federal Rule of Evidence 702 parallels *Daubert.* States that reject both *Daubert* and *Frye* (general acceptance) but selectively use elements of one or both (or similar parallels with Federal Rule of Evidence 702 either before or after the 2000 revision) are Georgia, Idaho, Nevada, New Jersey, North Dakota, South Dakota, Utah, Virginia, and Wisconsin.

Attorney John Parry[214] offers a slightly different breakdown. He indicates that 13 states still essentially follow *Frye,* 20 states have adopted *Daubert,* 12 largely follow Federal Rule of Evidence 702 but have not adopted *Daubert,* and six states have unique rules for admissibility. Table 1 in Parry's article identifies the states in each category and indicates the cases and/or statutes that establish their rules for admissibility. Parry notes that, while many states have adopted either the criteria in *Daubert* or a rule equivalent to Federal Rule of Evidence 702, courts do not generally apply those requirements for reliability to testimony unless it is considered "scientific" or "highly specialized." Thus, a physician might testify regarding his or her patient based solely on training, experience, and knowledge of the patient.

§ 1.18 American Bar Association Center on Children and the Law: Child Custody Proceedings Reform

September 8 through 10, 2000, the American Bar Association Family Law Section and the Johnson Foundation co-sponsored an international conference at Wingspread Conference Center in Racine, Wisconsin, on "High-Conflict Custody Cases: Reforming the System for Children."

The purpose of the conference was to recognize that high-conflict custody cases cause serious harm to children. *High-conflict cases* were defined as those "marked by a lack of trust between the parents, a high level of anger and a willingness to engage in repetitive litigation."[215] The damage done by high-conflict custody cases is exacerbated by the fact that the parents must continue to deal with one another on some level until the child(ren) becomes a legal adult. The conference report identifies roles for judges, attorneys, and

---

[214] John W. Parry, *Expert Evidence and Testimony:* Daubert *versus* Frye, 28 Mental & Physical Disability L. Rep. 136–40.

[215] Wingspread Conference report, accessed at www.abanet.org/child/wingspread.html on July 9, 2004 [hereinafter, Wingspread Conference].

mental health professionals in reducing or preventing conflict in high-conflict cases. Mental health professionals are urged to ensure that courts and attorneys are aware of the ethical standards and rules of the professionals, to ensure that mental health professionals respect the boundaries between their roles as evaluators and the other roles a mental health professional could play, for example, as therapist, mediator, arbitrator, or parent coordinator.

Further, "child custody evaluations should be neutral and include evaluations of both parents and all children and be undertaken with the agreement of the parents and the children, if appropriate, or by court order." A "child custody evaluation" is defined as one that "is comparative and focuses on family relationships, parental capacities, and the needs of the children." The conference called for qualifications for child custody evaluators to be uniform throughout the United States. Evaluators "should distinguish among their clinical judgments, research-based opinions, and philosophical positions," should "summarize their data-gathering procedures, information sources and time spent and present all relevant information on limitations of the evaluation that result from unobtainable information, failure of a party to cooperate or the circumstances of particular interviews." It also calls for reports to "be written in plain English."

§ 1.19   American Law Institute's *Principles of the Law of Family Dissolution*

In 2002, the American Law Institute (ALI) published the 1,100-page text that resulted from a decade of discussion of family law, the *Principles of the Law of Family Dissolution: Analysis and Recommendations*.[216] Among the areas discussed are a revision of the "best interest of the child" standard," which the ALI workgroup considered to be too subjective; a proposal to replace the terms "custody" and "visitation" with "custodial responsibilities" and "decision-making responsibilities" with the intent of specifying the specific responsibilities of each parent; a requirement that the parents submit parenting plans to the court, to change the emphasis from "winning" to defining a continuing role for each parent in the child's life; and the assignment of custodial responsibility on the basis of the previous division of parenting and caretaking. This last, called the "approximation standard," is meant to increase the predictability of the outcome while permitting individualized solutions. When the parents can craft their own parenting plan for presentation to the court, that plan would generally be adopted by the court. If they cannot, the court would apportion time with the child on roughly the same basis as caretaking was apportioned prior to the separation, unless there was a good reason to use a different standard. Importantly, "caretaking" would include employment to support the child and other family members, doing financial planning for the family, and taking care of the family home. The goal is to reduce dependence on the conjectured best interests of the child and focus on the caretaking plan in place prior to the separation, including trying to ensure that both parents have a continuing role in raising a child.[217]

---

[216] Press Release, Michael Greenwald, American Law Institute Publishes *Principles of the Law of Family Dissolution* (May 15, 2002).

[217] Kathy T. Graham, How the ALI Child Custody Principles Help Eliminate Gender and Sexual Orientation Bias from Child Custody Determinations, accessed at www.law.duke.edu/journals/djglp/articles/gen8p323.htm on July 9, 2004.

The most controversial proposal in the text is in **Chapter 6,** in which "domestic part-nerships" are recognized whether consisting of two individuals of the same or opposite genders, and the role of such individuals as either "parents by estoppel" (having lived with the child for at least two years, seeing themselves as parents, and having provided care for the child) and "de facto parents" (who have resided with the child for at least six months prior to the filing for dissolution or who try to maintain a continuing relationship with the child). These changes would open the door to recognizing parenting by many individuals, including homosexual couples, grandparents, and others who are *in loco parentis.* The *Principles* clearly indicate that an individual's or child's gender, an individual's sexual ori-entation, race, religious practices, extramarital sexual conduct, and/or a parent's income may not be considered when crafting a parenting plan.[218] The degree to which these proposals will be accepted by various states is unknowable at this time, though Massachusetts and New Jersey have adopted the principle of "de facto parenting." To the degree that states adopt various of the ALI provisions, the nature of child custody evalua-tions, and the need for those evaluations, may change.[219] Domestic partner benefits, civil unions, and/or same-gender marriage have been approved in California, Hawaii, Maine, Massachusetts, New Jersey, and Vermont as of July 2004.[220]

§ 1.20   Evaluating the Expert's Training and Experience

Being a mental health professional does not make someone an expert on any particular topic.[221] The attorney must carefully review the individual's professional vita to identify what specific training and experience the individual has and any gaps in those areas:

1.   What training and experience does the expert have in evaluating children, and what ages of children is the expert qualified to evaluate?

2.   What training and experience does the expert have in family law matters? Does the expert understand the requirements of the statutes in custody or termination of parental rights matters? How many times has the expert testified in custody or ter-mination of parental rights cases? How many times in other family court or juvenile court matters? In other forensic matters?

3.   Has the expert been court appointed in the current type of case or any other cases? Is there anything else that might suggest that the expert either may be biased or is free from bias?

---

[218] *Id.*

[219] ALI Press Release dated May 12, 2002, accessed at www.ali.org/ali/pro051502.htm on July 9, 2004; Conference-Workshop on the American Law Institute's *Principles of the Law of Family Dissolution: Analysis and Recommendations*, a discussion for Judges and Practioners, Woodrow Wilson International Center for Scholars (May 20, 2003), accessed at wwics.si.edu/index.cfm? fuseaction-=events.print&event_id-39231&stoplayout=true on July 9, 2004.

[220] *N.J. Starts Issuing Domestic Partnerships to Same-Sex Couples*, Milwaukee J. Sentinel, July 11, 2004.

[221] Psychiatric and Psychological Evidence, 2d ed. (1994) at 8–2 to 8–8.

4. If alcohol or other drug abuse is a question the expert needs to address, what specific training and experience does the expert have in this area?

5. If any central individual has been in a psychiatric hospital or on a psychiatric ward, does the expert have specific training and experience relevant to drawing conclusions about that hospitalization?

6. If any central individual is retarded (developmentally disabled), does the expert have any specific training or experience in evaluating people who are retarded?

7. Is the expert to testify regarding medication? In general, nonphysicians should not testify about medication issues. Exceptions may be made under special circumstances for psychopharmacologists, nurses, or others with specialized knowledge. Psychologists can generally testify regarding treatment methods to supplement or supplant psychotropic medications—for example, behavior therapy, relaxation therapy, or biofeedback. Neuropsychologists and psychologists who primarily work in health care settings may have substantial knowledge regarding medication and its effects. Several psychologists who work for the Department of Defense are currently prescribing medication, and after appropriate training is completed some psychologists in New Mexico and Louisiana will be prescribing medication in the near future.

8. Does the expert have the training and experience to evaluate the presence and magnitude of any psychological disorders that a party is alleged to have currently or in the past? In general, this requires an expert who is a clinical psychologist or a psychiatrist, because other types of mental health professionals rarely have significant training or experience in diagnosis and treatment of serious disorders.

9. What evidence is there that the expert has undergone peer review and been found to be competent and/or meritorious? Competence may be assessed by certification as a diplomate in any specialty, by membership in a professional organization requiring more than the payment of dues, by status as a Fellow in an organization, and by membership on the regular or clinical faculty of any college, university, medical school, or professional school. Professional recognition may be measured, for example, by whether the expert has held elected office in any professional organizations, or has been appointed to an ethics committee or other specialized committee of such an organization.

10. Has the expert published articles in professional journals? Given invited addresses to professional organizations? Authored or coauthored any professional books?

§ 1.21   Expert Witness Liability and Immunity

Expert witnesses are generally protected from civil liability because testimony given in court is considered to be necessary in order for the court or court-like body to carry out its functions. The immunity generally exists whether the expert is appointed by the court or retained by one of the parties, but exceptions have been found. Courts have also generally found that no doctor-patient relationship is formed simply by virtue of the conducting of an evaluation. Two exceptions should be noted: First, the Supreme Court indicated that liability may be found if a state official commits perjury that infringes upon someone's constitutional rights.[222]

---

[222] Schever v. Rhodes, 416 U.S. 232 (1974).

Second, in *Howard v. Drapkin*[223] and *Susan A. v. County of Sonoma*,[224] California courts of appeal indicated that quasi-judicial immunity was based upon the expert's being retained as a neutral, independent party, and may not apply if the expert is retained by one side, even though the expert's actual testimony is protected by witness immunity and quasi-judicial or judicial immunity.[225] Other than these types of examples, a perjury prosecution is the only potentially viable legal remedy if an expert makes statements known to be untrue. However, in the words of the Illinois Supreme Court, "it is virtually impossible to prosecute an expert witness for perjury."[226] One result is that courts tend to be highly suspicious of what experts have to say.[227] See the case law summaries at the end of this chapter regarding rulings on the quasi-judicial immunity that most courts have afforded experts.

Psychologist Stuart Greenberg presented a detailed examination of the liability and immunity of the expert witness at the Annual Convention of the American Psychological Association on August 26, 2001.[228] According to Dr. Greenberg, courts consider two questions when determining whether to confer immunity on an expert: "to whom does the expert owe a legal duty," and "does the role or the activity of the expert confer immunity regardless of any legal duty that may exist?"

Experts potentially owe legal duties to the court, the retaining attorney, and third parties, with each involving a professional duty as well. The duty to the court involves the offering of testimony that is reliable, helpful, honest, and objective. The related professional (ethical) duty is to provide assistance to the finder of fact, and to perform that function in a way that is consistent with the highest standards of his or her profession.

The expert's duty to the retaining attorney includes providing services that are at or above the standard of practice while assisting the attorney in fulfilling his or her obligation to be a zealous advocate. The related professional (ethical) duty is to present information fairly and with sufficient foundation, and to resist any attempt to distort, misrepresent, or omit information that may be contrary to the position of the attorney.

Most courts have held that expert witnesses do not have a legal duty to third parties. In *Zamstein v. Marvasti*,[229] for example, a father sued a psychiatrist who withheld exculpatory evidence when the father was accused in the midst of a divorce proceeding of having sexually abused his children. The Connecticut Supreme Court ruled that, absent a special relationship between the expert and the father, there is no duty of care owed to the father. There is, however, a professional (ethical) duty of forensic psychologists to all parties in a case to present in a fair manner all evidence, findings, and conclusions. There also is a duty to behave in such a manner as to avoid diminishing or threatening the rights of any party.

---

[223] 271 Cal. Rptr. 893 (Ct. App. 1990).

[224] 3 Cal. Rptr. 2d 27 (Ct. App. 1991).

[225] Robert Weinstock & Thomas Garrick, *Is Liability Possible for Forensic Psychiatrists?*, 23 Bull. Am. Acad. Psychiatry & L. 183, 186–88 (1995).

[226] Sears v. Rutishauser, 466 N.E.2d 210, 212 (Ill. 1984).

[227] Saks at 300–01.

[228] Stuart Greenberg, Liability and Immunity of the Expert Witness, Symposium presented at the 109th Annual Convention of the American Psychological Association, San Francisco (Aug. 2001).

[229] 692 A.2d 781 (Conn. 1997).

Courts grant immunity to experts in order to ensure that the individual can freely express his or her information and opinions without fear of civil liability for statements made, or facing a potential civil lawsuit by an unhappy party. Immunity fosters candor, and the availability of expert witnesses facilitates the work of the trier of fact and increases judicial efficiency. The grant of immunity means that a civil suit against the expert would be dismissed even if the expert performed below the standard of care and harmed some person by so doing. Without such immunity, the expert could be sued and have to defend him- or herself, even though the expert could ultimately be vindicated at a trial. It is nearly always to the advantage of a retaining attorney to attempt to obtain a grant of immunity for his or her experts.

Immunity does not generally extend to protect the expert from criminal liability if he or she knowingly provides false testimony (perjury), commits criminal fraud (for example, by stating he or she has a license that is, in fact, nonexistent), or engages in a criminal conspiracy (for example, by agreeing to collude with someone to provide false testimony).

Courts, however, cannot grant immunity to an expert with regard to licensing board or ethics committee complaints. An expert who violates the licensing laws of his or her state can be charged with that violation in an administrative proceeding and, if found guilty, may receive anything from a reprimand to the revocation of his or her license. Although neither state nor national ethics committees can directly affect an individual's license to practice, they can revoke the expert's membership in the professional association and can discreetly publicize that fact through mailings to members. They may also notify the relevant state licensing board of their action, opening the possibility that the licensing board will initiate an action *sua sponte*. See the case digest for *Deatherage v. Examining Board of Psychology* in **§ 1.25.**

While it does not violate any ethics code or guidelines for custody evaluators to be retained by the attorney for one parent, it is generally preferable to be appointed by the court.[230] The expert may testify on the basis of examinations of one or more individuals (for example, members of a family in a child custody contest), or on abstract or hypothetical matters germane to a case without having conducted any examinations (for example, on the developmental needs of children at certain ages). The expert may assist one side in a case, or may be appointed by a court as a neutral expert to advise the court.

The latter role, that of a "treating expert," may also result from an appointment by a court or from being retained privately, and the expert may function either as a trial consultant or as a witness. The treating expert may not, however, function as an independent witness, because he or she owes a duty to the client as well as to the court and professional standards. The treating expert is ethically required to be primarily a fact witness, as discussed at length in **§ 2.7.**

It should also be noted that there is a difference between being "court ordered" and "court appointed." Being "court ordered" does not necessarily indicate that the evaluator has immunity for the evaluation. The court, for example, may order the couple to go to the father's psychologist for the evaluation. If appointed by the court, as the court's expert or the guardian *ad litem*'s expert, the psychologist will normally have judicial or quasi-judicial immunity for the evaluation.

---

[230] Otto, Buffington-Vollum, & Edens, 2003.

The expert who does not have a grant of immunity from the court opens him- or herself up to potential liability in several areas. One area is if an expert engages in activities that are not within the expert's role but that are not otherwise negligent. An example would be the expert who was retained to conduct an examination but who either performed psychotherapy instead of conducting the examination, or conducted the examination and then began a course of psychotherapy for one or more of the individuals examined. Another example is the expert who was appointed by the court to assist the court and/or both sides but who assists one side only.

A second area of potential liability is if the expert engages in activities that are both outside the expert's role and potentially negligent. Examples include committing fraud, perjury, or conspiracy, physically harming an individual while conducting an examination, violating confidentiality or privilege, or altering or destroying evidence (spoliation).

A third area of potential liability is if the expert engages in activities that are both within the expert's role and potentially negligent. Examples include misdiagnosing someone, misusing tests, failing to acquire important records, failing to conduct essential interviews, or accepting appointment without understanding the relevant legal theory and criteria.

In summary, experts face potential liability in some states when they provide services before litigation is filed, provide supportive services rather than acting as an expert witness, are retained by a party rather than appointed by the court, practice below the standard of care, do not stay within the role associated with their appointment, and/or accept a role that does not involve exercising judicial or quasi-judicial authority.

§ 1.22   Types of Bias

Noting that everyone is subject to bias in the manner in which information is processed, psychologist Arthur Williams describes several types of bias that the expert must avoid to the degree possible: (1) looking for and emphasizing information that supports the expert's position as opposed to information that does not; (2) giving excessive weight to initial information; (3) emphasizing things brought easily to mind, especially vivid or dramatic things; (4) claiming a relationship even though no objective data indicates that the relationship exists; and (5) concluding that the outcome of some event could have been identified in advance more easily than was actually possible.[231]

To this list, psychologists Randy Borum, Randy Otto, and Stephen Golding would add: (1) relying too heavily on people's memory rather than gathering sufficient objective data; (2) failing to judge the validity of the data from various sources and to weigh the more-valid data more heavily; (3) failing to consider base rates—that is, how prevalent a given characteristic is in a given population; (4) exhibiting overconfidence, leading to a failure to search sufficiently for disconfirming data; and (5) failing to consider the influence of regression to the mean (extreme outcomes are generally followed by less-extreme outcomes) and sampling bias (small samples—of people or behavior—may not be representative of the relevant population).[232]

---

[231] Arthur Williams, *Bias and Debiasing Techniques in Forensic Psychology*, 10 Am. J. Forensic Psychol. 19, 20–21 (1992) [hereinafter Williams].

[232] Randy Borum et al., *Improving Clinical Judgment and Decision Making in Forensic Assessment*, 21 J. Psychiatry & L. 35, 37–64 (1993).

Other experts have identified the following types of bias:

"Observer effects" refer to the fact that the thoughts, feelings, experiences, and expectations of people, including scientists, influence their perceptions and conclusions. This is why double-blind research is important in any area of science in which observer effects may bias the results—provided it is possible in the given research project. It is essential in research on medications but is often difficult or impossible in psychological research.[233]

"Anchoring bias" refers to research indicating that information received early in the diagnostic process is remembered better and is used more than information received later in the process. If the clinician begins the evaluation by getting information about the traumatic event and the individual's response to it, this may bias the whole evaluation.[234]

"Confirmation bias" refers to evaluators giving more weight to information that is consistent with their own beliefs. A clinician who believed that no one could go through a serious motor vehicle accident, or being a soldier in active combat, or some other major traumatic event without severe psychological consequences may selectively hear information confirming that bias, and disregard contrary information.[235]

"Overconfidence bias" results when the clinician feels certain of his or her conclusions and therefore assumes they are valid. Research, however, has found that confidence in and validity of conclusions are not correlated. Regardless of his or her level of confidence, the clinician must keep an open mind while examining all of the relevant data.[236]

"Attribution bias" involves "discounting contextual factors accounting for behavior and imputing it instead to a permanent characteristic of an individual."[237] For example, an individual may be aggressive in a situation in which he or she has been attacked, or passive in a situation in which he or she is fearful. In the other 99 percent of his or her life, however, neither is a common characteristic.

"Hindsight bias" occurs when people who are aware of how an incident turns out believe that that outcome was more likely than objective prediction would indicate. Because both experts and juries generally know how an incident turned out, their attempt to objectively judge foreseeability may be compromised.[238]

---

[233] D.M. Risinger, Michael J. Saks, W.C. Thompson, & R. Rosenthal, *The* Daubert/Kumho *Implications of Observer Effects in Forensic Science: Hidden Problems of Expectation and Suggestion*, 90 Cal. L. Rev. 1–56 (2002) [hereinafter Risinger et al.].

[234] M.L. Bowman, *Problems Inherent to the Diagnosis of Posttraumatic Stress Disorder*, *in* I.Z. Schulze & D.O. Brady eds., *Psychological Injuries at Trial* (820–49) American Bar Assn. (2003) [hereinafter Bowman].

[235] Bowman; Risinger et al.

[236] Bowman.

[237] M. Sageman, *Three Types of Skills for Effective Forensic Psychological Assessments*, 10 Assessment 321–28 (2003).

[238] Daniel W. Shuman, *Persistent Reexperiences in Psychiatry and Law*, *in* R.I. Simon ed., *Posttraumatic Stress Disorder in Litigation* (American Psychiatric Press 1995); T. Wayte, J. Samra, J.K. Robbennolt, L. Heuer, & W.J. Koch, Psychological Issues in Civil Law, *in* J.R.P. Ogloff ed., *Taking Psychology and Law into the Twenty-First Century* 323–69 (Kluwer/Plenum 2003).

While there is no unequivocal solution to these problems of possible bias, awareness is a significant part of the answer. The expert must be aware of these natural tendencies to bias the data, and guard against them. He or she might keep a log of hypotheses generated by various pieces of data, some leading toward one conclusion and some toward other conclusions. Together with a commitment to impartiality, this may or may not solve the problem, but it should at the least reduce the influences of these biases on the expert's conclusions.

Psychologist Stanley Brodsky concludes that biases like those described "constitute a far greater hazard to impartiality than the mythical bought witness. Their impact is gradual and beyond the immediate awareness of the expert. These influences are sufficiently powerful that they may be the single greatest threat to expert integrity."[239]

Psychologist Thomas Grisso agrees, noting that "the issue is not one of the 'hired gun.' Any well-meaning and reputable clinician can be seduced by collaborative relationships having a subtle and almost irresistible pull toward advocacy. Often this will be at the expense of the objective attitude for which clinicians must strive, as required by their professional ethical principles."[240]

To counter these biasing tendencies, it is recommended that experts use explicit decision rules (for example, the specific criteria for each disorder in DSM-IV, see **Chapter 17**) to make diagnoses, and that only the most valid data be used. One must also avoid making generalizations based on studies involving small numbers of subjects.[241] It is often vital to know the base rates in the population for the disorders or problems being addressed, because predictions for low base-rate disorders or events (for example, suicide) are very difficult to make.[242]

Furthermore, Williams suggests that the clinician identify potentially relevant diagnoses and then seek evidence for each one. The expert might also ask him- or herself how the data would be viewed if the expert were retained by opposing counsel in the case. Other possible explanations for the data should also be explored.[243]

Reliance on one's memory is a poor practice in most cases. Clinicians tend to "remember" symptoms that were not actually present but are consistent with their diagnosis. They also tend to forget symptoms that are not consistent with their diagnosis. To counter this problem, it is recommended that the expert list separately symptoms that were present and those that were not.[244]

The clinician must also know the "sensitivity" and the "specificity" of the tests used and diagnoses made, Williams indicates. Sensitivity is the ability of a test or a diagnostic process to identify those people who have a given condition. Specificity is the ability to avoid false positives—that is, identifying someone who does not have a given condition as having that condition.[245]

---

[239] Brodsky at 9.

[240] Grisso at 37.

[241] Williams at 21–22.

[242] *Id.* at 23.

[243] *Id.* at 22.

[244] *Id.*

[245] *Id.* at 23.

Quoting a study by Needell, psychiatrists Landy Sparr and James Boehnlein indicate that "inaccuracy and bias may assume three major forms: (1) experts who offer biased opinions, based on either calculated or unconscious prejudices; (2) physicians lacking in psychiatric sophistication who offer expert psychiatric testimony; or (3) fully qualified experts who, through inadvertence or laziness, perform examinations that do not serve as a professionally adequate basis for their conclusions."[246]

Needell also maintains that using unqualified experts may be more problematic in psychiatry because any physician can testify as a psychiatric expert; collateral impeachment of psychiatric witnesses is extremely difficult; indices of objective professional review are often inadequate; and psychiatry has no uniform standards that clearly demarcate a thorough clinical examination.[247]

With specific regard to custody evaluations, one may identify both theoretical and practical biases:

> Examples of theoretical bias include favoring a particular custody arrangement without research basis for the point of view, theoretical overreaching which ignores the family's social, economic and legal realities, lack of training in the dynamics of child sexual abuse and spouse abuse, [and] falling into countertransference traps. Practical biases include ignorance about the practical and legal consequences of the custody recommendations, failure to understand long-standing inequities between men and women in the court system, the assumption that both parents contribute equally to a custody dispute, and participating in dual relationships. Many of these pitfalls can be avoided if the custody evaluator takes care not to go beyond the data.[248]

§ 1.23   Non–Mental Health "Experts"

Attorneys sometimes rely on physicians without psychiatric training, on clergy, and on other trusted individuals as if those individuals were well-trained mental health professionals. With few exceptions, they are not. As a result, attorneys frequently receive inappropriate advice. Attorneys should ascertain what formal training and experience these individuals have and caution their clients against weighing advice from non–mental health experts more heavily than advice from mental health experts.

§ 1.24   Questions for Chapter 1

1. Does the expert have the credentials necessary for his or her profession? See §§ **1.6** through **1.10** and **1.20**.

---

[246] Landy Sparr & James Boehnlein, *Posttraumatic Stress Disorder in Tort Actions: Forensic Minefield*, 18 Bull. Am. Acad. Psychiatry & L. 283, 296 (1990) (citing J. Needell, *Psychiatric Expert Witness: Proposals for Change*, 6 Am. J.L. & Med. 425–47 (1980)).

[247] *Id.*

[248] M. Deed, *Court-Ordered Child Custody Evaluations: Helping or Victimizing Vulnerable Families*, 28 Psychotherapy 76, 80 (1991).

2. If the professional is a psychologist, is he or she listed or eligible to be listed in the *National Register of Health Service Providers in Psychology*? Has he or she qualified for a Certificate of Professional Qualification (CPQ) from the Association of State and Provincial Psychology Boards (ASPPB)? See § **1.6.**

3. If the professional is a social worker, does he or she have ACSW credentials? Is the expert a qualified clinical social worker or NASW diplomate? Listed in NOFSW *Register of Diplomates in Forensic Social Work*? See §§ **1.9** and **1.10.**

4. If a psychologist is testing children, does he or she have training in that area? Conversely, if a psychologist is testing adults, does he or she have the necessary training?

5. Has the expert reviewed all relevant materials?

6. Does the expert have experience in the area(s) about which he or she is testifying?

7. Has the expert shown bias? See § **1.22.**

8. How many times has the expert testified previously in similar matters? In other legal matters?

9. Has the expert ever been denied (or had suspended or revoked) licensure, accreditation, or membership in any professional organization? Ever received a formal reprimand?

10. Is the expert board certified in any relevant area? See § **1.10.**

11. Does the expert practice within the limits of his or her expertise? See §§ **1.5** through **1.9.**

12. If the expert is trained as a counseling psychologist, can he or she demonstrate competence in assessment techniques? See § **1.6.**

13. Was the expert straightforward in fee negotiations and open about fees if a question was raised? See § **1.16.**

§ 1.25   Case Digest

The source of information for many of the following cases is the *Mental and Physical Disability Law Reporter* (MPDLR), a publication of the American Bar Association. Complete information for any other sources appears in the relevant references below. The following are direct quotations from the identified source. Quotations from the *Mental and Physical Disability Law Reporter*: Excerpted from *Mental and Physical Disability Law Reporter*. Copyright © 1989–2004. American Bar Association. Reprinted by permission. Other than the introductions by the authors of this text, if no source is identified, it is a summary from the court ruling.

U.S. Supreme Court

Kumho Tire Co. v. Carmichael, 119 S. Ct. 1167 (1999). On March 23, 1999, the U.S. Supreme Court ruled that an individual may be considered an expert if the individual has any type of specialized knowledge or experience that may contribute to the factfinder's understanding of a case. See § **1.2** for a discussion of *Daubert, Joiner,* and *Kumho.*

General Electric Co. v. Joiner, No. 96-188 (U.S. Dec. 15, 1997). The U.S. Supreme Court held that "[a]buse of discretion—the standard ordinarily applicable to review of evidentiary rulings—is the proper standard by which to review a district court's decision to admit or exclude scientific evidence. . . . Daubert v. Merrell Dow Pharmaceuticals, Inc. . . . did not somehow alter this general rule. . . . Nothing in either *Daubert* or the Federal Rules of Evidence requires a district court to admit opinion evidence which is connected to existing data only by the *ipse dixit* ["because I said so"] of the expert. . . ." See § **1.2.**

Daubert v. Merrell Dow Pharmaceuticals, Inc., 509 U.S. 579, 113 S. Ct. 2786, 125 L. Ed. 2d 469 (1993). See § **1.2.**

Jaffe v. Redmond, 116 S. Ct. 1923 (1996). In the first case in which it recognized a psychotherapist-patient privilege, the U.S. Supreme Court greatly extended the psychotherapist-patient privilege by ruling that, under Federal Rule of Evidence 501, federal courts are prohibited from requiring disclosure of confidential discussions between a therapist and a patient, including notes on such discussions. The court indicated that disclosure is prohibited even when the trial court has determined that the evidentiary value of the information is greater than the privacy interest of the patient. The Court also extended the privilege to all licensed social workers. See the case law summary at the end of **Chapter 2** for excerpts from the Court's opinion.

Ninth Circuit

The Supreme Court remanded *Daubert* to the Ninth Circuit, which issued a ruling often labeled "*Daubert II.*" *Daubert v. Merrell Dow Pharmaceuticals, Inc.*, 43 F.3d 1311 (9th Cir. 1995). See § **1.2.**

Sixth Circuit

Crum v. Sullivan, 921 F.2d 642 (6th Cir. 1990). The Sixth Circuit held that psychologists are as capable as psychiatrists of assessing mental impairments in disability benefit cases. . . . Although psychologists are not medical doctors, their assessments of mental impairments should not be given less weight than a psychiatrist's. 15 *Mental & Physical Disability Law Reporter* 294 (1991).

Third Circuit

In re Centant Corp. Securities Litigation, 343 F.3d 658 (3d Cir. 2003), the appellate court ruled that the attorney work product privilege encompasses work done by a consultant to the attorney. Under Fed. R. Civ. P. 26(b)(3), the "mental processes of the attorney" are sheltered so that he may "analyze and prepare his client's case." The Rule "establishes two tiers of protection: first, work prepared in anticipation of litigation by an attorney or his agent is discoverable only upon a showing of need and hardship; second, 'core' or 'opinion' work product that encompasses the 'mental impressions, conclusions, opinions, or legal theories of an attorney or other representative of a party concerning the litigation' is 'generally afforded near absolute protection from discovery. . . .'" [Citation omitted.] "We . . . hold that the work product of Dr. McGraw is privileged and subject to only limited discovery. . . . In addition, Dr. McGraw's notes of these discussions may reflect the mental impressions, opinions, conclusions and legal theories of Ernst & Young's counsel. Discovery of this information goes to the core of the work product doctrine and, therefore, is discoverable only upon a showing of extraordinary circumstances. . . . Compelled disclosure of the substance of conversations between Wood, his counsel, and Dr. McGraw would require disclosure of communications protected by the work product doctrine. . . . As such, the communications are at the core of the work product doctrine and are only discoverable upon a showing of rare and exceptional circumstances. . . .

Hughes v. Long, 242 F.3d 121 (3d Cir. 2001). As part of an acrimonious child custody battle, Long, a licensed clinical social worker, was appointed to conduct an evaluation. While Long was court-appointed, she contracted privately with the parties, with each agreeing to pay 50 percent of the cost. Hughes, not liking the outcome, retained his own expert. Hughes alleged that Long, and two psychologists with whom she consulted, destroyed their raw data and manufactured new data that supported Long's recommendation. The court accepted Long's report in spite of the allegation, and awarded Hughes and his wife joint custody. Hughes appealed to the United States District Court for the Eastern District of Pennsylvania, alleging violations of his familial rights in violation of the Fourteenth Amendment and his civil rights under 42 U.S.C. § 1983 and 1985(3). He also alleged a number of state law violations. The appellees filed motions to dismiss. The District Court granted those motions under the Rooker-Feldman doctrine that a federal court does not have subject-matter jurisdiction to evaluate constitutional claims that are "inextricably intertwined" with a state court custody proceeding. It did not rule on the merits of appellees' motions to dismiss. The appellate court reversed the District Court regarding the Rooker-Feldman doctrine, and also refused to affirm the dismissal on the basis of an alternative argument that appellees are entitled to absolute prosecutorial immunity pursuant to *Ernst v. Child & Youth Servs.*, 108 F.3d 486 (3d Cir. 1997). The appellate court held that the trial record was not sufficiently developed regarding appellees' precise functions and participation in the proceedings. On remand, the District Court granted appellees' motions for summary judgment on the basis of their being entitled to absolute prosecutorial immunity. Alternatively, the court held that they were entitled to witness immunity. It also ruled that Long and the psychologist were immune to state law claims. Hughes appealed. The Third Circuit indicated that social workers and other child care workers may have absolute immunity for actions involving the initiation and prosecution of proceedings involving child custody or dependency. In the instant case, however, contrary to the District Court ruling, it is not prosecutorial immunity that is relevant. Instead, Long and the psychologist are entitled to judicial immunity on the basis of their acting under court appointment and having performed functions central to the court process. The District Court's grant of summary judgment was affirmed.

Federal District Courts

Akbarnia v. Deming, 845 F. Supp. 788 (D. Kan. 1994). A Kansas federal court held that psychologists were entitled to judicial immunity for performing court-ordered evaluations. . . . [T]he [trial] judge placed a child in the custody of the Department of Social and Rehabilitation Services. The parents sued the psychologists, alleging that they negligently recommended that the father have no contact with the child and contending that the psychologists were not immune from suit because they performed either a ministerial act or an informative discretionary act. The court awarded summary judgment to the psychologists based on *Cook v. City of Topeka*, 654 P.2d 953 (Sup. Ct. Kan. 1982) in which the state supreme court interpreted the Kansas Tort Claims Act . . . to mean that a "judicial function" is discretionary and not ministerial in nature and determined that immunity should be based on a job's substantive duties rather than on the title of the person claiming immunity. The federal court concluded that the psychologists, who exercised considerable discretion in performing the examinations, qualified for judicial function immunity. 18 *Mental & Physical Disability Law Reporter* 435–36 (1994).

Hulsey v. Stotts, Barclay, Pettus, Moore, Whipple, & Dugan, Inc., 155 F.R.D. 676 (N.D. Okla. 1994). An Oklahoma federal court determined that a man who participated in joint counseling with a former girlfriend did not waive patient-psychotherapist privilege with respect to these sessions or to individual sessions he underwent during the same course of treatment. Susan Hulsey sought to depose the psychotherapist who conducted the counseling, but questions arose as to whether her former boyfriend's presence in the joint sessions waived his confidentiality rights for those sessions or for the individual sessions. The court followed the reasoning of *Mrozinski v. Pogue*, 423 S.E.2d 405 (Ga. Ct. App. 1992) . . ., which declared, "The strongest public policy considerations militate against allowing a psychiatrist to encourage a person to participate in joint therapy, to obtain his trust and extract all his confidences and place him [in] the most vulnerable position, and then to abandon him on the trash heap of lost privilege." With respect to joint and individual counseling, "no division may be made as to where one therapy ends and another's begins," so each patient in joint counseling retains the right to prevent disclosure by another—including the joint counselee—of confidential communications related to diagnosis and treatment. 19 *Mental & Physical Disability Law Reporter* 83–84 (1994).

Miller v. Gentry (In re Miller), No. 93-4221-SAC (D. Kan. June 3, 1994). The U.S. District Court for the District of Kansas ruled that a woman may not discharge through bankruptcy the fees owed to the guardian ad litem appointed to represent her children or those owed to the psychologist appointed to evaluate the family. [The guardian ad litem and psychologist] "argued that her debts to each of them were non-dischargeable under 11 U.S.C. § 523(a)(5). . . ." After considering cases from the Second, Fifth, and Eighth Circuits, the 10th Circuit held "that the term 'support' as used in 523(a)(5) is entitled to a broad application." 9 F.3d at 981. The 10th Circuit concluded that court-ordered attorney's fees arising from post-divorce custody actions are deemed in the nature of support under 523(a)(5). . . . [T]he court is compelled to conclude that [the debts to the guardian ad litem and psychologist] are non-dischargeable under 523(a)(5). It appears clear that the fees charged . . . are in the nature of "support" under the 10th Circuit's interpretation of 523(a)(5).

Williams v. Rappeport, 699 F. Supp. 501 (D. Md. 1988). The Maryland federal district court found a court-appointed psychiatrist and psychologist entitled to absolute quasi-judicial immunity for their assistance in a child custody dispute.

States

Alabama

Mitchell v. Mitchell, 830 So. 2d 755 (Ala. Civ. App. 2002). The Alabama Court of Appeals reversed a trial court ruling that a psychologist who was not licensed in Alabama could not testify as an expert in a child visitation case. The appellate court indicated that the statute that defines the practice of psychology does not list testifying as a function of the practice of psychology. Therefore, while practicing psychology without a license is a crime in the state, the legislature did not intend to prevent psychologists licensed in another state from offering expert testimony. 27 *Mental & Physical Disability Law Reporter* 214–15 (2003).

Alaska

Lythgoe (Wellman) v. Guinn, 884 P.2d 1085 (Alaska 1994). The Alaska Supreme Court recognized quasi-judicial immunity for the first time in a case involving allegations of misconduct by a psychologist in a child custody case. With virtual uniformity, courts have granted absolute immunity to persons who perform functions analogous to those performed by Guinn [the psychologist]. . . . Guinn was appointed by the court to provide professional advice and expertise regarding the custody of Lythgoe's child. Lythgoe's allegations stem directly from Guinn's role in the custody proceeding. In acting pursuant to her court-appointment, Guinn served as an "arm of the court" and performed a function "integral to the judicial process." . . . Thus, we conclude that the court did not err in granting Guinn absolute quasi-judicial immunity. . . . In *Lavit* [*v. Superior Court*, 839 P.2d 1141 (Ariz. 1992)], the court identified several grounds supporting absolute judicial immunity:

> (1) the need to save judicial time in defending suits; (2) the need for finality in the resolution of disputes; (3) to prevent deterring competent persons from taking office; (4) to prevent the threat of lawsuit from discouraging independent action; and (5) the existence of adequate procedural safeguards such as change of venue and appellate review. . . .

In extending absolute judicial immunity to quasi-judicial officers such as court-appointed psychotherapists, most courts have relied in particular on the fear that "[e]xposure to liability could deter their acceptance of court appointments or color their recommendations." *Id*. Similarly, courts have consistently recognized that the threat of civil liability may affect the manner in which such court-appointed experts perform their jobs. . . . Certainly it is undeniable that a psychotherapist appointed by the court to conduct a child custody investigation exercises discretionary judgment in rendering an evaluation. . . . The *sine qua non* of the exercise of such discretion is the freedom to act in an objective and independent manner. Thus, the extension of absolute judicial immunity to quasi-judicial officers such as court-appointed psychotherapists is a proper recognition of the "possibility that a professional who is delegated judicial duties to aid the court will become a 'lightning rod for harassing litigation.'" *Lavit*, 839 P.2d at 1144. . . . The U.S. Supreme Court has noted an additional rationale underlying the distinction between absolute judicial immunity and qualified executive or public official immunity. In *Forrester v. White*, 484 U.S. 219, 226 (1988), it recognized that

> [T]he nature of the adjudicative function requires a judge frequently to disappoint some of the most intense and ungovernable desires that people can have. . . . [T]his is the principal characteristic that adjudication has in common with legislation and with criminal prosecution, which are the other two areas in which absolute immunity has most generously been provided.

The concerns expressed in *Forrester* certainly apply in the emotional and often inflammatory divorce and child custody context.

Arizona

Logerquist v. McVey, 1 P.3d 113 (Ariz. 2000). The Arizona Supreme Court rejected the *Daubert* standard due to concern about judicial power, and ruled that Arizona would not reject the *Frye* standard. The concern of the court was that the U.S. Supreme Court had, in *Kumho v. Carmichael* (526 U.S. 19 (1999)), extended the gatekeeping function of the trial court judge to all expert testimony, not just scientific testimony. This, the court feared, would permit the trial judge to make decisions that were the proper province of the jury, for example, whether an expert witness was credible or whether the expert's credentials were adequate. The Arizona constitution, the court indicated, was not consistent with the *Kumho* extension of *Daubert*. The court indicated that judges should remain responsible for determining that testimony is relevant, but that the reliability of the expert is a matter for the jury to decide.

Lavit v. Superior Court, 839 P.2d 1141 (Ariz. Ct. App. 1992). The Arizona Court of Appeals has indicated that a psychologist retained by a divorcing couple to facilitate the resolution of child custody arrangements is entitled to absolute immunity from a suit based on his participation in the divorce case. The court said that a nonjudicial professional such as the psychologist may have quasi-judicial immunity when fulfilling quasi-judicial functions. This is in accord with the public policy of ensuring that professionals can participate in court proceedings without fearing liability. The court noted that other courts have similarly granted absolute immunity to psychologists who conduct custody evaluations as court-appointed experts. The psychologist fulfilled his role of helping the court decide upon the custody arrangement that would best serve the interests of the child.

California

Laborde v. Aronson, 92 Cal. App. 4th 459, 112 Cal. Rptr. 2d 119 (Sept. 21, 2001). A man sued a psychologist, Dr. Aronson, who had been retained to do a custody evaluation by the attorneys for the parties, and who was later appointed by the court as its expert. When the father learned the result of the evaluation, he threatened to sue the psychologist if she testified in the case, and refused to pay her bill. He also filed a complaint accusing the psychologist and his wife's attorney of conspiring against him. The psychologist and the attorney moved for and were granted summary judgment, with Dr. Aronson's based upon the litigation privilege. Both the psychologist and the attorney were awarded expenses on the bases that the action was frivolous, had no merit, and was filed in bad faith. The father appealed. The appellate court affirmed. Although Dr. Aronson was initially retained by the parties, she was court-appointed prior to her testimony, and her report was accepted *nunc pro tunc* [after the fact, retroactively] by the court at the trial. Citing *Gootee v. Lightner*, 224 Cal. App. 3d 587 (1990), the appellate court indicated that the suit against Dr. Aronson was barred by absolute privilege. The $24,000 award to Dr. Aronson was also affirmed.

Howard v. Drapkin, 222 Cal. App. 3d 843, 271 Cal. Rptr. 893 (1990). The court held that absolute quasi-judicial immunity is extended to neutral third parties for their conduct in performing dispute resolution services in connection with the judicial process, if the services include the making of binding decisions; the making of findings and recommendations to a court; or arbitration, mediation, conciliation, or evaluation. In this case, the court found that the psychologist defendant was acting in the capacity of a neutral third party engaged in efforts to effect a resolution of a family dispute and therefore was entitled to quasi-judicial immunity. Timothy B. Walker, "Family Law in the 50 States: An Overview." Paper presented at the 10th Annual Divorce Law Update, Vail, Colo. (Jan. 1992).

Gootee v. Lightner, 224 Cal. App. 3d 587 (Cal. Ct. App. Sept. 24, 1990). Alleging that an independent expert was negligent in the administration and interpretation of psychological tests, and that the expert had destroyed tapes of the assessment sessions, a custodial father sued the expert. The suit was dismissed on the basis that courtroom testimony enjoys a testimonial privilege and, the court indicated, activities preparatory to that testimony are also therefore covered. Expert witnesses must be certain that their testimony will not result in costly litigation, in order to ensure that the witness is completely open and honest regarding his findings and opinions.

Roe v. Superior Court, 280 Cal. Rptr. 380 (Ct. App. 1991). A husband and wife were involved in a custody battle, and the wife told her therapist she believed her husband was abusing their child. The therapist reported the incident, as required under California's Child Abuse and Neglect Reporting Act. A court found no evidence of abuse, and the husband sued his wife for defamation, malicious prosecution, negligent and intentional infliction of emotional distress, negligence, interference with visitation rights, and conspiracy. He attempted to depose his wife's therapist, but the therapist refused, citing the psychotherapist-patient privilege. A trial court granted the husband's motion to compel discovery, finding the therapist already had disclosed the information under the Child Abuse Act, and the wife appealed. The appeals court ruled that the husband's need for disclosure outweighed the wife's privacy rights. Moreover, the information already had been disclosed to several parties, including at least two social workers. The court felt it necessary to give the husband an opportunity to show that his wife supplied the information in the therapist's report. In addition, the state needs to ensure that child abuse cases are reported. The appeals court noted, however, that the legislature never intended to provide immunity to patients who recklessly cause their therapists to file false child abuse reports. 15 *Mental & Physical Disability Law Reporter* 393 (1991).

Colorado

Ryder v. Mitchell, 54 P.3d 885 (Colo. Sept. 16, 2002). A mother sued her children's therapist, Gloria Ryder, for breach of fiduciary duty and negligence after Ryder formed an opinion that the mother was engaging in behavior designed to alienate her ex-husband from the children, with Ryder sending the ex-husband a copy of a letter to that effect. The trial court dismissed all of Mitchell's claims, indicating that the children were not parties to the action, and that the law created no duty from Ryder to Mitchell. The court of appeals reversed, holding that Ryder did owe Mitchell a duty of due care. The supreme court reversed, affirming the trial court's order of summary judgment and dismissing all claims. In examining the legal question of whether a duty exists, the court looks to the risk involved, the foreseeability and likelihood of injury as weighed against the social utility of the defendant's conduct, the magnitude of the burden of guarding against the harm and the consequences of placing the burden on the defendant. On balance, the court concludes that the duty the therapist owes the children themselves is primary and may, under certain circumstances, require disclosure to the parents or other involved parties. . . . [T]he possibility of liability to the children for breach serves as an adequate safeguard against negligent treatment by the therapist.

Dalton v. Miller, 984 P.2d 666 (Colo. Ct. App. Apr. 29, 1999). Patricia Dalton sued her insurance company for failure to renew her coverage, and alleged various emotional and other damages. The insurance company asked the court to order a psychiatric evaluation. The psychiatrist, Dr. Miller, evaluated Ms. Dalton, issued a report, and testified in a video-taped deposition. Ms. Dalton settled with the insurance company, but then sued Dr. Miller for "alleged discrepancies between his written report to the insurer and his videotaped deposition testimony," and "alleged numerous claims for relief, including: misrepresentation and deceit; intent to cause loss of improved chances for recovery and increased risk of harm . . . ; invasion of privacy by intrusion upon seclusion; abuse of process; intentional infliction of emotional distress and outrageous conduct; and civil conspiracy." The trial court granted the defendant's motion to dismiss and for summary judgment. Ms. Dalton appealed. The appeals court noted that, in *Awai v. Kotin*, a court-appointed psychologist was granted "absolute immunity because [his] activities were intimately related to the judicial process of finding facts and rendering decisions" and he was appointed by the trial court. "Such an appointee acts as an officer of the court." [fn218] Most courts recognize quasi-judicial immunity only when an examiner is appointed by and reports directly to the court, the appeals court indicated. An examiner retained by one of the parties does not normally receive such immunity. Therefore, "we hold that professionals conducting an independent medical or psychiatric examination pursuant to a [request of a party] are not entitled to absolute quasi-judicial immunity for their activities." The defendant also contended that he was entitled to witness immunity for his actions in this case. The United States Supreme Court has held that trial witnesses are entitled to absolute immunity from subsequent civil liability for their trial testimony. *Briscoe v. LaHue*, 460 U.S. 325, 103 S. Ct. 1108, 75 L.Ed.2d 96 (1983). . . . Witness immunity has been held to extend to statements and opinions offered in deposition testimony and advisory reports prepared in the course of litigation [by both federal and state courts]. . . . We find the rationale of these cases persuasive. If shadowed by the threat of liability, a witness might testify in a manner that would prevent a potential lawsuit, but would deprive the court of the benefit of candid, unbiased testimony. . . . [W]itness reliability is otherwise ensured by oath, cross-examination, and the threat of criminal prosecution for perjury. . . . Thus, we hold that defendant is entitled to absolute immunity from civil liability for any statements he made during the course of his videotaped trial preservation deposition testimony that would have been played at trial in lieu of actual testimony from the defendant. In addition, he is entitled to immunity for the contents of the report he prepared for counsel for insurer, which detailed his conclusions from his examination of plaintiff. The appellate court indicated that it did not have sufficient information from the record regarding whether the psychiatrist may be liable for harm the plaintiff incurred during the psychiatric evaluation, on the basis that he violated a duty to the plaintiff. That question was remanded to the trial court for further proceedings.

Awai v. Kotin, 872 P.2d 1332 (Colo. Ct. App. 1993). The Colorado Court of Appeals indicated that court-appointed psychologists who provide treatment do not have the quasi-judicial immunity given to court-appointed psychologists who do evaluations and make recommendations. According to the court:

> The same concerns that support judicial immunity justify the grant of absolute immunity to persons other than judges when conducting activities judicial in nature. . . . Court-appointed therapists have been afforded immunity for their evaluations and recommendations. . . .

And, because the claim against a supervisor is dependent upon the claim against the therapist, immunity has also been extended to the supervisor of a therapist making evaluations and recommendations. . . .

In each of these cases, the therapist's functions were intimately related and essential to the judicial process of finding facts and rendering decisions. . . . However, treatment, unlike reports or evaluations and recommendations, is not intimately related and essential to the judicial decision-making process. Rather, it is a separate remedial function in which full disclosure may be contrary to the best interests of the patient and improper. . . . The need for absolute immunity for treatment is therefore not as compelling as the need for immunity for evaluations and recommendations.

Connecticut

Cabrera v. Cabrera, 580 A.2d 1227 (Conn. App. Ct. 1990). When marital problems developed, the wife agreed to her husband's suggestion of joint marriage counseling (and she later saw the psychologist individually for therapy). The wife filed for divorce, and the trial court dissolved the marriage, awarded the wife custody of the couple's minor children, and made certain financial awards. The husband appealed. The appeals court held that the trial court properly granted the wife's motion to exclude the psychologist's testimony. Because the wife's communications were privileged and she had not waived the privilege . . . the psychologist could not testify about her sessions with the wife or her sessions with both the husband and the wife. The court rejected the husband's argument that his ex-wife's disclosures in her counseling sessions before filing for divorce should have been admitted at trial. The husband claimed that any disclosures made during those sessions were marital counseling rather than psychological counseling, and not privileged. "It would make no sense . . . to divide visits to a psychologist in a case such as this into marital counseling versus psychological counseling and assign privileged status to the latter but not the former." 15 *Mental & Physical Disability Law Reporter* 173–74 (1990).

Florida

Attorney ad Litem for D.K. v. Parents of D.K., 780 So. 2d 301 (Fla. Dist. Ct. App. 2001). A psychologist appointed by the court to evaluate a family in a custody action requested D.K.'s medical and mental health records. Through the child's attorney ad litem, D.K. asserted the psychotherapist-patient privilege. The trial court denied the motion for a protective order, indicating that D.K.'s parents had waived such privilege. The District Court quashed the trial court's order, indicating that the statutory definition of "patient" includes "children." The child's privilege, therefore, was protected by statute. The court indicated that there was no Florida case law addressing who may waive privilege for a child. The weight of decisions in other jurisdictions is that, when the child's mental status may be relevant to litigation involving the parents, the parents are not permitted to either assert or waive the child's privilege. In the instant case the child, age 17, was considered old enough to assert the privilege on the child's own behalf.

Oswald v. Diamond, 576 So. 2d 909 (Fla. Dist. Ct. App. 1991). A Florida appeals court ruled in a child custody case that the psychotherapist-patient privilege protects from discovery the records a physician made to diagnose or treat a mother's mental or emotional condition. The trial court erred in permitting discovery of all of the mother's medical records. While Florida does not recognize a general doctor-patient privilege, it does protect communications or records made for the purpose of diagnosis or treatment of mental or emotional conditions. Although psychologists are not medical doctors, their assessments of mental impairments should not be given less weight than a psychiatrist's. 15 *Mental & Physical Disability Law Reporter* 393 (1991).

Illinois

In re Marriage of Markey, 586 N.E.2d 350 (Ill. App. Ct. 1991). Despite the objection of a mother who had joint custody, an Illinois appeals court held that a father's written consent was sufficient to permit the disclosure of a clinical psychologist's confidential records regarding the child. The mother argued that she had equal rights to make decisions regarding the child, and invoked the confidential records and communications privilege on the child's behalf. . . . The trial court erred in finding that the confidentiality statute required both parents' consent, where the statute used the word "parent," not "parents," in outlining who can give consent. Moreover, allowing the court to examine all mental health reports involving a child in a custody proceeding was consistent with the legislative intent to protect the child's best interests, and allowing one parent to block this exam would frustrate this goal. 16 *Mental & Physical Disability Law Reporter* 429 (1992).

Renzi v. Morrison, 618 N.E.2d 794 (Ill. App. Ct. 1993). An Illinois appeals court held that a psychiatrist who voluntarily disclosed confidential information about a patient while testifying for the patient's spouse during a child custody hearing was liable for damages. Dr. Helen Morrison evaluated Diane Renzi, administered psychological tests, and gave her marriage counseling. . . . Renzi informed Morrison that she intended to exercise her right to keep her communications with Morrison privileged. . . . At the custody hearing, the court overruled Renzi's objection and allowed Morrison to testify about Renzi's communications, Renzi's psychological test results, and Morrison's opinion of Renzi's emotional health. Based on Morrison's testimony, the court awarded temporary custody of Renzi's child to her husband. Renzi brought suit for damages, claiming that Morrison's testimony violated Renzi's right to keep their communications privileged. . . . The court agreed, noting that [the statute] allows a therapist to reveal a patient's confidences only after a court examines the testimony in camera and determines it is relevant, admissible, and more important to the interest of justice than a patient's right to confidentiality. Furthermore, the party seeking to disclose confidential information must establish a compelling need for its production. 18 *Mental & Physical Disability Law Reporter* 74–75 (1994).

Iowa

In re Marriage of Peck, 2001 WL 194918 (Iowa Ct. App. Feb. 28, 2001). A former wife sought to modify the divorce decree that awarded her ex-husband physical placement of their two daughters. She called her ex-husband to testify at the trial and introduced mental health records of his that she had obtained from his previous wife with neither his knowledge or consent. On the basis of information from those records, the trial court transferred placement of the children to the wife. The appeals court ruled that his mental health records should not have been admitted. He had given the records to his previous wife for safekeeping, trusting that she would maintain their confidentiality. He testified about the information in the records only after they had erroneously been admitted. Neither factor constitutes a waiver of privilege, and the ex-husband therefore may assert the psychotherapist-patient privilege.

Louisiana

Louisiana v. Atterberry, 664 So. 2d 1216 (La. Ct. App. 1995). A Louisiana appeals court affirmed a preliminary injunction prohibiting a licensed professional counselor from administering certain psychological tests. Boyd Atterberry held a master's degree in clinical psychology. For the purpose of counseling mental disorders such as autism, attention deficit disorder, and mental retardation, Atterberry used various tests, including: the Wechsler Intelligence Scale for Children-Revised; the Bender Visual Motor Gestalt Test; the Woodcock-Johnson Psycho-Educational Battery Test of Achievement; the Gordon Diagnostic System; the Achenbach Child Behavior Checklist; Incomplete Sentences Blank; the Kinetic Family Drawing Test; and the Draw-A-Person Test. The Department of Health and Human Services' Louisiana State Board of Examiners advised Atterberry that he was engaged in the practice of psychology without a license and that he should cease all independent activities. When Atterberry refused, the board filed suit to enjoin him from using these various diagnostic tests. A trial court issued a preliminary injunction, and Atterberry appealed. The appeals court affirmed. . . . Under Louisiana law, a licensed professional counselor could engage in mental health counseling, consulting, referral and research activities, and appraisals, which included the use or administration of certain kinds of tests for certain purposes. . . . Here, Atterberry administered and interpreted tests for the purpose of treating a mental and emotional disorder, a personality disorder, and a neurological impairment. This violated La. Rev. Stat. Ann. 37:2352(5), which prohibits someone who is only licensed as a professional counselor from engaging in the practice of psychology. 20 *Mental & Physical Disability Law Reporter* 120 (1996).

Maine

Seider v. Board of Examiners of Psychologists, 762 A.2d 551 (Me 2000). The Maine Board of Examiners of Psychologists was justified in sanctioning a psychologist who released records without the patient's consent or a court order. A mother consulted a clinical psychologist, Dr. Seider, regarding the possibility her son was being sexually abused. After the mother terminated the relationship with Dr. Seider, Dr. Seider began a professional relationship with the mother's ex-husband and the couple's daughter. Dr. Seider disclosed that the son had been and was still being sexually abused, and disclosed her concerns about the daughter's risk of abuse. A custody dispute began. Dr. Seider also contacted the children's pediatrician to discuss the possibility the daughter was being sexually abused. She did not, however, immediately report her beliefs about the sexual abuse to the state Department of Human Services (DHS), as required by law. When DHS was made aware and investigated the allegations, Dr. Seider furnished all family treatment records and a 51-page report that contained a great deal of confidential information. The mother complained to the Board of Examiners of Psychologists. The Board found 12 violations of the 1992 American Psychological Association's Ethical Principles of Psychologists and Code of Conduct, and violation of three rules of the Association of State and Provincial Psychology Boards' (ASPPB) Code of Conduct. Dr. Seider's 51-page report disclosed more information than necessary to comply with the DHS subpoena. Also, she did not obtain consent to release the information and did not do an adequate evaluation to justify some of her conclusions. She also disclosed information that should have remained confidential. The fact that the mother had disclosed much of the information to the father and the pediatrician did not lessen the violation, because the privilege belonged to the mother and could not be waived except by the mother or by a court order.

Maryland

In re Adoption/Guardianship No. CCJ14746, 759 A.2d 755 (Md. Ct. App. 2000). A mother in a termination of parental rights case asserted that a licensed clinical social worker was engaging in the practice of medicine by assigning her a diagnosis from the American Psychiatric Association's *Diagnostic and Statistical Manual of Mental Disorders, Fourth Edition (DSM-IV)*. The appellate court ruled that social workers are, by statute, permitted to make "a diagnosis based on a recognized manual of mental and emotional disorders," and were not practicing medicine in so doing.

Laznovsky v. Laznovsky, 745 A.2d 1054 (Md. Ct. App. 2000). The Maryland Court of Appeals held that a person seeking an award of child custody that claims to be a fit parent, does not, without more, waive the confidential psychiatrist/psychologist patient privilege in respect to his or her past mental health "diagnosis and treatment" communications and records. . . . An assertion that one is fit is merely an assertion that one meets the qualifications to be awarded custody. It does not serve to place their mental condition in issue. [*Id.* at 1073.] The court noted that the states are divided regarding whether a party seeking sole custody automatically permits disclosing privileged mental health records. The Indiana Supreme Court has held that the mere filing of a custody suit places a parent's mental health at issue, thereby waiving the privilege. Florida courts, in contrast, have held that merely filing for custody does not place one's mental health at issue. If a trial court determines that the mental health of a parent is of concern, the court may order evaluations of the parties. Release of confidential psychiatric/psychological records is not essential when adequate information can be obtained through the evaluation process.

Rosenberg v. Helinski, 616 A.2d 866 (Md. 1992). Maryland's highest court held that a psychologist in a sex abuse case who repeated his in-court testimony to a TV reporter could not be sued for defamation. [The] psychologist testified that the child feared her father because he had hurt her in the genital area, and she was afraid he might do so again. . . . When the hearing ended, the psychologist left the courthouse and summarized his testimony for a TV reporter, repeating the child's allegations about being hurt in the genital area by her father, and declaring that the child's fear and anxiety of further abuse were genuine. The father sued the psychologist for defamation. A trial court determined that the psychologist's comments were protected by the privilege for those who recount in-court testimony and granted the psychologist's motion for summary judgment. An intermediary appeals court reversed. . . . The state's highest court held that the psychologist "enjoyed a legal privilege to defame" and that his statements to the reporter were not actionable. First, all of the psychologist's testimony at the hearing was absolutely privileged and could not serve as the basis for a defamation action. Second, operating in tandem with the absolute privilege accorded participants in court proceedings was a lesser privilege given to people who repeat the defamatory statements uttered during the course of such proceedings. "Reports of in-court proceedings containing defamatory material are privileged if they are fair and substantially correct or substantially accurate accounts of what took place." Here, the father conceded that the psychologist's remarks on the courthouse steps essentially repeated what he had said in court. 17 *Mental & Physical Disability Law Reporter* 187 (1993).

Massachusetts

LaLonde v. Eissner, 539 N.E.2d 539 (Mass. 1989). This may be the first time a state's highest court has granted judicial immunity to a forensic psychiatrist performing an evaluation in the absence of a specific court order for the evaluation. In the context of a visitation dispute, the probation department was ordered by the probate court to conduct an investigation and to arrange for a psychiatric evaluation of the LaLonde family. Pursuant to this order, the probation department engaged Dr. Eissner, who interviewed the family and arranged for separate psychological testing for the minor child. The mother and child brought action against Dr. Eissner alleging that he was negligent in performing his evaluation and that as a result continued contact by the father was allowed which brought harm to the child. The superior court granted summary judgment in favor of Dr. Eissner and mother and child appealed. The Supreme Judicial Court identified the salient issue as to whether a psychiatrist chosen by the probation department to conduct a court-ordered evaluation is entitled to quasi-judicial immunity. It ruled that when acting under a judge's order these people enjoy the same absolute immunity as does the judge. The court further recognizes that barring such protection it would be difficult to obtain experts to assist the court in conducting evaluations and would enhance the chances of obtaining the disinterested objective opinion that the court seeks. Accordingly, the court finds that "persons appointed to perform essential judicial functions are entitled to absolute immunity." 16 *Newsletter of the American Academy of Psychiatry & the Law* 40 (1991).

Minnesota

Meyers v. Price, 463 N.W.2d 773 (Minn. Ct. App. Dec. 4, 1990). Parents who were being prosecuted for child sexual abuse filed a federal civil rights suit against a therapist appointed by the court who had examined their children. The Minnesota Court of Appeals ruled that the therapist was protected by quasi-judicial immunity, indicating that he was entitled to the same protection in the parents' state law tort suit. The parents had commenced the federal § 1983 suit after the criminal charges against them were dropped. The federal court had ruled that the therapist was given immunity as a consequence of his appointment by the court. 618 F. Supp. 1434 (D. Minn. 1985). The court stated that there was no evidence that the therapist or any of his associates acted beyond the scope of the court appointment. The court also ruled that a psychologist was shielded by quasi-judicial immunity from a claim that she was negligent for failing to supervise the therapist. The court indicated that the psychologist's liability is dependent upon the therapist's conduct in the role of a court-appointed official. There was no evidence that the psychologist acted beyond the scope of that appointment.

Mississippi

Lauderdale County Department of Human Services v. T.H.G., No. 90CA-0713 (Miss. 1992). The Mississippi Supreme Court ruled that the doctor-patient privilege for psychologists and psychiatrists under Mississippi's rules of evidence does not permit information about treatment received by the parents of a five-year-old girl to be introduced in the termination of parental rights proceeding without the consent of the parents. The trial court's ruling, which excluded the testimony and records of a psychologist and a psychiatric nurse, was upheld. Although the court acknowledged the importance of decision making in the best interests of the child, the court ruled that it was also extremely important and in the public interest to facilitate access to mental health professionals by eliminating a fear that confidential information might some day be used in a court proceeding.

Nevada

Duff v. Lewis, 958 P.2d 82 (Nev. 1998). The Nevada Supreme Court held that a court-appointed psychologist in a child custody action was entitled to absolute quasi-judicial immunity. Dr. Lewis was appointed by the court to evaluate a family as part of a post-judgment action. He recommended that the children permanently remain in the custody of their mother and her new husband. The father reported Dr. Lewis to the Nevada Board of Psychological Examiners, which concluded that Dr. Lewis's evaluation had been deficient in three areas: (1) he had not given an opinion regarding the effect of the father's medications on his psychological test performance; (2) he had selectively reported his findings, giving an impression that the father was of below-average intelligence; and (3) he misled the court by failing to indicate that the father's IQ was in the average range. A private letter of reprimand was issued to Dr. Lewis. The father then sued Dr. Lewis for negligence. The district court dismissed the suit on the basis that the doctor had quasi-judicial immunity. The father appealed, and the state Supreme Court affirmed. On this issue of first impression, the state supreme court indicated that the common law doctrine of absolute immunity extends to anyone who is a central part of a judicial proceeding. This preserves the independence of the witness and fosters truthfulness by eliminating any fear that the witness may be threatened with personal liability. It also increases the pool of experts willing to accept court appointments and prevents experts from shading their feedback to the court in order to limit liability. Safeguards that hold experts accountable include cross-examination and the ability of a litigant to appeal a trial court verdict.

New Jersey

Runyon v. Smith, 730 A.2d 881 (N.J. Super. Ct. App. Div. 1999). A woman received a temporary restraining order (TRO) against her husband. The husband sought an immediate hearing to contest the TRO. He called his wife's treating psychologist to testify. The psychologist testified that the wife had an obsessive-compulsive personality disorder and abused her children. The psychologist also submitted a written report to the court. A friend of the wife also testified that she was abusive toward the children. The court granted temporary custody of the children to the father. The wife sued the psychologist and her employer, alleging violation of the psychologist-patient privilege. The trial court granted summary judgment to the defendants. The appeals court reversed. The trial court, it indicated, had not applied *In re Kozlov*, 298 A.2d 882 (N.J. 1979), which established that a party may avoid the privilege if (1) there is a legitimate need for the evidence, (2) the evidence is relevant and material to the issue to be decided, and (3) the information sought cannot be secured from any less intrusive source. The appellate court indicated that had the trial court applied the third prong, it would have found that the testimony of the husband and friend were far less intrusive than the testimony and records of the psychologist, as well as sufficient to deny giving her custody. There was also other evidence that could have been considered as an alternative to the psychologist's testimony. In addition, the appeals court indicated that the wife had a cause of action against the psychologist for revealing confidential information without her consent or a court order.

In re Guardianship of B.L.N., 250 N.J. Super. 113 (N.J. Super. Ct. Ch. Div. Apr. 11, 1991). A New Jersey trial court ruled in a termination of parental rights proceeding that an indigent mother is entitled to appointment, at public expense, of a psychological expert as well as an attorney. The court noted how important psychological experts are in defense of actions to terminate parental rights.

New York

Ochs v. Ochs, 749 N.Y.S.2d 650 (Sup. Ct. 2002). In a custody dispute between Mitchell and Stacy Ochs, a forensic psychologist appointed by the court recommended that custody be awarded to Mitchell. Stacy made a request for the psychologist's notes and raw test data prior to cross-examination. The court denied the request. The "court found that court-appointed neutral psychologists differ from experts retained by litigants in other matters in that their reports are not used to advocate a party's position. Instead, these psychologists provide the court with an unbiased professional opinion." While the conclusions of an expert are subject to cross-examination, and the expert's notes and raw data are subject to discovery, "courts must discard or limit procedures for litigating custody disputes if they are not likely to improve the result sufficiently to justify their financial and emotional costs. . . . Before allowing discovery in custody cases, New York courts require a showing of some specific need for disclosure. . . . Here . . . the psychologist's raw data and notes may add to the relevant information before the court, but at a significant cost. Because the parties will continue to interact after the litigation, disclosure may make their future relationship more difficult. . . ." Disclosure would permit a party to attempt to discredit the testimony of the psychologist by criticizing the psychologist's methodology, while failing to test the psychologist's conclusions. This process would be of limited value, while increasing the emotional and financial costs to the parties, including the children. In addition, if psychologists expect litigants to review their data and notes they may be less willing to state impressions they form during the interviews they conduct. Only a showing of bias or another basis for questioning the credibility of the report would be sufficient to cause disclosure. 27 *Mental & Physical Disability Law Reporter* 55, at 55 (2003).

Deed v. Condrell, 568 N.Y.S.2d 679 (Sup. Ct. 1991). A New York court dismissed a mother's malpractice and fraud action against a court-appointed psychologist. In 1977, the mother was divorced and received joint custody of her daughter. The mother's ex-husband petitioned for sole custody, and both parents and the daughter submitted to counseling by a court-appointed psychologist. Based on the psychologist's recommendations, the court awarded sole custody to the girl's father. The mother's suit alleged that the psychologist exceeded the bounds of his professional role as a court-appointed evaluator, and established a deeper, more significant relationship in which he counseled the mother about her relationship with her daughter. The court held that a civil action could not be based on the psychologist's treatment, exam, evaluation, recommendations, and opinion, since he rendered them pursuant to a judicial directive and in the course of a judicial proceeding. 15 *Mental & Physical Disability Law Reporter* 402 (July–Aug. 1991).

Tolisano v. Texon, 550 N.E.2d 450, 551 N.Y.S.2d 197 (1989). The New York State Court of Appeals ruled that there existed no doctor-patient relationship when a forensic evaluation is performed. In so doing, the court acted to protect expert witnesses. 16 *Newsletter of the American Academy of Psychiatry & the Law* 40 (1991).

Ohio

In re Jones, 2001 WL 1607732 (Ohio Ct. App. Dec. 18, 2001). The Ohio Court of Appeals ruled that a trial court did not err when it admitted a psychological assessment of the mother in a child dependency case. Because the psychological assessment was for forensic rather than treatment purposes, the psychologist-patient privilege does not apply.

Elling v. Graves, 640 N.E.2d 1156 (Ohio Ct. App. 1994). An Ohio appeals court ruled that a court-appointed psychologist who examined a family involved in divorce proceedings was not liable for making allegedly defamatory and fraudulent statements during these proceedings. Peter Elling sued Dr. Wayne Graves, claiming Graves's faulty opinions caused the court to award custody of Elling's children to Elling's ex-wife. Graves was entitled to absolute immunity for any defamatory or false testimony or reports presented for the judicial proceedings, as "Ohio courts have long recognized that freedom of speech is essential in a judicial proceeding in order to ascertain the truth and to achieve justice," and thus have prohibited civil actions based on witnesses' or parties' statements, e.g., *Willitzer v. McCloud*, 453 N.E.2d 693 (Ohio Sup. Ct. 1983). Under *Willitzer*, Graves would have retained this immunity even if he had knowingly made false statements, and only would have faced liability if his examination procedures had been negligent, which Elling did not allege. 19 *Mental & Physical Disability Law Reporter* 93 (1995).

Pennsylvania

Althaus v. Cohen, 756 A.2d 1166 (Pa. 2000). A teenager alleged that she was sexually abused by her father, and she was removed from the family home. She underwent more than a year of psychotherapy with a psychiatrist, Dr. Cohen. Dr. Cohen attended, but did not testify at, several proceedings. As the allegations became increasingly fanciful, she indicated that the teenager could not distinguish fact from fiction, and the charges against the parents were later dropped. The parents sued Dr. Cohen and her employer, alleging negligent diagnosis and treatment. A jury and an appeals court found for the plaintiffs. The supreme court reversed. To determine whether a duty exists, several factors must be weighed: the relationship between the parties; the social utility of the actor's conduct; the nature of the risk imposed and the foreseeability of the harm incurred; the consequences of imposing a duty on the actor; and the overall public interest in the proposed solution. . . . Applying those factors . . ., the relationship between Cohen and [the parents] does not weigh in favor of imposing a duty of care. Cohen had minimal contact with the parents and did not participate in the original criminal investigation, which gave rise to the criminal charges, or testify against the parents at any court proceeding related to those charges. Second, the social utility of effective therapeutic treatment of child victims of alleged sexual abuse by parents, when weighed against the nature and foreseeability of harm of a false accusation of sexual abuse, also does not support imposing a duty of care. Cohen did not create the harm suffered by the parents, did not participate in the original criminal investigation, played no legal role in the child's initial accusations against the parents, and was not called as a witness against the parents in the criminal proceedings. . . . Third, imposing a duty of care would alter the important therapeutic relationship between victims and professionals, and perhaps, cause such professionals to avoid providing treatment in sexual abuse cases. Finally, society's interest in encouraging treatment of child abuse victims and maintaining the trust and confidentiality within the therapist-patient relationship weighed against imposing a duty. Victims may become reluctant to seek treatment if confidentiality of treatment is not guaranteed and conflicting duties arose.

Tennessee

Guity v. Kandilakis, 821 S.W.2d 595 (Tenn. Ct. App. 1991). A Tennessee appeals court held that a psychologist was immune from a lawsuit alleging that he breached the duty not to disclose privileged communications made during joint marital counseling sessions. While the husband and wife had individual sessions with the psychologist, both of them participated in most of the sessions. The wife called the psychologist as a witness in the divorce trial, the husband objected, and the judge instructed the psychologist to testify only about the joint sessions. The wife was awarded a divorce, and the husband sued the psychologist for the tortious disclosure of confidential information and breach of an implied contract. A trial court granted summary judgment to the psychologist. The appeals court held that the trial court had erred in allowing the psychologist to testify and that the wife's presence in the joint counseling sessions did not constitute a waiver of the privilege. The court nevertheless concluded that the psychologist was immune from suit because he would have been found in contempt if he had refused to testify. 16 *Mental & Physical Disability Law Reporter* 314 (1992).

Texas

B.K. v. Cox, 116 S.W.3d 351 (Tex. Ct. App. 2003). A mother filed a negligence suit against a psychologist for failing to report his suspicion of child abuse during a child custody evaluation. The trial court granted summary judgment on the basis of absolute immunity due to experts functioning as an arm of the court. The appellate court affirmed. Because their function is intimately linked to the judicial process, and they use their discretion much like the judge, they have judicial immunity if any part of their work is considered a judicial function. Since the psychologist was assisting the court in evaluating the family, the judicial immunity prevented any civil liability.

Macurak v. Doyle, 2002 WL 1263900 (Tex. Ct. App. June 7, 2002). Randal Macurak brought claims on his own behalf and that of his son against a psychologist and psychiatrist who had treated his son. The trial court granted summary judgment for both defendants, indicating that they owed no duty of care to Macurak, a third-party non-patient. During their bitter 1993 divorce, Macurak's wife alleged that their four-year-old son had seen a pornographic movie while with his father. The trial court ordered a psychological evaluation. The clinical assessment indicated that the child had been sexually traumatized, but that the father's involvement could neither be confirmed nor refuted. The trial court ordered that the child's treatment by a team that included psychologist Doyle and psychiatrist Lewis continue. The parents were also ordered to obey instructions by the treatment team, unless modified by order of the court or agreed upon in writing by the parties. The father was initially given supervised one-hour-per-week visitation, with expansion of visitation left to the discretion of the treatment team. In October 1994, the child's condition deteriorated. The treatment team temporarily suspended the father's visitation. There was little contact between father and son for the next two and a half years. In 1997 the family court ordered limited visitation resumed. A jury trial in family court in 1998 led to the father being appointed "joint managing conservator" with unsupervised visitation involving up to 45 percent of the child's time. In 1999, Macurak sued the members of the treatment team and their hospital, alleging negligence, gross negligence, deceptive trade practices, civil conspiracy, breach of a duty of good faith and fair dealing, breach of fiduciary duty, and loss of consortium. The appellate court, citing *Bird v. W.C.W.*, 868 S.W.2d 767 (Tex. 1994), affirmed the decision of the trial court that Doyle and Lewis "owed no duty to Macurak, a third-party non-patient, to provide competent medical health care to his son."

Abrams v. Jones, 35 S.W.3d 620, 2000 WL 890385 (Tex. July 6, 2000). The Texas Supreme Court ruled that a divorced father did not have a right to detailed notes regarding his daughter's sessions with her psychologist, because release of the notes would have been harmful to his daughter's emotional health. The court indicated that (1) a mental health professional need not provide confidential records to a parent who is not acting "on behalf of" the child, according to Texas law, and (2) even if a parent is acting on the child's behalf, the records may be refused if the professional believes that releasing them would be harmful to the patient's physical, mental, or emotional health. It was noted that professionals may limit the release of records to a patient when such release is believed to be harmful to the patient's physical, mental, or emotional health, and that a parent who is standing in the patient's stead has no greater right to the records than does the patient. 24 *Mental & Physical Disability Law Reporter* 729, at 729–30.

Vermont

Politi v. Tyler, 751 A.2d 788 (Vt. 2000). This Vermont case underscores the recommendation that experts get a court appointment to conduct a custody evaluation rather than be directly retained by the parties for that purpose. The parents divorced in 1990. A custody and placement dispute came to a head in 1993. The family court issued an order for an evaluation in a custody action and directed the parties to recommend the psychologist who would do the evaluation. The parents contracted with Dr. Janet Tyler, a psychologist, and split her fees evenly. The psychologist wrote a report, which she gave to the parents and about which she testified in court. The parents stipulated to a modified custody agreement in 1994. In 1997, the mother sued Dr. Tyler for slander, malpractice, and intentional infliction of emotional distress. Dr. Tyler moved dismissal on the grounds that she had absolute judicial immunity as a court-appointed expert or, in the alternative, that she had immunity as a witness in a judicial proceeding. She also asserted that the suit was barred by the statute of limitations, and that she did not owe a duty to the plaintiff that would justify a malpractice claim. The trial court held that Dr. Tyler was not entitled to a judicial immunity defense, that she did owe a duty of care, and that the statute of limitations for this duty was six years. The other two claims were dismissed. Dr. Tyler appealed. The Vermont Supreme Court affirmed the trial court. It concluded that Dr. Tyler was not a court-appointed expert because she contracted directly with the parties rather than having received an appointment by the family court. The court's order that a forensic evaluation be done was not sufficient to permit Dr. Tyler to claim to be a court-appointed expert. Further, Dr. Tyler's contract with the parents contained no language suggesting that she was acting as an arm of the family court. The contract also specified that the evaluation and testimony was predicated upon payment by the parties rather than upon authority granted by a court order. The Vermont Supreme Court agreed that Dr. Tyler was entitled to witness immunity for statements made during her actual court testimony. She was, however, not entitled to such immunity for the acts of conducting a forensic evaluation or preparing a report. The court further held that Dr. Tyler owed a duty of care predicated upon her contract with the parties.

Virginia

Hall v. Sykes, 164 F.R.D. 46, 33 Fed. R. Serv. 3d 428 (Va. 1996). [A] federal magistrate judge in Virginia ruled that while treating physicians are not usually considered retained experts who must file written reports with the court under the Federal Rules of Civil Procedure, there are several exceptions. . . . [T]he magistrate ruled that "These medical care providers are required to prepare an expert written report because the court concludes that when an attorney selects the physician for treatment as well as testimony, it is presumed that the physician was selected for expert testimony." Thus physicians to whom attorneys refer clients for treatment may be considered "retained experts," as are physicians who render opinions based in part on information not learned during the course of treatment. 21 *Newsletter of the American Academy of Psychiatry & the Law* 72–73 (1996).

Washington

Gustafson v. Mazer, 54 P.3d 743, 113 Wash. App. 770 (2002). A mother in a child custody dispute sued a psychologist and her employer, claiming that the psychologist negligently and defamatorily reported to the guardian ad litem (GAL) that the mother may suffer from Munchausen Syndrome by Proxy (MSBP). At the request of the GAL, Dr. Mazer had been retained by the parents to conduct an evaluation of the parents and child. She prepared a memorandum giving the basis for her suspicions. The GAL brought an *ex parte* motion seeking a transfer of custody. She attached Dr. Mazer's memorandum to the motion. The court commissioner granted the motion immediately transferring custody to the father. Three days later, Dr. Mazer testified in support of her memorandum at an emergency hearing to vacate the transfer of custody. The motion was denied. However, a superior court judge returned the child to the mother's custody 17 days later. Seven months later, Dr. Mazer submitted a report indicating that her allegations of MSBP were not substantiated. Dr. Mazer moved for summary judgment in the mother's malpractice suit, and the superior court granted it based on witness immunity. Gustafson appealed. The appellate court found that Dr. Mazer had no professional relationship with Gustafson because she assisted the GAL and she functioned much like an expert appointed by the court. Further, Dr. Mazer was entitled to witness immunity for her report to the GAL, in part because she had prepared it in anticipation of testimony. The appellate court affirmed the decision of the superior court.

Deatherage v. Examining Board of Psychology, 134 Wash. 2d 131, 948 P.2d 828 (1997). The question presented is whether an expert witness is absolutely immune from the disciplinary action of a state licensing board when the board initiates the proceeding based upon work performed as an expert witness in child custody cases. . . . The State of Washington, Examining Board of Psychology (Board) brought disciplinary proceedings against Edward Deatherage alleging Deatherage failed to meet professional ethical standards in work that formed the basis of his expert testimony in several child custody suits. The Board found Deatherage's failure to qualify statements, his mischaracterization of statements, his failure to verify information, and his interpretation of test data were adequate grounds for initiating disciplinary proceedings. . . . His conduct was also found to violate regulations of the Board. . . . After an extensive hearing, the Board found Deatherage had committed misconduct in three custody evaluations, and suspended his license for 10 years. In this case, the State subjected Deatherage to a professional disciplinary proceeding for Deatherage's alleged negligent rendering of professional opinion in child custody cases. Deatherage has raised the defense of absolute witness immunity. . . . The defense of absolute privilege generally applies to statements made in the course of judicial proceedings and acts as a bar to any civil liability. . . . The absolute privilege of witness immunity is well stated by the RESTATEMENT (SECOND) OF TORTS § 588 (1977):

> A witness is absolutely privileged to publish defamatory matter concerning another in communications preliminary to a proposed judicial proceeding or as a part of a judicial proceeding in which he is testifying, if it has some relation to the proceeding.

The comments to the Restatement emphasize that the privilege does not provide blanket immunity to all statements, and the comments limit the scope of the privilege to statements that have some relation to the proceeding or to a party to the proceeding. . . . The privilege of immunity is a judicially created privilege founded upon the belief that the administration of justice requires witnesses in a legal proceeding be able to discuss their views without fear of a defamation lawsuit. . . . In 1989, the privilege was extended, and we held an expert witness cannot be found civilly liable for any action done as part of a judicial function. . . . Immunity was extended beyond eyewitnesses to include expert witnesses because courts realized that forcing an expert witness to face retaliatory lawsuits by those who disagree with the expert's opinion may cause an expert to be reluctant to appear in litigation. . . . We felt the benefits gained by extending witness immunity were counterbalanced by safeguards inherent in the judicial system. We noted witness reliability is ensured by oath, cross examination, and the threat of criminal prosecution for perjury. . . . [A] disciplinary proceeding is not a civil suit against the expert, and the policies that underscore witness immunity do not apply. Disciplinary actions are different in character to civil actions. . . . Case law from other jurisdictions supports the conclusion that while civil liability is not available, professional discipline may be appropriate. . . . Permitting a professional to be subjected to discipline for unprofessional conduct is consistent with *Bruce*, serves to advance the court's goal of accurate testimony from expert witnesses, and furthers the disciplinary board's goal of protecting the public. . . . Witness immunity is traditionally available in defamation cases and other related tort actions. However, the privilege is not so broad as to extend to a professional disciplinary proceeding. We reverse the Court of Appeals and hold absolute witness immunity does not exist in the context of a professional disciplinary proceeding.

Wisconsin

Snow v. Koeppl, 159 Wis. 2d 77, 464 N.W.2d 215 (Ct. App. 1990). Koeppl, in the course of preparing a court-ordered psychological evaluation of Snow for use in a family court action, obtained and delivered to the court excerpts from earlier counseling records of the Northern Wisconsin Psychological Associates (hereafter "the clinic"), Koeppl's place of employment. . . . The circuit court dismissed Snow's claims on grounds that Koeppl was immune from liability as a quasi-judicial officer and court-appointed expert witness. . . . The trial judge in that action met with the parties, neither of whom was represented by legal counsel, and verbally ordered the entire family to undergo psychological evaluation. The court advised Koeppl of the order via telephone. The order and its exact provisions were never recorded or reduced to writing. . . . In the course of her task, Koeppl learned of Snow's previous counseling sessions. Koeppl examined the clinic files and incorporated some information from them in her report to the court. . . . Snow's complaint in this action alleges that Koeppl "revealed and disclosed this information to the general public, without the authorization of the plaintiff," that Koeppl's conduct was negligent, reckless and wanton, violated an implied contract as well as various laws protecting against breach of confidentiality and invasion of privacy, and she sought both compensatory and punitive damages for her injuries. . . . "Because we conclude that a judicial order creating official duties directly and closely connected to court proceedings should be broadly construed in favor of the person required to act, we accord Koeppl absolute immunity. . . ." Statements made in the course of judicial proceeding are absolutely privileged and insulate the speaker from liability so long as the statements "bear a proper relationship to the issues. . . ." The rule extends to attorneys, witnesses and physicians appointed to examine a person in connection with judicial proceedings. . . . When making this inquiry, all doubts should be resolved in favor of relevancy. . . . Here, a directive to perform a psychological evaluation should, in keeping with the sound reasons for immunity, be liberally construed to protect the court official from liability for the examination and use of reports of earlier psychological counseling or therapy. 159 Wis. 2d at 78–81.

CHAPTER 2

ETHICAL ISSUES

§ 2.1   Codes of Ethics

Ethics guidelines, propounded by all professions, are essential to maintaining the integrity and cohesiveness of a profession. They are a primary ingredient in the professionalization of an occupation, in part because society accords professionals special privileges that it does not offer to commercial enterprises. It does so because professionals have mastered a large body of specialized information, use their judgment in application of that information, and evidence a commitment to the welfare of the public.[1] Not only do people expect professionals to be more trustworthy, competent, and error-free than the average businessperson, there is also a fiduciary relationship between professionals and their patients and clients.[2] The trust given to professionals by society and by patients and clients is a source of power,[3] as is the requirement that most professionals be licensed. Licensed professionals are permitted to provide services that people who are not licensed may not provide. Codes of ethics were instituted to help balance the self-interest of the professional against the interests of the people to whom the professional provides services by offering guidelines for decision making, educating each generation of professionals, and providing rules by which allegedly unethical behavior may be judged.[4]

---

[1] Samuel Knapp & Leon VandeCreek, A Guide to the 2002 Revision of the American Psychological Association's Ethics Code (Professional Resources Press (2003) [hereinafter Knapp & VandeCreek].

[2] K. Pope & M. Vasquez, Ethics in Psychotherapy and Counseling, 2d ed. at 40–42 (1998) [hereinafter, Pope & Vasquez].

[3] Ethical Principles of Psychologists and Code of Conduct, Principle A (2002) [hereinafter Ethics Code].

[4] Gerald Koocher & Patricia Keith-Spiegel, Ethics in Psychology (Oxford 1998).

§ 2.2   New American Psychological Association Code of Ethics

A major revision of the *Ethical Principles of Psychologists and Code of Conduct* (hereinafter "Ethics Code") went into effect on June 1, 2003. The revised Ethics Code is designed to give the psychologist a greater ability to exercise professional judgment regarding the appropriate response to a variety of situations, in part by increased use of terms like "reasonably," "appropriate," and "potentially," and decreased use of "must" or "should." The general directive is to do what a "reasonable psychologist" would do.[5] The complete revision of the Code of Ethics can be found in **Appendix B.**

There are a number of changes that directly affect the forensic work of psychologists. The most significant changes include the following:

1.   There is no longer a section of the Code labeled "Forensic Activities." Forensic ethics standards are now interspersed among the other standards. According to the Chair of the Ethics Code Task Force, this change was made because of evidence that many psychologists with little or no forensic training have entered the forensic arena as either expert or fact witnesses. By interspersing the forensic ethics standards with other areas addressing professional practice, it is hoped that these psychologists will become aware of the ethical issues they must bear in mind before they become involved in a legal case or some aspect of the legal system.

2.   Changes were made to better align the Ethics Code with the Supreme Court ruling in *Daubert v. Merrell Dow Pharmaceuticals, Inc.*[6]

3.   The change that may be of greatest interest to attorneys is with regard to the release of raw test data. As discussed in **§ 2.26,** raw test data has generally been considered to include both the test questions or other test-related material *and* the individual's responses to the questions/material. That is no longer the case: test data and test materials are now clearly differentiated:

Ethical Standard 9.04 Release of Test Data

(a) The term *test data* refers to raw and scaled scores, client/patient responses to test questions or stimuli, and psychologists' notes and recordings concerning client/patient statements and behavior during an examination. Those portions of test materials that include client/patient responses are included in the definition of test data. Pursuant to a client/patient release, psychologists provide test data to the client/patient or other persons identified in the release. Psychologists may refrain from releasing test data to protect a client/patient or others from substantial harm or misuse or misrepresentation of the data or the test, recognizing that in many instances release of confidential information under these circumstances is regulated by law.

(b) In the absence of a client/patient release, psychologists provide test data only as required by law or court order.[7]

---

[5] Knapp & VandeCreek at 12.

[6] 509 U.S. 579, 113 S. Ct. 2786 (1993).

[7] American Psychological Ass'n, *Ethical Principles of Psychologists and Code of Conduct*, 57 Am. Psychol. 1060–73, at 1071–72 (2002) (hereinafter Ethics Code).

This Ethical Standard must be considered along with Ethical Standard 9.11, maintaining Test Security:

> The term *test materials* refers to manuals, instruments, protocols, and test questions or stimuli, which do not include test data as defined in Standard 9.04, Release of Test Data. Psychologists make reasonable efforts to maintain the integrity and security of test materials and other assessment techniques consistent with law and contractual obligations, and in a manner that permits adherence to this Ethics Code.[8]

Thus, *test data* refer to a specific client/patient and to the responses of that particular individual, while test materials refer to the instrument or test to which the client/patient was responding. Test material, therefore, contains nothing that is unique to a given individual.[9] Taken together, these two Ethical Standards indicate that:

a. Psychologists may provide test data, as defined, to attorneys, provided that the client/patient has given informed consent, in writing, to that release.

b. However, the psychologist may withhold test data from the client/patient, from the attorney, and/or from others if the psychologist believes that release of the test data may cause substantial harm to the client/patient or others, or if the psychologist believes that the test data that are released may be misused or misrepresented.

c. Psychologists are required to follow statutory law related to release of information. Thus, if a state law prohibits release under conditions or circumstances that exist in a given case, the law would take precedence, and the psychologist would not release the test data. The same would be true if release of the test data was believed by the psychologist to violate the federal Health Insurance Portability and Accountability Act (HIPAA). It is also important to note that "HIPAA does not require release of records to clients/patients when information is compiled in reasonable anticipation of, or for use in, civil, criminal, or administrative actions or proceedings."[10]

d. If the client/patient has not provided a written, informed consent for release, the psychologist is not permitted to release the test data without specific statutory authority or a court order. A subpoena from an attorney is not a sufficient basis for the release of test data.[11] Attorneys are not trained to understand or evaluate most of the raw data obtained from an evaluation. Therefore, intentional or not, it is likely that they will be unable to validly use or present the data without the assistance of a psychologist retained for that purpose.[12] A psychologist who releases test data with neither a

---

[8] *Id.* at 1072.

[9] Stephen Behnke, *Release of Test Data and APA's New Ethics Code*, 34 Monitor on Psychol. 70–72 (2003) [hereinafter Behnke].

[10] Celia B. Fisher, Decoding the Ethics Code: A Practical Guide for Psychologists 29 (Sage 2003) [hereinafter Fisher].

[11] Behnke at 72.

[12] Personal communication with Solomon Fulero (May 4, 2003); Jeanne J. Johnson & Jeffrey L. Helms, *Test Security in the Twenty-First Century*, 21 Am. J. Forensic Psychol. 19–32, at 25–26 (2003).

signed, informed consent from the client/patient nor a court order is likely to be in violation of Standard 9.04.[13]

e. "Test materials" are defined as the test instruments themselves. If the client/patient responds by writing on the test materials, or if the psychologist writes the individual's responses on the test materials, the test materials *become* test data, because of the presence of those client/patient responses. If, however, the responses are recorded on a separate document or paper, it is only the responses, not the test questions or stimuli, that may be released.

f. If the psychologist has been retained by an attorney, appointed by a court, or otherwise retained by an organization rather than by the individual who is being evaluated, the test data do not have to be released to that individual because he or she is not the client.

g. Whenever possible, psychologists have a responsibility to avoid releasing test materials, due to the need to maintain the integrity and security of those test materials, the contractual agreements between the psychologist and the test publisher, and the need to minimize entry of the test materials into the public domain.[14]

h. Ethical Standard 9.04 specifies that "test data" includes "psychologists' notes and recordings concerning client/patient statements and behavior during an examination." "The term 'notes' in this standard is limited to the assessment context and does not include psychotherapy notes documenting or analyzing the contents of conversation during a private counseling session."[15]

4. The revised Code modified the Standard related to "multiple relationships (Ethical Standard 1.17 in the 1992 Code). Ethical Standard 3.05(a) reads, in part, that

[a] psychologist refrains from entering into a multiple relationship if the multiple relationship could reasonably be expected to impair the psychologist's objectivity, competence, or effectiveness in performing his or her functions as a psychologist, or otherwise risks exploitation or harm to the person with whom the professional relationship exists.[16]

This strongly reinforces the prohibition, discussed in § 2.8 of this book, against a psychologist's acting as an evaluator or expert witness (rather than solely as a fact witness) when his or her psychotherapy patient/client is a participant in the legal process.

5. Ethical Standard 3.10, Informed Consent, has been expanded to make it clear that the autonomy of the patient/client is to be maximized. If the patient/client is permitted to either accept or refuse the psychological services, he or she must receive an explanation sufficient to permit a knowing and voluntary choice to be made, "using language that is reasonably understandable to that person. . . ."[17]

---

[13] Behnke at 72.

[14] Jeanne J. Johnson & Jeffrey L. Helms, *Test Security in the Twenty-First Century*, 21 Am. J. Forensic Psychol. 19–32, at 24 & 27–28 (2003).

[15] Fisher at 192.

[16] Ethics Code at 1065.

[17] *Id.*

According to Ethical Standard 3.10(b),

> For persons who are legally incapable of giving informed consent, psychologists nevertheless (1) provide an appropriate explanation, (2) seek the individual's assent, (3) consider such persons' preferences and best interests, and (4) obtain appropriate permission from a legally authorized person, if such substitute consent is permitted or required by law. When consent by a legally authorized person is not permitted or required by law, psychologists take reasonable steps to protect the individual's rights and welfare.[18]

Further, according to Ethical Standard 3.10(c),

> When psychological services are court ordered or otherwise mandated, psychologists inform the individual of the nature of the anticipated services, including whether the services are court ordered or mandated and any limits of confidentiality, before proceeding.[19]

According to Cecilia Fisher, Ph.D., the Chair of the Ethics Code Task Force,

> Psychologists conducting a court-ordered forensic assessment must inform the individual tested: why the assessment is being conducted; that the findings may be entered into evidence in court; and if known to the psychologist, the extent to which the individual and his or her attorney will have access to the information. The psychologist should not assume the role of legal advisor, but can advise the individual to speak with his or her attorney when asked about potential legal consequences of noncooperation.[20]

When the psychological service is an assessment, Ethical Standard 9.03(a) reinforces the above requirements by indicating that informed consent "includes an explanation of the nature and purpose of the assessment, fees, involvement of third parties, and limits of confidentiality, and sufficient opportunity for the client/patient to ask questions and receive answers."[21] Finally, for individuals who are court-ordered to be evaluated, or who are not legally competent to give informed consent, which would include children in child custody matters, psychologists are required by Ethical Standard 9.03(b), which is new, to inform them "about the nature and purpose of the proposed assessment services, using language that is reasonably understandable to the person being assessed,"[22] as well as telling them who is expected to receive copies of the psychologist's report.

Ethical Standard 6.04(d) indicates that "if limitations to services can be anticipated because of limitations in financing, this is discussed with the recipient of services as early as is feasible."[23] That is, if the psychologist does not believe that he or she can reasonably perform the requested service due to limitations on finances, this must be discussed with the retaining attorney, the Court, or another appropriate party as early in the process as

---

[18] *Id.*

[19] *Id.*

[20] Fisher at 80.

[21] Ethics Code at 1071.

[22] *Id.*

[23] *Id.* at 1068.

possible. If the limitations due to finances will prevent the psychologist from doing every-thing necessary to provide an adequate assessment, the psychologist should generally withdraw from the case. If the psychologist only becomes aware that the actual cost of an assessment or other services will be greater than the amount agreed upon when well into the process, the psychologist must discuss any limitations with the party(ies) with whom he or she contracted as soon as possible, and try to work out limitations on the services provided or another equitable solution.

The present authors recommend that the informed consent (or assent, if it is a child or if the evaluation is court-ordered) statements be given both orally and in writing, and that the signature of the person being evaluated (or his/her guardian, if relevant) be obtained whenever possible. The limits of confidentiality and the foreseeable ways in which the information will be used should be repeated at subsequent assessment sessions, or expanded if circumstances change over time.

   6.   While a court-ordered evaluation is not confidential, per se, since it is done in antic-ipation of a court proceeding and a number of people, including the parties themselves, the attorneys, a guardian ad litem, and a judge, at minimum, would be expected to review the report, psychologists still "have a primary obligation and take reasonable precautions to protect confidential information obtained through or stored in any medium, recognizing that the extent and limits of confidentiality may be regulated by law. . . ."[24] This includes ensuring that the computer on which test data or a report is stored is adequately protected from access by unauthorized individuals, including encryption, password protection, and use of an effective firewall. The same holds true for confidential information sent via e-mail, because e-mail that is not encrypted is accessible to knowledgeable individuals ("hackers"). Further, the psychologist has an obligation to ensure that the recipient of con-fidential information by e-mail, fax, or other electronic transmission has an adequate con-fidentiality policy and that individuals who are not authorized to view the confidential information do not have access to it.[25]

   7.   While psychologists do not often make audio or video records of assessments, a psychologist who does so is required by Ethical Standard 4.03, Recording, to get permis-sion from each individual who is recorded, or from his or her legal representative, or a court order. "[U]nder Standard 4.03, no . . . exceptions are permissible for service providers."[26] As will be discussed in the context of "third parties" being present at an eval-uation (see § **2.13**), there are a number of reasons that it is of questionable ethics to either tape an assessment or permit a third party to be present.

   8.   Ethical Standard 6.01, Documentation of Professional and Scientific Work and Maintenance of Records, indicates that psychologists must "maintain, disseminate, store, retain, and dispose of records and data relating to their professional . . . work"[27] in ways that facilitate provision of services and ensure compliance with the law. "Creating or main-taining records that are illegible to others would be a violation of this standard."[28]

---

[24] Ethical Standard 4.01 Maintaining Confidentiality, *id.* at 1066.

[25] Fisher at 86.

[26] *Id.* at 93.

[27] Ethics Code at 1067.

[28] Fisher at 115.

9. While Ethical Standard 6.04(a), Fees and Financial Arrangements, is not significantly different from 1992 Ethical Standard 1.25(a), Dr. Fisher's commentary indicates that forensic psychologists must make a financial arrangement as early in the professional relationship as is feasible:

> In specifying compensation, psychologists must include a description of all reasonably anticipated costs. For forensic . . . services this might include charges for telephone conversations; client, employee or participant interviews; library or computer research; statistical analysis; court preparation time; travel; postage; and/or duplication. Psychologists arranging compensation for assessment services should provide information about fees for test administration, scoring, interpretation, and report writing.[29]

10. Ethical Standard 9.01, Bases for Assessment, addresses the requirements for an assessment to be considered adequate. Ethical Standard 9.01(a) indicates that psychologists must provide opinions that are adequately substantiated by the information reviewed and/or the methods used, a slight modification of 1992 Ethical Standard 2.01(b). A more significant change is Ethical Standard 9.01(b), which indicates that

> [e]xcept as noted in 9.01(c), psychologists provide opinions of the psychological characteristics of individuals only after they have conducted an examination of the individuals adequate to support their statements or conclusions. When, despite reasonable efforts, such an examination is not practical, psychologists document the efforts they made and the result of those efforts, clarify the probable impact of their limited information on the reliability and validity of their opinions, and appropriately limit the nature and extent of their conclusions or recommendations.[30]

The recommended meaning of "reasonable efforts" is tied to the standard of practice, that is, the prevailing professional practice and judgment of psychologists engaged in similar activities regarding the minimum effort necessary if the psychologist is to be able to state an opinion to a reasonable degree of psychological/scientific certainty.

Ethical Standard 9.01(c) is new:

> When psychologists conduct a record review or provide consultation or supervision and an individual examination is not warranted or necessary for the opinion, psychologists explain this and the sources of information on which they based their conclusions and recommendations.[31]

Dr. Fisher's commentary specifies that

> Standard 9.01(b) specifically addresses the importance of in-person evaluations of individuals about whom psychologists will offer a professional opinion. Under this standard, with few exceptions psychologists must conduct individual examinations sufficient to obtain personal verification of information on which to base their professional opinions and refrain from providing opinions about the psychological characteristics of an individual if they themselves

---

[29] *Id.* at 124.

[30] Ethics Code at 1071.

[31] *Id.* at 1071.

have not conducted an examination of the individual adequate to support their statement or conclusions.[32]

Legal scholar Daniel Shuman indicates that "the mental status examination remains a standard component of a thorough diagnostic workup. Thus, an in-court opinion not based on a personal examination of the patient, when it is possible to do so, violates accepted practice. This failure should bear on the weight given the resulting opinions."[33]

In summary, if a psychologist, despite reasonable efforts, is unable to conduct a personal interview, the psychologist is obligated to state in both written and oral opinions the limitations that lack of a personal interview has on the validity and reliability of his or her opinions. The psychologist must also limit any conclusions or recommendations to those that are based upon information that the psychologist has personally verified, and to specify the source and nature of that information.

This does not, in our opinion, preclude an attorney from asking a psychologist a hypothetical question that involves the specific allegations in a case, and to ask for an opinion based upon the assumption that those allegations are true. The court, of course, may limit or exclude such testimony.

Dr. Fisher also notes that some forensic opinions only require that records be reviewed. Examples include a determination as to whether an assessment that was conducted was both appropriate and sufficient, recommendations in disability or professional liability cases in which there is a sufficient record available, or other cases in which a personal interview is not generally considered essential. As indicated above, the psychologist must still specify any limitations and identify why an interview is not essential to the opinion being offered.[34]

11. Ethical Standard 9.02, Use of Assessments, has been expanded beyond what was in the 1992 Code. Ethical Standard 9.02(a) indicates that "[p]sychologists administer, adapt, score, interpret, or use assessment techniques, interviews, tests, or instruments in a manner and for purposes that are appropriate in light of the research on or evidence of the usefulness and proper application of the techniques."[35]

Ethical Standard 9.02(b) is new:

> Psychologists use assessment instruments whose validity and reliability have been established for use with members of the population tested. When such validity or reliability has not been established, psychologists describe the strengths and limitations of test results and interpretation.[36]

Thus, a psychologist should ensure that a test or other instrument has been validated for use with individuals the age, ethnicity, language, gender, and/or disability or other characteristics of the client/patient. Some of this information will come from the test/instrument manual. The psychologist also needs to be sufficiently familiar with the research literature

---

[32] Fisher at 181.

[33] Daniel W. Shuman, Psychiatric and Psychological Evidence, 2d ed. (West 1994, 2003 Supp.) at 9-7 [hereinafter Psychiatric and Psychological Evidence].

[34] Fisher at 183.

[35] Ethics Code at 1071.

[36] *Id.* at 1071.

on the test/instrument to be able to assess whether new research supports or questions particular uses of the test or instrument or specific interpretations of the results. If a test or other instrument is used despite the lack of research-based support for the particular use, the psychologist is required to specify why it was used, the advantages of using it, and any limitations on interpretations and recommendations as a result of its use.[37]

A psychologist who violates the Ethical Standards of the American Psychological Association faces sanctions ranging from educational advisories regarding errors at minimum, to expulsion from the Association (if he or she is a member) at maximum. A California appellate court has upheld the right of the American Psychological Association to censure a member who provided false testimony in a child custody proceeding.[38]

More significant, because most of the statutes licensing psychologists make reference to the APA Ethics Code, the psychologist could be sanctioned by his or her licensing board, including the potential for having his or her license revoked if the misconduct is especially egregious.

While the Ethical Principles of Psychologists and Code of Conduct were substantially revised, there have been no changes made in either the *Guidelines for Child Custody Evaluations in Divorce Proceedings*[39] or the *Specialty Guidelines for Forensic Psychologists*.[40] The *Specialty Guidelines for Forensic Psychologists* is undergoing review at the present time, however, and a revision is expected to be published in 2006.

HIPAA and the New APA Code of Ethics

There is no reason to believe that the provisions of HIPAA control any aspect of a forensic psychological evaluation, with one exception. HIPAA explicitly excludes "release of records to clients/patients when information is compiled in reasonable anticipation of, or for use in, civil, criminal, or administrative actions or proceedings."[41] Furthermore, the forensic services are provided in order to respond to a legal question or issue, not a psychotherapeutic question or issue. The forensic psychological services are also provided at the behest of a third party, not the client/patient him- or herself, and the services are not provided within the health care system. Finally, because the services fall outside the health care system, they are not covered by health insurance.[42]

The exception is that a forensic psychological evaluation may involve the psychologist receiving protected health information (PHI), including medical and/or psychological records. A request for records is often a part of a custody evaluation, and if there is an allegation of abuse or neglect, the records take on particular importance. Thus, the forensic

---

[37] Fisher at 186.

[38] Budwin v. American Psychological Ass'n, 24 Cal. App. 4th 875, 29 Cal. Rptr. 2d 453 (3d Dist. 1994).

[39] American Psychological Ass'n (1994). See **Ch. 3.**

[40] Committee on Ethical Guidelines for Forensic Psychologists, 15 Law & Hum. Behav. 655–65 (1991) [hereinafter Specialty Guidelines]. See **App. C.**

[41] Fisher at 29.

[42] Mary Connell & Gerald P. Koocher, *Expert Opinion: HIPAA and Forensic Practice*, 23 Am. Psychol.-L. Soc'y News 16–19, at 18–19 (2003).

psychologist must maintain the security of any PHI he or she receives. The psychologist may also get the informed consent of the client/patient to a waiver of any expectation that he or she will have access to the PHI.

Standards under *Daubert, Joiner,* and *Kumho*

Several Ethical Standards have particular relevance to the requirements set down by the Supreme Court in *Daubert v. Merrell Dow Pharmaceuticals, Inc.*,[43] *General Electric Co. v. Joiner*,[44] and *Kumho Tire Co. v. Carmichael*[45] (see **Chapter 1** for an extensive discussion of these cases):

Ethical Standard 2.04: Psychologists' work is based upon established scientific and professional knowledge of the discipline.[46]

Ethical Standard 9.01(a): Psychologists base the opinions contained in their recommendations, reports, and diagnostic or evaluative statements, including forensic testimony, on information and techniques sufficient to substantiate their findings.

(b) Except as noted in 9.01(c), psychologists provide opinions of the psychological characteristics of individuals only after they have conducted an examination of the individuals adequate to support their statements or conclusions. When, despite reasonable efforts, such an examination is not practical, psychologists . . . clarify the probable impact of their limited information on the reliability and validity of their opinions, and appropriately limit the nature and extent of their conclusions or recommendations.

(c) When psychologists conduct a record review or provide consultation . . . and an individual examination is not warranted or necessary for the opinion, psychologists explain this and the sources of information on which they based their conclusions and recommendations.[47]

Ethical Standard 9.02(a): Psychologists administer, adapt, score, interpret, or use assessment techniques, interviews, tests, or instruments in a manner and for purposes that are appropriate in light of the research on or evidence of the usefulness and proper application of the techniques.

(b) Psychologists use assessment instruments whose validity and reliability have been established for use with members of the population tested. When such validity or reliability has not been established, psychologists describe the strengths and limitations of test results.[48]

Ethical Standard 9.06: When interpreting assessment results . . ., psychologists take into account the purpose of the assessment as well as the various test factors, test-taking abilities, and other characteristics of the person being assessed, such as situational, personal, linguistic, and cultural differences, that might affect psychologists' judgments or reduce the accuracy of their interpretation. They indicate any significant limitations of their interpretations.[49]

---

[43] 509 U.S. 579, 113 S. Ct. 2786, 125 L. Ed. 2d 469 (1993). *See also* Daubert v. Merrell Dow Pharms., Inc., 43 F.3d 1311 (9th Cir. 1995).

[44] 522 U.S. 136 (1997).

[45] 119 S. Ct. 1167 (1999).

[46] Ethics Code at 1064.

[47] *Id*. at 1071.

[48] *Id*.

[49] *Id*. at 1072.

Ethical Standard 9.08(a): Psychologists do not base their assessment or intervention decisions or recommendations on data or test results that are outdated for the current purpose.

(b) Psychologists do not base such decisions or recommendations on tests and measures that are obsolete and not useful for the current purpose.[50]

The psychologist who adheres to these requirements should have no significant difficulty passing judicial muster under the *Daubert* requirements.[51]

Specialty Guidelines for Forensic Psychologists

In addition to the *Ethical Principles of Psychologists and Code of Conduct*, forensic psychologists are expected to follow the aspirational rules of the *Specialty Guidelines for Forensic Psychologists.* "Forensic psychology" is defined as "all forms of professional psychological conduct when acting, with definable foreknowledge, as a psychological expert on explicitly psycholegal issues, in direct assistance to courts, parties to legal proceedings, correctional and forensic mental health facilities, and administrative, judicial, and legislative agencies acting in an adjudicative capacity."[52]

Portions of the *Guidelines* that relate to the *Daubert* requirements include

III.B. Forensic psychologists have an obligation to present to the court, regarding the specific matters to which they will testify, the boundaries of their competence, the factual bases (knowledge, skill, experience, training, and education) for their qualification as an expert, and the relevance of those factual bases to their qualification as an expert on the specific matters at issue.

IV.A. During initial consultation with the legal representative of the party seeking services, forensic psychologists have an obligation to inform the party of factors that might reasonably affect the decision to contract with the forensic psychologist. These factors include, but are not limited to . . . 3. their areas of competence and the limits of their competence; and 4. the known scientific bases and limitations of the methods and procedures that they employ and their qualifications to employ such methods and techniques.

IV.G. When conflicts arise between the forensic psychologist's professional standards and the requirements of legal standards, a particular court, or a directive by an officer of the court or legal authorities, the forensic psychologist has an obligation to make those legal authorities aware of the source of the conflict and to take reasonable steps to resolve it. Such steps may include, but are not limited to, obtaining the consultation of fellow forensic professionals, obtaining the advice of independent counsel, and conferring directly with the legal representatives involved.

VI.A. Because of their special status as persons qualified as experts to the court, forensic psychologists have an obligation to maintain current knowledge of scientific, professional and legal developments within their area of claimed competence. They are obligated to also use

---

[50] *Id.*

[51] Frederick Rotgers & Deidre Barrett, Daubert v. Merrell Dow *and Expert Testimony by Clinical Psychologists: Implications and Recommendations for Practice*, 27 Prof. Psychol.: Res. & Prac. 467, 471 (1996).

[52] Specialty Guideline, I.B.1.b.

that knowledge, consistent with accepted clinical and scientific standards, in selecting data collection methods and procedures for an evaluation, treatment, consultation, or scholarly/empirical evaluation.

VI.B. Forensic psychologists have an obligation to document and be prepared to make available, subject to court order or the rules of evidence, all data that form the basis for their evidence or services. The standard to be applied to such documents or recording *anticipates* that the detail and quality of such documentation will be subject to reasonable judicial scrutiny. . . . When forensic psychologists conduct an examination or engage in the treatment of a party to a legal proceeding, with foreknowledge that their professional services will be used in an adjudicative forum, they incur a special responsibility to provide the best documentation possible under the circumstances.

VI.C. In providing forensic psychological services, forensic psychologists take special care to avoid undue influence upon their methods, procedures, and products, such as might emanate from the party to a legal proceeding by financial compensation or other gains. As an expert conducting an evaluation, treatment, consultation, or the scholarly/empirical investigation, the forensic psychologist maintains professional integrity by examining the issue at hand from all reasonable perspectives, actively seeking information that will differentially test plausible rival hypotheses.

VI.F. Forensic psychologists are aware that hearsay exceptions and other rules governing expert testimony place a special ethical burden upon them. When hearsay or otherwise inadmissible evidence forms the basis of their opinion, evidence, or professional product, they seek to minimize sole reliance upon such evidence. Where circumstances reasonably permit, forensic psychologists seek to obtain independent and personal verification of data relied upon as part of their professional services to the court or to a party to a legal proceeding.

1. . . . When using hearsay data that have not been corroborated, but are nevertheless utilized, forensic psychologists have an affirmative responsibility to acknowledge the uncorroborated status of those data and the reasons for relying upon such data.

VI.H. Forensic psychologists avoid giving written or oral evidence about the psychological characteristics of particular individuals when they have not had an opportunity to conduct an examination of the individual adequate to the scope of the statements, opinions, or conclusions to be issued. Forensic psychologists make every reasonable effort to conduct such examinations. When it is not possible or feasible to do so, they make clear the impact of such limitations on the reliability and validity of their professional products, evidence, or testimony.

VII.B. Forensic psychologists realize that their public role as "experts to the court" or as "expert representing the profession" confers upon them a special responsibility for fairness and accuracy in their public statements. . . .

VII.C. . . . [P]ublic statements are designed to assure accurate representation of their role or their evidence, not to advocate the positions of parties in the legal proceeding. . . .

VII.D. When testifying, forensic psychologists have an obligation to all parties to a legal proceeding to present their findings, conclusions, evidence, or other professional products in a fair manner. This principle does not preclude forceful representation of the data and reasoning upon which a conclusion or professional product is based. It does, however, preclude an attempt, whether active or passive, to engage in partisan distortion or misrepresentation. Forensic psychologists do not, by either commission or omission, participate in a misrepresentation of their evidence, nor do they participate in partisan attempts to avoid, deny, or subvert the presentation of evidence contrary to their own position.

VII.E. Forensic psychologists, by virtue of their competence and rules of discovery, actively disclose all sources of information obtained in the course of their professional services; they actively disclose which information from which source was used in formulating a particular written product or oral testimony.

VII.F. Forensic psychologists are aware that their essential role as expert to the court is to assist the trier of fact to understand the evidence or to determine a fact in issue. In offering expert evidence, they are aware that their own professional observations, inferences, and conclusions must be distinguished from legal facts, opinions, and conclusions. Forensic psychologists are prepared to explain the relationship between their expert testimony and the legal issues and facts of the instant case.

As indicated above, the *Specialty Guidelines for Forensic Psychologists* are in the process of revision.

Other Relevant Codes of Ethics

The Principles of Medical Ethics with Annotations Especially Applicable to Psychiatry   The code of ethics for **psychiatrists** is *The Principles of Medical Ethics with Annotations Especially Applicable to Psychiatry.* Because the American Medical Association revised its ethical code in 2001, the psychiatric code underwent some revision in 2001, some amendments in November 2003, and revised annotations are expected to be approved in 2004. Among the AMA changes, the phrase "a physician must recognize responsibility to patients first and foremost" was added to the Preamble; "respect for human . . . rights" added to Principle 1; "upholding the standards of professionalism" added to Principle 2; "safeguarding patient . . . privacy" to Principal 4; maintaining "a commitment to medical education" to Principle 5; and a responsibility to contribute to "the betterment of public health" to Principle 7. Two new principles were added:

> Principle 8. A physician shall, while caring for a patient, regard responsibility to the patient as paramount.

> Principle 9. A physician shall support access to medical care for all people.

Because of these changes, the code of ethics for psychiatrists has undergone some revision, with final changes anticipated to be approved in 2004.[53]

Ethics Guidelines for the Practice of Forensic Psychiatry   Also relevant is the *Ethics Guidelines for the Practice of Forensic Psychiatry* of the American Academy of Psychiatry and the Law, last revised in 1995. Although the *Ethics Guidelines* indicate that they are considered supplemental to the *Annotations*, the *Guidelines* are not necessarily binding on psychiatrists who are not members of the American Academy of Psychiatry and the Law (AAPL). They can, however, be considered an aspirational code against which the practice of a given psychiatrist can be compared. It is unfortunate that the AAPL has decided not

---

[53] Howard Zonana, *AMA Adopts New Ethics Principles*, 26 Newsl. Am. Acad. Psychiatry & L. (2001); American Psychiatric Ass'n Principles of Medical Ethics with Annotations Especially Applicable to Psychiatry (2001 ed., including Nov. 2003 amendments). The Principles . . . with Annotations may be accessed at www.psych.org/psych_pract/ethics/ethics.cfm.

to try to enforce its *Ethics Guidelines*, primarily because of a fear of costly litigation.[54] The AAPL *Ethical Guidelines* may be found at *www.aapl.org/ethics.htm.*

Ethics complaints against AAPL members are referred to the Ethics Committee of the American Psychiatric Association, to state licensing boards, and to psychiatric organizations in other countries if the complaint is about a foreign member.[55] This referral of ethics matters to the American Psychiatric Association suggests that "certain aspects of a physician-patient relationship still are applicable."[56]

It should be noted that at least one court, the Supreme Judicial Court of Massachusetts, has indicated that any psychiatrist engaged in forensic psychiatry is to be held to the AAPL standards, whether or not a member of that organization.[57]

Code of Ethics of the National Association of Social Workers   The **NASW** *Code of Ethics* was last revised in 1999. A copy of the Code may be accessed at *www.naswdc.org/pubs/ code/default.asp.*

National Federation of Societies for Clinical Social Work   Clinical social workers may also belong to the National Federation of Societies for Clinical Social Work, which has its own code of ethics, which may be accessed at *www.cswf.org/www/CSWF%20Ethics % 20Code%20Prtctd.pdf.*

National Organization of Forensic Social Workers   The National Organization of Forensic Social Workers also has its own code of ethics, last revised in 1997, which may be accessed at *www.nofsw.org.*

This chapter describes some of the ethical problems that psychologists, other mental health professionals, or attorneys may confront in the course of an evaluation and subsequent testimony. Although the specific references are primarily to psychologists, most comments apply to all mental health experts.

§ 2.3   Competency of Experts

No expert can claim to know everything of possible relevance to a case, nor to have done all possible research in the course of an evaluation. Therefore,

> [f]orensic psychologists have an *obligation* to present to the court, regarding the specific matters to which they will testify, the bundaries of their competence, the factual bases (knowledge,

---

[54] R.D. Miller, *Professional versus Personal Ethics: Methods for System Reform?*, 20 Bull. Am. Acad. Psychiatry & L. 163, 171 (1992).

[55] Larry Strasburger et al., *On Wearing Two Hats: Role Conflict in Serving as Both Psychotherapist and Expert Witness*, 154 Am. J. Psychiatry 448–56 (1997) [hereinafter Strasburger et al.].

[56] Robert Weinstock et al., *Ethics and Forensic Psychiatry*, 13 Am. Psychiatric Press Rev. Psychiatry 379 (1994) [hereinafter Weinstock et al.].

[57] Board of Registration in Medicine, 662 N.E.2d 1020 (Mass. 1996), *reported in* Howard V. Zonana, *AAPL Ethical Guidelines in Appellate Decision*, 22 Am. Ass'n Psychiatry & L. Newsl. 3 (1997).

skill, experience, training and education) for their qualifications as an expert, and the relevance of those factual bases to their qualification as an expert on the specific matters at issue.[58]

A psychologist who claims to have special expertise must have achieved it through "education, training, supervised experience, consultation, study or professional experience." (Ethical Standard 2.01(a).) Furthermore, according Ethical Standard 2.01(c), psychologists planning to provide services for which they are not yet trained must obtain those skills through those same means. If there are not yet standards of practice in an area in which psychologists wish to practice, they must "take reasonable steps to ensure the competence of their work and to protect clients/patients . . . and others from harm." (Ethical Standard 2.01(e).)

§ 2.4   Expert's Openness and Honesty with the Retaining Attorney

An attorney who retains an expert not only relies on the expert to be competent in doing the evaluation but, also, expects that the expert will do nothing to harm the case. The expert has an ethical duty to inform the attorney about anything known to the expert that may interfere with these expectations. Of particular concern are "skeletons in the closet" and philosophical beliefs that may prevent the expert from doing an objective evaluation.

"Skeletons" include any matter that might have an adverse impact upon the expert's credibility in court. Current allegations of professional ethics violations, sanctions by a licensing board or ethics committee, criminal convictions, and so forth are matters about which the attorney must know prior to the expert's being retained to do an evaluation. Although attorneys are generally not required to report these kinds of information about themselves, mental health experts are, for several reasons. Depending on the type of violation at issue, the nature of the case at hand, and the attorney's evaluation of any offsetting factors (for example, qualities that may make the past allegation or problem seem irrelevant or unimportant), the attorney may choose to retain the expert in spite of those matters or to find another expert with no such obvious drawbacks. It must be assumed that the opposing side will discover the information and potentially use it to discredit the expert. Allowing this to happen well into a case would be highly unethical and would damage both the litigant and the attorney. With advance knowledge, the attorney is able to decide how the matter should be handled—for example, through a plan to bring the matter out in direct examination—and the evaluation can proceed.[59]

Philosophical beliefs or personal beliefs may interfere with the expert's ability to be highly objective in conducting an evaluation. Because everyone has some of these biases, the original *Ethical Guidelines for the Practice of Forensic Psychiatry* of the American Academy of Psychiatry and the Law was changed in 1989 by replacing "impartiality" with "honesty" in guideline IV.[60]

For example, many experts would have difficulty objectively evaluating an alleged perpetrator of sexual harassment, or of child abuse, or of spouse abuse, because of strong

---

[58] Specialty Guidelines, III.B (emphasis added).

[59] *Skeletons in the Closet Haunt Experts*, 2 Testifying Expert 1, 4 (1994).

[60] Weinstock et al. at 377.

negative feelings about people alleged to have done those things. When such beliefs and biases are relevant, experts who have them must reveal them to the attorney prior to being retained. The attorney can then determine whether a particular belief or bias would be a hindrance or a help in the instant case. One of the authors of this text, for example, has evaluated a number of victims of sexual misconduct by professionals, and was involved in helping to pass a statute making such misconduct a felony in Wisconsin. Most attorneys for alleged perpetrators have, not surprisingly, failed to consider retaining this psychologist to evaluate their clients—but a few have sought him out, believing that his credibility as an opponent of exploitation by professionals would aid their cases.

§ 2.5   Rights and Responsibilities of Test Takers

The Joint Committee on Testing Practices of the American Educational Research Association, the American Psychological Association, and the National Council on Measurement in Education has published a set of "guidelines and expectations" on "the rights and responsibilities of test takers," "the rights of test takers: guidelines for testing professionals," and "the responsibilities of test takers: guidelines for the testing professionals." The Guidelines establish that test takers have a right to be tested with instruments that are based upon high professional standards, and that are appropriate for the purpose for which they are being used. Tests are to be administered and interpreted by individuals with appropriate training who adhere to a professional ethical code. They have a right to accommodations if they meet the specifications of the Americans with Disabilities Act. They usually have a right to information about the purpose of the testing and to whom the results will be reported. They have a right to informed consent, unless the test has been ordered by a court or other relevant authority. Under most circumstances, they have a right to some feedback regarding the results of the testing. The complete text of the *Rights and Responsibilities of Test Takers* is available at *www.apa.org/science/ttrr.html.*

§ 2.6   Preserving Legal and Civil Rights

Forensic psychologists are required to make a reasonable effort to ensure that their services are used in a manner that promotes the preservation of the legal rights of the parties to a legal proceeding.[61] They are also obligated to understand the civil rights of parties to those proceedings, and in no way to diminish or endanger those rights.[62]

§ 2.7   Promoting Client and Patient Welfare

Most professional codes of ethics mandate that the welfare of the consumer is paramount and that the services of the professional must be used in a responsible manner. It would

---

[61] Specialty Guidelines, IV.E.

[62] Ethics Code, Preamble, Principle E; Specialty Guidelines, III.D.; Canadian Code, Principle I, Ethical Standard I.5 [hereinafter Canadian Code].

be a violation of these requirements to simply point out the nature of the problems in the person or people being evaluated, without also identifying strengths and recommending means of improvement. Principle A of the *Ethical Principles of Psychologists and Code of Conduct*, headed "Beneficence and Nonmaleficence," indicates that "[p]sychologists strive to benefit those with whom they work, and take care to do no harm. . . ." In a child custody case, for example, the expert should analyze the strengths of each parent, the developmental needs of the children, and the requirements for promoting new family structures. In so doing, the advantages and disadvantages of various alternatives must be weighed. If treatment is seen as necessary for any family member, the expert should recommend types of treatment that may be helpful, and, if known, some places where that treatment is available.

The evaluator should not actually *provide* the treatment, however, as that is outside the evaluator's role, and it could establish a doctor-patient relationship. See the discussion on dual/multiple relationships in the next section.

§ 2.8   Avoiding Dual or Multiple Relationships

Psychologists must "avoid improper and potentially harmful dual relationships."[63] In other words, they must avoid situations wherein loyalty is owed to more than one person or institution, or that may otherwise compromise the quality of the psychologists' judgment by involving a conflict of interest. In a custody case, the primary loyalty is owed to the "best interests of the child," but loyalty is also owed to the psychologist's other clients: the court, each person evaluated, and, unless the psychologist is court-appointed, to one or more attorneys. The psychologist is, therefore, required to abide by ethical obligations regarding informed consent (or assent, if court-ordered) for those assessed, confidentiality, clarification of any matters related to fees, and so forth. "As adjuncts to the fact-finding process, psychologists must internalize the court's concern for objectivity, fairness, and the well-being of the child."[64]

Evaluators are automatically cast into dual or multiple relationships by virtue of the conflicts between their professional and legal roles. Evaluators have a responsibility to the person who retained them and, if not one and the same, also have a separate responsibility to the individual or individuals being evaluated.[65] They have responsibilities to their codes of ethics, which may be in conflict with statutes, case law, and rulings by judges in the specific case. They also have responsibilities to those who may be harmed by the person being evaluated, under the *Tarasoff* principle. See **§ 2.24.**

It is always better for the expert to evaluate both parents, whether the expert is appointed by the court, retained by the guardian ad litem, or jointly retained for that purpose by agreement of both parents. Part of the reason is that the clinician is likely to feel "a subtle and almost irresistible pull toward advocacy . . . at the expense of the objective attitude for which clinicians must strive." In addition,

---

[63] Ethics Code, Principle C. *See also id.* Ethical Standards 3.05, 3.06, 3.07, 3.08, 6.05, 7.07. Specialty Guidelines, IV.D.1., IV.D.2; Association of State and Provincial Psychology Boards Code of Conduct B.2.a. [hereinafter ASPPB Code]; Canadian Code, III.32.

[64] Weithorn & Grisso, Psychological Consultation in Divorce Custody Litigation 193 (1987) [hereinafter Weithorn & Grisso].

[65] Weinstock et al. at 369.

some of the most important information obtained in custody cases is about the relationships between the parents. An arrangement that often does not give us access to both parents and the child places severe limits on what we can offer the court. . . . It is not clearly unethical for an examiner to be retained by one side, as long as the examiner restricts testimony to the narrow opinions formed with such limited information.[66]

Combining Therapist and Evaluator Roles

There are many reasons why a therapist should not be retained or appointed as an expert to evaluate his or her own patient/client. If the evaluation favors the patient/client, for example, the therapist could be accused of favoritism. If it does not, the therapeutic relationship could be seriously harmed and the therapy accomplished up to that point may become relatively worthless. Furthermore, in therapy, an individual has a right to expect confidentiality, to expect the therapist to do only what is in the person's best interest (beneficence), and to avoid doing anything harmful (nonmaleficence), except in a "duty to warn or protect" situation. See **§ 2.24.** The trust relationship between the therapist and patient may lead the therapist to exert undue influence on the patient, to the patient's detriment.[67] The need for confidentiality in therapy is the basis for the Supreme Court's recognition of the psychotherapist-patient privilege in *Jaffee v. Redmond*.[68] See **§ 2.35.**

In contrast, the evaluator's task is to seek the truth, whether that helps or harms the patient/client. It is therefore rarely possible for a therapist to ethically become an evaluator for a patient/client.[69] The only significant exception may be in rural areas where the therapist is the only expert available to provide the necessary forensic services.[70]

This is directly addressed by the *Ethics Guidelines for the Practice of Forensic Psychiatry* of the American Academy of Psychiatry and the Law: "A treating psychiatrist should generally avoid agreeing to be an expert witness or to perform an evaluation of his patient for legal purposes because a forensic evaluation usually requires that other people be interviewed and testimony may adversely affect the therapeutic relationship."[71]

Ethical Standard 3.05 of the American Psychological Association's *Ethical Principles of Psychologists and Code of Conduct* indicates that psychologists must be careful to avoid

---

[66] Grisso, *Evolving Guidelines for Divorce/Custody Evaluations*, 28 Fam. & Conciliation Cts. Rev. 37 (1990) [hereinafter Grisso].

[67] Grant L. Iverson, *Dual Relationships in Psycholegal Evaluations: Treating Psychologists Serving as Expert Witnesses*, 18 Am. J. Forensic Psychol. 79–87 (2000) [hereinafter Iverson].

[68] 116 S. Ct. 1923 (1996).

[69] Iverson at 79–87.

[70] Paul S. Appelbaum, *Ethics in Evolution: The Incompatibility of Clinical and Forensic Functions*, 154 Am. J. Psychiatry 445–46 (1997); Strasburger et al.; Stuart Greenberg & Daniel Shuman, *Irreconcilable Conflict between Therapeutic and Forensic Roles*, 28 Prof. Psychol.: Res. & Prac. 50–57 (1997) [hereinafter Greenberg & Shuman]; David Shapiro, Standard of Care in Forensic Assessments, Paper presented at the Annual Convention of the American Psychological Association, New York (Aug. 1995); Steven Golding, *Expert Opinion*, 14 Am. Psychol. L. Soc'y News 5 (1994).

[71] AAPL Ethics for the Practice of Forensic Psychiatry § IV, para. 7 (1995) [hereinafter AAPL Ethics]; Paul S. Appelbaum, *Ethics in Evolution: The Incompatibility of Clinical and Forensic Functions*, 154 Am. J. Psychiatry 445–46 (1997).

multiple relationships that may involve conflicting roles, especially if there is a potential to harm the patient/client. Sometimes, however, there is no realistic alternative to the therapist's also serving in an expert capacity. Standard 3.05 therefore notes that, when multiple and potentially conflicting roles cannot be avoided, the ethical mandate is to "take reasonable steps to resolve it with due regard for the best interests of the affected person and maximal compliance with the Ethics Code." Further, "[w]hen psychologists are required by law, institutional policy, or extraordinary circumstances to serve in more than one role in judicial or administrative proceedings, at the outset they clarify role expectations and the extent of confidentiality and thereafter as changes occur."

Part of a therapist's role when there is a potential for litigation involving a patient/client is to help the person look at the pros and cons of proceeding toward litigation. The primary advantage is that legal actions may be both therapeutic and empowering, helping an individual to feel less victimized. Major disadvantages include the potential that therapy may plateau during the life of the legal action, as issues related to the lawsuit keep the person from resolving other issues, and the difficulty both the patient/client and the therapist have in addressing issues that could impact positively or negatively on the litigation. If the therapist testifies, the patient/client may see the vulnerability of the therapist during a tough cross-examination, and a legally naive therapist could potentially do real harm to the patient/client's case.[72]

The situation is further confused by multiple-role demands on therapists:

> [W]ith many patients' problems being seen as manifestations of extrapsychic (environmental, institutional, economic, legal, or political) conditions, the therapist is becoming a social worker, mobilizing dual resources on the patient's behalf; a gatekeeper, unlocking the doors of managed care; a detective, obtaining useful information; or an agent of social control, protecting others from the patient. The therapist, thus placed in an advocate's or case manager's role, is expected to influence external outcomes rather than simply accompany the patient on an inner exploration.[73]

Furthermore, an evaluator must be objective and neutral, while the therapist's task is to learn to see the world through the patient/client's eyes and to be an advocate for the patient/client. The therapist does not, therefore, have the type or depth of psycho-legal foundation usually required to form a forensic opinion to a reasonable degree of certainty. In addition, if the therapist became an evaluator for his or her patient, it could also destroy any gains made in therapy, given the need of the evaluator to be open regarding problems identified—whether or not the patient/client is ready to hear the complete, unadulterated truth.[74]

In addition, if the therapist-cum-evaluator recommends further psychotherapy, it may be seen as an attempt to feather the therapist's nest rather than an objective statement of the individual's needs. Similarly, if the independent evaluator recommends psychotherapy *and* volunteers to become the therapist, the same conclusion may be drawn. While there are

---

[72] Strasburger et al. at 452–53.

[73] *Id*. at 450.

[74] Robert I. Simon & Robert M. Wettstein, *Toward the Development of Guidelines for the Conduct of Forensic Psychiatric Examinations*, 25 J. Am. Acad. Psychiatry & L. 17, 19–20 (1997) [hereinafter Simon & Wettstein]; Strasburger et al. at 451; Greenberg & Shuman at 51.

some circumstances in which the evaluator could agree to become the therapist if strongly requested by the individual who was evaluated, this request should not be given any consideration until the evaluation is complete[75] and the case is closed—and, even then, it is not recommended under most circumstances, but neither is it forbidden.[76] Becoming the therapist would require that the patient/client clearly understands that the evaluator would never be able to serve as an evaluator in the patient/client's case again, and the individual's signed informed consent to that effect should be obtained.[77]

While the evaluator must carefully consider whether there is malingering or at least distortion of the facts, the therapist's task is to see the world through the patient/client's eyes and to suspend a portion of the therapist's own "reality orientation" in order to do so. The evaluator consults medical records, family members, and various other sources of collateral information in an attempt to establish the accuracy of statements made by the patient/client. The therapist, on the other hand, largely takes the person's word for what has happened and gives the benefit of the doubt as part of the process of learning how the patient/client thinks and perceives the world. These evaluator vs. therapist orientations are clearly in conflict.[78]

In an emergency—for example, if the person being evaluated becomes acutely suicidal—an evaluator may have to take on a therapeutic role. If this occurs, the evaluator should, if reasonably possible, provide no further forensic services, to prevent the individual being evaluated from being confused by the dual roles and revealing things that may be appropriately said to a therapist but not to an evaluator.[79] If it is not reasonably possible to end the forensic evaluation, the evaluator should continually remind the individual that the relationship is forensic and not therapeutic, to try to prevent problems from occurring.

Further, in child custody matters, if either parent is the psychologist's patient/client, the psychologist may have a conflict of interest in that the best interests of the child and those of the patient/client may not be the same. If the psychologist believes the patient/client *would* be a good custodial parent, this potential conflict of interest may be avoidable. If the *child* is the patient/client, it may irreparably damage the progress of therapy if the psychologist is required to testify in open court regarding his or her knowledge and opinions. Doing so could create a conflict between the role of the child as patient/client on the one hand and the obligation of the psychologist to advocate for the best interests of the child on the other, and also raises confidentiality concerns. This conflict may be resolvable only by having the psychologist meet in chambers with the judge and the attorneys, with the psychologist's testimony being unavailable to the parents until therapy ends.[80]

Having pointed out in an evaluation that one or more parties to a custody action should have individual or conjoint psychotherapy, it is not unusual for the independent or court-

---

[75] Bruce Bennett et al., Professional Liability and Risk Assessment 93 (1990).

[76] Weinstock et al. at 384.

[77] Simon & Wettstein at 19; Strasburger et al. at 449.

[78] Simon & Wettstein at 19; Strasburger et al. at 451.

[79] Gary B. Melton et al., Psychological Evaluations for the Courts 661 (2d ed. 1997) [hereinafter Melton et al.].

[80] L. Weithorn, *Psychological Consultation in Divorce Custody Litigation: Ethical Considerations, in* Psychology and Child Custody Determinations 193 (L. Weithorn ed., 1987) [hereinafter Weithorn].

appointed evaluator to be asked to be the therapist for the party or parties, given that he or she already knows the individual(s) well. If the request is for therapy to begin prior to the end of the legal matter, it would be unethical (as a dual relationship problem) for the psychologist to agree. If therapy is to begin after the court matter is settled, and particularly "if the subsequent therapeutic request is wholly unanticipated,"[81] there would be a lesser dual relationship problem, and therapy could proceed *if* all parties and attorneys agree in writing that the psychologist's role as an independent evaluator has terminated and that the psychologist will no longer be required to ever fulfill the role of an independent expert in the case.[82] Nevertheless, it is recommended that the evaluator refuse to take on the role of therapist because it could give the appearance that the recommendation for therapy was made in order to provide the evaluator with future business. Because it would preclude the evaluator from doing a future evaluation of an individual, becoming the therapist for any party could also detract from future court actions. Only in exceptional circumstances, therefore, should an evaluator become the therapist for a party to a custody matter.

In summary, psychologist Stuart Greenberg and law professor Daniel Shuman identify 10 differences between therapeutic and forensic relationships, shown in **Table 2–1.**[83]

It should be noted that no court is known to have excluded a forensic assessment by a psychologist or psychiatrist on the basis that the individual also served as the litigant's therapist.[84] Courts also have the prerogative under Federal Rule of Evidence 701, or an equivalent rule at the state level, of treating a therapist as an expert who can state opinions and inferences, even if the therapist was presented only as a fact witness.[85]

Therapists who must testify for some reason need to proceed cautiously. Given the expectation that a patient/client is likely to disclose more information to a therapist (who is expected to maintain confidentiality) than to a forensic evaluator (who is not), the therapist who considers testifying as an expert must discuss at length with the patient/client the nature of potentially embarrassing or otherwise harmful information that could come out at a deposition or trial and, with the patient/client's consent, discuss the same information with the litigant's attorney. These discussions should, of course, be carefully documented, and the patient's acknowledgment of proceeding on the basis of informed consent should be in writing and signed.[86]

---

[81] Melton et al. at 86.

[82] Lyn R. Greenberg, David A. Martindale, Jonathan W. Gould, & Dianna J. Gould-Saltman, *Ethical Issues in Child Custody and Dependency Cases: Enduring Principles and Emerging Challenges*, 1 Journal of Child Custody 7–30 (2004).

[83] Greenberg & Shuman at 52. Copyright © 1997 by the American Psychological Association. Reprinted with permission.

[84] *Id.* at 55.

[85] Jane Goodman-Delahunty, *Forensic Psychological Expertise in the Wake of* Daubert, 21 L. & Hum. Behav. 121, 125 (1997).

[86] Greenberg & Shuman at 55–56.

Table 2–1

Ten Differences between Therapeutic and Forensic Relationships

	Care provision	Forensic evaluation
1. Whose client is patient/litigant?	The mental health practitioner	The attorney
2. The relational privilege that governs disclosure in each relationship	Therapist-patient privilege	Attorney-client and attorney work privilege
3. The cognitive set and evaluative attitude of each expert	Supportive, accepting, empathetic	Neutral, objective, detached
4. The differing areas of competency of each expert	Therapy techniques for treatment of the impairment	Forensic evaluation techniques relevant to the legal claim
5. The nature of the hypotheses tested by each expert	Diagnostic criteria for the purpose of therapy	Psycholegal criteria for the purpose of legal adjudication
6. The scrutiny applied to the information utilized in the process and the role of historical truth	Mostly based on information from the person being treated	Litigant information, supplemented with that of collateral sources and scrutinized by the evaluator and court
7. The amount and control of structure in each relationship	Patient-structured and relatively less structured than forensic evaluation	Evaluator structured and relatively more structured than therapy
8. The nature and degree of "adversarialness" in each relationship	A helping relationship; rarely adversarial	Frequently adversarial
9. The goal of the professional in each relationship	Therapist attempts to benefit the patient by working within the relationship	Evaluator advocates for the results and implications of the evaluation for the benefit of the court
10. The impact on each relationship of critical judgment by the expert	The basis of the relationship is the therapeutic alliance, and critical judgment is likely to impair that alliance	The basis of the relationship is evaluative, and critical judgment is unlikely to cause serious emotional harm

Informal Discussions

There are no official procedural or ethics guidelines that prevent an expert from consulting with a peer or even talking with an attorney for "the other side" about a case in which the expert has been retained as an educator or a testimonial witness. Informally, however, attorneys have a norm that requires that the attorney who retained the expert be consulted prior to any discussions with that attorney's expert by opposing counsel. If an attorney used information from an informal encounter with an expert against the adverse party, any sanctions that may be imposed would normally be imposed on the attorney or the parties, not the experts. If a specific jurisdiction differs in any way from these conclusions, it is important for attorneys to so advise any experts they retain.[87]

Acting as Mediator

Similar to the above discussion of an evaluator considering becoming a therapist for one or more family members after the case is settled (that is, the court has ruled on custody and placement), the authors of this text do not believe that it is a dual-relationship conflict for the psychologist to act as a mediator in a custody matter *once the evaluation process is complete*. Because the ethical imperative is to serve the best interests of the child, the individual who conducted the evaluation may be in a particularly good position to help avoid having to go to court, which should decrease the animosity between the parents, which in turn will certainly benefit the child. Certain precautions must be taken for this to work, however.

All parties and all attorneys must be aware that psychologists who become mediators in cases are unlikely to be sufficiently independent to be evaluators who could subsequently be available for court testimony. All attorneys and all parties should sign a statement acknowledging that they understand and accept the psychologist's change of roles and, further, understand that the psychologist will no longer be available to testify in the case—and that the attorneys will not ask the psychologist to do so.

Appearance of Duality

The expert must also avoid the appearance of a dual relationship as much as possible. One way to do so is to limit telephone calls from litigants, requesting that any information to be added to what has been said during the evaluation should be written down and mailed to the expert. Any expressed need for counseling should, of course, be referred to another professional. The expert should make notes on all calls received because they are part of the relevant clinical record. By taking these steps, it should not appear as if the expert is favoring one of the parents over the other in a custody suit.[88]

---

[87] Saks, *Expert Witnesses, Nonexpert Witnesses, and Nonwitness Experts*, 14 L. & Hum. Behav. 291, 309 (1990).

[88] D. Martindale et al., *Providing Expert Testimony in Child Custody Litigation, in* 10 Innovations in Clinical Practice: A Source Book 482 (P. Keller & S. Heyman eds., 1991) [hereinafter Martindale et al.].

Evaluator as a Consultant to an Attorney

The expert who is retained by an attorney is acting as the agent of the attorney and is bound by the attorney-client privilege. In most states, this means that the attorney and the attorney's agents do not have to report child abuse or most other threats to public safety.[89]

As a consultant, the professional is also likely to be acting as a researcher, identifying information from the professional literature that is relevant to the process of determining whether each of the parents would be a suitable custodial parent for the specific children in the family.

Although there is no dual relationship between the role of researcher and the professional's other roles, the expert witness role and the consultant role are mutually exclusive.[90] The expert who is to render an opinion, in a report or in court, needs to strive to be impartial and objective,[91] while a consultant tries to help the attorney build the case.

There are at least two exceptions, however. The primary one is if the client requests the attorney's services to help the client commit a future crime. The second requires or recommends that an attorney provide sufficient information to prevent a death or serious bodily harm, whether or not the attorney's services were requested for that purpose.[92] The expert retained by the attorney may have the same obligation to report under these circumstances. The expert should determine the standards he or she is required to adhere to under state law and licensing codes, and act accordingly. It should be noted that if the expert is asked to testify, the attorney-client privilege is waived in most jurisdictions, and the "professional may be compelled to disclose all relevant information disclosed by the client."[93]

An evaluator who cannot accept this restriction must so inform the attorney prior to agreeing to this evaluation. If this is not acceptable to the attorney, the psychologist should decline to do the evaluation. If the attorney still chooses to retain the expert, the expert next needs to specify to the client, prior to the evaluation, that the expert will not hold confidential any information regarding a danger to public safety, as defined above, and should get the client to sign an acknowledgment that this has been explained and is understood. This would permit the evaluator to adhere to his or her ethical and often statutory requirement to report behavior that is dangerous to self or others.

If an expert is asked to evaluate one parent and one or more children in an actual or potential custody case, the psychologist should determine whether it is both legal and ethical to do so in each particular case. See § 2.7. "In some states, a noncustodial parent may not legally seek services from a psychologist for a child without permission from the

---

[89] Simon & Wettstein at 23; Daniel Shuman, *Reporting of Child Abuse during Forensic Evaluations*, 15 Am. Psychol. L. Soc'y News 3, 5 (1995); Personal communication with Donald Bersoff, Ph.D., J.D. (Feb. 6, 1998).

[90] Warren, *Roles and Dilemmas of Mental Health Professionals in Child Custody Evaluations*, 4 Am. J. Fam. L. 251, 253 (1990).

[91] Schetky, *Ethical Issues in Forensic Child and Adolescent Psychiatry*, 31 J. Am. Acad. Child & Adolescent Psychiatry 403, 403 (1992) [hereinafter Schetky].

[92] American Bar Association Model Rules of Professional Conduct, Rule 1.6, *discussed in* Melton et al. at 659.

[93] Daniel Shuman, *Reporting of Child Abuse during Forensic Evaluations*, 15 Am. Psychol. L. Soc'y News 3, 5 (1995).

custodial parent or by court order. However, to avoid a charge of unethical behavior, the psychologist should notify the custodial parent, regardless of the statute."[94] If the parents are informally separated, getting the consent of the other parent is still strongly recommended. If formally separated, it is critical to obtain that consent. Prior to agreeing to conduct the evaluation, the noncustodial parent should be informed of the need for notice to the custodial parent. Even though not required by law, ethics codes generally require that the expert clarify the nature of relationships when multiple parties are involved. Because the custodial parent could be affected by the results of the evaluation, that parent is a party to the request for the evaluation and should be notified.[95]

§ 2.9   Avoiding Iatrogenic Harm

"Iatrogenic illness" refers to "a disorder precipitated, aggravated, or induced by the physician's attitude, examination, comments, or treatment."[96] In the course of conducting an evaluation, a mental health expert could do a number of things that would harm the individuals involved in the process. The expert must be cognizant of ways in which this could occur and should make every effort to avoid doing harm.[97]

Forensic psychologists are required to "ensure that their services and the products of their services are used in a forthright and responsible manner"—that is, a manner that minimizes the probability of an iatrogenic injury.[98]

In a custody battle, it is likely that each family member is going through a personal crisis engendered by the divorce and custody dispute. It is therefore essential that the evaluator do everything possible to minimize the stress involved in the process. One means of doing so is to discuss the nature of the evaluation process, so that the individual has some feeling for what to expect. Another is to avoid probing in areas that are only marginally relevant to the questions that must be answered in the evaluation.[99]

In the custody evaluation, it would also be harmful in most cases to directly ask a child which parent the child wishes to live with, implying that the choice belongs to the child. "Assigning a child this responsibility invariably provides the child a destructive misperception of omnipotence and potentiates a sense of betrayal and ultimately guilt."[100] Care should also be taken in general to try to keep from subjecting children to unnecessary distress, confusion, or guilt.[101]

---

[94] Boyer, *Assuming Risk in Child Custody Evaluations*, 16 Reg. Rep. 8, 8 (1990).

[95] *Id.* at 8–9.

[96] American Psychiatric Glossary 103 (J.E. Edgerton & R.J. Campbell eds., 1994).

[97] Stone & Shear, *The Boundaries of Mental Health Expertise in Dependency and Family Law: A Proposal for Standards of Practice*, 26 Conciliation Cts. Rev. 49, 54 (1988) [hereinafter Stone & Shear].

[98] Specialty Guidelines, II.B.

[99] Stone & Shear at 54.

[100] Steven B. Bisbing et al., Sexual Abuse by Professionals: A Legal Guide 517 (1995) [hereinafter Bisbing et al.].

[101] Lois B. Oberlander, *Ethical Responsibilities in Child Custody Evaluations: Implications for Evaluation Methodology*, 5 Ethics & Behav. 311, 325 (1995).

It would also be destructive of the relationship between a parent and a child to indicate, unless absolutely necessary, that negative conclusions about the parent are based directly on statements made by the child.

Although experts have the obligation to disclose the bases of their conclusions and recommendations, discretion must be used in an attempt to effect the best outcome for the child and the family, and to avoid this type of iatrogenic injury.[102]

If the evaluator is seeing only one of the parents, along with the children, it is likely that the anxiety of the children will be increased. This is true whether the other parent is aware of the evaluation but refuses to participate, or is unaware of the evaluation and the children are being asked to keep it a secret from that parent. In either case, the relationship between the children and the noninvolved parent will be strained, with the psychologist as a "party to the crime."

A dilemma can arise when an expert is asked to evaluate a child or parent who has been victimized, with the knowledge that discussion of the victimization could precipitate a negative psychological reaction that could be as severe as suicidal acting out. The expert must ethically respond first as a mental health professional, protecting the individual from harm, and only secondarily as an expert retained in a legal matter.

OBTAINING DATA

§ 2.10   The Expert's Need for Data and Time to Collect It

A psychologist is obligated to identify all the major factors that need to be addressed prior to stating an opinion and to refuse to do an evaluation (or to limit the scope of an evaluation) if those factors cannot, for whatever reason, be addressed adequately.[103] This would apply to the situation discussed in **§ 2.20,** where the psychologist may not have access to all the parties involved in the custody action. It would also apply if any medical, school, social service, or other records were refused. For the evaluation to be adequate, it is essential that many sources of data be consulted, including these records, psychological tests, and interviews of the parties and others who have potentially relevant input. In addition, a low and arbitrary limit placed on the number of hours a psychologist may devote to data gathering and analysis would mean that some important factors may not be adequately addressed. Although there need not be a blank check, any limits on time need to be liberal if the best interests of the child are to be served. "[P]roviding information to one's expert is not a place for attorneys to be cutting corners for the sake of saving money, time, or presumably reducing their exposure for deposition and cross-examination."[104] A 1997 study by one of the authors of this text found that the average time required for a custody evaluation has increased to 21.1 hours.[105]

---

[102] Stone & Shear at 60.

[103] Ethics Code, Ethical Standards 9.01(a), (b); Specialty Guidelines, VI.C; Bisbing et al. at 517 (1995).

[104] Bisbing et al. at 517.

[105] Marc J. Ackerman & Melissa C. Ackerman, *Custody Evaluation Practice: A Survey of Experienced Professionals (Revisited)*, 28 Prof. Psychol.: Res. & Prac. 137, 138 (1997) [hereinafter Ackerman & Ackerman].

Because it is also important not to allow fatigue to play a significant role in the results of the evaluation, the amount of time the parties should be asked to participate in a single day should be limited. The psychological assessment, including interviews, should occur on two or more separate occasions, at least several days apart.

A psychologist who cannot devote the amount of time necessary to do an evaluation correctly, or whose client is unwilling to retain the psychologist for enough hours to do the job right, or whose attempt to evaluate a party is limited by that person's attorney, has an ethical obligation to refuse the task or to limit the scope of the evaluation and clearly state in the report why the scope was so limited.[106]

§ 2.11   Requirement to Use Best Methods Available

Evaluators have enormous power over and influence on the lives of the people who are evaluated. It is therefore essential that the best methods available be utilized to conduct the evaluation.

> The best methods are those that do two things: (1) they promote the principles of objectivity and scientific competence, and (2) they provide data that are as relevant as possible for the questions faced by the court. . . . [In general,] standardized methods promote objectivity better than non-standardized methods. . . . Among other things, standardization means that the examiner has less opportunity to be swayed by personal bias or simple error in seeking information about a parent or child.
>
> A method does not have to be a "test" to be standardized. There are standardized interview schedules that may be used. . . . Moreover, a method does not have to be "published" in order to be standardized. . . . If [used] consistently from one case to another, then they can be said to have this quality of standardization. . . . On the other hand, the most common standardized methods now used in custody evaluations are our traditional clinical psychological tests.[107]

When a test designed for one purpose is used in a different setting, it may not satisfy the requirement to use best methods.[108]

Some newer methods may provide more obviously relevant information than do common psychological tests, but these newer methods also lack the time-tested validity and reliability of the psychological tests. The expert must weigh all these factors, selecting those tests and other instruments that are as valid, reliable, and relevant as possible to the task at hand.

> Relevancy is the underlying predicate for all expert testimony . . . .
>
> Courts have not seemed inclined to limit the use of forensic instruments or psychological tests, so long as their relevance to the legal standard can be demonstrated. Such demonstration could be made in the report itself or during direct testimony. This could be considered part of the ethical obligation incurred by a psychologist, working in a forensic context, to

---

[106] Simon & Wettstein at 28.

[107] Grisso at 38–39.

[108] *Id.*

provide a "full explanation of the results of tests and the bases for conclusions . . . in language that the client can understand."[109]

Ethical Standard 9.08(a) of the 2002 revision of the *Ethical Principles of Psychologists and Code of Conduct* requires that "[p]sychologists do not base their assessment or intervention decisions or recommendations on data or test results that are outdated for the current purpose." Similarly, 9.08(b) indicates that "[p]sychologists do not base such decisions or recommendations on tests and measures that are obsolete and not useful for the current purpose." Thus, when the MMPI-2 had been independently researched sufficiently to demonstrate that it in fact functioned as a replacement for the MMPI, the MMPI became obsolete. Similarly, with each revision of an intelligence test, for example, the Wechsler Adult Intelligence Scale, the old version becomes obsolete when the new version (currently the WAIS-III) has been sufficiently independently researched to demonstrate its validity and reliability.

Using the best methods also includes the need both to use instruments that are appropriate for the specific evaluation and to avoid using instruments that are not relevant. Many psychologists have a "standard test battery" that they use for virtually every evaluation, even if some of the instruments are not appropriate to the task at hand.[110] And, being so comfortable with their "standard battery," they may avoid utilizing instruments that are especially appropriate to the task. An example of an appropriate specialized instrument is the Ackerman-Schoendorf Scales for Parent Evaluation of Custody (ASPECT) for child custody evaluations.

When scoring of a test or other instrument is complicated, the "best method" includes using a computer for scoring the test if possible. The advantage of doing so is that scoring errors should be nonexistent, particularly if the test was computer administered as well. There is also no need for concern that numbers may have been transferred incorrectly from the test sheet to the summary profile. See **§ 2.32.**

One means of identifying the "best methods" is to use instruments that are utilized by a substantial percentage of psychologists for the given purpose. For child custody evaluations, the definitive research was done by one of the authors of this text.[111] It indicates, for example, that 92 percent of psychologists surveyed used the MMPI or MMPI-2 with adults, with 48 percent using the Rorschach. A psychologist who does not administer commonly used instruments, or who uses instruments that are rarely administered, should be asked to explain why. See **Chapter 3** for further discussion of tests used in custody evaluations.

Effect of Costs

The requirement to use the best methods must be part of what the examiner considers when initially determining whether to do the evaluation and when estimating the cost of doing

---

[109] Kirk Heilbrun, *The Role of Psychological Testing in Forensic Assessment*, 16 L. & Hum. Behav. 257, 260 (1992).

[110] James N. Butcher & Kenneth S. Pope, *Seven Issues in Conducting Forensic Assessments: Ethical Responsibilities in Light of New Standards and New Tests*, 3 Ethics & Behav. 267, 271 (1993) [hereinafter Butcher & Pope].

[111] Ackerman & Ackerman.

the evaluation correctly. If it does not appear that sufficient funds are available to pay the expert for the amount of time it is expected to take to do the evaluation correctly, the examiner may ethically choose to charge a lesser fee or even to do the evaluation *pro bono*, but the examiner does *not* have the option of doing less than a competent evaluation.[112] Nor does the expert have the option of failing to be familiar with the most up-to-date information regarding any area in which he or she practices, particularly if one testifies in court.[113]

§ 2.12   Need for a Personal Interview

The evaluator cannot do a complete evaluation without doing a personal interview. No amount of records review and consultation with collaterals will provide sufficient data for the evaluator to claim that a complete evaluation has been performed. Many statements in the professional literature and professional codes indicate the necessity of an interview.

> A psychologist rendering a formal professional opinion about a person, for example about the fitness of a parent in a custody hearing, shall not do so without direct and substantial professional contact with or a formal assessment of that person.[114]
>
> . . . [P]sychologists provide opinions of the psychological characteristics of individuals only after they have conducted an examination of the individuals adequate to support their statements or conclusions. When, despite reasonable efforts, such an examination is not practical, psychologists document the efforts they made and the results of those efforts, clarify the probable impact of their limited information on the reliability and validity of their opinions, and appropriately limit the nature and extent of their conclusions or recommendations.[115]
>
> [U]nless there is a compelling reason for not doing so, a personal interview of the individual in question is regarded as an essential part of a forensic assessment. Rendering a conclusion about someone whom one has not had the opportunity to examine would be regarded as a deviation from the standard of care. Were someone to be injured . . . as a result of a psychologist rendering conclusions without interviewing the individual, the potential for a malpractice action would certainly loom quite large.[116]

While slightly less strong, a statement in the American Academy of Psychiatry and the Law's *Ethics Guidelines for the Practice of Forensic Psychiatry* (1995) indicates that

> [h]onesty, objectivity and the adequacy of the clinical evaluation may be called into question when an expert opinion is offered without a personal examination. While there are authorities who would bar an expert opinion in regard to an individual who has not been personally examined, it is the position of the Academy that if, after earnest effort, it is not possible to conduct

---

[112] Simon & Wettstein at 26–27.

[113] Kirk Heilbrun, Substance and Style of Expert Testimony: Ethics and Effectiveness, Paper presented at the 112th Annual Convention of the American Psychological Association, Honolulu (July 28, 2004).

[114] ASPPB Code, Rule III.A.6.

[115] Ethics Code, Ethical Standard 9.01(b).

[116] David Shapiro, Standard of Care in Forensic Assessments, Paper presented at the Annual Convention of the American Psychological Association, New York (Aug. 1995).

a personal examination, an opinion may be rendered on the basis of other information. However, under such circumstances, it is the responsibility of forensic psychiatrists to assure that the statements of their opinion and any reports of testimony on those opinions, clearly indicate that there was no personal examination and the opinions expressed are thereby limited.[117]

The *Specialty Guidelines for Forensic Psychologists*, Guideline 6H, indicates that

> Forensic psychologists avoid giving written or oral evidence about the psychological characteristics of particular individuals when they have not had an opportunity to conduct an examination of the individual adequate to the scope of the statements, opinions, or conclusions to be issued. Forensic psychologists make every reasonable effort to conduct such examinations. When it is not possible or feasible to do so, they make clear the impact of such limitations on the reliability and validity of their professional products, evidence, or testimony.

Thus, if for some reason—the patient/client's refusal, lack of physical availability (for example, the person lives out of state)—the personal interview cannot be conducted, the ethical responsibility of the evaluator is to state that the evaluation has been limited to some degree and that some conclusions could be different if the individual had been available for an interview. Because this may detract significantly from the weight of the expert's statements, every possible effort should be made to conduct a personal interview.

§ 2.13   Requirement That Tests and Interviews Be Correctly Administered

Psychologists are responsible for ensuring that tests and other instruments are correctly administered. They must ensure that the correct instructions are used, that the environmental conditions are appropriate, and that the patient/client personally responds to all of the test items. The "Casebook for Providers of Psychological Services" indicates that

> [w]hen the psychologist does not have direct, firsthand information as to the conditions under which a test is taken, he or she is forced . . . to assume that the test responses were not distorted by the general situation in which the test was taken (e.g., whether the client consulted others about test responses). Indeed, the psychologist could have no assurance that this test was in fact completed by the client. In the instance where the test might be introduced as data in a court proceeding, it would be summarily dismissed as hearsay evidence.[118]

Further, according to the *Standards for Educational and Psychological Testing* (1999),

> **Standard 1.4.** If a test is used in a way that has not been validated, it is incumbent on the user to justify the new use, collecting new evidence if necessary.[119]

---

[117] AAPL Ethics, para. 4.

[118] *Casebook for Providers of Psychological Services*, 39 Am. Psychologist 663, 664 (1984).

[119] Joint Committee on Standards for Educational and Psychological Testing of the American Educational Research Association, the American Psychological Association, and the National Council on Measurement in Education, Standards for Educational and Psychological Testing 18 (American Educational Research Ass'n 1999) [hereinafter Joint Committee].

Standard 5.1. Test administrators should follow carefully the standardized procedures for administration and scoring specified by the test developer, unless the situation or a test-taker's disability dictates that an exception should be made.[120]

Standard 5.6. Reasonable efforts should be made to assure the integrity of test scores by eliminating opportunities for test takers to attain scores by fraudulent means.[121]

To be absolutely certain that tests are correctly administered, the psychologist should administer the tests personally. This ensures that correct procedures are used, that extra-test behavior (reactions, expressions, and side comments, for example) is noted, and that the entire realm of test-taking behavior is considered in the interpretation done by the psychologist.[122]

> If any circumstances might have affected the results of psychological testing, such as dim lighting, frequent interruptions, a noisy environment, or medication, or if there is doubt that the person being tested shares all relevant characteristics with the reference groups on which the norms are based, these factors must be taken into account when interpreting test data and must be included in the formal report.[123]

The same may be said of the interview(s). The interview needs to be conducted in a private place with a reasonably quiet environment if at all possible—and any exceptions to this rule need to be noted in the report. In addition, people must not be asked to fill out forms in busy waiting rooms or other places where the environment is somewhat likely to interfere with concentration.

According to the July 1993 *American Psychological Association Monitor*, the APA's Ethics Committee was requested "to address whether it is a *per se* violation of the *Ethical Principles of Psychologists and Code of Conduct* to send a Minnesota Multiphasic Personality Inventory home for administration." The response of the Ethics Committee was that this would not automatically be an ethics violation, and that each case would be considered individually. In the past, however, the Committee has found it to be a violation to write a report based on information from a test that was sent home. "The reasons for the violation involved failure to protect the security of the test, failure to adequately supervise the testing, particularly when reservations about reliability and validity are not stated [in the report], and impairment of the welfare of the client."

The Committee endorsed the following points in its response to the question:

- Nonmonitored administration of the MMPI generally does not represent sound testing practice, and may result in invalid assessment for a variety of reasons (e.g., influence from other persons, completion of the test while intoxicated, etc.).

- Test security cannot be guaranteed when the MMPI is allowed outside the clinical setting.

- There is debate as to whether there are ever any circumstances in which it might be reasonable and appropriate to allow an MMPI to be completed away from the clinical setting.

---

[120] *Id*. at 63.

[121] *Id*. at 64.

[122] Berman, *The Expert at Trial: Personality Persuades*, 9 Fam. Advoc. 11–12 (1986). *See also* Nissenbaum, *The Expert at Trial: Tests Tell All*, 9 Fam. Advoc. 14–19 (1986).

[123] K. Pope & M. Vasquez, Ethics in Psychotherapy and Counseling, 2d ed. at 154 (1998).

If the psychologist allows an MMPI to be completed away from the clinical setting, the burden lies with the psychologist to demonstrate that the welfare of the client, or other extenuating circumstances, necessitated the nonmonitored administration, and reasonable efforts were made to maintain test security [2002 Ethical Standard 9.11]. Furthermore, in such circumstances, it would be incumbent upon the psychologist to consider the non-standard conditions under which the test was completed in interpreting and reporting the results [2002 Ethical Standard 9.06]

- These issues are not unique to the MMPI, but must be considered in conducting any assessment.

- In judging the ethicality of at-home administration of tests, it is important to consider such things as the nature and purpose of the test and available information regarding reliability, validity, and standardization procedures. Relevant statements of the test authors and other experts in this regard must be considered seriously. However, the final responsibility for the appropriate use of any assessment instrument lies with the psychologist who administers it.

The above statements are entirely consistent with earlier comments in this section. In any evaluation, the psychologist should, if possible, administer the tests personally, should certainly have tests administered in the professional office, and should note in the report any variations from normal procedure.

Presence of Third Parties during Evaluations

While some attorneys want to observe the evaluations of their clients, this poses an ethical dilemma for the psychologist because there is no psychological instrument that was standardized under circumstances involving an attorney or other nontrained individual observing the administration of the instrument. It is therefore not possible for the psychologist to state, to a reasonable degree of certainty, that the administration was valid, since there is no extant data to support that conclusion—or the opposite conclusion. The same is true of an evaluation that is tape-recorded or videotaped. In each situation, the presence of a third party or a recorder may influence the responses of the person being evaluated, potentially invalidating the evaluation.

The individual being assessed should be alone with the examiner, since assessment instruments are standardized under this condition and there is no research literature indicating whether, and to what degree, the results of a nonstandardized administration may change the results of a particular instrument. This is also true with regard to audio- or videorecording. There is some research indicating that there is an adverse impact on the validity of an assessment when a third party is present or the assessment is recorded. There is no research indicating that the assessment is as valid when a third party is present or the assessment is recorded as when it is not.[124]

---

[124] C.A. Kehrer, P.N. Sanchez, U. Habif, J.G. Rosenbaum, & B.D. Townes, *Effects of a Significant-Other Observer on Neuropsychological Test Performance*, 14 Clinical Neuropsychologist 67–71 (2000); M. Constantinou, M.L. Ashendorf, & R.J. McCaffrey, *When the 3rd Party Observer of a Neuropsychological Evaluation Is an Audio-Recorder*, 16 Clinical Neuropsychologist 407–12 (2002); M. Constantinou & R.J. McCaffrey, *The Effects of 3rd Party Observation: When the Observer Is a Video Camera*, 18 Archives Clinical Neuropsychology 788–89 (2003).

Ethical standards also suggest that there may be serious problems with validity if there is a third party present or if other nonstandard conditions are present. Ethical Standard 9.02(a) of the *Ethical Principles of Psychologists and Code of Conduct* (2002) states that "[p]sychologists administer, score, interpret, or use assessment techniques, interviews, tests, or instruments in a manner and for purposes that are appropriate in application of the techniques." Ethical Standard 9.06 indicates that "[w]hen interpreting assessment results . . ., psychologists take into account . . . various test factors. . . . They indicate any significant limitations of their interpretations." Ethical Standard 9.11 states that "[p]sychologists make reasonable efforts to maintain the integrity and security of test materials and other assessment techniques consistent with law and contractual obligations, and in a manner that permits adherence to this Ethics Code."

Similarly, Standard 1.4 of the *Standards for Educational and Psychological Testing* (1999) indicates that "if a test is used in a way that has not been validated, it is incumbent on the user to justify the new use, collecting new evidence if necessary." Standard 5.4 refers to a need for "minimal distraction." Standard 12.19 indicates that the examiner "should take cognizance of the many factors that may influence a particular testing outcome."

There are only two circumstances, to our knowledge, in which there is a benefit to the presence of a third party and/or audio- or videotaping. One is when a child is interviewed as part of the investigation of alleged sexual or other abuse, if a given child will not speak without a parent or other significant adult present. When that is the case, it is much better to have the third party present than to lose access to the information from the child. Children should also have the fewest number of interviews possible, so an interview by a skilled interviewer or interviewers should be taped (preferably videotaped) so that the interview data is available to all parties. The videotape may also make it unnecessary for the child to testify in person in some jurisdictions. For these and other reasons, the American Academy of Child and Adolescent Psychiatry endorsed videotaping of interviews of children when sexual abuse is alleged. (See *www.aacap.org/publications/policy/ps22htm.*)

The second circumstance in which the presence of a third party may be beneficial is when any individual refuses an interview without that third party present, whether it is a family member, a therapist, an attorney, or someone else. If it is deemed better to permit the third party's presence than to request a court order, that may be done. While the data from the interview may be open to some question regarding its validity, it is generally better to have an interview with the individual rather than have information only from secondary sources or under the duress of a court order.

If the court orders that the attorney may be present, he or she must remain as invisible as possible—in other words, out of the client's sight (for example, behind the client), and entirely silent. Although these caveats are less important during a clinical interview by a mental health professional than they are during psychological testing, the same concerns are present in that situation as well.[125] The U.S. Supreme Court, in *Estelle v. Smith,*

---

[125] Robert I. Simon, *"Three's a Crowd": The Presence of Third Parties during the Forensic Psychiatric Examination*, 24 J. Psychiatry & L. 3–25 (1996); Robert Lloyd Goldstein, *Consequences of Surveillance of the Forensic Psychiatric Examination: An Overview*, 145 Am. J. Psychiatry 1243–47 (1988); Norman E. Zinberg, *The Private versus the Public Psychiatric Interview*, 142 Am. J. Psychiatry 889–94 (1985); Bruce Bennett et al., Professional Liability and Risk Assessment 93 (1990).

indicated that the physical presence of an attorney during an evaluation "could contribute little and might seriously disrupt the examination."[126]

§ 2.14   Revision of the *Standards for Educational and Psychological Testing*

The Joint Committee on the Standards for Educational and Psychological Testing, consisting of representatives of the American Psychological Association, the American Educational Research Association, and the National Council on Measurement in Education, has revised the *Standards for Educational and Psychological Testing*, last revised in 1985. They invited more than 700 organizations to appoint advisors to the Joint Committee.[127] The revision was completed, and endorsed by the three organizations, in 1999. It is the intent of the sponsoring organizations to offer guidelines that are based upon the most up-to-date studies of test construction, validation, and administration.[128] The authors indicate that "each standard should be carefully considered to determine its applicability to the testing context under consideration. In a given case there may be sound professional reason why adherence to the standard is unnecessary."[129] However, they indicate, test developers or users are not expected to have documentation of their decision making regarding each standard routinely available.[130]

The *Standards* define "test" as "an evaluative device or procedure in which a sample of an examinee's behavior in a specified domain is obtained and subsequently evaluated and scored using a standardized process. While the label 'test' is ordinarily reserved for instruments on which responses are evaluated for their correctness or quality and the terms 'scale' or 'inventory' are used for measures of attitudes, interest, and dispositions, the *Standards* uses the single term 'test' to refer to all such evaluative devices." They also note that there is a distinction between the terms "test" and "assessment," with the latter "referring to a process that integrates test information with information from other sources (e.g., information from the individual's social, educational, employment, or psychological history). The applicability of the *Standards* to an evaluation device or method is not altered by the label applied to it (e.g., test, assessment, scale, inventory)." Finally, they note that the field of test development continues to evolve, and that it is not the intent of the *Standards* to prescribe the use of any particular technical methodology.[131]

---

[126] Estelle v. Smith, 451 U.S. 454, 470 n.14 (1981).

[127] Jo-Ida Hansen, Practitioner Concerns regarding the Standards for Educational and Psychological Testing, Paper presented at the Annual Convention of the American Psychological Association, Chicago (Aug. 16, 1997).

[128] Beth Azar, *Changes Will Improve Quality of Tests*, 30 APA Monitor 30 (1999).

[129] Joint Committee 3.

[130] *Id.*

[131] *Id.*

A new type of validity is being included in the revised Standards: "consequential validity":

> Consequential validity is essentially a consideration of the social consequences of the use of a test. The rationale behind consequential validity is that if validity is established through evidence that supports inference regarding specific uses of a test, then intended and unintended consequences of test interpretation and use should be considered in evaluating validity. . . . [T]he traditional forms of validity (criterion, content, and construct) would be the evidential bases of validity, and appraisals or judgments about the value implications and social consequences would comprise the consequential bases of validity.[132]

Thus, while a test may have criterion, content, and construct validity, the test developer or user also has an obligation to try to ensure that there are not unintended consequences of the use of the test. A test that accurately measures variables directly related to, for example, job or school performance or qualities of parenting, and does not also measure extraneous variables that do not directly relate to job or school performance or qualities of parenting, would have consequential validity as well. If, however, the test measured characteristics of the individual not directly related to the stated goal, potentially causing the individual to get a higher or lower score than is justified, the consequential validity would be in question.[133] A test of parenting on which every item related to some aspect of parenting demonstrated by the professional literature to be relevant to good parenting would likely have substantial consequential validity. Any items that were extraneous to that goal, for example, questions that measure socioeconomic status, political viewpoints, gender roles, or other extraneous variables, would have questionable consequential validity. Particularly if something unexpected occurs, the researcher or clinician is to try to determine why it occurred—for example, whether it was the result of something that was done, or something that was omitted.[134]

Other changes in the revised *Standards* include increased emphasis on the use of multiple methods in assessments (tests plus collateral information, observations, interviews, reviews of personal diaries, notes by other professionals, and so forth); increased emphasis on cautionary statements if one's data is limited; and a requirement that any accommodations made for the test taker be described and justified.[135]

Correct test administration, the authors indicate, also includes ensuring that the test is appropriate for the individual being evaluated. If there is any question about the individual's reading ability, a test such as the reading subtest of the Wide Range Achievement Test-3 (WRAT3) should be administered. If English is not the individual's primary language, or if the individual is from a different culture and not well-assimilated into this culture, tests may have to be used that are either culture-fair or that have been validated for the specific cultural group. Failure to choose culturally appropriate test instruments and to

---

[132] Dianne C. Brown, *Joint Committee Report: Standards Revision Is Underway*, 17 The Score 8, 8 (1994).

[133] Joint Committee at 16.

[134] Bert Green, Validity Arguments in the Standards for Educational and Psychological Testing (Revised), Paper presented at the Annual Convention of the American Psychological Association, Chicago (Aug. 16, 1997).

[135] *Id.*

institute culturally appropriate assessment procedures may invalidate much, if not all, of the evaluation.[136]

Examples of standards that may be particularly relevant to child custody matters include

Standard 1.3: If validity for some common or likely interpretation has not been investigated, or if the interpretation is inconsistent with available evidence, that fact should be made clear and potential users should be cautioned about making unsupported interpretations.

Standard 1.4: If a test is used in a way that has not been validated, it is incumbent on the user to justify the new use, collecting new evidence if necessary.

Standard 5.1: Test administrators should follow carefully the standardized procedures for administration and scoring specified by the test developer, unless the situation or a test taker's disability dictates that an exception should be made.

Standard 5.2: Modifications or disruptions of standardized administration procedures or scoring should be documented.

Standard 5.4: The testing environment should furnish reasonable comfort with minimal distractions.

Standard 5.7: Test users have the responsibility of protecting the security of test materials at all times.

Standard 8.4: Informed consent should be obtained from test takers, or their legal representatives when appropriate, before testing is done except (a) when testing without consent is mandated by law or governmental regulation, (b) when testing is conducted as a regular part of school activities, or (c) when consent is clearly implied.

Standard 11.2: When a test is to be used for a purpose for which little or no documentation is available, the user is responsible for obtaining evidence of the test's validity and reliability for this purpose.

Standard 11.3: Responsibility for test use should be assumed by or delegated only to those individuals who have the training, professional credentials, and experience necessary to handle this responsibility. Any special qualifications for test administration or interpretation specified in the test manual should be met.

Standard 11.4: The test user should have a clear rationale for the intended uses of a test or evaluation procedure in terms of its validity and contribution to the assessment and decision-making process.

Standard 11.6: Unless the circumstances clearly require that the test results be withheld, the test user is obligated to provide a timely report of the results that is understandable to the test taker and others entitled to receive this information.

Standard 11.7: Test users have the responsibility to protect the security of tests, to the extent that developers enjoin users to do so. When tests are involved in litigation, inspection of the instruments should be restricted—to the extent permitted by law—to those who are legally or ethically obligated to safeguard test security.

Standard 11.8: Test users have the responsibility to respect test copyrights.

Standard 11.15: Test users should be alert to potential misinterpretations of test scores and to possible unintended consequences of test use; users should take steps to minimize or avoid foreseeable misinterpretations and unintended negative consequences.

---

[136] Hansen, APA Convention.

Standard 11.20: In educational, clinical, and counseling settings, a test taker's score should not be interpreted in isolation; collateral information that may lead to alternative explanations for the examinee's test performance should be considered.

Standard 12.1: Those who use psychological tests should confine their testing and related assessment activities to their areas of competence, as demonstrated through education, supervised training, experience, and appropriate credentialing.

Standard 12.5: The selection of a combination of tests to address a complex diagnosis should be appropriate for the purposes of the assessment as determined by available evidence of validity. The professional's educational training and supervised experience also should be commensurate with the test user qualifications required to administer and interpret the selected tests.

Standard 12.11: Professionals and others who have access to test materials and test results should ensure the confidentiality of the test results and testing materials consistent with legal and professional ethics requirements.

Standard 12.13: Those who select tests and draw inferences from test scores should be familiar with the relevant evidence of validity and reliability for tests and inventories used and should be prepared to articulate a logical analysis that supports all facets of the assessment and the inferences made from the assessment.

Standard 12.14: The interpretation of test results in the assessment process should be informed when possible by an analysis of stylistic and other qualitative features of test-taking behavior that are inferred from observations during interviews and testing and from historical information.

Standard 12.15: Those who use computer-generated interpretations of test data should evaluate the quality of the interpretations and, when possible, the relevance and appropriateness of the norms upon which the interpretations are based.

Standard 12.16: Test interpretation should not imply that empirical evidence exists for a relationship among particular test results, prescribed interventions, and desired outcomes, unless empirical evidence is available for populations similar to those representative of the examinee.

Standard 12.18: The interpretation of test or test battery results generally should be based upon multiple sources of convergent test and collateral data and an understanding of the normative, empirical, and theoretical foundations as well as the limitations of such tests.

Standard 12.19: The interpretation of test scores or patterns of test battery results should take cognizance of the many factors that may influence a particular testing outcome. Where appropriate, a description and analysis of the alternative hypotheses or explanations that may have contributed to the pattern of results should be included in the report.

Finally, the *Standards'* authors address "testing for judicial and governmental decisions." It is noted that participation in the assessment may not be voluntary, and admonishes the clinician to "clarify the purpose of the evaluation, who will have access to the test results and reports, and any rights that the client may have to refuse to participate in court-ordered evaluations." Further, the professional is responsible for accurately relating the assessment results to the legal criteria by which the factfinder will make decisions. It is also "important to assess the examinee's testtaking orientation including response bias to ensure that the legal proceedings have not affected the responses given."[137]

---

[137] Joint Committee at 129.

It is further noted that

> [s]ome tests are intended to provide information about a client's functioning that helps clarify a given legal issue (e.g., parental functioning in a child custody case . . .). However, many tests measure constructs that are generally relevant to the legal issues even though norms specific to the judicial or governmental context may not be available. Professionals are expected to make every effort to be aware of evidence of validity and reliability that supports or does not support their inferences and to place appropriate limits on the opinions rendered. Test users who practice in judicial and government settings are expected to be aware of conflicts of interest that may lead to bias in the interpretation of test results. Protecting the confidentiality of a client's test results and of the test instrument itself poses particular challenges for professionals involved with attorneys, judges, jurors, and other legal and quasi-legal decision makers. The test taker does have a right to expect that test results will be communicated only to persons who are legally authorized to receive them and that other information from the testing session that is not relevant to the evaluation will not be reported. It is important for the professional to be apprised of possible threats to confidentiality and test security (e.g., releasing the test questions, the examinee's responses, and raw and scaled scores on tests to another qualified professional) and to seek, if necessary, appropriate legal and professional remedies.[138]

Paul Sackett, Ph.D., of the University of Minnesota, indicated that the Joint Committee tried to word the *Standards* to make it clear that the *Standards* are not meant to be a checklist that a psychologist should follow to the letter. Rather, "[d]epending on the context and purpose of test development or use, some standards will be more salient than others."[139]

Sackett also indicated that the definition of "validity" has been changed by the committee that drafted the *Standards*. While it used to be said that a test itself was valid or invalid, or that the test possessed construct- and/or content- and/or criterion-based validity, one now addresses whether the test is valid for the specific purpose for which it is being used. The presence or absence of construct-, content-, and/or criterion-based validity is now considered evidence regarding whether the test is valid for its intended purpose. "Test developers and users need to start with the question: What are the inferences we wish to draw from the test score. . . . Then they accumulate evidence to support that." Thus, there are no valid tests, there are valid uses of tests. The psychologist's task is to provide evidence to support the validity of the inference made rather than the test itself, according to Sackett.[140]

§ 2.15   Requirement to Report Relevant Data

Psychologists are ethically obligated to report all relevant data they have that relate directly to the purpose of an evaluation. They are obligated to discuss the limitations of the data, may not suppress disconfirming data, and must acknowledge alternative hypotheses and explanations for their results.[141] For this reason, "we have an affirmative obligation to

---

[138] *Id.*

[139] Quoted in Beth Azar, *Changes Will Improve Quality of Tests*, 30 APA Monitor 30, at 30 (1999).

[140] *Id.*

[141] Ethics Code Principle C, Ethical Standards 9.01(b), 9.02(b), 9.06; Specialty Guidelines, II.B., VI.C., VII.B., VII.D.; ASPPB Code, III.H.3.; Canadian Code, III.8, III.9, III.11.

document everything in our reports. . . . Reports should be long and detailed."[142] "If a psychologist is appointed by the court, he may feel more independent. Nevertheless, an expert is professionally obligated to state his or her findings and opinions truthfully and without bias—regardless of who engaged him."[143] The psychologist is also obligated to try to prevent distortion of his or her views.[144]

Similarly, section IV of the AAPL *Ethics Guidelines for the Practice of Forensic Psychiatry* (1995) states that "practicing forensic psychiatrists enhance the honesty and objectivity of their work by basing their forensic opinions, forensic reports and forensic testimony on all the data available to them . . ., [and distinguish], to the extent possible, between verified and unverified information as well as among clinical 'facts,' 'inferences' and 'impressions.'"

Thus, the expert's task may be seen as the utilization of special skills to generate a representative sample of data to supplement and complement data the parties will produce. The evaluator might also indicate whether various factual allegations of the parties are consistent with the data developed in the evaluative process. The court may then assign relative weights to these independent sources of data to arrive at an ultimate decision.[145]

§ 2.16   Limits on Going Beyond the Data

As clinicians and scientists, psychologists are well trained to gather and interpret data, whether from observations, interviews, psychological testing, medical or school records, or other sources. The data gathered and analyzed may relate to abilities, attitudes, thoughts, feelings, behavior, and relationships. The psychologist is also trained to organize the data from disparate sources into a meaningful whole, which may then be presented as part of the legal inquiry. In addition, psychologists are trained to be able to elaborate on those aspects of functioning of each parent that relate to the unique needs of each child. Ethically, however, psychologists must limit how far beyond the data they go in predicting the future, and must clearly distinguish between those conclusions that are based on hard data and those that are not.[146]

A different way to address the same question is with reference to how validly the psychologist can make statements in response to each of several types of questions asked. If the question is about the individual's current psychological functioning, existing psychological tests permit a number of statements to be made validly and reliably. Examples

---

[142] Kirk Heilbrun, Substance and Style of Expert Testimony: Ethics and Effectiveness, Paper presented at the 112th Annual Convention of the American Psychological Association, Honolulu (July 28, 2004).

[143] The Psychologist's Legal Handbook at 646; *see also* David L. Shapiro, *Problems Encountered in the Preparation and Presentation of Expert Testimony, in* The Encyclopedic Handbook of Private Practice 739–58, at 752 (Eric Margenau ed., 1990); Heilbrun, 1992, at 48; Heilbrun et al. at 64–65 & 73.

[144] Psychologist's Legal Handbook at 663; Ethics Code, Principles B, C; Ethical Standards 1.01, 9.04(a); Specialty Guidelines, VI.B., VII.A.1., VII.D.; ASPPB Code, III.F.6; Canadian Code, III.6, III.13.

[145] Stone & Shear at 54.

[146] Ethics Code, Principle B, Ethical Standards 9.01(b), 9.06, Specialty Guidelines, VI.C., VI.F., VI.F.1., VI.F.3., VI.H.; ASPPB Code, III.A.5; Canadian Code, II.13.

would include statements regarding an individual's level of intelligence as measured by the Wechsler Adult Intelligence Scale-III (WAIS-III) or personality as described by the Minnesota Multiphasic Personality Inventory, Second Edition (MMPI-2). More difficult are questions regarding the presence of a particular state or condition—for example, a formal diagnosis of a mental disorder—because the criteria for making the diagnosis are less explicit than are test results; that is, the psychologist must infer rather than simply report. More difficult yet are responses to questions involving potential dangerousness to self or others or future parenting quality. Here the inference is clouded by the substantial influence that environmental factors can have on the way an individual responds to future situations. The quality of possible predictions is at best equivocal and must be made with a variety of qualifying statements to have any validity at all. In other words, the psychologist should not claim certainty about these tenuous factors.[147]

Equally important, psychologists and other experts must qualify statements by identifying whether the basis for a conclusion is their clinical expertise, moral sense, or common sense.[148] Many conclusions on ultimate issues (for example, who is the better custodial parent, is a dangerous individual, and so forth) are based as much or more on moral sense or common sense as on clinical expertise.

DRAWING CONCLUSIONS

§ 2.17   Drawing Conclusions on Matters of Law

Being relatively naive about the legal process, a psychologist may draw conclusions on matters of law rather than solely provide data and recommendations that can be used by the judge in making the determination of what would be in the best interests of the child. Although psychologists can and should provide data regarding the positive and negative aspects of parenting by each parent, and the quality of the "fit" between the needs of the child and the abilities of the parents, it goes beyond the present ability of any psychologist to predict with certainty which parent would be the better custodial parent in all circumstances and over a period of years. In stating their opinions, psychologists are obligated to acknowledge this lack of a threshold below which custodial rights should be denied. That judgment belongs to the court.[149] This does not necessarily mean that a psychologist must not render an opinion regarding type of custody arrangement, visitation, or similar issues—only that the opinion must be labeled as an opinion. Some state laws oppose recommendations from experts regarding the ultimate disposition of the case, while laws of other states permit or require such recommendations to be made.[150]

---

[147] Weiner, *On Competence and Ethicality in Psychodiagnostic Assessment*, 53 J. Personality Assessment 827, 828 (1989).

[148] Melton et al. at 17.

[149] Weithorn & Grisso, *Psychological Evaluations in Divorce Custody: Problems, Principles, and Procedures, in* Psychology and Child Custody Determinations 157–61 (1987) [hereinafter Weithorn & Grisso].

[150] Melton et al. at 540.

These points are underscored by Judge David Bazelon's statement that

> conclusory statements are bad enough when they merely propound the scientific gospel. They become positively dangerous when they verge into naked pronouncements on the ultimate issue faced by the decision maker. . . . What the public needs most from any expert, including the psychologist, is a wealth of intermediate observations and conceptual insights that are adequately explained. Only then can his or her contributions be combined with the communal sense of right and wrong to produce a decision.[151]

As indicated in **Chapter 1,** some judges feel that they need the expert's opinion on the ultimate issue in order to come to a fair decision. Experts are expected to have such opinions and to offer them if asked.[152] Sixty-five percent of experts in a recent survey of child custody evaluators strongly felt that they *should* give an opinion on the ultimate issue.[153] None of the major mental health professional organizations has formulated a position regarding whether an evaluator should make a recommendation regarding the ultimate issues.[154] The attorney should advise the psychologist regarding what the relevant statute in the particular state requires or permits. If ultimate issue opinions are not forbidden by law, however, it is ethical for psychologists to state such opinions, qualifying the conclusions to the degree necessary to ensure clarity regarding any limitations on the opinions given.[155]

§ 2.18   Limits on Predictions

Although the body of research regarding the effect of divorce on children is substantial and growing, there is a "lack of any methodologically sound empirical evidence allowing psychological predictions as to the effects of various types of custodial placements on children, or whether joint custody, in general, is a better option than single-parent custody."[156] Thus, psychologists may use the data from their evaluations to make statements "to a reasonable degree of psychological certainty" about the past and present; however, any statements about the future must be stated as opinions, the psychologist noting the limitations of the opinions and the willingness and ability to identify the bases for those opinions.[157]

---

[151] David Bazelon, *Veils, Values and Social Responsibility*, 37 Am. Psychologist 115, 116 (1992).

[152] Slovenko, *The Role of the Expert (with Focus on Psychiatry) in the Adversarial System*, 16 J. Psychiatry & L. 333, 353 (1988).

[153] Ackerman & Ackerman at 143.

[154] Martindale et al. at 485.

[155] Lyn R. Greenberg, David A. Martindale, Jonathan W. Gould, & Dianna J. Gould-Saltman, *Ethical Issues in Child Custody and Dependency Cases: Enduring Principles and Emerging Challenges*, 1 J. Child Custody 7–30 (2004) [hereinafter Greenberg et al.].

[156] Weithorn & Grisso at 161.

[157] Ethics Code, Ethical Standards 9.01(b), 9.06; Specialty Guidelines, VI.B., VI.F.3., VII.E.

§ 2.19   Limits on Predictions from Tests

Very few of the tests used by psychologists have been specifically validated for use in custody proceedings, making it necessary for the psychologist to report (1) what the test *does* validly address, and then (2) how that intermediate factor would be expected to impact both the ability of an individual to parent well and the needs of the child. For example, if a child is determined to have a very substantial need for nurturing, while a given parent is found to have a severe narcissistic personality disorder or frequent, ongoing major depressive episodes, it is reasonable to conclude that there is a poor fit between this need of the child and the ability of the parent to address the need—not because the test showed the degree of fit, but because the test yielded information that could be analyzed and addressed in drawing this conclusion.[158]

§ 2.20   Limits on Custody Recommendations

Because the recommendations made by the expert may be given great weight by the judge, the life of the individual and possibly others (for example, family members) will be affected for years by the recommendations made. With such great power, experts must be cautious in their conclusions and recommendations.[159]

Psychologists should consider all factors that may potentially affect their opinions and recommendations and try to avoid situations wherein there is a significant potential for misuse of those opinions and recommendations.[160] Similarly, it would very likely be an ethical violation to indicate that *either* parent would be the better custodial parent unless the expert has evaluated each child for whom that statement is to be made, because the better custodial parent for one child may not be better for another child.[161]

However, Guideline 13 of the APA *Guidelines for Child Custody Evaluations in Divorce Proceedings* (see **Chapter 3**) specifies that "[t]his guideline, however, does not preclude the psychologist from . . . addressing theoretical issues or hypothetical questions, so long as the limited basis of the information is noted." While the *Guidelines* are noted to be "aspirational," the authors of this text believe the more conservative and reasonable approach is to treat them as though they are requirements (see **Chapter 3**) since both courts and attorneys are likely to see guidelines promulgated by the profession's parent organization as representing the standard of practice.

Furthermore, the primary responsibility of the psychologist is to the child (by virtue of the requirement that the decision ultimately made be in the best interest of the child), a fact that may become cloudy if the psychologist is retained by only one parent. It does not serve the best interests of the child if the psychologist appears to be a "hired gun," and even

---

[158] Weithorn & Grisso at 162–63.

[159] Deed, *Court-Ordered Child Custody Evaluations: Helping or Victimizing Vulnerable Families*, 28 Psychotherapy 76, 82 (1991).

[160] Ethics Code, Ethical Standards 9.01(b), 9.04(a), 9.06; Specialty Guidelines, VII.A.1, VII.D; Canadian Code, II.5, II.28, III.1, III.6, IV.23.

[161] Ethics Code, Ethical Standards 9.01(a), (b); Specialty Guidelines, VI.H.

the most ethical psychologist may feel some pressure to shade the results of the evaluation in the direction of the parent who is paying the bill. "Even merely the fact of being employed by one side or the other will create a tendency toward bias or somewhat diminished objectivity, sometimes, even without awareness on the part of the expert that such a tendency is operating."[162] To counter this, forensic psychiatrists are cautioned that "[a]lthough they may be retained by one party to a dispute in a civil matter . . ., they adhere to the principle of honesty and they strive for objectivity."[163]

These factors do *not* preclude a psychologist from being retained by one parent in a custody matter. They *do*, however, point out the ethical traps inherent in doing so, and the extreme caution a psychologist must exercise in making any statements at all when one or some, but not all, of the parties involved in the custody action have been evaluated. Tentative conclusions and recommendations may, however, be predicated upon information in hypothetical questions from the attorney.[164]

§ 2.21   Sharing Draft Report with Attorney

While some sources would permit the retaining attorney to see the evaluator's report only when it was finalized, in order to avoid any appearance that the attorney influenced the content of the report, this practice involves several dangers. The evaluator may have drawn conclusions not supported by facts known to the attorney, may have addressed one or more incorrect questions, may have failed to address some important issue(s), may have misunderstood some legal issue(s), or may have failed to consider legal rulings in the case.[165] Justice is better served, in the opinion of the authors of this text, if the evaluator submits a semi-final draft to the retaining attorney with a request for feedback regarding "errors and omissions." The evaluator must refuse to make *any* changes that do not fall under one of these two headings, however.

DISCOVERY AND DISSEMINATING INFORMATION

§ 2.22   Informed Consent

Psychologists and other mental health professionals are ethically obligated to obtain informed consent for nearly all professional activities.[166] See **§ 2.2** and **Chapter 3** for discussions of informed consent requirements in various contexts.

---

[162] J. Ziskin, Coping with Psychiatric and Psychological Testimony 37 (1981).

[163] AAPL Ethics § IV (1995).

[164] Daniel W. Shuman, Psychiatric and Psychological Evidence, 2d ed. (2003 Supp.) at 9-7.

[165] Simon & Wettstein at 21.

[166] Ethics Code, Principles D, E, Ethical Standards 1.07(a)–(b), 1.21(a)–(b), 1.25(a), (e), 4.01(a), (d), 4.02, 5.01(a)–(b); Specialty Guidelines, IV.E.1; ASPPB Code, Rules III.C.1, III.E.3, III.G.1; Canadian Code, I.11–.20, I.22–.23, I.29–.31, III.14.

Ensuring Ongoing Awareness of the Assessment Process

A skilled examiner may create an environment that feels therapeutic—an environment in which the individual may forget that he or she has been warned about the lack of confidentiality. The evaluator must, therefore, avoid being too empathetic or cordial, while still establishing enough rapport to get an accurate reading of the litigant. If rapport is *not* adequately established, many people will consciously or unconsciously exaggerate their usual defenses, reducing the quality of the information obtained through the evaluation.[167] Psychologist Gary Melton and his coauthors note that the use of empathetic questioning may be the most reasonable way to obtain essential information, the major alternative in forensic evaluations being far more coercive. So long as the clinician does not deceive the litigant, and makes it very explicit that the purpose of the evaluation is not treatment, an empathetic approach may be the most ethical one to take.[168]

To reduce the likelihood that the individual will feel that a confidential assessment relationship has been formed, implying that things that are said will remain confidential, the examinee should be told explicitly that no doctor-patient relationship confidentiality exists, and should further acknowledge that understanding by signing a "consent for an evaluation" form that states the limits on confidentiality and that there is not a doctor-patient relationship.

§ 2.23   Confidentiality and Privilege

The American Psychological Association clearly sets forth guidelines for confidentiality in its *Ethical Principles of Psychologists and Code of Conduct*. See **Appendix B.** However, when an individual is involved in a custody dispute, the aspects of confidentiality change substantially. If the evaluation is court ordered, individuals must understand that what occurs during the evaluation will not be confidential. At minimum, the attorneys, guardian ad litem, and judge will receive the expert's report.

Generally, communication that takes place between a psychologist and a client is considered privileged. When an individual is seen in psychotherapy, and chooses not to have the content of that therapy process disclosed in the custody dispute, that individual may invoke privilege, and the therapist, in most states, may invoke it on behalf of the patient (at least if the therapist is a psychologist or psychiatrist). Social workers seldom have privileged communication status in state courts, though the Supreme Court, in *Jaffe v. Redmond*,[169] indicated that social workers have privileged communication status in federal courts (see the case digest at the end of **Chapter 2**). It is important for the individual to realize that privilege is an all-or-nothing situation—the therapist may not be allowed to disclose certain information and withhold other information. If the individual's psychological status is at issue, the court will generally order that records be made available.

Psychologists Samuel Knapp and Leon VandeCreek, experts in the area of privileged communication, point out many concerns that have surfaced around the issues of

---

[167] Schetky at 406; Daniel Shuman, *The Use of Empathy in Forensic Examinations*, 3 Ethics & Behav. 289–302 (1993).

[168] Melton et al. at 85.

[169] 116 S. Ct. 1923 (1996).

confidentiality and privileged communication. Laws regarding privileged communication
vary from state to state. Knapp and VandeCreek indicate that

> only doctors can practice medicine, and only lawyers can practice the law. Psychiatrists,
> psychologists, social workers, mental health counselors and pastoral counselors, however, all
> provide psychotherapy. . . . Privileged communication laws often apply to psychiatrists and
> psychologists qualified for private practice, but less frequently for other mental health profes-
> sionals who are likely to work in community mental health centers.[170]

Knapp and VandeCreek also point out that there needs to be a balance between what the
court requires and what the psychotherapist requires. Both are working for the best interests of the children. However, at times attorneys and judges feel pressure to discover everything about a particular case, while psychotherapists may be reluctant to disclose certain
pieces of information because of the therapeutic harm that could come to the child or family. In sensitive situations, it can be suggested that the judge screen records privately in
chambers before allowing open testimony in court. This may protect individuals from
being required to expose irrelevant, potentially harmful information.[171]

Release of Information

Privileged information may be supplied to others if a *release of information* form is signed
by the parties involved. A patient/client can legally waive privilege, and, in many circumstances, a court can order the removal of privilege. Information is generally either privileged
or not privileged; the patient/client cannot pick which information to release. A psychologist
should be careful about release authorizations that attempt to limit disclosure to one person.

When utilizing a release of information form as part of a legal case, it is generally a good
idea to have each individual sign a release, officially allowing the psychologist to talk with
all the attorneys and any other evaluators. If other significant individuals need to be contacted, releases for these individuals should also be signed. This allows the psychologist to
speak to all parties involved in the custody matter, maximizing the accuracy and thorough-
ness of the evaluation. The release of information form should be drafted such that it allows
for an *exchange* of information between the evaluator and the other parties. Furthermore,
the release of information form should state whether and when the release expires, and that
the individual has the right to withdraw the release at any time in writing. State laws may
designate the maximum time a consent for release of information may be in effect.

§ 2.24   Duty to Warn or Protect (*"Tarasoff"* Duty)

Case law has firmly established the responsibility of psychotherapists to at least warn
responsible parties if a patient or client makes a threat, if not take a number of actions to

---

[170] Samuel Knapp & Leon VandeCreek, *Psychotherapy and Privileged Communications in Child
Custody Cases*, 16 Prof. Psychol.: Res. & Prac. 405, 405 (1985). *See also* Daniel W. Shuman,
Psychiatric and Psychological Evidence, 2d ed. (1994, 2003 Supp.) at 10.01–10.05.

[171] *Id.*

try to protect the threatened party. Even if no release of information form has been signed, the psychologist may have an ethical responsibility to breach confidentiality when, in his or her judgment, an individual is dangerous to himself or herself, or someone else, through abuse, acts of violence, or other criminal acts.[172]

In particular, the California Supreme Court opinion in *Tarasoff v. Regents of the University of California*[173] is considered the landmark decision on this area of law. A considerable amount of litigation has since centered around a therapist's "failure to warn."

In December 1974, the California Supreme Court indicated that

> [W]hen a doctor or psychotherapist in the exercise of his professional skill and knowledge, determines, or should determine, that a warning is essential to avert danger arising from the medical or psychological condition of his patient, he incurs a legal obligation to give that warning.[174]

In a second *Tarasoff* ruling, in 1976, the California Supreme Court went further, ruling that the therapist must not only warn, he or she must also *protect:*

> When a therapist determines, or pursuant to the standards of his profession should determine, that his patient presents a serious danger of violence to another [person], he incurs an obligation to use reasonable care to protect the intended victim against such danger. The discharge of this duty may require the therapist to take one or more of various steps, depending on the nature of the case. Thus it may call for him to warn the intended victim or others likely to apprise the victim of the danger, to notify the police, or take whatever other steps are reasonably necessary under the circumstances.[175]

> [W]hen the avoidance of foreseeable harm requires a defendant to control the conduct of another person, or to warn of such conduct, the common law has traditionally imposed liability only if the defendant bears some special relationship to the dangerous person or to the potential victim. . . . [T]he relationship between a therapist and his patient satisfied this requirement. . . .[176]

> We recognize the difficulty that a therapist encounters in attempting to forecast whether a patient presents a serious danger of violence. Obviously, we do not require that the therapist, in making that determination, render a perfect performance; the therapist need only exercise "that reasonable degree of skill, knowledge, and care ordinarily possessed and exercised by members of [that professional specialty] under similar circumstances.". . .[177]

> We realize that the open and confidential character of psychotherapeutic dialogue encourages patients to express threats of violence, few of which are ever executed. Certainly a therapist should not be encouraged routinely to reveal such threats; such disclosures could seriously disrupt the patient's relationship with his therapist and with the persons threatened. To the contrary, the therapist's obligations to his patient require that he not disclose a confidence

---

[172] Ethics Code, Ethical Standard 4.05(a); Canadian Code, I.40, II.36; ASPPB Code, Rule III.E.2.; Principles of Medical Ethics with Annotations Especially Applicable to Psychiatry § 4, annot. 8.

[173] 13 Cal. 3d 177, 529 P.2d 553, 118 Cal. Rptr. 129 (1974).

[174] 118 Cal. Rptr. at 131.

[175] 17 Cal. 3d 425, 431, 551 P.2d 334, 131 Cal. Rptr. 14 (1976).

[176] 17 Cal. 3d at 435.

[177] *Id.* at 438 (citations omitted).

unless such disclosure is necessary to avert danger to others, and even then that he do so discreetly, and in a fashion that would preserve the privacy of his patient to the fullest extent
compatible with the prevention of the threatened danger. . . . [However,] [w]e conclude that
the public policy favoring protection of the confidential character of patient-psychotherapist
communications must yield to the extent to which disclosure is essential to avert danger to
others. The protective privilege ends where the public peril begins.[178]

Thus, the *Tarasoff* court employed the law of "rescue," which essentially says that an
individual has no common-law duty to rescue someone in danger even if the individual is
the only one in a position to save the imperiled person and could do so with no risk or
inconvenience, *unless* there is a special relationship between the rescuer and the person in
peril. The *Tarasoff* court indicated that such a special relationship does exist between the
psychotherapist and the patient. In utilizing this theory, the court ignores the usual area of
professional-patient concern—that is, whether there has been malpractice.[179] However, "in
cases in which therapists have prevailed on the merits, they have done so by showing that
they provided reasonable care and treatment for the patient under the circumstances" and
adequately documented the care that was given and the thinking that went into it.[180]

According to law professor Michael Perlin, on the other hand, some courts have placed
limits on therapist liability

where the victim was neither identified nor identifiable. Similar results were reached where
the therapist lacked sufficient control over the patient in question, where the therapist could
have reasonably believed that the patient's fantasies did not pose a danger to an identifiable
victim, where the foreseeable victim had pre-existing knowledge of the patient's potential
danger, where a separate statutorily-created privilege protected the therapist from disclosing
the patient's actual confidential communication, [or] where, by the time of the disclosure, the
communication was no longer confidential. . . .[181]

The difficulty with *Tarasoff* and similar court decisions is that they are highly ambiguous.
For example:

1. There is no professional standard regarding the prediction of dangerousness; on the
    contrary, research indicates that professionals are no better than laypersons at pre-
    dicting it except perhaps in the very short-term.
2. No court has defined whether "violence" refers to criminal or civil acts, damage to
    property or to persons, felonies or misdemeanors, or whether the duty is invoked if a
    patient with AIDS is indiscriminately having sexual relationships.

---

[178] *Id.* at 441–42.

[179] Peter C. Carstensen, *The Evolving Duty of Mental Health Professionals to Third Parties: A
Doctrinal and Institutional Examination*, 17 Int'l J.L. & Psychiatry 1, 8–9 (1994) [hereinafter
Carstensen]; David L. Shapiro, *Problems Encountered in the Preparation and Presentation of
Expert Testimony, in* The Encyclopedic Handbook of Private Practice 739, 748 (Eric Margenau
ed., 1990).

[180] Carstensen at 15–16.

[181] Perlin at 477–78.

3. It is not evident how the therapist may discharge his or her duty. Warning the victim appears to be part of it, but there may be no identified or identifiable victim. Telling the police may be part of it, though the police may have no obligation to follow up. Hospitalizing and/or medicating the patient may be relevant, including consideration of involuntary civil commitment.[182]

4. "Unless one is dealing with repeat offenders, the behaviors in question tend to have low base rates, thus creating circumstances in which predictions must necessarily (by Bayesian logic) produce a large proportion of false positives and . . . the behaviors probably represent the consequences of an interaction between person and situational variables, with the latter being difficult to assess in many clinical assessment contexts."[183]

5. The therapist has a fiduciary responsibility to the patient/client to do what is in the individual's best interest, and to do no harm. The *Tarasoff* warning to the patient/client may interfere with the professional relationship and therefore breach the fiduciary relationship. If a third party must be warned, the probable breach increases, especially if the police are also notified. "Therefore, the therapist must malpractice on the patient in order to protect society."[184]

There is at present only one state in which there is no "*Tarasoff*" duty: The Supreme Court of Texas, in *Thapar v. Zelulka*,[185] ruled that therapists in Texas do not have a duty to warn or protect third parties.[186]

Professor Robert Howell suggests that the same responsibility to warn or protect may be present if an expert is doing an evaluation in which a threat is made against someone. The basis for this responsibility is that a special relationship exists between the evaluator and the people who are evaluated, much as there is a special relationship between a therapist and a patient or client. Further, Howell cites the well-known fact that violence in family disputes, including custody battles, is not uncommon. It is therefore a small step, he suggests, from the requirement to warn or protect in psychotherapy to the same requirement when evaluations are done.[187] For psychologists, this responsibility could fall under the ethical requirement to "respect and protect human and civil rights."[188] The requirement to notify the appropriate authorities may also occur in the circumstances discussed in the next section.

---

[182] Egley, *Defining the* Tarasoff *Duty*, 19 J. Psychiatry & L. 99–133 (1991) [hereinafter Egley].

[183] T. Grisso, *Clinical Assessments for Legal Decisionmaking: Research Recommendations, in* Law & Mental Health: Major Developments and Research Needs 49, 66–67 (S. Shah & D. Sales eds., 1991).

[184] Carstensen at 3.

[185] 994 S.W.2d 635 (Tex. 1999).

[186] Deborah B. Reed, *Therapist's Duty to Protect Third Parties: Balancing Public Safety and Patient Confidentiality*, 1 Community Mental Health Rep. 1–3 (2001).

[187] Robert J. Howell, *Duty to Warn: A Case Study in Child Custody*, 6 Psychotherapy in Private Prac. 37, 43 (1988); Personal communication with Robert J. Howell (Jan. 10, 1998).

[188] Ethics Code, Preamble. *See also* Ethics Code Principles A, E; Ethical Standard 4.05; Specialty Guidelines, III.D, IV.E; ASPPB Code, Rule III.E.2; Canadian Code, II.36.

§ 2.25   Reporting Child Abuse

The laws in all states require psychologists to report suspected child abuse.[189] The *Ethical Principles of Psychologists and Code of Conduct*[190] and the *General Guidelines for Providers of Psychological Services*[191] reinforce that requirement. A psychologist conducting any part of an evaluation who suspects child abuse must report that suspicion to the designated social services agency. However, as noted in **§ 2.8,** some sources indicate that the examiner who is retained by an attorney must abide by the attorney-client privilege, and in most states attorneys do not have a duty to warn or protect, nor a mandate to report child abuse.[192]

Every expert should determine the standards that must be followed under state law and licensing codes, and act accordingly. While Wisconsin statutes, for example, mandate reporting of child abuse only if the information comes directly from provision of services to the child,[193] the state Psychology Examining Board has indicated that it considers it gross negligence for a psychologist to fail to report even if the information comes solely from the alleged perpetrator of the abuse.[194]

§ 2.26   Test Integrity

Psychologists are obligated to maintain the integrity of the tests they use, both by ethical requirements[195] and by contractual agreements with the publishers who hold the copyrights on those tests. It would be a violation of those ethical and contractual requirements for the psychologist to submit to an attorney or to the court raw data, answer sheets, or other information that would compromise both the validity of the test and its utility for others, though (with patient/client consent or a court order) the information could be released to another psychologist.[196]

According to an editorial in the *American Psychologist*, it should be assumed that "all tests are protected by copyright, even if the work does not contain copyright notice. Copyright vests in a work from the moment it is created, and neither a formal copyright notice nor registration at the U.S. Copyright Office in Washington, D.C., is required." Permission to reproduce any portion of a test requires contacting the publisher to

---

[189] Daniel W. Shuman, Psychiatric and Psychological Evidence, 2d ed. (1994, 2003 Supp.) at 13–17.

[190] Ethics Code, Preamble; Principles A, E; Ethical Standard 4.05.

[191] General Guidelines for Providers of Psychological Services 2.24 (1987).

[192] Simon & Wettstein at 23.

[193] Wis. Stat. § 48.981(2).

[194] Barbara Van Horne, 8 Wis. Regulatory Dig. (Dec. 1995).

[195] Ethics Code, Principle B; Ethical Standards 9.04(a), 9.11 (2002); Specialty Guidelines, VII.A.2.a; Standards for Educational and Psychological Testing 5.6, 5.7, 11.7, 12.11 (1999); ASPPB Code, Rule III.H.4; Canadian Code, IV.9.

[196] General Guidelines for Providers of Psychological Services 2.3.7 (1987); Ethics in Psychology at 159–60 (1998); Samuel Knapp & Leon VandeCreek, *An Overview of the Major Changes in the 2002 APA Ethics Code*, 34 Prof. Psychol.: Res. & Prac. 301–08 (2003).

determine if the test is protected by copyright and to request permission to copy it if there is a copyright.[197]

According to psychologist Daniel Tranel, there are two primary reasons for limiting the release of raw data (test questions/materials and answers). The first is that laypersons may misunderstand the content and context of psychological test stimuli and administration, and may therefore reach incorrect conclusions about items and tests. The second is that the release of raw data could place psychological test stimuli in the public domain, accessible to nearly anyone. It could become difficult to find anyone who is naive regarding test content, making it necessary to discard test items quite frequently and substitute new (but research-demonstrated to be equally valid and reliable) items—an impossible task. In effect, psychological testing as a reasonable and useful procedure would be eliminated.[198]

The American Psychological Association's *Ethical Principles of Psychologists and Code of Conduct* offers some direction. The Code's Introduction indicates that "if the Ethics Code establishes a higher standard of conduct than is required by law, the psychologist must meet the higher ethical standard." Its Preamble indicates that the Ethics Code "has as its goals the welfare and protection of the individuals and groups with whom psychologists work. . . ." Principle B states that "[p]sychologists uphold professional standards of conduct. . . ." Ethical Standard 1.01 indicates that psychologists "take reasonable steps to correct or minimize the misuse or misrepresentation" of their work. According to Ethical Standard 4.01, indicates that "psychologists have a primary obligation and take reasonable precautions to protect confidential information obtained through or stored in any medium. . . ." Ethical Standards 9.04 and 9.11 are discussed at length in **§ 2.2.** Ethical Standard 9.07 indicates that "[p]sychologists do not promote the use of psychological assessment techniques by unqualified persons. . . ."

Similarly, the Association of State and Provincial Psychology Boards' *Code of Conduct* (see **Appendix I**), Rule of Conduct III H.4, states:

> *Protection of integrity of assessment procedures.* The psychologist shall not reproduce or describe in popular publications, lectures, or public presentations psychological tests or other assessment devices in ways that might invalidate them.[199]

The *Canadian Code of Ethics for Psychologists* (see **Appendix H**), Ethical Standard IV.11, requires psychologists to "protect the skills, knowledge, and interpretation of psychology from being misused, used incompetently, or made useless (e.g., loss of security of assessment techniques) by others."[200]

Psychologists also have contractual obligations to test distributors as well as an obligation to honor copyrights for test materials. In general, psychologists are prohibited from copying or otherwise utilizing materials for nearly any purpose other than assessment without the written consent of the publisher. The reason, according to correspondence

---

[197] Editorial, *Test Security: Protecting the Integrity of Tests*, 54 Am. Psychol. 1078 (1999).

[198] Daniel Tranel, *The Release of Psychological Data to Nonexperts: Ethical and Legal Considerations*, 25 Prof. Psychol.: Res. & Prac. 33–38 (1994).

[199] Association of State and Provincial Psychology Boards, Montgomery, Ala. (1991, 2001).

[200] Canadian Psychological Ass'n, Canadian Code of Ethics for Psychologists, Third Edition (2000).

from the legal counsel for The Psychological Corporation,[201] is that "any leakage of test items severely compromises the value of the test," both to the psychologist and to the publisher, and "any copying of the test protocols also constitutes an infringement of the copyright and other proprietary rights." Some tests cost millions of dollars to develop and standardize, yet could be made nearly worthless if the contents of the test became widely known.

Steven Stein, Ph.D., and Rita Chadda, J.D., of Multi-Health Systems (MHS) presented the current position of most test publishers at the 2004 Annual Convention of the American Psychological Association.[202] The release of test materials, they indicate, involves disclosure of trade secrets, copying of test items that are copyrighted, infringement on the owner's property rights, compromising the investment of hundreds of thousands of dollars spent in the development and validation of each test, potential harm to the author's reputation, and is a violation of the psychologist's contract with the test publisher.

Further, they indicated, test data can be misinterpreted and misused easily by untrained individuals, who may make harmful decisions based on those misinterpretations. Public disclosure of test items can also lead to manipulation of an individual's performance on a test, and will generally prevent the individual from being tested with that instrument for a lengthy period of time, if ever. Test publishers have also begun removing some validation information from test manuals, depriving psychologists of full knowledge regarding the validation process, in order to safeguard the test. Many test publishers do not provide copies of tests to the Library of Congress in order to protect the text instruments.

HIPAA does not require release of information gathered in anticipation of litigation, they also indicated.[203] Further, test materials are to be used solely by individuals who have an ethical obligation to protect the security of the test, a category that does not include attorneys. Stein and Chudda cited examples of attorneys using test materials to coach their clients. The Department of Health and Human Services has also officially stated to MHS that HIPAA does not require release of test materials or data. Finally, test publishers have begun going to court to protect their tests, Stein and Chudda indicated, with Houghton Mifflin and Harcourt Assessments currently involved in such litigation. MHS invites psychologists to consult with their legal staff (privacyofficer@mhs.com or 800-456-3003) if an attempt is made to force a psychologist to furnish test materials that MHS has developed.

It should also be noted that

> HIPAA's preemption clause . . . provides that when HIPAA conflicts with state law, the law (HIPAA or state) more protective of privacy governs. Because many, perhaps all, state laws are more protective of privacy than HIPAA regarding release pursuant to a subpoena, a preemption analysis will likely indicate that test data cannot be released on the basis of a subpoena alone.[204]

---

[201] Personal communication with Yvette A. Beeman (Jan. 22, 1996).

[202] Steven Stein & Rita Chadda, Revised Ethics Code—Release of Test Information to Nonpsychologists, Paper presented at the 112th Annual Convention of the American Psychological Association, Honolulu (Aug. 1, 2004).

[203] See also Fisher at 97 & 195.

[204] Stephen Behnke, *Release of Test Data and APA's New Ethics Code*, 34 Monitor on Psychol. 70–72, at 72 (2003).

In theory, there is a potential exception under the "fair use" section of the law, on the basis of (1) the nature of the use (for example, commercial versus educational), (2) the nature of the copyrighted work, (3) the amount of material used, and (4) the effect of the use in a potential market for the material. It was suggested by The Psychological Corporation's attorney, however, that release of test materials would fail the fair use test on the basis of the last three criteria, and that test materials do not therefore fall under an exception to the copyright, trade secrets, or other proprietary rights.[205]

An editorial in the *American Psychologist* indicates that, "[a]lthough the use of copyrighted material without permission . . . may be regarded by law as 'fair use' under certain circumstances, it may not be safe to rely on fair use when dealing with test materials because secure tests enjoy heightened protection under the fair use analysis." It is recommended that any request to disclose test materials be followed by a request to the court to limit disclosure to "psychologists or other professionals who are bound by the same duty to protect them." It is also recommended that a protective order be sought forbidding parties from copying the materials, requiring that test materials be returned to the psychologist when the case ends, and asking that the record be sealed if either test answers or questions are made part of the record. Protection of secure test materials, the editorial indicates, "helps ensure that these materials are used in a manner that best serves the community at large."[206]

In response to "a large number of inquiries," the Committee on Legal Issues of the American Psychological Association issued a document in 1995 to address "strategies for private practitioners coping with subpoenas or compelled testimony for client records and/or test data."[207]

With regard to testing data and materials, the document notes, the issues are more complicated. The psychologist may have an obligation to withhold these data and materials because of a duty to the client and/or the public ("e.g., to avoid public dissemination of test items, questions, protocols, or other test information that could adversely affect the integrity and continued validity of tests") and/or test publishers ("e.g., contractual obligations between the psychologist and test publishers not to disclose test information") and requirements of copyright laws and/or other third parties (for example, employers).

The Committee recommended (1) identifying whether the psychologist has received a legally valid subpoena; (2) discussing the subpoena with the client (or parent or guardian); (3) considering consulting with an attorney; (4) considering contracts with and trade secrets and property rights of test publishers; (5) exploring ways to address the subpoena that do not involve giving confidential and protected materials; if there is no other solution, consider requesting a ruling from the court.

> [T]he psychologist . . . may request that the court consider the psychologist's obligations to protect the interests of the client, the interests of third parties (e.g., test publishers or others), and the interests of the public in preserving the integrity and continued validity of the tests

---

[205] Personal communication with Yvette A. Beeman (Jan. 22, 1996).

[206] Editorial, *Test Security: Protecting the Integrity of Tests*, 54 Am. Psychol. 1078 (1999).

[207] Committee on Legal Issues, American Psychological Ass'n, *Strategies for Private Practitioners Coping with Subpoenas or Compelled Testimony for Client Records or Test Data*, 27 Prof. Psychol.: Res. & Prac. 245–51 (1996).

themselves. . . . The letter might also attempt to provide suggestions such as the following, to the court on ways to minimize the adverse consequences of disclosure if the court is inclined to require production at all:

1. Suggest that, at most, the court direct the psychologist to provide test data only to another appropriately qualified psychologist. . . .

2. Suggest that the court limit the use of client records or test data to prevent wide dissemination. . . .

3. Suggest that the court limit the categories of information that must be produced. For example, client records may contain confidential information about a third party, such as a spouse, who may have independent interests in maintaining confidentiality, and such data may be of minimal or no relevance to the issues before the court. . . .

4. Suggest that the court determine for itself, through in camera proceedings . . . whether the use of the client records or test data is relevant to the issues before the court or whether it might be insulated from disclosure, in whole or in part, by the therapist-client privilege or another privilege.

5. If . . . guidance cannot be sought through the informal means of a letter to the court, it may be necessary to file a motion seeking to be relieved of the obligations imposed by the demand for production of the confidential records. . . . [T]he possible motions include a motion to quash the subpoena, in whole or in part, or a motion for a protective order. . . . Courts are generally more receptive to a motion to quash or a motion for a protective order if it is filed by the client about whom information is sought (who would be defending his or her own interests). . . . If the client has refused to consent to disclosure of the information, his or her attorney may be willing to take the lead in opposing the subpoena. . . . Grounds may exist for asserting that the subpoena or request for testimony should be quashed, in whole or in part. . . .

Possible grounds for opposing or limiting production of client records or test data [include]:

1. The court does not have jurisdiction over the psychologist, the client records, or the test data, or the psychologist did not receive a legally sufficient demand . . . for production of records or test data testimony.

2. The psychologist does not have custody or control of the records or test data that are sought. . . .

3. The therapist-client privilege insulates the records or test data from disclosure. . . . The psychologist is under an ethical obligation to protect the client's reasonable expectations of confidentiality. . . .

4. The information sought is not relevant to the issues before the court, or the scope of the demand for information is over-broad. . . .

5. Public dissemination of test information such as manuals, protocols, and so forth may harm the public interest because it may affect responses of future test populations. This effect could result in the loss of valuable assessment tools to the detriment of both the public and the profession of psychology.

6. Test publishers have an interest in the protection of test information, and the psychologist may have a contractual or other legal obligation (e.g., copyright laws) not to disclose such information. . . .

7. Psychologists have an ethical obligation to protect the integrity and security of test information and data and to avoid misuse of assessment techniques and data. Psychologists are also ethically obligated to take reasonable steps to prevent others from misusing such information. In particular, psychologists are ethically obligated to refrain from releasing raw test results or raw data to persons other than the client . . . who are not qualified to

use such information. . . . This prohibition has the force of law in many jurisdictions where state boards of psychology or boards with similar responsibilities have either adopted the APA Ethics Code or a code of ethics with similar provisions.

8. Refer to ethical and legal obligations of psychologists as provided for under ethics codes; professional standards; state, federal or local laws; or regulatory agencies.[208]

The document suggests that if the psychologist is asked to disclose confidential information during testimony, either during a deposition or in court, that privilege be invoked if there is a legitimate basis for doing so. The suggestions from the APA's Committee on Legal Issues parallel and reinforce those made earlier in this section, adding weight to the conclusion that psychologists must ethically and legally refuse to comply with demands to release client information or raw test data in the absence of appropriate consent from the client or a court order.

In most published cases in which a psychologist refused to furnish raw data to anyone other than another psychologist, the court has honored the psychologist's request and ethical duty.[209]

§ 2.27   Personal Notes

Many evaluators believe, in error, that the notes they write during or following an evaluation are not subject to discovery. In some jurisdictions the psychologist may be able to identify hypotheses or areas to pursue as "psychologist work product." The safest assumption, however, is that everything the psychologist does is subject to discovery. See the section on work product discovery in § 1.15.

§ 2.28   Hearsay

Experts may generally testify regarding things told to them in the course of their evaluations and research. However,

[w]hile hearsay or otherwise inadmissible evidence may form the partial basis of their opinion, evidence or professional product, [psychologists] actively seek to minimize their reliance upon such evidence. Where circumstances reasonably permit, forensic psychologists seek to obtain independent and personal verification of data relied upon as part of their professional services to the court or to a party to a legal proceeding. . . . When data . . . has not been corroborated, but is nevertheless utilized, the forensic psychologist has an affirmative responsibility to clarify its evidentiary status and the reasons for relying upon such data.[210]

---

[208] *Id.* Copyright © 1996 by the American Psychological Association. Reprinted with permission.

[209] David Shapiro, APA (1995); Melton et al. at 112; Jeanne J. Johnson & Jeffrey L. Helms, *Test Security in the Twenty-First Century*, 21 Am. J. Forensic Psychol. 19–32 (2003).

[210] Specialty Guidelines, VI.F.

OTHER CONCERNS

§ 2.29   Providing Quality Services

Although it is possible for an evaluator to be competent without being ethical, it is not possible to be ethical without being competent. Experts who wish to perform their role in an ethical manner have an obligation to do so in a competent manner, and to refuse participation in an evaluation if this cannot be done.

The requirement for quality services includes the "right and responsibility of psychologists to withhold an assessment procedure when not validly applicable [and a] right and responsibility of psychologists to withhold services in specific instances in which their own limitations or user characteristics might impair the quality of the services."[211]

This requirement includes the need for assessments to take significant cultural issues into consideration.[212] While a high percentage of people who are evaluated are either white Anglo-Saxons or have been assimilated into mainstream American culture, many are from different cultural backgrounds and maintain their cultural diversity, often having English as their second, not primary, language. When this is the case, adjustments must be made in the evaluation to take the cultural differences into consideration. Interviews may have to be conducted in the individual's primary language, and tests may be limited to those that have been validated as either culture-free or valid for the specific population being addressed. In addition, the evaluation format may need to be altered. While Anglo and assimilated populations generally exhibit an immediate orientation to the task, culturally different individuals may require that the social etiquette of their culture be followed. Many Hispanic-Americans, for example, need a substantial emphasis on rapport-building (including some informality and the conveying of a sense of warmth and acceptance) before being able to trust the evaluator enough to permit the evaluation to proceed.[213] The evaluator who does not speak the language of the evaluatee, or who cannot alter the evaluation procedures in ways needed by the evaluatee, or who is not sufficiently expert in the administration and interpretation of culture-fair or culture-validated tests cannot ethically do the evaluation.[214]

§ 2.30   Contingency Fees and Insurance Billing: Dangerous Practices

The expert needs to be independent to maximize his or her objectivity. This independence is seriously compromised if the expert is not paid for each phase of the evaluation process as it is completed, and would be even more seriously compromised if the expert worked on

---

[211] General Guidelines for Providers of Psychological Services 3.1 (1987).

[212] APA Office of Ethnic Minority Affairs, *Guidelines for Providers of Psychological Services to Ethnic, Linguistic, and Culturally Diverse Populations*, 48 Am. Psychologist 45–48 (1993).

[213] Richard H. Dana, *Culturally Competent Assessment Practice in the United States*, 66 J. Personality Assessment 472, 476 (1996).

[214] Ethics Code, Ethical Standards 9.02(b), (c).

the basis of a contingency fee. Thus, the *Specialty Guidelines for Forensic Psychologists* state[215] that

> forensic psychologists do not provide professional services to parties to a legal proceeding on the basis of "contingent fees," when those services involve the offering of expert testimony to a court or administrative body, or when they call upon the psychologist to make affirmations or representations intended to be relied upon by third parties.

Similarly, the AAPL *Ethics Guidelines for the Practice of Forensic Psychiatry* state that contingency fees interfere with objectivity, and should not be accepted. Retainers, however, may be accepted, since they do not interfere with objectivity.[216]

The Council on Ethical and Judicial Affairs of the American Medical Association has also stated that contingency fees are not ethical.[217] If a retainer has not covered the cost of producing a written report, the report should not be furnished until the expert has been paid for all the work that led to its production.[218] The 2002 APA Ethics Code also permits withholding of records when payment is not received for a psychological assessment.[219]

> The purpose of the retainer is not simply to ensure payment but also to provide protection from financial pressures or the appearance of pressure. If the forensic clinician has been paid prior to submitting the report, he or she is less likely to be concerned about the financial implications of the opinion. In a worst-case scenario, if the attorney does not like the opinion, the forensic clinician will not be paid at all.[220]

It should also be noted that APA Ethics Code Principle A (Beneficence and Nonmaleficence) and Principle B (Fidelity and Responsibility) emphasize the importance of awareness of potential or actual conflicts of interest. Ethical Standard 3.05 addresses "multiple relationships," including any relationships that may adversely impact the psychologist's objectivity, competence, or effectiveness. Ethical Standard 3.06 addresses "conflicts of interest" directly, prohibiting psychologists from taking on professional roles involving such conflicts because they may impair the psychologist's objectivity, competence, or effectiveness.

Some experts bill a client's health insurance for forensic evaluations and even for testimony. Such billing may be both unethical and illegal, as it may be considered a fraudulent practice (see the exceptions below). Ethical Standard 6.04(b) of the APA Ethics Code states that "Psychologists' fee practices are consistent with law." Ethical Standard 6.04(c) indicates that "[p]sychologists do not misrepresent their fees." Ethical Standard 6.06 states that "in their reports to payors for services . . ., psychologists take reasonable steps to ensure the accurate reporting of the nature of the service provided . . ., the fees, charges, or payments. . . ." Similarly, the ASPPB Code of Conduct, Rule III.F.4, indicates that the

---

[215] Specialty Guidelines, IV.B.

[216] AAPL Ethics, Guideline IV.

[217] Simon & Wettstein at 26.

[218] T. Blau, The Psychologist as Expert Witness 336 (1984).

[219] Fisher at 122.

[220] Kirk Heilbrun, Geoffrey R. Marczyk, & David DeMatteo, Forensic Mental Health Assessment: A Casebook 45 (Oxford 2002).

psychologist "shall not include false or misleading information in public statements concerning professional services offered." Health insurance contracts generally specify that they cover "medically necessary" services. Since child custody evaluations do not fall under that heading, they cannot be legitimately billed to an individual's health insurance as if one was billing for a clinical evaluation for the purpose of treatment.

There are three *possible* exceptions to this rule:

1. If the evaluator specified on the statement that "the following services were provided as part of a child custody evaluation," with each service fully described. Some health insurance companies will provide at least partial payment, most likely predicated on the proposition that the policyholder gained psychological benefit from the service. There is an ICD-9-CM code, V62.5, covering "sociolegal problems," including "forensic: civil" problems. "If the company recognizes that some part of a test battery given for forensic purposes would have been administered if the litigant were beginning treatment and chooses to reimburse on that basis, . . . it is free to do so." It is recommended, however, that the psychologist be paid by the attorney who retained him or her, or by court order, and that any payment received directly from an insurance company be returned to the insurance company with a request to reissue it to the policyholder, the psychologist having been paid already.[221]

2. If the person evaluated became the patient of the evaluator after the evaluation was completed, or if the individual's therapist did the evaluation because the situation fit one of the rare exceptions to the rule that a therapist should not act as an expert witness for his or her own patient (see § 2.8).

3. If the individual is convinced to seek psychotherapy by the results of the evaluation (and the results of the evaluation are given to the therapist), or if the evaluation was given to the individual's current therapist in order to facilitate ongoing psychotherapy.

In each circumstance, the evaluation *does* get used for clinical purposes, making it legitimate to bill health insurance in most cases. There is *no* circumstance that would permit the evaluator to bill health insurance for deposition or court testimony under the guise of, for example, an "environmental intervention"—that is, assisting the patient in interacting with an agency, employer, or institution. Even when there is a legitimate basis for billing health insurance, however, it is recommended that the expert be paid for his or her evaluation by the retaining attorney or the court, and that the person request reimbursement from his or her insurance.

§ 2.31   Interplay between the Guardian ad Litem and Psychological Expert

The role of the guardian ad litem in a divorce case cannot be underestimated or ignored. However, states define guardians ad litem in different ways. Some states allow only attorneys to be guardians ad litem, while other states allow nonattorneys such as psychologists or social workers to be guardians ad litem. If an attorney is used as a guardian ad litem, some

---

[221] Mary A. Connell, *Expert Opinion: Are Forensic Evaluations Eligible to Be Reimbursed by Health Care Providers?*, 20 Am. Psychol.-L. News 16–17 (2000).

states define the guardian ad litem as an individual who is to represent the best interest(s) of the child(ren), while other states will indicate that the attorney represents the child in court.

As in other types of legal representation, when a child is represented by the guardian ad litem, individuals are not allowed to communicate with the child about the case without the permission of the guardian ad litem. In particular, this extends to the psychologist acting as a therapist or evaluator of a child, when an attorney guardian ad litem is involved in a case as the child's attorney. If a psychologist sees a child for therapy or performs an assessment of the child and does not seek the permission of the guardian ad litem, that psychologist could be removed from the case or even sanctioned by the court. This removal could be damaging to the child, if the psychologist has developed an ongoing therapeutic relationship with the child, or damaging to the case itself.

When a psychologist and a guardian ad litem are both involved in a case, it becomes necessary for both the psychologist and the guardian ad litem to know the legal requirements of the state in which the case is venued. It is incumbent upon the psychologist and the guardian ad litem to know what state law requires of each of these individuals for the following issues:

1. Does the state require that the guardian ad litem be an attorney?
2. If the guardian ad litem is an attorney, does the state allow the attorney to represent the child's wishes as well as the child's best interests, or one without the other?
3. When a state does not require a guardian ad litem to be an attorney, what will the interplay between the guardian ad litem and the psychological expert be?
4. What authority does the guardian ad litem have with regard to placement issues and time with parents, grandparents, and significant others?

Theoretically, the guardian ad litem and the court-appointed expert should operate as a team. Because both of them are considered to be neutral and working for the best interest(s) of the child(ren), it is expected that they will work together. To this end, the guardian ad litem and the psychological evaluator should meet and discuss the case before either writes a report. The assumption is that the guardian ad litem will know things about the case that the psychologist does not and the psychologist evaluator will know things about the case that the guardian ad litem does not. A meeting would facilitate an exchange of information and an exchange of ideas. Engaging in such practice can be a valuable component of the evaluation process, which is lost if the guardian ad litem and psychologist do not work as a team.

§ 2.32   Computerized Scoring and Computer-Generated Reports

Research indicates that errors are common when an instrument is hand-scored. In one recent study, psychologists had error rates in excess of 5 percent on four tests, and lower rates on three other tests. The resulting profiles were significantly different in 42.3 percent of the tests psychologists scored incorrectly.[222]

---

[222] Roland Simons, Richard Goddard, & Wendy Patton, *Hand-Scoring Error Rates in Psychological Testing*, 9 Assessment 292–300 (2002).

Computer-generated test *interpretation* may be acceptable as a means of providing the evaluator with a primary clinical and diagnostic formulation, but that must be only the starting point for interpretation of the test. The computer-generated interpretation of the MMPI-2, for example, gives an interpretation based on the two highest clinical scales, though there may be a number of elevated clinical scales that must be considered for a valid interpretation. Therefore, computerized interpretations are less important than is scoring, and carry a danger as well.[223] Unsophisticated evaluators may take the computer-generated report at face value, and may even use it as the primary means of interpreting the results of the test. Since doing so will often lead to a significant misrepresentation of the test results, however, it is unethical for the evaluator to do so.

A survey of a sample of the membership of the Society for Personality Assessment found that more than 80 percent of the respondents considered it ethical to use computer-based software to score tests, and to use computer-based printouts to supplement the clinician's usual clinical methods. In contrast, more than 80 percent of the respondents indicated that it was unethical to use computer-based interpretations as the primary source of data for formulation of a case.[224] Therefore, while there is no problem *per se* with generation of a computer-based report, there is a serious problem if the evaluator makes that report the primary basis for interpretation of the MMPI-2. A further problem is likely to develop, however, if the cross-examining attorney obtains a copy of the computer-generated report. If the evaluator has used that report as the primary or exclusive basis of his or her MMPI-2 analysis, the attorney can point out that the evaluator failed to consider other scale elevations, including two-point and three-point code types (see **Chapter 9**). If the evaluator does—correctly—go beyond the computer-generated report to include all other significant data from the MMPI-2, the cross-examining attorney may then question the evaluator regarding why he or she did not include each point indicated as significant in the computer-generated report. The computer-generated report, the attorney may indicate, is the product of the work of James Butcher, Ph.D., based on decades of experience with the MMPI/MMPI-2 and Butcher's familiarity with the thousands of research studies on the test. How, the attorney might ask, can the psychologist on the stand know more than Dr. Butcher? While the answer is that the computer-generated report lacks considerable, important detail from other MMPI-2 scales, the credibility of the psychologist may suffer as a result.

The present authors therefore recommend that psychologists score the MMPI-2 and other appropriate tests using the computer program, to maximize the accuracy of the scoring, but that the computer-generated report not be utilized in the interpretation of the test except as supplementary support.

§ 2.33   Concluding Remarks

There are a number of areas where the needs of the psychologist may limit or conflict with the needs of the attorney. It is essential that these potential or actual problems be anticipated and understood by both, so that unnecessary conflict can be avoided. The psychologist needs to find ethical ways to address the questions and requests from the

---

[223] Butcher & Pope at 281.

[224] Mark R. McMinn, Brent M. Ellens, & Erez Soref, *Ethical Perspectives and Practice Behaviors Involving Computer-Based Test Interpretation*, 6 Assessment 71–77 (1999).

attorney. The attorney needs to find ways of obtaining important information from the psychologist without compromising the psychologist's ethical and legal obligations. With a spirit of cooperation, it should be possible to accomplish both tasks, thereby serving both the best interests of the child and justice.

§ 2.34   Questions for Chapter 2

1. Has the expert recognized the limitations of the tests? See § **2.19.**
2. Has the expert limited the custody recommendations? See § **2.20.**
3. Has the expert gone beyond the data presented? See § **2.16.**
4. Has the expert reported all relevant data? See § **2.15.**
5. Has the expert avoided becoming involved in dual/multiple relationships? See § **2.8.**
6. Has the expert done anything to compromise the integrity of tests? See § **2.26.**
7. Has the expert followed the correct administration procedures for all tests? See § **2.13.**
8. Has the expert ever worked on a contingency fee basis? See § **2.30.**
9. Does the expert use idiosyncratic tests? See § **2.13.**
10. Has an opposing expert violated the affirmative requirement to promote patient/client welfare? See § **2.7.**
11. Has the expert made a custody recommendation without evaluating all the parties? See § **2.18.**
12. Has iatrogenic harm resulted from the expert's intervention? See § **2.9.**
13. Has the expert been candid with the retaining attorney regarding any skeletons in the expert's closet, any relevant strong personal opinions, and any possible conflicts of interest? See § **2.4.**
14. If the expert has been in a "duty to warn or protect" ("*Tarasoff*") situation, has he handled it ethically? See § **2.24.**
15. Has the expert been open about the limits of his or her expertise? See § **2.4.**
16. Has the expert reviewed all relevant materials? See § **2.10.**
17. Did the expert clearly advise anyone interviewed regarding the role of the expert, the nature and purpose of the evaluation, and that information relevant to the instant case would not be confidential? Has the expert kept confidential information that has no relevance to the instant case but that would be embarrassing or otherwise harmful to the litigant or another party? See §§ **2.5, 2.6, 2.7, 2.22,** and **2.23.**
18. Has the expert conducted an interview of all parties to the custody suit? If not, has the expert been candid about the limitations this places on his or her conclusions and testimony? See § **2.12.**

§ 2.35   Case Digest

The source of information for many of the following cases is the *Mental and Physical Disability Law Reporter* (MPDLR), a publication of the American Bar Association.

Complete information for any other sources appears in the relevant references below. The following are direct quotations from the identified source. Quotations from the *Mental and Physical Disability Law Reporter:* Excerpted from *Mental and Physical Disability Law Reporter.* Copyright © 1989–2004. American Bar Association. Reprinted by permission. Other than the introductions by the authors of this text, if no source is identified, it is a summary from the court ruling.

U.S. Supreme Court

Jaffee v. Redmond, 116 S. Ct. 1923, 64 U.S.L.W. 4490 (1996). In the first case in which it recognized a psychotherapist-patient privilege, the U.S. Supreme Court, by a vote of seven to two, greatly extended the psychotherapist-patient privilege by ruling that, under Federal Rule of Evidence 501, federal courts are prohibited from requiring disclosure of confidential discussions between a therapist and a patient, including notes on such discussions. The Court indicated that disclosure is prohibited even when the trial court has determined that the evidentiary value of the information is greater than the privacy interest of the patient. The Court also extended the privilege to all licensed social workers, in addition to the licensed psychiatrists and psychologists already covered by the privilege.

Justice Stevens delivered the opinion of the Court:

> After a traumatic incident in which she shot and killed a man, a police officer received extensive counseling from a licensed clinical social worker. . . . Petitioner is the administrator of the estate of Ricky Allen. Respondents are Mary Lu Redmond, a former police officer, and the Village of Hoffman Estates, Illinois. . . . Redmond shot and killed Allen while on patrol duty . . . on June 27, 1991. . . . Petitioner filed suit in Federal District Court alleging that Redmond had violated Allen's constitutional rights by using excessive force during the encounter. . . . Petitioner learned that after the shooting Redmond had participated in about 50 counseling sessions with Karen Beyer, a clinical social worker licensed by the State of Illinois. . . . Petitioner sought access to Beyer's notes concerning the sessions for use in cross-examining Redmond. Respondents vigorously resisted the discovery. . . . In his instructions at the end of the trial, the judge advised the jury that the refusal to turn over Beyer's notes had no "legal justification" and that the jury could therefore presume that the contents of the notes would have been unfavorable to respondents. . . . The jury awarded petitioner $45,000 on the federal claim and $500,000 on her state-law claim.
>
> The Court of Appeals for the Seventh Circuit reversed and remanded for a new trial. Addressing the issue for the first time, the court concluded that "reason and experience," the touchstones for acceptance of a privilege under Rule 501 of the Federal Rules of Evidence, compelled recognition of a psychotherapist-patient privilege . . . 51 F.3d 1346, 1355 (1995). "Reason tells us that psychotherapists and patients share a unique relationship, in which the ability to communicate freely without fear of public disclosure is the key to successful treatment." Id., at 1355–1356. As to experience, the court observed that all 50 States have adopted some form of the psychotherapist-patient privilege. Id., at 1356. . . .
>
> The United States courts of appeals do not uniformly agree that the federal courts should recognize a psychotherapist privilege under Rule 501. . . . Because of the conflict among the courts of appeals and the importance of the question, we granted certiorari. . . . We affirm.
>
> The common-law principles underlying the recognition of testimonial privileges can be stated simply. " 'For more than three centuries it has now been recognized as a fundamental maxim that the public . . . has a right to every man's evidence. . . . We start with the primary

assumption that there is a general duty to give what testimony one is capable of giving, and that any exemptions which may exist are distinctly exceptional, being so many derogations from a positive general rule.' " [Citation deleted.] Exceptions from the general rule disfavoring testimonial privileges may be justified, however, by a " 'public good transcending the normally predominant principle of utilizing all rational means for ascertaining the truth.' " [Citation deleted.] . . . The question we address today is whether a privilege protecting confidential communications between a psychotherapist and her patient "promotes sufficiently important interests to outweigh the need for probative evidence. . . ." 445 U.S., at 51, 100 S.Ct., at 912. Both "reason and experience" persuade us that it does. . . .

Treatment by a physician for physical ailments can often proceed successfully on the basis of a physical examination, objective information supplied by the patient, and the results of diagnostic tests. Effective psychotherapy, by contrast, depends upon an atmosphere of confidence and trust in which the patient is willing to make a frank and complete disclosure of facts, emotions, memories, and fears. Because of the sensitive nature of the problems for which individuals consult psychotherapists, disclosure of confidential communications made during counseling sessions may cause embarrassment or disgrace. For this reason, the mere possibility of disclosure may impede development of the confidential relationship necessary for successful treatment. As the Judicial Conference Advisory Committee observed in 1972 when it recommended that Congress recognize a psychotherapist privilege as part of the Proposed Federal Rules of Evidence, a psychiatrist's ability to help her patients

> is completely dependent upon [the patients'] willingness and ability to talk freely. This makes it difficult if not impossible for [a psychiatrist] to function without being able to assure . . . patients of confidentiality and, indeed, privileged communication. Where there may be exceptions to this general rule . . ., there is wide agreement that confidentiality is a sine qua non for successful psychiatric treatment. . . .

By protecting confidential communications between a psychotherapist and her patient from involuntary disclosure, the proposed privilege thus serves important private interests. . . . The psychotherapist privilege serves the public interest by facilitating the provision of appropriate treatment for individuals suffering the effects of a mental or emotional problem. The mental health of our citizenry, no less than its physical health, is a public good of transcendent importance. . . . In contrast to the significant public and private interests supporting recognition of the privilege, the likely evidentiary benefit that would result from the denial of the privilege is modest. . . . Without a privilege, much of the desirable evidence to which litigants such as petitioner seek access—for example, admissions against interest by a party—is unlikely to come into being. This unspoken "evidence" will therefore serve no greater truth-seeking function than if it had been spoken and privileged. . . .

That it is appropriate for the federal courts to recognize a psychotherapist privilege under Rule 501 is confirmed by the fact that all 50 States and the District of Columbia have enacted into law some form of psychotherapist privilege. . . . Because state legislatures are fully aware of the need to protect the integrity of the factfinding functions of their courts, the existence of a consensus among the States indicates that "reason and experience" support recognition of the privilege. In addition, given the importance of the patient's understanding that her communications with her therapists will not be publicly disclosed, any State's promise of confidentiality would have little value if the patient were aware that the privilege would not be honored in a federal court. . . .

Because we agree with the judgment of the state legislatures and the Advisory Committee that a psychotherapist-patient privilege will serve a "public good transcending the normally predominant principle of utilizing all rational means for ascertaining truth," [citation deleted] we hold that confidential communications between a licensed psychotherapist and her patients in the course of diagnosis or treatment are protected from compelled disclosure under Rule 501 of the Federal Rules of Evidence.

All agree that a psychotherapist privilege covers confidential communications made to licensed psychiatrists and psychologists. We have no hesitation in concluding in this case that the federal privilege should also extend to confidential communications made to licensed social workers in the course of psychotherapy. . . .

We part company with the Court of Appeals on a separate point. . . . Making the promise of confidentiality contingent upon a trial judge's later evaluation of the relative importance of the patient's interest in privacy and the evidentiary need for disclosure would eviscerate the effectiveness of the privilege. . . . [I]f the purpose of the privilege is to be served, the participants in the confidential conversation "must be able to predict with some degree of certainty whether particular discussions will be protected. An uncertain privilege, or one which purports to be certain but results in widely varying applications by the courts, is little better than no privilege at all." 449 U.S., at 393, 101 S.Ct., at 684. . . . The judgment of the Court of Appeals is affirmed.

In addition to the recognition of the testimonial privilege, the Supreme Court decision is significant in that it equates mental health with physical health, and recognizes both the value of mental health treatment and how essential confidentiality is to the success of psychotherapy. The only exception explicitly noted is in a footnote, in which Justice Stevens indicated that "we do not doubt that there are situations in which the privilege must give way, for example if a serious threat of harm to the patient or to others can be averted only by means of a disclosure by the therapist.[FN19]" Thus, confidentiality may be breached *only* as a last resort, and only when necessary to protect someone from serious harm.

Second Circuit

Fraser v. United States, 83 F.3d 591 (2d Cir. 1996). The Second Circuit held that under Connecticut state law, a Veterans Administration (VA) hospital did not owe a duty to control a psychiatric care outpatient, and thus, the United States was not liable for the death of an unidentified third party. 21 *Mental & Physical Disability Law Reporter* 131 (1997) [See below for the Connecticut Supreme Court ruling.]

Fifth Circuit

Standeford & Standeford v. Winn-Dixie of Louisiana, Inc., No. 95 C 207 (5th Cir. 1995). It is ordered that the trial judge permit Dr. Antionette Appel to testify and that portions of the record dealing with proprietary psychological testing manuals and/or materials be sealed. We note that defense attorneys did not object to the sealing of parts of the record relating to trade secrets. [Quoted from court summary, Mar. 16, 1995.]

Federal District Courts

United States ex rel. Patosky v. Kozakiewicz, No. Civ. A. 96-451 (W.D. Pa. Mar. 24, 1997). A Pennsylvania federal court denied the *habeas corpus* petition of a defendant challenging a trial court's refusal to allow his attorney pre-trial access to a victim's psychiatric records, and upholding the constitutionality of a state statute creating an absolute privilege for communications between patients and their psychiatrists and psychologists. . . . Patosky's due process rights were not violated because the statutory privilege was narrowly tailored to achieve the compelling interest in protecting victims' privacy so that treatment and recovery would be expedited. *U.S. Const. Amend. XIV.* The interests protected by the statute outweigh defendants' interest in searching through a victim's psychotherapy records for helpful evidence. 21 *Mental & Physical Disability Law Reporter* 377 (1997).

Moye v. United States, 735 F. Supp. 179 (E.D.N.C. 1990). The federal district court for the Eastern District of North Carolina ruled that a therapist did not have a duty to warn:

> The decedent was fully aware that his son was dangerous and had been for some time. Through his consultations with medical personnel and through his own personal observation, the decedent understood his son's record of violent and aberrant behavior. Consequently, in this situation where the foreseeable victim knew of the danger associated with the patient, the [defendant medical facility] had no duty to warn the decedent.

States

Connecticut

Fraser v. United States, 236 Conn. 625 (Apr. 16, 1996). On a question certified from the Second Circuit, the Connecticut Supreme Court held that psychotherapists do not have a duty to control outpatients from harming unidentified third parties.

The Connecticut court ruled that there was no such duty where the outpatient was not known to be dangerous and the victim was not a foreseeable victim. Neither Connecticut case law, policy reasons, nor precedents from other jurisdictions extend any duty to control mental patients to encompass harm to unidentifiable third parties. Connecticut law only imposes a limited duty to prevent injury to a third person unless there is a special relationship of custody or control such as where a patient has made specific threats against a specific victim. . . . Proof that the victim was an identifiable target is an essential element of a negligence action in general, and the state legislature had not enlarged that scope of liability for injuries to third persons. In balancing public policy interests, the interests of the mental health profession in maintaining the confidentiality of patient-therapist relationships . . ., and in respecting due process limitations on involuntary hospitalizations . . ., outweighed those of unforeseeable third persons injured by psychiatric outpatients with no history of dangerous conduct. Many other states have either rejected the psychotherapist's duty to control outpatients altogether . . ., or limited the duty to situations where victims are specifically identifiable or within a class of foreseeable victims. 20 *Mental & Physical Disability Law Reporter* 419 (1996). [See above for the federal appeals court decision.]

Florida

Green v. Ross, 691 So. 2d 542 (Fla. Dist. Ct. App. 1997). A Florida appeals court held that a mental health worker does not have a duty to warn a potential victim when a patient presents a serious threat of violence to that victim. . . . Florida does not recognize such a common-law cause of action. . . . Florida law . . ., which waives the patient-mental health worker privilege when there is a clear and immediate probability of physical harm to a third party, does not create an affirmative duty to warn. 21 *Mental & Physical Disability Law Reporter* 392 (1997).

Leonard v. Leonard, 673 So. 2d 97 (Fla. Dist. Ct. App. 1996). A Florida appeals court quashed and remanded a trial court's denial of a woman's motion for a protective order to prevent the release of her psychotherapist-patient records. . . . Although the mental health of both parents is a factor to be considered in a child custody dispute, this does not mean that a spouse places his or her mental health at issue thereby triggering a waiver of psychotherapist-patient privilege. Neither allegations of mental instability nor denial of such allegations on the part of either parent causes a waiver of psychotherapist-patient privilege. . . . To do so would " 'eviscerate the privilege.' " . . . Waiver may occur in a child custody proceeding only when an adverse event about one party's mental health status occurs, such as an attempted suicide . . . or a voluntary commitment. . . . The appeals court noted that the proper approach to resolving any mental health issues in child custody proceedings—which the trial court ordered—is to have both parties undergo independent psychological evaluations, as these evaluations will provide the court with relevant information while maintaining the confidentiality required by the psychotherapist-patient privilege. 20 *Mental & Physical Disability Law Reporter* 548 (1996).

Boynton v. Burglass, 590 So. 2d 446 (Fla. Dist. Ct. App. 1991). After Lawrence Blaylock fatally shot Wayne Boynton, Boynton's parents brought a malpractice action against Dr. Burglass, a psychiatrist who had treated Blaylock as an outpatient. The Boyntons alleged that Dr. Burglass knew or should have known that Blaylock had threatened Wayne Boynton with serious harm, and that Dr. Burglass had failed to warn their son of the threatened harm. The trial court dismissed the case for failure to state a cause of action. The appeals court declined to follow *Tarasoff v. Regents of Univ. of California*, 551 P.2d 334 (Cal. Sup.Ct. 1976). . . .

Imposing a duty to warn third parties would also require the psychiatrist to foresee a patient's dangerousness, which is virtually impossible, due to the inexact nature of psychiatry, and would undermine psychiatrist-patient confidentiality and trust. The court also noted the common law rule that one person has no duty to control the conduct of another, and the exception that exists when the defendant has a special relationship with the person who needs to be controlled or the foreseeable victim. The exception did not apply here, however, where the doctor did not have the right or the ability to control Blaylock, who was a voluntary outpatient. . . . The court further noted that there was no statute mandating a duty to warn. 16 *Mental & Physical Disability Law Reporter* 318–19 (1992).

Georgia

Mrozinski v. Pogue, 423 S.E.2d 405 (Ga. Ct. App. 1992). Dr. Pogue treated Mrozinski's 14-year-old daughter for drug addiction and mental health problems which began while she was in her mother's custody. After Mrozinski was awarded legal custody, he participated in therapy with Dr. Pogue. Mrozinski contended that Dr. Pogue gave privileged information to his ex-wife's attorney for use in a subsequent custody suit. . . . A trial court granted summary judgment to Dr. Pogue. The appeals court [indicated] there was evidence that Mrozinski sought assurance from Dr. Pogue that the therapy sessions would be confidential and that he relied on these assurances by joining in the therapy with his daughter. . . . The court rejected Dr. Pogue's argument that Mrozinski's communications to him lost their privileged status because he treated Mrozinski and his daughter jointly. "The strongest public policy considerations militate against allowing a psychiatrist to encourage a person to participate in joint therapy, to obtain his trust and extract all his confidences and place him in the most vulnerable position, and then abandon him on the trash heap of lost privilege." . . . "What is protected is not merely words spoken, but 'disclosures made in confidence.' " 17 *Mental & Physical Disability Law Reporter* 186 (1993).

Illinois

Renzi v. Morrison, 241 Ill. App. 3d 5 (Ill. App. Ct. 1993). The Illinois Appellate Court for the First District ruled that a woman could sue her psychiatrist for damages on the basis of the psychiatrist's having voluntarily disclosed her confidential communications and psychological test results without her consent. The psychiatrist's testimony was a significant factor in the trial court's award of temporary custody to the father. The appellate court agreed with the lower court that Illinois's common-law witness immunity did not protect the psychiatrist's testimony, because the statutory confidentiality act gives a patient the power to prevent disclosure of communications with a psychiatrist. A psychiatrist may break confidentiality only when his or her testimony would be more critical to the interests of justice than is the patient's privilege. The court held that because the psychiatrist had voluntarily testified on behalf of the husband in the divorce action, she did not come under the protection of witness immunity, because her "function was to treat [her patient], not to advise the court."

Indiana

Hayes v. Indiana, 667 N.E.2d 222 (Ind. Ct. App. 1996). An Indiana appeals court held that statements made to a therapist by a man who was subsequently charged with sexually abusing his 12-year-old step-daughter were not protected by Indiana's therapist-client privilege. . . . Indiana's Abrogation Statute specifically excludes from the privilege statements reported by a health care provider about a child who may be [a] victim of child abuse or neglect. . . . Patrick Hayes filed an interlocutory appeal from the trial court's denial of his motion to suppress statements he made to therapist Karen Peterson that he sexually abused his step-daughter. Peterson notified Child Protective Services, as required under Indiana's Reporting Statute. . . . The court rejected Hayes' argument that the Abrogation Statute only applies when the abused child reports the abuse. It also rejected Hayes' contention that a therapist must advise a client of the existence of the Reporting Statute prior to counseling. 20 *Mental & Physical Disability Law Reporter* 735 (1996).

Iowa

Leonard v. Iowa, 491 N.W.2d 508 (Iowa 1992). The Iowa Supreme Court held that a state mental hospital did not have a duty to protect an unforeseeable third party whom a patient assaulted shortly after his release from the hospital. . . . The patient was diagnosed with bipolar affective disorder and alcohol dependency. . . . [T]he hospital determined that the patient was in remission and discharged him. Two weeks later, he assaulted a co-worker, and was convicted of kidnapping and attempted murder. The co-worker sued the state, claiming that the hospital failed to provide the patient with proper care and treatment and discharged him knowing that he posed a threat to others. . . . The state appealed a trial court's denial of summary judgment. The court . . . granted summary judgment to the state, because the duty to refrain from negligently releasing the patient extended only to the "reasonably foreseeable victims of the patient's dangerous tendencies," not to the public at large. . . . "We believe that the risks to the general public posed by the negligent release of dangerous mental patients would be far outweighed by the disservice to the general public if treating physicians were subject to civil liability for discharge decisions." 17 *Mental & Physical Disability Law Reporter* 85 (1993).

Louisiana

Louisiana v. Rupp, 614 So. 2d 1323 (La. Ct. App. 1993). A state appeals court, in affirming a child molestation conviction, held that the state's therapist-patient privilege did not apply in child abuse prosecutions. The state law . . . mandates that no privilege will apply in child sex abuse cases except the attorney-client and religious privileges. Here the mother had sought professional counseling for herself, her husband who was the defendant in this case and their daughter who was the victim. In those sessions, the defendant admitted having abused his daughter and that evidence was used against him at trial. 17 *Mental & Physical Disability Law Reporter* 417–18 (1993).

Maryland

Hartford Insurance Co. v. Manor Inn, 617 A.2d 590 (Md. Ct. Spec. App. 1992). A Maryland appeals court affirmed the dismissal of an insurer's claim for reimbursement from the State of Maryland and a hotel for injuries an insured sustained in a car accident with an escaped psychiatric patient because the insured was not a readily identifiable victim. On August 20, 1988, the patient was involuntarily committed to a state mental health facility. On October 28, 1988, staff discovered him missing and reported his escape to the state police. Three days later, county police found the patient wandering around the streets. Believing that he was homeless and in need of emergency shelter, the county police took him to a hotel that had an agreement with the county social service agency to provide overnight shelter to homeless people. The county police did not notify the state hospital or state police of their contact with the patient. The next day, a hotel employee left a van unlocked with the keys in the ignition. The patient drove the van and struck the insured's car. After compensating the insured . . ., the insurer sued the state and the hotel seeking reimbursement. A trial court granted summary judgment to the defendants, and the insurer appealed. The appeals court held that the state did not owe a duty of care to the insured because he was not a readily identifiable victim. Even if the state knew that the patient was inclined to steal a car and to negligently crash it into another driver, the state had no way to warn the insured prior to the incident. . . . [T]he insured [also] failed to prove that the hotel had a duty of care to the insured because he was not a readily identifiable victim. 17 *Mental & Physical Disability Law Reporter* 292 (1993).

Massachusetts

Sugarman v. Board of Registration in Medicine, 662 N.E.2d 1020 (Mass. 1996). Muriel Sugarman was retained as an expert witness by the attorney for the mother in a custody dispute. . . . A court nondisclosure order against any media publicity was in effect. . . . Sugarman leaked to the press selected portions of the report. . . . The Board charged Sugarman with undermining public confidence in the medical profession by knowingly disregarding the gag order, undermining the orderly administration of justice, and failing to adhere to the warning that continued publicity was detrimental to the child's best interests. . . . The Board based its decision on standards of conduct promulgated by the American Academy of Psychiatry and the Law, the *Ethical Guidelines for the Practice of Forensic Psychiatry*, and the American Psychiatric Association's *Principles of Medical Ethics with Annotations Especially Applicable to Psychiatry*. 21 *Mental & Physical Disability Law Reporter* 667 (1997).

Michigan

Michigan v. Adamski, 497 N.W.2d 546 (Mich. Ct. App. 1993). Criminal defendant's sixth amendment right to confront his daughter who accused him of having sexual intercourse with her took priority over daughter's statutory right to keep her mental health records private. A Michigan court of appeals held the trial court committed harmful error when it excluded the defendant's daughter's prior inconsistent statements made to her mental health counselor that her father had not engaged in sexual intercourse with her. The trial court excluded the evidence under [state statute] which provides that a patient's communications made in connection with obtaining counseling are privileged unless the patient waives the privilege. After the defendant was convicted of first degree criminal sexual conduct, the trial court determined it should have admitted the complainant's prior inconsistent statement for impeachment purposes, but concluded the error was harmless. The court of appeals disagreed. . . . [T]he daughter's testimony was of paramount importance to the prosecutor's case and there was no corroborating evidence to her statements. In addition to simply showing that the daughter had a bias against her father, the excluded statements called into question the daughter's credibility and veracity. . . . The court's failure to allow the complainant's father to use his daughter's prior statements that he had not had sexual intercourse with her was not harmless error and violated his sixth amendment right of confrontation by limiting his right to cross-examination. 17 *Mental & Physical Disability Law Reporter* 414 (1993).

Navarre v. Navarre, No. 130123 (Mich. Ct. App. Oct. 7, 1991) (released Feb. 3, 1992). The Michigan Court of Appeals ruled that the statutory physician-patient relationship provisions are not subject to waiver in child custody evaluations. The court held that it is essential to protect the physician-patient relationship, even if it means sacrificing potentially important evidence. Information about the parents is available from other sources, and may be admitted for this purpose. The mother's agreeing to a court-ordered psychological evaluation and the introduction of testimony by the psychologist did not constitute waiver of her physician-patient privilege.

Minnesota

Culbertson v. Chapman, 496 N.W.2d 821 (Minn. Ct. App. 1993). A Minnesota appeals court held that, without evidence of malice, a chemical dependency counselor who disclosed a client's threats to the client's employer was immune from liability. Minnesota law grants practitioners immunity for failing to predict, warn of, or take reasonable precautions to provide protection from a patient's violent behavior . . . unless the patient has communicated to the practitioner a specific, serious threat of physical violence against a specific, clearly identified or identifiable potential victim. . . . Where no specific victim is identified, Minnesota law grants immunity to practitioners who erroneously disclose a patient's confidences to third parties in a good faith effort to warn against or take precautions against a patient's violent behavior. . . . Culbertson brought an action alleging his chemical dependency counselor negligently disclosed threats he made about an unnamed third party to his former employer. Based on previous conversations in which Chapman told her that he distrusted his former employer and blamed him for his termination, she assumed the comment he made that "he would kill 'him' if he could get away with it" was about his former employer. She disclosed the threat to the former employer. Culbertson filed suit alleging he would have gotten his job back if Chapman had not told his employer of his threats. Chapman appealed the trial court's denial of her motion for summary judgment based on qualified immunity. . . . The appeals court reversed. . . . The court noted that immunity for acts made in good faith is applicable even when there would otherwise be negligence or other fault. The court construed "good faith" to mean absence of actual malice. 17 *Mental & Physical Disability Law Reporter* 414 (1993).

Mississippi

Lauderdale County Department of Human Services v. T.H.G., 614 So. 2d 377 (Miss. 1992). The Mississippi Supreme Court held that parents' statements to their therapists could not be disclosed in a parental termination proceeding without the parents' consent. The couple's daughter was placed with foster parents by court order when she was six months old because the daughter was failing to thrive and the mother gave a delusional response when asked why her daughter was crying. The Department of Human Services (DHS) petitioned for termination of parental rights. . . . The statute provides for termination when a parent is unable to provide minimally acceptable care of a child and when the parent has a condition such as mental illness which is unlikely to change within a reasonable time. At the termination hearing, the parents objected to the use of their psychiatric records, the testimony of a psychiatric nurse and the deposition of a psychologist, both of whom had recently treated the parents. The chancery court sustained the parents' objections based on the therapist-patient privilege . . . which makes such evidence inadmissible unless a party has filed pleadings which put her or her mental condition at issue, or the party has waived the privilege. The court rejected DHS's argument that it could not provide [the] clear and convincing evidence required in a termination of parental rights hearing unless it could admit the disputed testimony and medical records. The state has a strong public policy of encouraging persons to seek help without the fear that their statements may be used against them, and creating an exception for termination of parental rights proceedings could open the floodgate for other exceptions. The case was remanded to the chancery court for a final determination on whether the parents' rights should be terminated. 17 *Mental & Physical Disability Law Reporter* 416 (1993).

Missouri

Bradley v. Ray, 904 S.W.2d 302 (Mo. Ct. App. 1995). A Missouri appeals court held that psychologists owed a common-law duty to take steps to protect a child once it became apparent that their client, the child's stepfather, presented a serious danger of sexually abusing the child. On Kelly Pope's behalf, a friend brought an action against Kelly's stepfather, Lester Pope, and his psychologists, Drs. Ray and Strnad, for injuries sustained as a result of alleged sexual abuse by the stepfather. It was alleged that Ray and Strnad were aware that Pope was sexually abusing Kelly but failed to report it to any law enforcement authorities as required by the Child Abuse Reporting Act. . . . The trial court dismissed the suit.

The appeals court reversed. Whether a common-law duty for a psychologist or other professional exists to warn a readily identifiable intended victim that their patient presents an imminent danger to them was an issue of first impression for the Missouri court. . . . A majority of other jurisdictions have considered this issue of a psychologist's duty to warn foreseeable third parties and have imposed a similar duty to warn as was set forth in *Tarasoff*. These courts in large part have established a common-law duty, which requires a psychotherapist to warn readily identifiable victims of the violent intentions of their patients. Thus, they have judicially imposed a duty to warn or control such behavior. Other jurisdictions have statutorily imposed a duty to warn in similar situations. . . . [T]he court concluded that Missouri public policy favors imposing such a duty to warn when a special relationship between physician and patients exists and there is foreseeability of harm. 20 *Mental & Physical Disability Law Reporter* 109 (1996).

New Jersey

Kinsella v. Kinsella, 696 A.2d 556 (N.J. 1997). [T]he supreme court [found] that John did not waive the psychologist-patient privilege against disclosure by alleging extreme cruelty as grounds for divorce. . . . [W]hile stressing that courts must maintain a proper balance between the need to determine the parents' mental health for custody and visitation determinations in order to act in the child's best interests, and to protect the psychologist-patient privilege, the court remanded the psychologist records access issue about custody and visitation. However, it appears that the trial court "in this case has an alternative tool [compulsory psychiatric examinations] which may accomplish both purposes." 21 *Mental & Physical Disability Law Reporter* 650 (1997).

Ohio

Whiteman v. Whiteman, No. CA94-12-229 (Ohio Ct. App. June 26, 1995). The Ohio Court of Appeals indicated that a divorcing husband who seeks custody of his children must permit disclosure of his medical records, including records of psychiatric treatment received during the marriage. The court indicated that all factors potentially relevant to the welfare of the children must be investigated and that the husband had made his mental condition a matter for consideration by the trial court. The court further found that the Ohio statute on physician-patient privilege indicates that a patient who files any civil action waives the privilege, including when the patient files for divorce.

Oklahoma

Ellison (Eldridge) v. Ellison, No. 86696 (Okla. May 21, 1996). The Oklahoma Supreme Court ruled that a custodial parent may not prevent testimony by a child's psychotherapist regarding allegations of abuse by invoking the statutory psychotherapist-patient privilege on the child's behalf. The court indicated that the basis for the state's Child Abuse Reporting and Prevention Act supersedes the basis for the privilege.

Texas

Thapar v. Zezulka, 994 S.W.2d 635 (Tex. 1999). The Texas Supreme Court refused to impose a duty on mental health professionals to warn third parties of a patient's threats. Renu K. Thapar, a psychiatrist, treated Freddy Ray Lilly with psychotherapy and medication for Posttraumatic Stress Disorder, alcohol abuse, and paranoid and delusional beliefs concerning his stepfather, Henry Zezulka, and people of certain ethnic backgrounds. Dr. Thapar's notes from August 23, 1988, indicated that Lilly "feels like killing" Henry Zezulka, but that he "has decided not to do it but that is how he feels." Lilly then spent seven days in the hospital and was discharged. Less than a month later he shot and killed Henry Zezulka. Thapar had never warned Zezulka or any member of Zezulka's family, nor any law enforcement agency. Lyndall Zezulka, Henry's wife and Lilly's mother, sued Thapar for negligence.

The trial court granted summary judgment for Thapar based on the Supreme Court's decision in *Bird v. W.C.W.*, 868 S.W.2d 767 (Tex. 1994) that "no duty runs from a psychologist to a third party to not negligently misdiagnose a patient's condition." Zezulka appealed. The Texas court of appeals "held that the no-duty ground asserted in Thapar's motion for summary judgment was not a defense to the cause of action pleaded by Zezulka. . . ." [W]e are asked whether a mental-health professional owes a duty to warn third parties of patient's threats. . . . The Legislature has chosen to closely guard a patient's communications with a mental-health professional. . . . Zezulka complains that Thapar was negligent in not warning members of the Zezulka family about Lilly's threats. But a disclosure by Thapar to one of the Zezulkas would have violated the confidentiality statute because no exception in the statute provides for disclosure to third parties threatened by the patient. . . . Under the applicable statute, Thapar was prohibited from warning one of his patient's potential victims and therefore had no duty to warn the Zezulka family of Lilly's threats.

Zezulka also complains that Thapar was negligent in not disclosing Lilly's threats to any law enforcement agency. There is an exception in the confidentiality statute that provides for disclosure to law enforcement personnel in certain circumstances. The statute, however, permits these disclosures but does not require them. . . . Because of the Legislature's stated policy, we decline to impose a common law duty on mental-health professionals to warn third parties of their patient's threats.

Virginia

Nasser v. Parker, 455 S.E.2d 502 (Va. 1995). While some courts have expanded [the duty to warn or protect] beyond that enumerated in the original *Tarasoff* case, other courts have narrowed or rejected such a duty. The most common reason for the latter . . . has been that *Tarasoff* doctrine places an unfair burden on therapists when such harm isn't foreseeable. The Supreme Court of Virginia . . . has gone a step further, rejecting the fundamental notion that the doctor-patient relationship in itself places special obligations on physicians. . . .

Under ordinary circumstances one person does not have a duty to take precautions to protect another person from harm by a third party. An exception to this rule is provided by section 315 of the Second Restatement of Torts, which states that such a duty does exist when a "special relationship" exists between the defendant and the third party. . . . [T]he Court found the [*Tarasoff*] analysis of the "special relationship" unpersuasive. This analysis failed to consider section 315 in the context of section 319, which states that (with emphasis added) "one who *takes charge* of a third person whom he knows or should know to be likely to cause bodily harm to others if not controlled is under a duty to exercise reasonable care to control the third person to prevent him from doing such harm." . . . [T]he court argued . . . that—in itself—the doctor-patient or hospital-patient relationship involves an insufficient degree of control over the patient to constitute a "special relationship." While the plaintiffs had argued that the degree of control necessary to issue a warning (as opposed to confining the patient) is "minimal," the Court argued that to accept this "minimal" standard would be to render all but meaningless the standard of responsibility set by the "takes charge" language of section 319. 20 *American Academy of Psychiatry & The Law Newsletter* 104–05 (1995).

Washington

Niece v. Elmview Group Home, 929 P.2d 420 (Wash. 1997). [T]he Washington State Supreme Court expands the duty to protect patients from the foreseeable actions of third parties. The Court held that, due to the "special relationship" that exists between the care provider and the developmentally disabled, there is an obligation to protect residents from the "foreseeable consequences" of the residents' impairments. This includes protecting them from sexual assault by staff. . . . [S]exual assault was a potential harm that was foreseeable. The presence of the special relationship and the foreseeable nature of the assault signal Elmview's duty to protect Niece from the assaults she suffered. 25 *Journal of the American Academy of Psychiatry & Law* 418 (1997).

Redding v. Virginia Mason Medical Center, 878 P.2d 483 (Wash. Ct. App. 1994). A Washington appeals court held that the psychologist-patient privilege did not protect statements made by one spouse during joint counseling sessions from being disclosed in a later custody dispute between the couple. Michell Redding had agreed to attend joint counseling with her husband Tracy as part of his court-ordered anger-management counseling. . . . During the joint sessions with Dr. Arden Snyder of the Virginia Mason Medical Center . . ., Michell's drinking problem was discussed. Dr. Snyder's report to the court mentioned the problem as a factor contributing to Tracy's anger. After Michell petitioned for divorce and custody, Tracy asked the Center for copies of the records of the joint sessions in order to show Michell had admitted her alcohol problem. The Center released the records without a subpoena and without Michell's consent. The trial court granted the Center's motion for summary judgment and this court affirmed on the ground that in litigation arising between joint patients, the psychologist-patient privilege . . . does not protect statements made by one party during a joint counseling session. . . . The marital privilege was also inapplicable because the statements were made in the presence of a third party. Dr. Snyder's release of the records without a subpoena was irrelevant in this case because the records were not privileged in the suit between Michell and Tracy and a subpoena would have been enforced had it been resisted. Since Michell's drinking problem would be significant to a court deciding the custody dispute, the records were not privileged in the context they were released, and the trial court did not err in granting summary judgment. 19 *Mental & Physical Disability Law Reporter* 361 (1995).

CHAPTER 3

WHAT CONSTITUTES A PSYCHOLOGICAL EVALUATION?

§ 3.1   Stages of the Psychological Evaluation

A psychological evaluation of adults or children is generally performed in three stages: gathering data, processing the information, and communicating results.

Gathering Information

The first stage involves gathering information. During this stage, it is important for the evaluator to identify the questions that should be answered during the evaluation process. In a custody dispute, the overriding question in determining the best interests of the child is which parent would make the better custodial/placement parent. Questions asked of all parents would include, for example, "What do you most like to do with your child(ren)?" "What do you see as your deficiencies as a parent?" and "How are your child(ren) doing in school?" When there is a known problem area for a parent, the evaluator should ask additional, specific questions, such as the following:

1. Will the parent's alcoholism adversely affect the child(ren)?
2. Does the parent have the personality of a physical abuser?
3. Although the parent has a history of psychiatric hospitalizations, is the person currently stable enough to be considered as a custodial parent?

As part of the information-gathering stage, the evaluator decides which tests and other instruments to administer, what collateral information to gather, and whom to interview. At this point, the tests and other instruments are administered and scored, the individuals are interviewed, and collateral information is gathered. Collateral information could include, for example,

1. Police reports
2. Letters from attorneys
3. Previous psychological evaluations
4. Medical reports/physicians
5. School information
6. Mental health records/therapists

7. Previous arrest records (charges or convictions)

8. Interviews of objective third parties (teachers, day care staff, etc.).

Processing the Information

The second step of the evaluation is the processing stage. During this stage, all the information gathered through interviews, tests, or collateral sources is synthesized and processed by the examiner. It is the examiner's responsibility to score and interpret all the tests administered. This information is then integrated with information obtained through interviews and supporting documents. The examiner should separate the more important information from the extraneous or irrelevant material. Then the examiner is ready to write a report.

§ 3.2   Test Administration

Questions have been raised about the efficacy of administering psychological tests. In 2001, Gregory J. Meyer and his associates wrote an article for the American Psychological Association in which they concluded, "We have also demonstrated that distinct assessment methods provide unique sources of data and have documented how sole reliance on clinical interview often leads to an incomplete understanding of patients."[1]

Before administering the evaluation, the evaluator should find an appropriate setting—one that is quiet, free from distractions, and comfortable. It is also important that the evaluator establish rapport with the individual being tested. As part of this process, the evaluator can briefly describe the evaluation process in a manner that is designed to put the individual at ease. An experienced examiner can usually establish rapport in a relatively short period of time. However, it may be difficult to establish rapport with young children who are fearful. In such instances, occasionally a parent or attorney requests permission to sit in the evaluation room with a child during the evaluation. This is generally not recommended, because a parent or attorney or other individual not involved in the evaluation may unknowingly provide additional stress for the child or may inadvertently attempt to help the child. If the examiner notes a significant amount of reticence on the part of the child, the examiner can invite the parent to accompany the child to the testing room and to leave shortly after the child is settled. (See also Chapter 2 discussion on third-party observers.)

The most important requirement for the examiner during a psychological evaluation is that the tests be administered correctly. With tests that are standardized, individuals who read or interpret the results of an evaluation assume that the exact instructions were followed. Whether the examiner agrees or disagrees with the prescribed instructions for the individual being tested, they must be followed verbatim. If examiners use their own stylized version of the directions, the standardization of the test will be in jeopardy and the

---

[1] Gregory J. Meyer, Stephen E. Finn, Lorraine D. Eyde, Gary G. Kay, Kevin L. Moreland, Robert R. Dies, Elena J. Eisman, Tom W. Kubiszyn, & Geoffrey M. Reed, *Psychological Testing and Psychological Assessment: A Review of Evidence and Issues*, 56 Am. Psychol. 155 (2001).

results will need to be interpreted with skepticism. When an examiner deviates from the established directions for any legitimate reason, the reason must be indicated in the report, along with a statement regarding whether the nonstandard instructions are believed to have affected the test results in any way, and, if so, how. Acceptable reasons for deviation include visual, auditory, physical, or mental impairment. Some psychologists permit individuals to take certain tests home to be answered at the subject's leisure. This procedure may work when individuals are coming in solely for therapy, though it is not recommended. However, in a custody evaluation, it is essential to ensure that the answers were provided by the subject and were not the result of collaborative work. This can be a particular problem when both a parent and a stepparent are filling out the same instruments at home. The *American Psychological Association Case Book for Providers of Psychological Services* addresses this issue. It states:

> When the psychologist does not have direct, firsthand information as to the conditions under which a test is taken, he or she is forced (in the above instance, unnecessarily) to assume that the test responses were not distorted by the general situation in which the test was taken (e.g., whether the client consulted others about the test responses). Indeed, the psychologist could have no assurance that this test was in fact completed by the client. In the instance where the test might be introduced as data in a court proceeding, it would be summarily dismissed as hearsay evidence. Although the psychologist should be free to exercise judgment as to the trustworthiness of the client, it is generally not a good professional practice to surrender direct monitoring of test administering.[2]

(See also **§ 2.13,** "Requirement That Tests and Interviews Be Correctly Administered.")

§ 3.3   Distortion of Test Results

It should be kept in mind that test results, while relatively objective evidence, can be distorted, consciously or unconsciously, by the professional using them, including the psychologist who administers and interprets the test, and the psychiatrist, social worker, or other professional who may use information from tests in forming or defending an opinion. The distortion can range from the choice of tests to the specific operations necessary to administer and score the test.[3]

   John Podboy and Albert Kastle write about "the misuse of psychological testing in complex trial situations." They point out that there are both unintentional and intentional misuses of psychological instruments.[4] Psychologists can *unintentionally* misuse psychological tests when the psychologists lack the knowledge necessary to administer

---

[2] American Psychological Association Case Book for Providers of Psychological Services 664 (1984).

[3] Melendez & Marcus, *Mental Distress Claims: Testing the Psychological Tests*, 11 Am. J. Forensic Psychiatry 19, 19 (1990).

[4] John Podboy & Albert Kastle, The Intentional Misuse of Psychological Tests in Complex Trials, Paper presented at the 8th Annual Symposium in Forensic Psychology of American College of Forensic Psychology 8, San Francisco (Apr. 1992).

and interpret the test appropriately. Unintentional errors can also occur when psychologists place undue reliance on a single, relatively brief test. A third typical error arises when an intelligence test is only partially administered, thus reducing the validity of the results.

The authors also address *intentional* misuse that can occur at the hands of psychologists. They point out that outright fraud appears to be rare; however, some intentional misuses still need to be addressed. One such misuse occurs when a psychologist, or other mental health professional, has inadequate training in the field of assessment and relies on computerized interpretations without fully understanding the information. A second source of error occurs when overgeneralizations are used in interpreting Rorschach data.

In a study in which 120 psychological reports in mental disability cases were reviewed, only five (4 percent) of the reports "were considered to be free of errors, biases, or slanted points of view."[5] Twenty-three of the reports evidenced problems because the evaluator did not have adequate credentials to administer the tests used. Seventy-six had problems with the specific test battery used, including utilization of batteries inadequate to the task, violation of standardization norms, violation of test instructions, violation of scoring procedures, or other problems. Eighty-seven had problems involving test interpretation, including interpreting selective data, making contradictory statements, making errors in interpretations, and ignoring indicators of invalidity of results. Seventy-one of the reports were judged to offer exaggerated or biased diagnoses, and 10 others used diagnoses that did not meet DSM-III-R criteria.[6] Therefore, it is critical that the evaluator be carefully chosen, and that all tests used be properly administered and interpreted.

§ 3.4   Criteria for the Use of Testing

Psychologist Kirk Heilbrun suggests a very conservative set of criteria for the use of psychological testing in forensic assessment:

(1) The test is commercially available and adequately documented in two sources. First, it is accompanied by a manual describing its development, psychometric properties, and procedure for administration. Second, it is listed and reviewed in *Mental Measurements Yearbook* or some other readily available source. . . .

(2) Reliability should be considered. The use of tests with a reliability coefficient of less than .80 is not advisable. The use of less reliable tests would require an explicit justification by the psychologist. . . .

(3) The test should be relevant to the legal issue, or to a psychological construct underlying the legal issue. . . . Such justification should be made in the report, clarifying the evaluator's reasoning for selecting a given test on relevancy grounds. A justification can be made on theoretical grounds; if there is no research evidence with which to evaluate the accuracy or strength of the connection between psychological construct and legal issue, then the court should be so informed. . . .

(4) Standard administration should be used, with testing conditions as close as possible to the quiet, distraction-free ideal. . . .

---

[5] *Id.* at 20.
[6] *Id.* at 21–22.

(5) Applicability to this population and for this purpose should guide both test selection and interpretation. . . . The closer the "fit" between a given individual and the population and situation of those in the validation research, the more confidence can be expressed in the applicability of the results. . . .

(6) Objective tests and actuarial data combination are preferable when there are appropriate outcome data and a "formula" exists. . . . If no "formula" exists, that means we have no alternative but to use our heads. . . .

(7) Response style should be explicitly assessed using approaches sensitive to distortion, and the results of psychological testing interpreted within the context of the individual's response style. When the response style appears to be malingering, defensive, or irrelevant rather than honest/reliable, the results of psychological testing may need to be discounted or even ignored and other data sources emphasized to a greater degree. . . . The only psychological test with extensive empirical support in reassuring response style is the MMPI. . . . Unless response style is explicitly measured and demonstrated to be honest . . . the interpretation of the results of psychological tests may be impossible.[7]

In an ideal world, all Heilbrun's criteria could be fully met. In practice, psychologists may use a test that does not quite meet the ideal—for example, a test that, although the best test, is relatively new, too new to appear in the *Mental Measurements Yearbook* or published research. The psychologist is responsible for acknowledging this fact, however, and for indicating how a given test addresses the psychological and legal issues.

§ 3.5   The Interview

A complete evaluation must include some form of interview, often referred to in the psychological report as the *clinical interview.* The interview process can follow several different formats. The psychologist could spend a considerable amount of time in a question-and-answer format with each of the individuals. This approach is often facilitated by the use of a questionnaire to provide background information. When such a questionnaire is used, the interview time with the psychologist is often reduced. Alternatively or in addition, a social worker could obtain a social history from the individuals.

Whatever method is used, many questions need to be addressed in the interview. They include the following:

1. Place of residence
2. Place of employment
3. Employment history
4. Educational history
5. Names and ages of children, and whether children are living at home
6. Status of children (educational, occupational, marital, or other)
7. Previous or current psychological or psychiatric treatment

---

[7] Kirk Heilbrun, *The Role of Psychological Testing in Forensic Assessment*, 16 Law & Hum. Behav. 257, 264–68 (1992). Copyright 1992 by Plenum Publishing Corp. Reprinted with permission.

8. Whether the treatment was inpatient or outpatient

9. Any psychiatric medication previously taken or currently being taken

10. Satisfaction with life (job, friends, relatives, others)

11. Alcohol or other drug use history

12. Problems with the law—past and present

13. Organizations belonged to

14. Hobbies, skills, or interests

15. Information about the family of origin

16. Whether parents are living or deceased

17. Types of occupations or professions the parents have or had

18. Ages and marital status of, and closeness with, siblings

19. Any problems with developmental milestones

20. Any history of sexual assault

21. Any current medical problems

22. Major stressors in their lives

23. Histories of previous marriages

24. If previously married, whether there were children, and, if so, who received custody

25. Reasons for divorce in the previous marriages, if applicable.

In custody cases, in addition to these background personal-history-type questions, several questions need to be asked about the current divorce situation. They would include questions addressing the following issues:

1. Problems with visitation, access or periods of physical placement

2. Reasons why the individual feels that he or she would make the best custodial/placement parent

3. Reasons why the individual feels the other parent would not make the best custodial/placement parent

4. Concerns the individual feels the other parent has about him or her

5. Views about the ideal placement schedule

6. Reason for the current divorce

7. Amount of time with the child(ren) the parent is willing to allow the other parent to have

8. Living environment that the parent will provide for the child(ren), including place of residence, school, use of day care, and use of baby sitters

9. Additional concerns that the other parent has.

When the children are interviewed, either a direct interview technique or a diagnostic interview technique can be used. As part of the child's interview, the child should be asked why he or she thinks the divorce is taking place and how he or she feels about it, as well as questions regarding any areas of concern that have been raised (e.g., physical abuse, sexual abuse, alcoholism, psychological abuse, mental illness, and criminal histories). Additional questions would include, "When you do something bad, how does your mother/father punish you? Did your mother ever hurt you? Did your father ever hurt you? Did your mother ever hurt your father? Did your father ever hurt your mother?" The child should not be asked which parent he/she prefers to live with. Instead, the questions should be framed in a format such as, "How would you feel if the judge said you should live with your father/with your mother?" "What did your mother/father tell you to be sure to tell me today?" "When your mother/father talks about your father/mother, what does your mother/father say about your father/mother?"

A relatively new approach to interviewing children involves structured diagnostic interviews. One of the most prominent diagnostic interview techniques developed is the Diagnostic Interview Schedule for Children (DISC), developed by the National Institute for Mental Health (NIMH). The work was performed by Dr. Barbara Herjanic, Dr. Joaquim Puig-Antizh, and Dr. Keith Connors. An outgrowth of this instrument is the Diagnostic Interview for Children and Adolescents (DICA). The other major diagnostic review instrument is popularly referred to as the Kiddie-SADS (K-SADS). It is adapted from the original Schedule for Affective Disorders and Schizophrenia. The structured diagnostic interviews hold promise for future assessment of children but are not used as much as would have been expected. It is not likely that a diagnostic interview would answer all the questions relevant to a custody evaluation.

§ 3.6   Order of Administration of Psychological Tests

In general, the least-structured psychological tests should be administered first—for example, the Thematic Apperception Test (TAT) and sentence completion tests. The somewhat-structured tests—for example, the Minnesota Multiphasic Personality Inventory-2nd Edition (MMPI-2)—should be given next. The last to be given should include the most-structured tests, those that clearly have right and wrong answers—for example, the intelligence tests.[8]

The Rorschach may be an exception to the above rule. John Exner Jr. indicates that the Rorschach should normally be given last, as it "is usually the most ambiguous test given in a battery and for this reason may prove to be the most threatening and disruptive to the subject."[9] He indicates that differences have been found in intelligence test performance when the Rorschach precedes the intelligence test. Some psychologists disagree, feeling that the Rorschach should be first so that there is minimal interference from other tests and procedures.

If one test is administered a significant period of time before another—for example, a week or more before—the order of administration is much less likely to be significant. So, for example, the Wechsler Adult Intelligence Scale-3rd Edition (WAIS-III) could be administered during the first evaluation session without necessarily having a negative effect on the results of tests administered a week later. Within a single session, however, the effect can be substantial if the administration of structured tests precedes that of unstructured ones.

---

[8] Lundy, *Instructional Set and Thematic Apperception Test Validity*, 52 J. Personality Assessment 309, 318 (1988); A. Anastasi, Psychological Testing 437 (7th ed. 1997).

[9] John Exner Jr. & B. Clark, The Rorschach in Clinical Diagnosis of Mental Disorders 155 (B. Wolman ed., 1978).

§ 3.7   Factors Affecting the Examinee

There is a phenomenon in psychological testing that is referred to as the *practice effect.* The more frequently an individual takes a specific test, the more familiar that individual becomes with the items, and the more that familiarity could affect the outcome. One who has been through a significant number of psychological evaluations will undoubtedly benefit from practice effect on some tests. To prevent the practice effect from distorting results, intelligence tests generally should not be administered more frequently than once per year with adults and older children, or once per six months with younger children. It should also be noted that individuals who are more outgoing and those more likely to guess are more likely to score higher on tests of cognitive functioning than those who are more passive and introverted. Results of evaluations must be interpreted with this in mind.

Because many, perhaps most, examinees attempt to manage the impression the examiner has of them in some ways, the examiner must assess what kinds of attempts are made, if any, including any attempts at malingering or other forms of falsification.

§ 3.8   Factors Affecting the Examiner

Many factors may affect the examiner during the evaluation process, including race, gender, and experience.

Race.   It has been hypothesized that examiners of one race testing people of another race could adversely affect the results of the evaluation. This includes black subjects tested by white examiners and white subjects tested by black examiners. John Graham and Ries Lilly tell of a researcher, Jensen, who reviewed 30 studies done between 1936 and 1977 that addressed this issue.[10] Jensen indicated that only 17 of the studies were adequately designed to properly measure the variable of race. All 17 studies concluded that the race of the examiner is not an important variable in determining performance on tests of cognitive functioning. Data for the effect of race on other types of tests is not available, but we would not expect a problem.

Gender.   It has been hypothesized that individuals tested by examiners of the same sex would perform better than individuals tested by examiners of the opposite sex. Researchers have conducted many studies in this area.[11] Although some studies indicate that the sex of the examiner can have a small effect on the results, most conclude that there is no significant difference in results based on the sex of the examiner.[12]

Experience.   One might expect that the evaluator with more training and more experience in assessment techniques will generate more accurate results. However, one study

---

[10] John Graham & Ries Lilly, Psychological Testing 75 (1984).

[11] *Id.*

[12] *Id.*

suggests that medium-experience examiners have higher accuracy than high- or low-experience examiners.[13] The most experienced examiner can become stale in evaluation skills without appropriate continuing education. As a result, it is important to make sure that experienced examiners also maintain their skills through continuing education.[14]

§ 3.9   Communicating Results

The results of the psychological evaluation are generally communicated in report form. It is important to know that the clients have a right to receive information about the tests they have taken.[15] However, it is the psychologist's responsibility to communicate the information so that it is not misunderstood, misused, or misrepresented by the clients. As a result, it is usually important not to provide actual scores or to share raw data with the individuals.

Because it is essential that the psychologists not do anything to compromise the integrity of the tests administered, they cannot share raw test data with attorneys. It is not unethical for the attorney to receive a copy of information-gathering forms. The American Psychological Association's *Guidelines for Providers of Psychological Services* states, "Raw psychological data (e.g., test protocols, therapy or interview notes, or questionnaire returns), in which a user is identified are ordinarily released only with the written consent of the user or the user's legal representative, are released only to a person recognized by the psychologist as competent to interpret data."[16] The 2002 APA code of ethics makes two important statements about this issue at Ethical Standards 9.04b and 9.11. Each person or institution purchasing a test must agree to comply with these basic principles of minimum test security. Attorneys are generally not in the position to be able to fully understand the materials received, and, consequently, the information could be inappropriately used. It is far more appropriate to share the raw data with another psychologist of the attorneys' choice. Then the information is likely to be used accurately and with discretion. It can be very disconcerting for a psychologist to go into a deposition or trial and find that the raw data from an evaluation has been shared with the attorney by another psychologist, forcing the psychologist to consider filing an ethics complaint against the psychologist who disclosed the data. It is equally disconcerting to hear an attorney reading from a test manual that is supposed to be protected by the psychologist, given the ethical and contractual responsibility of the psychologist to protect the tests. See **Chapter 2** on ethical issues for an extensive discussion of these concerns.

Each psychologist signs an agreement with the major test-publishing companies not to share test materials with nonpsychologists. An example comes from the Psychological Corporation's 2004 Catalog:

1. Test takers must not receive test answers before beginning the test.
2. Test questions are not to be reproduced or paraphrased in any way.

---

[13] *Id.* at 342.

[14] *Id.* at 367.

[15] *Id.*

[16] Ethical Principles of Psychologists and Code of Conduct, Ethical Standards 9.04b and 9.11 (2002).

3. Access to test materials must be limited to qualified persons with a responsible, professional interest who agree to safeguard their use.

4. Test materials and scores may be released only to persons qualified to interpret and use them properly.

5. If a test taker or the parent of a child who has taken a test wishes to examine the test responses or results, the parent or test taker may be permitted to review the test and the test answers in the presence of a representative of the school, college or institution that administered the test. Such review should not be permitted in those jurisdictions where applicable laws require the institution to provide a photocopy of the test subsequent to review. If you are not certain of the effect of the laws in your state, please contact your state's professional organization.

6. No reproduction of test materials is allowed in any form or by any means, electronic or mechanical.

7. Requests to copy any test materials must be in writing and directed to the:

    Legal Affairs Department
    Harcourt Assessment
    19500 Bulverde Rd.
    San Antonio, Texas 78259-3701
    Or sent via online to legalaffairs@harcourt.com. Our policy on confidentiality.

8. Release of test materials to unqualified individuals can be viewed at www. HarcourtAssessment.com.

9. Test materials may not be resold or distributed for any purpose.[17]

If the psychologist is put in the position of divulging specific test items or specific interpretations of various responses, the tests could be rendered invalid. Anyone in the court reading the transcript of the case could know what types of answers to give and what types to avoid. As a result, none of those individuals could ever take the tests again and obtain valid results. With all the civil and criminal cases in the country that utilize psychologists, the test would quickly become useless and would not be available to provide the necessary information to the courts, wasting sometimes millions of dollars spent to develop the tests. A dilemma arises when the psychologist's need to protect the data conflicts with the attorney's need to discover. However, in the experience of the authors of this text, courts tend to uphold the psychologist's position, recognizing that the attorney's needs can be adequately addressed by the attorney's retaining a psychologist to review the test results.

§ 3.10   *Guidelines for Child Custody Evaluations in Divorce Proceedings*

The American Psychological Association adopted and published *Guidelines for Child Custody Evaluations in Divorce Proceedings* in 1994. They describe the guidelines as

---

[17] Psych Corp. 167 (2004).

being aspirational in intent: "As guidelines they are not intended to be either mandatory or exhaustive. The goal of the guidelines is to promote proficiency in using psychological expertise in conducting child custody evaluations."[18]

As noted above, it is not mandatory for psychologists to follow these guidelines. However, when an organization such as the APA develops guidelines of this nature, they become the standard of practice or standard of care for the profession. As a result, it may not technically be mandatory for psychologists to follow the guidelines, but psychologists who do not will be operating outside the standard of practice or care as set forth by the parent organization for psychologists. Guidelines 7, 9, 10, 12, and 15 and 16 of the *Guidelines for Child Custody Evaluations in Divorce Proceedings* are based upon the American Psychological Association Code of Ethics. For the American Psychological Association to say that the guidelines are not mandatory, when the standards in the ethics code are, is contradictory.

The APA Guidelines for Child Custody Evaluations in Divorce Proceedings collects in one document many standards of practice that psychologists generally have been encouraged to follow in the past but are now much more strongly urged to follow. Furthermore, it clarifies areas that have been problematic in divorce cases involving custody disputes. It does not, however, address the specific procedures to be used in carrying out the recommended guidelines.

The guidelines themselves are divided into three major categories. The first is "Orienting Guidelines: Purpose of a Child Custody Evaluation." The second major area is "General Guidelines: Preparing for a Child Custody Evaluation," and the last is "Procedural Guidelines": Conducting a Child Custody Evaluation." The guidelines cover only five pages of material, although there is an introduction and a supplementary reference list. Because of the brevity of some of the guidelines, it becomes essential for psychologists to use their expertise to expand on what is stated to adequately practice within the standards of the profession.

Psychologists Lois Oberlander and Marion Gindes both wrote articles supporting the use of the guidelines in child custody evaluations. Oberlander stated:

> The application of the Guidelines to practice enriches discussion about important issues such as anticipating ethical issues in high-conflict cases, defining and measuring relevant psycholegal constructs in valid and reliable ways and learning how to correspondingly protect children and adolescents from distress while giving them a voice concerning custody and visitation preferences. . . . The application of guidelines for child custody evaluations and high-conflict custody disputes is an area of concern for psychologists who must grapple with how to identify and uphold the best interest of the children when complex and relatively intractable conflicted family dynamics are in play.[19]

---

[18] Guidelines at 677.

[19] Lois Oberlander, *Ethical Responsibilities in Child Custody Evaluations: Implications for Evaluation Methodology,* 5 Ethics & Behav. no. 4, at 311, 330 (1995). *See also* Marion Gindes, *Guidelines for Child Custody Evaluations for Psychologists: An Overview and Commentary*, 29 Fam. L.Q., no. 1, at 39–62 (1995).

§ 3.11   —Orienting Guidelines: Purpose of a Child Custody Evaluation

Best Interests Standard

The first section of the APA guidelines is divided into three subsections. First, *"The primary purpose of the evaluation is to assess the best psychological interest of the child."*[20] This indicates that the Committee on Professional Practice and Standards (COPPS) adopted the best interests standard that has been used by psychologists in courts for years, and that is the standard in state laws and case law.

Second, *"The child's interest and well-being are paramount."*[21] This standard states that, although parents competing for custody may have legitimate concerns, it is essential that the best interests of the child(ren) prevail and that the parents' interests become secondary.

Third, *"The focus of the evaluation is on parenting capacity, the psychological and developmental needs of the child, and the resulting fit."*[22] An interesting distinction is made in this subsection. It states that although any psychopathology of the parent may be of interest as it relates to the parent's ability to function as a parent, it is not the primary focus of the evaluation. The primary focus is to assess (1) the adult's capacity for parenting; (2) the psychological functioning and developmental needs of the child, and the wishes of each child, when appropriate; (3) the functioning ability of each parent to meet these standards; and (4) the interaction between each adult and each child. This subsection informs the psychologist that it is necessary to look at the parents' knowledge, attributes, skills, and abilities; to understand the developmental needs of the child; and to evaluate the interaction between each parent and each child. This closely follows the standards set forth in the Uniform Marriage and Divorce Act (UMDA) of 1979. The best interests standard was codified in the UMDA, which was passed by Congress in 1979 and has since been adopted by every U.S. jurisdiction:

> The court shall determine custody in accordance with the best interest of the child. The court shall consider all relevant factors including: 1) The wishes of the child's parent or parents as to his custody; 2) The wishes of the child as to his custodian; 3) The interaction and interrelationship of the child with his parent or parents, his siblings and other persons who may significantly affect the child's best interest; 4) The child's adjustment to his home, school, and community; 5) The mental and physical health of all individuals involved; and 6) The physical violence or threat of physical violence by the child's potential custodian, whether directed against the child or directed against another person, but witnessed by the child.

Although the guidelines are clear in identifying concepts such as "best interest," "parenting capacity," and "resulting fit," they do not provide guidance to the evaluator regarding how to assess and satisfy those requirements. Numerous variables must be addressed in performing a custody evaluation to respond to the issues raised by the first three statements in the APA *Guidelines for Child Custody Evaluations in Divorce Proceedings.*

---

[20] Guidelines at 677.

[21] *Id.*

[22] *Id.* at 678.

Factors to Consider

One of the first areas to be addressed is how the parent presents himself or herself for the evaluation. The parent's level of cooperation, hygiene, and interaction must be assessed. Identifying whether parents are able to set appropriate limits and have realistic perceptions of their capabilities as parents is also important. A primary concern is whether the parents are aware of their motivation for seeking custody and understand the effect of divorce on the child.

A second major area involves each parent's interaction with the environment. The evaluator must ascertain whether each parent purchases clothes for the children, feeds the children, attends school conferences, runs errands for the children, takes the children to medical appointments, and generally supports their activities of daily living. When addressing the issue of whether an appropriate home environment is available, the evaluator is primarily concerned with whether there is sufficient sleeping space for all the children, whether the kitchen and bathroom areas are sanitary, and whether privacy is available.

The parents' ability to identify social support networks and community support has been demonstrated to be an important component of effective parenting. Research also indicates the ability to identify age-appropriate development milestones, current and future needs of children, and relevant school information as important factors. Provision of appropriate discipline, sex education, and hygiene training are also necessary.

In the legal area, the parents' arrest records must be evaluated, specifically with regard to abuse allegations and alcohol- or other drug-related offenses. In addition, the parents' cooperation with previous court orders and placement schedules is important. Last, the recency and frequency of any criminal complaints must be addressed. Many states have online access to court information.

Anger between parents and children, threats by parents, and positive attitudes of parents and children toward one another are all factors that affect the issue of parent-child interaction. Furthermore, the parents' participation in the child's education and the placement preference of the child, if stated, should also be considered especially if the child is over 15 years old.

As for the psychological or emotional issues of placement, psychological test results should be considered in addition to inpatient and outpatient treatment histories, history of substance abuse, and any use of psychiatric medications. The frequency and recency of mental health contacts cannot be ignored. A parent who has been hospitalized 12 times in the past five years in psychiatric units is certainly in much worse shape than the parent who had one psychiatric hospitalization at 19 years of age during a significant adjustment period. Outpatient therapy may indicate either major problems or that the parent has matured and grown, resulting in his or her being a better parent.

Custodial or placement parents engage in many appropriate and inappropriate behaviors. A parent who is engaging in most of the recommended appropriate behaviors and only a few of the inappropriate behaviors is in a more favorable position to obtain custody or placement than a parent who is performing only a few of the appropriate behaviors and most of the inappropriate behaviors. **Chapter 5** details these behaviors.

It can easily be seen that the task of measuring parenting capacity is quite involved. For an evaluator to be able to perform all the tasks necessary to address all of the preceding issues, many areas of competence are required.

Observing Parent and Child

The first section of the APA guidelines also addresses the issue of observations involving each parent and each child. There are probably as many different ways to perform observations as there are evaluators. Some evaluators prefer to utilize structured observations with each parent and each child alone. Others prefer to see all of the children together with one parent and then the other, and still others prefer to see all the children together with both parents. There are advantages and disadvantages to each approach.

Another decision made by the evaluator is whether to have a structured task available for the parents and children to engage in during the evaluation or to have the observation be an unstructured event. The age of the children must be considered, in addition to whether the observation should be formal or informal.

Many evaluators feel that it is not necessary to observe the interaction between parents and older children, as the observations are likely to be stilted, unproductive, and biased in the direction of the children's wishes. The research by Marc J. Ackerman *et al.*[23] demonstrates that a majority of family law judges and family lawyers expect psychologists to observe children of all ages, especially those 12 years of age and younger.[24]

One of the other questions raised is whether observations should be required between children and alleged abuse perpetrators or between children and parents when a restraining order is in place. These evaluations are often requested in an effort to determine whether the abuse has indeed occurred, whether there is sufficient bonding between the child and the parent to warrant continued contact, and/or whether supervised or unsupervised visitation should be commenced after a hiatus. In spite of the fact that many attorneys will strongly object to their clients' children being required to be in the company of a parent when there are these types of concerns, there is no other way to adequately evaluate the interaction between parents and children—one must observe them together. Attorneys must recognize that the evaluator is a mental health professional who is obligated to act in the children's best interests. As such, the evaluator will not allow the interaction to be harmful to the child psychologically or physically, if possible. Therefore, if the attorney truly wants to determine what is in the children's best interests, observations under the circumstances are essential.

§ 3.12   —General Guidelines: Preparing for a Child Custody Evaluation

Importance of Impartiality

The second section of the APA guidelines begins by imploring the psychologist to act neither as a judge nor as an advocating attorney. It begins, "*4. The role of the psychologist is*

---

[23] Marc J. Ackerman, Melissa C. Ackerman, Linda J. Steffen, & Shannon Kelley-Poulos, *Psychologists' Practices Compared to the Expectations of Family Law Judges and Attorneys in Child Custody Cases*, 1 J. Child Custody 41–60 (2004).

[24] Marc J. Ackerman, Melissa C. Ackerman, Shannon Kelley-Poulos, & Linda J. Steffen, Child Custody Evaluation: Comparing Survey of Psychologists, Judges, and Lawyers, Paper presented at the 109th Annual Meeting of the American Psychological Association, San Francisco (Aug. 2001).

that of a professional expert who strives to maintain an objective impartial stance."[25] It is essential for the psychologist to remain balanced and impartial, and to serve as an adviser to the court. This section also states that *"the psychologist should be impartial regardless of whether he or she is retained by the court or by a party to the proceedings. If either the psychologist or the client cannot accept this neutral role, the psychologist should consider withdrawing from the case.*[26] This section states that psychologists retained for court-ordered or for second-opinion evaluations must not serve as advocates but in an impartial role.

The most important issue related to this guideline is whether the psychologist can remain impartial or will act as (or appear to be) a "hired gun." The guidelines specifically state that if the psychologist is hired by one side or the other, it is still essential for him or her to remain impartial. Being appointed by the court, however, is the best situation for the psychologist. It is clearly to the psychologist's benefit to have a court order stating the appointment. From a liability standpoint, a psychologist who is court-ordered is likely to have either absolute or quasi-judicial immunity from malpractice lawsuits. When the psychologist is hired by one side or the other, this immunity may not apply. Furthermore, when a psychologist is court-appointed, courts have ruled the fees for the psychological evaluation cannot be discharged in bankruptcy court.

The best practice, when performing a second-opinion evaluation, is to perform it in the same manner that would be utilized if a first-opinion evaluation were occurring. In other words, the attorney who is engaging the psychologist is informed that the report will be sent to the court, the guardian ad litem, and both parents' advocate attorneys. If the attorney states that he or she wants the evaluation performed but will decide later whether the information will be disseminated, the psychologist should assert that the information will get disseminated regardless of the outcome. The obvious concern is the appearance of being a hired gun in the case.

Psychologists may argue they are not merely paid advocates but serve as rebuttal witnesses to rebut the testimony of the court-appointed psychologist without performing an evaluation. There are many forensic psychologists who serve in this capacity. Care must be taken to not give the appearance of looking like a hired gun.

§ 3.13   —General Guidelines: Sexual Abuse Allegations

One issue implicitly covered by the guidelines is sexual abuse allegations. The *Guidelines for Psychosocial Evaluation of Suspected Sexual Abuse in Young Children* from the American Professional Society on the Abuse of Children are recommended to be followed in child sexual abuse allegation evaluations. See **Appendix J.**

When a psychologist is called upon to aid the trier of fact in determining whether sexual abuse has taken place, many different variables must be addressed in addition to the ones previously described. The behavior and demeanor of the victim should be evaluated in an effort to determine whether it is similar to that of an individual who has been abused.

---

[25] Guidelines at 678.

[26] *Id.*

In addition, the behavior and demeanor of the alleged perpetrator should be evaluated in an effort to determine whether it is similar to the behavior of known perpetrators. Furthermore, the behavior and demeanor of the non-perpetrating parent should also be evaluated in an effort to determine how similar it is to the behavior of other non-perpetrating parents. Having performed all of these tasks, it may still be difficult for the psychologist to definitely state that abuse did or did not take place, in the absence of physical findings. Instead, it may be possible for the psychologist to state only that the behavior of the child is or is not similar to that of a sexually abused child; the behavior of the alleged perpetrator is or is not similar to that of sexual abuse perpetrators; and/or the behavior of the non-perpetrating parent is or is not similar to that of parents with bona fide or fabricated allegations. Having to answer this way is particularly likely when a child's therapist is asked to testify regarding whether abuse has or has not taken place.

§ 3.14   —Handling Biases

The next section—which begins, "*6. The psychologist is aware of personal and societal biases and engages in nondiscriminatory practice.*"[27]—lists a number of areas where biases can occur and suggests that psychologists be aware of these biases as they apply to age, gender, sexual orientation, and other areas. Having biases is not necessarily bad, and everyone has them. It is important, however, for the psychologist to be aware of his or her own biases. For example, one of the writers of this book favors joint custody, whenever possible, and opposes alternating 50-50 placement schedules, except when the parents cooperate and communicate exceptionally well. Other psychologists may have different biases in areas about which reasonable people can disagree. However, if a psychologist is going to allow personal biases to enter into the evaluation process, it is essential that the psychologist not only be aware of those biases but also state them openly, preferably in the report, but at least in court testimony.

§ 3.15   —Sexual Orientation

Considerable research indicates that a parent's sexual orientation should not be a primary consideration in making a placement recommendation. As in all cases, it is necessary to assess parenting capacity, best interests of the child, and resulting fit. More important than one's sexual orientation is how parents have accepted their sexual orientation. If homosexual parents have recently "come out of the closet" and are unsure of themselves and their sexual orientation, this emotional instability may have a detrimental effect on the children. However, when such parents have fully explored and accepted their sexual orientation, and are leading a well-adjusted life, and the sexual preference does not interfere in any way, then it should not be an issue in the placement decision process. See **Chapter 4** for detailed discussion of homosexuals as parents.

---

[27] Guidelines at 678.

§ 3.16   —Multiple Relationships

Next, the guidelines state: "*7. The psychologist avoids multiple relationships.*"[28] The first item mentioned in this section states that "[p]sychologists generally avoid conducting a child custody evaluation in a case in which the psychologist served in a therapeutic role. . . . In addition, during the course of a child custody evaluation, a psychologist does not accept any of the involved participants in the evaluation as a therapy client."[29]

Lois Oberlander stated a major concern in her presentation at an APA convention when she indicated that this guideline does not address the issue that "divorce is a process, not an event." There is life before and after the custody evaluation during the divorce process. Although multiple relationships must be assiduously avoided, there are times when exceptions are clearly in the best interests of the children and/or the family. This may be especially true in rural areas.[30]

Because the custody evaluation process and the court proceedings are adversarial in nature, it is important for psychologists to remember that, as trained mental health professionals, they are in a helping profession. As part of being a custody evaluator, there are many cases in which it is desirable for the parents to work out some form of child placement schedule that will allow for relatively equal time with each of the parents. In these cases, it is frequently recommended that the parents become involved in a mediation/negotiation/arbitration process that would allow for this outcome. It is not unusual, under these circumstances, for an attorney, or both attorneys, to turn to the psychologist who performed the evaluation and ask the psychologist to perform the mediation/negotiation/arbitration. Clearly, if the psychologist decided to perform this role, it would represent multiple relationships in the same case. However, attorneys convincingly argue that starting with a new individual will be time-consuming and costly; who could possibly know the parties' needs, desires, and idiosyncrasies better than the evaluating psychologist?

There are a few occasions when an exception may be made that permits an evaluator to switch from the role of evaluator to the role of mediator/negotiator/arbitrator, with several important qualifications. All attorneys, including the guardian ad litem, both parents, and the court, must be apprised of the fact that if the evaluator becomes the mediator, the evaluator's role as an evaluator ceases at that moment and can never be resumed. Furthermore, in the future, if it becomes necessary for additional psychological testing to be performed, a psychological evaluation report to be written, or an updated evaluation to be conducted, the mediating psychologist could no longer perform these tasks, and it would be necessary to find a new psychologist for that purpose. If all three attorneys and both parents are in agreement with this change in role, and are willing to sign statements indicating that it is acceptable to them, then the psychologist's change in roles can conceivably be in the best interests of the children and may be pursued.

---

[28] *Id.*

[29] *Id.*

[30] Lois Oberlander, The Utility of Ethical Standards in Specialty Guidelines in Child Custody Evaluations, Paper presented at the 102d Annual Convention of the American Psychological Association, Los Angeles (Aug. 1994).

§ 3.17   —Procedural Guidelines: Conducting a Child Custody Evaluation

Scope of Evaluation

The next category of sections in the guidelines begins as follows: "*8. The scope of the evaluation is determined by the evaluator, based on the nature of the referral question.*"[31] This section points out that, generally, a child custody evaluation requires an evaluation of all of the parents or guardians and all of the children, but may be limited to evaluating the parental capacity of one parent "without attempting to compare the parents or *make recommendations*."[32]

A number of different types of inappropriate requests are made of psychologists, either out of naiveté or a desire to cut costs. These include asking the evaluator to evaluate only the parents, only the children, or one parent and the children without the other parent. These approaches may save time and money but do not allow the psychologist to render a complete opinion with regard to who would make the most appropriate placement parent. Before engaging in this partial evaluation approach, the attorney must be informed of the limitations of the possible recommendations. When evaluating only one parent, the psychologist can state whether the parent is psychologically stable or unstable, and whether or not that parent recognizes the role of effective parenting, but cannot state to any level of certainty that the parent would make a better placement or custodial parent than the other parent. When evaluating both parents without the children, neither the children's developmental needs nor the children's interaction with each parent can be taken into consideration. When evaluating the children without the parents, parenting capacity cannot be considered. Because the interaction of parenting capacity and developmental needs of each child must be addressed for the custody evaluation to be adequate, each of these is an essential component of an appropriate custody evaluation.

§ 3.18   —Informed Consent

The next provision has the following requirement: "*9. Psychologist obtains informed consent from all adult participants and, as appropriate, informs child participants.*"[33] Each adult should sign a statement indicating that informed consent for the evaluation has been given. When the parents are ordered to participate by the court, informed consent is technically irrelevant. The parents should still be given all the same information, however, and asked to consent to the evaluation ("it has been explained and I understand . . ."). See **§§ 2.2** and **2.22.**

---

[31] Guidelines at 678.

[32] *Id.* (emphasis added).

[33] *Id.* at 679.

Informed consent should address the purpose, nature, and method of evaluation, who has requested the psychological services, and who will be paying the fees. Further information would include

- Nature and purpose of the evaluation at the beginning of an evaluation
- Extent of the evaluation
- Cost of the evaluation
- Amount of time the evaluation will take
- Any fee arrangements in writing (if the participant is not paying for the evaluation, inform the participant who is paying for the evaluation and what the relationship is between the evaluator and the payor)
- Who will receive the report and how the information will be used
- Concept of confidentiality and whether the results of the evaluation will be confidential
- "Duty to warn or protect" if applicable.[34]

Fee arrangements.   In most cases, the court or the parents pay the fees for the custody evaluation. In many jurisdictions, in cases in which the parents cannot afford a custody evaluation, the courts will advance the funds for the evaluation and allow the parents to pay the court system back over an extended period of time. Courts usually find some way of dividing the cost of the evaluation between the parents on an equitable basis, or by ability to pay. However, in some cases, the court may require that the parent who brought the action be solely responsible for the cost of the entire evaluation. All adult parties involved in the evaluation process must be made aware of who will be paying for the services. In setting up fee structures, attorneys must be aware that it is unethical for psychologists to work on a contingency fee basis. See **Chapter 2.**

Description of the process.   As part of the informed consent process, the individuals involved should be informed of what will constitute the evaluation process. This does not necessarily mean that the psychologist must identify each test that will be administered and explain the purpose of each test. However, in general, a description of psychological testing and its purpose is important. In addition, if collateral contacts will be used, the psychologist should indicate what collateral contacts will be made, what additional documentation will be necessary, and how the information will be reported. If a psychologist plans to meet with any or all of the attorneys, the participants in the evaluation should be notified. Furthermore, participants should be made aware of who will and who will not ultimately receive the final reports. The latter should be part of the informed consent statement(s) signed by each adult.

§ 3.19   —Confidentiality and Disclosure of Information

The next section begins, "*10. The psychologist informs participants about the limits of confidentiality and the disclosure of information*."[35] The participants in the evaluation must be aware

---

[34] Marc J. Ackerman, Clinician's Guide to Child Custody Evaluations 15 (2d ed. 2001).
[35] *Id.*

that in consenting to participate in the evaluation, they are also consenting to disclosure of the findings in the context of litigation. As part of this process, the psychologist should obtain a written waiver of confidentiality from all adults or their legally authorized representatives.

It is the practice of the authors of this text to have each of the parents sign a document indicating that they understand that the results of the evaluation will *not* be confidential and *will* be shared with the court, attorneys, and other individuals relevant to the evaluation process.

Privilege.   When a parent has been involved in individual psychotherapy prior to the evaluation process, that parent may not desire to have the content of those therapy sessions become part of the divorce process. This can occur if the individual invokes privilege. In this manner, the parent is stating that the content of the therapy session is privileged communication and that the parent will not sign a release for that information. Several risks are associated with taking this posture, however. The obvious first question in a situation of this nature is, "What is the person trying to hide?" Second, if the individual's mental health is being called into question as part of the custody evaluation process, the judge may not allow the parent to invoke privilege and may order that parent to sign a release for the relevant information, or order the therapist to release the records.

When invoked, all interested parties must understand that privilege is an all-or-none situation. If the information is truly to be confidential, the parent cannot select some people to receive the information and others who should not, nor can the parent select which information is to be released. When the information has been released in any fashion to anyone, privilege has already been waived and cannot subsequently be invoked as part of the custody evaluation process.

§ 3.20   —Gathering Data

Some psychologists have been criticized in the past for limiting the scope of their evaluation by including only one or two psychological instruments and no collateral information. The guidelines state: "*11. The psychologist uses multiple methods of data gathering.*"[36] The multiple methods of data gathering should normally include interviews, observations, and psychological assessments. In addition, psychologists are encouraged to review potentially relevant documents, interview extended family and objective third parties, and corroborate information gained from significant others.

This section of the guidelines deals with the heart of the evaluation process. Psychological testing, significant others, collateral sources, behavioral observations, and contact with attorneys are all part of the evaluation process. A number of studies have been performed in this area and will be discussed later in this chapter.[37]

---

[36] *Id.*

[37] Marc J. Ackerman & Melissa C. Ackerman, *Child Custody Evaluation Practices: A Survey of Experienced Professionals (Revisited)*, 28 Prof. Psychol.: Res. & Prac. 137–45 (1997); James Bow & Francella Quinnell, *Psychologists' Current Practices and Procedures in Child Custody Evaluations: Five Years after American Psychological Association Guidelines*, 32 Prof. Psychol.: Res. & Prac. 261–68 (2001); Marc J. Ackerman, Melissa C. Ackerman, Linda J. Steffen, & Shannon Kelley-Poulos, *Psychologists' Practices Compared to the Expectations of Family Law Judges and Attorneys in Child Custody Cases*, 41 J. Child Custody 41–60 (2004).

Collateral contacts.   The use of collateral contacts in the custody evaluation is important. Generally speaking, it is appropriate to obtain information from objective collateral contacts. Such contacts include school records, legal records, police records, and/or records. Testimonials from relatives of a parent generally are of little value. However, if a relative of a parent is willing to provide negative information about that parent, it is generally weighed in the evaluation process.

School records.   School records should be utilized in an effort to determine whether a child has performed better while living with one parent or the other, whether there has been a substantial change in academic performance during the pendency of the divorce, or whether teacher comments on school reports suggest any concerns.

Medical records.   Medical records, especially in abuse cases, should also be reviewed. When one parent is taking the child to the doctor much more frequently than the other parent, for no identifiable reason, this too must be taken into consideration. Likewise, if the children are more frequently getting sick in the company of one parent than the other, that too should be investigated.

Mental health records.   The mental history of an individual is also important as part of the medical records review. The extent of the outpatient and inpatient history, the frequency of the contacts, and recency of the episodes must be considered. As stated earlier, one psychiatric hospitalization 10 years prior to the evaluation, for a problem that has been completely resolved, cannot carry the same weight as a number of hospitalizations in recent years.

Criminal records.   The issue of recency and frequency is also important when reviewing criminal records. In an illustrative case, the stepfather was found to have a 14-year criminal history, including felony convictions for crimes against both property and person. This history weighed much more heavily than another individual's history of one property offense occurring many years ago. See **Chapter 16** for discussion of the significance of a criminal history of a parent.

It is the preference of the authors of this text to request as much collateral information as possible in all custody evaluations, to avoid the possibility of being confronted with surprise information during court testimony. Even though a considerable amount of extraneous material may be provided, at least it is the evaluator who determines what will be reviewed in the attempt to ensure that all essential information is reviewed.

§ 3.21   —Interpretation of Data

The next section begins: "*12. The psychologist neither overinterprets nor inappropriately interprets clinical or assessment data.*"[38] In this section, the psychologist is encouraged to refrain from drawing conclusions that are not supported by the data, and to acknowledge to the court any limitations of methods or data uses. The American Psychological Association's

---

[38] Guidelines at 679.

Ethical Principles of Psychologists and Code of Conduct have a number of references to data-related issues. Psychologists are not to go beyond the test data, must report all relevant data, and should discuss the limitations of the data presented (see **Chapter 2**).

The family law section of the American Bar Association tendered a document as part of the 2000 Wingspread Conference entitled "Child Custody Proceedings Reform." Within that document they suggest "in addition, mental health professionals should summarize their data-gathering procedures, information sources and time spent and present all relevant information on limitations of the evaluations that result from unobtainable information, failure of a party to cooperate or the circumstances of particular interviews."[39]

§ 3.22   —Rendering Opinion about Individual Not Evaluated

Next, the guidelines provide, "*13. The psychologist does not give any opinion regarding the psychological functioning of any individual who has not been personally evaluated.*"[40] The important implication of this section is that a psychologist cannot make a custody recommendation without evaluating both of the parents. However, psychologists are allowed to address theoretical issues or hypothetical questions even when they have not evaluated all parties.

An example of recommendations taken from a report submitted to a court by a psychologist illustrates this problem:

> The following recommendation is made with the awareness that the mother was evaluated without evaluating the father. Nevertheless, I am quite confident and comfortable in stating that the mother has the intellectual and emotional resources to be a competent parent to her two young sons. . . . Therefore, it is my recommendation that the mother be granted primary placement, although in joint custody, with the father of her two young sons.

The first two statements do not exceed appropriate limits. The psychologist has informed the reader that he evaluated the mother without evaluating the father and that the mother has the intellectual and emotional resources necessary to be a competent parent. However, when the psychologist recommends placement be given to the mother, based on this limited information, acceptable boundaries have been transcended.

§ 3.23   —Recommendations by Psychologists

With regard to recommendations given by psychologists, the next section begins, "*14. Recommendations, if any, are based on what is in the best psychological interests of the child.*"[41] This section also points out that the profession of psychology "has not reached

---

[39] American Bar Association, Child Custody Proceedings Reform, Wingspread Conference, Racine, Wis. (2000).

[40] *Id.*

[41] Guidelines at 679.

consensus about whether psychologists ought to make recommendations about the final custody determination to the court."[42] In addition, psychologists must not primarily rely on their own biases or unsupported beliefs when rendering opinions.

Although psychologists are generally not allowed to testify to the ultimate issue in criminal proceedings, they are frequently requested to do so in civil proceedings. It is unusual for a court to refer a case to a psychologist for a custody evaluation and to be content without receiving a recommendation as to the ultimate issue. In a number of instances, when one of the authors of this book felt that cases were too close to call in making a recommendation, considerable pressure was brought to bear to make a "close-call" recommendation, as opposed to just leaving the issue to the trier of fact.

Supervised visits. There are times when supervision is necessary, usually when there have been substantiated abuse allegations or when a parent is actually mentally ill. A stepwise procedure, moving from supervised visits to unsupervised visits, is generally acceptable in these situations. The initial contacts should be therapeutic supervised visits in a therapist's office. The second step involves supervised visits with a disinterested third party; these ultimately lead to supervised visits with an interested third party, for example, an adult family member. Last, after all of these steps have been completed to the satisfaction of the supervisor, guardian ad litem, court, and/or court-appointed psychologist, unsupervised visits should be embarked upon. When moving from supervised to unsupervised visits, a relatively short transition period of monitoring should be considered. This should include a mental health professional meeting with the children and parent just prior to, and immediately following, the supervised visit. This is referred to as a closely monitored visit. Closely monitored visits are followed by loosely monitored visits with the child, and a supervised/monitored parent meeting with the therapist approximately once per week to determine how the contacts have gone during the past week. After loosely monitored visits have occurred, daytime unsupervised visits can take place, eventually leading to overnight unsupervised visits.

Therapeutic intervention. The necessity of therapy is recognized in most custody evaluation reports. When the acrimony in a divorce situation reaches sufficient magnitude that a custody evaluation is required, it is likely that significant adjustment problems will need to be addressed. This may require individual therapy for some or all of the children, individual therapy for either or both of the parents, and/or family therapy to deal with pre- or post-divorce family issues. A cry that often comes from parents is that all this therapy is very costly. However, it is the parents who escalated the disharmony and dysfunction to the level of requiring therapeutic intervention, and, unfortunately, this is one of the prices to be paid. In selecting the therapists, it is essential that the same therapist not serve in more than one role. A party's therapist should not be the supervisor of the visits. A parent's therapist should not be the children's therapist, and the family therapist should not be the therapist for any of the individuals.

Results of the evaluation. One of the issues that is raised after the evaluation is performed is, "Who owns the results?" Generally, if the evaluation has been court-ordered,

---

[42] *Id.* at 7.

the court owns the results and decides to whom they will be disseminated. However, if the psychologist is retained by one side and paid by that side, technically that attorney and/or parent owns the results, unless some other arrangement has been clarified in advance. Therefore, the psychologist must be very careful to make sure that everyone knows in advance who will or will not receive the results.

It is counterproductive for attorneys to hand the complete reports to the parents. It is often the case that a parent uses the reports as a way of demonstrating to other people the incompetency or other deficiencies of the other parent. One alternative is to include with the complete report a brief report that summarizes the feelings and recommendations, which may then be disseminated to the parents.

§ 3.24   —Financial Arrangements

The next section begins, "*15. The psychologist clarifies financial arrangements*."[43] Not only must the psychologist explain the financial arrangements prior to commencing the child custody evaluation, but he or she also may not misrepresent services for reimbursement purposes. It is generally recommended that a psychologist have a custody evaluation agreement form or a custody evaluation contract that covers all financial information. This agreement should include a disclosure of the full cost of the evaluation, who will be paying for the evaluation, and what services are included in that cost. If additional services are not included in the cost of the usual evaluation, the agreement should identify the psychologist's hourly rate and what arrangements will be needed to cover the additional services.

Generally speaking, psychologists do not include the cost of testimony in court or deposition as part of the evaluation fee. Most psychologists require that all of the evaluation and testimony fee be paid prior to the evaluation or testimony, well in advance of the court date. If the court date is canceled, a psychologist generally is willing to refund the portion of the fee that represents reserved time that can be filled by other income-generating professional activity. See **Chapter 2** for discussion of these issues.

The U.S. District Court for the District of Kansas ruled that a bankruptcy debtor is not entitled to the discharge of court-ordered obligations to pay fees to the guardian ad litem and the psychologist appointed in a divorce proceeding.[44]

§ 3.25   —Maintaining Records

The final section of the guidelines begins, "*16. The psychologist maintains written records*."[45] This section requires psychologists performing child custody evaluations to maintain records in accordance with the APA Record Keeping Guidelines published in 1993 (see **Appendix F**). It also states that "[a]ll raw data and interview information are

---

[43] *Id.* at 679.

[44] Miller v. Gentry (*In re* Miller), No 93-4221-SAC (D. Kan. June 3, 1994). See Case digest at end of **Chapter 1.**

[45] *Id.*

recorded with an eye toward their possible review by other psychologists or the court, where legally permitted. Upon request, appropriate reports are made available to the court.[46] See **Chapter 2.**

Psychologists often attempt to discriminate between personal notes and the records in the file. The most conservative approach that a psychologist can take in a case is to assume that anything in the file is discoverable and that there is no such thing as a personal note. More often than not, when a psychologist attempts to keep something out of court on the basis that it is a personal note, the court will require disclosure of the information.

Although in most states a specific standard has not been statutorily set for maintaining records, the American Psychological Association Committee on Professional Practice has suggested guidelines.[47] They state that the complete record should be kept for three years after the last contact with the client. After that time, the complete record or a summary must be kept for another 12 years. Records involving minor children must be kept for three years after the child reaches the age of majority. The content of these records should include identifying data, dates of service, types of services, fees, assessment plans, and summary reports. The guidelines were adopted in 1993.

§ 3.26   —Association of Family and Conciliation Courts Model Standards

The October 1994 issue of *Family and Conciliation Courts Review* includes the Association of Family and Conciliation Courts (AFCC) *Model Standards of Practice for Child Custody Evaluation.* These 10 pages of standards are not discussed in detail in this section, as many of the provisions are redundant in light of the American Psychological Association *Guidelines for Child Custody Evaluations in Divorce Proceedings* (but see **Appendix G**). The AFCC standards of practice for child custody evaluation were formulated for AFCC members. This organization includes psychologists, psychiatrists, social workers, court evaluators, judges, mediators, and attorneys. As a result, the guidelines are much more broad-based and general than are the American Psychological Association guidelines. However, because only psychologists are obligated to work within the American Psychological Association guidelines, the AFCC guidelines are not only useful for all custody evaluations but also essential for nonpsychologist practitioners.

The AFCC *Model Standards of Practice for Child Custody Evaluation* are divided into six sections. The first section discusses initiating the process, which involves choosing the evaluator and making arrangements with the parties. The second section, entitled "Evaluator Standards," addresses the education and training of the evaluator. It further discusses supervision of the evaluator, when necessary, and the requirement for knowledge of the statutes and case law governing child custody. It also states that psychological testing should be performed only by a licensed or certified psychologist.

---

[46] *Id.*

[47] American Psychological Association Committee on Professional Practice, A*merican Psychological Association Record Keeping Guidelines*, 48 Am. Psychologist 640–41 (1993). See **App. G.**

The third section deals with evaluation procedures and is divided into nine subsections. These sections include interviewing and testing, collateral sources, home visits, and procedures to be used with children. The fourth section identifies areas that should be evaluated. Such areas include quality of relationship between the contesting parents or potential caretakers, ability of each parent or caretaker to parent the child, psychological health of each parent or potential caretaker, psychological health of each child, and patterns of domestic violence. In the fifth section's discussion of the evaluation report, style, contents, and distribution of the report are addressed. In the "Ethical Principles," section six of the standards, mental health professionals are instructed to adhere to the ethical principles of their own professions. In addition, the standards require that any prior relationship between the evaluator and family members be disclosed, and that the evaluator be cautious in changing roles after the evaluation has been completed. Last, limitations of the evaluator's recommendations and expertise are discussed.

§ 3.27   Written Report

Psychologists Joann Ondrovik and David Hamilton recommend the following structure for the written report on the results of the psychological evaluation:

> A written forensic report should initially name the source of the referral, detailing the circumstances and setting forth the legal issue to be addressed. It may also be important to present any circumstances which may be relevant to this particular evaluation, such as ongoing involvement with social service agencies in a custody/termination evaluation. If the referral is court ordered, the circumstances of the referral should be succinctly stated. Frequently, the judge has reduced the objectives of such an evaluation to a written order and the practitioner should quote or refer to this order. It is important to remember that orders from judges are generally prepared by attorneys representing parties in the case. Typically, therefore, the orders will be either loosely worded and open-ended or extremely specific, again requiring practitioner interpolation.
>
> A chronological listing of the dates and all of the contacts, including missed appointments, should be included. This is most easily handled by merely listing the dates and the individuals contacted chronologically.
>
> The written report should refer to data which were acquired in addition to information elicited in the patient interview. The source of this data, as well as the nature and date of the information, should be indexed appropriately.
>
> An extensive social history and background information concerning the client should be included as is relevant to the legal question to be addressed. This may include family of origin information, history of criminal or antisocial behaviors or physical disabilities which may be present.
>
> The report should detail all of the special assessment techniques, including all psychometric testing. Video or audio taping should be noted and the recording preserved for evidence. The results or conclusions of each psychometric technique should be detailed in the report, as well as validity, reliability and standardization statistics.
>
> Finally, the forensic practitioner should present clinical findings, summarizing significant observations and providing a DSM-IV and ICD-10 [see **Chapter 17**] diagnosis as well as other statements concerning mental functioning, global functioning and stressors. . . .

[In addition,] remaining within the scope of the referral question is of paramount importance. . . . Avoid offering gratuitous opinions on unpresented issues. . . . Limiting the amount of information included in a written report is an important goal. . . . Conclusions and opinions should be substantiated and supported through observation and information; however, the report should not contain a detailing of all of the facts or all observations. Rather, only those observations essential to the theories advanced should be included. . . . A forensic report should limit the use of clinical terms and phrases. . . . Importantly, the practitioner must be able to explain phrases, diagnoses and scale interpretations in court.[48]

In the written report, the expert presents the major data and conclusions that can be drawn from the data. Careful differentiation must be made between those conclusions that are made tentatively and those made "to a reasonable degree of medical/psychological/scientific" certainty. Although the expert will have amassed a great deal of information, only the most salient information should be included in the report. And, although the expert must provide support for his or her conclusions, only data that is essential to that task should be included.[49]

It is important to realize that a report is a summary of the findings. In one court case, a psychologist had to review approximately 600 pages of materials generated from previous reports and the six evaluations performed for the case. The report for the evaluation was approximately 25 to 30 pages long. However, when the psychologist testified in court, the cross-examining attorney kept asking why specific minor pieces of information were left out of the report. It is not possible to distill 600 pages of materials down to 30 pages and include every piece of potentially relevant information. As a result, there is much information from the evaluation process not included in the report. In most psychological evaluations, the information will include both positive and negative information about an individual. If a report appears to be slanted in one direction or the other, it becomes that attorney's responsibility during cross-examination to uncover salient information not included in the report. The report should not be written to include only that information that supports the examiner's conclusion. This is referred to as confirmatory bias. The authors only include information that confirms the points they are making. It should also include nonsupporting material and the rationale for why the supporting material was weighed more heavily than the nonsupporting material. If the psychologist has not done this, then the attorney must bring this fact to the court's or jury's attention on cross-examination.

Attorneys have an ethical responsibility upon receiving reports of psychological evaluations on their clients and their opponent's clients. As indicated in **§ 3.23,** it is inappropriate and potentially dangerous to share the reports with clients, since clients are likely to disseminate the information or may misinterpret the information given. There have been too many times that clients have taken the psychological evaluations and freely shown them to friends, neighbors, or relatives. They use the reports as a way to substantiate their position and demonstrate their concerns about the opposing parent. The best way to avoid such a situation may be for the attorney to have a conference with the client and provide a summary of the results and recommendations, rather than giving a copy of the actual report to the client. If

---

[48] Joann Ondrovik & David Hamilton, *Forensic Challenge: Expert Testimony,* 10 Am. J. Forensic Psychol. no. 1, at 15, 21–23 (1992).

[49] *Id.*

the individual is in psychotherapy, it may be appropriate and helpful for the evaluator to send a copy of the report to the treating therapist, who can go over it with the individual.

§ 3.28   Custody Evaluation Practices

Dr. H.D. ("De") Kirkpatrick identified 26 standards that are defined as a set of minimum practice standards that go beyond aspirational goals of existing guidelines. According to Kirkpatrick, an argument could be made that the 26 are existing standards of minimum practice of performing child custody evaluations. They are represented in **Table 3–1.**

Table 3–1

Minimum Standards of Practice in Conducting Child Custody and Visitation Evaluations

Standard	Foundation
1. Child custody evaluations are by definition"forensic" evaluations.	AACAP (1997); Galatzer-Levy & Kraus (1999); Gould (1998); Heilbrun (2001); Melton et al. (1997); Otto et al. (2003).
2. The purpose of the evaluation is to assess the psychological best interests of the child.	APA (1994); California Rules of Court (2003); Martindale (2001); North Carolina Psychological Association, NCPA (1994).
3. The court is the evaluator's primary client.	AACAP (1997); AFCC (1995); Melton et al. (1997); NCPA (1994).
4. The evaluator is either court-appointed or assigned by consent order.	AACAP (1997); AFCC (1995); Committee on Ethical Guidelines for Forensic Psychologists (1991); Gould (1998); Heilbrun (2001); Melton et al. (1997); New Jersey State Board of Psychological Examiners (1993); NCPA (1994); Ackerman (2001).
5. The scope of the evaluation is anchored to specific referral questions.	APA (1994); Gould (1998); Heilbrun (2001); NCPA (1994); Ackerman (2001).
6. The evaluator obtains informed consent from all parties.	AACAP (1997); APA (1994); AFCC (1995); California Rules of Court (2003); Committee on Ethical Guidelines for Forensic Psychologists (1991); Heilbrun (2001); Martindale (2001); New Jersey State Board of Psychological Examiners (1993); NCPA (1994).

Table 3–1

(continued)

Standard	Foundation
7. The skills, knowledge, and expertise needed to conduct a competent evaluation require that the evaluator gain specialized forensic competence.	American Academy of Psychiatry & Law (AAPL) (1995); APA (1994); AFCC (1995); Committee on Ethical Guidelines for Forensic Psychologists (1991); Gould (1998); Heilbrun (2001); Ackerman (2001).
8. Record keeping is of the highest standard and one's records should be retained.	Committee on Ethical Guidelines for Forensic Psychologists (1991); Gould (1998); Martindale (2001); NCPA (1994).
9. The evaluator uses multiple avenues of data gathering.	APA (1994); California Rules of Court (2003); Galatzer-Levy & Kraus (1999); Heilbrun (2001); Melton et al. (1997); NCPA (1994); Ackerman (2001).
10. Opinions are not given about the psychological functioning of any individual who has not been personally evaluated.	AAPL (1995); APA (1994); AFCC (1995); Committee on Ethical Guidelines for Forensic Psychologists (1991).
11. The evaluator clarifies with the parties in advance her contractual arrangements for conducting the evaluation.	AFCC (1995); California Rules of Court (2003); NCPA (1994).
12. The evaluator avoids multiple relationships, which can create role conflicts.	APA (1994); California Rules of Court (2003); Committee on Ethical Guidelines for Forensic Psychologists (1991); Martindale (2001); Melton et al. (1997); Stahl (1999); Strassburger, Gutheil, & Brodsky (1997); Ackerman (2001).
13. The evaluator acknowledges any implicit or explicit limitations of psychological knowledge and techniques used in the evaluation.	APA (1994); Heilbrun (2002); Melton et al. (1997).
14. The evaluator avoids *ex parte* communication with counsel or the judge.	California Rules of Court (2003); NCPA (1994); Stahl (1999).
15. The evaluator avoids accepting allegations as facts.	Gould (1998); Melton et al. (1997); NCPA (1994).
16. The evaluator recognizes a high probability of re-litigation and that judicial decisions do not mark a definitive end to a custody dispute.	New Jersey State Board of Psychological Examiners (1993); NCPA (1994).
17. It is important to assess the family factors that affect the child(ren).	APA (1994); AFCC (1995); Otto et al. (2003).

Standard	Foundation
18. Parent B is aware of the children's relevant school information.	AFCC (1995); California Rules of Court (2003).
19. The evaluator shall be knowledgeable about the relevant statutes and case law governing child custody.	AACAP (1997); AFCC (1995); Heilbrun (2001); Melton et al. (1997); Ackerman (2001).
20. Parent A uses physical punishment and Parent B does not.	AFCC (1995); Gould (1998); Ackerman (2001).
21. Appropriate and relevant collateral information is obtained.	APA (1994); AFCC (1995); Gould (1998); Heilbrun (2001); Melton et al. (1997); NCPA (1994); Otto et al. (2003); Skafte (1985); Ackerman (2001).
22. The quality of the relationship between parent/care taker and child should be assessed.	AFCC (1995); Galatzer-Levy & Kraus (1999); Gould (1998); Stahl (1999); Ackerman (2001).
23. Evaluators should adhere to the ethical principles of their own professions.	AACAP (1997); AFCC (1995); Galatzer-Levy & Kraus (1999); Martindale (2001); Melton et al. (1997); Ackerman (2001).
24. There are essential differences between traditional clinical practice and the performance of child custody evaluations.	AACAP (1997); Galatzer-Levy & Kraus (1999); Gould (1998); Melton et al. (1997).
25. Evaluators need to be aware of and knowledgeable about special considerations in child custody evaluations.	AACAP (1997); APA (1994); Gould (1998); Stahl (1999); Ackerman (2001).
26. Evaluators must be aware of relevant law, local rules, and rules of discovery.	Committee on Ethical Guidelines for Forensic Psychologists (1991); Heilbrun (2001); Melton et al. (1997).

Adapted and reprinted with permission of H.D. Kirkpatrick and Hayworth Press, Inc.

Source: Kirkpatrick, H.D. (2002). A Floor, Not a Ceiling: Beyond Guidelines—An Argument of Minimum Standards of Practice in Conducting Child Custody and Visitation Evaluations. 1 *Journal of Child Custody* 65–66 (2004).

§ 3.29   A Potentially Dangerous Book

A number of books have been written on the subject of performing child custody evaluations and the practices of doing so. The most prominent books in this area have been published by Phil Stahl (*Conducting Child Custody Evaluations—A Comparison Guide*), Marc Ackerman (*Clinician's Guide to Child Custody Evaluations–Second Edition*), and Jonathan Gould (*Conducting Scientifically Crafted Child Custody Evaluations*). However, the American Psychological Association recently published a book by G. Andrew Benjamin and Jackie K. Gollan. The book is entitled *Family Evaluation in Custody Litigation: Reducing Risks of Ethical Infractions and Malpractice*. Published in 2003, it has been the center of a raging professional controversy since the date of its publication. Ordinarily, when a book is published by a parent organization, that suggests the content of said book is endorsed by that organization. However, the Benjamin and Gollan book recommends many practices that run contrary to policies of the American Psychological Association as endorsed in its guidelines, code of ethics, and position papers. Psychologists and attorneys alike have been critical of this book. Attorney Leslie Ellen-Shear reviewed the book in the inaugural issue of the *Journal of Child Custody*. She states, "Because so many evaluators will turn to an APA publication for a definitive template for the evaluations process, Benjamin & Gollan's (2003) work represents serious risks to the community.[50] She also reports, "Some of *Family Evaluation*'s controversial recommendations have triggered a fire-storm within the child custody community of evaluators and family lawyers."[51] Recommendations made by Benjamin and Gollan include advising evaluators not to make eye contact with a parent; recommending that information from collateral sources be provided in the form of a declaration under penalty of perjury; recommending that pre-adolescent children not be individually interviewed or assessed; using an allegation-based model; securing written permission to destroy records made during the evaluation; and other violations of state laws, and procedures endorsed by APA and AFCC.

Kathryn Kuehnle, Lyn Greenberg, and Michael Gottlieb point out that "these authors appear to move beyond the scientific literature . . ."[52] i.e., drawing conclusions not supported by science. Benjamin and Gollan themselves state that the erasure of tapes made during interviews "prevents the opposing counsel from using contemporaneous material out of context during a later cross-examination at deposition or trial."[53]

In summary, David A. Martindale, Ph.D., Kathryn Kuehnle *et al.*, and Leslie Shear very strongly advise against using the Benjamin and Gollan book. Leslie Shear concludes by saying, "Where tapes exist, the failure of the evaluator to preserve them is unconscionable. . . . Evaluators should not rely upon this book as a template, and should be wary about adopting many of these protocols. . . . The book is an unreliable map through the complexities and challenges of child custody evaluation.[54] The authors of this text strongly concur.

§ 3.30   Child Custody Evaluation Research

W.G. Keilin and L.J. Bloom undertook in 1986 the task of attempting to identify the practices and procedures of mental health professionals in child custody evaluations.[55] They

---

[50] Leslie Ellen-Shear, J.D., *When Form Fails to Follow Function: Benjamin & Gollan's Family Evaluation in Custody Litigation*, 1 J. Child Custody 129 (2003).

[51] *Id.* at 130.

[52] Kathryn Kuehnle, Lyn Greenberg, & Michael Gottlieb, *Incorporating the Principles of Scientifically Based Child Interviews into Family Law Cases*, 1 J. Child Custody 97 (2004).

[53] Benjamin & Gollan, Family Evaluation in Custody Litigation 35 (American Psychological Ass'n, Washington, D.C., 2003).

[54] Shear at 139–40.

[55] W.G. Keilin & L.J. Bloom, *Child Custody Evaluation Practices: A Survey of Experienced Professionals*, 17 Prof. Psychol.: Res. & Prac. 338–46 (1986) [hereinafter 1986 study or Keilin & Bloom study].

surveyed 302 psychologists, psychiatrists, and masters-level practitioners, but only 82 fit their selection criteria and were included in their study. Of the 82 represented in their sample, 64 or 78.1 percent were doctoral-level psychologists.

Marc Ackerman and Melissa Ackerman performed a study, published in 1997, to replicate and extend the Keilin and Bloom study.[56] The 1997 study included the 70 original items from the Keilin and Bloom study and added another 42 items representing variables that have become part of child custody evaluation practices during the past decade, according to a literature review, as well as items addressed by the Ackerman-Schoendorf Scales for Parent Evaluation of Custody (ASPECT).

Marc Ackerman, Melissa Ackerman, Linda Steffen, and Shannon Kelley-Poulos combined studies performed by Ackerman and Ackerman (A&A) in 1997, Ackerman and Steffen (A&S) in 2001, and Ackerman and Kelley-Poulos (A&K) in 2001. The Ackerman *et al.* 2004 study compares psychologists' practices with judges' and attorneys' expectations as previously reported in the above studies. Psychologists, judges, and attorneys were more alike than different in their practices, with notable exceptions reported below. The Ackerman *et al.* study included 201 psychologists, 159 family law judges, and 153 family law attorneys, resulting in a combined total of 513 professionals involved in custody cases.

Table 3–2 summarizes the demographics of the participants in the three studies.

Table 3–3 addresses the issue of conditions of retainment. It should be noted that both attorneys and judges rate court-appointed, mutually agreed-upon, or guardian ad litem–appointed psychologists significantly higher than second-opinion or rebuttal witness psychologists. The court-appointed, mutually agreed upon, and GAL-appointed psychologists are all given approximately the same weight, while the second-opinion and rebuttal witness psychologists are given the same weight, but significantly lower than the court-appointed, mutually agreed-upon, and GAL-appointed psychologists.

Table 3–4 summarizes the time psychologists spend in each of the activities required as part of a custody evaluation.

Table 3–5 compares the results of the family law judges' and the family law attorneys' expectations about evaluation procedures that psychologists use. Judges and attorneys alike

Table 3–2

Demographics

	A&A Psychologists	A&S Judges	A&K Attorneys
N	201	159	153
Age	49.1	53.5	51.6
% Males	69.0	73.9	70.9
% Females	31.0	26.1	29.1

---

[56] Marc J. Ackerman & Melissa C. Ackerman, *Child Custody Evaluation Practices: A Survey of Experienced Professionals (Revisited)*, 28 Prof. Psychol.: Res. & Prac. no. 2, at 137–45 (1997) [hereinafter 1997 study or Ackerman and Ackerman study].

Table 3–3

Conditions of Retainment

	A&S Judges	A&K Attorneys	Grand Mean
Court-appointed	4.19	3.93	4.06
Mutually agreed	3.94	4.22	4.08
GAL-appointed	3.89	3.50	3.70
Second-opinion	2.94	2.89	2.92
Rebuttal witness	2.90	2.81	2.86

Table 3–4

Evaluation Activities

Activity	Mean Number of Hours Spent in Activity
Observation	2.6
Reviewing material	2.6
Collateral contacts	1.6
Psychological testing	5.2
Report writing	5.3
Interviewing parents	4.7
Interviewing children	2.7
Interviewing significant others	1.6
Consulting with attorneys	1.2
Testifying in court	2.2

Ackerman & Ackerman, 1997, at 138.

expect psychologists to observe children of all ages; review mental health records; review children's school and medical records; perform psychological testing of parents, children, and significant others; consult with the guardian ad litem; interview parents, children, and significant others; and write a report along with testifying in court. However, attorneys feel that psychologists should review criminal records and contact collateral sources, while judges do not expect psychologists to perform these tasks. Neither judges nor attorneys expect psychologists to review pleadings of family law cases, review legal records, review parents' medical records, perform home visits, or consult with the parties' attorneys.

The frequency of psychological test usage with children and adults in child custody evaluations by psychologists is reported in Ackerman and Ackerman.[57] It should be noted that neither attorneys nor judges have much knowledge about the use of psychological tests. The only test family law judges were able to identify with any frequency was the MMPI-2, and

---

[57] Ackerman & Ackerman study at 139–40.

Table 3–5

Evaluation Procedures

	Do Not Expect		Neutral		Expect	
	A&S Judges	A&K Attys.	A&S Judges	A&K Attys.	A&S Judges	A&K Attys.
Observation of children under 6 with parent(s)	2.6%	0.0%	9.0%	6.0%	88.4%	94.0%
Observation of children 6–12 with parent(s)	1.9	0.8	11	6.5	87.1	92.7
Observation of children over 12 with parent(s)	7.7	5.0	23.2	26.0	69.0	69.0
Review mental health records	1.9	3.0	7.7	11.0	90.3	86.0
Review pleadings of family law cases	27.1	38.0	42.6	21.0	30.3	41.0
Review legal records	32.9	46.6	44.5	26.7	22.6	26.7
Review criminal records	21.9	21.3	35.5	18.0	42.6	60.7
Review children's school records	3.9	1.6	18.7	19.5	77.4	78.9
Review children's medical records	5.2	5.7	24.7	27.6	70.1	66.7
Review parents' medical records	17.4	16.4	52.2	45.9	30.3	37.7
Contact collateral sources	15.5	13.8	40.6	30.9	43.9	55.3
Perform psychological testing on parents	3.2	3.2	19.9	16.9	76.9	79.8
Perform psychological testing on children	2.6	1.6	23.5	12.9	73.9	85.5
Perform psychological testing on significant others	13.7	14.5	35.9	31.5	50.3	54.0
Home visit	31.4	35.5	39.7	32.2	28.8	27.3
Consult with GAL	13.0	8.6	24.7	28.4	62.3	62.9
Consult with parties' attorneys	30.7	14.6	42.5	39.8	26.8	45.5
Interview parent	3.6	2.4	1.4	1.6	95.0	96.0
Interview children	0.0	0.8	1.8	1.6	98.2	97.6
Interview significant others	8.7	5.6	17.8	15.2	73.5	79.2
Write a report	0.6	0.0	7.2	4.0	92.2	96.0
Testify in court	3.9	2.5	29.6	13.4	66.4	84.1

then only 34.6 percent of the time. Attorneys' understanding of psychological tests was a little more broad-based than that of judges. However, for the most part, they were also unfamiliar with tests other than the MMPI-2. Although attorneys tended to recognize custody-related tests more frequently than judges, none of the custody specialty tests were recognized by a majority of the groups. The Bricklin Perceptual Scales (BPS) and Ackerman-Schoendorf Scales for Parent Evaluation of Custody (ASPECT) are most recognized by judges and attorneys, just as they are by psychologists. The highest ratings by attorneys were 31.8 percent and 37.7 percent for the BPS and ASPECT, respectively. It should be noted that all of the judges' ratings were in the teens and twenties. See **Table 3–6**.

Psychologists' attitudes toward single/sole custody were assessed by having the subjects respond to 40 9-point Likert-type scales addressing a number of custody decisionmaking areas. Furthermore, for each variable the respondents were asked to determine whether they would endorse "Parent A, Parent B, or Neither Parent" based on that item. **Table 3–7** compares the ratings of the three groups and rank orders the items from most important to least important.

Table 3–6

Familiarity with Custody Tests

		% Familiar with		
	Test	A&S Judges	A&K Attorneys	Mean
1	Bricklin Perceptual Scales (BPS)	26.8%	38.1%	32.4%
2	Ackerman-Schoendorf Scales for Parent Evaluation of Custody (ASPECT)	19.9	37.7	28.8
3	Parent-Child Relationship Inventory (PCRI)	28.6	22.9	25.7
4	Parent Awareness Skills Survey (PASS)	24.1	25.0	24.6
5	Custody Quotient	12.9	24.4	18.6
6	Perception of Relationships Test (PORT)	17.0	16.1	16.5

Table 3–7

Mean Ratings of Sole- or Single-Parent Custody Decisionmaking Criteria

		Ranks			Means			
	Rank Item	A&A Psych.	A&S Judges	A&K Attys.	A&A Psych.	A&S Judges	A&K Attys.	Grand Mean
1	Parent B is an active alcoholic.	1	1	1	8.35	8.14	8.41	8.30[*ac]
2	Parent B often attempts to alienate the children from the other parent by negatively interpreting the other parent's behavior.	2	2	3	8.12	7.87	7.95	7.99[*a]

		Ranks			Means			
Rank	Item	A&A Psych.	A&S Judges	A&K Attys.	A&A Psych.	A&S Judges	A&K Attys.	Grand Mean
3	Parent A exhibits better parenting skills than Parent B.	3	4	2	7.94	7.73	7.95	7.88
4	Parent A has not been cooperative with previous court orders.	6	3	4	7.62	7.74	7.81	7.71
5	Parent B appears to be more psychologically stable than Parent A.	5	6	7	7.70	7.47	7.44	7.55*ab
6	The child appears to have a closer emotional bond with Parent B.	4	7	9	7.70	7.42	7.32	7.50*ab
7	Parent A actively participates in the children's education.	9	5	6	7.33	7.51	7.51	7.44
8	Parent B has a history of psychiatric hospitalizations.	14	8	5	7.14	7.38	7.64	7.36*b
9	Parent B is more tolerant of other parent visitation.	8	11	12	7.52	7.24	7.23	7.35
10	The 15-year-old child would prefer to live with Parent A.	12	12	8	7.15	7.22	7.39	7.24
11	Parent A exhibits a great deal of anger and bitterness about the divorce.	10	13	13	7.24	7.18	7.19	7.21
12	Physical abuse allegation has been made against Parent B.	11	10	14	7.15	7.29	7.16	7.20
13	Sexual abuse allegation has been made against Parent A.	13	9	15	7.14	7.31	7.14	7.19
14	Before the divorce, Parent A had primary caretaking responsibility.	17	14	10	7.00	7.10	7.25	7.11
15	Parent A is threatening to move to another state with the children.	7	18	11	7.53	6.93	6.37	7.00*ac
16	Parent A is aware of the children's future needs.	16	15	16	7.03	7.06	6.81	6.97
17	Parent A has a criminal record.	15	19	18	7.06	6.78	6.67	6.86*b

Table 3–7

(*continued*)

		Ranks			Means			
Rank Item		A&A Psych.	A&S Judges	A&K Attys.	A&A Psych.	A&S Judges	A&K Attys.	Grand Mean
18	The child appears to have a closer emotional bond with Parent B.	19	16	19	6.83	7.03	6.58	6.81*[bc]
19	Parent B is aware of the children's developmental milestones.	21	17	22	6.74	7.02	6.53	6.76*[ac]
20	Parent A appears to be much more economically stable than Parent B.	18	22	21	6.86	6.38	6.54	6.62*[ab]
21	Parent B is significantly less intelligent than the children.	22	20	23	6.57	6.52	6.51	6.54
22	Parent A has significantly worse MMPI-2 results.	20	23	26	6.77	6.33	6.40	6.52*[ab]
23	Parent A is a recovering alcoholic.	23	21	27	6.38	6.40	6.37	6.38
24	Parent A's schedule would require placing the child in day care; Parent B's would not.	26	26	24	6.22	6.26	6.50	6.32
25	Parent B is taking psychiatric medication.	27	24	25	6.20	6.32	6.42	6.30
26	Parent A has remained living in the original family home, while Parent B has moved to a home in a different school district.	28	27	20	6.15	6.22	6.57	6.30*[bc]
27	Parent B has more extended family available.	25	25	29	6.23	6.26	6.23	6.24
28	Before the divorce, Parent B had the primary responsibility for disciplining the child.	24	28	30	6.26	6.21	6.17	6.22
29	Parent B is currently involved in a homosexual relationship.	32	29	17	5.41	5.99	6.71	5.97*[d]

		Ranks			Means			
Rank Item		A&A Psych.	A&S Judges	A&K Attys.	A&A Psych.	A&S Judges	A&K Attys.	Grand Mean
30	Parent A appears to be much more economically stable than Parent B.	29	33	34	5.97	5.58	5.72	5.77*[a]
31	Parent A's new partner has children living with him/her.	31	34	28	5.52	5.57	6.27	5.76*[bc]
32	The 10-year-old child would prefer to live with Parent A.	29	30	33	5.70	5.80	5.79	5.76
33	Parent B is cohabiting with a person of the opposite sex (without marriage), while Parent A has remarried.	36	31	31	4.87	5.73	6.04	5.50*[ab]
34	Parent B is cohabiting with a person of the opposite sex (without marriage), while Parent A lives alone.	35	32	32	4.93	5.63	5.97	5.46*[ab]
35	Parent A is much more socially active than Parent B.	33	35	36	5.25	5.15	5.19	5.20
36	Parent A has remarried; Parent B lives alone.	38	36	35	4.66	4.70	5.22	4.84*[bc]
37	Parent B is the same sex as the child.	34	37	37	5.06	4.49	4.68	4.77*[a]
38	The 5-year-old child would prefer to live with Parent B.	37	38	38	4.84	4.45	4.06	4.49*[d]
39	Parent A is the mother, Parent B is the father.	39	39	39	4.19	4.02	3.75	4.01
40	Parent A is 10 years older than Parent B.	40	40	40	3.28	3.51	3.72	3.49

*—Significant difference

[a]—psychologists and judges significantly different

[b]—psychologists and attorneys significantly different

[c]—judges and attorneys significantly different

[d]—all three groups significantly different from each other

_—sole criterion for decisionmaking

Source: Marc J. Ackerman, Melissa C. Ackerman, Linda J. Steffen, & Shannon Kelly-Poulos, Psychologists' Practices Compared to the Expectations of Family Law Judges and Attorneys in Child Custody Cases, 1 J. Child Custody 41–60 (2004).

The asterisks after the grand mean represent significant differences, with the letters "a" through "d" designating which pairs were significantly different from one another. An "a" signifies that psychologists and judges were significantly different from one another, but neither were significantly different from attorneys. A "b" indicates that psychologists and attorneys were significantly different from each other, but neither group was significantly different from the judges. A "c" indicates that judges and attorneys were significantly different from one another, but neither were significantly different from psychologists. A "d" represents that all three pairs were significantly different from one another. It should be noted that for the most part, psychologists, judges, and attorneys tended to rate the same items as high, the same items in the middle, and the same items at the lower end of the continuum, with some exceptions. All three groups saw active substance abuse as being the greatest concern, with alienation being the second greatest concern. All groups also agreed that the wishes of 5- and 10-year-olds were not to be given major consideration. Both attorneys and judges felt that lack of cooperation with previous court orders was more important than psychologists did. On the other hand, psychologists did not see a history of psychiatric hospitalizations as being as great a concern as judges and attorneys viewed it to be. Psychologists took a parent's threatening to move to another state with the children as being a much greater concern than did judges or attorneys. Emotional bonding to one parent over the other was more important to psychologists than it was to judges or attorneys. One of the more noteworthy differences among these groups was with regard to the question of sexual preference. Psychologists and judges rated sexual preference as 32nd and 29th out of 40, respectively, whereas family law attorneys rated it at 17th out of 40.

Table 3–8 addresses the issue of joint-custody placement, comparing the three groups on 30 items. The asterisks and a, b, c, and d represent the same types of significance as in **Table 3–7.** Both judges and attorneys found substance abuse to be the greatest concern in making a joint-custody recommendation, while psychologists found the ability to separate interpersonal difficulties as being more important. Psychologists also found the quality of the relationship that each parent has with the children more important than judges and attorneys did. On the other hand, judges and attorneys found cooperation with previous court orders more important than psychologists did. Additionally, attorneys weighed the expressed wishes of a 15-year-old more than did psychologists or judges. Judges ranked current state law much higher than psychologists and attorneys did. As with sole custody, whether an individual was involved in a homosexual relationship or not was of much greater concern to attorneys than it was to judges or psychologists. All three groups rated the age of the parents, the wishes of a five-year-old, the number of children in the family, and the gender of the child at the bottom of the list.

All three groups were asked reasons for supporting or ordering sole custody and reasons for supporting or ordering joint custody. See **Table 3–9.** All three groups rated the mental stability of the parents, inability to cooperate or communicate, and the presence of physical or sexual abuse as the top three areas of concern that would result in recommending sole custody.

Table 3–8

Rank Ordering of Joint-Custody Decisionmaking Criteria

Rank	Item	Ranks			Means			
		A&A Psych.	A&S Judges	A&K Attys.	A&A Psych.	A&S Judges	A&K Attys.	Grand Mean
1	Problems with substance abuse	3	1	1	8.15	8.06	8.19	8.13
2	Ability of parents to separate their interpersonal difficulties from their parenting	1	2	3	8.33	7.90	7.92	8.07*ab
3	The quality of relationship the child has with each parent	2	5	7	8.28	7.74	7.70	7.94*ab
4	The amount of anger and bitterness between the parents	5	6	5	7.98	7.73	7.77	7.84
5	Psychological stability of the parents	4	7	6	7.99	7.66	7.72	7.81*ab
6	Cooperation with previous court orders	8	3	2	7.42	7.89	7.94	7.72*ab
7	Expressed wishes of the child, age 15	7	8	4	7.65	7.41	7.77	7.61*c
8	The parents' willingness to enter joint-custody arrangements	6	9	9	7.79	7.28	7.31	7.49*ab
9	Current state law (in your state)	10	4	12	7.24	7.75	6.80	7.27*d
10	Whether the child exhibits behavior problems at home or school	12	10	8	6.86	7.18	7.45	7.14*ab
11	Problems with the law	9	12	11	7.35	6.84	6.86	7.05*ab
12	Each parent's previous involvement in caretaking responsibilities	11	11	10	7.11	6.92	6.91	6.99
13	The geographic proximity of parental homes	13	13	14	6.81	6.62	6.54	6.67
14	Amount of flexibility in parents' work schedules	15	14	15	6.45	6.47	6.43	6.45
15	Differences between parental discipline styles	14	15	17	6.64	6.36	6.28	6.45*b

Table 3–8

(*continued*)

Rank Item	Ranks			Means			
	A&A Psych.	A&S Judges	A&K Attys.	A&A Psych.	A&S Judges	A&K Attys.	Grand Mean
16 Influences of extended family members (e.g., in-laws and close relatives)	17	19	18	6.20	6.06	6.23	6.17
17 Economic stability of the parents	16	18	21	6.23	6.08	6.12	6.15
18 Intelligence of parents	21	17	16	6.05	6.14	6.29	6.15
19 Whether or not one parent is involved in a homosexual relationship	22	21	13	5.98	5.97	6.55	6.15*[d]
20 Expressed wishes of the child, age 10	18	20	20	6.19	5.99	6.18	6.13
21 Age of the children	19	22	19	6.17	5.94	6.20	6.11
22 Availability of extended family members	20	16	23	6.09	6.19	6.03	6.10
23 Whether or not the child is placed in day care while the parent works	22	23	24	5.98	5.73	5.91	5.88
24 Economic and physical similarities or differences between parental homes	24	26	26	5.57	5.38	5.64	5.53
25 Differences between parents' religious beliefs	25	25	22	5.25	5.39	6.04	5.53
26 Marital status of each parent: remarried, single, or cohabiting	26	24	25	5.19	5.55	5.75	5.47*[b]
27 Number of children in the family	27	27	27	5.18	5.14	5.20	5.17
28 Gender of the child	29	30	29	4.91	4.41	4.56	4.65*[a]
29 Age of the parents	30	28	28	4.36	4.69	4.88	4.62*[b]
30 Expressed wishes of the child, age 5	28	29	30	4.94	4.46	4.31	4.60*[ab]

*—Significant difference

[a]—psychologists and judges significantly different

[b]—psychologists and attorneys significant different

[c]—judges and attorneys significantly different

[d]—all three groups significantly different from each other

Table 3–9

Reasons for Sole Custody

	A&A Psychologists	A&S Judges	A&K Attorneys	Grand Mean
Physical/sexual abuse	3	1	1	1
Inability to communicate/ cooperate	2	2	2	2
Parents psych./mentally ill	1	3	3	3
Substance abuse	4	4	4	4
Domestic violence	6	5	5	5
Geographical distance	5	7	6	6

There was some discrepancy among these three groups with regard to recommending or ordering joint custody. See **Table 3–10.**

All three groups rated the ability to cooperate and communicate and the children's attachment to both parents as being the top two areas of concern. However, judges and attorneys ranked geographical proximity of the two parents much higher than psychologists did. The psychological health of both parents was rated much higher among psychologists than it was among family law judges and family law attorneys.

The three groups were asked what they considered to be the most appropriate conditions of placement, or the percentage of times that they recommended, ordered, or supported various placement plans. All three groups preferred the joint-custody arrangement with primary placement to one parent over sole custody with visits. Shared 50/50-type placement schedules were preferred in only 15.47 percent of the participants across all three groups. Sole custody without visits, splitting the children, and placing the children in foster placement were recommended, ordered, or preferred in 5 percent or less of the cases for each category. See **Table 3–11.** Lastly, these groups were asked about whether mediation should or should not be used, the use of binding arbitration, at what age children should be allowed to choose which parent they live with, and at what age they should be allowed to choose whether they visit or not. [**Table 3–13** summarizes the results.]

Table 3–12 reports on evaluation issues. Psychologists preferred mediation more than the other two groups. However, the lower number for ordering mediation by judges may be a reflection of the fact that by the time the judges see a case, it is likely to be beyond the ability to mediate. There appears to be considerable agreement among all three groups with regard to what age children should be allowed to choose with whom they live and the age at which they are permitted to choose whether to visit the other parent. The grand mean of 15.17 was very close to the means of each of the three groups separately. Furthermore, the grand mean for when children should be able to choose to visit or not is 15.95. It is somewhat peculiar that ratings indicate that children should be allowed to choose with whom they live at a younger age than they can choose whether they have placement time with a parent.

Table 3–13 addresses the preferred placement schedules of judges and attorneys. There is considerable difference in the favored schedules between these two groups. Judges are

Table 3–10

Reasons for Joint Custody

	A&A Psychologists	A&S Judges	A&K Attorneys	Grand Mean
Cooperation/ Communication	1	1	1	1
Attachment to both	2	2	2	2
Contact with both	4	2	2	3
Geographic proximity	6	3	3	4
Psychologically healthy	3	5	6	5
Desire of parents	5	4	5	5
Child's choice	7	6	4	7

Table 3–11

Conditions of Placement

	A&A Psychologists	A&S Judges	A&K Attorneys	Grand Mean
Sole custody without visits	2.71	3.91	2.69	3.08
Sole custody with visits	32.35	36.33	33.02	33.78
Joint-custody primary placement	46.38	45.00	52.40	47.75
Shared placement	17.52	12.27	16.10	15.47
Splitting children	6.41	4.45	3.78	5.02
Foster placement	2.90	2.17	0.71	2.02

Table 3–12

Evaluation Issues

	A&A Psychologists	A&S Judges	A&K Attorneys	Grand Mean
Mediation	49.00	41.19	33.88	
Arbitration	N/A	2.25	0.33	
Live with	15.10	15.14	15.29	15.17
Visit	N/A	15.79	16.11	15.95

much more favorable to the traditional alternating weekend schedule, allowing for two overnights every two weeks. They preferred this in a total of 70 percent of the cases, combining those who would include a midweek dinner with those who would exclude a midweek dinner. On the other hand, the most favored schedule for attorneys was the

Table 3–13

Preferred Placement Schedule

	A&S Judges	A&K Attorneys
12/2 without midweek dinner	39.2%	14.0%
12/2 with midweek dinner	30.4	16.8
11/3	8.8	4.2
10/4	7.2	9.8
9/5	4.0	19.6
8/6	2.4	2.8
50/50	6.4	12.6
No favorite	20.0	21.0

9/5 schedule,[58] which allows for a four-day expanded alternate weekend, and one midweek overnight every two weeks. This schedule was preferred by approximately 20 percent of attorneys.

A number of conclusions can be drawn from these three studies.

1. Psychologists, judges, and attorneys prefer psychologists to be court appointed, mutually agreed upon, or GAL appointed as opposed to being hired as second-opinion or rebuttal experts.

2. Both judges and attorneys expect psychologists to observe children of all ages; review mental health records; review children's school and medical records; perform psychological testing of parents, children, and significant others; consult with the guardian ad litem; interview parents, children, and significant others; and write a report along with testifying in court.

3. Only attorneys expect psychologists to review criminal records and contact collateral sources.

4. Judges and attorneys do not expect psychologists to review pleadings of family law cases, review legal records, review parents' medical records, perform home visits, or consult with the parties' attorneys.

5. Judges and attorneys are not knowledgeable about the wide variety of psychological tests used in custody cases, with a majority of them indicating that they did not know which tests they would rely on (or not responding to the question).

6. The only test that had any level of familiarity for attorneys and judges was the MMPI-2, but not by a majority.

7. The majority of judges were not familiar with the specialized custody instruments that had been developed. However, the two instruments that had the highest level of familiarity were the BPS and the ASPECT.

---

[58] Ackerman & Ackerman at 57.

8.   When a forced choice is presented concerning sole-custody orders or recommendations, substance abuse, parental alienation, lack of cooperation with previous court orders, parenting skills, participation in the child's education, and parental stability are the most important for all three groups.

9.   When an open-ended question is asked about sole custody, physical or sexual abuse, inability to communicate or cooperate, the parents' psychological instability or mental illness, and substance abuse were the most frequently mentioned areas of concern.

10.   When a forced choice was presented concerning joint-custody orders or recommendations, problems with substance abuse, ability to separate interpersonal conflicts from parenting, quality of the relationship with the children, and the amount of anger and bitterness were the highest-rated areas of concern.

11.   In the open-ended question about the same issue, cooperation and communication, attachment to both parents, contact with both parents, and geographical proximity were the highest-rated areas of concern.

12.   All three groups preferred joint custody with primary placement to one parent over sole custody with placement time with the other parent.

13.   The overall mean age at which these groups feel that children should be allowed to determine with whom they live is 15.17.

14.   According to these judges and attorneys the mean age at which children should be allowed to choose to have placement is 15.95.

15.   Alcoholism is a major negative variable, but being in recovery is not.

16.   Sexual preference is not a major issue, but it is significantly more of an issue for attorneys than it is for judges or psychologists, who perceive it as a non-issue.

17.   Psychologists appear to be more concerned about mental-health-related issues than attorneys and judges are.

18.   Attorneys and judges appear to be more concerned about law-related issues than psychologists are.

Discussion

When looking at the sole-custody criteria, 33 significant differences were found. Twenty-six of those 33 significant differences were psychologists differing from attorneys or judges, whereas only seven of the 33 were judges differing from attorneys. On the joint-custody questions, there were 23 significant differences; 22 of those 23 significant differences involved psychologists differing from judges or attorneys, while only one represented attorneys differing from judges.

Alcohol- and other substance-abuse-related concerns consistently ranked the number one concern with psychologists, judges, and attorneys, whether they were addressing joint-custody issues, sole-custody issues, or placement concerns. As a result, when a psychologist is involved in a custody case where active substance abuse is an issue, it can be demonstrated to the court that this area is the number one concern among psychologists, family law judges, and family law attorneys and as a result should be given considerable weight in custody and placement decisionmaking.

The area of alienation ranked second by these three groups. There has been considerable controversy within the professional community regarding the issue of Parental

Alienation Syndrome, the concept of alienation, and whether these concerns occur, do not occur, and if they do occur, to what extent. Further research must be performed in the area of alienation, its prevention, and its effects on families.

Several mental health issues should be addressed. With regard to psychiatric hospitalizations, psychologists do not use this criterion to endorse either parent (ranked 14th), whereas judges and attorneys rank it 8th and 5th, respectively, and would use this criterion to endorse one parent over the other. This suggests a better understanding of mental illness by psychologists. It also may be related to the stigma associated with mental illness and psychiatric hospitalizations as viewed by judges and attorneys.

Although it does not rank as high as substance abuse and alienation-related issues, physical and sexual abuse issues are also prominent in custody and placement decisionmaking. There tends to be a cautious reluctance on the part of these groups to rank the abuse areas as high as other areas.

A number of interesting points are identified with regard to custody and placement issues. Judges are far more conservative than attorneys and psychologists in recommending placement issues. They prefer the traditional, somewhat archaic, alternating weekend placement schedule from Friday evening to Sunday evening with or without a midweek dinner. However, attorneys prefer the more liberal 9/5 schedule, which allows for alternate weekends from Thursday after school until Monday morning when school starts. It was anticipated that based on societal pressures and recent research, there would be a greater drive for 50/50 placement schedules. This clearly was not the case.

One of the more interesting points was with regard to the overall mean age at which these groups felt that children should be allowed to determine with whom they live is 15.17. In contrast, the mean age at which children should be allowed to choose to have placement or not is 15.95. At first blush it may appear to be unusual that children would have to be almost a year older to decide whether they visit or not than they would have to be to choose with whom they live. However, the decision of whom they live with assumes the continuation of a relationship with both parents. In contrast, the decision of whether to visit or not assumes the possibility of ending the relationship with one of the parents. As a result, the groups felt that a child needed to be older to make the latter decision.

There are a number of limitations to these studies. The samples of the three groups were primarily Caucasians. There is also a skew in the population of individuals who are able to afford custody evaluations, which are becoming more costly over time and not generally available to the public. Furthermore, although 800 questionnaires were sent to each group, there was a relatively small response among family law judges (N=159) and family law attorneys (N=153) even following two reminders.

In conclusion all three groups agree more than they disagree on factors that are important in sole- or joint-custody decisionmaking. However, judges and attorneys are more similar to each other, and psychologists differ more from these two groups. The areas in which judges and psychologists tend to agree are areas in which attorneys may be attempting to engage in case building (homosexuality, psychiatric hospitalizations). Although judges are likely to be seen as more neutral than attorneys, thus aligning themselves with psychologists, they are nonetheless more like attorneys than they are like psychologists.

The data from these studies have been very useful in pointing out to courts and guardians ad litem what psychologists, family law attorneys, and family law judges perceive as being important. With the comparisons that have been made among these three groups, it is clear that substance abuse, alienation, and physical/sexual abuse are the most important areas of concerns. As a result, psychologists can assert in legal settings that these issues need to be given more weight than other issues that are deemed to be less important.

Although the Ackerman, Ackerman, Steffen, and Kelley-Poulos study is the largest study performed making these comparisons, other researchers have added meaningful work to the area of establishing standards of practice within the field of child custody evaluation practices. James Bow and Francella Quinnell have become leading contributors to this area. They have published several articles since 2000 addressing components of the child custody evaluation process. In 2001, they published an article entitled "Psychologists' Current Practices and Procedures in Child Custody Evaluations: Five Years after American Psychological Association Guidelines."[59] They surveyed 198 psychologists nationally. They found that most psychologists preferred joint custody, with the mother being the custodial parent and the father having regular contact, that the consensus was to not provide reports to the parents, that full payment was required prior to the release of the report, that data should only be forwarded to a licensed psychologist selected by the attorney, and that the average evaluation currently costs $3,335. The latter figure represents greater than a threefold increase in the last 15-plus years.

Quinnell and Bow also published a study in 2001 addressing the issue of the use of psychological tests in child custody evaluations.[60] They found that while the ASPECT was the most commonly used battery of tests in child custody evaluations, it still only represented 16 percent of those using tests. However, those using it used it almost 75 percent of the time. A significant finding with regard to the reduction of the number of tests used is a decrease from 92 percent to 60 percent in the number of children who were tested in child custody evaluations.

Bow and Quinnnell along with colleagues Mark Zaroff and Amy Assemany studied the assessment of sexual abuse allegations in child custody cases.[61] The authors conclude that a comprehensive model should be used in assessing sexual abuse allegations in child custody cases. They suggest that the evaluator must understand his/her role; review records; assess the nature, sequence, and circumstances of the allegation(s); use multiple sources of data; interview the alleged victim; test the accusing parent and alleged perpetrator along with the alleged victim; assess the alleged perpetrator's sexual history; do parent-child observations; make collateral contacts; and formulate findings.

In 2002 Bow and Quinnell published an article critically reviewing child custody evaluation reports.[62] Although this study represents a relatively small N of 52, Bow and Quinell found that most of the reports followed what was suggested by previous research performed by Ackerman and Ackerman and Bow and Quinell. However, they found a

---

[59] James N. Bow & Francella A. Quinnell, *Psychologists' Current Practices and Procedures in Child Custody Evaluations: Five Years after American Psychological Association Guidelines*, 32 Prof. Psychol.: Res. & Prac. 261–68 (2001).

[60] Francella A. Quinnell & James N. Bow, *Psychological Tests Used in Child Custody Evaluations*, 19(4) Behav. Sci. & Law 491–501 (2001).

[61] James A. Bow et al., *Assessment of Sexual Abuse Allegations in Child Custody Cases and Practice*, 33 Psychol. Res. 566–75 (2001).

[62] James A. Bow & Francella A. Quinnell, *A Critical Review of Child Custody Evaluation Reports*, 40 Fam. Cts. Rev. 164–76 (2002).

number of areas that needed improvement, including documentation of informed consent, provision of clinical descriptions of the parties, listing of documents reviewed, identification and documentation of contact with school personnel, detailed description of parent-child interactions, inclusion of child history, and addressing relevant legal criteria.

William Austin addressed partner violence and risk assessment in child custody evaluations, providing a list of questions that need to be asked when partner violence is raised as a relevant issue in child custody evaluations. They are

1.   Was there partner violence or other types of family violence?

2.   Are the facts in dispute on the violence issue?

3.   When did the allegations of violence first surface?

4.   If the allegations are verified, what is the subtype of partner violence? This will yield information on the pattern, type, severity, causal pattern (who initiates), and if children were exposed. What does the subtype imply for future harm or emotional security to the child?

5.   If the allegations are in dispute, what system will be used to sort out the potential bias in the data?

6.   Is the violence likely to recur in the new family living arrangements?

7.   What risk and protective factors are present in the family system?

8.   What custody and access arrangement will work best to lower the risk of harm to the child in light of the violence?

9.   What is the likelihood of change? Is the perpetrator or perpetrators amenable to treatment? Are they taking responsibility for the misconduct? Are the relevant risk factors mostly static or dymamic?[63]

Last, William Austin discussed guidelines for utilizing collateral sources in child custody evaluations. He supports the use of collateral sources for important issues that are in dispute to move from the "he-said-she-said." He states, "Objective records and credible persons who have the opportunity to observe critical behaviors provide the evaluator with the means to discriminate the validity of disputed issues between the parties. . . . It is suggested the evaluator must describe to the court what method was used to assess the credibility of the sources of data gathered."[64]

Mary Connell, Marsha Hedrick, Daniel Schuman, Stanley Brodsky, and Beth Clark participated in a symposium titled "Expert Witness Expertise—Three Vantage Points" at the 2001 American Psychologist Association Conference. During the presentation, Marsha Hedrick addressed the issue of what judges want from psychologists in custody cases. Her presentation was titled, "What Judges Want to Hear from the Experts." She reported that judges want psychologists to state the basis for their opinions succinctly. Judges tend to be "lukewarm" about psychological tests. When psychological tests are administered, they do not want psychologists to report endlessly about the results. They look for psychologists to

---

[63] W.G. Austin, *Assessing Credibility in Allegations of Marital Violence in the High-Conflict Child Custody Case*, 38 Fam. & Conciliation Cts. Rev. 462–77 (2000).

[64] W.G. Austin, *Guidelines for Utilizing Collateral Sources of Information in Child Custody Evaluations*, __ Fam. Cts. Rev. 18, § 3 (in press).

make realistic recommendations and are upset by recommendations that, for example, require parents to hire a secretary and a driver. Furthermore, diagnostic statements must be tied to the issues before the court. Although psychologists are trained to make a diagnosis or provide diagnostic impressions, judges generally are not interested in the diagnosis of the parents in that they do not perceive these diagnoses to be particularly helpful in family law cases. Dr. Hedrick also reported that judges are not interested in hearing about ethical violations of other psychologists involved in the case, unless the ethical violations directly affect placement recommendations. They want psychologists to state why the ethical violations matter to the court and the case at hand, not why the violation is a violation in and of itself. Judges also are not impressed when a psychologist's demeanor changes during cross-examination, when a psychologist exaggerates data, or when a psychologist responds in a hostile manner under cross-examination. Judges perceive the psychologist's job as teaching them, not persuading them. Psychologists must remember that judges have good conceptual ability but may not have the vocabulary necessary to understand psychological concepts. Judges want confident, intelligent, well-prepared testimony but do not like cleverness on the witness stand. Furthermore, they like visual aids to be utilized in helping explain issues.

Law professor Daniel Schuman addressed similar issues when he reported on juror assessments of the believability of expert witnesses. For jurors, qualifications are important. They perceive the more qualified expert as being the more believable expert. As a result, when juries are involved, considerable time should be taken to address an expert's qualifications. However, testifying to the ultimate issue did not persuade jurors in reaching their conclusions. Also, the more familiar the psychologist was with the facts of the case, the more credible the psychologist was. If a psychologist is asked a question that begins with, "Oh, Dr., you didn't know about . . . ," the credibility of the psychologist is lessened. Last, jurors look for psychologists to be disinterested and impartial. As a result, if an opposing expert is able to demonstrate partiality or bias on the part of a psychologist, that psychologist's credibility is lessened.

As the discussant for this symposium, Dr. Beth Clark summarized and addressed many of the issues raised. Clark pointed out that preparation needs to be a mutual process, with the attorneys preparing the psychologist and the psychologist preparing the attorneys. She also pointed out that psychologists do not benefit from impugning the ethics or morals of the other expert. If there are ethical or licensure issues that need to be addressed, they should be directed to the ethics committees or licensure boards and should not be part of the case in court. It is also essential for the psychologist to know the case backward and forward. One way to do this is to obtain all of the discovery materials and review them prior to court. It can be costly to have the psychologist read all of the discovery materials; however, it can be more costly if the psychologist is ill prepared and has not had the opportunity to review the materials.

§ 3.31   Second-Opinion Evaluations

Philip Stahl, a well-known author in the area of child custody evaluations, addresses the concern of second-opinion evaluations:

> [T]o give a second opinion, it is important for the reviewer of a child custody evaluation to maintain a neutral, objective stance in the review, just as the original evaluation does. Reviews

should be done by court order or by stipulation of the parties, after the reviewer has a release of information signed by all relevant parties. It is best to have a list of the disgruntled parents' objections to the evaluation as direction for the review. I recommend that the reviewer have all the data originally available to the evaluator when making the review, and it is best if the reviewer speaks with the evaluator and understands the evaluator's view of the family before completing the review.[65]

It is not unusual for an individual who has received an unfavorable opinion from the court-appointed or guardian ad litem–appointed psychologist to seek a second opinion. However, this request should not be treated as a birthright but rather something granted at the judge's discretion. It becomes the psychologist's responsibility to inform the parties seeking a second-opinion evaluation that, in a large majority of cases, the second-opinion results should agree with the first-opinion results, especially when the initial evaluation was performed by a competent psychologist. There is always room for the concept of "reasonable people can disagree," and there is also the possibility that there may be disagreement on minor points, but it is unlikely that there would be any significant disagreements on major points in a majority of cases when a standard, competent evaluation is performed. However, there are times when a second-opinion evaluation is warranted. These include

1. When it has been more than one year since the first-opinion evaluation has been performed, and there has been a substantial change of circumstances;
2. When a first-opinion expert performs an evaluation outside the standard of practice; or
3. When it can be demonstrated that inappropriate tests were administered, grossly inappropriate interpretations were given to the results, or if significant criminal, mental health, and/or substance abuse history affecting parenting skills was ignored.[66]

Substantial Change

Unfortunately, in some circumstances, it can take more than a year for a custody case to reach court based on adjournments or other problems. It is also not unusual for the initial recommendations of the psychologist to be incorporated into temporary orders between the time of the evaluation and the start of the custody trial, and then for changes of circumstances to occur. For example, if a temporary order awarded placement of the children to the father, and during the ensuing year, the child dropped from being an A/B student to being a D/F student and if there were numerous absences, and/or if homework was not being completed, this would represent a substantial change from when the mother was caring for the children. There are certainly other areas where substantial change can be identified, for example, medical care, parental responsibility, dangerousness, anger management, school problems, hygiene problems, and/or neglect-related problems.

---

[65] Philip Stahl, *Second Opinions: An Ethical and Professional Process for Reviewing Child Custody Evaluations*, 35 Fam. & Conciliation Cts. Rev. no. 3, at 386 (July 1996).

[66] Marc J. Ackerman, Clinician's Guide to Child Custody Evaluations 105 (2d ed. John Wiley & Sons 2001).

Standard of Practice

There has been sufficient literature published in the last decade and a half about what represents an appropriate custody evaluation, in addition to the publication of the American Psychological Association *Guidelines for Child Custody and Divorce Proceedings*.[67] These research findings combined have helped form what is now identified as the standard of practice in performing custody evaluations. If these standards have not been met, then a second-opinion evaluation would be warranted.

Inappropriate Tests or Interpretations

With the advent of managed care plans, the ensuing reduction of therapy case referrals for psychologists, and the overall tightening of the health care market, more and more psychologists who lack adequate training or experience have started to engage in performing custody evaluations. If an individual who may be a very competent neuropsychologist administers a battery of neuropsychological tests for a custody evaluation, that would represent an example of the use of inappropriate tests. Furthermore, if the testing that is administered is inadequate, such as the Peabody Picture Vocabulary Test as a measure of cognitive functioning and the Bender-Gestalt as a personality measure, this would represent inadequate testing procedures. In addition, when extremely outdated tests are used to form the basis of an opinion, and research has demonstrated that those tests are not useful in custody cases anymore, this would represent an additional concern. Gross misinterpretations can be found on occasion where people are using their own stylized interpretations of the MMPI-2, the MMPI, or Rorschach without professional literature supporting the interpretations. It may be necessary to utilize a psychologist as a consultant to determine if this is indeed the case.

When it has been demonstrated that a second opinion is warranted, it becomes essential for the second-opinion psychologist to not appear as a "hired gun" who is hired solely for the purpose of opposing the first evaluation and is not as independent as would be desired. It is difficult to completely avoid the appearance of being a hired expert. However, there are ways to overcome this problem. When this author performs a second-opinion evaluation, the attorney hiring this psychologist is informed that the evaluation will be handled in the same manner as a first-opinion evaluation. This means that the results of the evaluation will be disseminated to all three, both attorneys and the GAL (who may not be an attorney), whether they are favorable or unfavorable to the hiring attorney's client, that the report will be addressed to the guardian ad litem, and that consultation will be held with

---

[67] William G. Keilin & Larry J. Bloom, *Child Custody Evaluation Practices: A Survey of Experienced Professionals*, 17 Prof. Psychol.: Res. & Prac. 338–46 (1986); American Psychological Ass'n, *Guidelines for Child Custody and Divorce Proceedings*, 49 Am. Psychologist 677–80 (1994); Marc J. Ackerman & Melissa C. Ackerman, *Child Custody Evaluation Practices: A Survey of Psychologists*, 30 Fam. L. Q. 565–86 (1996); Marc J. Ackerman & Linda J. Steffen, *Child Custody Evaluation Practices: A Survey of Family Law Judges* (in preparation, 2000); Marc J. Ackerman, Melissa C. Ackerman, Linda J. Steffen, & Shannon Kelley-Poulos, *Psychologists' Practices Compared to the Expectations of Family Law Judges and Attorneys in Child Custody Cases*, 1 J. Child Custody no. 1, at 41 (2004).

the guardian ad litem prior to writing the report. Thus, if the second-opinion evaluation renders results contrary to the first-opinion evaluation, it will give more of an appearance of a neutral evaluation than a "hired gun" evaluation. When the report is written on the second-opinion evaluation, it is explained that the second-opinion evaluation was handled in this manner, and the reasons for doing so. If the attorney will not agree to these requirements for performing the second-opinion evaluation, then this author will not do it and will suggest that another psychologist be sought.

Another form of second-opinion evaluation can occur when the aggrieved parent hires a second-opinion evaluator and the non-aggrieved parent also hires a second-opinion evaluator in an attempt to counter the perception that the first second-opinion evaluator will agree with the aggrieved parent. Thus, a battle of the experts among mom's expert, dad's expert, and the court-appointed expert results. However, it is important to understand that there is a dynamic operating under these circumstances that will affect the results of the second-opinion evaluations. Understand that when the mother and father go to her expert, she will be in what is perceived as "friendly territory," and the father will be in what is perceived as "hostile territory." When the two go to the father's expert, the father will be in what is perceived as "friendly territory," and the mother will be in what is perceived as "hostile territory." As a result, both sets of evaluations carry with them different dynamics. It would not be expected, under those circumstances, that the mother's results and the father's results in each of these settings would be identical. Therefore, the mother is likely to look better with her expert, and the father better with his expert. The psychological evaluators may naively interpret this to mean that there are substantial differences between the mother and the father, with the mother's expert recommending for the mother and the father's expert recommending for the father, with each asserting the other expert is wrong. Instead, what we have is a comparison between how the parents perform on psychological testing in comfortable environments and how they perform on psychological testing in uncomfortable environments. Therefore, the results of the mother's evaluation with her expert should be compared with the father's evaluation with his expert. This will allow the examiners to compare the parents in comfortable environments. Then the father's results with the mother's expert should be compared with the mother's results with the father's expert to understand how the parents react under stress. (See **Table 3–14**). Unfortunately, experts who are not aware of this cutting-edge method of interpreting these results will naively battle this out in court with the mom's expert saying mom is better, and the father's expert saying dad is better, each saying that the other expert is wrong.

Table 3–14

Compare 1 & 2 and 3 & 4

Mother's Expert	Father's Expert	
1. Mother's findings: performance positive	2. Father's findings: performance positive	Parents when comfortable
3. Father's findings: performance negative	4. Mother's findings: performance negative	Parents when under stress

For psychologists to make the type of comparison that is discussed above, it is essential for them to exchange raw data. When the court order is obtained requiring that the second-opinion evaluations be performed, it should also include the requirement that the raw data be exchanged between the first-opinion expert and the second-opinion expert, or among the first-opinion expert and the two second-opinion experts. Attorneys should not get caught up in the professional controversy of requiring psychologists to provide raw data to attorneys, when this exchange of information among psychologists can easily be accomplished by the raw datas being sent directly to each psychologist.[68] In the case of a psychologist with a history of being noncompliant with either meeting deadlines or exchanging data on a timely basis, the court order should indicate that if the raw data have not been exchanged by a certain date, or the reports have not been written by a certain date, then that psychologist will not be allowed to testify in the matter or the report will not be utilized.

When a second-opinion evaluation is warranted, some of the psychological tests may be repeated while others should not. Tests of cognitive functioning, which include intelligence tests and achievement tests, should not be repeated less than six months (but preferably 12) after the original evaluation is performed due to what is referred to as "practice effect." Practice effects occur when an individual is exposed to a unique task in a first-opinion evaluation. Having engaged in the task on one occasion, the individual will be educated to the task and will perform better the second time, not because he or she is more intelligent but because of having practiced the task. Thus, he/she will end up with an inflated IQ score. There is no identifiable reason other than incompetence on the part of the first-opinion psychologist to repeat tests of cognitive functioning in less than 6 to 12 months. However, personality tests, such as the MMPI-2 and Rorschach, can easily be repeated based on the fact that if the individual chooses to be cooperative and open, the results will be valid, and if the person chooses to be guarded and defensive, there will be questions about validity, whether they are the results of the first-opinion or a second-opinion evaluation. Personality tests also respond to changes in circumstances, while intelligence tests and achievement tests generally do not. Without this updating of testing and interviewing, the evaluator will only be able to speak about the status of each individual(s) at the time of the original evaluation but may not be able to make many statements "to a reasonable degree of psychological certainty" at the time of trial.

The issue of practice effects not only involves a particular test but also the evaluation as a whole. The first-opinion evaluation educates the participants about how to respond the second time around. For example, if a parent's MMPI-2 shows a significant amount of depression, and the examiner indicated that the depression was a factor in recommending placement to the other parent, when reading the MMPI-2 items during the second-opinion evaluation, the party would likely try to not answer the depression questions in a scoreable direction as had occurred the first time. Therefore, the parent who is seeking the second-opinion evaluation is likely to look better the second time around, not because the first-opinion evaluator was incorrect but because the party has been educated by the results of the first-opinion evaluation. Again, the second-opinion evaluator often naively interprets these results to mean the first-opinion evaluator was wrong, ignoring the educative aspect

---

[68] Marc J. Ackerman, The Essentials of Forensic Psychological Assessment 14–22 (John Wiley & Sons 1999).

of the first-opinion evaluation for one parent and the negative impact of the second-opinion evaluation on the other parent.

The attorney is left with helping the client make the difficult decision of whether a second-opinion evaluation should be performed or not. There is not only a significant financial cost to performing a second-opinion evaluation, there is also the psychological cost of subjecting the parties, especially the children, to the stress of additional evaluations. There is no birthright that necessarily gives the aggrieved parent the right to seek a second-opinion evaluation if the first-opinion evaluation does not suit their liking. It should be the judge's and the guardian ad litem's responsibility to determine whether there is sufficient reason to allow for a second-opinion evaluation. It is this author's opinion that second-opinion evaluations are used far too frequently and, in many cases, unnecessarily. As a result, the second-opinion evaluation is likely to be of little value in standard cases with standard evaluations, and is likely to be given little weight except for the above noted concerns. In a recent national survey, family court judges reported that they give significantly less weight to second-opinion evaluations than neutral court- or guardian ad litem–appointed evaluations.[69]

§ 3.32   Questions for Chapter 3

Attorneys should not expect to merely go into court and ask all the following questions. Preparation is necessary, referring to the content of the chapter to determine whether the question applies in a particular case. The section number at the end of a question refers to the place in this chapter where the reader can find an explanation of why the question may be important.

1. Who did the psychologist interview other than those individuals tested? (See **§ 3.1.**)

2. Was the client allowed to take any tests home? (See **§ 3.2.**)

3. Was the setting appropriate? If not, why not? (See **§ 3.2.**)

4. Was rapport easily established? If not, why not? (See **§ 3.2.**)

5. Did the psychologist use standard administration procedures? If not, why not? (See **§ 3.2.**)

6. Did the tests used meet the Heilbrun criteria for use of testing? (See **§ 3.4.**)

7. Were there significant others who were excluded from the interview process? If so, why? (See **§ 3.5.**)

8. Was there any practice effect? (See **§ 3.7.**)

9. Does the evaluator consider the factors of the Uniform Marriage and Divorce Act, and other factors the research support drawing conclusions? (See **§ 3.11.**)

10. Did the evaluator follow the American Psychological Association's *Guidelines for Child Custody Evaluations?* (See **§§ 3.10** to **3.25.**)

---

[69] Marc J. Ackerman & Linda J. Steffen, *Child Custody Evaluation Practices: A Survey of Family Law Judges*, 15 Am. J. Family Law 12–16 (2001).

11. Did the examiner handle bias appropriately? (See § **3.14.**)

12. Did the examiner avoid multiple relationships? (See § **3.16.**)

13. Did the examiner make recommendations without evaluating all of the parties? (See § **3.22.**)

14. Did the examiner obtain informed consent? (See § **3.18.**)

15. Did the examiner explain and follow the rules of confidentiality? (See § **3.19.**)

16. Were the financial arrangements explained to the parties? (See § **3.24.**)

17. What type of information was left out of the report and why? (See § **3.27.**)

18. Did the examiner follow the evaluation procedures recommended in **Table 3–5**? (See § **3.28.**)

19. If the examiner performed a second-opinion evaluation, was it for one of the reasons outlined? (See § **3.31.**)

§ 3.33   Case Digest

The source of information for most of the following cases is the *Mental and Physical Disability Law Reporter* (MPDLR), a publication of the American Bar Association. Complete information for any other sources appears in the relevant references below. The following are direct quotations from the identified source. Quotations from the *Mental and Physical Disability Law Reporter:* Excerpted from *Mental and Physical Disability Law Reporter*. Copyright (c) 1989–2004. American Bar Association. Reprinted by permission. If no source is identified, it is a summary from the court ruling.

Massachusetts

Sugarman v. Board of Registration in Medicine, 662 N.E.2d 1020 (Mass. Sup. Jud. Ct. 1996). Muriel Sugarman was retained as an expert witness by the attorney for the mother in a custody dispute. . . . A court nondisclosure order against any media publicity was in effect. . . . Sugarman leaked to the press selected portions of the report. . . . The Board charged Sugarman with undermining public confidence in the medical profession by knowingly disregarding the gag order, undermining the orderly administration of justice, and failing to adhere to the warning that continued publicity was detrimental to the child's best interest. . . . The Board based its decision on standards of conduct promulgated by the American Academy of Psychiatry and the Law, the Ethical Guidelines for the Practice of Forensic Psychiatry, and the American Psychiatric Association's Principles of Medical Ethics with Annotations Especially Applicable to Psychiatry. 21 *Mental & Physical Disability Law Reporter* 667 (1997).

Michigan

Navarre v. Navarre, 191 Mich. App. 395 (Mich. Ct. App. Oct. 7, 1991) (released Feb. 3, 1992). A Michigan Court of Appeals ruled that the statutory physician-patient relationship provisions are not subject to waiver in child custody evaluations. The court held that it is essential to protect the physician-patient relationship, even if it means sacrificing potentially important evidence. Information about the parents is available from other sources, and may be admitted for this purpose. The mother's agreeing to a court-ordered psychological evaluation and the introduction of testimony by the psychologist did not constitute waiver of her physician-patient privilege.

New Jersey

Kinsella v. Kinsella, 696 A.2d 556 (N.J. 1997) [T]he supreme court [found] that John did not waive the psychologist-patient privilege against disclosure by alleging extreme cruelty as grounds for divorce. . . . [W]hile stressing that courts must maintain a proper balance between the need to determine the parents' mental health for custody and visitation determinations in order to act in the child's best interests, and to protect the psychologist-patient privilege, the court remanded the psychologist records access issue about custody and visitation. However, it appears that the trial court "in this case has an alternative tool [compulsory psychiatric examinations] which may accomplish both purposes." 21 *Mental & Physical Disability Law Reporter* 650 (1997).

Virginia

Nasser v. Parker, 455 S.E.2d 502 (Va. 1995). The Virginia Supreme Court found a psychiatrist and a psychiatric hospital did not owe a duty to protect prospective victims of a former patient because the necessary special relationship never existed between the psychiatrist and his former patient.

Angela Nasser Lemon was involved in a relationship with George Edwards, which she attempted to terminate. Edwards, who had a history of committing violent acts against women who rejected him, held a gun to Lemon's head and threatened to kill her. Lemon obtained a warrant for Edwards' arrest and left her home to conceal her whereabouts. Edwards consulted his treating psychiatrist, who was aware of Edwards' violent history and his recent threat to Lemon. The psychiatrist concluded that Edwards' deteriorating mental condition warranted prolonged therapy in a psychiatric hospital and arranged for Edwards' admittance to Peninsula Psychiatric Hospital "on a voluntary basis." Learning of Edwards' admittance and that it was for a prolonged period, Lemon returned home. However, the day after his admittance, Edwards left the hospital. Neither his psychiatrist nor the hospital notified Lemon of Edwards' departure. Edwards again visited his psychiatrist who prescribed medication for his mental condition. A few days after, Edwards shot and killed Lemon and then himself. Lemon's father filed suit against Edwards' psychiatrist and the hospital alleging they had a duty to notify Lemon of Edwards' departure from the hospital. When the trial court sustained Defendants' demurrer to Lemon's father's motion for judgment, Lemon's father appealed.

In affirming the trial court's decision, the Virginia Supreme Court rejected the holding of *Tarasoff v. Regents of the Univ. of Calif.*, 551 P.2d 334 (Cal. Sup. Ct. 1976) . . . , and stated that the mere existence of either a doctor-patient relationship, or of a hospital-patient relationship was not enough to establish a "special relationship" under § 315(a) of the Restatement (Second) of Torts. Rather, "to establish a 'special relationship' under Restatement § 315(a), . . . a plaintiff must allege facts, which, if proven, would show that the defendant had `taken charge' of a third person within the meaning of § 319." Here, the facts did not show that either the hospital or the psychiatrist had taken charge of Edwards, and thus had a duty to control his conduct. In particular, Edwards had entered the hospital on a voluntary basis, and neither the psychiatrist's treatments and arrangements for admittance nor the hospital's admittance of Edwards was enough "to assert custody in the sense that the [patient] is in the personal care and control of the [doctor or hospital]." 19 *Mental & Physical Disability Law Reporter* 520–21 (1995).

Washington

Redding v. Virginia Mason Medical Center, 878 P.2d 483 (Wash. Ct. App. 1994). The Washington Court of Appeals held that it was not a breach of the psychologist-patient relationship for a father to use records from a joint counseling session with the mother in which she admitted having a problem with alcohol. The court cited *Cummings v. Sherman*, 132 P.2d 998 (Wash. 1943): "[I]f two or more persons consult an attorney at law for their mutual benefit, and make statements in his presence, he may disclose those statements in any controversy between them." Analogously, a therapist is free to disclose statements of the mother during custody litigation with the father.

CHAPTER 4

HOW DIVORCE AFFECTS FAMILIES

§ 4.1   Decisions to Divorce

It appears that during the past two decades there has been a breakdown in the commitment of individuals to long-term relationships: fewer people are staying with the same employer for the duration of their working years; moves from neighborhood to neighborhood and city to city are far more common; and there has been a steady increase in the divorce rate.

Today's laws make it relatively easy to obtain a divorce; in fact, many states have no-fault divorce laws. Unfortunately, the children of today's marriages are modeling their parents' behavior and are likely to reflect the same feelings their parents have toward interpersonal and marital relationships.

Whether a couple should stay together for the sake of the children is a question that often arises. More than a generation ago, the notion was that people should remain married for the sake of the children no matter how bad the marriage was. However, research has indicated that couples who stayed together for the sake of the children often ended up with maladjusted children. As a result, divorcing couples are likely to be less concerned about how their divorce affects the children. Unfortunately, research has shown that children can suffer maladjustment as a result of their parents' divorce as well.

Today, the question must be asked, when is it better to stay together for the sake of the children and when is it better to get divorced for the sake of the children? When answering this question, parents must realize that divorce adversely affects children. When the parents' relationship is destructive, staying married has a greater adverse effect on the children than terminating the marriage. Examples of destructiveness in a marriage include verbal, physical, and/or sexual abuse, frequent inappropriate expressions of anger, and continually involving the children in unresolved conflicts. Although parents may have fallen out of love, if they can cohabitate without exhibiting destructive behavior, staying in a home with parents who do not love each other will generally have a less adverse effect on the children than breaking up the home.[1] Consequently, the parents' ability to control their behavior determines the extent to which a divorce will adversely affect the children.

---

[1] Judith Wallerstein, 1986 Cape Cod Institute, Institute for Psychological Study, Inc.

§ 4.2   Adversarial versus Cooperative Divorce

Once parents have decided to divorce, many concerns must be addressed. The first concern is whether the divorce will be cooperative or adversarial. A *cooperative divorce* is one in which the parents are willing to meet, discuss, and resolve the issues without requiring a court battle. In cooperative divorces, attorneys generally encourage the mediation or collaboration process, facilitate reaching a stipulation, and participate in negotiations when necessary. An *adversarial divorce* is one that leads to a legal contest or a court battle and forces attorneys to assume opposing positions in court. The adversarial divorce generally occurs when individuals are initially unwilling to enter into a cooperative process or when the cooperative process breaks down. It is important for attorneys today to be able to participate in both cooperative and adversarial divorce processes. A cooperative divorce will help children adjust; an adversarial divorce will be harmful.

Bruce Sales has long been an advocate of looking at public policy issues in relation to psychology and the law. Dr. Sales, along with Connie Beck, wrote a critical appraisal of divorce mediation in 2000. They conclude by stating that "the goals of divorce mediation may be overly optimistic."[2] They point out that one of the difficulties with assessing mediation research is the fact that research designs, outcome studies, and confounding variables make it difficult to assess that research.

§ 4.3   —Divorce Mediation

Divorce mediation has become relatively popular in recent years. Because many individuals present themselves as divorce mediators, it is important for anyone seeking mediation to select an individual who is qualified to be a divorce mediator. At this time, the Academy of Family Mediators accredits individuals based on their training and experience as mediators. Criteria for admission to the Academy of Family Mediators include at least 40 hours of mediation training, review of mediation agreements from at least 15 successfully completed mediations, and documentation from an already experienced mediator that the individual is qualified.

The mediation process can involve either one or two mediators. A divorce can be either fully mediated—resolving custody and placement issues, financial issues, division of property, and other related issues—or partially mediated.

The advantages of the mediation process include that it resolves divorce issues quickly, it costs a fraction of the adversarial approach, and it leaves far fewer scars on the immediate family members than does the adversarial approach.[3] Furthermore, mediated divorces are much less likely to be relitigated than adversarial divorces.[4]

It is important to note that the mediation process is not designed to exclude attorneys from the divorce process; indeed, most mediators are either attorneys or psychotherapists

---

[2] Connie J.A. Beck & Bruce D. Sales, *A Critical Re-Appraisal of Divorce Mediation Research and Policy*, Psychol. Pub. Pol'y & L. 989 (2000).

[3] Ellison, *Issues Concerning Parental Harmony and Children's Psychosocial Adjustment*, 53 Am. J. Orthopsychiatry 73 (Jan. 1983).

[4] S. Erickson, Divorce Mediation Workshop, Wisconsin Psychological Association (Fall 1984).

with some level of specialized training. However, some attorneys perceive the role of mediator to violate the ABA Code of Professional Responsibility, because they view it as providing legal representation to both parties.

When a mediation agreement is reached, the parents submit it to their respective attorneys. The attorneys then advise their clients as to the legality of the items agreed to and ensure that the agreement is read into the court order as agreed upon. The court then accepts or rejects the agreement.

Several long-term studies have been performed to identify how mediated and litigated divorces affect parents' outlooks. Katherine Kitzman and Robert Emery evaluated the differences between parents who had used mediation and those who had used litigation to settle custody disputes. They found that one year after settlement, parents who had used mediation showed a greater similarity in their perceptions of the problems their children were having. Child outcomes seemed to depend more on the extent of parental conflict than on whether the parents were involved in mediation versus litigation.[5]

Peter Dillon and Robert Emery studied the same issue nine years postjudgment. Parents who had used mediation nine years earlier reported more frequent contact with their children and greater involvement in decisionmaking. They also reported greater communication about the children. The authors concluded that the study supported the hypothesis that "families using mediation have a more positive outcome than those using litigation."[6] This study also demonstrates the benefits of mediation beyond two years, which was previously the maximum follow-up period.

§ 4.4   —Collaborative Divorce

In recent years, a new concept in resolving divorce conflicts has been developed—*collaborative divorce.* The collaborative divorce process has taken many mental health concepts and applied them to the divorce setting. During the collaborative divorce process, both parties hire attorneys who will attempt to work together with the parties to reach a resolution. Mental health professionals may be brought into the process to serve as "coaches." In the event that the collaborative process is not successful, the attorneys and mental health professionals must withdraw from the case, and new attorneys and mental health professionals enter for the purpose of litigation. As a result, the only interest that the attorneys and mental health professionals have in the collaborative process is to reach resolution. Under other systems, the attorneys may attempt to resolve the case but later take the case to trial themselves if the case is not resolved.

§ 4.5   —Arbitration

Another approach that can be used to aid conflict resolution is arbitration. Arbitration can be either binding or nonbinding. *Binding arbitration* obligates the parties to follow the

---

[5] Katherine Kitzman & Robert E. Emery, *Child and Family Coping One Year after Mediated and Litigated Custody Disputes*, 8 J. Fam. Psychol. no. 1, at 150–59 (1994).

[6] Peter Dillon & Robert E. Emery, *Divorce, Mediation, and Solution of Child Custody Disputes: Long-Term Effects,* 1 Am. J. Orthopsychiatry 131–41 (Jan.1996).

arbitrator's recommendations, while *nonbinding arbitration* allows the parties to disagree with the arbitrator and find remedies for their disagreement through other avenues. The authors of this book consider binding arbitration to be the better approach.

An arbitrator can be used in a number of different ways in cases. For example, a retired judge may be appointed as an arbitrator to resolve small technical issues and avoid the necessity of going to court. Non-judges can also serve as arbitrators for a number of different issues.

Sometimes, the mediation process allows resolution to a certain point, only to break down with a few minor details left unresolved. This may result when the parties need to continue to fight with one another, unconsciously battling each other as a way of being able to maintain their relationship. The mediation process may need to end in arbitration when small issues cannot be resolved. For example, when all of the major marital property has been divided, but a list remains of items valued at less than $1,000 total, an arbitration approach can be used productively. The mediator may state, for example, that these issues will be mediated for three more sessions. If resolution has not been reached after the three sessions, the mediator becomes the binding arbitrator and determines who gets which pieces of property.

Although this approach can be used to wind up the mediation process, it can also be court-ordered when the small issues remain unresolved and would take up unnecessary court time. This approach alerts the parties that unless they find a way to reach a resolution themselves, the decisionmaking power will be taken out of their hands and given to someone else. As a result, this almost always serves to increase the parties' motivation to reach a resolution.

§ 4.6   Joint versus Sole Custody

Another issue that must be decided is whether to enter into a joint custody agreement or designate one of the parents as sole custodian. In a *joint custody* arrangement, both parents have equal legal rights with regard to their children's education, religious upbringing, and medical treatment. Joint custody, however, does not necessarily mean that the children will spend an equal amount of time with each parent. It is the *placement* decision that determines how much time children will spend with each parents. In a *sole custody* arrangement, the sole custodian holds all of the legal rights to decisionmaking about the children's development and future.

Joint custody is generally best for the parents and the children because it keeps both parents actively involved in the development of their child(ren).[7] Jessica Pearson and Nancy Thoennes report that parents with joint custody felt they had better cooperation with ex-spouses and greater financial resources available to them than those with sole custody.[8]

---

[7] V. Schiller, *Joint versus Maternal Custody for Families with Latency Age Boys: Parent Characteristics and Child Adjustment*, 56 Am. J. Orthopsychiatry 486 (1986).

[8] Jessica Pearson & Nancy Thoennes, Custody after Divorce: Demographic and Attitudinal Patterns 233 (1990).

Joint custody works most effectively when the parents can communicate with one another. Practically speaking, it is likely that the couple were unable to communicate effectively while they were married; otherwise, they may not have divorced. When parents demonstrate that, despite a considerable amount of effort and intervention, they cannot cooperate with each other even for the sake of their children, it may become necessary to designate a sole custodian. If a custody dispute ensues, it often forces the parents to become adversaries to demonstrate the incompetence of the other parent and the expertise of their own parenting skills. This process is usually destructive and tends to leave wounds that are very difficult to heal. It is ironic that, following an extended custody dispute that may include a considerable amount of mudslinging, judges often conclude a case by stating, "The parties must now cooperate with one another for the sakes of the children."

Several factors need to be considered when deciding whether joint or sole custody should be sought:

1. Can the parents sustain the communication that is necessary to maintain joint custody?
2. What kinds of children do well in a joint custody arrangement?

Joint custody generally benefits younger children because of the ongoing issues that need to be discussed between the parents. Parents who can separate their own needs from those of their children are much more likely to make good joint custodial parents. Joint custody should not be used as a compromise when no other solution can be achieved.

Marsha Kline and her associates found that there was no difference between children's adjustment to sole custody versus joint custody arrangements. However, they did find that "joint custody children had contact with both parents significantly more often than sole custody children."[9] They concluded that, despite having more access to both parents, joint custody children show neither less disturbance nor better social and emotional adjustment after divorce than in sole custody divorces.

Joseph Goldstein is one author who dealt with the concept of "the best interest of the child" in works he coauthored in 1973 and 1979. He later took a retrospective look at the concept of "best interest," based on the years of study since his original works were written.[10] He believes that courts should not force visitation, should leave the decision of whether visits take place up to the noncustodial parents, and should not forcibly remove children from the custodial parent who refuses to cooperate with court orders. His conclusion is that, although judges may believe they are making decisions in the best interest of children, they may actually be putting children in harmful situations.

Robert Bauserman[11] performed a meta-analytic study on 33 studies between 1982 and 1999 on the topic of joint versus sole custody. These 33 studies had a combined sample size of 1,846 sole custody children and 814 joint custody children. Previous research argued the topic in both directions. Some research unequivocally supported joint custody, while other research argued that the amount of parental conflict was more important than

---

[9] Marsha Kline et al., Children's Adjustment in Joint and Sole Custody Families 435 (1989).

[10] Joseph Goldstein, *In Whose Best Interest?*, *in* J. Folberg, Joint Custody and Shared Parenting 11–25 (1991).

[11] Robert Bauserman, *Child Adjustment and Joint-Custody versus Sole-Custody Arrangements: A Meta-Analytic Review*, 16 J. Fam. Psychol. 91–102 (2002).

the custodial arrangement.[12] As would be predicted, the meta-analysis indicated that the joint custody groups were better adjusted than the sole custody groups. Joint custody children showed better adjustment in parental relationships and spent significant amount of time with the father, allowing the opportunity for authoritative parenting. This is deemed important, because nonresident father involvement and authoritative parenting by the father were positively associated with behavioral adjustment.[13] Bauserman goes on to indicate that parental conflict remains an important confounding variable in research. Conflict was found to be highest with mid-level-type visitations and lower when father contact was very high or very low. The meta-analytic study also concluded, as hypothesized, that intact-family and joint custody children did not differ in adjustment because such an arrangement provides children with ongoing contact with both parents.[14]

Identifying Appropriate Placement Parent

When parents cannot agree on custody and/or placement arrangements, it is often left to professionals to determine who would make the best custodial parent. **Chapter 3** is devoted to these issues.

See §§ **4.30** through **4.36**, Judith Wallerstein's research, for further discussion.

§ 4.7 Physical Placement and Visitation Schedules

In divorce situations, another important issue to decide is the physical placement of the child(ren). Even when joint custody is awarded, one parent generally becomes the primary placement parent and the other the alternate placement parent. Sometimes, *shared placement* is arranged, which allows the parents to have substantially equal amounts of time with their children. Traditionally, a placement parent and a "visiting parent" are designated. Because the term "visitation" has certain connotations that have become distasteful over the years, the new terminology is "periods of physical placement," "access," "companionship," or other similar terms.

Psychiatrist William Hodges has presented guidelines for helping determine the most appropriate visitation patterns that still apply today. He states that, although they are not exhaustive, the guidelines can be very helpful:

1. If the child is an only child and there are no special considerations, consider the developmental guidelines.
2. If the parents have tried a developmentally inappropriate pattern with apparent success over some reasonable period of time, consider that the child may be very adaptable. Evaluate whether there are symptoms or problems that are ignored by parents, such as difficulty at transfer, unusual levels of dependency, unusual levels of detachment or spaciness. If no symptoms are present, and the pattern is not widely divergent from the guidelines, acceptance of the deviation might be appropriate.

---

[12] *Id.* at 92.

[13] *Id.* at 98.

[14] *Id.* at 98–99.

3. If the child shows symptoms of attachment problems, consider evaluation by a mental health professional.

4. If the child shows symptoms at transition from leaving one parent's, consider (a) that visitation problems may exist (e.g. psychological abuse, sexual abuse, neglect, conflict): (b) that the child may attempt to please the parent who is being left; and (c) that the child may find leaving the parent less painful if everyone is upset and angry.

5. If the child shows symptoms at transition from leaving both parents, consider that the child (a) has difficulty with loss; (b) is trying to please both parents; and (c) has a difficult temperament and has difficulty with any change.

6. If an older sibling is present for parent access times and the child has bonded with the sibling, consider longer duration visits.

7. If the child is not bonded with the sibling(s) consider the developmental guidelines.

8. If the parents have chronic conflict, consider (a) third party transfer; (b) sole custody; (c) regular predictable visits; and (d) reduced frequency of transfers.

9. If the non-primary parent is psychopathological, consider reducing visitation frequency and duration. Also consider supervision or termination.

10. If the non-primary parent is an abuser, consider supervision or termination of parent access.

11. If the child has a difficult temperament, consider longer visitation duration and fewer changes. Consider providing stability in terms of where the visitation occurs.

12. If the child is severely alienated from the parent, consider very brief visits (one half hour to one hour) with or without supervision.

13. If there is a great geographic distance between parents, consider frequent visits if the child is young, provided such visits are financially feasible. Half the time, have the primary parent take the child to the non-primary for visits with nightly return to the primary parent. Half the time, have the non-primary parent travel to the city of the primary parent. Avoid long visits for very young children. For children over seven, long visits tend to be better tolerated.

14. If there has been a long break in parent access with a wish to reinstate contact, consider phasing in a schedule to let the child get used to the formerly absent parent and rebuild trust. If trust is absent in the child or the primary parent, consider a phase-in with supervision.

15. If the custodial parent is socially isolated, is under stress, has few friends or relatives available to share child care, and has low income, consider increasing visitation duration with the non-custodial parent to relieve the custodial parent from constant child care responsibilities.

16. If the child has an easy temperament and the parents want to change the guidelines, consider such compromises, but evaluate the effect on the child. Often visitation schedules are related to convenience rather than to the child's welfare.[15]

Hodges provides developmental guidelines to help in the determination of an appropriate amount of visitation. He states:

For infants from birth to six months, a frequent and predictable visitation pattern is recommended. The more frequently the non-custodial parent can be available, the longer the

---

[15] William Hodges, Interventions for Children of Divorce: Custody, Access, and Psychotherapy 171–72 (2d ed. John Wiley & Sons 1991). Reprinted by permission of John Wiley & Sons, Inc.

duration should be. For infants who can be visited only once or twice a week, visitations should not exceed one or two hours.[16]

He also concludes, "If the six to 12 month old child has had little prior contact with the non-custodial parent, visitations should be short and frequent to provide familiarity and comfort for the infant."[17] When the children are 18 months to three years of age, they can handle less frequent visits than can infants, "but consistency and frequency are still important. Long visitations during summer vacations are not recommended. Although the exact length of long visitation for this age child is not known, a child familiar with and bonded to the noncustodial parent can handle three to four days."[18] Hodges believes that "for pre-school children, professionals should take into account that conflict between parents and high-quality parenting may be more important than the pattern of visitation. . . . Children from three to five benefit from highly predictable visits. Support of more frequent visitation should be the next level of priority after consistency."[19]

There has been much written in recent years about developing parenting and placement plans for young children. This debate has been played out with numerous articles in *Family Court Review* since 2000. In 1998, Mary Whiteside pointed out that there are three models in the research literature. They include the notion that very young children need a primary and stable attachment to their mother—one primary parent, one bed to sleep in.[20] The second model places importance on children having a father or father figure in the household, while the third model takes the family systems perspective and looks at the full network of relationships surrounding children.[21] Whiteside addresses the issue with regard to attachment theory and indicates that children with insecure attachments have more difficulty coping with the separation process. She points out that of primary importance is the caregiver's interactions with the children, which must be predictable, responsive, affectionate, and warm.[22]

Michael Lamb and Joan Kelly[23] have been prominent in attachment and placement literature for decades. In two articles they address the issue of placement of young children. They take the position that overnights for young children with the non-placement parent do not affect the child's psychological adjustment. However, they do not indicate how they define children in terms of their age. They point out that the two "residential beds or environments" do not need to be the same, but the feeding and sleep routines should be similar to maintain stability.[24]

---

[16] *Id.* at 174.

[17] *Id.* at 175.

[18] *Id.* at 177.

[19] *Id.*

[20] Mary F. Whiteside, *Custody for Children Ages 5 and Younger*, 36 Fam. Conciliation Cts. Rev. no. 4, at 479–502 (Oct. 1998).

[21] *Id.* at 482.

[22] *Id.* at 495.

[23] Michael J. Lamb & Joan B. Kelly, *Using the Empirical Literature to Guide the Development of Parenting Plans for Young Children: A Rejoiner to Solomon & Biringen*, 39 Fam. Ct. Rev. 365–71 (2001).

[24] *Id.* at 307.

Judith Solomon and Zeynep Biringen[25] responded to the position that Lamb and Kelly took by stating that Lamb and Kelly go too far in their interpretation of the literature. They support the position that repeated overnight separations from the primary attachment figure provide developmental challenges for the infant.

Not to be outdone, Lamb and Kelly respond to Solomon and Biringen by stating that Solomon and Biringen are far too conservative in their interpretation of the literature and that delaying overnights as long as Solomon and Biringen want is detrimental to the children.

The most recent writing on this topic has been provided by Marsha Kline-Pruett, Rachel Ebling, and Glendessa Insabella.[26] They reviewed the points made by previous authors and studied parenting plans for children under six years of age. A solid piece of research, their work utilized psychometrically valid instruments to measure children's responses to various parenting plans. They take the position that looking at the issue of overnights alone is not appropriate, but, instead, the evaluator should include the child's social, cognitive, and emotional behavior with caregivers and schedule consistency as being more important than overnights.[27]

And so goes the controversy. The problem with much of the literature that has been written on the subject is the lack of discrimination between infants, toddlers, and preschool children. The authors of this book state that there is no developmental research that would indicate that children between two and three years of age should not have overnights. The research also supports that children should not be away from the primary attachment figure for more than three days at a time when they are one to three years of age. However, the research does not specifically segregate out how children from birth to 12 months of age fare under these conditions. As a result, we are taking the position that repeated overnights are ill-advised for children birth to 12 months of age. Instead, frequent visits of short duration, two to three hours at a time, four to five times a week at various times of the day, should be considered.

Richard Warshak[28] concludes by stating, "I believe that the data show that overnights should be among the options considered for infants, toddlers, and older children. Overnights should neither be made mandatory nor routinely excluded."[29]

When addressing the issue of older children, Hodges states:

> As children move into the primary school age, Hodges believes that the visitation pattern should minimize the interference with peer relations. . . . If the parents have a reasonably cordial relationship, visitation more frequent than every other weekend may be desirable. At

---

[25] Judith Solomon & Zeynep Biringen, *"Another Look at the Developmental Research: Commentary on Kelly & Lamb's "Using Child Development Research to Make Appropriate Custody and Access Decisions for Young Children,* 39 Fam. Ct. Rev. 355–364 (2001).

[26] Marsha Kline-Pruett, Rachel Ebling, & Glendessa Insabella, *Critical Aspects of Parenting Plans for Young Children: Interjecting Data into the Debate about Overnights,* 42 Fam. Ct. Rev. 39–59 (2004).

[27] *Id.* at 57.

[28] Richard Warshak, *Who Will Be There When I Cry? Revisited Overnights—A Rejoinder to Biringer et al.,* 40 Fam. Ct. Rev. 208–19 (2002).

[29] *Id.* at 217.

seven or eight years of age, children who have contact with non-custodial parents several times a week are the most content with visitation. . . . At ages 10 to 11, boys in particular seem to prefer less contact, perhaps only every other week with the non-custodial parent. . . . Long visitations during the summer are acceptable, but some contact with the noncustodial parent either through visitation or phone is desirable.[30]

Finally, Hodges states that "visitation for adolescents should take into account that teenagers do not need contact for long duration with either parent. Weekend visitation may interfere with developmental needs to separate from both parents. Contact once or twice a week for an hour or more may be enough contact."[31]

Hodges addresses the issue of long visitation for young children. Although it may be ideal for children under seven years of age to have shorter visits, it is not always practical. When long visitations are necessary, Hodges provides several guidelines. He indicates that an increase of object constancy is necessary for the young child. "[W]ith long separations, the child has increasing difficulty in maintaining an image of the absent parent. Photographs of the parent, cassette tapes of the favorite bedtime stories in the parent's voice, and frequent phone calls can help bridge the memory of the absent parent for the young child."[32] This object constancy can also be maintained by bringing familiar objects such as dolls, toys, and blankets when the child is placed with the other parent. Whenever possible, the receiving parent should maintain the same routines for mealtimes, bedtimes, and discipline.

Periods of physical placement can vary. The traditional arrangement allows for an 11/3 split. This generally allows the primary parent to have the child(ren) 11 of every 14 days and the nonprimary placement parent to have them 3 of every 14 days. Generally, the 3 days involve a Friday night through Saturday afternoon one week and a midweek contact the alternate week. However, placement can also be on an 11/3, 10/4, 9/5, 8/6, or 7/7 basis. These decisions generally depend on the availability of parents, the input from professionals, and the parents' desire to be involved in the upbringing of their children.

One of the more popular recent arrangements is the 9/5 split, which gives the alternate placement parent one overnight one week and a four-day weekend the alternate week. The four-day weekend is generally from Thursday night to Monday morning or Friday night to Tuesday morning. This allows the alternate placement parent to do more than visit with the children and to become actively involved with child rearing. It also requires active communication between parents. This plan is nothing more than an extension of the traditional visitation schedule of alternating weekends. However, instead of the weekend being a Friday night to Sunday afternoon, it is a four-day weekend. With the long weekend, the parent will be required to help with homework, take children to lessons, taken children to sporting activities, and discipline children when appropriate. This also reduces the likelihood that a parent will become a "Disneyland parent." The 8/6 and 7/7 (or other 50-50

---

[30] William Hodge, Interventions for Children of Divorce: Custody, Access, and Psychotherapy 171–72 (2d ed. John Wiley & Sons 1991). Reprinted by permission of John Wiley & Sons, Inc.

[31] William Hodges, Interventions for Children of Divorce: Custody, Access, and Psychotherapy 180 (2d ed. John Wiley & Sons 1991).

[32] *Id.* at 185.

schedules) should not be considered unless parents communicate well, live near one another, and do not exhibit acrimonious behavior.

§ 4.8 Nesting

"Nesting" is a relatively new concept in shared placement schedules. In this plan, the children remain in the house, but the parents move in and out for their periods of placement. Although theoretically a good plan, as time progresses, the process often breaks down due to the parents' inability to communicate effectively or cooperative optimally with one another. It should only be considered when parents communicate well with each other. It is recommended that this be used as a short-term solution, perhaps during the pendency of the divorce, and not as an ultimate placement schedule. As parents move on to new relationships, the nesting schedule can become very cumbersome and impractical.

§ 4.9 Forced Visitation

The issue of mandatory visitation, forced visitation, or refusal to visit has long plagued those professionals who are engaged in child custody work. The issue of "forced visitation" goes in both directions. It can involve forcing the non-custodial parent to visit the children or forcing children to visit with a parent they have no desire to be with.

Daniel Pollack and Susan Mason[33] addressed the issue of parents who do not spend placement time with their children. They conclude that parents' visiting with children confirms that they still have two loving, caring parents even though the parents are not living with each other. They state that "visitation rights should instead be viewed as an obligation owed by non-custodial parents to their children."[34] Pollack and Mason suggest that if parents choose not to visit with their children, the courts should order mandatory counseling for the non-visiting parent.

Janet Johnston[35] points out that there are a number of reasons why children may choose not to visit with a particular parent. This is especially true when there is a history of abuse. Johnston suggests that young children who resist visitation need help feeling safe. Children who have been traumatized by witnessing or being victims of abuse need to be involved in therapy to resolve these issues. She concludes by stating that "the overall thesis of this paper is that children's resistance and refusal to visit a non-custodial parent may have their origins in diverse and multiple psychological, developmental, and family system factors that require careful differential assessment by experienced clinicians."[36]

---

[33] Daniel Pollack & Susan Mason, *Mandatory Visitation in the Best Interest of the Child*, 42 Fam. Ct. Rev. 74–84 (2004).

[34] *Id.* at 74.

[35] Janet Johnston, Children of Divorce Who Refuse Visitation, 109–135.

[36] *Id.* at 133.

§ 4.10   Relocation/Move-Away Cases

Sanford Braver[37] and his associates wrote a scholarly work in 2003 that has caused considerable controversy. They performed a study based on concerns about Judith Wallerstein's controversial 1995 *amica curiae* brief. The *amica curiae* brief basically supported the notion of move-away and indicated that in general what is good for the custodial mother is good for the child. However, Braver and his associates conclude that "on most child outcomes, the ones whose parents moved are significantly disadvantaged."[38] Students and families where one parent moved "received less financial support from their parents, worried more about the support, felt more hostility in their interpersonal relations, suffered more distress related to their parents' divorce, perceived their parents less favorably as sources of emotional support and as role models, believed the quality of their parents' relation with each other to be worse, and rated themselves less favorably on their general physical health, their general life satisfaction, and their personal and emotional adjustment."[39]

Joan Kelly and Michael Lamb[40] addressed the same issue from the perspective of attachment relationships with parents. They state that "the age and developmental needs of the children, the quality of the parent-child relationships, the psychological adjustment of the parents, and the likely effects of moving on the children's social relationships, as well as cultural and educational opportunities in both locations" need to be addressed in deciding relocation.[41] They also state concerns about very young children's attachment relationships deteriorating or terminating with the non-moving parent. They further suggest that this could create psychological risks and long-term consequences.[42]

Removal Cases: Different Cities

There will be occasions when one parent needs to move to another city for legitimate reasons, other than just trying to spirit the children away from the other parent. Parents living in different cities can implement a multitude of schedules to maximize the amount of contact between the non-placement parent and the children. School schedules are such that much contact time is available during the school year. Teacher conferences, teacher planning days, teachers' convention, Presidents' Day weekend, mid-winter and spring breaks, and traditional holiday times allow for the opportunity for long weekends or extended time out of school. Any four-day weekend should be made available to the non-placement parent.

---

[37] Sanford Braver, Ira M. Ellman, & William V. Fabrucius, *Relocation of Children after Divorce and Children's Best Interest: New Evidence and Legal Considerations*, 17 J. Fam. Psychol. 206–19 (2003).

[38] *Id.* at 206.

[39] *Id.* at 214.

[40] Joan B. Kelly & Michael E. Lamb, *Developmental Issues in Relocation Cases Involving Young Children: When, Whether, and How?*, 17 J. Fam. Psychol. 193–205 (2003).

[41] *Id.* at 202.

[42] *Id.*

In addition, the non-primary placement parent should be allowed to travel to where the children reside during the school year for up to four one-week periods of placement during the school year, provided he or she is willing to take the children to all scheduled activities. Furthermore, the non-primary placement parent should have the lion's share of summertime, which is operationally defined as one week after school is out until two weeks before school begins.

In 1996, the California Supreme Court decided, in *In re Marriage of Burgess*[43] that a primary placement parent who wishes to relocate shall be permitted to do so without having to prove that the move is necessary. This was a substantial change in policy from previous court decisions in most jurisdictions around the country. The California Supreme Court further ruled that it was not a substantial change of circumstances for the custodial parent to relocate. So long as the custodial parent has a "sound, good faith reason" to change his or her place of residence, that parent may do so unless, as a direct result, there will be significant detriment to the child. The ultimate decision of the trial court also needs to consider this, as it does all child custody matters, in the context of the best interests of the child.

This case has taken on particular importance in part because a number of courts in other states have made similar decisions that cited *Burgess*, and in part because of the major split in the mental health community regarding the probability that this policy would be harmful to the best interests of the child whose parent chooses to relocate.

The decision of the California Supreme Court was consistent with the recommendations of an amica curiae brief filed on behalf of Judith Wallerstein, Ph.D, *in Burgess*. Wallerstein's brief was based in large part on her extensive longitudinal research with children in the San Francisco Bay area, as well as two relocation cases that were studied in depth. Wallerstein notes that children are limited in their ability to travel to visit a distant parent, that children should not be made to travel a great deal during their developmental years, and that some parents relocate in bad faith, and should be enjoined from doing so. Her bottom line, however, is predicted on the principale that

> [i]t is altogether reasonable to assume that a parent and child who have been living together as a family unit and sharing the same household for several years are likely to have a close attachment to each other that promotes a healthy sense of security and self-esteem in the child. It is reasonable to assume that more guidance and discipline from that parent will prepare the child for responsible participation in society.[44]

The best interests of the child, she indicates, are "best served within the nurture and protection provided by high-quality parent-child relationships—the relationships, rather than geographical convenience, should be paramount in custody case."[45]

Over the past several years, a substantial backlash has developed against the *Burgess* decision, culminating in the filing of amici briefs by psychologist Richard

---

[43] 913 P.2d 473, 51 Cal. Rptr. 2d 444 (Cal. 1996).

[44] Judith Wallerstein & Tony J. Tanke, *To Move or Not to Move: Psychological and Legal Considerations in the Relocation following Divorce*, 30 Fam. L. Q. 305–32, at 319 (1996). This article is an adaptation of Dr. Wallerstein's brief in *Burgess*.

[45] *Id.* at 320.

Warshak *et al.*,[46] and family law attorney Leslie Ellen Shear *et al.*[47] in a case currently before the California Supreme Court, *In re Marriage of Navarro (LaMusga v. LaMusga)*.[48] The essential position of both the Warshak *et al.* and Shear *et al.* briefs is that (1) Wallerstein's briefs in both *Burgess* and *LaMusga*[49] do not represent the views of the majority of experts on child development and child custody; (2) the California Supreme Court's decision in *Burgess* does not adequately permit trial courts to consider the individual needs of each child and what is in the best interests of that child; (3) the *Burgess* decision grossly underestimates the profound effect that relocation can have on a child and his or her development and welfare; and (4) relocation should be among the factors that are considered a change of circumstances requiring the trial court to make an assessment in the context of the best interests of the child.

The authors of the present text have a great deal of respect for Dr. Wallerstein, as witnessed by our lengthy discussion below of her pioneering research. However, we are also impressed by the arguments of Warshak *et al.* and Shear *et al.* and by the fact that many prominent experts in child development and child custody are signers of one or both of those amicus briefs.

We do not have a problem with the principles in *Burgess* requiring a decision that is sound, in good faith, without significant detriment to the child, and in the best interest of the child. We do have a concern regarding the manner in which some court's have interpreted *Burgess,* permitting the primary placement parent to move away without the trial court's carefully reviewing all four of these factors. We also believe that relocation should be considered as a possible change of circumstances requiring the trial court to make a formal assessment in the context of the best interests of the child. It is our position that each case should be evaluated on its own merits, and we have not supported positions that state that any placement decision that could have a major negative impact on a child should "always" or "never" be permitted.

---

[46] Amici, along with Warshak, in *LaMusga* are Sanford L. Braver, Ph.D.; Joan B. Kelly, Ph.D.; James H. Bay; and William G. Austin, Ph.D.

[47] Amici, along with Shear, in *LaMusga*, are Marjorie G. Fuller, J.D.; Nancy Williams Oleson, Ph.D.; Mamela Panasti Stettner, J.D. CFLS; Michael E. Lamb, Ph.D.; Dawn Gray, J.D., CFLS; Joan B. Kelly, Ph.D.; Lawrence E. Leone, J.D., CFLS; William G. Austin, Ph.D.; Constance R. Ahrons, Ph.D., M.S.W.; Harold J. Cohn, J.D., CFLS; Sanford L. Braver, Ph.D.; Frieda Gordon, J.D., CFLS; James M. Hallett, J.D., CFLS, CFCLS; Sidner J. Brown, Ph.D.; Lynette Berg Robe, J.D., CFLS; Michael Gottlieb, Ph.D.; Tammy-Lyn Gallarini, J.D., CFLS; Richard A. Warshak, Ph.D.; Kenneth C. Cochrane, J.D., CFLS; Neil S. Grossman, Ph.D.; David R. Lane, J.D., CFLS; Maureen Stubbs, J.D., CFLS; Fred Norris, Ph.D.; Dianna Gould-Saltman, J.D., CFLS; Carol Silbergeld, LCSW, BCD; Susan Ratzkin, J.D.; Jeffrey M. Lulow, Ph.D.; Dale S. Frank, J.D.; Leslye Hunter, M.A., LPC, LMFT; Ronald S. Granberg, CFLS; James R. Flens, Psy.D.; Rebekah A. Frye, J.D.; Renee A. Cohen, Ph.D.; Tracey Duell-Cazes, J.D., CFLS; Marnee W. Milner, J.D.; Jacqueline Singer, Ph.D.; Erica L. Hedlund, J.D.; James Livingston, Ph.D.; Josephine A. Fitzpatrick, J.D., CFLS; Michael A. Fraga, Psy.D.; Timothy C. Wright, J.D.; CFLS; Avery Cooper, J.D.; CFLS; and Lawrence W. Thorpe, J.D., CFLS.

[48] Supreme Court Case No. S107355.

[49] Amici, along with Wallerstein, in *LaMusga*, are Pauline F. Kernberg, M.D.; Joyanna Lee Silberg, Ph.D.; Julia M. Lewis, Ph.D.; John B. Sikorski, M.D.; and Stephanie Joan Dallam, R.N., M.S.N., F.N.P. *Amici*, along with Wallerstein, in *Burgess* are Trevor C. Thorpe, J.D.; Steven R. Liss, J.D.; Mark J. Warfel, J.D.; and John R. Schiller, J.D., CFLS.

Lawyers and psychologists must watch this issue as it evolves. We urge the readers of this text to review all of the briefs in *LaMusga*, as well as related research on the question of the effect of relocation on children. Those briefs, and some of the research articles, may be found at *http://psych.la.asu.edu/people/faculty/sbraver.html*.

§ 4.11   The Ackerman Plan: Joint Custody/Shared Placement

When parents divorce, they often both qualify as reasonable custodial parents who desire placement of the children. Unfortunately, in making decisions about sharing placement, judges sometimes fail to consider what is psychologically best for the children. Judges have issued orders requiring children to spend the first half of the week in one household and the second half of the week in the other household; alternating every three days; alternating weeks; alternating every two weeks; alternating months; even alternating years. Orders have been issued allowing the mother to have the children on Monday, Wednesday, and Friday of one week, on Sunday, Tuesday, Thursday, and Saturday of the following week, and alternating that plan every two weeks. The problem with all of these alternating plans is that they do not provide the children with a sense of having a home and a secure base from which to operate. The reader must also keep in mind that the most important job children have is their education, and the most important job divorced parents have is to develop a schedule that interferes with their children's education as little as possible. However, there is a plan that provides the parents with relatively equal time with the children throughout the year, and at the same time, allows the children a sense of security. The plan is a 9/5-10/4 "flip-flop" arrangement. Deciding that this was a mouthful, Judge Patrick Madden in Milwaukee County Circuit Court labeled it the *Ackerman Plan*, after the author of the plan. It should be noted that this plan has been successfully utilized in thousands of cases throughout the country during the past decade, and has become the favored plan of attorneys around the country.

This plan allows one parent to have primary placement during school time (approximately September 1 to June 1) on a 9/5 basis, as described in **§ 4.7.** The other parent then would have the children for primary placement on a 10/4 basis during nonschool time. In this way the alternate placement parent would have the children 10 out of every 14 days, during which time the first parent has the children for a three-day weekend one week and an overnight the alternate week. *Nonschool time* is defined as the time from approximately June 1 to September 1, a week at Thanksgiving, two weeks at Christmas, and a week at Easter. This allow the 10/4 parent to have the children on a 10/4 basis 4 out of the 12 months of the year, and the 9/5 parent to have the children on a 9/5 basis 8 of the 12 months of the year. When all is tallied, the 9/5 parent has the children approximately 20 days more than the 10/4 parent.

One objection to the Ackerman Plan is that the 10/4 parent always has the children during holiday times. It must be noted that the 9/5 parent still has four days during these blocks of time in which to spend holiday time with the children. In addition, each parent can be allowed two or three weeks of uninterrupted time during the course of the year to allow for vacation.

When deciding which parent will have the children 9/5 during school time and who will have the children 10/4 during nonschool time, several things must be considered.

Generally, the parent who is better able to support the children academically would be the 9/5 parent during school time, and the one who can better provide and support recreational activities would be the 10/4 parent during nonschool time. Child support would be established to reflect that the parents have the children on a nearly equal basis.

§ 4.12   Holidays

When working out an arrangement for placement schedules, the common practice is to alternate holidays. The present authors' preference, however, is to share rather than to alternate holidays. When holidays are alternated, the children miss spending the holiday with half of their extended family. Not only do they miss visiting with one parent, they also miss spending time with the aunts, uncles, cousins, and grandparents on that side of the family. Provided the parents are living in the same city, most major holidays provide an opportunity for sharing. We recommend the following plan for sharing holidays.

Thanksgiving

If one family has Thanksgiving dinner early in the day, the other family can schedule its meal later in the day. Or the children can eat Thanksgiving dinner with one family and have dessert with the other family. The parents can alternate having the children for dinner from year to year. This, of course only works if the parents live in the same city or very near one another.

Christmas

The children can spend Christmas Eve with one parent and Christmas Day with the other parent. If both parents wish to have Christmas Eve or Christmas Day, then the other Christmas Eve/Christmas Day placement can be rotated annually. This allows the children to spend part of Christmas with each family.

When children reach school age, the issue of Christmas/winter break becomes part of the holiday planning. Parents may wish to take a vacation with their children at Christmastime but be unable to do so because of the restrictions of the placement schedule. One alternative allows the parents to share the winter break each year. For example, in odd-numbered years, the mother could have the children from the beginning of the vacation through Christmas Eve, and the father would have the children from Christmas Day until school starts again. During even-numbered years, this would reverse. Thus, each year one parent would have a majority of the break and the other would have a shorter portion, but they would both be able to spend holiday time with their children.

Easter

The children can spend Easter morning and Easter brunch with one family, and Easter dinner with the other family.

Fourth of July

Many activities take place on the Fourth of July, generally starting the evening of July 3 or in the morning of the July 4, and ending with evening fireworks. The day can be divided so that the children go to a morning parade and have a picnic lunch with one family, then have dinner and fireworks with the other family. If both parents have the same preference, the arrangement can be rotated on an annual basis.

Jewish Holidays

Jewish holidays can be divided the same way. One parent could have Erev Rosh Hashanah, the other parent could have Rosh Hashanah day. The same plan can be used for Yom Kippur. If both parents want the same day, it could be alternated from year to year. With Passover, one parent could have the first Seder, and the other the second Seder. This could remain constant from year to year or alternated. Chanukah is a long holiday that can be shared easily.

Other Holidays

The children should spend Mother's Day with their mother and Father's Day with their father, regardless of the established placement schedules. On each parent's birthday, the children should also be available to visit that parent.

Because children's birthdays are seldom celebrated on the actual birth date, one parent can plan a birthday celebration for the child on the weekend prior to the actual birth date, with the other parent arranging a celebration for the weekend following the actual birth date.

Memorial Day and Labor Day, considered minor holidays, and can either be alternated or shared as the parents desire. These holidays also provide a three-day weekend with each parent.

Several rules of thumb should be utilized as part of visitation and holiday schedules:

1. Holiday placement supersedes regular placement schedules.
2. Whoever has the children at 6:00 P.M. is responsible for feeding the children.
3. The receiving parent will transport the children. This reduces concerns about parents' being late in dropping off or picking up children.
4. Flexibility is necessary, with no requirement for parents to balance out hours that have been gained or lost. Parents must understand that throughout the course of their children's minority, the time will even out.

§ 4.13   Families' Adjustments to Divorce

The divorce process necessitates a complex adjustment for both parents and children. Parents who think life will be much simpler when the divorce is final must remember that they will be required to maintain a relationship with her/his former spouse as long as their children are minors. In addition, adjusting to the demands of the divorce itself may take six months to a year.[50]

The adjustment period after the divorce is just as important for the children as it is for the parents.

In a meta-analysis, Paul Amato and Bruce Keith reviewed 92 studies that evaluated how divorce affects children. They addressed the issues of parental absence, economic disadvantage, family conflict, and other related issues, with several interesting results. The authors concluded that "children who experience parental death tend to be better off than children who experience divorce."[51] When examining socioeconomic factors, the hypothesis that children are better off living with stepfathers than with single mothers was not supported for girls, but was for boys. However, "some support was found for the hypothesis that children have a higher level of well-being in father-custody families than mother-custody families."[52] The authors' meta-analysis supported the conclusion that family conflict remains a significant factor in how children function. The impact of post-divorce conflict between parents was strongly associated with children's maladjustments, receiving the widest support among the general concerns.

Bonnie Barber and Jacquelynne Eccles reviewed divorce research literature, looking at a number of different variables, and concluded:

> [I]n summary, past research that has focused on the negative outcomes of divorces has been inconclusive. Although there seemed to be some small differences between children of divorced and intact families [in] cognitive performance, delinquency, and self-esteem, these differences frequently disappear when confounding and mediating variables are controlled. The research on children of divorce is frequently flawed by serious methodological problems, reducing the generalized reliabilities of findings and leading to the possibility that the negative outcome attributed to divorce may, in fact, be due to economic struggle or parent conflict. Although it may be generally true that two parents can do a better job of raising children than one parent, it does not follow that all children are better off if their parents stay together. First, the negative consequences of being raised in a conflictual family may be averted if parents separate. Second, there may be some advantages to the socialization experienced by children growing up with their single mothers. Children in single-parent, female-headed families may develop a greater sense of personal responsibility and self-esteem, and girls and boys may develop less gender-role stereotyped occupational aspirations and family values, which could lead to their increased success in the labor market.[53]

Neil Kalter and his associates discussed the predictors of postjudgment adjustment.[54] They found that parents' adjustment directly affects children's adjustment. They also

---

[50] J. Wallerstein, 1986 Cape Cod Institute, Institute for Psychological Study, Inc.

[51] Paul Amato & Bruce Keith, Parental Divorce and the Well-Being of Children: A Meta-Analysis 39 (1991).

[52] *Id.* at 40.

[53] Bonnie L. Barber & Jacquelynne S. Eccles, *Long-Term Influence of Divorce in Single Parenting and Adolescent Families and Work-Related Values, Behaviors, and Aspirations*, 111 Psychol. Bull. 108–26 (1992).

[54] Neil Kalter et al., *Predictors of Children's Post-Divorce Adjustment*, 59 Am. J. Orthopsychiatry no. 4, at 605–18 (Oct. 1989).

report that negative changes in the mother's life negatively affect boys' adjustment to divorce, and severity of problems negatively affects girls' adjustment to divorce.

Research performed by David Demo and Alan Acock[55] determined that a child's emotional adjustment, gender role identification, and antisocial behavior appeared to be affected by the divorce process. However, other dimensions of a child's well-being remain unaffected. Like other authors, Demo and Acock concluded that the level of family contact may also be a factor in the adjustment of children.

Parents should be aware of several distinct problems that their children may confront following a divorce. It is unusual for children to experience divorce without some degree of difficulty. Guilt and withdrawal of affection often cause children particular difficulty.[56]

Furthermore, both parents and children must deal with the concerns of moving to a new neighborhood, going to a new school or job, getting used to new relationships, and becoming familiar with the visitation schedules.[57] Children, especially those five to seven years of age, may believe they caused the divorce.[58] A child may think, "If only I had been better," of "If only I had not made Mommy or Daddy scream so much, they would not be getting divorced." If children have been told that Mom and Dad divorced because they no longer love each other, they may reason that Mom and Dad no longer love them. They should be assured that their parents have *always* loved them and will not fall out of love with them.

Undoubtedly, divorce has a financial impact on a family. It may be necessary for a parent who had not previously worked outside the home to do so after the divorce. Research clearly demonstrates that if the mother has worked before divorce, continuing to work after the divorce will not negatively affect the children.[59] However, when a mother who did not work prior to the divorce is forced to get a job after the divorce, it will affect the children negatively.[60] They will perceive this as a second loss; first Dad left, and now Mom is leaving also.

§ 4.14   Grandparents' Visitation

All 50 states had passed laws giving grandparents the right to petition the court for legally enforced visitation privileges with their grandchildren, even over parental objections, under certain conditions. However, with *Troxel v. Granville* (see case digest in § **4.39**) the U.S. Supreme Court ruled that grandparent visitation laws unconstitutionally infringed on the fundamental right of parents to raise their children. Research, however, indicates that grandparents affect the development of their grandchildren by caregiving and providing both cognitive and social stimulation. In addition, they serve as an important source of

---

[55] David Demo & Alan Acock, *The Impact of Divorce on Children*, 50 J. Marriage & Fam. 619–48 (Aug. 1988).

[56] J. Wallerstein, 1986 Cape Cod Institute, Institute for Psychological Study, Inc.

[57] *Id.*

[58] *Id.*

[59] *Id.*

[60] *Id.*

social support for the parents. Grandparents can act as historians, transmitting family values and traditions to succeeding generations. They also influence the grandchildren through their relationships with the adult children. Interestingly, the relationship between grandparents and grandchildren is shaped by the grandparents' relationship with their children. When separation and divorce occur, maternal grandparents tend to see the children more frequently and assume more of a parental role in their child's life by assisting the mother both financially and in other ways. By contrast, the paternal grandparents generally experience less contact with their grandchildren.

Grandparents' visitation may need to be restricted or eliminated altogether if they use their visitation time to denigrate the other parent. Grandparents should not engage in destructive comments like, "Why does your mother keep accusing your father of . . . ," or "Things would be much better if your father would pay the child support he's supposed to." The very special relationship between grandparents and their grandchildren should be unencumbered by unwarranted pressure on the children.

The role of grandparents in the divorce process can be very important. When grandparents are committed to helping their grandchildren, it is a tremendous support during the divorce process. However, if grandparents choose to become part of the fight, it has an even greater adverse effect on their child(ren) and grandchildren. Grandparents can help counterbalance the problems occurring between the parents. They can help maintain a sense of family and self-esteem. Unfortunately, grandparents are available for support in only 25 percent of divorces.

§ 4.15   Problems Confronting Children following Divorce

Parents should be aware of several distinct problems that their children may confront following a divorce. It is unusual for children to experience divorce without some degree of difficulty. Guilt and withdrawal of affection often cause children particular difficulty.[61] As noted above, children, especially those five to seven years of age, may believe they caused the divorce.[62] A child may think, "If only I had been better," or "If only I had not made Mommy or Daddy scream so much, they would not be getting divorced." If children have been told that Mom and Dad divorced because they no longer love each other, they may reason that Mom and Dad no longer love them. They should be assured that their parents have *always* loved them and will not fall out of love with them.

Following are a number of factors that affect children during and following divorce:

1. Abandonment and rejection: Children often feel abandoned by or rejected by the departing parent.

2. Powerlessness and helplessness: Children often feel like they have no control over their lives.

3. Insecurity: Not knowing where they are going to live, who they are going to live with, what school they will attend, and who their friends will be, children of divorce often feel insecure about their future.

---

[61] J. Wallerstein, 1986 Cape Cod Institute, Institute for Psychological Study, Inc.
[62] *Id.*

4. Regressive behavior: Because of the stress associated with the divorce problem, children may revert to behaviors they left behind developmentally, such as bed-wetting, thumb sucking, baby talk.

5. Acting-out behavior: Children of divorce often engage in acting-out behavior (fighting, lying, being oppositional) as a function of their frustration and anger over the changes in their lives.

6. Guilt: Children may feel guilty because their parents are getting divorced, believing that they somehow caused the divorce by their own inappropriate behavior.

7. Unresolved anger: Children can be angry about whatever their departing parent did that resulted in the need to leave, whatever their remaining parent did to require the departing parent to leave, and/or all of the changes that they will experience in their lives as a result of the divorce.

8. Depression: All of the above stated concerns together can result in significant feelings of depression on the part of the child.

When any of these behaviors last for a month or less, the parent can generally consider the behavior as "a stage" the child is going through as a function of the divorce. However, when these behaviors last longer than a month or so, therapeutic intervention is necessitated to prevent long-term negative sequelae and these behaviors' becoming habitual.

Christy Buchanan addressed the issue of children's adjustment to interparental conflict. She found that interparental conflict pressured children to choose to side with one parent or the other. She reports that "asking a child to carry messages, denigrating the other parent, asking questions about the other parent, comparing homes, questioning the child's love, and making it difficult for a child to talk about the other parent were all strongly related to feelings of being caught" between parents.[63] James Twaite and Anya Luchow point out that interparental conflict appears to be the most powerful influence on children's adjustment.[64]

James Bray and E. Mavis Hetherington address the issues of families in transition, stating that "there is a considerable body of research that indicates that, on the average, children from divorced and remarried families show more problems with achievement, social relations, internalizing behaviors such as depression and anxiety disorders, and externalizing behaviors such as aggression, resistance to authority, noncompliance, delinquency, and substance abuse."[65]

§ 4.16   Preschool Years

Although Linda Franke's work is somewhat dated, it still provides excellent characterizations of how divorce affects children at various ages. In establishing the placement

---

[63] Christy Buchanan, Patterns of Children's Response to Parent's Marital Conflict, Paper presented at Children and Marital Conflict: Process of Effects Symposium, Annual meeting of the Midwestern Psychological Ass'n, Chicago (May 1994).

[64] James A. Twaite & Anya K. Luchow, *Custodial Arrangements and Parental Conflict following Divorce: The Impact of Children's Adjustment*, 24 J. Psychiatry & L. 58 (Spring 1996).

[65] James H. Bray & E. Mavis Hetherington, *Families in Transition: Introduction and Overview*, 7 J. Psychol. no. 1, at 3–8 (1993).

arrangements for children in their preschool years, several considerations must be taken into account in light of the difficulties such children often experience. Children under one year of age should generally not have overnight visitations. Linda Franke states, "In visitation, a baby under two should not be moved back and forth between the homes of the divorced parents, for example, but should stay put in one place and have the parents visit him."[66]

> "It's too hard for the young mind to integrate that lack of constancy," says Frank Williams at Thaliens Community Mental Health Center in Los Angeles. "A baby needs not only the familiar shapes of the room [but also] his own crib to make him feel secure. Not until the child is at least two years old does he or she have the maturity to tolerate spending alternate weekends or a summer stint as long as two weeks away from the familiarity of 'home.' In the interim, the baby will benefit from as much visitation as possible from the noncustodial parent."[67]

The concern for very young children has been addressed by Ciji Ware, who points out that children under two years of age should sleep in the same home to establish a home base. She suggests that the other parent visit on Monday, Wednesday, and all day Saturday.[68]

Franke looks at the way children of different ages respond to the process of divorce. She refers to the preschool years as the "age of guilt."[69] During this period children feel guilty about their parents' divorce. They may think, "If I had been a better child, my parents would not have gotten divorced." It is important for parents of preschool children to explain the process of divorce in simple terms. In doing so, make sure that they understand that their behavior did not cause the divorce. Parents must strive to act in an adult-like manner in the presence of their children. If their anger causes them to react childishly, it will only confuse their preschool-age children and make their adjustment to the divorce more difficult.

John Gottman and Lynn Fainsilber Katz performed research on four- and five-year-old children in an effort to determine how divorce affected the children's behavior. The researchers found that marital discord negatively affected the children's level of play, their peer interaction, and their physical health, and increased children's susceptibility to physical illness.[70]

As has been pointed out previously in this book, meta-analytic studies are not only popular in the literature today but also provide the reader the opportunity to understand the state of the art in a particular field at the time the meta-analysis is performed as opposed to just one author's point of view. Three meta-analytic studies were performed in the early 2000s to address the topic of children's adjustment to divorce. Joan Kelly[71] reviewed the empirical studies done between 1990 and 1999 and found that children of divorce certainly

---

[66] Linda Franke, Growing Up Divorced 70 (1983).

[67] *Id.*

[68] Ciji Ware, Sharing Parenthood after Divorce (1982).

[69] Linda Franke, Growing Up Divorced 70 (1983).

[70] John M. Gottman & Lynn Fainsilber Katz, *Effects of Marital Discord on Young Children's Peer Interaction and Health*, 25 Dev. Psychol. 373–81 (1989).

[71] Joan B. Kelly, *Children's Adjustment to Conflicted Marriage and Divorce: A Decade Review of Research*, 39 J. Am. Acad. Child & Adolescent Psychiatry 963–73 (2000).

have more adjustment problems than children from never-divorced parents. However, the newer research supports the notion that not all of these adjustment problems are a function of the divorce.[72] Kelly reports that her reading of the research suggests that education and nonadversarial approaches are viable alternatives. She supports the use of alternative dispute resolution techniques, except in cases of child abuse and neglect, substance abuse, violence, reduced mental capacity, and mental illness. In those cases she believes that the adversarial system is an effective process for protecting children and parents.[73]

The article written by Mary Whiteside and Betsy Jane Becker[74] reviewed the research from 1970 to 1994 for children who had experienced divorce when below five years of age. They indicate that the analysis suggests that the discussion with parents needs to shift from a preoccupation with the number of overnights to a more complicated assessment of the parenting environment. They also point out that the co-parenting relationship is critical, indicating that positive co-parenting relationships involve a supportive, cooperative environment, while negative co-parenting arrangements provide hostile, problematic, destructive patterns that leave the children at risk.[75] Last, they point out that poor parenting skills on the part of the less experienced parent can contribute to higher conflict between parents.[76]

Jenifer Kunz also performed a meta-analysis in 2001[77] and found that more recent studies show a reduction in the quality of the mother-child relationship with younger children.[78] The research suggests that parental divorce was negatively associated with mother-child, father-child, family, peer, and dating relationships.[79]

§ 4.17   Elementary School Years

Linda Franke refers to the years between six and eight as the "age of sadness."[80] Children at this age have come to rely on the security of the family structure and interpret disruption of that structure as a collapse of their entire protective environment. Their emotional immaturity prevents these children from protecting themselves against these losses. The child's survival is threatened because "loss of one parent implies the loss of the other as well." Franke states that

> [a]nger, fear, betrayal, in the disruptive post-divorce household, and a deep sense of deprivation are the characteristic responses of children this age to divorce. But above all, the children

---

[72] *Id.* at 963.

[73] *Id.* at 972.

[74] Mary Whiteside & Betsy Jane Becker, *Parental Factors and the Young Child's Post-Divorce Adjustment: A Meta-Analysis with Implications for Parenting Arrangements*, 14 J. Fam. Psychol. 5–26 (2000).

[75] *Id.* at 21.

[76] *Id.* at 22.

[77] Jenifer Kunz, *Parental Divorce and Children's Interpersonal Relationships: A Meta-Analysis*, 34 J. Divorce & Remarriage 19–47 (2001).

[78] *Id.* at 19.

[79] *Id.* at 39.

[80] Linda Franke, Growing Up Divorced 112 (1983).

feel sad, a persistent and sometimes crippling sadness that, even a year after the divorce, they have only been able to mute to resignation.[81]

The following example shows how this sadness pervades the child's life:

> Jacob is kicking a soccer ball around his backyard. In the garage he can see the oil stain where his father's car used to be and the hook where his father's golf bag used to hang. There are still a lot of tools on his father's workbench, but Jacob isn't allowed to touch them unless his father is there. And his father hasn't been there for six months. They were going to build a bicycle rack together, but that was before his father left. Now, they probably never will. Jacob halfheartedly kicks the ball again. But it isn't fun. Nothing seems to be fun these days.[82]

Sanford Braver and his associates found that "the most powerful factor in the [visitation] model was the noncustodial parent's perception that he/she had some control over the child's upbringing. Among fully employed noncustodial parents who reported high per-ceived control, there was an excellent record of involvement and child support payment."[83]

E. Mark Cummings, Patrick Davies, and Kelly Simpson point out that

> appraisals of coping efficiency and the threat posed by marital conflict predicted adjustment in boys, whereas self-blame was linked with externalizing problems for girls. The appraised destructiveness of conflict was significantly related to perceived threat in boys and self-blame in girls. Boys appeared more attuned or, alternatively, less shielded from marital conflict.[84]

§ 4.18   Middle School Years

The period from 9 to 12 years of age has been called the "age of anger."[85] This is a par-ticularly crucial period of time in the child's life. It is essential to resolve the anger that is experienced during this period. Otherwise, it will be carried forward into later childhood and early adulthood and be extremely disruptive to relationships. Franke states:

> The bad news follows naturally from much of the good news. As team players, children have a very strict sense of fairness, of what is right and what is wrong. . . . Children live by a rigid code of ethics that stresses black and white definitions of loyalty and behavior. When the very parent who taught the child these rules does not abide by them, the child becomes angry—very angry. It is this deep and unrelenting anger that most characterizes the reaction to divorce of late latency-age children. Unlike younger children, who fight against feelings of anger

---

[81] *Id.* at 90.

[82] *Id.* at 90–91.

[83] Sanford Braver et al., *A Longitudinal Study of Noncustodial Parents: Parents without Children*, 7 J. Fam. Psychol. no. 1, at 9–23 (1993).

[84] E. Mark Cummings et al., *Marital Conflict, Gender, and Children's Appraisals and Coping Efficiency as Mediators of Child Adjustment*, 8 J. Fam. Psychol. no. 2, at 141–49 (1994).

[85] Linda Franke, Growing Up Divorced 112 (1983).

toward a parent, these children often seek it out. Often the child chooses between the "good" and "bad," reserving so much hostility for the latter that visitation with the noncustodial parent sinks to an all-time low, especially for boys.[86]

Defusing the anger the child feels toward the parent is extremely important. Although it is tempting for the angry custodial parent to take advantage of the child's angry feelings, creating an alliance that may make the parent feel triumphant may prevent the child from resolving issues relating to the divorce and moving on. Furthermore, this approach has a tendency to backfire in adolescence. The child may become angry with the custodial parent for encouraging his anger toward the noncustodial parent during the late latency years. He may even go as far as accusing the custodial parent of preventing a relationship with the other parent. Psychotherapy can help deal with these extraordinarily volatile feelings. It is during this period that the seeds of alienation are often sewn.

Daniel Shybunko researched the effect of divorce on middle school children. He found that "for this particular age group, after a period of at least two years, the divorce process does not necessarily produce impaired parent-child relationships or impaired child adjustment."[87] The results did suggest, however, that children of divorced families were more inattentive, aggressive, and/or socially unpopular in school settings.

Irwin Sandler and his co-researchers studied 206 children between the ages of 8 and 15. They concluded, "In predicting children's self-reported maladjustment (a) stable, positive events but not changes in positive events were related to lower maladjustment; (b) increased negative events were related to high maladjustment; and (c) change for the worse was related to higher maladjustments."[88] Thomas Smith reports that children's school grades, but not their overall academic achievement, are affected by divorce and parental separation.[89]

§ 4.19   High School Years

Linda Franke refers to the teenage years as the "age of false maturity."[90] She feels that the developmental tasks of adolescence are both exaggerated and blurred by the divorce process. It is "during the teens, when a child begins to act and think as an adult, that the lasting effect[s] of a badly resolved divorce—parental abandonment, inattention, or overdependence suddenly jump to the fore."[91] It is less difficult to help teenage children through divorce than younger children, because teens have already begun gaining independence

---

[86] *Id.* at 113.

[87] D.E. Shybunko, *Effects of Post-Divorce Relationship on Child Adjustment, in* Children of Divorce: Developmental and Clinical Issues 299–313 (1989).

[88] Irwin Sandler et al., *Stability and Quality of Life Events and Psychological Symptomotology in Children of Divorce*, 19 Am. J. Community Psychol. 501–20 (1991).

[89] Thomas Evin Smith, *What a Difference Measure Makes: Parental-Separation Effect on School Grades, Not School Achievement*, 23 J. Divorce & Remarriage no. 3/4, at 151–65 (1995).

[90] Linda Franke, Growing Up Divorced 150 (1983).

[91] *Id.* at 152.

from their parents and have some stability of their own. Nevertheless, it is important to be totally honest with the teenage children as to why the marriage failed. If it was caused by extramarital affairs, alcoholism, mental illness, or abuse, the teenagers should be told, although they should be spared the gruesome details. If they sensed that any of these issues had become a problem, they will be glad to know that their perceptions were accurate. Because teenagers are entering the age when meaningful interpersonal relationships are likely to develop, it is extremely important to handle these issues properly at the time of divorce. If teenagers emerge from the divorce feeling that interpersonal relationships are not worth the effort, their own meaningful relationships will be disrupted. On the other hand, if teenagers realize that the dissolution of the parents' marriage was related only to the relationship between the two and is not a generalization applicable to all relationships, they are more likely to be able to sustain meaningful relationships. It is especially important, even with teenagers, to reassure them that their parents still love them and that the children did not cause the divorce.

Rex Forehand and his associates studied the functioning of adolescents for a two-year period after divorce. They studied 112 adolescents and found that adolescents from divorced families did not function as well as adolescents from intact families. The study examined the relationships in these adolescents' lives and found that the more conflict that existed between the children's parents, the greater the likelihood of problems in the parent-adolescent relationship. In turn, problems in the parent-adolescent relationship were predictors of difficulties in adolescent functioning.[92]

Abbie Frost and Bilge Pakiz studied 382 15-year-olds. They found that "those who experienced parental separation more recently were most likely to be adversely affected, and that girls from recently disrupted families were more likely than boys to experience problems in emotional and behavioral functioning and were likely to express dissatisfaction with available levels of social support."[93]

Bonnie Carlson specifically addressed how observing marital violence can affect adolescents. She studied 101 adolescents from residential treatment centers, approximately half of whom had witnessed marital violence. She found that many of the adolescents who had witnessed marital violence reported being depressed, running away, hitting their parents, and being struck by a parent's dating partners.[94]

Seminal research by E. Mavis Hetherington reports:

> [F]irst, gender differences in adverse responses to parents' marital transitions disappeared as children moved into adolescence. Second, early adolescence was a time of increased problem behaviors in children. . . . Adolescence often triggers problems in children of divorce and remarried families who have previously seemed to be coping well. Third, early adolescence was an especially deleterious time in which to have a remarriage occur and is still applicable today.[95]

---

[92] Rex Forehand et al., *Parental Divorce and Adolescent Maladjustment: Scientific Inquiry versus Public Information*, 30 Behav. Res. & Therapy no. 4, at 319–27 (1992).

[93] Abbie K. Frost & Bilge Pakiz, *The Effects of Marital Disruption on Adolescence: Time as a Dynamic*, 60 Am. J. Orthopsychiatry 544–50 (Oct. 1990).

[94] Bonnie E. Carlson, *Adolescent Observers of Marital Violence,* 5 J. Fam. Violence 285–99 (1990).

[95] E. Mavis Hetherington, *Divorce: A Child's Perspective*, 34 Am. Psychol. 851 (1979).

Eleanor Macoby and her co-researchers found that most fathers remained substantially involved in their children's lives, but that the parents' roles differed substantially after divorce. Mothers were still most likely to be responsible for residential care.[96]

§ 4.20   College and Young Adult Years

Cain is one of the few early researchers to examine the effects of parental divorce on college-age children.

> Preliminary findings suggest that young adult offspring are likely to deny their parents' impending divorce, are more likely to ascribe blame to one parent than blame themselves, to use aggressive morality as a conduit for rage, to experience a series of role realignments post-parental divorce, and to demonstrate altered attitudes toward romantic love and marriage following their parents' mid-life divorce.[97]

Bonkowski studied young adults between 18 and 21 years of age. She reported that when young adult children experienced their parents' divorce, they had difficulty establishing a separate relationship with each of the parents. Furthermore, they had a greater difficulty establishing a relationship with the father than the mother, possibly because fathers tended to be blamed for the divorce more frequently than mothers. Bonkowski concludes that although there was a lingering sadness in these adult children, most of them were able to overcome these concerns and progress in a developmentally appropriate way.[98]

Kathryn Franklin, Ronnie Janoff-Bulman, and John Roberts performed two studies with college-age children. They concluded that, although college-age children of divorce did not differ from intact family children on measures of depression and eight hypotheses tested, they were less optimistic about the success of their own future marriages and reported less trust in their future spouses.[99]

Jennifer Weiner and her associates found that "paternal indifference, lack of paternal caring, and maternal indifference were significant negative predictors of adjustment for college students from divorced families. Age at the time of divorce, gender, parental conflict, social support, and negative life events were not significant predictors."[100] They concluded, "The findings of this investigation may have implications for research and clinicians. First, young adult children of divorced families appear to present a different portrait of adjustment than short-term studies of young children indicate."[101]

---

[96] Eleanor Macoby et al., *Co-parenting in the Second Year after Divorce*, 52 J. Divorce & Fam. 141–55 (1990).

[97] B.S. Cain, *Parental Divorce during the College Years*, 52 Psychiatry 135–46 (1989).

[98] S.E. Bonkowski, *Lingering Sadness: Young Adults' Response to Parental Divorce*, 17 J. Contemp. Soc. Work 219–23 (1989).

[99] Kathryn Franklin et al., *Long-Term Impact of Parental Divorce on Optimism and Trust: Changes in General Assumptions or Narrow Beliefs?*, 59 J. Personality & Soc. Psychol. 743–55 (1990).

[100] Jennifer B. Weiner, *On Competence and Ethicality in Psycho-Diagnostic Assessment*, 53 J. Personality Assessment 827–31 (1989).

[101] *Id.*

Nicholas Zill and his co-researchers found that

> among 18 to 22 year-olds from disrupted families, 65% had poor relationships with their fathers and 30% with their mothers, 25% had dropped out of high school, and 40% had received psychological help. Even after controlling for demographic and socioeconomic differences, youths from disrupted families were twice as likely to exhibit these problems as youths from nondisrupted families. A significant effect of divorce on mother-child relationships was evident in adulthood, whereas none was found in adolescents. Youths experiencing disruption before six years of age showed poorer relationships with their fathers than those experiencing disruption later in childhood. Overall, remarriage did not have a protective effect, but there were indications of amelioration among those who experienced early disruption.[102]

Patricia Kozuch and Teresa Cooney present some very interesting data about young adult's attitudes as affected by the divorce process. They report that "youth reporting high parent conflict and those from recently divorced families were significantly more likely to favor cohabitation prior to marriage than those who were not. Young adults reporting high parental conflict were less likely than those reporting low parental conflict to agree that marriage is a life long commitment."[103] When addressing the issue of marriage as a lifelong commitment, "young from both intact and divorced families were more likely to agree with this item if the parents had low levels of parental conflict."[104]

§ 4.21   Academic Performance

Steven Kaye performed research with 234 children of divorce, comparing them with 223 children from intact families. Grades and achievement test scores in a variety of academic areas were recorded for five consecutive years. He reports:

> [T]he results showed that children had poor achievement test scores in the immediate aftermath of divorce. Their grades, on the other hand, did not seem to be adversely affected. By the fifth year following divorce, sex differences were pronounced with divorce adversely affecting the grades and achievement test scores of boys but not girls.[105]

Kaye also found that the poor academic performance in children of divorce lasted approximately two to three years. In addition, the research showed that the younger the child, the more likely divorce would adversely affect academic performance. Looking at content-specific areas, Kaye found that children of divorce showed poorer quantitative skills than did children from intact families.

---

[102] Nicholas Zill et al., *Long-Term Effects of Parental Divorce and Parent/Child Relationships, Adjustment and Achievement in Young Adulthood*, 7 J. Fam. Psychol. 91–103 (1993).

[103] Patricia Kozuch & Teresa M. Cooney, *Young Adults' Marital and Family Attitudes: The Role of Recent Parent Divorce, and Family and Parental Conflict*, 23 J. Divorce & Remarriage no. 3/4, at 45–62 (1995).

[104] *Id.*

[105] S. Kaye, *The Impact of Divorce on Children's Academic Performance, in* Children of Divorce: Development and Clinical Issues 283 (1989).

Lise Bisnaire, Philip Firestone, and David Rynard studied factors that affected academic achievement in children following parental separation:

> Elementary school children who maintained their academic performance following separation of their parents were compared with levels of those who declined. No single measure could accurately predict children's academic adjustment. Those who maintained performance level spent significantly more time with both parents. . . . In summary, 30 percent of the children in the present study experienced a marked decrease in their performance following parental separation, and this was still evident three years later. Access to both parents seemed to be the most predictive factor, in that it was associated with better adjustment.[106]

In addition, they found that the less time the mother spent at work and the more time the child spent with the noncustodial parent, the more academically competent the child was.

Debra Japzon Mulholland, Norman Watt, Anne Philpott, and Neil Sarlin reported similar results. They found that children of divorce showed academic deficits when compared with children from intact families even several years after the separation. They found "significant performance deficits in academic achievement, as reflected in grade point average and scholastic motivation in the middle school, but not in nationally normed tests of scholastic aptitude and other less direct measures of behavioral conformity."[107]

§ 4.22   Parents' Relationship after Divorce

Carol Masheter wrote two papers on the relationship between ex-spouses following divorce. In one study, she looked at friendly versus hostile feelings toward the ex-spouse and found that "contact was friendlier and quarreling was less frequent for those without children than with children. Lower well-being was associated with quarreling and preoccupation, whereas contact frequency and affect had no relationship to well-being."[108] Masheter concludes:

> Children of divorced couples need on-going contact with both parents. Therefore, divorced parents, though they may dislike or be indifferent to each other, must not let these feelings interfere with their children's relationships with both parents. The implication is that former marriage partners must cooperate sufficiently to permit on-going contact between each parent and the children. Such cooperation implies some sort of relationship between ex-spouses, though it may not be pleasant or easy.[109]

---

[106] Lise Bisnaire et al., *Factors Associated with Academic Achievement in Children following Parental Separation*, 60 Am. J. Orthopsychiatry 75 (1990).

[107] Debra J. Mulholland et al., *Academic Performance of Children of Divorce: Psychological Resilience and Vulnerability*, 54 Psychiatry 268 (1991).

[108] Carol Masheter, Post-Divorce Relationships between Ex-Spouses: The Roles of Attachment and Interpersonal Conflict 103 (1991).

[109] Carol Masheter, Post-Divorce Relationship Between Ex-Spouses: A Literature Review 118 (1990).

Eleanor Macoby and her co-researchers examined co-parenting dynamics during the second year after divorce. It is generally agreed that the first year after divorce involves a significant number of adjustment problems. They looked at children living either with mothers or fathers, or having dual residences. They reported that the residential placement of the children had little bearing on the amount of conflict between the divorced parents. They did note that although the residential arrangement did not appear to affect the amount of acrimony between parents, the initial level of discord between parents had a noticeable impact on the subsequent quality of co-parenting.[110]

§ 4.23   Parental Alienation Syndrome

Parental Alienation Syndrome: Does It Really Exist, and If So, What Is It?

The concept of "Parental Alienation Syndrome" (PAS) has been in the public arena for more than a decade. There has been considerable controversy generated regarding the use or misuse of this term. A distinction needs to be made between the concept of alienation and the possible existence of Parental Alienation Syndrome. If alienation occurs in a case, the reader must be aware that there are three possibilities for why the alienation occurs. The first is embodied in Gardner's lengthy explanations, which follow. However, children can also be alienated from the disfavored parent because of that parent's behavior. Last, the alienation could be occurring as a combination of both. Thus, it becomes the professional's responsibility to determine which of these factors is operative in each alienation case.

Gardner points out that mothers may program their children against their fathers in subtle and unconscious ways. By using the subtle manner, she can then proclaim innocence to any accusations of brainwashing. These subtle criticisms often take the form of indirect communications, such as, "There are things I could say about your father that would make your hair stand on end: but I am not the kind of person who criticizes a parent to his children."[111] Or "What do you mean you are going to your father's house? Oh, what am I saying, what's wrong, I shouldn't have said that. I shouldn't discourage you from seeing your father."[112] Parents who allow children to make the decision regarding visitation may indirectly tell them not to visit. A mother may say, "You have to go see your father. If you don't, he'll take us to court."[113] This is all done without mentioning any positive benefits that may result from visiting with the father. Another indirect way of alienating the child from the father occurs when the mother moves a considerable distance away for no other reason than to be far from the father.

Gardner identifies emotional factors within the child that may lead to Parental Alienation Syndrome. For instance, the child's psychological bond with the loved parent

---

[110] Eleanor Macoby et al., *Co-Parenting in the Second Year of Divorce*, 52 J. Divorce & Fam. 141–55 (1990).

[111] Richard Gardner, Family Evaluation and Child Custody, Mediation, Arbitration, and Litigation 226 (1989) [hereinafter Gardner].

[112] *Id.* at 239.

[113] *Id.* at 240.

may simply be stronger than the bond with the hated parent. If the child fears that this bond will be disrupted and that the preferred parent will become angry, the child may love the "loved" parent more and hate the "hated" parent more. Because he already feels abandoned by one parent, the child is unwilling to risk being abandoned by the other parent. "This fear of the loss of mother's love is the most important factor in development of the symptoms . . . of Parental Alienation Syndrome."[114]

What fathers do not realize is that this obsession with hatred is really a disguise for deep love; the child does not hate the father but rather is afraid of losing the mother's affection. Although Gardner does not use the term, this is often described as a loyalty issue.

Finally, Gardner identifies situational factors that can contribute to Parental Alienation Syndrome. He points out that the longer a child remains with a particular parent, the more the child will resist moving to the other parent. Another common situation is one "in which the child will develop complaints about the 'hated' parent in which the child has observed a sibling being treated harshly or even being rejected for expressing his/her affection for the 'hated' parent."[115]

In severe cases, "the mothers of these children are often fanatic. They use every mechanism at their disposal (legal and illegal) to prevent visitation. They are obsessed with antagonism towards their husbands. In many cases they are paranoid."[116] Unfortunately, these mothers do not respond to logic or appeals to reason. Children of these mothers end up being equally fanatic as a result of modeling their behavior. As a result, they can become panic-stricken when asked to visit their fathers. These panicked states become so severe as to render the possibility of visitation improbable. Unfortunately, cases of severe Parental Alienation Syndrome do not respond to traditional therapeutic approaches. Traditional therapy for the children is also not beneficial because the

> therapeutic exposure represents only a small fraction of the total amount of time of exposure to the mothers' denigrations of the father. This is a sick psychological bond here between the mother and children that is not going to be changed by therapy as long as the children remain living with the mother.[117]

Gardner believes that the first step in the treatment of children in this situation is to remove them from the mother's home and place them with the father. He also identifies very structured and drastic recommendations to facilitate this process:

> [F]ollowing this transfer, there must be a period of decompression and debriefing in which the mother has no opportunity at all for input to the children. The hope here is to give the children the opportunity to re-establish the relationship with the alienated father without significant contamination of the process by the brainwashing of the mother. Even telephone calls must be strictly prohibited for at least a few weeks, and perhaps longer. Then, according to the therapist's judgment, slowly increasing contacts with the mother may be limited.[118]

---

[114] *Id.* at 246.

[115] *Id.* at 249.

[116] *Id.* at 361.

[117] *Id.* at 362–63.

[118] *Id.* at 363.

Gardner notes that in some cases, the children may eventually be returned to the mother. However, if the mother continues to alienate the children, it may be necessary to consider never returning the children to the mother.

The fathers in these situations also need to be involved in individual therapy. The fathers must understand that the children do not sincerely hate them. A strong, healthy bond was established when the children were much younger, and the current allegations of hatred are merely a facet of a loyalty issue.

In moderate cases of Parental Alienation Syndrome, the mothers are not as fanatic:

> [T]hey are able to make some differentiation between allegations that are preposterous and those that are not. There is still, however, a campaign of denigration and a significant desire to withhold the children from the father as a vengeance maneuver. They will find a wide variety of excuses to interfere with or circumvent visitation.[119]

Children in this category are also less fanatic than those severely affected. Although they are likely to vilify the father in the presence of the mother, they are also likely to give up this attitude in the father's presence.

Gardner believes that these families should be seen in family therapy by one therapist rather than involving several therapists. The likelihood of manipulation may actually increase if several therapists take part. The therapist involved in this case must not succumb to the notion of "respecting the wishes" of the children and may actually have to be quite directive. The therapist must also be aware that "the older children may promulgate the mother's programming down to the younger ones.[120] The pathology extends itself when the mother relies on the older children to make sure that the younger children act accordingly with their father. If this becomes an ongoing problem, it can be recommended that the older children visit separately from the younger children.

If transition from the mother to the father becomes difficult, a neutral place, such as the therapist's office, the guardian ad litem's office, or a social service agency office, can be used for the transfer of the children.

It is also important for the therapist to understand that the mother may be continuing the acrimony in the relationship as a way of remaining in a relationship with the former husband. Although it may appear to be a perverted reason for doing so, it allows the mother to continue a relationship with the father. It becomes the therapist's obligation, if this is occurring, to help the mother move beyond that type of thinking. In cases of moderate Parental Alienation Syndrome, the fathers must learn not to take the children's vilifications too seriously. When the children engage in this type of denigration, the father must be encouraged to help avert their attention to healthier interchange. The entire therapy process can be aided if a therapist can "find some healthy 'insider' on the mother's side of the family."[121] Last, Gardner suggests that with moderate cases the therapist must be a strong individual who can be directive and structuring when necessary.

In mild cases of Parental Alienation Syndrome, mothers are generally more psychologically healthy than mothers in the moderate or severe cases. They recognize that alienation

---

[119] *Id.* at 365.

[120] *Id.* at 368.

[121] *Id.* at 372.

from the father may not be in their children's best interest and they are less likely to become involved in ongoing litigation. These mothers also recognize that protracted litigation could cause everyone in the family to suffer. Nevertheless, there may still be some minor acts of programming, but without paranoia. These children tend to be more interested in strengthening their position with their mother than in openly denigrating their father. When a final court order results in primary placement with the mother, the fear of being transferred to the father is reduced and the Parental Alienation Syndrome generally disappears.

Gardner points out "that without the proper placement of the child (for which a court order may be necessary) treatment may be futile."[122]

Gardner states that the guardian ad litem's role in these cases can be very important. He sees the guardian ad litem as being a potentially powerful ally for the therapist in working with the families where Parental Alienation Syndrome is present. However, he also points out that if the guardian ad litem is not familiar with the consequences of Parental Alienation Syndrome, the guardian ad litem may become manipulated into supporting the children's positions to their actual detriment. Because guardians ad litem are assigned to act in the best interest of their wards, they may have great difficulty supporting "coercive maneuvers" such as "insisting that the children visit with the father who they profess they hate" because "it goes so much against the traditional orientation to clients in which they often automatically align themselves with their client's cause."[123]

In 1998, Richard Gardner wrote an article addressing the issue of recommendations that should be made for dealing with parents who induce Parental Alienation Syndrome in their children. He stated then, as previously, that in severe Parental Alienation Syndrome cases it is likely to be necessary to transfer the children from the alienating parent at the "transitional site" during this transfer period. He suggests that the transitional site could be the home of a friend or relative, a community shelter, or hospitalization, depending upon how restrictive the environment would need to be. He also suggests a six-phase process for this transition. Phase 1 involves placement of the child in the transitional site. Following Phase 1, the child will begin to visit with his/her father for short periods of time at their home (Phase 2), eventually leading to the child's leaving the transitional site to live with his/her father on an ongoing basis (Phase 3). During this time, there would be no contact with his/her mother. During Phase 4, carefully monitored contact with the mother could commence on a trial basis, leading to monitored visits with the mother in the father's home (Phase 5). Eventually, these monitored visits can be attempted in the mother's home (Phase 6).

In his concluding remarks, Gardner states, "the *diagnosis* PAS is not made on the basis of the programmer's efforts, but the degree of the 'success' in each child. The *treatment* is based not only on the degree to which the child has been alienated but also on the mother's degree of attempted indoctrinations. In most cases the mother will remain the primary custodial parent. It is only when she cannot, or will not, inhibit herself from such indoctrinations that custodial transfer and the transitional site program should be implemented."[124]

---

[122] *Id.* at 374.

[123] *Id.* at 375.

[124] Richard Gardner, *Recommendations for Dealing with Parents Who Induce Parental Alienation Syndrome in Their Children,* 28 J. Divorce & Remarriage 22–23 (1998).

A number of authors have written about Parental Alienation Syndrome in recent years. Several of those authors' comments are addressed below.

In 1997, Deirdre Conway Rand wrote a two-part article talking about the spectrum of Parental Alienation Syndrome.[125] Dr. Rand offered a thorough review of the literature and provided case studies that support the diagnosis of Parental Alienation Syndrome. Much of the literature that she quotes does not directly address the issue of Parental Alienation Syndrome but deals with parallel issues from which she generalizes. Many of the supportive articles that are discussed are anecdotal reports as opposed to complete research studies. Rand points out that one of the by-products of Parental Alienation Syndrome, in some cases, is parents' making false sexual abuse allegations. She also makes a connection between Parental Alienation Syndrome and Munchausen Syndrome by Proxy.

A very through discussion in Rand's article about how children respond to high-conflict divorce is valuable, but not necessarily supportive of the existence of a Parental Alienation Syndrome. It is difficult to determine why Rand generalizes Garbarino's descriptors (see **Chapter 12**) for childhood maltreatment as being adapted to describe Parental Alienation Syndrome. When Rand discusses the involvement of third parties, the reader is made aware of the fact that additional parties can promote, foster, or expand the alienation process. New partners, mental health professionals, and therapists can all directly or indirectly foster the alienation process. However, the fact that attorneys may have written such articles does not necessarily add to the credibility or the validity of the concept. The author relies too heavily on using professional writings that reference Parental Alienation Syndrome as an indication of its acceptance. She also quotes a study by Nicholas that utilized 21 complete surveys. The results of a survey that utilizes such a small sample are put in question.

In summary, Rand relies on anecdotal information, studies with small samples, and the inclusion of Gardner's Parental Alienation Syndrome concept in literature as being equivalent to acceptance and validity of the concept. Individually or collectively, these sources do not adequately validate evidence of PAS.

Dr. Lowenstein, a consulting psychologist in the United Kingdom, addresses the use of mediation in dealing with Parental Alienation Syndrome as an alternative. He points out that "warring parents are a problem and that little can be achieved through this approach, and certainly those who suffer the most as a result are likely to be the children who are confused by warring parents, or who are poisoned by one parent against the other."[126] He suggests that engaging in the mediation process takes the case out of the legal arena and puts it into the mental health arena. However, in the United States this may not be the case as some states do not exempt mediators from subpoena for testimony.

Kathleen Coulborn Faller has written extensively on sexual-abuse-related issues. Her 1998 article addresses the use of Parental Alienation Syndrome in various settings. She points out that the "Parental Alienation Syndrome offers an explanation for reports of sexual abuse when parents are divorcing or are divorced."[127] Faller is highly critical of

---

[125] Diedre Conway Rand, *The Spectrum of Parental Alienation Syndrome (Part 1)*, 15 Am. J. Forensic Psychol. 53–92 (1997b).

[126] L.F. Lowenstein, *Parental Alienation Syndrome: A Two-Step Approach toward a Solution*, 20 Contemp. Fam. 514 (1998).

[127] Kathleen Coulborn Faller, *The Parental Alienation Syndrome: What IS It and What Data Support It?*, 3 Child Maltreatment 100–15 (1998).

Gardner's claims, indicating that Gardner uses many percentages that are not supported by research, stating, for example, that "90 percent of the time the accusing parent is the child's mother."[128]

Faller spends a considerable portion of her article addressing Gardner's Sexual Abuse Legitimacy Scale (SALS). She states that "the SALS has been used by Gardner and others who accept his idea, in conjunction with the Parental Alienation Syndrome."[129] Faller postulates that "further examination of the 84 factors in the SALS indicates that its primary function is diagnosis of the Parental Alienation Syndrome." [130] She further states, "[B]ecause the SALS has not been validated and, in fact, had not been the subject of any research; because it was based on Gardner's assumption about divorce allegations; and because its language lacked neutrality, it has been the subject of considerable criticism."[131]

Faller further states that "Gardner does not provide research findings to substantiate his assertions about the proposed characteristics and dynamics of the Parental Alienation Syndrome. . . . It is important to appreciate the consequences of the fact that Gardner published the vast majority of his work himself. His own press, Creative Therapeutics, only published his material and no works of other writers. . . . Thus, his ideas are not critically evaluated by others knowledgeable in the field before they appear in print."[132] Although there is a body of literature that exists on false sexual allegations, little or none of it references Gardner's work.

Much of the Faller article is devoted to research findings that do not support Gardner's points of view. Faller states, "[A]gain, the research findings from large samples with defined methodology do not support Gardner's assertion that large numbers of mothers (or others) involved in divorce make false allegations, either by design or because they are mentally ill."[133] She later states, "[T]herefore, it appears that experts in sexual abuse disagree with Gardner's (1991) assertion that sexual statements and sexualized behavior are characteristic of nonabused children and can be spontaneously generated by sexual fantasy."[134] Furthermore, she states, "[T]here are no data that support a conclusion that because children have sexual knowledge, they will use this information to make false allegations of sexual abuse."[135]

Faller concludes by dealing with the diagnostic label "Parental Alienation Syndrome" itself, pointing out that the *Diagnostic and Statistical Manual of Mental Disorders-Fourth Edition* (DSM-IV) does not include a diagnosis of Parental Alienation Syndrome. She states that "Parental Alienation Syndrome is a nondiagnostic syndrome. It only explains the behavior of the child and the mother, if the child has not been sexually abused."[136] She goes on to state, "[A]n additional problem described with Parental Alienation Syndrome is

---

[128] *Id.*

[129] *Id.* at 105.

[130] *Id.*

[131] *Id.*

[132] *Id.* at 106.

[133] *Id.* at 108.

[134] *Id.* at 110.

[135] *Id.*

[136] *Id.* at 111.

that virtually every symptom described by Gardner is evidence of its presence, and consequent false charges against the accused parent are open to opposing interpretations."[137]

As further substantiation of the concerns generated by Kathleen Faller, the present author experienced Gardner's approach firsthand in a divorce case that included a sexual abuse allegation. Gardner provided more than 100 criteria that could be used for evaluating whether sexual abuse had occurred or not. He provided no scientific research support, validation studies, or replication by other researchers to support his contentions of the more than 100 criteria. As a result, we were faced with "the gospel according to Dr. Richard Gardner." The 100 criteria were clearly supportive of findings of false allegations. Some representative examples included Gardner's statement that sexual abuse perpetrators are often intellectually impaired. Because the father was not intellectually impaired, this would be an indication of a false allegation. Merely because the allegation was part of a child custody dispute, Gardner gave an additional false rating. Because the child did not tell the story exactly the same way each time, there was further indication to Gardner that it was a false allegation. He stated that victims of sexual abuse will show depersonalization, dissociation, attitude toward one's genitals, sexual organ anesthesia, and stigmatization. Because the four-year-old victim did not report any of these types of symptomotology, these would be five additional indications that it was a false allegation, according to Gardner. Eight of the items were also considered to be indications of false allegations because of Gardner's interpretation of the projective drawings. Furthermore, because the four-year-old victim did not run away from home, and victims often run away from home, this would be a further indication of a false allegation. He also used mutually exclusive criteria, stating that perpetrators are coercive and dominating, as well as passive and having impaired self-assertion. A person cannot be both of these. Therefore, at least one of them would be rated an indicator of a false allegation. The judge found that the weight of the evidence was that Gardner functioned as a "hired gun" in this case.

When Gardner finished his evaluation, he indicated that 52 criteria suggested a false allegation, two criteria suggested a true allegation, and four of the criteria were equivocal. When those same variables were scrutinized separately by two other mental health professionals, one rated 12 of them as indicating false allegations, and 19 of them as indicating true allegation, with 23 being equivocal, and six nonapplicable, while the other found 30 of the criteria to suggest a true allegation.

Gardner was an accomplished mental health professional in the area of divorce-related issues. He has published many books, developed therapeutic techniques, and been innovative in his approaches. However, some feel he went astray in the past 5 to 10 years with his work in the area of sexual abuse allegations, especially as it relates to the concept of Parental Alienation Syndrome. Furthermore, there has been an "unholy alliance," whether developed through conscious efforts or accident, between the concept of False Memory Syndrome and Parental Alienation Syndrome. There are divorce cases in which a professional's opinions have been rendered that a false sexual abuse allegation is false because of Parental Alienation Syndrome and/or the False Memory Syndrome.

In addition, criticism has been leveled against Gardner for using the term "diagnosis" in relation to Parental Alienation Syndrome. Authors have written about the fact that there is no diagnostic manual that lists Parental Alienation Syndrome and/or its symptoms, thus

---

[137] *Id.*

stating that Parental Alienation Syndrome does not exist. This may be a rather hollow argument in that parents do alienate children from the other parent and the concept of alienation exists, whether we give it a diagnostic label of Parental Alienation Syndrome or not. Gardner has raised the level of consciousness of psychologists, attorneys, and courts to recognize the fact that alienation occurs. The danger, however, is when it becomes the answer every time a parent is concerned that visitation or placement is not going as he/she would like it to. Research and therapeutic efforts need to focus on how to identify when alienation is or is not occurring, therapeutic interventions when it does occur, and outcome studies instead of embroiling psychologists in the controversy whether a diagnostic label exists or does not.

Case Studies

Three different case studies follow. Case Study #1 demonstrates how the father's initial behavior could alienate the children from him but is followed by the mother's alienating behavior. Case Study #2 is a case where, although the father is accused of alienating the children from the mother, the mother's behavior has clearly alienated the children from her. Case Study #3 is an example of a situation in which the mother's behavior has exclusively alienated the children from their father, and she seriously interfered with their being able to see their father.

Case Study #1

Tom and Helen Garrison were married to one another for 10 years. Their children, Nancy and Edward, lived with them throughout the marriage. Tom, a professor in the community, became addicted to prescription medications through a number of illegal activities. His behavior became erratic, abusive, and withdrawn. As a result, Helen decided to divorce Tom. There is no question at the time that Nancy and Edward would live with their mother.

Over a four-year period of time, Helen engaged in an unending campaign against the father, identifying how bad a person he was, how abusive he had been, and that he was nothing more than a drug addict. Although Tom's professional license had been suspended, he had his license returned, had been clean and sober for more than five years, and was back to functioning as a professor in the community.

One contempt motion after another was brought against Helen by Tom for interfering with his placement rights. He had not seen his children for four years. Finally, after many contempt warnings, the court issued an order that essentially said, "[F]or every time your children do not visit with father at the prescribed times, you will be found in contempt and spend three days in jail." This author was appointed as the therapist to help reunite Tom with his children and help foster a relationship among them. It should be noted that once the "jail" order was issued, the children never missed a placement period with their father.

During the four-year period of time that the children did not see their father, Helen would require the children to write letters to their father in their own handwriting, which she dictated, indicating they did not want to see their father. On other occasions, she would write the letters herself and ask the children to copy them in their own handwriting. On still other occasions, she perjured herself in court when giving testimony about what the children had said their father had done.

When therapy commenced in fall of 1996, the children's denigration of their father during the sessions was merciless and very hard to listen to. As time went on, visits with their father at the office were commenced; followed by several-hour visits that commenced at the office, moved into the community, and terminated at the office; followed by all-day visits; followed by overnight visits; followed by visits with their father in an adjacent city. As time passed, the children came to realize that their father was not the ogre their mother had portrayed, that he was not still a drug addict, and that he was actually quite pleasant. Nancy and Ed became more integrated into their father's life, spent more time with their father, and eventually traveled with their father, his new wife, and their new stepsister.

When Nancy reached 16 years of age, she was unable to handle being with her mother and stepfather anymore, and requested to live with Tom. In the process of doing so, she disclosed to this author and the guardian ad litem all of the lies that had been perpetrated by her mother and carried out by her, all the manipulations that had occurred, and how she needed to leave that environment. She shook and sobbed uncontrollably as she described this entire set of circumstances. An immediate emergency transfer placement was made, and Nancy went to live with her father, stepmother, and half-sister.

Unfortunately, the damage had already been done. Moving in with her father did not appear to be the "magical" answer that Nancy had hoped it would be. She eventually ended up going through a series of mental health interventions, including inpatient hospitalizations, day hospital, and residential treatment. To this date, she is not fully recovered from the adverse effect of the alienation that her mother fostered toward her father.

Although in this case the father initially engaged in behavior that could result in being alienation against him, it was the mother's incessant need to punish the father for his previous "sins" and her ongoing alienation that adversely affected the children. Unfortunately, one of the factors that parents do not consider when they are alienating their children against the other parent is the long-term negative psychological impact of requiring their children to engage in such behavior.

Case Study #2

Kelly is an accountant and Michael a dentist. Both have reached the upper levels of professional competence and respect within the community. They have been divorced for seven years. As of the writing of this chapter, Kelly has not spent any meaningful time with her children in the last seven-and-a-half years, and claims that it is a function of alienation of the children by Michael against her. When the divorce was originally granted, Kelly was given primary placement of the children (two boys and two girls), and Michael was seeing them on an alternating-weekend basis. As time passed, Kelly's behavior became more erratic and of concern to the guardian ad litem. By mutual agreement of the attorneys, this author was appointed the therapist for the children to help them deal with the fallout of divorce and the acrimony that existed between their parents. As a result of this therapy, it quickly became apparent that Kelly's erratic behavior had a psychotic-like or dissociative quality about it. There were times that she would go into incoherent screaming rages, call her children by non-family member names, not provide food for the children, lock the children out of the house, leave town for the weekend, leave a six-year-old to wander the neighborhood, and other similar behaviors. After approximately six months of attempting to work with this problem, the guardian ad litem, with this author's help, filed a motion to transfer placement of the children from the mother to the father.

As part of the court order, Kelly was required to engage in therapy prior to being allowed to have visits with her children. She indicated that she did not need therapy and that it was her ex-husband who had the psychological or psychiatric problems. As a result, a considerable period of time passed before Kelly was willing to engage in therapy and before the process of reuniting Kelly with her children was commenced. A series of meetings were held with Kelly and her therapist, the attorney, the guardian at litem, and this author.

The mother had not seen the children for four months. She was informed that the ground rules for the meetings would include no discussion about substance abuse, physical abuse, the legal matters, or name-calling. She was also informed that she would be warned twice if she engaged in these types of behavior, and after the third occurrence the visit would be terminated.

The visit commenced with the mother complaining about the fact that the contact started four minutes late. All of the children crowded on a small sofa designed to seat two people in an effort to prevent their mother from sitting on the sofa with them. She asked for hugs from the children, they refused, and she began forcibly pulling them off the sofa in an attempt to get them to hug her. She brought a deck of cards with her to play a game with the children. She had a specific game in mind; the children did not want to play the game, wanted to play a game of their own, and she was unable to be flexible enough to defer to their wishes.

Five minutes into the visit, the mother found it necessary to tell the children that she did not trust this psychologist and that this psychologist had lied to her. It was apparent that this behavior on the mother's part upset three of the children, two of them asking to leave, and one sitting in a corner with her back to her mother. With the remaining child, the mother walked over to about four inches from her face and started berating her about something she said. The topic again turned to this psychologist and accusing the children of having misinformation. At this point, one of the children reported that she felt like she was going to throw up, and two of the others begged to have their mother stop saying what she was saying. After several warnings about her yelling at the children, criticizing her ex-husband, and other inappropriate behaviors, it was announced that the visit would end 19 minutes after it started. The children literally ran out of the room to leave the session when they were told they could. Following the termination of the visit, the mother was out of control, yelling, making accusatory statements, and telling people in the waiting room how "cruel" this psychologist was.

In the middle of this process, Kelly decided to sue the guardian ad litem and the therapist for malpractice for prohibiting contact with the children. The suit was found to be frivolous and was dismissed on a summary judgment. Unfortunately, the filing of the suit delayed the time for reconnecting the children with their mother.

After a delay of a year and a half, the process was reinstituted and a series of meetings with the same set of children was commenced. These meetings resulted in a schedule of sessions between the mother and her children in this therapist's office, with the mother's therapist present to help out with the process. The contacts were so stressful that the children all suffered adversely. One of the children became suicidal, one developed an eating disorder, and two had to repeat a grade in school. As a result, it was decided by all of the professionals that these contacts should once again be terminated.

Following these failed contacts, it was decided that each child, upon reaching 16 years of age, would be free to contact their mother if they chose. Because, at 16 years of age, each of the children would have a driver's license, it was felt that this freedom of contact should be acknowledged, instead of requiring a child to sneak to see his or her mother in an attempt to make a contact, if they desired to do so.

During the period of time between transfer of placement and the writing of this chapter (approximately seven and a half years), there have been hundreds, if not thousands, of violations of the court order by the mother. There were times that she would call the children's home as many as 25 times in an evening; she showed up at children's activities, drove past the house, tried to intercept one of the children at a school bus stop, and wrote inappropriate letters to the children, among many other damaging activities, all of which were prohibited by the existing court orders.

It should be understood that Michael was not without fault in the way that he handled these matters. There were times that he lost his temper with Kelly and called her names in front of the children. He was not as encouraging as he could have been in having the children send pictures of themselves, report cards, and presents to their mother. In addition, although he recognized that Kelly was in contempt of court dozens of times, he refused to file contempt motions; he did not want to put his children through potentially seeing their mother arrested and jailed for these offenses, since they had already been through enough. Although not perfect, Michael's inappropriate behaviors, for the most part, were a reaction to Kelly's aberrant behavior and not a function of his desire to alienate the children from their mother. On more than one occasion, he sat in this therapist's office lamenting the fact that his children did not have a healthy mother or a healthy relationship with their mother, and was distressed over same.

This is clearly a case where any alienation that the children have toward their mother is a function of her own behavior and not a function of the father's trying to keep them from their mother.

Case Study #3

Todd and Carol divorced after seven years of marriage, with three children, ages one, three, and five years old. Four years later, this author was asked by the court to review the case since serious allegations of alienation had been made. Unlike many cases of this nature, neither party had funds to pursue an extended court battle. As a result, any services performed would be paid by the County Court. Two years prior to my involvement, another psychologist performed an evaluation, opined that there was severe alienation, and recommended that the children be transferred from the mother to the father with no contact between the mother and the children for an extended period of time (a la Gardner).

During the four-year period of time during which the father had not seen the children, the children accused their father of engaging in a whole myriad of inappropriate behaviors, including physical abuse, sexual abuse, psychological abuse, substance abuse, manipulation, and other behaviors. The children had assumed the last name of their stepfather, informed their father that he was not their father, and called their stepfather "Dad." The mother had not sent pictures, medical records, school records, or other important documents to the father since the time of the divorce. Furthermore, the five-year-old daughter claimed that she remembered being sexually abused by her father four years earlier. She reported that her mother had told her about the sexual abuse. The nine-year-old boy threatened suicide if required to spend any time with his father. Upon observation of the children with their father in my office, there was a nonstop litany of denigrating statements toward the father, stated in a matter-of-fact, even-tempered, nonemotional manner.

They all told the father that he was not their father, that they wished that he was dead, and that they never wanted to see him again.

The school social worker from the school the children attended had been drawn into the fray and became an ally of the mother's. A relative neophyte to the profession, the social worker gleefully reported to the psychologist that the children verified everything that the mother had said about the father. Carol also came to the school the first day of school and provided the social worker with the negative litany about the father. Last, the social worker felt it should be the children's choice as to which last name they used, and saw no problem with their selecting their stepfather's last name.

The guardian ad litem recognized a significant amount of alienation had occurred but was fearful of forcing any contact between the father and the children for fear that the nine-year-old would follow through in his threat to attempt or commit suicide. This psychologist felt that although suicidal ideation should always be taken seriously, it was more a manipulation on the nine-year-old's part than an actual thought, let alone a plan. The fact that he was able to sit in the room with the father without being upset, and express no suicidal ideation, during or after the contact, made this psychologist question the veracity of the suicidal claims.

A team comprising me, another psychologist, and a psychology intern pored over the records, performed evaluations, and interviews, and contacted collateral sources. There were a handful of behaviors that the father engaged in that could have alienated him from the children. On the other hand, close to 50 alienating behaviors that the mother had engaged in during the past four years were identified through this process. As a result, it was concluded that the mother had engaged in an extraordinary ongoing campaign to alienate the children from their father. It was also apparent that the children could not live with their mother without hating their father. Furthermore, it was opined that if the father magically dropped out of the children's lives, they would not automatically become adjusted. They already learned that the negative behaviors in which they were engaging would get attention and provide secondary gains for them. As a result, it was further stated that these negative behaviors would follow them into adulthood whether the father was present or not.

In conclusion, there were five options available to be recommended to the court in this case:

1. Children remain with the mother and never see the father.
2. Children remain with the mother and be engaged in forced visitation with the father.
3. Children are transferred to the father without seeing the mother for an extended period of time.
4. Children are transferred to the father and have weekend supervised contacts with the mother.
5. Children are placed in foster care.

The report was made to the court that some drastic measure would be necessary to facilitate this process. As a result, the court was left with the choice of either transferring the children to the father without seeing their mother for an extended period of time, or having the children remain with the mother with forced visits with the father, coupled with severe sanctions against the mother, as in Case Study #1 above, for every time the children did not visit with their father. Because the children's therapist, the guardian ad litem, and the school social worker are concerned about the suicidal ideation, the choice of remaining with the mother and having forced visitation with the father, coupled with severe sanctions, is the one the court will likely endorse.

Concluding Remarks on Parental Alienation Syndrome

The label of Parental Alienation Syndrome has been around for slightly more than a decade. It was initially greeted with enthusiasm by both the mental health and legal professionals in the late 80s and early 90s as being a descriptor of loyalty-related issues. However, since that time, many authors and other mental health professionals throughout the country have been unable to find empirical studies that validate many of the notions presented by Gardner. There are many mental health professionals who are disheartened by their perception of his misuse of the Parental Alienation Syndrome concepts as being indicators of false sexual abuse allegations.

As a result, it is suggested that Parental Alienation Syndrome be used by attorneys as nothing more than a descriptor for loyalty issue problems. This author is not aware of any judges who have embraced the harsh recommendations that Gardner suggest for resolving severe Parental Alienation Syndrome.

Gardner[138] published his last article about Parental Alienation Syndrome shortly before he died. It appears as if the article was written based on the significant criticism that had been leveled against Gardner's description of Parental Alienation Syndrome and the radical interventions that he recommended. He points out that many professionals prefer to use the term parental alienation instead of Parental Alienation Syndrome. However, he continues to defend the term Parental Alienation Syndrome and argues that the full term "Parental Alienation Syndrome" should be utilized and not simply parental alienation. However, with all due respect to Gardner's position, a majority of professionals feel that the use of the term parental alienation is preferable to Parental Alienation Syndrome.

Carol Bruch[139] addresses the Parental Alienation Syndrome concept as a loyalty issue concern. She states, "PAS as developed and purveyed by Richard Gardner has neither a logical nor a scientific basis. It is rejected by responsible social scientists and lacks solid grounding in psychological theory or research."[140]

Jayne Major[141] discussed the issue of how parents can successfully fight Parental Alienation Syndrome. She suggests using parenting courses, managing anger, not giving up, getting legal representation, using a forensic evaluator, keeping the best interests of children at heart, understanding the nature of alienation, keeping a diary or journal of key events, always calling or showing up when a parent is supposed to, focusing on enjoying the child's company, not violating court orders, and making sure the children know that they are loved.

---

[138] Richard A. Gardner, *Parental Alienation Syndrome verses Parental Alienation: Which Diagnosis Should Evaluators Use in Child-Custody Disputes*, 30 Am. J. Fam. Therapy 93–115 (2002).

[139] Carol Bruch, *Parental Alienation Syndrome and Alienated Children—Getting It Wrong in Child Custody Cases*, 14 Child & Fam. L.Q. 381–400 (2002).

[140] *Id.* at 399.

[141] A. Jayne Major, *Parents Who Have Successfully Fought Parent Alienation Syndrome, at* www.livingmedia.com 1–9 (2000).

§ 4.24   Added Problems of Divorce

This section reflects a combination of 30 years of experience by one of the authors of this book, in working with divorce cases. Many of the problems reported are also reported by other therapists and research.

During the divorce process, it is not only the parents who are getting divorced. The child gets divorced, too, even though the legal document does not specifically record the children's names. Interest in normal childhood activities decreases at this time. It is almost as if the child is saying, "What's the use? Mom and Dad are getting divorced, so why should I worry about something as trivial as school?" The child becomes preoccupied with the divorce and, as a result, may be distracted easily. This preoccupation is manifested in feelings of anger, helplessness, and insecurity. The child's teacher may be trying to explain an important concept, but the child is wondering how much longer he will be in that school or neighborhood. Often, academic performance can be a barometer of how the divorce is affecting the child. When a former A or B student suddenly becomes a C or D student, and there are no other major problems, the divorce is obviously having a dramatic effect on the child.

A wish for reconciliation.   Children of divorce often carry with them the magical wish that their parents will reconcile. In a significant number of cases, this wish is carried into adulthood. Unfortunately, the issue is frequently ignored by the parents. As a result, it remains unresolved in adulthood. When one of the parents decides to date or to remarry, this unresolved issue may cause problems. A child may try to interfere with the parent's decision, not because of a dislike for the new person or the inability to get along, but because the new person is interfering with the fantasy that the natural parents will get back together. The child reasons, "If Mom marries this man, then she cannot remarry Dad." In this situation, children may consciously or unconsciously act inappropriately in an effort to sabotage the upcoming marriage.

Details of placement.   The post-divorce adjustment period involves working out the details of placement. It remains to be seen if the custodial and non-custodial parents are going to be reasonable about visitation. Often, the non-custodial parent will see the children twice a week at first. However, four years later the children may be lucky to see this parent twice a year.

With younger children, it is important for the non-custodial parent to see the children more, rather than less, frequently. It is equally important for the custodial parent to be flexible. When the custodial parent becomes too rigid in the visitation schedule, it is difficult for the children to handle. Flexibility is important because of special events or simply unexpected changes in scheduling.

Availability of appropriate role models.   Another problem associated with divorce is that the child may not have an appropriate gender role model. This tends to be a problem more often with male children than with female children. Most frequently the mother becomes the custodial or primary placement parent, and the female child has an appropriate gender role model. It is very important for a male child also to have a strong male role model available. This is particularly true during the onset of pubescence and adolescence. An uncle, an older cousin, or an organization like Boy Scouts or Big Brothers can provide this type of role model. Although the Big Brother organization can be beneficial, there is one key concern with this group—it requires only a one-year commitment. Consequently, just as the child is becoming comfortable with his new big brother, the big brother may leave his life, which may be experienced as additional abandonment or rejection that the child must resolve.

In addition to not having an appropriate gender role model, the child may not have an appropriate heterosexual relationship model. It is important for children to see their parents hug or kiss other adults within a meaningful relationship. After the divorce it can also be important for children to see their parents experience anger and then resolve it. The process of resolving disagreement is often absent in a divorce situation. Immediately prior to the divorce, children may see only the arguing but no resolution. They do not have the opportunity to see their mother and father interacting positively as husband and wife. As a result, their last male-female relationship model has been a negative one.

When this type of positive model is absent, children may have difficulty establishing their own relationships as they approach adulthood. They may not know how to establish good, healthy heterosexual relationships because they have never witnessed one during their childhood. Typically, divorce begets divorce. Their parents got divorced, and often the children never saw an appropriate model for establishing a meaningful heterosexual relationship. When these children get married and have difficulties within their own marriages, they see divorce as the means of resolving these difficulties rather than developing the interpersonal communication skills that could affect resolution of the problems.

Minimizing the Problems

Parents can do several things at the outset of divorce to prevent some of the problems. These problems can be minimized by following the suggestions in **Chapter 5.**

Spring Dawson-McClure[142] and her associates performed a six-year longitudinal study examining the effects of prevention programs that had been developed for children of divorced families. A risk index was used involving the variables of environmental stressors and externalizing problems. This index was highly predictive of internalizing and externalizing problems, competence, substance use, and mental disorders six years later. The study indicated that children who had higher risk scores showed greater program effects than those who had lower risk scores. The study clearly confirms that intervention programs are useful for children who have at-risk behaviors.

§ 4.25   Parental Factors

Fathers

A number of researchers have evaluated the specific effect of divorce on fathers' roles. These studies looked at the differences between joint custody and non-custodial fathers,

---

[142] Spring R. Dawson-McClure, Irwin N. Sandler, Sharlene A. Wolchik, & Roger E. Millsap, *Risk as a Moderator of the Effects of Prevention Programs for Children from Divorced Families*, 32 J. Abnormal Child Psychol. 175–90 (2004).

frequency of visitation, the attitudes of the single custodial father, and the relationships between single fathers and their children.

Geoffrey Greif and Alfred DeMaris studied 1,132 single fathers in an effort to identify their characteristics.[143] They concluded that single fathers should be considered in the same context as single mothers. The same social dynamic issues must be addressed with single fathers as with single mothers. In another study, Greif and DeMaris concluded that fathers no longer must have significant financial means to obtain custody. Furthermore, fathers should not be discouraged from pursuing placement of children based exclusively on the age of the children.

Dennis Facchino and Arthur Aron found that "single parent fathers were likely to be better adjusted if they were older and had completed college, if they had older children and had greater percentages of custody, and if they were dating."[144] Joyce Arditti found that joint custody fathers "saw their children more frequently, showed greater satisfaction with their custody arrangement, and had more education than fathers without custody."[145]

Judith Seltzer looked at the relationships between fathers and children who live with their mothers.[146] She found that fathers who visit with their children are more likely to pay child support and be influential in child-rearing decisions.

Joseph Healy and his co-researchers found that both frequency and regularity of fathers' visits positively correlate with their children's self-esteem.[147] A reduction in the frequency or regularity is also related to behavior problems for young children.

Constance Ahrons and Richard Miller studied the effect of post-divorce relationships based on paternal involvement. They concluded that the quality of the post-divorce relationships between mothers and fathers had a significant impact on the father's relationship with the children. "These results also suggest that the woman's perception of the quality of the relationship has a greater impact on the men's perception of the level of father involvement and contact."[148]

Hetherington, Bridges, and Insabella[149] reported that non-custodial fathers were more likely to see their children regularly and to make regular support payments when mediation occurred. However, non-custodial fathers generally became more permissive after the divorce by relaxing rules and consequences for inappropriate behavior, perhaps in an

---

[143] Geoffrey Greif & Alfred DeMaris, *Single Parents with Custody*, 18 J. Contemp. Hum. Services 259–66 (1990).

[144] Dennis Facchino & Arthur Aron, Divorced Fathers for Custody: Method of Obtaining Custody and Divorce Adjustment 45 (1990).

[145] Joyce Arditti, Differences between Fathers with Joint Custody and Non-Custodial Fathers 186 (1992).

[146] Judith Seltzer, *Relationships between Fathers and Children Who Live Apart: The Father's Role after Separation*, 53 J. Marriage & Fam. 79–101 (Feb. 1991).

[147] Joseph Healy et al., *Children of Their Fathers after Parental Separation*, 60 Am. J. Orthopsychiatry no. 4, at 531–43 (Oct. 1990).

[148] Constance Ahrons & Richard Miller, *The Effect of the Post-Divorce Relationship on Paternal Involvement: A Longitudinal Study*, 63 Am. J. Orthopsychiatry no. 3, at 441–50 (July 1993).

[149] E.M. Hetherington, M. Bridges, & G.M. Insabella, *What Matters? What Does Not? Five Perspectives on the Association between Transitions and Children's Adjustment*, 53 Am. Psychologist no. 2, at 167–84 (1998).

attempt to maintain a good relationship with their children.[150] Pruett and Pruett[151] indicate that when fathers are perceived as visitors rather than parents, their parental functioning is likely to deteriorate.

Nehami Baum[152] wrote a paper suggesting that men respond to the divorce process differently from women. He stated, "[T]hey start the mourning process later than women, mourn the loss of their home and children more than the loss of their wives, and tend to express their mourning through actions rather than in words or obvious emotional manifestations of grief."[153]

A meta-analysis of 63 studies was performed by Paul Amato and Joan Gilbreth,[154] addressing the issue of nonresident fathers and children's well-being. They report that how often fathers see the children is less important than what fathers do when they are with their children.[155] Engaging in authoritative parenting is an important component to the relationship between nonresident fathers and children. Authoritative parenting includes support, limit-setting, and non-coercive discipline. Amato and Gilbreth further point out that because men are fearful that their relationships with their children are tenuous, they often are reluctant to set firm rules or to discipline their children.[156] The research appears to indicate that fathers are less reluctant to engage in authoritative parenting in recent years than they had been in the past. The research still supports the fact that nonresident fathers with joint legal custody visited their children more often and had more overnight visits than nonresident fathers where sole custody rested with the mothers.[157]

Mothers

A number of researchers have specifically looked at the effect of divorce on mothers and their children. Geoffrey Greif surveyed 517 mothers without custody. He found that non-custodial mothers needed to improve their self-esteem, define themselves in roles broader than that of being a mother, and provide children with models when appropriate.[158] Karen Schachere researched the relationships between working mothers and their infants. She concluded, "Poor marital quality compounded by long working hours has produced the problems in attachment between working mothers and their infants."[159] Susanne Denham,

---

[150] E.M. Hetherington, *An Overview of the Virginia Longitudinal Study of Divorce and Remarriage with a Focus on Early Adolescence*, 7 J. Fam. Psychol. 39–59 (1993).

[151] M. Pruett & K. Pruett, *Fathers, Divorce and Their Children*, 7 Child & Adolescent Psychiatric Clinics of N. Am. 389–407 (1998).

[152] Nehami Baum, *The Male Way of Mourning Divorce: When, What and How*, 31 Clinical Soc. Work J. 37–50 (2003).

[153] *Id.* at 37.

[154] Paul R. Amato & Joan G. Gilbreth, *Non-Resident Fathers and Children's Well-Being: A Meta-Analysis*, 61 J. Marriage & Fam. 557–73 (1999).

[155] *Id.* at 569.

[156] *Id.*

[157] *Id.*

[158] Geoffrey Greif, *Mothers without Custody*, Soc. Work, Jan.–Feb. 1987, at 11–16.

[159] Karen Schachere, Attachment between Working Mothers and Their Infants: The Influence on Family Processes 31 (1990).

not too surprisingly, found that maternal emotions affected the emotions of their toddlers. The lower the mother's psychosocial functioning, the more negative the toddler's behavior.[160] Robert Green and Leigh Leslie studied the mother-son relationship following divorce. They found that "a mother's attitude towards her former mate is related to how supportive and coercive her son reports her to be in their relationship." Likewise, how coercive the mother is perceived to be is related to the son's level of aggression in school.[161] Clark-Stewart *et al.*[162] found that single and divorced mothers compared to married mothers have greater anxiety and are less capable as parents. After the marital disruption it was found that separated mothers had lower incomes, higher depression, and provided children with less support and stimulation than married mothers. Kathryn Wilkox and her associates studied the issue of maternal preference regarding sole versus joint custody. The only factor that they found to be significant was the mother's perceptions of her ex-husband's parenting competence. Those who felt the ex-husband was more competent were more likely to prefer joint custody, while those who felt the ex-husband was incompetent were more likely to prefer sole custody.[163]

§ 4.26 Homosexual Parents

Until recent years, a parent's acknowledged homosexuality led to almost immediate exclusion from consideration as a placement parent. As society in general and courts in particular have become more open-minded and understanding, the sexual preference of the parents has become less an issue. At the current time, however, psychologists and family law judges perceive a parent's sexual preference to be largely irrelevant in matters of custody and placement.[164] Most assertions promulgated in the past about the negative aspects of having a child raised by a homosexual parent have been demonstrated to be in error. Instead of looking at sexual preference as a primary issue, the parent's acceptance of their own sexual preference, how the sexual relationship is presented to the children, and the children's overall response to the homosexual parent's sexual preference are more important indicators. These parents today tend to be evaluated more on general factors than on sexual preference factors.

As further discussed in **§ 4.27,** most of the studies have addressed the relationships between lesbian mothers and their children. Few studies have addressed homosexual fathers and their children. Studies that have been performed indicate that sons of homosexual fathers tend not to become homosexual themselves.

---

[160] Susanne Denham, *Maternal Affect and Toddlers' Social-Emotional Competence*, 59 Am. J. Orthopsychiatry no. 3, at 368–76 (July 1989).

[161] Robert Green & Leigh Leslie, Mother's Behavior and Son's Adjustment following Divorce 235 (1989).

[162] K.A. Clark-Stewart, D.L. Vandell, D.L. McCartney, M.T. Owens, & C. Booth, *Effects of Parental Separation and Divorce on Very Young Children*, 14 J. Fam. Psychol. 304–26 (2000).

[163] Kathryn L. Wilkox, Sharlene A. Wolchik, & Sanford Braver, *Predictors of Maternal Preference of Joint or Sole Custody*, 47 Fam. Relations 93–101 (1998).

[164] Marc J. Ackerman, Melissa C. Ackerman, Linda J. Steffen, & Shannon Kelly-Poulos, *Psychologists' Practices Compared to the Expectations of Family Law Judges and Attorneys in Child Custody Cases*, 1 J. Child Custody 41–60 (2004).

In William Hodges's book on custody evaluations, he states that in any family, it is important to evaluate that a child is not being exposed to sexually explicit material or to adults' sexual behavior. Questioning may need to be more explicit in an evaluation with a homosexual parent, because norms concerning parenting behavior are less well defined and the "coming-out" behavior (and concomitant increase in self-esteem) may conflict with "hiding" something about the homosexuality from the children.[165]

Charlotte Patterson and Richard Redding performed a study with gay and lesbian families. In reviewing the literature extensively, their conclusion was that parental sexual orientation should be considered irrelevant in disputes involving child custody and visitation. They pointed out that research has demonstrated heterosexual/lesbian mothers do not end up with lesbian children with any greater or lesser frequency than other mothers. The authors concluded:

> This review of the scientific literature reveals no evidence suggesting that psychosocial development among children of gay men or lesbians is compromised in any significant respect relative to that among offspring of heterosexual parents. Not a single study has found children of gay or lesbian parents to be disadvantaged in any important way relative to children of heterosexual parents.[166]

Dan McPherson, in a 1994 presentation to the American Psychological Association Convention, pointed out in his study that gay parenting couples report a more equitable performance of parental tasks than heterosexual couples, report greater satisfaction with parental task arrangements than heterosexual couples, and showed no difference in relationship satisfaction.[167]

Nanette Gartrell and her colleagues studied prospective lesbian mothers. The research demonstrated that the children of these conceptions were highly desired and thoughtfully conceived.[168] Buxton[169] states that there is no research that indicates that sexual orientation of a lesbian couple significantly influences the sexual orientation of the children. Cameron and Cameron[170] report on American Psychological Association briefs that indicate that there is insufficient knowledge to justify a policy recommendation concerning children raised by homosexual parents in relation to any adjustment problems they may experience.

---

[165] William Hodges, Interventions for Children of Divorce: Custody, Access, and Psychotherapy 118 (2d ed. John Wiley & Sons 1991).

[166] Charlotte J. Patterson & Richard E. Redding, *Lesbian and Gay Families with Children: Implications of Social Science Research for Policy*, 52 J. Soc. Issues no. 3, at 29–50 (1996).

[167] Dan McPherson, Gay Parenting Couples: Parenting Arrangement Satisfaction, and Relationship Satisfaction, Symposium presented at the American Psychological Assn's 102d Annual Convention, Los Angeles (Aug. 1994).

[168] Nanette Gartrell et al., *The National Lesbian Family Study: Interviews with Prospective Mothers*, 6 Am. J. Orthopsychiatry no. 2, at 272–81 (Apr. 1996).

[169] A. Buxton, *The Best Interest of the Children of Gay and Lesbian Parents, in* R. Galatzer-Levy, L. Kraus, & B. Leventhal eds., The Scientific Basis of Custody Decisions in Divorce 319–56 (John Wiley & Sons 1999).

[170] P. Cameron & K. Cameron, *Did the APA Misrepresent the Scientific Literature to Courts in Support of Homosexual Custody?*, 13 J. Psychol. 313–32 (1997).

§ 4.27   Effect of Homosexuality

Although it is treated as such by many courts, homosexuality is *not a mental disorder*[171] and is not listed in DSM-IV. Research has not shown that lesbians are likely to have any mental illness.[172]

It has been estimated that from 1.5 million to 5 million lesbian mothers live with their children. It is therefore essential that courts deal realistically with the impact (or lack thereof) a homosexual parent has on a child.[173]

Most allegations about the negative aspects of having a child raised by a homosexual parent have proved to be in error. Studies of parenting by homosexuals, mostly of lesbian mothers, have not found any consistent detrimental effects upon children nor any evidence of increased homosexuality among those children.[174] Although less is known about gay fathers, available research indicates that they are as nurturing and supportive as are heterosexual fathers. It is possible that children may have some distress regarding their parent's homosexuality.[175]

According to David Kleber, Robert Howell, and Alta Lura Tibbits-Kleber, research has found that lesbian mothers were much more likely to encourage play with a varied mixture of masculine and feminine sex-typed toys than were heterosexual mothers. Boys raised by lesbian mothers rated themselves as more gentle and aware of others' feelings, and girls raised by lesbian mothers rated themselves as higher in leadership and adventurousness, when compared with either boys or girls raised by heterosexual mothers. An investigation of gender identity in two groups of children of lesbian and single heterosexual mothers found no significant differences between groups. Lesbian parents were, however, found to demonstrate greater concern for providing male figures for their children.[176]

Kleber and colleagues also note that children may be "viewed as a stigma in [the] male homosexual culture, with few if any men willing to couple with a gay father." This could be an obstacle to gay parenting.[177]

The expert doing the evaluation should address the same issues as in any custody evaluation: the quality of parenting, the quality of the parent-child relationship, and the best interests of the child(ren).[178]

---

[171] Falk, *Lesbian Mothers: Psychosocial Assumptions in Family Law*, 44 Am. Psychol. 941, 942 (1989) [hereinafter Falk].

[172] *Id.* at 943.

[173] *Id.* at 941; David Kleber et al., *The Impact of Parental Homosexuality in Child Custody Cases: A Review of the Literature*, 14 Bull. Am. Acad. Psychiatry & L. 81, 81 (1986) [hereinafter Kleber et al.].

[174] Falk at 944, 946; Herman, *Special Issues in Child Custody Evaluations*, 29 J. Am. Acad. Child & Adolescent Psychiatry 969, 970 (1986) [hereinafter Herman]; Kleber et al. at 83–84.

[175] Herman at 970.

[176] Kleber et al. at 83

[177] *Id.* at 85–86.

[178] Herman at 971; Kleber et al. at 86; Falk at 947.

Although psychologists in 1986[179] found homosexuality to be the 9th greatest concern in determining custody, in 1997[180] it was the 32nd greatest concern. Family law judges[181] and family law attorneys[182] also did not rate sexual preference as an important issue.

Most research supports the notion that children of homosexuals do not differ appreciably from children who live with married parents; however, Paul and Kirk Cameron[183] take a different approach. They state that 94 percent of the children of homosexual parents attributed problems they had to their homosexual parents. Furthermore, 27 percent of the older daughters and 20 percent of the older sons of homosexual parents describe themselves as homosexual or bisexual.[184]

§ 4.28 Positive Adjustment following Divorce

Many factors have been identified as leading to a relatively positive adjustment to the divorce process. Seminal works were published by researchers Wallerstein and Kelly,[185] and Stolberg and Anker[186] report that little change in financial stability leads to a positive adjustment. Wallerstein and Kelly, and E. Mavis Hetherington and associates,[187] identify several variables, including the emotional adjustment of the custodial parent, low levels of conflict between parents prior to and during the divorce process, and cooperative parenting following the divorce process.[188] In addition, Wallerstein and Kelly[189] believe that the approval and love from both parents and the availability of regular visitation from the non-custodial parent are also important factors.

---

[179] W.G. Keilin & L.J. *Bloom, Child Custody Evaluation Practices: A Survey of Experienced Professionals*, 17 Res. & Prac. 338–46 (1986).

[180] Marc J. Ackerman & Melissa C. Ackerman, *Child Custody Evaluation Practices: A Survey of Experienced Professionals (Revisited)*, 28 Prof. Psychol.: Res. & Prac. 137–45 (1997).

[181] Marc J. Ackerman, Melissa C. Ackerman, Linda J. Steffen, & Shannon Kelly-Poulos, *Psychologists' Practices Compared to the Expectations of Family Law Judges and Attorneys in Child Custody Cases*, 1 J. Child Custody 41–60 (2004).

[182] *Id.*

[183] Paul Cameron & Kirk Cameron, *Children of Homosexual Parents Report Childhood Difficulties*, 90 *Psychol. Rep.* 71–82 (2000).

[184] *Id.* at 71.

[185] Judith Wallerstein & Joan Kelly, *Surviving the Breakup: How Children and Parents Cope with Divorce* (1980) [hereinafter Surviving the Breakup].

[186] A.L. Stolberg & M. Anker, *Cognitive and Behavioral Changes in Children Resulting from Parental Divorce and Consequent Environment Changes*, 7 J. Divorce 23–40 (1984).

[187] Surviving the Breakup; E. Mavis Hetherington et al., *The Aftermath of Divorce, in* Mother-Child, Father-Child Relations (1978) [hereinafter The Aftermath of Divorce].

[188] The Aftermath of Divorce.

[189] Surviving the Breakup.

§ 4.29   Research

A considerable amount of research has been performed on how divorce affects children. A very comprehensive pioneering study was performed by John Guidubaldi and his associates at Kent State University and formed the basis for much of the research performed in the future.[190] The study included 699 children from 38 states and was designed as a two-year longitudinal examination. All of the children were evaluated with regard to the effect of divorce at least two years after it occurred (Time 1); two years later, the same children were reevaluated to determine their level of adjustment (Time 2).

The Time 1 study indicated that the physical health of children was significantly poorer in divorced homes than in intact homes, and that divorced-family male children were most adversely affected by the time they reached fifth grade. These children had significantly greater anxiety, were significantly more withdrawn, physically acted out behavior, had feelings of blame, were impulsive, talked irreverently, had significantly poorer reading and spelling achievement, had significantly greater referrals to the school psychologist, and had significantly greater nonregular classroom placements. Divorced-family male and female children in first grade showed these same differences when compared with intact families. However, by fifth grade, divorced-family females were similar to intact family males and females at the same age levels. In other words, between first grade and fifth grade, divorced-family female children were able to adjust, but divorced-family male children were not.[191]

Two years later (Time 2), the average time since the divorce was 6.2 years. The results were relatively similar. Divorced-family boys achieved significantly lower scores on 10 of the 46 variables measured, but girls were significantly lower on only one variable. When the children's adjustment was compared with intelligence, those individuals with lower intelligence had significantly poorer adjustment. When adjustment was compared to mental health variables, male children were significantly lower on six mental health variables. These studies suggest that girls are more stable over time and that boys manifest greater variability.[192]

The children's home environment was evaluated to determine its effect on their adjustment. Higher-income families showed significantly better adjustment than did lower-income families. In addition, the quality of the relationship with the non-custodial parent predicted adjustment better than did the quality of the relationship with the custodial parent. Permissive child-rearing styles yielded better adjustment for girls but significantly poorer adjustment for boys.[193]

---

[190] John Guidubaldi et al., Longitudinal Effects of Divorce on Children, Report from NASP-KSU Nationwide Study, Paper presented at the Meeting of the American Psychological Ass'n (Aug. 1984) (cited in *Recent Psychological Research* at 30).

[191] *Recent Psychological Research* at 30–31.

[192] *Id.* at 31.

[193] *Id.*

§ 4.30   Judith Wallerstein's Research

Perhaps the most widely known research in the area of how divorce affects children has been performed by Judith Wallerstein.[194] Criticisms have been leveled against some of Wallerstein's research, claiming that she has generalized too much from the data presented, has used too small a sample to support her conclusions, and has not been entirely in step with the generalizations she has made. It must be noted that Wallerstein is a pioneer in the area of longitudinal studies, having presented the only information on a group of children who have been followed for up to 15 years. Certainly, more recent research has been performed that may demonstrate tighter research design models. However, Wallerstein is a pioneer in the field, whose conclusions are nonetheless extremely important to understanding the effects of divorce on children.

Wallerstein's research is summarized below:

- At the one-year mark, the girls had recovered, but many boys had gotten worse.
- At the five-year mark, the boys were still much worse, with significantly higher learning and social problems.
- At the 10-year mark, this changed directions, with the most psychologically vulnerable group at the entry into young adulthood being young women.
- Children who are older at the time of the marital rupture typically respond worse than those who are younger.
- What affects the children most is not the marital rupture itself but rather the post-marital course in the partial family.
- Eighty percent of preschool children are not told that their parents are divorcing: they just wake up one morning to find the parent gone.
- Boys seek to be with fathers when they are living with a psychologically deteriorating mother or perceive a lack of warmth from the mother.
- As girls grow older, they experience a greater degree of anxiety because they are concerned about repeating their parents' experiences.
- Girls are afraid they would end up marrying men like their fathers and were concerned about the problems associated with it.
- Boys need more contact with their fathers during adolescence.

§ 4.31   Diminished Capacity of Parent

Diminished capacity goes hand in hand with the crisis in the adult. This diminished capacity can exhibit itself in many ways, including reduced sensitivity, poorer judgment, and less awareness of the children. It is difficult to maintain discipline in a family because parents do not want the child to become angry and reject them. There is an unconscious

---

[194] Judith Wallerstein, *Children of Divorce: Preliminary Report of a Ten-Year Follow-up of Older Children and Adolescents*, 24 J. Am. Acad. Child Psychiatry 545–53 (1985).

feeling that because the marriage contract has been broken, the parent does not have to be as attentive to the concerns of the children. This diminished capacity occurs at the time when the children's needs are greater and much more important than before. Diminished capacity can also lead to either a wish to abandon the children or a greater dependency on them. This is one reason that many separations and divorces are precipitated by the birth of a child and the unconscious need to abandon the responsibility.

§ 4.32   Overburdened Child

The concept of being overburdened refers to children who are required to deal with more, psychologically and developmentally, than they are prepared for at their stage of development. Wallerstein's work on the overburdened child is based on research performed with 700 individuals.

There are three types of overburdening:

1.   Children are required to take too much responsibility for growing up. The parent generally reneges on many of the parenting roles and leaves children to fend for themselves.

2.   Children are responsible for maintaining the psychological functioning of the parent. They often end up having to parent the parent. Children in this category feel that it is their responsibility to ward off the parent's loneliness, depression, fear of disintegration, and other serious psychological concerns. This is known as parentification.

3.   Parents fight over the children and their affection, time, and alliance.

Overburdening often occurs when parents cannot reconcile the fact that being divorced means they will spend less time with the children, whether or not they are the primary placement parent. The overburdening remains unresolved as more litigation and relitigation occur.

Young children are more vulnerable to overburdening than are older children. A child is more likely to become overburdened if he or she is an only child. Parents also contribute to overburdening the child when they distort the child's role by taking the child to adult functions and even allowing the child to sleep with the parent.

Partly because of the experience of being overburdened, there is a 45 percent chance that children of divorce will also divorce. There is a 30 percent chance that these children of divorce will remarry and a 20 percent chance that they will be divorced a second time.

§ 4.33   College Education

College education is something that is generally not included in the divorce agreement. There are so many issues that need to be resolved at the time of divorce that attorneys are generally reluctant to add issues that are not relevant until the children reach adulthood. Unfortunately, as a result, college education is often not planned for in divorce situations. Even though the fathers could afford to pay for college, they often respond, "I have been an honorable man and paid my child support all these years and fulfilled my legal obliga-tions. As a result, it is now the mother's responsibility to pay for the college education." This is often impossible, because the mother's earning capacity is generally significantly less than the father's.

Wallerstein studied 49 college-age children from upper-middle to upper-class families. Only half the children attended college. Forty-two percent ended their education with a two-year degree. Only 20 percent of the children attended college with full support. The children tended to feel bitter and betrayed and a victim of their parents' divorces.

Wallerstein also performed 5-, 10-, 15-, and 25-year follow-up studies. The findings are summarized below.

§ 4.34   Five-Year Follow-up Study

- At the five-year mark, those children who did poorly were generally in families in which the fighting between the parents continued as if the divorce had never occurred.
- The children also did poorly when parenting skills remained diminished.
- The children who did well at the five-year mark were those in families where the dimin-ished parenting had improved, and the parental fighting had declined significantly.
- Thirty percent of the children five years after the divorce were still somewhat fixated at the developmental stage they were in at the time of the divorce.
- There was an increase in suicidal ideation at the five-year mark, with 37 percent of the children being clinically depressed.

§ 4.35   Ten-Year Follow-up Study

- The children who were young at the time of divorce were doing better because the post-divorce course for these children was easier.
- Younger children did not have vivid memories of the divorce process.
- The older group tended to feel that their entire childhood and adolescence was spent in the shadow of their parents' divorce.
- Women were generally economically worse off than their former husbands.
- When girls reach young adulthood, they have trouble trusting the reliability of their partner.

§ 4.36   Fifteen-Year Follow-up Study

- It is apparent that the third decade of life of many of these young people is critical for working out issues of male-female relationship.
- Half the children emerged as compassionate and competent people.
- Half were worried, underachieving and self-deprecating.

There is no long-term study of patterns of overnight visiting for infants and toddlers, although the courts have issued orders for these very young children, including nursing babies. There is no long-term study of the psychological effects of the major divorce-related economic issues: the decline in primary parent family income; greater economic insecurity of the child; child support that ends when the child reaches age 18; and significant economic discrepancies between the parents' households over the post-divorce years. Further, much of the psychological research in divorce has dealt with white middle-class families. There is a pressing need to expand the database to include families at different socioeconomic levels from diverse ethnic and racial populations.[195]

§ 4.37   Parting Comment

Repeatedly, research cited in this chapter, as well as the present authors' experience, indicates that the quality of the interpersonal relationship between the parents has an extraordinary effect on the adjustment of the children. Children virtually always do better when their parents have adequate communication and a cordial relationship. Anything that courts, attorneys, and mental health professionals do to improve communication and cordiality between parents will serve the best interests of the children.

§ 4.38   Questions for Chapter 4

Because the content of this chapter provides essential ancillary information to aid in an understanding of how divorce affects families, no specific questions are suggested for examination or cross-examination. However, any mental health professional whom holds himself or herself out to be an expert in the area of child custody and placement should be familiar with all of the information in this chapter. When conducting voir dire on an expert, an expert can be asked about the various areas in this chapter. If he or she does not have sufficient knowledge about these areas, it may be advantageous to ask the judge not to qualify the mental health professional as an expert.

§ 4.39   Case Digest

The source of information for most of the following cases is the *Mental and Physical Disability Law Reporter* (MPDLR), a publication of the American Bar Association. Complete information for any other sources appears in the relevant references below. The following are direct quotations from the identified source. Quotations from the *Mental and Physical Disability Law Reporter.* Excerpted from *Mental and Physical Disability Law Reporter.* Copyright © 1989–2004. American Bar Association. Reprinted by permission. If no source is identified, it is a summary from the court ruling.

---

[195] *Id.*

National

In *Troxel v. Granville*, 530 U.S. 57, 120 S. Ct. 2054, 147 L. Ed. 2d 49 (2000), the U.S. Supreme Court ruled on June 5, 2000, that a Washington state law that gives grandparents and others broad rights for visitation unconstitutionally infringes on the fundamental right of parents to raise their children. The Court wrote:

> The Fourteenth Amendment's Due Process Clause has a substantive component that "provides heightened protection against government interference with certain fundamental rights and liberty interests . . . , including parents' fundamental right to make decisions concerning the care, custody, and control of their children. . . . Washington's breathtakingly broad statute effectively permits a court to disregard and overturn any decision by a fit custodial parent concerning visitation whenever a third party affected by the decision files a visitation petition, based solely on the judge's determination of the child's best interest. A parent's estimation of the child's best interest is accorded no deference. . . .

> A combination of several factors compels the conclusion that [the state law], as applied here, exceeded the bounds of the Due Process Clause. . . . There is a presumption that fit parents act in their children's best interests, *Parham v. J.R.*, 442 U.S. 584, 602; there is normally no reason for the State to inject itself into the private realm of the family to further question fit parents' ability to make the best decisions regarding their children. . . . The problem here is not that the Superior Court intervened, but that when it did so, it gave no special weight to Granville's determination of her daughter's best interests. More importantly, that court appears to have applied the opposite presumption, favoring grandparent visitation. In effect, it placed on Granville the burden of *disproving* that visitation would be in her daughter's best interest and thus failed to provide any protection for her fundamental right. . . .

In two other cases, the U.S. Supreme Court has ruled in favor of the right of grandparents to visit their grandchildren, even against the wishes of the grandchildren's parents. In a case from Kentucky (*King v. King*, 828 S.W.2d 630 (Ky.), *cert. denied*, 113 S. Ct. 378 (1992)), the Supreme Court let stand a decision of the Kentucky Supreme Court granting a paternal grandfather visitation against the wishes of his son and daughter-in-law. 7 *Speak Out for Children* 11 (1992). In a similar case from Wisconsin (*T.F. & D.L. v. H.F. & F.F.* (*In re C.G.F.*), 168 Wis. 2d 62, 483 N.W.2d 803, *cert. denied*, 113 S. Ct. 408 (1992)), the Supreme Court let stand a Wisconsin law that permits visitation by grandparents even when the parent objects. In the specific case, the grandchild's father died, the mother remarried, the stepfather adopted the child, and the mother and stepfather denied the natural father's parents visitation. The Wisconsin Supreme Court ruled that visitation could be ordered even after the adoption, if in the best interests of the child. *Milwaukee Journal*, Nov. 2, 1992.

Alaska

Kelly v. Joseph, 46 P.3d 1014 (Alaska 2002). The Alaska Supreme Court ruled that when a custodial parent substantially interferes with the visitation rights of a non-custodial parent, that is sufficient to constitute a change of circumstances. One type of "substantial interference" is when the custodial parent engages in a detrimental, well-established pattern of behavior designed to erode the relationship between the non-custodial parent and the child(ren). In the instant case, the father had custody of the children, and did not take actions to ensure that the mother's rights under the visitation agreement were fulfilled, nor did he honor the spirit of the visitation agreement. The context for the modification of custody remains the best interests of the child(ren). A lack of compliance with court orders, by itself, is not sufficient to modify custody. That change requires a "best interests" analysis.

West v. West, 21 P.3d 838 (Alaska 2001). A trial court gave primary custody to a father, primarily because the father was about to remarry, while the mother remained single. When the parents separated the mother moved to Oregon, while the father remained in Alaska. The boy, of kindergarten age at the time of trial, moved between parental homes every few months. The custody evaluator found both parents to be appropriate and about equally positive, and recommended joint custody. She indicated her belief that the boy could flourish in either home, and that the boy remain in one home for the school year. Because of the distance between homes, she had to recommend one as preferred. She picked the mother, because the mother had a 16-year-old daughter who helped care for the boy, and other relatives nearby who would be available as needed. The trial court considered the recommendations, but found that the greatest stability for the boy would come from being with his father, who was "likely" to marry a woman with 12 years of experience as a nurse who would not be employed outside the home, providing a home with two adults present.

   The state Supreme Court held that it was improper to award primary physical custody on the basis of the anticipated marriage. In the required context of the best interests of the child, the trial court found the parents to be essentially equal. The father's anticipated remarriage tipped the scale in his favor. The court indicated that other courts ruling on similar situations had generally indicated that custody should not be determined on the basis of a presumption of an advantage of a two-parent household. A custody determination may not be based on a presumption, without scientific evidence, that a working mother would not provide care equal to that of a father with a wife not employed outside the home. There was also no evidence that the convenience of in-home care would be better for the boy than being with his mother, stepsister, and maternal grandparents. The trial record contained no objective information that would indicate that either household would necessarily be better than the other. The case was remanded for a determination of custody on the basis of the current best interests of the child.

Arizona

Pollock (Kay) v. Pollock, 889 P.2d 633 (Ariz. Ct. App. 1995). The Arizona Court of Appeals held that a custodial parent who wishes to move out of state has the burden of showing that relocation is in the child's best interest. The court also identified a number of factors that should be taken into consideration when a trial court decides what is in the child's best interests in these situations, noting "that no single factor is controlling and that all of them should be weighed collectively":

> A very important factor is whether the request to move is made in good faith and not simply to frustrate the other parent's right to maintain contact with the child. . . . Another factor is the prospective advantage of the move for improving the general quality of life for the custodial parent and the child. . . . A trial court should also consider the likelihood that the custodial parent will comply with modified visitation orders when that parent is beyond the jurisdiction

of the court. . . . It should consider whether the move will allow a realistic opportunity for visitation for the non-custodial parent . . . and if not, the possible adverse effect of the elimination or curtailment of the child's association with the non-custodial parent. . . . The court should also take into account the extent to which moving or not moving will affect the emotional, physical, or developmental needs of the child. . . . It must also assess the integrity of the non-custodial parent's motives in resisting the move and consider the extent to which, if at all, the opposition is intended to secure a financial advantage in respect to continuing support obligations. . . . [I]t is not a prerequisite for the custodial parent who wants to move to show that the move will result in a "real advantage" for the custodial parent and child.

Arkansas

Hollandsworth v. Knyzewski, 353 Ark. 470 (2003). Hollandsworth, the mother of the couple's two children, wished to relocate 500 miles to Tennessee in order to live with the man she had married who lives in that state. Knyzewski filed a petition for change of custody to him, arguing that there had been a material and substantial change in circumstances. The trial court ordered a change of custody to the father on the basis that the mother had failed to show a real advantage to herself and to the children, and that it would be harmful to the children's relationship with their father and the strong ties the children had with family in Arkansas. The mother appealed, and the appellate court reversed. The father appealed to the Arkansas Supreme Court.

The Supreme Court of Arkansas indicated that the factors to be considered when a custodial parent seeks to relocate with his or her child are "(1) the reason for the relocation; (2) the educational, health, and leisure opportunities available in the location in which the custodial parent and children will relocate; (3) visitation and communication schedule for the noncustodial parent; (4) the effect of the move on the extended family relationships in the location in which the custodial parent and children will relocate . . . ; and (5) preference of the child, including the age, maturity, and the reasons given by the child as to his or her preference." All of these are to be considered in the context of the best interest of the child.

The Supreme Court opinion indicates that courts in Minnesota, Tennessee, California, Colorado, Wyoming, Illinois, and New Jersey have indicated a presumption that a custodial parent may relocate so long as he or she has any good faith reason to do so. The New York Court of Appeals held that the trial court needs to weigh the evidence that a proposed relocation would serve the child's best interests. Texas and North Carolina courts have held that relocation, regardless of distance, does not constitute a substantial change of circumstances.

The Arkansas Supreme Court held that the relocation of a custodial parent is not a material change in circumstances, and that there is a presumption favoring the relocation of a custodial parent with primary custody. The custodial parent has no obligation to prove there is a real advantage to him- or herself or the children. The burden is on the noncustodial parent to rebut the presumption. In the instant case, the Supreme Court found that the father could have adequate visitation and could maintain an adequate relationship with his children after the relocation, that there was no evidence the children would be harmed by the move, and that the mother has a valid reason to relocate. The appellate court decision was reversed and remanded. *Staab v. Hurst*, 868 S.W.2d 517 (Ark. Ct. App. 1994). The Arkansas Court of Appeals held, en banc, that, when a custodial parent wants to move out of state and the other parent objects, consideration must be given to the best interest of the family unit of custodial parent and child, not solely the best interest of the child. The court followed the framework of the New Jersey Superior Court in *D'Onofrio v. D'Onofrio*, 365 A.2d 27, indicating that several other states had already accepted that model. When the custodial parent moves a distance sufficient to make weekly visitation by the other parent difficult or impossible, the custodial parent bears the burden of demonstrating that the move is in the best interest of the new family unit. The trial court may consider such factors as the ways the move may be advantageous, the custodial parent's history of good faith, evidence the custodial parent may not comply with visitation orders, the reasons why the non-custodial parent is resisting the move, and the effect of the move on the relationship of the child with the non-custodial parent.

California

In re Guardianship of Z.C.W., 71 Cal. App. 4th 524. 84 Cal. Rptr. 2d 48 (1999). The California First District Court of Appeal held that a lesbian partner does not have standing to sue for guardianship of her partner's children. One of the children was from a prior relationship of the partner, one was the product of a decision of the two that the partner be artificially inseminated. When they parted, the partner adhered to an agreement for visitation to four years, then terminated the agreement unilaterally. The court held that a non-parent does not have standing to obtain guardianship of or visitation with a partner's children.

In re Robin N., 7 Cal. App. 4th 1140, 9 Cal. Rptr. 2d 512 (1992). De facto parents may have visitation rights over a custodial parent's objections where loss of the contact would be detrimental to the child, there is a substantial parental relationship with the child, and the child's emotional needs mandate visitation with the de facto parent. T. Walker & L. Elrod, "Family Law in the Fifty States: An Overview," 26 *Family Law Quarterly* 392 (1993).

Colorado

In re Dureno, 854 P.2d 1352 (Colo. App. 1992). The Colorado Court of Appeals held that a family court may grant visitation to an individual who is not the child's parent if so doing is in the child's best interest. The court noted that state law permits custody to be awarded to a stepparent or another non-parent, and that courts in other states have permitted stepparent visitation on the basis of the best interests of the child despite a lack of statutory language specifically permitting such visitation. The court indicated that visitation may be granted to a "stepparent or surrogate parent" when in the best interest of the child, with consideration given to the wishes of the parents, the age of the child, and the length and quality of the relationship with the child.

Connecticut

Knock v. Knock, 224 Conn. 776 (1993). The Connecticut Supreme Court held that evidence that the mother had been battered by the father was relevant to the determination of custody of the child. It noted that research has indicated that it is usually not in the child's best interest to give custody to a parent who has battered the other parent. The court also indicated that one parent's abuse of the other parent has been accepted as relevant to custody determinations by the U.S. Congress, the National Council of Juvenile and Family Court Judges, 38 states, and the District of Columbia. The court found that "it appears that the presence of battering in the household has, at a minimum, some effect on the parenting skills of both spouses and the child's response to the parents even after their separation."

District of Columbia

In re M.M.D., 662 A.2d 837 (D.C. App. 1995). The District of Columbia Court of Appeals ruled that nothing in the adoption statute precluded unmarried couples from adopting a child. When it is in the best interests of the child, the adoption may proceed. The committed partner of an adoptive parent may also adopt the nonmarital partner's adopted child. Both adoptive parents are male, and the child is female.

> The trial judge indicated that the adoption Bruce and Mark now seek would be in the child's best interests. . . . In this case, the proposed adoption by Mark very well may be in Hillary's best interests because it would formalize a parental relationship that she recognizes in fact, and would assure that both men are equally committed to her and continue to have a financial responsibility to her. . . .

The court also ruled that the adoption did not affect the original adoptive parent's parental rights, because "when a natural parent (by birth or adoption) is living in a committed personal relationship with the prospective adoptive parent, then the stepparent exception . . . applies to preserve the natural parent's rights after the adoption."

Florida

Kantaras v. Kantaras, Case No: 98-5375CA (Fla. Cir. Ct. Feb. 2003). In a massive (809-page) decision, a circuit court judge ruled that Michael Kantaras, who had been born as a female, is a male under Florida law, is the legal father of two children born to his wife, and should be awarded custody and primary placement of his children.

Michael had completed sex reassignment surgery in 1986, and met Linda in 1988. They married in 1989, when the older child was six weeks old. Linda was aware of the sex reassignment. The older child was conceived by Linda Kantaras prior to her relationship with Michael. The younger child was conceived by artificial insemination using sperm from Michael's brother.

The trial court ruled that the marriage was valid, that the parents have joint custody, that Michael has primary residential custody and Linda has visitation, and that Michael shall remain in the family residence until the younger child reaches 18, at which time the house is to be sold and the proceeds divided between the parties.

The complete transcript is available at *www.transgenderlaw.org/cases/kantarasopinion.pdf.*

Beagle v. Beagle, 678 So. 2d 1271 (Fla. 1996). The Florida Supreme Court ruled that a trial court may not impose visitation by grandparents upon an intact family when a parent objects, unless it finds that the child would be harmed by the disallowance of that visitation. The court found that the new statutory provision permitting grandparent visitation was unconstitutional.

Kuutti (Drecksel) v. Kuutti, 645 So. 2d 80 (Fla. Dist. Ct. App. 1994). Florida's Fourth District Court of Appeals met en banc to try to ensure uniformity in its opinions and to assert recognition that the Florida legislature has abolished the "tender years doctrine." The case involved a trial court that awarded custody of an 18-month-old girl to her father on the bases that the mother was less likely to promote visitation, the father's living situation was more stable, and the father had bonded strongly with the child. The court also noted that the relevant facts in a given case could still include reference to the sex or age of a child when relevant.

Caraballo v. Hernandez, 623 So. 2d 563 (Fla. App. 4 Dist. 1993) Florida's Fourth District Court of Appeals ruled that a trial court was in error when it ordered that the primary placement of an eight-year-old boy change from one parent's house to the other's on an annual basis. The parents received joint custody. The appellate court noted that rotating primary placements are rarely in the best interests of the child, particularly when the child would have to change schools with each change of primary placement. The appellate court upheld the joint custody awarded by the trial court.

Illinois

In re Petition of K.M. & D.M. to Adopt Olivia M., 653 N.E.2d 888 (Ill. App. Ct. 1995). The Illinois Appellate Court for the First District ruled that unmarried couples may petition the court jointly to adopt a child related to one of them by blood or marriage. The court also noted that sexual orientation is not an issue, that "lesbians and gay men are permitted to adopt in Illinois." "[The statute explicitly requires] that the welfare of the adoptee shall be of 'paramount consideration.' "

Indiana

Crafton v. Gibson, 752 N.E.2d 78 (Ind. Ct. App. 2001). Crafton was awarded custody of her two children after a divorce in 1997. Gibson, the paternal grandmother, sought visitation, saying that Crafton would not permit any meaningful contact. The trial court granted visitation. In 1999, the father's parental rights were terminated and the children were adopted by their stepfather, Crafton's husband.

When the U.S. Supreme Court decided *Troxel v. Granville*, 530 U.S. 57, 120 S. Ct. 2054, 147 L. Ed. 2d 49 (2000), Crafton filed a motion for relief on the bases that Gibson's grandparent visitation was no longer equitable and that the trial court had failed to apply a presumption that Crafton's decision to limit Gibson's visitation was in the children's best interests. The trial court denied the motion. Crafton appealed.

The appellate court first indicated that it had previously found Indiana's Grandparent Visitation statute to be constitutional. They also held that it is not overly broad, unlike the Washington statute in *Troxel*. In the absence of an allegation that the mother is unfit, deference must be given to the mother's decision to deny visitation to Gibson, with the grandparent having the burden of rebutting the presumption that the decision to deny visitation was made in the children's best interests. The record does not suggest that the trial court gave the requisite special weight to Crafton's decision. The case was remanded to the trial court to address the requirements (1) that a presumption be made that the parent's decision to deny visitation was on the basis of the best interests of the child, (2) that consideration be given to Crafton's offer of limited visitation, (3) that special weight be given to Crafton's decision regarding grandparent visitation. The burden is on the grandparent to demonstrate that visitation should be permitted.

Teegarden v. Teegarden, 642 N.E.2d 1007 (Ind. Ct. App. 1994). The Indiana Court of Appeals ruled that a trial court erred in imposing conditions upon a lesbian mother that she not cohabit with another lesbian, that she not engage in "lesbian activity" in front of the children, and that she get counseling for herself and her children. The appeals court indicated that the trial court lacked authority to impose these conditions and that there was no indication that the mother was unfit. Further,

> homosexuality standing alone without evidence of any adverse effect upon the welfare of the child does not render the homosexual parent unfit as a matter of law to have custody of the child. (We note that other states have adopted a similar view of homosexuality as it relates to parental fitness. . . .) [W]ithout evidence of behavior having an adverse effect upon the children, we find the trial court had no basis upon which to condition [the mother's] custody of her sons.

Pierce v. Pierce, 620 N.E. 2d 726 (Ind. App. 1993). The Indiana Court of Appeals affirmed a trial court's award of sole custody to the mother, terminating joint custody. The trial court found that the father failed to do his part to make the joint custody workable, making it difficult for the mother to have an active role in parenting. "Where a parent with physical custody voluntarily and unreasonably causes joint custody itself to become unreasonable, that parent may lose custody of the children altogether."

Iowa

In re Stange, No. 1-390/00-1886 (Iowa Ct. App. June 13, 2001). Curt and Tammy Stange were divorced in 1997. The parties agreed that Curt would be the primary care parent for their son, Jacob (11/84), and Tammy would be the primary care parent for Janae (05/88). In 2000, Tammy filed a petition for modification of visitation because she had accepted a teaching position in the state of Washington.

After a trial, the district court awarded primary care of Janae to Curt. It indicated that the loss of her relationship with her father, brother, and relatives on both sides of the family outweighed any benefit she would obtain by moving with her mother. The court indicated that Curt provided her with greater stability, and noted that Tammy often placed her own interests before her daughter's. The court also indicated that Tammy showed "flagrant disregard" for Curt's joint custodial interests by failing to consult him before deciding to relocate. Tammy appealed.

The appeals court reviewed the case *de novo*. It noted that the criteria for custody in modification proceedings are the same as those in initial custody determinations, that is, the best interests of the child(ren). It indicated that Curt had a substantial role in Janae's life, and she would suffer if denied that involvement. She would also lose regular and frequent contact with her brother and the families of both parents. Further, the appeals court found that Curt offered significantly greater stability for Janae. Tammy was often late to Janae's activities, had relocated on several occasions since the separation, and she did not investigate getting a teaching position in Illinois that would have given her a comparable salary to that in Washington state. She had also failed to support the relationship between

Janae and her father. She arranged for Janae to be out of town on two Father's Days, had withheld visitation on one occasion because she was being punished—though Curt went to the planned event anyhow, and found that Janae was there. She also informed other parents of her planned move well before informing Curt. The court of appeals therefore affirmed the decision of the trial court.

In re Rykhoek, 525 N.W.2d 1 (Iowa Ct. App. 1994). The Iowa Court of Appeals ruled that a mother with primary placement may not have the authority to veto decisions by the father regarding the people with whom he associates while with his children. The mother did not want her ex-husband to take the children to see her own parents. The court indicated that conditions may be placed on visitation rights of a parent only when required to prevent physical or emotional harm to a parent or the children. It specified that any conditions placed on visitation must be in the best interests of the children.

In re Quirk-Edwards, 509 N.W.2d 476 (Iowa 1993). The Iowa Supreme Court ruled that interference with the visitation rights of a child's father is adequate grounds for changing physical placement from the mother to the father. The parents shared joint custody. The supreme court agreed with the trial court that attempts by the mother to minimize contact between the father and child were an indication of an inability to provide proper parenting. The court also found that the mother's moving out of state served no evident purpose other than to limit contact between father and child. These findings constituted a material change of circumstances calling for a change of physical custody.

In re Wedemeyer (Maas), 475 N.W.2d 657 (Iowa App. 1991). The Iowa Court of Appeals ruled that a custodial mother who continually portrayed her ex-husband as an "insane sex addict who masturbates and performs sexual acts with animals" has caused a substantial change of circumstances that warrants modifying the provisions of the divorce decree regarding custody and placement. The trial court had ruled that her attempts to destroy the relationships between the three boys and their father was not in the children's best interests. The appeals court indicated that the statutes require consideration of the support each parent gives to the relationship with the other parent in determining custody. The court also noted that the mother seemed obsessed with ruining the relationship between her ex-husband and his sons, including telling the boys that if they emulated their father they would become sex addicts too.

Hodson v. Moore, 464 N.W.2d 699 (Iowa Ct. App. 1990). Physical custody was awarded to the mother despite her homosexual relationship with her roommate, because the mother and the roommate were discreet and did not engage in inappropriate behavior in the child's presence. 15 *Mental & Physical Disability Law Reporter* 148 (1991).

Kansas

Ward v. Ward, 30 P.3d 1001 (Sept. 14, 2001). Vanita and Stanley Ward were divorced on October 21, 1999. The mother was awarded sole custody and primary placement of their seven-year-old daughter, Jaclynn. The father had limited visitation (a maximum of three three-hour afternoon periods per week). On January 11, 2000, Vanita Ward was killed in an accident. Jaclynn then lived with her maternal grandmother and maternal aunt and uncle. Her father saw her briefly four times between January 11 and 23. On January 23 he asked for a three-hour visitation, but did not return Jaclynn to her grandmother and aunt and uncle. He filed a petition seeking to have his brother and sister-in-law appointed as co-guardians and co-conservators of Jaclynn. The trial court concluded that Jaclynn's father automatically received sole legal custody of Jaclynn upon the death of her mother. The maternal grandmother and aunt and uncle moved for reconsideration.

The appellate court initially noted the "admonition of Chief Justice Frank D. Celebrezze of the Ohio Supreme Court in *In re Wonderly*, 67 Ohio St.2d 178, 188, 423 N.E.2d 420 (1981), where, in a contest over a guardianship, he said:"

> While statutes can be amended and case law can be distinguished or overruled, we take judicial notice of the fact that children grow up only once. When a mistake is made in a custody dispute, the harmful effects are irrevocable.

The appellate court indicated that it was clear that custody of Jaclynn belonged to her father upon the death of her mother, affirming the decision of the trial court.

In re Debenham (Ellis), 896 P.2d 1098 (Kan. Ct. App. 1995). The Kansas Court of Appeals ruled that the "best interest of the child" standard should be used in deciding what school a child of joint custodial parents should attend. It rejected the notion that the parent with primary placement should solely decide where there was a dispute, indicating that this would give the primary custodian veto power in all decisions.

Kentucky

Fenwick v. Fenwick and Huck v. Huck, 114 S.W.3d 767 (Ky. 2003). The Kentucky Supreme Court addressed these two cases together because both involved a primary custodian wishing to relocate with the children of the parties over the objection of the other parent. In *Fenwick*, the wife wished to relocate to a county 35 miles from her current home. In *Huck*, the wife wished to relocate to an adjoining state.

Acknowledging that relocation of a custodial parent is a thorny and divisive issue, the Kentucky Supreme Court indicated that the issue had been resolved in the context of sole custody in 1992 in *Wilson v. Messinger*, 840 S.W.2d 203, noting that we live in a mobile society in which no one should be required to remain in a given location in order to retain custody. While earlier cases had placed the burden on the custodial parent who wanted to relocate, *Wilson* and the subsequent enactment of statute KRS 403.340 indicate that the custodial parent's relocation decision is presumptively permissible, and that a modification of the joint custody award is not necessary. The non-custodial parent would have to show that the child's present or proposed environment seriously endangers the physical, mental, moral, or emotional health of the child, and that a change of custody is therefore necessary. Accordingly, in both of these cases the custodial parent was permitted to relocate.

Newton v. Riley, 899 S.W.2d 509 (Ky. Ct. App. 1995). The Kentucky Court of Appeals ruled that the fact that a stepparent is infected with HIV is not sufficient, in itself, to call for a modification of custody in favor of the non-custodial parent. It was noted that courts in a number of other jurisdictions have ruled that a parent with an HIV infection is not a direct threat to a child's health, since there is no evidence that the child can become infected through casual contact with a parent or stepparent. It affirmed the trial court's decision that the children's best interests favored maintaining the current joint custody and placement.

Massachusetts

In re Adoption of Tammy, 416 Mass. 205 (1993). The Massachusetts Supreme Judicial Court ruled that a woman and her lesbian partner may adopt the woman's biological daughter, who was conceived through artificial insemination. The court noted that state statutes do not prevent adoptions because of either sexual orientation or gender. The court also indicated that the joint adoption could occur without terminating the mother's legal relationship with her child. The court noted that the child would be in "legal limbo" if the mother died without the adoption having occurred, and that it would therefore be in the child's best interest for the joint adoption to occur—particularly as the women had a committed relationship and had co-parented since the child's birth.

Michigan

Lombardo v. Lombardo, 507 N.W.2d 788 (Mich. Ct. App. 1993). The Michigan Court of Appeals ruled that, when parents with joint custody cannot make "important decisions" regarding a child's welfare, the trial court has the duty to make the decision in the child's best interests. Noting the absence of a statute in Michigan that would give the parent with primary placement the authority "to make child-rearing decisions in the absence of an enforceable agreement concerning the child's education," the court indicated that

> joint custody in this state by definition means that the parents share the decision-making authority with respect to the important decisions affecting the welfare of the child, and where the parents as joint custodians cannot agree on important matters such as education, it is the court's duty to determine the issue in the best interests of the child. . . . The controlling consideration in child custody disputes between parents is the best interests of the children. . . . [W]e hold that a court must determine the best interests of the child in resolving disputes concerning "important decisions affecting the welfare of the child" that arise between joint custodial parents.

Minnesota

Ayers v. Ayers (Kotz), 508 N.W.2d 515 (Minn. 1993). The Minnesota Supreme Court indicated that the "best interest of the child" standard, not the "endangerment" standard, applied to a situation in which the trial court refused to allow a mother to move out of state and transferred the children's "primary residence" to the father's home. The high court accepted the parties' characterization of their situation as one of joint legal and physical custody, and found that the best interests of the child would be served by affirming the rulings of the trial court.

Mississippi

Goodson v. Goodson, 816 So. 2d 420 (Miss. Ct. App. 2002). David and Judy Goodson were divorced in January 2001. Judy was awarded primary custody of their daughter, born in 1986, by the chancery court. A visitation schedule was set up by the court. The chancellor found Judy to be in contempt of court when she did not force her daughter to follow the court's visitation schedule.

Sheri, age 14, told both of her parents that she refused to visit her father. At the trial, Judy testified that she urged Sheri to visit with her father, and that, short of physically putting Sheri in David's car, she could not do more to comply with the order of the court.

A finding of contempt is appropriate when there is a willful and deliberate ignoring of a court order, the appellate court indicated. The fact that Judy had attempted to get her daughter to comply with the court order, and that Judy was not responsible for Sheri's refusal, indicates that Judy did not willfully violate the court's order. The appellate court therefore reversed the contempt order.

Missouri

Herndon v. Tuhey, No. 75184 (Mo. 1993). The Missouri Supreme Court ruled that Missouri's grandparent visitation statute, which permits courts to grant visitation by a grandparent even if the child's parents object, is not a constitutional infringement on parental rights, when visitation is in the child's best interest.

Montana

In re Marriage of Robinson, 2002 MT 207. Jill and Dixon Robinson divorced in 1999, after entering into a Final Parenting Plan that permitted Jill to live in the family home with their three children and set visitation and other conditions. The following year, Jill notified Dixon of her plan to move to Idaho and to remarry there. Dixon filed a motion to amend the parenting plan. A psychiatrist stipulated to by both parents indicated that both were fit parents and that the children needed regular contact with both parents. She also noted that Dixon's parents lived in Butte and had been involved with the care of the children. She recommended that Jill stay in close proximity to Dixon's home or work so that shared custody would be possible.

The trial court adopted the psychiatrist's recommendations, and concluded that the best interests of the children would be served by their remaining in Butte. Jill's residence would remain the children's primary residence if she remained in Butte, but if she moved to Idaho the children would remain with Dixon. Contrary to the court's order, Jill took the children to Idaho. Dixon went to Idaho and returned with the two youngest children, but the oldest refused to return with him. Jill was found in contempt for not returning the oldest child to Butte to live with her father. The parties later entered into a stipulation regarding the transportation of the children. Jill appealed the court's decision that the children must remain in Butte, alleging that she has a constitutional right to relocate with the children. Dixon argued that her right to travel does not supersede the best interests of the children.

The appellate court agreed that the "best interests of the child" was the standard upon which the decision rests. The district court had found that Dixon had a strong support system for the children in Butte, including the fact that his parents had a close relationship with the children. The support system also included neighbors, friends with children of similar ages, teachers, and day-care providers. In contrast, neither Jill nor her fiancè had any relatives in Idaho. The appellate court held that the best interests of the children outweighed Jill's constitutional right to travel. It further indicated that a parenting plan may be amended if there is a change in circumstances and an amendment is necessary to serve the best interests of the child. The district court order was affirmed.

In re Marriage of Converse, 252 Mont. 67, 826 P.2d 937 (1992). Although the Montana statute lists seven statutory factors, which include physical abuse or threat of physical abuse and chemical dependency, the court added the parents' ability to cooperate in their parental roles and the geographical proximity of the parents' residences. T. Walker & L. Elrod, "Family Law in the Fifty States," 26 *Family Law Quarterly* 380 (1993).

New Jersey

Wilde v. Wilde, 341 N.J. Super. 381 (App. Div. 2001). A father committed suicide. Some visitation occurred between the grandfather and grandchildren in the next few months, but was cut off by the mother four months after the suicide. The paternal grandfather and his second wife sued under the New Jersey Grandparent Visitation Statute. The mother filed a motion for dismissal on constitutional grounds. The trial court held the statute to be facially constitutional and constitutional as applied. The mother appealed.

The Appellate Division of the Superior Court of New Jersey declined to rule on the facial constitutionality of the statute. Citing *Troxel v. Granville*, 530 U.S. 57, 120 S. Ct. 2054, 147 L. Ed. 2d 49 (2000), the court held that the Due Process Clause of the Fourteenth Amendment protects the right of a parent to make decisions regarding the care, custody, and control of his or her children. The court further indicated that, when the fitness of the parent is not disputed, the grandparents have a responsibility to try to repair any breach between themselves and the parent before seeking a legal remedy. Litigation should also not be threatened prior to a denial of visitation with finality. The grandparents must also refrain from making severe criticisms of the parent, or impugning the parent's character. Since the grandparents had not proceeded according to these requirements, the Grandparent Visitation Statute was found unconstitutional as applied to the facts of this particular case.

In re Adoption by H.N.R., 285 N.J. Super. 1 (1995). The New Jersey appellate court ruled that the trial court was too restrictive in its interpretation of the state's adoption statute, and that the mother's lesbian partner could adopt twins conceived during the couple's relationship by artificial insemination.

New Mexico

Roth v. Bookert (In re Adoption of J.J.B.), 868 P.2d 1256 (N.M. Ct. App. 1993). The New Mexico Court of Appeals ruled that custody of a child may not be awarded to nonrelatives without a showing that the unwed father was an unfit parent. The court indicated that the state may not infringe upon constitutionally protected parental rights absent a compelling reason, and that there is a "constitutional requirement that parental unfitness must be first determined before independently considering the child's interests."

A.C. v. C.B., 113 N.M. 449, 829 P.2d 660, *cert. denied*, 113 N.M. 449, 829 P.2d 837 (1992). A New Mexico court allowed a woman to pursue her claim for custody of a child born to her former partner by artificial insemination. The court found that a continuing relationship between a woman and her former partner's child was in the child's best interest and that the trial court could consider a party's sexual activities only to the extent of whether and how they affect the child. A party's sexual orientation alone is not a permissible basis for denying that party custody or visitation. T. Walker & L. Elrod, "Family Law in the Fifty States: An Overview," 26 *Family Law Quarterly* 384 (1993).

New York

New York v. Fortin, 706 N.Y.S.2d 611 (N.Y. County Ct. 2000). A man who was charged with sex crimes involving his 13-year-old niece sought to introduce testimony about "Parental Alienation Syndrome" (PAS). Psychiatrist Richard Gardner, who coined the term, testified that

> PAS typically arises when one parent programs a child in a campaign of denigration of the other parent, although PAS may also occur when other family members are involved. Under cross examination, Gardner admitted that he previously had written that psychodynamic psychiatry is the most speculative of all alleged sciences and that the concept of scientific proof is less important in that field than in other sciences, particularly with respect to persons charged with committing sexual abuse.

The court ruled that testimony regarding PAS was inadmissible, because the defendant failed to establish that the scientific community generally accepts PAS, "given the lack of a clear consensus by psychologists of the existence of this syndrome." 24 Mental & Physical Disability Law Reporter 366 (2000).

J.D. v. N.D., N.Y. Fam. Ct. Westchester County, N.Y.L.J., Oct. 17, 1996. A New York family court ruled that "domestic violence" includes verbal, psychological, physical, and financial abuse, and awarded sole custody to the mother on the basis of domestic violence committed by the father.

In re Jacob (Roseanne M.A.), 86 N.Y.2d 651, 660 N.E.2d 397, 636 N.Y.S.2d 716 (1995); *In re Dana (G.M.)*, 85 N.Y.2d 809, 628 N.Y.S.2d 52, 651 N.E.2d 920 (1995). A New York appeals court considered together attempts by the lesbian partner of one mother and the male cohabitant of another mother to adopt the children of these mothers. The court noted that an unmarried individual, heterosexual or homosexual, can adopt a child, according to state statutes. It therefore ruled that both of the adoptions at issue "are fully consistent with the adoption statute." The appellate court noted that the principle behind adoption is to secure "the best possible home for a child. Our primary loyalty must be to the statute's legislative purpose—the child's best interest."

In re Yost (Douris), 542 N.Y.S.2d 279 (Fam. Ct. Dutchess County 1994). The New York Family Court for Dutchess County ruled that a father may terminate paying child support on the basis that his ex-wife facilitated the end of his relationship with their daughter. While state law precludes forgiveness of arrears on the basis of interference with visitation, the court was able to suspend future payments pending the end of the interference and of the refusal of the daughter to visit her father. The law guardian appointed to represent the daughter supported the suspension of child support payments. The court indicated that

> [b]ased upon a totality of the evidence, this court reaches the inescapable conclusion that the mother of this young child has created an aura that over the years has made it difficult if not impossible for there to be a father-daughter relationship established. From a very young age, the child was given the option of whether to control the manner in which she would relate to her father. There is very little question that the demise of the father-daughter relationship was facilitated if not encouraged by the mother. . . . It is axiomatic that unjustified refusal by a child to visit his or her parent should not be condoned by the courts.

In re Adoption of a Child Whose First Name Is Evan, 153 Misc. 454 (N.Y. Sur. Ct. 1992). In the first such application of its kind in New York State, a lesbian couple sought and were granted legal recognition of their status as parents of a six-year-old boy. . . . The court held that Evan's adoption by DF would be in the child's best interests for the following reasons: It would legalize a family which has been functioning well for the past six years; it would not disrupt the child's life in any way; it would grant him important legal rights including status as an heir to DF and her family and eligibility for social security benefits in the event of her death or disability; it would allow Evan to receive medical and educational benefits provided under DF's employment. The court also reasoned that in the event of the couple's separation, Evan would be able to maintain his ties with DF since she would be considered to have parental rights co-equal with those of VC, his biological mother. . . . The judge considered the couple to be in a marital relationship "at its nurturing supportive best." . . . The court lastly touched upon the issue of homosexual parenting. Citing mental health literature on homosexual parents and their offspring, Judge Preminger concluded, "The fact that the petitioners here maintain an open lesbian relationship is not a reason to deny adoption. . . . This is consistent with the more general principle that a parent's sexual orientation or sexual practices are presumptively irrelevant in resolving custody disputes and may be considered only if they are shown to adversely affect the child's welfare." Herman, "*In the Matter of the Adoption of a Child Whose First Name Is Evan:* First Legal Recognition of Lesbian Co-Parenting in New York State," 17 *Newsletter of the American Academy of Psychiatry and the Law* 43–44 (1992).

North Dakota

Zeller v. Zeller, 640 N.W.2d 53 (N.D. 2002). Jenny and Doni Zeller are both members of the United States Air Force, stationed in North Dakota. They have joint custody, and Jenny was awarded physical custody of their children, born in 1994 and 1995. The parties had stipulated in their 1997 divorce that, if Jenny was transferred out of North Dakota, it would be a material change of circumstances and that physical custody would transfer to Doni. In 2000, Jenny was transferred to Fort Leonard Wood, Missouri, for a four-year teaching assignment. Jenny moved for an order allowing her to take the children to Missouri. The trial court denied the motion. Jenny appealed.

The North Dakota statute on relocation is designed to protect the non-custodial parent's visitation rights by requiring either a court order or consent of the non-custodial parent.

The primary consideration is the best interests of the child. There are four factors to be considerd:

1. The prospective advantages of the move in improving the custodial parent's and child's quality of life,
2. The integrity of the custodial parent's motive for relocation, considering whether it is to defeat or deter visitation by the non-custodial parent,
3. The integrity of the non-custodial parent's motives for opposing the move,
4. The potential negative impact on the relationship between the non-custodial parent and the child, including whether there is a realistic opportunity for visitation which can provide an adequate basis for preserving and fostering the non-custodial parent's relationship with the child if relocation is allowed, and the likelihood that each parent will comply with such alternate visitation.

While finding that Jenny's relocation request met the above criteria, the trial court ruled that the parties' stipulation, incorporated in the divorce decree, "is the law of the case," and that "[i]t is in the best interest of the children to be in the physical custody of their father if plaintiff relocates to Fort Leonard Wood, Missouri."

The supreme court cited *Zarrett v. Zarrett*, 1998 N.D. 49, 574 N.W.2d 855, which indicates that "a stipulation by the parents prohibiting or limiting the power of the court to modify future child support is against public policy and invalid." Therefore, the court ruled, the stipulation for "an automatic change in custody upon the occurrence of a future event is unenforceable and the district court retains control over the rights of children. . . ." The case was remanded to the trial court, which had already found that Jenny met the statutory criteria for location, for an order permitting her to take the children to Missouri.

Seigneur v. Olson (In re Guardianship of Nelson), 519 N.W.2d 15 (N.D. 1994). The North Dakota Supreme Court ruled that, as the "psychological parent," the woman who was the primary caregiver for two girls while living for four years with their father prior to his death should be made their guardian. The contest was between the woman and the father's aunt. The mother had little contact with the children since the divorce. The court found that the care and custody of the psychological parent was an exceptional circumstance and ruled that it should prevail over the interests of the aunt, based on the best interests of the children. As in a proceeding for modification of custody, the court ruled, the status quo should be preserved absent strong evidence to the contrary.

In re D.R., 525 N.W.2d 672 (N.D. 1994). The North Dakota Supreme Court ruled that permanent foster care was not a reasonable alternative to the termination of a mother's parental rights where the subsequent adoption of the children was in their best interests. The mother had borderline intellectual functioning and their father had schizophrenia. Additionally, the mother was unable to control the children or protect them from their father's abuse. A lower court ordered that the parental rights of the parents be terminated. The appeals court stated that permanent foster care should only be considered as an option if adoption is not in the best interests of the children. The court agreed with the lower court's determination that the boys needed a stable and permanent place to live apart from the parents in order to help them recover from the effects of their prior home environment. Also, visitation even by the mother would be detrimental to the children. Therefore, termination of parental rights and subsequent adoption were in the children's best interests. 19 *Mental & Physical Disability Law Reporter* 318 (1995).

Ohio

In re Bonfield, 773 N.E.2d 507 (Ohio 2002). The Ohio Supreme Court addressed a request to recognize the lesbian partner of a mother of five children as equal to the parent in matters concerning the children.

Teri J. Bonfield and Shelly M. Zachritz have lived together since 1987 in a committed homosexual relationship. During that period, Teri adopted two children and gave birth to three children, conceived through anonymous artificial insemination. Shelly has actively participated in the planning and births of the children and in raising all five children. According to Teri, Shelly is the primary caregiver for the children, and is seen by the children as an equal parent with Teri. A licensed psychologist testified that Teri and Shelly are jointly raising the children and form a close, loving, committed family in which the children are strongly bonded to each of them. He opined that it would be devastating for the children to be separated from Shelly.

Unfortunately, under law Shelly has no legally recognized rights with regard to any of the children. She does not have equal access to medical or school records, and cannot authorize medical care or obtain medical insurance for the children. If Teri were to die, a relative of Teri's would have a greater right than Shelly to adopt the children.

In some states, but not Ohio, there is an option for a "second parent adoption." This is a mechanism for permitting a partner in a cohabiting, non-marital relationship to adopt the partner's biological or adoptive child without the parent having to relinquish any parental rights. In Ohio, Teri would have to lose her parental rights in order for Shelly to adopt the children.

The trial court concluded that it did not have jurisdiction to grant the petition to make Shelly a parent of the children. The appeals court indicated that the trial court does have jurisdiction, but ruled that the trial court does not have the authority to award parental rights or shared parenting to an individual who is neither a biological nor adoptive parent. The Supreme Court accepted the case on a discretionary appeal.

Appellants advocated a four-part test of whether an individual is a "psychological" or "second" parent, as is done in some other states:

> (1) whether the legal parent consents to and fosters the relationship between the "psychological" or "second" parent and the child, (2) whether the "psychological" or "second" parent has lived with the child, (3) whether the "psychological" or "second" parent performs parental functions for the child to a significant degree, and (4) whether a parent-child bond has been forged between the "second" parent and the child. *Bonfield* at 512.

However, the Supreme Court indicated that the word "parent" was used differently in existing statutes, and declined to accept that proposal. For similar reasons, the Supreme Court also rejected *in loco parentis* as a basis.

Noting its desire to honor the appellants' goal of providing a stable environment for the children, the supreme court indicated that the trial court has exclusive original jurisdiction to determine the custody of any child not a ward of another court. The court therefore held that the juvenile court has jurisdiction to determine the custody of the Bonfield children. Further, parents may waive the right to custody of their children, and are bound by an agreement to do so. Accordingly, the case was remanded to the juvenile court for proceedings to determine whether a shared custody agreement between Teri and Shelly is in the best interests of the children.

Pennsylvania

T.B. v. L.R.M., 786 A.2d 913 (Pa. 2001). T.B. and L.R.M., both females, had an exclusive, intimate relationship. They decided to have a child, and agreed that donor sperm would be used to impregnate L.R.M. The child, A.M., was born August 27, 1993. They raised the child together, but did not execute a formal parenting agreement. L.R.M. named T.B. as guardian of the child in her will. Both women did all of the things a parent would normally do in raising a child, including taking off work when the child was ill.

In May 1996, they purchased a new home together. T.B. left that home shortly thereafter, and entered a relationship with another woman. In August 1996, T.B. and L.R.M. formally separated. After T.B.'s visit with A.M. on September 4, 1996, L.R.M. refused all requests for visitation, all phone calls, and all gifts for A.M. On October 3, 1996, T.B. filed a "Complaint for Shared Legal and Partial Custody and Visitation." The hearing officer found that T.B. had standing to seek visitation and custody pursuant to the doctrine of *in loco parentis*, as well as finding that it would be in the child's best interests for T.B. to have partial custody for purposes of visitation. L.R.M. appealed. The *en banc* superior court agreed that T.B. stood *in loco parentis*, but indicated that the record did not provide an adequate basis to determine whether visitation was in A.M.'s best interests. The case was remanded for a full hearing. The Pennsylvania Supreme Court agreed to solely address whether the lower courts correctly applied the common law doctrine of *in loco parentis*. It noted that, while third parties are often refused standing, actions for custody have been permitted when that third party stands *in loco parentis* to a child.

> The phrase "*in loco parentis*" refers to a person who puts oneself in the situation of a lawful parent by assuming the obligations incident to the parental relationship without going through the formality of a legal adoption. The status of *in loco parentis* embodies two ideas; first, the assumption of a parental status, and, second, the discharge of parental duties. . . . The rights and liabilities arising out of an *in loco parentis* relationship are . . . exactly the same as between parent and child. . . . The third party in this type of relationship, however, can not place himself *in loco parentis* in defiance of the parents' wishes and the parent/child relationship.

T.B. at 916.

The Pennsylvania Supreme Court rejected L.R.M.'s contention that T.B. lacked standing because the law does not apply to former partners of a biological parent. Rather, it found that

> the nature of the relationship between Appellant and Appellee has no legal significance to the determination of whether Appellee stands *in loco parentis* to A.M. The ability to marry the

biological parent and the ability to adopt the subject child have never been and are not now factors in determining whether the third party assumed a parental status and discharged parental duties. What is relevant, however, is the method by which the third party gained authority to do so. The record is clear that Appellant consented to Appellee's performance of parental duties. She encouraged Appellee to assume the status of a parent and acquiesced as Appellee carried out the day-to-day care of A.M. . . . Appellant further contends that Appellee can not stand *in loco parentis* to A.M. because Appellee merely acted as a caretaker and because A.M. was never in Appellee's sole care. . . . [However,] the record supports the hearing officer's finding that Appellee lived with Appellant and A.M. as a family unit and that Appellee assumed the role of co-parent. . . . Appellee has demonstrated that she assumed a parental status and discharged parental duties.

T.B. at 918–19.

Finally, the Pennsylvania Supreme Court addressed L.R.M's contention that the court should adopt the position of the U.S. Supreme Court in *Troxel v. Granville*, 120 S. Ct. 2054 (2000). The Pennsylvania Supreme Court refused, indicating that the Pennsylvania statute was not overly broad, nor was there an abandonment of the presumption that a fit parent will act in the best interests of the child. Rather, the issue was whether the facts supported a determination that T.B. had standing to seek partial custody. The Pennsylvania Supreme Court indicated that she did, affirming the lower court order.

Myers v. DiDomenico, 657 A.2d 956 (Pa. Super. Ct. 1995). The Pennsylvania Superior Court held that the wishes of children are important considerations in determining the child's best interests, and that the wish of two teenage children to have custody transferred from their mother to their father should be granted. The children wanted to live with their father for some period prior to their becoming legal adults, and the court agreed that they should have that opportunity. The mother would have visitation rights, to be determined by the trial court.

Rowles v. Rowles, 542 Pa. 443 (1995). The Pennsylvania Supreme Court ruled that a natural parent does not always automatically receive custody when there is a dispute between parents and a third party. Rather, the question is what placement is in the best interests of the child. Parenthood remains a very significant factor, but is not an automatic basis for a decision.

Hill v. Divecchio, 425 Pa. Super. 355 (1993). The Pennsylvania Superior Court ruled that a child's maternal grandmother has standing to request partial custody or visitation of the child under Pennsylvania's grandparent visitation statute, even where the child's divorced mother objects.

Blew v. Verta, 420 Pa. Super. 528 (1992). The Pennsylvania Superior Court ruled that a trial court abused its discretion when it prohibited a mother from having her son with her when her lesbian partner was present. Their relationship was six years old, and the women lived together. The modified custody order required the mother's visitation to take place at her parents' home. The court found no evidence that the lesbian relationship had had an adverse effect on the boy. The court cited psychological studies that indicate that a parent's homosexuality does not, in itself, have a negative impact on children. The court drew an analogy with a case in which a trial court had denied custody to a parent on the basis of that parent's interracial relationship.

Rhode Island

Rubano v. DiCenzo, 759 A.2d 959 (R.I. Sept. 2000). The Rhode Island Supreme Court ruled that a woman may petition for visitation with the son she and her former lesbian partner raised together. The women agreed they wished to have a child, and one of them conceived via artificial insemination by an anonymous donor. They raised the child together for four years, then separated. The biological mother agreed to visitation by her former partner, then changed her mind. The former partner petitioned the family court, seeking to establish her *de facto* parental status and to obtain court-ordered visitation. The women entered a consent order establishing "permanent visitation." The mother reneged again, and alleged that the visitation was harmful to the child. The Family Court certified the case to the Rhode Island Supreme Court due to its uncertainty regarding how to resolve the matter.

In this case of first impression, the Supreme Court held that the biological parent does not have an "absolute right to prevent all third parties from ever acquiring any parental rights *vis-à-vis* the child." In the instant matter, the fact that the biological mother allowed her partner to take on an equal role as a parent, and agreed to and signed an order granting the partner "permanent visitation" because it is in the "best interests of the child," indicate that the mother had, by word and deed, allowed her former partner to establish a parental relationship with the child. The case was remanded to the Family Court for adjudication consistent with the holding of the Rhode Island Supreme Court.

Tennessee

Casby v. Hazlerig, W2001-02073-COA-R3-CV (Tenn. Ct. App. July 24, 2002). A couple were divorced, and, based on the wife's having engaged in "inappropriate marital conduct," emergency temporary custody of the two children was given to the father. After a hearing, joint custody was awarded to the father and to the maternal grandmother. After a trial, joint custody was awarded to the parents of the children, with the father as primary custodial parent. The mother, and later the father, filed motions to alter the custodial arrangement.

The trial court found that the mother had made allegations of abuse by the father that were without any factual basis, and that the mother had attempted to manipulate the children. The court also noted that the mother's psychological evaluation had found her to be

> "self-focused" and to have a "narcissistic personality, with an overt agenda to portray [Father] in a negative light. She accepted little responsibility for her actions, and made frequent use of denial, minimization, rationalization, and projection of blame onto others. Based on the court's prior dealings with the mother, the court concurred in the evaluation's conclusions.

The evaluation also suggested that the mother would not be an appropriate custodial parent, and that she needed long-term psychotherapy. In contrast, the evaluation cast the father in a positive light, indicating that he would be an appropriate and protective parent who had created a safe, stable, and nurturing environment for the children. The trial court awarded custody of the children to the father, giving the mother limited visitation. The mother appealed.

Indicating that "the courts' paramount concern in a custody case is the welfare and best interest of the parties' minor children," the appeals court affirmed the ruling of the trial court.

Texas

In re C.P.J. & S.B.J., 129 S.W.3d 573 (Tex. App. [5th Dist.] 2003). Marshall Jackson agreed to allow his former parents-in-law visitation with his two children, their grandchildren, after his wife died. Nearly two years after a trial court approved the agreement, Jackson filed a motion to terminate the visitation order on the basis of the U.S. Supreme Court decision in *Troxel v. Granville*, 530 U.S. 57 (2000). The trial court reduced the amount of visitation, but refused to terminate it. Jackson appealed, stating that the grandparent visitation statute was unconstitutional.

The appellate court determined that *Troxel* was limited to the special facts of the Washington statute, and did not apply to the Texas statute. It further acknowledged that a parent has a special liberty interest in the care, custody, and control of his or her child, and that the court is required by *Troxel* to accord some special weight to the wishes of the parent. However, it ruled that the trial court had accorded some special weight to the parent's own determination regarding visitation, and that the Texas statute was not unconstitutional on its face or as applied to the instant case.

Utah

Sigg v. Sigg, 905 P.2d 908 (Utah App. 1995). The Utah Court of Appeals held that a custodial parent who interferes with the visitation of the non-custodial parent may, by so doing, cause a change of circumstances sufficient to warrant a change of placement.

Vermont

Spaulding v. Butler, 782 A.2d 1167 (Vt. 2001). A trial court had ruled that, because a father had "a full parent/child relationship" with his son, while the mother was estranged from the boy, the father should be the "primary parent," with the mother having supervised visitation that would transition to unsupervised visitation. The mother appealed.

The Vermont Supreme Court reversed. While the facts supported the conclusion that the father had a full parent-child relationship with his son, that fact was undermined by the trial court's finding that the father had engaged in a long, persistent campaign to eliminate the mother-child relationship. Citing its decision in *Renaud v. Renaud*, 168 Vt. 306, 309, 721 A.2d 463, 465–66 (1998), the court indicated that "[a]cross the country, the great weight of authority holds that conduct by one parent that tends to alienate the child's affections from the other is so inimical to the child's welfare as to be grounds for a denial of custody to, or a change of custody from, the parent guilty of such conduct." The Supreme Court reversed and remanded the case to the trial court for further proceedings in the context of these rulings.

Virginia

Bottoms v. Bottoms, 444 S.E.2d 276 (Va. Ct. App. 1994). The Virginia Court of Appeals ruled that an open lesbian relationship is not, alone, sufficient to permit a court to remove a child and give custody to a nonparent, in this case a grandparent.

> The psychological evidence was that Sharon's lesbian relationship has had no discernible effect on her son. He and Sharon have had a close, loving relationship. She has not physically abused the child, neglected him, or endangered his well-being. . . . The trial court ruled that because Sharon lives in a sexually active lesbian relationship and engaged in illegal sexual acts (she admits she engages in oral sex in violation of Virginia's sodomy law), she is an unfit parent as a matter of law. It granted custody to [the child's grandmother].
>
> [I]n order for a third party, even a grandparent, to be awarded custody of a child in preference to the child's parent, the third party must prove by clear and convincing evidence that the parent is unfit or that special circumstances give an extraordinary reason for a transfer of custody. . . . No credible evidence proves that Sharon is an unfit parent or that her having custody of her son will be harmful to him. No evidence suggests that any of her actions resulted in psychological or physical harm to the child or that her actions constituted neglect or abuse. . . . The fact that a parent is homosexual does not per se render a parent unfit to have custody of his or her child. . . . The fact that a parent has committed a crime does not render a parent unfit, unless such criminal conduct impacts upon or is harmful to the child, or unless other special circumstances exist aside from the parent's conduct that would render continued custody with the parent deleterious to the child. . . . A parent's private sexual conduct, even if illegal, does not create a presumption of unfitness. . . . A court will not remove a child from the custody of a parent, based on proof that the parent is engaged in private, illegal sexual conduct or conduct considered by some to be deviant, absent proof that such behavior or activity poses a substantial threat of harm to a child's psychological or physical well-being. . . .
>
> Where a parent exposes a child to an illicit sexual relationship . . . , the supreme court has upheld denying a parent custody; however, where parents have shielded the child from illegal heterosexual adultery . . . , we have held the parents not to be unfit. . . .
>
> The supreme court has held that adverse effects of a parent's homosexuality on a child cannot be assumed without specific proof. . . . The psychological testimony was to the effect that a parent's homosexual relationship alone does not harm a child psychologically or make the parent an unfit custodian. The social science evidence showed that a person's sexual orientation does not strongly correlate with that person's fitness as a parent.

Washington

In re Kovacs, 121 Wn.2d 795 (1993), 854 P.2d 629. The Washington Supreme Court ruled that there is no statutory presumption that the parent who was the primary caretaker during the marriage will be the better primary placement parent, nor is there a presumption that placement with the former primary caretaker will be in the child's best interests, unless there has been evidence of harm to the child. The supreme court indicated that knowing which parent was the primary caretaker is a significant factor to consider in awarding custody, but other factors must be considered as well. The court reinstated the trial court's award of primary placement of the three children to the father, even though the mother had been their primary caretaker.

Wisconsin

Richard D. v. Rebecca G., 228 Wis. 2d 658, 599 N.W.2d 90 (Ct. App. 1999). The Wisconsin Court of Appeals held that the bond between a foster parent and a child must be considered as a critical element in determining with whom a child lives.

The case involved a four-year-old girl, who had seen her biological mother only twice during her first two years. The girl spent nearly all of her life with foster parents, who wanted to adopt her. The appellate court held that the trial court placed too much emphasis on the biological relationship with the mother rather than on the best interests of the child. The appellate court indicated that if a biological parent abdicates responsibility by abandoning the child or failing to fulfill "core parental responsibilities," it is up to the court to determine what is in the child's best interests. If there is determined to be "a strong bonding by a child with its caretakers," trial courts may "preserve the status quo and leave the child in a happy, nurturing home of a caring and loving non-parent." The appellate court further noted that "safety" and "best interests" are not synonymous, and that the latter governs the decision to be made by the trial court.

Holtzman v. Knott (In re H.S.H.-K), 533 N.W.2d 419 (Wis. 1995). The Wisconsin Supreme Court ruled that a trial court has the authority to grant visitation with a child born to a former lesbian partner. The court first determined that the legislature intended that visitation be granted to "a . . . person who has maintained a relationship similar to a parent-child relationship with the child" (Ch. 767, Wis. Stats), and that it was not intended that this be limited to situations involving the dissolution of a marriage. The court's power to act in the best interest of a child derives in part from its responsibility to protect minors. It also concluded that "public policy considerations do not prohibit a court from relying on its equitable powers to grant visitation apart from § 767.245 on the basis of a co-parenting agreement between a biological parent and another when visitation is in a child's best interest."

> Mindful of preserving a biological or adoptive parent's constitutionally protected interests and the best interests of a child, we conclude that a court has equitable power to hear a petition for visitation when it determines that the petitioner has a parent-like relationship with the child and that a significant triggering event justifies state intervention in the child's relationship with a biological or adoptive parent. To meet those two requirements, a petitioner must prove the component elements of each one. . . .
>
> To demonstrate the existence of the petitioner's parent-like relationship with the child, the petitioner must prove: (1) that the biological or adoptive parent consented to, and fostered, the petitioner's formation and establishment of a parent-like relationship with the child; (2) that the petitioner and the child lived together in the same household; (3) that the petitioner assumed obligations of parenthood by taking significant responsibility for the child's care, education and development, including contributing towards the child's support, without expectation of financial compensation; and (4) that the petitioner has been in a parental role for a length of time sufficient to have established with the child a bonded, dependent relationship parental in nature.
>
> To establish a significant triggering event justifying state intervention in the child's relationship with a biological or adoptive parent, the petitioner must prove that this parent has intervened substantially with the petitioner's parent-like relationship with the child, and

that the petitioner sought court ordered visitation within a reasonable time after the parent's interference.

H.F. v. T.F., 168 Wis. 2d 62, 483 N.W.2d 803 (1992). The Wisconsin Supreme Court said that a stepparent adoption did not terminate the paternal grandparents' visitation rights where the child's father had died. The court found that, after the father's death, the child was adopted by her stepfather, but that continued visitation with her deceased father's parents was in her best interest. The court distinguished cases involving the death of a parent from those cases where a parent voluntarily terminates his or her parental rights. The court stated that, unlike when a parent voluntarily terminates his or her parental rights, a deceased parent continues to be a parent, and thus grandparents continue to be grandparents. T. Walker & L. Elrod, "Family Law in the Fifty States: An Overview," 26 *Family Law Quarterly* 392 (1993).

CHAPTER 5

DO'S AND DON'T'S FOR DIVORCE CLIENTS

§ 5.1   Introduction

This chapter identifies and briefly discusses the recommendations for appropriate behaviors for parents during separation, court proceedings, and following divorce, as well as the inappropriate behaviors they should avoid. As an attorney, read through the list of Do's and Don't's and subjectively determine how well your client is complying with these recommendations. A parent who is following most of the recommended positive, appropriate behaviors (the Do's) and at most a few (preferably) of the identified negative (inappropriate) negative behaviors (the Don't's) is in a favorable position to obtain custody and/or primary placement. A parent who is exhibiting only a few of the appropriate behaviors and most of the inappropriate behaviors is less likely to obtain custody or placement of the children. This list of Do's and Don't's can be used as a subjective, informal guide to help determine who would make the more appropriate custody or placement parent. All the recommendations regarding behaviors (the Do's versus the Don't's) are based both on research and on the authors' experience in more than 2,000 divorce-related cases.

Have your client prepare a list of the Do's that his/her partner is not doing and the Don't's that his/her partner is doing. At the same time, encourage your client to be honest in describing what Do's your client is not doing and what Don't's your client is doing. Again, these can be used as a subjective guide in helping determine the likelihood of obtaining custody or placement.

§ 5.2   Do's

1. **Encourage your client to attempt mediation before litigation.** The research clearly demonstrates that mediated divorces result in fewer adjustment problems for

both children and parents, a shorter period required for resolution of problems, and less likelihood of re-litigation. It is generally a good idea to have an agreement among the parties and the attorneys that the mediator have immunity from testimony. As a result, each of the individuals can feel free to state concerns openly, without fearing the statements will be used in future litigation. Many states currently have legislation requiring mediation prior to litigation and guaranteeing immunity from testimony for the mediator.

2. **Help your client understand that two parents living apart will not see their child(ren) as often as will two parents living together.**

3. **Help your client understand that the expenses of two individuals, living apart, will be greater than those of two individuals living together.** In the authors' experience, items number two and three represent the issues most commonly encountered during postjudgment hearings. The typical scenario involves the father who believes that the mother has too much time with the children, while the mother must realize that time her ex-husband spends with the children is time no longer available to her. Furthermore, one parent having more bills to pay than before does not mean the other parent has excessive disposable income.

4. The client must be helped to realize that time spent with the children and financial support are two separate issues, neither of which has a legal effect on the other. Fathers may withhold support because they want more visitation, or the mother may withhold visitation because she does not receive support on a timely basis—but both actions are inappropriate. In an assessment of placement time and support, the two issues may become enmeshed.

5. **Help your client consider a joint custody arrangement rather than a sole custody arrangement.** Both joint custody and sole custody present problems. Parents who are granted sole custody often demonstrate behavior suggesting "ownership" of the children, which tends to lead summarily to the exclusion of the other parent. Even though two parents may not communicate effectively after the divorce, joint custody should be considered the optimal choice. Joint custody implies that the parents will be able to cooperate well enough to make joint decisions about such issues as the child(ren)'s education, religious upbringing, and medical treatment. In most cases, by the time the divorce has taken place, most of these decisions have already been made. The one exception is nonemergency medical treatment for problems unforeseen at the time of the divorce. It is in the best interests of the child(ren) if both parents can make medical decisions. As a result, religious upbringing and education decisions tend not to become a major part of joint custody communications. Sole custody should be considered only when one parent is clearly harmful to the children, is an active substance abuser, is chronically mentally ill and does not consistently take medication, is a habitual criminal, or has some other severe problem.

6. **Recommend that your client consider sharing holidays as opposed to alternating holidays.** The concept of alternating holidays may be an archaic concept in the new millennium. When parents live in the same city, it is important for the children to maintain contact with both sets of families during important holidays. For example, there is no reason why the children should be allowed to see only the father's relatives at Thanksgiving one year and the mother's relatives at Thanksgiving the next year. When families live in close proximity, important holidays such as Thanksgiving

and Christmas can be shared so the children have an opportunity to see both parents and their extended families for each of the holidays. These opportunities help provide children lifelong positive memories of holiday times. If possible, both extended families should celebrate together. If necessary, holidays can be divided between the families.

7.   **Encourage your client to tell the child(ren) in advance that the separation is going to take place and to do so** *with the other parent.* Unfortunately, all too often children come home from school to find that one of the parents has moved out of the house without prior explanation or an opportunity to discuss the matter. It is vitally important to prepare the children before the actual separation takes place. This information should be communicated to the children by the parents together. This tells children that even though their parents are getting divorced, they still have the capacity to work together in the children's best interests. At a minimum, children under six should be given several days' notice. Children over six should have at least a week's notice. The explanation should not be blameworthy nor pit one parent against the other. If one parent refuses to participate in the explanation process, the other parent should be as neutral as possible in the explanation.

8.   **Encourage your client to tell child(ren) often that they are still loved and that they are not getting divorced from their parents.** Parents all too often assume that their children understand this truth, even though they are not frequently reminded. During the separation period and shortly after the divorce, children may need to be told often that they are loved. Their concern may be, "You stopped loving Mom. How do I know you won't stop loving me?" One way to reassure children is to tell them that the love between spouses is different from the love between parent and child. Although the love between spouses can fade away, there is a permanency to the love between parents and their children, a love that began from the moment of birth. By contrast, the parents had to meet and fall in love, and therefore could fall out of love as well.

9.   **Do parents understand that they should not move more often than necessary?** Although several moves may be necessary during the divorce process and shortly thereafter, it is important to provide stability as soon as possible for the children. If may be necessary for the parent to engage in a first move at the time of the separation, then into temporary quarters after the divorce while looking for a permanent residence, and finally to a more permanent residence, all occurring within a year or two. However, moving children several times within two years, *especially* if doing so requires different school placements, is likely to have a detrimental effect on the children's psychological well-being.

10. **Encourage both parents to be sensitive to the child(ren)'s needs as well as the parent's own needs.** Unfortunately, parents often become bogged down in meeting their own needs, to the neglect of recognizing their children's needs. Parents who cannot be sensitive to their children's needs may find the children exhibiting maladaptive behavior in response.

11. **Encourage your client to plan and consult with the other parent, in advance, regarding activities of the child(ren).** This recommendation applies to many factors in the overall development of the children. When it comes to planning lessons, athletic activities, camp, recitals, extended medical treatment, out-of-town visits to

relatives, or other routine activities, it is essential for the parents to communicate with one another prior to implementation of these plans. It only serves to increase the acrimony if one parent makes the plans without consulting the other, then attempts to follow through with the plans without the other parent's input. When one parent does not incorporate the other parent in these areas, it raises a concern about the level of cooperation that will occur in the future, and may affect recommendations.

12. **Encourage your client to strictly observe time schedules with the child(ren).** The tardy parent should call, explaining the reason for being late and giving an estimated time of arrival. One way to reduce the likelihood of tardiness is to agree that the receiving parent will transport the children. For example, if the children are going to the mother's for the weekend visit, their mother would pick them up. When the visit is completed, their father would pick them up. As a result, there is less likelihood for tardiness unless it cannot be avoided. The placement schedule is a road map from which adaptations can be made with mutual parental consent. However, absent this, the schedule should be strictly followed.

13. **Encourage your client to be flexible with regard to visitation times for the other parent.** No placement schedule can take into account all the possible exceptions that may occur. As a result, flexibility is encouraged. It is important for parents not to count up the minutes, hours, or days that may be lost or gained as a result of this flexibility. The presumption should be that, over the course of the children's childhood, the time will balance out. One of the authors of this book is reminded of a mediation session during which a parent sat down and stated, "No mediation can take place until I get the three days' visitation time that my ex-wife owes me." The ex-wife responded that she had no knowledge of receiving three days of visitation she was not entitled to. At that point, the father pulled out a notebook covering three years of entries: the mother was 15 minutes late for a drop-off, was an hour late in arriving home, took the children to a parent-child school function during the father's time, and so on. He pointed out that all of this time over the three years added up to approximately 72 hours, and he wanted his three days before any mediation was going to take place. The author, as a mediator, was not able to convince the father that the amount of energy wasted in keeping track of these minutes could have been spent far more productively with the children. The father was also unable to recognize that he had been late occasionally and that his ex-wife could have docked him for those times but chose not to do so. Parents who count the minutes are not working in the best interests of their children.

14. **Encourage your client to do whatever is necessary to resolve the angry feelings toward the ex-spouse.** As mentioned in **Chapter 4**, research clearly demonstrates that there is a significant amount of depression in children whose parents are still fighting five years postjudgment. Ex-spouses do not have to love or even like one another. They *must*, however, be civil to one another in the presence of their children. Angry feelings will be conveyed to the children and can cause serious problems—in some cases, even clinical depression. Postjudgment parental communication counseling is often the best method to resolve these areas of concern.

15. **Ensure that your client works with the other parent to present a united front when handling any problems with the child(ren).** Children should not be allowed to manipulate the parents by playing one off against the other. If a problem arises and

the parents choose to respond to it in different ways, it presents an opportunity for the child to manipulate the situation. Discussions should take place and ground rules should be established for dealing with specific problems. It may be necessary for the parents to recognize that there is little likelihood that they will agree on how to handle some or all of the problems. Parents must not allow this to provide an opportunity for one parent to "bad mouth" the other parent.

16. **Do the parents permit their child(ren) to have too much decision-making power?** This applies especially to allowing preadolescent children to decide whether they will or will not have placement with the other parent. When children of that age are allowed to have this kind of decisionmaking power, they are more likely to demand excessive and inappropriate power during their teenage years, perhaps even become uncontrollable. Older teenagers may reasonably have some say in how much time they spend with the other parent and the timing of the placement. Research demonstrates that children should not have significant input in deciding where they live, or whether they visit the other parent, or not until they are 15 and 16 years old, respectively (see **Chapter 3**).

17. **Encourage your client to take the child(ren) to a therapist if the psychological adjustment appears too problematic.** Parents should not be running to a therapist whenever a child has an adverse reaction to divorce. However, adverse reactions that last for months rather than weeks may become habitual rather than transient. A difficult conflict results when one parent feels that psychotherapy is necessary and beneficial but the other parent says, "My kids aren't crazy and I'm not taking them to any shrink." In general, if either parent believes that therapy is warranted, a brief evaluation of the need for therapy should take place.

18. **Encourage your client to provide the child(ren) with an emotional environment that allows them to continue to love the other parent and spend time with that parent.** Children often realize that their parents got divorced because they neither like nor love each other. They also recognize the acrimony between their parents. As a result, they can be fearful that one parent may see them being too friendly with the other parent, and become angry. Children must be made aware that it is perfectly acceptable and appropriate to show love and positive regard for the other parent.

19. **Encourage a good relationship between the child(ren) and the parent's extended family.** The principle in item 18 also applies to the children's feelings about aunts, uncles, grandparents, and other members of the other parent's extended family. For one parent to criticize the other parent's extended family puts inappropriate pressure on the child and increases the problems between the divorced parents.

20. **Encourage the child(ren) to remember the other parent on special occasions, allowing the children to telephone on a reasonable basis (the time and length of the phone calls to be in accordance with family rules) and on special occasions.** If children are unable to purchase birthday cards, Father's or Mother's Day cards, or cards for special occasions without help, the parents should encourage and aid them as necessary to make sure these occasions are recognized. Each parent needs to understand that the other parent would enjoy receiving recognition on appropriate occasions just as much as he or she would, and that it is in the child(ren)'s best interest for the child(ren) to share in special occasions.

21. **Encourage your client to use discretion as to the time and frequency of calls to the child(ren).** Parents must recognize that when their children are with the other parent, they will be involved in family time, quiet time, homework time, and other forms of interaction. Frequent, unnecessary phone calls become intrusive and serve to agitate and aggravate the other parent. With children under six years of age, daily contact is desirable. With children over six years of age, daily contact is not necessary but if desired by the children should be allowed. In this age group, two to three times per week is sufficient. In any case, when daily contact is made, *once* per day is optimal.

22. **Encourage your client to recognize that child(ren) will feel powerless and helpless.** Children are subject to parents' decisions about where they will live, with whom they will live, what school they will attend, what neighborhood they will live in, and whom their friends will be, all with little consultation with them. Furthermore, if a judge is required to resolve conflicts, some decisions will be made by a complete stranger. As a result, the children are likely to feel both powerless and helpless about the outcomes of their lives.

23. **Make sure your client is aware that the child(ren) may feel insecure and exhibit regressive behavior.** Insecurity in children may occur for the same reasons identified in the previous recommendation. In addition, insecurity can be associated with concerns like, "Mom already left. How do I know that Dad won't leave too?" It is not unusual for children to exhibit regressive behavior when under stress. This behavior could include returning to thumb sucking, bed wetting, whining, tantrums, or other similar behaviors. If such behavior continues for a relatively short time, psychotherapeutic intervention is not necessary. However, if it appears for more than one or two months, therapy may be warranted.

24. **Encourage your client to provide an appropriate role model for the child(ren).** Parents should recognize that the behavior they exhibit serves as a model for their children and that they are actually teaching them how to respond. As a result, parents who are excessively angry, overreactive, or depressed (or who exhibit other extremes of behavior) are likely to have children who are excessively angry, overreactive, or depressed.

25. **Encourage your client to allow the child(ren) to see where the other parent is going to live after moving out of the house.** Children need to know that the parent who is leaving the house is having his or her primary needs met. This is done by showing the children that the departing parent will have a place to sleep, a place to eat, and a bathroom. By seeing this dwelling as soon as possible, children are assured that their parent has these necessities. It can be helpful to the child(ren) to pack a few of the boxes for the departing parent and help that parent move those boxes.

26. **Encourage your client to put aside differences with the other parent long enough for both parents to attend school conferences together.** When parents have a problem dealing with one another, it should not become the school's problem. Some school districts offer only one teacher conference, and the parents must decide whether to attend together or designate one parent to attend. When school systems are willing to provide two separate conferences for the parents, it makes the parents' problem the school's problem. Parents must also recognize that when their behavior is inappropriate in school, it will reflect negatively on their child(ren). Children need

assurance that their parents are willing to put aside their differences for the benefit of their children. Doing so is a powerful statement to the children of how much the parents care about them.

27. **Encourage your client to exercise the right and responsibility of both parents to consult with school officials concerning the child(ren)'s welfare and educational status, and the right to inspect and receive student records if state law allows.**

28. **Encourage your client to exercise the right of both parents to receive, or have forwarded promptly from the appropriate parent or school, copies of all school reports, calendar of school events, and notices of parent-teacher conferences.**

29. **Encourage your client to exercise the right of both parents to be notified in case of the child(ren)'s "serious illness," and to respond—and allow the other parent to respond—to these important circumstances.**

30. **Encourage your client to exercise the right of both parents to authorize emergency medical, surgical, hospital, dental, institutional, and/or psychiatric care. The parents should consult during or as soon as possible after the emergency.**

31. **Encourage your client to recognize the right of both parents to inspect and receive the child(ren)'s medical and dental records, and the right to consult with any treating physician, dentist, or mental health professional of the child(ren).** The previous five recommendations emphasize that each parent must continue to be aware of all of the above-stated areas of information. When this type of information is withheld, or when parents are excluded from participating in these processes, post-judgment visitation or support conflicts are likely to appear. When parents are kept fully informed, they will feel more a part of the children's lives and are less likely to feel the necessity for postjudgment actions. When one parent does not keep the other parent informed, it is likely to be held against that parent in a custody proceeding.

32. **Encourage your client to recognize that the child(ren) need substantial contact with the same-gender parent during adolescence.** Male children identify more closely with their fathers during adolescence, and female children identify more closely with their mothers during adolescence. As a result, it may be necessary to voluntarily alter placement time with parents based on these increased needs of the children. This should not be viewed as an attempt of one parent to sabotage the time of the other parent but rather as a normal developmental process.

33. **Encourage your client to allow all grandparents to continue to have contact with the child(ren).** Whether or not there is a state law, parents should recognize that the children are not getting divorced from the grandparents. There is a special place in children's hearts for their grandparents. When one parent denies contact with the ex-spouse's parents because of animosity, it serves only to remove another important component of the childhood experience and an important source of support for the child. Certainly, as part of this process, grandparents must be instructed not to criticize the other parent because it can undermine the relationship and heighten the acrimony.

34. **Encourage your client to communicate with the other parent openly, honestly, and regularly to avoid misunderstandings harmful to the child(ren).** Most of the child-rearing difficulties between divorced parents result from poor communication. When a child tells Mom what Dad said, or tells Dad what Mom criticized, it is important for

parents to be able to communicate about these concerns and "check it out." If the communication skills between parents are so poor that this is impossible, it allows children to continue manipulating their parents, increases the acrimony between parents, and teaches the children poor communication techniques. Unfortunately, we are asking the parents to do something outside the marriage that they were incapable of doing inside the marriage. Had they been able to communicate effectively inside the marriage, they may not have needed to get divorced in the first place. As a result of the current electronic age, e-mails can be used as a method to facilitate communication without parents' becoming frustrated over being unable to make contact by telephone, without the other parent hearing yelling, negative tone of voice, or frustration. This method only works if the e-mailing parent makes an effort to not include inflammatory or profane language in the e-mail.

35. **Encourage your client to make plans directly with the other parent rather than through the child(ren).** Anytime the children are caught in the middle of communication, it becomes burdensome for them. It is unfair to burden children with the role of middleman.

36. **Encourage your client to live as close to the other parent as is practical, convenient, and reasonable, especially if the child(ren) are young.** Children are more likely to feel that they have two homes if they can move conveniently between the houses, especially if they are old enough to do so on foot or by bicycle because the houses are near each other. Older children should be able to go to their "other house" to retrieve forgotten items, discuss matters with the other parent, interact with pets, and so on. However, it should be made clear to the children that they will eat and sleep at the placement home, not the other home. This reduces the likelihood of their playing one parent off against the other.

37. **Recommend that your client maintain household routines as much as possible.** There are already many changes occurring during a child's life at the time of separation and divorce. To the degree they are able, parents should maintain the basic structure of their lives. Chores, eating and sleeping routines, and regular schedules should be maintained as much as possible. Any changes should be discussed with the children in advance and kept to a minimum.

38. **Encourage your client to maintain the same set of rules as much as possible in both homes.** Although it may be a valuable lesson for children to learn that different rules can apply to different settings, when the basic routines at each home are too different from one another, it can increase the children's anxiety. As a result, it is beneficial to keep mealtime rules, bedtime rules, homework rules, and general rules as similar as possible between the two homes. At the same time, parents must realize that they cannot enforce rules or maintain discipline when the children are in the other parent's home. This recommendation may be difficult to follow, since many divorces occur because parents have different views of child-rearing techniques. For example, one parent often accuses the other of being too lax, while the other parent accuses the first of being too strict.

39. **Make sure your client realizes that winning against the other parent can never be more important than the well-being of the child(ren).** If your client remembers only one fact from this book, remember this: WINNING IS NEVER MORE IMPORTANT THAN THE WELL-BEING OF THE CHIDREN. *No one* wins a painful

custody battle, and the children are the biggest losers. In a custody dispute, it is not unusual for one parent to strongly believe that he or she is superior to the other parent, that the other parent is defective, and that placement with the other parent would be detrimental for the children. However, there is a point of diminishing returns. When the pursuit of winning endangers the mental health of the children, the parents must step back and recognize that the children's well-being is far more important than winning.

§ 5.3 Don't's

1. **Advise your client not to agree to any type of alternating, 50-50 arrangement unless there is nearly complete cooperation between the parents at all times, without acrimony.** As family law moved into the new millennium, it was recognized that traditional visitation/placement schedules did not allow both parents to have an extended, ongoing relationship with their children. Today, many states have enacted laws that posit the assumption that each parent should have "substantially equal" time with the children, allowing for exceptions when necessary. This replaces the previous concept that posited that a primary placement parent should be sought with exceptions being made when necessary. Consequently, many parents have attempted to develop "substantially" equal placement schedules on a 50-50 basis, such as a Sunday through Wednesday and Wednesday through Sunday schedule, alternating weeks, or alternating two-week segments. The problem with these schedules is that they may not allow children to feel like they have a home. For example, a 12-year-old girl, who was in therapy with one of the authors of this book, had been ordered by the court to spend two weeks with her mother followed by two weeks with her father on an alternating basis throughout the entire calendar year. During the therapy process, she talked about what she did at her mother's house and what she did at her father's house. The therapist asked her, "Where is *your* home?" The girl responded, "My mother has a house and my father has a house, but I don't have a house." When a child feels this way, it produces feelings of insecurity. When parents communicate effectively with one another, are flexible, and live within a short distance of one another, an alternating schedule may work because the children can move back and forth relatively easily to pick up their belongings or elicit emotional support from the other parent. However, parents must recognize that giving the children too much mobility could allow them to play one parent off against the other. Therefore, children must adhere to the established placement schedule.

2. **Do not allow repeated overnight placement for infants (birth to 12 months).** This concept is supported by research, but it is also controversial. The thought is to permit non-placement parents to have frequent daytime contacts (four to five times per week) of short duration (two to three hours at a time) with children, but not overnight contacts. Some believe it is essential for infants to sleep in the same crib every night even though the non-placement parent might have cared for the child during the day. Others may argue that this is not harmful when children spend overnights with

grandparents. This may certainly be accurate, but overnight visits with grandparents generally do not occur several times a week. The non-placement parent should be allowed to put the child to bed, go through the typical bedtime routine in the placement parent's home, bathe the child, feed the child, play with the child, and engage in other activities of daily living. Although this is an intrusion, children are not infants for long, and this temporary solution will provide the child with greater feelings of security.

3.   **Do not allow your client to make an excessive or prolonged effort to prove that the other parent is a "bad actor."** Your client does not have to prove that the other parent is a "bad actor." If the other parent is a bad actor, he/she will prove it without help. If your client attempts to prove that the other parent is a bad actor, and is unsuccessful, it will be held against your client. However, if the other parent is a bad actor, and engages in inappropriate behavior, it will be held against the other parent.

4.   **Do not allow your client to foster the child(ren)'s feelings of guilt over the divorce process.** Young children oftentimes believe they have caused the divorce. Parents who encourage these feelings of guilt will also be promoting long-term psychological problems.

5.   **Do not allow your client to let latency-age child(ren) (especially 9 to 12 years of age) refuse visitation with the former spouse or have too much decisionmaking power.** Giving a child of this age the power to make an important decision of this nature is likely to produce further problems during adolescence. When allowed to decide something as important as whether they will visit the other parent, children may get the false impression that they will have the power to make other major decisions. Keep in mind, children of this age are not allowed to choose whether or not they attend school or receive medical treatment. It is possible that a child who refuses visits at this age is caught up in a loyalty issue and cannot be objective about the situation. Older teenagers, however, may reasonably have some say in how much time they spend with the parent and in the timing of the placement.

6.   **Do not allow your client to let preteen or teenage child(ren) become too parental.** Teenage children will often attempt to fill the role of the same gender absent parent. The present parent will often feel good about being supported by this teenage child, who may assume false feelings of maturity. This is one type of "parentification" and is nearly always harmful. (See also items 18 and 19 below.)

7.   **Do not allow your client to misinterpret teenage child(ren)'s reluctance or refusal to visit.** Teenagers, by their nature, are working on individuating from their parents and are more interested in spending time with peers, at work, at school, and in extracurricular activities. Parents should not assume that because the placement schedule is being altered at this time that it is a function of the other parent's attempting to interfere with, manipulate, or sabotage placement time. Rather it is a function of typical teenage development.

8.   **Do not let your client allow the child(ren) to exhibit too much acting-out behavior in response to the divorce process.** It is not unusual for children of divorced parents to engage in acting-out or regressive behavior. It becomes a greater problem if parents allow the acting-out behavior to become excessive because they feel sorrow and guilt over what the children are going through. Parents who think, "He's having such a hard time, let's not make him follow the bedtime rules" will face even greater

acting-out behavior later. Children benefit when parents maintain consistent, fair structure in the home, including setting appropriate limits on the children's behavior.

9. **Encourage your client not to take sides or take issue with decisions or actions made by the other parent, especially in front of the child(ren).** When a child becomes involved in a dispute with one parent, it is important for the other parent to remain neutral if he or she was not part of the original problem or discussion. When one parent happens to disagree with what the other has done, this disagreement should be discussed privately with the other parent. When a resolution is reached, the children should be informed. If a resolution cannot be reached, the children can be told how that lack of resolution will affect them.

10. **Do not allow your client to put the child(ren) in the middle of arranging placement time.** Placement time should be arranged with the other parent. To put this kind of responsibility on the child adds to the child's burden.

11. **Do not allow your client to communicate with the other parent through the child(ren).** Unfortunately, parents often look to the children to carry messages to the other parent. Because the parents are not communicating effectively with one another, they use their children to convey these messages. This puts the children in an awkward and inappropriate position.

12. **Do not allow your client to fight or argue with or degrade the other parent in the presence of the child(ren).** It is too easy for an angry parent to make derogatory comments about the ex-spouse in the presence of the children. This only serves to polarize the parties involved and to put the children in a difficult position. Eventually, the children will grow tired of being caught in the middle of these degrading remarks and will become angry with the parent making them.

13. **Do not allow your client to plan placement time with the child(ren), and then arrive late or not at all.** An angry parent may arrive late for placement time as retaliation toward the other parent. After all, it would certainly disrupt the other parent's plans to be forced to wait around for the ex-spouse to arrive. However, it is the children who are hurt most by this action. Many stories have been told about children sitting and looking out the living room window, waiting for the other parent, only to end up feeling more rejected when the parent is late or fails to arrive.

14. **Do not allow your client to withhold time with the other parent as punishment for the child(ren) or the other parent.** It is certainly important for parents to follow through on discipline that the other parent has invoked. However, for one parent to withhold placement time with the other in order to punish the child is grossly inappropriate. It is equally inappropriate for one parent to withhold placement time as a way of punishing the other.

15. **Do not allow your client to discuss any of the financial aspects of the divorce process (support, maintenance, arrearages) with the child(ren).** Two parents cannot live as cheaply apart as together. It can become very frustrating for parents to try to make budgets balance when their funds are so limited. As part of this frustration they may express anger toward the other parent over financial issues. However, to discuss any financial issue with the children is inappropriate. It requires them to deal with an adult problem that they are not emotionally prepared to handle. Furthermore, it embroils children in the acrimony between the parents. When activities and purchases must be limited or postponed because of limited or late child support or

maintenance payments, the parent should explain the circumstances to the child in a nonderogatory, nonaccusatory manner. For example, a parent should not say, "We won't be able to go to the movie tonight because your father is such an ass and we can never count on him to give us the money he should." Instead, a parent might say, "It's frustrating to me and I'm sure it's frustrating to you that we don't have enough money to go to the movies," or "I'm trying to stretch the money we have as far as possible, but we can't afford everything we want to do."

16. **Encourage your client not to believe everything the child(ren) say about the other parent.** When a parent automatically believes what a child has said about the other parent, it often precipitates further legal battles or other problems. Even in intact families, children may tell preposterous stories to the parent. If one parent hears something from the child about the other parent that sounds unreasonable, before posturing for a battle it is appropriate to verify the child's statement with the other parent. If the other parent cannot provide a reasonable explanation for what the child has said, it may become necessary to pursue the issue in other ways. In most cases, however, unnecessary complications can be avoided merely by checking with the other parent.

17. **Do not allow your client to use child(ren) as pawns to express anger toward the other parent.** Bringing a child late for placement time, scheduling activities during placement time with the other parent, or not allowing the child to come to the phone to talk to the other parent may be inappropriate expressions of anger by the placement parent. This is unfair to the other parent and harmful to the child as well.

18. **Encourage your client not to overburden the child(ren) by requiring too much responsibility for growing up.** When parents become overwhelmed by the circumstances of their divorce, it becomes too easy to ignore the needs of the children. Certainly, children need to learn to be responsible for their behavior and to carry their weight in maintaining the household. However, when children are put in the difficult position of assuming too much responsibility, they can easily become overwhelmed. For example, children should not be required to decide which school to attend or whether to have elective surgery or otherwise be placed in an adult decisionmaking role. (Also, see item 6 above.)

19. **Recommend that your client never overburden the child(ren) by giving them the responsibility for maintaining the parent's psychological stability.** This problem is characterized by a role reversal: the child acts more like a parent (parentification) and the parent acts more like a child. The child is put in the position of continually having to console the parent, provide psychological support for the parent, or provide solutions for the parent's problems. This is an excessive burden on the child.

20. **Encourage your client not to overburden the child(ren) by making them the focus of arguments between the parents.** Children can become overburdened by being "caught in the middle" when parents argue, especially when the arguments are about the child(ren). Research clearly demonstrates that overburdened children have greater psychological problems and take longer to adjust to the difficulties associated with divorce. As a result, if your client is engaging in any of the three behaviors (items #18, 19, and 20) just described, they should desist for the good of the children.

21. **Do not require the child(ren) to spend more time than necessary with a parent who is out of touch with reality (psychotic).** Research has also demonstrated that

children who are required to spend a great deal of time with actively psychotic or severely depressed parents feel less stable. An appropriate way to deal with this difficulty is to require the mentally ill parent to undergo individual psychotherapy for as long as the therapist deems necessary. Furthermore, the therapist should be allowed to report to the guardian ad litem and/or the court-appointed psychologist. When all three feel that visits with the mentally ill parent can be increased, it should be done gradually. By following this approach, both the child's psychological need to maintain stability and the parental rights are maintained.

22. **Do not allow your client to separate the children if possible.** Except in very unusual circumstances, it is generally a bad idea to separate the children. When there are two children involved in a divorce, parents may treat them as property and state that the mother and the father should each have one child. This may satisfy the needs of the parents but certainly not those of the children because siblings generally need to remain together. For one thing, the sibling rivalry that occurs during childhood is a training ground for adulthood. It teaches children how to share, coexist, and deal with controversy. If the children are raised separately, "as only children," they will not be exposed to these components of development. Remaining together is also important because these children will probably survive their parents and need to maintain a relationship during adulthood. It should be noted that it may not be as much of a problem to separate children when there are many siblings, and it is more economically feasible for three of them to live with the mother and three of them with the father, for example. However, when children live separately, there should be periods of placement with all of the children together. An exception can also be made when the oldest minor child is nearing adulthood and would benefit from living apart from the other children.

23. **Recommend that your client not introduce the child(ren) to every person the client is dating.** It is hard enough for children of divorce to deal with the termination of the marital relationship between their parents. Their burden increases if they are exposed to every new person the parent dates. When a child is introduced to every new date, it can also result in false hopes and unrealistic expectations, and lead to recurrent feelings of rejection and abandonment. Once a relationship has progressed to the point of becoming a meaningful relationship, it can be advantageous to slowly introduce the children to that individual. If possible, each parent should date when the former spouse has the children. When this is not adequate or possible, parents should meet their dates away from the home. Lunch dates may be more desirable than evening dates because they do not involve the children. This is particularly important when the children are young (preteen) and when the divorce is recent (less than two years ago).

24. **Point out to your client that he or she should never allow the child(ren) to observe sexually intimate behavior.** This prohibition applies to both divorced parents and married parents. Although it may appear to be natural to expose children to intimate behavior, they are not psychologically ready to deal with these observations during childhood. Furthermore, divorced parents and their partners are more likely to be careless about preventing children from observing these behaviors because of the limitations imposed on the dating relationship. Divorced or divorcing parents often live on severely limited budgets in housing that cannot accommodate everyone.

Consequently, children and parents may be required to sleep in the same room. Parents may assume that the children are asleep and engage in sex, only then to find out that the child has observed the sexually intimate behavior. As a result, it is important to restrict sexually intimate behavior to times of complete privacy.

25. **Advise your client not to let school-age child(ren) sleep in the same bed with the client, except for occasional, unusual circumstances.** Parents may think they should allow younger children to sleep with them in order to reduce the trauma associated with the separation or divorce. Allowing children to sleep with their parents under these circumstances can result in unrealistic fantasies, expectations, and feelings about the parents.

26. **Encourage your client not to ask the child(ren) to keep secrets from the ex-spouse.** It is very disconcerting to a child to be told, "Whatever you do, don't tell your mother," or "Be sure not to let your father know." This places the child in the middle of the conflict, encourages the child to be deceptive, and engenders guilt feelings if the child feels pressured to keep secrets from the other parent or if the child has accidentally or intentionally divulged the secret he/she promised to keep. As always, innocent secrets about birthday presents or Christmas presents are acceptable but should probably be phrased in terms other than "secrets."

§ 5.4   Questions for Chapter 5

1. How many of the "Do's" is your client doing?
2. How many of the "Don't's" is your client avoiding doing?
3. How many of the "Do's" is your client's partner *not* doing?
4. How many of the "Don't's" is your client's partner engaging in?

CHAPTER 6

CHILDREN AS WITNESSES

§ 6.1 Overview of Issues

In recent years, there has been an ever-growing controversy about whether children should be subjected to live court testimony. One side of the argument addresses the issue of how victimizing in-court testimony can be to children, while the other side of the argument addresses the defendant's constitutional rights. These issues are discussed later in this chapter. Many alternatives to live testimony have been suggested, including in-camera testimony, videotaped testimony, audiotaped testimony, closed-circuit television testimony, and the use of screens in court. All of these approaches have advantages. Assuming that children will be required to testify in some cases, many issues must be addressed when considering their testimony.

Helen Dent has addressed the issue of the effects of age and intelligence on a child's ability to be an effective witness. A number of studies have been performed that suggest that children as young as six years of age can be as reliable as adults when answering questions. Research has also demonstrated that retarded children and children with learning disabilities provide less complete and less accurate responses. In addition, they are more susceptible to suggestion than are children of normal intelligence. Dent reports that female children tend to give more complete and accurate reports than do male children. She also reports, "[I]f child witnesses are allowed to relate their report with minimal prompting, either as free recall or response to general, open-ended questions, then the results of the present research suggest they would not be significantly less accurate than adult witnesses."[1]

Dent also indicates that the results of some of her research suggest that children's

> memory deteriorates sharply over a period of two weeks and then more gradually, up to two months, after witnessing the event. Reduced accuracy has been found in recall of children aged five to nine years after a five month delay. . . . [This] would suggest that evidence from witnesses should be obtained as early as possible. A video recording of the interview could fulfill the dual purpose of being a record of the witnesses' earliest and most vivid and complete memory and showing how the recall was elicited.[2]

In conclusion, Dent states, "The results indicated quite clearly that, though increased completeness could be obtained by use of specific questions, this was at the expense of accuracy, particularly for the two child groups."[3]

Beth Schwartz-Kenney's research on the competency of children as witnesses shows that the younger the child, the greater the number of errors that are made and the smaller the percentage of correct responses. She compared two groups of young children on free recall and police lineup conditions. She found that there are significantly more correct responses on lineup (52 percent) as compared to free recall (34 percent). There was also a decrease in the number of "do not know" responses in lineup (1 percent) versus free recall (26 percent). In all, younger children had more commission errors, fewer correct responses, and more "do not know" responses.[4]

§ 6.2   Interviewing Children

James Cook, Kimberly McClure, and Rebecca Birch suggest that some of the typical means of commencing interviews with children should be avoided. They state, "[I]nterviews should avoid introducing dolls or discussing truth/lie and the names of body parts

---

[1] Children as Witnesses 8 (H. Dent & R. Flin eds., 1992) [hereinafter Dent].

[2] *Id.* at 9.

[3] *Id.* at 10.

[4] Beth Schwartz-Kenney et al., Improving Children's Accuracy for Person Identification, Paper presented at the 100th Annual Convention of the American Psychological Association, Washington, D.C. (1992).

until after a child has given a statement about abuse. In our view, these activities are best saved until the end of the interview, when they will not interfere with rapport building."[5]

Amye Warren and her co-researchers studied 42 transcripts of sexual abuse interviews conducted by child protective services agencies and made recommendations on appropriate interview techniques. They point out that

> although the majority of interviewers attempted to establish rapport, they rarely conducted practice interviews regarding past, neutral events, and rarely informed children that "I don't know" "I don't understand", and "I don't remember" are acceptable answers to questions. Further, the majority of interviewers failed to begin their abuse-related questions with general, open-ended questions, instead relying primarily on specific yes/no questions throughout the interview.[6]

In light of research findings on children's suggestibility (see **§ 6.3**), L. Dennison Reed recommends that interviewers keep in mind the following six tips when conducting abuse-related interviews of children:

1. "Bear in mind that misleading can occur in any direction depending on the nature of the interviewer's suggestions."[7] This suggests that children can be influenced to say abuse occurred when it did not, and to say abuse did not occur when it did.

2. "Ask developmentally appropriate questions."[8] Questions should be asked in a manner that meets the children's level of vocabulary.

3. "Avoid using highly leading or coercive questions."[9] The concern about leading and coercive questions is discussed fully in other portions of this chapter.

4. "Avoid repetitive questions and multiple repetitive interviews."[10] When misleading questions are repeated, the risk of invalid content of the interview increases, especially with preschoolers. Coordinated interviews should be used instead of multiple interviews.

5. "Begin with open-ended questions and, after a free narrative is elicited, ask forced questions as needed and justified."[11] When the interviewer fails to get adequate information through open-ended questions, even the most qualified interviewer may end up asking focused questions that may be leading or misleading.

6. "Adequately document relative questions and responses."[12] Interviews of this nature should either be audiotaped or videotaped.

---

[5] James Cook et al.

[6] Amye Warren et al., *"It Sounds Good in Theory, But . . ."* *Do Investigators Follow Guidelines Based on Memory Research?*, 1 Child Maltreatment no. 3, at 231 (1996).

[7] L. Dennison Reed, *Findings from Research on Children's Suggestibility and Implications for Conducting Child Interviews*, 1 Child Maltreatment no. 2, at 117 (1996).

[8] *Id.*

[9] *Id.*

[10] *Id.*

[11] *Id.*

[12] *Id.*

Karen Saywitz has developed a method to help children report what happened to them, referred to as the *narrative elaboration procedure:*

> Narrative elaboration is an intervention package extrapolated from laboratory studies or memory development. It incorporates six experimental procedures that have enhanced the memory performance of school-aged children in the laboratory: memory strategy instructions, practice with feedback, rationale for strategy utility, organizational guidance according to category cues, external memory aids, and reminders to use new strategies on subsequent events.[13]

The narrative elaboration intervention includes six components:

> 1) Rationale for strategy utility: An explanation of the value of using new ways to remember better. 2) Instructions to be complete and accurate: "When you tell what happened to you, you tell as much as you can about what really happened, even the little things, without guessing or making anything up." 3) Strategy: Introduction of a strategy for organizing narratives into five categories and reporting on specified level of detail for each category. 4) Visual cues: Introduction of visual cues to remind self of each category. 5) Practice, modeling, and feedback: Practice using the new strategy and the visual cues on mock recall tasks with feedback on accuracy and with modeling with more detailed and relevant responses. 6) Reinstruction: Review of (2) though (4) above in the second session.[14]

Dr. Saywitz and her co-researchers concluded that

> if further studies of narrative elaboration continue to demonstrate its efficacy, perhaps the accuracy and detail of school-aged children's reports can be improved and meritorious cases of abuse more effectively investigated and prosecuted. A technique such as narrative elaboration reduces the need for leading and potentially misleading questions, because more information is initially provided by children themselves, and follow-up questions focus on clarifying children's statements rather than adult supposition. This could result in fewer false allegations. Obtaining more competent testimony from children earlier in the process could reduce the number of interviews children undergo.[15]

Lawyers are often put in the position of having to question children either through direct examination or cross-examination. A study addressing the effects of such questioning was performed by Nancy Perry and her co-researchers. As part of the study, 15 males and 15 females from each of four student populations (kindergarten, fourth grade, ninth grade, and college) were questioned by lawyers. The researchers found that "questions that included multiple parts with mutually exclusive responses were the most difficult to answer. Those that included negatives, double negatives, or difficult vocabulary, also posed difficult problems."[16] The researchers also concluded that the results of their research

---

[13] Karen Saywitz, Lynn Snyder, & Vivian Lamphear, *Helping Children Tell What Happened: A Follow-up Study of the Narrative Elaboration Procedure*, 1 Child Maltreatment no. 3, at 201–02 (Aug. 1996).

[14] *Id.* at 205.

[15] *Id.* at 211.

[16] Nancy Perry et al., *When Lawyers Question Children, Is Justice Served?*, 19 Law & Hum. Behav. no. 6, at 609 (1995).

strongly support the hypothesis that developmentally inappropriate language reduces both the witness's understanding of the question and the accuracy of the response.

Furthermore, they found that five- and six-year-olds could correctly answer most simply phrased questions. The results of the study also indicated that the ability to accurately repeat a question is related to the ability to correctly answer it.[17] The article concludes with three recommendations for lawyers:

> 1) The language of the courtroom should be simplified. . . . 2) Specifically, courts should require professionals to eliminate the use of negatives, double negatives, questions with multiple parts, and questions that employ difficult vocabulary. . . . 3) Lawyers and judges, as well as other professionals who work with child witnesses, should receive specialized training in developing appropriate questioning techniques.[18]

Karen Saywitz, in a presentation to the American Psychological Association in 1997, addressed three dilemmas that are unanswered at this point:[19]

1. When open-ended questions fail to give the information needed, there are few guidelines on how to proceed.

2. With regard to establishing rapport, moderate rapport is appropriate—too much or too little rapport is not. However, no studies on rapport exist.

3. The research is also silent on overcoming factors of anxiety, fear, and avoidance on the part of the child.

Kathleen Carter, Bette Bottoms, and Murray Levine also studied the linguistic and socioeconomic influences on the accuracy of children's reports.

> Results indicated that children were significantly less accurate in reporting the event when questioned with complex, developmentally inappropriate questions rather than simple questions, yet children rarely voice their comprehension failures. In addition, children interviewed by a warm supportive interviewer were more resistant to misleading questions about the event than were children interviewed in an intimidating manner.[20]

Anne Walker performed a linguistic study of young children being questioned in court. She found that the three major problem areas were age-inappropriate vocabulary, complex syntax, and general ambiguity.[21]

Additional Guidelines for Interviewers

Jerome Sattler, a prominent psychologist, states, "It is important to emphasize that you should not conduct an investigatory interview unless you have been trained to do so or

---

[17] *Id.* at 626.

[18] *Id.* at 627.

[19] Karen Saywitz, Improving the Reliability of Children's Reports, A Symposium presented at the 105th Convention of the American Psychological Association, Chicago (1997).

[20] Kathleen Carter, Bette Bottoms, & Murray Levine, *Linguistic and Socioeconomic Influences on the Accuracy of Children's Reports*, 20 Law & Hum. Behav. no. 3, at 335 (1996).

[21] Anne Walker, *Questioning Young Children in Court: A Linguistic Case Study*, 17 Law & Hum. Behav. no. 1, at 59 (1993).

unless you are directly supervised in this work.[22] The following are his suggested guidelines for interviewers of children in abuse cases.

Guideline 1. Allow sufficient time with the child to obtain relevant information.

Guideline 2. Discuss confidentiality, especially with older children and adolescents, and inform them of your obligation to report any situation in which the child is unsafe.

Guideline 3. Conduct a non-biased, noncoercive, and nonrepetitive interview.

Guideline 4. Ask open-ended questions, use prompts, and avoid leading questions.

Guideline 5. Avoid giving the child information given to you by someone else.

Guideline 6. Ask the child for important information in several different ways if she or he is reluctant to give you the information, especially if you believe the child knows the information.

Guideline 7. Listen to everything the child says, and follow up on all information the child gives you.

Guideline 8. Follow up leads by asking the child for more details using neutral probing questions and prompts as needed.

Guideline 9. Be alert to whether the child answers every question with a "yes" or "no." If the child answers every question with a "yes" or with a "no," you may be phrasing your questions so that only a "yes" or "no" response is acceptable.

Guideline 10. Help the child find words to express what took place when the child is reluctant to talk about the possible maltreatment or when the child does not know the words to describe the possible maltreatment.

Guideline 11. Give the child who is reluctant to talk directly about the maltreatment opportunities to draw on paper with pencils and crayons and to respond to direct questions.

Guideline 12. Probe any inconsistencies in the child's statements by explaining that you are confused, not by challenging the child.

Guideline 13. Ask preschool children about multiple incidents of possible maltreatment by asking specific or direct questions about time sequences.

Guideline 14. Use age-appropriate language.

Guideline 15. Avoid the use of pronouns because of potential ambiguity, unless the referent is clear.

Guideline 16. Use short sentences, few syllables per word, and concrete, visual words with young children.

Guideline 17. Use uncomplicated grammar with all children.

Guideline 18. Use simple and direct questions with all children.

Guideline 19. Use the active voice with all children.

Guideline 20. Use positive phrasing with all children.

Guideline 21. Avoid questions that may imply a child is guilty.

Guideline 22. Learn about the child's terminology for body parts and for sexual acts, and use the child's terms during the interview, as needed.

Guideline 23. Consider carefully what it means when a child changes her or his story.

---

[22] Jerome Sattler, Clinical and Forensic Interviewing of Children and Families 760 (1998).

Guideline 24. Accept what the child says when you are inquiring about the maltreatment, and do not offer interpretations.

Guideline 25. Attend carefully to the child's terminology for designating people in her or his world.

Guideline 26. Determine whom the child is talking about when there are several individuals who may assume similar roles.

Guideline 27. When you need to clarify whom the child is talking about, show the child photographs or draw faces of people in the child's life.

Guideline 28. Take note of the child's concepts (such as knowledge of time and numbers), the child's vocabulary and diction, and other characteristics about the child that may help you in conducting the interview.

Guideline 29. Determine whether the child knows the difference between the truth and a lie.

Guideline 30. Ask the child whom she or he has told about the maltreatment.

Guideline 31. Clarify any terms the child uses that appear to be based on experiences in therapy.

Guideline 32. Determine whether a young child or a developmentally delayed child knows basic concepts such as top, under, behind, inside, and outside.

Guideline 33. Keep interruptions to a minimum, allow the child to control the flow of information if at all possible, and take cues from the child about the speed of questioning and the length of silences.

Guideline 34. Help the child get past any fears that she or he may have about revealing the maltreatment.

Guideline 35. Give the child permission to break any secrets made between herself or himself and the abuser.

Guideline 36. Take special care to help the child express her or his feelings, reactions, and any painful experiences.

Guideline 37. Help the child be as open as possible in talking about the alleged maltreatment.

Guideline 38. Never promise the child what you cannot deliver.[23]

§ 6.3 Suggestibility

Many articles have been written about the suggestibility of children. Utilizing many different experimental designs, many different populations, and many different procedures, the consensus is that children are suggestible. In one set of experiments, performed by William Thompson and his associates, children witnessed a janitor play with toys. Subsequent interviews in a number of settings demonstrated that when the interviews were neutral, children consistently gave accurate accounts of the janitor's behavior. When these interviews were suggestive, children's accounts shifted strongly in the direction of suggestion as the interview progressed. By the end of the suggestive interviews, children's accounts uniformly corresponded to the interviewer's suggestion even when the suggestions were inconsistent with what actually happened.[24]

---

[23] *Id.* at 760–63.

[24] William Thompson et al., *What Did the Janitor Do? Suggestive Interviewing and the Accuracy of Children's Accounts*, 21 Law & Hum. Behav. no. 4, at 405 (1997).

Gail Goodman has become one of the more prominent researchers in the area of child testimony and has devoted a considerable amount of research time to the concept of suggestibility. She and Beth Schwartz-Kenney state:

> We conceive of suggestibility as a characteristic that varies as a function of a variety of factors including memory strength, feelings of power or powerlessness, extent of social pressure, and comprehension of what is being asked and why it is being asked. Because suggestibility is not viewed as a stable trait, our conception does not preclude the possibility that suggestibility varies in accordance with the circumstances of an interview.[25]

Some of the research performed by Goodman and her associates supports earlier research indicating that repeated interviewing does not reduce the child's accuracy, but on the contrary, actually improves it. Repeated interviewing, moreover, makes the children less resistant to false suggestions. In addition, Goodman's research supports previous findings that older children make fewer incorrect statements in free recall and are better able to answer both specific and misleading questions correctly.[26]

Goodman reports a study performed by Karen Saywitz and her associates that included children undergoing physical examinations. In half of the physical examinations, genital touching occurred, while in the other half of the evaluations, no genital touching occurred.

> Saywitz et al. found that children in the genital condition were unlikely to report the genital part of the examination in free-recall, even when using the anatomically detailed dolls. It was only when asked specific, leading questions that a majority of the children finally revealed genital touch had occurred. . . . For the children who did not have a genital examination, none falsely reported genital touch in free-recall or when using anatomically detailed dolls. When asked specific, leading questions, three of the children gave false information for one of the genital questions. . . . These findings indicate that the likelihood of obtaining a false report of genital contact by asking a leading question must be weighed against the likelihood of children not revealing genital contact unless they are directly questioned about it. . . . The data suggests that leading questions may at times be important in obtaining accurate information about genital touch from children. At the same time, there is some degree of obtaining a false report.[27]

In another study, Goodman reports that social influences have a powerful effect on the testimony of children. She points out:

> Although older children may at times be more capable than younger children of reporting an event, social influences can eliminate and sometimes even reverse the typical age advantage. . . . The children's willingness to report secret activities was not affected by the form of the question asked. Regardless of use of more or less leading questions, older children tended to withhold information about secret activities.[28]

---

[25] Gail Goodman & Beth Schwartz-Kenney, *Why Knowing a Child's Age Is Not Enough: Influences of Cognitive, Social and Emotional Factors on Children's Testimony*, in Dent at 19 (1992).

[26] *Id.* at 21.

[27] *Id.* at 22–25.

[28] *Id.* at 28.

In a presentation at the American Psychological Association Convention in 1991, Goodman addressed issues of children's testimony.[29] She stated that as part of children's testimony, their embarrassment and intimidation, and the effects of their memory, must be understood. In addition, research must look at children's suggestibility and their tendency to fantasize events. Goodman reports that most children exhibit a surprising resistance to abuse suggestions.

Concerns about the manipulation of children's testimony and the suggestibility of children have been raised quite frequently over the years. Paul Lees-Haley performed a research study involving a six-step technique to demonstrate that the children's responses could be reversed. Lees-Haley pointed out that the average five-year-old child cannot recall his phone number, does not know the day of the week, and cannot accurately answer the question, "What is your address?" He stated, "Yet young children are considered to be sufficiently knowledgeable to take an oath and testify on the complex matters that can lead to imprisonment of an innocent defendant."[30]

William Thompson and his associates studied children's susceptibility to suggestive interrogation. They found that "[c]hildren questioned in a neutral, nonsuggestive manner, gave accurate accounts of what occurred, while those questioned in a suggestive manner gave accounts that were more consistent with the suggestion than what had actually happened."[31] Furthermore,

> [c]hildren exposed to suggestive questioning did not fix immovably on a particular interpretation, but rather, were influenced by the interrogators' suggestions; the interpretations of children exposed to one suggestive interrogation followed by another in which counter-suggestion was made were malleable and changed according to the interrogator's suggestion. One explanation for children's susceptibility to suggestion is that they lack confidence in their ability to interpret adult actions. Children may be accustomed to looking to adults for cues as to how to interpret events.[32]

Amye Warren and her associates studied methods of inducing resistance to suggestibility in children. They found that they could reduce children's susceptibility to leading questions or misleading information. This study also "bolsters the arguments made by many who work with children in the legal system that repeated questioning by high-status interrogators has detrimental effects on children's testimony. Reducing the number of interrogations and the status of the questions is one but perhaps not the only solution.[33]

---

[29] Gail Goodman, Understanding Children's Testimony, Paper presented at the 99th Annual Convention of the American Psychological Association, San Francisco (1991).

[30] Paul Lees-Haley, *Innocent Lies, Tragic Consequences: The Manipulation of Child Testimony,* 10 Trial Dipl. J. 23–26 (Fall 1987).

[31] William Thompson et al., Children's Susceptibility in Suggestive Interrogation, Paper presented at the 99th Annual Convention of the American Psychological Association, San Francisco (1991).

[32] *Id.* at 13.

[33] Amye Warren, Katherine Hulse-Trotter & Ernest C. Tubs, *Inducing Resistance to Suggestibility in Children,* 15 Law & Hum. Behav. at 273, 283 (1991).

§ 6.4 Validity Checks

Steller and Koehnken suggest in rating the accuracy of a report that validity checks be done by considering certain psychological characteristics and other factors.

1. Note the child's language style and specific knowledge that are beyond the developmental level of a person.
2. Evaluate speech characteristics or descriptions that could be the result of an adult's influencing the child in preparing and organizing statements.
3. Observe behavioral indicators, such as inappropriate affect or the absence of appropriate affect.
4. Evaluate the relative suggestibility of the child.
5. Have a psychologist evaluate certain interview characteristics—for example, mistakes of prior interviews or inadequate interview techniques.
6. Conduct interviews according to the appropriate guidelines.
7. Evaluate the child's possible motivation including whether there are motivating factors for false allegations.
8. View the history of the statement made and determine whether any pressure to make false statements was brought to bear on the child.[34]

The last portion of the validity check deals with the investigation process. Descriptions that are contrary to the laws of nature raise questions about the validity of the allegations. Contradiction is another important aspect of the validity check. The evaluator must determine if earlier and later parts of the statements contradict one another. Furthermore, comparisons should also be made between statements that are made at different times. When looking at contradiction, elements of physical evidence must also be addressed.

Steller and Koehnken point out that this approach has generated some concern and that it may be used to discredit children who have actually experienced abuse.[35] It is important to recognize that this approach is not a test, but simply a systematic means of obtaining and analyzing data relevant to sexual abuse allegations.

§ 6.5 Credibility

Elizabeth Luus and Gary Wells studied the issue of the credibility of children as witnesses, looking at perceptions of child credibility by jurors and at how well children remember and can truthfully recount events they have witnessed.[36] The findings of their study suggest that jurors enter the courtroom with a negative bias toward child witnesses' speech style, an important factor in assessing the witnesses' credibility. Because the speech style of children is not as powerful as that of adults, they are perceived as being less credible than adults.

---

[34] Max Steller & G. Koehnken, *Criteria-Based Statement Analysis, in* Psychological Methods in Criminal Investigation and Evidence 138 (D.C. Raskin ed., 1989) [hereinafter Steller].

[35] *Id.*

[36] Elizabeth Luus & Gary Wells, *The Perceived Credibility of Child Eyewitnesses, in* Dent at 89 (1992).

Another factor that affects perceived credibility is the confidence of the witness. Children—who are generally awed by the courtroom and legal process—seldom express themselves well in such intimidating circumstances.

Gail Goodman and her associates found that jurors perceived children as being less credible in closed-circuit television testimony and more likely to be making up a story. Witnesses who were in courtroom settings were more believable and more attractive to jurors. The researchers concluded that even though some argue that closed-circuit television may bias the jury against the defendant, on the contrary, it appears to bias the jury against the child witness.[37]

Bette Bottoms looked at how the attitudes of individuals affect their perception of credibility in child sexual abuse cases. She found that females made significantly more pro-child or pro-victim judgments. In addition, people who tended to believe children outside courtroom settings were more believing of child witnesses. Individuals who were more pro-women as well as more empathetic were more pro-child credibility. In general, individuals who have biases against children will not convict, even in the face of overwhelming evidence.[38]

Judy Cashmore and Kay Bussey studied how judges perceive the competence of child witnesses. Children's honesty was not an issue for judges. However, children were perceived as being highly suggestible and susceptible to the influence of others and prone to fantasy.[39]

Linda Jones and Christopher Gordon performed another study with mock juries about the believability of children witnesses' reports. They stated:

> The results contain logical and consistent patterns indicating that, as in previous studies, child witnesses can influence jurors' verdicts but that their credibility and influence are fragile and do not stand up well against conflicting testimony from an adult. However, the data from the study do seem to indicate that child's testimony can be strengthened by the presence of detail and might for some jurors thus be seen as more persuasive than the testimony of an adult who does not give details.[40]

When Luus and Wells addressed the issue of the adequacy of children's memory, and its impact on perceived credibility, they found no differences in accuracy between child and adult witnesses under direct examination.

> However, [the children] only report their memories with the same degree of accuracy as adults if questioned in the direct, straightforward manner characteristic of direct examination.

---

[37] Gail Goodman et al., Impact of Innovative Court Procedures on Children's Testimony, Paper presented at the 100th Annual Convention of the American Psychological Association, Washington, D.C. (1992).

[38] Bette Bottoms, Attitudinal Determinants of Child Sexual Assault Victims: Perceived Credibility, Paper presented at the 100th Annual Convention of the American Psychological Association, Washington, D.C. (1992).

[39] Judy Cashmore & Kay Bussey, *Judicial Perceptions of Child Witness Competence*, 20 Law & Hum. Behav. 313 (1996).

[40] Linda Jones & Christopher Gordon, The Influence of Detail and Child Witness Testimony 7, Paper presented at the 100th Annual Convention of the American Psychological Association, Washington, D.C. (1992).

As expected, cross-examination presented more problems for the 8-year-old witness than for the 12-year-old or adult eyewitnesses on measures of actual testimony accuracy. The non-leading aspects of direct examination versus the leading aspect of cross-examination seems to account for this interaction between age and type of examination. . . . Despite the difficulty our 8-year-old witnesses had in providing accurate testimony under cross-examination, they were perceived as no less confident or believable than more accurate adolescent and adult counterparts.[41]

In studying how professionals perceive child witnesses, John Brigham and Stacey Spier found

professionals' views of child witnesses in a legal arena appeared to be strongly related to professional role. Defense attorneys evaluated child witnesses very differently from prosecuting attorneys, child protection workers and law enforcement personnel. For most issues, the latter three groups, despite differences in levels of education, gender representation and professional duties, view child witnesses in similar ways. In general, these groups had more confidence in child witnesses' ability to remember accurately, testify appropriately, and resist suggestion than did the defense attorneys. The defense attorneys state that children are likely to give completely inaccurate and distorted testimony about sexual abuse almost one-fifth of the time, but the other three groups believe this is to be a rare occurrence. The child protection workers were particularly sensitive to the possibility the children might underestimate the extent of the sexual abuse.[42]

When professionals were asked what cues they used in assessing the credibility of child witnesses, they felt the most important was the consistency of the child's statement. The second and third most frequently mentioned cues were body language and eye contact, respectively.[43]

Maggie Bruck and Stephen Ceci, two of the most prominent researchers in the area of children's memory, along with Helene Hembrooke, addressed the issue of the reliability of young children's reporting. They conclude, "[A]lthough we have shown that to some degree young children's false allegations that emerge as a result of suggestive interviewing practices reflect cognitive and social factors characteristic of young children, it is also the case that factors external to the children—those that characterize suggestive interviews— probably have a predominant influence on the emergence of children's false allegations. Thus, we do not view the young child as an incompetent witness. Rather, if questioned under the appropriate circumstances, the young witness may provide the court with forensically important evidence."[44]

Mark Everson discusses the issue that sometimes children's accounts of abuse will contain descriptions that seem bizarre, improbable, or even impossible. He states that improbable or fantastic children's accounts should not result in automatic dismissal of

---

[41] Elizabeth Luus & Gary Wells, *The Perceived Credibility of Child Eyewitnesses, in* Dent at 89 (1992).

[42] John Brigham & Stacey Spier, *Opinions Held by Professionals Who Work with Child Witnesses, in* Dent at 107 (1992).

[43] *Id.*

[44] Maggie Bruck, Stephen Ceci, Helene Hembrooke, *Reliability and Credibility of Young Children's Reports: From Research to Policy and Practice*, 53 Am. Psychologist 149 (1998).

the account. Instead, he proposes 24 possible explanations for why these accounts may occur:

I.   Interaction of abusive event with child characteristics
     Reflection of reality
          (1) Accurate description of reality
     Impact of perpetrator manipulation
          (2) Deception to confuse or discredit child
          (3) Drug-induced distortions
     Trauma or stress-induced processes
          (4) Treat incorporation
          (5) Traumagenic misperception or memory distortion
     Influence of coping mechanisms
          (6) Mastery fantasy
          (7) Expression of affect through metaphor or hyperbole
          (8) Misreports by child to deflect blame or deny victimization
     Impact of cognitive immaturity
          (9) Misperception or miscommunication due to developmental limitations
          (10) Distortion due to attempts to assimilate novel events into existing schemata
II. Interaction of assessment process with child characteristics system response errors
          (11) Distortion due to successive misapproximations
          (12) Miscommunication due to interviewer error
     Influence of interview process
          (13) Impact of leading or suggestive questioning techniques
          (14) Distortion induced by interview props
          (15) Confabulation
          (16) Distortion due to interview fatigue
     Deceptive processes
          (17) Exaggeration for attention or approval
          (18) Snowballing of an innocent lie
          (19) Deliberate exaggeration or lying
          (20) Fantasy lying
III. Interaction of extrinsic influences with child characteristics
     External source confusion
          (21) Cultural influences
          (22) Cross-tainting
     Internal source confusion

(23) Dream incorporation

(24) Delusions due to psychotic processes[45]

Reprinted with permission.

Christine Ricci, Carole Beal, and Dawn Dekle studied the impact on child witness recall of interviews by a parent versus by an unfamiliar person. They found "children showed poorer recall of the event when interviewed by their parent in an unstructured interview. However, no differences were observed when parents and experimenters followed the same script. Overall, the results indicate that interviewers can influence the accuracy and consistency of children's eyewitness identification."[46]

John Myers, a law professor who has written extensively in the area of forensic psychology and psychiatry, concludes his review of children's credibility by stating:

> [S]ociety is seldom more than half-willing to believe children's claims of sexual abuse. Thus, advocates for children were encouraged during the 1980's, when society entertained a relatively high regard for children's credibility. Unfortunately, as the 20th century draws to a close, the long tradition of skepticism appears once again to be gaining the upper hand. It will be sad indeed if the century closes with the same high level of skepticism that existed when it opened. This discouraging possibility is made all the more likely by articles in the popular and professional literature that exaggerated children's weaknesses, and by court decisions that institutionalized disbelief.[47]

§ 6.6   Eyewitness Testimony

Julien Gross and Harlene Hayne studied 34 five- and six-year-old children and found that they were accurate in identifying individuals with whom they had had prolonged contact, and those who were present briefly. However, their performance was very poor when the target individual to be identified was absent in lineups.[48]

Carole Beal and her associates found that children made false-positive identification errors when viewing a target-absent lineup even though they had initially recognized and previously identified the perpetrator. The results emphasize the strength of young witnesses' tendency to guess.[49]

Gail Goodman and her associates studied the relationship between children's eyewitness memory and maltreatment. They once again supported the previous research that older

---

[45] Mark Everson, *Understanding Bizarre, Improbable, and Fantastic Elements in Children's Accounts of Abuse*, 2 Child Maltreatment 135 (1997).

[46] Christine Ricci et al., *The Effect of Parent versus Unfamiliar Interviewers on Children's Eyewitness Memory and Identification Accuracy*, 20 Law & Hum. Behav. no. 5, at 483 (1996).

[47] John Myers, Evidence of Child Sexual Abuse and Neglect Cases 398 (2d ed. 1992).

[48] Julian Gross & Harlene Hayne, *Eye Witness Identification by 5-to-6-Year-Old Children*, 20 Law & Hum. Behav. 359–73 (1996).

[49] Carole R. Beal, Kelly L. Schmitt, & Dawn J. Dekle, *Eyewitness Identification of Children: Effects of Absolute Judgment, Non-Verbal Response Options and Event Encoding*, 19 Law & Hum. Behav. 197–216 (1995).

children compared to younger children's reports were more complete and accurate. They also report "importantly, abused and non-abused children did not differ in accuracy or suggestibility in response to questions that were relevant to abusive actions."[50]

Bette Bottoms and her associates address the issue of eyewitness testimony under the influence of secrecy. Half the children were told to keep a secret about an event, and the other half were not. The researchers found that "older children who were instructed to keep events secret withheld more information than did older children not told to keep events secret. Younger children's reports were not significantly affected by the secret manipulation."[51]

§ 6.7 Legal Reforms

A number of legal reforms have been suggested as a result of legislation and Supreme Court rulings. The Victims of Child Abuse Act of 1990[52] also endorsed a number of rights and protections for child victims and child witnesses. They included the following:

1. Alternatives to live court testimony, whether by two-way closed-circuit television at trial or by videotaped depositions

2. Presumption of children's competency as witnesses

3. Privacy protection from public identification

4. Closing the courtroom during children's testimony

5. Victim impact statements from children

6. Use of multidisciplinary teams to provide medical and mental health services to child victims, expert testimony, case management, and training for judges and courtroom personnel

7. Appointments of guardians ad litem to protect the best interests of child victims

8. Appointment of a child's attendant to provide emotional support for children during judicial proceedings

9. Speedy trials

10. Extension of the statute of limitations for commencing prosecution of child sexual and physical abuse allegations until the child reaches the age of 25

11. Technical aids, such as dolls, puppets, and drawings.[53]

Certain reforms have addressed the issue of whether videotape or closed-circuit television can be used in cases. Broadcasting a child's live testimony to a courtroom via

---

[50] Gail S. Goodman, Bette L. Bottoms, Leslie Rudy, Suzanne L. Davis, & Beth M. Schwartz-Kenney, *Effects of Past Abusive Experiences in Children's Eye Witness Memory*, 25 Law & Hum. Behav. 269 (2001).

[51] Bette L. Bottoms, Gail S. Goodman, Beth M. Schwartz-Kenney, & Sherilyn N. Thomas, *Understanding Children's Use of Secrecy in the Context of Eye Witness Reports*, 26 Law & Hum. Behav. 285 (2002).

[52] Pub L. No. 101-647, tit. II, 104 Stat. 4792 (codified in scattered sections of 18 U.S.C. and 42 U.S.C.).

[53] Whitcomb, *Legal Reforms on Behalf of Child Witnesses: Recent Developments in the American Courts, in* Dent at 152.

closed-circuit television, videotaping the child's testimony, or erecting a screen between the child and the defendant in the courtroom are all techniques that involve physical separation. By interfering with "direct face-to-face" confrontation between the victim and the accused, a potentially serious threat is made to the accused's Sixth Amendment Rights. In *Coy v. Iowa,*[54] the Supreme Court acknowledged "that the right of confrontation is not absolute, and may give way to 'other important interests.'"[55] In *Maryland v. Craig,*[56] "the Supreme Court found that the Maryland statute, which requires a determination that the child will suffer serious emotional distress such that the child cannot reasonably communicate, clearly suffices to meet constitutional standards."[57]

As part of its clarification, in *Maryland v. Craig,* the Court suggested that an alternative to direct confrontation is permitted when it can be demonstrated that the child will be traumatized and the child's emotional distress will be "more than de minimis."

The American Psychological Association's Psychology-Law Society wrote a brief on *Maryland v. Craig,* which states in pertinent part:

> For the foregoing reasons, APA respectfully submits, the State has a compelling interest in protecting a vulnerable child victim-witness; that determinations whether that interest is implicated must be made case-by-case for each particular child; and that it is not necessary in every case to subject a young child victim-witness to the ordeal of attempting testimony face-to-face with the defendant before allowing the child to testify by means of a one-way or two-way closed circuit television. Instead of adhering to the Maryland Court of Appeals' recommendation which would subject some vulnerable children to unnecessary emotional harm, multiple sources of information, including expert testimony should be sought in making an individualized determination whether there is a need to limit the defendant's right to face-to-face confrontation when a particular child victim testifies. A "trial run" with attendant traumatization should not invariably be required before the court makes an individualized determination.[58]

Many of the leading researchers in the area of forensic psychology published an article in 1995 addressing the research that has been performed on child maltreatment and the law. The authors include Gary Melton, Gail Goodman, Seth Kalichman, Murray Levine, Karen Saywitz, and Gerald Koocher.[59] They point out that little research has been performed on the effects of the legal process on children, the effects of child abuse reporting on service delivery, and the functioning of the child protection system itself. Their review of memory research and children's testimony demonstrates that children as young as three years of age can describe core features of some events, and information suggests that children's memory fades more quickly than does adult memory. The authors of the

---

[54] 487 U.S. 1012 (1988).

[55] Whitcomb, *Legal Reforms on Behalf of Child Witnesses: Recent Developments in the American Courts, in* Dent 153.

[56] 110 S. Ct. 3157 (1990).

[57] Whitcomb, *Legal Reforms on Behalf of Child Witnesses: Recent Developments in the American Courts, in* Dent at 154.

[58] Gail Goodman et al., *Child Witnesses and the Confrontation Clause,* 15 Law & Hum. Behav. no. 1, at 29 (1991).

[59] Gary Melton et al., *Empirical Research on Child Development and the Law,* 24 J. Clinical Child Psychol. 47–77 (1995).

article also point out that deception in young children is particularly easy to detect but less recognizable as children grow older. This may be related to negative biases that factfinders have about young children's testimony.

There are a number of reasons why increasing involvement of psychologists in the adjudicative process is controversial. The researchers warn that "a purely investigatory role or, worse, a mixture of investigatory and clinical roles may damage the integrity of the mental health system, or create violations of party's expectations and the related ethical duty to keep promises and maintain fidelity to role."[60] According to the article, "many defense attorneys and prosecutors believe that, as a practical matter, expert testimony at the adjudicatory phase of child abuse cases is helpful and uninfluential."[61] Furthermore, "there is a logical leap in moving from group probability data to determination of whether an event occurred, which has a probability of either zero or one."[62] The authors of the article also point out that "testimony about characteristics of sexually abused children may be inherently misleading and prejudicial, because base rates are likely not to be applied correctly."[63] Furthermore, "testimony about clinically derived syndromes is misleading and prejudicial because they have low scientific validity."[64]

§ 6.8   Hearsay Exceptions

As part of the issue of whether children should be required to testify in court, attention has been focused on whether hearsay information is admissible in cases of this nature, if the child is not required to testify. This issue was addressed in *Idaho v. Wright*,[65] a case in which the Supreme Court found that a child's statement to a pediatrician about the sexual abuse the child had experienced lacked sufficient trustworthiness to allow the hearsay testimony into evidence. This opinion was reversed in *White v. Illinios*.[66] Wisconsin Appellate Judge Charles B. Schudson writes:

> On January 15, 1992, in *White v. Illinois*, the Supreme Court confirmed the use of such hearsay evidence explicitly, for the first time in a child sexual abuse case. The defendant was convicted of the aggravated assault of a four-year-old girl. She did not testify, but her babysitter, her mother, a police officer, an emergency room nurse, and a doctor were allowed to testify about what she told them during the four hour period after the assault. Significantly, the Supreme Court concluded: 1. That unavailability had no bearing on the question of whether the hearsay should be allowed; the hearsay was admissible whether or not the child testifies; 2. that *Ohio v. Roberts* "unavailability" analysis is required "only" when the hearsay statement is from a prior judicial proceeding; 3. that although the statements in this case were admitted

---

[60] *Id.* at 66.

[61] *Id.* at 67.

[62] *Id.*

[63] *Id.*

[64] *Id.*

[65] 110 S. Ct. 3139 (1990).

[66] 112 S. Ct. 736 (1992).

under the "spontaneous declaration" and "medical diagnosis/treatment" exceptions, the decision is not limited.[67]

In summary, the Supreme Court implied that the Sixth Amendment's confrontation clause does not require, as a condition for the admission of "court statements" that qualify under the hearsay exception for spontaneous declarations or statements made in the course of securing medical treatment, that the proponent of the statements show that the declarant is "unavailable" to testify or that the proponent produce the declarant at trial. See **§ 6.17** for digests of these cases.

§ 6.9   Videotaped Testimony

Many states have enacted legislation allowing videotaped statements or interviews of children to be admitted into evidence under certain circumstances. As part of this process, however, reforms need to take place not only within the courtroom but also, because only a minority of cases go to trial, within the system itself—by assigning a guardian ad litem for the children, streamlining the court process, and reducing the number of interviews children are required to undergo. Because it has been demonstrated that continued interviewing revictimizes a child, there is growing support for designating one central location for an interview or videotape by all interested parties. This process is described more fully in **Chapter 13**, regarding sexual abuse.

Janet Swim and her associates studied the use of videotaped versus in-court testimony. They state, "Videotaping depositions may protect a child witness from the stress of testifying in court, but also may influence jurors' perception of the child and the defendant, and jurors' verdicts in systematic ways."[68] Of greatest concern is the likelihood that the jury may be prejudiced against the defendant by being told that the child needs to testify via videotape or closed-circuit television to protect the child from emotional trauma or damage. "Jurors may view the defendant more negatively because of the presumption that the child is being protected from the defendant; if protection is required, the defendant must be guilty."[69]

§ 6.10   Children Testifying

The issue of whether children should be required to testify in courts of law requires a balance between concern about the children's rights and recognizing that testifying places children in a powerful position. Gail Goodman points out that if children are required to testify, it is most

---

[67] Charles B. Schudson, *Escape from Wonderland, The United States Supreme Court Decision in* White v. Illinois, Fam. Violence & Sexual Assault Bull., Jan. 15, 1992, at 5.

[68] Janet Swim et al., Videotaped versus In-Court Witness Testimony: Is Protecting the Child Witness Jeopardizing Due Process?, Paper presented at the 99th Annual Convention of the American Psychological Association, San Francisco (1991).

[69] *Id.* at 5.

likely to take place in child sexual abuse allegation cases.[70] When Goodman refers to children's testimony, she is talking not only about court testimony but also the reports of events to police, social service workers, psychologists, and other people related to these cases.

In spite of court rulings and desires to the contrary, at times children will be required to testify in court. When this occurs, a number of steps can take place to aid the child. Most involve preparing the child. Louise Dezwirek-Sas is one of the individuals who participated in the London Family Court Clinic projects on helping prepare children for testimony in court. She and her colleagues identified nine criminal justice systems stressors:

1. Delays: Numerous unforeseen adjournments, lengthy delays which span many months, even years in a child's life.
2. Public exposure: Having to recount embarrassing and frightening incidents in a public room at an age where speaking publicly about oneself is difficult.
3. Facing the accused: Having to face the accused person when on the stand despite intense fear for personal safety.
4. Understanding complex procedures: Being exposed to court procedures that are foreign and easily misunderstood by children who do not know the legal terminology or the adversarial context.
5. Change of Crown Attorneys: Having changes in Crown Attorneys on their case just prior to or on the day of court, which undermines their sense of security and self-confidence. The lack of a supportive/comfortable relationship when entering into court with their counsel because insufficient time has been spent together.
6. Cross-examination: Being cross-examined by a defense lawyer, who can be very aggressive. At times withstanding cross-examination that can be downright harassing, in that it exploits the child's sensitivity and vulnerability.
7. Exclusion of witnesses: Being "alone" in the court because of the removal of witnesses results in the child finding himself/herself in court on the stand without significant adult figures in his/her life (family) present as support.
8. Apprehension and placement outside the home: Being removed for safety reasons from one's home while the accused is allowed to stay. Children are often the ones to leave and are then stripped of their family support while the accused remains home.
9. Lack of preparation for the role of witness: Not being aware of the expectations of them because they are child witnesses. Most children are totally unprepared to give testimony and do not understand the adversarial system.[71]

Dezwirek-Sas and her colleagues also identify factors related to the child's ability to testify. They include the child's level of cognitive social functioning, the child's level of anxiety and fear, the child's feelings of ambivalence and guilt, the availability of family support, the child's overall temperament and pre-morbid history, and the child's emotional sequelae related to the sexual abuse.[72]

The researchers involved children in a number of procedures to help them prepare for the courtroom setting. Courtroom models and dolls were used, and a judge's gown was worn during role-playing. Children were given homework assignments about the importance of

---

[70] Gail Goodman, Understanding Children's Testimony, Paper presented at the 99th Annual Convention of the American Psychological Association, San Francisco (1991).

[71] Louise Dezwirek-Sas, *Child Witnesses for Sexual Abuse Prosecutions, in* Dent at 184 (1992).

[72] *Id.* at 185.

telling the truth and were also taken on courtroom tours. Last, the children were exposed to stress reduction techniques. These techniques addressed the five greatest fears that child witnesses had, which included "facing the accused person; being hurt by the accused in the courtroom or outside; being on the stand or crying on the stand; being sent to jail; and not understanding the question."[73] The professionals who ran the London Family Court Clinic, Child Witness Project, found that court preparation offered by the Child Witness Project benefited the child witnesses in four distinct ways:

1. By educating them about court procedures.

2. By helping them deal with the stress and anxieties related to the abuse and to testifying.

3. By helping them tell their story competently on the stand in court.

4. By providing an advocacy role on their behalf with the other mandated agencies in the criminal justice system.[74]

A similar project was conducted in the United States at the National Children's Advocacy Center in Hunstville, Alabama. That highly structured program involved sessions over a four- to six-week period of time. The developers of the program concluded that

> Court Prep Group benefits the child and family in a number of ways. The group provides materials in a well-defined program for reinforcing reality while reducing anxiety, teaches improved coping skills, provides a safe setting to work through the effects of post-traumatic stress disorder, and allows the support of peers as additional "teammates" when court delays and occurrences occur.[75]

§ 6.11   False Memories

Elizabeth Loftus addressed the issue of false memories in legal situations. She speaks about an old experiment referred to as the *barn experiment.* Individuals viewed a film about an accident, in which there was no barn. However, following the film they were asked, "Did you see a barn?" Another group in the experiment was asked, "How fast was the white sports car going when it passed the barn while traveling along the country road?" A week later, 17 percent of the individuals recalled the nonexistent barn. Loftus concludes, "What this study is showing is by simply mentioning an object in the course of questioning, you can essentially add the object to someone's recollection."[76]

Loftus also refers to an experiment that she performed with fellow researchers. The actual scene involved a truck. However, the individuals were asked leading questions suggesting that the truck was actually a car. Loftus found that in recounting the story, some people reported that they saw a station wagon that was a melding of what was actually seen and what the leading questions suggested was seen.

---

[73] *Id.* at 187.

[74] *Id.* at 196.

[75] K. Kenney et al., *The Court Prep Group: A Vital Part of the Court Process, in* Dent at 207.

[76] Elizabeth Loftus, False Memories in a Court, Paper presented at the 99th Annual Convention of the American Psychological Association, San Francisco (1991).

Further evidence of individuals' melding information involved a case in which a victim immediately told a 911 operator and the police that the perpetrator of an assault was 16 years old and wore braces. The man who was arrested was 18 years old and never wore braces. However, she positively identified the 18-year-old as the perpetrator. When she was confronted about the fact that the perpetrator never wore braces, her response was, "I guess that must have been the glint of a knife against his teeth: the way the light was hitting it." Thus is an example of an individual's memory accommodating for contradiction of fact.

Loftus found that 5- and 10-year-olds were highly susceptible to misleading suggestions, as were individuals over 65 years of age. According to Loftus, in another experiment that required recall, the researchers concluded that when people are given misinformation, their responses were correct only 43 percent of the time. However, when misinformation was not given, their responses were correct 67 percent of the time.[77]

Kathy Pezdek and Danelle Hodge studied two groups of children, 5 to 7 years of age and 9 to 12 years of age. The experimenters read descriptions of two true events and two false events that reportedly happened to the children when they were four years old. They were given both a plausible and an implausible false event. Forty-six percent of the children recalled the plausible but not the implausible false event.[78]

Stephen Porter, John Yuille and Darrin Lehman encouraged 77 subjects to "recover" a memory of a false event. Twenty-six percent of the participants "recovered" the false experience, while another 30 percent recalled aspects of the false experience.[79]

Lenore Terr and her co-researchers studied children's memory in relation to their recollections of the Challenger spacecraft explosion. They compared latency-age children's responses with adolescents at five to seven weeks after the explosion and 14 months after the explosion.

> About 30 percent of all children in the study misunderstood something about Challenger and incorporated these misunderstandings into their memories as false details. Latency-age children continue to harbor false details for 14 months, as opposed to the adolescents. Childhood memories of the Challenger space shuttle explosion appeared predictable, were related to patterns of memory that have been observed following single, unrepeated traumas, and reflected age and stage differences.[80]

Karen Saywitz, who has been involved with child sexual abuse concerns for a number of years, addressed the use of memory research as a criterion for determining the veracity of a child's testimony by stating, "Memory research often involves learning lists of words, not remembering such things as sexual abuse."[81] In other words, laboratory research is very different from real-world trauma.

---

[77] *Id.*

[78] Kathy Pezdek & Danielle Hodge, *Planting False Childhood Memories in Children: The Role of Event Plausibility*, 4 Child Development 887–95 (1999).

[79] Stephen Porter, John C. Yuille, & Darrin R. Lehman, *The Nature of Real, Implanted, and Fabricated Memories for Emotional Childhood Events: Implications for the Recovered Memory Debate*, 23 Law & Hum. Behav. 517–37 (1999).

[80] Lenore Terr et al., *Children's Memories in the Wake of Challenger*, 153 Am. J. Psychol. no. 5, at 618 (1996).

[81] Karen Saywitz, Developmental Sensitivity in the Assessment of Child Sexual Abuse, Paper presented at the 99th Annual Convention of the American Psychological Association, San Francisco (1991).

§ 6.12   Perception of Lies

Jeffrey Haugaard and his colleagues studied the issue of children's definitions of truth and how the definitions affect their competency as witnesses in legal arenas.[82] Jean Piaget, whose work and writings are classic, studied children's perceptions of lies from ages five to seven. Children at this age of development possess a concept referred to as *moral realism*, a principle simply holding that if information is inaccurate, it is a lie, and if it is accurate, it is the truth. The intention of the speaker is not considered by the child before age seven. Haugaard and his associates noted that when a parent provides information, the information would be viewed as true simply because the parent made the statement. Nearly all the children between ages four and six knew that saying something untrue to the police is a lie, even if a child is prompted to do so by a parent.

Victoria Talwar and her associates studied the conceptual understanding of truth-telling versus lying in three experiments that totaled 403 subjects. They found that the act of promising to tell the truth had a stronger effect on children than discussions about the concept of moral implications of truth and lying. However, children who understood the moral implications of lying were no more likely to tell the truth than those who did not understand the moral implications. The researchers hypothesize that children should not be excluded from testifying because they fail certain conceptual questions about lie- and truth-telling.[83]

Holly Orcutt and her associates examined the influence of closed-circuit television on juror's ability to detect deception in children's testimony. Using mock juries, they concluded that there was no support for the notion that jurors are better able to reach the truth when children testify in open court versus closed-circuit television.[84]

§ 6.13   Courtroom Practices

Julie Lipovsky and other members of a grant project surveyed the common practices utilized with child witnesses in court settings today.[85] Three hundred sixteen adjudicated cases involving prosecuted witnesses were studied. In 80.1 percent of the cases, children were oriented to the courtroom. In 66 percent of the cases, children were allowed to wait their turn to testify in a separate area. In 68.1 percent of the cases, a victim/witness advocate was allowed in the courtroom during the child's testimony. One hundred forty-five

---

[82] Jeffrey Haugaard et al., *Children's Definitions of the Truth and Their Competency as Witnesses in Legal Proceedings*, 15 Law & Hum. Behav. no. 3, at 253–71 (1991).

[83] Victoria Talwar, Kang Lee, Nicholas Bala & R.C.L. Lindsay, *Children's Conceptual Knowledge of Lying and Its Relation to Their Actual Behavior: Implications for Court Competence Examinations*, 26 Law & Hum. Behav. 395–415 (2002).

[84] Holly K. Orcutt, Gail S. Goodman, Ann E. Tobey, Jennifer M. Batterman-Faunce, & Shelly Thomas, *Detecting Deception in Children's Testimony: Fact Finders' Abilities to Reach the Truth in Open Court and Closed-Circuit Trials*, 25 Law & Hum. Behav. 339–72 (2001).

[85] Julie Lipovsky et al., Children as Witnesses in Criminal Court: Examination of Current Practice, Paper presented at the 99th Convention of the American Psychological Association, San Francisco (1991).

defense attorneys were surveyed to discuss the specific practices that they use in calling child witnesses. Of the 46.2 percent who indicated they had called child witnesses, 71.2 percent had used child witnesses on three or more occasions in the past five years. In 94 percent of the cases, the attorneys explained courtroom procedures to the children and in 51.6 percent of the cases had a special place for the children to wait. In only 34.8 percent of the cases did they provide a tour of the courtroom, and a judge was used to orient the child to the proceedings in 27.3 percent of the cases.

Kay Saywitz and her colleagues studied the stress of the courtroom environment versus the non-courtroom environment. They evaluated children 8 to 10 years of age and found that the more stressful the children perceived the courtroom setting to be, the greater the errors in free recall. However, specific questions did not show a significant difference between the courtroom versus non-courtroom settings. The implication is the need to reduce the stress in the courtroom and therefore increase the accuracy. As a result, closed-circuit testimony may increase the quality of evidence that is available.[86]

§ 6.14   Preparing the Child for Testimony

In preparing a child for testimony, Karen Saywitz is most concerned that the assessor develop sensitivity toward the child's overall functioning. She identifies four areas that need to be addressed in looking at these issues:

1. Observe and assess the child's developmental status.
2. Match the task with the child's skill level.
3. Prepare the child for questioning.
4. Consider the need for follow-up questioning.[87]

Observe and assess the child's developmental status.   It is important that the assessor have a measure of the child's level of cognitive functioning. It becomes necessary to use appropriate language when communicating with a child. The assessor must look at communication skills, and cognitive academic skills, as well as social and emotional skills. Examples of inappropriate vocabulary include typical legal language that a child may not understand. For example, the phrase *point to* should be used instead of *identify*. Children often interpret the word *charges* to mean something having to do with a credit card, the word *court* to mean something involved with basketball to tennis, and the word *date* to mean a social engagement with someone. A child should also not be asked *how many times* if the child does not know how to count. These areas may be assessed with instruments discussed in **Chapter 8.**

---

[86] Karen Saywitz & Rebecca Nathanson, Effects of Environment on Children's Testimony and Perceived Stress, Paper presented at the 100th Annual Convention of the American Psychological Association, Washington, D.C. (1991).

[87] Karen Saywitz, Developmental Sensitivity in the Assessment of Child Sexual Abuse, Paper presented at the 99th Annual Convention of the American Psychological Association, San Francisco (1991).

Match the task with the child's skill level.   For a child to be appropriately interviewed in a sexual abuse allegation situation, the child will need to know a number of concepts. For example, the child must understand height, distance, weight, age, time, body parts, colors, location, and kinship terms. In addition, the basic concept of first, last, never, always, ever, before, after, above, and below must be understood. Therefore, the assessor must determine whether the child understands these basic concepts. If not, the completeness of the interview may be questioned.

When questioning a child, shorter sentences should be used. Whenever possible, one- or two-syllable words should be used in sentences that include simple tenses. Last, common terms the child is familiar with should be used.

Prepare the child for questioning.   Louis Sass and David Wolfe have spent considerable time addressing the issue of preparing the child for questioning and indicate that there was a tenfold increase in abuse allegations in the 20 years between 1970 and 1990.[88] Testimony utilizing closed-circuit television and videotape has taken the place of live testimony in many courtrooms.[89] Unfortunately, many courts remain adult-oriented places. Sass and Wolfe point out that one of the areas a child does not understand is why lengthy delays can occur when objections are made, when side bar conferences occur, or when the judge or attorneys are reviewing legal documents. The child must be prepared to understand that these delays can occur and have nothing to do with the child's own performance or competence. Secondary victimization can result from the need for the child to testify, the length of time before the trial commences, and the need for the child to recall the trauma long after completing significant therapeutic work toward resolving it.

Karen Saywitz, as the principal investigator of a report to the National Center on Child Abuse and Neglect, wrote about preparing children for the investigative and judicial process. She summarized the significant findings for this organization by indicating that

> school-aged children's spontaneous reports did not convey all of the relevant information they had stored in memory . . . ; those who did not receive preparation tried to answer linguistically complex questions they did not fully understand. . . . [D]emonstrated limited knowledge/experience with the task demands response options of the investigative and judicial process.[90]

She also reported that the method of "narrative elaboration" (See **§ 6.2**) and "resistance training" were helpful in obtaining more useful information. Furthermore, "instructing children to request that adults rephrase questions was successful in improving the accuracy of responses to complex questions about past events."[91] "The courtroom context was experienced as significantly more stressful than a private room adjacent to the courtroom, and was

---

[88] Louis Sass & David Wolfe, Preparing Sexually Abused Children for the Stress of Court, Paper presented at the 99th Annual Convention of the American Psychological Association, San Francisco (1991).

[89] *See* Maryland v. Craig, 110 S. Ct. 3157 (1990), discussed in **§ 6.7.**

[90] Karen Saywitz, Preparing Children for the Investigative and Judicial Process: Improving Communication, Memory and Emotional Resiliency, Final Report to the National Center on Child Abuse and Neglect at XIV (1993).

[91] *Id.*

associated with impaired recall during mock testimony in comparison to recall in an adjacent room."[92] Increased preparation did not lead to increase in errors in memory performance, and self-image and perceived social support were associated with court-related anxiety."[93]

Sass and Wolfe provide a synopsis of the typical victim.[94] Their research demonstrates that 80 percent of the victims are female, with 46 percent being subjected to intrafamilial abuse. Only 13 percent of the children were abused by strangers. In all, 74 percent of the children were involved in abuse that included genital touching. Nearly 20 percent of the victims had low cognitive functioning.

Sass and Wolfe stress that the level of cognitive functioning of the child must be taken into consideration when preparing the child for court.[95] As part of this process, the evaluator must assess the child's overall anxiety level. Sass and Wolfe point out that it can be very difficult for children under age seven to understand the court process. This difficulty can be alleviated somewhat by using a model of a courtroom with dolls, much as dollhouses are used in child's play, and by role-playing the various parts of the court case. In addition, a tour of the courtroom and the use of stress reduction techniques can be helpful. The suggestion that stress reduction techniques be used derives from the fact that 48 percent of the children in the study met the criteria for diagnosis of Posttraumatic Stress Disorder.

Last, the facts of the case should never be discussed as part of the preparation. Such issues need to be left for spontaneous testimony. The objective of preparing for court is only to familiarize the child with the setting. The credibility of a child's testimony can be severely damaged when a child is asked a question such as, "What did Attorney X [or what did your mother] talk to you about before coming to court today?" When the child subsequently provides a lengthy scenario of what the attorney or parent told the child to state in court, the opposing attorney will be able to use it to reduce the credibility of the child's testimony in cross-examination.

With older children, it is also important to have the child understand the court procedure. Legal terminology should be explained, the courtroom setting should be reviewed, and court procedures should also be understood. Vignettes about telling the truth and telling lies can also be used as part of preparation.

The research by Sass and Wolfe identified five common fears of children who are required to testify:

1. Facing the accused
2. Being hurt by the accused
3. Crying and losing control
4. Not understanding the questions asked on cross-examination
5. Being sent to jail themselves.[96]

---

[92] *Id.*

[93] *Id.*

[94] Louis Sass & David Wolfe, Preparing Sexually Abused Children for the Stress of Court, Paper presented at the 99th Annual Convention of the American Psychological Association, San Francisco (1991).

[95] *Id.*

[96] *Id.*

As a result, it becomes necessary to allay these fears in preparing the child for court testimony. The research done by Sass and Wolfe demonstrated that when children were prepared for testimony, they "were rated as better witnesses by the prosecuting attorney: had less generalized fear; had less specific fears; were more competent when they did not know the answer; and there were more findings of guilt."[97]

§ 6.15   Summary and Conclusions

One of the difficulties associated with the research that has been performed on abuse victims and witnesses is the fact that it is difficult to simulate what would actually occur in abuse testimony situations. Furthermore, loyalty issues, secrecy issues, motivation-to-lie issues, and a desire to gain attention via allegations have been minimally addressed in research. As a result, the ability to generalize from these results may be somewhat questionable.

There is no doubt that reform in the legal process and the courtroom setting needs to be made for protection of children. Although we tend to live in an adult-rights-oriented society more than a child's-rights-oriented society, legislation and Supreme Court rulings have leaned in the direction of protecting children. The courts have found ways to accomplish this without violating the defendants' Sixth or Fourteenth Amendment rights. Now that we are allowing children to testify in cases, the question of credibility is always an important issue. Research that identifies problems with memory, suggestibility, and distortion of fact has been performed. Although we are in a better place, questions still remain unanswered. Interview procedures like Steller's and the types of courtroom preparation used in London Family Court Clinics or Saywitz's narrative elaboration have gone a long way to help with this process and are recommended by the authors of this text.

§ 6.16   Questions for Chapter 6

Caution.   Attorneys should not expect to be able to go into court and ask all the questions listed below. Preparation is necessary, reviewing material in this chapter to determine whether the question applies to a particular case. The section or chapter number at the end of the question refers to where in this chapter readers can find an explanation of why that particular question may be important.

1. Has the expert followed the guidelines suggested for interviewing children? See § **6.2.**
2. Does the expert understand suggestibility? See § **6.3.**
3. If it is necessary for the child to testify, has the expert taken into account the research on suggestibility? See § **6.3.**

---

[97] *Id.*

4. Has the expert adequately protected the child by suggesting that the child not be required to be available for testimony?

5. Prior to requiring testimony by the child, has the expert explored alternatives to live court testimony? See § **6.7.**

6. Has the mental health professional adequately prepared the child for court testimony? See §§ **6.10, 6.13,** and **6.14.**

7. Is the expert conversant about the false memory/recovered memory controversy? See § **6.11.** See **Chapter 13.**

§ 6.17   Case Digest

The source of information for most of the following cases is the *Mental and Physical Disability Law Reporter* (MPDLR), a publication of the American Bar Association. Complete information for any other sources appears in the relevant references below. The following are direct quotations from the identified source. Quotations from the *Mental and Physical Disability Law Reporter:* Excerpted from *Mental and Physical Disability Law Reporter.* Copyright © 1989–2004. American Bar Association. Reprinted by permission. If no source is identified, it is a summary from the court ruling.

Supreme Court

White v. Illinois, 502 U.S. 346, 112 S. Ct. 736, 116 L. Ed. 2d 848 (1992).

> Decision: Admission of testimony against accused under Illinois hearsay exceptions for spontaneous declarations and medical-treatment statements held not to violate Sixth Amendment's confrontation clause.
>
> Summary: At the Illinois trial of an accused on charges arising out of an alleged sexual assault on a child, the child never testified, as (1) the state attempted on two occasions to call the child as a witness, but in each instance the child experienced emotional difficulty and left without testifying; and (2) the defense made no attempt to call the child as a witness. The trial court neither made, nor was asked to make, a specific finding that the child was unavailable to testify. Over the defense's objections, however, the trial court, under the state's hearsay exceptions for spontaneous declarations and for statements made in the course of securing medical treatment, permitted testimony by the child's babysitter, the child's mother, an investigating officer, an emergency room nurse, and a doctor, regarding prior, out-of-court statements made by the child to these individuals about the alleged assault. The accused was found guilty of aggravated criminal sexual assault, residential burglary, and unlawful restraint. On appeal, the Appellate Court of Illinois, Fourth District, in affirming the accused's conviction, ruled that (1) the trial court acted within its discretion under state law in admitting the child's hearsay statements; and (2) the admission of the statements did not violate the accused's right, under the confrontation clause of the Federal Constitution's Sixth Amendment, to confront the witnesses against him (198 Ill. App. 3d 641, 555 N.E.2d 1241). The Illinois Supreme Court denied discretionary review.
>
> On certiorari, the United States Supreme Court affirmed. . . . It was held that (1) the Sixth Amendment's confrontation clause applies to more out-of-court statements admitted under an accepted hearsay exception than those few statements in the character of ex parte affidavits— that is, where the circumstances surrounding the statements suggest that the statements were

made for the principal purpose of accusing or incriminating a defendant. . . . ; but (2) the confrontation clause does not require that before a criminal trial court, under the hearsay exceptions for spontaneous declarations and for statements made in the course of securing medical treatment, permits the prosecution to present testimony against an accused regarding a declarant's prior, out-of-court statements, either the prosecution must produce the declarant or the trial court must find that the declarant is unavailable, because (a) these two hearsay exceptions are firmly rooted, (b) the out-of-court statements admitted under the two exceptions are not themselves made in the course of a prior judicial proceeding, and have substantial probative value that cannot be duplicated simply by the declarant's later testifying in court, and (c) the establishment of a generally applicable unavailability rule would have few practical benefits while imposing pointless litigation costs; and (3) there is no basis under the confrontation clause to import a necessity requirement—to the effect that any confrontation restrictions must be necessary to protect a child's physical and psychological well-being— for in-court procedures once a child witness is testifying, to the much different context of a child's prior, out-of-court declarations admitted under established exceptions to the hearsay rule. . . .

The Chief Justice delivered the opinion of the court.

In this case we consider whether the Confrontation Clause of the Sixth Amendment requires that, before a trial court admits testimony under the "spontaneous declaration" and "medical examination" exceptions to the hearsay rule, the prosecution must either produce the defendant at trial or the trial court must find that the declarant is unavailable. The Illinois Appellate Court concluded that such procedures are not constitutionally required. We agree with that conclusion.

Petitioner was convicted by a jury of aggravated criminal sexual assault. . . . The events giving rise to the charges related to the sexual assault of S.G., then four years old. Testimony at the trial established that . . . S.G.'s babysitter, Tony DeVore, was awakened by S.G.'s scream. DeVore asked S.G. what had happened. According to DeVore's trial testimony, S.G. stated that petitioner had . . . "touch[ed] her in the wrong places." Asked by DeVore to point to where she had been touched, S.G. identified the vaginal area. . . . [S.G.'s mother] testified that S.G. repeated her claims that petitioner "put his mouth on her front part." . . . [The police officer's] summary of S.G.'s statement indicated that she had offered essentially the same story as she had first reported to DeVore and to [her mother]. . . .

S.G was taken to the hospital. She was examined first by . . . an emergency room nurse, and then by [a physician]. Each testified at trial and their testimony indicated that, in response to questioning, S.G. again provided an account of events that was essentially identical to the one she had given to [the others]. . . .

Petitioner objected [to all of this testimony] on hearsay grounds. . . .

We have been careful "not to equate the Confrontation Clause's prohibitions with the general rule prohibiting the admission of hearsay statements," *Idaho v. Wright*, (1990). . . .

We note first that the evidentiary rationale for permitting hearsay testimony regarding spontaneous declarations and statements made in the course of receiving medical care is that such out-of-court declarations are made in contexts that provide substantial guarantees of their trustworthiness. . . . A statement that has been offered in a moment of excitement—without the opportunity to reflect on the consequences of one's exclamation—may justifiably carry more weight with a trier of fact than a similar statement offered in the relative calm of the courtroom. Similarly, a statement made in the course of procuring medical services, where the declarant knows that a false statement may cause misdiagnosis or mistreatment, carries special guarantees of credibility that a trier of fact may not think replicated by courtroom testimony. . . .

The preference for live testimony . . . is because of the importance of cross examination, "the greatest legal engine ever invented for the discovery of truth." . . . [W]here proffered hearsay has sufficient guarantees of reliability to come within a firmly rooted exception to the hearsay rule, the Confrontation Clause is satisfied. . . .

And as we have also noted, a statement that qualifies for admission under a "firmly rooted" hearsay exception is so trustworthy that adversarial testing can be expected to add little to its reliability. *Wright*, . . . 110 S. Ct. 3139. . . .

[P]etitioner presses upon us two recent decisions involving child-testimony in child-sexual assault cases, *Coy v. Iowa* . . . and *Maryland v. Craig*. . . . Both *Coy* and *Craig* required us to consider the constitutionality of courtroom procedures designed to prevent a child witness from having to face across an open courtroom a defendant charged with sexually assaulting the child. . . . Petitioner draws from these two cases a general rule that hearsay testimony offered by a child should be permitted only upon a showing of necessity—i.e., in cases where necessary to protect the child's physical and psychological well-being. . . .

Petitioner's reliance is misplaced. *Coy* and *Craig* involved only the question of what in-court procedures are constitutionally required to guarantee a defendant's confrontation right once a witness is testifying. Such a question is quite separate from that of what requirements the Confrontation Clause imposes as a predicate for the introduction of out-of-court declarations. *Coy* and *Craig* did not speak to the latter question.

Six Justices joined the Chief Justice in the opinion. Two Justices concurred in part and concurred in the judgment. This is substantially different from the 5-4 votes in *Idaho v. Wright* and *Maryland v. Craig*.

Idaho v. Wright, 497 U.S. 805, 110 S. Ct. 3139, 111 L. Ed. 2d 638, 58 U.S.L.W. 5036 (1990).

Decision: Admission, at Idaho criminal trial for sexual abuse of child, of two-and-a-half-year-old declarant's hearsay statements made to examining pediatrician held to violate confrontation clause of Sixth Amendment.

Summary: A mother was charged, under Idaho law, with lewd conduct with her two minor daughters, who were 5-$\frac{1}{2}$ and 2-$\frac{1}{2}$ years old at the time that the crimes were charged. At trial, the court concluded, and the parties agreed, that the younger daughter, who was then 3 years old, was "not capable of communicating to the jury." However, under Idaho's residual hearsay exception . . . the trial court admitted certain statements that the younger daughter had made to a pediatrician who had examined her following the reporting of her mother's alleged offenses to the police. The pediatrician, who had extensive experience in child abuse cases, testified that the younger daughter had reluctantly answered questions about her own abuse but had spontaneously volunteered information about her sister's abuse. . . . The mother, who was convicted of lewd conduct with each daughter, appealed from only the conviction involving the younger daughter, asserting that the admission of the pediatrician's testimony violated her rights under the confrontation clause of the Federal Constitution's Sixth Amendment. The Supreme Court of Idaho [reversed] the mother's conviction and [ordered] the case to be remanded for a new trial. . . .

On certiorari, the United States Supreme Court affirmed. . . . It was held that the admission, at the mother's trial, of the younger daughter's statements to the pediatrician violated the mother's rights under the Sixth Amendment's confrontation clause, because (1) the state's residual hearsay exception was not a firmly rooted hearsay exception for confrontation clause purposes; (2) if the admission of hearsay statements under the residual exception automatically passed confrontation clause scrutiny, virtually every codified hearsay exception would assume constitutional stature; and (3) given the presumption of inadmissibility accorded accusatory hearsay statements not admitted pursuant to a firmly rooted hearsay exception, the state had failed to show that the younger daughter's statements possessed sufficient particularized guarantees of trustworthiness, for confrontation clause purposes, to overcome that presumption, since (a) viewing the totality of the circumstances surrounding the younger daughter's responses to the pediatrician's questions, there was no special reason for supposing that the statements were particularly trustworthy, and (b) to be admissible under the confrontation clause, hearsay evidence used to convict an accused must possess indicia of reliability by virtue of its inherent trustworthiness, not by reference to corroborating evidence at trial.

[The dissenting justices expressed] the view that (1) there was no constitutional justification for the Supreme Court's decision to prescind corroborating evidence from consideration of the question whether a child's hearsay statements are reliable, and (2) whatever doubt the court had with the weight to be given the corroborating evidence in the case at hand was no justification for rejecting the position of virtually the entire legal community that corroborating evidence is relevant to reliability and trustworthiness.

Justice O'Connor delivered the Court's opinion.

The Confrontation Clause . . . bars the admission of some evidence that would otherwise be admissible under an exception to the hearsay rule. . . . Reliability can be inferred without more in a case where the evidence falls within a firmly rooted hearsay exception. In other cases, the evidence must be excluded, at least absent a showing of particularized guarantees of trustworthiness. . . .

For purposes of deciding this case, we assume without deciding that, to the extent the unavailability requirement applies in this case, the younger daughter was an unavailable witness within the meaning of the Confrontation Clause.

The crux of the question presented is therefore whether the State, as the proponent of evidence presumptively barred by the hearsay rule and the Confrontation Clause, has carried its burden of proving that the younger daughter's incriminating statements to Dr. Jambura bore sufficient indicia of reliability to withstand scrutiny under the Clause. . . .

[B]ecause the younger daughter's hearsay statements do not fall within a firmly rooted hearsay exception, they are "presumptively unreliable and inadmissible for Confrontation Clause purposes . . . [and] must be excluded, at least absent a showing of particularized guarantees of trustworthiness." . . . Out-of-court statements made by children regarding sexual abuse arise in a wide variety of circumstances, and we do not believe the Constitution imposes a fixed set of procedural prerequisites to the admission of such statements at trial. . . .

We think the "particularized guarantees of trustworthiness" required for admission under the Confrontation Clause must likewise be drawn from the totality of circumstances that surround the making of the statement and that render the declarant particularly worthy of belief. . . .

The state and federal courts have identified a number of factors that we think properly relate to whether hearsay statements made by a child witness in child sexual abuse cases are reliable . . . [including] spontaneity and consistent repetition . . . mental state of the declarant . . . use of terminology unexpected of a child of similar age . . . [and] lack of motive to fabricate. . . . [W]e think the factors identified also apply to whether such statements bear "particularized guarantees of trustworthiness" under the Confrontation Clause. . . . [T]he unifying principle is that these factors relate to whether the child declarant was particularly likely to be telling the truth when the statement was made. . . .

To be admissible under the Confrontation Clause, hearsay evidence used to convict a defendant must possess indicia of reliability by virtue of its inherent trustworthiness, not by reference to other evidence at trial. . . .

We think the presence of corroborating evidence more appropriately indicates that any error in admitting the statement might be harmless, rather than that any basis exists for presuming the declarant to be trustworthy. . . .

We think the Supreme Court of Idaho properly focused on the presumptive unreliability of the out-of-court statements and on the suggestive manner in which Dr. Jambura conducted the interview. Viewing the totality of the circumstances surrounding the younger daughter's responses to Dr. Jambura's questions, we find no special reason for supposing that the incriminating statements were particularly trustworthy. The younger daughter's last statement regarding the abuse of the older daughter, however, presents a closer question. According to Dr. Jambura, the younger daughter "volunteered" that statement "after she sort of clammed-up. . . ." Although the spontaneity of the statement and the change in demeanor suggest that the younger daughter was telling the truth when she made the statement, we note that it is possible that "[if] there is evidence of prior interrogation, prompting, or manipulation by adults, spontaneity may be an inaccurate indicator of trustworthiness." *Robinson*, 153 Ariz. at 201, 735 P.2d at 811.

Commenting on this case, Professor Billie Wright Dziech and Wisconsin Appellate Court Judge Charles B. Schudson indicate that

For juries, the critical importance of hearsay evidence has become even clearer in recent years as an increasing number of defendants assert that the allegations are fabrications, resulting from the motives and manipulations of vengeful parents in custody disputes. In such instances, jurors want to know when the child first made the allegation, to whom, and under what circumstances. . . . If the trial presents competing theories about whether . . . interviews were objective or manipulative, jurors should know the details—including the exact words, whenever possible—and the nature, circumstances, timing, and substance of all the child's communications. Without the admission of hearsay, such knowledge is impossible. [B.W. Dziech & C.B. Schudson, *On Trial: America's Courts and Their Treatment of Sexually Abused Children* 191 (1991)] . . . [I]f carefully considered, *Idaho v. Wright* should establish that residual hearsay statements are admissible in most instances because children are "particularly likely to be telling the truth" about sexual abuse, and that virtually all other hearsay statements of abuse will be admissible under specific hearsay exceptions. [*Id.* at 194.]

Maryland v. Craig, 497 U.S. 836, 110 S. Ct. 3157, 111 L. Ed. 2d 666, 58 U.S.L.W. 5044 (1990).

Decision: Sixth Amendment's confrontation clause held not absolutely to prohibit Maryland from using one-way closed-circuit television for receipt of testimony by child witness in child abuse case.

Summary: A Maryland statute permitted a trial judge to receive, by one-way closed-circuit television, the testimony of a child witness who was alleged to be a victim of child abuse, if the judge determined that testimony by the child in the courtroom would result in the child's suffering serious emotional distress such that the child could not reasonably communicate. Under the statute, (1) the witness, prosecutor, and defense counsel withdrew to a separate room, while the judge, jury, and defendant remained in the courtroom; (2) the witness was then examined and cross-examined in the separate room, while a video monitor recorded and displayed the witness' testimony to those in the courtroom; and (3) during this time, the witness could not see the defendant, but the defendant remained in electronic communication with defense counsel, and objections could be made and ruled on as if the witness were testifying in the courtroom. . . . After the trial court found the alleged victim and three other children competent to testify and permitted them to testify using the statutory procedure, the jury convicted the accused on all counts. . . .

On certiorari, the United States Supreme Court vacated and remanded. . . . It was held that the confrontation clause did not absolutely prohibit the child witnesses from testifying through the statutory procedure, because (1) face-to-face confrontation with witnesses appearing at trial is not an indispensable element of the Sixth Amendment's confrontation guarantee, since (a) in certain narrow circumstances, competing interests, if closely examined, may warrant dispensing with confrontation at trial, and (b) the word "confront," as used in the confrontation clause, cannot simply mean face-to-face confrontation; (2) the Supreme Court, in prior cases, had held that other Sixth Amendment rights must be interpreted in the context of the necessities of trial and the adversary process; (3) the statutory procedure insured the reliability of the evidence by subjecting it to rigorous adversarial testing, and thereby preserved the essence of effective confrontation, when, under the procedure, the witnesses testified under oath, were subject to full cross-examination, and were able to be observed as they testified by the judge, jury, and defendant; and (4) a state's interest in the physical and psychological well-being of child abuse victims may be sufficiently important to outweigh, at least in some cases, a defendant's right to face his or her accusers in court.

[The dissenting justices expressed] the view that the confrontation clause of the Sixth Amendment guarantees, in a criminal prosecution, a defendant's right to meet face-to-face all those who appear and give evidence at trial, because "to confront" plainly means to encounter face-to-face, whatever else "to confront" may mean in addition.

Justice O'Connor delivered the opinion of the court. . . .

In October 1986, a Howard County grand jury charged respondent, Sandra Ann Craig, with child abuse, first and second degree sexual offenses, perverted sexual practice, assault, and battery. The named victim in each count was [Brooke], . . . a six-year-old child. . . .

In support of its motion invoking the one-way closed circuit television procedure, the State presented expert testimony that Brooke, as well as a number of other children who were alleged to have been sexually abused by Craig, would suffer "serious emotional distress such that [they could not] reasonably communicate," . . . if required to testify in the courtroom. . . . The Maryland Court of Appeals characterized the evidence as follows:

> The expert testimony in each case suggested that each child would have some or considerable difficulty in testifying in Craig's presence. For example, as to one child, the expert said that what "would cause him the most anxiety would be to testify in front of Mrs. Craig." . . . The child "wouldn't be able to communicate effectively." As to another, an expert said she "would probably stop talking and she would withdraw and curl up." With respect to two others, the testimony was that one would "become highly agitated, that he may refuse to talk or if he did talk, that he would choose his subject regardless of the questions" while the other would "become extremely timid and unwilling to talk.". . .

We observed in *Coy v. Iowa* that "the Confrontation Clause guarantees the defendant a face-to-face meeting with witnesses appearing before the trier of fact.". . .

We have never held, however, that the Confrontation Clause guarantees criminal defendants the *absolute* right to a face-to-face meeting with witnesses against them at trial. . . . The procedure challenged in *Coy* involved the placement of a screen that prevented two child witnesses in a child abuse case from seeing the defendant as they testified against him at trial. . . . In holding that the use of this procedure violated the defendant's right to confront witnesses against him, we suggested that any exception to the right "would surely be allowed only when necessary to further an important public policy"—i.e., only upon a showing of something more than the generalized, "legislatively imposed presumption of trauma" underlying the statute at issue in that case. . . . We concluded that "[s]ince there ha[d] been no individualized findings that these particular witnesses needed special protection, the judgment . . . could not be sustained by any conceivable exception.". . . Because the trial court in this case made individualized findings that each of the child witnesses needed special protection, this case requires us to decide the question reserved in *Coy*.

The central concern of the Confrontation Clause is to ensure the reliability of the evidence against a criminal defendant by subjecting it to rigorous testing in the context of an adversary proceeding before the trier of fact. The word "confront," after all, also means a clashing of forces or ideas, thus carrying with it the notion of adversariness. . . .

The combined effect of . . . elements of confrontation—physical presence, oath, cross-examination, and observation of demeanor by the trier of fact—serves the purposes of the Confrontation Clause by ensuring that evidence admitted against an accused is reliable and subject to the rigorous adversarial testing that is the norm of Anglo-American criminal proceedings. . . .

("[T]he Confrontation Clause is generally satisfied when the defense is given a full and fair opportunity to probe and expose [testimonial] infirmities [such as forgetfulness, confusion, or evasion] through cross-examination, thereby calling to the attention of the factfinder the reasons for giving scant weight to the witness' testimony.")

In sum, our precedents establish that "the Confrontation Clause reflects a *preference* for face-to-face confrontation at trial". . . , a preference that "must occasionally give way to considerations of public policy and the necessities of the case.". . .

Maryland's statutory procedure, when invoked, prevents a child witness from seeing the defendant as he or she testifies against the defendant at trial. We find it significant, however, that Maryland's procedure preserves all of the other elements of the confrontation right: the child witness must be competent to testify and must testify under oath; the defendant retains full opportunity for contemporaneous cross-examination; and the judge, jury, and defendant are able to view (albeit by video monitor) the demeanor (and body) of the witness as he or she testifies. . . . [T]he presence of these other elements of confrontation . . . adequately ensures that the testimony is both reliable and subject to rigorous adversarial testing in a manner functionally equivalent to that accorded live, in-person testimony. . . .

The critical inquiry in this case, therefore, is whether use of the procedure is necessary to further an important state interest. The State contends that it has a substantial interest in protecting children who are allegedly victims of child abuse from the trauma of testifying against the alleged perpetrator and that its statutory procedure for receiving testimony from such witnesses is necessary to further that interest.

We have of course recognized that a State's interest in "the protection of minor victims of sex crimes from further trauma and embarrassment" is a "compelling" one. . . .

We likewise conclude today that a State's interest in the physical and psychological well-being of child abuse victims may be sufficiently important to outweigh, at least in some cases, a defendant's right to face his or her accusers in court. That a significant majority of States has enacted statutes to protect child witnesses from the trauma of giving testimony in child abuse cases attests to the widespread belief in the importance of such a public policy. . . . Thirty-seven States, for example, permit the use of videotaped testimony of sexually abused children [Alabama, Arizona, Arkansas, California, Colorado, Connecticut, Delaware, Florida, Hawaii, Illinois, Indiana, Iowa, Kansas, Kentucky, Massachusetts, Michigan, Minnesota, Mississippi, Missouri, Montana, Nebraska, Nevada, New Hampshire, New Mexico, Ohio, Oklahoma, Oregon, Pennsylvania, Rhode Island, South Carolina, South Dakota, Tennessee, Texas, Utah, Vermont, Wisconsin, Wyoming], 24 States have authorized the use of one-way closed circuit television testimony in child abuse cases [Alabama, Alaska, Arizona, Connecticut, Florida, Georgia, Illinois, Indiana, Iowa, Kansas, Kentucky, Louisiana, Maryland, Massachusetts, Minnesota, Mississippi, New Jersey, Oklahoma, Oregon, Pennsylvania, Rhode Island, Texas, Utah, Vermont], and 8 States authorize the use of a two-way system in which the child-witness is permitted to see the courtroom and the defendant on a video monitor and in which the jury and judge is [*sic*] permitted to view the child during the testimony [California, Hawaii, Idaho, Minnesota, New York, Ohio, Virginia, Vermont].

Given the State's traditional and "transcendent interest in protecting the welfare of children,". . . and buttressed by the growing body of academic literature documenting the psychological trauma suffered by child abuse victims who must testify in court, . . . we hold that, if the State makes an adequate showing of necessity, the state interest in protecting child witnesses from the trauma of testifying in a child abuse case is sufficiently important to justify the use of a special procedure that permits a child witness in such cases to testify at trial against a defendant in the absence of face-to-face confrontation with the defendant.

The requisite finding of necessity must of course be a case-specific one: the trial court must hear evidence and determine whether use of the one-way closed circuit television procedure is necessary to protect the welfare of the particular child witness who seeks to testify. . . . The trial court must also find that the child witness would be traumatized, not by the courtroom generally, but by the presence of the defendant. . . . Finally, the trial court must find that the emotional distress suffered by the child witness in the presence of the defendant is more than de minimus [*sic*], i.e., more than "mere nervousness or excitement or some reluctance to testify," . . . . [T]he Maryland statute, which requires a determination that the child witness will suffer serious emotional distress such that the child cannot reasonably communicate, . . . clearly suffices to meet constitutional standards. . . .

[W]here face-to-face confrontation causes significant emotional distress in a child witness, there is evidence that such confrontation would in fact *disserve* the Confrontation Clause's truth-seeking goal. . . .

In sum, we conclude that where necessary to protect a child witness from trauma that would be caused by testifying in the physical presence of the defendant, at least where such trauma would impair the child's ability to communicate, the Confrontation Clause does not prohibit use of a procedure that, despite the absence of face-to-face confrontation, ensures the reliability of the evidence by subjecting it to rigorous adversarial testing and thereby preserves the essence of effective confrontation. Because there is no dispute that the child witnesses in this case testified under oath, were subject to full cross-examination, and were able to be observed by the judge, jury, and defendant as they testified, we conclude that, to the extent that a proper finding of necessity has been made, the admission of such testimony would be consonant with the Confrontation Clause. . . .

The Court of Appeals appears to have rested its conclusion at least in part on the trial court's failure to observe the children's behavior in the defendant's presence and its failure to explore less restrictive alternatives to the use of the one-way closed circuit television procedure. . . . Although we think such evidentiary requirements could strengthen the grounds for use of protective measures, we decline to establish, as a matter of federal constitutional law, any such categorical evidentiary prerequisites for the use of the one-way television procedure. The trial court in this case, for example, could well have found, on the basis of the expert testimony before it, that testimony by the child witnesses in the courtroom in the defendant's presence "will result in [each] child suffering serious emotional distress such that the child cannot reasonably communicate. . . ." So long as a trial court makes such a case-specific finding of necessity, the Confrontation Clause does not prohibit a State from using a one-way closed circuit television procedure for the receipt of testimony by a child witness in a child abuse case.

Oregon

Oregon v. Barkley, 315 Or. 420 (1993), 846 P.2d 390. The Oregon Supreme Court ruled that a trial court was not in error when it admitted into evidence a videotaped interview of a child at her father's trial for sexually abusing the girl. The videotaped interview was done by hospital personnel. The videotape showed the child describing and identifying, using dolls, her father's sexual behavior toward her. The supreme court ruled that the videotape fell under the state's exception to the hearsay exclusion for statements made for the purpose of medical care.

CHAPTER 7

STATISTICAL CONCEPTS

§ 7.1   Introduction

Because textbooks on statistics are often several hundred pages in length, this chapter is written to provide attorneys with some basic principles necessary to understand statistical concepts. The discussion does not delve in any depth into the theoretical underpinning of each of the statistical concepts. Instead, it provides the overview necessary for a basic understanding of the concepts and techniques utilized in research, test development, and test interpretation that can be used in cross-examination of an expert witness. Because the content of the chapter provides essential ancillary information to aid in understanding statistical concepts, there are no specific questions suggested for examination or cross-examination.

§ 7.2   Test Standardization

A standardized test is administered with a standard set of directions under uniform conditions. It is assumed that every examiner administering the test will follow the directions verbatim and the testing conditions recommended as closely as possible. The level of consistency among examiners is necessary if an individual's scores are to be compared with the normative sample. After administering the test, raw scores are obtained and converted to standard scores that can be compared with norms. The norms can be based on, for example, grade equivalents, age equivalents, or percentile ranks. The examiner has no choice about which norms are selected. There is only one acceptable set of norms for each person on each test based on age, gender, developmental level, or other important variables. Test manuals should include tables of norms that provide the examiner the opportunity to convert raw scores into normative scores.

§ 7.3   Norms

For test scores to be meaningful, the individual taking the test must be within the group that the norms reflect. The norms are established by the individual(s) who developed the test. For example, if there are norm tables for children ages 6 through 16 on a particular test, it would generally not be acceptable to test children below 6 or above 16 years of age. Doing so would not provide the examiner the opportunity to meaningfully compare the results with those of the individuals on which the test was standardized. A well-constructed test uses a broad-based sample. One of the most popular methods used is referred to as a *stratified* sample. A well-stratified sample includes individuals from all the age, gender, race, geographical, and socioeconomic groups who may take the test. Individuals in each stratum are included in proportion to their presence in the general population based on the United States census at the time the test is developed. For example, if 13 percent of the population is urban blacks, then 13 percent of the test sample should be urban blacks. If 43 percent of the population is from the northeastern quadrant of the United States, 43 percent of the test sample should be from that area. It is easy to see that establishing norms for a test, following appropriate standards, can be difficult and very costly.

The most familiar form of norming is through children's achievement scores. Whenever students take tests in school, the results are often reported as grade equivalents, age equivalents, and/or percentile ranks. They are also generally reported as national norms, local norms, and possibly independent school norms. The national norms would compare the student with all individuals in the country in the same norm groups (age and grade). The local norms would compare the student with the local population. Whether the students would compare to anyone in the city or suburb, or only to individuals in a particular school system, should be specified in the results.

§ 7.4   Measures of Central Tendency

Measures of central tendency[1] are designed to show a typical or average performance for a specified group on a particular test. This allows the reader to compare individuals and groups within and across tests.

---

[1] J. Spence et al., Elementary Statistics 39 (4th ed. 1983) [hereinafter Elementary Statistics]; R. Sprinthall, Basic Statistical Analysis 23 (2d ed. 1987) [hereinafter Basic Statistical Analysis]; T. Anderson & S. Sclove, An Introduction to the Statistical Analysis of Data 67 (1978) [hereinafter An Introduction to the Statistical Analysis of Data]; J. Graham & R. Lilly, Psychological Testing 14–15 (1984) [hereinafter Graham & Lilly, Psychological Testing].

Mean.   The most commonly used measure of central tendency is the *mean*.[2] To obtain the mean, all the scores are added together and the sum is divided by the number of scores. The result is referred to as an arithmetic mean and is designated by an *x* with a line over it: "$\bar{x}$."

Median.   The median is the score that falls in the middle of the distribution.[3] For example, if there were five scores in a distribution—9, 10, 11, 16, and 18—the median would be 11, whereas the mean would be 12.83.

Mode.   The mode is defined as the most frequently occurring score in the sample.[4] When two scores occur with equal frequency, the distribution is referred to as a *bimodal* distribution. It is important to know when a bimodal distribution occurs because the interpretation of the test data will be affected. The bimodal distribution will have two modes (the most frequently occurring scores): one at the lower end of the distribution and another at the upper end of the distribution. The mean (the average score) does not accurately reflect the distribution. In the bimodal distribution, the mean falls between the two modes and is of little statistical significance because it reflects one of the least frequently occurring scores. **Figure 7–1** reflects this. The modes in the figure are 5 and 15, thus a bimodal distribution. The mean is 10, which is an arithmetic average of all the scores but does not provide much meaningful data.

§ 7.5   Measures of Variability

Measures of variability deal with the spread of scores across the distribution. One of the most frequently used measures of variability is the *range*. The range represents the difference between the lowest score and the highest score. Looking at a distribution of 9, 10, 11, 16, and 18, the range would be 9 (18 minus 9). Perhaps the most widely used statistic, which also is a measure of variability, is the *standard deviation*.[5] The standard deviation allows an individual to understand what is the average deviation or difference from the mean. The greater the variability of scores, or the more spread out the scores are, the larger the standard deviation will be. By knowing nothing more than the mean and the standard deviation of a particular set of scores, a wealth of information can be obtained.

Looking at the top of **Figure 7–2,** the Gaussian, or normal, curve is represented. It should be noted that 68.26 percent of the scores fall between plus and minus 1 standard

---

[2] Elementary Statistics at 39–45; Basic Statistical Analysis at 23; An Introduction to the Statistical Analysis of Data at 75–78; Graham & Lilly, Psychological Testing, at 14.

[3] Elementary Statistics at 45–49; Basic Statistical Analysis at 27–29; An Introduction to the Statistical Analysis of Data at 71–72; Graham & Lilly, Psychological Testing, at 14–15.

[4] Elementary Statistics at 45–46; Basic Statistical Analysis at 29–32; An Introduction to the Statistical Analysis of Data at 67–71; Graham & Lilly, Psychological Testing, at 15.

[5] Elementary Statistics at 59–61; Basic Statistical Analysis at 41–45; An Introduction to the Statistical Analysis of Data at 118–19; Graham & Lilly, Psychological Testing, at 16–18.

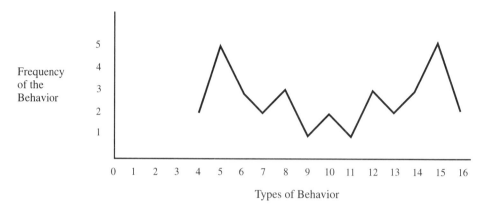

Figure 7–1. Bimodal distribution.

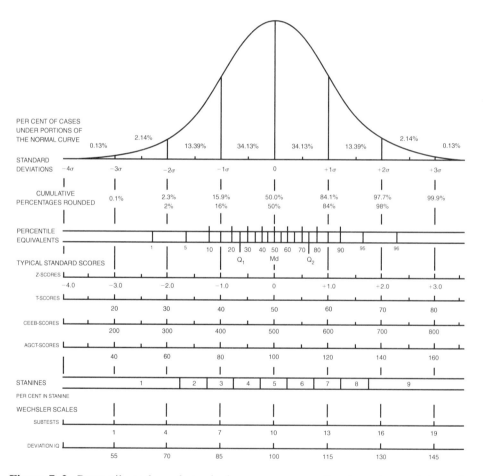

Figure 7–2. Percentile ranks and standard scores corresponding to various points on the baseline of a normal distribution of scores. Source: H.G. Seashore, "Methods of expressing test scores," *The Psychological Corporation Test Service Bulletin* No. 48 (1958).

deviation. This can be determined by adding together the 34.13 percent between 0 plus 1 standard deviation and the 34.13 percent between 0 and minus 1 standard deviation. Furthermore, more than 95 percent of the scores fall between plus and minus 2 standard deviations. Scores outside this range are usually considered significant. And last, 99.8 percent of the scores fall between plus and minus 3 standard deviations from the mean; any score that falls outside this group is considered to be very significant. Only one out of 1,000 people will score beyond 3 standard deviations above the mean and another one in 1,000 below 3 standard deviations below the mean. This would indicate that the individual has set him- or herself apart from the population at one extreme or another.

In the next section of the chart, the percentile equivalents are scored, giving the reader an opportunity to look at what percentile ranks fall within the different standard deviation groups.

The next group of scores reported on the chart are standard scores—the z-scores and T-scores.[6] The z-scores[7] are not used as frequently as the T-scores. However, a z-score allows the reader to understand how many standard deviations are represented by converting standard deviations of all distributions into a uniform score. For example, a z-score of plus 2 means that that number falls 2 standard deviations above the mean, or a z-score of minus 1.5 would indicate that that score falls 1½ standard deviations below the mean. A z-score of plus 2 would be 2 standard deviations above the mean on any distribution, no matter what the standard deviations of the variability of the distribution were.

The T-scores are much more frequently reported, as they are easier to understand. A T-score is a converted standard score with a mean of 50 and a standard deviation of 10. For example, one of the most popular instruments used in psychological testing is the Minnesota Multiphasic Personality Inventory–Second Edition (MMPI-2). The MMPI-2 has a mean of 50 and a standard deviation of 10. This corresponds with the distribution of the T-score on the chart. Looking at the T-score of 65, which is generally the cutoff score indicative of psychopathology on the MMPI-2, the reader will notice on the chart that it represents a cumulative percentage of approximately 92 percent. Scores above 70 show that the individual's scores are beyond more than approximately 98 percent of the population, indicating that only 2 percent of the population would fall in this area. A score of 80 on the MMPI-2 would represent a T-score of 80, which is three standard deviations beyond the mean and would indicate that 99.9 percent of the population would score below that score. Any time a score beyond 80 is obtained on the MMPI-2, it is of major concern because only 1 in 1,000 individuals would have scores that extreme, indicating a very significant score. For further discussion, see **Chapter 9.**

Interpreting Test Scores

The Wechsler Scales are the most frequently used intelligence tests. See **Chapter 8.** Subtest scale scores generally range from 0 to 19. It can be noted in looking at the Wechsler subtest

---

[6] Elementary Statistics at 68–73; Basic Statistical Analysis at 55–57.

[7] Elementary Statistics at 73; Basic Statistical Analysis at 85–89; An Introduction to the Statistical Analysis of Data at 432–33.

scale scores that they have a mean of 10 and a standard deviation of 3. Furthermore, the intelligence quotient (IQ) scores on these tests are reported as deviation IQs. They have a mean of 100 and a standard deviation of 15. Therefore, an individual who has an IQ of 130 would be two standard deviations above the mean, scoring at the 98th percentile. An individual with a score of 55 would be three standard deviations below the mean, and would be at the .1 percentile.

For tests that are not represented on **Figure 7–2,** an individual need only find out the mean and standard deviation of a particular test and apply them to these charts to obtain useful information. For example, if a test is reported to have a mean of 80 and a standard deviation of 16, with a score of 104 reported, the table can be used. One hundred four minus 80 (the mean) equals 24. The score is therefore 24 points above the mean. The standard deviation is 16. Twenty-four divided by 16 equals 1.5 (or $1\frac{1}{2}$ standard deviations above the mean). One and one-half standard deviations would be comparable to plus 1.5 z-scores. If a line is drawn up and down the point at 1.5 standard deviations above the mean, notice that the line would be approximately at the 93rd percentile and in the 8th stanine. The line would fall between the 90th and 95th percentile. A visual extrapolation would show the score to be approximately at the 93rd percentile.

The term *percentiles* and *percentile ranks* are used frequently in discussing these types of statistical analysis. A percentile score represents both the percentage of the population that falls below a particular score and the percentage that falls above a particular score. For example, if an individual had a percentile rank of 65, or was at the 65th percentile, 65 out of every 100 individuals would score below that person, while 35 out of every 100 individuals would score above that person. A percentile rank of 28 would indicate that 28 out of every 100 individuals would score below that person, while 72 out of 100 individuals would score above that person. When an individual achieves a rank of 99.9, this indicates that 999 out of 1,000 people score below that score, while 1 out of 1,000 would exceed that score.

§ 7.6   Levels of Confidence

It is not unusual for an expert witness to include testimony about research that has been performed. Psychology is not an exact science. As a result, there is almost nothing that occurs 100 percent of the time on a causal relationship basis as would be true in many cases of pure science. In psychology, results are reported based on *levels of confidence* or *confidence intervals.*

The measure that is used in determining the level of confidence is what is referred to as a "*p* (probability) value."[8] When psychological, educational, or sociological research is performed and results are obtained, the researcher uses tables to interpret the results in an effort to determine the *p* value. *P* values are reported anywhere from 1.0 to approaching 0.00. Generally, in research, an acceptable *p* value is one that is less than .05. When an individual performs research and ends up with a *p* value of less than .05, she can interpret it to

---

[8] Elementary Statistics at 153–55; Basic Statistical Analysis at 151–55; An Introduction to the Statistical Analysis of Data at 321–25; Graham & Lilly, Psychological Testing, at 26.

mean that the results will have occurred 95 times out of 100 as a product of the experimental manipulations in the research and the other 5 times out of 100 based on chance.
When a p value of less than .01 is reported, 99 times out of 100 the results are considered
caused by the experimental manipulations generated in the research, and 1 time out of 100
the results would have occurred by chance. In an extraordinary case, a p value may be less
than .0001. This would indicate that 9,999 times out of 10,000 the results would have
occurred based on the research, while 1 time out of 10,000 the results would have occurred
by chance. The smaller the p value, the better the results. Generally, psychology does not
accept a p value greater than .05 as being meaningful. The research may also report p values
by stating that the results were "significant at the .05 level" (p is less than .05) or
"significant at the .001 level" (p is less than .001). In research that is not meaningful,
a p value of .25 may be reported. This would indicate that 75 times out 100 the results
would occur based on the research, while 25 times out of 100 results would occur based
on chance. This outcome is not acceptable in most psychological research.

When cross-examining an expert witness on the results of research, it is important to
determine the p value, or the level of significance. Furthermore, it is important to determine whether the subject research has been replicated with the same or similar results as
the original research. If the p value is not .05 or less, or if the research has not been replicated with the same or similar level of success that was achieved in the original research,
the results of the research should not carry as much weight as would the research that
meets these criteria.

§ 7.7   Standard Error of Measurement

As stated in § 7.6, psychology is not an exact science. When results are obtained in norming a test or doing research, one of the useful statistics provided is the *standard error of
measurement*.[9] The standard error of measurement enables the interpreter to estimate the
limits within which the individual's true scores are expected to fall. For example, if the standard error of measurement on an intelligence test is 5, and the actual score obtained by the
individual is 112, the actual true score would likely fall between plus and minus 1 standard
error of measurement or 107 to 117. Therefore, many of those who interpret these tests
would report the intelligence score of 112 as 107 to 117. Basically, the smaller the standard
error of measurement in relation to the score, the more valid the exact score will be.

If, hypothetically, an IQ test had a standard error of measurement of 23, and a score of
112, plus and minus 1 standard error of measurement would be reported as 89 to 135.
It can readily be seen that this would not be a very useful test. It is important to note that
comparing test scores can be dangerous if one does not know the standard of measurement.
For example, with a standard error of measurement of 6 and scores of 112 and 115, it
would be inappropriate to state that one individual was more intelligent than the other.
Because both the scores fall within 1 standard error of measurement, they could be
considered to be statistically the same.

---

[9] An Introduction to the Statistical Analysis of Data at 319; Psychological Testing and Assessment
at 89–90; Graham & Lilly, Psychological Testing, at 38–39; A. Anastasi, Psychological Testing,
at 125–27 (5th ed. 1982) [hereinafter Anastasi, Psychological Testing].

§ 7.8   Reliability

When a test is constructed, the two most important factors that must be determined are the test's reliability[10] and validity. Unfortunately, the concepts of reliability and validity are often confused by those unfamiliar with statistical concepts. A test is considered to be reliable if it consistently produces the same results under varying conditions that could produce measurement errors.

Anytime two sets of scores are reported, they can be statistically correlated with one another. A quantitative measure of the relationship existing among two or more variables, called a *correlation coefficient,* is obtained. The correlation coefficient is denoted by the letter *r*. Generally, correlation coefficients vary from plus 1.0 to minus 1.0. A positive correlation of 1.0 would indicate that there is a perfect relationship between the two variables being measured. In other words, every time *A* happens, *B* happens. A correlation of minus 1.0 indicates that there is a perfect inverse relationship between the two sets of scores. In other words, any time *A* happens, *B* does not happen. A correlation of 0.0 indicates that the two variables are totally unrelated to one another. Generally, the further the correlation is from 0.0 in either direction, the stronger the relationship between the two variables.

It is important to understand that correlation does *not* imply a causal relationship. It only implies the relationship between the two scores, and not necessarily that *A* causes *B* to happen. For example, roosters crow at dawn but do not cause the sun to rise or vice versa.

Reliability Measures

There are many different types of reliability statistics, called *coefficients.* Reliability coefficients are sometimes referred to as the *coefficient stability*.[11] One type is referred to as *test-retest reliability.* In test-retest reliability, the same test is administered on two separate occasions to the same group of individuals. The scores are then statistically compared with one another and a correlation coefficient is obtained.

Another means of measuring reliability is the *parallel-forms procedure*.[12] In this case, parallel or equivalent forms of a test are administered to the same group of individuals. The correlation between the two sets of scores is then computed. In a situation where there is a high reliability on parallel forms, then different forms of the test can be administered at different times without concern about *practice effect.* Practice effect is not something that is measured statistically. It refers to an individual's ability to perform better on the re-administration of a test, when that test is given relatively shortly after the original administration. This improved performance is said to be based on practicing the task as part of the original administration, leading to a better performance on the second administration.

Another popular reliability measure is an internal consistency coefficient called *split-half reliability*.[13] In this case, the scores on arbitrarily selected halves of the test are

---

[10] Psychological Testing and Assessment at 84–92; Graham & Lilly, Psychological Testing, at 37–39, Anastasi, Psychological Testing, at 26–27.

[11] Psychological Testing and Assessment at 85–86; Anastasi, Psychological Testing, at 26.

[12] Psychological Testing and Assessment at 79–86; Anastasi, Psychological Testing, at 26.

[13] Psychological Testing and Assessment at 86–88.

statistically compared with one another, and a correlation coefficient is obtained. Split-half reliability could be performed by comparing the results on the items on the first half of the measure with the items on the second half of the measure. An alternative form of split-half testing would compare the results of the odd-numbered items with the even numbered items. This method of reliability testing can be used only when there is relative equality of items throughout the instrument. The Rorschach, for example, cannot be split into two equivalent halves.

Interscorer or interrater reliability is another method used to measure reliability.[14] With interrater reliability, two different examiners score the same test. The scores obtained are then correlated with one another.

Generally, reliability coefficients in intelligence tests need to be in the .80 range or above before a test is considered to be very useful. Some intelligence tests can have reliability coefficients of less than .80 on some of the subtests or some of the subscales, but, generally, overall the coefficients need to be higher than .80.

On personality tests, correlations will generally be lower. Research on the Rorschach, for example, often finds reliability coefficients of .30 to .40 (see **Chapter 10**). As a result, the Rorschach, standing alone, is not a very reliable instrument. However, because it is a personality test, the reliability coefficients do not need to be as high. Furthermore, as will be discussed in **Chapter 10,** the Rorschach is a much more subjective instrument. With regard to the MMPI-2, attorneys have often asked psychologists during direct- or cross-examination, "What is the reliability of the MMPI-2?" It is impossible to establish a reliability coefficient for the entire MMPI-2 because it is not an instrument that generates just one score. The reliability coefficient can be determined for the different scales of the MMPI-2 but not for the instrument as a whole. It is legitimate to question the reliability of the scores on specific scales, because some scales are more reliable than others. This subject will be discussed in greater detail in the chapter on the MMPI-2. See **Chapter 9.**

Daubert and "Reliability"

The Supreme Court's opinion in *Daubert*[15] added some confusion by requiring that there be "evidentiary reliability," using the term to mean roughly the same thing psychologists mean by "validity." The problem is partially clarified in footnote 9, in which it was indicated that, while scientists "distinguish between 'validity' and 'reliability' . . . our reference here is to evidentiary reliability—that is, trustworthiness." It is therefore necessary for attorneys to substitute "trustworthiness" for "reliability" in the legal context, while using the terms as defined in this chapter in the psychological context.

§ 7.9   Validity

The *validity* of a test is defined as how well the test measures what it is designed to measure. It is a way of stating how useful the test is. As is true of reliability, there are many

---

[14] Elementary Statistics at 80–81; Statistical Analysis at 184–86; An Introduction to the Statistical Analysis of Data at 183; Graham & Lilly, Psychological Testing, at 21.

[15] Daubert v. Merrell Dow Pharms., 509 U.S. 579 (1993).

different types of validity. It is important to note that a test can be reliable without being valid.[16] In other words, the first half of a test could measure the same thing as the second half of a test (split-half reliability), but the test itself may not measure what is was designed to test.

The first type of validity measure is referred to as *face validity*.[17] This refers to how well the specific items, on their face value alone, appear to reflect what the test is purported to measure. Face validity is not something that lends itself to statistical analysis. On a test designed to measure anxiety, a question like "do you often have butterflies in your stomach?" would be face valid. Someone looking at the question would be able to state that it appears to fit the nature of the test. However, a question on the same test that asks "would you like to be a mountain ranger?" would not appear to be face valid.

Content validity[18] is another type of validity than cannot be subjected to statistical analysis. Content validity applies more to achievement tests than to personality or other psychological tests. For a test on American history to be considered content valid, the test would need to include a wide variety of questions about all aspects of American history. If the test contained questions about Russian history or the periodic table, it would not be considered valid for an American history test.

There are several forms of validity measures that are referred to as *criterion-related validity*.[19] An example would be a comparison between test scores and school grades. If the test is considered to be valid, the higher the test scores were, the higher the school grades would be expected to be. Two types of validity fit into the category of criterion-related validity. The first is *concurrent validity*.[20] In concurrent validity, the criterion scores are immediately available. Again, returning to the school example, the individual school grades are available and can be compared with the results on the tests.

A second form of criterion-related validity is *predictive validity*.[21] In this case, the criterion scores are not available at the time of the testing. The criterion scores—for example, the grades—become available at a later date. Predictive validity has been very useful in trying to identify individuals who potentially have problems before the problems manifest themselves. For example, if a test has high predictive validity for potential sexual abusers, child abusers, or criminals, intervention could be undertaken prior to the commission of an actual offense.

Another form of validity is referred to as *construct validity*.[22] The construct validity of a test is the extent to which the test may be said to measure a theoretical construct or "trait." Validity is determined by defining the characteristics to be measured by a test and then relating this to measures of behavior in the environment where the characteristic is thought to be an important variable. It is a much more sophisticated and involved process of validity. The construct validity of a test is determined over time by gathering information from many research projects, observations, and studies.

---

[16] Psychological Testing and Assessment at 93; Graham & Lilly, Psychological Testing, at 46.

[17] Psychological Testing and Assessment at 94; Graham & Lilly, Psychological Testing, at 40.

[18] Psychological Testing and Assessment at 94; Graham & Lilly, Psychological Testing, at 40–41.

[19] Psychological Testing and Assessment at 94–95; Graham & Lilly, Psychological Testing, at 41–42.

[20] Psychological Testing and Assessment at 95; Graham & Lilly, Psychological Testing, at 41–42.

[21] Psychological Testing and Assessment at 95; Graham & Lilly, Psychological Testing, at 42.

[22] Psychological Testing and Assessment at 97–98; Graham & Lilly, Psychological Testing, at 42–43.

There are many factors that can influence the validity of a test. As is true of reliability, the more homogenous the variables, the more valid the result is likely to be. When a test is originally being developed, it should not be used for selection purposes until the predictive validity has been determined. Until concurrent or predictive validity of an instrument or both have been established, the user does not know if the test measures what it is designed to measure. *Therefore, unvalidated tests should not be used (except experimentally) until their validity has been demonstrated.* The reliability of a test will also affect its validity. The greater the reliability, the more likely the test will be valid. Reliability is necessary but is not the only criterion for a test to be valid.

§ 7.10   Practice Tips

Although the statistical concepts may seem confusing at first, understanding the basic concepts of the mean, standard deviation, and levels of confidence can go a long way in helping an attorney understand the usefulness of the information obtained. If under cross-examination the expert witness is talking about tests or research that is not covered in this book, it is essential to ask about the reliability and validity of the instrument, especially in this era of *Daubert*. Do not be satisfied if the psychologist simply reports that the test is reliable or valid if you are not familiar with the test. Ask for reliability and validity coefficients. As for the mean and standard deviation of the results, ask the psychologist how these reliability and validity coefficients compare with other tests, and how the specific individual scores fit into the distribution based on the mean and standard deviation. If the research that is being quoted does not sound familiar, ask the psychologist to tell you the p values or the level of significance of the research. A statement by the psychologist that the p value "approaches significance" is not sufficient because any time the p value is greater than .05, the results should be considered nonsignificant.

CHAPTER 8

INTELLIGENCE TESTING

§ 8.1   Classification Systems for Intelligence

There are probably as many different theoretical definitions of *intelligence* as there are individuals defining the term. When the question, "What is intelligence?" has been asked, psychologists have often coyly responded, "Intelligence is what intelligence tests measure." For the purposes of this book, the statistical analysis of intelligence is more important than the definition.

Many different classification systems for intelligence have been developed. Intelligence quotient (IQ) tests generally use the following classification system:

IQ	Classification	Percentage of Population
130 or above	very superior	2.2%
120–129	superior	6.7%
110–119	high average or above average	16.1%
90–109	average	50.0%
80–89	low average or below average	16.1%
70–79	borderline deficient or borderline retarded	6.7%
69 and below	mentally retarded or cognitively deficient	2.2%

The American Psychiatric Association's *Diagnostic and Statistical Manual of Mental Disorders* (DSM-IV) divides individuals with low intelligence into classifications of mildly, moderately, severely, or profoundly retarded:[1]

Classification	IQ
mild retardation	50–55 to 70
moderate retardation	35–40 to 50–55
severe retardation	20–25 to 35–40
profound retardation	less than 20 or 25

Other systems use the same labels with slightly different ranges.[2] These classifications are substitutes for the original classifications of imbecile, idiot, and moron, designated by Binet, the developer of the first major intelligence test. Unfortunately, these words had acquired such negative connotations in society that they were no longer useful. Today, mentally retarded individuals are often referred to as *cognitively disabled* or CD in some areas of the country.

Educational systems classify intelligence in other ways. A child with an IQ of 50 to 75 is often referred to as being in the EMR or *educable mentally retarded* range.[3] This individual would fall within the retarded range but would likely be able to learn basic academic

---

[1] American Psychiatric Ass'n, Diagnostic and Statistical Manual of Mental Disorders 40 (4th ed. 1994).

[2] J. Sattler, Assessment of Children 648 (3d ed 1988) [hereinafter Assessment of Children].

[3] *Id.*

information. Individuals in the EMR range are likely to be able to live on their own in either a supervised apartment or group home setting and to gain low-level, meaningful employment.

The next range, between and 25 and 50, is referred to as the TMR or *trainable mentally retarded* range. Individuals who fall within this range will not be able to acquire academic skills such as reading and arithmetic but can be trained to perform the activities of daily living (hygiene, nourishment, and self-care). Such individuals are likely to be able to work only in a sheltered workshop setting and to live in highly supervised, structured situations.

Individuals with IQs below 25 are considered to be in the *custodial mental retardation* (CMR) range. These are individuals who are likely to be institutionalized and may not be able to be trained to walk, talk, or carry on the activities of daily living.

§ 8.2 Mild Retardation

Mild retardation is referred to as the educable range for individuals with IQs between the low 50s and upper 60s, and a mental age of 8 years, 3 months (8–3) to 10 years, 9 months (10–9). During the first five years of life, mildly retarded individuals can develop social and communication skills. During the school-age years, they can achieve academic skills up to approximately a sixth-grade level. Mildly retarded individuals generally cannot learn high school subjects and require special education. During adult years, they are capable of social and vocational adequacy. They generally need frequent guidance during stressful situations.

§ 8.3 Moderate Retardation

Individuals who are moderately retarded are considered trainable, have IQs from the low 40s to the middle 50s, and generally function at the 5–7 to 8–2 range. During the preschool years, they learn to talk and communicate, have poor social awareness, and have only fair motor development. During the school-age years, they can function academically to approximately the fourth-grade level by the time they reach their late teens. They will require special education all the way through school. In adulthood, they are capable of maintaining themselves in unskilled or semiskilled occupations. They will, however, need continued supervision and guidance.

§ 8.4 Severe Mental Retardation

Individuals who are severely mentally retarded are considered to be "dependent trainables," having IQs from the low 20s to the middle 30s and ability to function at the 3–2 to 5–6 age range. During the preschool years, their motor development is poor, their speech is minimal, and they are unable to profit from training in the self-help areas. During the school-age years, they do learn to talk and communicate, and can be trained to perform the activities of daily living. During adulthood, they can contribute partially to self-support under complete supervision.

§ 8.5   Profound Mental Retardation

Profoundly retarded individuals fit into the category of custodial retardates. These individuals have IQs of less than 25 and a mental age development of less than three years. During the preschool years, they require constant care and demonstrate minimal capacity for functioning. During the school-age years, they continue to require total care with some motor skill development emerging. During their adult years, they are totally incapable of maintaining themselves and will continue to require complete care and supervision throughout their lives.[4]

§ 8.6   Mental Retardation and Intelligence Testing

It is important to note that retarded individuals who possess the same IQ can demonstrate a much wider variety of development than do individuals of average or above-average intelligence who possess the same IQ. For example, if, on an intelligence test, it takes only one-third of the items being correct to obtain an IQ of 60, three different individuals could obtain three different thirds of the questions correct and still have an IQ of 60. As a result, all three individuals would be very different, yet obtain the same IQ.

In addition, "[m]entally retarded persons tend to show less change in IQ when retested than do persons who are not mentally retarded."[5] The same instruments that have been developed for assessing non-retarded individuals are used with retarded individuals. However, the norms established are often not useful with retarded individuals. Although the Stanford-Binet Intelligence Scale–Fifth Edition and the Wechsler Intelligence Scale for Children–Fourth Edition are used for evaluating mentally retarded children, they are not designed to be used with severely and profoundly retarded individuals. As is true of other groups, more than one test should be utilized in measuring retardation. It is often helpful to give one of the major intelligence tests mentioned above in addition to the Kaufman Assessment Battery for Children–Second Edition (KABC-II) and one other.

Assessing severely and profoundly retarded individuals is a much more difficult task. These individuals often have other areas of deficit, including hearing, speech, vision, or motor integration.[6]

> Profoundly retarded children, in particular, have a high incidence of devastating motoric, sensory, and physical handicaps. Their mortality rate is high. Compared to severely retarded children, they tend to have a higher incidence of delayed puberty, institutionalization, seizures and enuresis, poor communications, pika (a strong craving to eat non-nutritional objects, such as paint, gravel or hair), self-biting, fecal smearing, mutism, echopraxia (a tendency toward autonomic imitation of the movements and gestures of others), lack of self-recognition, rumination, abnormal EEGs, and encopresis (involuntary defecation not due to local organic defect or illness), lack of socialization skills, and high-pain thresholds.[7]

---

[4] Assessment of Children at 649.

[5] *Id.* at 655.

[6] *Id.*

[7] *Id.* at 556 (quoting Switzky et al.).

Sattler points out that

> standardized norm-referenced tests are of limited use in the assessment of severely and profoundly handicapped children. These children have difficulty in following instructions, administrative procedures may be too inflexible to permit them to display the knowledge by unconventional means, and the small number of items at the extreme ranges of ability may restrict the sampling of their abilities. Extrapolated test scores are not appropriate for individual diagnosis because their reliability is unknown. . . . Criterion-referenced tests, which usually follow standard curriculum guidelines, may not be appropriate for severely and profoundly handicapped children, because these children are rarely candidates for instruction and the school's standard curriculum. These tests fail to take into account the children's handicapping condition, as the standardization groups for most criterion-referenced tests are composed of normal children. . . . The use of normal developmental scales with severely and profoundly handicapped children is also fraught with problems. These scales fail to take into account the limited opportunities the severely and profoundly handicapped children have to develop and refine concepts. . . . Although standardized, norm-referenced, criterion-referenced and developmentally based tests and scales have potentially serious shortcomings, they still have a role to play in the assessment of severely and profoundly retarded youngsters. Mental ages, test ages, and developmental ages from these scales provide useful indices which place the child's performance at an approximate developmental level.[8]

In addition to the above-identified methods, task analysis, systematic observation, diagnostic teaching, informal assessment of communication, adaptive behavior questionnaires, checklists, and interviews can be used to evaluate severely and profoundly retarded individuals.

§ 8.7   Stability of Intelligence Quotient

For decades, the IQ has been considered to be a relatively stable measure.[9] A number of studies have compared IQ scores of young children and have conducted retests 10 and 25 years later. A classic study by researchers K.P. Bradway, C.W. Thompson, and R.B. Cravens correlated IQs with a 10-year retest and a 25-year retest. After 10 years, they found correlation coefficients of .65 with the original measures, and after 25 years, correlations of .59 with the original measures. In addition, the correlation between the 10-year retest scores and the 25-year retest scores was .85[10]

However, some studies have indicated large upward or downward shifts in intelligence test scores for some people. These shifts tend to be related to "drastic changes in family structure or home conditions, adoption into a foster home, severe or prolonged illness and therapeutical remedial programs."[11]

---

[8] Assessment of Children at 657.

[9] D. Wechsler, The Measurement and Appraisal of Adult Intelligence 578 (4th ed. 1958).

[10] K.P. Bradway, C.W. Thompson, & R.B. Cravens, *Preschool IQs after 25 Years*, 49 J. Educ. Psychol. 278–81 (1958).

[11] A. Anastasi, Psychological Testing 326 (6th ed. 1988).

§ 8.8   Heredity versus Environment

There is a strong hereditary component in individuals' intelligence.[12] One of the best ways to predict the adult intelligence of a child under six years of age is to give his or her parents an intelligence test. Regarding the question of mental retardation as a hereditary factor, retardation could be the result of nonhereditary factors such as chromosomal anomalies or phenylketonuria (PKU), and other factors that result from prenatal organic brain dysfunction or are primarily hereditary in causation.[13]

Even though the hereditary factor is a strong component in determining a child's intelligence, environmental manipulations also have a great effect on an individual's measured IQ. It is not unusual for preschool children from educationally oriented families or children who have been exposed to a tremendous amount of early environmental stimulation to have disproportionately high intelligence test scores. These scores tend to even out over the years as the early intervention loses its impact. Children who are born retarded (cognitively disabled) also show fewer effects of retardation with greater environmental intervention than those who have little or no environmental intervention. The IQ is not raised per se. The individual's capacity to function is maximized, and tested IQ tends to increase with these factors.

§ 8.9   Evaluation of Giftedness

Dennis Saccuzo and his fellow researchers evaluated 4,546 gifted Afro-American, Caucasian, Filipino, and Hispanic children in grades one through nine. The subjects' verbal IQs were compared with their performance (nonverbal) IQs. As would be expected, gifted Caucasian and Afro-American children showed significantly higher verbal skills than performance or nonverbal skills. The Filipino and Hispanic children showed no significant verbal-performance differences. In all groups, with the exception of the Filipino children, verbal skills were higher than performance skills. In the case of the Filipino children, the performance skills were higher than the verbal skills. The authors conclude:

> As with so many psychological variables, test indices of giftedness cannot be considered independently of ethnicity. From such a realization, it follows that in identifying giftedness in a diverse population, the measures used must be tailored to the specific ethnic group under study. Furthermore, decisions about an individual child must be based on observed occurrence in the population, rather than on statistically significant group mean differences.[14]

§ 8.10   Stanford-Binet Intelligence Scale–Fifth Edition

The Stanford-Binet Intelligence Scale–Fifth Edition (SB5) is the latest revision of the 1960 Stanford-Binet Intelligence Scale: Form L-M. It was published in 2003 by Riverside

---

[12] A. Anastasi, Psychological Testing 350 (6th ed. 1988).

[13] *Id.*

[14] *Id.* at 244.

Publishing Company and authored by Gale Roid. The SB5 can be used with individuals from two years of age through adulthood. The examiner is required to determine a basal level and a ceiling level for each of the areas measured. The basal is the first age level at which all subtests are passed, while the ceiling is the first age level at which all subtests are failed.

The Stanford-Binet is the grandfather of intelligence tests. The original Stanford-Binet instrument was published more than 100 years ago. Its current edition is applicable for individuals from 2 through 85 years of age. Unlike the Wechsler Scales, which require three tests (WPPSI-III, WISC-IV, and WAIS-III) to cover this age range, all ages can be tested with one instrument with the SB5. As a result, the Stanford-Binet still remains the best single instrument for exceptionalities. For example, with a child over 6 years of age, functioning under 6 years of age, the WISC-IV could not be used. However, the SB5 could be used with both of these groups.

There are a number of changes between the fourth edition (SBiFE) and the fifth edition. A fifth factor has been added to the four factors of the fourth edition. The five factors of the SB5 are Fluid Reasoning, Knowledge, Quantitative Reasoning, Visual-Spatial Processing, and Working Memory. The "manipulative toys" from pre-SBiFE editions have been returned to the SB5. The authors have also expanded nonverbal assessments, with half of the subtests not requiring verbal responses, due to previous criticisms of the Stanford-Binet Intelligence Scales alleging them to be too verbally oriented. Additional breadth has been added to more adequately measure the very low functioning and very high giftedness of subjects.

The SB5 cautions against using an intelligence test solely to diagnose mental retardation, learning disabilities, attention deficit hyperactivity disorder (ADHD), giftedness, and cognitive decline in the elderly. [The professional standard now requires an assessment of functional ability as well.]

The entry level into each of the subtests varies based on the age of the individual being tested. Furthermore, an abbreviated form of the SB5 can be used and is explained in the manual.

The five factors on the SB5 are

1. *Fluid Reasoning*, which is the ability to solve verbal and nonverbal problems using inductive or deductive reasoning. Inductive reasoning is measured through Matrices or Verbal Analogies, while deductive reasoning is measured by the individual's ability to deduce underlying problems or situations.

2. *Knowledge* measures the general fund of knowledge that one requires in such settings as work, school, and/or home. Because for adults much of this information was acquired many years earlier, it is also a measure of acquired and stored memory, measuring fluid and crystallized intelligence.

3. *Quantitative Reasoning* utilizes the traditional arithmetic-reasoning-type subtests.

4. *Visual-Spatial Processing* measures the subject's ability to see patterns, relationships, and spatial orientations. These are acquired through administering the Form Board and Form Patterns subtests.

5. *Working Memory* utilizes a number of different tasks to measure short-term memory.

Each of these five factors is measured in the nonverbal and verbal domains. As a result, factor scores, domain scores, and a full-scale IQ can be measured through the SB5.

§ 8.11   McCarthy Scales of Children's Abilities

The McCarthy Scales of Children's Abilities was developed by Dorothea McCarthy in 1972. It can be used with children from two and a half to eight and a half years of age. However, for seven- or eight-year-old children of above-average or greater ability, it is inadvisable to use the McCarthy.[15] In such cases, it is more advantageous to use the Wechsler Intelligence Scale for Children–Fourth Edition (WISC-IV).

The McCarthy is divided into six scales. They include the following: Verbal, Perceptual-Performance, Quantitative, Memory, and Motor. The sixth scale is an overall measure of the Verbal, Perceptual-Performance, and Quantitative Scales, which is referred to as the General Cognitive Index (GCI). The overall McCarthy consists of 18 subtests that can be administered in 45 minutes to an hour.

The McCarthy is more than 30 years old at this time, without the publishers having any plans to revise it. As a result, it has reduced utility, and it should be used sparingly and as an adjunct, not a primary instrument.

§ 8.12   The Wechsler Scales

The Wechsler Scales are a series of tests developed over a period of several decades. The original Wechsler Intelligence Test—the Wechsler-Bellevue—was named for the hospital at which Wechsler worked when the instrument was developed. Today, there are three major Wechsler Scales in use: the Wechsler Adult Intelligence Scale–Third Edition (WAIS-III), the Wechsler Intelligence Scale for Children–Fourth Edition (WISC-IV), and the Wechsler Preschool and Primary Scale of Intelligence–Third Edition (WPPSI-III).

Scaled Score	Classification
0–2	severely retarded or severely deficient
3–4	retarded or deficient
5–6	borderline retarded or borderline deficient
7–8	below average or low average
9–11	average
12–13	above average or high average
14–15	superior
15–17	very superior
18–20	gifted

§ 8.13   —Wechsler Adult Intelligence Scale–Third Edition

The Wechsler Adult Intelligence Scale–Third Edition (WAIS-III) was developed in 1997 as a revision of the Wechsler Adult Intelligence Scale–Revised, which was developed in 1981. Like the other Wechsler Scales, it is divided into a Verbal Scale and a Performance Scale.

---

[15] Personal Communication with Dr. Alan Kaufman (1979).

The WAIS-III was developed to resemble its predecessors. However, there was a desire to replace outdated norms and biased items. In addition to the composite scores, the same indices that were developed for the WISC-III earlier are available on the WAIS-III. A new subtest called Matrix Reasoning was developed to replace the old, less reliable, Object Assembly Test. Furthermore, the WAIS-III was co-normed with the Wechsler Memory Scale–Third Edition (WMS-III) to aid clinicians in examining any IQ/memory discrepancies. It was also believed that there was an increased need to be able to test individuals 75 years of age and older since they represent 6 percent of the population, or 15 million people. Furthermore, an effort was made on the WAIS-III to eliminate as many references to the United States as possible, to facilitate use in other countries. There is also a European version of the WAIS-III.

The developers of the WAIS-III pointed out that studies have found that as much as 25 percent of the time, trained psychologists make significant errors in determining strengths and weaknesses on the Wechsler Scales. As a result, they support the use of their computerized program to overcome this concern.

As with all IQ tests, concerns about practice effects dictate using a different intelligence test if a person is retested within six to eight months of the administration of the original test. The 20-point rule for discrepancy between the Verbal IQ and Performance IQ applies both to the WAIS-III and to the WISC-III. When the Verbal and Performance IQs are more than 20 points apart, the Full Scale IQ is not reported, as it does not accurately represent these two ability areas. The authors of this text advise psychologists against using words like "trends/close trends" since they are not statistically meaningful.

Reliability and Validity

The reliability and validity coefficients on the WAIS-III are quite high. The WAIS-III correlates very well with the WAIS-R, the Stanford-Binet FE, and the WISC-III.[16] The correlation coefficients tend to be in the 80s and 90s.[17]

At times, concerns have been raised about whether administration errors on tests affect the overall results. Gary Moon and his associates studied administration errors on the WAIS-R given by graduate students. They found that individuals who participated in a structured training program to learn how to administer the WAIS-R performed with far fewer errors than those who taught themselves.[18]

§ 8.14   —Wechsler Intelligence Scale for Children–Fourth Edition

It is fairly standard within cognitive test development to provide a new edition to intelligence tests approximately every 10 to 15 years. The Wechsler Intelligence Scale for

---

[16] A. Anastasi, Psychological Testing 248 (7th ed. 1997).

[17] *Id.*

[18] Gary Moon, William A. Blakey, Richard Gorsuch, & John W. Fontuzzo, *Frequent WAIS-R Administration Errors: An Ignored Source of Inaccurate Measurement*, 22 Prof. Psychol.: Res. & Prac. no. 3, at 256–58 (1991).

Children–Third Edition (WISC-III) was published in September 1991. The WISC-IV was published in 2003.

The original Wechsler Scales were developed more than 50 years ago. Until now, all of the Wechsler family of intelligence tests have relied on a three-factor measure of intelligence that includes a Verbal Scale, a Performance Scale, and Full Scale. With the introduction of the Wechsler Intelligence Scale for Children–Fourth Edition (WISC-IV) the developers of the instrument have presented an entirely new format for measuring intelligence. Gone are the Verbal and Performance Scales and their comparisons. Gone are the Picture Arrangement, Object Assembly, and Mazes. The Arithmetic and Information subtests have been relegated to supplemental status, and five new measures of intelligence have been added.

Instead of the Verbal Scale and Performance Scale comprising the Full Scale of the WISC-IV, the composite is now made up of a Verbal Comprehension Index (VCI), a Perceptual Reasoning Index (PRI), a Working Memory Index (WMI), and a Processing Speed Index (PSI). The Verbal Comprehension Index is comprised of the Similarities, Vocabulary, and Comprehension subtests. The Perceptual Reasoning Index is composed of the Block Design, Picture Concepts, and Matrix Reasoning subtests. The Working Memory Index is made up of a Digit Span and Letter-Number Sequencing, while the Processing Speed Index includes Coding and Symbol Search.

The new subtests include Word Reasoning, Matrix Reasoning, Letter-Number Sequencing, Picture Concepts, and Cancellation. Word Reasoning is a supplemental Verbal Comprehension subtest measuring verbal reasoning by providing the subject with a series of clues. The task is designed to measure verbal comprehension, analogical and general reasoning ability, verbal abstraction, domain knowledge, the ability to integrate and synthesize different types of information, and the ability to generate alternative concepts. Picture Concepts is a core perceptual reasoning subtest designed to measure abstract, categorical reasoning ability. Matrix Reasoning is also a core perceptual reasoning subtest that is considered to be a good measure of fluid intelligence and a reliable measure of general intellectual ability. Letter-Number Sequencing is a core working memory subtest in which a sequence of numbers and letters is presented, with the requirement to recall them in ascending numerical order and alphabetical order. Cancellation is a supplemental processing speed subtest that measures processing speed, visual selection attention, vigilance, and visual neglect.

The interpretation process for the WISC-IV is much more involved than the WISC-III, including a 10-step procedure. The first five steps include reporting and describing the Full Scale IQ, the VCI, the PRI, the VMI, and the PSI. Step six evaluates the discrepancies between and among the various scales, followed by evaluating the relative strengths and weaknesses shown by the individual. Then subtest level discrepancies need to be compared, along with evaluating the pattern of scores within the subtests. Last, a process analysis is performed.

Unlike the WISC-III, prorating IQ scores is discouraged by the developers of the WISC-IV. Instead, an abbreviated instrument like the Wechsler Abbreviated Scale of Intelligence (WASI) could be used (see **§ 8.21**). The manual specifically discourages prorating based on the fact that there are only two or three subtests per index, making it difficult to achieve valid scores through prorating.

Generally, a new intelligence test should be incorporated into the psychologist's test battery within a year of development to comply with ethical standards. In the case of the

WISC-IV, with the number of new subtests that have been added, the number of old subtests that have been eliminated, and the restructuring of scales from the traditional Verbal and Performance Scales to the four new indices, the clinician must be cautious in rushing into the use of the WISC-IV until such time as research has been published on exactly what this instrument measures in comparison to what was measured by the WISC-III. As is always the case, Psychological Corporation has published some of its own research in its manual. However, it will be important to wait for independent research to be performed to address some of these issues. If this process follows its typical course, there should be sufficient information within the next year or so to know what the WISC-IV is measuring and what its utility will be.

§ 8.15   —Wechsler Preschool and Primary Scale of Intelligence–Third Edition

The Wechsler Preschool and Primary Scale of Intelligence was recently revised. Its original edition was oftentimes considered to be a "weak sister" of the other Wechsler Scales. The revised edition (WPPSI-R) was an attempt to make the instrument more broad-based and better able to provide a strong measure for intelligence for young children. The third edition (2002) is designed to further strengthen the measurement of intelligence in young children. Unlike the WISC-IV, it did not change its format and continued with the Verbal Scale, Performance Scale, and Full Scale IQs.

The WPPSI-III updated its theoretical foundation by incorporating additional composite scores, enhancing the measure of fluid reasoning, adding matrix reasoning, picture concepts, and word reasoning, and incorporating measures of processing speed with a Processing Speed Index. In addition, the WPPSI-III has divided early childhood into two age bands, 2–6 to 3–11 and 4–0 to 7–3. In all, the WPPSI-III was made more user friendly by simplifying instructions, adding prompts and teaching items, and revising the scoring criteria. Furthermore, the WPPSI-III updated testing materials in the stimulus books.

The clinical utility of the WPPSI-III was enhanced by increasing a number of special group studies incorporating achievement results in the analyses and extending the age range of the test down to two years six months from three years zero months.

The younger age band (2–6 to 3–11) utilizes two verbal and two non-verbal subtests to obtain a Full Scale IQ. However, the older age band (4–0 to 7–3) utilizes three verbal, three non-verbal, and one processing speed subtest to obtain a Full Scale IQ. A total of five subtests were deleted from the WPPSI-R: arithmetic, animal pegs, geometric design, mazes, and sentences. There were concerns that some of these subtests were confounded by the fact that they were measuring two different modalities, such as verbal and motor or spatial and verbal. In their place, five new subtests were added: word reasoning, matrix reasoning, picture concepts, coding, and symbol search. Matrix reasoning, coding, and symbol search were subtests that had previously been utilized on the WISC-III.

The manual gives strong information about reliability, validity, and relationships with other variables. Correlations with the WPPSI-R were .86, .70, and .85 for the Verbal, Performance and Full Scale IQs, respectively.

§ 8.16   —Wechsler Memory Scale–Third Edition

The Wechsler Memory Scale is in its third edition. However, the WMS-III has been elevated to a new level of prominence by being co-normed with the WAIS-III. The Wechsler Memory Scale measures a number of key concepts—immediate memory (less than 10 minutes), delayed memory (more than 10 minutes), and working memory—that address the auditory and visual modalities of memory. The subtests of the WMS-III include Information and Orientation. The scores on these scales may be caused by factors such as disorientation, aphasia, inattention, poor motivation, or a thought disorder.[19]

Additional information provided about the WMS-III and memory in general identifies the fact that information that has been presented several times will result in increased memory. The WMS-III score affected most by attention deficit disorder (ADD) was the single trial learning subtest. This certainly underscores the importance of re-presenting material several times.

§ 8.17   —Wechsler Individual Achievement Test–Second Edition

The Wechsler Individual Achievement Test–Second Edition was published in 2001. It has nine different subtests measuring the basic academic areas of reading, arithmetic measures, and spelling, in both the oral and written format. It is applicable for ages 4 to 85 and takes between 45 minutes and two hours to administer, depending upon the age of the recipient. The older the subject, the longer the instrument takes. Because it is a Wechsler Instrument, it can be statistically compared with the various Wechsler Intelligence Scales and/or the Wechsler Memory Scale. The WIAT-II is a carefully designed refined achievement test. Its strength is in being able to compare it with Wechsler intelligence or memory test results.

Gerald Tindal and Michelle Nutter reviewed the WIAT in the *Mental Measurements Yearbook*. They stated:

> The WIAT-II has several strong features. First, its comprehensive nature allows for a thorough examination of students' strengths and weaknesses within and across several academic domains. Second, the modifications made to the most recent edition are that sub-tests reflect current trends in research and curriculum. Third, the materials are well organized and very accessible for both administration and scoring or reporting. Finally, the link between assessment and instruction/intervention is explicit through the inclusion of an error analysis component and partial correct scoring.[20]

§ 8.18   Kaufman Assessment Battery for
Children–Second Edition

The Kaufman Assessment Battery for Children–Second Edition (KABC-II) assesses intelligence of children between 3 and 18 years of age and was published in 2004. This

---

[19] WAIS-III WMS-III Technical Manual 199 (1997) [hereinafter Technical Manual].

[20] Gerald Tindall & Michelle Nutter, *Wechsler Individual Achievement Test–Second Edition, in* Buros, The Fifteenth Mental Measurements Yearbook 1001 (Univ. of Neb. 2003).

particular intelligence scale is derived from theories of mental processing that are different from the traditional scales of cognitive ability. The Mental Processing Scales measure the child's ability to solve problems sequentially and simultaneously. The Kaufmans were concerned that tests like the Wechsler Scales were really achievement tests, which were more concerned with emphasizing the child's ability to produce correct solutions than with the specific content of the items. To deal with the achievement aspects of cognitive ability, the K-ABC also includes an achievement scale.

There are a number of factors that make the KABC-II a valuable instrument for cognitive assessment, addressing issues that other cognitive assessment instruments may not. The KABC-II measures a range of abilities, including sequential and simultaneous processing, reasoning, learning, and crystallized ability, that are relevant to understanding children's cognitive functioning. It also provides a non-verbal scale composed of subtests that may be administered in pantomime and responded to motorically. This scale can be administered to hearing-impaired, severe-speech- or language-disabled, or bilingual students. The administration of the KABC-II results in a Mental Processing Index (MPI), which provides a global overview of the child's cognitive ability.

The KABC-II utilizes a number of methods in its administration that are unique to this instrument. There are teaching opportunities to make sure that the child understands the task before it is administered, along with encouraging the examiner to modify wording, use gestures, and otherwise improvise on the introductory unscored items. Furthermore, verbal, fact-based, and traditional academic measures were included in a separate achievement scale, as opposed to within the measure itself. The KABC-II also allows for recording of "Qualitative Indicators (QIs)" to provide information about distractibility, perseveration, impulsive responding, and the like.

§ 8.19   Wide Range Achievement Test–Third Edition

A number of excellent achievement test batteries have been developed over the years. Perhaps the two most widely known and widely used are the Woodcock-Johnson–Third Edition (WJ-III) and the Peabody Individual Achievement Test–Revised Edition (PIAT-R). These batteries are most frequently used in educational or psycho-educational evaluations and provide more information than is necessary in a custody evaluation. As a result, a quick, easy-to-administer instrument like the Wide Range Achievement Test–Third Edition (WRAT3) is recommended for custody evaluation usage when achievement tests are administered.

The Wide Range Achievement Test–Third Edition (WRAT3) is an updated version of the original Wide Range Achievement Test. It is a relatively easy test to administer and provides a quick measure of achievement in the reading, spelling, and arithmetic areas. It is applicable for individuals from kindergarten age through adulthood. The WRAT3 is best used when a thorough educational diagnostic evaluation is not desired but a quick estimate is needed. In custody evaluations, the WRAT3 generally suffices as a measure of achievement.

The WRAT3 is the seventh revision of the Wide Range Achievement Test, which was initially published in 1936. Criticisms have been raised about the fact that over this period of time, the test has not been completely rewritten. Criticisms are also leveled at the test because of the fact that the norming procedure did not use the carefully stratified sample that is used in the development of most major instruments. It is suggested that caution should be used in overinterpreting the results of the WRAT3. However, it still provides a quick screen for achievement in three major academic areas. Certainly tests like the Peabody Individual Achievement Test-Revised (PIAT-R), Woodcock-Johnson, and other achievement tests mentioned at the beginning of this section are better for broad-based evaluation of cognitive ability.

§ 8.20   Kaufman Brief Intelligence Test–Second Edition

For years, the only brief intelligence tests available to clinicians were the Slosson Intelligence Test and the Shipley-Hartford. Because the Slosson is a paper-and-pencil test and verbally loaded, it was never widely accepted in the psychological community. The Kaufmans developed the Kaufman Brief Intelligence Test (K-BIT) in an effort to provide an individually administered measure of intelligence that was not as verbally loaded. Although it utilizes the same mean and standard deviation as other standardized intelligence tests, "it does not imply that the K-BIT may substitute for a more comprehensive measure of a child's or adult's intelligence."[21]

The Kaufmans state that the K-BIT "is designed for those circumstances in which a brief measure of intelligence will suffice."[22] Examples of situations in which the K-BIT may be used include the following:

1.   To provide large-scale screening to identify high-risk children
2.   To permit screening for educational diagnosis, job applicants, or for vocational or rehabilitation information, or screening of a large group
3.   To obtain an estimate of intelligence as part of a personality evaluation to provide for periodic rechecking of intellectual status in psycho-educational or neuropsychological batteries
4.   To be used when time is of the essence
5.   To measure groups of individuals in research projects.

Because the K-BIT is a brief instrument, it can be administered in approximately 15 to 30 minutes and is applicable for individuals 4 to 90 years of age. With younger children, it takes closer to 15 minutes to administer, and with adults it takes closer to one-half hour. Unlike a comprehensive intelligence test, the K-BIT can be administered by appropriately trained paraprofessionals. If paraprofessionals are used to administer the K-BIT, they must be trained by a qualified individual. It is important to understand that there is a difference between test administration and test interpretation. Even though the K-BIT can be administered by paraprofessionals, it must still be interpreted by a competent psychologist.

A number of features of the K-BIT make it very attractive. Not only does it cover a wide age range, it also allows for teaching during administration. It is divided into both verbal and non-verbal subtests, with scores that translate well with other major intelligence tests.

---

[21] A.S. Kaufman & N.L. Kaufman, Kaufman Brief Intelligence Test 11 (1990).

[22] *Id.*

The test itself is a fully standardized test with reliability and validity data presented on its representative normative sample. The same statistical procedures utilized in the major intelligence tests have been used in obtaining K-BIT scores.

It appears as though the K-BIT will provide the clinician with an opportunity to determine an estimate of an individual's intellectual potential through an appropriately standardized, individually administered test. Because there are only two subtests, vocabulary and matrices, it is possible that an individual may be unfairly penalized by the K-BIT if these are only two weakness areas an individual possesses. As long as the practitioner realizes that this is only an estimate that cannot substitute for traditional comprehensive individually administered intelligence tests, the K-BIT will add to the battery of tests that the clinician has in his or her possession.

Richard I. Naugle and his associates studied the validity of the K-BIT.[23] The researchers demonstrated that the K-BIT correlated well with other instruments. It was their view that because the K-BIT had both a non-verbal and a verbal intellectual measure, as is true of the WAIS-R, McCarthy, and the K-ABC, it provides a better alternative than unidimensional screening devices like the Slosson, Peabody Picture Vocabulary, and the Quick Test. The authors also point out that the user of the K-BIT must remember that it is a screening instrument and "cannot provide the wealth of information offered by the WAIS-R subtest profile."[24]

A number of studies have been performed comparing the K-BIT with WISC-III and WAIS-R results. They all point out that the Full Scale measure will provide a better estimate of the individual's intelligence than will the K-BIT. They also all point out that, as a screening instrument, it is well grounded, reliable, and valid. In summary, the review by David Miller in the *Twelfth Mental Measurements Yearbook* says that "the K-BIT is a well-constructed brief test measuring intelligence. State of the art procedures have been used in norming and measuring reliability and validity. The combined evidence, which is fairly extensive, points to a psychometrically sound measure of verbal, nonverbal, and composite intelligence."[25]

Norman Eisenstein and Charles Engelhart found that in a neuropsychological evaluation, the K-BIT did not do as well as the WAIS-R short forms. However, they noted that an advantage of the test was that it was motor-free and took only 15 to 30 minutes to complete.[26]

§ 8.21   Wechsler Abbreviated Scale of Intelligence

The Wechsler Abbreviated Scale of Intelligence (WASI) was developed in 1999 as Psychological Corporation's answer to the K-BIT. It was developed in an effort to establish a reliable short form for measuring intelligence. In all, there are two verbal and two

---

[23] Richard I. Naugle et al., Validity of the Kaufman Brief Intelligence Test, 5 Psychol. Assessment 182–86 (1993).

[24] *Id.* at 185.

[25] David Miller, *Review of the Kaufman Brief Intelligence Test, in* Twelfth Mental Measurements Yearbook 534 (1995).

[26] Norman Eisenstein & Charles Engelhart, *Comparison of the K-BIT with Short Forms of the WAIS-R in a Neuropsychological Population,* 9 Psychol. Assessment no. 1, at 57 (1997).

performance subtests. They include Vocabulary and Similarities as an estimate of verbal intelligence, and Block Design and Matrix Reasoning as an estimate of performance intelligence. These four subtests are utilized to establish a Full Scale IQ. The examiner has a choice of administering one verbal and one performance subtest or both verbal and both performance subtests, resulting in an FS IQ-2 or an FS IQ-4. The administration of the WASI takes 15 to 30 minutes depending upon how many subtests are administered.

Bradley N. Axelrod conducted a study comparing the WASI results with WAIS-III results and found correlations to be considerably lower than what the manual suggested. Axelrod concludes by stating, "The reader is encouraged to use caution when deciding to use any short form, as they are usually less stable than are the full versions of the same measure. . . . Finally, if the clinician's goal is to obtain an accurate estimation of general intellectual functioning, the current results suggest that the WASI should not be used in the assessment of individual patients."[27]

§ 8.22   Slosson Intelligence Test

The Slosson Intelligence Test, revised in 1991, is referred to as the SIT-R. It was developed as a quick estimate of general cognitive ability. In general, however, with the advent of the K-BIT, which is a better brief intelligence measure, the use of the SIT-R is questionable.

§ 8.23   Raven's Progressive Matrices

The Raven's Progressive Matrices (RPM) test was developed by Raven as a non-verbal measure of intelligence. The items consist of a set of matrices with a part missing. The subject must choose the missing piece that fills up the matrix from variety of options. Although it has use in obtaining a general measure of intelligence, it is not widely used by clinicians today.

§ 8.24   Shipley Institute of Living Scale

The Shipley-Hartford is the popular name for the Shipley Institute of Living Scale (SILS). Developed approximately 50 years ago, the test has been found to correlate relatively well with Full Scale IQs on the WAIS-R. It is a paper-and-pencil test that appears to have a relatively high verbal loading and, as a result, may penalize individuals whose verbal skills are not as high as their non-verbal (performance) skills. The conclusion reached by the authors of this text by reviewing hundreds of correlational studies was that the Shipley-Hartford measured verbal and overall intelligence better than non-verbal intelligence. Although the Shipley-Hartford was originally designed as a measure of both intelligence and cognitive deterioration, research has demonstrated very clearly that it is a

---

[27] Bradley N. Axelrod, *Validity of the Wechsler Abbreviated Scale of Intelligence and Other Very Short Forms of Estimating Intellectual Functioning,* 9 Assessment 22 (2002).

weak measure of cognitive deterioration. As a result, it should be used only as a screening measure of intelligence. Unlike the WAIS-III, which must be administered by a trained psychologist or psychometrist, the individual can work through the Shipley-Hartford on his or her own in a relatively few minutes. Scoring is also done quickly. When detailed intelligence information is not needed, the Shipley-Hartford is a good screening instrument, as long as updated scoring norms are used.

The Shipley Institute of Living Scale was reviewed in the *Eleventh Mental Measurements Yearbook* by William Deaton, Professor, College of Education, Auburn University.[28] Deaton notes that the test's manual has some apparent errors regarding calculation of "normalized T-scores" and conversion of scores to estimated Wechsler Adult Intelligence Scale-Revised (WAIS-R) IQ scores. The computer version of the test also uses a slightly different calculation procedure than that indicated in the manual. Use of the test for detection of intellectual impairment or deterioration is not appropriate, according to published research.[29]

The test is a valid and reliable indicator of level of intelligence, with a correlation with the WAIS and WAIS-R ranging from the mid .70s to mid .80s. Special tables are available in the test manual and from the research literature to estimate specific Wechsler Scale equivalents. The test remains appropriate in situations in which one requires an estimate of the individual's IQ level rather than the detailed information available from the WAIS-III.

§ 8.25   Questions for Chapter 8

Caution.   Attorneys should not expect to be able to go into court and ask all the questions listed below. Preparation is necessary, reviewing material in this chapter to determine whether the question applies to a particular case. The section or chapter number at the end of a question refers to where in this chapter readers can find an explanation of why that particular question may be important.

1. If the psychologist deviated from the standard administration procedures on any of the intelligence tests, how would that affect the reliability and validity of the scores? See **Chapter 3.**

2. What classification system did the psychologist use in determining the range of performance on the IQ test? See § **8.1.**

3. Why did the psychologist select the specific intelligence test that was administered? See §§ **8.10, 8.11, 8.13,** and **8.14.**

4. Did the psychologist take into account the weaknesses of the selected intelligence test when making the interpretations? See §§ **8.10, 8.11, 8.13,** and § **8.14.**

5. Did the psychologist administer all the subtests of the intelligence test administered? If not, why not? See **Chapter 3.**

---

[28] William Deaton, *Review of the Shipley Institute of Living Scale, in* Eleventh Mental Measurements Yearbook 821–23 (1992).

[29] *Id.*

6. How would the overall reliability and validity of the results be affected by those subtests that were not administered?

7. Did the psychologist address the limitations for the McCarthy, discussed in § **8.11**, the Wechsler Scales, discussed in § **8.13,** and the K-ABC, discussed in § **8.18?**

8. If one of the Wechsler Scales was administered, does the Full Scale IQ accurately represent the individual's overall intelligence, or is it merely a function of the average of the Verbal Scale and the Performance Scale? See § **8.13.**

9. Were any of the intelligence scores adversely affected by the level of anxiety that the individual presented at testing? See § **8.15.**

10. Was the Wechsler Intelligence Scale for Children–Fourth Edition (WISC–IV) used instead of the Wechsler Intelligence Scale for Children–Third Edition (WISC-III), or was the Wechsler Adult Intelligence Scale–Third Edition (WAIS-III) used instead of the Wechsler Adult Intelligence Scale-Revised Edition (WAIS-R)?

11. If the Kaufman Brief Intelligence Test (K-BIT), Slosson Intelligence Test, or the Shipley-Harford was used, did the expert use it as a screening device or mistakenly use it as if it was the equivalent of a full intelligence scale? See §§ **8.20, 8.22, 8.23,** and **8.24.**

12. Was an established achievement test used as part of the evaluation? See §§ **8.1, 8.17** and **8.19.**

§ 8.26   Case Digest

The source of information for most of the following cases is the *Mental and Physical Disability Law Reporter* (MPDLR), a publication of the American Bar Association. Complete information for any other sources appears in the relevant references below. The following are direct quotations from the identified source. Quotations from the *Mental and Physical Disability Law Reporter:* Excerpted from *Mental and Physical Disability Law Reporter.* Copyright © 1989–2004. American Bar Association. Reprinted by permission. If no source is identified, it is a summary from the court ruling.

Cases involving *both* mental disorders and mental retardation can be found in the listing in **Chapter 14.**

Alabama

S.J. v. Alabama Department of Human Resources, 579 So. 2d 640 (Ala. Civ. App. 1991). An Alabama appeals court affirmed a decision to terminate the parental rights of a mother with mild to moderate mental retardation. There was clear and convincing evidence the mother was unable to care for herself, and there was no less drastic alternative to termination. An expert testified that someone with the mother's degree of retardation cannot care for an 18-month-old because she cannot perceive the consequences of events, including those having to do with the child's protection and safety. 15 *Mental & Physical Disability Law Reporter* 481 (1991).

Alaska

In re J.L.F., 828 P.2d 166 (Alaska 1992). The Alaska Supreme Court held that a lower court should have considered the availability of relatives willing and able to care for the children, and made an explicit finding as to the reasonableness of a treatment plan for attempting to return the children to their home, before finding that the children were in need of aid and terminating their mother's parental rights. The lower court had based its finding on the fact that the mother, who had cognitive difficulties, a personality disorder, and developmental delays, admitted that she was unable to provide adequate care for her children. The lower court had also concluded that the mother would not be able to care for her children in the future because of her developmental disabilities. The supreme court remanded the case because the state had presented no evidence regarding the availability of relatives, and the mother had shown that her sister and aunt were interested in assuming custody of the children. Also, the lower court had not made a specific finding as to whether the state had provided reasonable remedial services to the mother in an attempt to return the children to their home. 16 *Mental & Physical Disability Law Reporter* 409 (1992).

Illinois

In re P.M., 581 N.E.2d 720 (Ill. App. Ct. 1991). An Illinois appeals court ruled that the state did not deny a mother equal protection by refusing to provide 24-hour supervision to enable her to live with her son. The mother's diminished mental capacity combined with the special needs of her son, who was at risk of developing cerebral palsy, supported the termination of her rights. . . . There was no equal protection violation, because the state did not treat the mother differently from other parents with mental retardation. 16 *Mental & Physical Disability Law Reporter* 167 (1992).

Indiana

Stone v. Daviess County Division of Children & Family Services, 656 N.E.2d 824 (Ind. Ct. App. Oct. 17, 1995). An Indiana appeals court held that the Americans with Disabilities Act (ADA) does not require the state to prove that it reasonably accommodated the special needs of parents with mental disabilities prior to terminating their parental rights. . . . Indiana law, consistent with the ADA, provides that parental rights may not be terminated solely on the basis of mental disability. Here, however, parental rights were terminated based on clear and convincing evidence that the conditions in which the children were living were inadequate. 19 *Mental & Physical Disability Law Reporter* 731–32 (1995).

Egly v. Blackford County (Indiana) Department of Public Welfare, 575 N.E.2d 312 (Ind. Ct. App. 2d Dist. July 23, 1991). An Indiana court of appeals ruled that the parental rights of a couple, both of whom were retarded, could not be terminated solely due to their difficulty learning to parent. Mental retardation, alone, may not be a basis for a termination of parental rights. It may, however, be among the factors considered. In this case, the other factors were not sufficient to justify termination. Indiana case law requires clear and convincing evidence that the parents are extremely inadequate before parental rights can be terminated. The children's survival would not be jeopardized in this particular case, so the parental rights may not be terminated.

Iowa

In re Interest of Rhode, 503 N.W.2d 881 (Iowa Ct. App. 1993). An Iowa appeals court affirmed a decision to deny maternal grandparents custody of a child residing with her widowed father. Rachel Kay Rhode lived with her parents—who both had mental retardation—although her maternal grandparents monitored, supervised, and substantially assisted them. Following the mother's death, the grandparents sought custody and guardianship of Rachel, arguing that the father . . . could not be expected to care for her adequately because he was unable to read, might not be able to keep Rachel on her restricted diet, and had failed to contact emergency services in a timely manner when their daughter experienced the seizures that killed her. The court rejected their request because Iowa's custody law provides a statutory presumption in favor of natural parents, and merely showing that the grandparents had assisted the couple or that Craig needed help from another adult to care for Rachel was insufficient to overcome this presumption. Craig and Rachel had moved into the home of his sister, who helped with Rachel's care. . . . No evidence showed that Rachel was in any danger or had been neglected or abused, or that Craig failed to meet her needs or lacked the skills necessary to care for her. 18 *Mental & Physical Disability Law Reporter* 41–42 (1994).

In re M.D.B., 475 N.W.2d 654 (Iowa Ct. App. 1991). An Iowa appeals court ruled that a child with mental retardation and a language disorder was properly placed in therapeutic foster care. The boy had special needs, including counseling and speech therapy, was afraid of his father and expressed a desire not to see him. There also was strong evidence that the father physically abused the boy. Based on all this evidence, the trial court correctly held that therapeutic foster care was the least restrictive placement for the child. The appeals court left open the possibility that the father could regain custody if he completed parental training and demonstrated an ability to assume a parental role. 16 *Mental & Physical Disability Law Reporter* 60 (1992).

Missouri

In re J.K.C., 841 S.W.2d 198 (Mo. Ct. App. 1992). In a case involving two parents with mental retardation, a Missouri appeals court held that the evidence did not support terminating the father's right to a son with mental retardation, but did warrant terminating both parents' rights to their daughter. Both parents had mild mental retardation. The son, who also had mild mental retardation, had lived with his parents for four years before being placed in a foster home. The daughter had been in foster care her entire life. A juvenile court terminated the mother's and the father's parental rights to both children. The appeals court reversed with regard to the son. A court must consider and make findings with respect to a parent's permanent and irreversible mental condition " 'which renders the parent unable to knowing [*sic*] provide the child the necessary care, custody and control.' " Mo. Rev. Stat. § 211.447.2. . . . Here, the father showed an understanding of child safety and discipline, the need for education, and emergency measures. The father and son had developed strong emotional ties . . . , and the father had earnestly attempted to comply with agency requirements to improve conditions in the family's house. Moreover, there was no evidence that the son's developmental regression was caused by his parents, or that foster care was an improvement. . . . The mother had emotional problems in addition to mental retardation and was less mature and responsible than the father. The parents were married, however, and lived together in a relatively stable environment. . . . Because the parents were likely to continue living together, the court saw no point in terminating the mother's rights to her son. . . . Because the daughter had never been in her parents' custody, there had been no opportunity for bonding. There also was evidence that the parents would be unable to care for two children. 17 *Mental & Physical Disability Law Reporter* 166 (1993).

In re R.I.H., 842 S.W.2d 200 (Mo. Ct. App. 1992). A Missouri appeals court affirmed the termination of a mother's parental rights, finding sufficient evidence that her mental retardation made her incapable of caring for her children. A clinical psychologist, the mother's father, and a social worker all testified that the mother was not mentally capable of keeping her house in a sanitary condition, even with frequent supervision. There also was evidence that the mother's husband sexually abused the two children in the mother's presence, but that she made no effort to stop the abuse. In addition, the trial court properly relied on a prior determination that the children had been abused and neglected. 17 *Mental & Physical Disability Law Reporter* 167 (1993).

New York

In re Loraida G., 183 Misc. 2d 126, 1999 WL 1292948 (N.Y. Fam. Ct. Nov. 16, 1999). A family court in New York denied a petition by the Department of Social Services (DSS) alleging that Lori G., who has mild mental retardation, would not be capable of parenting her child. The child was taken from Lori G. within days of birth. The court indicated that mild mental retardation is not *per se* or *ipso facto* child neglect. A finding of child neglect must be based upon evidence that there is impairment of a child's physical, mental, or emotional condition, or that the child is imminently in danger of impairment due to a parent's failure to exercise even minimally adequate care. The court granted Lori G. custody, with the proviso that she accept help from appropriate social services programs to ensure that the child will be properly cared for.

In re Joshua "O," 641 N.Y.S.2d 475 (App. Div. 1996). A New York appeals court affirmed a family court ruling terminating the parental rights of a mother with mild mental retardation and numerous emotional problems. In order to terminate parental rights on the grounds of mental illness, the petitioner must show, by clear and convincing evidence, that the respondent presently is—and for the foreseeable future will be—unable to provide proper and adequate care for his or her children because of the respondent's mental illness. . . . Here, there was clear and convincing evidence from an examining psychologist that the mother's mild mental retardation made it difficult for her to anticipate problems and plan for the future; that she had high levels of stress and anxiety and difficulty controlling her emotional outbursts; and that she showed no signs of being able to understand the complex needs of a child. 20 *Mental & Physical Disability Law Reporter* 498 (1996).

Pennsylvania

In re E.M., 620 A.2d 481 (Pa. 1993). The Pennsylvania Supreme Court reversed and remanded a decision terminating the parental rights of a mother with mental retardation because the lower court did not adequately consider the needs and welfare of the children. In

1983, appellant's two children, both of whom had disabilities, were placed with a foster family after the County's Children and Youth Services (CYS) petitioned the court to adjudicate the children dependent [*sic*]. CYS had observed that appellant fed the children spoiled and diluted milk in dirty bottles, left dirty diapers in the living area for days and was lax about providing the children medical care. . . . [I]n 1989 CYS obtained an order from the court of common pleas terminating the mother's parental rights. The superior court affirmed the decision. . . . Pennsylvania's supreme court noted that state law provides for termination of parental rights where a parent's incapacity cannot be remedied. . . . The law requires a court to give primary consideration to the needs and welfare of the child. The supreme court found that CYS did not meet its burden of showing by clear and convincing evidence that the termination would meet the needs and welfare of the children. The superior court erred in finding that there was no need to determine whether a beneficial bond existed between appellant and the children, or whether continuing the relationship with appellant would serve the needs and welfare of the children. . . . A CYS psychologist testified . . . that the children maintained an emotional bond with their mother, that they expressed their desire to live with their foster family and their mother, and that they had told her that they have " 'two mommies and daddies.' " 17 *Mental & Physical Disability Law Reporter* 379 (1993).

In re P.A.B., 570 A.2d 522 (Pa. Super. Ct. 1990). Finding that maintaining the status quo "would best serve the needs and welfare" of three children with mental or physical disabilities, a Pennsylvania appeals court reversed a trial court order terminating the rights of parents with mental retardation. While the trial court had found that the parents' inability to provide for their children's physical or developmental needs would not improve, the trial court should have considered the role the parental bond had in the children's lives. 14 *Mental & Physical Disability Law Reporter* 328 (1990).

In re G.D.G., 573 A.2d 612 (Pa. Super. Ct. 1990). Affirming the termination of parental rights of a mother with mental retardation, a Pennsylvania appeals court ruled that medical evidence on the extent of the mother's disability was not required where she consistently had failed to assume parental responsibilities. After the mother abandoned her infant daughter, the child remained in a foster home. In the five years since regular supervised visits began between mother and daughter, the mother had engaged in parallel play rather than interacting with the daughter, and had shown insufficient parenting or independent living skills. 14 *Mental & Physical Disability Law Reporter* 413 (1990).

South Dakota

In re M.K., 466 N.W.2d 177 (S.D. 1991). The social services department tried to help J.K. with her parenting and independent living skills after she gave birth to M.K. After two years of counseling, however, J.K. showed no significant change in her ability to follow instructions and improve her parenting skills. She provided her son with little stimulation, did not feed him food appropriate for his age, and did not seek medical treatment. J.K. appealed the termination of her parental rights, claiming she should have been given additional services and was prejudiced by the trial court's failure to order a medical exam for M.K. The supreme court affirmed, finding social services had given J.K. the benefit of all the available programs, but that all counseling had proven futile. The court found no prejudice . . . since, regardless of the outcome, she was unable to feed and stimulate M.K. properly. 15 *Mental & Physical Disability Law Reporter* 371–72 (1991).

CHAPTER 9

OBJECTIVE PERSONALITY TESTING: MMPI-2 AND OTHER OBJECTIVE PERSONALITY TESTS

§ 9.1   Minnesota Multiphasic Personality Inventory

Personality tests are generally classified in two broad categories: objective and projective. In reality, many tests fall more on a continuum between these poles. However, the traditional dichotomy is observed here for organizational purposes. The personality tests that fall in the objective category are those that demand a structured response from the subject and do not invite a free-form association or a projection of the subject's feelings into the test. The most important objective personality test is the Minnesota Multiphasic Personality Inventory–Second Edition (MMPI-2).

The MMPI-2 is a test that comprises 567 true-false questions. It is by far the most frequently administered personality test.[1] Its importance lies not only in its popularity but also in the vast amount of documented research verifying its reliability and validity.

Developed by Starke R. Hathaway and J. Charnley McKinley in the early 1940s, the early form of the MMPI contained 504 true-false items. It was replaced by the MMPI-2 in 1989. The MMPI-2 can be administered in group form, in booklet form, or by computer. It is currently used with individuals 18 years of age and older who have at least an eighth-grade reading level. Individuals with a reading level below the eighth-grade level might

---

[1] Marc J. Ackerman & Melissa C. Ackerman, *Child Custody Evaluation Practices: A 1996 Survey of Experienced Professionals (Revisited)*, 28 Prof. Psychol. Res. & Prac. 137–45 (1997).

need to respond to an oral form of the MMPI-2. Examined in more than 18,000 published articles and books to date, the MMPI/MMPI-2 is the best researched of all personality tests. Jim Butcher[2] reported that between 1970 and 2000 approximately 2,000 of these published research articles were in the area of forensic psychology. Almost every psychologist is taught the use of the MMPI-2 and would be expected to include it as a key part of any evaluation. Given its universal acceptance as a central part of evaluations, a psychologist who does not use it should be questioned about the omission, because reliance solely on subjective tests and interviews may permit erroneous conclusions to be drawn that might have been avoided if the research base available for use with the MMPI-2 had been utilized.

§ 9.2   Reading Levels

Much concern has been generated about the use of the MMPI-2 with individuals who have substandard reading skills. Anthony Paolo, Joseph Ryan, and Allen Smith raised considerable concern about some of the reading level items on the MMPI-2. They discovered that approximately 90 percent of the items required less than a ninth-grade reading level. However, 25 percent or more of the items appearing in nine subscales required greater than an eighth-grade reading level. These scales included the ASP (Antisocial Practice), TPA (Type-A), Hy2 (Need for Affection), Pa3 (Naivete), Se5 (Lack of Ego Mastery, Defective), Sc6 (Bizarre Sensory Experience), Ma1 (Amorality), Ma3 (Imperturbability), and Ma4 (Ego Inflation). The authors concluded, "These findings suggest that for persons with relatively low reading proficiency, interpretation of the above scales should be done cautiously, if at all, especially when the results are inconsistent with other available information."[3] They conclude that individuals with a reading level below the sixth-grade level should have the MMPI-2 read to them. It is important when the MMPI-2 is read to an individual that the reader provide no assistance to the individual beyond what would occur if the individual was reading it him- or herself. There is a standardized audiotape available for administration of the MMPI-2.

§ 9.3   Scoring and Interpretation

Whether hand scored or computer scored, the same profile should result on an MMPI-2. Differences do not come from the scoring form used but rather from the various methods of interpreting the profile that are used by different individuals. In this age of computers, psychologists who hand score the MMPI-2 should be questioned. Not only do they lose the subtlety of the subscales, but also there is an increased likelihood of error, as approximately 10 percent of hand-scored MMPI-2s have scoring errors, as reported by Roger Greene.[4]

---

[2] James N. Butcher, Assessment with the MMPI-2: Decisions in Diverse Applications, American Psychological Association Annual Meeting, San Francisco (Aug. 2001).

[3] Anthony Paolo et al., *Reading Difficulty of MMPI-2 Subscales*, 47 J. Clinical Psychol. no. 4, at 532 (1991).

[4] Roger Greene, Presentation before the American Bar Association/American Psychological Association Joint Conference, Los Angeles (Apr. 1997).

§ 9.4   Computerized Scoring

A number of computer programs that score and/or interpret the MMPI-2 are on the market. Some are usable in the psychologist's office, while others require the psychologist to mail or fax the answer sheet to a central computer service for scoring and interpretation. Although most, if not all, interpretations generated by these programs are acceptable, those preferred are the ones that are known to periodically update their programs in response to new research. Three that do so are the "Caldwell Report," the "Minnesota Report," and the programs from "Psychological Assessment Resources." Several learned treatises have suggested that psychologists need to be careful when using computerized interpretations. It is not appropriate to lift verbatim information from computerized printouts and put them directly into the report as if it was the psychologist's own work product.

Michael Finger and Deniz Ones[5] also point out that the results generated from a computer-administered MMPI-2 and a booklet MMPI-2 are virtually identical, as would be expected. Keith A. Campbell and his associates performed a study demonstrating that test-retest reliability was not affected by tests' being administered in a computer-based format.[6]

Scales are divided into three basic groups. The first group contains the *validity* scales, which help the examiner determine whether the profile is valid. The second group is referred to as the *clinical scales*. These scales present the information from which the clinical diagnosis is made and are the heart of the MMPI-2. The remaining scales are referred to as the *content scales* and the *supplementary scales*. These scales evaluate specific personality characteristics or measure specific problem areas.

The interpretation of an MMPI-2 involves several steps. In the first step, the computer categorizes test responses into the various scales. Many of the test items are scored on more than one scale. The computer then calculates responses and computes total scoreable responses for each scale. A *scoreable response* is one that is answered in the direction that represents potential pathology. This step produces a raw score.

The third step involves making a correction to some of the raw scores to account for defensiveness on the clinical scales. To accomplish this, the K Scale was developed to measure clinical defensiveness. A high score on the K Scale may indicate an attempt to maintain control and project an appearance of adequacy and effectiveness. These tendencies have been shown to predictably lower the scores on certain clinical scales. Thus, this aspect of responding has the potential to distort scores on other parts of the profile. To correct this potential distortion on the clinical scales, differing amounts of a K factor are added to those scales known to be distorted by defensiveness. The clinical scales to which a K factor is added are Scales 1, 4, 7, 8, and 9. The result of this third step is to obtain a raw score adjusted to reflect K factor loadings.

The fourth, and final step, before actual interpretation, is to convert the adjusted raw scores to standard scores called T-scores. See **Chapter 7.** The T-scores have a mean value of 50 and a standard deviation of 10. Thus, T-scores between 30 and 70 contain two

---

[5] Michael Finger & Deniz Ones, *Psychometric Equivalence of the Computer and Booklet Forms of the MMPI-2: A Meta-Analysis*, 11 Psychol. Assessment 58–66 (1999).

[6] Keith A. Campbell, Diane S. Rohlman, Daniel Storzman, Lawrence M. Binder, W. Kent Anger, Craig A. Covera, Kelly L. Davis, & Sandra S. Grossmann, *Test-Re-Test Reliability of Psychological and Neurobehavioral Tests Self-Administered by Computer*, Assessment 21–32 (1999).

standard deviations from the mean, or about 95 percent of the total. As a result, approximately 2 percent of the population falls below 30 and 2 percent above 70.

Last, the test results are interpreted. The interpretation involves a combination of comparing the results to the norms and to the many research findings published, and using professional judgment to assess the subject's background and possible reasons or explanations for tendencies shown in the results.

Most, if not all, of the available computerized scoring systems perform the first function—that is, they compare individual test scores to the norms determined by various research publications. The computer program generates a list of characteristics, tendencies, or personality traits that the subject is likely to exhibit. The task of the professional, then, is to interpret all these data in light of the clinical history, information from outside sources, other psychological tests administered, and the reason for the psychological evaluation.

The major problem with computerized interpretations is that they primarily interpret the test on the basis of the primary code type. (See § **9.8.**) Unfortunately, this often leaves out significant essential information that is available if there are elevations on clinical scales. Anyone who bases a report *solely* on the computer-generated report is failing to meet the standard of practice.

§ 9.5   Stability over Time

Roger Greene and his colleagues attempted to measure the stability of MMPI-2 administration over time. This was done by looking at individuals who received the MMPI-2 at two or more different times during forensic cases. In child custody evaluations, the MMPI-2 results were relatively consistent from the first administration to the second administration. Individuals tended to be somewhat more defensive during the second administration. With that exception, scores generally were lower during the second administration than the first administration. Furthermore, defensiveness continued to rise in those cases where a third administration was necessary. Some of the clinical scales returned to the same level where they were during the first administration. Greene *et al.* conclude by saying, "It does seem that forensic psychologists need to be very cautious about making long-term or characterological interpretations from any single interpretation of the MMPI-2 in any forensic setting. Instead the forensic psychologist should describe how this given MMPI-2 profile reflects the current circumstances of the individual."[7]

Patrick Munley[8] addressed the stability of MMPI-2 profiles over time. He found that the correlation coefficients were high enough to suggest similarity of profile shape across testing occasions. In addition, from scale to scale the mean scores ranged from no difference to less than a two-point difference from the initial test to the retest.[9]

---

[7] Roger L. Greene, Stuart A. Greenberg, Jeffrey Davis, Marc J. Ackerman, & Richard I. Frederick, MMPI-2 Stability within and across Forensic Settings, Paper presented at the Annual Meeting of the American Psychological Association, San Francisco (2001).

[8] Patrick Munley, *Comparability of MMPI-2 Scales and Profiles over Time*, 58 J. Personality Assessment 145–60 (2002).

[9] *Id.* at 152–53.

Note. The original name of scales is used in the following discussion, though the meaning of the scale may have changed over time. For example, the "L Scale" was originally the "Lie Scale," though the test taker is usually not *lying* per se.

§ 9.6   Validity Scales

? Scale ("Cannot Say Scale")

The ? Scale is the number of items left unanswered by the subject. This scale is not a psychometrically based scale but rather simply the number of items the individual has omitted. It is generally believed that when 30 or more items are omitted, there is probably an insufficient number of items to warrant interpretation.

David Berry and his associates performed a study in1997, wherein seven different levels of item omissions were investigated. Statistically reliable results were found on the MMPI-2 clinical scales up to 30 omitted items. Two-point code types were also relatively stable up to 30 omitted items. The authors recommended that item content of omitted items should be analyzed to determine whether they are clinically significant.[10]

When items are left blank, the individual can be asked to retake those items to allow them to be scored. If the subject is not available for administration of those items, one method proposed involves scoring the MMPI-2 with those items omitted and rescoring it with those items all answered as if they would have been answered in the scoreable direction. Both profiles are then compared, and the interpretation is said to be somewhere between the two profiles.

L Scale (Lie Scale)

The L Scale is a 15-item "perfection" scale designed to determine how much an individual is trying to make him- or herself look positive in an obvious manner. The higher the score on the L Scale, the more the individual is attempting to appear socially appropriate and virtuous. The lower the score, the more the individual is willing to admit to human weaknesses. Alexander Caldwell, the developer of one of the more popular methods of interpretation, believed this scale measures an individual's fears of shame or moral judgment.[11] A person with these fears will deny moral fault and therefore score higher. Most people will have a T-score below 50 and rarely above 60 on this scale.[12]

Robert Colligan's research reports that the L Scale score is negatively correlated with education.[13] In other words, the more education an individual has, the lower the L Scale score on average. The L Scale can also be elevated if the individual has a strict religious upbringing or religious occupation, is foreign-born, has below-average intelligence, is

---

[10] David Berry et al., *MMPI-2 Clinical Scales in 2-Codetypes: Impact of Varying Levels of Omitted Items*, 9 Psychol. Assessment no. 2, at 158 (1997).

[11] Alexander Caldwell, Presentation before the Wisconsin Psychological Association (Jan. 1996).

[12] J. Duckworth & W. Anderson, MMPI and MMPI-2 Interpretation Manual for Counselors and Clinicians 39 (4th ed. 1995) [hereinafter MMPI Interpretation Manual for Counselors and Clinicians].

[13] *Id.* at 41 (referring to Colligan's research).

applying for a job, or is involved in some kind of litigation and wants to look good. High L scores may also be the result of individuals' being highly moralistic, having an inability to gain self-insights, or having limited sophistication but attempting to look better than they really are.[14]

In summary, a T-score of 50 or below on the L Scale indicates an individual is willing to admit to his or her faults. A T-score of 50 through 60 indicates an individual who sees him- or herself as virtuous, conforming, and self-controlled. Finally, a T-score of 60 or more indicates that the individual is likely to repress or deny unfavorable traits.

Roger Greene[15] is one of the world's top experts in the use and interpretation of the MMPI-2. Greene reports that a person's educational level and socioeconomic class must be kept in mind when interpreting the L Scale.[16] He also points out that marked elevations on the L Scale occur with individuals who are very self-controlled and who lack insight into their own behavior, have very conservative religious and moralistic upbringing, are unsophisticated persons who are trying to create an unusually favorable impression, or could be overtly psychotic patients.[17]

F Scale (Frequency or Confusion Scale)

The higher the score on the F Scale, the more the individual is reporting confusion or unusual problems.[18] The F Scale is a 60-item scale. T-scores of 75 and above on the F-Scale may be a "cry for help." The items on the scale were chosen on the basis that fewer than 10 percent of the normative population answered the items in the scoreable direction. These individuals are hurting psychologically and want to make sure that the examiner is aware of the extent of their pain. As a result, they are likely overstating the unusual thoughts and experiences that may be occurring. When this score reaches 100 or more, it can be an indication that everything appears bad to the subject, and, as a result, he or she is overreacting in general.[19] This may also indicate malingering.

Timbrook and Graham[20] showed that the empirical correlates for MMPI-2 scales apply equally for blacks and whites. Several other studies show that the MMPI-2 performances of ethnic minorities are similar to those of Caucasians in a non-clinical sample.[21] McNulty, Graham, Ben-Porath, and Stein[22] found similar results with mental health outpatients.

---

[14] *Id.* at 40.

[15] Roger L. Greene, The MMPI-2; An Interpretive Manual (2d ed. Allen & Bacon, 2000) [hereinafter Greene].

[16] *Id.* at 91.

[17] *Id.* at 94.

[18] *Id.* at 50.

[19] MMPI Interpretation Manual for Counselors and Clinicians at 50.

[20] R.E. Timbrook & J.R. Graham, *Ethnic Differences on the MMP1-2?* 6 Psychological Assessment 211–217 (1994).

[21] *Id.*

[22] J.L. McNulty, J.R. Graham, Y.S. Ben-Porath, & L.A.R. Stein, Comparative Validity of MMP1-2 Scores of African American and Causasian Mental Health Center Clients, 9 Psychological Assessment 464–470 (1997).

A study of men undergoing court-ordered evaluations provided an empirical evaluation of the relative unimportance of ethnic group differences on the MMPI-2, at least for certain groups under certain circumstances.[23]

Marked elevations—T-score equaling 70 to 80—are found in individuals with an unusual and unconventional thinking style. They may be overly anxious and have a high need for help, or may actually have difficulty reading the items on the MMPI-2.[24]

When the T-scores on the F Scale are in the range of 80 through 90, according to W. Grant Dahlstom, author of one of the most widely used early textbooks on the MMPI, one must determine whether the individual is in contact with reality, has poor reading ability, or was purposely malingering. If these possibilities can be ruled out, the profile is considered valid, and a score this high usually indicates a cry for help, a severely disturbed subject, or an adolescent who is attempting to appear unconventional.[25]

T-scores in the range of 90 through 100 usually indicate a random marking of the test items. According to Carson's research, this may be the result of a person who is illiterate and does not want to admit it, someone who is confused, or someone who has brain damage.[26]

Generally, T-scores equal to 100 or above are an indication of error somewhere. There has been either an error in scoring the items, deliberate marking of the items in an all-true, all-false, or random format, or reading error. If these possibilities are ruled out, however, the score can reflect the severity of psychopathology in the person or the degree to which the individual feels the need to look pathological.[27] When a raw score of 30 or more is found, it generally suggests a random response set. A raw score of 23 or above indicates an extreme elevation and probably an invalid profile.

Roger Greene reports that marked elevation on the F Scale may be the function of an invalid profile. However, if the items have been endorsed accurately, the elevation reflects the severity of distress and the extent of psychopathology the client is experiencing that may be readily apparent in a clinical interview.[28]

Individuals with T-scores in the range of 45 or below are generally considered to be free from stress, honest, and conventional.[29]

F(B) (Back Page F or F-Back)

On the MMPI-2, the F Scale items are included in the first 370 items. F(B) starts at 300. This allows the examiner to determine whether there is a difference in responding between the first half of the MMPI-2 and the second half of the MMPI-2. Results on the F may be "normal" while results on the F(B) are not, because the individual is paying less attention to responding, responding inappropriately, or responding randomly. It is unlikely that an elevated F-Back would affect interpretation of the 3 main validity scales and the 10 clinical scales. However, it would affect interpretation of the supplementary scales.

---

[23] Id.

[24] Id.

[25] MMPI Interpretation Manual for Counselors and Clinicians at 53.

[26] Id.

[27] Id. at 55.

[28] Greene at 70.

[29] Id. at 58.

Variable Response Inconsistency

The Variable Response Inconsistency (VRIN) Scale looks at the consistency between pairs of items. For example, one item may be "I sleep well," while another item is "I sleep poorly." The assumption is that the individual will respond to one of these items as "True" and the other as "False." However, if the individual responds that both are true or both are false, this represents an inconsistency in responding. A high VRIN could measure self-contradiction, reading comprehension problems, or inattention to the test. It is not a measure of "fake good" or fake bad," as a person trying to fake is usually very consistent.

True Response Inconsistency (TRIN)

The True Response Inconsistency (TRIN) Scale score indicates the tendency of the individual to give "true" responses to the items indiscriminately. A very high TRIN is a warning that the individual may have been answering the inventory indiscriminately, and, as a result, the profile may be invalid or uninterpretable.

Mp and Sd

Two other scales have been developed that can be used in an effort to determine the validity of the profile. The Mp (Malingering Positive) Scale was developed in an effort to help pick up intentional "fake-good" distortions. The Sd (Social Desirability) Scale is different from the Mp in that it emphasizes high moral standards and "good citizen" qualities. It does, however, correlate highly with Mp. Mp has been renamed the Other Deception Scale (Odecp).

K Scale (Correction Scale)

The K Scale (30 items) measures the individual's defensiveness or guardedness. As a result, some of the same motivation that would go into raising the L Scale score could also go into raising the K Scale score. The K Scale was developed after the other validity scales. It is called a correction scale, as K loadings are added to the Scales 1, 4, 7, 8, and 9 of the clinical scales. See § 9.4. When adolescents are tested, K corrections are not used, research having shown that more accurate profiles are obtained without them.

Dahlstrom, Welsh, and Dahlstrom point out that high K scores are usually associated with lower scores on the clinical scales.[30] The K Scale is a much more subtle scale than is the L Scale and, as a result, can detect defensiveness in even sophisticated individuals. Kenneth Carson points out that the higher the score on the K Scale, the poorer the prognosis for therapy.[31] Average scores (T-scores equaling 45 through 60) are found with people who are generally demonstrating "a balance between self-disclosure and self-protection."[32]

---

[30] W.G. Dahlstrom et al., An MMPI Handbook: Volume 1 Clinical Interpretation 166 (rev. ed. 1982).

[31] MMPI Interpretation Manual for Counselors and Clinicians at 68 (citing Carson).

[32] Id.

A moderate elevation on the K Scale (T-scores equaling 56 to 64) is typical for individuals who are upper middle class or above or are college students. Individuals who are upper middle class or higher in socioeconomic status with scores in this range are usually living well-managed and controlled lives. However, with lower socioeconomic classes, this score would reflect a greater degree of defensiveness.[33] T-scores of 65 or higher usually mean that the person is impelled to present a psychologically healthy appearance to others.[34]

There are generally two reasons why an individual might have a low score (T-score of 35 to 45). Carson states that individuals with scores in this range have problems that they are quite willing to admit.[35] On the other hand, Dahlstrom, Welsh, and Dahlstrom point out that these individuals believe that life has been rough for them and they are accurately perceiving their difficult background.[36] T-scores of 35 or below indicate these individuals are too willing to admit their problems and may tend to exaggerate them.[37] The higher the K Scale score, the less value the clinical and content scales have. When K rises to about 60 to 65, there is likely to be little utility in the content scales, with most of them having raw scores of 0 or 1.

Scores of 65 or above "indicate clients who are consistently trying to maintain a facade of adequacy or control and are admitting to no problems or weaknesses despite their presence in a mental health setting. Such persons have a serious lack of insight into and understanding of their own behavior. They are being extremely defensive about some kind of inadequacy, which may not be directly discernable from the problems."[38] The prognosis for any form of psychological intervention is very poor.[39]

The research of Marc Ackerman and Scott Ackerman and Marc Ackerman and Una O'Leary demonstrate that the K Scale in custody cases is significantly elevated. As a result, when interpreting an MMPI-2 administered in a custody case, the same K interpretations that would be given to the general population should not be given in custody cases until the K Scale is at least above 60. David Medoff[40] discussed this issue by stating that "it is critical to note that, while elevations have reached levels of statistical significance, they fall short of clinical significance." He goes on to state, "Nevertheless, it has become commonplace for psychologists engaged in this line of work to tender false casual attributions of clinically significant defensiveness to the divorce or custody dispute context." Their position basically states that we must take the divorce context into consideration but cannot use it to excuse all defensiveness or lying.[41]

---

[33] Id. at 69.

[34] Id.

[35] Carson, cited in MMPI Interpretation Manual for Counselors and Clinicians at 70.

[36] Dahlstrom et al., cited in MMPI Interpretation Manual for Counselors and Clinicians at 71.

[37] Id.

[38] Roger Greene, MMPI-2/MMPI: An Interpretative Manual 117 (1991).

[39] Greene at 97.

[40] David Medoff, MMPI-2 Validity Scales in Child Custody Evaluations: Clinical versus Statistical Significance, 17 Behav. Sci. & L. 410–11 (1999).

[41] Id. at 410.

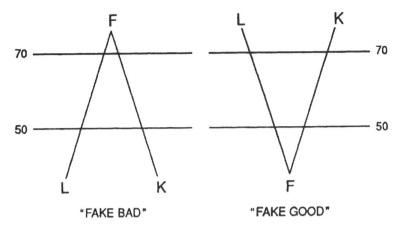

Figure 9–1. Validity Scale Profiles.

L-F-K Scales

The L-F-K Scales are seldom interpreted individually. A typical interpretation involves looking at combinations of these scales in pairs or taking them all together as well. Generally, as shown in **Figure 9–1,** a high F Scale score with low L and K Scale scores is an indication of a "fake-bad" profile. On the other hand, high L and K Scale scores and low F Scale score are indications of a "fake-good" profile.[42]

One of the indexes used in looking at the validity scales is called the F minus K Index. This is also referred to as the Dissimulation Index, or Gough Index. Generally, a fake-bad profile was considered if the F minus K Index was greater than 7, or if the F Scale score was greater than 15.[43] The Gough Index, developed by H.G. Gough in 1956, is found by subtracting the raw score of the K Scale from the raw score of the F Scale. T-scores should not be used for this index. Gough found that most normals on the MMPI had F minus Ks of minus 2 to minus 19.

Alexander Caldwell reported that when the F Scale raw score is equal to or less than 16, the test is considered valid regardless of what the K Scale score is.[44] If F is greater than 22 or 23, the test is considered invalid regardless of what K is. When F is 17 through 21, and the F minus K Index is equal to or greater than 11, then the test is invalid.[45]

Not every researcher feels that the criteria used by Caldwell or Gough are the appropriate cutoffs. N.C. Anthony wrote that a score of 19 or greater on the F minus K Index is an indication of invalidity.[46]

---

[42] MMPI Interpretation Manual for Counselors and Clinicians at 78.

[43] *Id.* at 82.

[44] Alexander Caldwell, Families of MMPI Code Types, Paper presented at the 12th Annual Symposium on the MMPI, Tampa, Fla. (1977).

[45] Roger Greene, The MMPI: An Interpretative Manual 50 (2001) [hereinafter R. Greene, The MMPI].

[46] N.C. Anthony, *Comparison of Client Standard, Exaggerated and Matching MMPI Profiles,* 36 J. Consulting & Clinical Psychol. 100–03 (1971), *cited in* R. Greene, The MMPI, at 50.

Elevations of L and F Scale Scores

Generally, simultaneous elevations of L and F Scale scores indicate a contradiction of problem areas. Individuals with these scores are denying inappropriate actions and thoughts or actions as measured by the L Scale, and at the same time acknowledging unusual thoughts as measured by the F Scale. This combination may actually be the function of "poor integration of diverse behavioral trends to characterize some psychotic processes."[47]

Elevations of F and K Scale Scores

Elevations of both F and K Scale scores imply the same type of contradiction that would be seen by joint elevations of L and F Scale scores. In addition to the possibility of psychotic processes, these individuals may have a pervasive lack of insight or difficulties grasping the reality of situations.[48]

David Berry and his associates studied the ability to detect random responses on the MMPI-2 using the F, F-Back, and VRIN Scales. They found that their research supported the use of the F, F-Back, and VRIN for determining random responses.[49]

Paul Lees-Haley used the MMPI-2 F and F minus K Index scores in an effort to identify malingering. He found that an F minus K score greater than zero generally indicates that there is a need to review the data for the possibility of faking. Even though up to 6 percent of the general population can have F minus K scores of greater than zero, it is still of concern when scores exceed zero.[50]

A number of studies were performed addressing the issue of faking on the validity scales. R. Michael Bagley and his co-researchers found that the F Scale was superior in detecting fake-bad profiles, and that the Mp and L Scales were equally effective in detecting fake-good profiles.[51] Ruth Baer and her associates concluded that coaching may enable the subjects to underreport symptoms without detection.[52] In another study, Ruth Baer and her associates found that fake-good individuals scored higher on all underreporting scales.[53]

---

[47] J.W. Dahlstrom et al., An MMPI Handbook: Volume 1 Clinical Interpretation 169 (rev. ed. 1982) [hereinafter An MMPI Handbook: Volume 1 Clinical Interpretation].

[48] *Id.* at 170.

[49] David Berry et al., *MMPI Clinical Scales in 2-Codetypes: Impact of Varying Levels of Omitted Items,* 9 Psychol. Assessment no. 2. at 158–60 (1997).

[50] Paul Lees-Haley, *Efficacy of MMPI-2 Validity Scales and MCMI-II Modifier Scales Detecting Spurious PTSD Claims: F, F-K, Fake-Bad Scale, Ego Strength, Subtle-Obvious Subscales, DIS and DEB,* 48 J. Clinical Psychol. no. 5, at 681–88 (Sept. 1992).

[51] R. Michael Bagley et al., *Relative Effectiveness of the Standard Validity Scales in Detecting Fake-Bad and Fake-Good Responding: Replication and Extension,* 7 Psychol. Assessment no. 1, at 84 (1995).

[52] Ruth Baer et al., *Effects of Information about Validity Scales on Underreporting of Symptoms on the MMPI-2: An Analogue Investigation,* 2 Investigation no. 2, at 189 (1995).

[53] Ruth Baer et al., *Sensitivity of MMPI-2 Validity Scales to Underreporting of Symptoms,* 5 Psychol. Assessment no. 4, at 419 (1995).

Jeeyoung Lim and James Butcher found that the new S Scale shows particular promise in detecting fake-good profiles.[54]

Invalidating Response Sets

At times, the way the individual responds on the entire MMPI-2 can invalidate the results. If the individual chooses to respond with all true responses, all false responses, all random responses, all deviant responses, or all nondeviant responses, the profile will be considered invalid. The four profiles shown in **Figures 9–2** through **9–5** demonstrate these various response patterns.

Robert Gallen and David Berry performed two studies addressing the issue of random responding. The results of their work indicated that validity scales differed significantly between random and valid profiles.[55] Furthermore, when random responding occurred after item 370 (all clinical scale items are within the first 370), delayed onset of random responding was both identifiable and partially interpretable, at least in reference to the clinical and validity scales.

§ 9.7 Clinical Scales

The clinical scales are the 10 main scales on the MMPI-2. Originally, there were eight basic clinical scales. In later years, two clinical scales (Masculinity-Femininity and Social Introversion) were added to reach the full complement of 10 scales used today. The 10 basic clinical scales are as follows:

Number	Abbreviation	Original Name
1	Hs	Hypochondriasis
2	D	Depression
3	Hy	Hysteria
4	Pd	Psychopathic Deviate
5	Mf	Masculinity-Femininity
6	Pa	Paranoia
7	Pt	Psychasthenia
8	Sc	Schizophrenia
9	Ma	Hypomania
0	Si	Social Introversion

Because the names of the scales do not always represent current or the full meaning of what the scales measure, the clinician generally refers to the scale by its number as opposed to its actual name.

---

[54] Jeeyoung Lim & James Butcher, *Detection of Faking on the MMPI-2: Differentiation among Faking-Bad, Denial and Claiming Extreme Virtue*, 67 J. Personality Assessment, 1–25 (1996).

[55] Robert Gallen & David Berry, *Partially Random MMPI-2 Protocols: When Are They Interpretable?*, 4 Assessment no. 1, at 6 (1997); Robert Gallen & David Berry, *Detection of Random Responding in MMPI-2 Protocols*, 3 Assessment no. 2, at 171 (1996).

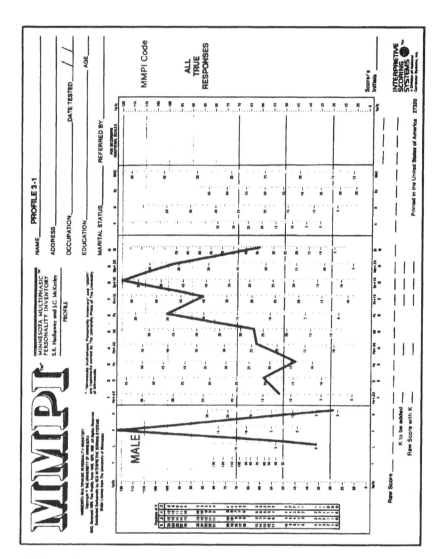

Figure 9–2. "All true" response set. Data obtained and reprinted with permission from Roger Greene, *The MMPI: An Interpretive Manual.* Copyright 1980, The Psychological Corporation. MMPI form reproduced with permission from the University of Minnesota. Copyright 1943, renewed 1970. This Profile Form 1948, 1976, 1982. All rights reserved.

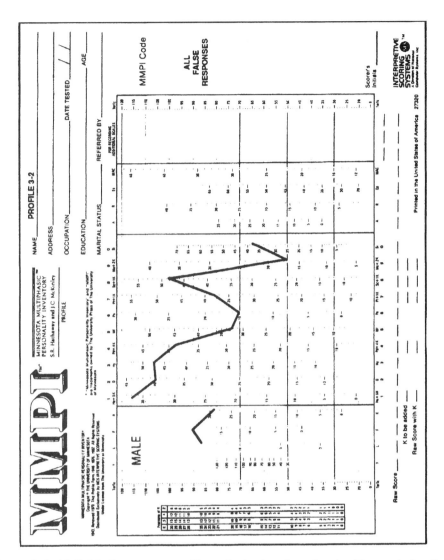

Figure 9–3. "All false" response set. Data obtained and reprinted with permission from Roger Greene, *The MMPI: An Interpretive Manual.* Copyright 1980, The Psychological Corporation. MMPI form reproduced with permission from the University of Minnesota. Copyright 1943, renewed 1970. This Profile Form 1948, 1976, 1982. All rights reserved.

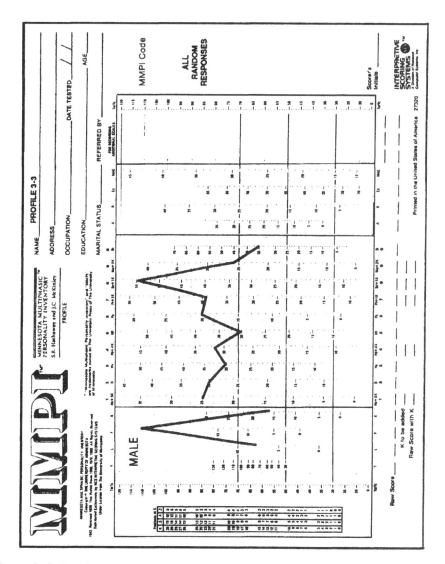

Figure 9–4. Random response set. Data obtained and reprinted with permission from Roger Greene, *The MMPI: An Interpretive Manual.* Copyright 1980, The Psychological Corporation. MMPI form reproduced with permission from the University of Minnesota. Copyright 1943, renewed 1970. This Profile Form 1948, 1976, 1982. All rights reserved.

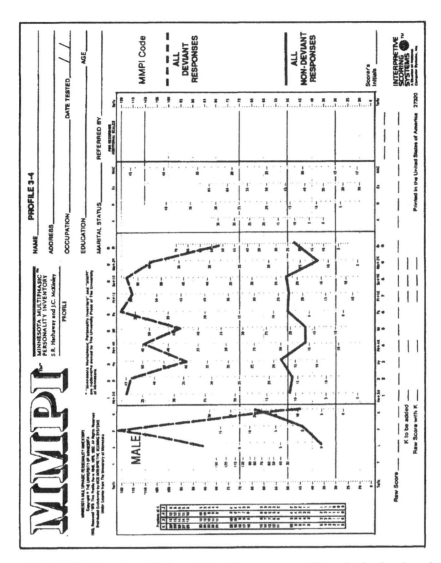

Figure 9–5. "All deviant" and "all nondeviant" response set. Data obtained and reprinted with permission from Roger Greene, *The MMPI: An Interpretive Manual.* Copyright 1980, The Psychological Corporation. MMPI form reproduced with permission from the University of Minnesota. Copyright 1943, renewed 1970. This Profile Form 1948, 1976, 1982. All rights reserved.

Most clinicians view the basic clinical scales of the MMPI-2 as indicating the extent of problems in the basic diagnostic category areas. Different authors have different opinions as to what emphasis should be placed on various scores. Generally, scores in the lower 60s are perceived as moderate elevations, while scores above 65 are considered to be significant.[56] In addition, very high scale scores (greater than 80) suggest serious psychopathology and incapacitating symptoms.[57] Scores below 45 are generally considered to be low scores. However, little research tends to be done in this area.

Scale 1: (Hs) Hypochondriasis

Scale 1 contains 32 items dealing with physical symptoms, attitudes about work, and daily activities, all of which are dependent upon physical health.

Descriptors.   Individuals with scores below 45 tend to have little concern about health functioning, tend to be frustrated when in ill health, and generally seem to have a high energy level. Their medical histories generally indicate that they have positive recoveries from past illnesses and tend to react negatively to other individuals who are hypochondriacal.[58]

Individuals with moderate elevations, but below 65, have concern about their bodily functions. Others may see them as being immature or lacking sufficient motivation. Marked elevations, scores above 65, are seen in individuals characterized by the following descriptors: these clients are excessively concerned about vague physical symptoms and may use them to manipulate and control others. They are cynical, whiny, demanding of attention, and generally negative and pessimistic.[59]

Elevations on the Scale 1 do not necessarily mean that the individual is hypochondriacal. They can be an accurate representation of the effects of physical illness or physical injury on the subject of the MMPI-2.

Alexander Caldwell suggests a number of questions that should be asked when evaluating the Hypochondriasis Scale. They include: "[H]ow much of the person's mental attention is occupied with problems of bodily functioning? How multiple and diverse are the health concerns that the person presents? To what extent is the person's life oriented towards securing medical care whether or not it is needed? To what extent does the person forgo activities or interests that others think are within his/her capacity lest the exertion or stress aggravate his/her physical health problems?"[60]

B.J. Hibbs, J.C. Kobas, and J. Gonzales found that men score significantly higher than women on this scale.[61] They suggest that this may be due to sex role sanctioning of somatizing behavior. Blacks and people with lower socioeconomic backgrounds tend to have higher scores on this scale also.[62] Some general rules that can be applied to interpreting

---

[56] MMPI Interpretation Manual for Counselors and Clinicians at 83.

[57] John Graham, The MMPI: A Practical Guide 52 (2d ed. 1987) [hereinafter Graham, The MMPI].

[58] A User's Guide at 16.

[59] Greene at 133.

[60] Alexander Caldwell, Forensic Questions and Answers on the MMPI/MMPI-2, at 9 (1997) [hereinafter Caldwell, Forensic Questions].

[61] B.J. Hibbs et al., Effects of Ethnicity, Sex and Age on MMPI Profiles 45 (1979).

[62] *Id., cited in* MMPI Interpretation Manual for Counselors and Clinicians at 91.

this scale are as follows; the more manipulative the client is with his or her physical complaints, the higher his or her score on this scale; the less the client is able to cope with life, the more he or she has an attitude of "you must take care of me"; the more the person uses his or her somatic complaints to get out of responsibility and to gratify dependency needs, the more immaturely the person behaves.[63]

It should be noted that an individual can have an elevated Scale 1 based on genuine physical maladies and not hypochondriacal thinking. For example, individuals with diabetes, survivors of open-heart surgery or cancer, or individuals with similar major illnesses are likely to have Scale 1 elevated in the absence of any psychopathology.

Scale 2: (D) Depression

Scale 2 is a 57-item scale that has some content overlap with Scales 1 and 3.

Descriptors.   Individuals with low scores on the Scale 2 are considered to be alert, outgoing, and active. Scores under 40 are found in individuals who would generally be described as cheerful, optimistic (possibly to the point of being unrealistic), and goal-oriented.[64] Individuals with moderate elevations (scores between 58 and 64) are dissatisfied with something or themselves but usually do not recognize this as a state of depression. Marked elevations of scores (above 65) indicate individuals who clinically present themselves as depressed. The higher the score above 65, the greater the pessimism, depression, and hopelessness. These individuals tend to be withdrawn, have feelings of guilt, and are self-deprecating.[65]

Significant elevations also are found in individuals who exhibit a general sadness and depressed mood either about life or themselves. As the scores increase, the pessimism, depression, and hopelessness begin to pervade the individual's entire life.[66]

Caldwell suggests several questions that should be asked when interpreting Scale 2. One such question is, "To what extent or level is the person feeling pessimistic or hopeless, dissatisfied with himself/herself, or persistently unhappy about his/her life or circumstances?"[67]

Scale 2 most frequently has the highest score of all the major clinical scales used in psychological profiles. It is the view of Robert Carson that the scale measures people's present attitudes about themselves in relationship to others, in addition to people's present feelings about contentment and security.[68] Alexander Caldwell perceives the scale as indicating the degree of fear of irretrievable loss that an individual experiences.[69]

---

[63] Jane Duckworth & Wayne Anderson, MMPI Interpretation Manual for Counselors and Clinicians 81 (3d ed. 1985).

[64] Hibbs et al., *cited in* MMPI Interpretation Manual for Counselors and Clinicians at 91.

[65] Roger Greene, MMPI/MMPI-A: An Interpretative Manual 144 (2000).

[66] *Id.* at 137.

[67] Caldwell, Forensic Questions, at 9.

[68] MMPI Interpretation Manual for Counselors and Clinicians at 96.

[69] *Id.* at 109.

When looking at Scale 2, one must consider suicidal risk. The risk tends to go up as the score on Scales 4 and/or 8 or 9 rise together with a high score on Scale 2.[70] An elevation on Scale 2 alone tends to be an uncomplicated depression.[71]

R.E. Harris and J.C. Lingoes developed five subscales from the Scale 2:

1. D1 (Subjective Depression)
2. D2 (Psychomotor Retardation)
3. D3 (Physical Malfunctioning)
4. D4 (Mental Dullness)
5. D5 (Brooding)

The D1 (Subjective Depression) Scale indicates the amount of pessimism, poor morale, and low self-esteem that the individual is feeling. When the D2 (Psychomotor Retardation) Scale is elevated, it measures the amount of non-participativeness in social relations and the immobility of the individual. The D3 (Physical Malfunctioning) Scale identifies the amount of physical malfunctioning and preoccupation with bodily functioning that the individual is demonstrating. The D4 (Mental Dullness) Scale looks at the client's nonresponsiveness and distrustfulness of his or her own psychological functioning. The D5 (Brooding) Scale indicates the amount of irritability and rumination the individual is experiencing.[72]

Scale 3: (Hy) Hysteria

Scale 3 is made up of 60 items. Many of the items deal with concerns about bodily functions and pain. Scale 3 is generally considered to be a measure of the dimension of pain—both emotional and bodily—that the individual is experiencing. It can include fear of physical pain, pain of rejection, pain of cruelty or mistreatment, and fear of pain as a result of devaluation or criticism.[73]

Descriptors. Low scores (below 44) on the Scale 3 can represent individuals who are caustic, sarcastic, and socially isolated. In contract, moderate scores (58 to 64) indicate individuals who are likely to be exhibitionistic, extroverted, and superficial. Such individuals are naïve and self-centered, and deny problems. When marked elevations are noted (65 and above), the client's naivete, suggestibility, and lack of insight come into play. In spite of an initial positive impression, psychological intervention with these individuals is difficult. They tend to look for simplistic solutions to problems that do not require introspection.[74] John Graham indicates that the descriptors of high 3 scores include the

---

[70] *Id.* at 107.

[71] R.E. Harris & J.L. Lingoes, Subscales for the MMPI: An Aid to Profile Interpretation (1955) (unpublished manuscript, University of Cal.) [hereinafter Harris & Lingoes], *cited in* Greene, The MMPI, at 140.

[72] Greene, The MMPI-2, at 139.

[73] A User's Guide at 17.

[74] Greene, MMPI-2: An Interpretative Manual 142 (2d ed. 2000).

following: symptoms of preoccupation with bodily functions, lack of insight, anxiety, egotism, narcissism, social involvement, tendency to be slow to gain insight, and tendency to have problems with authority figures.[75]

Robert Carson points out that these individuals tend to be naïve, self-centered, extroverted, and superficial in their relationship with others, and to lack insight into their own and others' motivations and actions. He also points out that these individuals cannot tolerate questioning of their way of looking at the world, make inordinate demands on counselors or therapists, and tend to want concrete solutions while resisting developing insight into their problems.[76]

Subscales. Harris and Lingoes developed five subscales for Scale 3:

1. Hy1 (Denial of Social Anxiety)
2. Hy2 (Need for Affection)
3. Hy3 (Lassitude-Malaise)
4. Hy4 (Somatic Complaints)
5. Hy5 (Inhibition of Aggression).[77]

An elevated Hy 1 (Denial of Social Anxiety) Scale score indicates that the client tends to be socially extroverted. Clients whose score on the Hy2 (Need for Affection) Scale is elevated obtusely deny that they have a critical or resentful attitude toward others. They are seen by others as being overly optimistic. A high Hy3 (Lassitude-Malaise) Scale score results in clients who complain about functioning below par physically and mentally. An elevation of the Hy4 (Somatic Complaints) Scale suggests repression and conversion of affect (converting psychological problems into physical problems). The Hy5 (Inhibition of Aggression) Scale is elevated for individuals who emphasize concurrence with others and disavow violence.

Triad Profiles

Scales 1, 2, and 3 together are referred to as the *neurotic triad*.[78] There are many different ways to interpret the triad. Generally, the highest of the three scores is listed first, the second highest second, and the lowest of the three scores third. For example, a 1, 2, 3 profile would indicate that the score on Scale 1 is higher than on Scale 2, and the Scale 2 score is higher than Scale 3. Generally, four common neurotic triads are reported. The first triad reported is the 1, 2, 3 triad. Individuals with this profile are generally seen to be avoiding their emotional problems. They tend to see themselves as being in declining health or "over the hill." This pattern is typical with long-term alcoholics and is unusual in females.[79] These individuals also "have

---

[75] Graham, The MMPI, at 60–61.

[76] Carson, *cited in* MMPI Interpretation Manual for Counselors and Clinicians at 146.

[77] Harris & Lingoes, *cited in* Greene, The MMPI-2, at 143.

[78] MMPI Interpretation Manual for Counselors and Clinicians at 158; Greene, The MMPI, at 148; 1 An MMPI Handbook: Clinical Interpretation, at 20.

[79] MMPI Interpretation Manual for Counselors and Clinicians at 159.

a long-standing somatic over-concern manifested by hypersensitivity to even the most minor dysfunction and have constant physical complaints without adequate physical pathology."[80]

A second common configuration is a 3, 1, 2 or 1, 3, 2 profile. This is generally referred to as a conversion V. Individuals with this profile tend to convert personal troubles into rational or socially acceptable problems—in other words, they convert psychological problems into somatic complaints. The greater the elevation of Scales 1 and 3 in comparison to Scale 2, the more severe and long-standing the resistance to change is likely to be on the part of these clients. These individuals tend to be poor candidates for psychological treatment.

A third common neurotic triad is the 2, 1, 3 or 2, 3, 1 triad. This is an inverted V on the profile on these scales. Individuals with this profile have multiple somatic complaints, common depression, and hysteroid features. They are generally emotionally over-controlled and report feeling bottled up. They are usually fatigued, anxious, and filled with self-doubts that prevent them from functioning.[81] In both men and women, this configuration reflects a mixed pattern of depression and somatization concerns.[82]

Scale 4: (Pd) Psychopathic Deviate

Scale 4 is made up of 50 items. It was originally designated as the *Psychopathic Deviate Scale*, based on the fact that many of the original criterion groups used in establishing this scale were prison inmates or psychiatric patients with histories of habitually transgressing social standards.[83] It is important to note, though, that not only does Scale 4 measure deviancy, it also measures the amount of independent thinking the individual possesses. As a result, well-educated college graduates may have high Scale 4 without demonstrating any social deviancy.[84] Furthermore, Scale 4 also identifies family problems and the amount of anger that one may be feeling at a particular time. Alexander Caldwell points out that individuals with high Scale 4s tend to feel parental indifference during childhood.[85] They need to turn off their resting arousal and emotionality so that they will not self-destruct. These individuals tend to describe themselves as being unwanted, unprotected, and unloved. As a result, they do not demonstrate the ability or have the opportunity to bond with their parents. These individuals tend not to show anticipatory arousal when they see trouble coming.

Scale 4 is most frequently interpreted with other scales. When Scale 9 is also elevated, the diagnosis is likely to be Antisocial Personality Disorder. These individuals are likely to be dangerous when they are upset. Individuals with both an elevated Scale 2 and an elevated Scale 4 tend to catastrophize or overexaggerate. Individuals with Scales 2 and 8 elevated along with Scale 4 tend to become suicidal when things go wrong.[86]

---

[80] Greene, The MMPI-2, at 144.

[81] *Id.* at 150.

[82] MMPI Interpretation Manual for Counselors and Clinicians at 162.

[83] Green, The MMPI, at 151.

[84] A User's Guide at 18.

[85] *Id.*

[86] Alexander Caldwell, Families of MMPI Code Type, Paper presented at the 12th Annual Symposium on the MMPI, Tampa, Fla. (1997) [hereinafter Families of MMPI Code Types].

Descriptors.   Low scores (below 44) on Scale 4 are generally found in individuals who are rigid and conventional. Moderate elevations (between 58 and 64) can be found in individuals who are generally concerned about social situations or may be responding to situational conflicts that they have adjusted to and that have become habitual. Significantly elevated scores on Scale 4 (65 or above) generally indicate an individual who is fighting against something, which is usually some form of conflict with authority figures. Although such individuals may not act out, they are viewed as rebellious and hostile toward authority figures. Furthermore, they are characteristically unreliable, egocentric, and irresponsible. They present themselves well with a good social façade but, following longer interactions, the sociopathic or psychopathic tendencies begin to surface.[87]

Graham listed the following characteristics of individuals with high Scale 4 scores:

> Difficulty in incorporating values in standards of society; asocial or antisocial behavior (lying, cheating, stealing, or sexual acting out); rebellion toward authority figures; stormy family relationships; blame of parents for problems; history of underachievement in school; poor work history; marital problems; impulsiveness; impatience; poor judgment; tendency not to profit from experience; immaturity; creation of a good first impression; shallow, superficial relationships; no definite goals; sarcasm and cynicism; resentment; tendency to feel little or no guilt over behavior; feigned guilt and remorse when in trouble; no disabling anxiety, depression, and psychotic symptoms; poor prognosis for change in psychotherapy or counseling; intellectualization; agreement to treatment to avoid jail or other unpleasant experiences.[88]

Individuals with scores higher than 70 who are over age 40 tend to be alcoholics or to be involved in embezzling or other financial types of crimes. These traits probably are unchangeable. Education needs to be taken into consideration when drawing conclusions about the individuals.

There are several questions that Caldwell suggests we ask about individuals with elevated 4 Scales, one of which is whether the person shows significant deficiencies of conscience in acts or behaviors that are seen as unsocialized or lacking in recognition of their adverse consequences to others.[89]

Researchers J. Kunce and Wayne Anderson state that an underlying dimension of this scale is the assertiveness and ego strength of the individual. Individuals with scores in the 60 to 70 range tend to be enterprising, frank, and adventurous, and show initiative and drive.[90] The "fighting out" pattern found in adolescents with high 4s reduces over time. These adolescents tend to have difficulty with family, school, and the law.

Looking at other variables, researchers J.E. Hokanson and G. Calden, and C. Mitler, C. Wertz, and S. Counts state that blacks score higher on Scale 4 than do whites.[91] In a

---

[87] Green, MMPI: An Interpretive Manual 150 (2d ed. 2000).

[88] Graham, The MMPI-2, at 71.

[89] Caldwell, Forensic Questions, at 9.

[90] J. Kunce & Wayne Anderson, *Perspectives on Uses of the MMPI in Non-Psychiatric Settings, in* Advances in Psychological Assessment 164 (P. McReynolds & G. Chelune eds., 1984).

[91] J.E. Hokanson & G. Calden, *Negro-White Differences on the MMPI,* 16 J. Clinical Psychol. 32–33 (1960); C. Mitler et al., *Racial Differences on the MMPI,* 16 J. Clinical Psychol. 140–59 (1961), *cited in* MMPI Interpretation Manual for Counselors and Clinicians at 168.

subsequent study, 44 percent of the heroin addicts showed the 4 Scale as the highest scale.[92]

Subscales. Roger Greene lists the five Harris and Lingoes subscales that have been developed for Scale 4:

1. Pd_1 (Familial Discord)
2. Pd_2 (Authority Conflict)
3. Pd_3 (Social Imperturbability)
4. Pd_{4a} (Social Alienation)
5. Pd_5 (Self-alienation)

The Pd_1 (Familial Discord) Scale measures the amount of struggle a person has against familial control and the perception that his/her home life is generally unpleasant. The Pd_2 (Authority Conflict) Scale not only indicates resentment toward socially acceptable norms, standards, and mores but also may be elevated in an individual who has had trouble with the law. The Pd_3 (Social Imperturbability) Scale measures how much the individual is comfortable in social situations based on being unconcerned about what others think about him or her. The Pd_4 (Social Alienation) Scale is elevated when an individual believes that no one understands him/her, feels regret for things he/she has done, and has the belief that others talk about him/her or have it in for him/her. The Pd_5 (Self-Alienation) Scale is elevated in individuals who may be depressed, regret things they have done wrong, or are pessimistic, and may indicate the excessive use of alcohol.[93]

Scale 5: (MF) Masculinity-Femininity Scale 5 is a 56-item scale that was not one of the original clinical scales. Starke Hathaway and J. Charnley McKinley originally intended Scale 5 to be a measure of homosexuality. However, they quickly realized that the homosexual population was too heterogeneous to be measured by one scale.[94] It is also the only scale that has different norms for males and females. It is not unusual for well-educated males to score high on the 5 Scale, as it acknowledges interest in things related to poetry, drama, and other cultural and aesthetic interests. Only a few items deal with overt homosexuality. As a result, this scale tends to measure interests that are considered to be stereotypically masculine or stereotypically feminine.[95]

The scoring of the scales tends to be reversed for the sexes. However, to say that a high score for a male is equivalent to a low score for a female is an oversimplification.

Descriptors. Men with low scores (less than 35) are individuals who tend to have "macho" self-images and present themselves as being extremely masculine, overemphasizing their

---

[92] Craig, *A Comparison of MMPI Profiles of Heroin Addicts Based on Multiple Methods of Classification,* 48 J. Personality Assessment 115–29 (1989), *cited in* MMPI Interpretation Manual for Counselors and Clinicians at 168.

[93] Greene, The MMPI-2, at 150.

[94] A User's Guide at 19.

[95] *Id.* at 20.

masculinity in a somewhat unsophisticated way. Women with similar scores identify with the stereotypical feminine roles but may doubt their own femininity.[96]

Greene points out that elevated scores on the Mf Scale for men (above 65) generally indicate men who are passive and inner-directed, and who have aesthetic interests and activities.[97] Such individuals tend not to identify with traditional masculine roles. Similar elevations on the Mf Scale for women are found in individuals who are definitely not interested in appearing or behaving according to traditional feminine roles. Aggressive behavior is probable.

In one of the most popular MMPI textbooks written, Jane Duckworth and Wayne Anderson point out that women who score above 50 on this scale tend to be uninterested in being seen as feminine.[98] They may or may not have masculine interests, but they are not interested in appearing or behaving as other women do.[99] In related studies, Colligan and colleagues indicate that Scale 5 is highly related to education.[100]

Graham states that males who score high on Scale 5 tend to show the following descriptors. They have conflicted thoughts about their sexual identity, are insecure in a masculine role, are effeminate, have aesthetic and artistic interests, are intelligently capable, are ambitious, are competitive, and are persevering. They tend to show good judgment and common sense, are curious, are creative as well as imaginative and individualistic, are social and sensitive to others, are tolerant, are capable of expressing warm feelings toward others, are passive and dependent as well as submissive, have good self-control, and rarely act out.[101]

Females who score high on the 5 Scale reject the traditional female role, have stereotypic masculine interests, are active, vigorous, and assertive, are competitive, aggressive, and dominating, are outgoing, uninhibited, and self-confident, are unemotional, and may be unfriendly.[102]

Usefulness.   Kathleen Long and John Graham studied the usefulness of the Masculinity/Femininity Scale on the MMPI-2. They reported:

> [T]his finding suggests the consideration of educational levels of normal men could be more important than Scale 5 scores in describing their behaviors and personality characteristics. In summary, the results of this study do not offer much support for the use of Scale 5 of the MMPI-2 for describing the behaviors and characteristics of normal men.[103]

---

[96] Kenneth Pope et al., MMPI, MMPI-2 and MMPI-A in Court (Second Edition): A Practical Guide for Expert Witnesses and Attorneys 343 (2000).

[97] Greene, MMPI/2: An Interpretative Manual 155 (2000).

[98] Jane Duckworth & Wayne Anderson, MMPI Interpretation Manual for Counselors and Clinicians 197 (3d ed. 1986).

[99] MMPI Interpretation Manual for Counselors and Clinicians 197 (3d ed. 1986).

[100] Colligan et al., *Development of Contemporary Norms,* 40 J. Clinical Psychol. 100–07 (1984), *cited in* MMPI Interpretation Manual for Counselors and Clinicians at 201 [hereinafter Development of Contemporary Norms].

[101] John Graham, MMPI-2: Assessing Personality and Psychopathology 68–69 (1990).

[102] Graham, The MMPI, at 69.

[103] Kathleen Long & John Graham, *The Masculinity/Femininity Scale of MMPI-2: Is It Useful for Men?*, 57 J. Personality Assessment 50 (1991).

Scale 6: (Pa) Paranoia

Scale 6 includes 40 items originally used to discriminate psychiatric patients with paranoid symptoms from nonpsychiatric patients.[104] The authors of this text have evaluated a number of individuals involved in custody disputes with elevated 6 Scales, even though the individuals do not have any other characteristics that would be considered paranoid. This is based on the fact that the adversarial custody dispute engenders suspiciousness and distrust on the part of the parties. Attorneys often indicate to their clients that certain pieces of information should not be disclosed. Furthermore, in the custody evaluation, each party is trying to demonstrate his or her own level of competence over the perceived incompetence of the other party. Individuals with high Scale 6s will be reflecting on the question, "Who is for and who is against me?" It is interesting to note that in custody disputes, when Scales 6 and 3 are elevated in a mother, she often adopts the attitude of "if he struck me, it is an unforgivable act and I can't let him anywhere near the children." When the 3 and 6 are elevated together and a parent adopts this posture, the interpreter must suspect the likelihood that the problem is being overstated.

Descriptors.   Those individuals with low scores on Scale 6 tend to be insensitive to and unaware of others' motives. Moderate elevations are generally found in individuals who are interpersonally sensitive and think clearly and rationally. Alexander Caldwell identifies individuals scoring under 50 on the Scale 6 as being balanced, trustful, and self-satisfied.[105] In contrast, Greene states that marked elevations (65 and above) tend to represent individuals who are suspicious, hostile, and overly sensitive. The higher the elevation, the greater the likelihood that a thought disorder is present.[106] It is unlikely that Scale 6 will elevate above 65 in a custody case unless there is some genuine underlying paranoia in addition to the above-stated situational concerns.

John Graham indicates the extreme elevations on Scale 6 (greater than 75) indicate the following descriptors: disturbed thinking, delusions of persecution, ideas of reference, anger, or resentment, and feelings of being mistreated or picked on.[107]

Individuals with elevations between 60 and 75 are described as follows: sensitive, suspicious, guarded, hostile, resentful, argumentative, moralistic and rigid, overly rational, having a poor prognosis in psychotherapy, and not open to talking about emotional problems.[108]

In evaluating this scale, Caldwell suggests that we ask, "Does the person show paranoid trends, and how are they expressed?"[109]

Subscales.   Roger Greene discusses the Harris and Lingoes subscales of Pa_1 (Persecutory Ideas), Pa_2 (Poignancy), and Pa_3 (Naivete). Elevations on the Pa_1 (Persecutory Ideas) Scale indicate that the individual tends to externalize blame for his or her problems and

---

[104] A User's Guide at 20.

[105] Families of MMPI Code Types.

[106] Greene, MMPI-2: An Interpretive Manual 159 (2000).

[107] Graham, The MMPI, at 75.

[108] *Id.*

[109] Alexander Caldwell, Forensic Questions, at 10.

frustrations and feels persecuted. High Pa$_2$ (Poignancy) Scale scores result when individuals are overly subjective, appreciate sensitive feelings, and tend to be high-strung. These individuals consider themselves to be different from other people. Elevated Pa$_3$ (Naivete) Scale scores occur in individuals who affirm moral virtues, tend to be righteous about ethical matters, and display obtuse naivetè. Although items on all these scales contribute to the overall Scale 6 score, it can be seen that different types of concern will be generated depending upon which of the Harris/Lingoes Scale 6 subscales are elevated.[110]

Scale 7: (Pt) Psychasthenia

Psychasthenia is a term used to describe a variety of psychoneurotic symptoms, including anxiety, excessive worry, obsessions, and compulsions. Scale 7 has 48 items. A few of the items overlap with Scales 1 and 2, especially those dealing with health and physical symptoms. The scale generally measures long-term neurotic symptomotology. However, it can be elevated due solely to a highly stressful situation that the individual may be experiencing.[111]

Descriptors.   Low scores on Scale 7 indicate individuals who are secure and comfortable with themselves and generally emotionally stable. A moderate elevation suggests that an individual easily worries and becomes anxious. When the elevations become marked (above 65), individuals are generally found to be worried, tense, and indecisive. The greater the anxiety, the greater the likelihood of agitation associated with it. When scores become extreme (greater than 85), agitated rumination and obsessions no longer control the anxiety. Disabling feelings of guilt may also be present.[112]

Graham lists the following descriptors for individuals with high Scale 7 scores: they experience turmoil and discomfort, are anxious, tense, and agitated, are worried and apprehensive, are high-strung and jumpy, have difficulties in concentrating, are introspective, ruminate, are obsessive in their thinking, are compulsive, feel insecure and inferior, lack self-confidence, are rigid and moralistic, are perfectionistic and conscientious, distort importance of problems, worry about popularity, and make slow but steady progress in psychotherapy.[113]

Caldwell suggests that we ask the following questions when evaluating Scale 7: "Is the person a repetitive, obsessive worrier? Is he or she filled with self-doubt, self-preoccupied, and pervasively anxious?"[114]

There are no separate subscales for the Scale 7.

Scale 8: (Sc) Schizophrenia

Scale 8 comprises 78 items, which makes it the longest of the 10 basic clinical scales. Although it was referred to as the Schizophrenia Scale, it actually measures the amount of

---

[110] Greene, The MMPI-2, at 159.

[111] A User's Guide at 21.

[112] Greene, MMPI-2: An Interpretative Manual 163 (2000).

[113] Graham, The MMPI-2, at 80–81.

[114] Caldwell, Forensic Questions, at 10.

mental confusion that an individual is experiencing at any one time, rather than diagnosing a specific disorder. The subject is essentially saying that he or she is having experiences that do not make sense at this point.[115] Although Scale 8 is sometimes elevated in individuals who are highly creative, it does not often give false-positives. The confusion demonstrated on Scale 8 can be a function of chronic or temporary disorientation. As a result, additional sophisticated interpretation is required by the examiner.

Descriptors. Low scores on the Scale 8 represent individuals who tend to be conventional, realistic, and unimaginative. They generally present as concrete thinkers. Alexander Caldwell points out that individuals with scores under 50 tend to be clear in their thinking, are involved in stable relationships, and deal with conflict relatively well.[116] Moderate elevations may characterize individuals who look like creative thinkers but may actually be avoiding reality through fantasy and daydreams. When elevations become marked (65 to 90), these individuals become alienated and remote from their environment, which may be representative of an actual schizophrenic process or simply personal distress. Poor judgment becomes apparent the higher the score on the Scale 8. Extreme elevations (91 and above) generally represent individuals who are under acute, severe situational distress but are typically not schizophrenic.[117]

Graham identifies the following descriptors of individuals with very high 8 Scales: blatant psychotic behavior, confusion, disorganization, disorientation, unusual thoughts or attitudes, delusions, hallucinations, poor judgment, feelings of not being a part of a social environment, feelings of unacceptance, withdrawal, seclusion, secretiveness, inaccessibility, shyness, aloofness, lack of involvement, inability to express feelings, self-doubt, feelings of inferiority, incompetence, dissatisfaction, nonconformance, unconventionality, and eccentricity.[118]

It is important to keep in mind that scores in the higher ranges must be interpreted in conjunction with the validity scales. It is not unusual for scores on Scale 8 to enter upper-level ranges when the F Scale is grossly distorted. As a result, as indicated in the F Scale discussion in § 9.6, the profile may actually be invalid because of faking rather than a genuine "schizophrenic" process. Scores on this scale may also be elevated because of "anxiety, homosexual panic, identity crisis or sudden personal dislocation such as divorce or cultural shock."[119]

Subscales. Harris and Lingoes developed three subscales for Scale 8, which they have further subdivided. The Schizophrenia Scale—is made up of the Sc_1 (the Social Alienation Scale), Sc_2 (The Emotional Alienation Scale), Sc_3 (Lack of Ego Mastery; Cognitive), Sc_4 (Lack of Ego Mastery, Conative), and Sc_5 (Lack of Ego Mastery, Defective Inhibition) Scales. The last Harris and Lingoes Scale is the Sc_6 (Scale of Bizarre Sensory Experiences).[120]

---

[115] MMPI Interpretation Manual for Counselors and Clinicians at 243.

[116] Families of MMPI Code Types.

[117] Greene, MMPI-2/MMPI: An Interpretative Manual 167 (2000).

[118] Graham, The MMPI, at 78–79.

[119] MMPI Interpretation Manual for Counselors and Clinicians at 244.

[120] Harris & Lingoes, *cited in* Greene, The MMPI-2, at 168.

The Sc_1 (Social Alienation) Scale measures the lack of rapport the individual feels with others and withdrawal from meaningful relationships. The Sc_2 (Emotional Alienation) Scale indicates a lack of rapport the individual feels with him- or herself, including experiences of seeing him- or herself as strange and alien.

The Sc_3 (Lack of Ego Mastery, Cognitive) Scale indicates the degree to which the individual admits autonomous thought processes, including strange and puzzling ideas. The Sc_4 (Lack of Ego Mastery, Conative) Scale indicates the amount of impaired decision-making ability, inertia, massive inhibition, and regression demonstrated. The Sc_5 (Lack of Ego Mastery, Defective Inhibition) Scale measures the individual's ability to control his or her impulses. The Sc_6 (Bizarre Sensory Experiences) Scale measures the amount of change in perception of self, feelings of depersonalization, and estrangement.[121]

Scale 9: (Ma) Hypomania

Scale 9 is made up of 46 items. It is believed that the higher the score on the scale, the more energetic the individual feels. Individuals with low scores on the Scale 9 are considered to have insufficient energy to sustain their efforts.[122]

Descriptors.   Low scores on Scale 9 are often related to individuals who have low energy and activity levels. However, normally functioning, aged, individuals can have scores in the low range. According to Alexander Caldwell, an individual with a score under 45 generally presents him- or herself as being easygoing, someone who can sit back and listen intently without feeling the need to respond. These individuals are careful not to overcommit and are realistic about their abilities. Moods tend to be very stable as such individuals stay easily focused on their tasks. This type of individual also tends to dislike chemical stimulation.[123]

Moderate elevations (58 to 64) are found with individuals who are energetic, outgoing, and active. However, they can become agitated when external restrictions are placed on their activity level. Marked elevations (65 and above) represent overactivity and emotional lability and individuals who may experience flight of ideas. They present themselves as euphoric, and can have outbursts of temper. They tend to be impulsive and have an inability to delay gratification. The higher the elevation, the greater the likelihood of narcissistic and grandiose features.[124]

Graham uses the following descriptors for a high 9 Scale scorer:

> May have manic episodes; may manifest successive purposeless activities; has accelerated speech; may have hallucinations and delusions of grandeur; is emotionally labile; may be confused; displays flight of ideas; is energetic and talkative; prefers action to thought; has a wide range of interests; does not utilize energy wisely; is creative, enterprising, and ingenious; has little interest in routine or detail; is easily bored and restless; has difficulty inhibiting expression of impulses; has episodes of irritability, hostility, and aggressive outbursts; has unrealistic and unqualified optimism; has grandiose aspirations; exaggerates self-worth and

---

[121] *Id.*

[122] MMPI Interpretation Manual for Counselors and Clinicians at 267.

[123] Families of MMPI Code Types.

[124] Greene, The MMPI-2, at 171.

self-importance; is unable to see his or her own limitations; is outgoing, sociable, and gregarious; creates a good first impression; is friendly, pleasant, and enthusiastic; has superficial relationships; is manipulative, deceptive, and unreliable; harbors feelings of dissatisfaction; feels upset, tense, nervous, and anxious; is agitated and prone to worry; has poor prognosis for therapy; attends therapy irregularly; may terminate psychotherapy prematurely; and becomes hostile and aggressive towards therapists.[125]

Subscales. Harris and Lingoes developed four subscales for the Scale 9. They are the Ma_1 (Amorality) Scale, the Ma_2 (Psychomotor Acceleration) Scale, the Ma_3 (Imperturbability) Scale, and the Ma_4 (Ego Inflation) Scale.[126]

The Ma_1 (Amorality) Scale identifies the individual's callousness about his or her own motives and goals. The individual is disarmingly frank and denies guilt feelings. The Ma_2 (Psychomotor Acceleration) Scale identifies how hyperactive and labile the individual is. It also measures the amount of anxiety and pressure for action. The Ma_3 (Imperturbability) Scale measures the individual's confidence in social situations, denial of sensitivity, and proclaimed independence from the opinion of others. The Ma_4 (Ego Inflation) Scale measures how self-important the individual feels, even to the point of unrealistic grandiosity.[127]

Scale 0: (Si) Social Introversion

Scale 0, along with Scale 5, is not one of the original scales. The 69 items on this scale cover the range from social extroversion to social introversion.

Descriptors. High Scale 0 scores tend to indicate shyness, whereas low Scale 0 scores are likely to indicate an individual who shows leadership and does not tolerate being alone.[128] With scores of 45 or below, Alexander Caldwell feels that individuals may have a certain amount of exhibitionism.[129]

Greene indicates that individuals with extremely high 0 Scales are introverted, shy, and socially insecure. They withdraw from and avoid significant others, which serves to exacerbate problems.[130]

John Graham summarizes descriptors of high Scale 0 scores as follows:

socially introverted; more comfortable alone; reserved, timid, shy, and retiring; uncomfortable around members of the opposite sex; self-effacing and lacking self-confidence; hard to get to know; sensitive to what others think; overcontrolled and not likely to display feelings openly; submissive and compliant; overly accepting of authority; serious, reliable, and dependable; cautious, conventional, and unoriginal; rigid and inflexible; indecisive, even for minor decisions; worrisome and irritable.[131]

---

[125] Graham, The MMPI, at 81–82.

[126] Harris & Lingoes, *cited in* Greene, The MMPI-2, at 172.

[127] *Id.*

[128] A User's Guide at 23.

[129] Families of MMPI Code Types.

[130] Greene, The MMPI-2, at 174.

[131] Graham, The MMPI-2, at 85–86.

Subscales.   Yossef Ben-Porath and his colleagues developed new subscales for the Social Introversion Scale. This was necessary because the Serkownek subscales from the MMPI could not be used on the MMPI-2 due to deletion of items in the re-standardization study. The three subscales that were developed are called the S_1 (Shyness), S_2 (Social Avoidance), and S_3 (Self-Other Alienation) Scales. The Shyness Scale indicates individuals who are feeling shy around others, feeling easily embarrassed, feeling ill at ease in social situations, and feeling uncomfortable in new situations.[132] The Social Avoidance Scale measures "a great dislike of group activities, concerns about group participation, active efforts to avoid being in a crowd, dislike for parties and social events, and avoidance of contact with other people."[133] The Self/Other Alienation Scale indicates "low self-esteem, lack of self-confidence, a tendency to be self-critical, questioning of one's own judgment, and feeling ineffective at determining one's fate. In women, high scores may also reflect nervousness, fearfulness, indecisiveness, suspicion of others, viewing others as malevolent, and suspicion of being talked about by others."[134]

§ 9.8   Common Code Types

MMPI-2 results are often interpreted by pairing the two or three highest-scoring clinical scales into dyads as code types. This section describes the code types most frequently found. In most cases, it makes little difference which of the two scales in the dyad is higher. Caution should be used when interpreting T-scores below 65.

1-3/3-1.   See § 9.7.

2-3/3-2.   Individuals with this code type are usually significantly depressed, with symptoms of apathy and helplessness.

2-4/4-2.   When interpreting a 2-4 profile, the examiner must determine whether the depression is coming from internal or from external (situational) causes. This dyad is often found in individuals who have been caught in some type of illicit or illegal activity, indicating external depression. When the depression is internal, these individuals tend to be immature, dependent, and egocentric.

2-7/7-2.   Clients with this profile are tense, anxious, and depressed, and would be characterized as being constant worriers. Suicidal ideation should be assessed.

2-8/8-2.   Individuals with this code type are likely to be experiencing severe depression associated with anxiety and agitation. As a result, they may appear to be more angry than depressed. However, the observer should not be fooled by this appearance.

---

[132] Yossef Ben-Porath et al., *New Subscales of the MMPI-2 Social Introversion (S_I) Scale,* 1 Psychol. Assessment: J. Consulting & Clinical Psychol. 172 (1989).

[133] *Id.*

[134] *Id.*

3-4/4-3.   See § **9.16.**

3-6/6-3.   See § **9.16.**

4-6/6-4.   See § **9.16.**

4-7/7-4.   Although these two scales would seem to be contradictory, what this profile suggests is cyclical behavior or acting out followed by guilt and remorse.

4-8/8-4.   These individuals are often marginally functioning and have difficulty maintaining close emotional relationships. Their dissatisfaction with these relationships can lead to anger and resentment.

4-9/9-4.   Clients with this code type generally display some type of acting-out behavior or another. They tend to be impulsive, irresponsible, untrustworthy, and manipulative. Interpersonal relationships are generally superficial, and they may use these relationships to their benefit. Their high need for excitement results in their frequently acting out. It may be difficult for the observer to recognize the negative characteristics in such individuals, because they are likely to make a good first impression. However, once the superficiality of the relationship is gone, the pathology surfaces.

6-8/8-6.   When these two scales are elevated, the likelihood of a thought disorder needs to be considered. These individuals tend to be socially isolated and withdrawn, and establish poor interpersonal relationships. They tend to be isolated and preoccupied, and will often ruminate. Even if the level of pathology has not escalated to the level of a thought disorder, these clients are likely to be severely and chronically maladjusted.

6-9/9-6.   Angry, hostile, and potentially grandiose, these individuals also tend to be irritable, excitable, and energetic. They may have difficulty concentrating and will likely exercise poor judgment.

8-9/9-8.   Individuals with this code type evidence serious pathology. They may exhibit a rapid onset of excitement, confusion, disorientation, and hyperactivity. Their unpredictability leads to acting out unexpectedly.

4, 6, 8 and/or 9.   An elevation of 4, 6, 8, and/or 9 together indicates individuals who are extremely disturbed and likely to be extremely dangerous. It is no surprise that this is the profile mass murderer Jeffrey Dahmer displayed. When any three of these four scales are elevated together, concerns about extreme pathology and dangerousness are not diminished. The absence of an elevated Scale 7 demonstrates in these individuals a lack of guilt, worry, and/or anxiety about their behavior, thus increasing their dangerousness.

§ 9.9   Critical Items

Although the MMPI-2 is generally interpreted through combinations of items referred to as scales, clinicians are generally unwilling to ignore the clinical information that can be derived from specific items. The original concept of critical items was to select those items that were "highly indicative of severe psychopathology." It becomes the examiner's responsibility to review those critical items answered in the scoreable direction with each individual. The clinician then uses his or her clinical judgment to determine whether the explanation for the answer is reasonable or indeed represents serious psychopathology. When the explanation of the critical items answers is reasonable, the concern about elevated clinical scales should be reduced. On the other hand, if the explanation for the answers on the critical items represents serious psychopathology, the score on the clinical scales would more likely be accurate. For example, an item like "I believe I'm being followed" is a critical item. However, if the subject's spouse has hired a private investigator to follow the individual, it would be a legitimate concern. On the other hand, if the subject's response to this item is "no matter where I go there are people in bushes taking pictures of me, standing on rooftops drawing sketches of me, and hiding in my kitchen cupboards," this would be a representation of severe psychopathology. As a result, it is essential that the clinician identify the source of the concern that leads to the response given.

Four commonly used sets of critical items have been developed over the years. H.M. Grayson identified 38 items in 1951. Alexander Caldwell listed 78 different items in nine content areas in 1969. In 1973 M.P. Koss and James Butcher selected 73 items to be used as critical items. The most recent list was developed by David Lachar and Nancy Wrobel in 1979. Through a complicated research process, they identified 11 content areas representing 111 items. Today, the Koss and Butcher and Lachar and Wrobel lists of critical items are most frequently used by clinicians.[135]

As of 1992, the Lachar-Wrobel and Caldwell sets of critical items had not incorporated the new MMPI-2 items into their critical item sets. However, the Koss and Butcher list had. It is Roger Greene's interpretation that use of MMPI-2 critical items can "yield high rates of false positive and negative errors, and [the clinician should] not assume that the patient's endorsement or lack thereof for a specific item is a veridical response."[136]

Greene found that normal men and women endorsed approximately 12 of the 78 Koss-Butcher critical items. He further pointed out that endorsement of any particular item is often an idiosyncratic response that requires further investigation.

Caldwell suggests reading the critical items to the client, in part to give the interpreter feedback regarding whether the client read the items carefully enough or not.

> For the MMPI-Pattern-Sophisticated Psychologist, such item by item questioning is often, as noted, an annoying digression. . . . One can stress that, (1) because one would have to ask the person what each and every item meant to him/her, as well as considering (2) their unexpected contributions to different scales and (3) their changeability over time (items get changed much more than the scores change). Single items cannot be independently interpreted.[137]

---

[135] Greene, MMPI-2: An Interpretative Manual 269 (2000).

[136] Roger Greene et al., MMPI-2 Critical Items: How Critical Are They?, Paper presented at the 100th Annual Convention of the American Psychological Association 5, Washington, D.C. (Aug. 1992).

[137] Caldwell, Forensic Questioning, at 80.

In effect, critical items are "clues" that the evaluator should follow up on during interview.

§ 9.10   Supplementary or Research Scales

After the original MMPI was developed, a group of individual scales were developed that are referred to as *supplementary scales, research scales*, or *frequently scored scales*. These scales tend to identify certain aspects of an individual's personality as opposed to the global measures indicated by the clinical scales.

A Scale (First Factor-Anxiety Scale)

The 39-item First Factor-Anxiety Scale, originally developed by George Welsh, generally reflects conscious emotional upset about questions concerning thinking and thought process, negative emotional tone, lack of energy, pessimism, and personal sensitivity.[138]

Individuals with scores below 45 on this scale are considered to not be consciously anxious. Individuals with scores above 60 on the scale are consciously anxious, easily upset, and pessimistic.[139]

The major content areas in the A Scale are problems in attention and concentration; negative emotional tone and dysphoria; lack of energy; negative self-evaluation and hypersensitivity; and obsessions and ruminations.[140]

R Scale (Repression Scale)

The Repression Scale includes 37 items that are designed to measure "health and physical symptoms, emotionality, violence in activity, reaction to other people in social situations; social dominance, feelings of personal adequacy and personal appearance; and personal and vocational interests."[141] The scale measures whether the individual is consciously denying these negative traits. Scores below 45 on the R Scale indicate that the individual is not consciously repressing feelings and attitude, while scores above 60 on the R Scale indicate that the individual prefers to avoid unpleasant topics or situations.[142]

The A Scale and the R Scale are often interpreted in combination with one another. When an individual has a high A Scale score and a low R Scale score, the person would be considered to be anxious and open and is probably motivated to work in therapy. When both A and R Scale scores are high, not only is the person consciously anxious, he or she is also consciously attempting to work within a therapeutic environment.[143]

---

[138] MMPI and MMPI-2 Interpretation Manual for Counselors and Clinicians 306 (4th ed. 1995).

[139] MMPI Interpretation Manual for Counselors and Clinicians at 241.

[140] Greene, The MMPI-2: An Interpretation Manual, 2nd ed. 220 (2000).

[141] *Id.* at 314.

[142] *Id.* at 315.

[143] *Id.*

Es Scale (Ego Strength Scale)

The Ego Strength Scale was made up of 68 items reported by F. Barron in 1953.[144] Only 52 remain on the MMPI-2. The higher the score on the Ego Strength Scale, the more likely it is that the individual is to recover from problems without long-term negative effects. The lower the Ego Strength Scale, the more likely the individual is going to have difficulty coping with everyday problems and recovering from identified concerns. Individuals with high Ego Strength Scale scores tend to return to homeostasis rapidly, and will succeed better in therapy. Individuals with very low Ego Strength Scale scores often have sufficient difficulty functioning that they may require hospitalization.[145]

Do Scale (Dominance Scale)

The Dominance Scale is a 25-item scale developed in 1951 by H.G. Gough, H. McClosky, and Paul Meehl.[146] The higher the score, the more the individual feels in charge of his or her life, while the lower the score, the more the individual feels not in charge.

Re Scale (Social Responsibility Scale)

The Social Responsibility Scale, also developed by H.G. Gough, H. McClosky, and Paul Meehl, contains 32 items on the MMPI-2.[147] Individuals receiving high scores on this scale are generally considered to be socially responsible and willing to accept the consequences of their behavior. Low scores are indicative of lack of social responsibility. With individuals under 25 years of age, a low score may be a function of rejection of parental values rather than a reflection of social irresponsibility.[148]

MAC-R Scale (MacAndrew Alcoholism Scale-Revised)

The MacAndrew Alcoholism Scale, originally developed by MacAndrew in 1965, contains 49 items. Although it is one of the more recently developed MMPI-2 scales, it is used widely today in making a differential diagnosis of alcoholism or other chemical dependence.[149] A cutoff raw score of 24 is frequently indicative of alcoholism or other chemical dependence, with every point higher increasing the probability the diagnosis is accurate.[150]

Even alcoholics sober for years do not generally score below 24. High scores are generally predictive of opiate or alcohol abuse or both, but not necessarily predictive of

---

[144] A User's Guide at 25.

[145] MMPI Interpretation Manual for Counselors and Clinicians at 323.

[146] Id. at 340.

[147] A User's Guide at 27.

[148] MMPI Interpretation Manual for Counselors and Clinicians at 279.

[149] Id. at 374.

[150] Families of MMPI Code Types.

tobacco, cocaine, or marijuana use.[151] It is also a very difficult scale to fake, as most of the items do not directly relate to substance use or abuse. They instead relate to characteristics that alcoholics tend to indicate in answering MMPI-2 items. Often individuals with high scores feel the "pull" of substance abuse but work hard to control this pull. Individuals with scores in the high range on this scale who are not alcoholics or other substance abusers have a much greater propensity to become alcoholics or substance abusers.[152]

One question that always remains about the MAC-R is, "What raw score cutoff should be used for identifying whether an individual is or is not a substance abuser as measured by the MAC-R?" As indicated above, consensus states that the minimum raw score that should be used as a cutoff is 24. However, conservative evaluators prefer to use a cutoff score of 28 or greater. When raw scores are between 24 and 28, substance abuse should be suspected, but the reader must be aware that there will be a considerable number of false-positives in this range. When using the MAC-R with adolescents, it is advisable not to use a cutoff below 28, as there will be too many false-positives.

Roger Greene and his associates evaluated the use of two new scales on the MMPI-2 that are designed to assess substance abuse-related problems. They are the Addiction Potential Scale (APS) and the Addiction Acknowledgement Scale (AAS). "Results replicated earlier findings that both scales discriminate between psychiatric and substance abuse samples and do so more effectively than other substance abuse scales designed for use with the MMPI."[153] They also report that these scales appear to discriminate between psychiatric and substance abuse samples better than does the MacAndrew Alcoholism Scale-Revised.

Greene and his co-researchers were impressed with the stability of the Addiction Acknowledgement Scale (AAS), Addiction Potential Scale (APS), and MacAndrews Alcoholism Scale-Revised (MAC-R) to provide valuable information. They point out that there is a practical difference (one that may not be statistically significant but would be clinically significant) between individuals who have a high AAS and high APS scales and those who have low AAS and high APS scores.

Richard Clements and JoAnn Heintz[154] recently addressed the diagnostic accuracy of the Addiction Acknowledgement and Addiction Potential Scales. They found that the Addiction Acknowledgement Scale was very useful in identifying current alcohol dependence. However, the Addiction Potential Scale did not fare as well, being outperformed by the MAC-R and the Addiction Acknowledgment Scale.[155]

O-H Scale (Overcontrolled Hostility Scale)

The Overcontrolled Hostility Scale was developed in 1967 by Edwin Magargee, P.E. Cook, and G.A. Mendelsohn. The scale is used to differentiate between undercontrolled

---

[151] *Id.*

[152] *Id.*

[153] Roger L. Greene et al., A *Cross Validation of MMPI-2 Substance Abuse Scales*, 58 J. Personality Assessment 405 (1992).

[154] Richard Clements & JoAnn M. Heintz, *Diagnostic Accuracy and Factor Structure of the AAS and the APS Scales of the MMPI-2*, 79 J. Personality Assessment, 564–82 (2002).

[155] *Id.* at 564.

and overcontrolled assaultive individuals. The undercontrolled individuals are felt to have failed to learn to control their aggressive impulses, whereas the overcontrolled individuals rigidly defend against expression of impulsive aggressiveness. However, in those cases in which these overcontrolled individuals do express anger, it tends to come out in extreme forms, including severe physical assaults.[156] High scores on the O-H Scale are described as displaying excessive control of their hostile impulses and feeling socially alienated. They also tend to be reluctant to admit any psychological symptomotology.

This scale basically assesses the personality style of overcontrolled hostility or the possibility that the individual represses conflict to the extent that explosive behavior could occur.[157]

Concerns have been generated about the fact that the original Overcontrolled Hostility Scale was developed for male inmates and may not be applicable to the custody evaluation population. That was true of the original MMPI. However, the standardization of the MMPI-2 was far more broad based and can be interpreted with both males and females outside corrections settings.

Relevant Research

Edwin Megargee developed a classification system using the original MMPI on prison inmates. His classification system followed the "Able, Baker, Charlie" labeling system. He found that, with the exception of the Baker classification, most all other classifications had agreements between the original MMPI and the MMPI-2. This would suggest that the original Megargee code types can be used with the MMPI-2.[158]

Megargee provided a continuing education workshop at the 2001 American Psychological Association Annual Meeting in which he discussed the use of the MMPI-2 with the corrections classification code types that were originally developed for the MMPI, confirming the appropriateness of using the classifications with people taking the MMPI-2.

§ 9.11   Content Scales

The original MMPI has a set of content scales referred to as the Wiggins Content Scale. Because many of the items on the Wiggins Content Scales were among the items that were changed or eliminated on the MMPI-2, a new set of content scales were developed for the MMPI-2. The content scales for the MMPI-2 are designed to assess four general clinical areas: (1) Internal Symptomatic Behaviors; (2) External Aggressive Tendencies; (3) Negative Self-Views; and (4) General Problem Areas: Social, Family, Work, and Treatment. Internal symptomatic behaviors are examined by six content scales on the MMPI-2: Anxiety, Fears, Obsessiveness, Depression, Health Concerns, and Bizzare Mentation.

---

[156] Greene, The MMPI-2, at 243.

[157] Kenneth Pope et al. MMPI, MMPI-2 and MMPI-A in Court: A Practical Guide for Expert Witnesses and Attorneys 261 (1993).

[158] Edwin Mergargee, *Using the Mergargee MMPI-Based Classification Systems with MMPIs of Male Prison Inmates*, 6 Psychol. Assessment no. 4, at 337–42 (1994). See also **Ch. 15.**

Anxiety (ANX: 23 items). "High scores on the ANX report general symptoms of anxiety, including tension, somatic problems (i.e., heart pounding and shortness of breath), sleep difficulties, worries and poor concentration. They fear losing their minds, find life a strain, and have difficulty making decisions. They appear to be aware of these symptoms and problems, and admit to them."[159]

Fears (FRS: 23 items). "A high score on the FRS indicates an individual with many specific fears. These may include the sight of blood, high places, money, animals (i.e., snakes, mice or spiders) leaving home; fire, storms and natural disasters; water, the dark, being indoors, the dirt."[160]

Obsessiveness (OBS: 16 items). "High scorers on the OBS have tremendous difficulty making decisions and are likely to ruminate excessively about issues and problems, causing others to become impatient. Having to make changes distresses them, and they report compulsive behaviors like counting or saving important things. They are excessive worriers who frequently become overwhelmed by their thoughts."[161]

Depression (DEP: 33 items). "High scores on this scale characterize individuals with significant depressive thoughts. They report feeling blue, uncertain about their future, and uninterested in their lives. They are likely to brood, be unhappy, cry easily and feel hopeless and empty. They may report thoughts of suicide or wishes that they were dead. They may believe that they are condemned or have committed unpardonable sins."[162]

Health Concerns (HEA: 36 items). "Individuals with high scores on the HEA report many physical symptoms across several body systems. Included are gastrointestinal symptoms (i.e. constipation, nausea and vomiting, stomach trouble), neurological problems (e.g. emotions, dizzy and fainting spells, paralysis), sensory problems (e.g. poor hearing or eyesight), cardiovascular symptoms (e.g. heart or chest pains), skin problems, pain (e.g. headaches, neck aches), respiratory troubles (e.g. coughs, hay fever, or asthma). These individuals worry about their health and feel sicker than the average person."[163]

Bizarre Mentation (BIZ: 24 items). "Psychotic thought processes characterized individuals high on the BIZ Scale. They may report auditory, visual or olfactory hallucinations and may recognize that their thoughts are strange or peculiar. Paranoid ideation (e.g. the belief that they are being plotted against or that someone is trying to poison them) may be reported as well. These individuals may feel that they have a special mission or powers."[164]

---

[159] Williams, *Introducing the New MMPI-2 Content Scales, in* Topics in MMPI-2 Interpretation 15 (J. Butcher & Graham eds., 1991) [hereinafter MMPI-2 Content Scales].

[160] *Id.* at 16.

[161] *Id.*

[162] *Id.*

[163] *Id.* at 17.

[164] *Id.*

External Aggressive Tendencies

There are four content scales on the MMPI-2 that characterize the external aggressive tendencies type of behavior. They are Anger, Cynicism, Antisocial Practices, and Type A.

Anger (ANG: 16 items).   "High scores on the ANG Scale suggest anger-control problems. These individuals report being irritable, grouchy, impatient, hot headed, annoyed and stubborn. They sometimes feel like swearing or smashing things. They may lose self-control and report having been physically abusive towards people and objects."[165]

Cynicism (CYN: 23 items).   "Misanthropic beliefs characterize high scores on CYN. They expect hidden, negative motives behind the acts of others (e.g. believing that most people are honest simply because they fear being caught). Other people are to be distrusted because people use each other and are friendly for selfish reasons. They are likely to hold negative attitudes about those close to them including fellow workers, family, and friends."[166]

Antisocial Practices (ASP: 22 items).   "In addition to having misanthropic attitudes similar to those of high scorers on the CYN Scale, high scores on the ASP Scale report problem behaviors during the school years and antisocial practices such as being in trouble with the law, stealing, or shoplifting. They report sometimes enjoying the antics of criminals, and even if not explicably endorsing unlawful conduct, they believe it is all right to get around the law."[167]

Type A (TPA: 19 items).   "High scorers on the TPA are hard driving, fast moving, and work oriented individuals who frequently become impatient, irritable and annoyed. They do not like to wait or be interrupted. There is never enough time in a day for them to complete their tasks. They are direct and may be overbearing in their relationships with others."[168]

Negative Self-Views

One's negative self-views are characterized by the Low Self-Esteem Scale.

Low Self-Esteem (LSE: 24 items).   "High scores on the LSE characterize individuals with low opinions of themselves. They do not believe that they are liked by others or that they are important. They hold many negative attitudes about themselves including thinking they are unattractive, awkward and clumsy, useless, and a burden to others. They certainly lack self-confidence, and find it hard to accept compliments from others. They may be overwhelmed by faults they see in themselves."[169]

---

[165] *Id.*

[166] I MMPI-2 Content Scales at 18.

[167] *Id.*

[168] *Id.*

[169] *Id.* at 19.

General Problem Areas: Social, Family, Work, and Treatment

The general problem areas that one encounters in life are characterized by the last four MMPI content scales. They are Social Discomfort, Family Problems, Work Interference, and Negative Treatment Indicators.

Social Discomfort (SOD: 24 items).   "SOD high scorers are very uneasy around others, preferring to be by themselves. When in social situations, they are likely to sit alone rather than joining in the group. They see themselves as shy and dislike parties and other group events."[170]

Family Problems (FAM: 25 items).   "Considerable family discord is reported by high scorers on FAM. Their families are described as lacking in love, quarrelsome and unpleasant. They even may report hating members of their families. Their childhood may be portrayed as abusive, and their marriages as unhappy and lacking in affection."[171]

If someone in a custody case battle has an average or lower score on FAM, the evaluator should inquire about that seeming inconsistency. Some individuals think of their family of origin, or of themselves and their children without their spouse.

Work Interference (WRK: 33 items).   "A high score on WRK is indicative of behaviors or attitudes likely to contribute to poor work performance. Some of the problems relate to low self-confidence, concentration difficulties, obsessiveness, tension and pressure, and decision-making problems. Others suggest lack of family support for their career choices, personal questioning or career choice and negative attitudes towards co-workers."[172]

Negative Treatment Indicators (TRT: 26 items).   "High scorers on the TRT indicate individuals with negative attitudes toward doctors and mental health treatment. High scorers do not believe that anyone can understand or help them. They have issues or problems that they are not comfortable discussing with anyone. They may not want to change anything in their lives, nor do they feel that change is possible. They prefer giving up to facing a crisis or difficulty."[173]

Relevant Research

Douglas Jackson, Maryann Fraboni, and Edward Helms were concerned about how much content the MMPI-2 Content Scales really measured. They pointed out that when response style factors were removed, the uniqueness of the content of these scales was reduced.[174] Christine Brems and Pamela Lloyd concluded that the Low Self-Esteem Content Scale

---

[170] *Id.*

[171] *Id.*

[172] *Id.*

[173] *Id.* at 20.

[174] Douglas Jackson et al., *MMPI-2 Content Scales: How Much Content Do They Measure?*, 4 Assessment no. 2, at 112, 117 (1994).

renders a good global assessment of an individual's self-esteem.[175] Scott Lilienfeld found that the Antisocial Practices Content Scale and the Psychopathic Deviate Clinical Scale (Scale 4), both measures of deviant behavior, appear to measure somewhat different facets of psychopathy.[176] As a result, the interpreter cannot assume that they are measuring the same thing.

Yossef Ben-Porath and his colleagues studied the use of the content scales on the MMPI-2 to help make a differential diagnosis between Schizophrenic patients and patients with Major Depression. They concluded that the new content scales of the MMPI-2 were useful in making this type of differential diagnosis.[177]

§ 9.12   Usefulness of the Content Scales

Alexander Caldwell, a prominent researcher in the area of the MMPI/MMPI-2, reviewed the work done by the authors of the MMPI-2 in establishing the new content scales. Caldwell stated, "The multiple stages in the development of the new scales reflect an unusual mixture of judgmental decisions and careful statistical analysis . . . It is this reviewer's opinion that claims of substantial validity must await further research."[178] It was Caldwell's view that "the writing is occasionally self-serving and probably propagandistic."[179] He states this is due to the author's reporting low correlations as being meaningful.

David Nichols addressed the issue of whether the content scales are useful in determining what causes elevations in the clinical scales. He had some concerns about the Antisocial Practice Scale (ASP), stating that a score above 70 could be achieved without endorsing any antisocial practices on the MMPI-2. Nichols answered this concern by developing his own Psychopathy Scale (PSP), which he reports measures antisocial practices better than does the MMPI-2 ASP Scale. Nichols also felt that the Negative Treatment Indicators Scale (TRT) was a problem because only one-third of the items were truly reflective of treatment indicators. As a result, he concluded that a T-score of 80 could be achieved without endorsing any treatment indicator items.[180]

Robert Archer, one of the researchers on the MMPI-A (adolescent MMPI), looked at the use of the MMPI-2 content scales with adolescents and found there was a high correlation

---

[175] Christine Brems & Pamela Lloyd, *Validation of the MMPI-2 Low Self-Esteem Content Scale*, 65 J. Personality Assessment no. 3, at 550 (1995).

[176] Scott Lilienfield, *The MMPI-2 Antisocial Practice Content Scale: Construct Validity and Comparison with the Psychopathic Deviate Scale*, 8 Psychol. Assessment no. 3, at 281–93 (1996).

[177] Yossef Ben-Porath et al., *Contribution of the MMPI-2 Content Scales to the Differential Diagnosis of Schizophrenia and Major Depression*, 3 Psychol. Assessment: J. Consulting & Clinical Psychol. 634–40 (1991).

[178] Alexander Caldwell, *MMPI-2 Content Scales: What You Say Is What You Get?*, 36 Contemp. Psychol. no. 7, at 560 (1991).

[179] *Id.*

[180] David Nichols, The MMPI-2 Content Scales: In Interim Clinical Assessment, Paper presented at the American Psychological Association Convention, San Francisco (Aug. 1991).

between the MMPI-A content scales and the Wiggins Content Scales on nine of the scales, a moderate correlation on the Hypomania, Poor Morale, and Psychoticism Scales, and no significant correlation on the Religious Fundamentalism and Psychoticism Scales.[181]

Robert Colligan analyzed the relationship between the MMPI and MMPI-2 content scales and found that the correlation between the full-length Wiggins Content Scales of the MMPI and the remaining Wiggins Content Scales items of the MMPI-2 was very high.[182]

The conclusions reached by these studies on the content scales suggest that the developers of the MMPI-2 may have been too hasty in discarding the MMPI Wiggins Content Scales and suggest that a second look be taken at the efficacy of continuing the use of the Wiggins Content Scales on the MMPI-2.

§ 9.13   MMPI-2 and Faking

Richard Rogers and his colleagues performed another study about individuals' faking tendencies and the ability to identify such faking.[183]

Numerous authors have studied deception, malingering, feigning, and faking on the MMPI-2. David Nichols and Roger Greene point out that considerable advances have been made in the study of deception in the past 50 years. However, there is considerable concern about the fact that the complexity of deception was largely unforeseen and research to date has not fully explained what occurs during this process.[184]

§ 9.14   Studies on Various Groups

Military Personnel

James Butcher and his associates studied the MMPI-2 profiles of individuals in the active military. They found that active military personnel responded to the MMPI-2 items in a manner similar to that of those in the normative sample. These results differ from the original MMPI, where there were differences between military personnel and the MMPI standardization sample. This study also found clear age differences on the MMPI-2 in military settings, with younger subjects having higher MMPI-2 profile elevations than did older subjects.[185]

---

[181] Robert Archer, MMPI-A: Assessing Adolescent Psychopathology (2d ed. 1997).

[182] Robert Colligan, Relationships between MMPI/MMPI-2 Content Scales: A Preliminary Study, Paper presented at the American Psychological Association Convention, San Francisco (Aug. 1991).

[183] Richard Rogers et al., *Feigning among Chronic Outpatients on the MMPI-2: A Systematic Examination of Fake Indicators*, 2 Assessment 81–89 (1995).

[184] David S. Nichols & Roger L. Greene, J. Personality Assessment 264 (1997).

[185] James N. Butcher et al., *A Study of Active Military Personnel with the MMPI-2*, 2 Mil. Psychol. 47, 58 (1990).

College Students

Butcher and another group of colleagues studied the MMPI-2 profiles of college students. They compared the responses of 1,312 college students with the overall normative sample of the MMPI-2. College students demonstrated scores of 1 to 1½ standard deviations (10 to 15 points) above the mean on the original MMPI. However, "the results of the study show that college students scored at or very near the mean on most validity and clinical scales, within ½ of a standard deviation on the MMPI-2 norms on all of the scales."[186] They conclude that the MMPI-2 can be used for college students without concern about its applicability.

Aging Population

Butcher and a third set of colleagues studied the effect of aging on the MMPI-2. The study was performed in an effort to determine whether special age-related norms for the MMPI-2 would be needed. They conclude, "The results of this study indicate that there are few MMPI-2 differences between older persons' responses in the normative sample on the validity, clinical, and content scales. . . . Thus, our findings indicate rather clearly, that separate norms are *not* required for using the MMPI-2 with older men."[187]

Other Settings

A large study was done involving more than 300 subjects in outpatient psychiatric settings, Veterans' Administration (VA) settings, college campus settings, and a sample of peace officers.

Outpatients.   Herbert Weissman and Thomas L. Morrison reported that, in their study of 200 outpatient subjects, there were very similar raw scores between the MMPI and the MMPI-2, but very different T-scores, even after five score points were subtracted from each of the MMPI T-scores to adjust them to the new MMPI-2 cutoffs.[188] They also found a gender difference on the MMPI-2. Females had significantly higher scores on Scale 1, and males had significantly lower scores on Scales 2, 4, 5, and 8, when comparing the MMPI-2 with the MMPI.

VA population.   When Daniel Edwards and Ronald Allen replicated this study with the VA population, they reached the same basic conclusions. That is, they also found that the raw scores for the MMPI and the MMPI-2 were comparable, while the T-scores were

---

[186] James N. Butcher et al., *The MMPI-2 with College Students*, 54 J. Personality Assessment I, 14 (1990).

[187] James N. Butcher et al., Personality and Aging: A Study of the MMPI-2 among Older Men, Paper presented at the 98th Annual Convention of the American Psychological Association 15, Boston (Aug. 1990).

[188] Herbert N. Weissman & Thomas L. Morrison, Implications of Differences (Code-types, T-scores) for Clinical and Forensic Practice, Paper presented at the 100th Annual Convention of the American Psychological Association, Washington, D.C. (Aug. 1992).

not. They also concluded that the MMPI-2 raw scores should be plotted on the MMPI profile form.[189]

College students. Arnold de la Cruz replicated this same study with University of California-Davis students and got the same results.[190]

Peace officers. Last, George Hargrave and his associates replicated this study with peace officers. They tested 166 peace officers, who took both the MMPI and MMPI-2. They found the typical profiles for this group were 4-3/3-4, or 4-9/9-4. These are the same typical profiles that have been found with the MMPI in the past. Their results were the same as those for outpatients, VA patients, and college students, in that raw scores for the two tests were about the same, but T-scores were not.[191]

§ 9.15 Low MMPI-2 Scores

Scott Keiller and John Graham addressed the issue of low scores on the MMPI-2.[192] There are many individuals who feel that low scores should not be interpreted on MMPI-2s. Others feel that such scores represent the opposite of high scores. For example, a low Depression Scale score would indicate happiness, whereas a high score would indicate depression. Still others feel that low scores are to be interpreted completely differently from the opposite end of the score. Keiller and Graham identify six different possible interpretations of low scores:

1. "They could indicate favorable characteristics that are at the opposite of characteristics typically attributed to high scores on the scale."

2. "Low scores could represent unfavorable characteristics that also are related conceptually to characteristics of high scores."

3. "Low scores could indicate good general adjustment that is not limited to characteristics conceptually related to high scores on a scale."

4. "Low scores could indicate general maladjustment that is not conceptually related to the meaning of high scores on a scale."

5. "Low and high scores on a scale could be associated with similar characteristics."

---

[189] Daniel W. Edwards & Ronald Allen, Replication and Unique Considerations in a V.A. Outpatient Population, Paper presented at the 100th Annual Convention of the American Psychological Association, Washington, D.C. (Aug. 1992).

[190] Arnold de la Cruz, Replication and Unique Considerations in a Student Counseling Center Population, Paper presented at the 100th Annual Convention of the American Psychological Association, Washington, D.C. (Aug. 1992).

[191] George Hargrave et al., Replication and Unique Consideration for a Sample of Peace Officers, Paper presented at the 100th Annual Convention of the American Psychological Association, Washington, D.C. (Aug. 1992).

[192] Scott Keiller & John Graham, *The Meaning of Low Scores on the MMPI-2: Clinical Scales of Normal Persons*, 3 MMPI-2 News & Profiles 2–3 (Oct. 1992).

6.   "Low scores could have no meaning at all. Persons with low scores might not differ at all from persons with average scores on a scale."[193]

The authors point out that at this time, we are not able to determine which of these meanings should be attributed to low scores. In their study, they demonstrated that

> low scores on a particular scale typically were rated as having less than an average amount of negative characteristics that were associated with high scores on that scale. . . . Our study provided little support for interpreting MMPI-2 low scores as indicating greater than average maladjustment or other negative characteristics. Quite to the contrary, our low scorers were rated as being better adjusted than medium scorers on most scales.[194]

§ 9.16   MMPI-2 Use in Child Custody Evaluations

Scale Patterns

It has been stated for years that there is no good-parent/bad-parent profile on the MMPI-2. However, over the past decade, a number of large studies have looked at the mean profiles of various parent groups on the MMPI/MMPI-2: Ackerman & Ackerman, 1992;[195] Ackerman & O'Leary, 1995;[196] Bathurst, Gottfried, & Gottfried, 1997;[197] Hoppe & Kennedy, 1995;[198] Ollendick & Otto, 1984;[199] Schenk, 1997.[200] All of these studies have identified the same basic profile for individuals in custody cases with the highest mean scale on scores 3, 4, and 6. Because the 3, 4, and 6 scales are the most frequently elevated scales, the interpretation of these three scale combinations is most important in custody evaluation cases.

The Marc Ackerman and Scott Ackerman study in 1992, using the MMPI, looked at 262 parents who were divided into nine different groups. These groups were identified as all parents, all mothers, all fathers, all placement parents, all placement mothers, all placement fathers, all non-placement mothers, and all non-placement fathers. The mean K score

---

[193] *Id.* at 2.

[194] *Id.*

[195] Marc J. Ackerman & Scott Ackerman, *Comparison of Different Subgroups on the MMPI of Parents Involved in Custody Litigation* (1992) (unpublished).

[196] Marc J. Ackerman & Una O'Leary, Comparison of Different Subgroups on the MMPI-2 of Parents Involved in Custody Litigation, Paper presented at the 103d Annual Convention of the American Psychological Association, New York (1995).

[197] Kay Bathurst, A. Gottfried, & A. Gottfried, *Normative Data on the MMPI-2 in Child Custody Litigation*, 9 Psychol. Assessment 205–11 (1997).

[198] Carl Hoppe & L. Kennedy, Integrating MMPI, Rorschach and Other Test Data in Custody Evaluations, Paper presented at the 103d Annual Convention of the American Psychological Association, New York (1995).

[199] D.G. Ollendick & B.J. Otto, *MMPI Characteristics of Parents Referred for Child Custody Studies*, 152 J. Psychol. 571–78 (1984).

[200] Paul Schenk, *MMPI-2 Norms and Child Custody Litigants*, Custody Newsl. no. 15, Jan. 1997, at 1.

for these parent groups ranged from 59.1 to 61.2. The three most frequently elevated scales were the 3, 4, and 6 Scales, with Scale 4 being the highest scale in all of the groups. The range on the 4 Scale was 59.2 to 63.7, with an overall mean of 61.2.

The Marc Ackerman and Una O'Leary study, using the MMPI-2, looked at 122 parents with mean K scores of 55.6 to 60.7. The study also found the 3, 4, and 6 Scales to be the most frequently elevated, with 3 and 6 being elevated more frequently than 4.

The Ackerman and Ackerman study (1992) showed significant elevations on the Dominance, MacAndrew Alcoholism, and Overcontrolled Hostility Scales on the MMPI-2, generally in the lower 60s. However, when comparing these scores to the MMPI-2 results found by Ackerman and O'Leary, almost all content scale mean scores were below 50, with very few exceptions, the most notable being the Repression Scale (see § **9.10**). Research has demonstrated that the higher the K Scale is elevated on the MMPI-2, the less information one gets from the content scales. Because we are dealing with mean K scores in the low 60s, the utility of the content scales basically disappears. As a result, one can generally not rely on the content scales to provide much useful information on the MPPI-2 when K scores are over T-60.

The difference in the results on the MMPI MacAndrews Alcoholism Scale-Revised is notable. The three highest means on the MAC for the MMPI were non-placement mothers (61.9), all mothers (60.9), and placement fathers (60.8). The three highest means on the MAC-R for the MMPI-2 study were non-placement mothers (51.3), non-placement parents (50.5), and non-placement fathers (48.5). This is greater than a 10-point difference in the mean T-scores. It may be that the Addiction Potential Scale of the MMPI-2 will provide more useful information than does the MAC-R.

Because the 3, 4, and 6 Scales are the most frequently elevated scales in all of the MMPI-2 custody evaluation studies, an analysis of what the elevations mean together is important. Alexander Caldwell states that when interpreting multiple elevations, the elevations should be looked at as dyads. Therefore, to interpret elevations on these scales, one would need to look at the single elevations, as described earlier for the clinical scales, plus the 3-4/4-3, 3-6/6-3, and 4-6/6-4 combinations.

3-4 elevations.   These people tend to be very immature and may satisfy their own aggressions and hostilities through indirect acting out. They are often described as excitable, may have physical complications, and may be passive-aggressive.

4-3 elevations.   The elevation of the Scale 4 indicates the amount of aggressive or hostile feelings present. When Scale 4 is higher than Scale 3, the behavioral control is not always adequate. As a result, these individuals tend periodically to have violent episodes.

3-6 elevations.   These individuals tend to deny their hostilities, aggressions, and suspicions. They are hard to get along with because of their underlying egocentricity. Although their anger is seen by others, the individual is typically unaware of the level of anger.

6-3 elevations.   When Scale 6 is higher than Scale 3, suspiciousness and acting-out behavior increases.

4-6/6-4 elevations.   These individuals may be hostile, resentful, and suspicious. They tend to transfer blame for their problems onto others. They are litigious, and may threaten lawsuits. They have poor impulse control, are explosive, and have a propensity toward violence. Seriously disruptive relationships occur with the opposite sex. They also tend to have poor work records and demonstrate poor judgment.

Individual Clinical Scales in Custody Cases

Scale 1.   When Scale 1 (Hypochondriasis) is elevated, it is not likely to interfere with parenting skills unless the parent is significantly preoccupied with the physical symptomotology. In recent years, Chronic Fatigue Syndrome (See **Chapter 14**) is a diagnostic label that has been used with greater frequency. It is not unusual to see elevations on the 1 Scale in chronic fatigue patients. These patients often engage in behavior that will interfere with their parenting skills.

Scale 2.   Scale 2 (Depression) is the most frequently elevated scale in clinical referrals. When this scale is elevated in conjunction with Scale 7 (Psychasthenia), the parent is relatively unlikely to be able to support the child's self-esteem development. Furthermore, if the depression has reached a vegetative state, it is likely that the parent will not be able to function adequately in parenting tasks.

Scale 3.   An elevation on Scale 3 (Hysteria) is likely to be found when an individual overreacts to and overinterprets events. As a result, reports of incidents that have occurred are likely to be overstated and must be weighed against tendencies to overreact and over-interpret. These individuals also tend to have an unforgiving aspect to their personality.

Scale 4.   Generally speaking, there is little "good news" associated with an elevation on Scale 4 (Psychopathic Deviate). An elevation on Scale 4 represents deviance in thinking and often in behavior. This elevation can be acceptable in highly educated individuals. However, the lower the education level, the greater the concern about an elevated Scale 4. In addition, when a 4-9 profile is found, it represents individuals who are likely to demonstrate antisocial tendencies and transfer these tendencies to their children through teaching and modeling. The 4-9 profile individual typically does not do well with children who need structure. Their lack of ability to connect interpersonally with other individuals will also interfere with child rearing. It is important to interpret the 4-9 profile in conjunction with the First Factor-Anxiety Scale, a supplementary scale. The lower the score on the First Factor-Anxiety Scale, the greater the likelihood that the individual is demonstrating anti-social tendencies. However, if the Anxiety Scale is elevated in conjunction with the 4-9 profile, it is likely that there will be concerns associated with it. Individuals with elevated 4-9 profiles have a considerable amount of difficulty accepting responsibility for their own behavior. They tend to blame others. In custody cases, a person with an elevated 4-9 who loses the custody litigation is not going to be able to accept responsibility for the fact that his or her behavior is what led to losing custody. Instead, the claim will be made, for example, "My ex lied about me in court, and that's why I lost." "The judge didn't know what he/she was doing." Or "if my attorney had done a better job, we would have won the case." Because 4-9 individuals are not likely to accept responsibility for their own behavior and may blame the attorney for the loss of placement, attorneys should make sure they have collected their fees in advance. The elevated 4-9 individual is likely to think, "I lost custody, and it was my attorney's fault; therefore, there is no need to pay him/her for the work, because the job wasn't done right."

When the 4 and 6 Scales are elevated together, there should be concern about the amount of anger and hostility that may be present and how the anger will interfere with the individual's ability to function with children and interact with the ex-partner. It may be necessary, as a result, to evaluate the safety level of the child(ren) in the presence of individuals with high 4-6, 4-6-8, 4-6-9, or 4-6-8-9 profiles. These generally represent the most dangerous of the elevations.

Scale 6.   Elevations on Scale 6 (Paranoia) are not unusual in child custody cases. Many activities occurring during divorce litigation can engender feelings of paranoia. The other side may be hiring someone to follow the individual and in fact plot against that individual, leading to legitimate suspiciousness. However, it is unlikely that the 6 Scale will elevate much above 65 unless there was already an underlying component of paranoia present in the individual's personality.

Scale 7.   Because elevations on Scale 7 (Psychasthenia) result from lack of confidence, feelings of insecurity and inferiority, anxiety, and worrying, these characteristics may interfere with the parent's ability to interact with the child(ren) effectively.

Scale 8.   An elevation on Scale 8 (Schizophrenia) can represent confusion in thinking on the part of the parent. The greater the confusion on the part of the parent, the greater the unpredictability, which will lead to difficulty in having the child understand the parent's wishes or desires. This could result in overburdening or parentifying the child.

Scale 9.   The elevated Scale 9 (Hypomania) individual is likely to be impulsive, need excitement, and not recognize the consequences of his or her own behavior. Obviously, all of these represent a potential danger to the child. This is particularly dangerous when the scale is elevated along with 4, 6, and/or 8.

Scale 0.   An individual with an elevated Scale 0 could be so introverted that he or she will be unable to appropriately model prosocial behavior.

Supplementary Scales in Custody Cases

The three most relevant supplementary scales evaluated in custody cases are the Anxiety (A) Scale, Repression (R) Scale, and MacAndrews Alcoholism Scale-Revised (MAC-R).

Anxiety Scale.   An individual with an elevated Anxiety Scale may suffer from debilitating anxiety. This would suggest that the parent's anxiety could interfere with his or her ability to adequately provide stability in the child's life. This can lead to the child's feeling overburdened, with resulting psychological problems on the part of the child.

Repression Scale.   Individuals with high Repression Scales, who use the unconscious psychological defense mechanism of denial, are probably not dealing with their problems adequately, and they may deny concerns that other people have about them. When the

Repression Scale is elevated in conjunction with the L and K Scales, it further supports the notion that the individual may be unconsciously downplaying those aspects of his or her personality that are viewed as being detrimental.

MacAndrews Alcoholism Scale-Revised.   An individual with an elevated MacAndrews Alcoholism Scale-Revised score is not necessarily an active alcoholic. This scale can be elevated in alcoholics or other drug abusers who have been "dry" for years. In addition, adult children of alcoholics often have elevated MacAndrews Scales, even if they are not alcoholics or drug abusers themselves. Nevertheless, any time that the MacAndrews Alcoholism Scale is elevated, it is incumbent upon the clinician to adequately evaluate the reasons for the elevation and to consider the likelihood of an alcoholic or addictive personality.

In addition, the following supplementary scales may be relevant.

Ego-Strength Scale.   Individuals with low Ego-Strength (Es) Scales may not have the psychic energy necessary to deal with crises, problem solving, and child rearing. These individuals also show a relatively low likelihood that they will be able to take advantage of therapeutic intervention.

Overcontrolled Hostility Scale.   When the Overcontrolled Hostility (O-H) Scale is elevated, the parent may have a considerable amount of underlying, unresolved anger that has not been dealt with adequately. As a result, these individuals should be recommended for individual psychotherapy. It should also be noted that elevations on the Overcontrolled Hostility Scale are not just present in individuals who are angry all of the time but may be elevated in individuals who infrequently show excessive anger. These people also tend to lack self-confidence and find it difficult to accept compliments from others.

Content Scales in Custody Cases

Among the most relevant content scales are the following.

Family Problems Scale.   It would be expected that scores on the Family Problems (FAM) Scale would be elevated, since the individuals are going through a custody determination dispute and/or custody litigation. As a result, an elevated score does not necessarily mean that the family is abusive, lacking in affection, or otherwise inappropriate under these circumstances.

Work Interference Scale.   The Work Interference (WRK) Scale provides the evaluator with an opportunity to determine whether there are characteristics in the subject's personality that would contribute to poor work performance. These variables can include low self-esteem, difficulty with concentration, obsessiveness, difficulty making decisions, and problems with tension and pressure.

Negative Treatment Indicators Scale.   Therapy is often recommended for parents following child custody evaluations. The Negative Treatment Indicators (TRT) Scale can help discern whether the parent is likely to benefit from psychotherapy. High scorers on the Negative Treatment Scale do not believe that anyone can understand them or help them. In addition, they may not feel that it is necessary to change anything in themselves.

Effect of Child Custody Litigation

Many MMPI-2 studies have been performed looking at the results of child custody litigation. The results of the Ackerman and Ackerman study have been reported previously. Jeffrey Segel found that custody litigants are likely to have elevated L and K Scales that look like a fake-good profile.[201] Studies by Kay Bathurst, Carl Hoppe, and Allen and Adelle Gottfried,[202] and Paul Schenk,[203] as well as the two Ackerman studies described above all demonstrate the most elevated scales on the MMPI-2 in custody evaluations are the 3, 4, and 6 Scales.

Yossef Ben-Porath also reported correlations between scores on various scales of the MMPI-2 and custody determination. Relatively high correlations were found between the "paranoia" and "depression" scales for parents who lost legal custody of their children—in other words, parents with high scores on Scales 2 and 6 were likely to fail to get custody. Moderate correlations were found between the Depression Scale (2), the Social Introversion Scale (0), the Anxiety Content Scale (ANX), the Low Self-Esteem Content Scale (LSE), and the Family Problems Scale (FAM), and whether parents lost custody of their children. When looking at the validity scales, people motivated to "fake-good" or "fake-bad" were unable to avoid elevating the F Scale score, the F-K score, and the Ds (Dissimulation Index) score. However, the faking did not elevate the VRIN score.

§ 9.17   Ethnic, Gender, and Other Differences

Vinston Goldman, Arlene Cook, and W. Grant Dahlstrom studied black-white differences among college students on the MMPI-2. They found that there were significant differences between black and white groups on the MMPI-2. They concluded, "[T]he findings of this investigation strongly suggest that the MMPI-2 version of this inventory provides a more suitable basis for evaluating the emotional status and personality characteristics of young black adults from the original version.[204]

Patricia Fantoni-Salvador and Richard Rogers found that the Spanish version of the MMPI-2 had only moderate hit rates. As a result, until further research is done, the use of the Spanish version of the MMPI-2 may not be efficacious.[205]

---

[201] Jeffrey Segel, *Traditional MMPI-2 Validity Indicators and Initial Presentation of Custody Evaluations*, 14 Am J. Forensic Psychol. no. 3, at *55–63 (1996)*.

[202] Kay Bathurst et al., *Normative Data on the MMPI-2 in Child Custody Litigation*, 9 Psychol. Assessment no. 3, at 205–11 (1997).

[203] Paul Schenk, *MMPI-2 Norms and Child Custody Litigants*, Custody Newsl. no. 15, Jan. 1997, at 33.

[204] Vinston Goldman et al., *Black-White Differences among College Students: A Comparison on the MMPI and the MMPI-2 Norms*, 2 Assessment no. 3, at 293–99 (1995).

[205] Patricia Fantoni-Salvator & Richard Rogers, *Spanish Version of the MMPI-2 and PAI: An Investigation of Concurrent Validity with Hispanic Patients*, 4 Assessment no. 1, at 29–39 (1997).

Denise Shondrick and her colleagues wrote about the use of the MMPI-2 in forensic settings.[206] The authors found that 32.2 percent of men and 21.3 percent of women had invalid profiles based on F, F-Back, and/or VRIN scores. They also report that, unlike other research, Afro-Americans and Caucasians did not score differently on the F, 4, 6, and 8 Scales, as had been predicted by others. They further found that mental retardation correlated with elevations on the L Scale, whereas mental illness correlated significantly with elevations on the F, 6, and 8 Scales.

§ 9.18   MMPI-2 and the Rorschach

In recent years, there has been an increase in interest in comparing MMPI-2 and Rorschach results. For the past five decades, research generally indicates that the Rorschach and MMPI-2 do not have a meaningful direct relationship with one another. Therefore, if a comparison is to be made of the Rorschach and MMPI-2 results, it is necessary to identify the specific variables that are being compared.[207]

David Nichols points out that there have been intellectual arguments about which instrument provides a more in-depth view of an individual's personality.[208] He suggests that this is a fruitless exercise and that it is more beneficial to recognize the differences and to use them collaboratively. Ronald Ganellen also agrees that the current literature does not permit any firm conclusions about these two instruments. Ganellen becomes concerned about these two instruments when the indicated level of pathology differs between the two instruments.[209] When the Rorschach shows more pathology than does the MMPI-2, it could be stated that the individual is coping with underlying problems. However, when the MMPI-2 shows more pathology than does the Rorschach, it is a possible indication of a "cry for help." These two instruments assess personality in different ways, one objectively with forced choices (MMPI-2) and the other in an open-ended subjective manner (Rorschach).

Gregory Meyer addressed the issue in both a 1996 and a 1997 article.[210] He, too, recognizes the differences in results between the two instruments but hypothesizes that such differences may, in part, be the result of differences in response style to the instrument. Roger Greene points out that for meaningful research to be done in this area, a number of variables must be considered. Greene supports what Archer says, that "human nature may

---

[206] Denise Shondrick et al., *Forensic Applications of the MMPI-2*, 3 MMPI News & Profiles 6–7 (Oct. 1992).

[207] Robert Archer, *MMPI-Rorschach Interrelationship: Proposed Criteria for Evaluating Explanatory Models*, 67 J. Personality Assessment no. 3, at 504–15 (1996).

[208] David Nichols, *Remarks on Method for MMPI-Rorschach Studies*, 67 J. Personality Assessment no. 3, at 516–28 (1996).

[209] Ronald Ganellen, *Exploring MMPI-Rorschach Relationships*, 67 J. Personality Assessment no. 3, at 529–43 (1996).

[210] Gregory Meyer, *The Rorschach and MMPI: Toward a More Scientific Differentiated Understanding of Cross-Method Assessment,* 67 J. Personality Assessment no. 3, at 558–78 (1996); Gregory Meyer, *On the Integration of Personality Assessment Methods: The Rorschach and MMPI,* 68 J. Personality Assessment no. 2, at 297–330 (1997).

be slightly more complex than a single linear correlation between two variables or scales."[211]

§ 9.19   MMPI-2 and Personality Disorders

Borderline, antisocial, and narcissistic personality disorders are grouped together and referred to as Cluster B Personality Disorders on Axis II of DSM-IV. See **Chapter 17.** The results of the research performed by Frank Castlebury and his coworkers suggest that the MMPI-2 personality disorder scales can be used to screen for the presence of personality disorders. The use of the Antisocial Personality Disorder Scales was found to be positive for both the presence and absence of these disorders. However, the Narcissistic Personality Disorder Scale was only valuable in negative predictive powers.[212]

§ 9.20   Status of MMPI-2 Research

Roger Greene and his associates studied the current status of MMPI-2 research between 1990 and 1997.[213] They concluded that

1. The use of short forms of the MMPI-2 is not appropriate due to the lack of research to support their use.

2. A more conservative cutting score of 10 or more omissions is more appropriate than the "official" 30 items on the ? Scale.

3. Typical cutting scores for F and F-Back range from 20 to 23 and T-scores of 100 to 110 to identify invalid profiles.[214]

Short Forms

As pointed out above, Roger Greene believes that short forms should not be used with the MMPI-2, although it was a popular method with the original MMPI. Grant Dahlstrom and Robert Archer developed a short form of the MMPI-2 in 2000.[215] Their short form is

---

[211] Roger Greene, Critical Issues in the Integration of the MMPI-2 and Rorschach, Paper presented as part of Symposium at the Annual Meeting of the American Psychological Association, Chicago (1997).

[212] Frank Castlebury et al., *The Use of the MMPI-2 Personality Disorder Scales in the Assessment of the DSM-IV Antisocial, Borderline, and Narcissistic Personality Disorders*, no. 2, at 155 (1997).

[213] Roger Greene et al., *The Current Status of MMPI-2 Research: A Methodologic Overview*, J. Personality Assessment no. 1, at 20–36 (1997).

[214] *Id.* at 20.

[215] Grant Dahlstrom & Robert Archer, *A Shortened Version of the MMPI-2*, 7 Assessment 131–37 (2000).

referred to as the MMPI-2-180. Carlton Gass and Cheryl Luis[216] performed research with this short form and found limited utility.[217] Robert McGrath studied another short form referred to as the MMPI-2-297 and found that it provided a reasonable estimate when the full MMPI could not be administered. Also, administering the first 370 items will permit all of the major clinical scales and the original validity scales to be scored. The consensus appears to be that short forms are not an adequate substitute for the full MMPI-2. Although it can be cumbersome for the client to take the MMPI-2, due to its length, the results are of much greater utility and validity than those of any of the short forms.

MINNESOTA MULTIPHASIC PERSONALITY INVENTORY–ADOLESCENT EDITION

§ 9.21   Background

It has long been recognized that adolescents have a higher range of scores on the MMPI than do adults. Phillip Marks originally developed a separate set of norms for adolescents' MMPI scores. The developers of the MMPI-2 decided on a separate adolescent MMPI, the Minnesota Multiphasic Personality Inventory–Adolescent Edition (MMPI-A), to be used exclusively with adolescents, instead of having separate norms for the MMPI-2. As stated earlier, the MMPI-2 manual specifically states that the MMPI-2 should not be used with adolescents.

The sample for the adolescent MMPI comprised 1,625 subjects. Yossef Ben-Porath suggested that initial analysis of the MMPI-A should be limited to adolescents age 14 through 18.[218] Like the MMPI-2, the MMPI-A uses uniform T-scores. Analysis of the MMPI-A T-scores indicated the scores in the range of 61 to 65 were of potential clinical significance. "Thus, a decision was made to draw a gray, shaded area within the range to indicate that MMPI-A T-scores in the range of 61 to 65 should be considered as representing initial signs of clinical elevations."[219]

There were no item changes between the MMPI and the MMPI-A on the K, 1, 2, 3, 6, 7, or 9 Scales. Developmentally inappropriate items were eliminated on the L and 4 Scales (for example, "Sometimes in elections, I vote for people about whom I know very little" or "my sex life is satisfactory"). Many deletions occurred on the F, 5, and 7 Scales because the items were objectionable, developmentally inappropriate, or of limited face or content validity (for example, I used to play drop the handkerchief"). New items (for example, "my teacher has it in for me" or "sometimes I make myself throw up after eating so I won't gain weight") were added due to the timeliness of these kinds of concerns.

---

[216] Carlton S. Gass & Cheryl A. Luis, *MMPI-2 Short Form: Psychometric Characteristics in a Neuropsychological Setting*, 8 Assessment 213–19 (2001).

[217] *Id.* at 213.

[218] Yossef Ben-Porath, Standardization and Interpretation of Scores on the MMPI-A, Paper presented at the American Psychological Association Convention 4 (Aug. 1991).

[219] *Id.*

§ 9.22   Validity Scales

? (Cannot Say) Scale

The ? Scale consists of the total number of items that the respondent fails to answer or answers in both true and/or false directions. A majority of adolescents would be expected to omit 10 or fewer items. When 11 to 30 items are omitted, one must look at reading ability or limitations of life experience.[220]

L. (Lie) Scale

The L Scale is made up of 14 items from the original MMPI L Scale. Scores of 60 to 65 are related to an emphasis on conformity and perhaps represent denial. Marked elevations (above 65) raise questions about possible "nay-saying" or an unsophisticated attempt to portray oneself in a favorable light.[221]

F (Frequency) Scale and F[1] and F[2] Subscales

The F Scale had to be revised for the MMPI-A, as adolescents did not respond with the same frequency to the same items as did adults. The F Scale is the only basic scale with substantially different item content from the MMPI-2. MMPI-A items were selected when items were endorsed in the deviant direction by more than 20 percent of the adolescent normative sample. As with adults, high F Scale responding in adolescents can be a result of reading problems, faking bad, random responding, or serious psychopathology. The F Scale is divided into two subscales on the MMPI-A—F[1], assessing the front half of the test booklet, and F[2], assessing the back half of the test booklet.[222]

K (Defensiveness) Scale

The MMPI-A K Scale consists of 30 items. K correction is not used with adolescent profiles on either the MMPI or the MMPI-A. Elevations on the K Scale are often produced by adolescents who are defensive and who underreport psychological problems and symptoms.[223]

---

[220] Robert Archer, MMPI-A: Assessing Adolescent Psychopathology 98 (2d ed. 1997).

[221] Robert Archer, *Future Directions of the MMPI-A: Research in Clinical Issues,* 68 J. Personality Assessment no. 1, at 95–105 (1997) [hereinafter Archer, *Future Directions*].

[222] Carolyn Williams, An Examination of the Changes in the Descriptors of the MMPI-A Validity and Standard Scales, Paper presented at the American Psychological Association Convention (1991).

[223] Archer, *Future Directions,* at 107.

Additional Validity Scales: Variable Response Inconsistency (VRIN) and True Response Inconsistency (TRIN) Scales

Both VRIN and TRIN provide information about the adolescent's tendency to respond to MMPI-A items in a consistent manner. TRIN was developed to determine whether the adolescent was responding in a false or true direction.

Robert Archer and his colleagues[224] addressed the utility of the MMPI-A validity scales for detecting random responding. They found that the validity scales could detect random responding if the entire item pool was responded to in that manner. However, when less than half of the total items were randomly responded to, the validity scales were not able to make that discrimination.[225]

§ 9.23   MMPI-A Clinical Scales

Scale 1 (Hs: Hypochondriasis).   Reports concerning physical functioning on Scale 1 would be expected to be influenced by the adolescent's actual physical condition. The adolescent Hypochondriasis Scale includes 32 items that measure a preoccupation with bodily functioning, illness, and/or disease.[226]

Scale 2 (D: Depression).   High Depression Scale adolescents are most likely to be diagnosed with depression, but they are also less likely to engage in rebellious, deceitful, manipulative, or hostile behavior.[227]

Scale 3 (Hy: Hysteria).   The MMPI-A Scale 3 consists of 60 items. As the scale suggests, high scores are likely to demonstrate hysterical symptomotology. Low scores are associated with lower academic achievement and lower socioeconomic background than for high-scoring adolescents.[228]

Scale 4 (Pd: Psychopathic Deviate).   The MMPI-A Pd Scale consists of 49 items. Normal samples of adolescents tend to endorse more Scale 4 items than do adults. As a result, elevated 4 Scales must be interpreted with caution. However, all of the adult indicators of high 4 Scales should be considered, in addition to poor school adjustment, school conduct problems, and an increased probability in delinquency.[229]

---

[224] Robert P. Archer, Richard W. Handel, Kathleen D. Lynch, & David E. Elkins, *MMPI Validity Scale Uses and Limitations in Detecting Varying Levels of Random Responding*, 78 J. Personality Assessment 417–31 (2002).

[225] *Id.* at 417–18.

[226] Robert Archer, MMPI-A: Assessing Adolescent Psychopathology 160 (2d ed. 1997) [hereinafter Archer, MMPI-A]. Used with permission of Lawrence Erlbaum Associates, Inc.

[227] *Id.* at 161.

[228] *Id.* at 167–68.

[229] *Id.* at 172–73.

Scale 5 (Mf: Masculinity-Femininity Code Types).   Elevated scores on this 44-item scale generally represent less likelihood of acting out.[230]

Scale 6 (Pa: Paranoia).   The MMPI-A Paranoia Scale consists of 60 items that involve symptomotology of suspiciousness, feelings of persecution, moral self-righteousness, and rigidity. Adolescents tend to score somewhat higher on Scale 6 than do adults.[231]

Scale 7 (Pt: Psychasthenia).   The Psychasthenia Scale consists of 48 items that look basically at neurotic symptomotology. These individuals tend to be angry, tense, and indecisive, along with being self-critical and perfectionistic.[232]

Scale 8 (Sc: Schizophrenia).   This 77-item scale is the largest scale on the MMPI-A. Individuals with elevated scores are often thought of as feeling alienated, confused, or potentially delusional.[233]

Scale 9 (Ma: Hypomania).   There are 46 items on the Hypomania Scale. High scores on this scale relate to impulsivity, excessive activity, narcissism, social extra-version, and a preference for action in contrast to thought and reflection.[234] The 4-9 profile occurs in 10 percent of males taking the MMPI-A. Their referrals are marked with concerns about defiance, disobedience, impulsivity, provocativeness, and truancy.

Scale 0 (Si: Social Introversion).   The Si Scale consists of 62 items. Elevated 0 scores are likely to reflect social introversion, insecurity, and marked discomfort in social situations. Such individuals are shy, timid, and submissive, and lack self-confidence. High scorers on the 0 Scale are less likely to act out or engage in impulsive behaviors.[235]

Jennifer Fontain and her research associates[236] addressed the issue of classification accuracy of the MMPI-A. Using a T-score cut-off of 65 resulted in higher levels of accurate classification while minimizing the misclassification of both clinical and normal cases.[237]

§ 9.24 MMPI-A Supplementary Scales

MacAndrews Alcoholism Scale-Revised (MAC-R).   This scale contains 49 items. When raw scores are 28 or greater, there is an increased likelihood of alcohol or other drug

---

[230] *Id.* at 180.

[231] *Id.* at 184–85.

[232] Archer, MMPI-A, at 187–88.

[233] *Id.* at 190–91.

[234] *Id.* at 193.

[235] *Id.* at 195–96.

[236] Jennifer Lee Fontain, Richard P. Archer, David E. Elkins, & John Johansen, *The Effects of MMPI-A T-Score Elevation on Classification Accuracy for Normal and Clinical Adolescent Samples*, 76 J. Personality Assessment 264–81 (2001).

[237] *Id.* at 264–65.

abuse problems. The individual is likely to be interpersonally assertive and dominant, self-indulgent and egocentric, unconventional and impulsive.[238]

Alcohol/Drug Problem Acknowledgement (ACK) Scale.   This scale was developed exclusively for the MMPI-A to assess an adolescent's willingness to acknowledge alcohol- or other drug-related problems.[239]

Alcohol/Drug Problem Proneness (PRO) Scale.   This 36-item scale corresponds to the Addiction Potential Scale on the MMPI-2. T-scores of 65 or greater are associated with increased potential to develop alcohol or other drug problems.[240]

Immaturity (IMM) Scale.   The Immaturity Scale was also developed as a supplementary scale exclusively for the MMPI-A. High scorers on the IMM Scale are likely to be easily frustrated, quick to anger, impatient, loud and boisterous, not trustworthy or dependable, defiant and resistant, and have a history of academic and social difficulties.[241]

Welsch's Anxiety (A) and Repression (R) Scales.   These scales were originally developed for the MMPI. The MMPI-A Anxiety Scale measures individuals' tenseness and anxiety along with fearlessness, maladjustment, self-critical tendencies, and guilt behaviors.[242] An elevated R Scale is found in individuals who are overcontrolled, show little feelings, are inhibited and constricted, feel pessimistic, and feel defeated.[243]

§ 9.25   MMPI-A Content Scales

There are 15 MMPI-A Content Scales, which have a substantial overlap with the MMPI-2 Content Scales.

Adolescent-Anxiety (A-anx) Scale.   This 21-item scale produces high scores for individuals who are angry, tense, nervous, and ruminative. These individuals also tend to have difficulty concentrating, have low endurance, and fatigue easily. Sadness and depression, along with the probability of suicidal thoughts and ideation, are often also present.[244]

Adolescent-Obsessiveness (A-obs) Scale.   This 15-item scale measures excessive worrying and rumination in making decisions, and the occurrence of intrusive thoughts and problems in concentration.[245]

---

[238] Robert Archer, MMPI-A: Assessing Adolescent Psychopathology 98 (2d ed. 1997).

[239] *Id.* at 217.

[240] Archer, MMPI-A, at 218.

[241] *Id.* at 220.

[242] *Id.* at 221.

[243] *Id.* at 222.

[244] *Id.* at 234.

[245] *Id.* at 235.

Adolescent-Depression (A-dep) Scale.   This 26-item scale, as the name would suggest, measures sadness, depression, and despondency, as well as fatigue and apathy. Pervasive thoughts of hopelessness may include suicidal ideation.[246]

Adolescent-Health Concerns (A-hea) Scale.   This 37-item scale reflects concerns about physical symptoms and complaints along with tiredness and fatigue.[247]

Adolescent Alienation (A-aln) Scale.   The Alienation Scale has 20 items that measure the adolescent's feelings of interpersonal isolation, alienation, and frustration, along with social withdrawal.[248]

Adolescent-Bizarre Mentation (A-biz) Scale.   The Bizarre Mentation Scale consists of 19 items that can reflect poor reality testing, deficits in impulse control, and the occurrence of a thought disorder or psychotic thought processes, possibly elevating to the level of hallucinations or delusions.[249]

Adolescent-Anger (A-ang) Scale.   Individuals on the 11-item scale are angry, hostile, and irritable, and generally display impatience along with poor anger control, and have a potential for physical aggressiveness.[250]

Adolescent-Cynicism (A-cyn) Scale.   Guardedness and suspiciousness of others' motives, along with unfriendliness and hostility in relationships, are noted with adolescents scoring high on this 22-item scale.[251]

Adolescent-Conduct Problems (A-con) Scale.   High scorers on this 23-item scale are likely to be in trouble because of their behavior, exhibit poor impulse control, and demonstrate antisocial behavior. Their attitudes and beliefs often conflict with societal norms and standards as evidenced by problems with authority figures. There is increased likelihood that these adolescents will be diagnosed with a conduct disorder.[252]

Adolescent-Low Self-Esteem (A-lse) Scale.   There are 18 items on the Low Self-Esteem Scale that measure, as would be expected, poor self-esteem and low self-confidence. In addition, these individuals feel inadequate and incompetent, and are passive and uncomfortable in interpersonal relationships.[253]

---

[246] Archer, MMPI-A, at 236.

[247] *Id.* at 237.

[248] *Id.* at 238.

[249] *Id.* at 239.

[250] *Id.* at 241.

[251] *Id.* at 242.

[252] Archer, MMPI-A, at 243.

[253] *Id.* at 244.

Adolescent-Low Aspirations (A-las) Scale. Poor academic performance, low frustration tolerance, and persistent pattern of underachievement are measured with this 16-item scale.[254]

Adolescent-Social Discomfort (A-sod) Scale. This scale is made up of 24 items that measure social discomfort, withdrawal, shyness, and social introversion.[255]

Adolescent-Family Problems (P-fam) Scale. There are 35 items on this scale. Adolescent scoring high on this scale see the family environment as being unsupportive, hostile, unloving, or punitive. There is also an increased likelihood of acting out, including running away from home. Resentment, anger, and hostility toward family members are likely to be present.[256]

Adolescent-School Problems (A-sch) Scale. This 20-item scale was created specifically for the MMPI-A and does not exist on the MMPI-2. High scores generally have a negative attitude toward academic activities and achievement. This is also reflected in poor school performance, including behavioral and academic problems. However, the possibility of a learning disability or significant developmental delay must be evaluated before interpreting this scale.[257]

Adolescent-Negative Treatment Indicators (A-trt) Scale. There are 21 items on this scale. Individuals scoring high are likely to have negative attitudes toward treatment, along with a pessimistic view of their ability to change. They are also likely to perceive talking about problems with others as not only not helpful, but also a potential sign of weakness.[258]

Usefulness of Scales

Psychologist John Graham reports that the Adolescent-Anxiety, Adolescent-Depression, Adolescent-Bizarre Mentation, and Adolescent-Social Discomfort Scales are not particularly useful because they correlate highly with the concomitant clinical scales. However, the Adolescent-Anger, Adolescent-Conduct Problems, and Adolescent-School Problems Scales are very useful because they do not correlate highly with clinical scales, indicating that they provide information not available through the clinical scales. The usefulness of the remaining content scales cannot yet be measured, as there are no relevant correlates available at this time.[259]

---

[254] *Id.* at 245.

[255] *Id.* at 246.

[256] *Id.* at 247.

[257] *Id.* at 248.

[258] Archer, MMPI-A, at 250.

[259] John Graham, Development and Validation of MMPI-A Content Scales, Paper presented at the American Psychological Association Convention (Aug. 1991).

§ 9.26   Additional Content Scales

Immaturity (Imm) Scale

Psychologist Robert Archer developed an additional Content Scale referred to as the Immaturity Scale (Imm), which is related to a lack of self-confidence, lack of insight and self-awareness, and interpersonal and social discomfort. A high score on the Immaturity Scale is correlated with greater academic difficulties and antisocial behavior as well as less involvement in school activities.[260]

Gender-Related Scales

Archer also developed the Gender Communality Masculine (GCm) and Gender Communality Feminine (GCf) Scales. There are 38 items on the GCm Scale (for example, "I like science" (True) and "I would like to be a nurse" (False). There are 57 items on the GCf Scale (for example, "I like poetry" (True) and "I like to cook" (True). Generally, individuals with a high GCm score are interested in stereotypical masculine interests and occupations and deny stereotypical feminine interests and occupations. Individuals with high GCf scores have a high interest in stereotypical feminine interests and occupations and deny stereotypical masculine interests and occupations. The GCf scale correlates negatively with the L and K Scales. Individuals with high scores on both GCg and GCm Scales were achievement-oriented and successful. Individuals with low scores on these scales had the greatest problems at school, both academically and behaviorally. It was found that females with high GCm scores had greater acting-out problems and antisocial behaviors, including problems with the law. Boys with high GCf scores sought out adults for approval and had a tendency to be dominated. In addition, they had greater dependency needs, and suicidal ideation.[261]

§ 9.27   Research on the MMPI-A

L.A.R. Stein and his co-researchers found that the MMPI-A validity scales are able to differentiate clinical from nonclinical adolescents who are faking.[262] Ruth Baer and her associates found that most adolescents acknowledged one or more random responses during the administration of the MMPI-A.[263] However, "validity scales are sensitive to all or partially random protocols, and produced high classification rates when discriminating among groups."[264]

---

[260] Robert Archer, Development of the Immaturity Scale and Gender Community Scales for the MMPI-A, Paper presented at the American Psychological Association Convention (Aug. 1991).

[261] *Id.*

[262] L.A.R. Stein et al., *Detecting Fake-Bad and Fake-Good MMPI-A Profiles,* 65 J. Personality Assessment no. 3, at 415–27 (1995).

[263] Ruth Baer et al., *Detection of Random Responding on the MMPI-A,* 68 J. Personality Assessment no. 1, at 139–51 (1997).

[264] *Id.* at 139.

Nicholas Galucci looked at a number of MMPI-A scales identified as substance abuse predictors.[265] He found that the Alcohol/Drug Problem Proneness Scale (PRO), the Alcohol/Drug Acknowledgement Scale (ACK), the MacAndrews Alcoholism Scale-Revised (MAC-R), the Substance Abuse Proclivity Scale (SAP), and the Psychopathy Scale (PSP) were all "reliable and positively correlated with therapists' rating of behavioral undercontrol and substance abuse, and negatively correlated with ratings of behavioral overcontrol."[266]

Bradley Shaevel and Robert Archer compared MMPI-2 and MMPI-A results with 18-year-olds.[267] They found that T-score elevations for 18-year-olds on the validity scales were generally lower on the MMPI-2, and with clinical scales generally higher on the MMPI-A.

Liana Pena and her associates addressed the issue of MMPI-A patterns with male juvenile delinquents.[268] The most frequently elevated scales were 4, 6, and 9, with the 4-9/9-4 profile being the most frequent 2-point code type. The least common elevations were in the 3, 5, and 0 Scales. Elevations of the 4, 6, and 9 Scales together are often indicators of dangerousness.

Redhika Krishnamurthy, Robert Archer, and Joseph House failed to find an interrelationship between the MMPI-A and the Rorschach.[269] The results have also been found in comparing the MMPI-2 and the Rorschach.

Cassandra Newsom and her research associates[270] addressed response patterns on the MMPI/MMPI-A for adolescents over a four-decade period of time. They found that the current MMPI-A normative sample produced higher scale scores on all basic clinical scales and lower scores on the validity scales than the earliest studies with adolescents. They interpret some of the results to suggest that contemporary adolescents have a more rapid personal tempo, greater psychological energy, and may feel more restless and impulsive.[271]

Need for Critical Items?

Robert Archer addressed the issue of whether critical items were needed on the MMPI-A. He concluded, "Findings suggest that it may be difficult to construct critical item lists for

---

[265] Nicholas Galucci, *Correlates of MMPI-A, Substance Abuse Scales*, 4 Assessment no. 1, at 87–94 (1997).

[266] *Id.* at 87.

[267] Bradley Shaevel & Robert Archer, *Effects of MMPI-2 and MMPI-A Norms on T-Score Elevations for 18 Year Olds*, 67 J. Personality Assessment no. 1, at 72–78 (1996).

[268] Liana Pena et al., *MMPI-A Patterns of Male Juvenile Delinquents*, 8 Psychol. Assessment no. 4, at 388–97 (1996).

[269] Radhika Krishnamurthy et al., *The MMPI-A and Rorschach: A Failure to Establish Conversion Validity*, 3 Assessment no. 1, at 179–91 (1996).

[270] Cassandra Rutledge Newsom, Robert P. Archer, Susan Trumbetta, & Irving I. Gottsman, *Changes in Adolescent Response Patterns on the MMPI/MMPI-A across Four Decades*, 81 J. Personality Assessment 74–84 (2003).

[271] *Id.* at 79.

adolescents based on the type of empirical methodology used with adults, because of the high frequency of endorsement of critical samples.[272]

Future Considerations

In a recent publication, Robert Archer addressed future considerations for the MMPI-A.[273] Archer points out that there is no sufficient 2-point code type literature on the MMPI-A at this point. He also addressed the issue of profile elevations in clinical samples as it relates to those samples and the development of new scales. He suggests that relevant research in the area of administrating the MMPI-A to 12- and 13-year-olds would be valuable. Last, he suggests that an MMPI-A structural summary approach to interpretation would be valuable and should be developed.

§ 9.28   Millon Inventory Tests

Psychologist Theodore Millon and his colleagues have developed several tests that are used by many psychologists for clinical assessments as part of diagnostic workups and treatment evaluation. The tests are based upon Millon's personal theory of personality types. When used for the purpose of assessing people in treatment, and particularly when used to identify any personality disorders that may be present in those people, they do the job fairly well. Millon describes the Millon Clinical Multiaxial Inventory (MCMI, MCMI-II, MCMI-III) as an "objective psychodynamic instrument," in that it has a format and administration like the MMPI but is to be interpreted like the Rorschach and Thematic Apperception Test on the basis of test results combined with the evaluator's clinical experience.[274]

It is problematic when the Millon Inventory tests are used in forensic evaluations rather than as an adjunct to clinical treatment. Millon's tests were standardized on people in outpatient or inpatient treatment for various psychological disorders, rather than on a normal population. As a result, the Millon instruments tend to overdiagnose psychopathology, especially personality disorders. While an advantage when diagnosing disorders, since it makes it likely a given diagnosis will not be missed, this makes them largely inappropriate for use in forensic evaluations, since they are very likely to make an individual seem more pathological than he or she actually is.

Nevertheless, because psychologists do often use the Millon instruments in their evaluations, it is necessary for the attorney to be aware of the nature of those instruments and the pros and cons of each.

---

[272] Robert Archer, Are Critical Items "Critical" for the MMPI-A?, Paper presented at the 100th Annual Meeting of the American Psychological Association 1, Washington, D.C. (1992).

[273] Archer, *Future Directions,* at 95–109.

[274] Theodore Millon & Roger Davis, Disorders of Personality: DSM-IV and Beyond 157 (1996) [hereinafter Millon & Davis, Disorders of Personality].

§ 9.29   Millon Clinical Multiaxial Inventory

The Millon Clinical Multiaxial Inventory (MCMI) was published by Millon in 1983 and was modeled after MMPI-type inventories. It was designed to coordinate its diagnostic categories with the third edition of the *Diagnostic and Statistical Manual of Mental Disorders* (DSM-III). As indicated, it tended to overpathologize, leading psychologist Scott Wetzler to write that "the MCMI should not be given to normal subjects. The test was intended to differentiate psychiatric patients from one another. To make discriminations among psychiatric patients, it is necessary to have a level of resolving power that overpathologizes certain personality disorders."[275]

§ 9.30   Millon Clinical Multiaxial Inventory–II

While psychologists ordinarily stop using an older form of a test within at most a few years of the publication of a new edition, that principle does not apply to the MCMI-II. Because the MCMI-III is so different from the MCMI-II (over half of the items were changed), many psychologists continue to use the MCMI-II rather than the MCMI-III. We are therefore presenting a substantial amount of information on both the MCMI-II and the MCMI-III.

The MCMI-II was a 1987 revision of the MCMI, designed to address some of the published criticisms of the MCMI and to coordinate its diagnostic categories with the 1987 revision of the *Diagnostic and Statistical Manual of Mental Disorders*, DSM-III-R. Because it both replaced and improved on the MCMI, and because it continues to be used by a number of psychologists (including 34 percent of psychologists surveyed regarding tests used in child custody evaluations who used the MCMI-II or III[276]), it will be discussed at greater length.

The MCMI-II has 22 measures of personality disorders and clinical syndromes, an increase of two over the MCMI. Although it still consists of 175 items, 45 are new or reworded. Five of the clinical scales are new, as are three correction scale scores. An item-weighting system has also been added. The normative data are based on inpatients and outpatients in clinics, hospitals, and private practices throughout the United States. The minimum age group is people over 17 years of age. The required reading level is at the eighth-grade level.

Among the findings of research on the MCMI-II are the following:

*   It significantly underdiagnosed Major Depression.[277]
*   It was relatively accurate in the diagnosis of Borderline Personality Disorders.[278]

---

[275] Scott Wetzler, *The Millon Clinical Multiaxial Inventory (MCMI): A Review*, 55 J. Personality Assessment 458 (1990).

[276] Marc J. Ackerman & Melissa C. Ackerman, *Custody Evaluation Practices: A Survey of Experienced Professionals*, 28 Prof. Psychol.: Res. & Prac. 137, 140 (1997).

[277] Harry L. Piersma, *The MCMI-II Depression Scales: Do They Assist in the Differential Prediction of Depressive Disorders?*, 56 J. Personality Assessment 478–86 (1991).

[278] Joseph McCann et al., *MCMI-II Diagnosis of Borderline Personality Disorder: Base Rates vs. Prototypic Items*, 58 J. Personality Assessment 105, 110–11 (1992).

- A high score on a scale is not, *per se*, an indication of a disorder. Rather, it is an indication of a personality *style*, which may be either functional or dysfunctional for the individual. If a personality style suggested by the MCMI has not led to distress and/or dysfunction, it should not be considered evidence of a disorder.[279]

- While the MMPI was better at discriminating Axis I (see **Chapter 17**) clinical syndromes, the MCMI-II's clinical syndrome scales correlated highly with the analogous scales of the MMPI except in the case of the Delusional Disorders Scale.[280]

- The personality disorder scales of the MCMI-II (except for the Obsessive-Compulsive Scale) have convergent validity with the MMPI, but the MMPI scales corresponded better to DSM-III-R categories. Even so, while the MMPI should be used to diagnose Axis I disorders, the MCMI-II may be more useful in addressing personality disorders.[281]

- Of the validity scales (Validity (VI), Disclosure Scale (DIS), Desirability Gauge Scale (DES), Debasement Measure (DEB)), none does well at identifying "fake-good" malingerers, the pattern that would be most important in custody evaluations.[282] Using a cutoff of one for the Validity Scale leads to a large error rate, but using a VI of 0 reduces the error rate to 7 percent.[283]

- Two reviews of the MCMI-II appear in the *Eleventh Mental Measurements Yearbook*. The first indicates that the test has a number of virtues, but the validation data is dated, the construct validity is "unclear," and technical difficulties remain.[284] The second finds good construct validity and praises its thorough evaluation of Axis II disorders but indicates concern that full use of the test requires knowledge of Millon's approach to personality, and that the test was normed on people referred for clinical evaluation rather than on the general population. Furthermore, the reference groups of those age 56 or older, or black, or Hispanic may be too small to permit the test to be used with these populations. The test also focuses exclusively on weaknesses, and there is no database that would permit the test to be used with nonclinical populations. "Clinicians must be extremely careful in using the MCMI-II with nonclinical populations such as in child custody evaluations, foster-parent studies, employment testing in all settings . . . , and in criminal forensic work."[285]

---

[279] Gary Groth-Marnat, Handbook of Psychological Assessment 313 (John Wiley & Sons 2003).

[280] Joseph McCann, *A Multitrait-Multimethod Analysis of the MCMI-II Clinical Syndrome Scales*, 55 J. Personality Assessment 465–76 (1990).

[281] Joseph McCann, *Convergent and Discriminant Validity of the MCMI-II and MMPI Personality Disorder Scales*, 3 Psychol. Assessment: J. Consulting & Clinical Psychol. 9–18 (1991).

[282] Paul Retzlaff et al., *MCMI-II Report Style and Bias: Profile and Validity Scales Analyses*, 56 J. Personality Assessment (1991).

[283] R. Michael Bagby et al., *Effectiveness of the Millon Clinical Multiaxial Inventory Validity, in the Detection of Random Responding,* 3 Psychol. Assessment: J Consulting & Clinical Psychol. 285–87 (1991).

[284] Thomas Haladyna, *Millon Clinical Multiaxial Inventory–II, in* Eleventh Mental Measurements Yearbook 530 (Jack Kramer & Jane Close Conoley eds., 1992).

[285] Cecil Reynolds, *Millon Clinical Multiaxial Inventory–II, in* Eleventh Mental Measurements Yearbook 533–34 (Jack Kramer & Jane Close Conoley eds., 1992).

- The test is "normed on and intended to be used for a clinical population. When used for other assessment purposes, the MCMI-II must be interpreted extremely cautiously because of its tendency to . . . greatly [exaggerate] psychopathology."[286]

- The MCMI-II has higher convergent validity than did the MCMI, but good discriminant validity was found for only five scales.[287]

- Despite the above concerns, researchers Joseph McCann and Frank Dyer note that the MCMI-II can offer the psychologist useful information in a child custody evaluation regarding the personality and clinical symptoms of the parents that may affect the psychological environment of the child.[288] They respond to the criticism that the MCMI-II was standardized on a clinical rather than normal population by noting that many parents in custody battles do have identifiable psychopathology, and that some couples with relationship difficulties were present in the normative samples. They also indicate that Millon's caution against using the MCMI-II "with normals refers to applications as a self-exploration tool and in personnel selection." They also note that no particular codes or scale elevations are directly translatable into parenting styles or abilities, and that parents are expected to try to present themselves positively by minimizing disclosure and giving answers with a high degree of social desirability.[289] The authors of this text continue to believe that the MCMI-II is inappropriate for use in child custody evaluations.

§ 9.31   Millon Clinical Multiaxial Inventory–III

The MCMI-III was published in 1994, to coordinate with the publication of the fourth edition of the *Diagnostic and Statistical Manual of Mental Disorders* (DSM-IV). Based on research since the MCMI-II was published, 90 of the 175 items were changed, the weighting of items was changed, and the number of items per scale was reduced. According to psychologist Thomas Will, the MCMI-III should not be used in child custody evaluations, as the test will make the parents appear more pathological than they likely are. The only exception would be if other data clearly indicated psychopathology, in which case the MCMI-III could be used with great caution.[290] Similarly, the test manual states that "[t]he MCMI-III is not a general personality instrument to be used for normal populations or for any purpose other than diagnostic screening or clinical assessment."[291] Some research with

---

[286] Hollida Wakefield & Ralph Underwager, *Misuse of Psychological Tests in Forensic Settings: Some Horrible Examples,* 11 Am. J. Forensic Psychol. 55, 61 (1993).

[287] Richard Rogers et al., Convergent and Discriminant Validity of the Millon Clinical Multiaxial Inventory for Axis II Disorders: Time for a Moratorium?, Paper presented at the 105th Annual Convention of the American Psychological Association, Chicago (Aug. 1997).

[288] Joseph T. McCann & Frank J. Dyer, Forensic Assessment with the Millon Inventories 118 (1996).

[289] *Id.* at 118–19.

[290] Thomas Will, The MCMI-III and Personality Disorders, Paper presented at the 1994 Fall Conference of the Wisconsin Psychological Association, Madison, Wis. (Nov. 18, 1994).

[291] Theodore Millon et al., MCMI-III Manual: Millon Clinical Multiaxial Inventory–III 5 (1994).

normal subjects has found that they score higher than psychiatric patients on some scales, further indicating that the test should not be administered to normals.[292]

A 1996 study by psychologist Paul Retzlaff found that the predictive validity (the percentage of patients with scores above the cutoff who in fact have the indicated disorder) of the MCMI-III was poor, ranging from .00 to .32 for personality disorders and from .15 to .58 for Axis I disorders.[293]

In a paper presented at the 1997 Convention of the American Psychological Association, psychologists Richard Rogers, Randall Salekin, and Kenneth Sewell reviewed Millon's study of the convergent and discriminant validity of the MCMI-III. They found that the MCMI-III has very low convergent and discriminant validity, as well as corresponding poorly to clinical diagnosis; and they recommend against *any* use of the test outside research projects, given the ethical mandate that only adequately validated instruments be used in clinical practice.[294]

There is insufficient validity data on the MCMI-III to use it in forensic evaluations, according to two of the most active MCMI researchers, McCann and Dyer, who have written a book entitled *Forensic Assessment with the Millon Inventories.*[295] Instead, the MCMI-II should be used until validity data on the MCMI-III becomes sufficient to justify its use.

The Millon Clinical Multiaxial Inventory-II and III (MCMI-II, MCMI-III) continue to be among the most frequently used tests in evaluation of adults in child custody actions.[296] Research continues to raise substantial questions regarding the appropriateness of this use. The *Thirteenth Mental Measurements Yearbook* includes two reviews of the MCMI-III. The first is by psychologist Allen Hess, Distinguished Research Professor and Department Head, Department of Psychology, Auburn University at Montgomery, Montgomery, Alabama. He indicates that the MCMI-III is not psychometrically sound, because of (1) a lack of information on the true base rates of personality disorders in the general population and about the clinicians who did ratings, raising questions regarding the reliability and validity of the categories utilized in the test; (2) numerous problems with the item content, including too many items keyed "true" and having too many items appear on more than one scale, compromising statistical analysis of the data; and (3) inadequate differentiation

---

[292] Anne Anastasi & Susan Urbina, Psychological Testing 369 (1997) [hereinafter Anastasi & Urbina].

[293] Paul Retzlaff, *MCMI-III Diagnostic Validity: Bad Test or Bad Validity Study*, 66 J. Personality Assessment 431–37 (1996).

[294] Richard Rogers et al., Convergent and Discriminant Validity of the Millon Clinical Multiaxial Inventory for Axis II Disorders: Time for a Moratorium?, Paper presented at the 105th Annual Convention of the American Psychological Association, Chicago (Aug. 1997).

[295] Joseph T. McCann & Frank J. Dyer, Forensic Assessment with the Millon Inventories 3 (1996).

[296] Marc J. Ackerman & Melissa Ackerman, *Child Custody Evaluation Practices: A 1996 Survey of Psychologists*, 30 Fam. L.Q. 565–86 (1996); Marc J. Ackerman & Melissa Ackerman, *Custody Evaluation Practices: A Survey of Experienced Professionals (Revisited)*, 28 Prof. Psychol.: Res. & Prac. 137–45 (1997); K.A. LaFortune & B.N. Carpenter, *Custody Evaluations: A Survey of Mental Health Professionals*, 16 Behav. Sci. L. 207–24 (1998); James N. Bow & Francella A. Quinnell, *Psychologists' Current Practices and Procedures in Child Custody Evaluations: Five Years after American Psychological Association Guidelines*, 32 Prof. Psychol.: Res. & Prac. 261–68 (2001); Margaret A. Hagen & Nicole Castagna, *The Real Numbers: Psychological Testing in Custody Evaluations*, 32 Prof. Psychol.: Res. & Prac. 269–71 (2001).

among disorders, with a low sensitivity (ability to correctly identify people who have a disorder, with scales ranging from 12.5 percent to 53.1 percent and a mean sensitivity of 36.26 percent, i.e., error rates from 46.9 to 87.5 percent and a mean error rate of 63.74 percent) at the lowest level of pathology (the "trait" or "features" level), and worse at a diagnostic level of severity.[297] Given the test's inability to accurately diagnose, its strong tendency to exaggerate psychopathology, its minimal likelihood of identifying anyone taking it as "normal," and its poor psychometric soundness, Hess concludes that "the user of the MCMI-III does so at his or her own risk."[298]

The second review is by psychologist Paul Retzlaff, Professor, Psychology Department, University of Northern Colorado, Greeley, Colorado. Retzlaff's review is nearly 180 degrees opposite that of Hess's. He indicates that the test is "not only clinically useful but psychometrically the most sophisticated of any available product."[299] He does indicate that there is a problem associated with having only 175 items when the test derives 24 content scales, a reference to the number of items that appear on more than one scale. Retzlaff indicates that the internal consistency and reliability of the test are very high, as is the criterion validity. He also indicates that the positive predictive power of the test, based on the research done for the 1997 revision of the manual, ranges from the .50s to the .70s (i.e., error rates from the .30s to the .50s). He concludes that "the MCMI-III is a clinically useful, well-constructed, and sophisticated test. It is particularly useful to diagnose the relatively difficult personality disorders."[300]

Psychologist Anita Lampel evaluated the use of the MCMI-III in child custody evaluations. The test protocols of 50 couples were analyzed. It was found that 64 of the 100 parents had significant elevations on the defensiveness scale. Despite their defensiveness, 84 had elevations on one or more of the clinical scales. The author notes[301] that "litigating parents test with personality difficulties at a high rate compared to a nonclinical population."[302]

Psychologist Robert Craig wrote about testimony based on the MCMI-II and III. He notes that the "the MCMI was normed on patients being treated or evaluated in mental health settings. The normative clinical groups included about 10% of patients in forensic settings, but this does not mean that the MCMI was normed or validated for use in forensic settings."[303] The only forensic areas for which there is a literature base, he indicates, are with regard to substance abuse and Post-Traumatic Stress Disorder. He further indicates that "the test was not intended for use with nonclinical (e.g., normal) patients, and using the MCMI with this population tends to inaccurately describe and to overpathologize these

---

[297] Allen Hess, *Millon Clinical Multiaxial Inventory–III, in* James C. Impara & Barbara S. Plake, The Thirteenth Mental Measurements Yearbook 667 (Univ. of Neb.-Lincoln 1998) [hereinafter Hess].

[298] *Id.* at 665–67.

[299] Paul Retzlaff, *Millon Clinical Multiaxial Inventory–III*, in James C. Impara & Barbara S. Plake, The Thirteenth Mental Measurements Yearbook 667 (Univ. of Neb.-Lincoln 1998).

[300] *Id.* at 667–68.

[301] Anita Lampel, *Use of the Millon Clinical Multiaxial Inventory–III in Evaluating Child Custody Litigants,* 17 Am. J. Forensic Psychol. 19–31 (1999).

[302] *Id.* at 27.

[303] Robert J. Craig, *Testimony Based on the Millon Clinical Multiaxial Inventory: Review, Commentary, and Guidelines*, 73 J. Personality Assessment 290–304, at 291 (1999).

groups."[304] He indicates that the limited research with a normal population finds that "non-clinical patients usually attain their highest elevations, often in 'clinical ranges' . . . on the Histrionic (4), Narcissistic (5) and Compulsive (7)" scales. That is, people with no known psychopathology may still score in the pathological range on the test.[305]

Psychologist James Schutte discussed the use of the MCMI-III in forensic evaluations. He indicates that "it is worth noting that unlike the MMPI-2 there are no non-clinical norms for the MCMI-III, and as such, the instrument's use is not recommended for individuals for whom assessment of pathology is not of interest (e.g., career choice counseling, self-exploration, executive coaching)."[306] He cautions that "assessing individuals who are likely to vary greatly from the normative sample runs the risk of overpathologizing. . . . [C]aution is advised in child custody . . . litigation."[307] He also notes that most of the MCMI-III test questions are "keyed positive," so that an individual must endorse many pathological traits in order to get a high score. He suggests mentioning this fact and that the individual being evaluated may be similar to the normative sample when a psychologist is questioned regarding the test's overdiagnosing of pathology.[308]

Psychologists Richard Rogers, Randall Salekin and Kenneth Sewell addressed whether the MCMI meets the *Daubert*[309] standard. They note that other authors have recommended against using the MCMI-III in forensic assessments, and indicate that they concur, while adding "serious concerns about the diagnostic accuracy and construct validity of the MCMI-III."[310] They discuss the very substantial differences in content of the MCMI, the MCMI-II, and the MCMI-III, and indicate that each test is a new instrument, not simply a revision of the previous version. They indicate that research has established a false-positive rate for the MCMI-III of 82 percent—that is, of 100 tests administered, 82 will indicate psychopathology that is in fact not present. False-negatives, in contrast, are rare: only 7 percent of individuals for whom the test indicates a lack of psychopathology will in fact have serious psychological problems. The authors also indicate that the MCMI-III does not meet established standards for construct validity. Although the MCMI-II (the previous version of the test) has some limited utility for diagnosing three personality disorders (Avoidant, Schizotypal, and Borderline Personality Disorders), it has virtually no database of research in forensic areas, and should not be utilized in forensic matters.[311]

The article by Rogers *et al.* was commented upon by three articles in a later issue of the same journal. In the first, psychologists Frank Dyer and Joseph McCann indicate that Rogers *et al.* missed some important published research, particularly research contained in the 1997 revision of the MCMI-III manual, and suggest that MCMI-II and III have more

---

[304] *Id.* at 292.

[305] *Id.* at 295.

[306] James W. Schutte, *Using the MCMI-III in Forensic Evaluations*, 19 Am. J. Forensic Psychol. 5–20, at 6 (2000).

[307] *Id.* at 15.

[308] *Id.* at 16.

[309] Daubert v. Merrell Dow Pharms., 509 U.S. 579 (1993).

[310] Richard, Rogers, Randall T. Salekin, & Kenneth W. Sewell, *Validation of the Millon Clinical Multiaxial Inventory for Axis II Disorders: Does It Meet the* Daubert *Standard?*, 23 Law & Hum. Behav. 425–43 (1999).

[311] *Id.* at 439.

validity than Rogers *et al.* identified.[312] Dyer and McCann also identify criminal case law that refers to personality disorders as relevant to an individual's culpability for a crime. They suggest that the MCMI-III can provide "very useful data that can inform consideration of forensically related issues, including substance abuse, posttraumatic stress disorder, domestic violence, [and] violence risk assessment."[313]

The second article is by psychologist Paul Retzlaff. He was concerned that Rogers *et al.* had not included information from the 1997 revision of the MCMI-III manual that supported the validity of the test. He also indicated that the number of scales with "positive predictive power" has risen from the three indicated by Rogers *et al.* to 11 of the 14 personality disorder scales.[314]

The third article is a rejoinder by Rogers *et al.*[315] They indicated that Dyer and McCann appear to accept that the MCMI, MCMI-II, and MCMI-III are substantially different instruments, so that conclusions about one cannot be generalized to the others. Dyer and McCann also appear to have accepted the conclusions of Rogers *et al.* about the MCMI falling below the standards of the *Daubert* requirements, and did not argue with the allegations regarding the lack of content validity of the MCMI-III.

With regard to the 1997 revision of the MCMI-III manual, Rogers *et al.* indicate concern that (1) clinicians were free to decide whether to participate in the research, free to decide which of their cases to refer for inclusion, and free to decide whether to consult other clinicians to ensure the reliability of their conclusions—each a violation of normal research protocols. Rogers *et al.* indicate that none of the six studies cited by Dyer and McCann as "forensic studies" are in fact forensic studies. Rogers *et al.* acknowledge their oversight in failing to include a review of the revised MCMI-III manual. They indicate that a review of that revision indicates that (1) their previous statement regarding a lack of construct validity remains accurate, (2) there is a new concern about the normative group, with the original group of 998 patients being eliminated and a much smaller sample of 321 patients replacing it, and, therefore, (3) some of the diagnostic categories now have too few patients to permit great generalizability. Rogers *et al.* note that the revised manual claims an increase in "positive prediction" from .18 in the original manual to .70 in the new manual. The reason, they indicate, is that the test author eliminated the objective criterion of a base rate equal to or greater than 85, substituting a criterion of the "percentage of patients having a particular MCMI-III personality scale as the highest in their profile."[316] This criterion could allow an MCMI-III score that falls well below the cutoff for significance to be accepted as correct so long as it is the highest score. Recalculating the positive predictability from the data in the manual, Rogers *et al.* indicate that the correct figure is

---

[312] Frank J. Dyer & Joseph T. McCann, *The Millon Clinical Inventories, Research Critical of Their Forensic Application, and Daubert Criteria*, 24 Law & Hum. Behav. 487–97 (2000).

[313] *Id.* at 490.

[314] Paul D. Retzlaff, *Comment on the Validity of the MCMI-III*, 24 Law & Hum. Behav. 499–500 (2000).

[315] Richard Rogers, Randall T. Salekin, & Kenneth W. Sewell, *The MCMI-III and the* Daubert *Standard: Separating Rhetoric from Reality*, 24 Law & Hum. Behav. 501–06 (2000).

[316] T. Millon, R. Davis, & C. Millon, The Millon Clinical Multiaxial Inventory–III Manual 98 (2d ed.) National Computer Sys. (1997).

.31—that is, the test is wrong two out of three times. Further, Rogers *et al.* indicate that Millon *et al.* violated a fundamental rule of test validation by encouraging contributing clinicians to include MCMI-III protocols already in those clinicians' files, so that the clinicians may recall aspects of the test results while attempting to render an "independent" opinion regarding the validity of the test. Permitting a rater to have any knowledge of test scores is called "criterion contamination." Rogers *et al.* reassert their conclusion that the MCMI-III is not appropriate for forensic work and does not meet the *Daubert* criterion for admissibility in court.[317]

Psychologist Robert Halon notes that the highest MCMI-III scales for child custody litigants tend to be Scales Y (Desirability), 4 (Histrionic), 5 (Narcissistic), and 7 (Compulsive). These must be interpreted in the context of the individual's life circumstances, that is, involvement in litigation in which each parent wants to be seen as the "best" parent. These litigants would be expected to be defensive, to give socially desirable responses, to be self-centered, to put their best feet forward, and to toot their own horns. Rather than indicating psychopathology, the elevation of these scales may be due to the custody litigation rather than to any long-term personality characteristics of the litigants. Yet the MCMI-III implies that psychopathology is present by virtue of the way it is scored and interpreted.[318]

Joseph McCann, a psychologist and attorney, indicates that the MCMI-III *does* meet the *Daubert* criteria for admissibility. He cites one 1989 court case that accepted the MCMI under the *Frye* test and indicates that other courts have also accepted versions of the MCMI. He also notes that Ackerman and Ackerman (1997) indicated that the MCMI-II or III was widely used in custody litigation. He also notes that there has been substantial peer review, some positive and some negative, regarding these tests. The tests also have a standardized method for administration and scoring. He indicates that the MCMI-III has been demonstrated to have both validity and clinical utility, though indicating that research is still needed to address alleged criterion contamination. He acknowledges that in a prior study,[319] he and his co-authors had investigated whether the MCMI-III overpathologizes child custody examinees. They found that Scales 4, 5, and 7 did overpathologize, and they recommended adjustments that evaluators can make to make false-positive errors less likely. That study also found significant elevations on Scale Y, indicating socially desirable responding. No published research to date has indicated whether child custody evaluators who use the MCMI-III in fact make those adjustments, or even recognize the need for making them. He also recommends that forensic evaluators should never rely solely on MCMI-III results, that conclusions should be drawn only after integrating that data with other test data, clinical history, third-party reports, and various records that may be reviewed in a given case. He also recommends against using the computer-generated

---

[317] Richard Rogers, Randall T. Salekin, & Kenneth W. Sewell, *The MCMI-III and the* Daubert *Standard: Separating Rhetoric from Reality*, 24 Law & Hum. Behav. 501–06 (2000).

[318] Robert L. Halon, *The Millon Clinical Multiaxial Inventory–III: The Normal Quartet in Child Custody Cases*, 19 Am. J. Forensic Psychol. 57–75 (2001).

[319] Joseph T. McCann, Jay R. Flens, Vicky Camnpagna, P. Collman, T. Lazzaro, & E. Connor, *The MCMI-III in Child Custody Evaluations: A Normative Study*, 1 J. Forensic Psychol. Prac. 27–44 (2001).

interpretive reports, which sometimes include "incorrect or misleading" information about the test taker.[320]

Psychologist Daniel J. Hynan indicates that, while there is no significant difference between the raw scores of men and women on the MCMI-III on the Desirability, Histrionic, Narcissistic, and Compulsive Scales, there *are* significant differences in the Base Rate scores assigned to the raw scores on the latter three of those scales. As a result, women will score as significantly more pathological on those three scales than will men. Hynan concludes that "practitioners need to be particularly cautious about using the MCMI-III personality disorder scales in custody evaluations. . . . Also, the likelihood that an individual will be found normal on the MCMI-III is relatively small."[321]

Psychologist Gary Groth-Marnat reviewed the MCMI-II and MCMI-III and the arguments for and against use of the tests in various settings. He concludes that "the MCMI is intended for psychiatric populations and should not be used with normal persons or those who are merely mildly disturbed."[322] Further concerns are that the MCMI "overdiagnoses and overpathologizes," and that the computerized interpretation of the tests suggests that moderate scale elevations (less than BR=75) may be interpreted and that DSM diagnoses (see **Chapter 17**) can be made on the basis of MCMI scores. "Thus, the MCMI [tests] should be used only with clinical populations."[323]

We know some excellent clinicians for whom we have a great deal of respect who continue to use the MCMI-II or III in child custody evaluations. We trust that they are very careful in their interpretations, and that they do not mischaracterize the people they evaluate. Even so, the overwhelming weight of the evidence is that the MCMI (all forms) is not appropriate for a normal (non-patient) population. Further, given the continued evidence that the MCMI-II and MCMI-III overpathologize, the continued lack of a normal comparison group, and the evidence that the test does not meet the *Daubert* criterion for admissibility in court, the present authors continue to strongly recommend against using the MCMI in any of its versions in a child custody evaluation.

§ 9.32   Millon Adolescent Clinical Inventory

The Millon Adolescent Clinical Inventory (MACI) was developed as a revision of the Millon Adolescent Personality Inventory (MAPI), with 111 of the 160 items being new or rewritten. The MAPI was used in child custody evaluations by 11 percent of psychologists surveyed by Ackerman and Ackerman.[324] The MACI was published in 1993. Unfortunately, unlike the

---

[320] Joseph T. McCann, *Guidelines for Forensic Application of the MCMI-III*, 2 J. Forensic Psychol. Prac. 55–69 (2002).

[321] Daniel J. Hynan, *Unsupported General Differences on Some Personality Disorder Scales of the Millon Clinical Multiaxial Inventory-III*, 35 Prof. Psychol.: Res. & Prac. 105–110, at 108 (2004).

[322] Gary Groth-Marnat, Handbook of Psychological Assessment 313 (John Wiley & Sons 2003).

[323] *Id.* at 323.

[324] Marc Ackerman & Melissa Ackerman, *Child Custody Evaluation Practices: A Survey of Experienced Professionals (Revisited)*, 28 Prof. Psychol.: Res. & Prac. no. 2, at 137–45 (1997) [hereinafter Ackerman & Ackerman (1997)].

MAPI, which was standardized on both clinical and normal samples, the MACI is standardized only on "adolescents in various clinical treatment settings." It is to be used solely for adolescents (ages 13 to 19) in clinical settings. It consists of 160 true-false items, written at a sixth-grade reading level, and was designed to be compatible with the DSM-IV.[325]

The MACI was reviewed in the *Twelfth Mental Measurements Yearbook*. The first review, by psychologist Paul Retzlaff of the University of Northern Colorado, indicates that the MACI "is intended for 'disturbed' adolescents who have come to the attention of clinical professionals. It is not appropriate for screening or for the assessment of 'normal' personality."[326] The second review, by psychologist Richard Stuart of the University of Washington, indicates that all of the adolescents in the standardization sample "were in treatment programs. Adolescents who were not identified as patients were not included in the normative sample, thus limiting the utility of the MACI for use as a screening tool with general adolescent populations."[327] There is some useful literature regarding juvenile offenders,[328] but it is not of value in child custody evaluations.

§ 9.33   Millon Index of Personality Styles–Revised

Millon *has* made an attempt to measure the normal personality, in contrast with the above clinical inventories. However, there is no data presently available regarding its potential for use in forensic cases. It is not discussed at all in McCann and Dyer's book, *Forensic Assessment with the Millon Inventories*. We cannot recommend that the Millon Index of Personality Styles (MIPS) be used in forensic evaluations but do want readers to know that it exists.

The MIPS was published in 1994 and is designed to assess the "normal range" personality. It is designed to be used with adults age 18 and older, and was normed on both college students and adults. It is designed to assess "clients in general counseling but without diagnosable psychopathology . . . , undergoing career, transition, outplacement, or personnel selection . . . , and individuals who need screening for general maladjustment (e.g., testing military recruits for emotional fitness for duty)." It is designed to appraise personality styles rather than psychopathology.[329] No assertions have been made regarding its potential for use in forensic cases.

The MIPS-R came out in 2003. It has updated scale names and is meant to be easier to use than the MIPS. It continues to be recommended for individuals 18 and

---

[325] National Computer Systems, *MACI: Millon Adolescent Clinical Inventory,* Winter 1997 Catalog 54–55.

[326] Paul Retzlaff, *Millon Adolescent Clinical Inventory, in* Twelfth Mental Measurements Yearbook 621 (Jane Close Conoley & James C. Impara eds., 1995).

[327] Richard Stuart, *Millon Adolescent Clinical Inventory, in* Twelfth Mental Measurements Yearbook 620, 622 (Jane Close Conoley & James C. Impara eds., 1995).

[328] *E.g.,* Randall Salekin *Factor-Analysis of the Millon Adolescent Clinical Inventory in a Juvenile Offender Population: Implications for Treatment,* 34 J. Offender Rehabilitation 15–29 (2002).

[329] MIPS: Millon Index of Personality Styles, Brochure from The Psychological Corporation (1994); Millon & Davis, Disorders of Personality, at 163–64.

older, who have at least an eighth-grade reading level. Normative groups include adults in general or college students, and are available with genders combined or separate. The normative sample consisted of 1,000 adults ages 18 to 65, following the U.S. Census indications of race and educational level. Because the test is new, it should not be used in forensic evaluations.[330]

§ 9.34   Millon: Conclusion

Although the Millon tests may have significant utility when used by clinicians in clinical settings for clinical purposes, their lack of a normal standardization sample makes them generally inappropriate for use in a forensic evaluation. The present authors cannot, therefore, recommend their use in civil forensic evaluations.

§ 9.35   California Psychological Inventory–Third Edition

The California Psychological Inventory (CPI) draws nearly half its items from the MMPI but is designed to be used with a normal population. The current edition is the third, published in 1996. It has 434 items, which are answered "true" or "false." This is a decrease from the 462 in the previous edition, with items having been deleted that were found objectionable to many respondents or that were thought to violate the Americans with Disabilities Act of 1990. There are 20 scales, including three validity scales and 17 that assess such personality dimensions as Dominance, Sociability, Responsibility, Empathy, and Independence. As with the MMPI-2, scores are presented as standard scores with a mean of 50 and a standard deviation of 10. The normative sample consisted of 3,000 each of males and females, and is representative of the general population with regard to age, socioeconomic status, and geography. Norms are offered for females, for males, and for both genders combined.[331]

The CPI was used by fewer than 3 percent of psychologists in the survey of child custody practices conducted by Ackerman and Ackerman.[332] Although it may have some utility in forensic evaluations by virtue of its being standardized on a normal population, it does not appear that it has much to add to the MMPI-2 and other tests more regularly used in these evaluations.

§ 9.36   Sixteen Personality Factor Questionnaire

The Sixteen Personality Factor Questionnaire (16 PF) is now in its fifth edition, with updated language, a reduction in gender, cultural, and racial bias, and normative data

---

[330] MIPS-Revised, accessed at publisher's web site, www.personassessments.com/tests/mips.htm, on Aug. 23, 2004.

[331] Anastasi & Urbina at 359–60.

[332] Ackerman & Ackerman (1997).

reflective of the 1990 U.S. Census regarding gender, age, and race. It is for use with individuals age 16 and older, and has a reading level of fifth grade. It yields five Global Factors
(Extraversion, Anxiety, Tough-Mindedness, Independence, and Self-Control), as well as
individual factors such as warmth, reasoning ability, emotional stability, and dominance.[333]
The fifth edition has improved internal consistency and test-retest reliability, and has added
three scales identifying response styles (acquiescence, random responding, and social
desirability).[334] There is an updated normative sample of more than 10,000 adults, based
on the 2000 U.S. Census, available from the test publisher.[335] The 16 PF is primarily used
in business and career assessments, though it was also used by 8 percent of the psychologists who reported on child custody evaluation practices in the Ackerman and Ackerman
study.[336] Although its standardization on a normal population gives it some potential to be
used in forensic evaluations, it is far less useful than are the MMPI-2 and other objective
and projective tests.

§ 9.37   Questions for Chapter 9

An attorney should not expect merely to go into court and ask all of the questions listed
below. Preparation is necessary, referring to the content of the chapter to determine
whether a particular question applies to the case. The section number at the end of some
of the questions refers to the place in this chapter where readers can find an explanation of
why the particular question may be important.

1. Did the psychologist ask the subject for an explanation of the critical items on the
   MMPI-2? See § **9.9.**

2. Did the examiner look at the L-F-K Profile? See § **9.6.**

3. During interpretation, did the examiner take into account the fact that Scales 3, 4, and
   6 are the most frequently elevated scales on the MMPI-2 in child custody cases? See
   § **9.16.**

4. Were the Harris-Lingoes subscales examined to determine why the underlying
   clinical scale was elevated? See § **9.7.**

5. Is there a "real life" explanation for elevations on any of the clinical scales? See
   § **9.16.**

6. If Scale 6 (Paranoia) was elevated, is it in any way related to how the custody dispute has been handled (private investigators used, funds cut off, ongoing negative
   communication, etc.)? See § **9.16.**

7. Did the examiner look at how elevations on the content scales may be related to what
   is occurring in the custody case? See § **9.16.**

---

[333] 16 PF: Fifth Edition, Pamphlet from IPAT, the publisher (undated).

[334] Anastasi & Urbina at 364.

[335] Thanos Patelis, *What's New*, 24 The Score 8–9 (2002).

[336] Ackerman & Ackerman (1997).

8. If the OH (Overcontrolled Hostility) Scale was elevated, what are the inferences that can be drawn from this elevation? See § **9.16.**

9. Did the examiner appropriately interpret the MacAndrews Alcoholism Scale–Revised? See § **9.10.**

10. Was the MMPI-2 administered in the office or taken home? See **2.13?**

11. Is the examiner conversant about MMPI-2 research specifically in custody cases? See § **9.16.**

12. If computerized scoring was utilized, did the examiner do so appropriately? See § **9.4.**

13. Did the examiner understand ethnic differences on the MMPI-2? See § **9.17.**

14. If both the MMPI-2 and the Rorschach were administered, does the examiner understand the relationship between the two? See § **9.18.**

15. Has the examiner administered the MMPI-A only to individuals ages 14 through 18? See § **9.21.**

16. If the examiner has administered any of the Millon Instruments, is the examiner familiar with their limitations? See §§ **9.28** through **9.34.**

CHAPTER 10

PROJECTIVE PERSONALITY TESTING

§ 10.1   Overview

Projective tests are "psychologic diagnostic tests in which the test material is unstructured so that any response will reflect a projection of some aspect of the subject's underlying personality and psychopathology."[1] Prior to the availability of projective tests, psychologists relied on personality questionnaires or inventories for information. These "tests" asked the individual to indicate "yes," "no," or "uncertain" regarding specified thoughts or feelings— for example, "Are your feelings easily hurt?" Because the meaning of the items was readily apparent, it was easy for individuals to falsify their responses to present the picture they wanted to be seen. This changed with the advent of projective tests, wherein the individual taking the test had to respond to ambiguous, unstructured stimuli by providing his or her own structure. Because in projective tests it is not generally obvious which responses are normal or abnormal, the individual is likely to be less self-conscious while taking the test and is much less able to manipulate the test.[2]

---

[1] American Psychiatric Dictionary 168 (Jane E. Edgerton & Robert J. Campbell III eds., 7th ed. 1994).

[2] Bernstein, *Psychological Testing: II. The Rorschach Test*, 1 J. Children's Asthma Res. Inst. & Hosp. (Sept. 1961) [hereinafter *Psychological Testing: II*]; Anne Anastasi & Susan Urbina, Psychological Testing 411 (7th ed. 1997) [hereinafter Anastasi & Urbina].

Although many existing tests and instruments would fit under the definition of projective tests, three particular tests are widely used: the Rorschach inkblot test (Rorschach), the Thematic Apperception Test (TAT), and the Children's Apperception Test (CAT). In addition, many psychologists use projective drawings and sentence completion tests as additional sources of information and hypotheses.

Interpretation of Projective Tests

Projective tests tend to be interpreted in either of two different ways. In the first, specific criteria can be applied to most tests to elicit quantitative information about the content of the individual's responses—in other words, the tests can be scored. This is sometimes helpful in defining how common or uncommon the individual's responses are, or how much certain themes or tendencies occur in a response protocol. The quantifiability of this method has made it possible to computerize the analysis of some tests.

In the second, the psychologist uses the test as a means of generating global information and hypotheses about the individual, focusing on the content of the responses rather than the statistical criteria that could be applied. A survey of Rorschach users,[3] for example, found that one-fifth of the examiners did not score the test at all, and 75 percent of those who did score it personalized the scoring in some manner—for example, combining elements of two or more scoring systems. Psychologist Sidney Blatt indicates, "The Rorschach has begun to be viewed not so much as a perceptual test but rather as an experimental procedure that systematically presents an individual with ambiguity and allows us to observe and study how the individual constructs meaning from relative ambiguity."[4]

Similarly, psychologist E. Jerry Phares indicates that

> it often seems that the Rorschach comes off best when it is viewed as a kind of controlled interview. That is, the clinician can observe how the patient behaves in response to the test stimuli. . . . Its value does not reside in the instrument itself but in its use in conjunction with the skill and sensitivity of the clinician.[5]

"Basically, the focus of concern for Rorschach interpretation may be placed either on the content of the responses or on their formal characteristics . . . and the various quantitative summaries derived from the responses."[6] Neither approach is more correct than the other. Psychologists who score tests will nearly always also analyze the content of the tests, but the converse may not hold: many psychologists forgo scoring and use the tests entirely as sources of more global information and hypotheses through content analysis. What matters for purposes of evaluation of the psychologist's work is how accurate and reasonable the analysis is, rather than whether the psychologist used one or both of these methods.

---

[3] Exner & Exner, *How Clinicians Use the Rorschach,* 36 J. Personality Assessment 403–08 (1972).

[4] Sidney Blatt, *The Rorschach: A Test of Perception or an Evaluation of Representation*, 55 J. Personality Assessment 394, 401 (1990). See § **10.6** for further information about interpretation of the Rorschach.

[5] E. Jerry Phares, Clinical Psychology: Concepts, Methods & Profession 246 (1988).

[6] Anastasi & Urbina at 412.

§ 10.2   Evaluation of Projective Techniques

Perhaps the best review of the validity and reliability of psychological tests in general is *Psychological Testing,* by Anne Anastasi and Susan Urbina, now in its seventh edition. Anastasi and Urbina initially note that

> the differences between projective techniques and standardized tests are not as large or as fundamental as may appear at first sight. . . . [I]t has been argued convincingly that projective techniques and self-report inventories differ in degree rather than in kind. . . . Individual instruments fall into a continuum; although at the extremes the differences are easily recognizable, overlapping in several features is evident at the center.[7]

Next they note some specific, extra-test purposes for projective tests. Such tests are a good way to break the ice when beginning an evaluation, in part because there are no "wrong" answers, in part because the tasks are inherently interesting, and in part because attention is diverted away from the patient or client. Anastasi and Urbina also suggest that special populations—for example, children, illiterates, and those with language or speech handicaps—may be able to articulate things through projective tests that they could not through interviews or through more objective tests.[8]

One advantage of projective tests is that "in general, projective instruments are less susceptible to faking than are self-report inventories," in part because the purpose, scoring, and interpretation of the projective tests are generally not evident.[9] This is furthered as the individual becomes more involved in the task. Even so, these tests are not immune to faking, and research amply demonstrates that both "faking good" and "faking bad" are possible. The examiner must be alert to the possibility of faking and must look for it both through the individual responses and response patterns and through inconsistencies with other sources of information about the individual. The Minnesota Multiphasic Personality Inventory–Second Edition (MMPI-2) may be of particular value in making this determination because it offers the only readily available, objective means of identifying the credibility, attitude, and intent of the individual taking the test.

A potentially significant source of contamination of results is the relative lack of standardization of administration of most projective techniques, in the face of research evidence that, for example, different instructions and the quality of examiner-examinee relationships can make a significant difference in performance. Examiners must be careful to identify any such factors that may affect the examinee's productivity, defensiveness, or other performance characteristics.[10] Meaningful interpretation of projective tests is possible only when the examiner has "extensive information about the circumstances under which they were obtained and the aptitudes and experiential background of the respondent."[11]

Anastasi and Urbina conclude that, if seen as "tests," the projective techniques will be found wanting. If seen, however, as "clinical tools," to be used as interviewing aids and combined with other data before major conclusions are drawn, the projective techniques

---

[7] Anastasi & Urbina at 433.

[8] *Id.*

[9] *Id.*

[10] *Id.* at 434.

[11] *Id.* at 439.

may have significant utility in the hands of a skilled clinician. "The special value that projective techniques may have is more likely to emerge when they are interpreted by qualitative, clinical procedures than when they are quantitatively scored and interpreted as if they were objective psychometric instruments."[12] "These techniques serve best in sequential decisions, by suggesting leads for further exploration or hypotheses about the individual for subsequent verification."[13]

The general lack of objective scoring may be equally serious. Nearly all projective techniques depend, ultimately, on the examiner's skill at interpretation. There is a real potential for the tests to be interpreted according to the personal biases (such as theoretical orientation and favorite hypotheses) of the examiner rather than strictly according to the data about the examinee's personality dynamics.[14]

Many projective techniques also lack substantial normative data, forcing the clinician to fall back on his or her own "general clinical experience" of whatever quality and with whatever biases the clinician may have. There is also the potential that the clinician, whose personal data bank is primarily filled with data on psychopathology, will overinterpret the data received or will make other errors based on selective or incomplete recall.[15]

Reliability and Validity of Projective Tests

Given these potential problems, scorer reliability becomes an important question. That reliability question extends not only to the formal scoring, where there may be a high degree of consistency among examiners, but also to the meaning given to the data, where research has shown much less consistency. Even skilled clinicians may interpret the same data differently, to a degree.[16]

Common tests of reliability—for example, "split-half" or "test-retest" (see **Chapter 7**)—do not apply well to projective tests, Anastasi and Urbina indicate. In the former, reliability testing is hampered by the fact that individual items are often designed to measure different variables, so no manner of splitting will result in equivalent halves. Some tests are also designed to be progressive, with stimuli responded to in a context created in part by previous stimuli and responses, together with the natural rise and fall of behavioral tendencies throughout the administration of a test.[17]

Similarly, test-retest reliability can be a problem to assess. In the short run, the individual may recall previous responses and give them (or give something different) intentionally, rather than responding directly to the stimuli.[18] If there has been a longer interval between tests, the test should respond to any real personality changes that have taken place—but each time it does, the reliability coefficient goes down. See **Chapter 7**.

---

[12] *Id.* at 440–41.

[13] Anastasi & Urbina at 442.

[14] *Id.* at 434.

[15] *Id.* at 435.

[16] *Id.* at 435–36.

[17] *Id.* at 436.

[18] *Id.*

With regard to validity, Anastasi and Urbina conclude that "the large majority of published validation studies on projective techniques are inconclusive because of procedural deficiencies in either experimental controls or statistical analysis, or both."[19] They also indicate that even clinicians carry stereotypes of various kinds and may apply these rather than sticking strictly to clinical evidence in interpreting test results. People (including clinicians) tend to notice and recall data that coincides with their own expectations, and to ignore and forget data that does not.[20] Poor experimental design will often lead to an underestimate of validity.[21] For example, the TAT has been criticized for being a poor predictor of real-life aggression on the basis of the presence or absence of aggression in the stories. The research evidence, Anastasi and Urbina note, is that "high aggression in fantasy may be associated with either high or low overt aggression" depending on characteristics of the person and the situation. Further, some subjects' scores will be positive and some negative because of the interaction between fantasized aggression and real-life aggression—but the appearance when scores are added together for statistical analysis will be that the test is not shown to be a valid predictor of aggressive tendencies.[22]

RORSCHACH PSYCHODIAGNOSTIC TEST

§ 10.3   Rorschach Psychodiagnostic Test

The Rorschach inkblot test is perhaps the best-known of the projective techniques.[23] Although standardized series of inkblots had been used previously in the study of imagination and other functions, Rorschach pioneered the application of inkblots to personality diagnosis and description as a whole.[24] Development of the Rorschach inkblot test was

---

[19] Anastasi & Urbina at 437.

[20] *Id.* at 437–38.

[21] *Id.* at 438.

[22] *Id.* at 439.

[23] Carr, *Psychological Testing of Personality, in* Comprehensive Textbook of Psychiatry/IV 522 (H. Kaplan & B. Sadock eds., 1985) [hereinafter *Psychological Testing of Personality*]; Lubin et al., *Patterns of Psychological Test Usage in the United States: 1935–1982*, 39 Am. Psychologist 451-54 (1984) [hereinafter *Patterns of Psychological Test Usage in the United States: 1935–1982*]; Keilin & Bloom, *Child Custody Evaluation Practices: A Survey of Experienced Professionals,* 17 Prof. Psychol.: Res. & Prac. 338-46 (1986) [hereinafter *Child Custody Evaluation Practices*]; Chris Piotrowski & John Keller, *Psychological Testing in Outpatient Mental Health Facilities: A National Study,* 20 Prof. Psychol.: Res. & Prac. 423, 424 (1989); Paul R. Lees-Haley, *Psychodiagnostic Test Usage by Forensic Psychologists,* 10 Am. J. Forensic Psychol. 25, 26 (1992); C. Edward Watkins Jr. et al., *Contemporary Practice of Psychological Assessment by Clinical Psychologists,* 26 Prof. Psychol.: Res. & Prac. 54, 57 (1995) [hereinafter Watkins et al.]; Marc J. Ackerman & Melissa C. Ackerman, *Custody Evaluation Practices: A Survey of Experienced Professionals (Revisited),* 28 Prof. Psychol.: Res. & Prac. 137, 140 (1997) [hereinafter Ackerman & Ackerman].

[24] Anastasi & Urbina at 411.

begun by Hermann Rorschach in 1911, with most of his major work published between 1917 and 1921. His major monograph, *Psychodiagnostik,* appeared in 1921.[25] With Rorschach's untimely death in 1922, others were left to carry on his work. Although a number of interpretive systems have been developed, three stand out: those of Samuel Beck, Bruno Klopfer, and John E. Exner Jr. When referring to any of the interpretive and scoring systems, the last name of the author is used to identify which system is being discussed.

Beck published the first major treatise on the Rorschach in the United States in the early 1930s and several books on the test in later years.[26] His approach was cautious and empirical. Klopfer, who began publishing on the Rorschach in the mid-1930s, was at the other end of the continuum, emphasizing subjective rather than objective interpretation of responses.[27] Although both systems incorporate aspects of psychoanalytic theory in their interpretation of responses, they differ in technique of administration, instructions, scoring categories, how far to go in ascertaining why an individual responded as he or she did, and how to interpret the data received.

It was not until the late 1950s that John E. Exner Jr. published the first of a number of works that compared and contrasted the Beck, Klopfer, and other systems of Rorschach administration and interpretation, and began a systematic study of the test and the means of using it, designed to maximize the reliability and validity of test protocols. The result is an attempt to integrate the best aspects of the various systems into one comprehensive system.[28] The vast majority of psychologists who formally score the Rorschach use Exner's method. Some use Beck's or Klopfer's methods, however, so information regarding all three is presented herein.

In describing his system, Exner begins with a caution against overinterpretation, saying that "the technique was never designed to answer all types of diagnostic or descriptive questions, just as it was never designed to predict all or most types of behavior."[29] Rather, he writes,

> the test gives a representative view of the person as he is behaving at the present. . . . Specifically, a description of a person based on the Rorschach data can include statements about a subject's affective world, his cognitive and response styles, how he related to his interpersonal sphere and to the rest of the environment as a whole, what motivates him and what are his response styles.[30]

He cautions against making predictions about the individual's future behavior based solely on the Rorschach, because one lacks information about the subject's future environment. He also cautions against using the Rorschach as a primary source of conclusions about intelligence or organic mental disorders (organicity).

---

[25] John Exner Jr. & Beth Clark, *The Rorschach, in* Clinical Diagnosis of Mental Disorders 148 (B. Wolman ed., 1978) [hereinafter Clinical Diagnosis of Mental Disorders].

[26] *Id*. at 149.

[27] *Id*.

[28] *Id*. at 153–54.

[29] *Id*. at 154.

[30] *Id*.

Psychologist Philip Erdberg indicates that the Rorschach can productively be used to address a number of important clinical questions, including:

1. "How does the person prefer to cope with need states?"
2. "Is the person's style likely to work? What kinds of problems will it meet?"
3. "What is the quality of the person's reality testing?"
4. "How mature and complex are the person's psychological operations?"
5. "How frequently does the person attempt to organize the environment? Does the person tend to 'coast' through life or to control his environment?"
6. "How efficient are the person's attempts?"
7. "What is the extent and quality of the person's self-focus?"
8. "How actively or passively does the person interact with the world?"
9. "How does the person respond to 'emotional' experience?"
10. "What is the quality of interpersonal function?"
11. "Is it likely that the person is schizophrenic?"
12. "Is it likely that the person is suicidal?"[31]

A slightly different approach is taken by psychologist Irving Weiner, who prefers to refer to the Rorschach as a *method*, rather than a *test*:

> The Rorschach is more than a test . . . because its utility is not limited to applications of the scores and indices that it yields or to interpretive strategies rooted in any one theoretical frame of reference. Rather . . . , the Rorschach is a multifaceted method of generating structural, thematic, and behavioral data that can be applied in both quantitative and qualitative terms and can be interpreted from many different theoretical perspectives. Accordingly, to recognize that the Rorschach functions not only as a personality test but as a method of generating useful information in other ways as well, it seems appropriate to refer to it as the RIM [Rorschach Inkblot Method].[32]

Utilizing this method, Weiner indicates, one can describe an individual's personality, can make behavioral predictions (on the basis of relatively stable personality traits), can determine diagnoses, and can plan and evaluate treatment.[33]

§ 10.4   Description of the Rorschach

The Rorschach test consists of 10 cards, each about 7 by 9½ inches in size. On each is printed a standardized, bilaterally symmetrical inkblot. Cards I, IV, V, VI, and VII are gray and black. Cards II and III add a bright red to the grays and blacks. Cards VIII, IX, and X

---

[31] Philip Erdberg, *Rorschach Assessment, in* Handbook of Psychological Assessment 387, 390–97 (G. Goldstein & M. Hersen eds., 2d ed. 1990).

[32] Irving B. Weiner, *Current Status of the Rorschach Inkblot Method*, 68 J. Personality Assessment 5, 6 (1997).

[33] *Id.*

are in pastel colors. The subject is shown each card, in numerical order. On the average, administration of the test takes 45 to 60 minutes.

There may be some deviation in the manner of presentation, depending in part on the system the examiner ascribes to. Each of the major systems (Beck, Klopfer, and Exner) has a different approach, and each may, therefore, yield slightly different data. For example, Beck wrote that the subject "sits in front of and with his back to" the examiner;[34] Klopfer preferred side-by-side seating;[35] and Exner[36] wrote that any position *except* face-to-face is acceptable, suggesting that side-by-side seating may be best. The purpose, in all cases, is to prevent the individual from getting visual cues of any kind from the examiner or from concentrating on what the examiner is writing down rather than on the blots.

The introduction to the test is very general, because the subject needs nearly complete freedom to react to the cards if the test is to be meaningful. The examiner might inquire whether the subject has heard about the "Rorschach" or "the inkblot test," and might tell the subject that the cards are "only inkblots," so that there are no right or wrong answers. It is critically important that the subject *not* have the impression that the test is a measure of intelligence or a test of imagination, because the former gives a mind-set that there are right and wrong answers, and the latter that one is to associate to the inkblots rather than telling what one *sees*. "It is what the subject sees that constitutes the Rorschach response."[37] If a test battery is given, Exner also suggests that the Rorschach be administered at or near the end.[38] The test taker should be as relaxed as possible, to minimize anxiety.[39]

The instructions to the subject vary to some degree depending on the system and the examiner, though all specify that the subject is to report exactly what he or she *sees*. Beck's introduction is relatively long and emphasizes that the examinee should "tell the examiner what you see on each card, or anything that might be represented there."[40] The examiner may vary from that exact language, so long as the essence of the message is the same.

In contrast, after the brief introduction, Exner hands the subject the first card, saying, "What might this be?" and not another word. "Those four words are very important and should not be altered or added to in any way," Exner stresses.[41] These four words are the same recommended by Rorschach and by Klopfer.[42] Exner's research found that Beck's instructions led to relatively long protocols, Klopfer's to relatively short ones.[43] Exner chose to limit his instructions to try to minimize the impact of instructional sets on

---

[34] Samuel Beck et al., Rorschach's Test 2 (3d ed. 1961) [hereinafter Rorschach's Test].

[35] John E. Exner, Jr., *cited in* Gary Groth-Marnat, Handbook of Psychological Assessment 421 (4th ed. John Wiley & Sons 2003).

[36] John E. Exner Jr., A Rorschach Workbook for the Comprehensive System 3 (3d ed. 1990) [hereinafter A Rorschach Workbook for the Comprehensive System].

[37] *Id.* at 4.

[38] Clinical Diagnosis of Mental Disorders at 155.

[39] Gary Groth-Marnat, Handbook of Psychological Assessment (4th ed. John Wiley & Sons 2003) [hereinafter Groth-Marnat (2003)].

[40] Rorschach's Test at 2.

[41] A Rorschach Workbook for the Comprehensive System at 5.

[42] Clinical Diagnosis of Mental Disorders at 157.

[43] *Id.*

an individual's responding as well as to adhere to the rule that "the primary task of the examiner is to remain silent as much as possible so as not to contaminate the testing session with unnecessary remarks that might influence the subject."[44]

As noted above, the cards are handed to the subject in numerical order, from I to X, in the standard, upright position. The examiner repeats the "What might this be?" statement in handing over each card, though if the subject clearly understands the task, that statement need not be repeated after the first four or five cards. Although the subject is free to turn the card if he or she wishes, the examiner may not suggest that the subject do so.

Questions from the subject, regardless of the system preferred by the examiner, are answered as briefly and generally as possible. If the subject asks about turning the card, Beck would have the examiner say that the subject "is free to do so,"[45] while Exner recommends answering this and similar questions with, "It's up to you."[46] Beck urges the examiner to encourage the subject to give more than one response if only one is elicited by cards I through V. Klopfer and Exner recommend that the examiner encourage the subject only on the first card, never thereafter, so long as even a single response is made for each card. Both Beck and Exner urge the examiner not to permit the subject to reject a card (give no response at all) if possible, Beck writing that he tries to make the subject hold the card at least two minutes,[47] with both Beck and Exner recommending making statements like, "We're in no hurry" or "Everyone can find something."[48] If the subject gives a great many responses, Exner writes that "research . . . has shown that the interpretive yield is essentially no different if only the first five answers to each blot are used as compared to using the entire record."[49] However, he cautions that as soon as the subject gives fewer than five responses to any blot, the examiner should not intervene again even if more than five are later given. The intent is to preserve the spontaneity of responding as much as possible.

Exner notes that brief records, with fewer than 14 answers, are not interpretively valid and should not be accepted. He indicates that the examiner should interrupt the standard procedure to explain to the subject:

> Now you know how it's done. But there's a problem. You didn't give enough answers for us to get anything out of the test. So we will go through them again and this time I want you to make sure to give me more answers. You can include the same ones you've already given if you like but make sure to give me more answers this time.[50]

Responses are recorded verbatim under all systems. The intent is to record every word used by the subject in describing what he or she sees, to maximize the likelihood that the examiner can perceive the same thing. This includes not only what parts of the inkblot were used for the percept but also what made it look the way it did to the subject, including the shape, shading, color, and so forth.

---

[44] *Id.* at 158.

[45] Rorschach's Test at 4.

[46] A Rorschach Workbook for the Comprehensive System at 6.

[47] Rorschach's Test at 4.

[48] A Rorschach Workbook for the Comprehensive System at 7.

[49] A Rorschach Workbook for the Comprehensive System at 8.

[50] *Id.* at 7–8.

The examiner also records comments the subject makes, facial expressions, gestures, laughter, changes in voice, exclamations, and any other behavior that may indicate that the subject is having a special reaction to something in the test. Particularly in a protocol with a small number of responses, the extra-test behavior may tell as much or more about the individual's perceptions than do the verbal responses to the blots. Finally, the examiner records the time it takes the individual to give the first response (reaction time) and the total time the individual holds the card (response time).

After the administration of the test (the *free association*) is completed, an *inquiry* is conducted. The inquiry has great importance under all systems of interpretation, though those examiners who do not formally score the test will conduct only a very brief one. The purpose of the inquiry is to try to ensure that the examiner's understanding of responses is accurate—that the examiner understood what the subject perceived at the time the response was initially given. No new responses are permitted, only clarification of responses already given. Exner suggests the following introduction:

> Now we are going to go back through the cards again. It won't take very long. I want to see the thing that you saw and make sure that I see them like you do. We'll do them one at a time. I'll read what you said and then I want you to show me where it is in the blot and then tell me what there is there that makes it look like that to you, so that I can see it too, just like you did. Is that clear?[51]

The examiner then reads back, verbatim, what the subject said during the initial administration of the cards, requesting the subject to indicate where the percept is located and what made it look as it did. The examiner must continue to be nondirective to ensure that he or she learns what made the blot look the way it did to the subject and does not put words or ideas in the subject's mind. Thus, the examiner asks questions such as, "What made it look like a _____?" rather than, "Did the color/shading/shape help make it look like a _____?" Exner indicates that the questions should be as brief as possible, should seek only information essential to the scoring of the test, should keep the inquiry as short as possible, and should be as nondirective as possible.[52]

§ 10.5   Scoring of the Rorschach

For a number of years now, the primary scoring system taught to psychology graduate students has been the Comprehensive System(s) of John Exner, Ph.D. However, psychologists trained prior to the widespread use of the Comprehensive System are likely to use a scoring system devised by either Beck or Klopfer.

Unlike the scoring of an IQ test, which entails counting right and wrong answers, scoring on the Rorschach refers to coding the data in various ways to facilitate an understanding of the categories of information, which must be considered in context to be meaningful. The examiner explores several areas, including the following: location, determinants, content, and Popular responses. The discussion that follows describes each system of scoring, followed by an interpretation of the information scored, in **§ 10.6**.

---

[51] John E. Exner, Jr., *quoted in* Groth-Marnat (2003) at 422.

[52] Clinical Diagnosis of Mental Disorders at 159.

Beck's System

Under Beck's system of scoring, initial consideration is given to *location*: whether the individual has used the whole inkblot, a major detail, a minor detail, or space (the white area around or within the blot) for each response. Whether the detail is major or minor is determined from frequency tables based on research by Beck and others.

Next, the examiner studies and records the *determinants* of the responses—the features of the blots that led the subject to respond as he or she did. The primary determinants are form, color, movement, and shading.

Then, the examiner records the *content* of the responses. Five categories encompass the majority of percepts: human, human detail, animal, animal detail, and anatomy, though Beck identifies a total of 34 categories.[53]

Next, the examiner identifies "*Popular*" responses, those given very commonly, with Beck listing 21 such responses.[54]

Finally, the examiner determines the total number of responses. The average record has 20 to 30 associations.

Examiners who do not do formal scoring may still make use of the categories above, recognizing the importance of identifying gross overproduction or underproduction of any type of response determinant. Their greatest emphasis, however, is usually on the content of the responses and hypotheses that may be generated about the individual from the types of content the individual identifies.

Klopfer's System

The Klopfer scoring system's first consideration is scoring the *locations*. Klopfer looks at whole responses, large details, small details, unusual details, and space responses. After the location is scored, the *determinants* are scored. There are four main categories of determinants: form, movement, shading, and color. After the determinants are scored, the scorer looks at the *content* of the responses. Klopfer identifies 24 categories as the most frequently used content areas. They include human responses, animal responses, anatomical responses, food, nature, geography, and abstract concepts. Next, Popular responses are recorded. In Klopfer's scoring system, only 10 responses are scored as Populars, compared with 21 in Beck's system.

Exner's Comprehensive System

In slight contrast to the 20 to 30 responses expected with Beck's system, Exner indicates that an average of 22 responses are expected with the Comprehensive System.[55]

---

[53] Rorschach's Test at 217–21.

[54] *Id.* at 208–11.

[55] John E. Exner, Jr., *cited in* Groth-Marnat (2003) at 460.

While acknowledging that the Rorschach cannot be scored in the same way many objective tests could be scored, Exner notes that there are four sets of data that may be derived from the test:

[1.]   Quantitative data which can be compared across other records. . . .

[2.]   Internal comparisons among the subject's own productions. It is here where the most valuable idiographic information is obtained . . . [the subject's] own unique style of responding, his needs and motivations, and his weaknesses and strengths.

[3.]   The sequence of the scores can be examined. This helps to illustrate how the subject approaches the testing situation, how a response may be related to a previous response, and how the performance varies as the test progresses.

[4.]   The subject's own words, which are subjected to a qualitative analysis.[56]

Exner's Comprehensive System has two basic rules that must be followed:

1.   [O]nly what was perceived during Free Association can be scored. . . . [The Free Association and Inquiry] represent two different thought processes. . . . [Thus,] the Free Association should be read in its entirety first, and then the Inquiry.

2.   [T]o make sure that all determinants given in the Free Association are scored and are given equal weight.[57]

Like Beck, Exner scores for location, determinants, content, and popularity. To these, Exner adds *blends, organizational activity, form quality,* and two special scorings: *perseveration* and *unusual verbalizations.*

Location

Like Beck, Exner's location criteria primarily involve looking at the subject's use of the whole inkblot, of major details, of minor details, and of space.

Determinants

As in Beck's system, one then looks at the determinants, which Exner and Clark indicate are "the most complex and most important scoring category, involving the perceptual-cognitive process that the individual employs in order to select and to organize the various elements in his stimulus world."[58] Exner and Clark also note that there is some filtering of responses by most individuals, citing research finding that, when asked to give as many responses as they could in 60 seconds, subjects averaged six per card rather than the two that subjects average in the actual test.[59] Exner's system uses seven major categories of determinants: form, movement, chromatic color, achromatic color, shading, form dimension, and "pairs and reflections."[60]

---

[56] Clinical Diagnosis of Mental Disorders at 163–64.

[57] *Id.* at 164.

[58] *Id.*

[59] Clinical Diagnosis of Mental Disorders at 167.

[60] *Id.* at 166–68.

Content

Next, as with Beck and Klopfer, the examiner identifies the content of the responses. Exner identifies 26 categories, most of which are the same as in Beck's and Klopfer's systems. Exner stresses that many responses include two or more contents and that all should be identified. Unique contents that do not fit into any of the 26 categories are identified as "ideographic contents."[61]

Popular responses

Like Beck, Exner identifies *Popular* responses, which he defines as those occurring in at least one-third of the protocols in the research base. This led to the identification of 13 Populars.[62]

Special scorings

Exner's system adds two categories of responses to those used in the systems of Beck and Klopfer, identifying these as *special scorings*. The first is *perseveration*.[63] The second is *unusual verbalizations*, which indicate that a response is strange in some way.[64]

§ 10.6   Interpretation of the Rorschach

Method Used by Beck and Klopfer

Beck and Klopfer and their followers primarily base their interpretations on clinical data, including both the personal experience of the examiner and the limited research on the Rorschach protocols of people with diagnosed mental disorders.[65] Each type of scoring yields hypotheses about the individual's functioning, to be tested against what is known about the individual's case history and information from other parts of the test battery.

1. *Form.* In a normal record, 30 to 50 percent of responses are based exclusively on form.[66] The examiner compares an individual's responses with statistical norms regarding accuracy of perceptions.[67] A normal record will show at least 70 percent of the form responses to be accurate based on that comparison.[68]

---

[61] A Rorschach Workbook for the Comprehensive System at 47–50.

[62] *Id.* at 171.

[63] *Id.*

[64] *Id.* at 171–72.

[65] L. Phillips & J. Smith, Rorschach Interpretation: Advanced Techniques at v–vii (1953) [hereinafter Rorschach Interpretation].

[66] *Psychological Testing: II* at 5.

[67] Rorschach's Test at 134–207.

[68] Brent Willock, *Projection, Transitional Phenomena, and the Rorschach*, 9 J. Personality Assessment 99, 111 (1992).

2. *Color.* The color responses reveal a person's emotional relationship with the environment.[69]

3. *Movement.* The examiner scores movement when the subject describes people engaged in some activity—for example, "people bowling"—or when animals are seen in a human-like activity—for example, "bears dancing." Form is necessarily implied by movement responses.

4. *Shading.* Shading refers to use of the gray areas of the blots.

Content

As indicated in **§ 10.5**, Beck's system has 34 categories of percepts, though five categories (human, human detail, animal, animal detail, and anatomy) cover the majority of percepts.[70]

As with the other categories of information, hypotheses can be formed about subjects on the basis of how their responses compare with normative data collected on people who have taken the test. Of particular interest in custody evaluations are those Rorschach indicators of difficulty with interpersonal relationships.

The ambiguity of the Rorschach sometimes allows the examiner to detect psychotic processes that an individual is able to keep under control during other parts of the psychological evaluation.[71]

Exner particularly cautions against drawing strong conclusions from individual responses. Rather, "it is the classes of projected material that generate the greatest interpretive yield. Some responses that appear to have projected features may be nothing more than straightforward translations of the blot stimuli."[72]

A given individual may have responses covering a range of personality descriptions. These responses are likely to be to some degree inconsistent with one another because individuals are not generally narrow, unitary creatures. An examiner identifies the primary hypotheses on the bases of (1) how frequently a given type of content is given during the test, (2) whether an individual exhibited "shock" on particular cards, (3) whether the individual's responses to certain blots are of unusually poor quality compared with his or her other responses, and/or (4) whether the response to a particular blot is unique. The examiner also compares the hypotheses with what is known about the individual, looking for evidence that the hypothesis is or is not supported by other data.

Populars

As indicated above, Beck identifies 21 responses considered *Populars,* meaning responses that are particularly commonly given. A normal (that is, statistically average) record has seven to nine populars.[73]

---

[69] *Psychological Testing: II* at 5.

[70] *Id.*

[71] Arthur C. Carr, *Psychological Testing of Personality, in* Kaplan & Sadock, Comprehensive Textbook of Psychiatry 524–25 (1985).

[72] J. Exner Jr., *Searching for Projection in the Rorschach,* 53 J. Personality Assessment 530 (1989).

[73] *Psychological Testing: II* at 6.

Unusual responses

Anything unusual about the individual's responses is taken into consideration. Everything an individual does has some potential to give insight into his or her personality, so no data is excluded from that available for forming hypotheses.

Exner's Methods

Exner's interpretations are based on the same types of data as those used by Beck and Klopfer, but the conclusions offered by Exner are supported by far greater research. It is of particular note that most of the development of the Rorschach has been through the study of abnormal personalities, which has biased interpretation in the direction of maladjustment.[74] To offset this, Exner includes a table of "Descriptive Statistics for [700] nonpatient Adults"[75] and for 1,390 nonpatient children and adolescents by age[76] in his *Rorschach Workbook,* to permit analysis of responses of a given subject in the context of normal subjects as well as abnormal ones.

Total number of responses

Exner indicates that protocols containing 13 or fewer responses are generally not reliable, according to test-retest research he conducted. Interpretation of such "brief" protocols should therefore be done cautiously, and should not be interpreted based on its CS summary scores. Individual responses may be interpreted, however.[77] Exner suggests that, when a brief protocol occurs, the examiner should either discard the Rorschach and rely solely on other data, or that the examiner immediately (during the same session, if possible) retest the individual, instructing the subject to give more answers than he or she did on the first test administration.[78]

§ 10.7   Malingering on the Rorschach

One of the reasons the Rorschach is included in many test batteries is that it is believed to be resistant to faking.[79] Nevertheless, research on this question suggests that it is sometimes possible for sophisticated subjects to fool even highly skilled Rorschach interpreters, at least with regard to the presence or absence of psychosis.[80] Although there is no specific pattern of

---

[74] *Id.* at 13.

[75] A Rorschach Workbook at 158.

[76] *Id.* at 167–90.

[77] Irving Weiner, Principles of Rorschach Interpretation 65–66 (2d ed. Erlbaum 2003).

[78] J. Exner Jr., *Problems with Brief Rorschach Protocols,* 52 J. Personality Assessment 645–46 (1988).

[79] Perry & Kinder, *The Susceptibility of the Rorschach to Malingering: A Critical Review,* 54 J. Personality Assessment 47, 47 (1990); Gary Groth-Marnat, Handbook of Psychological Assessment (John Wiley & Sons 2003).

[80] *Id.* at 52.

faking that would reliably indicate that an individual is definitely malingering,[81] it is possible for an individual to alter his or her responses to try to prevent the evaluator from learning a great deal about him or her. An individual may also reduce the number of responses he or she produces in order to avoid giving the psychologist useful data, though a low number of responses may also result from the person's having a below-average IQ.[82] Therefore, the psychologist needs to be aware of indications that a given person may be trying to falsify the test protocol.

> Characteristics that should alert the clinician to possible faking include reduced number of responses, slow reaction times, . . . vague or poor form responses, dramatic contents . . . , an attitude of pained compliance, frequent card rejections, inconsistency (e.g., failures to give easy, popular responses while recognizing more difficult ones), and expressions of perplexity or repeated questions about the test directions.[83]

§ 10.8   Validity and Reliability of the Rorschach

The Rorschach and other projective tests have been criticized with regard to the lack of predictive ability of projective tests, the fact that it is common for different examiners to administer the test with minor and not-so-minor differences in approach, the many studies showing poor validity of the tests, and the problems engendered by having numerous systems for scoring the tests. It is also often noted that projective tests are substantially more subjective than, for example, the MMPI-2, and validity and reliability are therefore harder to demonstrate.

By the mid-1970s, psychologists increasingly looked to the Rorschach as an information source, in effect a structured interview, rather than as a stand-alone diagnostic instrument.[84] "Whenever the Rorschach is used as an information resource per se, the resultant psychological reports are useful and valuable," Psychology Professor Richard Dana, Ph.D., concludes.[85] Dana cautions that taking the Rorschach test is a stressful experience for most people and that research continues to indicate that the examiner's behavior can have a significant effect on the outcome of the test.[86]

To address the validity question, researchers collected a sample of Rorschach validation studies from every fifth year of *Psychological Abstracts* between 1930 and 1980, totaling 120 studies.[87] They found that

> the success of conceptual research demonstrates both criterion validity, insofar as scores correlate with some concurrent or predicted aspect of behavior, and construct validity, insofar

---

[81] *Id.* at 53.

[82] Gary B. Melton et al., Psychological Evaluation for the Courts 47 (2d ed. 1997).

[83] Schretlen, *The Use of Psychological Tests to Identify Malingered Symptoms of Mental Disorder,* 8 Clinical Psychol. Rev. 451, 465 (1988).

[84] Richard Dana, *Rorschach, in* Eighth Mental Measurements Yearbook 1040 (1978) [hereinafter Eighth Mental Measurements Yearbook]; H. Lerner & P. Lerner, *Rorschach Inkblot Test,* 4 Test Critiques 525 (1984); Irving B. Weiner, Principles of Rorschach Interpretation (Erlbaum 2003).

[85] Eighth Mental Measurements Yearbook at 1040–41.

[86] *Id.* at 1041.

[87] Atkinson et al., *Rorschach Validity: An Empirical Approach to Literature,* 42 J. Clinical Psychol. 360–62 (1986).

as the theoretical formulation accounts for the relationship between the Rorschach score(s) and some condition or behavior. . . . This study suggests that inadequate research methodology, rather than the Rorschach itself, is at least partly culpable for condemnation of the technique.[88]

According to psychologists Franklin Shontz and Patricia Green, between 1983 and 1988 there were "four major meta-analyses on the psychometric properties of the Rorschach. All concluded that the Rorschach is reliable and valid when it is properly used."[89]

Further, Rorschach variables believed to identify traits (long-term characteristics) have been found to have high test-retest reliability, while those associated with states (short-term or situational) have been found to have low test-retest reliability.[90] The ability of the Rorschach to reliably identify traits permits valid statements to be made regarding an individual's personality style and, to the degree behavior is based on that personality style, his or her future behavior.[91]

It should be noted that Exner indicates that the Rorschach is inappropriate for use in deriving a DSM-III-R (and presumably DSM-IV) diagnosis. It is to be used as part of a test battery in a psychological assessment, he holds—not as a means of generating a specific diagnosis.[92]

Because not all psychologists use the Exner system, however, law professor Daniel Shuman cautions that the multiplicity of scoring systems and differences in reliability and validity among systems make it imperative that any challenge to Rorschach testing testimony be specific, as general attacks on the Rorschach may be irrelevant to the scoring system used. Given the sophistication necessary to mount this challenge properly, consultation with a forensic or clinical psychologist may be necessary.[93]

Finally, Exner and colleagues Eugene A. Thomas and Barbara Mason caution that the Rorschach does *not* have long-term reliability for children until at least the age of 14.[94] "Even an interval of nine months is sufficient to find very significant structural changes in the re-tests of seven-year-olds," they indicate.[95]

In a review of the published research on use of the Rorschach with African-Americans, George Frank found that the seven extant studies from the past 60 years yielded little information other than that African-Americans tend to give fewer responses than do white Americans. He notes that this has been found with other minority groups as well. It is his conclusion that African-Americans have learned to limit their degree of self-disclosure to strangers.[96] More recent research has found that there are few differences between

---

[88] *Id.* at 361–62.

[89] Franklin Shontz & Patricia Green, *Trends in Research on the Rorschach: Review and Recommendations,* 1 Applied & Preventive Psychol. 149, 149–50 (1992).

[90] Irving Weiner, Principles of Rorschach Interpretation 27 (2d ed. Lawrence Erlbaum Associates 2003) [hereinafter Weiner (2003)].

[91] *Id.* at 29.

[92] John Exner Jr., The Rorschach in the '90's, Paper presented at the 100th Annual Convention of the American Psychological Association, Washington, D.C. (Aug. 1992).

[93] Daniel Shuman, Psychiatric and Psychological Evidence 53 (1986).

[94] John Exner et al., *Children's Rorschachs: Description and Prediction,* 49 J. Personality Assessment 13–20 (1985).

[95] *Id.* at 13.

[96] George Frank, *The Response of African Americans to the Rorschach: A Review of the Research,* 59 J. Personality Assessment 317–25 (1992).

Caucasian and non-Caucasian adults (including European-Americans, African-Americans, Hispanic-Americans, Asian-Americans, and Native Americans on the CS scoring of the Rorschach.[97]

In summary, research since the early 1980s has substantially increased the evidence that the Rorschach is both valid and reliable, particularly when it is used as part of a test battery and in the context of a complete evaluation of an individual. In the hands of a skilled clinician, it can provide data and hypotheses that few other tests or interviews can.

§ 10.9   Intended Audience for the Rorschach

Exner provides data on children's responses starting with age five,[98] so the Rorschach can be administered to anyone five or older. Miriam G. Siegel writes that very young children have difficulty with the Rorschach procedures, but, "although the scoring of his responses may lack finesse, the experienced examiner can usually catch the drift of things. The administration of the Rorschach to the school-age child can usually be conducted along traditional procedures used with adolescents and adults."[99]

§ 10.10   Acceptance of the Rorschach by Mental Health Professionals

A 1989 survey of psychological testing trends in outpatient mental health facilities by Chris Piotrowski and John Keller found that the Rorschach was the fifth-most-popular projective test, and the eighth-most-popular test overall.[100]

A 1991 study by Robert Archer and his colleagues found that the Rorschach was the most popular projective test, and the second-most-popular test overall, for use with adolescents, according to a survey of 165 psychologists. For the 139 respondents who utilize a standard test battery, the Rorschach was again in second place, with 75 percent of the psychologists including it in their standard batteries.[101]

A 1992 report by Paul Lees-Haley on tests used by forensic psychologists indicates that the Rorschach was the third-most-frequently-used test, behind the MMPI/MMPI-2 and the WAIS-R, among the 69 forensic psychologists who responded.[102]

---

[97] Weiner (2003) at 51–52.

[98] A Rorschach Workbook for the Comprehensive System at 167–90.

[99] Miriam G. Siegel, *Cognitive and Projective Test Assessment, in* Handbook of Clinical Assessment of Children and Adolescents 74 (C. Kestenbaum & D. Williams eds., 1988).

[100] Chris Piotrowski & John Keller, *Psychological Testing in Outpatient Mental Health Facilities: A National Study,* 20 Prof. Psychol.: Res. & Prac. 423, 424 (1989).

[101] Robert Archer et al., *Psychological Test Usage with Adolescent Clients: 1990 Survey Findings,* 22 Prof. Psychol.: Res. & Prac. 247, 248–50 (1991).

[102] Paul Lees-Haley, *Psychodiagnostic Test Usage by Forensic Psychologists,* 10 Am. J. Forensic Psychol. 25, 26 (1992).

A 1995 study by C. Edward Watkins Jr. and colleagues found that the Rorschach was the sixth-most-frequently-used psychological test by clinical psychologists, with 82 percent using it.[103]

A 1997 study of child custody evaluation practices of forensic psychologists by Marc Ackerman and Melissa Ackerman found that the Rorschach was the second-most-widely-used test with adults, with 92 percent of forensic psychologists using it. It was also the sixth-most-frequently-used test with children, with 27 percent of the psychologists surveyed using it.[104]

In a 2001 article, psychologists Francella Quinell and James Bow indicated that the Rorschach remains the most-frequently-used projective test in child custody evaluations. Forty-four percent of the survey respondents used the Rorschach, and they used it in 64 percent of their evaluations.[105]

A New Rorschach Controversy

A 1999 study by psychologists Thomas W. Shaffer, Philip Erdberg, and John Haroian had an impact far beyond the intent of the researchers. Noting that the professional literature has relatively few articles that indicate the response patterns of nonpatients on the Rorschach, the Wechsler Adult Intelligence Scale-Revised (WAIS-R), and the Minnesota Multiphasic Personality Inventory, Second Edition (MMPI-2), they set out to provide data to address this need. Individuals were excluded who had a major medical illness in the past six months, who had ever been hospitalized in a psychiatric facility, who had been in psychological treatment in the past two years, who had ever been convicted of a felony, or who had psychological testing within the past year. The results of administration of these three tests to 123 nonpatient adults were very similar to the standardization samples for the WAIS-R and the MMPI-2, but not extremely similar to those of the Comprehensive System (CS) for the Rorschach. Rather, the Comprehensive System identified these adults as having significant psychopathology, despite all the contrary indicators from other sources.[106]

A study by psychologists Mel Hamel, Thomas W. Shaffer, and Philip Erdberg[107] found similar problems in the assessment of children aged six to 12 years. One hundred children were identified who had never been referred for psychological or psychiatric treatment, had never been arrested, convicted, or put on probation for any offense, had no more than one suspension or expulsion from school, had never used alcohol or other drugs, and had a GPA of at least 2.0 for the current school year. To further ensure that this was a "normal" sample, the Conners Parent Rating Scale-93 (CPRS-93) was used to identify whether any

---

[103] C. Edward Watkins Jr. et al., *Contemporary Practice of Psychological Assessment by Clinical Psychologists*, 26 Prof. Psychol.: Res. & Prac. 54, 57 (1995).

[104] Ackerman & Ackerman at 139–40.

[105] Francella A. Quinell & James N. Bow, *Psychological Tests Used in Child Custody Evaluations*, 19 Behav. Sci. L. 491–501 (2001).

[106] Thomas W. Shaffer, Philip Erdberg, & John Haroian, *Current Nonpatient Data for the Rorschach, WAIS-R, and MMPI-2*, 73 J. Psychol. Assessment 305–16 (1999).

[107] Mel Hamel, Thomas W. Shaffer, & Philip Erdberg, *A Study of Nonpatient Preadolescent Rorschach Protocols*, 75 J. Personality Assessment 280–94 (2000).

of the children had significant behavioral problems. The parents of these children clearly indicated that the children did not have behavioral problems. Since these were mentally healthy children, from all indications, it was expected that the Comprehensive System would support that conclusion. It did not. The interpretive guidelines collectively described the children as "grossly misperceiving and misinterpreting their surroundings and having unconventional ideation and significant cognitive impairment. Their distortion of reality and faulty reasoning approach psychosis."[108]

Numerous articles addressing the Shaffer *et al.* and Hamel *et al.* results and other issues have been published in the past few years. Much of the criticism of the Comprehensive System has come from psychologists James M. Wood, M. Teresa Nezworski, Howard N. Garb, and Scott O. Lilienfeld. In articles published in 2000–2001,[109] they indicated that the norms for the Comprehensive System are not accurate, and that using those norms makes an individual appear to have more psychopathology than he or she actually has. All 14 variables they studied were found to differ significantly for nonpatients in the Comprehensive System's normative groups and nonpatients tested by other researchers. They also found that the reliability of some Comprehensive System scores is far below acceptable levels. As a result, the authors "recommend that psychologists not use the present CS norms in clinical or forensic work, with either children or adults. Psychologists who use these norms run the risk of attaching false and negative labels to clients and thereby potentially harming them," an ethical violation. Any psychologists who continue to use the Comprehensive System norms, they indicate, have at the least an ethical obligation to describe the controversy and the possible limitations of those norms.[110] In another article, one of these authors, Howard Garb, has called for a moratorium on use of the Comprehensive System in clinical and forensic evaluations until further research has established new, valid norms for the System. The problem, Garb *et al.* indicate, is not that all Comprehensive System scores are invalid; rather, at this point in time no one knows with certainty which norms are valid and which are not. They criticize articles by other Rorschach researchers on various methodological grounds, indicating that none of the "pro-Comprehensive System" authors has produced methodologically sound data thus far. The authors also note that their own research supports the use of several Comprehensive System scales, though they also recommend further research on those scales.[111]

---

[108] *Id.* at 291.

[109] James M. Wood, Theresa M. Nezworski, Howard N. Garb, & Scott O. Lilienfeld, *The Misperception of Psychopathology: Problems with the Norms of the Comprehensive System for the Rorschach*, 8 Clinical Psychol.: Sci. & Prac. 350–73 (2001); James M. Wood, Scott O. Lilienfeld, M. Teresa Nezworski, & Howard N. Garb, *Coming to Grips with Negative Evidence for the Comprehensive System for the Rorschach: A Comment on Gacono, Loving, and Bodholdt; Ganellen; and Bornstein*, 77 J. Personality Assessment 48–70 (2001); James M. Wood, M. Teresa Nezworski, Howard N. Garb, & Scott O. Lilienfeld, *Problems with the Norms of the Comprehensive System for the Rorschach: Methodological and Conceptual Considerations*, 8 Clinical Psychol.: Sci. & Prac. 397–402 (2001); Scott O. Lilienfeld, James M. Wood, & Howard N. Garb, *The Scientific Status of Projective Techniques*, 1 Psychol. Sci. in Pub. Int. 27–66 (2000).

[110] Wood et al., *Misperception of Psychopathology*, at 363.

[111] Howard N. Garb, James M. Wood, M. Teresa Nezworski, William M. Grove, & William J. Stejskal, *Toward a Resolution of the Rorschach Controversy*, 13 Psychol. Assessment 433–48 (2001).

In addition to the above conclusions, Wood *et al.* indicate their belief that the Comprehensive System is no longer widely accepted by the scientific community, given the controversy regarding it, and, to a degree, the Rorschach itself is brought into question given that most psychologists now use the Comprehensive System norms. Questions regarding the accuracy of scoring the test using the Comprehensive System, in particular, make most of the CS scales highly inappropriate in forensic settings, they indicate. At minimum, they say, if the Comprehensive System's scoring is to be used in a forensic context, it should be scored independently by at least two experts on the test, to try to ensure the accuracy of the results. Finally, they indicate that there is substantial evidence that some variables in the Comprehensive System yield significantly different results for Caucasians, Blacks, Hispanics, and other minorities, as well as non-Americans. Their recommendation is that the Comprehensive System (and perhaps Rorschach) not be used in court or, if used, that only the few well-validated Comprehensive System scales be utilized until new research produces the valid and reliable results that are essential to the forensic arena.[112]

Psychologists John Hunsley and J. Michael Bailey caution that *many authors confuse criticisms of the Comprehensive System with criticisms of the Rorschach Inkblot Test* (or Method) itself. While some researchers criticize aspects of the Rorschach, it is the Comprehensive System that is the object of most concerns. They note that many psychologists do not attempt interpretations utilizing the Comprehensive System norms, preferring other systems or using idiographic (case-specific) interpretations. They also suggest that the reputation of the Rorschach for identifying psychopathology may be based to a substantial degree on the apparent tendency of the Comprehensive System to overpathologize. They recommend great caution in use of the Comprehensive System at this time, while calling for a great deal of research to establish clearly for whom the Rorschach is an appropriate test, what outcome criteria are valid and reliable, and in what circumstances the Rorschach is an appropriate instrument (forensic, clinical, other).[113] Hunsley, in an article authored with Gina Di Giulio, finds the arguments of Wood *et al.* "compelling," and urges that new research be done as soon as possible to determine which Comprehensive System scales are valid and reliable and which are not.[114]

Psychologists R.K. McKinzey and Victoria Campagna asked 30 psychologists with extensive experience using the Comprehensive System to score a single Rorschach protocol. The Rorschach was also scored with the Rorschach Interpretation Assistance Program: Version 4 (RIAP4). Three of the psychologists considered the protocol unscoreable, while 27 scored it. Of that 27, 19 made from one to seven scoring errors each, as identified by RIAP4. Many of the scoring errors changed the interpretation of the test results, in some cases dramatically. As a result of these findings, McKinzey and Campagna recommend against use of the Comprehensive System for scoring and interpretation.[115]

---

[112] James M. Wood, M. Teresa Nezworski, William Stejskal, & R.K. McKinzey, *Problems of the Comprehensive System for the Rorschach in Forensic Settings: Recent Developments*, 1 J. Forensic Psychol. Prac. 89–103 (2001).

[113] John Hunsley & J. Michael Bailey, *Whither the Rorschach? An Analysis of the Evidence*, 13 Psychol. Assessment 472–85 (2001).

[114] John Hunsley & Gina Di Giulio, *Norms, Norming, and Clinical Assessment*, 8 Clinical Psychol.: Sci. & Prac. 378–82 (2001).

[115] R.K. McKinzie & Victoria Campagna, *The Rorschach, Exner's Comprehensive System, Interscorer Agreement, and Death*, WebPsychEmpiricist (Apr. 27, 2002), retrieved from www.wpe.info/papers table on Aug. 14, 2002.

Similarly, Vincent Guarnaccia, Charles A. Dill, Susan Sabatino, and Sarah Southwick had 21 graduate students and 12 psychologists score 20 Rorschach responses using the Comprehensive System. Nearly all scorers made errors.[116] In contrast, Gregory Meyer, Mark J. Hilsenroth, Dirk Baxter, John E. Exner Jr., J. Christopher Fowler, Craig C. Piers, and Justin Resnick examined scoring of the Rorschach by large samples of students, researchers, and clinicians, all using the Comprehensive System. They found a high level of accuracy across, and reliability among, the groups of scorers, particularly for summary (rather than individual) scores. Meyer *et al.* recommend that clinicians continually update the accuracy of their scoring, to ensure that errors do not occur.[117]

Several Comprehensive System proponents have responded to the above articles. Psychologist Irving B. Weiner, one of the foremost Rorschach experts, wrote that the Comprehensive System calls for a standardized administration and scoring, and that the test can be reliably scored. Further, the Comprehensive System does have reasonable norms, even if some of those about which questions have been raised are included, and the CS scoring of the Rorschach remains valid for most scoring purposes, he indicates. Further, he writes, the CS adds incremental validity in situations in which decisions must be made, including forensic evaluations. It must also be noted, he indicates, that many psychologists use the CS recommendations for administration and scoring of the Rorschach but use different interpretive strategies from those recommended by John Exner, the primary author of the Comprehensive System. Even if all the criticisms of the CS norms were valid, use of these other interpretive strategies would not be affected. In addition, many psychologists use primarily or exclusively idiographic interpretations that are case-specific rather than comparing an individual's CS scores with Exner's or any other normative group. This method circumvents all of the criticisms of the Comprehensive System, since each Rorschach protocol is individually addressed, with or without formal scoring. Weiner also suggests that Exner's normative groups may be better-adjusted than is a representative sample of the U.S. population, which would also lead to the finding that more representative samples would appear more pathological. Weiner's suggestion is that both the MMPI-2 and the Rorschach should be used in most evaluations, because each may yield data that is missed by the other test, as well as helping to confirm hypotheses based on either test.[118] Similar statements are made by other authors.[119]

Prominent researchers Gregory Meyer and Robert Archer indicate that no single measure of personality or psychopathology is so comprehensive that it may reasonably be used alone. Rather, one should look for incremental validity based on several overlapping

---

[116] Vincent Guarnaccia, Charles A. Dill, Susan Sabatino, & Sarah Southwick, *Scoring Accuracy Using the Comprehensive System for the Rorschach*, 77 J. Personality Assessment 464–74 (2001).

[117] Gregory J. Meyer, Mark J. Hilsenroth, Dirk Baxter, John E. Exner Jr., J. Christopher Fowler, Craig C. Piers, & Justin Resnick, *An Examination of Interrater Reliability for Scoring the Rorschach Comprehensive System in Eight Data Sets*, 78 J. Personality Assessment 219–74 (2002).

[118] Irving B. Weiner, *Advancing the Science of Psychological Assessment: The Rorschach Inkblot Method as Exemplar*, 13 Psychol. Assessment 423–32 (2001).

[119] Robert Rosenthal, Jordan B. Hiller, Robert F. Bornstein, David T.R. Berry, & Sherrie Brunell Neuleib, *Meta-Analytic Methods, the Rorschach, and the MMPI*, 13 Psychol. Assessment 449–51 (2001); Donald J. Viglione & Mark J. Hilsenroth, *The Rorschach: Facts, Fictions, and Future*, 13 Psychol. Assessment 452–71 (2001); Ronald J. Ganellen, *Weighing Evidence for the Rorschach's Validity: A Response to Wood et al. (1999)*, 77 J. Personality Assessment 1–15 (2001).

measures. They indicate that research evidence has established that the Rorschach is a valid test, with validity coefficients similar to those of other frequently used instruments such as the MMPI-2 and the Wechsler intelligence scales. They acknowledge that the Comprehensive System may appear to overpathologize, because the reference group is made up of people who are both relatively healthy and functioning well, and recommend that a sample representative of the U.S. population be collected. They recommend an approach to test interpretation that places the greatest weight on those factors that have been empirically replicated, and the avoidance of conclusions based on factors with little or no empirical support. They also caution against drawing inferences regarding whether a child was sexually abused from Rorschach results.[120] Dr. Meyer, in another article, indicates that the coding for the Comprehensive System form categories ("good" vs. "bad" form) has changed substantially over time on the basis of ongoing research, and will change in the future on the same basis. Rather than dismissing the CS, he asserts, one should foster research to further improve it. He also compares the continuing improvements in the CS with the periodically changed norms of intelligence tests, on which an individual whose tested IQ two generations ago was 100 would score at or below 84 based on current norms. Meyer also reports that analysis of data based on thousands of Rorschachs from non-clinical settings around the world that were scored utilizing the CS norms found that there was little difference from Exner's nonpatient data. Further, data on the first 100 people in the new nonpatient sample were analyzed, with the result that they evidence very slightly more psychopathology than Exner's earlier nonpatient sample but less than Exner's patient sample. He characterizes the differences as trivial.[121]

Psychologist Thomas Widiger, who was the research coordinator for the DSM-IV Task Force, seeks a middle ground. While noting that the Comprehensive System was a major advance over other, less concrete systems, he acknowledges that the problems identified must be rectified. The Rorschach itself, he indicates, "does provide useful and valid information and, as a projective test, it is a very intriguing instrument that might be helpful in the assessment of dispositions, needs, or conflicts that the person is unable or reluctant to acknowledge."[122] He questions, however, making it the primary source of data indicating whether an individual should have custody of his or her child. He also indicates that the current debate about the Comprehensive System, and, to a lesser degree, the Rorschach, may be predicated in part on a larger dispute among psychologists regarding the use of projective tests at all, despite the Rorschach's being characterized by the American Psychological Association's Board of Professional Affairs in 1998 as the "single, most powerful psychometric instrument ever developed."[123] He suggests that the Rorschach remains both useful and effective as a source of hypotheses regarding intrapsychic problems that may then be explored and validated by data from other sources.

---

[120] Gregory J. Meyer & Robert P. Archer, *The Hard Science of Rorschach Research: What Do We Know and Where Do We Go?*, 13 Psychol. Assessment 486–502 (2001).

[121] Gregory J. Meyer, *Evidence to Correct Misperceptions about Rorschach Norms*, 8 Clinical Psychol.: Sci. and Prac. 389–96 (2001).

[122] Thomas A. Widiger, *The Best and Worst of Us?*, 8 Clinical Psychol.: Sci. & Prac. 374–77, at 375 (2001).

[123] *Id.* at 376.

Psychologist Edward Aronow recasts the dispute by indicating that the error may be placing too much emphasis on the Rorschach as a psychometric instrument rather than as a rich source of clinical data and hypotheses. He urges that the primary use of the Rorschach be projective analysis, with the psychometric characteristics a secondary consideration.[124]

Psychologist John Exner Jr., primary developer of the Comprehensive System, also responded to the criticisms by various authors. He acknowledges that there are differences between the data presented by Shaffer *et al.* and the nonpatient data for the CS. He is critical of the methodology of Wood *et al.* and other CS opponents, and questions the validity of comparing samples that have widely disparate populations, ages, and other characteristics. With regard to the Shaffer *et al.* study, he notes that the nonpatient sample appears to have been unusually defensive, thereby skewing the results. This would not explain all of the differences, however, so he indicates that a new nonpatient sample is being developed to address various issues. He is also critical of the notion that psychopathology is diagnosed based on the differences between the scores of the nonpatient sample and those of an individual taking the test. Rather, he indicates, interpretation using the Comprehensive System involves reviewing seven clusters of data, developing hypotheses, and evaluating these hypotheses against data gathered from other sources regarding the individual.[125]

Exner has also published data on the first 175 individuals in the new nonpatient sample he and his colleagues are developing. He indicates that the data from these individuals are quite similar to that from the original sample of 600 people, collected between 1973 and 1986. He notes that a major revision of the CS was undertaken in 1990 because it was determined that Rorschach records with fewer than 14 responses were likely to be invalid. From a database with some 1,100 records, 700 met criteria for number of responses and distribution of gender, geography, and socioeconomic level. Exner also acknowledges that a serious error was made: it was discovered in 1999 that 221 records were included twice among the 700, skewing the data. The "700" records represented only 479 individuals. Those duplicate records have since been replaced with others that maintained the gender, geographic, and socioeconomic balance of the sample. The current normative group consists of 300 men and 300 women, with 120 individuals from each of five geographic areas of the United States, with partial stratification for socioeconomic level. In addition, data collection is proceeding for the new normative sample. Unfortunately, Exner indicates that data collection is proceeding at about the same rate as the original normative sample, which took 10 years to complete. That would put the end of the data-gathering in 2009, followed by publication of the results (though partial data could continue to be presented, as did this article).[126] Exner is periodically revising certain tables in *A Rorschach Workbook for the Comprehensive System, Fifth Edition*, published

---

[124] Edward Aronow, *CS Norms, Psychometrics, and Possibilities for the Rorschach Technique*, 8 Clinical Psychol.: Sci. & Prac. 383–85 (2001).

[125] John E. Exner, Jr., *A Comment on "The Misperception of Psychopathology: Problems with the Norms of the Comprehensive System for the Rorschach*, 8 Clinical Psychol.: Sci. & Prac. 386–88 (2001).

[126] John E. Exner, Jr., *A New Nonpatient Sample for the Rorschach Comprehensive System: A Progress Report*, 78 J. Personality Assessment 391–404 (2002).

in 2001. The latest revision is available for downloading from the Rorschach Workshops web site.[127]

The primary Comprehensive System critics (Garb, Wood, Lilienfeld, and Nezworski) published a 2002 article with several recommendations for current utilization of the Rorschach and other projective techniques:

> Clinical Guideline 1: Exercise caution when using the CS norms, as research indicates that their use is related to the overperception of psychopathology. In many instances, it may be best not to use the CS norms.[128]
>
> Clinical Guideline 2: Use scores that are valid for their intended purposes. Scores should be validated in well-designed studies, results should be consistent, and positive findings should be replicated by independent investigators.[129]
>
> Clinical Guideline 3: Do not use the Rorschach, TAT, or human figure drawings to detect child physical or sexual abuse.[130]
>
> Clinical Guideline 4: Use projective techniques differently depending on whether one is testifying in court as an expert witness, evaluating a client in clinical practice, or using a projective technique as an aid for exploration in psychotherapy.[131]

They also have some recommendations for assessments in general. With children, they recommend that data primarily be gathered via interviews with the children, with teachers, and/or with parents. The screening instruments they recommend are the Child Behavior Checklist or the Draw a Person: Screening Procedure for Emotional Disturbance (DAP: SPED). To diagnose children or adults, they recommend primary reliance on interviews and historical information, "but results from psychological tests, including self-report personality inventories and projective techniques, can sometimes be helpful," including careful use of the Rorschach with certain Comprehensive System variables or with criteria from non-CS methods. Behavioral predictions should primarily be predicated on interview and historical data, but projective techniques may help with prediction in certain areas. For assessment of psychiatric disorders and personality characteristics, they recommend reliance on history and interview information, brief self-report measures, and, if necessary, projective techniques. They again note the success of the Rorschach at identifying thought disorders and dependency tendencies. Finally, they recommend use of the Washington University Sentence Completion Test, which has extensive validation research behind it, but is not used by many clinicians as a source of data.[132]

---

[127] Rorschach Workshops web site, accessed Sept. 27, 2002.

[128] Howard N. Garb, James M. Wood, Scott O. Lilienfeld, & M. Teresa Nezworski, *Effective Use of Projective Techniques in Clinical Practice: Let the Data Help with Selection and Interpretation*, 33 Prof. Psychol.: Res. & Prac. 454–63, at 455 (2002).

[129] *Id*. at 457. The authors also indicate that the Rorschach has demonstrated validity at detecting thought disorders, e.g., a psychosis, as well as evaluating dependent personality traits. They also recommend it as a method for generating hypotheses in psychotherapy, for the purpose of identifying and addressing an individual's problems. They do not believe it valid at this time for other purposes.

[130] *Id*. at 459.

[131] *Id*. at 460.

[132] *Id*. at 461.

Three of the experts cited above presented papers at a seminar at the 2002 Convention of the American Psychological Convention: Gregory Meyer, Howard Garb, and Thomas Widiger. Dr. Meyer began by noting that the degree of interrater reliability in medicine tends to fall between .21 and .57, with examples being the .42 agreement on abnormalities in mammograms, .45 agreement on the meaning of cardiac arrhythmias, and .42 agreement on the meaning of PAP smears. In comparison, interrater agreement on the scoring of the Rorschach exceeds .80 in several studies, far better than most reliability ratings in medicine. Further, test-retest reliabilities have been found to average .79 for intelligence testing of adults ages 18 to 24; .85 for the Rorschach, .82 for the Wechsler Adult Intelligence Scale, and .74 for the Minnesota Multiphasic Personality Inventory. Validity coefficients for the Rorschach also compare favorably with other psychological tests, he indicated.[133]

Dr. Garb began by indicating that clinicians should not draw any conclusions about the presence or absence of sexual abuse from the Rorschach. He also questioned the validity of several of the Comprehensive System scales, noted Exner's error in double-counting 221 Rorschach protocols among the 700 protocols in the normative study, and criticized Exner for refusing to give independent evaluators access to his raw data. He emphasized the tendency of the Comprehensive System interpretation guidelines to overpathologize, the CS often being the only data source that indicates psychopathology, even when numerous other sources clearly indicate that there is none.[134]

Dr. Widiger indicated that projective techniques do have validity, reliability, and usefulness *when used appropriately and conservatively*. Most problems associated with prominent psychological tests are problems related to the competence of test users rather than problems with the tests. He emphasized that the Rorschach is very good at generating hypotheses, which may then be validated or invalidated by other data. It is not unusual for the Rorschach to identify significant issues that are not identified by other tests or lengthy interviews, he indicated.[135]

Psychologists Jeffrey M. Lohr, Katherine A. Fowler, and Scott O. Lilienfeld wrote, in a 2002 article, about what they call "pseudoscience," which they characterized as involving use of various means of shielding hypotheses from falsification; rigidity in the face of negative findings; use of language that sounds scientific but is not; relying on anecdotes rather than on systematic scientific methodology; trying to place the burden of proof on critics, rather than providing evidence that a methodology is valid and reliable; and use of alleged experts rather than systematic data to "prove" their case. They note that "clinical techniques, per se (e.g., the Rorschach Inkblot Test) are not pseudoscientific. Instead, the concept of pseudoscience applies to the ways in which certain proponents of these techniques deal with evidence, particularly evidence that contradicts their hypotheses."[136] They

---

[133] Gregory J. Meyer, *Overview of Evidence on the Rorschach and TAT*, Paper presented at the 110th Annual Convention of the American Psychological Association, Chicago (Aug. 25, 2002).

[134] Howard N. Garb, *Validity of Projective Techniques and Self-Report Tests*, Paper presented at the 110th Annual Convention of the American Psychological Association, Chicago (Aug. 25, 2002).

[135] Thomas A. Widiger, *Training Implications of Empirically Supported Assessments*. Paper presented at the 110th Annual Convention of the American Psychological Association, Chicago (Aug. 25, 2002).

[136] Jeffrey M. Lohr, Katherine A. Fowler, & Scott O. Lilienfeld, *The Dissemination and Promotion of Pseudoscience in Clinical Psychology: The Challenge to Legitimate Clinical Science*, 55 Clinical Psychologist no. 3, at 5 (2002).

indicate that, with the primary exception of indices relevant to detecting thought disorder, the indices derived from the Rorschach CS have been found to exhibit low or negligible construct validity. For example, although the Rorschach CS possesses some validity for detecting schizophrenia and related conditions, its validity for detecting depression, Post-traumatic Stress Disorder, psychopathy, and other psychiatric conditions appears to be weak. Nor is there compelling evidence that the CS is helpful for the detection of child sexual abuse, even though it is used frequently for this purpose.[137]

The authors end with a recommendation that "[t]he APA and other professional organizations must be willing to impose stiff sanctions, including expulsion if necessary, on practitioners who routinely use therapeutic and assessment practices that are devoid of scientific support."[138]

In response, psychologists Irving B. Weiner, Charles D. Spielberger, and Norman Abeles indicate that "the psychometric soundness of an assessment instrument is defined by stan-dardized procedures, intercoder agreement, reliability, normative data, and validity."[139] They proceed to indicate that "meta-analytic reviews and studies with patient and non-patient samples have identified mean Kappa coefficients [degree of agreement among multiple raters] across various Comprehensive System coding categories, ranging from .79 to .88, which is in the excellent range for Kappa." In addition, researchers have "found median and mean interrater coefficients of .92 and .90, respectively, for 164 structural summary variables in two independent ratings of 219 protocols containing 4,761 responses. . . . Without doubt, then, the RIM [Rorschach Inkblot Method] can be reliably coded using the Comprehensive System."[140]

Next, they indicate that "almost all of the variables coded in the Comprehensive System and conceptualized as relating to trait characteristics show substantial short-term and long-term stability, with retest correlations in excess of .75."[141] They further note that the claim of critics that the CS overpathologizes is largely based on poor-quality research. The current restandardization project, they indicate, yields data that "closely resemble the ear-lier reference data and dispel any concerns about overpathologizing."[142] With regard to validity, the authors indicate that meta-analytic studies have produced unweighted mean validity coefficients similar to those for MMPI variables. Finally, while Lohr *et al.* criticized the CS for failing to provide specific diagnoses, the authors indicate that the Rorschach is not meant to be a diagnostic test; it addresses personality processes. It does well at addressing thought disorders, which could lead to a diagnosis of a psychosis. It does well at addressing mood dysfunctions, which could lead to a diagnosis of depression. Thus, they indicate, the Rorschach, and the Comprehensive System, do well at identifying processes that con-tribute to diagnoses, but neither is meant to lead, per se, to a specific diagnosis, without data from other sources.[143]

---

[137] *Id.*

[138] *Id.* at 8.

[139] Irving B. Weiner, Charles D. Spielberger, & Norman Abeles, *Scientific Psychology and the Rorschach Inkblot Method*, 55 Clinical Psychologist no. 4, at 7 (2002).

[140] *Id.*

[141] *Id.* at 8.

[142] *Id.*

[143] *Id.*

Psychologist Stephen Hibbard criticized a paper by Lilienfeld, Wood, and Garb,[144] referenced at the beginning of this subsection, as making statements that are too broad considering the relatively narrow bases they have for those statements, and for ignoring the fact that at least some of the Comprehensive System norms that Lilienfeld *et al.* indicate "overpathologize" may, in fact, reflect accurately on the general level of psychopathology in the normative sample. Hibbard concurs with Lilienfeld *et al.* that the CS should be used with caution—or not used—with non-Caucasian populations, because there is minimal normative data for these groups. He is critical of Lilienfeld *et al.*'s claim that other researchers get lower test-retest coefficients for many scales than those reported by Exner. Three of the four studies cited by Lilienfeld *et al.* appear in peer-reviewed journals. None of those three studies actually provides test-retest data, Hibbard indicates. He does not comment on the fourth study.[145]

Psychologist Cato Gronnerod did a literature search for all journal articles, books, and dissertations that reported test-retest data from the Rorschach in English, Norwegian, Swedish, or Danish. He found 158 studies, with 23 studies providing 36 samples usable in meta-analyses. The average test-retest interval was just over three years. Eleven studies provided data on the Comprehensive System. Gronnerod found that "[t]he CS was consistently associated with higher temporal stability levels than other systems. Furthermore, the CS variable reliability coefficients were generally more consistent across samples than variables from other systems."[146]

The authors of the present text continue to believe that the Rorschach Inkblot Test has much to offer in child custody and other forensic evaluations. In our experience it has often yielded hypotheses about an individual that led to areas of inquiry that might have been missed without the input from this instrument. Test-taking attitude is also a valuable clinical component.

As indicated by most of the authors above, the Rorschach, like any single instrument, should not be used in isolation. There is strong evidence for its validity and reliability, and it can be a critical part of a complete evaluation. Its primary purpose should be to generate hypotheses regarding the individual taking the test, so that other sources of information (other tests, interviews with parent/child, collateral interviews, historical information, and so forth) may be used to confirm or deny the hypotheses formed.

Given the difficulty with accurate scoring of the Comprehensive System, as documented above, we recommend that all Rorschach protocols scored with the Comprehensive System be scored by the current version of the computer program designed for that purpose: the Rorschach Interpretation Assistance Program: Version 5 (RIAP5).[147] The available evidence indicates that the computer program is more accurate than the vast majority of clinicians at scoring the test.

---

[144] Scott O. Lilienfeld, James M. Wood, & Howard N. Garb, *The Scientific Status of Projective Techniques*, 1 Psychol. Sci. in Pub. Int. 27–66 (2000).

[145] Stephen Hibbard, *A Critique of Lilienfeld et al.'s "The Scientific Status of Projective Techniques,"* 80 J. Personality Assessment 260–71 (2003).

[146] Cato Gronnerod, *Temporal Stability in the Rorschach Method: A Meta-Analytic Review*, 80 J. Personality Assessment at 287 (2003).

[147] John E. Exner & Irving Weiner, Psychological Assessment Resources, Odanna, Fla.

While the Rorschach remains a valuable tool, the evidence that there are significant problems with interpretations based on the Comprehensive System is compelling, and psychologists should avoid making strong statements, including predictions, predicated on CS-based interpretive criteria until the research has established new guidelines. We recommend that psychologists use the CS interpretive guidelines with extreme caution or not at all, recognizing that there is now a substantial body of research indicating that those interpretations are likely to exaggerate the level of psychopathology actually present. In particular, if the conclusions based on the CS guidelines are the *only* source of evidence of psychopathology, even after careful investigation utilizing other tests, interviews, and reviews of historical information, the CS results should generally be given less weight or ignored. Interpretations *not* based on the Comprehensive System may continue to be made using other criteria.

§ 10.11   The Rorschach in Court

Psychologists Irving B. Weiner, John E. Exner Jr., and Anthony Sciara surveyed 93 psychologists who actively used the Rorschach in 7,934 federal and state court cases in which they had testified over a five-year period. This included 4,024 criminal cases, 3,052 custody cases, and 858 personal injury cases. Testimony was presented in courts in 32 states and many federal districts. Of these 7,934 cases, in only six was the integrity of the Rorschach seriously challenged, they indicate, and in only a single case was Rorschach testimony declared inadmissible.[148]

Psychologists J. Reid Meloy, Trayce L. Hansen, and Irving B. Weiner addressed the weight given to the Rorschach in 247 cases in federal, state, and military courts of appeal between 1945 and 1995. Of these, only 26 involved questions regarding the reliability or validity of the test—and these focused more on the interpretations made by psychologists than on the Rorschach itself. In some cases, the psychologist had gone beyond his or her data, in some the psychologist had focused on too narrow a portion of the data, and in some the Rorschach data was irrelevant to the legal matter before the court. In only two cases was the Rorschach "completely devalued as a psychological measure." The authors conclude that "the Rorschach has authority, or weight, in higher courts of appeal throughout the United States."[149]

Law professor Daniel Shuman writes, "The Rorschach is frequently used in expert witness testimony and forensic psychology, and Rorschach testimony is almost always admitted into evidence."[150]

---

[148] Irving B. Weiner et al., *Is the Rorschach Welcome in the Courtroom?*, 67 J. Personality Assessment 422–24 (1996).

[149] J. Reid Meloy et al., *Authority of the Rorschach: Legal Citations during the Past 50 Years*, 69 J. Personality Assessment 53, 60–61 (1997).

[150] Daniel W. Shuman, Psychiatric and Psychological Experts 2-31 (2d ed. 1994, Supp. 2000).

THEMATIC APPERCEPTION TEST

§ 10.12 Thematic Apperception Test

Although clinicians and researchers published various reports on the use of free association and stories as adjuncts to psychotherapy or personality research, there was no widely used method for doing so prior to the publication in 1935 of "A Method for Investigating Fantasies: The Thematic Apperception Test," by C.D. Morgan and Henry A. Murray in the *Archives of Neurology and Psychiatry*.[151] This was followed in 1938 by the publication, by psychologist Henry Murray and the staff of the Harvard Psychological Clinic, of *Explorations in Personality*, their report of research that led to the Thematic Apperception Test (TAT).[152] Today, the TAT is one of the most widely used and researched projective tests.[153]

According to the manual for the test, the TAT is

> a method of revealing to the trained interpreter some of the dominant drives, emotions, sentiments, complexes and conflicts of a personality. Special value resides in its power to expose the underlying inhibited tendencies which the subject, or patient, is not willing to admit, or can not admit because he is unconscious of them. . . . The technique is especially recommended as a preface to a series of psychotherapeutic interviews or to a short psychoanalysis.[154]

§ 10.13 Description of the TAT

The TAT consists of 31 cards, of which 30 are pictures in black and white and one is blank. Each card is approximately $9\frac{1}{4}$ by 11 inches in size. There are cards that were originally intended especially for men, some for women, some for boys, and some for girls (4 to 14 years of age).[155] The cards currently in use reflect the third revision of the test.[156]

The original instructions for the test called for the examiner to administer two series of 10 cards each, at least one day apart, with the cards chosen on the basis of the individual's gender and age. The examiner was to sit in back of the subject or patient and to note all verbalizations of the subject/patient. Each of the two sessions was to last about one hour.[157]

---

[151] C.D. Morgan & Henry A. Murray, *A Method for Investigating Fantasies: The Thematic Apperception Test,* 34 Archives Neurology & Psychiatry 289–306 (1935).

[152] Henry Murray, Explorations in Personality (1938).

[153] Richard Ryan, *Thematic Apperception Test, in* 2 Test Critiques 799 (D. Keyser & R. Sweetland eds., 1984) [hereinafter Ryan, *Thematic Apperception Test*]; Groth-Marnat (2003) at 477–78.

[154] Henry Murray, Thematic Apperception Test Manual 1 (1943) [hereinafter Murray, Thematic Apperception Test Manual].

[155] Morris Stein, *Thematic Apperception Test and Related Methods, in* Clinical Diagnosis of Mental Disorders 179–235 (B. Wolman ed., 1978) [hereinafter Stein, *Thematic Apperception Test and Related Methods*].

[156] Murray, Thematic Apperception Test Manual, at 2; Stein, *Thematic Apperception Test and Related Methods,* at 183–84.

[157] Murray, Thematic Apperception Test Manual, at 2–3.

However, clinicians commonly use fewer than 20 cards and administer the test in a single one-hour session.[158] The examiner selects those cards most likely to provide information germane to the purpose of the examination[159] or that "elicit themes that are thought to be pertinent to a given examinee's conflicts or concerns."[160]

Psychology Professor Richard Ryan writes that

> the single most important consideration in TAT administration is the creation of a psychological atmosphere in which the examinee feels relaxed, comfortable, and freely available to respond to the situation. Examiner rigidity or lack of friendliness or evaluative attitude is likely to result in constriction or discouragement of the subject, an unwanted situational contribution to the results. A quiet, comfortable physical setting is most suitable for the session.[161]

The instructions in the manual are as follows:

> This is a test of imagination, one form of intelligence. I am going to show you some pictures, one at a time; and your task will be to make up as dramatic a story as you can for each. Tell what has led up to the event shown in the picture, describe what is happening at the moment, what the characters are feeling and thinking; and then give the outcome. Speak your thoughts as they come to your mind. Do you understand? Since you have fifty minutes for ten pictures, you can devote about five minutes to each story.[162]

Although few psychologists use these exact instructions, psychologists can use them as a guide for the general content of the instructions. A parallel but simpler set of instructions, "suitable for children, for adults of little education or intelligence, and for psychotics" is also offered in the manual.

Murray added that the exact words of the instructions may be altered to suit the age, intelligence, personality, and circumstances of the subject.[163] He cautioned against using terms like *free imagination,* because this could lead the subject/patient to assume responses will be interpreted. "[The subject] should believe that the examiner is solely interested in his literary or creative ability."[164] After the first story, the examiner is to ask questions to bring out any of the key elements that are lacking (what is happening, what led up to what is happening, what is the person or are the people thinking and feeling, and what is the outcome?). Thereafter, the examiner speaks only to note whether the subject/patient is well ahead of or behind the five-minutes-per-story-average schedule, to provide some encouragement, or to bring out any of the key elements that are missing or inadequate. The examiner does not discuss the story at all. If a story is too long or rambling, the examiner may ask, for example, "How does it turn out?" Inquiries about details by the subject/patient are to be answered, "You may make it anything you please." The average story length is about 300 words for adults and 150 words for 10-year-old children.

---

[158] Korchin, Modern Clinical Psychology, at 242.

[159] Groth-Marnat (2003) at 478.

[160] Ryan, *Thematic Apperception Test,* at 801.

[161] *Id.* at 804.

[162] Murray, Thematic Apperception Test Manual, at 3.

[163] *Id.* at 4.

[164] *Id.*

Since Murray's 1943 manual was written, much research has been done on test-related variables. For example, Morris Stein, Ph.D., of the New York University Department of Psychology, notes that "there is no research evidence as to the effect of any [seating] position on TAT responses. The position selected has to suit the individual subject, the examiner, and the conditions of the examination."[165] Research has suggested "that Murray's instructions [with regard to imagination] result in stories of sadder emotional tone and outcome than is true of instructions designed specifically to be mental or intellectual."[166] Stein also cites two studies indicating that, "even without specific instructions to do so, subjects seem to be generally predisposed to appear at their best when telling TAT stories."[167] Research has supported Murray's statement that average story length is 300 words for adults and 150 words for children, except that in clinical situations the average is about 100 words.[168]

Some examiners conduct an *inquiry* at the end of the test in an effort to obtain additional information about the thoughts, feelings, and interactions of characters in particular stories. This inquiry is reserved for the end, so that the subject/patient is not cued as to what might be a desirable story.[169]

Recording the Stories

There are pros and cons to each of several methods of recording the stories. An examiner who can write quickly enough may write everything down him- or herself, taking note of both what is said by the subject/patient and the examiner's own questions and observations. If the examiner writes slowly, or has to ask the individual to repeat something, however, it can interfere with rapport and cause the subject to feel frustrated. Many examiners, therefore, tape-record the stories, transcribing them later. This also allows the examiner to note facial expressions, body language, and other non-verbal information during the test. The potential problem with this method is the loss of the material if the recorder fails for any reason. The examiner may, as a third alternative, ask the subject/patient to write down his or her own stories. This is the only possible method when the TAT is administered in a group (and slides of the pictures are available for that purpose). There is a potential, however, for the stories to be more formal, more controlled, and less spontaneous than verbalized stories, as well as lacking data on pauses, changes in tone of voice, and so forth. No research indicates which method is best.[170]

§ 10.14   Analysis and Interpretation of the TAT

"Unlike the Rorschach, there are no generally accepted systems of TAT scoring and interpretation."[171] Although several psychologists have attempted to formulate such

---

[165] Stein, *Thematic Apperception Test and Related Methods,* at 185–86.

[166] *Id.* at 186.

[167] *Id.*

[168] *Id.* at 187.

[169] *Id.*

[170] *Id.* at 188; Groth-Marnat (2003) at 488.

[171] Groth-Marnat (2003) at 478.

a system, most clinicians proceed to analyze the results impressionistically, as Murray did.[172]

> The data from the TAT can be scored according to a variety of existing quantitative systems. However, more commonly in clinical use the stories are interpreted in accord with general principles of inference derived from psychodynamic theory. Its use in clinical assessment is generally part of a larger battery of tests and interview data, which provide the background and convergent information necessary for appropriate interpretation. . . . [T]he strength of the "test" is no better than the . . . interpretive skills of the examiner in dealing with the material. . . . In this sense the TAT is more a method than a "test."[173]

In the manual, Murray indicates that, first, one must have basic facts about the subject: "the sex and age . . . whether his parents are dead or separated, the ages and sexes of his siblings, his vocation and his marital status."[174] The TAT was not meant to reveal those details, and analysis without basic background information, he suggests, is a "stunt" rather than acceptable clinical practice.

Next, the interpreter reads and rereads the stories, looking for significant elements. Murray recommends that the interpreter analyze each story into "the force or forces emanating from the hero, and . . . the force or forces emanating from the environment."[175] The *hero* is the character in each story with whom the subject/patient has identified him- or herself. The interpreter then looks at the *motives, trends, and feelings of the heroes* in each story, hypothesizing that these are projections of the thoughts and feelings of the subject/patient.

Then the interpreter looks at the *forces of the hero's environment,*[176] noting which elements of the pictures are emphasized and which are ignored, as well as which elements not shown in the picture are included in the stories. The interpreter evaluates how the hero relates to people and other aspects of the environment.

Fourth, the interpreter looks at *outcomes.*[177] What are the successes and failures of the heroes? How hard do the heroes fight? Do the heroes make things happen or have things happen to them? Does punishment follow transgression?

On one or more pictures the subject may misperceive significant elements—for example, misidentifying the sex of the characters or missing objects that most subjects/patients include in their stories. In many cases, these data indicate that the picture evokes particularly significant feelings.

Finally, the interpreter combines all the elements to look at the *themas* (themes) in the stories—the interactions among the heroes, the environments, and the outcomes. The interpreter hypothesizes about things the subject/patient has done or wishes to do, aspects of the subject/patient's personality, his or her feelings and desires, possible future behavior, relationships with people in general and significant people in particular, and so forth. Test-related behavior that may be significant is also noted—which stories were hardest to

---

[172] *Id.* at 478, 482–83.

[173] Ryan, *Thematic Apperception Test,* at 799–800.

[174] Murray, Thematic Apperception Test Manual, at 6.

[175] *Id.* at 7–10.

[176] *Id.* at 10–12.

[177] *Id.* at 12–13.

begin or resolve, which involved the greatest intensity of voice or other clear signs of emotion, and so forth.[178] Psychology Professor Richard Ryan notes that *response latency*—the time it takes the subject to begin telling a story—may yield information about which cards the subject responds to most strongly, emotionally, because those are likely to have response times significantly longer or shorter than the average for that individual.[179]

Murray again cautions that "the conclusions that are reached by an analysis of TAT stories must be regarded as good 'leads' or working hypotheses to be verified by other methods, rather than as proved facts."[180]

Psychology Professor Jon D. Swartz, of the University of Texas at Odessa, notes that "almost any dynamic theory of personality, particularly psychoanalysis and its various derivations, can be used as a basis for analysis of stories."[181] Thus, knowing which particular structure the interpreter utilizes is not crucial—the crucial element is that the interpreter have an appropriate structure with which to analyze the stories.

§ 10.15   Reliability and Validity of the TAT

Because of the lack of a generally agreed-upon scoring and analysis system, the reliability and validity of the TAT are harder to demonstrate than for the Rorschach.

> Reliability and validity seem especially hard to establish for the TAT due to the open-ended free response nature of the task, the high degree of interaction between situational factors and personality, the great difficulty in obtaining suitable independent criteria against which to validate inferences about unconscious aspects of personality, and the problems encountered in trying to develop meaningful, quantitative measures from stories.[182]

Ryan particularly cautions, as did Murray, against predictions of behavior based solely on the TAT. According to Ryan "[t]he TAT is most appropriate for looking at psychological processes that may or may not have direct behavior correlates,"[183] making it necessary for the examiner to find convergent data from other sources before drawing conclusions. Used properly, Ryan notes that "the TAT method can be used for special purposes and can provide credible, sometimes impressive, results."[184]

Professor of Law Daniel Shuman concludes that "the TAT is designed to be used for diagnosis of mental disorders as well as for understanding the patient's attitudes. This information may be useful, even crucial, to diagnosis and treatment planning when combined with other test data and the history."[185]

---

[178] *Id.* at 6.

[179] Ryan, *Thematic Apperception Test,* at 805.

[180] Murray, Thematic Apperception Test Manual, at 14.

[181] Jon D. Swartz, *Thematic Apperception Test, in* The Eighth Mental Measurements Yearbook 1128 (1978) [hereinafter Swartz, *Thematic Apperception Test*].

[182] Groth-Marnat (2003) at 482–83.

[183] Ryan, *Thematic Apperception Test,* at 810.

[184] *Id.* at 812.

[185] Daniel Shuman, Psychiatric and Psychological Evidence 53 (1986).

A series of studies by Allan Lundy, Ph.D., of the Marshall University Psychology Department, have found that the conditions of test administration are significantly related to the test results. A 1984 study Lundy presented to the American Psychological Association indicated that results were less accurate if the experimenter came on as an authority figure, if students were tested in their classrooms, or if the TAT was presented as a "test."[186] A 1985 study found that reliability was markedly higher when the TAT was given as a first test rather than later in a test battery, and that a test-retest method indicated reliability coefficients at about the level of those for the MMPI and 16PF.[187] In a 1988 study, Lundy used four sets of instructions, one set designed to be neutral, according to Murray's criteria, and the other three to be more stressful. He found that the neutral instructions produced a substantial validity coefficient, while the other instructions produced zero or negative validity coefficients.[188] Lundy suggests that the "best way to give the TAT is in as relaxed, friendly, and approving a manner as one can manage. Also, a TAT should never follow an objective test or cognitive task, as these evoke a verbal, task-oriented approach which is likely to persist and spoil the TAT."[189]

In summary, although reliable and valid scoring systems exist for the TAT, there is no widely used system at present. Most clinicians use the TAT as part of a test battery and as a form of structured clinical interview to gather data that can be combined in an attempt to fully understand the individual. Used in this manner, the reliability and validity of the interpretation are dependent on the ability of the interpreter to evaluate the data in the context of the other information available about the individual. To maximize the validity and reliability of the instrument, it should be administered at the beginning of a battery of tests, in a relaxed, positive environment.

§ 10.16 Intended Audience for the TAT

According to Ryan, "[a]ppropriate subjects [for the TAT] are those who range in age from 4 through adult. However, since projective story tasks more pertinent to childhood issues are available, the TAT is most widely used for subjects who are late adolescents or older."[190]

---

[186] Allan Lundy, Testing Conditions and TAT Validity: Meta-Analysis of the Literature through 1983, Paper presented at the 92d Annual Convention of the American Psychological Association, Toronto (Aug. 1984).

[187] Allan Lundy, *The Reliability of the Thematic Apperception Test*, 49 J. Personality Assessment 141–45 (1985).

[188] Allan Lundy, *Instructional Set and Thematic Apperception Test Validity*, 52 J. Personality Assessment 309–20 (1988).

[189] *Id.* at 318.

[190] Ryan, *Thematic Apperception Test*, at 804.

§ 10.17   Acceptance of the TAT by Mental Health Professionals

A 1989 study by Chris Piotrowski and John Keller found that the TAT was the sixth-most-popular projective test and the ninth-most-popular test overall in outpatient mental health clinics.[191]

The results of a study in 1991 by Robert Archer and his colleagues showed that the TAT was the third-most-popular projective test, and the fourth-most-popular test overall, for use with adolescents, according to a survey of 165 psychologists. For the 139 respondents who utilize a standard test battery, the TAT was in third place, with 63 percent of the psychologists including it in their standard batteries.[192]

A 1992 report by Paul Lees-Haley on tests used by forensic psychologists indicated that the TAT was the fifth-most-widely-used projective test, and the 10th-most-frequently-used test, among the 69 forensic psychologists who responded.[193]

A 1995 study by C. Edward Watkins Jr. and colleagues found that the TAT was the fifth-most-frequently-used assessment procedure by clinical psychologists, with 82 percent using it.[194]

The 1997 study of custody evaluation practices of psychologists by Marc Ackerman and Melissa Ackerman found that the TAT was the fifth-most-frequently-used test for adults, with 29 percent of the psychologists using the test.[195]

According to psychologist Gary Groth-Marnat, the TAT is the fourth-most-researched psychological test, behind the MMPI/MMPI-2, the Wechsler intelligence scales, and the Rorschach.[196]

CHILDREN'S APPERCEPTION TEST

§ 10.18   Children's Apperception Test

Leopold Bellak and Sonja Bellak developed the Children's Apperception Test (CAT) in 1949, using anthropomorphic animals instead of human beings. These animals were presented in pictures that paralleled human activities that the child may experience in everyday life. Originally, the CAT was developed to look at specific problem areas such as feeding problems, oral problems, problems about acceptance in the adult world, and

---

[191] Chris Piotrowski & John Keller, *Psychological Testing in Outpatient Mental Health Facilities: A National Study,* 20 Prof. Psychol.: Res. & Prac. 423, 424 (1989).

[192] Robert Archer et al., *Psychological Test Usage with Adolescent Clients: 1990 Survey Findings,* 22 Prof. Psychol.: Res. & Prac. 247, 248–50 (1991).

[193] Paul Lees-Haley, *Psychodiagnostic Test Usage by Forensic Psychologists,* 10 Am. J. Forensic Psychol. 25, 26 (1992).

[194] Watkins et al. at 57.

[195] Ackerman & Ackerman at 140.

[196] Groth-Marnat (2003) at 485.

problems related to loneliness, toilet behavior, and masturbation. Animals were chosen because research supports the theory that children identify more readily with animals.[197]

§ 10.19   Description of the CAT

The CAT employs 10 cards approximately 8½ by 11 inches in size. The picture on each card is a black-and-white cartoon-like depiction of anthropomorphic animals. The cards are used for children 3 to 10 years of age, or for older, developmentally delayed children. The original instructions suggested by Bellak and Bellak stated:

> For actual instruction, it may be best to tell the child that we are going to engage in a game in which he has to tell a story about pictures; that he should tell what is going on, what the animals are doing. At suitable points, the child may be asked what went on in the story before and what will happen later.[198]

Bellak and Bellak suggest that the examiner may need to encourage the child. However, it is important for the examiner not to be suggestive in his or her prompting. As part of the process, the examiner should ask the child with regard to each of the cards why the subjects of the story were performing certain tasks, how they felt, what they were thinking about, or other related important variables.

During the course of the test, the examiner should record all extraneous activities and comments. All pictures except the one being utilized at the moment should be kept out of sight. The Bellaks suggest that all 10 cards be administered in the same order in which they are numbered.

After general test administration, some examiners prefer to do an additional inquiry. The instructions for this additional inquiry would be, "Now I would like you to go back through the cards and put them in two piles. Put all of the cards that you like in this pile and all of the cards that you didn't like in this pile." After the separation is made, the examiner states, "Now look through the pile of cards that you liked, and choose the one that you liked the most. After that, look through the pile of cards that you didn't like and choose the one that you liked the least." The examiner then asks the child why he or she chose each of the cards.

§ 10.20   Analysis and Interpretation of the CAT

When interpreting the CAT, Leopold Bellak suggests that 10 different variables be assessed. They are

1. Main themes
2. Main hero

---

[197] L. Bellak, T.A.T., C.A.T. and S.A.T. in Clinical Use 242 (4th ed. 1986) [hereinafter T.A.T., C.A.T. and S.A.T. in Clinical Use].

[198] L. Bellak & S. Bellak, Children's Apperception Test 2 (1949).

3. Main needs and drive of the hero

4. Conception of the world

5. Relationship to others

6. Significant conflicts

7. Nature of anxiety

8. Main defenses utilized

9. Superego structure

10. Integration and strength of the ego.[199]

These variables are evaluated for each of the stories given on each of the 10 cards. The examiner then looks for a pattern or consistency across the stories to further the interpretation process.

§ 10.21   Reliability and Validity of the CAT

As is true of the TAT, because of the lack of a consistent scoring system for the CAT, the reliability and validity are much more difficult to demonstrate than on other tests. In the section of Bellak's book on the CAT, there is no report of any reliability or validity studies.[200]

Clifford V. Hatt, in *The Ninth Mental Measurements Yearbook,* states, "There is little, if any normative data available, poor coefficients of internal consistency and retest reliability, and inconclusive validation. In sum, the CAT is psychometrically inadequate."[201] Accordingly, the CAT, like the TAT, is addressed much like a structured clinical interview.

§ 10.22   Intended Audience for the CAT

The CAT is for use with children 3 to 10 years of age who are able to verbalize. It can be used with children beyond 10 years of age who are developmentally delayed but who function at the 3- to 10-year-old level.

§ 10.23   Acceptance of the CAT by Mental Health Professionals

Marcie B. Shaffer, in *The Ninth Mental Measurements Yearbook,* states, "Like most projective techniques, [the CAT] provides dubious psychometric data, but rich information regarding the unique emotional reactions of an individual child. . . . Despite the

---

[199] L. Bellak, The TAT, CAT and SAT in Clinical Use 75 (5th ed. 1993).

[200] TAT, CAT and SAT in Clinical Use.

[201] Clifford V. Hatt, *Children's Apperception Test, in* Ninth Mental Measurements Yearbook 315 (J. Mitchell Jr. ed., 1985).

shortcomings mentioned above, the CAT remains what it has been for decades, 'a classic of its genre.' "[202] Morris I. Stein states, "[T]he CAT may be superior for use with disturbed children with respect to the problems specifically tested for in the CAT."[203] Hatt points out that considerable training and skill are required in the administration and interpretation of the CAT.[204]

A 1992 report by Paul Lees-Haley on tests used by forensic psychologists indicates that the CAT was the seventh-most-widely-used projective test, and the 21st-most-frequently-used test, among the 69 forensic psychologists who responded.[205]

A 1995 report on assessment procedures used by clinical psychologists, by C. Edward Watkins Jr. and colleagues, indicated that the CAT was the fifth-most-frequently-used projective test, and 21st-most-frequently-used test, among the 412 psychologists who responded to the survey.[206]

As reported in **Chapter 3**, the Ackerman and Ackerman study found the CAT to be the most-widely-used children's projective technique in custody evaluations.

§ 10.24   Children's Apperceptive Story-Telling Test

A new children's apperception test was published in 1989, entitled the Children's Apperceptive Story-Telling Test. The instrument is referred to as the CAST and is used with 6- to 13-year-old children. It was developed by Mary Schneider and has an advantage over the CAT in that the stimuli cards are in color and are more contemporary. Seventeen cards are administered to all subjects. Three of the cards are given to everyone, and 14 of the cards have separate male and female versions available.

A scoring system has been thoroughly developed that measures 19 different variables, resulting in T-scores. A review in the *12th Mental Measurements Yearbook* by Psychology Professor Edward Aronow states, "In short, the CAST represents the most serious and psychometrically sound effort thus far to develop an apperceptive story-telling technique for use with children."[207] He goes on to state, "[T]he CAST is strongly recommended for use in preference to the CAT because of the greater neutrality of the stimuli presented, the modernity of the pictures, the use of color, and use of White, African-American, Hispanic and Asian children in the test stimuli."[208] An additional review by psychologist Martin

---

[202] Marcie B. Shaffer, *Children's Apperception Test, in* Ninth Mental Measurements Yearbook 316–17 (J. Mitchell Jr. ed., 1985).

[203] Morris I. Stein, *Thematic Apperception Test and Related Methods, in* B. Wolman, Clinical Diagnosis of Mental Disorders 214 (1978).

[204] Clifford V. Hatt, *Children's Apperception Test, in* Ninth Mental Measurements Yearbook 316 (J. Mitchell Jr. ed., 1985).

[205] Paul Lees-Haley, *Psychodiagnostic Test Usage by Forensic Psychologists,* 10 Am. J. Forensic Psychol. 25, 26 (1992).

[206] Watkins et al. at 57.

[207] Edward Aronow, *Children's Apperceptive Storytelling Test (CAST), in* Twelfth Mental Measurements Yearbook 181 (1995).

[208] *Id.*

Weise states, "In summary, the CAST successfully meets its objective to be a valid, reliable, theory-based, objectively scored apperceptive instrument, supported by a nationally standardized representative sample of children, ages 6 through 13."[209]

PROJECTIVE DRAWINGS AND OTHER TECHNIQUES

§ 10.25   Projective Drawings

As long as psychologists have been doing assessments, they have recognized that some of the information they desired could not be gained through verbal interactions. Children, by nature, do not possess the ability to express themselves fully in a verbal manner. Developmentally, children lack the vocabulary and the communication skills to which adults have access. In order to present thoughts and feelings about their experiences, children need to be provided with a suitable means of expression. Self-expression through drawing offers children a familiar, non-threatening way to talk.[210]

Because children start drawing before they learn to talk, drawing techniques can be very useful in assessing children's intellectual and personality functioning. Many researchers have asserted that for children, drawing is a language. Koppitz, a developer of research in drawings, identified 30 characteristics of human figure drawing as important emotional indicators. He looked at the quality of drawings, features that were omitted, and features that were included, though not typically present in the actual human figure.[211]

Wohl and Kaufman pointed out that there are limitations to using drawings for children. "Drawings uncover what children *will not* tell us or what they *cannot* tell us because they dare not reveal certain feelings even to themselves."[212]

§ 10.26   Draw-a-Person Test

Although drawings have been used for the past century as projective techniques, it was not until the 1920s that a standardized measure of drawings was developed by Goodenough. Goodenough developed the Draw-a-Man Test in 1926. It was initially developed for children between 3 and 15 years of age as a quick estimate of a child's intellectual development. Goodenough developed a 50-item scoring scale.

---

[209] Martin Weise, *Children's Apperceptive Storytelling Test (CAST), in* Twelfth Mental Measurements Yearbook 182–83 (1995).

[210] S. Tritell, Diagnostic and Therapeutic Uses of Drawings of Children Who Have Been Sexually Abused, A Review of the Literature 12 (1988) (unpublished doctoral dissertation, Wisconsin School of Professional Psychology) (on file with authors) [hereinafter Diagnostic and Therapeutic Uses of Drawings of Children Who Have Been Sexually Abused].

[211] Koppitz, The Psychological Evaluation of Children's Human Figure Drawings (1968).

[212] Wohl & Alan Kaufman, *cited in* Diagnostic and Therapeutic Uses of Drawings of Children Who Have Been Sexually Abused at 12.

In 1949, Machovers changed the technique from a "Draw-a-Man" to a "Draw-a-Person" (DAP) technique.[213] The Draw-a-Person Test was the first to formally extend drawing techniques from tests of cognitive development into personality interpretation based on projective testing theory.[214] The DAP is the most-frequently-used drawing technique. "Within clinical settings, quantitative scoring systems for cognitive development, emotional disturbance, impulsiveness, or cognitive impairment are rarely used, despite their greater levels of reliability and validity."[215] Much of the research that has been performed with these instruments is anecdotal and of little use. Psychologist Gary Groth-Marnat states:

> One major criticism of the projective drawings is the frequent subjectivity involved in their interpretation. This happens primarily when interpretations are made from intuitive judgments based on assumed isomorphy between the drawings and the person or his or her world. . . . It might be speculated that subjectivity is doubled, in that not only might the client subjectively project portions of self into the drawing, but the interpreter might project self into his or her interpretations.[216]

§ 10.27   Goodenough-Harris Drawing Test

In 1963, Harris updated the Goodenough Draw-a-Man Test to include a drawing of the self and of a woman. Scoring criteria were presented for each of the drawings. Harris added 22 items to Goodenough's original criteria.

Jerome Sattler, one of the foremost experts in intelligence testing, pointed out that "the Goodenough drawing test is an acceptable screening instrument for use as a non-verbal measure of cognitive ability, particularly with children under 10 or 11 years of age."[217] However, because of its reduced validity, Sattler felt that the drawing test should not be used as the only measure of intelligence.

§ 10.28   House-Tree-Person Drawing Test

In working with noncompliant children, J.N. Buck, out of desperation, requested subjects to draw a house, a tree, and a person. He chose these three items because they represented the items most frequently spontaneously drawn by children. In this drawing test, the subject is first asked to draw a house, a tree, and a person on separate pages. After the drawing of a person has been completed, the subject is asked to draw a person of the opposite sex.[218]

---

[213] Machovers (1949).

[214] Gary Groth-Marnat, Handbook of Psychological Assessment 501 (1997) [hereinafter Groth-Marnat (1997)].

[215] Id. at 502.

[216] Id. at 505.

[217] Jerome Sattler, Assessments of Children's Intelligence and Special Abilities 250 (2d ed. 1982).

[218] J.N. Buck & E. Hammer, Advances in the House-Tree-Person Technique: Variations and Applications (1969).

Although a thorough discussion of the interpretation of the House-Tree-Person Drawing Test is not possible in a book of this nature, "the house is thought to represent the environment, the tree depicts growth, and the person represents the integration of the subject's personality."[219]

The House-Tree-Person Drawing Test has advantages over the Draw-a-Person Test in that it includes a greater variety of objects drawn, resulting in a greater number of areas of interpretation. However, the lack of extensive research on the instrument is a major concern.[220]

§ 10.29   Draw-a-Family Test

The Draw-a-Family Test was originally developed by Appel and later elaborated on by Wolfe.[221] There are generally two acceptable methods of presenting this test. One method requires the subject to "draw a picture of your whole family" and the other requests the subject to "draw a picture of *a* family." Some examiners prefer the more ambiguous request to draw *a* family, as it provides the examiner with the opportunity to measure the subjects' identification with their own families. Family constellation, placement of individuals in the family, relative sizes of the family members, and other variables are used in interpreting the Draw-a-Family Test.

§ 10.30   Kinetic Family Drawing Test

The Kinetic Family Drawing (KFD) Test was developed by R.C. Burns and S.H. Kaufman in 1970. "The Approach of Using Kinetic (Action) instructions—i.e., asking the child to produce a drawing of figures *moving* or doing something—has been found to produce much more valid and dynamic material in the attempt to understand the psychopathology of children in a family setting."[222]

The instructions given by the examiner state, "I would like you to draw a picture of everybody in your family doing something." Of particular importance in the interpretation of this picture is noting whether the family is doing something together or whether each individual is doing something separately.

The Kinetic Family Drawing Test is a more popular variation of the Draw-a-Family Test in that it reduces the rigidity and noninteractive effect of the traditional Draw-a-Family Test.[223] A number of different objective scoring systems have been developed for the Draw-a-Family Test and Kinetic Family Drawing Test. However, the success of these systems is questionable, due to their variable reliability and validity.

---

[219] J. DiLeo, Children's Drawings as Diagnostic Aids (1973), *cited in* Diagnostic and Therapeutic Uses of Drawings of Children Who Have Been Sexually Abused at 35.

[220] Groth-Marnat (1997) at 524.

[221] Wolfe et al., *Early Intervention for Parents at Risk of Child Abuse and Neglect: A Preliminary Investigation,* 6 J. Consulting & Clinical Psychol. 40–47 (Feb. 1988).

[222] R.C. Burns & S.H. Kaufman, Kinetic Family Drawings (KFD): An Introduction to Understanding Children through Kinetic Drawings 17–18 (1970).

[223] Groth-Marnat (1997) at 530.

§ 10.31   Other Drawing Techniques

Many minor drawing techniques have been developed for use in interpreting specific kinds of personality concerns. The number of drawing techniques developed is limited only by the creativity of the examiner. Examples include:

1. Draw-a-Person-in-the-Rain Task, to measure how the individual deals with unpleasant environmental stress.
2. Draw-a-Dream Test, designed to depict a dream that the child actually has had or one that the child would like to have.
3. Representational family drawing, developed by Violet Oaklander in an effort to measure how the child representationally perceives each family member. The instruction "draw a picture of something that represents each member of your family" is given.
4. Draw a picture of an island and include all the things that the individual would need to live on the island, suggested by Gary Groth-Marnat.[224]

Although projective drawings have been used since the inception of psychological assessment, the authors who take a narrow, "scientific" stand on assessment issues object to projective drawings because it is difficult to demonstrate their validity and reliability. As a result, there is doubt that projective drawings would meet the *Daubert* standard. While projective drawings can be a good source of clinical hypotheses that can be addressed through interviews and other means, their scientific limitations should be acknowledged.

§ 10.32   Bender Visual Motor Gestalt Test

The Bender Visual Motor Gestalt Test is commonly referred to as the Bender-Gestalt Test. It is widely used by clinical psychologists as a screening device for the detection of brain damage. Nine simple designs are shown to the subject, one at a time, and the subject is instructed to copy each design. Many clinicians still interpret the Bender-Gestalt subjectively. However, several objective scoring systems have been developed by matching drawing errors resulting from reproducing the simple designs. Koppitz developed the most extensive scoring system for use of the Bender-Gestalt with children. Although fairly reliable for children under 10 years of age, the Bender-Gestalt does not correlate significantly with intelligence test scores or age for individuals beyond 10 years of age.

Some clinicians use the Bender-Gestalt as a subjective personality test. As a personality test, it has questionable validity.[225] Age effects begin to show up in the 60s. The Bender-Gestalt remains one of the best screening tests for organic brain damage.[226]

---

[224] *Id.* at 533.

[225] A. Anastasi, Psychological Testing 486–89 (6th ed. 1988).

[226] Muriel Deutsch Lezak, Neuropsychological Assessment 567 (3d ed. 1995).

§ 10.33   Roberts Apperception Test for Children

The Roberts Apperception Test for Children (RATC) was developed by Glen E. Roberts in 1982 for children between 6 and 15 years of age. It involves the use of 27 stimulus pictures, 11 for boys, 11 for girls, and five for both boys and girls. As a result, each subject receives 16 cards to respond to. "The pictures all represent common interpersonal situations of childhood and pull for such themes as aggression, sibling rivalry, parental support, and relationships to maternal figures."[227]

Although several apperception tests have been developed previously, the RATC is the first to provide an objective scoring system. The scoring criteria are divided into three major categories—the Adaptive Scales, Clinical Scales, and Critical Indicators:

1. The Adaptive Scales address reliance on others, support-other, support-child, limit setting, problem identification, and problem resolution.

2. The Clinical Scales measure anxiety, aggression, depression, rejection, and unresolved problems.

3. The Critical Indicators address atypical responses, maladaptive outcomes, and refusal to participate.

In response to the lack of stimulus pictures for black children, Glen Roberts published a supplementary RATC with pictures of black children. In specific response to that version of the RATC, Ron Cambias and his coauthors state:

> The addition of a set of stimulus pictures targeting black populations is part of a growing movement to develop apperception tests that show sensitivity to ethnic differences while addressing the need for psychometric rigor. . . . However, with the lack of normative reliability and validity data, test users would be unwise to use this additional set for anything other than research purposes. When and if psychometric rigor is attained, the Supplementary Test Picture for Black Children will take its place among the more sound apperception tests developed in recent years, of which the original RATC was a significant forerunner.[228]

Although it has been criticized for "pulling" for certain types of stories, the Roberts Apperception Test for Children represents a serious effort to combine the flexibility of projective techniques with a valid scoring system. Further research and clinical use will determine how valid an instrument this will become over time.[229]

The Ackerman and Ackerman study in 1997 demonstrated that the RATC is used by 10 percent of the respondents and ranked 14th among tests used with children in child custody evaluations.[230] This compared to 9 percent and a ranking of 12th 10 years earlier in the Keilin and Bloom study.[231] This indicates that, during the past 10 years, the

---

[227] Ron Cambias et al., *Roberts' Apperception Test for Children: Supplementary Test Pictures for Black Children, in* 9 Test Critiques 431–37 (D. Keyser & R. Sweetland eds., 1992).

[228] *Id.* at 436.

[229] *Id.* at 605.

[230] Ackerman & Ackerman at 139.

[231] Child Custody Evaluation Practices at 341.

acceptance and utilization of the RATC has not increased, suggesting that it has not gained the foothold that the authors would have anticipated. It is not even mentioned in Gary Groth-Marnat's *Comprehensive Handbook of Psychological Assessment–Fourth Edition* (2003).

§ 10.34 Acceptance of Drawing and Other Techniques by Mental Health Professionals

A 1989 study by Piotrowski and Keller found that the Bender-Gestalt was the most popular projective test, and the third-most-popular test overall, in outpatient mental health clinics surveyed. Human figure drawings ranked as fifth-most-popular overall, sentence completion tests as sixth, the House-Tree-Person Drawing Test as seventh, and the Children's Apperception Test as 14th.[232]

A 1991 study by Robert Archer and colleagues found, for use with adolescents, the Bender-Gestalt ranked as the third-most-frequently-used test, Human Figure Drawings ranked was seventh, the House-Tree-Person Drawing Test was eighth, the Kinetic Family Drawing Test was 10th, and the Roberts Apperception Test was 23d, according to a survey of 165 psychologists. For the 139 respondents who utilize a standard test battery, the Bender-Gestalt was fourth, with 49 percent of the psychologists including it in their standard batteries. The Kinetic Family Drawing Test was seventh, used by 41 percent of those responding to the survey. Human figure drawings ranked eighth, used by 33 percent. The House-Tree-Person Drawing Test was ninth, used by 30 percent.[233]

A 1992 report by Paul Lees-Haley on tests used by forensic psychologists indicates that the Bender-Gestalt was the fourth-most-frequently-used test among the 69 forensic psychologists who responded. Human figure drawings ranked seventh, the House-Tree-Person Drawing Test was 13th, and the Children's Apperception Test was 21st.[234]

A 1995 study by C. Edward Watkins and colleagues found that the Bender-Gestalt was the seventh-most-frequently-mentioned test, and the most-frequently-mentioned drawing technique, among the 412 psychologists who responded to their survey. A general "projective drawings" category was ranked eighth.[235]

The 1997 study by Ackerman and Ackerman found that "miscellaneous projective drawings" ranked seventh among tests administered to children, the Kinetic Family Drawing Test was ranked 10th, and the Bender-Gestalt was ranked 13th among the 201 respondents.[236]

---

[232] Chris Piotrowski & John Keller, *Psychological Testing in Outpatient Mental Health Facilities: A National Study,* 20 Prof. Psychol.: Res. & Prac. 423, 424 (1989).

[233] Robert P. Archer et al., *Psychological Test Usage with Adolescent Clients: 1990 Survey Findings,* 22 Prof. Psychol.: Res. & Prac. 247, 248–50 (1991).

[234] Paul Lees-Haley, *Psychodiagnostic Test Usage by Forensic Psychologists,* 10 Am. J. Forensic Psychol. 25, 26 (1992).

[235] Watkins et al. at 57.

[236] Ackerman & Ackerman at 139.

Gary Groth-Marnat indicates that, in spite of questions about its research and utility, the Bender-Gestalt has been one of the half-dozen most frequently used tests for many years.[237]

VINELAND ADAPTIVE BEHAVIOR SCALES

§ 10.35   Vineland Adaptive Behavior Scales

The Vineland Social Maturity Scale, originally developed by E.A. Doll, was more recently revised by American Guidance Service. Its name has been changed to the Vineland Adaptive Behavior Scales. The Vineland focuses on what the person usually or habitually does. Four major *domains* are explored by the Vineland. They are

1. Communication
2. Daily living skills
3. Socialization
4. Motor skills.

These domains allow the examiner to compare the level at which a child is functioning with reference to the general population. Supplementary norms have been established for retarded, emotionally disturbed, visually handicapped, and hearing-impaired individuals.[238] The test is designed for use with children from birth through 18 years 11 months. According to psychologist Jerome Sattler, who reviewed the instrument in the *Tenth Mental Measurements Yearbook,* it is a "potentially useful tool for the assessment of adaptive behavior, [but] the fluctuations in the means and [standard deviations] of the standard scores from age group to age group are a problem, particularly with mentally retarded individuals."[239] The Vineland Adaptive Behavior Scales and Vineland Social Maturity Scale were ranked 21st and 22d, respectively, in the 1990 survey of assessment instruments used with adolescents by Robert Archer and colleagues.[240] The Vineland Social Maturity Scale was ranked 22d on the list of assessment procedures of psychologists in the study by C. Edward Watkins and colleagues,[241] and also 22d among the forensic psychologists surveyed by Lees-Haley in 1992.[242] Neither instrument was among the 20 most-frequently-used instruments in the Ackerman and Ackerman study.[243]

---

[237] Groth-Marnat (2003) at 529.

[238] Ron Cambias et al., *Roberts' Apperception Test for Children: Supplementary Test Pictures for Black Children, in* 9 Test Critiques 287–90 (D. Keyser & R. Sweetland eds., 1992).

[239] Jerome M. Sattler, *Vineland Adaptive Behavior Scales, in* Tenth Mental Measurements Yearbook 881 (Jane Close Conoley & Jack J. Kramer eds., 1989).

[240] Robert P. Archer et al., *Psychological Test Usage with Adolescent Clients: 1990 Survey Findings*, 22 Prof. Psychol.: Res. & Prac. 249 (1991).

[241] Watkins et al. at 57.

[242] Paul Lees-Haley, *Psychodiagnostic Test Usage by Forensic Psychologists*, 10 Am. J. Forensic Psychol. 25, 26 (1992).

[243] Ackerman & Ackerman at 139.

CHAPTER QUESTIONS

§ 10.36   Questions for Chapter 10

Attorneys should not expect to be able to go into court and ask all the following questions. Preparation is necessary, referring to the content of the chapter to determine whether a particular question applies to a specific case. The section number at the end of several of the questions refers to the place in this book where readers can find an explanation of why a particular question may be important.

1.   What projective techniques were administered?

2.   What is the reliability and validity of the test used? Ask the psychologist to produce evidence of reliability and validity of any test that is not discussed fully in this book. Use the criteria in **Chapter 7** to determine whether the test is reliable or valid.

3.   If the psychologist used only projective methods for testing, why? This would especially be an important question if the MMPI-2 or an intelligence test was not administered.

4.   Were the instructions for the specific projective tests followed according to the manual? Ask the examiner to repeat the instructions that were given. If the instructions varied from those indicated in this chapter, ask the psychologist why.

5.   Were the projective instruments administered prior to objective instruments? If not, why not? See **§§ 10.3** and **10.5**.

6.   If the individual used an experimental test, did the test follow the APA guidelines for psychological tests? See **Chapter 2**. See **Appendix B**, Ethical Principles of Psychologists and Code of Conduct. See also *Standards for Educational and Psychological Testing*.

7.   If the Rorschach was administered, what was the seating arrangement? See **§ 10.4**.

8.   On the Rorschach, were both a free association and inquiry used? If an inquiry was not used, ask why. See **§ 10.4**.

9.   On the Rorschach, what scoring method was used, if any? If a scoring method was not used, ask why. See **§ 10.5**. If the Comprehensive System (Exner) was used, ask about the controversy about scoring of many parts of the CS.

10.   Did a psychologist identify a scoring method other than those discussed in this chapter? If so, ask for professional literature that substantiates the use of that other scoring method.

11.   Were the Rorschach cards administered in order? If not, why not?

12.   How many TAT cards were administered? See **§ 10.13**.

13.   Did the examiner use any philosophical system or psychological theory when interpreting the TAT? See **§ 10.14**.

14.   Were all 10 cards of the CAT administered? If not, why not? See **§ 10.19**.

15.   Were any of the additional practices in administering the CAT used? See **§ 10.19**.

16.   What projective drawings were used? See **§§ 10.25** through **10.33**.

17. If projective drawings were not used, why not?

18. How did the interpretations of the projective drawings tie into the results of the other instruments administered? Ask the psychologist for this information.

19. Were any drawings other than those identified in this chapter used? If so, ask the psychologist to explain the purpose for use of the drawings and how their interpretations apply to the overall results.

CHAPTER 11

OTHER TESTS USED IN CHILD CUSTODY EVALUATIONS

§ 11.1   History of Custody Decisionmaking

The Ackerman-Schoendorf Scales for Parent Evaluation of Custody (ASPECT)

The ASPECT is an instrument that utilizes a battery of information that is designed specifically to provide information for child custody evaluations. It attempts to identify those characteristics that are reported in psychological literature as being determinative of fitness for custody (Chasen & Gruenbaum, 1991;[1] Emery, 1988;[2] Gardner, 1982;[3] Hetherington, 1979;[4] Karras & Berry, 1985;[5] Wolfe, 1985;[6] Barnard & Jenson, 1984;[7] Berkman, 1984;[8]

---

[1] R. Chasen & H. Gruenbaum, *A Model for Evaluation in Custody Disputes*, 9 Am. J. Fam. Therapy no. 3, at 43–47 (1991).

[2] R.E. Emery, Marriage, Divorce and Children's Adjustment (1988).

[3] Richard A. Gardner, Family Evaluation in Child Custody Litigation (1982).

[4] E.M. Hetherington, *Divorce: A Child's Perspective* 34 Am. Psychologist 851–58 (1979).

[5] D. Karras & K. Berry, *Custody Evaluations: A Critical Review*, 16 Prof. Psychol.: Res. & Prac. 76–85 (1985).

[6] David A. Wolfe, *Child-Abusive Parents: An Empirical Review and Analysis*, 97 Psychol. Bull. 462–82 (1985).

[7] C.P. Barnard & G. Jenson, *Child Custody Evaluations: A Rationale Process for an Emotion-Laden Event*, 12 Am. J. Fam. Therapy no. 2, at 61–67 (1984).

[8] C.F. Berkman, *Psychodynamic and Family Issues in Post-Divorce Child Custody Litigation*, 23 J. Am. Acad. Child Psychiatry 708–12 (1984).

Lowery, 1984;[9] Wallerstein, 1983;[10] Keilin & Bloom, 1986;[11] Rae-Grant & Award,[12] 1977; McDermott et al., 1978;[13] Beaber, 1982;[14] Goldstein, Freud, & Solnit, 1973;[15] Belsky, Robbins & Gamble, 1984;[16] Guidubaldi, Cleminshaw, Perry, Nastasi, & Adams, 1984;[17] Hetherington, Cox, & Cox, 1978;[18] Camara & Resnick, 1989;[19] Johnston, Kline, & Tschann, 1989;[20] Exner, 1974;[21] Klopfer & Kelley, 1942),[22] and it was developed in the late 1980s and published in 1992 by Western Psychological Services (WPS). The ASPECT was developed by the authors out of frustration generating from questions asked in court during an examination and cross-examination about recommendations that psychologists were making regarding custody and placement of children. Judges and attorneys typically asked questions about how psychologists were able to determine which parent would make a better placement or custodial parent. The authors reviewed the psychological literature at that time and found 63 different variables identified as being related to parenting ability and fitness for parental custody or placement. After a pilot study with 25 couples, this number was reduced to 56 variables that were utilized in formulating the ASPECT that was eventually published, as seven of the variables were found to be non-discriminators. Some of the 56 items were empirically based and some were rationally based. The manual for the ASPECT explains each of these items in greater detail.

---

[9] C.R. Lowery, *Parents and Divorce: Identifying the Support Network for Decisions about Custody*, 12 Am. J. Fam. Therapy no. 3, at 26–32 (1984).

[10] Judith S. Wallerstein, *Children of Divorce: The Psychological Tasks of the Child*, 53 Am. J. Orthopsychiatry 230–43 (1983).

[11] W.G. Keilin & L.J. Bloom, *Child Custody Evaluation Practices: A Survey of Experienced Professionals*, 17 Prof. Psychol. Res. & Prac. 338–46 (1986).

[12] Q. Rae-Grant & G. Award, *The Effects of Marital Breakdown, in* P.D. Steinhauer & Q. Rae-Grant eds., Psychological Problems of the Child in the Family 565–91 (1977).

[13] J.F. McDermott, T. Wem-Shing, W.I. Char, & M.A. Fukunaga, *Child Custody Decisions Making*, Am. Acad. of Child Psychiatry (1978).

[14] R.J. Beaber, *Custody Quagmire: Some Psychological Dilemmas*, 10 J. Psychiatry & L. 309–26 (1982).

[15] Joseph Goldstein, Anna Freud, & A.J. Solnit, Beyond the Best Interests of the Child (Free Press 1973).

[16] J. Belsky, J. Robbins, & W. Gamble, *The Determinants of Parental Competence: Toward a Theory, in* Beyond the Dyad 251–75 (1984).

[17] J. Guidubaldi, H. Cleminshaw, J. Perry, B. Nastasi, & B. Adams, Longitudinal Effects of Divorce on Children: A Report from the NASP-KSU Nationwide Study, Paper presented at the meeting of the American Psychological Association, Toronto, Canada (Aug. 1984).

[18] E.M. Hetherington, M. Cox, & R. Cox, *The Aftermath of Divorce, in* J. Stevens & M. Mathews eds., Mother-Child, Father-Child Relations 149–76 (National Ass'n for the Educ. of Young Children 1978).

[19] K.A. Camara & G. Resnick, *Styles of Conflict Resolution and Cooperation between Divorced Parents: Effects on Child Behavior and Adjustment*, 59 Am. J. Orthopsychiatry 560–75 (1989).

[20] Janet R. Johnston, Marsha Kline, & Jeanne M. Tschann, *Ongoing Postdivorce Conflict: Effects on Children of Joint Custody and Frequent Access*, 59 Am. J. Orthopsychiatry 576–92 (1989).

[21] John E. Exner, The Rorschach: A Comprehensive System (1974).

[22] Bruno Klopfer & D.M. Kelley, The Rorschach Technique (1942).

The initial stage of using the ASPECT involves each parent's completing a Parent Questionnaire, which is composed of questions regarding preferred custody arrangements, living and child-care arrangements, the children's development and education, the relationship between the parent and the children, and the relationship between the parents. Questions are also included about information derived from collateral sources, about the parent's background, mental health history, substance abuse concerns, and legal history. The original ASPECT placed a heavy emphasis on testing. Each parent was administered an intelligence test, the MMPI-2, the Rorschach, Projective Questions, and achievement testing. In addition each parent was observed with the children. Children completed an intelligence test, the CAT/TAT, and projective drawings. After all data are gathered from the parents, children, and collateral sources and reviewed, the examiner rates each parent on a total of 56 items. Twelve of the items are described as "critical items" because they represent significant indicators of parenting deficits. The 56 items are equally weighted based on a rational approach and are combined to form a Parental Custody Index (PCI) for each parent.

§ 11.2   Important Parental Characteristics

In an effort to clarify the best interests test, numerous psychologists have attempted to define specific environmental and parental characteristics that best serve the interests of the child. J.A. Goldstein, Ann Freud, and A.J. Solnit suggested that the child should be placed with a *psychological parent*, defined as the parent or other person who provides continued companionship in a stable environment.[23] They focused on the "least detrimental alternative" and stressed the need for continuity in the child's life. R. Chasin and H. Gruenebaum attempted to further specify precisely which characteristics the custodial parent should possess.[24] They emphasize the following factors:

1. A favorable attitude toward the non-custodial parent
2. Ability to maintain continuity in the child's relationship to peers, school, and relatives
3. Skilled parenting (empathy, knowledge of the child's daily routine, appreciation of developmental levels, ability to communicate, competent guidance, and discipline)
4. Humane, flexible, but consistent child management
5. Attachment to the child that is not based on the parent's own needs.

C.P. Barnard and G. Jenson added to this already lengthy list, focusing on the emotional security and mental stability of the parent as well as the parent's ability to realistically perceive future problems and to solve them effectively. The parent's awareness of and access to community supports and services, and insights into the children, self, and the non-custodial parent are also important factors.[25]

---

[23] J.A. Goldstein et al., Beyond the Best Interests of the Child 73 (1973).

[24] R. Chasin & H. Gruenebaum, *A Model for Evaluation in Custody Disputes*, 9 Am. J. Fam. Therapy no. 2, at 43–47 (1981).

[25] C.P. Barnard & G. Jensen, *Child Custody Evaluations: A Rational Process for an Emotion-Laden Event*, 12 Am. J. Fam. Therapy at 61–67 (1984).

Other variables deemed important by various researchers include affection, ability to stimulate, parents' ability to maintain good relationships with their own parents, appreciation of the effects of divorce on the children, and ability to encourage positive character traits and good health habits.[26]

Clearly, the above list of variables considered to be important when determining the child's best interests is so lengthy as to be unmanageable. Not only are some of these variables as vague as the initial "psychological parent" concept, but also they are difficult to test. For example, how does one measure "appearance" and "ability to encourage good character traits" or "ability to solve problems" in the future? A further difficulty with this list of variables is that they do not come directly from research on the effects of divorce and various custody arrangements on children, but rather from either theoretical models of parenting or research in the general area of child development. Although such concepts may be helpful, it has been argued that when trying to determine the best interests of the child in a custody dispute, one should stay close to findings from empirical studies on children of divorce.

Two major long-term studies have been done with children of divorce. These are the Virginia Longitudinal Study of Divorce[27] and the California Children of Divorce project.[28] The results of these two studies indicate that family disorganization, anger, conflict between parents, and impaired coping ability of the custodial parent negatively affected the child's adjustment to the divorce. Positive outcome was related to availability of the non-custodial parent in a conflict-free parental relationship. The results offer some support for children doing better if in the custody of the same-sex parent.[29] However, both studies emphasize that overall adjustment of the children of divorce is a highly individual phenomenon. It may be more closely related to the developmental level of the child, the child's previous coping strategies, and successes with regard to other idiosyncratic variables within the individual family than to any overriding characteristics of the parents or the environment. Thus, we come full circle, back to the notion of examining each individual family, case by case, within the vague framework of "best interests of the child" to determine which custody arrangement is best in each particular case. See **Chapter 4** for a discussion of the needs of children.

The reader is referred back to **Chapter 3** of this book to review the typical procedure used in custody disputes, which was reported by Ackerman and Ackerman.[30] Besides the data that come from the psychological tests recommended in the Ackerman and Ackerman study, other pertinent information for making custody decisions must be gleaned from interviews and observations.

Interviews, psychological testing, and observation of interactions between parent and child can provide needed information about the members of the family and the relationships between them. Still needed, however, is information regarding the social support

---

[26] *Id.*

[27] Hetherington, *Divorce: A Child's Perspective*, 34 Am. Psychologist 851–58 (1979).

[28] Judith Wallerstein, *Children of Divorce: The Psychological Tasks of the Child*, 53 Am. J. Orthopsychiatry 230–45 (1983).

[29] *The Father's Case in Child Custody Disputes.*

[30] Marc J. Ackerman & Melissa C. Ackerman, *Child Custody Evaluation Practices: A Survey of Experienced Professionals (Revisited)*, 28 Prof. Psychol: Res. & Prac. (1997).

system of each parent. Although this aspect of parenting is often overlooked, researchers J. Belsky, J. Robins, and W. Gamble suggest that the social support system of the parent often makes the difference between good and poor child development.[31] They propose a theoretical model, referred to as the "buffered" system, wherein parental competence includes not only the personal characteristics of the parent but also the characteristics of the child and the social support system of the parent. They suggest that personal resources of the parent are not enough, in some cases, to ensure good development of a child.

The review of the current psychological literature provides a seemingly lengthy and unmanageable number of variables deemed important by researchers, and presents a wide range of methods used to assess these variables. Clearly, what is needed is a clinical tool that assesses all variables deemed important and provides a measure that can be used to compare one parent to another and to compare parents across studies.

THE ASPECT

§ 11.3   ASPECT Subscales

The ASPECT has three subscales, which form the combined Parental Custody Index (PCI). The Observational Scale (9 items) assesses the self-presentation and appearance of the parent. The Social Scale (28 items) addresses the parent's social conduct and interaction with others, including children, the other parent, and the community. The Cognitive-Emotional Scale (19 items) reflects the psychological health and emotional maturity of the parents. Data derived from psychological testing are primarily considered on items found on the Cognitive-Emotional Scale. At the time of the development of the ASPECT, the items were divided into the three scales based on face validity. It was hoped at the time that there would be subscale analyses of each of these areas. However, the research never supported the use of looking at the subscales exclusively. As a result, the total PCI is the only measure that should be used for interpretation.

§ 11.4   Principles of Use

The ASPECT is intended for use with parents who are disputing custody of one or more of their children. It employs a self-report format and should not be utilized with individuals who are unable or unwilling to cooperate in responding to the Parent Questionnaire. This would include parents who choose to stop after part of the Parent Questionnaire has been completed, who are unable to read the questionnaire, or who are unable to understand the questions when read to them. Evaluators must be cautious when examining subjects who have had prior exposure to the questions on the Parent Questionnaire in that they may have been educated on how to respond to the items by their previous experience

---

[31] J. Belsky et al., *The Determinants of Parental Competence: Toward a Theory, in* Beyond the Dyad (M. Lewis ed., 1984).

with the instrument. Because of its standardization, the ASPECT should not be used in cases involving placement with non-parent relatives, cases involving same-sex couples, couples who are cohabiting but not married, or grandparents. Furthermore, the ASPECT should not be used with parents who only have children under two years of age since 10 percent of the items are not applicable.

§ 11.5   Standardization Sample

The standardization sample consisted of 200 parents and their children. The mean age of the parents was 34.4 years, while the mean number of children per family was 2.28. The distribution of occupations among the participants approximated the statistical break-downs of individuals working in the United States at the time of standardization. Two major differences were noted between the standardization sample and the United States norms. While 20 percent of those in the United States had less than a high school diploma, only 6 percent of this sample did. Furthermore, 96.9 percent of the participants were Caucasian. This skewed number is representative of the fact that the lower socioeconomic groups tend to not have access to custody evaluations or are unable to afford custody evaluations.

§ 11.6   Validity and Reliability

The ASPECT is considered to be content and face valid, because the questions used in the Parent Questionnaire are derived from the literature on custody-related issues. The questions on the Parent Questionnaire were derived from the 56 variables that the literature demonstrated were related to parenting or custody as indicated earlier in this chapter. The gender study as well as the intercorrelation matrix give evidence of construct validity. The gender study was performed in an effort to ensure that the ASPECT was measuring parenting and not mothering and fathering. There was not a significant difference between the mean scores of mothers on the PCI and fathers on the PCI. Any difference between mothers and fathers was found on the Social Scale, where mothers had a significantly higher mean score than fathers. However, on the overall PCI there was no significant difference. The original research performed by WPS indicated that the PCI summary score had an adequate internal consistency reliability of .76 (Cronbach alpha). The overall interrater reliability on the PCI was .96 with a standard error of measurement of 4.90. The interrater reliability coefficients on the Observational, Social, and Cognitive-Emotional Scales were .92, .94, and .94, respectively.

   Some gender differences were noted utilizing a chi square analysis of each item. Mothers were found to be significantly better at identifying age-appropriate developmental milestones ($p < .05$), having an awareness of the child's relevant school information ($p < .05$), more actively participating in the child's education, and providing sex education ($p < .05$), oral hygiene training ($p < .01$), and general hygiene training ($p < .01$). On the other hand, fathers had a significantly higher arrest record ($p < .01$) and significantly higher incidents of being charged with sexual abuse and physical abuse ($p < .01$). This information is also useful for child custody evaluations outside the use of ASPECT.

Predictive validity was originally assessed by comparing the outcome of a child custody case with the PCI score after the case had been competed. Criticism has been leveled against using judge's orders as a basis for predictive validity, which will be discussed later in this chapter. Since that time, other research has been performed to address these issues. These studies were all performed post-publication of the original ASPECT but are included in the most recent revision of the manual. Because of the nature of the new studies, the criterion contamination concern was not an issue as was the case with the "judge's orders" study.

In a sample of 200 parents Ackerman and Ackerman[32] subdivided ASPECT scores into a number of categories postjudgment. They included all parents; all placement parents; all non-placement parents; all placement fathers; all placement mothers; all non-placement fathers; all non-placement mothers. The overall mean on the ASPECT was 78.1, which was not significantly different from the standardization sample. All placement parents had a significantly higher mean of 81.8 compared to a mean of 74.3 ($p < .01$) for all non-placement parents. The highest mean (83.1) was found among all placement mothers, while the lowest mean (73.6) was found in all non-placement fathers ($p < .01$).

These means were all calculated with ASPECT after each case was concluded. This study was performed almost simultaneously with the publication of the ASPECT. Since it was a new instrument, the study was designed to demonstrate that the PCI could adequately discriminate between placement and non-placement parents, placement and non-placement mothers, and placement and non-placement fathers.

Gordon Hubbard compared the ASPECT results with the then newly developed Parent-Child Relationship Inventory (PCRI) (N=60). The PCRI assesses parents' attitudes toward parenting and toward their children. At the time, it was used with about the same frequency as the ASPECT by psychologists conducting child custody evaluations.[33] When correlating mothers' scores on the PCRI and ASPECT and fathers' scores on the PCRI and PCI of the ASPECT, the results were very low. The correlations for mothers generally ran in the .2 to .3 range, while the correlations for fathers were around 0. This clearly demonstrates that the PCRI and PCI are measuring different variables. Since the PCRI and PCI are measuring different variables, it may be advantageous to administer both instruments when performing a child custody evaluation since neither of these tests is designed to stand alone in custody or placement decisionmaking. As is true of any battery of tests, the utilization of more than one instrument adds to the overall validity of the recommendations being made.

Pamela Beyer[34] examined the relationship between the parents' PCI scores and their children's satisfaction living in each parent's home using the Life Satisfaction Post Divorce (LSPD) Questionnaire (1996). All of the subjects in this study were postjudgment and not currently involved in any custody-related litigation. The subjects were an average of three years post-divorce. An average of three years after the divorce, 67 percent of the

---

[32] Marc J. Ackerman & Scott D. Ackerman, Comparison of Different Subgroups on the MMPI of Parents Involved in Custody Litigation (1992).

[33] Marc J. Ackerman & Melissa C. Ackerman, *Child Custody Evaluation Practices: A Survey of Experienced Professionals*, 28 Prof. Psychol. Res. & Prac. 137–45 (1997).

[34] Pamela Beyer, The Development and Preliminary Validation of the Life Satisfaction in Children: Post Divorce (1996) (unpublished doctoral dissertation, Wisconsin School of Professional Psychology).

children who found life with their fathers to be more satisfying had fathers with higher PCIs than their mothers at the time of the divorce, while 73 percent of the children who considered living with their mothers to be more satisfying than living with their fathers had higher PCIs than their fathers at the time of the administration. Although this study had a relatively low sample size (N=22), its implications for predictive validity are strong. Replications with a larger total sample would be desirable.

Susan Schoendorf[35] performed a study investigating the relationship between the PCI of the Ackerman-Schoendorf Scales for Parent Evaluation of Custody-Short Form (ASPECT-SF) and various scales of the Minnesota Multiphasic Personality Inventory–Second Edition (MMPI-2). The sample size of this study was 100 pairs of divorced parents who were no longer involved in a custody dispute but who had been previously. Because six scores from the MMPI-2 are utilized to determine the PCI on the ASPECT, the ASPECT-SF was used for this study as it does not rely on psychological testing. Schoendorf found that a significant inverse correlation existed between the PCI of the ASPECT-SF and Scales 4, 6, and 9, Content Scales ASP, FAM, and WRK, and the MAC-R. The only significant positive correlation existed between the Responsibility Scale and the PCI of the ASPECT-SF. When looking at the Clinical Scales, Content Scales, Subscales, and Supplementary Scales, there was no best single predictor of a lower PCI-SF score on the MMPI-2.

Caldwell and Ackerman are currently working on a project comparing the ASPECT scores with the interpretation program that Alex Caldwell has developed for the use of the MMPI-2 in custody cases.

§ 11.7   ASPECT-Short Form (ASPECT-SF)

In 2000 the ASPECT-SF was developed for two reasons. In the 10 years since the ASPECT had been developed, there appeared to be less of an emphasis being placed on psychological testing in making custody and/or placement recommendations. Second, the ASPECT-SF can be used by all mental health professionals since no testing is required. The ASPECT-SF consists of the 41 ASPECT items that are not tied to test results. ASPECT-SF scores are highly correlated with ASPECT scores (r =.93). The logical question that evolves from these data is why would one give the full ASPECT when the PCI-SF correlates .93 with the PCI?[36]

§ 11.8   Interpretation

The ASPECT has a mean of approximately 78 and a standard deviation of 10. This mean and standard deviation have held up over a half-dozen different research projects cited above. Since the standard deviation is 10, it is suggested that when the PCIs are within 10 points of

---

[35] Susan Schoendorf, A Correlation Study of Parental Custody Index (PCI) of the Ackerman-Schoendorf Scales for Parental Evaluation of Custody-Short Form (ASPECT-SF) and Selected Scales from the Minnesota Multiphasic Personality Inventory-2 (MMPI-2) (2001) (unpublished doctoral dissertation).

[36] Marc J. Ackerman & Susan Schoendorf, *The Ackerman-Schoendorf Scales for Parent Evaluation of Custody–Short Form*, Western Psychological Services 1 (2000).

one another, the parents are relatively equal in their parenting capacity. As a result, joint custody with substantially equal placement with both parents is recommended. When the PCIs are more than 20 points apart it suggests that the parent with the higher PCI is substantially more fit to parent and that primary placement with the possibility of sole custody should be explored for the parent with the higher score. The authors decided that when there is more than one child and the scores are different for specific items, the ASPECT items would be scored in the majority direction. When the scores are between 10 and 20 points apart, more careful scrutiny should be given to the collateral information to help determine whether the difference in scores indicates it would be better to pursue a joint-custody substantially equal placement schedule or a primary sole-custody type of arrangement instead. As is true of all tests that are administered in child custody evaluations, there is no single instrument that should "rule the day." A combination of all factors must be considered. One of the values of the ASPECT is that it summarizes these variables in helping make the custody and placement decisions.

§ 11.9   Usage

Between 1992 and 2004, 2,300 ASPECT kits were sold by Western Psychological Services.[37] Of course, purchase of the ASPECT does not necessarily mean its use. Marc Ackerman and Melissa Ackerman[38] reported that 11.4 percent of the psychologists they surveyed who conducted child custody evaluations indicated use of the ASPECT. Those psychologists who employed the measure reported using it in the large majority (90 percent) of the custody evaluations they performed. Quinell and Bow[39] report about the use of custody batteries in child custody evaluations. They indicate that 16 percent of those surveyed used the ASPECT 74 percent of the time. Although this still represents a relatively small percentage of psychologists, it is approximately a 50 percent increase in use as reported in the Marc Ackerman and Melissa Ackerman study.[40] The authors also indicate that it is the most "commonly used battery"[41] even with this limited use. The ASPECT was used twice as frequently as any other custody battery approach. Twenty percent of 156 family law judges throughout the country who were surveyed by Marc Ackerman and Linda Steffen[42] reported familiarity with the ASPECT, while 38 percent of the 15 family law attorneys surveyed by Marc Ackerman and Shannon Kelly-Poulos[43]

---

[37] Personal communication with Louis Warren (Apr. 23, 2004).

[38] Marc J. Ackerman & Melissa C. Ackerman, *Child Custody Evaluation Practices: A Survey of Experienced Professionals (Revisited)*, 28 Prof. Psychol. Res. & Prac. (1997).

[39] F.A. Quinell & J.N. Bow, *Psychological Tests Used in Child Custody Evaluations*, 19 Behav. Sci. L. 491–501 (2001) [hereinafter Quinell & Bow].

[40] Marc J. Ackerman & Melissa C. Ackerman, *Child Custody Evaluation Practices: A Survey of Experienced Professionals (Revisited)*, 28 Prof. Psychol. Res. & Prac. 137–45 (1997).

[41] Quinell & Bow at 498.

[42] Marc J. Ackerman & Linda J. Steffen, *Family Law Judge's Expectations of Psychologists Performing Child Custody Evaluations*, 15 Am. J. Fam. L. 12–16 (2001).

[43] Marc J. Ackerman & Shannon Kelly-Poulos, Child Custody Evaluation Practices: A Survey of Family Law Attorneys (2001) (unpublished doctoral dissertation, Wisconsin School of Professional Psychology).

reported familiarity with the measure. In general, the attorneys were about as familiar with the ASPECT as any other specialized test developed for the purpose of performing child custody evaluations.

§ 11.10   Criticism

When the ASPECT was originally developed, it was reviewed in the *Mental Measurements Yearbook* and in other literature. David Brodzinsky[44] reviewed a number of instruments that have been used for custody evaluations. He states, "Two interesting and more quantitative approaches to the assessment of custody and visitation disputes have been developed by Barry Bricklin[45] and Marc Ackerman and Kathleen Schoendorf."[46] He concludes:

> Despite the limitations of these alternative assessment procedures, they represent a valuable addition to the field of child custody evaluations. Most important, they shift the focus from a more traditional clinical assessment to one in which the evaluator is focusing more on a functional analysis of the parties' competencies within specific childcare roles. As such, these instruments are likely to provide information that is particularly relevant to the issues before the court.[47]

Wellman[48] wrote a critique of the ASPECT indicating that "the terms making up the ASPECT relate closely to the current literature on appropriate criteria for custody decisions. Further the measure uses criteria from many sources (intellectual, personality, and academic achievement tests, interviews, and observations) creating a comprehensive database."[49]

Randy Otto and J.F. Edens[50] and Otto, Edens, and E.H. Barcus[51] provide thoughtful critiques of the ASPECT. Otto, Edens, and Barcus report three primary concerns. The basic concern that is identified throughout the literature is with regard to basic psychometric properties, as indicated in the work by Joyce Arditti,[52] Gary Melton,[53] and

---

[44] David Brodzinsky, *The Use and Misuse of Psychological Testing in Child Custody Evaluations*, Prof. Psychol. Res. & Prac. 213–18 (1993).

[45] Barry Bricklin, Bricklin Perceptual Scales (Village Publ'g 1984).

[46] M.J. Ackerman & K. Schoendorf, The Ackerman-Schoendorf Scales for Parent Evaluation of Custody (ASPECT) (Western Psychological Servs. 1992).

[47] Brodzinsky at 218.

[48] M. Wellman, *Ackerman-Schoendorf Scales for Parent Evaluation of Custody, in* D. Keyser & R. Sweetwater eds., 10 Test Critiques 13–19 (1994).

[49] *Id.* at 18.

[50] Randy K. Otto & J.F. Edens, *Parenting Capacity, in* T. Grisso, *Evaluating Competencies*, Forensic Assessments and Instruments (2d ed. 2003).

[51] Randy K. Otto, J.F. Edens, & E.H. Barcus, *The Use of Psychological Testing in Child Custody Evaluations*, 38 Fam. & Conciliation Cts. Rev. 312–40 (2000).

[52] Joyce A. Arditti, *Ackerman-Schoendorf Scales for Parent Evaluation of Custody, in* J.C. Conoley & J.C. Impara eds., The Twelfth Mental Measurements Yearbook 20–22 (1995).

[53] Gary B. Melton, *Ackerman-Schoendorf Scales for Parent Evaluation of Custody, in* J.C. Conoley & J.C. Impara eds., The Twelfth Mental Measurements Yearbook 22–23 (1995).

M. Wellman.[54] In addition, concerns are generated that some of the items have "no clear relation to custody outcomes," that some "key factors" relevant to the final custody decision are not incorporated into the assessment process, and that the PCI "encourages clinicians to offer ultimate issue opinions."[55]

Otto and Edens[56] point out another common criticism with regard to using judges' decisions as a criterion for predictive validity. They state, "Moreover, although the PCI results apparently were not presented to the judges, it is unclear exactly what (if any) mental health information they were provided about the parents and whether or not this had any impact on their custody determinations."[57]

Joyce Arditti[58] reviewed the ASPECT, stating, "The ASPECT represents an important effort to quantify elements associated with parental effectiveness, as well as provide a sophisticated interpretation of test results. Its major shortcomings are its lack of internal validity and cumbersome administration, given the battery of tests deemed necessary."[59]

Gary Melton et al.[60] state,

> In short, the ASPECT was ill-conceived: An instrument that results in a score showing the parent who should be preferred in a custody decision necessarily results in over-reaching by experts who use it. Even if the idea had merit, though, the psychometric properties of the ASPECT remain essentially unknown, and the item selection and scoring procedures appear to pull for often irrelevant conclusions.[61]

Gary Melton and his associates raise several concerns about the ASPECT addressed later in the Otto and Edens and Otto et al. works. Melton et al. raise concerns about psychometric properties, item selection, averaging scores, and ignoring some factors.[62] While accurate, item-related concerns reflect less than five of the 56 items on the ASPECT. Psychometrically, these few items could be eliminated and the overall reliability of the PCI would not be affected. Although some of the psychometric concerns that Melton et al. raise may have merit, it does not seem prudent to "throw out the baby with the bath water" because few items may not be as reflective of parental capacity as once thought.

It is not surprising that Melton takes this position. In previous publications, Melton has indicated that he does not believe that psychologists should be testifying to the ultimate issue in custody cases. Because the ASPECT is specifically designed to help the

---

[54] M. Wellman, *Ackerman-Schoendorf Scales for Parent Evaluation of Custody, in* Keyser & Sweetwater eds., 1 Test Critiques 13–19 (1994).

[55] Otto, Edens, & Barcus at 331.

[56] Randy K. Otto & J.F. Edens, *Parenting Capacity, in* Tom Grisso, *Evaluating Competencies, Forensic Assessments and Instruments* (2d ed. 2003).

[57] *Id.* at 267.

[58] Joyce A. Arditti, *Ackerman-Schoendorf Scales for Parent Evaluation of Custody, in* J.C. Conoley & J.C. Impara eds., The Twelfth Mental Measurements Yearbook 20–22 (1995).

[59] *Id.* at 23.

[60] Gary Melton, *Ackerman-Schoendorf Scales for Parent Evaluation of Custody, in* J.C. Conoley & J.C. Impara eds., The Twelfth Mental Measurement Yearbook 22–23 (1995).

[61] *Id.* at 23.

[62] *Id.* at 503.

psychologist answer the ultimate issue for the court, it would be surprising if Melton supported use of the instrument. Furthermore, Arditti's comments are well taken. However, the authors of the ASPECT do not apologize for a "cumbersome administration given the battery of tests deemed necessary."[63] It is felt that one of the strengths of the ASPECT is its broad-based database that requires information from a wide battery of instruments. The best interest of the child criterion requires that the assessments be comprehensive.

Otto *et al.* and Otto and Edens raise some of the issues that Arditti, Wellman, and Melton had previously raised in their writings. They also address new issues. It must be remembered that there are 56 items on the ASPECT that were judged to be relevant to custody decisionmaking in the early 1990s when the instrument was developed. Some of these issues may not be as relevant in 2005 as they were in 1990. However, as the manual points out, five of the 56 items can be eliminated without affecting the overall PCI. Therefore, if several items are not as relevant today as they were 15 years ago or are deemed not to be related to parental competencies as suggested by Melton *et al.* and Otto *et al.*, the overall PCI is not affected until the research or criticism reaches the level of demonstrating that more than five items are not relevant.

Otto and Edens correctly point out that third-party interviews are not incorporated into the assessment process on the PCI. However, they state that "key factors" are not incorporated. They do not identify factors other than third-party interviews that are not included. Last, they address the issue of psychologists' offering ultimate-issue opinions. Marc Ackerman, Melissa Ackerman, Linda Steffen, and Shannon Kelley-Poulos indicate that approximately 70 to 75 percent of family law judges, family law attorneys, and psychologists support psychologists' testifying to the ultimate issue. Those not supporting psychologists' testifying to the ultimate issue are espousing a minority opinion not representing the standard of practice within the profession.

§ 11.11   Current Usage

Daubert v. Merrell Dow Pharmaceuticals[64] changed the landscape of expert testimony, which had relied on the *Frye*[65] standard for 70 years. A number of states have officially adopted the *Daubert* standard by law, while others have encouraged its use and still others have not adopted the *Daubert* standard. However, as forensic psychologists, it is this author's position that the *Daubert* standard should be followed whether the practitioner's state has adopted it by law or not. Kirk Heilbrun[66] established criteria for the use of tests in forensic settings. When taken together, the ASPECT meets the *Daubert* standard and the Heilbrun criteria with the exception of a measure of response style. As suggested by Heilbrun, the ASPECT is commercially available, has a manual, has been reviewed in the

---

[63] Marc J. Ackerman & Andrew W. Kane, Psychological Experts in Divorce Actions (3d ed. Aspen Law and Business 1998).

[64] 509 U.S. 579 (1993).

[65] Frye v. United States, 293 F. 1013 (D.C. Cir. 1923).

[66] Kirk Heilbrun, *The Role of Psychological Testing in Forensic Assessment*, 16 *Law & Hum. Behav.* 257–72 (1992).

Mental Measurements Yearbook, is found in the literature, has standard administration, has a formula, has high correlation coefficients, is developed for use in the setting within which it is used, and has a standard error of measurement. As a result, the ASPECT has met the *Daubert* standard and has been accepted in many states where the *Daubert* standard has been adopted by law, as reported by psychologists who use the instrument.

The ASPECT was developed in the late 1980s. It is now more than 15 years later, and the items that were selected for use in the ASPECT are still purported by the literature today to be those variables that should be addressed when making recommendations for parental fitness, parental capacity, and placement-related questions. It has clearly been recognized that the ASPECT is test laden and can be cumbersome to use. However, the ASPECT-SF alleviates that concern and can be used by all mental health professionals involved in child custody and placement decisions without the need for psychological testing. It has also been reported to the author that there are a number of mental health professionals who find the Parent Questionnaire of the ASPECT to be useful as a comprehensive structured interview of parents in child custody cases. Because child custody evaluations are about decisionmaking and because the more information gathered in our decisionmaking process, the better the decision will be, the ASPECT provides three different levels of information gathering that can be useful to child custody evaluators and those performing child custody studies.

The PCI of the ASPECT relies on other tests that have been solidly validated in the past. It is a useful way to organize data as a supplemental instrument. It is not the "end all, cure all." Psychologists should feel comfortable using it with the understanding of what it is, what its strengths are, and what its shortcomings are. There is enough data to support its use, and the authors still believe that it is a strong supplement to the entire child custody evaluation process.

BRICKLIN FAMILY OF INSTRUMENTS

§ 11.12   Bricklin Instruments

Barry Bricklin and Gail Elliot have constructed a number of Bricklin instruments, including the Bricklin Perceptual Scales (BPS), Perception of Relationships Test (PORT), Parent Awareness Skill Survey (PASS), and Parent Perception of Child Profile (PPCP). In addition, they have incorporated a number of interview techniques into a system they refer to as ACCESS, which stands for "A Comprehensive Custody Evaluation Standard System."

Bricklin and Elliot do not subject their instruments to traditional statistical techniques. However, they state they have strong support for the efficacy of using these instruments based on percentages that can be reported.

§ 11.13   Bricklin Perceptual Scales

The BPS was developed by Barry Bricklin, Ph.D., a clinical psychologist, for the purpose of identifying a child's "unconscious or nonverbal perception of each parent in the areas of competence, supportiveness, follow-up consistency, and possession of admirable traits."[67] It was Bricklin's intent to operationally define the best interests of the child criterion as well as to offer an objective means of assessing that criterion by identifying which parent, in the child's perception, would make the best primary caretaking parent. This would maximize the child's involvement in the ultimate custody decision. Bricklin also wished to address his experience that parents tend to accept nonbiased test data as inherently more fair than decisions that are made solely through adversarial testimony.[68]

Bricklin also identified three particular reasons why, he believed, a test like the BPS is a necessary part of custody evaluations:

> (1) Even parents *not* engaged in adversary battles often misrepresent themselves when observed, while parents actively engaged in custody battles *almost always* do; (2) Even if one could secretly observe competing parents there is no clear way to recognize behavior in a child's best interests, since what is most important is not what parents do but how a particular child at a particular time *utilizes* what the parents do; and (3) Children often reveal their reactions to parental behavior unconsciously, in *nonverbal* behaviors, rather than in what they say.[69]

The BPS was used as a research instrument from the early 1960s until its publication in 1984 as a test for use in custody evaluations.

§ 11.14   —Description of the BPS

The BPS consists of 64 questions, half pertaining to the child's perceptions of his or her mother and half to the perceptions of his or her father. Two responses are given by the child to each item: a verbal response that is recorded; and then a non-verbal response that the child supplies by making a hole on a continuous line at one end of which is printed "VERY WELL" and at the other end of which is printed "NOT SO WELL."

The examiner sits across a table from the child. On the table is a *card holder*, a box (part of the equipment purchased with the test) approximately $8^3/4$ inches long, $3^3/4$ inches wide, and $1^3/4$ inches deep. In the box is a rigid styrofoam pad slightly smaller than the box. The box is aligned with a dot placed on the table, so it will always be in the same place when the child makes a response. If the child moves the box, the examiner replaces it at the mark.

The examiner holds a pack of 64 cards, which are about $8^1/2$ inches long and $3^1/2$ inches wide. Each card has on its back the statements the examiner makes to the child, together with small rectangular boxes numbered 1 to 60, so that a numerical score can readily be assigned to each non-verbal "statement" by the child. On the front of each card is a heavy black line approximately $7^1/2$ inches long, at the left of which is printed

---

[67] Barry Bricklin, Bricklin Perceptual Scales 6 (1984) [hereinafter Bricklin Perceptual Scales].

[68] *Id.* at 7–10.

[69] *Id.* at 11.

"NOT SO WELL" and at the right is printed "VERY WELL." For Card 1, the examiner states to the child:

> We are going to do something where all you have to do is answer some questions and make a pinhole with this. [Hand child the stylus.] For example, if you were having a fight with some-one, say some friends or your brothers or sisters over some toys, how well would Dad do at solving this in a way that would be fair to everyone?[70]

The examiner records the verbal response verbatim, then holds the card so that its long edge rests on the card holder, with the front facing the child, and says: "If this [point to Very Well side] is Dad doing very well at solving a fight over toys, and this [point to Not So Well side] is Dad doing not so well at solving a fight over toys, where on this line would Dad be?"[71] The examiner then immediately places this card in the card holder, so that the child can make a hole in the black line with the stylus. That hole shows up on the opposite side as a numerical score. Without looking at the numerical score, the examiner places that card aside and proceeds to the next one.

Each question is repeated for the parent of the opposite sex 32 questions later—for example, question 33 asks the same about Mom as question 1 did about Dad. The questions alternate, so that the first is about Dad, the second about Mom, and so forth. Bricklin cautions that the examiner must clarify whom the child calls "Mom" and "Dad," because each title could refer to more than one individual in a given child's environment.[72] He also notes that young children tend to respond at the extremes and that a small proportion of children at any age give only very positive responses to a particular parent. The latter case Bricklin refers to as "the child with the mind-made-up, or as we abbreviate it, MMU. The child with the MMU is the child who perhaps has been programmed or bribed."[73] These children tend to give verbal answers that seem rehearsed, volunteer unasked information, answer very quickly (often before the question has been fully asked and before gut-level responses have a chance to proceed to consciousness), give non-verbal responses that are almost all at the "very well" end of the line, fail to relax as the testing session proceeds, avoid eye contact, and resist overtures of friendliness. Marc Ackerman suggests that children with an MMU profile may not be a reliable reporter of information. It is up to the evaluator to validate this hypothesis in other areas of the evaluation.[74] For these MMU children, Bricklin indicates that the examiner may as well ask directly whom the child prefers be the primary custodian, write it down, and then tell the child something to the effect of, "You have told me who you want to be with and that is very, very important infor-mation. This [the BPS] is simply designed to give us *more* information."[75] The examiner may also challenge responses felt to be suspect by, for example, asking for concrete exam-ples (that will not be readily available), and may watch for involuntary hand movements as the child starts to indicate one part of the black line but makes him- or herself alter the

---

[70] Bricklin Perceptual Scales at 22.

[71] *Id.*

[72] *Id.*

[73] Bricklin Perceptual Scales Test Manual Supplement no. 6, at 1 (June 30, 1988).

[74] Marc J. Ackerman, Clinician's Guide to Child Custody Evaluations (John Wiley & Sons 2001).

[75] *Id.* at 5.

unconscious response and indicate another, better, part. The test normally proceeds with-out a break through the 64 cards. Depending on the speed with which the child responds, administration takes about 20 to 30 minutes.

§ 11.15   —Scoring of the BPS

As indicated, each parent ends up with scores on 32 variables within the categories of "Perception of Competency," "Perception of Supportiveness," "Perception of Follow-Up Consistency," and "Perception of Admirable Traits." The parent with higher scores on the largest number of the 32 paired cards is the "parent of choice"—"the parent more fre-quently able to serve the child's vital needs."[76] Bricklin suggests that the greater the dis-parity of scores for the parents, the more definite the preference of the child for the parent of choice. Bricklin currently labels his approach "Access to Parental Strengths," and the purpose of the evaluation is explained to the parents as a quest to make available to the child the best of what each parent has to offer.[77]

The authors of this book have added one scoring procedure, after consultation with Bricklin, to try to ensure optimal validity: Bricklin scores a *win* when either parent has a score even a point higher than the other, but we do not score a win if the disparity is less than three points. Although this is a small deviation from the official instructions, it has not led to a change in direction for any custody evaluations we have performed and has increased the strength of the conclusions we could draw about the child's preferences.

With each parent getting from zero to 60 points per card, a given parent can range from zero to 1,920 points (60 points x 32 cards). Bricklin proposes that a difference of 40 or more is rare on a single card and that it is likely to signal an area of particular importance for the child when it occurs. He also recommends that an item-by-item comparison be done for the entire test, in an effort to find areas of particular significance for the child, particularly when the point score difference between the parents is 300 or more.[78]

§ 11.16   —Validity and Reliability of the BPS

Bricklin, in addressing reliability of the BPS, notes that "there are no reasons to expect the measurements reported here to exhibit any particular degree of stability, since they should vary in accordance with changes in the child's perceptions."[79] A particular change in a par-ticular parent may lead to a change in the child's responses, or it may not. And a given parental behavior may elicit a change in the child's perception of that parent one time and similar behavior have minimal impact another time. "What matters," Bricklin indicates, "is how these parental behaviors impact a given child at a given time."[80]

---

[76] Bricklin Perceptual Scales at 46.

[77] Personal communication with Barry Bricklin (Sept. 27, 1988).

[78] Bricklin Perceptual Scales at 46.

[79] Bricklin Perceptual Scales at 36.

[80] Bricklin Perceptual Scales Test Manual Supplement no. 3, at 1 (Mar. 28, 1986).

Bricklin does offer some data on the reliability of the test. In one study, 12 children in custody cases were retested on the BPS within seven months of the original testing. None of the results changed significantly. In another study, six children in a nonadversary population were retested. The only change was for a child who was in family therapy, an expressed purpose of which was to increase the quality of parenting of the new parent of choice.[81] Studies with samples that small are generally not accepted within the scientific community. In a test-retest reliability study of the BPS, 20 subjects ages 12 to 17 years (mean equal to 14.6) were tested one week apart. Fourteen were Caucasian, five were black, and one was Hispanic. Ten lived with both parents, 10 with the mother (but with frequent contact with the father). The subjects were each paid five dollars for their participation. A correlation of .84 was found between the two test administrations.[82]

Validity of the BPS has been tested in several ways.[83] One method involved validation against another, previously validated instrument, the Perception of Relationships Test (PORT)—another instrument developed to facilitate custody evaluations. See §§ **11.17** and **11.18**. In 40 of 45 cases, or 89 percent, the judge picked as best primary caretaker the same parent who was chosen by the PORT.[84] Of 23 cases in which both the BPS and PORT were given within a three-month time span, 19 (83 percent) identified the same winner. In two of the four where the tests disagreed, the item difference scores were less than two points apart.[85]

A second validity measure involved two kinds of child questionnaires. The first child questionnaire asked each child to "name the parent more likely to lend assistance, support or control in a wide variety of circumstances."[86] The questionnaire agreed with the BPS 70 percent of the time—consistent with the contention that consciously generated data is *less* accurate than the non-verbal responses of the BPS. The second child questionnaire described both practical and fantasy situations (for example, a shipwreck on a deserted island), and asked what each parent would do in the situation. It was anticipated that these "would" questions would access a less-conscious part of the child's personality when compared to the other questionnaire. The results confirm this: the "would" questionnaire agreed with the BPS 87 percent of the time.[87]

A third validity measure was a "Parent Questionnaire," which asked questions about whom the child would go to for various kinds of information or help, about which parent goes to school conferences, and so forth. Tested on "normal" families—that is, those not involved in an adversarial process—it was found that concord with their children's perceptions (as measured by the BPS) was 76 percent for mothers and 88 percent for fathers. Because adversary parents do not respond honestly to questionnaires, it was not also tested on an adversary population.[88]

---

[81] Bricklin Perceptual Scales at 37.

[82] E. Speth, Test-Retest Reliability of Bricklin Perceptual Scales (May 1992) (unpublished doctoral dissertation, Hahnemann University, Philadelphia, Pa.); Personal communication with Barry Bricklin (Sept. 24, 1992).

[83] Bricklin Perceptual Scales at 37–46.

[84] *Id.* at 40.

[85] *Id.* at 42.

[86] *Id.* at 43.

[87] *Id.*

[88] *Id.* at 44–45.

A fourth method for testing the validity of the BPS involved having two mental health professionals independently rate family clinical and life history data generated over a two- to seven-year period. The raters reviewed the massive amount of data and indicated which parent would make a better primary caretaking parent for the tested child. The raters agreed with each other on 20 of 21 cases. The magnitude of their judgment (close, considerable, or overwhelming) was highly correlated with the magnitude of the Item Difference Scores from the BPS.[89]

Bricklin also offers data on the outcome of adversarial cases that went to court. Of 29 cases that went to court in his initial sample, in 27 (93 percent) the judge—who used life histories, vocational data, school and medical records, and testimony—chose the winner as predicted by the BPS.[90] In a sample of 27 psychologists who offered data on 141 cases, "the agreement rate between the parent selected by the BPS as better able to be the primary caretaking parent (PCP) and the choice arrived at by a judge in a formal hearing" was 89 percent.[91] The same source indicated that

> the agreement rate between the choice arrived at by the psychologist's interpretation of other psychological tests and the BPS . . . was again 89%. The agreement rate between the BPS choice and the psychologist's interpretations of clinical/life-history data was 91%. . . . The agreement rate between the PCP selected by the BPS and the psychologist's choices as arrived at based on all information available (tests, clinical and/or life-history data) was 97%.[92]

Thus, several methods of validating the BPS yielded measures that indicate that the BPS is a valid and reliable measure of the best interests of the child—as perceived by the child, by nonadversarial parents, and by independent psychologists and jurists. However, some of these research projects cross-validate with instruments that are themselves of questionable validity (PORT, judge's decisions). Thus, Bricklin's validity research is also called into question. "There is some debate about the wisdom of asking a child for a parental preference directly, but the use of family drawings and a recently developed projective psychological test, the Bricklin Perceptual Scale, are helpful in determining the person the child considers to be the psychological parent."[93]

Bricklin has offered results of a survey he conducted of mental health professionals who have used the BPS.[94] As of December 1993, he had data from 36 individuals who had used the BPS in 1,730 evaluations. Data from these evaluations indicate that

1. In 89 percent of the evaluations, the BPS "parent of choice" was the same individual the evaluator would have independently chosen on the basis of all other data.

2. In 72 percent, the BPS and/or PORT added information not readily available from other sources.

---

[89] *Id.* at 45.

[90] *Id.* at 46.

[91] Bricklin Perceptual Scales Test Manual Supplement no. 5, at 1 (Feb. 15, 1988).

[92] *Id.*

[93] Daniel Shuman, Psychiatric and Psychological Evidence 13-8 (2d ed. 1994) [hereinafter Psychiatric and Psychological Evidence].

[94] B. Bricklin, Custody News, Dec. 1993, at 1.

3. In 21 percent, the BPS or PORT was critical to the final recommendation made.

4. In 3 percent, the BPS or PORT was "markedly in conflict" with the "parent of choice" who would have been chosen independently.

Concerns about the Bricklin Family of Scales

The Bricklin family of scales have been critiqued in the *Mental Measurements Yearbook.* Rosa Hagin, Professor of Psychological and Educational Services, Graduate School of Education, Fordham University-Lincoln Center, criticized the small amount of reliability and validity data available for the BPS.[95] She noted, however, that it may be that conventional expectations of reliability and validity cannot, as the *BPS Test Manual* suggests, be applied appropriately. "The BPS is an interesting approach that draws upon many years of distinguished clinical practice. However, insufficient data are present to justify its use as an independent measure in what must be regarded as a major decision in a child's life, the selection of the parent who will be the primary caretaker."[96]

Marcia Shaffer, a school psychologist, indicates that she was impressed by the manual and its supplements, but she urges caution in using the scales. She is concerned that (1) "The Scales rest on too many assumptions"; (2) "The Scales really have no more than face validity. Numbers tested are small and the external criteria are shaky: judges' decisions; parents' opinions"; (3) "The instructions for administering and scoring the Scales are obfuscating, wordy, and somewhat prone to error."[97] She also notes that the test is expensive and contains some inconsistencies.

> One must conclude that, contrary to Bricklin's hopes, the Scales may be of clinical rather than statistical help. It would, in this reviewer's opinion, be more appropriate to refer to the results as trends rather than thinking of them as hard data. . . . [Dr. Bricklin] has set himself a well-nigh impossible task: he has tried to quantify information which may not yield itself to quantification.[98]

Tami Yanez and William Fremouw addressed the applicability of the *Daubert* standard to the Bricklin Perceptual Scales. Their analysis concluded that standardization procedures utilized in the development of the BPS are not given, that normative data are not published, that there is no support for concluding that the BPS is internally consistent, temporally stable, or has interrater reliability, that the BPS does not have published data documenting concurrent, content, or discriminative validity, and that it lacks a structured indication of valid responding. They conclude that the Bricklin Perceptual Scales do not meet any of the four *Daubert* criteria.[99]

---

[95] Rosa Hagin, *Bricklin Perceptual Scales, in* Eleventh Mental Measurements Yearbook 117–18 (1992).

[96] *Id.*

[97] Marcia Shaffer, *Bricklin Perceptual Scales, in* Eleventh Mental Measurements Yearbook 118–19 (1992).

[98] *Id.*

[99] Y. Tami Yanez & William Fremouw, *The Application of the* Daubert *Standard to Parental Capacity Measures*, 22 Am. J. Forensic Psychol. 5–28 (2004).

Psychologists Randy Otto and John Edens evaluated the Bricklin Perceptual Scales and other instruments assessing parenting capacity. They state that the conceptual basis for the BPS is unclear and that its content domains are too limited to be considered a comprehensive measure of either parenting ability or the fit between the child's needs and the parent's abilities. They did note that the BPS does identify some of the important issues in assessing parenting capacity. They further conclude that the BPS is "loosely" standardized, that interrater reliability is not established, and that the normative sample is not evident.

They further suggest that construct validity is not adequately demonstrated and that factor analyses have not been done to determine what factors the instrument addresses. They indicate that the predictive validity of the BPS remains unknown. Finally, they conclude that the BPS should not be used in custody evaluations until greater empirical support is demonstrated.[100]

The authors of this text are concerned that very little formal data regarding the validity of the BPS has been made available during the 15 years since we first wrote about the test. If it is used, a greater-than-ever emphasis must be placed on the importance of using it as part of a battery of tests and other procedures. It appears that it has more usefulness as a form of structured interview than as a formal "test."

§ 11.17   Perception of Relationships Test

The Perception of Relationships Test (PORT) was developed by Barry Bricklin, Ph.D., and published in January 1990. The PORT is designed to maximize the examiner's ability to objectively identify the parent better able to be the primary caretaking parent. It does so in a manner very different from the Bricklin Perceptual Scales, purportedly providing an additional basis for making that judgment.

The PORT measures:

> [t]he degree to which a child seeks psychological "closeness" (Positive interactions with) [*sic*] each parent, and the types of action tendencies (dispositions to behave in certain ways, e.g., assertively, passively, aggressively, fearfully, etc.)—adaptive as well as maladaptive—the child has had to develop to permit or accommodate interaction with each parent.[101]

The PORT consists of seven tasks, several of which involve drawing tasks. (See **Chapter 10** for concerns about drawing tests.) The *parent of choice* is the parent whom the child has unconsciously *chosen* through his or her responses to the seven tasks. Although this will usually indicate one parent as a clear choice, it is possible for the parents to tie, an indication that the child chooses them equally.

When there has been very limited contact with one of the parents, Bricklin cautions that "the less a child interacts with a person, particularly a parent, the more [positively]

---

[100] Randy F. Otto & John F. Edens, *Parenting Capacity, in* Thomas Grisso ed., Evaluating Competencies 229–307 (2d ed. Kluwer/Plenum 2003) [hereinafter Otto & Edens].

[101] Barry Bricklin, PORT Handbook: Perception of Relationships Test 3 (1990) [hereinafter Bricklin].

wish-oriented the child's perceptions of this person become."[102] The examiner must be aware of how much contact there has actually been with each parent, so that a judgment may be made regarding when the threshold has been reached for a particular child. Bricklin notes that common custody arrangements—for example, where the child sees the non-primary custodial parent on alternate weekends and for a few weeks during the summer—will *not* introduce a significant "wish" factor. Less contact than this *may* introduce one.

§ 11.18   Validity and Reliability of the PORT

Prior to 1981, in 37 of 42 cases that went to court, the judge picked the same parent as primary caretaker as was chosen by the PORT. This is an 89 percent success rate (40 of 45 total cases). With improvements in the scoring system of the PORT, the success rate rose to 95 percent (40 of 42 cases) between 1981 and 1985.[103] During the same period, and for the same reason, the agreement rate between the PORT and the BPS rose to 90 percent.[104]

Between 1986 and 1990, Bricklin indicates that the PORT was utilized in 76 cases in which a judge used expert and lay testimony, medical and school records, and so forth to make custody decisions. Their decisions were the same as that recommended by the PORT 93 percent of the time.[105]

Bricklin notes that one would not expect a test like the PORT to have great reliability, given that the results should change in accordance with changes in the child's perceptions. Those perceptions would be expected to change as each parent changes, and to change on the basis of changes of circumstances in the child's life. The PORT is appropriate for children ages three years, two months and older.[106]

Concerns about the PORT

The PORT was reviewed by Janet Carlson in the *Mental Measurements Yearbook*. She states:

> [I]n summary, the PORT was developed to assist in custody decisions by assessing "gut level" perceptions of the child in question regarding his or her relationship with each parent. . . . But, the PORT has serious flaws regarding its psychometric properties. . . . At this time, the PORT is probably best suited for research purposes, including those that may address validation and reliability issues. For psychologists with considerable clinical experience and expertise, it may serve as a useful adjunctive source of interview data, as might other projective measures for which little support of psychometric viability exists.[107]

---

[102] *Id.* at 43.

[103] Bricklin at 63.

[104] *Id.* at 64.

[105] Personal communication with Barry Bricklin (Sept. 29, 1990).

[106] Bricklin at 20.

[107] Janet Carlson, *Perception-of-Relationships-Test, in* Eleventh Mental Measurements Yearbook 747 (1992).

Psychologists Randy Otto and John Edens also evaluated the PORT. They indicate that the PORT, like the BPS, lacks clear relevance to legal standards, though to the degree it is successful at identifying a child's perception of his or her parents it would be relevant to child custody evaluations. They indicate that guidelines for administration and scoring are "inconsistent and difficult to comprehend." They conclude that there is little evidence of reliability, and that no normative data are available. They indicate that there is little support for the construct validity of the PORT, thereby limiting the justification for its use in evaluations. While well-controlled studies of the PORT could be conducted, they indicate, no such studies have been done. As with the BPS, they conclude that the PORT is not appropriate for use as a test in evaluations.[108]

§ 11.19   Validity and Reliability of Other Bricklin Instruments

Parent Perception of Child Profile

The Parent Perception of Child Profile (PPCP), another Bricklin instrument, was reviewed by Robert Hiltonsmith. He summarizes by stating, "[T]he PPCP is a potentially useful instrument for assessing a parent's knowledge of his or her child."[109] He also concludes that "the PPCP includes little or no information on scoring, norms, reliability, or validity, and therefore, can only be considered a clinical tool rather than a psychometric instrument."[110]

Mary Kelly, in her review of the PPCP, says, "[T]hus, in an area that is very much lacking valid and reliable assessment instruments, the PPCP does, at least, represent an attempt at objectifying and standardizing data obtained from parents during clinical interviews. However, psychometric data on the instrument are minimal and, therefore, the validity of data derived from the PPCP is unknown."[111]

Otto and Edens evaluated the PPCP and the PASS (below) together. They indicate that both instruments are face valid, and both appear to assess domains of parenting relevant to the legal questions, though not tied to legal issues or any particular parenting model. Neither instrument is standardized, and there is no indication that results are reliable. There is no data supportive of the construct validity of either instrument, nor is there data that support the predictive validity of either instrument. Otto and Edens recommend that the PPCP and PASS be used only as structured interviews, rather than as scored tests.[112]

---

[108] Otto & Edens.

[109] Robert Hiltonsmith, *Parent Perception of Child Profile, in* Eleventh Mental Measurements Yearbook 738 (1992).

[110] *Id.*

[111] Mary Kelly, *Parent Perception of Child Profile, in* Eleventh Mental Measurements Yearbook 739 (1992).

[112] Otto & Edens.

Parent Awareness Skill Survey

In addition to the review by Otto and Edens, above, the Parent Awareness Skill Survey (PASS) was reviewed by Lisa Bischoff. She concludes that although the PASS presents an interesting format for assessing parent awareness of factors important to consider in reacting to and dealing with typical childhood problems, and may provide the clinician with relevant information for planning and implementing intervention programs with parents, the lack of information concerning test construction and psychometric properties of the PASS are serious limitations.[113] Debra Cole states,

> [U]nfortunately, the author does not present supporting empirical data. . . . The PASS is an interesting attempt to quantify an often complicated assessment process. Until the measure is better substantiated, however, it has limited usefulness to the evaluator for whom it has been designed.[114]

Concluding Remarks

In summary, serious concerns are stated by independent reviewers regarding the validity, reliability, usefulness, and empirical data regarding all of the Bricklin instruments. The present authors concur with Otto and Edens's conclusion that all these instruments are more useful as structured interview instruments than as tests useful in child custody evaluations.

SENTENCE COMPLETION TESTS

§ 11.20   Sentence Completion Tests

A great many tests use a format wherein individuals are asked to make sentences by completing sentence stems that are presented to them. In effect, the tests are a special type of projective technique, because it is expected that the individual will project into his or her responses deeply personal statements about needs, fantasies, and so forth. Examples of sentence stems could include "I want . . . ," "Lawyers are . . . ," "Children make me . . . ," and so forth. Although some examiners make up sentence stems for a particular use, most use one of the existing formats.

This type of instrument consists of a list of incomplete sentence stems that the individual is instructed to complete with any response. The incomplete stimulus sentence stem has varying content that deals with the individual's self-perception, perception of extended family members, and perception of the environment.

---

[113] Lisa Bischoff, *Parent Awareness Skills Survey, in* Eleventh Mental Measurements Yearbook 736 (1992).

[114] Debra Cole, *Parent Awareness Skills Survey, in* Eleventh Mental Measurements Yearbook 736 (1992).

First use of a sentence completion test for personality assessment is attributed to psychologist A.F. Payne in 1928.[115] Others began to use similar instruments, but not until World War II did the sentence completion method become popular. There was a need for quick, easily administered psychological tests that could be given to large groups of people, and "the sentence completion method soon became a part of psychological batteries in military settings. It was used in the Air Corps as a screening device . . . but was probably best known for its use in the Office of Strategic Service (OSS)."[116]

In nearly all settings, a sentence completion test was part of a battery of tests or part of a larger set of data about a person, and it often served as an aid in subsequent interviews. In military hospitals, the test was used as a screening device to help decide who should be given more thorough psychological testing.

One such test, developed to be used in Air Force hospitals, was adopted for civilian use after the war: the Rotter Incomplete Sentences Blank (RISB),[117] one of the most widely used sentence completion tests,[118] in part because it is one of the few that allows both qualitative and quantitative assessment of responses.[119] The RISB will be used herein as an example of sentence completion tests, with the understanding that most, but not all, comments about it can be generalized to other similar tests.

§ 11.21   Rotter Incomplete Sentence Blank

The Rotter Incomplete Sentence Blank (RISB) was originally published in 1950. Although the test was not seen as exposing extremely deep levels of personality, it was anticipated that information not readily available during an interview would often be brought out.[120] By placing some distance between the examiner and examinee via the use of the test, the test allows the examinee to respond more freely than he or she might in a face-to-face interview. The examiner can take the information at face value, yielding a quick overview of some of the issues for the given individual. The ease of administration and initial interpretation are among the reasons for the popularity of the test.[121]

In 1992, a second edition of the Rotter Incomplete Sentence Blank was published. Both the original and RISB-2nd Edition require completion of 40 sentence stems. An objective scoring method has been developed for use with the RISB. According to Gregory Boyle, "The revised instrument remains essentially unchanged from the earlier version, and provides direct information on personality conflicts. The original 40 sentence stems are

---

[115] Watson, *The Sentence Completion Method, in* Clinical Diagnosis of Mental Disorders 256 (B. Wolman ed., 1978) [hereinafter *The Sentence Completion Method*].

[116] *Id.*

[117] J. Rotter & J. Rafferty, Manual of the Rotter Incomplete Sentences Blank (1950) [hereinafter Manual of the Rotter Incomplete Sentences Blank].

[118] *The Sentence Completion Method* at 257.

[119] Cosden, *Rotter Incomplete Sentences Blank, in* 2 D. Keyser & R. Sweetland, Test Critiques 658 (1984) [hereinafter Cosden, *Rotter Incomplete Sentences Blank*].

[120] Cosden, *Rotter Incomplete Sentences Blank*, at 658.

[121] *Id.* at 654.

retained with only two slight modifications."[122] Boyle also reports, "[O]verall, the revised RISB should serve a useful role within the clinical psychology armamentarium, although clearly, and unnecessarily to some extent, the accompanying manual still retains a number of the deficiencies of the earlier edition."[123]

The RISB has three forms available: for college, adult, and high school populations. The instrument takes approximately 20 to 40 minutes to administer.

Concerns about the RISB

Mary J. McLellan reviewed the RISB-2nd Edition in the *Twelfth Mental Measurements Yearbook*.[124] She reports that the instrument is easy to administer and that the objective scoring criteria are well developed with excellent examples. However, concerns are generated about arbitrary cutoff scores and the fact that no specific examples are provided for the adult and high school forms of the instrument. McLellan states, "In conclusion, the RISB has an objective scoring system that appears to have reliability and validity. When applied to the uses specified in the manual, the test administrator has a good tool to assess overall adjustment of high school and college students, and adults."[125]

§ 11.22   Other Sentence Completion Tests

While the RISB is the most widely used form of these tests, many others exist. Among them, the most popular is the Sack's Sentence Completion Test.

Sacks Sentence Completion Test

The Sacks Sentence Completion Test (SSCT) consists of 60 items that are relatively structured compared to most sentence completion tests. The SSCT suggests that an inquiry also be conducted at the end of the test to maximize understanding of the responses. The test is organized around 15 attitudes, with four stems per attitude—for example, attitude toward women, toward mother, toward colleagues, and so forth. The degree of disturbance regarding each attitude is rated on a three-point scale, from none to severely disturbed.[126]

---

[122] Gregory Boyle, *Rotter Incomplete Sentences Blank-2nd Edition, in* Twelfth Mental Measurements Yearbook 881 (1995).

[123] *Id.*

[124] Mary J. McLellan, *Rotter Incomplete Sentences Blank-2nd Edition, in* Twelfth Mental Measurements Yearbook 883 (1995).

[125] *Id.*

[126] *The Sentence Completion Method* at 272–73.

§ 11.23   Acceptance by Mental Health Professionals

In a report presented at the meeting of the American Psychological Association in 1983, psychologists Bernard Lubin, Reed M. Larsen, and Joseph D. Matarazzo[127] indicate that "sentence completion tests (all kinds)" ranked 7.5 among psychological tests in their survey of psychologists. The RISB by itself ranked 12th and is the only sentence completion test mentioned by name in their survey. Sentence completion tests also ranked 7.5 in a 1982 survey, up from 8.5 in a 1969 survey. The RISB also ranked 12th in the 1982 survey, down from 10th in the 1969 survey but up from 61st in a 1959 survey.

In a 1997 article, Marc Ackerman and Melissa Ackerman indicate that, for adults in custody evaluations, sentence completion tests were used by 22 percent of psychologist/ respondents, who used them in 88 percent of their evaluations. For children, sentence completion tests were used by 29 percent of psychologist/respondents, who used them in 76 percent of their evaluations.[128]

A 1990 survey found that sentence completion tests were the fourth-most-popular projective test, and the fifth-most-popular test overall, for use with adolescents, according to a survey of 165 psychologists. For the 139 respondents who utilize a standard test battery, sentence completion tests were in sixth place, with 46 percent of the psychologists including it in their standard batteries.[129]

A 1992 report on tests used by forensic psychologists indicates that sentence completion tests were the third-most-widely-used projective test, and the fifth-most-frequently-used test, among the 69 forensic psychologists who responded.[130]

BECK DEPRESSION INVENTORY

§ 11.24   Beck Depression Inventory

The Beck Depression Inventory (BDI) was initially introduced in 1961 by psychiatrist Aaron Beck and his associates and copyrighted in 1978. It has gone through several revisions, including the BDI-IA (amended) version (1993) and the current version, the BDI-II, published in 1996. The BDI-IA was published to bring the BDI closer to the criteria for depression in the revised third edition of the *Diagnostic and Statistical Manual of Mental Disorders* (DSM-III-R) and the fourth edition (DSM-IV). The BDI-II is an "upgraded"

---

[127] Bernard Lubin et al., *Patterns of Psychological Test Usage in the United States: 1935–1982*, 39 Am. Psychologist 452–53 (1984).

[128] Marc J. Ackerman & Melissa C. Ackerman, *Child Custody Evaluation Practices: A Survey of Experienced Professionals (Revisited)*, 28 Prof. Psychol.: Res. & Prac. no. 2, at 137–45 (1997).

[129] R. Archer et al., *Psychological Test Usage with Adolescent Clients: 1990 Survey Findings*, 22 Prof. Psychol.: Res. & Prac. 423, 424 (1990).

[130] Paul Lees-Haley, *Psychodiagnostic Test Usage by Forensic Psychologists*, 10 Am. J. Forensic Psychol. 25, 26 (1992).

version of the BDI-IA, with 18 of the 21 BDI-IA items replaced or reworded.[131] It has been used to assess depression in both psychiatric patients and normals and has been the subject of more than 1,000 research reports.[132]

The test consists of 21 items, each of which is to be self-rated for the intensity of the symptoms on a scale of zero to three. The items address:

> sadness, pessimism, past failure, loss of pleasure, guilty feelings, punishment feelings, self-dislike, self-criticalness, suicidal thoughts, crying, irritability, loss of interest, indecisiveness, loss of energy, change in sleeping, tiredness or fatigue, change in appetite, [and] loss of interest in sex.

The total score is the sum of the highest ratings for each of the items, with a possible range from zero to 63. Totals from zero through 13 indicate "Minimal Depression," 14 through 19 indicate "Mild Depression," 20 through 28, "Moderate Depression," and 29 through 63, "Severe Depression."[133] High scores in nonclinical populations may be seen as indicative of similar maladaptive unctioning.[134] These cutoff scores may be altered under special circumstances. If one wishes to have fewer false-positives, higher cutoff scores should be used. If one wants to ensure that few depressed people are missed, lower cutoffs could be used.[135]

The test was standardized on a sample of 500 psychiatric patients and 120 undergraduates. Reliability and validity are good. Administration takes about five minutes. The age range for the test has been extended down to 13 years of age.[136]

The original version of the BDI asked about the individual's mood on the day the test was taken. The 1978 revision asked the individual to describe "the past week, including today." The time frame for the BDI-II was changed to two weeks, to be consistent with DSM-IV criteria for major depressive disorders. It is important to identify the time frame about which the test taker was asked, because various forms of the test are still used.

A 1996 study by Beck and colleagues found that the BDI-II total score was, on average, about two points higher than the BDI-IA total. They concluded that "the rewording of these items had detected more potentially depressed outpatients than the old wording would have,"[137] at least for this sample.

---

[131] Aaron T. Beck et al., *Comparison of Beck Depression Inventories -IA and -II in Psychiatric Outpatients*, 67 J. Personality Assessment 588, 588–90 (1996) [hereinafter Beck et al., 1996].

[132] G. Groth-Marnat, Handbook of Psychological Assessment 124 (3d ed. 1997) [hereinafter Groth-Marnat].

[133] Beck et al., 1996, at 590.

[134] Groth-Marnat at 126; Aaron T. Beck et al., *Psychometric Properties of the Beck Depression Inventory: Twenty-Five Years of Evaluation*, 8 Clinical Psychol. Rev. 79, 79 (1988) [hereinafter Beck et al., 1988].

[135] Beck et al., 1988, at 80.

[136] The Psychological Corporation: 1997 Catalog 82.

[137] Beck et al., 1996, at 593–94.

Acceptance by Mental Health Professionals

A 1989 study by Chris Piotrowski and John Keller of tests used in outpatient mental health clinics found that the BDI was the 12th-most-popular test utilized.[138] A 1992 study by Paul Lees-Haley found that it was the 11th-most-used test in evaluations by forensic psychologists.[139] It was used by 71 percent of the clinical psychologists in a 1995 study by C. Edward Watkins Jr., Vicki L. Campbell, Ron Nieberding, and Rebecca Hallmark, making it the 9th-most-frequently-mentioned instrument.[140] It was used by 6 percent of the psychologists surveyed by Marc J. Ackerman and Melissa C. Ackerman in child custody evaluations.[141]

PARENTING STRESS INDEX

§ 11.25   Parenting Stress Index

The Parenting Stress Index (PSI) was designed by Richard Abidin, Ed.D., as a self-report instrument that parents could fill out to offer a measure of the level and type of stress in a parent-child relationship. It is Abidin's belief that "stress in the parenting system during the first three years of life is especially critical in relation to the child's emotional/behavioral development and to the developing parent-child relationship."[142] The PSI addresses three major areas of stressors: child characteristics, mother characteristics, and situational/demographic life stress. It is designed to identify parents who are experiencing stress related to dysfunctional parenting.

The PSI was initially made up of items specifically based on research findings regarding dysfunctional parenting, including child abuse and stress research. "This procedure resulted in over 95% of the items included on the PSI being directly related to specific research findings."[143] The test went through five revisions, yielding the form presently used, Form 6.70.[144] The test manual was last revised in 1990. The normative sample for the current form was 534 people, consisting "predominantly of white mothers."[145] Of

---

[138] Chris Piotrowski & John Keller, *Psychological Testing in Outpatient Mental Health Facilities: A National Study*, 20 Prof. Psychol.: Res. & Prac. 423, 424 (1989).

[139] Paul R. Lees-Haley, *Psychodiagnostic Test Usage by Forensic Psychologists*, 10 Am. J. Forensic Psychol. 25, 26 (1992).

[140] C. Edward Watkins Jr. et al., *Contemporary Practice of Psychological Assessment by Clinical Psychologists*, 26 Prof. Psychol.: Res. & Prac. 54, 57 (1995).

[141] Marc J. Ackerman & Melissa C. Ackerman, *Custody Evaluation Practices: A Survey of Experienced Professionals (Revisited)*, 28 Prof. Psychol.: Res. & Prac. 137, 140 (1997).

[142] Richard Abidin, Parenting Stress 1 (2d ed. 1986) [hereinafter Abidin, Parenting Stress].

[143] *Id.* at 4; Barbara McKinney & Rolf A. Peterson, *Parenting Stress, in* 1 D. Keyser & R. Sweetland, Test Critiques 504 (1984) [hereinafter McKinney & Peterson, *Parenting Stress*].

[144] Abidin, Parenting Stress, at 5; McKinney & Peterson, *Parenting Stress*, at 505.

[145] Abidin, Parenting Stress, at 13.

them, 92 percent were white and 6 percent black, 25 percent of the families had incomes under $10,000 and 25 percent over $20,000, about one-third were college graduates, their ages ranged from 18 to 61 with a mean of 29.8, and the children who were the focus of the PSI ranged from one month to 19 years, with a mean age of 14 months and a median age of 9 months.[146]

§ 11.26   Description of the PSI

The PSI is a self-report questionnaire with 120 questions. The directions ask the subject to think about the child he or she is most concerned about and to indicate, for questions 1 to 101, the answer that is closest to describing his or her feelings along a continuum from 1 (strongly agree) to 5 (strongly disagree). Items 102 to 120 are optional and ask the subject to mark those life events that have occurred in the past 12 months. Abidin reports that the language of the test is understood by parents with at least a fifth-grade reading ability.[147]

The PSI items are divided into three main sources of stressors. In the Child Characteristics Domain, the six subscales are as follows:

- Child Adaptability/Plasticity
- Acceptability of Child to Parent
- Child Demandingness
- Child Mood
- Child Distractibility/Activity
- Child Reinforces Parent.

The Parent Characteristics Domain has seven subscales:

- Parent Depression
- Parent Attachment
- Restrictions Imposed by Parental Role
- Parent's Sense of Competence
- Social Isolation
- Relationship with Spouse
- Parental Health.

The Life Stress Domain looks directly at the amount of stress the parent is experiencing outside the parent-child relationship.

Raw scores are readily converted to percentiles on a profile sheet, allowing comparison with the normative group. Because they are simple and straightforward, neither the

---

[146] *Id.*

[147] McKinney & Peterson, *Parenting Stress*, at 505.

administration nor the interpretation of the test need be done by a psychologist. The administrator should ensure that each individual understands the directions, especially if the parents lack formal education or are inexperienced with answer sheets. Most parents complete the answer form in 30 minutes or less.

§ 11.27   Scoring and Interpretation of the PSI

The PSI form is multipage. The top page is the answer sheet, and what follows are pages on which answers are grouped according to subscales, and subscales grouped into domains. Each subscale is scored by adding the weights of the numbers above the answer selected. The domain scores are obtained by adding the subscale scores for a given domain. Scoring takes a few minutes to learn and about five minutes to complete.

Interpretation involves use of the Clinical Interpretation part of the manual. It is suggested that interpretations be seen as working hypotheses, requiring additional information prior to their acceptance as facts.

The PSI has a normal range from the 15th to the 75th percentiles, with scores outside these boundaries considered interpretable for total scores, domain scores, and subscale scores. Cutoff scores are also suggested for particular actions or interpretations.

The interpretations suggested are relatively superficial and need to be seen in the light of the whole body of clinical data for the individual. "Detailed interpretation should be made by a clinician."[148]

§ 11.28   Reliability and Validity of the PSI

Reliability and validity data for the PSI are primarily from unpublished research that is presented in the manual. Test-retest reliability correlations are reported to be from .55 to .82 for the Child Domain, .69 to .91 for the Parent Domain, and .65 to .96 for the total stress score. "Generally, the test-retest stability of the PSI appears sufficiently high to assume the test provides stable measurement and can be used to assess change. Additionally, internal consistency of items and factors appears adequate based on correlational and factor analytic data reported in the manual."[149]

Validity data comes primarily from three sources:

> correlation of PSI scores with other child problem checklists and/or measures of parental anxiety; effects of intervention on PSI scores; and comparison of parent groups expected to have a high frequency of stressors . . . with norm groups. The results from all three of these sources of validity information suggest the PSI is measuring an important aspect of parent perceptions which are related to child characteristics, parent stress, and child rearing problems. Additionally, the PSI appears to be a useful tool for the study of stressors and possible stress

---

[148] McKinney & Peterson, *Parenting Stress*, at 508.

[149] McKinney & Peterson, *Parenting Stress*, at 509.

reactions on parent and child behavior. . . . For clinical purposes, a high total stress score appears to represent a system with both excessive stressors and stress.[150]

It needs to be noted that the cut-off scores are not validated for level of correct classification and/or interpretation. . . . The total score cut-off, like the domain score cut-offs, needs to be further evaluated to determine frequency of correct prediction. However, for the time being the cut-off does serve to suggest the need for further assessment.[151]

§ 11.29   Intended Audience for the PSI

In their review of the PSI, Barbara McKinney and Rolf A. Peterson indicate that

[t]he PSI is appropriate for all parents with the ability to read English at a minimum fifth-grade level. Although the norm group includes only mothers, the current form of the PSI is appropriately worded for fathers and has been given to fathers in some research studies. . . . Based on the normative sample the PSI is most applicable for use with mothers of a target child aged three and under. Use with parents with a target child over three are [sic] not well represented in the norms and thus should be used with caution and preferably with the development of more appropriate norms and/or comparison groups.[152]

However, the test manual and the *Ninth Mental Measurements Yearbook*[153] indicate the test is applicable to both parents of children below 10 years of age. Because most of the research has been conducted on mothers and on children under 3 years of age, however, increased caution is appropriate when addressing results for fathers and for children between 3 and 10 years of age. It should especially be noted that "fathers earn significantly low stress scores on all components of the PSI when compared to mothers."[154]

§ 11.30   Acceptance of the PSI by Mental Health Professionals

The PSI is more often used by physicians, especially pediatricians, than by mental health professionals, though it has been used by many psychologists as a diagnostic tool and in research since 1979.[155]

The PSI was reviewed by psychologists Randy Otto and John Edens. They indicate that the PSI has a clear conceptual basis and good content validation procedures. They also note that the items on the test have been derived from empirical research. They indicate that the test appears to have a sound psychometric basis, though they would like to see an expansion of the normative sample and a breakdown of PSI scores into relevant categories

---

[150] *Id.*

[151] *Id.* at 508.

[152] *Id.* at 507.

[153] Ninth Mental Measurements Yearbook 920 (J.V. Mitchell Jr. ed., 1985).

[154] Abidin, Parenting Stress, at 13.

[155] McKinney & Peterson, *Parenting Stress*, at 507.

such as race/ethnicity. While they take issue with the factor structure that is reported, they conclude that the PSI does function as a global measure of stress. Finally, they indicate that parental stress is clearly associated with negative outcomes, and that the PSI appears able to identify parents who, due to stress, may demonstrate behavior that is adverse to their children. They suggest that the stress levels of the two parents be compared to try to identify the degree to which the parents attribute stress to the child.[156]

CHAPTER QUESTIONS

§ 11.31   Questions for Chapter 11

1. Was the ASPECT used? If not, why not? See § **11.3.**
2. Was the individual allowed to take the ASPECT home? See § **11.6.**
3. Were all the personality and cognitive tests necessary to support the ASPECT administered, if the ASPECT was used? See § **11.5.**
4. If the difference in scores on the ASPECT is 10 points or greater and did not result in a specific custody recommendation, why is this so? Ask the examiner to explain. See § **11.8.**
5. If the scores on the ASPECT were less than 10 points apart and the examiner did not recommend relatively equal placement, why was this so? See § **11.8.**
6. If both scores on the ASPECT were below 55, did the examiner recommend safeguards for protecting the children? Make sure safeguards are in place. See § **11.8.**
7. Did the examiner look at the specific items that made up the differences between the parents to determine whether they were non-substantial differences? See § **11.8.**
8. If both parents had scores on the ASPECT that were above 85, did the examiner avoid interpreting the difference? See § **11.8.**
9. Was the BPS used? If not, why not? See § **11.13.**
10. Did the examiner make sure there was no mind-made-up (MMU) profile? See § **11.14.**
11. Were other Bricklin instruments used? If so, were they administered in conjunction with other instruments?
12. Were sentence completion or projective questions–type tests used?
13. Did the examiner avoid an overreliance on these types of techniques? See § **11.23.**

---

[156] Otto & Edens.

CHAPTER 12

PHYSICAL ABUSE, DOMESTIC VIOLENCE, AND EMOTIONAL ABUSE

§ 12.1   Overview

Abuse can take a number of forms as is discussed in this chapter and the next. Regardless of any guarantees of confidentiality, psychologists, and essentially all other health care professionals who reasonably suspect abuse or neglect of children, are required to report their suspicions to state protective services, which has the responsibility of investigating and intervening when necessary. Failure to report suspected abuse or neglect is an offense, and those professionals who report suspected abuse in good faith, and without malice, are immune from suit or liability.

Reports of physical maltreatment showed a dramatic increase during the 25 years between 1974 and 2001. In 1974, 669,000 cases of child maltreatment were reported, while in 1985, there were 1,928,000, and 2,935,000 cases were reported in 1994. Of these, 56 percent were not substantiated, 31 percent were substantiated, 6 percent were considered suspicious, and 5 percent had other dispositions.

The most recent statistics were reported by the Department of Health and Human Services in 2001. They show that approximately 3,000,000 referrals affecting 5,000,000 children were made to child protective services agencies throughout the United States. Approximately two-thirds of these referrals were screened for further investigation. Fifty-seven percent of the screened-in referrals came from professionals, while 43 percent came from family members or neighbors. Of those where child maltreatment was identified, 57 percent suffered from neglect, 19 percent from physical abuse, 10 percent from sexual abuse, and 7 percent from psychological maltreatment. Half the victims were white, a quarter were African-American, and 15 percent were Hispanic. Fifty-nine percent of the perpetrators were women, with a median age of 31, and 41 percent of the perpetrators were men, with a median age of 34. Eighty-four percent of the victims were abused by a parent or parents, and 41 percent were abused by their mother. Nineteen percent were maltreated by both their mother and father. Children died from maltreatment at the rate of 1.81 children per hundred thousand children in the population.

When looking at the trend over the years, approximately one-half of maltreated children are neglected, a quarter of maltreated children are physically abused, and one-tenth of maltreated children are sexually abused.

One of the problems associated with reporting is attempting to define what constitutes "physical abuse." Most definitions of physical abuse include behaviors that, in the past, were considered acceptable punishment. Basically, any type of physical intervention that causes injury or harm to the victim is considered *physical abuse*. Punishment involving the use of wooden spoons, paddles, switches, and belts that leave bruises or other marks is considered physical abuse today. Abusiveness in the family does not take place just between parents and children. It also occurs among other family members.

The Child Abuse Prevention and Treatment Act defines *child abuse and neglect* as physical or mental injury (sexual abuse or exploitation, negligent treatment, or maltreatment)

> of a child (a person under the age of 18, unless the child protection law of that State in which the child resides specifies a younger age for cases not involving sexual abuse) by a person (including any employee of a residential facility or any staff personnel providing out-of-home care) who is responsible for the child's welfare under circumstances which indicate that the child's health or welfare is harmed or threatened thereby.[1]

---

[1] Pub. L. No. 108-36, June 25, 2003. Keeping Children and Families Safe Act of 2003.

Physical abuse is characterized by inflicting physical injury by punching, beating, kicking, biting, burning or otherwise harming a child. Although the injury is not an accident, the parent or caretaker may not have intended to hurt the child. The injury may have resulted from over-discipline or physical punishment that is inappropriate to the child's age.[2] . . .

Child neglect is characterized by failure to provide for the child's basic needs. Neglect can be physical, educational or emotional. The latest incidence study defines these three types of neglect as follows: Physical neglect includes refusal of or delay in seeking health care, abandonment, expulsion from home, or not allowing a runaway to return, and inadequate supervision. Educational neglect is permission for chronic truancy, failure to enroll a child of mandatory school age, and inattention to a special educational need.[3]

§ 12.2   Psychological Effect of Physical Abuse

Robin Malinosky-Rummell and David Hansen performed a meta-analysis of the long-term consequences of physical abuse.[4] Some of their findings and other researcher's findings include the following:

Aggressive and Violent Behavior

- Adolescents who exhibit aggressive and violent behaviors, including extra-familial and dating violence, demonstrate higher rates of maltreatment than the general population.[5]
- Violent adolescent boys in residential facilities demonstrate higher rates of physical abuse than do less violent and nonviolent comparison groups.[6]
- Overall, these findings imply that violent inmates and outpatients, particularly males, report higher rates of child physical abuse than do less violent comparison groups.[7]
- Studies that use several different self-report methodologies demonstrate a relationship between child physical abuse and abuse while dating college students.[8]
- Of men whose parents did not hit each other, those who had been physically abused as teenagers had twice the rate of violence toward their wives than non-abused men.[9]
- Physically abused alcoholic men describe significantly more marital violence toward their wives during treatment than do non-abused alcoholic comparisons.[10]

---

[2] *Id.*

[3] *Id.*

[4] Robin Malinosky-Rummell & David Hansen, *Long-Term Consequences of Childhood Physical Abuse*, 114 Psychol. Bull. 68–79 (1993) [hereinafter Malinosky-Rummell & Hansen].

[5] *Id.* at 70.

[6] *Id.*

[7] *Id.*

[8] *Id.* at 71.

[9] *Id.* at 71–72.

[10] *Id.* at 72.

Nonviolent Criminal Behavior

- Physically abused children demonstrate significantly more noncompliance, non-aggressive conduct disorders, and other externalizing behaviors than do non-abused comparison groups.[11]

Substance Abuse

- Evidence exists to support a relationship between childhood physical abuse and substance abuse in adolescence.[12]
- A high rate of parental substance abuse (75 percent) has been reported by the abused group, a finding supported by other research in adolescent inpatients.[13]

Suicidal and Self-Injurious Behavior

- Maltreatment has been linked to adolescent self-injurious and suicidal behaviors.[14]
- Physical abuse appears to be related to self-injurious and suicidal behaviors in male and female inpatients as well as female college students.[15]

Emotional Problems

- Physically abused youths who are 6 to 16 years old and from violent or distressed families display significantly more emotional problems, including anxiety and depression, than do non-abused community children.[16]
- Physical abuse has been associated with a variety of emotional problems, including somatization, depression, anxiety, hostility, paranoid ideation, psychosis, and disassociation in female inpatient and community samples.[17]
- Higher levels of internalizing symptoms have been found among abused preschoolers and adolescents.[18]
- 36 percent of maltreated children and youth met the criteria for a PTSD diagnosis.[19]

---

[11] *Id.*

[12] *Id.* at 72–73.

[13] *Id.* at 73.

[14] *Id.*

[15] *Id.*

[16] *Id.*

[17] *Id.*

[18] J. Fantuzzo, W. DelGaudio, M. Atkins, R. Meyers, & M. Noone, *A Contextually Relevant Assessment of the Impact of Child Maltreatment on the Social Competencies of Low-Income Urban Children*, 37 J. Am. Acad. Child & Adolescent Psychiatry 1201–08 (1998).

[19] D. Pelkovitz, S. Kaplan, B. Goldenberg, & F. Mandel, *Posttraumatic Stress Disorder In Physically Abused Adolescents*, 33 J. Am. Acad. Child & Adolescent Psychiatry no. 3, at 305–12 (1994).

- 33 percent of those with PTSD were later found to have retained the diagnosis in a two-year follow-up.[20]
- A history of maltreatment is associated with a diagnosis of borderline personality disorder, attention deficit hyperactive disorder (ADHD), and oppositional defiant disorder.[21]

Interpersonal Relationships

- There is a relationship between childhood physical abuse and negative findings about interpersonal relationships in adulthood.[22]
- Maltreatment is associated with having an insecure disorganized/disoriented attachment.[23]
- Abused children displayed less overall intimacy, were more conflicted, and demonstrated more negative affect.[24]
- Social withdrawal, academic underachievement, psychopathology including depression, Conduct Disorder, Attention Deficit Hyperactive Disorder, Oppositional Defiant Disorder, Post-traumatic Stress Disorder, insecure and atypical attachment patterns, and impaired relationships involving increased aggression were demonstrated in abused children.[25]

Academic and Vocational Abilities

- Academic and vocational abilities are affected by physical abuse during childhood.[26]

Health

- Retrospective cross-sectional studies document heightened health problems, including poor current health status, associated with being victims of physical abuse.[27]

---

[20] R. Famulario, T. Fenton, M. Augustyn, & B. Zukerman, *Persistence of Pediatric Post Traumatic Stress Disorder after 2 Years*, 20 Child Abuse & Neglect no. 12, at 1245–48 (1996).

[21] R. Famulario, R. Kinschereff, & T. Fenton, *Posttraumatic Stress Disorder among Children Clinically Diagnosed as Borderline Personality Disorder*, 170 J. Nervous & Mental Diseases 428–31 (1991).

[22] Malinosky-Rummell & Hansen at 74.

[23] D. Barnett, J. Ganiban, & D. Cicchetti, *Maltreatment, Negative Expressivity, and the Development of Type D Attachments from 12 to 24 Months of Age*, 64 Momographs Soc' Res. in Child Dev. no. 3, at 97–118 (1991).

[24] J.G. Parker & C. Herrera, *Interpersonal Processes in Friendship: A Comparison of Abused and Nonabused Children's Experiences*, 32 Development Psychol. 1025–38 (1996).

[25] D. Ciccherri & S.L. Toth, *Child Maltreatment and Attachment Organization: Implications for Intervention*, in S. Goldberg, R. Muir, & J. Kerr eds., Attachment Theory (Analytic Press 1995).

[26] Malinosky-Rummell & Hansen at 74.

[27] J. Lesserman, Z. Li, D. Drossman, T.C. Tooney, G. Nachman, & L. Glogan, *Impact of Sexual and Physical Abuse Dimensions on Health Status: Development of an Abuse Severity Measure*, 59 Psychomatic Med. no.2 at 152–60 (1997).

- There are increased hospital admissions and surgical procedures in adulthood of individuals who have been abused as children.[28]
- There is an increase in the reporting of chronic pain in victims of physical abuse.[29]

Other Conclusions

Judith Becker and her coauthors reviewed the research in child abuse treatment and issued a report by the Child Abuse and Neglect Treatment Working Group of the American Psychological Association.[30] Their conclusions were similar to research reported by Robin Malinosky-Rummell and David Hansen.

They provided a number of recommendations of areas that needed to be addressed in research in this area.

1. Intervention and services should be made available to all individuals if they have either been victims of child abuse or neglect or acted in an abusive or neglectful manner toward children.

2. Incidence and prevalence rates should be determined for major ethnic minority groups.

3. Intervention should range from primary prevention programs to direct services to children and their parents.

4. More effort must be made to define the behaviors that are being studied, with multiple measures being administered on repeated occasions.

5. Longitudinal studies are needed.

6. Major efforts should be undertaken to discover the factors that are prophylactic with respect to abuse.

7. Variables that moderate or mediate treatment effectiveness should be identified.

8. Follow-up assessments are needed to determine the stability of therapeutic change.

9. Any intervention should look at risk as well as protective factors.[31]

Cathy Spatz Widom and Robin Shepard studied the accuracy of adult recollections of being physically victimized as children.[32] They performed a 20-year follow-up study by interviewing individuals about their recollection of childhood physical abuse. The abuse was substantiated by reviewing existing police records and official court records of the abuse. The researchers found

---

[28] P. Salmon & S. Calderbank, *The Relationship of Childhood Physical and Sexual Abuse to Adult Illness Behavior*, 40 J. Psychosomatic Res. 329–36 (1996).

[29] R. Goldberg, W. Pachas, & D. Keith, *Relationship between Traumatic Events in Childhood and Chronic Pain*, 21 Disability & Rehabilitation: Int'l Multidisciplinary J. 23–30 (1999).

[30] Judith Becker et al., *Empirical Research on Child Abuse Treatment: Report by the Child Abuse and Neglect Treatment Working Group*, 24 J. Clinical Child Psychol. 23–46 (1995).

[31] *Id.* at 39–40.

[32] Cathy Spatz Widom & Robin Shepard, *Accuracy of Adult Recollections of Childhood Victimization: Part I, Child Physical Abuse*, 9 Psychol. Assessment no. 4, at 412–21 (1996).

at the same time, there is a problem in underreporting physical abuse. A substantial group of individuals who were physically abused do not report having been physically abused in childhood. Of 110 people in the sample who had documented cases of physical abuse in childhood, 60 to 62 percent reported abuse. . . . [T]his means that approximately 40 percent of the individuals with documented histories of physical abuse did not report . . . but these findings suggest that a substantial minority would not be included in retrospective self-report assessments of childhood physical abuse.[33]

They go on to report that one of the possible explanations is that the individual was too young at the time of abuse to have accurately remembered what occurred. The caution brought about by this report is concern about the reliability of retrospective studies, which are likely to underreport the actual level of abuse.

§ 12.3   Characteristics of Abusers

Although it can be difficult to predict who will be a child abuser, certain characteristics are present in many of these individuals.

> Parents may be more likely to maltreat their children if they use drugs or alcohol (alcoholic mothers are three times more likely and alcoholic fathers eight times more likely to abuse or neglect their children than are non-alcoholic parents); are isolated, with no family or friends to depend on; were emotionally deprived, abused, or neglected as children; feel worthless and have never been loved or cared about; or are in poor health. Many abusive and neglectful parents do not intend to harm their children and often feel remorse about their maltreating behavior. However, their own problems may prevent them from stopping their harmful behavior and may result in resistance to outside intervention. It is important to remember that diligent and effective intervention efforts may overcome the parent's resistance and help them change their abusive and neglectful behavior.
>
> Children are more likely to be at risk of maltreatment if they are unwanted, resemble someone the parents dislike, or have physical or behavioral traits which make them different or especially difficult to care for.[34]

Environmental conditions can affect the likelihood of an increase in the incidence of physical abuse. These include "changes in financial condition, employment status, or family structure."[35]

Joel Milner and Chinni Chilamburti identify several characteristics of physical abuse perpetrators. They found that the most frequent characteristic is having been physically abused during the perpetrator's own childhood. According to Milner and Chilamburti, the research demonstrates that physical abuse perpetrators

1. Show more physiological reactivity to child-related stimuli than do non-perpetrators

2. Have more physical symptom-related complaints than do non-abusive parents

---

[33] *Id.* at 418.

[34] U.S. Dep't of Health & Human Servs., Child Abuse and Neglect 3, 5 (1992).

[35] *Id.*

3. Tend to have poor self-concepts and lower ego-strengths than do non-abusing parents
4. Have a greater external locus of control, which suggests that they look for control from outside themselves as opposed to from within
5. Are more likely to see their children as being intentionally disruptive or disobedient
6. Have a greater expectation for the children to engage in appropriate behavior.[36]

Milner and Chilamburti report that the relationship between physical abuse and alcohol consumption is complex. However, there is a relationship between the two. Abusing parents feel more socially isolated and have lower rates of interaction with their children. These interactions tend to be more negative than positive. Abusing parents are more likely than non-abusing parents to rely on power as a form of discipline intervention.

William Downs, Nancy Smyth, and Brenda Miller studied the relationship between childhood violence and alcohol problems among men who batter.[37] They concluded that

> experiences of childhood violence are associated with mediator variables, including anti-social behaviors and depressive symptomatology that are themselves associated with development of alcohol problems and perpetration of partner violence for men in adulthood; (b) experiences of childhood violence, more strongly, observation of interparental violence during childhood predict perpetration of partner violence in adulthood for males; and (c) presence of partner violence associated with certain types of alcohol problems for men.[38]

Yuriko Egami and his associates report that 58.5 percent of adults who reported abuse of children, and 69.3 percent of those who have neglected a child, had a lifetime diagnosis of mental disorder.[39] They also reported that low socioeconomic status was a risk factor for neglecting, but not abusing.[40]

An interesting study was performed by Roy Herrenkohl, Brenda Egolf, and Ellen Herrenkohl.[41] This 16-year longitudinal study followed preschool children who had been maltreated and those who had not, in an effort to determine how this would affect adolescent assaultive behavior. The researchers found that "severity of physical discipline, negative quality of the mother's interaction with the child, and the experience of sexual abuse were related to adolescent assaultive behavior."[42]

Susan Zuravin and her fellow researchers looked at intergenerational cycles of maltreatment. They found that the more severe forms of sexual abuse (those involving

---

[36] Joel Milner & Chinni Chilamburti, *Physical Abuse Perpetrator Characteristics: A Review of the Literature*, 6 J. Interpersonal Violence no. 3, at 345–66 (Sept. 1991).

[37] William Downs et al., *The Relationship between Childhood Violence and Alcohol Problems among Men Who Batter: An Empirical Review and Synthesis*, 1 Aggression & Violent Behav. no. 4, at 327–44 (1996).

[38] *Id.* at 327.

[39] Yuriko Egami et al., *Psychiatric Profiles and Sociodemographic Characteristics of Adults Who Report Physically Abusing or Neglecting Children*, 153 Am. J. Psychiatry no. 7, at 921–28 (July 1996).

[40] *Id.* at 921.

[41] Roy Herrenkohl et al., *Preschool Antecedents of Adolescence Assaultive Behavior: A Longitudinal Study*, 67 Am. J. Orthopsychiatry no. 3, at 422–32 (1997).

[42] *Id.* at 422.

intercourse) increase the probability that the maltreatment will be passed on to the second generation, but less severe forms do not.[43]

Dr. Wiehe studied the effects of personality characteristics of physically and emotionally abusive parents on the likelihood of their being perpetrators.[44] He concluded that perpetrators may experience the aversive behavior in children differently, provoking them to physically and/or emotionally abuse their children, based on their own self-centeredness and low empathy.[45]

The best single predictor of whether an adult will abuse a child is whether or not he or she was abused as a child him- or herself. Therefore, it becomes incumbent upon psychologists to do whatever is necessary to break the intergenerational cycle of maltreatment.

§ 12.4 Substantiation

When a child abuse allegation is made it becomes necessary for the court, the psychologist, the child protective services workers, and therapists to determine whether the allegation is substantiated. The number of suspected abuse or neglect reports that have been substantiated has decreased.[46] Eckenrode *et al.* reported that in 1974 50 percent of cases were substantiated, while in 1984 only 25 percent of cases were substantiated.[47] In 2002 26.8 percent of child protective services investigations resulted in a finding of childhood maltreatment source. As a result, the number of substantiated cases has leveled off in the last 15 to 20 years. Although the number of substantiated cases has remained relatively the same, the number of unsubstantiated cases has been increasing since 2000, reaching 60.4 percent in 2002. Nearly one-quarter (24.6 percent) of substantiated reports were referred by legal, law enforcement, or justice personnel. Half of the unsubstantiated reports came from school personnel, social service personnel, unanimous reporters, and legal, law enforcement, or justice personnel.[48] Diminishing substantiation rates are due, in part, to understaffing of state protective agencies. Although many states require that abuse allegations be investigated within 24 hours by the state or local protective services agency, with staffing problems and staffing issues, in many jurisdictions it can be a week or more before the report is actually investigated. By that time, bruises have healed, young children may have been coached to not report events, and there is a general reduction of memory of the events. Concern is also raised about the stress that families experience during maltreatment allegation investigations when only approximately one-third of the cases are substantiated.

---

[43] Susan Zuravin et al., *The Intergenerational Cycle of Maltreatment Continuity versus Discontinuity*, 11 J. Interpersonal Violence no. 3, at 315–34 (Sept. 1996).

[44] Vernon R. Wiehe, *Empathy and Narcissism in a Sample of Child Abuse Perpetrators and a Comparison Sample of Foster Parents*, 27 Child Abuse & Neglect 541–55 (2003).

[45] *Id.* at 541.

[46] U.S. Dep't of Health & Human Servs., Child Abuse and Neglect: A Shared Community Concern (Nat'l Ctr. on Abuse & Neglect 1992).

[47] J. Eckenrode, J. Powers, J. Doris, J. Munsch, & N. Bolger, *Substantiation of Child Abuse and Neglect Reports*, 6 J. Consulting & Clinical Psychol. 9–16 (1988).

[48] U.S. Dep't of Health & Human Servs. Administration for Children and Families (2002).

§ 12.5   Child Abuse Potential

Over and over again through the decades, research has demonstrated that the best single predictor of whether an individual will be abusive is if the individual was abused as a child. Many researchers have attempted to develop child abuse risk assessments.

An instrument referred to as the Child Abuse Potential Inventory (CAP or CAPI) has been developed as a screening questionnaire for suspected adult perpetrators of physical child abuse. In a validation study performed using this particular instrument, 73.8 percent of the abusers and 99.1 percent of the non-abusers were correctly identified. A cutoff score developed with this instrument helps categorize people as having a high or low level of child abuse potential.

Developed by Joel Milner, this instrument has been studied by many researchers. A study performed by Wayne Holden and his associates using both the CAPI and the Parenting Stress Index indicated that the two instruments appeared to measure relatively similar constructs.[49]

§ 12.6   Intervention

Even though it is difficult to predict the at-risk families for abuse potential, it has been demonstrated that early intervention for parents at risk is beneficial. David Wolfe and his colleagues report that "case worker ratings of clients, risk of maltreatment and abilities to manage their families at a one year follow-up significantly favored the families who received parent training in addition to information."[50] They conclude:

> Early intervention for child abuse and neglect is in its infancy, and selection of the most beneficial treatment modalities will require ongoing evolvement. We must learn how to measure a reduction in the risk of maltreatment, and must gain an understanding of the appropriate timing and selection of intervention targets.[51]

§ 12.7   Munchausen Syndrome by Proxy

One of the more insidious forms of child abuse is referred to as Munchausen Syndrome by Proxy. Baron Von Munchausen was known for his skills in telling phenomenal stories about his military exploits. Thus, the name Baron Munchausen became associated with telling stories for the attention that one receives for doing so. Munchausen Syndrome

---

[49] E. Wayne Holden, Diane J. Willis, & Linda Foltz. *Child Abuse Potential and Parenting Stress: Relationships in Maltreating Parents*, 1 Psychol. Assessment: J. Consulting & Clinical Psychol. 64–67 (1989).

[50] David Wolfe, Betty Edwards, Ian Manion, & Catherine Koverola, *Early Intervention for Parents at Risk of Child Abuse and Neglect: A Preliminary Investigation*, 6 J. Consulting & Clinical Psychol. 40 (Feb. 1988).

[51] *Id.* at 46.

(telling stories for attention) has generalized to the concept of Munchausen Syndrome by Proxy, a disorder in which a caretaker, oftentimes a mother, systematically fabricates information about his or her child's health or intentionally makes his or her child gravely ill, and seeks repeated contacts with medical professionals as a result. Munchausen Syndrome by Proxy has two components involving the child victim and the adult perpetrator. When referring to the child victim, the condition is sometimes referred to as pediatric condition (illness, impairment, or symptom) falsification. This a form of child abuse in which the adult falsifies physical and/or psychological signs and/or symptoms in a victim, causing the victim to be regarded by others as ill or impaired.[52] Individuals who intentionally falsify history, medical test results, or symptoms in a child to meet their own self-serving psychological needs are diagnosed with Factitious Disorder by Proxy. "Some individuals appear to need or thrive on attention or recognition that results from being perceived as being the devoted parent of a sick child. Others appear to be motivated by the need to covertly control, manipulate or deceive authority figures or those perceived to be powerful."[53] These children usually are subjected to extensive medical attention, often entailing serious and dangerous invasive medical procedures, surgeries, intravenous medicines or multiple x-rays. Well-versed in medical conditions, these parents seemingly stop at nothing to gain access to doctors and the inner circle of care in hospitals.[54] Parents who engage in Munchausen Syndrome by Proxy may fabricate their children's medical histories, alter laboratory specimens, or even induce or inflict physical injuries. The majority of perpetrators do not acknowledge what they have done when they are first confronted, and they portray themselves as wrongly accused parents who are only interested in the welfare of their sick children. Spouses are almost always initially supportive of the abusing parent, whom they see as highly focused on and dedicated to their ailing child. The child victims themselves, as well as their siblings after learning of the allegations, frequently become champions for their parents.

Day identified factors that might be indicative of Munchausen Syndrome by Proxy:

1. A child who has one or more medical problems that do not respond to treatment or that follow an unusual course that is persistent, puzzling, and unexplainable.

2. Physical or laboratory findings that are highly unusual, discrepant with history, or physically or clinically impossible.

3. A parent (usually mother) who appears medically knowledgeable and/or fascinated with medical details and hospital gossip, appears to enjoy the hospital environment, and expresses interest in the details of other patients' medical problems.

4. A highly attentive mother who is reluctant to leave her child's side and who herself seems to require constant attention.

5. A mother who appears to be unusually calm in the face of serious difficulties in her child's medical course while being highly supportive and encouraging of the physician, *or* one who is angry, devalues staff, and demands further interventions and procedures.

6. The mother may work in the health care field or profess interest in a health-related job.

---

[52] APSAC Task Force 106 (2002).

[53] *Id.* at 106–07.

[54] Herbert Schreier & Jay Libow, *Munchausen Syndrome by Proxy: Diagnosis and Prevalence*, 63 Am. J. Orthopsychiatry no. 2, at 318–21 (1993).

7. The signs and symptoms of a child's illness do not occur in the mother's absence (hospitalization and careful monitoring are often needed to establish this causal relationship).

8. A family history of unusual or numerous medical ailments that has not been substantiated and raises questions about the mother's veracity.

9. A family history of similar sibling illness or unexplained sibling illness or death.

10. A mother with symptoms similar to the child's medical problems or an illness history that itself is puzzling and unusual.

11. A mother with an emotionally distant relationship with her spouse; the spouse often fails to visit the child and has little contact with physicians even when the child is hospitalized with serious illness.

12. A mother who reports dramatic, negative events, such as house fires, burglaries, car accidents, and the like, that affect her and her family while her child is undergoing treatment.

13. A mother who seems to have an insatiable need for adulation or who makes self-serving efforts at public acknowledgment of her abilities.[55]

When a psychologist evaluates a person for possible Munchausen Syndrome by Proxy, several factors are considered. They include

> evidence of induction of symptoms, evidence of feigning of symptoms, recurrent illness that appears unusual, lack of continuity of care or appropriate communication, and inconsistencies. Inconsistencies include reported symptoms that do not match objective findings; reported medical history that does not match previous medical records; diagnoses that do not match objective findings; behavior of parents that does not match expected distress or report of symptoms; other history reported that is determined to be false; medical record names and numbers that do not match.[56]

Mary Sheridan reviewed the literature on Munchausen Syndrome by Proxy and found that "the average victim was usually under 4 years of age with 21.8 months elapsing from the onset of symptoms to diagnoses. Six percent of the victims were dead, and 7.3 percent were judged to have suffered long-term or permanent injury. Twenty-five percent of the victims' known siblings are dead, and 61.3 percent of siblings had illnesses similar to those of the victim."[57] Mothers were perpetrators in 76.5 percent of the cases.

Diagnosing illnesses in young children is a difficult task for physicians. They cannot communicate directly with their patient and have to rely on the report of the parent. There are problems associated with inferring behaviors in the caregiver based on the physician's inability to diagnose a condition. It may be convenient, but dangerous, to infer that Munchausen Syndrome by Proxy exists just because a diagnosis cannot readily be made.

---

[55] D. Day, Personality Evaluation of the Perpetrator, Spouse, Siblings, and Victims of Munchausen by Proxy Syndrome, Paper presented at the 103rd Annual Convention of the American Psychological Association, Washington, D.C. (Aug. 1995).

[56] Mary J. Sanders & Brenda Bursch, *Forensic Assessment of Illness Falsification, Munchausen by Proxy, and Factitious Disorders, NOS*, Child Maltreatment 112–23, at 115–16 (2002).

[57] Mary S. Sheridan, *The Deceit Continues: An Updated Literature Review of Munchausen Syndrome by Proxy*, 27 Child Abuse & Neglect 431–51 (2003).

Although profiling a Munchausen Syndrome by Proxy abuser is not fail-safe, a number of factors help identify when this malady occurs. Among them are the parent whose life revolves around the child's illness, who does not appear to be relieved with normal test findings, and who promotes invasive tests or procedures. Perpetrators tend to be overly familiar with physicians or staff members, seem to enjoy the excitement of being in the spotlight, and have an interest or expertise in medicine. In addition, they are likely to predict deterioration or relapses, and the signs and symptoms of the child's illness are related to the presence of the suspected abuser. Furthermore, the father is rarely or briefly seen.[58]

Herbert Schreier and Jay Libow conclude, "Infants are damaged for life, if they survive. Enormous energies are required by child protective workers, the police, lawyers, and the courts. Doctors are often scarce and increasingly scarce medical resources are wasted."[59]

Richard Rogers has brought a new dimension to the issue of Munchausen Syndrome by Proxy. Munchausen Syndrome by Proxy is looked at in conjunction with Factitious Disorder by Proxy (FDBP). FDBP is a more encompassing diagnosis than Munchausen by Proxy. Rogers has done a considerable amount of work in his professional career studying malingering and deceit. He suggests that the research in the area of malingering and deceit can be generalized to making the diagnosis of Munchausen Syndrome by Proxy or Factitious Disorder by Proxy. He suggests developing tailored measures that explore specific detection strategies to help with this diagnostic process. Future research should be watched to look for these advancements and developments.

§ 12.8   Domestic Violence

Family violence can take the form of spouse abuse and is sometimes referred to as domestic violence. It is defined as

> the use or threat of physical violence by the abuser to gain control and power over the victim. It occurs in households of both married and cohabiting couples. Although either party may be the victim, most victims are women. The three types of spouse abuse (physical abuse, sexual violence, and psychological/emotional abuse) often occur in combination.[60]
>
> . . . Physical abuse can take many forms including kicking, hitting, biting, choking, pushing, and assaults with weapons. Sometimes particular areas are targeted, such as the abdomen of a pregnant woman.[61]

Family violence incidence rates are as reported by women. Sixteen percent of women report physical assault by their partner. Each year, 28 percent of women report physical assault sometime during their relationship with their partner, while 22 percent report being forced to do things sexually that they did not want to do. Eight to 11 percent report physical violence or sexual assault during pregnancy. Forty-six percent of women report that

---

[58] Sanders & Bursch at 117.

[59] Herbert Schreier & Jay Libow, *Munchausen Syndrome by Proxy: Diagnosis and Prevalence*, 63 Am. J. Orthopsychiatry no. 2, at 318–21 (1993).

[60] U.S. Dep't of Health & Human Servs., Family Violence 3 (1991).

[61] *Id.*

they were in love with their perpetrator at the time of the domestic violence. Seventy-nine percent were divorced or separated from the men who were perpetrators, while in 21 percent of the cases the husbands were the perpetrators.[62]

Victims stay in physically abusive relationships for many reasons. "Some victims stay because they blame themselves, believe the spouse will stop, are financially dependent, or feel that they or their children will be seriously injured or killed if they attempt to leave. Victims also stay because they have, or feel they have no other place to go."[63]

When *sexual violence* occurs in a domestic situation, it is sometimes referred to as *marital rape*. These attacks can include assaults on the victim's breasts or genitals, sexual sadism, or forced sexual activity.

> Similar to rape occurring outside the family, marital rape appears to be mainly an act of violence and aggression in which sex is the method used to humiliate, hurt, degrade, and dominate the woman. The violence and brutality in the sexual relationship seem to escalate with time. The sexual violence is frequently accompanied by life-threatening acts or threats.[64]

Psychological or emotional abuse in domestic situations can take many forms. It is more than the typical verbal arguments that can occur in any family. Instead, it results in a systematic destruction of the individual's self-esteem. It is not unusual for psychological or emotional abuse to occur in accompaniment with physical abuse or sexual violence.

Psychological or emotional abuse can take the form of *economic domination*, where "men who abuse attempt to control their partners by having complete power over the household finances. They try to keep the victim from working and therefore encourage the victim's economic dependence upon them." They can

> use the children to maintain power and control over their partners. For example, they belittle or degrade the children as a means of harassing the victim. Abusers may frighten their victims by using looks, actions, gestures, or loud voices; by smashing things; by destroying the victim's property. Abusers may threaten to take the children away from their spouse, to harm the children, or commit suicide. Such threats add to the anxiety and fear experienced by victims and children. Men who [use this form of] abuse may control their partner's activities, companions, or whereabouts. [They] often control what their victims do, whom they see, and where they go. Many abusers feel threatened by anyone with whom their victims have contact.[65]

§ 12.9   Some Facts about Domestic Violence

Although statistics on domestic violence are not complete, here are some important facts.

*According to the American Medical Association, 25 percent of the women in the United States, or 12 million women, will be abused by a current or former partner during their lives.

---

[62] *Id.*

[63] *Id.*

[64] *Id.*

[65] *Id.* at 4.

*The incidence of domestic violence is estimated at 4 million cases annually, or one assault every 15 seconds.

*Women in the United States are more likely to be victimized by a current or former male partner than by all other assailants combined. More than 50 percent of all women murdered are killed by male partners, and 12 percent of murdered men are killed by female partners.

*Over half of the defendants accused of murdering their spouses had been drinking alcohol at the time of the offense. Nonfamily murder defendants were even more likely to have been drinking. Also, almost half of the victims of spousal murder had been drinking alcohol at the time of the offense—about the same proportion as for the victims of nonfamily murder.

*Conditions associated with domestic violence include miscarriages, alcohol and other drug abuse, attempted suicide and other forms of mental illness, low birth weight babies, pain, injuries, and permanent physical impairment.

*Forty-seven percent of men who beat their wives do so three or more times a year. Battering may start or become worse during pregnancy; more than 23 percent of pregnant women are abused during pregnancy.

*Twenty-one percent of all women who use hospital emergency and surgical services are battered.

*One in four married couples experience one or more incidents of domestic violence, and repeated severe episodes occur in one marriage out of every four.[66]

Abusers tend to live in urban areas characterized by high rates of social problems and high unemployment.[67] As a group, abusers have high rates of histories of juvenile aggression, criminal behavior, mental illness, and substance abuse.[68]

§ 12.10 Myths about Domestic Violence

1. **Myth:** It doesn't happen to someone like me. It happens to poor and uneducated people.
    Fact: Victims are from all socioeconomic groups.

---

[66] Jerome Sattler, Clinical and Forensic Interviewing of Children and Families 698 (1998).

[67] J.M. Healy & C. Smith, *Batterer Programs: What Criminal Justice Agencies Need to Know,* Reseach in Action (Nat'l Inst. of Justice (NCJ171683) July 1988).

[68] S. Keilitz, P. Hannaford, & H. Efkman, *The Effectiveness of Civil Protection Orders, in* Legal Interventions in Family Violences: Research Findings and Policy Implications, Project of the American Bar Association's Criminal Justice Section, Commission on Domestic Violence, Center on Children and the Law, and Commission on Legal Problems of the Elderly presented to the National Institute of Justice, NCJ 171666, at 47–48 (July 1998); A. Klein, *Re-Abuse in a Population of Court Restrained Male Batterers: Why Restraining Orders Don't Work, in* Legal Interventions in Family Violence: Research Findings and Policy Implications, Project of the American Bar Association's Criminal Justice Section, Commission on Domestic Violence, Center on Children and the Law, and Commission on Legal Problems of the Elderly presented to the National Institute of Justice (1998); L.M. Simon, *A Therapeutic Jurisprudence Approach to the Legal Processing of Domestic Violence Cases,* 1 Psychol. Pub. Pol. & L. 43–79 (1995).

2. **Myth:** Pregnant women are not battered.

   Fact: Obstetrics and gynecology departments frequently see women who have been battered. Between 25 percent and 45 percent of battered women are battered during pregnancy.

3. **Myth:** Battering is a private affair. It isn't appropriate for health care providers to assess or intervene.

   Fact: Health care providers are legally and morally compelled to help by diagnosing victims of battering and informing them of their rights and how to get help.

4. **Myth:** If they wanted the abuse to end, they would leave or seek help.

   Fact: This myth exacerbates the situation. Most women seek outside help from clergy, police, family, and health care providers. A recent Texas study found the women contacted an average of five sources of help, without success, prior to leaving home. Battered women are often encouraged to return home, by people not trained to recognize the signs and ramifications of domestic violence, to keep the family together.

5. **Myth:** The battered woman is masochistic.

   Fact: A woman only stays when she is economically and emotionally dependent, embarrassed, lonely, afraid of retaliation, or guilt-ridden. Many abused women leave as many as seven times before they leave for good. Tragically, 70 percent of the women killed in domestic violence situations have already left or are in the process of leaving.

6. **Myth:** Only alcoholics and drug addicts abuse their partners.

   Fact: Batterers do demonstrate high usage of alcohol, but that use is separate from violent behavior. Domestic violence is an issue of control and dominance over another person. Alcohol or other drugs do not cause violence or abuse but are contributing factors.

7. **Myth:** Battering only occurs in heterosexual relationships.

   Fact: Battering can occur and has been reported among gay and lesbian couples.

8. **Myth:** Only women are battered.

   Fact: In approximately 5 percent of the total number of spousal abuse cases, men are battered by women.[69]

§ 12.11   Indicators and Contributing Factors of Domestic Violence

Lane Veltcamp and Thomas Miller divided signs of domestic violence into three sections: physical indicators, behavioral indicators, and psychological indicators.[70] However, forensic psychologists must be careful when making diagnostic statements based on the signs and indicators listed below. They should be viewed as indicators of concerns that need to be investigated more thoroughly by mental health and legal professionals since many of them can exist for reasons other than domestic violence.

---

[69] Sattler at 699.

[70] Lane Veltcamp & Thomas Miller, *Clinical Strategies in Recognizing Spouse Abuse*, 61 Psychiatric 179–87 (1990).

Physical indicators included unexplained bruises and welts on the face, lips, mouth, torso, back, and buttocks. In addition, unexplained fractures to the skull, nose, or facial area that were in various stages of healing, along with multiple or spiral fractures, are indicative of possible domestic violence. Furthermore, if the explanation for the injury does not fit the injury, there is reason for suspicion.[71]

Behavioral indicators include emotional constrictions or blunted affect, along with extreme withdrawal, apprehension, and fearfulness. Depression accompanied by regressive behavior, inhibition, and possible eating disorders are also indicators. Aggressiveness and compulsive behavior may also be present.[72]

Psychological indicators include sleep disorders, irritability, restlessness, difficulty concentrating, exaggerated startle responses, apprehension, anticipatory anxiety, phobias, obsessions, depression, and anxiety.[73]

Veltcamp and Miller also discuss the *spouse abuse accommodation syndrome* and suggest that there are several stages to this syndrome. Initially, the individual is likely to feel overwhelmed and intimidated during the acute state of trauma. This is followed by a state of cognitive disorganization and confusion. The third stage generally involves avoidance, which can take two directions. There may be conscious inhibitions or an avoidance involving unconscious denial. The perpetrator feeds into this cycle and reinforces the desire to continue the relationship. The men who perform this abuse generally do so as a result of their own lack of communication skills, fear of intimacy, and dependency upon the women they batter.[74]

Veltcamp and Miller summarize by stating:

> [T]he long-term effects of experiencing family violence suggest the following: (1) There tend to be self-destructive tendencies in victims, (2) Women who have been abused show significant adjustment difficulties and problems related to both interpersonal and sexual relationships with males and females, (3) Abuse victims tend to abuse their offspring, thus perpetuating abuse to the next generation, and (4) The most significant diagnostic profile for adults who are physically and sexually abused includes the following symptomatology: depression, self-destructive behavior, anxiety, and traumatic stress, feeling of isolation, poor self-esteem, a tendency towards re-victimization, substance abuse, difficulties in trusting others, and sexual maladjustment in adulthood.[75]

Contributing Factors

The likelihood of family violence.   Roland Maiuro and his associates reported on a study looking at the differences between anger, hostility, and depression in domestically violent men as compared to generally assaultive men. They found that

---

[71] *Id.* at 180.

[72] *Id.* at 181.

[73] *Id.*

[74] *Id.* at 182–83.

[75] *Id.* at 184.

the anger and hostility scores were very similar in the domestically violent and the generally assaultive men. However, the domestically violent men were more likely to be significantly depressed. The findings support the idea that anger dyscontrol is a key issue in the psychological profile of domestically violent men and indicates a need for clinical attention to depression as well as anger.[76]

One of the most prominent researchers in this area, David Finkelhor, reported many abuse-related factors.[77] In homicide, wives are more likely to attack husbands. In aggravated assault, the opposite is true. Intergenerational prevalence of familial violence is not as likely as expected. Transition across generations is not inevitable according to Finkelhor's research. He also reports that alcoholics do not simply become violent when they drink—the purpose of their drinking is to become violent. Alcohol is related to, but not predictive of, intrafamilial abuse.

Other researchers, Bolton and Bolton, report many factors that contribute to the likelihood of family violence. They include repeated exposure to crises; the poverty level of individuals; reduced amount of support available; absence of the nuclear family working together in a crisis; a lower level of education; problematic employment patterns; overreliance and physical punishment; rigidity and inflexibility; and lack of involvement of extended family members.[78]

Bolton and Bolton also identified those factors that contribute to appropriate family functioning. They include

1.   Willingness to nurture and protect family members
2.   Ability to make needs known
3.   Absence of obvious mental illness
4.   Children's ability to elicit caregiving from parents
5.   Reciprocal relationships in the family
6.   Manageable levels of competition within the family
7.   Supportive environment
8.   Lack of totally dominant family member
9.   No nagging sense that something is wrong with the family interaction.[79]

§ 12.12   Effects of Domestic Violence on the Victim and Children

Early research in the area of the effects of domestic violence on victims and their children suggest that "victims of all types of family violence share a common experience of

---

[76] Id. at 194.

[77] David Finkelhor et al., *Anger, Hostility and Depression in Domestically Violent versus Generally Assaultive Men and Nonviolent Control Subjects*, 6 J. Consulting & Clinical Psychol. 17 (Feb. 1988).

[78] F. Bolton & S. Bolton, A Guide for Clinical and Legal Practitioners: Working with the Violent Family 34 (Sage Publ'g 1987).

[79] Id. at 33

denigration of self that results in diminished self-esteem. The shame and feeling of worthlessness, so often expressed by battered woman, is shared by maltreated children as well as maltreated elderly parents."[80] David Finkelhor indicated that depression, suicidal feelings, self-contempt, and an inability to trust and develop intimate relationships in later life are the fallout associated with living in a family where family abuse has occurred. Severely assaulted women had higher rates of psychological distress, including four times the rate of depression and five and one-half times the number of suicide attempts.[81] Bolton and Bolton also indicated that victims had repeated exposure to crises, poverty, reduced amounts of support available, absence of the nuclear family working together in crisis, a lower level of education, problematic employment patterns, overreliance on physical punishment, rigidity and inflexibility, and lack of involvement of extended family members.[82]

Although the above citations are more than 15 years old, they demonstrate that these concerns remain the same over time. David Wolfe and his colleagues performed a meta-analysis on the effects of exposure of children to domestic violence. They identified 41 studies to include in this meta-analysis. Forty of the studies indicated that the children's exposure to domestic violence was related to emotional and behavioral problems. Co-occurence of child abuse increased the level of emotional and behavioral problems above and beyond exposure to domestic violence alone.[83] More recent research demonstrates that 30 to 60 percent of children living in domestic violence homes are abused and in 30 to 60 percent of families where children are the victims of abuse, mothers are also abused.[84] The issue of how domestic violence affects school-age children is reported by numerous researchers. School-age children demonstrate high rates of internalizing and externalizing behavior problems, low self-esteem, and more difficulty in school than children raised in non-violent families.[85] Children raised in violent homes demonstrate problems in interpersonal relationships, including fear and worry about those in the home and difficulty establishing and maintaining friendships with individuals outside the home.[86] Boys from violent families have a risk for abusive tactics in their teenage and young adult relationships.[87] Battering is the leading cause of injury in American women.[88] Spousal abuse contributed to one-fourth of all suicide

---

[80] M.D. Pageloe, Family Violence (Praeger 1984).

[81] David Finkelhor, The Dark Side of Families: Current Family Violence Research (Sage Publications 1983).

[82] F.G. Bolton & S.R. Bolton. A Guide for Clinical and Legal Practitioners, Working with the Violent Family (Sage Publications 1987).

[83] David Wolfe, Claire V. Crocks, Vivien Lee, Alexandra McIntyre-Smith, & Peter G. Jaffe, *The Effects of Children's Exposure to Domestic Violence: A Meta-Analysis and Critique*, 6 Child Clinical & Fam. Psychol. Rev. 171 (2003).

[84] J.L. Eddelson, Problems with Children's Witnessing of Domestic Violence, National Resource Center on Domestic Violence (1997), available at www.vaw.umn.edu.

[85] H.M. Hughes, *Impact of Spouse Abuse on Children of Battered Women*, 2 Violence Update 8–11 (1992).

[86] S.A. Graham-Berman, *Family Worries: The Assessment of Interpersonal Anxiety in Children from Violent and Nonviolent Families*, 25 J. Clinical Child Psychol. 280–87 (1996).

[87] E.N. Jouriles & W.D. Norwood, *Physical Aggression toward Boys and Girls in Families Characterized by the Battering of Women*, 9 J. Fam. Psychol. 69–78 (1995).

[88] A. Jones, Next Time She'll Be Dead: Battering and How to Stop It (Beacon Press 1994).

attempts by women.[89] Fifty percent of homeless women and children in the United States are fleeing from male violence.[90]

Lenore Walker has spent considerable time developing the concept of the Battered Woman Syndrome. Walker suggests that there are several types of batterers, including the "power and control" batterer, who uses violence to get his partner to do what he wants: the "mentally ill" batterer, who has a distorted sense of power; and the "anti-social personality disorder" batterer, who has psychopathic tendencies. She reports:

- 15 percent of the batterers were reported as unemployed during the battering relationship.
- The violence escalated in frequency and severity over time.
- Battered women held attitudes toward women's roles that were more liberal than most of the population.
- Battering was present in two-thirds of the battered women's childhood homes, four-fifths of the batterers' homes, and one-quarter of the non-batterers' homes.
- One-half of the battered women reported being sexually molested or abused as children.
- There was a high rate of arrest and conviction for batterers for offenses other than family violence.
- Women were more likely to be married to their batterers.
- Women were at high risk to be battered during pregnancy.
- Sex was used by the batterer as a power weapon to dominate the women in the same manner as they used physical violence.
- The batterer's unreasonable jealousy was almost always reported by the women.
- Battered women believed that their batterer would kill them.
- Children in battering-relationship homes were at high risk for physical child abuse and almost all were psychologically abused by living in the violent atmosphere.
- Battered women report experiencing more anger when living with a batterer than with a non-batterer.
- Eight times as many women report using physical discipline on their children when living with their batterers than when living alone or in a non-battering relationship.
- Battered women are more socially and financially isolated when living with a batterer than those who do not.
- Violence escalates over time. Use of weapons during battering incidents increases over time.
- The probability that women will seek help increases over time.
- There is more alcohol abuse reported than other drug abuse in battering relationships.
- The trend was that batterers who abuse alcohol were from lower socioeconomic status homes.
- Battered women reported themselves as high on depression indices.[91]

---

[89] *Id.*

[90] *Id.*

[91] Lenore Walker, The Battered Woman Syndrome (2d ed. Springer Publ'g 2000).

§ 12.13   Children Who Witness Domestic Violence

One of the startling features of spousal abuse is that in 45 percent of the cases, the children were also being abused. Gelles and Strauss report that child victims were two to three times more likely to have failing grades in school, difficulty forming friendships, disciplinary problems in school, physically assaultive behavior in school and the home, incident of vandalism and theft, and alcohol and other drug-abuse-related problems.[92] In addition, abused children had been arrested four times more often than non-abused children.

Matthew Reynolds and his co-researchers report that there are higher levels of symptoms of Post-traumatic Stress Disorder, greater number of depressive symptoms, and lower self-esteem for boys who had witnessed domestic violence.[93] These variables were not evident in girls who witnessed domestic violence. The authors conclude that this may be a function of boys' exhibiting a stronger emotional reaction to the domestic violence than girls.[94] Children raised in abusive households learn that violence toward a loved one is acceptable behavior; they exhibit fear, emotional symptoms such as psychosomatic complaints, school phobias, enuresis (bed-wetting), and insomnia. Young children may put themselves at risk by attempting to stop the violence, or they try to deny it by hiding. Very young children tend to identify with the aggressor and lose respect for the victim.[95] Memory for violent events witnessed in childhood may last a lifetime.[96] These children tend to feel worthless, mistrust intimate relationships, exhibit aggression themselves, and may be delayed intellectually.[97] Children who witnessed domestic violence are at increased risk for maladaption.[98] Preschool children exposed to parental violence had many more behavior problems, exhibited significantly more negative affect, responded less appropriately to situations, were more aggressive with peers, and had more ambivalent relationships with their caregivers than those from nonviolent families.[99] More than 80 percent of the children who observed violence between parents were also physically abused by one or both parents.[100] Small children have nightmares, insomnia, headaches, stomachaches, asthma, and enuresis (bed-wetting). Older children often feel guilty that they cannot prevent the violence. Boys tend

---

[92] R. Gelles & M. Strauss, Intimate Violence: The Causes and Consequences of Abuse in the American Family (Simon & Schuster 1988).

[93] Matthew W. Reynolds, Joanna Wallace, Tyra F. Hill, Mark D. Weist, & Laura A. Nebors, *The Relationship between Gender, Depression, and Self-Esteem in Children Who Have Witnessed Domestic Violence*, 25 Child Abuse & Neglect 1201–06 (2001).

[94] *Id.* at 1204.

[95] C. Crites & Coker, *What Therapists See That Judges Miss*, 27 Judges' J. 9–12, 40–41 (1988).

[96] Gayle S. Goodman & M. Rosenberg, *The Child Witness to Family Violence: Clinical and Legal Considerations, in* Domestic Violence on Trial 97–125 (Daniel J. Sonkin ed., Springer Publ'g Co. 1991).

[97] *Id.* at 97.

[98] Jeanne R. Kolbo, Eleanore H. Blakely, & David Engleman, *Children Who Witness Domestic Violence: A Review of the Empirical Literature*, 11 J. Interpersonal Violence, 282–93 (1996).

[99] Sandra A. Graham-Berman & Alytia A. Levendosky, *The Social Functioning of Preschool-Age Children Whose Mothers Are Emotionally and Physically Abused*, J. Emotional Abuse 59–84 (1998).

[100] Mildred D. Pageloe, *Effects of Domestic Violence on Children and Their Consequences for Custody and Visitation Agreements*, Mediation Q. 347–63 (1990).

to act out, showing aggression and disruptive behavior, while girls are more likely to become clinging, withdrawn, passive, and anxious.[101] Children, especially boys who witness mothers being abused, have an elevated rate of emotional, developmental, and behavioral problems.[102] The percentage of youth who report that they acted violently increases as the number of different types of violence in their family increases.[103]

B.B. Robbie Rosman, a leading expert in domestic violence, H.M. Hughes, and Mindy Rosenberg performed a meta-analysis (reviewing a large number of articles in the same area of research to find common or consistent findings) of 28 age and gender studies of domestic violence. The samples were largely drawn from the community or shelters and dealt with children from three years of age through adolescence. They concluded, "in some, both boys and girls show behavioral disruption associated with exposure. This appears to be more evident for boys during school age and, perhaps, for girls following school age."[104] They found that gender issues and the effect of abuse were related to "the development of emotional security; being the recipient of personal abuse; children's reactions to battered and depressed mothers and attitudes toward women more generally; selection of coping strategy; and children's perceptions of internal conflict."[105] The authors summarize the findings by stating that when children who are exposed to parental violence are compared with those who are not exposed, the following characteristics are found more frequently than in other cultural or ethnic groups:

1. greater internalizing (i.e., depression, anxiety, or social withdrawal) behavior problems;
2. greater externalizing (e.g., hyperactivity, aggression) behavior problems;
3. more aggressive social problem solving strategies;
4. lower social competence;
5. lower self-esteem;
6. lower school performance and school achievement;
7. poorer informational intake capacities, lower levels of curiosity and distortion of neutral information;
8. poorer performance on intelligence tests;
9. greater PTSD symtomatology;
10. more frequent attributions of self-blame and guilt for the domestic violence;
11. less secure attachments with caregivers;
12. lower sense of personal control.[106]

---

[101] *Id.* at 348.

[102] John Fantuzzo & W. Mohr, *Prevalence and Effects of Child Exposure to Domestic Violence: The Future of Children*, 9 Domestic Violence & Children no. 3 at 21–32 (1999).

[103] T. Thornberry, Violent Families and Youth Violence, Office of Juvenile Justice and Delinquency Prevention, Fact Sheet #21 (Dec. 1994).

[104] B.B. Robie Rosman, Honore M. Hughes, & Mindy S. Rosenberg, Children and Interparental Violence, The Impact of Exposure (Brunner/Mazel 2000).

[105] *Id.* at 44.

[106] *Id.* at 67–68.

§ 12.14   Issues of Cultural Diversity

Research has been conducted on domestic violence in reference to specific ethnic groups. Similarities and differences occur within ethnic groupings.

African-American Families

The greatest amount of research has been performed on African-American families. African-American families frequently use physical punishment.[107] Although acceptable within the African-American culture, these physical discipline methods can elevate to the level of domestic violence or physical abuse. Hampton and Gelles reported that 17 percent of mothers in African-American families reported at least one violent incident of spousal abuse within the past 10 years, and 7 percent had experienced severe violence.[108] They were 1.23 times more likely to experience minor violence and 2.36 times more likely to experience severe violence than Anglo wives. Even when controlling for demographic variables, African-American females were most likely to report being victims and perpetrators of spousal abuse.[109] Sorenson, Upchurch, and Shen found that being younger, less educated, lower-income, and African-American were risk factors for being more violent toward a spouse.[110]

Amy Koenig and her associates reported a study on 1,197 African-Americans.[111] They found that 54 percent of the sample reported being subjected to physical discipline by their caregivers. The study showed that lower family income and younger caregiver age were related to physical discipline on the part of the parents. These children had a significantly increased risk for psychopathology and were more than twice as likely to have experienced a history of suicidal ideation than those reporting a lower exposure to physical abuse.[112]

Latino Families

Culturally, the Latino family is different from other ethnic groups in that there is a strong emphasis on extended family. In addition, there is a high emphasis on respect for authority, with the father being superior and the head of the family. Kantor, Jasinski, and Aldarondo found that, as a group, Latino families have similar rates of domestic violence as Anglo

---

[107] M.K. Ho, Minority Children and Adolescents in Therapy (Sage 1992).

[108] R.L. Hampton & R. J. Gelles, *Violence toward Black Women in a Nationally Representative Sample of Black Families*, 25 J. Comparative Fam. Stud. 105–19 (1994).

[109] J.A. Neff, B. Holamon, & T.D. Schluter, *Spousal Violence among Anglos, Blacks, and Mexican-Americans: The Role of Demographic Variables, Psychosocial Predictors, and Alcohol Consumption*, 10 J. Fam. Violence 1–21 (1995).

[110] S.B. Sorenson, D.M. Upchurch, & H. Shen, *Violence and Injury in Marital Arguments: Risk Patterns and Gender Differences*, 86 Am. J. Pub. Health 35–40 (1996).

[111] Amy L. Koenig, Nicholas Ialongo, Barry M. Wagner, Jeanne Poduska, & Sheppard Kellam, *Negative Caregiver Strategies and Psychopathology in Urban, African American Young Girls*, Child Abuse & Neglect 1211–33 (2002).

[112] *Id.* at 1211.

families.[113] There is, however, considerable variation within different Hispanic ethnic groups. For example, about 20.4 percent of Puerto Rican wives, 10.5 percent of Mexican wives, 17.9 percent of Mexican-American wives, 2.5 percent of Cuban wives, and 9.9 percent of Anglo wives reported husband-to-wife violence in the Kantor *et al.* survey.[114]

Asian Families

Asian families highly value the family and perceive any negative actions of a family member as reflecting negatively on the family as a whole. Self-control, humility, and inconspicuousness are values of Asian families.[115] The expectation that would be based on the portrayal of a harmonious family is that physical and verbal abuse would be discouraged. However, C.K. Ho suggests that these activities occur in the privacy of the Asian family's home and that there is an emphasis on hiding such problems.[116] Reported rates of family violence in Asian-American families is low. However, it cannot be determined if the reported rates are low because of actual low frequencies or the emphasis on hiding such problems. It is reported that the Chinese culture perpetuates exploitation of women.[117] Twenty to 30 percent of Chinese husbands hit their wives, with at least 60 percent of Japanese women reporting some type of physical abuse.[118] Yoshihama concluded that domestic violence perpetrated by Japanese men against their partners was not only condoned but also was not viewed as a social problem.

Native American Families

While other cultures' identities are tied to their extended families, Native Americans' identities are also tied to their tribe. Chester, Robin, Koss, Lopez, and Goldman estimated between 50 percent and 55 percent of Native American women are physically abused by their partners at some point in their lives, and this number may be as high as 80 percent in urban areas.[119]

---

[113] G.K. Kantor, J.L. Jasinski, & E. Aldarondo, *Socioeconomic Status and Incidence of Marital Violence in Hispanic Families*, 9 Violence & Victims 207–22 (1994).

[114] B.B. Robbie Rossman, H.M. Hughes, & M.S. Rosenberg, Children and Interparental Violence, The Impact of Exposure (Brunner/Mazel 2000).

[115] *Id.*

[116] C.K. Ho, *An Analysis of Domestic Violence in Asian American Communities: A Multicultural Approach to Counseling, in* K.P. Monterio ed., Ethinicity and Psychology 138–51 (Kendall-Hunt 1996).

[117] M.Y. Lee & P. Au, *Chinese Battered Women in North America: Their Experience and Treatment, in* A.R. Roberts Ed., Battered Women and Their Families 448–82 (2d ed. Springer 1998); C.K. Ho, *An Analysis of Domestic Violence in Asian American Communities: A Multicultural Approach to Counseling, in* K.P. Monterio (ed., Ethnicity and Psychology 138–51 (Kendall-Hunt 1996).

[118] M. Yoshihama & S.B. Sorenson, *Physical, Sexual and Emotional Abuse by Male Intimates: Experiences of Women in Japan*, 9 Violence & Victims 63–77 (1994).

[119] B. Chester, R.W. Robin, M.P. Koss, T. Lopez, & D. Goldman, *Godmother Dishonored: Violence against Women by Male Partners in American Indian Communities*, 9 Violence & Victims 248–58 (1994).

Native Americans in an urban Indian Health Center reported approximately 56 percent of their parents engaged in violence toward each other.[120]

§ 12.15   The Psychologically Battered Child

A child is considered to be emotionally or psychologically abused when he or she is the subject of acts or omissions by the parents or other persons responsible for the child's care that have caused, or could cause, a serious behavioral, cognitive, emotional, or mental disorder. In some cases of emotional/psychological abuse, the acts of the parents or other caretakers alone, without any harm to the child's behavior or condition, are sufficient to warrant intervention by child protective services. An example would be if the parents/caretakers use extreme or bizarre forms of punishment, such as torture, or confinement of the child in a dark closet. For less severe acts, such as habitual scapegoating, belittling, or rejecting treatment, demonstrable harm to the child is often required before child protective services is able to intervene.[121]

Emotional neglect includes "such actions as chronic or extreme spouse abuse in the child's presence, permission for alcohol use by the child, and refusal of or failure to provide needed psychological care."[122] Today, the most frequently occurring form of abuse is that of emotional or psychological abuse. However, only 136,300 of such cases were reported in 1994.[123]

Behaviors on the part of parents who "jeopardize the development of self-esteem, of social competence, of the capacity for intimacy, and positive healthy interpersonal relationship"[124] are all aspects of psychological maltreatment. James Garbarino and colleagues give five examples of psychological maltreatment:

1. Each morning a mother threatens her four-year-old son with abandonment: "Maybe today is the day I go away and leave you alone. You better be good today, boy, or you'll never see me again."

2. A father restricts his seven-year-old daughter to her room every day after school: "I don't want you getting involved with any other kids; they're not good enough for you."

3. Each time a 10-year-old boy brings home his report card from school, his parents look it over with expressions of disgust: "No son of ours could be such a dummy; we wish you weren't around all the time reminding us of the mistake we make."

4. A three-year-old boy's father suspects that he's not the boy's father, that the boy's mother had an affair while he was away on business. Now he refuses to speak to the boy: "He's not mine; I don't want anything to do with him."

---

[120] I.M. Norton & S.M. Manson, *A Silent Minority, Battered American Indian Women*, 10 J. Fam. Violence 307–17 (1995).

[121] U.S. Dep't of Health & Human Servs., Child Abuse and Neglect 3 (1992).

[122] *Id.* at 2.

[123] *Id.*

[124] James Garbarino et al., The Psychologically Battered Child 1 (1987) [hereinafter Garbarino et al.]

5. A mother persuades her 13-year-old daughter to earn some money by having sex with the mother's "extra" boyfriends: "You're a little slut anyway, and I might as well get something out of being your mother."[125]

The accepted definition of *child maltreatment* reported by Garbarino came from the *Interdisciplinary Glossary on Child Abuse and Neglect:* "The definitions of emotional abuse include verbal or emotional assault, close confinement and threatened harm. The definitions of emotional neglect include inadequate nurturance/affection, knowingly permitting maladaptive behavior (for example, delinquency) and other refusal to provide essential care."[126]

Stuart Hart, Nelson Binggeli, and Marla Brassard point out that psychological maltreatment not only stands alone but is often embedded in other forms of maltreatment.[127] They identify six major types of psychological maltreatment:

1. Spurning, which includes belittling, shaming, and public humiliation

2. Terrorizing, which includes caretaker behavior that threatens or is likely to physically hurt, kill, abandon, or place the child in a dangerous situation

3. Isolating, which generally involves placing unreasonable limitations on the child's freedom of movement

4. Exploiting/corrupting, which includes modeling, permitting, or encouraging antisocial behavior, or developmentally inappropriate behavior

5. Denying emotional responsiveness, which is generally considered to be ignoring the child's needs

6. Mental, health, medical and educational neglect, which involves ignoring the need for, or failing or refusing to allow or provide treatment for serious emotional/behavioral problems, physical health problems, and/or educational problems.[128]

The authors indicate that a considerable amount of additional study needs to be done in the area of child maltreatment.

Joan Vondra, Anne Kolar, and Barbara Radigan point out that one of the difficulties in intervening in psychological maltreatment cases is determining what constitutes psychological maltreatment.[129]

§ 12.16   Parental Factors Related to Psychological Maltreatment

Garbarino and coauthors identify several parental factors related to maltreatment:

Parents' unavailability to respond to the children's needs. Such parents mainly ignore and reject their children. When they are unavailable to meet their children's physical needs, they

---

[125] *Id.*

[126] *Id.* at 4–5.

[127] Stuart Hart, Nelson Binggeli, & Marsha Brassard, *Evidence of the Effects of Psychological Maltreatment*, 1 J. Emotional Abuse no. 1, at 27–58 (1998).

[128] *Id.* at 32–33.

[129] Joan Vondra, Anne Kolar, & Barbara Radigan, *Psychological Maltreatment of Children*, *in* Assessment of Family Violence: A Clinical and Legal Source Book (1992).

fail to feed the children appropriately, to dress them as needed, or to enable them to get enough sleep or health care.[130]

[W]hen parents give partial and inappropriate responses to the children's needs, mainly rejecting or corrupting the children. For example, the parents try to meet the child's physical and psychological needs, yet they lack sufficient resources, knowledge, and skills for doing so effectively. . . . Another inappropriate response is infantilization. Instead of placing excessively high demands on the children, the parents underestimate the children's physical abilities and mental capabilities and consistently prevent the children from actualizing their potentials. . . . A third type of inappropriate response, corrupting or missocializing, occurs when parents teach the children values that deviate from normative community values. In some instances, children are raised on values that differ markedly from those of the community—for example, values favoring drug abuse, sexual misconduct, or delinquent activity—and therefore place the child in jeopardy.[131]

Parents are abusive when they make harsh and destructive responses to the needs of their children, mainly terrorizing, but also degrading, threatening, and exploiting their children.[132]

§ 12.17   Effects of Psychological Maltreatment

There are a number of psychological effects that are associated with being psychologically maltreated. They include emotional instability, impulse control problems, Borderline or Narcissistic Personality Disorder, unresponsiveness, substance abuse, anxiety, depression, low self-esteem, suicidal ideation, and/or eating disorders.[133]

- The greater the amount of verbal aggression by parents, the more likely the child would be physically aggressive or delinquent, or experience interpersonal problems.[134]
- Verbal aggression by parents was more strongly related to negative child outcomes than physical aggression unaccompanied by verbal aggression.[135]

---

[130] Garbarino et al. at 53.

[131] *Id.* at 54–55.

[132] *Id.* at 56.

[133] M. Braver, J. Bumberry, K. Green, & R. Rawson, *Childhood Abuse and Current Psychological Functioning in a University Counseling Center Population*, 39 J. Counseling Psychol. 252–57 (1992); P. Crittenden, A. Claussen, & D. Sugarman, *Physical and Psychological Maltreatment in Middle Childhood and Adolescence*, Dev. & Psychopathology 145–164 (1994); M. Engels & D. Moisan, *The Psychological Maltreatment Inventory: Development of a Measure of Psychological Maltreatment in Childhood for Use in Adult Clinical Settings*, 74 Psychol. Rep. 595–604 (1994); P. Mullen, J. Martin, J. Anderson, S. Romans, & G. Herbison, *The Long-Term Impact of the Physical, Emotional, and Sexual Abuse of Children: A Community Study*, 17 Child Abuse & Neglect 623–40 (1996); M. Rorty, J. Yager, & E. Rossotto, *Childhood Sexual, Physical, and Psychological Abuse in Bulimia Nervosa*, 151 Am. J. Psychiatry 1122–26 (1994); A.B. Gross & H.R. Keller, *Long-Term Consequences of Childhood Physical and Psychological Maltreatment*, 18 Aggressive Behav. 171–85 (1992); J. Briere & M. Runtz, *Differential Adult Symptomatology Associated with Three Types of Child Abuse Histories*, 14 Child Abuse & Neglect 357–64 (1990).

[134] Y.M. Vissing, M.A. Straus, R.J. Gelles, & J.W. Harrop, *Verbal Aggression by Parents and Psychosocial Problems of Children*, 15 Child Abuse & Neglect 223–38 (1991).

[135] *Id.*

- Psychological abuse was a stronger predictor than physical abuse for both depression and low self-esteem.[136]
- Social competency problems and anti-social functioning may result from psychological maltreatment, in addition to self-isolating behavior, low empathy, sexual maladjustment, and delinquency/criminality.[137]
- There is a relationship between psychological maltreatment and physical health problems as related to an increase in somatic complaints.[138]

§ 12.18   Treatment and Protection

Physical and emotional abuse and domestic violence remains a significant problem that results in life-long adjustment concerns affecting relationships and self-esteem, and requiring psychotherapy. Considerable research has been performed on how to treat psychological maltreatment within families. Individuals who reduce environmental stressors in the family, resolve problems among family members, and mobilize community resources are most likely to be effective. Melton developed eight concepts that should be addressed in forming the foundation of child protection:

1. The state has a profound duty to protect children from harm. He states that it is not a constitutional duty, but it is a moral duty. The basic duty is to protect the integrity of persons.

2. The child protection system is in a state of emergency. He points out that there are 2.7 million reports of child abuse per year. He also indicates that child protective services agencies are understaffed, undertrained, provide insufficient treatment, and have access to insufficient foster care. His figures indicate that $5.3 billion is being spent on a system that does not work.

3. The emergency in child protective services is because of a lack of a coordinated program. Unfortunately, the focus is on investigation and not on what needs to be done to protect and treat children.

4. The flaws in the current child protection policy are driven by the legal system.

---

[136] *Id.*

[137] R. Herrenkohl, B. Egolf, & E. Herrenkohl, *Preschool Antecedents of Adolescent Assaultive Behavior: A Longitudinal Study*, 67 Am. J. Orthopsychiatry 422–32 (1997), and *Circumstances Surrounding the Occurrence of Child Maltreatment*, 51 J. Consulting & Clinical Psychol. 424–31 (1983); H.M. Hughes & S.A. Graham-Berman, *Children of Battered Women: Impact of Emotional Abuse on Adjustment and Development*, J. Emotional Abuse no. 2, 23–50 (1998); J. Briere & M. Runtz, *Differential Adult Symptomatology Associated with Three Types of Child Abuse Histories*, 14 Child Abuse & Neglect 357–64 (1990); B. Egeland & M.F. Erickson, *Psychologically Unavailable Caregiving, in* M. Brassard, B. Germsin, & S. Hart eds., Psychological Maltreatment of Children and Youth 110–20 (Pergamon 1987).

[138] Honore M. Hughes, *Impact of Spouse Abuse on Children of Battered Women*, 2 Violence Update 8–11 (1992); R.D. Krugman & M.K. Krugman, *Emotional Abuse in the Classroom*, 138 Am. J. Diseases of Children 284–86 (1984).

5. Child protection would be facilitated by de-emphasizing the legal system's involvement. Because of the legal system's intervention and child protective services' approach, it has absolved the public from doing anything but reporting child abuse. One of the concerns raised about the reporting system is that 25 percent of therapy clients drop out of treatment when a report has been made by the therapist. Child protection ought to be part of everyday life; it should be a function of neighbor helping neighbor. Melton feels that this would decrease the opportunity for abuse and vulnerability of children. He also points out that prevalence rates are directly related to poverty rates, indicating that there is a six-times higher incidence rate in families with incomes under $15,000 per year.

6. Maltreatment of children is so abhorrent it warrants criminal punishment. Punishment for child sexual abuse should be more severe than for physical abuse because the sexual abuser is deriving sexual gratification as perpetrator, whereas it is rare for a physical abuser to derive gratification from the abuse.

7. There is a conflict of interest between the protection of children and the present reporting system (the emphasis on intervention without prevention and treatment). In some cases, removal of children from the home may be necessary.

8. A coercive authority should be applied to force treatment of the abuser. Court-ordered participants are more likely to complete treatments than are voluntary participants.[139]

When recognizing the adverse effects associated with abuse-related issues, it becomes the mental health professional's moral and ethical obligation to provide appropriate treatment interventions. Most of the treatment approaches currently in use have been developed as a result of necessity, or trial by fire. Carlson recommended 10 elements that should be included in treatment programs for children of battered women. They include (1) individual assessments; (2) individual counseling; (3) referrals; (4) advocacy; (5) group work for children; (6) regular, structured recreational activities for children; (7) aftercare and follow-up services; (8) prevention services; (9) parenting education and support groups for mothers; and (10) evaluation of all aspects of the program.[140] In a survey, Carlson found that on average, shelters for battered women provide 3.8 of these 10 components in their intervention programs. It is recognized by almost all researchers in the area that multifaceted approaches are necessary. These approaches need to include both individual and group work with children, therapy with the mother, therapy with the father, and recognition of developmentally appropriate interventions. Therapy needs to involve modeling and social learning, resolution of stress and trauma-related symptoms, and psychoeducational training.[141]

Treatment is one important intervention in dealing with domestic-violence-related circumstances. However, prevention activities may be more important because preventing abuse from occurring would result in not needing intervention programs. Unfortunately,

---

[139] Gary Melton, *The Improbability of Prevention of Sexual Abuse, in* D. Willis, E.J. Holden, & M. Rosenberg eds., Child Abuse Prevention 168–92 (John Wiley & Sons 1992).

[140] Bonnie E. Carlson, *Children's Beliefs about Punishment*, 56 Am. J. Orthopsychiatry 308 § 12 (1996).

[141] B.B. Robbie Rossman, Honore M. Hughes, & Mindy S. Rosenberg, Children and Interparental Violence: The Impact of Exposure (Brunner/Mazel 2000).

both the intervention and prevention programs require financial resources. Since more socioeconomically depressed families are abusers, they are less likely to have the resources available to take advantage of these services. Wolf and Jaffe report that home visitor programs have been effective not only in promoting healthy child development but also in reducing abusive behavior within the home for infants and preschool children.[142] School-age children can be reached by including education about domestic violence issues within the social studies or social science curricula. An effective curriculum will include "defining violence and its impact; develop safety plans; learn to express feelings and opinions based on values of equality, respect, and sharing of power; learn non-violent conflict resolution; and gain a sense of worth regardless of family difficulties."[143] When working with teens, Wolf and Jaffe report that emphasis needs to be on healthy relationships and alternatives to violence and abuse. These approaches are particularly helpful to teens who have grown up in families where family violence has occurred. Prevention at this age level focuses on dating and partner relationship building.

Treatment for female victims, batterers, and abusive environments can involve in-home prevention programs, outpatient therapy, and/or inpatient therapy. William McGuigan, Aphra Katzev & Clara Pratt worked with 1,093 "at-risk" families in a home-visiting child abuse prevention program. They found that families were less likely to remain in the program if they lived in a community with a high level of violence.[144] Older mothers and Hispanic mothers were more likely to remain in the program than younger mothers or white non-Hispanic mothers. It was also found that the more supervision the caseworker received, the more likely the family was to stay in the program.[145]

David Wright and his associates studied 132 adult survivors of childhood abuse with post-traumatic Stress Disorder in inpatient treatment programs.[146] All participants met the diagnosis of PTSD upon admission. Analyses revealed that treatment gains were maintained at the one-year post-discharge follow-up. The authors concluded that intensive inpatient group treatment appears to be effective in reducing PTSD symptomatology.[147]

Diane DePanfilis and Susan Zuravin studied 434 families randomly selected from a sample of 2,092 families with substantiated reports of child abuse or neglect.[148] They found that actively engaging families in a helping or therapeutic relationship was related to helping them accept the services which in time reduced the likelihood of future

---

[142] D.A. Wolf & P.G. Jaffe, Prevention of Domestic Violence: Emerging Initiatives, Paper presented at the Asilomar Conference on Children and Intimate Violence, Pacific Grove, Cal. (1999).

[143] B.B. Robbie Rossman, Honore M. Hughes, & Mindy S. Rosenberg, Children and Interparental Violence: The Impact of Exposure (Brunner/Mazel 2000).

[144] William M. McGuigan, Aphra R. Katzev, & Clara C. Pratt, *Multi-level Determinants of Retention in a Home-Visiting Child Abuse Prevention Program*, 27 Child Abuse & Neglect, 363–80 (2003).

[145] *Id.* at 363.

[146] David C. Wright, Wendy L. Woo, Robert T. Muller, Cheryl B. Fernandes, & Erin R. Craftcheck, *An Investigation of Trauma-Centered Inpatient Treatment for Adult Survivors of Abuse*, 27 Child Abuse & Neglect 393–406 (2003).

[147] *Id.* at 393.

[148] Diane DePanfilis & Susan J. Zuravin, *The Effect of Services on the Recurrence on Child Maltreatment*, Child Abuse & Neglect 187–205 (2002).

maltreatment.[149] These authors also found in another study that "increasing social supports may help families cope with life events that increase stress and risk of continued maltreatment; that collaborations between CPS and Domestic Violence Agencies are needed; and that screening maltreated children for mental health problems and other disabilities and assuring that children with these needs and their families get effective treatment may reduce the likelihood of continued maltreatment."[150]

§ 12.19   Legal Intervention

In conclusion, Dr. Melton identifies three types of situations in which legal intervention should be used:

1. When the danger to the child is high enough that the child cannot otherwise be protected
2. When there is a greater possibility of a positive outcome by involving legal authorities
3. In cases of depravity.

J. Davis and his co-researchers report that psychologists' willingness to report abuse cases is a function of the abuse indicators and what parental actions have been taken. They also report that another study indicated the most significant differences in reporting were based on the education that professionals had received about child abuse.[151]

When it becomes necessary for legal intervention, Dr. Melton recommends that the intervention should be child-centered and that children should be made partners in the justice process. In addition, children should be treated with dignity within the legal system. In response, the legal process itself should mitigate harm to the children. A strong, speedy trial provision and a strong case consolidation provision would go a long way toward reducing harm to children. He points out that the greatest harm comes from the length of time that resolution requires. Speediness and case consolidation would reduce this harm.[152]

Melton and several other prominent researchers in the area of child maltreatment and the law wrote a survey article in 1995. They point out that little research has been performed to examine the effects of the legal process on children and the functioning of the child protective services systems.[153]

---

[149] Id. at 187.

[150] Diane DePanfilis & Susan J. Zuravin, *Predicting Child Maltreatment Recurrences during Treatment*, 23 Child Abuse & Neglect 729 (2002).

[151] J. Davis, P. Petretic-Jackson, L. Pitman, J. Waitzman, L. Clark, M. Justice, & V. Simpson, Impact of Abuse Indicators and Reporting Criteria on Mandated Reporting, Paper presented at the 100th Annual Convention of the American Psychological Association, Toronto (Aug. 1996).

[152] Gary Melton, Can Caring and Coercion Coexist? Child Protection and the Law, Paper presented at the Annual Meeting of the American Psychological Association, Washington, D.C. (1992).

[153] Gary Melton et al., *Empirical Research on Child Maltreatment and the Law*, 24 J. Clinical Child Psychol. 47–77 (1995).

§ 12.20   Questions for Chapter 12

Caution.   Attorneys should not expect to be able to go into court and ask all of the following questions. Preparation is necessary, reviewing material in the book to determine whether the question applies to a particular case. Section numbers at the end of some of the questions indicate where to find an explanation of why the question is important. Not all questions have references to specific sections.

1.   Did the examiner evaluate the role of alcohol or other substance abuse in the physical abuse allegations? See § **12.9.**

2.   Is any evidence of "spouse abuse accommodation syndrome" present? See § **12.11.**

3.   Did the examiner determine whether physical abuse took place during the marriage in any combination (parent to parent, parent to child)? See § **12.3.**

4.   Did the examiner determine whether physical abuse took place during any of the parents' childhoods?

5.   Ask the same questions for psychological/emotional abuse.

6.   If physical abuse, sexual abuse, and/or psychological abuse took place during the childhood of either of the parents, what therapeutic steps have taken place to resolve the conflicts associated with experiencing such trauma during childhood? See § **12.6.**

7.   If the parent has experienced any of these kinds of abuse and has not undergone extensive psychotherapy, how does the psychologist performing the evaluation justify considering this parent as an appropriate custodial parent? See § **12.6.**

8.   If the parent or child reports any form of abuse, has the psychologist obtained detailed descriptions of the abuse in an effort to determine whether the allegations are overstated or exaggerated? See § **12.2.**

9.   If allegations of physical abuse have been made, is there any official documentation from an objective third party (police department, social services agency, or other professional)?

10.   Is there any evidence that the child who is the alleged victim of physical abuse has been coached by either parent, any other adult, or a sibling?

11.   If one of the parents was a victim of abuse during childhood, does he or she still act as a victim during adulthood? If so, how will this affect his or her ability to be an effective custodial parent?

12.   If there have been abuse allegations, has the mother handled them appropriately? Has the mother been able to put the issue to rest at an appropriate time?

13.   Has a convicted perpetrator of any form of abuse sought treatment? Has that treatment been successful?

14.   Did the examiner attempt to preserve the rights of both the alleged victim and alleged perpetrator?

15.   If there was domestic violence, has the evaluator taken into account the effects of children witnessing domestic violence? See § **12.13.**

§ 12.21 Case Digest

The source of information for most of the following cases is the *Mental and Physical Disability Law Reporter* (MPDLR), a publication of the American Bar Association. Complete information for any other sources appears in the relevant references below. The following are direct quotations from the identified source. Quotations from the *Mental and Physical Disability Law Reporter:* Excerpted from *Mental and Physical Disability Law Reporter.* Copyright © 1989–2004. American Bar Association. Reprinted by permission. If no source is identified, it is a summary from the court ruling. The following summaries are based on the official opinions rendered.

Iowa

Op. Att'y. Gen. 93-6-2 (June 1, 1993). The Iowa Attorney General said that children under spiritual treatment by their parents or guardians remain subject to the state's child abuse reporting, investigation, and treatment requirements, regardless of statutory exemption provisions. The attorney general indicated that the state's mandatory reporting, investigation, and treatment laws must be uniformly applied to ensure that all Iowa children receive proper medical care and treatment. If a parent is alleged to have failed to provide essential medical treatment for any reason, including religious beliefs, there must be an investigation to ensure that proper medical treatment is received and that the parent or guardian actually holds religious beliefs that preclude the child's getting proper medical care. If the parents do not hold such beliefs, or if their beliefs do not prohibit the specific treatment planned, the parents or guardian could be found in violation of child abuse statutes.

Missouri

Dickerson v. Dickerson, 55 S.W.3d 867 (Mo. Ct. App. 2001). Brent Dickerson filed for divorce from his wife, Tamera. The wife alleged that the husband had physically abused her and physically and sexually abused the children. The court appointed a guardian ad litem (GAL) for the children. Each parent sought sole custody. Testimony by the wife and a number of other witnesses established the husband's history of physical and sexual abuse. The guardian ad litem, the husband, and the wife presented testimony from three psychologists who did custody evaluations, each of whom recommended joint custody, with the wife having primary residential custody and the husband initially having supervised visitation. At the close of twelve days of testimony, the court invited the guardian ad litem to make a final recommendation. Rather than limiting her remarks to that recommendation, the GAL gave unsworn testimony that included a statement that two of the three psychologists had changed their minds and now agreed with the GAL's recommendation that the husband should have primary physical custody of the children. The judge refused to permit the GAL to be cross-examined, indicating that she was an officer of the court. The trial court granted sole legal and physical custody to the husband. The wife appealed.

The appellate court held that (1) the trial court failed to make specific findings of fact regarding allegations of domestic violence, as required by Missouri statute, and (2) the trial court failed to make necessary written findings of fact and conclusions of law to justify awarding custody to the abusive parent and how that would serve the child's best interest. The court further ruled that the trial court committed error when it allowed the GAL to give unsworn testimony and recommendations based on hearsay medical opinions that were not admissible. The trial court could not accept those statements without applying the required procedural and evidentiary rules regarding competency and reliability, and admitting them was prejudicial error. The case was remanded for a new trial on the custody issue and related matters.

Rhode Island

Duffy v. Reeves, 619 A.2d 1094 (R.I. 1993). The Rhode Island Supreme Court ruled that a trial court properly exercised emergency jurisdiction under the Uniform Child Custody Jurisdiction Act when it granted a divorced resident temporary custody of his son on the basis of allegations of unwarranted spankings by the mother's present husband while the child lived with his mother in New York. The court dismissed the mother's contention that spanking, per se, does not constitute abuse or mistreatment under the UCCJA's emergency section. The supreme court indicated that the trial judge's decision regarding whether an emergency exists must be made separately for each case. In the present case, the court felt that there was enough evidence of abuse to justify holding a full hearing on the custody question.

CHAPTER 13

SEXUAL ABUSE

§ 13.1   What Is Sexual Abuse?

One of the critical issues associated with proceeding with a sexual abuse allegation is trying to define sexual abuse. Is it sexual abuse when a child catches a glimpse of an exhibitionist? There is disagreement over this. Most people would not consider it abuse if a child is shown *Playboy* magazine by an older playmate. But what if a young child is shown hard-core pornography? Does a mother's sleeping with her child constitute sexual abuse in the absence of sexual touching? What if the child is a teenager who becomes aroused by this? Most people would agree that it is sexual abuse if a 19-year-old woman has sexual contact with a six-year-old boy, but not if the boy is 16. However, what if the boy is 14? What if the 14-year-old boy initiates the experience with the woman and later views the experience as positive?

This is not to say that all sexual abuse allegations fit into a gray area of definition. The U.S. Department of Health and Human Services defines *sexual abuse* to include

> fondling a child's genitals, intercourse, incest, rape, sodomy, exhibitionism, and sexual exploitation. To be considered child abuse, these have to be committed by a person responsible for the care of the child (for example, a parent, a baby sitter, or a day care provider). If a stranger commits these acts, it would be considered sexual assault and handled solely by the police and criminal courts.

Many experts believe that sexual abuse is the most underreported form of child maltreatment because of the secrecy or "conspiracy of silence" that so often characterizes these cases.[1] The *Diagnostic and Statistical Manual of Mental Disorders–Fourth Edition* (DSM-IV) defines *sexual abuse* in a number of ways. Pedophilia, for example, is defined as follows:

Diagnostic Criteria for 302.20 Pedophilia

A.   Over a period of at least six months, recurrent intense sexually arousing fantasies, sexual urges or behaviors involving sexual activity with a prepubescent child or children (generally 13 or younger).

B.   The fantasies, sexual urges, or behaviors cause clinically significant distress or impairment in social, occupations, or other important areas of functioning.

C.   The person is at least 16 years old and at least 5 years older than the child or children in Criterion A.

NOTE: Do not include an individual in late adolescence involved in an ongoing sexual relationship with a 12- or 13-year-old

Specify if:

   Sexually Attracted to Males

   Sexually Attracted to Females

   Sexually Attracted to Both

Specify if:

   Limited to incest.

---

[1] U.S. Dep't of Health & Human Servs., Child Abuse and Neglect 2–3 (1992).

Specify Type:
    Exclusive Type (attracted only to children)
    Nonexclusive Type.[2]

David Finkelhor states that "child sexual abuse is most commonly used in reference to sexual activity involving a child that has at least one or two characteristics: It occurs within a relationship where it is deemed exploitive by virtue of an age difference or caretaking relationship that exists with the child; it occurs as a result of threat or force."[3]

Incidence

The number of cases of child sexual abuse has increased dramatically in the last three decades. There were 139,599 cases in 1994, 133,600 cases (or 2.1 per thousand) cases of sexual abuse reported in 1986, and 7,559 in 1976. This certainly does not mean that there are more than 18 times as many incidents today as there were in 1976. Instead, it means that the public is more aware of sexual abuse-related concerns and that abuse is being reported more frequently.

An article by Timothy Wynkoop, Steven Capps, and Bobby Priest indicates that "[i]t is clear from this analysis that we remain uncertain as to the true incidence and prevalence of CSA (child sexual abuse) in our society. This is quite surprising, given the amount of effort directed toward uncovering the extent of this phenomenon."[4]

Frank Putnam reports in 2003 that there was a 67 percent increase of all forms of child abuse reports from 1986 to 1993 according to U.S. Department of Health and Human Services. However, officially reported cases declined during that same period.[5]

PROFILES OF ABUSER AND ABUSED

§ 13.2   Profiles of Abuser and Abused

With regard to characteristics of abusers, David Finkelhor points out that

> although good research is scarce, there is some reasonable empirical support for propositions that are consistent with some of these theories: (1) Some groups of abusers do have an unusual need for power and domination which may be related to their offender behavior; (2) most groups of offenders who have been tested using physiological monitors do show unusual levels of deviant sexual arousal to children; (3) many offenders have histories of being victims of sexual abuse themselves; (4) many offenders have conflict over adult heterosexual

---

[2] Diagnostic and Statistical Manual of Mental Disorders 528 (4th ed. 1994).

[3] David Finkelhor, *The Sexual Abuse of Children: Current Research Reviewed*, 17 Psychiatric Annals 233–41 (1987) [hereinafter Finkelhor].

[4] Timothy Wynkoop et al., Incidents and Prevalence of Child Sexual Abuse: A Critical Review of Data Collection Procedures (1995).

[5] Frank Putnam, *Ten-Year Research Update Review: Child Sexual Abuse*, 42 Am. Academy of Child & Adolescent Psychiatry at 269 (2003).

relationships or are experiencing disruption in normal adult heterosexual partnerships at the time of the offense; and (5) alcohol is connected to the commission of the acts in a large number of the offenses.[6]

He also states,

> According to recent community studies, the following factors are consistently associated with higher risk of abuse: (1) a child who is living without one of the biological parents; (2) a child whose mother is unavailable either as a result of employment outside of the home, disability or illness; (3) a child who reports that the parents' marriage is unhappy or conflictful; (4) a child who reports a poor relationship with the parents or being subject to extremely punitive discipline or child abuse; (5) a child who reports having a stepfather.[7]

Although not all child molesters are pedophiles, current research demonstrates that pedophiles rarely have a diagnosis of psychotic disorders, but often have mood disorder diagnoses.[8] Child molesters who prefer boys or younger children are generally of lower intellectual functioning.[9] Child molesters frequently abuse alcohol during the offense or in general.[10] Marshal states that offenders rarely accept full responsibility for their offense.[11] They demonstrate deficits in empathy in general, and empathy toward their victim,[12] lack self-esteem,[13] lack intimacy and experience loneliness,[14] and have inadequate attachment styles.[15]

Kathleen Faller, a prominent researcher in the area of sexual abuse, studied a sample of women who have sexually abused children.[16] After studying the 72 women, it was concluded that those children abused by female offenders underreport the abuse, and one-third of the female offenders continue to have access to their victims. There is some question whether women must be more deviant than men to perform sexual abuse, since three-quarters of the cases involved intrusive activity. These women also had significant

---

[6] Finkelhor at 234–35.

[7] *Id.* at 235.

[8] N.C. Raymond, E. Coleman, F. Ohlerking, G.A. Christenson, & M. Minor, *Psychiatric Co-Morbidity in Pedophilic Sex Offenders*, 156 Am. J. Psychiatry, 786–88 (1999).

[9] R. Blanchard, M.S. Watson, A. Choy, R. Dickey, P. Klassen, M. Kuban, & D.J. Ferren. *Pedophiles: Mental Retardation, Maternal Age, and Sexual Orientation*, 28 Archives Sexual Behav. 111–27 (1999).

[10] Callnuf, Bradford, Greenburg, & Currey (1996).

[11] W.L. Marshal, F. Champagne, C. Brown, & S. Miller. *Empathy, Intimacy, Loneliness, and Self-Esteem in Non-Familial Child Molesters: A Brief Report*, 6 J. Child Sexual Abuse 87–98 (1997).

[12] W.L. Marshal, S.M. Hudson, R. Jones, & Y.M. Fernandez, *Empathy in Sex Offenders*, 15 Psychol. Rev. 99–113 (1995).

[13] W.L. Marshal, D. Anderson, & F. Champagne, *The Importance of Self-Esteem in Sexual Offenders*, 3 Psychol. Crime & Laws 81–106 (1996).

[14] K.M. Bumby & D.J. Hansen. *Intimacy Deficits, Fear of Intimacy, and Loneliness among Sexual Offenders*, 24 Crim. Just. Behav. 315–31 (1997).

[15] A. Ward, S.M. Hudson, & W.L. Marshal, *Attachment Style in Sex Offenders: A Preliminary Study*, 33 J. Sex Res. 17–26 (1996).

[16] Kathleen Faller, *A Clinical Sample of Women Who Have Sexually Abused Children*, 4 Child Sexual Abuse no. 3, at 13–30 (1995).

problems in functioning, higher rates of mental illness, mental retardation, substance abuse, and other forms of maltreatment of their children. Despite the severity of the sexual abuse, few women suffered serious consequences, and there were no successful criminal prosecutions among the sample.

Hollida Wakefield and Ralph Underwager specifically addressed characteristics of women who sexually abused children. Although the vast majority of sexual abuse occurs at the hands of men, approximately 14 percent of perpetration against boys and 6 percent of perpetration against girls was performed by females acting alone. There are several conclusions that they draw from the literature about female perpetrators. They are (1) that awareness about female perpetrators of sexual abuse has greatly increased in recent years; (2) child sexual abuse by females does occur and may not be as rare as the earlier literature indicates; and (3) there is a great range in the estimated frequency of sexual abuse by women from different studies, and the definition of sexual abuse used, sample selected, and methodology employed must be considered.

Some of the literature that discusses female perpetrators is likely to have included cases of false allegations, which gives a misleading picture of both the frequency with which females abuse children and the characteristics of such women. Female child sexual abusers are less likely than men to fit the psychiatric definition of pedophile. There are widely different circumstances in which females may engage in behavior that is defined as child sexual abuse, and the circumstances that lead women to sexually abuse children can often be differentiated from those causing men to do so. Many studies depict women who sexually abuse children as being loners, socially isolated, alienated, likely to have had abusive childhoods, and apt to have emotional problems. However, most are not psychotic.[17]

Edward Rowan and his associates studied the fact that because females tend to be more embedded in family systems, their abuse of children may be more difficult to detect. This may lead to some underreporting of sexual abuse by females. Women also have more opportunities to touch than do men, and, as a result, may not receive the same level of attention associated with inappropriate sexual contact. Rowan and his colleagues conclude, "The most important factor seems to be disinhibition due to personality disorder and/or borderline intelligence and, perhaps more significantly, offending in the company of a dominant male."[18]

§ 13.3   Recidivism

Hanson, Steffy, and Gauthier examined the long-term recidivism rates of 197 child molesters who were released from prison between 1958 and 1974.[19] They report:

> Our results support previous research that child molesters are at risk for reoffending for many years. . . . The greatest risk appears to be the first 5 to 10 years and that child molesters appear

---

[17] Hollida Wakefield & Ralph Underwager, *Female Child Sexual Abusers: A Critical Review of the Literature,* 9 Am. J. Forensic Psychol. no. 4, at 63–64 (1991).

[18] Rowan & Rowan, Women Who Molest Children 83 (1990).

[19] R.K. Hanson, R.A. Steffy, & R. Gauthier, *Long-Term Recidivism of Child Molesters,* 64 J. Consulting & Clinical Psychol. 646–52 (1993).

to be at significant risk for reoffending throughout their life. Forty-two percent of this sample was eventually reconvicted, with 23% of the recidivists being reconvicted more than 10 years after they were released.[20]

They concluded by stating:

> Our findings of substantial long-term recidivism suggest that any short-term treatment, no matter how well conceived and how well delivered is unlikely to effectively control any child molesters. Sexual offense recidivism is most likely to be prevented when interventions attempt to address the life-long potential for reoffenses and do not expect child molesters to be permanently "cured" following a single set of treatment sessions.[21]

Dr. Way and his associates examined perpetrator recidivism and found

> that alleged perpetrators who are not substantiated at the index event do not disappear; they return to the system at alarming rates. . . . It is interesting to note that unsubstantiated sexual abuse perpetrators were re-reported at a significantly higher rate than those whose index events were substantiated. This may be because of the fact that substantiated perpetrators of sexual abuse are provided more intrusive services, which may help reduce recidivism.[22]

Overall the recidivism rate was 42.4 percent for all areas of abuse.

Melissa Johnson-Reid and her colleagues studied cross-type recidivism among child maltreatment victims and perpetrators.[23] Cross-type recidivism is a function of a child's being maltreated or at risk for one form of maltreatment at one time in his life, and at risk or suffering another form of maltreatment at a later time in his life. The researchers found that cross-type recidivism is common among re-reported cases of maltreatment. They found that the majority of recidivism events involve cross-type recidivism as opposed to within-type. They specifically point out that children who are neglected at an earlier age are more likely to be victims of physical and/or sexual abuse at a later age.[24]

Although it can be risky business for psychologists who try to predict dangerousness and the likelihood of recidivism, Quincy et al, found that they could correctly classify 178 sex offenders as recidivists or non-recidivists with 76 percent accuracy.[25] If psychology is able to accurately predict these types of concerns in a number of different ways, this will certainly aid the corrections system in determining how to handle this population.

---

[20] *Id.* at 650.

[21] *Id.* at 651.

[22] Ineke Way, Sulki Chung, Melissa Jonson-Reid, & Brett Drake, *Maltreatment Perpetrators: A 54 Month Analysis of Recidivism*, 25 Child Abuse & Neglect 1093–1108 (2001).

[23] Melissa Jonson-Rein, Brett Drake, Sulki Chung, & Ineke Way, *Cross-Type Recidivism among Child Maltreatment Victims and Perpetrators*, 27 Child Abuse & Neglect 899–917 (2003).

[24] *Id.* at 899.

[25] V.L. Quincy, M.E. Rice, & G.T. Harris, *Actuarial Prediction of Sexual Recidivism*, 10 J. Interpersonal Violence 85–105 (1995).

MMPI Profiles

Ronald Scott and David Stone examined the effects of father-daughter incest through use of the Minnesota Multiphasic Personality Inventory (MMPI). They found that elevations on the 4 and 8 Scales were most frequent with victims of father and daughter incest. Elevated 7-8 and 6-8 were the next most frequent scoring profiles. MMPI researchers Scott and Stone conclude:

> These findings suggest that father-daughter incest victimization results in lower psychological adjustment for both age groups (adults and adolescents) and indicate the probability that the adjustment problems of child victims do, indeed, persist over time. . . . There is also evidence of "schizoid process" with deficits in ego strength (psychic energy) and serious identity confusion, as well as possible sexual preoccupation with concerns of vulnerability and inadequacy.[26]

> A summary of these striking similarities and differences between the two groups leads to the speculation that being sexually victimized by the father produces an arrestment of ego development and related identity confusion at the core of the personality. However, the variable amount of time since the molestation seems to determine how this core disturbance is expressed. Shorter time and less development is exemplified by the adolescent victim and seems to produce more of an identity crisis, while the long-term effects from living for years with the core damage may result in a more chronically depressed and "an at odds with the environment" resignation.[27]

In another study, Scott and Stone examined the personality characteristics of father and stepfather perpetrators. They state that "approximately one-third of the stepfather group obtained 4-9/9-4 MMPI codes, indicating deficits in moral conscience with energized, narcissistic, and rationalized behaviors. The natural fathers tended to show a more passive-aggressive style, including immaturity, unrecognized dependency needs, and egocentrism with respect to their adult sexuality."[28] Gordon Hall and colleagues studied 406 sex offenders who had sexually abused children. They found that the 4-8 profile on the MMPI was the most common profile.[29] These results were replicated by Hall in 1989 and 1992. Byron Egeland and his associates studied 154 women who had a high potential for abusing their children. The MMPI-2 was used in an effort to determine whether there were any specific profiles that developed with these women. Like many of the studies performed with the original MMPI, significant elevations were found on the F, 4, and 9 Scales with women who showed a high risk for child abuse. Egeland and his colleagues conclude, "Perhaps the most significant new finding emerging from this study is the clear relationship between antisocial personality factors and child abuse potential. The significant difference between the (experimental group) and other women on the MMPI-2 content scale ASP (Antisocial

---

[26] Ronald Scott & David Stone, *MMPI Measures of Psychological Disturbance in Adolescent and Adult Victims of Father-Daughter Incest*, 42 J. Clinical Psychol. 257 (Mar. 1986)

[27] *Id.* at 258.

[28] *Id.* at 267.

[29] Gordon Hall et al., *The Utility of the MMPI with Men Who Have Sexually Assaulted Children*, 54 J. Consulting & Clinical Psychol. 493–96 (1986).

Practices) suggests that this variable should be taken into consideration when assessing potential for child abuse."[30]

William Follette, Amy Naugle, and Victoria Follette studied the MMPI-2 profiles of women with child sexual abuse histories. There were five different clusters of MMPI-2 profiles, suggesting that women who had been sexually abused are not a homogeneous group.[31] In cluster 1 the most elevated scales were 6, 2, and 7, while with cluster 2, the most elevated scales were 8, 7, and 2. Scales 4, 8, and 3 were the most elevated scales in cluster 3, and 8, 7, and 2 the most elevated scales in cluster 4. Cluster 5 was not representative of any specific pathology. It should be noted that 2, 7, and 8 were the most prominently featured across these clusters. The amount of depression, worrying, and confusion associated with being victims is demonstrated by these elevations.

John Graham, one of the world's leading MMPI-2 experts, reported in 2000 that several studies have indicated elevations on Scale 5 for sexual offenders. However, he states "relationships between Scale 5 scores and sexual aggression or other kinds of sexual problems are not established well enough to permit prediction of these problem behaviors in individual cases"[32] Graham also reports that the 4-8/8-4 profiles are still the most frequently found profiles with individuals exhibiting sexual deviancy.

John Graham also looked at the MMPI-A scores for adolescents who have been physically or sexually abused. Elevations on the 4 and Family Problems Scales suggest the possibility that physical abuse be considered for boys. He also reported "high scores on Scales 8 (boys and girls), 4 (girls), and 7 (boys) suggest the possibility of sexual abuse should be considered carefully. Histories of sexual abuse may be associated with high scores on the Family Problems Content Scale for girls and with high scores on the Depression, Anger, Low Self-Esteem, or School Problems Content Scales for boys."[33]

Sean Leonard and his co-researchers studied the MMPI-A results in adolescents who have been sexually abused.[34] Scales 1 and 3 significantly differentiate adolescents who reported both physical and sexual abuse from those reporting only one form of abuse. This suggests that adolescents are likely to somatize the psychological concerns associated with abuse. They point out that since 91 percent of the adolescents reporting abuse were females, the differences may be gender related.

Research on MMPI profiles of abusers was also performed by Evelyn Yanagida and June Chin.[35] They evaluated 183 abusers and found, as had previous research, that a 4-8 or 4-9 profile was most typical in sexual abuse perpetrators.

---

[30] Byron Egeland et al., MMPI-2 Profiles of Women at Risk 263 (1991).

[31] William Follette et al. MMPI-2 *Profiles of Adult Women with Child Sexual Abuse Histories: Cluster-Analytic Findings*, 65 J. Consulting & Clinical Psychol. no. 5, at 858 (1997).

[32] John R. Graham, MMPI-2 Assessing Personality and Psychopathology 73 (3rd ed. Oxford Univ. Press 2000).

[33] *Id.* at 343.

[34] Sean Leonard et al., Assessing Sexual and Physical Abuse in Adolescents Using the MMPI-A, Paper presented at the Annual Convention of the American Psychological Association, Toronto (Aug. 1996).

[35] Evelyn Yanagida & June Chin, *MMPI Profiles of Child Abusers*, 49 J. Clinical Psychol. 569–76 (1993).

§ 13.4   Gender-Related Characteristics of Abuse Survivors

A number of studies have been performed to examine specific gender-related concerns associated with child sexual abuse allegations. Michael Gordon studied the differences between males' and females' responses to the abuse. He used a sample of 585 respondents (416 females and 169 males). He found that

> abusers were overwhelmingly male; however, differences were apparent among their victims. Males were more likely to report being victims of non-relatives with the abuse taking place outside their home. Males were older than females at the time of the first abuse and their abuser tended to be rather close to them in age. Their abuse was more likely to be more severe than that of females, but they were less likely to have reported it. He also found that male and female victims related differently to perpetrators that were their relatives.[36]

Sandra Sigmon and her co-researchers studied differences between males and females as survivors of childhood sexual abuse. Although they found no significant difference in coping strategies, males tended to use acceptance more often as a method of coping, and females were more emotion focused. In addition, females reported more related distress.[37] Doris Shui Ying Mok and Diana Elliott compared gender differences in child sexual abuse victims. They found that of the 452 child sexual abuse victims studied, males were younger, more likely to be victimized by a juvenile offender, more likely to witness the abuse of others, and more likely to exhibit sexual reactive perpetrating behavior than were females. Females were more likely to disclose the abuse.[38] Genie Lenihan also studied gender differences. Boys reported higher prevalence of abusive sexual experience, were less involved with family members, and were more likely to report group sexual experiences. Girls showed stronger negative emotional reactions, feelings of victimization were more prominent, and they felt more threatened.[39]

Guy Holmes, Liz Offen, and Glenn Waller discussed why male victims are less willing to report sexual abuse. They offer four explanations. First,

> [I]t is shown that childhood sexual abuse has a similar psychological impact on males and females. . . . Therefore the severity of impact cannot account for the imbalance of unidentified cases. . . . Second, boys who are sexually abused may go on to develop characteristics that lead them to be seen in adulthood by services other than helping professionals (e.g. the criminal justice system). . . . Third, it has been shown that males disclose their experiences of childhood sexual abuse less often than females. . . . Finally, it has been demonstrated that

---

[36] Michael Gordon, Males and Females as Victims of Childhood Abuse 321 (1990).

[37] Sandra Sigmon et al., *Coping and Adjustment in Male and Female Survivors of Childhood Sexual Abuse*, 5 J. Child Sexual Abuse no. 3, at 57–75 (1996).

[38] Doris Shui Yink Mok & Diana Elliott, Gender Comparison of Child Sexual Abuse, Paper presented at the Annual Meeting of the American Psychological Association, Toronto (1996).

[39] Genie Lenihan, Childhood Sexual Abuse: Gender Differences in Prevalence, Experience, and Outcomes, Paper presented at the Annual Convention of the American Psychological Association, Toronto (Aug. 1996).

clinicians are less likely to suspect and enquire about histories about childhood sexual abuse in adult male clients.[40]

Studies have been performed with adult males who were sexually molested as children. Deloris Roys and Robert Timms studied male survivors of abuse by female caregivers and reported that the survivors have more complaints about psychological problems. Males who were not offenders but who were abused by females showed the most distress out of all the groups evaluated.[41] Gurmeet Dhaliwal and his co-researchers also studied adult male survivors. Three suggested long-term effects are homosexuality, homophobia, and sexual offense.[42]

Female survivors were also studied by Debra Peters and Lillian Range, who noted that female survivors often experienced self-blame, self-destruction, and stigmatization. They point out that self-blame is a crucial variable to consider in understanding issues facing female adult sexual abuse survivors.[43] Clair Draucker studied adult female survivors in relation to families of origin. Adult survivors retrospectively described their childhood families as more troubled than did non-abused individuals. The severity of the abuse influenced the adult's level of disturbance.[44]

§ 13.5   Incest Families

Richard Kluft reports that

> one-fifth to one-third of all women have experienced some form of childhood sexual encounter with an adult male, that between 4 and 12 percent have had some sort of sexual experience with a male relative, and that 1 in 100 have had a sexual experience with her father or stepfather. . . . A high incidence of incest victims among psychiatric patients ranging from 8 percent to 33 percent is reported.[45]

The effects of father-daughter incest were studied by researchers Lisa Swanson and Mary Kay Biaggio. They report that the oldest daughter in the family is most likely to be

---

[40] Guy Holmes et al., See No Evil, Hear No Evil, Speak No Evil: Why Do Relatively Few Male Victims of Childhood Sexual Abuse Receive Help for Abuse-Related Issues in Adulthood, Paper presented at the Annual Meeting of the American Psychological Association 69, 83, Toronto (1996).

[41] Deloris Roys & Robert Timms, *Personality Profile of Adult Males Sexually Molested by Their Maternal Caregivers: Preliminary Findings*, 4 J. Child Sexual Abuse no. 4, at 63–77 (1995).

[42] Gurmeet Dhaliwal et al., *Adult Male Survivors of Child Sexual Abuse: Prevalence, Sexual Abuse Characteristics, and Long-Term Effects*, 16 Clinical Psychol. Rev. no. 7, at 619–39 (1996).

[43] Debra Peters & Lillian Range, *Self-Blame and Self-Destruction in Sexually Abused Children*, 5 J. Child Sexual Abuse no. 4, at 19–33 (1996).

[44] Clair Draucker, *Family-of-Origin, Variables, and Adult Female Survivors of Childhood Sexual Abuse: A Review of the Research*, 5 J. Child Sexual Abuse no. 4, at 35–63 (1996).

[45] Richard Kluft, Incest and Adult Psychopathology: An Overview and Study of the "Sitting Duck Syndrome," 3 (Inst. of Pa. Hosp. 1988) [hereinafter Kluft].

the first victim of incestuous assault. The pressure for secrecy is generally a component of the incestuous relationship and adds to the burden placed on the child, resulting in fear and guilt on the part of the child. When the child reports the incest, the delicate balance in the family is generally disrupted. In a treatment setting, the first job of the therapist is to listen to the child in a believing manner and to reassure her that she will be protected from the perpetrator. Once the victim has disclosed the incest, she generally feels a deep sense of having betrayed her parents and feels increasing ambivalence about her father. Swanson and Biaggio report:

> The incest victim often expresses a desire to confront her parents, hoping that they will accept the responsibility for the incest and acknowledge that they have harmed her. . . . The incest secret is not fully laid to rest until the victim is able to talk about the incest with someone other than her therapist.[46]

William Samek provides significant information regarding the effects of sexual abuse allegations on incest families. Several issues need to be addressed as part of the evaluation process, including questions on the sanity of the alleged victim, witness credibility, visitation and custody, and treatment needs, and whether the family should be reunited or kept apart. Samek opposes using sexually anatomically correct (SAC) dolls on a regular basis. He states they are too distracting, add to the confusion of the child, and create ideas that may not have been present.[47]

§ 13.6   Incest Fathers

Samek points out that incest fathers typically have a close relationship with their children and lack psychological intimacy with their wives. They tend to be controlling in their interpersonal relationships and often come from dysfunctional families. Incest fathers have a greater than average problem with substance abuse, approaching 20 to 25 percent in research samples. Although these fathers present themselves as being honest, they are generally smooth and dishonest. They generally make an extreme effort to convince the listener that the mother is hysterical. These fathers lack insight and empathy, and focus on how they are being hurt—not on how their behavior is affecting others. They generally present themselves as good father figures when disciplining and handling children in general. Problems presented by these fathers include their inability to verbalize their feelings, portrayal of themselves as victims, and psychological naivete.[48]

---

[46] Lisa Swanson & Mark Kay Biaggio, *Therapeutic Perspectives on Father-Daughter Incest*, 142 Am. J. Psychiatry 673 (1985).

[47] William Samek, Forensic Assessment of Incest Families, Paper presented at the American Psychological Association Convention, San Francisco, CA (Aug. 1991) [hereinafter Samek, Forensic Assessment of Incest Families].

[48] Samek, Forensic Assessment of Incest Families.

§ 13.7   Mothers of Incest Victims

Mothers of incest victims are generally either inadequate in their roles as mothers or attempt to care for everybody's needs by taking the posture of a "super mom." They tend to be highly dramatic and appear to have Hysterical Personality Disorders. They are also overprotective of others and under-protective of themselves. Like incest fathers, mothers of incest victims often come from dysfunctional, abusive families. Initially they are reluctant to believe the allegations. These mothers have trouble disciplining their children and feel weak and powerless. In addition, they present themselves as being naïve and easy to manipulate, and as having low self-esteem.[49]

§ 13.8   Incest Victims

Generally, incest victims are slow to report the abuse. When they do report the abuse, they tend to underreport it in an effort to test the waters to determine how much they will be believed. Attorneys are likely to conclude, as a result, that the allegations are false. However, attorneys must understand that this is fairly typical of abuse victims. The victims themselves often feel responsible for the abuse and do not want to show that the behavior that occurred was abusive. Along with low self-esteem, they present sexual knowledge and behavior inappropriate for their chronological age. Incest victims as teenagers tend to be promiscuous and/or drug users, and to act out in other ways (for example, opposition, truancy, or vandalism).[50]

§ 13.9   Family Dynamics

In the incest family, the mother is often distant, while the father and daughter are enmeshed with one another. Secrecy is a significant component of the relationship, suggesting that the issues cannot be shared with anyone else. There are many types of family secrets that are kept. As a result, the boundaries with the community are high while the boundaries within the families themselves are low. The family, as a result of its feelings toward the accuser, often attempts to reintegrate without the child who "told the secret." They are likely to blame that child for the problems. The mother presents herself as knowing nothing, while the father knows whether he did or did not perpetrate. It is possible that the child may or may not be able to state whether the abuse took place, depending upon the age of the child. Even when abuse takes place, the mother of the incest victim often overreacts and presents herself poorly. The father's response will be to say, "There's nothing wrong with me. It's all her fault." Initially, the daughter usually presents the information reluctantly and understates it. When she finally does disclose the information, she is likely to assume responsibility for the acts that have occurred.[51]

---

[49] Samek, Forensic Assessment of Incest Families.

[50] Samek, Forensic Assessment of Incest Families.

[51] Samek, Forensic Assessment of Incest Families.

Pamela Alexander and Cindy Schaeffer found that female adult incest survivors could be classified into three different clusters. Women with the least severe abuse, with no severe physical violence, and the least family pathology; women with moderate abuse severity, more serious family problems, and more serious family problems characterized by father dominance; and a small group of women with severe and traumatic abuse living in conflicted and controlling families with extremely violent parents.[52]

Rizwan Shah and associates found that parental substance abuse, divorced family structure, being a female child, and sexual abuse history were significant factors associated with child sexual abuse in the family setting.[53]

In recent years there has been considerable research addressing the issue of cultural differences among child maltreatment perpetrators and child maltreatment victims. The three ethnic groups that have been studied most frequently are African-Americans, Latino or Hispanic Americans, and Native Americans. Jon Shaw and his associates found that Hispanic girls waited longer to disclose their abuse than African-American girls, but African-American girls were more likely to have experienced vaginal penetration.[54] The perpetrators of Hispanic girls were older and more likely to be fathers or stepfathers and the Hispanic girls were more likely to see their families as dysfunctional. In conclusion, the authors point out that Hispanic girls experienced more emotional and behavioral problems than African-American girls.[55]

Heather Taussig and Ayelet Talmi studied ethnic differences in risk behaviors. They found few differences between Caucasion, Hispanic, and African-American youth on levels of engagement and risk behaviors.[56] Lemyra DeBruyn and associates addressed child maltreatment in the Native American culture.[57] They point out that awareness of the communities' culture and history must be incorporated in the treatment and interventions for child maltreatment. Lisa Fontes, Mario Cruz, and Joan Tabachnick studied the differences of the cultural community's views of childhood sexual abuse in the African-American and Latino communities. They point out that both the Latino and African-American communities perceive child sexual abuse as being a significant problem within their communities.[58]

---

[52] Pamela Alexander & Cindy Schaeffer, *A Typology of Incestuous Families Based on Cluster Analysis*, 8 J. Fam. Psychol. no. 4, at 458 (1994).

[53] Rizwan Shah et al., *Familial Influences on the Occurrences of Childhood Sexual Abuse*, 4 J. Child Sexual Abuse no. 4, at 45–61 (1995).

[54] Jon A. Shaw, John K.E. Lewis, Andrea Loeb, James Rosado, & Rosemarie A. Rodriguez, *A Comparison of Hispanic and African American Sexually Abused Girls and Their Families*, 25 Child Abuse & Neglect 1363–79 (2001).

[55] *Id.* at 1363.

[56] Heather N. Taussig & Ayelet Talmi, *Ethnic Differences in Risk Behaviors and Related Psychosocial Variables among a Cohort of Maltreated Adolescents in Foster Care*, 6 Child Maltreatment 180–92 (2001).

[57] Lemyra DeBruyn, Michelle Chino, Patricia Serno, & Lynne Fullerton-Gleason, *Child Maltreatment in American Indian and Alaska Native Communities: Integrating Culture, History, and Public Health for Intervention and Prevention*, 6 Child Maltreatment 89–102 (2001).

[58] Lisa A. Fontes, Mario Cruz, & Joan Tabachnick, *Views of Child Sexual Abuse in Two Cultural Communities: An Exploratory Study among African Americans and Latinos*, 6 Child Maltreatment 103–17 (2001).

PSYCHOLOGICAL EFFECTS

§ 13.10   Psychological Effects of Sexual Abuse

Kendell-Tackett, Williams, and Finkelhor performed a meta-analysis of 45 studies designed to examine the psychological effects of sexual abuse.[59] They found:

- The symptomatology most frequently presented in sexually abused children included Post-traumatic Stress Disorder (PTSD), which was found in 32 percent of the cases, poor self-esteem (35 percent), promiscuity (38 percent), and general behavior disorders (37 percent).

- For preschoolers, the most common symptoms were anxiety, nightmares, general PTSD, internalizing, externalizing, and inappropriate sexual behavior. For school-age children, the most common symptoms include fear, neurotic and general mental illness, aggression, nightmares, school problems, hyperactivity, and regressive behavior. For adolescents, the most common behaviors were depression; withdrawn, suicidal, or self-injurious behavior; somatic complaints; illegal acts; running away; and substance abuse.

- Among symptoms that appear prominently for more than one age group were nightmares, depression, withdrawn behavior, neurotic mental illness, and aggressive and regressive behavior.[60]

- They further concluded that depression, school and learning problems, and behavior problems were the most prevalent symptoms across ages. The studies reviewed concluded that from 21 percent to 49 percent of those studied were asymptomatic. These individuals may have been symptomatic in ways that were not measured, they may not have yet manifested symptoms, or they may truly have been asymptomatic.

- Molestations that included a close perpetrator, a high frequency of sexual contact, a long duration, the use of force, and/or sexual acts that included oral, anal, or vaginal penetration led to a greater number of symptoms for victims.

- The lack of maternal support at the time of disclosure and a victim's negative outlook or coping style also led to increased symptoms. The influence of age at the time of assessment, age at onset of molestation, number of perpetrators, and time elapsed between the end of abuse and the assessment is somewhat unclear at the present time and should be examined in future studies on the impact of intervening variables.[61]

- As time progressed, symptoms abated or improved in 55 percent to 65 percent of children. However, depending on the study, from 10 percent to 24 percent of the children appeared to have symptoms that worsened.

- Court involvement was also found to influence the effect of sexual abuse on children. Children involved in court proceedings demonstrated less resolution and required

---

[59] K.A. Kendell-Tackett, L.M. Williams, & D. Finkelhor. *Impact of Sexual Abuse on Children: A Review and Synthesis of Recent Empirical Studies*, 113 Psychol. Bull. 164–80 (1993).

[60] *Id.* at 167.

[61] *Id.* at 171.

a longer time to reach resolution. It has long been felt that children required to testify in court suffer the adverse effects of these proceedings.

- Testimony provided by children in protected settings can mitigate the trauma, with children who testified via closed-circuit television, videotape testimony, or closed courtrooms demonstrating fewer symptoms than children who were required to testify in open court.[62]

Briere and Runtz identified six areas of concern presented in reviewing sexual abuse cases.

- The first area of concern, as identified in other studies, is Post-traumatic Stress Disorder. These individuals also suffer from cognitive distortions as a result of their abuse. Their perceptions tend to reflect an overestimation of danger or adversity.

- Survivors of sexual abuse often experience altered emotionality, with depression being the most common symptom.

- Disturbed relatedness is found with survivors of sexual abuse. They tend to have fewer friends and less closeness and satisfaction from their friends, report poor social adjustment, and see themselves as being unworthy of healthy relationships. They also demonstrate difficulties with sexual intimacy.

- Avoidance through dissociative reactions is also common, as is a relationship between childhood sexual abuse and later substance abuse and an increase in suicidal ideation.

- Sexually abused individuals are often involved in tension-reducing activities such as sexual promiscuity, binging and purging, and self-mutilation.

- Impaired self-reference is a problem area. This is accompanied by an inability to soothe or comfort one's self.[63]

Frank Putman reviewed the literature during the past 10 years to discuss what has happened with the status of sexual-abuse-related issues. Putman reported that approximately 10 percent of officially substantiated child maltreatment cases are child sexual abuse cases. His review indicated that the risk of child sexual abuse rises with age, is greater for disabled children, and is greater for lower socioeconomic children, and that the presence of a stepfather doubles the risk for girls. The most frequent symptomatology outcome is depression for adults and sexualized behavior for children.[64]

Although the above two studies are important in understanding the psychological effects of abuse on children, there are a number of other studies that are important. Histories of physical, and especially sexual abuse, are associated with severe psychological disturbances, Borderline Personality Disorder in particular.[65]

---

[62] Arthur D. Williams, *Bias and Debiasing Techniques in Forensic Psychology*, 10 Am. J. Forensic Psychol. 19–26 (1992).

[63] J. Briere & M. Runtz, *Child Sexual Abuse, Long-Term Sequelae and Implications for Psychological Assessment*, 3 J. Interpersonal Violence 312–30 (1993).

[64] Frank Putnam at 269.

[65] Melissa Polusny & Victoria Follette, *Long-Term Correlates of Child Sexual Abuse: The Theory and Review of the Empirical Literature*, 4 Applied & Preventive Psychol. 143–66 (1995).

Caron Zlotnick, Jill Mattia, and Mark Zimmerman studied the effects of sexual abuse on psychiatric diagnoses. They found that "patients with sexual abuse compared to those without sexual abuse histories had higher rates of co-morbidity, primarily Borderline Personality Disorder, Post-traumatic Stress Disorder, and multi Axis I diagnoses. Those with sexual abuse history had a longer duration of depressive episodes."[66] Jenny Macfie, Dante Cicchetti, and Sheree Toth found that sexually abused individuals had higher dissociation rates than the non-maltreated group.[67] Moreover, maltreatment severity and chronicity were each related to dissociation. Anne Buist and Helen Janson performed a three-year follow-up study. Women with histories of sexual abuse had higher anxiety and depression scores, greater life stressors than those who did not have histories of sexual abuse, and had greater difficulty recovering from post-partum depression, and failed to improve as much as the non-abused group.[68] Heather Cecil and Steven Matson found that females with a history of childhood sexual abuse scored significantly lower on measures of self-esteem and mastery and significantly higher on measures of physical and emotional abuse.[69] Linda Lewin and Christie Bergin found that non-offending mothers of child sexual abuse victims had heightened levels of depression and anxiety and diminished maternal attachment behaviors.[70]

Abused women had lower ratings on measures of body satisfaction than non-abused women.[71] Sixteen percent to 41 percent of children who had been sexually abused manifested overt sexual behavior problems.[72] Survivors of sexual victimization need to be aware that, without understanding the effect of past experiences, "they are at risk for being victimized again."[73] An increase in suicidality, eating disorders, and self-mutilation was found in adult survivors of childhood sexual abuse.[74] Almost half of low-income child abuse survivors perceive benefit from having been sexually abused in the form of protecting their children from abuse, self-protection, increased knowledge of child sexual abuse,

---

[66] Caron Zlotnick, Jill Mattia, & Mark Zimmerman, *Clinical Features of Survivors of Sexual Abuse with Major Depression*, 25 Child Abuse & Neglect 357–67 (2001).

[67] Jenny Macfie, Dante Cicchetti, & Sheree L. Toth, *Dissociation in Maltreated versus Nonmaltreated Pre High School-Aged Children*, 25 Child Abuse & Neglect 1253–67 (2001).

[68] Anne Buist & Helen Janson, *Childhood Sexual Abuse, Parenting and Postpartum Depression—A 3-Year Follow-up Study*, 25 Child Abuse & Neglect 909–21 (2001).

[69] Heather Cecil & Steven C. Matson, *Psychological Function and Family Discord among African American Adolescent Females with and without a History of Childhood Sexual Abuse*, 25 Child Abuse & Neglect 973–88 (2001).

[70] Linda Lewin & Christie Bergin, *Attachment Behaviors, Depression, and Anxiety in Non-Offending Mothers of Child Sexual Abuse Victims*, 6 Child Maltreatment 365–75 (2001).

[71] M.C. Sexton, C.D. Grant, & M.R. Nash, Sexual Abuse and Body Image: A Comparison of Abused and Non-Abused Women, Paper presented at the 98th Annual Convention of the American Psychological Association, Boston (Aug. 1990).

[72] D. Tharinger, *Impact of Child Sexual Abuse on Developing Sexuality*, 21 Prof. Psychol.: Res. & Prac. 331–37 (1990).

[73] G.E. Wyatt, D. Guthrie, & C.M. Notgrass, *Differential Effects of Women's Child Sexual Abuse and Subsequent Sexual Revictimization*, 60 J. Consulting & Clinical Psychol. 167–73 (1992).

[74] Melissa Polusny & Victoria Follette, *Long-Term Correlates of Child Sexual Abuse: The Theory and Review of the Empirical Literature*, 4 Applied & Preventive Psychol. 143–66 (1995).

and having a stronger personality.[75] Abused children have more depressive and anxiety symptoms and lower self-esteem than non-abused children.[76] Sexually abused children report higher levels of PTSD symptomatology,[77] with more than half the children reaching the diagnostic criteria for PTSD.[78] Sexually abused adolescents report more problems with their teachers[79] and are less socially competent.[80] Between 10 and 24 percent of child victims either do not improve or deteriorate.[81]

Tina Goodman and her associates studied why children report sexual abuse.[82] They found that the child's age, type of abuse, fear of negative consequences, and perceived responsibility for the abuse all contributed to predicting time of disclosure. The fear of negative consequences was more influential for older children than younger children. Older children were more likely to feel responsible for the abuse. Children whose abuse was intrafamilial took longer to disclose than children whose abuse was extra-familial. Children were less likely to report if they felt responsible for the abuse. Last, they took longer to report if they felt there would be negative consequences for reporting.[83]

One of the prime areas of concern in sexual abuse allegation reporting is what is referred to as delayed disclosure. It is not uncommon for children to delay reporting the sexual abuse because of shame, fear, guilt, and/or embarrassment. It is also not unusual for the victim to provide a partial report as a "trial balloon" and later add to the report. It is a mistake for people to assume that delayed disclosure and/or partial reporting that is addended later is representative of a false abuse allegation. Eli Somer and Sharona Szwarcberg provide a thorough review of delayed disclosure concerns. They report that the literature has clearly demonstrated that the delayed disclosure can be a function of accommodation, guilt, self-blame, helplessness, emotional attachment to the perpetrator, idealized self-identity, mistrust of others, dissociation, burden of the secret, successful/ego-strengthening experiences, and concern for others.[84] They also report family variables that contribute to delayed disclosure, including loyalty to the family, cultural norms reinforcing obedience,

---

[75] C. McMillen, S. Zuravin, & G. Rideout, *Perceived Benefit from Child Sexual Abuse*, 63 J. Consulting & Clinical Psychol. 1037–43 (1995).

[76] S. Boney-McCoy & D. Finkelhor, *Psychosocial Sequelae of Violent Victimization in a National Youth Sample*, 63 J. Consulting & Clinical Psychol. 726–36 (1995).

[77] *Id.*

[78] A.E. Dubner & R.W. Motta, *Sexually and Physically Abused Foster Care Children and Post-Traumatic Stress Disorder*, 62 J. Consulting Clinical Psychol. 367–73 (1999).

[79] S. Boney-McCoy & D. Finkelhor, *Psychosocial Sequelae of Violent Victimization in a National Youth Sample*, 63 J. Consulting & Clinical Psychol. 726–36 (1995).

[80] A.P. Mannarino & J.A. Cohen, *Abuse-Related Attributions and Perceptions, General Attributions, and Locus of Control in Sexually Abused Girls*, 11 J. Interpersonal Violence 246–60 (1996).

[81] I. Berliner & B.E. Saunders, *Treating Fear and Anxiety in Sexually Abused Children: Results of a Controlled 2 Year Follow-up Study*, 1 Child Maltreatment 294–309 (1996).

[82] Tina B. Goodman, Robin S. Edelstein, Gail S. Goodman, David P.H. Jones, & David S. Gordon, *Why Children Tell: A Model of Children's Disclosure of Sexual Abuse*, 27 Child Abuse & Neglect 525–40 (2003)

[83] *Id.* at 536–37.

[84] Eli Somer & Sharona Szwarcberg, *Variables in Delayed Disclosure of Children's Sexual Abuse*, 71 Am. J. Orthopsychiatry 333–34 (2001).

concern for family integrity, conservative sexual morality, and fear of blame.[85] Social variables include rejection and avoidance of victims, stigma mistrust of the judicial system, and publicity in the media.[86]

There is also significant literature on the psychological effects on adult survivors of childhood sexual abuse. There is a relationship between childhood sexual abuse and adult depression[87] and adult anxiety disorders.[88] Adult survivors of childhood sexual abuse often have somatically related symptoms such as headaches, gastrointestinal problems, back and pelvic pain, and muscle tension.[89] Problems with anger control, chronic irritability, unexpected feelings of rage, and fear of their own anger are found in this group.[90] Feelings of anger are expressed either internally through self-blame and self-injury[91] or externally, resulting in perpetration of violence toward-others. As many as 36 percent of adult survivors of childhood sexual abuse experience PTSD symptomatology.[92] Highly traumatic events may lead to dissociative disorders.[93] This group provides less satisfaction in their relationships, greater discomfort and sensitivity, and more maladaptive interpersonal patterns.[94] External emotional responses manifest through a variety of activities, including self-mutilation, such as cutting, burning, or hitting oneself or pulling out

---

[85] *Id.* at 334.

[86] *Id.* at 334–35.

[87] R.D. Levitan, S.V. Parikh, A.D. Lesage, K.M. Hegaforen, M. Adams, S.H. Kennedy, & P.N. Goering, *Major Depression in Individuals with History of Childhood Physical or Sexual Abuse: Relationship to Neurovegetative Features, Mania, and Gender*, 155 Am. J. Psychiatry no. 12, at 1746–52 (1998).

[88] S. Lombardo & R. Pohl, *Sexual Abuse History of Women Treated in Psychiatric Outpatient Clinic*, 48 Psychiatric Serv. 534–36 (1997).

[89] L.C. Maynes & L.L. Feinauer, *Acute and Chronic Dissociation and Somatized Anxiety as Related to Childhood Sexual Abuse*, 22 Am. J. Fam. Therapy 165–75 (1994); P. Salmon & S. Calderbank, *The Relationship of Childhood Physical and Sexual Abuse to Adult Illness Behavior*, 40 J. Psychosomatic Res. 329–36 (1996).

[90] J. Briere & M. Runtz, *Post-Sexual Abuse Trauma: Data and Implications for Clinical Practice*, 2 J. Interpersonal Violence 367–79 (1993).

[91] J. Briere & E. Gil, *Self-Mutilation in Clinical and General Population Samples: Prevalence, Correlates, and Function*, 68 Am. J. Orthopsychiatry 609–20 (1998).

[92] B.E. Saunders, D.G. Kilpatrick, R.F. Hanson, H.S. Resnick, & M.E. Walker, *Prevalence, Case Characteristics, and Long-Term Psychological Correlates of Child Rape among Women: A National Survey*, 4 Child Maltreatment: J. Am. Prof. Soc'y on Abuse of Children 187–200 (1999); Melissa K. Runyon & Maureen C. Kenny, *Relationship of Attributional Style, Depression, Post-Trauma Distress among Children Who Suffered Physical or Sexual Abuse*, Child Maltreatment 254–64 (2002).

[93] D.M. Elliott & J. Briere, *Sexual Abuse Trauma among Professional Women. Validating the Trauma Symptom Checklist-40 (TSG-40)*, 16 Child Abuse & Neglect 391–98 (1992); J.A. Chu & D.L. Gill, *Dissociative Symptoms in Relation to Childhood Physical and Sexual Abuse*, 147 Am. J. Psychiatry 887–92 (1990).

[94] M.G. Bartoi & B.N. Kinder, *Effects of Child and Adult Sexual Abuse on the Adult Sexuality*, 24 J. Sex & Marital Therapy 75–90 (1998); D.M. Elliott, *Impaired Object Relations in Professional Women Molested as Children*, 21 Psychotherapy 79–86 (1994).

hair;[95] binging and purging to deal with feelings of emptiness;[96] and alcohol or other drug abuse. There is generally an increase of alcohol consumption among victims of abuse.[97]

§ 13.11   Re-victimization

Banyard, Williams, and Siegel studied re-victimization among adult women who were sexually abused as children.[98] They found that the factor of re-traumatization differed for women depending upon their marital status. Unmarried women had greater poverty and homelessness, greater family of origin difficulties, and greater depression and dissociation. On the other hand, married women had greater alcohol use, with relationship satisfaction being a protection against a more severe level of traumatization. Arata found that child sexual abuse victims have a two to three times greater risk of adult re-victimization than women without a history of child sexual abuse.[99] Repeated victims had more symptoms of Post-traumatic Stress Disorder and dissociation than women with only a history of child sexual abuse.[100] Gibson and Leitenberg studied 1,050 undergraduate women.[101] They found that sexually assaulted young women with a history of childhood sexual abuse used more disengagement as a coping mechanism than adult sexual assault victims without a history of childhood sexual abuse.

§ 13.12   Sitting Duck Syndrome

One of the other effects of childhood sexual abuse is what Kluft referred to as the "Sitting Duck Syndrome."[102] Children who are abused learn to be victims as part of their childhood

---

[95] J. Briere & E. Gil, *Self-Mutilation in Clinical and General Population Samples: Prevalence, Correlates, and Function*, 68 Am. J. Orthopsychiatry 609–20 (1998); B.A. Van der Kolk, J.C. Perry, & J.L. Herman, *Childhood Origins of Self-Destruction Behavior*, 148 Am. J. Psychiatry 1665–71 (1991); B.W. Walsh & P.M. Rosen, Self-Mutilation: Theory, Research and Treatment (Guilford 1988).

[96] N. Piran, P. Learner, P.E. Garfinkel, S.H. Kennedy, & C. Brouilletee, *Personality Disorders in Anoretic Patients*, 7 Int'l J. Eating Disorders 589–99 (1988); H. Stieger & M. Zanko, *Sexual Trauma among Eating Disordered, Psychiatric and Normal Female Groups: Comparison, of Prevalences and Defense Styles*, 5 J. Interpersonal Violence 74–86 (1990).

[97] Shanta R. Dube, Robert F. Anda, Vincent J. Felitti, Janet B. Croft, Valerie J. Edwards, & Wayne H. Giles, *Growing Up with Parental Alcohol Abuse: Exposure to Childhood Abuse, Neglect, and Household Dysfunction*, 25 Child Abuse & Neglect 1627–40 (2001); Wait M. Schuck & Kathy Spatz Widom, *Childhood Victimization and Alcohol Symptoms in Females: Causal Inferences and Hypothesized Mediators*, 25 Child Abuse & Neglect 1069–92 (2001).

[98] V.L. Banyard, L.M. Williams, & J.A. Seigel, *Validity of Women's Self-reports of Documented Child Sexual Abuse*, 14 J. Traumatic Stress 697–715 (2001).

[99] C.M. Arata, *Child Sexual Abuse and Sexual Re-Victimization,* 9 Clinical Psychol. Sci. & Prac. 135–64 (2002).

[100] *Id.* at 135.

[101] Laura E. Gibson & Harold Leitenberg, *The Impact of Child Sexual Abuse and Stigma on the Methods of Coping with Sexual Assault among Undergraduate Women*, 25 Child Abuse & Neglect 1343–61 (2001).

[102] R. Kluft, Incest and Adult Psychopathology: An Overview and Study of the "Sitting Duck Syndrome" (Inst. of Pa. Hosp. 1988).

development. If they are young when the abuse occurs, they assume that all children experience the abuse that they are subjected to. As a result, they demonstrate an ongoing vulnerability to exploitation and inappropriate relationships. Without realizing it, they look for relationships that will fulfill their childhood role of victimization. They are more likely to be involved with husbands who are abusive, more likely to be victims of sexual misconduct, and are more likely to tolerate sexual harassment. Kluft refers to this process as the "Sitting Duck Syndrome" since these individuals are "sitting ducks" to be re-victimized over and over again throughout their lives, unless there is successful therapeutic intervention.

§ 13.13   Intervention

When child sexual abuse occurs, there are many interventions that have been suggested. They include the possibility of removing the child from the home, forbidding contact between the alleged perpetrator and the alleged victim, forbidding contact between the alleged perpetrator and all the children in the family, successful completion of therapy by the alleged perpetrator before contact is allowed, having both parents attend sexual abuse parenting classes, having the victim attend age-appropriate incest therapy groups, and/or having the perpetrator's visits supervised by a disinterested party who knows the nature and the extent of the abuse circumstances.[103]

The issue of whether children should or should not be required to testify in court has been hotly contested in recent years. There is concern that not requiring testimony prejudices the case against the defendant. However, requiring the child to testify may be even more victimizing than the abuse itself.

Sylvia Clute addresses the issue of adult survivor litigation, maintaining that this litigation can be a healing process.[104] Not only can it be empowering to the victim by reducing the individual's feelings of victimization, but also it can reduce the threat of the perpetrators victimizing other children.

§ 13.14   Psychologist's Role

Risen and MacNamara suggest that "because psychologists are capable of performing complex evaluations, it is recommended that they be involved early in the investigations of sexual abuse allegations, either by performing the initial evaluation or by training other mental health workers to gather relevant information."[105]

Hall states, "[T]here are many ways in which the well-qualified child psychologist can assist courts and/or the parties at the pretrial preparation stage during trial procedure.

---

[103] Jon Briere & John R. Conte, *Self-Reported Amnesia for Abuse in Adults Molested as Children*, 6 J. Traumatic Stress 21–31 (1993).

[104] Sylvia Clute, *Adult Survivor Litigation as an Integral Part of the Therapeutic Process*, J. Sexual Abuse 121–27 (1993).

[105] Leslie Risen & Regio MacNamara, *Validation of Child Sexual Abuse: The Psychologist's Role*, 45 J. Clinical Psychiatry 175–284 (1989).

The model presented here, the expert as the behavioral scientist-clinician, acting as a consultant, has implications for broadening the information base, improving interview and assessment procedures, stimulating more relevant research and in the end, helping the legal system to understand the psychological aspects of sexual abuse of children."[106] Hall also points out that psychologists are familiar with developmental issues, are trained in interview techniques, obtain objective data through testing, and can serve as effective consultants.

According to Gary Melton and Steven Limber, "whether the defendant shows characteristics of abusers or the victim shows characteristics of abused children tells little about whether the defendant perpetrated the specific offense of which he or she is accused."[107] Concerns are raised by Melton and Limber about psychologists' overstepping their bounds, and they warn that "intrusions on the privacy of victims should be no greater than necessary to meet the demands of justice."[108] They conclude by saying "no matter what the role, though, psychologists must keep in mind the compelling purposes of the legal process. They must show respect for the participants in the process and the authorities charged with decision making. Doing so is fully consistent with the high professional and personal duties of psychologists to promote human dignity."[109]

The area of sexual abuse allegations is fraught with concerns about iatrogenic harm to a much greater extent than most other areas. Children have been traumatized, adult survivors of childhood abuse have carried this trauma, sometimes for decades, and there is an extra degree of resolution necessary because of the psychological closeness that often occurs between the victim and the perpetrator.

The issue of whether or not the alleged victims should be allowed to testify is a difficult one. However, in some cases when the victim is forced to testify, it can precipitate feelings of continued victimization, a breakdown of psychological defenses, and result in the necessity for additional therapy.

It is important for professionals to know what happened in the abusive situation. Unfortunately, all too often the victim is interviewed and re-interviewed many times by psychologists, psychiatrists, social workers, attorneys, police officers, child protective services workers, parents, and others. This serves more as a re-victimization than resolution of the problem. One way to reduce this concern is to allow one interview, with the selected interviewer sitting on one side of a two-way mirror with the alleged victim and all of the other potential or interested professionals' interviewers on the other side of the mirror observing the interview. Toward the end of the interview, a break is taken and the selected interviewer determines if any of the other interviewers have any questions they would like to have included.

The issue of to "believe or not to believe" the allegation may also result in iatrogenic harm. When it is suggested that the abuse did not take place, but it actually did, the victim could be reunited with the perpetrator and additional victimization would be likely. Furthermore, when the victim knows that the abuse has occurred, and is unable to get the

---

[106] Miriam Hall, *The Role of Psychologists as Experts in Cases Involving Allegations of Child Sexual Abuse*, 23 Fam. L.Q. 451–64 (1989).

[107] Gary B. Melton & Steven Limber, *Psychologist's Involvement in Cases of Child Maltreatment*, 44 Am. Psychologist no. 9, at 1225–33 (1989).

[108] *Id.* at 1226.

[109] *Id.* at 1232.

professionals to believe him or her, the child's development of trust and interpersonal relationship skills can be adversely affected.

§ 13.15   Measuring Extent of Psychological Harm

Lane Veltkamp and Thomas Miller identify several factors that are useful in determining the extent of psychological harm associated with sexual abuse. The criteria are as follows:

1. *Age of the child.* The younger child may not actually realize what is going on, but may experience physical pain, which makes the initial sexual experience an emotionally and physically painful one, and contributes to an overall negative attitude regarding sex. More confusion is seen in the older child, who is bewildered, angry, depressed, and guilt-ridden.

2. *Duration.* The longer the abuse continues, the more traumatic it becomes.

3. *Aggression.* The greater the level of aggression, the more physically and psychologically traumatic its effects become.

4. *Threat.* The abusing parent often threatens the child. The greater the threat, the more traumatic the event is to the child. Examples include threat of removal of the child from the family, physical abuse to the child, or the parents being imprisoned.

5. *Kind of adult.* If the perpetrator is known to the child, the child is more confused and guilt-ridden than if the perpetrator is a stranger. In addition, knowing the perpetrator has a profound impact on the child's ability to trust.

6. *Degree of activity.* The more frequent the activity, the more psychologically traumatic it is to the child.

7. *Reaction of adults.* If adults do not believe or protect the child, the experience of abuse becomes more traumatic. If the parent overreacts, the child may feel guilty and responsible for the abuse.[110]

Psychotherapeutic Interventions

Debra Poole and her co-researchers studied psychotherapeutic interventions with children of sexual abuse. The survey they conducted of trained practitioners in the United States and Great Britain indicated the following:

> (a) Some clinicians believe they can identify clients who were sexually abused as children even when those clients deny abuse histories, (b) Some clinicians use a variety of techniques to help clients recover suspected memories of child sexual abuse, (c) Such clinicians are often successful in these attempts, and (d) These interventions can have serious implications for clients (e.g. some clients do terminate relationship with their fathers).[111]

---

[110] Lane J. Veltkamp & Thomas W. Miller, Clinical Handbook of Child Abuse and Neglect 28 (1995).

[111] Debra Poole, Stephen Lindsay, Amina Meman, & Ray Bull, *Psychotherapy and the Recovery of Memories of Childhood Sexual Abuse: U.S. and British Practitioners' Opinions, Practices and Experiences*, 63 J. Consulting & Clinical Psychol. 434 (1995).

The therapists questioned were asked to identify the five most frequently presenting problems that they found in their adult female survivors of sexual abuse during the past two years. The problems were reduced to four categories:

1. Relationships/intimacy/marital partner problems
2. Depression/mood disorder
3. Anxiety
4. Self-esteem/identity/autonomy and sexual abuse.

Candace Grosz[112] and her associates studied treatment for victims of extrafamilial sexual abuse. They reported a need for intervention and community-based programs for several reasons: "(1) The significant disruption in functioning that occurred in child victims of extrafamilial sexual abuse (ESA) and their families, (2) the risk of long-term sequelae, (3) the high incidence of extrafamilial sexual abuse, and (4) the consistent, large number of requests for services."[113] The authors place a special emphasis on providing group treatment for both the children and the parents of abused children.

§ 13.16   Post-traumatic Stress Disorder

Dr. Robert Geffner talked about general characteristics associated with credible allegations of child sexual abuse and the "child sexual abuse accommodation syndrome."[114] He also addressed the issue of Post-traumatic Stress Disorder (PTSD) as a diagnosis in sexual abuse cases. He states that the diagnosis of PTSD is the most frequently given diagnosis in child sexual abuse cases. However, he felt that with true child sexual abuse cases, there will also be child dissociative disorders associated with the PTSD. Symptoms include not remembering the abuse, "spacing out," denying obvious evidence, and engaging in self-mutilation.

John Briere and Marsha Runtz reviewed the long-term sequelae of childhood sexual abuse cases.[115] The authors identify six different areas of concern in reviewing these cases. The first area is post-traumatic stress symptomatology. They state:

[C]hild sexual abuse has been shown to produce both immediate and long-term post-traumatic symptoms in individuals. . . . Especially prominent for sexual abuse survivors are PTSD-related flashbacks, sudden intrusive memories, sensory memories, often including visual, auditory, olfactory, and/or tactile sensations reminiscent of the sexual assault. Triggers of flash-backs include sexual stimuli or interactions, abusive behavior by other adults, disclosure of one's abuse experiences, or reading or seeing sexually violent media depictions. . . . Other

---

[112] Candace Grosz, Ruth S. Kempe, & Michele Kelly, *Extrafamilial Sexual Abuse: Treatment of Child Victims and Their Families*, 24 *Child Abuse & Neglect 9–23 (1999).*

[113] *Id.* at 9.

[114] Robert Geffner, Characteristics of Victims of Sexual Abuse: Relevance for Child Witnesses, Paper presented at the 98th Annual Meeting of the American Psychological Association, Boston (1990).

[115] Briere & Runtz at 312–30.

intrusive PTSD symptoms involve repetitive, often ego-dystonic thoughts and/or memories of childhood sexual victimization, difficulties that many survivors of sexual abuse find both distressing and disruptive. . . . Nightmares with violent abuse-related themes are also commonly associated with sexual abuse-related PTSD.[116]

Amy Diehl and Maurice Prout studied the effect of PTSD on self-efficacy of victims of childhood sexual abuse. Self-efficacy is defined as the child's belief in his/her ability to perform certain actions successfully. Because the child's self-efficacy is negatively impacted by childhood sexual abuse, the suggestion is that treatment for PTSD focus on the child's self-efficacy.[117]

§ 13.17   Child Sexual Abuse Accommodation Syndrome

Child sexual abuse accommodation syndrome was formally presented in the literature in 1983, by Dr. Summit. He described characteristics commonly known in sexually abused children, including secrecy, helplessness, entrapment, delayed disclosure, and retraction. This syndrome was developed, assuming the abuse had occurred, to explain the child's reaction to the abuse. In the courtroom setting, it helps explain why children may delay reporting their abuse and why they may recant their stories of abuse.

Arthur Garrison[118] reports that child sexual abuse accommodation syndrome should be admissible under the *Daubert* standard, especially as rebuttal information if the defense asserts deceit.

§ 13.18   Rape Trauma Syndrome

Not all sexual abuse involves child victims. Rape is one of the most devastating forms of sexual impropriety with adults. A syndrome is a term that describes a constellation of symptoms that may imply a disorder or disease. A syndrome is somewhat elusive in that it does not always consist of the same criteria for each individual said to be experiencing the syndrome. Syndromes are not listed in the *Diagnostic and Statistical Manual of Mental Disorders* and thus have not obtained the general acceptance by the mental health community that disorders and diseases have obtained. Thus, it is relevant that rape trauma syndrome (RTS) is in fact a syndrome and not a disorder or disease.

Rape trauma syndrome is a term coined by a psychiatric nurse and a sociologist.[119] Burgess and Holstrom noted great similarity among women's responses to a sexually traumatic event that each had experienced. Burgess and Holstrom further noted that others, such as psychotherapists, social workers, and family members of these attacked women, had

---

[116] *Id.* at 313.

[117] Amy S. Diehl & Maurice F. Prout, *Effects of Post-traumatic Stress Disorder and Child Sexual Abuse on Self-Ethicacy Development*, 72 Am. J. Orthopsychiatry 262 (2002).

[118] Arthur Garrison, *Child Sexual Abuse Accommodation Syndrome: Issues of Admissibility in Criminal Trials*, 10 IPTG J. 1–19 (1998).

[119] Ann Wolbert Burgess & Lynda Lytle Holmstrom (1974).

described these women as experiencing similar symptoms in response to their sexually traumatic events.

Burgess and Holmstrom divided RTS into two phases, an acute crisis phase and a long-term reactions phase. The acute crisis phase may last for days or weeks, and consists of reactions that are severe in nature. During this phase, one's life can be affected physically, psychologically, socially, and sexually. In contrast, the long-term reaction phase entails a healing component, in which the victim attempts to deal with the emotional and psychological pain resulting from her attack.

Victim's self-reports of their reactions to the assault often have great similarity and collectively comprise the acute crisis phase of RTS. According to Veronen, Kilpatrick, and Resnick,[120] within hours of an assault, more than 90 percent of their sample of victims reported fear, anxiety, and confusion. Victims also reported physiological reactions such as trembling (96 percent of victims), racing heartbeat (80 percent), pain (72 percent), tight muscles (68 percent), rapid breathing (64 percent), and numbness (60 percent). Depression is another common acute crisis phase reaction.[121]

The long-term reactions phase of RTS consists of a healing component. During this phase, the survivor regains order and predictability in her life by developing feelings of mastery of her world and a sense of equilibrium.[122] This reconstruction process can last from a few months to years, depending upon the individual and the severity of the attack. Greatest recovery usually occurs between one and three months after the assault,[123] with 20 percent to 25 percent reporting no symptoms one year after the assault. However, Burgess and Holmstrom reported that 25 percent of their sample did not significantly recover even several years after the rape.[124] Thus, some symptoms may reoccur, such as specific anxieties, guilt, shame, helplessness, isolation, catastrophic fantasies, feelings of dirtiness, and physiological symptoms. Part of the recovery process during the long-term phase is for survivors to develop an understanding of what has happened to them and what they are feeling. While this process is occurring, life activities are often resumed, but they are "undertaken superficially or mechanically.[125]

§ 13.19   Normal Sexual Behavior and Knowledge

When trying to discriminate bona fide from fabricated sexual abuse, one must understand what is typical behavior for children in various age groups. Sharon Lamb and Mary Culinen

---

[120] L.J. Veronen, L.J., D.G. Kilpatrick, & P.A. Resnick, *Treatment of Fear and Anxiety in Rape Victims: Implications for the Criminal Justice System, in* W.H. Parsonage ed., Perspectives on Victimology 148–59 (1979).

[121] E. Frank & B.D. Stewart, *Depressive Symptoms in Rape Victims: A Revisit*, 7 J. Affective Disorders 77–85 (1984).

[122] A.W. Burgess & L.L. Holmstrom, *Rape Trauma Syndrome and Post-Traumatic Stress Response, in* Burgess ed., Research Handbook on Rape and Sexual Assault 46–61 (1985).

[123] D.G. Kilpatrick, P. Resnick, & L. Veronen, *Effects of a Rape Experience: A Longitudinal Study*, 37 J. Social Issues 105–112 (1981).

[124] Burgess & Holmstrom (1985).

[125] M.P. Koss & M.R. Harvey, *The Rape Victim: Clinical and Community Interventions* (2nd ed. Sage 1991).

addressed these issues by surveying 128 undergraduate women about their recollections of childhood sexual games. They responded by identifying five basic groups of sexual play and games. Fifteen percent recalled "playing doctor"; 15 percent recalled exposing themselves to other children; 15 percent involved experimentation with stimulation; 6 percent were involved in kissing games; 31 percent were involved in sexual fantasy games (such as imitation of adult sex and love scenes). Thirty percent of the participants indicated that they were persuaded or coerced into playing, and 44 percent reported that their experiences involved cross-gender play.[126]

Lamb and Culinen also discussed the physical sexuality in the games. Thirteen percent reported nongenital touching; 24 percent reported exposure; 15 percent reported clothed genital touching, while 19 percent reported unclothed genital touching.[127]

Betty Gordon and her associates addressed the age and social class differences in understanding children's knowledge or sexuality. They studied the sexual knowledge of 130 children between two and seven years of age.[128]

Significant differences were found for all areas of knowledge (gender, sexual and non-sexual body parts and functions, sexual behavior, pregnancy, and abuse prevention). Younger children generally knew less than older ones. None of the children demonstrated much understanding of adult sexual behavior. Lower-class children had less knowledge than did middle-class and upper-class in the areas of sexual body parts, pregnancy, and abuse prevention. Lower-class parents reported more restrictive attitudes toward sexuality, had given their children less sex education, and reported that their children had less sexual experience.[129]

William Friedrich, a well-known author in the area of sexual abuse, and his associates studied normative sexual behavior. In a sample of 287 two- to five-year-olds, they found that 43.8 percent touched sex parts at home, 43.7 percent touched breasts, 26.9 percent tried to look at people when they are nude, 25.8 percent stand too close, and 15.8 percent masturbate with a hand. When looking at 6- to 9-year-olds, they found that 20.7 touched sex parts at home, 20.5 percent tried to look at people when they are nude, 18.8 percent stand too close, 15.9 percent touched breasts, and 15.5 percent know more about sex. The focus changes considerably with 10- to 12-year-olds. In a group of 96 10- to 12-year-olds, 28.7 percent were very interested in the opposite sex, 17.9 percent knew more about sex, 14.8 percent stand too close, 12.8 percent want to watch TV nudity, and 11.6 percent touch sex parts at home.[130]

§ 13.20   Comparing Abused with Non-abused Children

Authors Betty Gordon, Carolyn Schroeder, and J. Michael Abrams expected that abused children would have more knowledge about adult sexual behavior than non-abused

---

[126] Sharon Lamb & Mary Culinen, Normal Childhood Sexual Play and Games 1 (1991).

[127] Id.

[128] Betty Gordon et al., Age and Social Class Differences in Children 3 (1990).

[129] Id.

[130] William N. Friedrich, Jennifer Fisher, Daniel Droughton, Margaret Houston, & Constant R. Shafran, *Normative Sexual Behavior in Children: A Contemporary Sample*, 101 Pediatrics 1–8 (1998).

children. They concluded:

> [W]e were surprised to find that within the range of knowledge about sexuality thought to
> be appropriate for young children, sexually abused and non-abused children did not differ. . . .
> The data from this study that looked specifically at sexual knowledge appear to contradict the
> results of other studies which may have found differences in sexual behavior between sexu-
> ally abused children and non-abused controls. We did not find evidence of precocious sexual
> knowledge in the abused children.[131]

The authors did note that the abused children responded in "unusual" ways reflecting their distress during the interview. They also surmised that it was possible that the abused children knew more about sexuality than they were revealing.

SEXUAL ABUSE ALLEGATIONS

With an increase in concerns about child sexual abuse, there has also been an increase in concern about whether the sexual abuse allegations that are being made are bona fide or fabricated.

§ 13.21   Bona Fide versus Fabricated Abuse Allegations

Over the past several years, research has been performed in an effort to help clinicians discriminate bona fide sexual abuse allegations from fabricated sexual abuse allegations. It has been the hope that this research would provide clinicians with a clearer understanding of these issues. Instead of the issues becoming more black and white, however, they have become more gray. Unfortunately, in almost all sexual abuse allegation cases when the alleged perpetrator has not admitted the offense, experts can be found to testify about those components of the case that suggest the allegations are bona fide and other experts to simultaneously testify about those aspects of the case that suggest the allegations are fabricated. As a result, at an increasing rate the triers of fact are left with contradictory testimony from experts and are required to make their own conclusions without the benefit of clear expert testimony.

In the past, evaluators relied on the amount of detail that the child was able to provide and the description of the abuse as indicators of whether the allegation was bona fide or fabricated. Children today have access to much more information about sex and sexuality than in the past. A child watching the six o'clock news can hear stories about day care workers who have been charged with sexual abuse. Premium cable channels all show explicit sexual behavior as early as seven o'clock in the evening. Even X-rated home videos

---

[131] Betty Gordon et al., *Children's Knowledge of Sexuality: A Comparison of Sexualy Abused and Nonabused Children*, 60 Am. J. Orthopsychiatry 250, 255 (1990).

are much more available to children, and long-favored soap operas have become sexual showcases during the daytime. Both general sex education and sexual abuse education occur in the schools starting as early as the preschool years. In the past, the only source of information that a child may have had about sexual abuse was when he or she had actually been abused. However, this information now could come from being abused or from any of the above-identified sources.

Barbara Mara, of the Child Protection Team of Central Florida, also addresses this issue.[132] She pointed out some of the concerns that are raised when children four to seven years of age are involved in sexual abuse allegations. Children from ages four to seven tend to overgeneralize from information they are given. They will fabricate in an effort to fill in the blanks if the facts are not there. Children in this age group who are repeatedly interviewed will begin to believe what they have said whether it is true or not. Mara also supported the contention that sexually abused children suppress their concerns about the sexual abuse after it has been disclosed, as opposed to continuing to talk about it.

Patricia Bresee and her co-researchers describe components found in mothers who are child-focused and are not fabricating or exaggerating the stories of sexual abuse. The components are as follows:

- Testimony

  Bona Fide—In a bona fide allegation the nonperpetrating parents will not want the child to testify because of the trauma.

  Fabricated—In a fabricated allegation the reporting parent will want the child to testify, as it will help support his or her position.

- Substantiation

  Bona Fide—The parent will feel relieved if none of the professionals are able to substantiate the allegation.

  Fabricated—If none of the professionals are able to substantiate the allegation, the reporting parent will continue to shop around for a professional who will support his or her opinion.

- Interview

  Bona Fide—In a bona fide allegation, the nonperpetrating parent will willingly allow the child to be interviewed without that parent being present.

  Fabricated—In a fabricated allegation, the reporting parent will either insist on being present during the interview or display considerable discomfort when not allowed to do so.

- Disclosure

  Bona Fide—In the bona fide allegation, the nonperpetrating parent will feel shame and guilt over not protecting the child and will be reluctant to disclose what has occurred to anybody other than when absolutely necessary.

  Fabricated—In a fabricated allegation, the parent is likely to want to tell the whole world.

- Alternatives

  Bona Fide—In a bona fide allegation, the nonperpetrating parent is willing to consider alternative possibilities.

---

[132] Barbara Mara, Child Sexual Abuse, A Workshop presented at the Southeastern Psychological Association Convention, Orlando, Fla. (Mar. 1986).

Fabricated—In the fabricated allegation, the parent is not willing to consider alternative possibilities because of a need to convince people that the abuse has actually occurred.

- Feelings

Bona Fide—In bona fide allegations, the nonperpetrating parent expresses remorse over not protecting the child sufficiently to prevent the abuse.

Fabricated—In fabricated situations, the parent does not show remorse, shame, or guilt.[133]

Bresee and her co-researchers also talk about the difference between a child who has been molested on one occasion and a child who has experienced long-term chronic molestation. A child who has been assaulted only once is likely to demonstrate increased clinging to parents, refusal to leave home, social withdrawal, sleep disturbances, and crying. However, a child who has been the victim of chronic molestation has a greater tendency to identify with the aggressor. These children typically show symptoms including pseudomaturity, role reversal with adults, acting-out behavior, depression, precocious sexual knowledge, and sexual advances toward adults and other children.[134]

Bresee and her co-researchers also point out that, whether or not the sexual abuse has occurred, counseling is necessary. If the allegations are unverified, the counseling is necessary to deal with the aftermath of the allegations. If the allegations are verified, the child needs to be in therapy to deal with the aftermath of the allegations. If the allegations are verified, the child also needs to be in therapy to deal with the abuse. The perpetrator needs to be in therapy to deal with whatever is wrong with him or her, and the nonperpetrating parent needs to be in therapy to help the child.

Linda Ruben studied false accusations and false memory. She states that the reasons abusers developed false memories include denial, the nature of secrecy in incest, the experience of having been victimized themselves, alcohol-related blackouts, and outright lying.[135]

Mark Everson and his collaborators studied what professionals believe about false allegations.[136] Two hundred forty-four judges, law enforcement officers, mental health practitioners, and child protective services workers were surveyed regarding their beliefs of credibility of alleged sexual abuse victims. CPS workers and mental health professionals were more likely to believe the child's statements, as were those who had dealt with more child abuse cases in the past. All four groups perceive that female adolescents were less believable than all other groups of children. District court judges and law enforcement officers expected higher rates of lying than did the other two groups.

---

[133] Patricia Bresee, Jeffrey Stearns, Bruce Bess, & Leslie Pevker, *Allegations of Child Sexual Abuse in Child Custody Disputes: A Therapeutic Assessment Model*, 56 Am. J. Orthopsychiatry 559, 564 (1986).

[134] *Id.* at 566.

[135] Linda Ruben, *Childhood Sexual Abuse: False Accusations of "False Memory,"* 27 Prof. Psychol.: Res. & Prac. no. 5, at 447 (1996).

[136] Mark Everson, Barbara Beck, Sherrie Bourge, & Kevin Robertson. *Beliefs among Professionals about Rates of False Allegations of Child Sexual Abuse*, 1 J. Interpersonal Violence no. 4, at 541–53 (1996).

§ 13.22   Case Examples

The following two case examples are presented to demonstrate what occurs in bona fide cases and fabricated cases. Following the portion of the interview that provides information about the alleged sexual abuse incident, it can be helpful to ask more specific questions as part of the interview process in an effort to further substantiate the concerns about whether the allegations are bona fide or fabricated. In the bona fide case, the victim is generally able to answer all the additional detailed questions with reasonable responses. In the fabricated case, the child has generally been coached by someone. The coach cannot anticipate all the questions that are likely to be asked in the interview. As a result, when the child is asked additional detailed questions, there is no basis from which to answer. Therefore, responses are likely to be vague, preposterous, or lacking altogether. The following case examples represent these two situations.

Case No. 1

Nancy is a four-year-old girl who was brought to a psychologist's office by her mother following visits with her father. The mother reported that the daughter claimed that her father, her aunt, and her sister, as well as Nancy herself, would take off their clothes and play kissing games. The evaluator asked the child to describe the kissing games. The four-year-old girl said, "Daddy and auntie take off all their clothes and auntie kisses daddy's pee-pee and then daddy goes pee-pee on auntie's face." The evaluator followed up with additional questions, such as "Where did this happen?" The child responded, "Auntie was lying on the floor when she kissed daddy's pee-pee. And you know what, when daddy went pee on auntie's face, it wasn't yellow, it was white and gooey." The evaluator asked the child, "What did daddy's pee-pee look like when auntie was kissing it?" The child responded, "It was hard and about this long (holding her hands about six inches apart)." The evaluator asked the child, "What did auntie look like with her clothes off?" The child stated, "It's funny cuz when auntie has her clothes on, her boobies are up here (pointing at nipple level) and when she has her clothes off, her boobies are way down here (pointing at navel level)." These are the types of detailed descriptions that make it very apparent that the child's report is bona fide. The detail was accurate and descriptive of actual sexual activity, and the child was able to respond to additional questions that in all likelihood a "coach" would not have anticipated.

Case No. 2

A five-year-old girl reported that her daddy "stuck his pee-pee in my bucky." In an effort to determine what the child meant by "bucky," the therapist/evaluator asked the child where her bucky was. She pointed to her vaginal area. At the end of the interview, through the use of sexually anatomically correct (SAC) dolls, the child also pointed to the vaginal area. When the child was asked if her daddy had his clothes on or off when he put his pee-pee in her bucky, she stated, "on." When asked what her daddy's pee-pee looked like, she stated, "It was this big" (stretching her arms as wide as they would go). When asked if her daddy's pee-pee was hard or soft when he put it in her bucky, she stated, "Soft." And when asked if it hurt or did not hurt when her daddy put his pee-pee in her bucky, she stated, "No." Certainly it is possible that something sexually inappropriate may have occurred between this father and child. However, by virtue of the child's responses to the specific detailed questions, it is unlikely that the father gained vaginal entry with his penis.

§ 13.23   False Abuse Allegations

A representative example of what courts may do when false sexual abuse allegations are made is found in an Illinois case, *Mullins v. Mullins*. The court found

> evidence that the mother had refused to use father's surname as children's surname, had filed false sexual abuse complaints against father and had limited and/or denied him visitations were [*sic*] sufficient to support findings that the mother had engaged in a scheme to terminate father's parents rights and to destroy the children's relationship with him, warranting transfer of custody of the children to the father.[137]

The case was heard originally by Cook County Circuit Court Judge Ellen F. Rosin. The appellate court affirmed the original decision.

Edwin Michelson and his associates reviewed the literature on false abuse allegations by children and adolescents.[138] The authors found four basic subtypes of false allegations resulting from the accuser's psychological disturbance, and Subtype III involved false allegations that result from contamination errors, inappropriate evaluation processes, and similar interfering variables.

§ 13.24   Preschool Children's Erroneous Allegations

Authors Elaine Yates and Tim Musty report on erroneous allegations made by preschool children:

> Occasionally, a preschool child may erroneously accuse a parent of molestation. When this occurs, the child usually believes that his/her story is correct. A false accusation can be made when: an adult has persuaded a child that these sexual events actually occurred; when a child in the Oedipal stage has misinterpreted caregiving ministrations; when a child's thought processes are confused by primary process material; or when a child is secondarily involved in the projective identifications of a dominant care giver. More than one of these mechanisms may operate in a given case.[139]

The authors also point out that children often change their attitudes and stories about the accused parent when they are moved from the accusing parent and placed in the presence of the accused parent.

---

[137] Kluft at 4.

[138] Edwin Michelson, Thomas Gutheil, & Margaret Emens, *False Sexual Abuse Allegations by Children and Adolescents: Contextual Factors and Clinical Subtypes*, 46 Am. J. Psychotherapy 557 (1992).

[139] Elaine Yates & Tim Musty, *Preschool Children's Erroneous Allegations of Sexual Molestation*, 145 Am. J. Psychiatry 989–92 (1988).

§ 13.25   Generalizations about Sexual Abuse Allegations

Kathleen Dillon examines 10 generalizations that have been made about child sexual abuse allegations.[140] She points out that although they are not invariably false, they can be false.

Generalization 1.   *Nightmares, infantile behavior, excessive masturbation, and depression are signs of sexual abuse in children.* Although these characteristics can be a sign of sexual abuse, they also can exist independently of sexual abuse in all children.

Generalization 2.   *When children say they were touched on their genitals, they mean sexual touching.* Children under the age of five may describe acceptable hygiene in a manner that sounds like sexual abuse.

Generalization 3.   *If a child has presocial sexual knowledge, he or she gained that knowledge from direct sexual contact.* This may certainly be the case, but the child "may have witnessed the parents during sexual activity, may have examined hidden pornographic magazines . . . may have watched explicit sexual acts on cable television, or may have been exposed to another child who educated him/her about sexual language and behavior."[141]

Generalization 4.   *Children do not lie about sexual abuse.* Research has been done that indicates that there are cases in which children have lied about sexual abuse.

Generalization 5.   *Children of any age can be tested reliably for sexual abuse.* In fact, children under age five usually lack the verbal and conceptual abilities necessary for a full interview.

Generalization 6.   *The use of anatomically correct dolls is a valid procedure for sexual abuse assessment.* Research was performed on 19 normal, non-abused children ranging in age from two to (four years, nine months). "Three children fled the testing situation. Half of the remaining 16 exhibited unusual interactions with the dolls' genitals, similar to interactions described by examiners in sexual abuse investigations."[142] (See also **§ 13.26.**)

Generalization 7.   *The more times the child is tested, the more reliable the results will be.* In actuality, the opposite is more likely to be true.

Generalization 8.   *Knowing about the relationship between the parents is not necessary to ascertain whether sexual abuse has occurred.* One research study reported that all seven cases in which false accusations were made involved parents in family law litigation.

Generalization 9.   *Anyone with appropriate training in sexual abuse assessment can test accurately for sexual abuse of children.* Being trained in sexual abuse assessment does not

---

[140] Kathleen Dillon, False Sexual Abuse Allegations: Causes and Concerns 540 (1987).

[141] *Id.*

[142] *Id.*

guarantee that the examiner has adequate knowledge of child development or child interview techniques or a lack of bias in sexual-abuse-related matters.

Generalization 10.   *It is better to err in falsely accusing someone of sexual abuse than to fail to confirm that a child has been sexually abused.* As stated in the context of the book itself, the human and civil rights of both the alleged victim and alleged perpetrator must be considered. Although the above list was published more than 15 years ago, it still applies today and is still supported by current literature.

David Mantel reviewed several hundred court cases involving alleged child sexual abuse. He found that both children and adults made some false reports. The false reports are grouped into several different categories. They include:

Misunderstandings

Misreporting

Distortion through illness

Distortion by design

Professional error

Misrepresentation.[143]

Simple misunderstanding was often a function of the adults' misunderstanding the language that the child was using. Simple misreporting was often a result of an individual's exaggeration of reports. Mantel felt that distortion through illness may be a function of preoccupation with sexually bizarre content that may even represent a pre-psychotic state. Distortion by design involves such areas as revenge, alienation, and divorce-related circumstances. Professional error can include suggestive questioning, inappropriate use of sexually anatomically correct dolls, and impassioned statements on the part of the professional. Misrepresentation can come from individuals who are opportunistic, have hidden agendas, or are looking for secondary gain associated with sexual abuse allegations. They can also adversely affect the presentations of suggestible children.

INVESTIGATION

§ 13.26   Sexually Anatomically Correct Dolls

The issue of the use of sexually anatomically correct dolls was addressed at a panel at the 1993 American Psychological Association Convention in Toronto, Canada. The panel raised many of the concerns addressed in this chapter.

Linda J. Skinner and Kenneth K. Berry reviewed concerns about the use of sexually anatomically correct dolls in child sexual abuse allegation cases.[144] The authors point out

---

[143] David Mantel, *Clarifying Erroneous Child Sexual Abuse Allegations*, 58 Am. J. Orthopsychiatry 618–21 (Oct. 1988).

[144] Linda J. Skinner & Kenneth K. Berry, *Anatomically Detailed Dolls and the Evaluation of Child Sexual Abuse Allegations: Psychometric Considerations*, 17 Law & Hum. Behav. 399–421 (1993).

that the users of anatomically detailed (AD) dolls must be cognizant of the psychometric properties of such dolls. They also note that, in one survey, 92 percent of evaluating professionals used the AD dolls. They identify two problem areas in using dolls to validate child sexual abuse allegations.

> The first of these areas focuses on the inappropriate substitution of personal data for scientific data. With the lack of standardized materials, administration procedures, and scoring, and the absence of normative doll-play patterns, each doll user is apt to develop personal administration and scoring guidelines and norms that not only may not generalize across practitioners, but may also reveal more about the practitioner than the child being addressed. . . . Secondly, given the equivocal evidence for the validity of the dolls, mental health professionals may need to rethink the proposition that sexual play or knowledge in young children is an indicator of sexual abuse. The lack of discriminative validity evidence is not restricted to the analysis of AD doll play patterns.[145]

The authors conclude:

> The lack of sufficient evidence supporting the psychometric properties of AD dolls calls into question the use of those dolls in the validation of child sexual abuse allegations. Being ethically responsible for ensuring the tests employed meet adequate psychometric standards, it appears that a psychologist who uses AD dolls in sexual abuse validation interviews is operating in a professionally risky and, perhaps, indefensible manner. Moreover, given that validity is the principal issue underlying the admissibility of psychological evidence in the courtroom . . . and the inadequate evidence for the construct and criterion-related validity of AD dolls, evidence collected using AD dolls should not be admitted in court in child sexual abuse cases at this time. Presently, the use of dolls in validation interviews fails to meet scientific test criteria and, consequently, it can only be concluded that AD dolls should not be used as the basis for expert opinions or conclusions.[146]

One of the interesting changes reported in a study by Mary Haskett and her co-researchers involved the use of *sexually* anatomically correct (SAC) dolls.[147] The research, performed in the late 1980s, showed that the use of such dolls was widespread. However, those cases reviewed in this study showed a relatively low rate of use of dolls but, as expected, a higher rate with younger children. The child's affect and behavior during interview and disclosure were also important factors in decisionmaking. However, the authors warn that using affect as an indicator to substantiate allegations can be problematic.

The use of SAC dolls in forensic evaluations has raised quite a controversy. As a result, the American Psychological Association Council of Representatives adopted a statement on February 8, 1991, with regard to the use of anatomically detailed dolls. The statement adopted is as follows:

Statement on the Use of Anatomically Detailed Dolls in Forensic Evaluations

Anatomically detailed dolls are widely used in conducting assessments in cases of alleged child sexual abuse. In general, such dolls may be useful in helping children to communicate

---

[145] *Id.* at 417–18.

[146] *Id.* at 417.

[147] Mary Haskett, Kathleen Weiland, James Hutcheson, & Teirsa Tavana, *Substantiation of Sexual Abuse Allegations: Factors Involved in the Decision-Making Process*, 4 J. Child Sexual Abuse 19–47 (1995).

when their language skills or emotional concerns include direct verbal responses. These dolls may also be useful communication props to help older children who may have difficulty expressing themselves verbally on sexual topics.

These dolls are available from a variety of vendors and are readily sold to anyone who wishes to purchase. The design, detail, and the nature of the dolls vary considerably across manufacturers. Neither the dolls, or their use, are standardized or accompanied by normative data. There are currently no uniform standards for conducting interviews with the dolls.

We urge continued research in quest of more and better data regarding the stimulus properties of such dolls and normative behavior of abused and non-abused children. Nevertheless, doll-centered assessment of children, when used as part of a psychological evaluation, and interpreted by experienced and competent examiners, may be the best available practical solution for a pressing and frequent clinical problem (i.e. investigation of the possible presence of sexual abuse of a child).

Therefore, in conformity with the *Ethical Principles of Psychologists and Code of Conduct*, psychologists who undertake the doll-centered assessment of sexual abuse should be competent to use these techniques. We recommend that psychologists document by videotape (whenever possible), audiotape, or in writing the procedures used for each administration. Psychologists should be prepared to provide clinical and empirical rationale (i.e. published studies, clinical experiences, etc.) for procedures employed and for interpretation of results derived from using ADDs (anatomically detailed dolls).[148]

§ 13.27   Responses of Abused versus Non-abused Children

Gary Melton and Susan Limber also discuss the use of SAC dolls in sexual abuse allegation investigations. They state:

Use of SAC dolls has been mischaracterized as a "test" for sexual abuse, rather than a means for children to clarify their verbalizations through demonstration. The former conceptualization, which is based on a misunderstanding of the proper role of the clinicians in the fact-finding process, leads to exclusion of interview material altogether because of reliance on a scientifically unproven technique.[149]

William McGivor and his associates compared the response of abused and non-abused children to SAC dolls. Their study demonstrated that "non-abused and abused children did not differ in their comments about the dolls or their behaviors and play with them. . . . Children frequently demonstrated aggressive and sexual acts that had occurred; this was particularly marked when the interviewer asked leading questions and cued and

---

[148] Statement on the Use of Anatomically Detailed Dolls in Forensic Evaluations, American Psychological Association Council of Representatives (Feb. 8, 1991). Copyright, 1991 by the American Psychological Association. Reprinted with permission.

[149] Gary B. Melton & Susan Limber, *Psychologists' Involvement in Cases of Maltreatment: Limits of Role and Expertise*, 44 Am. Psychologist 1225, 1231 (1989).

encouraged the child."[150] They suggest that the use of SAC dolls may provide misleading information. They support what Melton and Limber reported when suggesting that psychologists be careful when using these dolls, as inappropriate use of them may constitute unethical conduct on the part of the psychologist.

Finally, Brenda Dawson and her associates published a study in 1992 about the use of SAC dolls with non-abused children. There were several conclusions of interest from this research. The authors report:

> There were no instances in which the children acted out or described sexual intercourse or sexual fondling. . . . Additionally, there were very few instances of sexual aggression displayed by the children when exposed to SAD (Sexually Anatomically Detailed) dolls. . . . In contrast to the low incidence of sexual aggression that was displayed, there was a high incidence of sexual exploratory play. . . . Aggressive, non-sexual responses to the SAD dolls also occurred frequently.[151]

Barbara Boat, Mark Everson, and their colleagues have done a number of studies over the years on the use of SAC dolls. In a 1996 pilot study they were interested in the consistency of behaviors of children using anatomically correct dolls over time. They found that the children's behavior changed in both the experimental and control groups over a 16-month period of time. One of the conclusions drawn is that this has a direct implication on using dolls as part of the interview process based on the inconsistencies of reportings that were found.[152]

Lane Geddie and his associates addressed the socioeconomic and ethnic differences in how children interacted with sexually anatomically detailed dolls. Nine percent of the non-abused children demonstrated behaviors that professionals often associate with sexual abuse. They found that low socioeconomic status, African-American children were more likely to demonstrate sexualized behavior with the dolls. The authors urge caution in the use of anatomically correct dolls with all preschoolers but specifically with low socioeconomic African-American children.[153]

Robin Weill and her associates also looked at non-abused children's behavior with SAC dolls. They specifically studied "externalizing" children. They found that these behaviorally acting-out children showed more sexual aggression with the anatomically detailed dolls than the non-externalizing children, once again suggesting that inconsistent results can be found when using anatomically detailed dolls as part of sexual abuse allegation evaluations and/or interviews.[154]

---

[150] William McIver, Hollida Wakefield, & Ralph Underwager, Behavior of Abused and Non-Abused Children in Interviews with Anatomically Correct Dolls, Paper presented at the 98th Annual Meeting of the American Psychological Association, Boston (1990).

[151] Brenda Dawson, Allyson R. Vaughn, & William G. Wagner, Normal Responses to Sexually Anatomically Detailed Dolls 148–49 (1992).

[152] Barbara Boat, Mark Everson, & Lisa Amaya-Jackson, *Consistency of Children's Sexualized or Avoidant Reactions to Anatomical Dolls: A Pilot Study*, 5 J. Child Sexual Abuse 61 (1996).

[153] Lane Geddie, Brenda Dawson, & Kare Weinsch, *Socioeconomic Status and Ethnic Differences in Pre-Schoolers' Interactions with Anatomically Detailed Dolls*, 3 Child Maltreatment 43 (1998).

[154] Robin Weill, Brenda L. Dawson, & Lillian M. Range, *Behavioral and Verbal Responses of Unabused Externalizing Children to Anatomically Detailed Doll Interviews*, 14 J. Fam. Violence 61 (1999).

§ 13.28   Gender Differences in Responses

The authors of this study noticed that there were gender differences in the responses to the dolls. They report:

> Girls showed more behavioral affection and verbal sexual exploratory play than did boys, overall. . . . When the dolls were undressed, the girls exhibited more behavioral sexual exploration (touching, looking, and examining the dolls) and verbal sexual exploration (making statements concerning the breasts or penis on the dolls). . . . In contrast to the boys, playing with the dolls, particularly when the dolls were undressed, had a general activating effect on the girls' behavior.[155]

Jan Aldridge and numerous associates who are very experienced in sexual abuse allegation evaluations and investigations performed a study on the use of human figure drawings. They used the National Institute of Child Health and Human Development investigative interview protocol. They found that the use of human figure drawings elicited an average of 86 new forensically relevant details. They were especially productive of four- to seven-year-olds and provided an average of 95 additional details after the drawings were introduced, even when the memories of the children had been previously "exhausted." They warn about the fact that the use of drawings may elicit recognition memory prompts and that use of the drawings should only be introduced late in the interview process.[156]

§ 13.29   Interview Process

The American Academy of Child and Adolescent Psychiatry outlined a six-page procedure of practice parameters that should be used in the forensic evaluation of children and adolescents when physical or sexual abuse allegations have been made. The major categories include role definition and clarification, diagnostic assessment, possible explanations of denials of abuse, possible explanations of allegations of abuse, issues regarding child's testimony, recommendations regarding placement and treatment, and a written report. A full copy of this protocol can be obtained by contacting the American Academy of Child and Adolescent Psychiatry at 3615 Wisconsin Avenue Northwest, Washington, D.C., 20016, or www.aacap.org.

The interview process should focus on several factors, including the abuse allegations themselves, family of choice (foster or adoptive), previous families of choice, family of origin, and the spouses' families. When discussing the allegations, it is important to know exactly what happened, when it happened, why it happened, to whom it happened, who knew about it, what was done after the abuse occurred, and what was done after the abuse was disclosed. As part of this assessment process, it is important to obtain information from as many sources as possible, including police department reports, department of social services reports, and treatment reports.[157]

---

[155] Id. at 149.

[156] Jan Aldridge, Micahel E. Lamb, Kathleen J. Steinberg, Yael Orbach, Phillip W. Epstein, & Lynn Bowler, *Using a Human Figure Drawing to Elicit Information from Alleged Victims of Child Sexual Abuse*, 72 J. Consulting & Clinical Psychol. 304 (2004).

[157] Samek, Forensic Assessment of Incest Families (1991).

The issue of the effect of the interview process on the alleged victim has been discussed by many prominent researchers in recent years. Kathleen Faller and her associates discuss the practice of parent-child interviews in alleged sexual abuse cases. They point out that parent-child interviews are not only potentially traumatic but also can be misleading. As a result, they suggest that the use of such interviews should be reevaluated.[158] The guidelines by the American Professional Society on the Abuse of Children recommend against such interviews. See **Appendix J.**

Kathleen Mayers addresses the issue of using nonleading questions in the assessment of alleged abuse victims.[159] As part of the interview process, it is important to identify the terminology the child uses to describe genitalia. In addition, it is appropriate to ask questions like, "Has anyone told you what are the private parts of your body?" and "Has anyone helped you understand that it is wrong for someone else to touch you on your private parts?" In addition, it is important when soliciting a child's description of the molestation to ask questions like, "Did that really happen?" or "What were you told to tell me today?" Like other researchers, Mayers cautions against the overuse of SAC dolls.

Because some states require the alleged victim to be able to identify the "time and place" that the alleged abuse took place, it is helpful in the interview process to ascertain when the incident likely happened. When the child is unable to give specific dates, to help identify the date, ascertain whether the alleged abuse took place near a particular season, holiday, or family event. It is also far more appropriate to ask questions like, "Did he put anything in your mouth?" than to ask, "Did he put his penis in your mouth?"

Dr. Leonard Gries and co-researchers suggest that when asking children to disclose information about sexual abuse, less-structured and more traditional methods lead to fewer disclosures than the assessment protocol Gries and his colleagues suggest. They found a 50 percent recantation rate. They also found that females made significantly more disclosures than males, and that older males were significantly more likely to report abuse than younger males. The authors were also surprised to find out that 30 percent of the disclosures included reports of genital penetration.[160]

Kay Keary and Carol Fitzpatrick sampled 231 children. They found that children under five years of age were least likely to disclose abuse during formal investigation, whether they had disclosed it before or not. The majority of children over age five, who had previously disclosed, did re-disclose the abuse during formal questioning.[161]

It is important for the interviewer in child sexual abuse allegation cases to ask specific, detailed questions of the child following the explanation of the abuse, in an effort to determine whether the abuse was bona fide or fabricated. If a child states, "Mommy took her shirt off and made me kiss her boobies," ask the child, "What did mommy's boobies look like when her shirt was off?" When a child states, "Daddy made me kiss his pee-pee," ask

---

[158] Kathleen Faller, Mary Froning, & Julie Lipovsky, *The Parent-Child Interview: Use in Evaluating Child Allegations of Sexual Abuse by Parent*, 61 Am. J. Orthopsychiatry no. 4, at 552–57 (1991).

[159] Kathleen Mayers, *Non-leading Techniques in the Assessment of the Alleged Child Molest Victim*, 9 Am. J. Forensic Psychol. 37–39 (1991).

[160] Leonard Gries, David Goh, & Jeanne Cavanah, *Factors Associated with Disclosure during Child Sexual Abuse Assessment*, 5 J. Sexual Abuse no. 3, at 1–19 (1996).

[161] Kay Keary & Carol Fitzpatrick, *Children's Disclosure of Sexual Abuse during Formal Investigation*, 18 Child Abuse & Neglect no. 7, at 543–48 (1994).

the child what the father's pee-pee looked like: "Was it hard or soft?" "How big was it?" If a child states, "My daddy made me kiss his pee-pee until he went to the bathroom," ask the child what the pee-pee or ejaculate looked like when he went pee-pee. A child who is not coached will be able to provide information that is relatively reasonable. However, a child who is coached will not have the knowledge base to fill in appropriate information. As a result, the responses of such a child are likely to be unrealistic.

§ 13.30 Clinical and Legal Concerns

Milton Schaefer and Melvin Geier suggest that "use of anatomical dolls as diagnostic devices be curtailed until their efficacy has been demonstrated in clinical trials subject to guidelines similar to those for any reported new medical or diagnostic device."[162] They also point to the importance of "maintaining or restoring the relationship between the child and the alleged perpetrator during the evaluation process."[163] The concern of the authors is that sometimes all contact between the alleged perpetrator and alleged victim is terminated when the allegation occurs in the context of a custody dispute. They state, "Unfortunately, whether unfounded or confirmed, the enforced parent-child separation and the exposure of the child to the angry perceptions and projections of the accusing parent create a rupture between the accused parent and the child so severe that a positive relationship may never be fully restored."[164]

The authors also point out two types of behavior on the part of the children that can lead to allegations. The first is "any sexualized behavior of the child, such as masturbation, or insertion of objects into the vagina or anus."[165] The scenario that follows can involve the mother questioning the behavior, which may lead to the child responding that she had done this "at daddy's." This typical exploratory behavior, as a result, may be misconstrued as sexual abuse. The other type of behavior involves regressive behavior on the part of the child, such as bed-wetting, masturbation, separation anxiety, oppositional behavior, or withdrawal. Although these behaviors can be the result of sexual abuse, they "are also common behaviors of preschoolers' reactions to divorce."[166] Unfortunately, with both types of behavior, "experts" can be found to testify that they would only occur as the result of sexual abuse, when in fact research has concluded that they can occur for other reasons. Finally, the authors suggest that we must be concerned about the limited memory capacity of very young children. One of the reasons that different stories are told at different times is the poor memory of the child, and this is more likely the cause than the possibility of a false allegation. Unfortunately, the interview and the actual event can occur more than a year apart. Although the parent may remember the events the same from one time to the next, a preschool child will have considerable difficulty doing so. As a result, recantation, or a change in the story, cannot be used as evidence that the abuse did or did not occur.

---

[162] Milton Schaefer & Melvin Geier, Allegations of Sexual Abuse and Custody and Visitation Disputes: A Level and Clinical Challenge, Paper presented at the American Psychological Association Convention (Aug. 1988).

[163] Id. at 10.

[164] Id.

[165] Id. at 3.

[166] Id. at 4.

§ 13.31 Child as Witness

The issue of whether children should be required to testify in court has been hotly contested in recent years. Although it is felt that requiring a child to testify in court can be as victimizing or even more victimizing than the abuse itself, there are times that it becomes necessary for children to testify. See **Chapter 6** for a discussion of the child as a witness.

The American Professional Society on the Abuse of Children developed a set of guidelines in 1990 that addresses concerns associated with evaluating children who have allegedly been sexually abused. The guidelines address the evaluators, components of the evaluation, interviews, child interview, and conclusions. These guidelines encompass standards that should be followed by evaluators in these cases. They can be found in **Appendix J.**

§ 13.32 Recantation

After a period of time, recantation is often used by the alleged perpetrator as "evidence" that the abuse did not actually take place. Recantation is a typical component of sexual abuse allegations. In the case of a bona fide sexual abuse allegation, the allegation may have been made by the child for a number of reasons, including desiring the abusive behavior to terminate. However, when the allegation was made, the child was not aware of the fact that his or her mother or father might be prohibited from seeing him or her, sent to jail, handcuffed and carried away, or required to have a supervisor during visits. The child may recant the allegation, not because the abuse did not occur but rather in an effort to have the return of a more normalized relationship with the mother or father.

§ 13.33 Investigating Likelihood of Abuse

Kathleen Faller's book, *Understanding Child Sexual Maltreatment,* identifies several areas that must be investigated in determining the likelihood of sexual abuse occurrence. They include

1. The child's ability to describe the sexual behavior
2. The child's ability to describe the context of the sexual abuse
3. The child's affect when recounting the sexual abuse
4. Medical evidence
5. Confession of the offender.[167]

In investigating these five areas, consider the following:

1. When a child describes sexually explicit behavior such as "Snot came out of my daddy's dinky," or "He put his ding-dong in my mouth and I choked," it is unlikely that this type of description would have occurred in a false allegation.

---

[167] Kathleen Faller, Understanding Child Sexual Maltreatment 128–31 (1990).

2. The child's ability to identify where the abuse occurred, what the offender said to obtain the child's involvement, where other family members were, what the victim and offender were wearing, what, if any, clothing was removed, and whether the offender said anything about telling or not telling is evidence that is likely to increasingly support the likelihood that the abuse occurred. A childs merely stating, "He stuck his finger in my butt," without being able to voluntarily provide any of the above information, is more likely to be falsely alleging abuse than if all the above information is available. However, in preschool children, the lack of this information may be a function of immature cognitive abilities, and not false allegations.

3. Reluctance to disclose, embarrassment, anger, anxiety, disgust, and fear are all examples of affect that is seen in children during descriptions of bona fide sexual abuse. It is common for very young children to engage in self-sexual arousal while describing these events.

4. Faller points out that in only about 10 to 20 percent of the cases are medical findings available.

5. Faller also points out that in only about 10 percent of the cases does the offender confess.[168]

Cassia Spohn reported on the comparison of children and adult victims in sexual abuse cases. She found that cases of child victims were more likely to be dismissed and less likely to result in conviction or incarceration than those with adult victims. Child victims were also less likely to be involved in aggravated sexual assaults.[169]

§ 13.34   Police Involvement following Sexual Abuse Allegations

The role of police in sexual abuse allegations has been addressed in some informative articles.[170] Edward Maguire reports that "when police receive the initial abuse report, they are significantly more likely than social workers to remove children from the home and place them in an emergency shelter."[171] Research also reports that police attitudes toward sexual abusers tend to be more punitive in nature. Maguire also points out that there is no medium available to disseminate knowledge to police officers as is available to other professionals in the child protective services area. He reports that the police department's "initial response can make a lasting impression on victims, parents, witnesses and others important to the case. If their initial response is problematic, they risk further traumatizing the victim, or frightening the parents into removing the child from further criminal justice system involvement."[172] "[P]olice know how to investigate crime, but often fail to apply

---

[168] *Id.*

[169] Cassia Spohn, *A Comparison of Sexual Assault Cases with Child and Adult Victims*, 3 J. Child Sexual Abuse no. 4, at 59–78 (1994).

[170] Edward Maguire, *The Professionalism of Police in Child Sexual Abuse Cases*, 2 J. Sexual Abuse 107–16 (1993).

[171] *Id.* at 109.

[172] *Id.* at 114.

this knowledge to child sexual assault cases. This is not acceptable. They must utilize the same skills and techniques they employ in other criminal investigations."[173]

§ 13.35   Recommended Interventions

There are many interventions that can be suggested. They include the possibility of removing the child from the home, the possibility of forbidding contact between the alleged abuser and specific children, the possibility of forbidding contact with all the children, the successful completion of a treatment program by the abuser before contact is allowed, both parents' attending non-abusing parents classes, the victims attending age-appropriate incest survivors groups, and/or having the abuser's visits supervised by a disinterested party who knows the nature and extent of the situation.[174]

MEMORIES

§ 13.36   Sexual Abuse Memories: Repressed, False, or Confabulated

Impact of Self-Help Books

Although the issue of repressed memories, false memories, and confabulated memories did not become a "hot topic" until the 1988 publication of *The Courage to Heal* by Ellen Bass and Laura Davis, William James, a pioneer in psychology, had discussed false memories and suggestibility in a 1910 publication entitled *Psychology*.

By 1994, *The Courage to Heal* had sold more than 700,000 copies, although neither of the authors is a trained therapist. The authors make some strong statements about repressed memories, such as, "If you think you were abused, and your life shows the symptoms, then you were."[175] They also state, "If you are unable to remember any specific instances like ones mentioned above, but still have a feeling that something abusive happened to you, it probably did."[176] Last, "There are nonviolent means of retribution you can seek. Suing your abuser and turning him in to the authorities are just two of the avenues open."[177] Taking these statements and applying them to a vulnerable populace has led to an explosion of sexual abuse allegations that purportedly come from repressed or recovered memories. *The Courage to Heal* goes so far as to provide checklists that identify symptoms resulting from

---

[173] Bill Walsh, *The Law Enforcement Response to Child Sexual Abuse Cases*, 2 J. Sexual Abuse 117–21 (1993).

[174] John Briere & John Conte, *Self-Reported Amnesia for Abuse in Adults Molested as Children*, 6 J. Traumatic Stress 21, 29 (1993).

[175] Ellen Bass & Laura Davis, The Courage to Heal 22 (1988).

[176] *Id.* at 21.

[177] *Id.*

incest. Unfortunately, although the items on the checklist could be a result of sexual abuse, the same symptoms could also be caused by many other sets of circumstances. The checklist includes symptoms such as low self-esteem, lack of motivation, phobias, and perfectionism, each of which could be the result of abuse or many other problems.

Kenneth Pope and Laura Brown, two prominent authors in the area of repressed memories, quote the past president of the American Psychiatric Association's statement about therapists using *The Courage to Heal* and similar books with their patients. He said, "[T]here's a name for this—Bibliotherapy. . . . [T]o give a book that espouses a narrow thesis of mental functioning is malpractice."[178]

Attorney Ralph Slovenko addressed the issue of people blaming *The Courage to Heal*. He believes that the courts, in general, do not support making authors and publishers liable for what has been written based on First Amendment rights. As a result, he believes that Bass and Davis should not be held liable for the content of their book.[179]

Tina Stern and her colleagues studied self-help books on recovering memories of childhood abuse. The reviewers reported a wide range of quality among the books that were surveyed. Although the information presented in most books was accurate, the reviewers felt that the books did not provide enough information about the nature of memory. They caution about the use of self-help books and say that individual therapists must maintain a knowledge of the content of these books.[180]

The issue of recovered memories, false memories, and repressed memories was a "hot topic" in the 1990s. Today the consensus is that people can forget things and remember them later and that their memories can be distorted through suggestibility. The energy is being put into what is occurring in a particular case, instead of trying to prove which theory is correct.

§ 13.37 Popular Cases Involving Recovered Memories

Many cases involving recovered memories have appeared in the popular press in recent years. One of the most widely reported cases involved Joseph Cardinal Bernardin, who was accused by a 34-year-old man of sexual abuse 17 years earlier. The man stated that he had recovered the memory of the abuse as a result of hypnosis used during therapy. However, three months later, the charges were dropped when the alleged victim stated that he felt unable to rely on the accuracy of his recovered memories.

Another famous case from several years ago was the McMartin preschool case in California, in which the McMartins and their staff were accused of molesting 360 children over a 10-year period. These accusations included accounts of animal sacrifice, sexual rituals in churches, and digging up coffins in cemeteries. In addition, satanic rituals and

---

[178] Kenneth Pope & Laura Brown, *Recovered Memories of Abuse, Assessment, Therapy*, Forensics 96 (1996) (quoting D. Sifford, *Perilous Journey: The Labyrinth of Past Sexual Abuse*, Phila. Inquirer, Feb. 13, 1992, at D6).

[179] Ralph Slovenko, *Blaming a Book,* 22 J. Psychiatry & L. 437–51 (Fall 1994).

[180] Tina Stern, Kudy Marx, & Royality Georgia, Study of Self Help Books on Recovering Memories of Childhood Sexual Abuse: Preliminary Findings, Paper presented at the American Psychological Association 104th Annual Convention, Toronto (Aug. 1996).

their involvement in sexual abuse have been the subject of many television talk shows. Virtually all allegations against the McMartins and their staff were eventually found to be false, with few or none found to be true.

There is also the case of Paul Ingram in Washington state. Ingram pleaded guilty to raping and sexually abusing his children, based on their "recovered memories" and his belief that his children would not concoct a story of that nature if it was not true, even though he was not able to recall any abuse. After pleading guilty and being sentenced to 20 years in prison, a false memory was planted in Ingram's mind by sociologist Richard Ofshe. As time progressed, Ingram began to believe that these planted false allegations had actually taken place.

Another popular media example of sexual abuse allegations is the one put forth by Roseanne Barr Arnold, in which she stated recollection of being sexually abused by her father when she was less than two years old. However, due to developmental limitations, it would be virtually impossible for anyone to remember events that occurred prior to two years of age.

§ 13.38   Possible Interpretations of Allegations

When a sexual abuse allegation is ultimately made, a number of possibilities exist. These possibilities, as outlined by John Watkins, include the following:

1. The abuse did not occur; the allegation is false and the accuser(s) deliberately lied.
2. The allegation is false but is based on pseudo-memory without intent to lie.
3. The abuse actually occurred, but the abuser is knowingly lying to deny it.
4. The accusation is partly true based on incomplete memory.
5. The abuse occurred, but the perpetrator has simply forgotten.
6. The process of "normal" forgetting may well have been carried further, into the actual defense of repression.
7. The abuser, like the victim, may have dissociated memories of the abuse.[181]

It is important to note that in more than 90 percent of the cases, sexual abuse perpetrators do not admit to their abuse. As a result, the professionals involved in the cases are left with the task of determining whether the abuse actually occurred or not.

§ 13.39   Memory

With regard to literature on memory, Stephen Lindsay and J. Don Read report, "The memory literature suggests that incautious use of memory recovering techniques may lead

---

[181] John Watkins, *Dealing with the Problem of "False Memory" in Clinic and Court*, 21 J. Psychiatry & L. 297, 302–03 (Fall 1993).

some adult clients, who were not abused, to come to believe that they were."[182] The literature is filled with well-known anecdotes describing errors in autobiographical memory. These include psychologist Jean Piaget's memory of being kidnapped as a child, which did not occur. Mark Twain once said, "It isn't as astonishing the number of things I can remember, as the number of things that I remember that aren't so." We also know that people's beliefs and expectations can distort their recollections.

§ 13.40   Suggestibility

One of the greatest areas of concern regarding memory is the concept of suggestibility. Much research has been performed that demonstrates how individuals' memories can be affected by suggestibility. Lindsay and Read report, "In the typical experiment in this area, people witness an event, and later take a memory test concerning the event. People in these experiments often claim to have seen things in the event that were in fact merely suggested to them."[183] These authors also identify five factors that affect suggestibility:

1. As the time between the event and the questioning about the event increases, the effect of suggestibility increases.
2. Suggestibility is also affected by the perceived authority of the individual providing the misleading information.
3. The more the suggestions are repeated, the greater the impact.
4. Suggestibility is also increased when the suggestions are more plausible to the individual than implausible.
5. Memory confusions increase the more vague the questions are about the individual's memory.

In 1995, Maggie Bruck spoke to the Wisconsin Judicial Conference on the issue of suggestibility as it relates to children's memories.[184] In addition to the concerns raised by Lindsay and Read, she reports several other factors that affect suggestibility. The most obvious of these factors would be asking leading questions. Furthermore, repeating misinformation across interviews eventually leads the child to believe that the information is correct. As part of this, Bruck states that "stereotype induction" can take place with the use of questions like "tell us about Dr. Fred: he's a bad man?" Interviewers also often use bribes, without the interviewer's necessarily being aware of it. For example, an interviewer may say, "You may leave as soon as you answer my questions." This leads the child to know that going home is made contingent upon providing answers to the adult's questions. When peer pressure is used in the interview process, it can also affect suggestibility. The interviewer who says, "Your friend told us about Dr. Fred, so you might as well" again puts

---

[182] Stephen Lindsay & J. Don Read, *Psychotherapy and Memories of Childhood Sexual Abuse: A Cognitive Perspective*, 8 Applied Cognitive Psychol. 281 (1994) [hereinafter Lindsay & Read].

[183] *Id.* at 287.

[184] Maggie Bruck, Suggestibility and Credibililty of Child Witnesses: Research Findings, 1995 Annual Meeting of the Wisconsin Judicial Conference, Lake Geneva, Wis. (Sept. 1995).

pressure on the child to provide an answer even though one may not be available in the child's experience. Last, Bruck states concerns about the use of visualization procedures. When the interviewer states, "Close your eyes and try to remember," this encourages fantasy on the part of the child and, again, may result in a suggested answer.

Daniel Schacter and his co-researchers studied memories of children from a cognitive psychology perspective in response to the professional controversy that had developed regarding "true" and "false" memories.[185] They point out that

> the young child has difficulty separating what was actually experienced in the past—the background event—from the thoughts and ideas that are generated by the suggestions of others. . . . The preschool child typically lacks a standard that dictates a concern with accuracy. As a result, the child is not motivated to implement a reflective style in the service of evaluating the validity of a response.[186]

They also point out that the temperament of the child at the time the memory is being elicited can affect the susceptibility to suggestion. Last, they hypothesize that an inhibited child will be more likely to respond to suggestion than an uninhibited child.

§ 13.41   Sources of Memory Error

E.K. Johnson and Robert Howell identified potential sources of error in memory. They include:

1. *Encoding.* Children's memories tend to be more fragmented and less complete than adult memories.
2. *Retention.* The longer the memory has existed, the more malleable it is over time.
3. *Retrieval.* Although children's retrieval is accurate, it is more limited than adult memories. They tend to omit details unless they are prompted to provide them.[187]

J. Douglas Bremner and three of his colleagues from the Department of Psychiatry at Yale University discussed the "neural mechanism" into dissociative amnesia in childhood abuse. The article basically examines the neurobiology of memory at times of extreme stress or trauma. The researchers point out that research shows that trauma enhances memory of central details but lessens peripheral memory. Children are more reliable and resistant to suggestion than might be expected, but they do show the tendency to accommodate to authority figures. This is especially true in very young children. Stressful events appear to cause more accurate memories that are very resistant to suggestion. Memories can be altered by stress-related psychiatric disorders, memory deficits, and retrieval deficits.

---

[185] Daniel Schacter, Jerome Kagan, & Michelle Leichtman, *True and False Memories in Children and Adults: A Cognitive Neuroscience Perspective*, 1 Psychol. Pub. Pol'y & L. 411–28 (1995).

[186] *Id.* at 423.

[187] E.K. Johnson & Robert Howell, *Memory Processes in Children: Implications for Investigation of Alleged Child Sexual Abuse*, 21 Bull. Am. Acad. Psychiatry & L. no. 2, at 213 (1993).

Exposure to a stressor amplifies the response whenever that stressor is again encountered. In addition, emotional states can cause fragmented memories.[188]

Two Stories, Two Sides of the Issue

A young woman reported that her therapist insisted that she had been sexually abused as a child. In addition, the therapist said the terrible memories of this abuse were in her unconscious and needed to be exhumed. Although the patient was uncomfortable with these allegations, after a few sessions she reported that her father had raped her when she was four years of age. As time progressed, the memories of the abuse became more violent and haunted her more. After being hospitalized, the patient enlisted the help of new therapists, who concluded with her that the abuse had never occurred.

In a second case, a patient reported flashbacks of physical and sexual abuse committed by her older brother when she was four years old, including being handcuffed, burned, and forced to submit to other sexual acts. Fifteen years prior to her recollection of these events, her brother had died in combat. From the time of his death, the patient's parents had left his room intact. The patient searched his room and closet and found handcuffs and diary extensively reporting the sexual abuse acts.

These two stories demonstrate that there is credibility to both sides of the issue. The following materials discuss supporting research for both points of view.

§ 13.42   Repressed Memory

John Briere is a research psychologist and one of the leading proponents of the concept that repressed memories can and do exist. These memories are interchangeably referred to as *repressed memories, recovered memories,* or *dissociated memories.* Several research studies are cited regularly to support the contention that memories of traumatic events actually can be repressed. Briere quotes a study performed by J.L. Herman and E. Schatzow in 1987, in which 64 percent of 53 women involved in group therapy for sexual abuse reported some level of amnesia concerning their abuse. The largest study performed to date was done by Briere and John Conte, in which 59 percent of 450 men and women, in outpatient treatment for sexual abuse-related problems, reported having some period of time, prior to 18 years of age, during which they had no knowledge of having been sexually abused.[189] More recently, Dr. Linda Meyer Williams interviewed 100 women who had been seen in emergency rooms for sexual abuse, 18 to 20 years after their emergency room visits. Thirty-eight percent of these women reported not having been sexually abused, despite hospital records indicating that the abuse had occurred.[190]

---

[188] J. Douglas Bremner et al., *Neural Mechanisms in Dissociative Amnesia Childhood Abuse: Relevance to the Current Controversy Surrounding the "False Memory Syndrome,"* 153 Am. J. Psychiatry no. 7, at 71–82 (July 1996).

[189] John Briere & John Conte, *Self-Reported Amnesia for Abuse in Adults Molested as Children,* 6 J. Traumatic Stress no. 1, at 21 (1993).

[190] Linda Meyer Williams, *Recall of Childhood Trauma: A Prospective Study of Women's Memories of Child Sexual Abuse,* 62 J. Consulting & Clinical Psychol. 1167–75 (1995).

One of the other areas Briere has investigated is the accuracy of self-reports of abuse. He concludes that amnesia for childhood sexual abuse may be a relatively common phenomenon (see § 13.44) and may be associated more with violence and early abuse. Previous amnesia may be associated with greater current psychological symptomatology.[191]

§ 13.43   Repressed Memory or Suggestibility?

One of the criticisms leveled against the research performed to demonstrate that repressed memories are really a function of suggestibility—such as those by Elizabeth Loftus[192]—points out that these studies do not address the difference between memories in traumatic situations and memories in non-traumatic situations. A psychologist cannot ethically perform research that induces trauma in a subject. Therefore, some individuals are willing to discount the conclusions drawn from this research as being inapplicable to trauma-related memories.

In the judgment of the authors of the present text, it is time for researchers to stop disagreeing with one another about whether repressed memories or suggestibility occurs. Both do occur. Energy now needs to be put into performing research to help psychologists and other mental health professionals, attorneys, and courts discern whether the report made is that of a legitimate repressed memory or whether it is a function of suggestibility.

§ 13.44   Amnesia in Child Sexual Abuse Cases

Judith Sherman addresses the issue of amnesia in child sexual abuse cases.[193] She reports that children can use dissociation as a way of protecting themselves from the overall psychological trauma that they have experienced during the assault. This is a way of separating themselves from the event. Amnesiac survivors and those who dissociate often have a sense that *something* has occurred, without being aware of exactly what it may be. Sherman used an instrument called the Dissociative Experiences Scale (DES). She found that scores above 30 on the DES "have been associated with Multiple Personality Disorder or Post-traumatic Stress Disorder, and scores above 50 have rarely been found without a concomitant diagnosis of Multiple Personality Disorder."

John Briere and John Conte studied a sample of 450 subjects who had reported sexual abuse histories. They looked at the extent to which the subjects may have repressed some of the material from that abuse. They report:

> [T]he current data offered information with regard to each of four questions introduced earlier: (1) Amnesia for abuse (partial or otherwise) appears to be a common phenomenon among clinical sexual abuse survivors; 59 percent of abused subjects in the present study

---

[191] *Id.*

[192] Elizabeth Loftus, *Memory Distortion and False Memory Creation*, 24 Bull. Am. Acad. Psychiatry & L. no. 3, at 281–95 (1996).

[193] Judith Sherman, *I've Always Wondered If Something Happened to Me: Assessment of Child Sexual Abuse Survivors with Amnesia*, 1 J. Child Sexual Abuse 13–21 (1993).

reported some time, before age 18, when they could not recall their first molestation experience, (2) sexual-abuse specific amnesia was associated with violent abuse (e.g., involving physical injury multiple perpetrators, fear of death if the abuse was disclosed) as opposed to abuse that might be expected to increase psychological conflict (e.g., psychological or physical enjoyment of the abuse experience, receipt of bribes, feelings of guilt or shame), (3) early molestation onset (i.e., at a mean of 5.8 years in this study) and longer abuse duration were both related to the increased likelihood of amnesia and (4) amnesia about sexual abuse experiences was associated with greater current symptomatology.[194]

The authors indicate that because some of the material is repressed, the credibility of the reporting survivor tends to be reduced.

§ 13.45   Recovered Memories

Joel Paris, a psychiatrist at McGill University, provided a critical review of recovered memories. He points out that in both clinical and normal populations, memories of past events are surprisingly inaccurate and that memory does not function like a tape recorder. The mind remembers events selectively. "There is also no objective method, short of corroborating data, which can determine whether memory is either true or false."[195] Furthermore, the belief that hypnosis makes memories more accurate is false. Paris also points out that repression of traumatic events can occur but is unusual. These events are not readily forgotten even when individuals consciously attempt to do so. Last, he points out that the more severe the trauma, the more likely it is to be remembered.

Marc Nesca addressed both sides of the recovered memory controversy. He stated, "[O]verall it is concluded the adoption of extreme positions with regard to this controversy is not supported by available data."[196] Furthermore, Laura Brown indicated that if we are to resolve the false memory debate in the arena of science instead of the courtroom or in the news media, we need more willingness to conduct experimental studies on comparative memory performance in normal and traumatized individuals.[197]

Elizabeth Loftus and Laura Rosenwald address the issue of recovered memories with regard to the hundreds of lawsuits that were filed in the 1990s.[198] They point out that today researchers view memory as a process of reconstruction rather than a "video replay" technique. Even when it can be demonstrated that memories are inaccurate, people are still extremely confident of their memories. Much attention has been paid to research performed

---

[194] John Briere & John Conte, *Self-Reported Amnesia for Abuse in Adults Molested as Children*, 6 J. Traumatic Stress 21–31 (1993).

[195] Joel Paris, *A Critical Review of Recovered Memories in Psychotherapy: Part 1—Trauma and Memory*, 41 Can. J. Psychiatry no. 4, at 201, 202 (1996).

[196] Clark Neska, *Seeking a Middle Ground on the Recovered Memories Controversy*, 15 Am. J. Forensic Psychol. no. 3, at 3 (1997).

[197] Laura Brown, *Pseudomemories: The Standard of Silence and the Standard of Care in Trauma Treatment*, 37 Am. J. Clinical Hypnosis no. 3, at 1, 15 (1995).

[198] Elizabeth Loftus & Laura Rosenwald, *Recovered Memories: Unearthing the Past in Court*, 3 J. Psychiatry & L. at 281, 293 (1996).

on how college students remember the Challenger explosion. One study demonstrated that only 21 percent reported learning of the explosion from television at the time of the explosion. However, two and a half years later, 45 percent claimed they first learned of the news from television. In another article, Elizabeth Loftus reports that "we should be able to concede that it is possible for people to forget about traumatic experiences and later remember them without having to agree that every memory so recovered is an accurate one."[199]

§ 13.46   False Memory Syndrome Foundation

The False Memory Syndrome Foundation (FMSF) is an artifact of the 1990s and is not considered a credible organization at this time. It was founded and supported by many people who claimed to have been falsely accused of sexual abuse. After years of publicity and attempts to establish its credibility, the FMSF is no longer a force in the professional community.

§ 13.47   Hypnosis

Hypnosis is the technique most frequently utilized in memory recovery therapy. It is the experience of the authors of this text that most individuals who believe that repressed/recovered/dissociated memories can occur advocate against using hypnosis as a means of recovering those memories. John Briere also states this specifically in his works.

This writer was involved as an expert in a personal injury suit in which a high school instructor was accused of physically abusing a student. After four years of individual therapy, and no disclosure of sexual abuse, the alleged victim's therapist took a weekend workshop in hypnosis. Following that workshop, she hypnotized the alleged victim as her first subject. Following hypnosis, this subject disclosed that she had been both physically and sexually abused. A high degree of skepticism must be associated with claims of sexual abuse by a therapist as inexperienced as this one, with the minimal amount of training in hypnosis that this therapist had, and following four years of individual therapy that yielded no disclosures.

Jeffrey Schneider addresses the issue of legal admissibility of memories refreshed by hypnosis. Some states disallow such testimony, whereas other states deem it admissible. It is necessary for an attorney to check case law and statutes in her or his own state to determine the level of admissibility of such evidence. Still other courts have indicated the "view that hypnotically refreshed memories are admissible, since the jury can decide how much weight to give such testimony."[200] When this approach is utilized, the court should review the hypnotic procedures used, and the consistency of pre- and post-hypnotic

---

[199] Elizabeth Loftus, *Memory Distortion and False Memory Creation*, 24 Bull. Am. Acad. Psychiatry & L. no. 3, at 281, 293 (1996).

[200] Jeffrey Schneider, *Legal Issues Involving "Repressed Memory" of a Childhood Sexual Abuse, in* The Psychologist's Legal Update (National Register of Health Serv. Providers in Psychology Aug. 1994),.

recollection.[201] Still other states have indicated that hypnotically refreshed memories are admissible as long as certain safeguards have been employed. These safeguards include

> 1) The hypnotist must be a qualified psychiatrist or psychologist who has experience in the use of hypnosis; 2) The hypnotist should be working independently of either side involved in the litigation; 3) All the information given to the hypnotist, prior to the hypnosis session, must be recorded; 4) The subject must describe the facts to the hypnotist as he or she remembers them before hypnosis; 5) All contact between the hypnotist and subject must be recorded, preferably on videotape; and 6) No person besides the hypnotist and the subject should be present during any contact between the two.[202]

§ 13.48   Guidelines on How to Handle "False Memory" Cases

Briere states that "memory comes back in pieces. People do not get better because they remember painful things. They get better and it allows them to recover memories that have been previously dissociated. Therefore, there is no need to try to recover memories."[203] This statement contends that it is not necessary to engage in recovered memory therapies, because, as the patient gets better, the memories will surface. Read and Lindsay state that recovered memory therapies are used too often, too indiscriminately, and without sufficient safeguards.[204]

Thomas Nagy provided guidelines that therapists should use in treating individuals with repressed memories.[205] Nagy identifies 10 different areas that should be addressed.

1. Informed consent should be obtained prior to beginning therapy, which includes how the therapy will proceed, any specialized techniques to be used, and the potential benefits and risks of these techniques.

2. All professional activities should be documented according to the American Psychological Association Record Keeping Guidelines.

3. Specialized techniques such as hypnosis and guided imagery should be used only by highly qualified individuals.

4. No assumptions should be made about the historical accuracy of recalled events.

5. Uncovering techniques should not be utilized until an extensive history has been taken.

6. The client should be educated as to what occurs in any of these specialized activities, using handouts and other materials.

7. When conducting any of these exploratory sessions, it is wise to use audio- and/or videotape.

---

[201] *Id.* at 8.

[202] *Id.* at 9.

[203] John Briere, Repressed Memories and False Memory Syndrome—Memory: True or False?, Paper presented at the Wisconsin Psychological Association Spring Meeting (Apr. 6, 1994).

[204] Don Read & D. Stephen Lindsay, *Moving Toward a Middle Ground in the "False Memory" Debate: Reply to Commentaries on Lindsay and Read*, 8 Applied Psychol. 407 (1994).

[205] Thomas Nagy, *Guidelines and Direction When Treating Clients with Repressed Memories*, Nat'l Psychologist, July–Aug. 1994, at 8–9.

8. Consent forms should be signed for the specialized technique.

9. Sufficient time should be allowed for debriefing after the specialized technique has been used.

10. The American Psychological Association Code of Ethics should be consulted when necessary.

Both the American Psychological Association and the American Psychiatric Association have addressed the issue of memories of sexual abuse. In a "Statement on Memories of Sexual Abuse" disseminated in 1994, the American Psychiatric Association cautions the psychiatrist against using information about recovered memories indiscriminately. The APA points out that a balance is necessary, indicating that many individuals who have experienced sexual abuse have a history of not being believed by people they have trusted. The clinician must carefully discern the believable from the less believable. The APA also advises against using hypnotic or amytal-type interventions without specialized training in these areas.

The American Psychological Association established a working group on the investigation of memories of childhood abuse. The panel's responsibility was to address the controversy over adult memories of childhood abuse. The key conclusions were as follows:

• Controversies regarding adult recollections should not be allowed to obscure the fact that child abuse is a complex and pervasive problem in America, which has historically gone unacknowledged.

• Most people who were sexually abused as children remember all or part of what happened.

• However, it is possible for memories of abuse that have been forgotten for a long time to be remembered. Mechanisms by which such delayed recall occur are not currently well understood.

• It is also possible to construct convincing pseudo-memories for events that never occurred. The mechanisms by which these pseudo-memories occur are not currently well understood.

• There are gaps in our knowledge about the process that leads to accurate and inaccurate recollections of child abuse.[206]

A position paper published by the Canadian Psychiatric Association in 1996 concluded that, while sexual abuse is a real, deplorable problem, lasting trauma may or may not occur and recovered memories may or may not be valid.[207] The group cautions therapists against leading patients into recovery of memory and potential action against alleged perpetrators.

These well-measured statements point out that it is inappropriate for a well-trained mental health professional to identify with any one camp in this controversy, to the exclusion of the recognition that there is plausibility and accuracy in the other camp's position.

---

[206] American Psychological Ass'n, Questions and Answers about Memories of Childhood Abuse (Oct. 1995).

[207] *Position Statement: Adult Recovered Memories of Childhood Sexual Abuse,* 41 Can. J. Psychiatry no. 5, at 305–06 (1996).

Stated simply, people do forget and later recall important events in their lives, and people do create recollections of experiences that are distorted or did not exist. It becomes the mental health professional's charge over the next decade to help clients/patients, the courts, and the public in general to discern the difference between false memories and accurate but repressed memories.

§ 13.49   Creation of False Beliefs

Maggie Bruck and colleagues studied the use of anatomically detailed dolls in investigating the creation of false beliefs in sexual abuse allegation cases.[208] In this particular study, half of the three-year-old children received a genital examination and half did not.

> Children were inaccurate in reporting genital touching, regardless of how they were questioned, and regardless of whether they had received a genital examination. The dolls increased inaccurate reporting because some of the children falsely showed that the doctor had inserted a finger into the anal or genital cavity. The results indicate that anatomically detailed dolls should not be used in forensic or therapeutic interviews with three-year-old children.[209]

§ 13.50   Research Findings regarding Memory Cases

Steven Ceci and Maggie Bruck discussed several interesting factors about research in the area of sexual abuse memories.[210] They point out that, in 1991, of the 21.7 million cases of suspected child maltreatment, approximately 130,000 cases were substantiated or indicated cases that were sexual in nature. Only 3 to 10 percent of all cases of sexual abuse that are eventually filed with the police result in a trial. They also point out that preschool children are more likely to be abused than older children. They mention that research has demonstrated that seven-year-olds, in one project, never made a false report of abuse and only four five-year-olds did.

§ 13.51   Impact of the Interview Process

Ceci and Bruck point out that the interview process is a significant component to these allegations. It is rare for a child to be interviewed only once, or by one interviewer. Children have generally been interviewed between 4 and 11 times before a case has gone

---

[208] Maggie Bruck et al., *Anatomically Detailed Dolls Do Not Facilitate Pre-Schoolers' Reports of a Pediatric Examination Involving Genital Touching,* 1 J. Experimental Psychol.: Applied 95–109 (1995).

[209] *Id.* at 95.

[210] Steven Ceci & Maggie Bruck, *Social Policy Report for the Society for Research and Child Development in 1993,* 7 Child Witnesses: Translating Res. into Pol'y 1–30 (1993).

to trial. On average, children were interviewed 2.3 times before being taken to a mental health professional. Only 27 percent of professionals indicated that they were the first person to talk with the child about abuse. This certainly raises the issues of possible contamination in these types of cases.

Karen Saywitz, a leading expert on child interview techniques, developed the concept of narrative elaboration, which is an intervention package extrapolated from laboratory studies of memory development. It incorporates six experimental procedures that have enhanced the memory performance of school-age children in the laboratory and included memory strategy instruction, practice with feedback rationales for strategy utility, organizational guidance according to category cues, external memory aids, and reminders to use new strategies on subsequent events. The narrative elaboration intervention as outlined includes these six components:

1. *Rationale for strategy utility.* An explanation of the value of using new ways to remember better.

2. *Instructions to be complete and accurate.* "When you tell what happened to you, tell as much as you can about what really happened, even the little things without guessing or making anything up."

3. *Strategy.* Introduction of a strategy for organizing narratives into five categories and reporting on specific level of detail for each category.

4. *Visual cues.* Introduction of visual cues to remind self of each category.

5. *Practice, modeling, and feedback.* Practice using the new strategy and the visual cues on mock recall tasks with feedback on accuracy and with modeling with more detailed and relevant responses.

6. *Reinstruction.* Review of items 2 through 4 in the second session.

Using a technique like narrative elaboration reduces the likelihood of leading and potentially misleading questions, and it is likely to result in fewer false allegations.[211]

Ceci and Bruck point out that expert witnesses in these cases must tell the courts several important pieces of information. They suggest that courts need to know

1. Preschoolers are more vulnerable to suggestibility than older children.

2. Young children do make mistakes.

3. A child's report is less likely to be distorted after one interview than after several interviews.

4. Interviewers who ask nonleading questions are more likely to obtain accurate reports from children.

5. There is a complex interrelationship between children's testimony and factors of suggestibility.

---

[211] Karen Saywitz & Lynn Snyder, *Narrative Elaboration: Test of a New Procedure for Interviewing Children*, 64 J. Consulting & Clinical Psychol. 1347–57 (1996).

HOW COMMON IS FORETTING?

§ 13.52   Surveys of Mental Health Professionals

Shirley Feldman-Somers and Kenneth Pope surveyed psychologists about their own experience with sexual abuse. Three hundred thirty individuals reported that approximately one-quarter had been abused themselves as children, and 40 percent of those individuals claiming to have been abused as children stated that at some point they had forgotten about the abuse. The major findings of this study were "1) both sexual and nonsexual abuse were subject to forgetting; 2) being in therapy was the most common factor related to recall; 3) half of those who forgot also report corroboration of the abuse; and 4) forgetting was not related to gender or age, but did vary with the severity of abuse."[212]

In the past several years, a number of surveys have been performed addressing the issue of what various mental health professionals believe about repressed and recovered memories. Kenneth Pope and Barbara Tabachnick surveyed 382 [*sic*] therapists (205 female, 173 male). Seventy-three percent of the therapists stated that they had patients claiming recovered memories. There was a substantial gender difference, with 71 percent reporting having a female patient with recovered memories and 36 percent claiming to have a male patient with recovered memories. However, this gender difference did not hold up with alleged perpetrators, recovering memories of their perpetration.[213] Melissa Polusny and Victoria Follett surveyed 223 psychologists. More than a quarter of the psychologists regularly employ memory retrieval techniques with clients without abuse memories. Therapists who themselves had been victims of childhood sexual abuse placed a greater emphasis on these issues in performing therapy.[214]

ROLES OF PROFESSIONALS

§ 13.53   Psychologist's Role

Marian Hall points out that the psychologist is familiar with developmental issues, knows how to interview the child, has objective information available through testing, and can serve as an effective consultant. She also points out that the psychologist's role should be limited to the extent that the psychologist should not be pressured into declaring guilt or innocence of the alleged offender or declaring whether the abuse actually occurred.

Even though tests like the Child Abuse Potential (CAP) Inventory have been developed and demonstrated a high hit rate in discriminating abusers from non-abusers, psychologists

---

[212] Shirley Feldman-Somers & Kenneth Pope, *The Experience of "Forgetting" Childhood Abuse: A National Survey of Psychologists,* 62 J. Consulting & Clinical Psychol. no. 3, at 636 (1994).

[213] Kenneth Pope & Barbara Tabachnick, *Recovered Memories of Abuse among Therapy Patients: A National Survey,* 5 Ethics & Behav. no. 3, at 237–48 (1995).

[214] Melissa Polusny & Victoria Follett, *Long-Term Correlates of Child Sexual Abuse: Theory and Review of the Empirical Literature,* 4 Applied & Preventive Psychol. 143–66 (1995).

should take care not to use such tests exclusively in attempting to substantiate abuse allegations. Collaboration from as many sources as practicable should be the norm.

Hall concludes by saying, "No matter what the role, though, psychologists must keep in mind the compelling purposes of the legal process. They must show respect for the participants in the process and the authorities charged with decision making. Doing so is fully consistent with the high professional and personal duties of psychologists to promote human dignity."[215]

Kenneth Pope and Laura Brown addressed the rule of the evaluator in repressed memory cases. They state, "[T]he evaluator's job is to assist the triers of fact by presenting information about a person's mental state that will inform the decision-making process in the litigation. It is clearly not the job of the treating therapist."[216] They go on to say, "[W]e suggest that, similar to child custody evaluations, which require that the evaluator have a broad information base in a number of topic areas, in this field, the evaluator must be familiar with specialized knowledge."[217] They state that this special knowledge should include "familiarity with the field of child sexual abuse, broadly, trauma, the field of interpersonal violence, memory and suggestibility, developmental psychopathology . . . literature on perpetrators of sexual abuse . . . as well as repression, dissociation, forgetting, and amnesia, . . . in addition to other factors that may lead to delayed recall."[218]

The American Psychological Association Committee on Professional Practice and Standards, as a committee of the Board of Professional Affairs, published an article dealing with 24 questions about the professional practice in the area of child abuse. They indicated that psychologists need to be aware of applicable legislation in the state in which they are located. In addition, the committee recommends that psychologists ask themselves the following questions:

1. What constitutes child abuse and neglect?
2. Who has to report child abuse and neglect?
3. If I report, am I breaking confidentiality?
4. Under what circumstances do I have a duty to report child abuse?
5. How do I report? And what information am I required to disclose in a child abuse report?
6. Will I get in trouble if I do not report child abuse as required under state laws of my state?
7. Will I get in trouble if I do report? And can I be sued by the person I report?
8. Do I have to report every instance of child abuse?
9. Do I have to report if the suspected abuser is in treatment or I believe the reporting would do more harm than good?
10. What will be the response to my report?
11. Are there issues I should consider for disclosure?
12. How shall I handle a child's disclosure of abuse by a parent?

---

[215] Marian Hall, *The Role of Psychologists as Experts in Cases Involving Allegations of Sexual Abuse,* 23 Fam. L.Q. 451, 464 (1989).

[216] Kenneth Pope & Laura Brown, *Recovered Memories of Abuse, Assessment, Therapy,* Forensics 234 (American Psychological Ass'n 1996).

[217] *Id.* at 235.

[218] *Id.* at 235–36.

13.   How shall I handle a child's disclosure of abuse by a non-family person?

14.   What are some possible effects for the child, the family, and treatment when a disclosure and report are made?

15.   What are possible beneficial effects of reporting for the child and family?

16.   What are some of the possible personal issues I should be aware of in handling disclosure and reporting?

17.   What are the characteristics and symptoms of a child who has been abused?

18.   How do I recognize and verify what abuse had occurred?

19.   Are there psychological measures to assist in evaluations of victims of child abuse?

20.   What special considerations are there in the assessment of victims of child abuse?

21.   What are the emotional demands of providing intervention services to victims of child abuse?

22.   What roles can I play in supporting and providing intervention services to victims of child abuse?

23.   How do I provide treatment to a child who has been abused?

24.   What are the therapeutic issues, reasonable goals, and special considerations when providing treatment to a child who has been abused?

All of these issues need to be addressed and understood by psychologists practicing in the area of child abuse.[219]

§ 13.54   Factors Influencing Professionals' Perceptions

Kathleen Kendall-Tackette and Malcolm Watson performed research involving interviewing 201 professionals participating in child sexual abuse cases. They found that "professionals' perceptions of indicators of sexual abuse were influenced by expectation, profession and sex of the interviewer. . . . Expectation created the strongest effect of perception of behavioral indicators."[220] They also found that law enforcement professionals were more convinced than mental health professionals about whether abuse had taken place. Similarly, women were more convinced by general indicators than were men.

CHAPTER QUESTIONS AND CASES

§ 13.55   Questions for Chapter 13

Caution: Attorneys should not expect merely to go into court and ask all the following questions. Preparation is necessary, referring to the content of the chapter to determine

---

[219] American Psychological Ass'n, *Twenty-Four Questions (and Answers) about Professional Practice in the Area of Child Abuse,* 26 Prof. Psychol.: Res. & Prac. no. 4, at 377–85 (1995).

[220] Kathleen Kendall-Tackette & Malcolm Watson, Factors That Influence Professionals' Perceptions of Behavioral Indicators in Child Sexual Abuse 392 (1991).

whether a particular question applies to a case. The cross-reference at the end of many of the questions refers to the location in this book where readers can find an explanation of why a particular question may be important.

1.   Is the examiner aware of the recidivism rates of sexual abuse perpetrators? See **§ 13.3.**

2.   Is the examiner aware of the dynamics of incest families? See **§§ 13.5** to **13.9.**

3.   Is the examiner aware of the psychological effects of being victims of sexual abuse? See **§§ 13.10** and **13.15.**

4.   Did the examiner evaluate the role of alcohol or other substance abuse in sexual abuse allegations? See **Chapter 14.**

5.   Has the examiner considered child sexual abuse accommodations syndrome where applicable? See **§ 13.17.**

6.   Is the examiner aware of "normal" sexual behavior of children? See **§ 13.19.**

7.   During a child sexual abuse allegation evaluation interview, did the examiner follow the guidelines set forth by the American Professional Society on the Abuse of Children? See **Appendix O.**

8.   Does the examiner understand the difference between the behavior of abused and non-abused children? See **§ 13.20.**

9.   Is the examiner aware of the difference between mothers' behavior when making a bona fide allegation versus a fabricated allegation? See **§ 13.21.**

10. If sexual abuse took place during the childhood of either of the parents, what therapeutic steps have taken place to resolve the conflicts associated with experiencing such trauma during childhood?

11. If the parent has experienced any of these kinds of abuse and has not undergone extensive psychotherapy, how does the psychologist performing the evaluation justify considering this parent as an appropriate custodial parent?

12. If the parent or child reports any form of abuse, has the psychologist obtained detailed descriptions of the abuse in an effort to determine whether the allegations are overstated or exaggerated? See **§§ 13.5** and **13.29.**

13. If sexual abuse allegations have been made against one of the parents by one of the children, did the psychologist or other professional use the criteria discussed in this chapter to discriminate bona fide from fabricated sexual abuse allegations? See **§§ 13.21** and **13.22.**

14. If allegations of sexual abuse have been made, is there any official documentation from an objective third party (police department, social services agency, or other professional)?

15. Is there any evidence that the child who is the alleged victim of sexual abuse has been coached by either parent, any other adult, or a sibling?

16. If one of the parents was a victim of abuse during childhood, does he or she still act as a victim during adulthood? If so, how will this affect his or her ability to be an effective custodial parent?

17. If there have been abuse allegations, has the mother handled them appropriately? See **§ 13.2.**

18. Has a convicted perpetrator of any form of abuse sought treatment? Has that treatment been successful? If not, why not?

19. In sexual abuse cases, were sexually anatomically correct dolls used? Were conclusions drawn that went beyond the data available from the use of such dolls? See **§ 13.26.**

20. Does the examiner understand the dynamics of recantation? See **§ 13.32.**

21. Is the psychologist familiar with the research on the repressed memory/recovered memory controversy? See **§§ 13.39, 13.41, 13.42,** and **13.49.**

22. Did the examiner understand and take into account the concept of suggestibility? See **§ 13.40.**

23. If hypnosis was used, did the psychologist use appropriate guidelines? See **§ 13.47.**

§ 13.56   Case Digest

The source of information for most of the following cases is the *Mental and Physical Disability Law Reporter* (MPDLR), a publication of the American Bar Association. Complete information for any other sources appears in the relevant references below. The following are direct quotations from the identified source. Quotations from the *Mental and Physical Disability Law Reporter:* Excerpted from *Mental and Physical Disability Law Reporter.* Copyright © 1989–2004. American Bar Association. Reprinted by permission. If no source is identified, it is a summary from the court ruling.

Supreme Court

Two cases decided by the United States Supreme Court in 1990 and one in 1992 have had a profound effect upon the process used when a perpetrator of child abuse is brought to court: *Idaho v. Wright* and *Maryland v. Craig,* both in 1990, and *White v. Illinois,* in 1992. Digests of these three cases appear in **Chapter 6.**

Federal

Mindombe v. United States, 795 A.2d 39 (D.C. 2002). The Court of Appeals for the District of Columbia ruled that the testimony of a clinical psychologist about the behavior of children who have been sexually abused was properly admitted with limitations that prevented the psychologist from stating conclusions regarding whether the victim was honest or the defendant was guilty.

The prosecution presented testimony by a clinical psychologist to provide the jury with a profile of the range of behaviors exhibited by victims of child sexual abuse. The victim was six or seven at the time of the abuse and eight at the time she testified. The psychologist testified that child victims do not always report abuse promptly, that children react with a range of responses that can include no visible reaction, and that children that age may not remember events in sequential order.

This expert testimony was appropriately admitted because significant evidence at trial is likely to be inconsistent with the expectations of a lay juror regarding how a victim of child sexual abuse should react to such abuse. Without such expert testimony, the jury may conclude from the secrecy, inconsistency, or recantation of the child that the testimony has been fabricated. Without the expert's testimony, the jury may not be able to judge the credibility of the victim.

Finally, the court indicated that experts are not permitted to make ultimate conclusions regarding the truthfulness of witnesses, whether a person was in fact abused, or whether the defendant is guilty. Those conclusions belong to the factfinder. 26 *Mental and Physical Disability Law Reporter* 614–15 (2002).

United States v. Rouse, 100 F.3d 360 (8th Cir. 1996). The defendants . . . claimed, in part, that the district court erred in not allowing the jury to hear expert testimony from a psychologist who would have testified that the investigators used techniques that resulted in a "practice of suggestibility." . . . The district court held that the psychologist's testimony was not scientific evidence as described in *Daubert*. . . . The Eighth Circuit reversed . . . and remanded the case for a new trial in part because of the exclusion of that part of the psychologist's testimony. . . . In reviewing the literature pertaining to children's suggestibility the court relied heavily on Stephen Ceci and Maggie Bruck, Suggestibility of Child Witnesses: A Historical Review and Synthesis, *Psychological Bulletin* (1993). The court concluded that testimony based on this literature was reliable and relevant to the facts of the *Rouse* case. Provided that the psychologist was not going to tell the jury whether or not the children's testimony was based on false memories, testimony about whether a "practice of suggestibility" was employed in the investigative techniques should have been admitted. 28 *American Psychological Association Monitor* 45 (1997).

Vanderbilt v. Town of Chilmark, No. 95-12403-JLT (D. Mass. June 18, 1997). A Massachusetts federal court decided that the content of the psychiatric care received by an employee filing a sex discrimination claim for emotional distress was protected by psychiatrist-patient privilege. The court found that for the purpose of the privilege to be served—to encourage patient confidence and trust in the health care relationship in order to effectuate treatment—decisions to remove the privilege's protection cannot be determined by balancing the patient's interest with the proposed evidence's value. See *Jaffe v. Redmond*, 116 S. Ct. 1923 (1996). . . . To waive the privilege, one must use the specific privileged communication as evidence. . . . "The fact that a privileged communication has taken place may be relevant. But, the fact that a communication has taken place does not necessarily put [its] content at issue." 21 *Mental & Physical Disability Law Reporter* 651 (1997).

Corbett v. Morgenstern, 934 F. Supp. 680 (E.D. Pa. 1996). A Pennsylvania federal court denied a psychiatrist's motion to dismiss a suit brought by a former patient who alleged that he committed malpractice by initiating and continuing a sexual relationship with her during the course of her therapy. . . . The court agreed with Corbett that Morgenstern owed her a professional duty of care in the nature of a fiduciary duty and that her allegations supported her claim for negligent infliction of emotional distress. The court also found that Morgenstern's conduct was so outrageous as to permit recovery for intentional infliction of emotional distress. . . . Pennsylvania courts have found that symptoms of severe depression, nightmares, stress, and anxiety, requiring psychological treatment and ongoing mental, physical, and emotional harm, may sustain a cause of action for infliction of emotional distress. 21 *Mental & Physical Disability Law Reporter* 113–14 (1997).

Wilkinson v. Balsam, 885 F. Supp. 651 (D. Rt 1995). The U.S. District Court for the District of Vermont ruled that a psychiatrist owed a legal duty to a father to not falsely accuse the father of sexually abusing his son and stepson, and that two social work staff members violated the father's constitutional right to be free from arbitrary interference in his family relationships.

> Vermont law requires a physician who reasonably suspects child abuse to report [that suspicion]. One who files a report in accordance with this provision is entitled to good faith immunity. . . . Problematic for Balsam [the psychiatrist], however, is the limitation of the grant of immunity to those who report "in good faith." A genuine issue of fact exists as to whether Balsam acted in good faith in reporting his beliefs. . . . Given Balsam's involvement in the matter as . . . therapist and, perhaps, advocate, this evidence . . . suggests that Balsam was deceitful—in short, that his actions were undertaken without good faith. Further, the statute grants good faith immunity only with respect to liability incurred "as a result of making a report." Balsam's actions in this case were not limited to making a report. He rendered a diagnosis . . . and offered his opinions to Wiegand, the police, and others. There is evidence that his diagnosis is the result of gross negligence. To the extent the plaintiff's damages flow from the flawed diagnosis, independent of the SRS [Department of Social and Rehabilitation Services] report, Balsam cannot benefit from the immunity granted by [statute]. . . .
>
> Balsam next contends that, as he treated only the boys and their mother, he owed no duty as a matter of law to Wilkinson. . . . [However], the Vermont Supreme Court recognized that under certain circumstances a therapist owes a duty of care to potential victims of the therapist's patient. Foreseeability is the key factor in such a case. Here, the issue is not harm to a third party perpetrated by a patient of the psychiatrist, but harm to the third party arising *directly* from the psychiatrist's negligent evaluation and treatment of his patient. . . . If the factfinder determines that harm to Wilkinson was foreseeable in the circumstances, then Balsam owed a legal duty to Wilkinson to conform his conduct to the appropriate standard of care. . . .
>
> The two SRS employees . . . contend that they are immune from suit under the doctrine of qualified official immunity. . . . I am satisfied that the evidence submitted by the plaintiffs, *if proved*, is sufficient to support a finding that the SRS employees violated the clearly established constitutional rights of the plaintiffs and that they did not have an objectively reasonable basis to believe that their conduct did not violate such rights. Plaintiffs have submitted evidence that defendant Adams conducted an extraordinarily shoddy and unprofessional investigation of the report of child sexual abuse . . . , that the record before him did not reasonably support the finding that Wilkinson had abused his sons, that defendant Russell knew or should have known that the abuse finding was not reasonably supported, that both Adams and Russell ignored and concealed exculpatory evidence, and that both Adams and Russell substantiated and reported to others their finding . . . knowing that the probable result would include the criminal prosecution of Wilkinson and his loss of custody over the children. Taking this evidence as true . . . it is more likely than not that Russell and Adams violated the clearly established constitutional rights of the plaintiffs to be free of the state's arbitrary interference in their familial relationships.

California

Ramona v. Superior Court of Los Angeles County, 66 Cal. Rptr. 2d 766 (Ct. App. 1997). A California appeals court ruled that alleged repressed memory testimony of sexual abuse recalled after undergoing psychotherapy and a sodium amytal ("truth serum") interview was inadmissible. . . . [P]rior to being interviewed under sodium amytal Holly was undisputedly uncertain whether any abuse had occurred. In addition, with the exception of Holly's proposed recovered memory testimony, there was no other substantial evidence to support her claims. . . . Although sodium amytal is accepted as a drug that can break down inhibitions . . . , the scientific consensus about the reliability of information extracted remains "overwhelmingly negative." Before being admitted, the scientific principle or theory from which the evidence is derived must be "sufficiently established to have gained general acceptance in the particular field in which it belongs." *Frye v. United States*. 21 *Mental & Physical Disability Law Reporter* 652 (1997). [See also the following digest of the original *Ramona* lawsuit.]

Ramona v. Isabella, C61898 (Cal. Super. Ct. Napa 1994). [A] California jury in May awarded Gary A. Ramona $500,000 in damages. . . . Ramona alleged that he lost his $500,000-a-year job, his wife, his family and his reputation after the defendants implanted false memories of incest in his daughter's mind. . . . In a landmark procedural decision, the trial judge held that as a family member of the patient and one substantially affected by the therapists' alleged malpractice, Ramona did have standing to sue the defendants . . . . At trial . . . , Ramona denied abusing his daughter. His daughter, now 23 . . . , repeated her allegations that her father had raped her repeatedly between the ages of 5 and 8. Family counselor Marche Isabella, who had treated Ramona's daughter for bulimia, acknowledged telling the young woman and her mother that 80 percent of women suffering from eating disorders have been sexually abused. Then, after psychiatrist Richard Rose, M.D., interviewed the daughter after administering sodium amytal to her, the purported abuse was revealed. . . . Psychologist, psychiatrist and hypnosis authority Martin T. Orne, Ph.D., M.D., testified that sodium-amytal interviews are "inherently untrustworthy and unreliable," and that "Holly Ramona's memory has been so distorted that [she] no longer knows what the truth is." Charles Patrick Ewing, "Plaintiff Awarded $500,000 in Landmark 'Recovered Memories' Lawsuit," 25 *American Psychological Association Monitor* 22 (1994).

Colorado

Dill v. Colorado, 927 P.2d 1315 (Colo. 1996). The Colorado Supreme Court held that a man convicted of sexual assault on a child was not improperly denied access to the child's psychologist's notes made by the psychologist in the course of treating the child for post-traumatic stress disorder (PTSD). . . . The Colorado Supreme Court agreed with the trial court and appeals court that the child had not waived her privilege to keep information about her treatment sessions privileged. . . . Colorado public policy strongly favors promoting psychotherapy for sexual assault victims, and the statutory waiver of privilege in [the statute] is designed to protect the best interest of the child by preventing further harm to the abused child. . . . Colorado's statutory psychologist-patient privilege is to aid in the effective diagnosis and treatment of mental illness by encouraging full disclosure without fear of embarrassment or humiliation, and the statute's exceptions to the privilege are very limited. 21 *Mental & Physical Disability Law Reporter* 101 (1996).

Connecticut

Zamstein v. Marvasti, 692 A.2d 781 (Conn. 1997). The Connecticut Supreme Court decided that a psychiatrist hired to evaluate children for evidence of sexual abuse does not owe a duty of care to the person suspected of committing the abuse. . . . After Zamstein was acquitted of the charges, he sued Marvasti for negligence in the psychiatric evaluation of the children and in aiding the prosecution. The trial court dismissed the claims, ruling that Marvasti owed no duty of care to Zamstein. The supreme court affirmed. There was no special relationship between Marvasti and Zamstein on which to base a duty of care. 21 *Mental & Physical Disability Law Reporter* 524 (1997).

Florida

Hadden v. Florida, 690 So.2d 573 (Fla. 1997). Some experts have used the child sexual abuse accommodation syndrome (CSAAS), developed by Roland Summit, as a framework for describing their clinical observations of alleged abuse victims and for determining whether a child has been sexually abused. Other psychologists have argued that the relationship between sexual abuse and a well-defined cluster of behavioral symptoms is unclear. They argue, as does Summit, that CSAAS was not intended for use as a diagnostic tool and that there is no compelling evidence that the presence of the syndrome discriminates between abused and nonabused children. . . .

In [this case], the court handed down a consolidated ruling of two appeals: *Hadden v. State*, 670 So.2d 77 (Fla. App. 1st Dist. 1996) and *Beaulieu v. State*, 671 So.2d 807 (Fla. App. 5th Dist. 1996). . . . The court opined that CSAAS was inadmissible and remanded both cases back to the lower courts for retrial. . . . The court . . . argued that syndrome evidence must be generally accepted by the psychological community to be admissible in Florida courts and that the CSAAS evidence does not meet this standard. 28 *American Psychological Association Monitor* 25 (1997).

Michigan

Michigan v. Regts, 555 N.W.2d 896 (Mich. Ct. App. 1996). A Michigan appeals court held that a psychologist who sexually abused patients provided "medical treatment" . . . pursuant to criminal patient sexual abuse statutes even though he was not a physician. The broad definition of the "practice of medicine" under state public health codes focused on the treatment or advice provided as opposed to the qualifications of the practitioner, thus supporting a broad application of [the statute]. Further, a narrow interpretation excluding psychologists would have contradicted the legislative intent to provide protection from professionals who sexually abuse vulnerable patients under the guise of treatment. 21 *Mental & Physical Disability Law Reporter* 114 (1997).

New York

In re Guardianship of Charles Frederick Eugene M., 577 N.Y.S.2d 253 (App. Div. 1991). A New York appeals court held that a lower court erred in refusing to terminate the parental rights of a mother who was incarcerated for sexually abusing her child and did not obtain psychological counseling. The lower court had dismissed the termination petition after finding that counseling services were not " 'readily accessible' " in prison, and determining that the mother could obtain treatment upon release. The appeals court found that while the mother stated an intention to obtain mental health treatment upon release, this was nothing more than a "dim hope" and did not represent a concrete plan. The court found no evidence that the mother had taken steps to recognize her problem or to alter her behavior despite the fact that the prison had psychiatric services. 16 *Mental & Physical Disability Law Reporter* 291 (1992).

North Carolina

Doe v. Holt, 332 N.C. 90 (1992), 418 S.E. 2d 511. The North Carolina Supreme Court ruled that an unemancipated child is precluded from suing a parent for ordinary negligence, but not when there is willful and malicious conduct. The court noted a trend in other states to permit children to recover damages for injuries caused by a parent's willful misconduct. The court indicated that the father's sexual abuse of his two daughters over a period of nine years, for which the father was serving a prison term, constituted willful and malicious acts.

Oklahoma

Paulson v. Sternlof, 15 P.3d 981, 2000 WL 1810920 (Okla. Ct. App. Dec. 12, 2000). The Oklahoma appeals court ruled that a parent could not sue a psychologist for conducting an allegedly negligent evaluation of his child, because no doctor-patient relationship existed between the psychologist and the father.

A father won custody of his son in Virginia in 1991, based on the trial court finding that the mother had made continual and unsupported allegations of abuse of the child by the father. In 1993, the mother moved to Oklahoma with her son, but without consent of the father or a court. The mother's attorney got a recommendation of a psychologist, Dr. Sternlof, to evaluate the boy and then to testify at a custody hearing that the boy may have been sexually abused. The trial court granted summary judgment to the defendant.

The court of appeals affirmed. In this matter of first impression, the court adopted *Bird v. W.C.W.*, 868 S.W.2d 767 (Tex. Sup. Ct. 1994), which held that a psychologist has no professional duty to a third party for failing to properly diagnose the condition of a child, based on the lack of a physician-patient relationship.

South Dakota

State v. Edelman, 593 N.W.2d 419 (S.D. 1999). A father convicted of child sexual abuse of his stepdaughter argued that the trial court erred in admitting a psychologist's testimony regarding behavioral characteristics of sexually abused children and about the Child Sexual Abuse Accommodation Syndrome (CSAAS), on the basis that such testimony did not meet the *Daubert* standard. The South Dakota Supreme Court unanimously ruled that other courts have accepted such testimony under the *Daubert* standard. In addition, the psychologist made the points that care must be taken not to overinterpret, and that behavior typical of the CSAAS did not prove that sexual abuse had occurred. The psychologist also did not directly compare the child's behavior with the CSAAS. Fairness was ensured, the court indicated, by virtue of the adversarial nature of the proceedings and the opportunity to demonstrate problems with expert testimony on cross-examination.

Texas

Bird v. W.C.W., 868 S.W.2d 767 (Tex. 1994). The Texas Supreme Court ruled that a psychologist who misdiagnosed child sexual abuse may not be sued by the falsely accused father.

> First, we address whether a mental health professional owes a duty to a parent to not negligently misdiagnose a condition of the child. . . . We acknowledge that the harm to a

parent accused of sexual abuse is foreseeable. However, foreseeability alone is not a sufficient basis for creating a new duty. . . . A claimant's right to sue a mental health professional must be considered in light of countervailing concerns, including the social utility of eradicating sexual abuse. Evaluating children to determine whether sexual abuse has occurred is essential to that goal. Young children's difficulty in communicating sexual abuse heightens the need for experienced mental health professionals to evaluate the child. Because they are dealing with such a sensitive situation, mental health professionals should be allowed to exercise their professional judgment in diagnosing sexual abuse of a child without the judicial imposition of a countervailing duty to third parties. . . . We hold that [the psychologist] owed no professional duty to W.C.W. to not negligently misdiagnose the condition of his child. . . .

Communications made during the course of judicial proceedings are privileged. . . . The privilege also extends to pre-trial proceedings, including affidavits filed with the court. . . . The privilege afforded against defamation actions is founded on the "theory that the good it accomplishes in protecting the rights of the general public outweighs any wrong or injury which may result to a particular individual." *Reagan*, 166 S.W.2d at 913. . . . Any injury caused to W.C.W. by denying him the ability to bring a negligence cause of action . . . is outweighed by the need to encourage the reporting of child abuse. . . . Furthermore, the administration of justice requires "full and free disclosure from witnesses unhampered by fear of retaliatory lawsuits." *James*, 637 S.W.2d at 917. . . . We hold that a mental health professional owes no professional duty of care to a third party to not negligently misdiagnose a condition of a patient.

Virginia

Plummer v. Center Psychiatrists, Ltd., 476 S.E.2d 172 (Va. 1996). In a split decision, the Virginia supreme court ruled that a psychologist who had sexual intercourse with a patient may have acted within the scope of his employment, thus making his employer liable. . . . Plummer sued the Center under a *respondeat superior* theory. . . . The trial court granted the Center demurrer. Plummer appealed. The supreme court found that the test for whether *respondeat superior* applied was not Gerald's [the psychologist's] motive in having relations with Plummer, but " 'whether the activity that gave rise to the tortious act was within or without the . . . scope of employment.' " . . . *Respondeat superior* liability could apply even if an employee's tortious conduct was outrageous, violated company rules, and advanced the employee's rather than the employer's interests—as long as the injurious acts were committed while the employee was performing the duties of his employment. Thus, if Plummer proved her allegation that Gerald had sexual intercourse with her at the Center during therapy, a jury could find that Gerald was acting within the scope of his employment. 21 *Mental & Physical Disability Law Reporter* 112–13 (1997).

Wisconsin

Wisconsin v. Locke, 502 N.W.2d 891 (Wis. Ct. App. 1993). A Wisconsin appeals court ordered a case retried because the testimony of a social worker that was protected by physician-patient privilege had been admitted erroneously.

Murray Locke was convicted of five counts of first-degree sexual assault on a minor. . . . At trial, a social worker Locke had voluntarily seen several times at a community mental health center testified over objection that during therapy Locke had told her he had problems with an uncontrollable sex drive and pedophilia. The social worker had assured him of confidentiality as long as he did not tell her anything she was required by law to report. She claimed that in the course of the interviews with Locke she had noted that it was her duty to report child sexual abuse, but Locke testified that he had believed his discussion of this issue was to be confidential.

Locke appealed, claiming that the interviews were subject to physician-patient privilege. . . . The appeals court reversed, holding that Locke's objectively reasonable expectation of confidentiality brought his revelations within the requirements for privilege, that the error of admitting the social worker's testimony was harmful, and that a retrial was necessary. The court noted that a social worker's obligation to report child abuse only arises when the allegedly abused child is the source of such information. 18 *Mental & Physical Disability Law Reporter* 24 (1994).

Wisconsin v. Maday, 507 N.W.2d 365 (Wis. Ct. App. 1993). A Wisconsin appeals court held that a trial court may order psychological evaluations of an alleged child sexual abuse victim by defense experts, but must balance the defendant's right to obtain all relevant evidence against any potential harm to the victim, including privacy violations. . . .

The appeals court . . . [indicated that] the responsive mechanisms available . . . in lieu of pretrial discovery—such as cross-examination and the use of non-examining experts—may not be an adequate substitute for pretrial clinical examinations of the children. An expert who has personally examined an alleged victim is in a better position to offer a credible opinion than one who has not.

The appeals court held that if a trial court is confronted with a motion for a psychological examination of an alleged sexual assault victim in response to the state's intention to introduce expert evidence that the alleged victim's behavior is consistent with that of other victims, the trial court should consider the following:

(1)   the nature of the examination requested and the intrusiveness inherent in that examination;
(2)   the victim's age;
(3)   the resulting physical and/or emotional effects of the examination on the victim;
(4)   the probative value of the examination to the issue before the court;
(5)   the remoteness in time of the examination to the alleged criminal act;
(6)   the evidence already available for the defendant's use; and
(7)   the necessity for a personal interview with the victim is essential before the court can form an opinion that the victim's behaviors are consistent with the behaviors of other victims of sexual abuse.

If a court determines that examination of the alleged victim by defense experts is warranted but the victim refuses to be examined, the prosecution's examining experts should be prohibited from testifying. 18 *Mental & Physical Disability Law Reporter* 154–55 (1994).

Wisconsin v. S.H., 159 Wis. 2d 730 (Ct. App. 1990), 465 N.W. 2d. 238. A father ("S.H.") charged with sexually assaulting his three minor children sought to compel the Directions Counseling Center ("DCC") to provide him with copies of his children's treatment records to aid his defense. The children were seen by a clinical social worker who met regularly with a licensed psychologist to discuss the children's therapy. S.H. executed authorizations for the release of his children's records, but their mother opposed the release and the children's guardian ad litem asserted the psychologist-patient privilege on behalf of the children, so a trial court ruled that the records were privileged and ordered DCC not to release the records. S.H. appealed. The appeals court found that a state statute on communications between patients and physicians, section 51.30(6), Wis. Stats. was ambiguous and that the claim of privilege invoked by the children's guardian superseded the authorization for release executed by S.H. The court was satisfied that the privilege extended to the children's communications with the social worker who met regularly with, and was supervised by, the psychologist. . . . Although S.H. asked the trial court to review the children's treatment records in camera, citing numerous types of information material to his defense that he felt were or might be contained in the treatment records, the trial court denied this request and since the issue was not preserved for appeal, it was deemed by the court to have been abandoned. 18 *Register Reports* 19 (1992).

CHAPTER 14

SPECIAL CONCERNS: MENTAL DISORDERS

§ 14.1   Introduction

A *normal* family has two parents, both of whom are in adequate touch with themselves and with the external world, and who can consistently and accurately perceive what is going on in each realm and cope adequately with their own needs and the needs of their children. When a psychological disorder is present, however, these abilities will be impaired to some degree. Those individuals who have a severe impairment will usually be considered *psychotic*, while those with less impairment will be considered to be *neurotic* or to have a *personality* or *character* disorder. This chapter will address the need of children for *normal* parenting and the potential results if they do not receive it.

An Overriding Concern

A serious problem with the testimony of many experts is that it addresses psychological or psychiatric issues that have no obvious relationship to legal issues, and is therefore irrelevant to the legal issues before the court. Diagnoses, in particular, have been problematic, since many experts either suggest that all people with a given diagnosis behave in the same manner, or that the presence of a given diagnosis tells a great deal about the functional ability of the individual, neither of which is correct (see **Chapter 17**). What is needed is for the expert to "present the logic that links these observations to the specific abilities and capacities with which the law is concerned."[1] Benjet, Azar, and Kuersten-Hogan emphasize similar points. Specifically, they indicate that (1) diagnosis (current or past) does not accurately predict the quality of parenting or risk for mistreatment of a child; diagnosis does not predict success of parenting interventions; and that (2) parents who are determined to do poorly at caring for their children do not necessarily remain poor caretakers indefinitely. Consequently, it is essential that evaluations focus on parenting skills rather than diagnosis or other secondary factors.[2]

---

[1] Randy K. Otto & John F. Edens, *Parenting Capacity, in* Thomas Grisso, ed., Evaluating Competencies 229–307, at 250 (2d ed. Kluwer/Plenum 2003) [hereinafter Otto & Edens].

[2] Corina Benjet, Sandra T. Azar, & Regina Kuersten-Hogan, *Evaluating the Parental Fitness of Psychiatrically Diagnosed Individuals: Advocating a Functional-Contextual Analysis of Parenting*, 17 J. Fam. Psychol. 238–51 (2003).

§ 14.2   Children's Needs

For children to develop normally, they need a number of things from their parents. Among these, "parental affection, protection, and guidance are necessary to promote the child's development of social and learning skills, self-control, socially oriented values, positive self-esteem, and a coherent sense of self."[3] According to the Task Force on Clinical Assessment in Child Custody of the American Psychiatric Association, children need to feel valued and cared for, and need parents who can set limits and model coping techniques.[4] "Children need parents to model and teach a value system which accommodates self-interest to social realities. . . . Parental awareness and acceptance of the child as a unique person is essential to the development of positive self-esteem and a sense of autonomy."[5]

Law professor Joseph Goldstein and psychoanalysts Anna Freud and Albert Solnit indicate that

> unlike adults, children have no psychological conception of relationship by blood-tie until quite late in their development. . . . What registers in their minds are the day-to-day interchanges with the adults who take care of them and who, on the strength of these, become the parent figures to whom they are attached.[6]

Goldstein and his colleagues indicate that dysfunctional families may provide too little or too great attention to the physical care of the child, in both cases paying too little attention to the substantial psychological and emotional needs of the child, whether the family is intact or not. One result is that the child may not have appropriate models for identification.[7] When the parent has an "impoverished" or "unstable" personality, and may therefore not be able to provide adequate parenting, "unbroken closeness to them, and especially identification with them, may cease to be a benefit and become a threat. In extreme cases this necessitates state interference."[8]

Goldstein *et al.* propose that the "best interests of the child" doctrine be replaced with a new standard:

> the least detrimental available alternative for safeguarding the child's growth and development. . . . The least detrimental alternative, then, is that specific placement and procedure for placement which maximizes . . . his or her opportunity for being wanted and for maintaining on a continuous basis a relationship with at least one adult who is or will become his psychological parent.[9]

---

[3] Derdeyn et al., Child Custody Consultation, Report of the Task Force on Clinical Assessment in Child Custody 21 (American Psychiatric Ass'n 1981).

[4] *Id.* at 21–22.

[5] *Id.* at 22.

[6] Joseph Goldstein et al., Beyond the Best Interests of the Child 12–13 (1973).

[7] *Id.* at 15.

[8] *Id.* at 19–20.

[9] *Id.* at 53.

On the basis of the book by Goldstein and his colleagues and two related books by the same authors, "much custody litigation now seeks to ascertain and turns upon the identity of the psychological parent."[10] It has been suggested that the "least detrimental alternative" standard fits well with the actual practices and expertise of psychologists, whose psychological tests are largely designed to detect psychopathology, not positive psychological qualities.[11]

Psychologist Eleanor Maccoby discusses research on "child rearing and the growth of competence."[12] Among the findings of that research are the following:

- "The children who were happy, self-reliant, and able to meet challenging situations directly . . . had parents who exercised a good deal of control over their children and demanded responsible, independent behavior from them but who also explained, listened, and provided emotional support. . . . The parents of the immature children were moderately nurturant but conspicuously low in exercising control."[13]

- "When parents consistently enforce their rules and demands and do not let their children's noncompliance or resistance divert them, their children have been found to be: (1) Able to control aggressive impulses and not [be] coercive toward parents . . . (2) Adequately controlled (as distinct from undercontrolled or overcontrolled) . . . (3) High in self-esteem at age ten or eleven . . . (4) Competent . . . that is, able to approach new situations with confidence, to take initiative and persist in tasks once begun—generally positive in mood and not withdrawn or immaturely impulsive. . . . An important element in enforcement of demands and rules is parental vigilance: Parents must notice whether children have complied. . . . Only the reasonably vigilant parent can enforce rules firmly and consistently."[14]

- While parents need to be in charge, "children must also be able to exercise some degree of control over the events impinging on them. . . . Apparently, a responsive environment— especially a responsive *human* environment—is one of the first requisites for a sense of control. . . ."[15] If the parents are unable, for whatever reason, to pay attention to and respond to the child's needs, the child is likely to "suffer a sense of loss of control—what Seligman . . . has called 'learned helplessness.' If this situation occurs consistently, the child is likely to become increasingly apathetic, passive, and even depressed."[16]

Psychologist Sandra Scarr indicatesthat "all children deserve supportive environments that nurture their development and enable them to be the best and happiest people they can

---

[10] Daniel Schuman, Psychiatric and Psychological Evidence 13-4 (2d ed. 1994) [hereinafter Psychiatric and Psychological Evidence].

[11] Daniel A. Krauss & Bruce D. Sales, *Legal Standards, Expertise, and Experts in the Resolution of Contested Child Custody Cases*, 6 Psychol. Pub. Pol'y & L. 843–79 at 874 (2000).

[12] Eleanor Maccoby, Social Development: Psychological Growth and the Parent-Child Relationship 368 (1980).

[13] *Id.* at 374–75.

[14] *Id.* at 381–82.

[15] *Id.* at 386–87.

[16] *Id.*

become. Beyond loving support, children need opportunities to develop their own individual abilities, talents and personalities. Parents' most important job, therefore, is to provide support and opportunities."[17]

Social worker F. Givelber identifies five parental tasks that he deems crucial to the evolution of self-esteem:

1. Winnicott's term, *"good enough"* mothering . . . describes a quality of parenting that responds to the basic physiological and emotional needs of the infant. These essential features of mothering include acceptance, responsiveness, sensitivity, and tolerance of the infant and his particular needs.

2. *Separateness* describes the parent's ability to differentiate a child's needs and feelings from his own and to acknowledge and support the child as a separate person.

3. *Anxiety mastery* refers to the parent's capacity to teach the child that anxiety can be tolerated. A parent, given his own ability to handle anxiety, empathically encourages the child to meet and triumph over new and frightening experiences.

4. *Mirroring of affect and achievement* reflects the parent's understanding of the child's feelings and pleasurable responsiveness to his achievements.

5. *Promotion of growth and maturation* refers to the parent's effort to guide the child toward an increasingly realistic sense of himself and the world.[18]

Givelber considers these five parenting tasks to be necessary for the development of an ability to regulate *self-esteem*, which he defines as "a highly sophisticated evaluative function that develops in the context of a successful reciprocity between parent and child."[19] If the parent cannot adequately address these tasks because of the presence of a psychological disorder, the child's development will suffer substantially.

Psychologist Ronald Rapee reviewed several dozen research studies that addressed the perceptions of anxious and/or depressed adults of the parenting they received while growing up. He concluded that "there appears to be strong and consistent evidence to support the conclusion that current feelings of anxiety and depression are associated with perceived parental rejection and perceived parental control." In other words, adults who are depressed and/or anxious tend to perceive their parents as having rejected them and/or tightly controlled them, preventing them from learning adequate coping skills and causing affective symptoms that carried into adulthood.[20]

Psychologist Craig Shealy reviewed the professional literature on parental and familial factors that correlate with psychopathology in children. He found that "parents with [mental] disorders produce children with disorders in greater proportions than the 'normal' populations, but that children's disorders are not necessarily of the same type as their parents." This indicates, he said, that certain kinds of parental behaviors and family environments

---

[17] Sandra Scarr, *How People Make Their Own Environments: Implications for Parents and Policy Makers*, 2 Psychol. Pub. Pol'y & L. 204, 204 (1996).

[18] F. Givelber, *The Parent-Child Relationship and the Development of Self-Esteem, in* The Development and Sustenance of Self-Esteem in Children 163–64 (1983).

[19] *Id*. at 164.

[20] Ronald M. Rapee, *Potential Role of Childrearing Practices in the Development of Anxiety and Depression*, 17 Clinical Psychol. Rev. 47, 61 (1997).

correlate with the presence of mental, emotional, and behavioral problems in children. Specific correlates of children's psychopathology include hostility, criticism, mixed messages, blurred boundaries, rigidity, lack of conflict resolution, inconsistency, coercion, demandingness, affective inhibition, enmeshment, and disengagement.[21]

Numerous studies have shown that children must bond with a caretaker as infants if they are to develop good coping skills. Children who bond with mothers or other caretakers tend to do better with friends, be more successful in school, have greater self-esteem, have a lower rate of psychopathology, and deal better with new, possibly stressful, situations. With that bonding, or attachment, children have a safe base from which to explore the world. Psychologist Carollee Howes found in a series of research studies that secure attachment to primary caregivers other than mothers (for example, day care providers) occurred about half the time, while secure bonding with natural mothers occurred in 70 percent of cases. Howes attributed this difference to the reduced quality and closeness of the non-mother caretaking relationships. Many researchers have used this kind of data as a basis for calling for high-quality day care for children.[22]

Psychologists Randy Otto and John Edens address parenting competency in the two contexts in which it is commonly addressed: divorce proceedings and dependency (allegations of abuse and/or neglect, termination of parental rights) proceedings. In both types of cases, they indicate, the concern is the ability of the parent(s) or other caretakers to adequately take care of a child or children. While it is presumed in custody cases that both parents are fit parents, the court addresses the comparative abilities of the parents to address the best interests of the child(ren), primarily in the contexts of decisionmaking authority and the physical placement of the child(ren). In order to adequately parent a child, the parent must understand the child's needs, and must have the ability to adequately address those needs. Anything that seriously impedes a parent's ability to both understand and address children's needs is important for the factfinder to consider.[23] One of the factors that *may* impede understanding and/or ability to address children's needs is a mental disorder.

Specific Needs of Children

In summary, children need many things from their parents and families if they are to have a childhood that provides a strong base for normal psychological development. The authors of this text consider the following needs to be among the most important:

1. Parental affection, protection, and guidance
2. A need to feel valued and cared for
3. Parents who can set limits and model coping techniques
4. A value system that accommodates both self-interest and social realities

---

[21] Craig N. Shealy, *From* Boys Town *to* Oliver Twist: *Separating Fact from Fiction in Welfare Reform and Out-of-Home Placement of Children and Youth*, 50 Am. Psychologist 565, 569 (1995).

[22] Beth Azar, *The Bond between Mother and Child*, 26 Am. Psychol. Ass'n Monitor 28 (1995).

[23] Thomas Grisso, *Advances in Assessments for Legal Competencies, in* Thomas Grisso, ed., Evaluating Competencies 229–307 (2d ed. Kluwer/Plenum 2003).

5. Parental awareness and acceptance of the child as a unique person

6. Physical care that is individualized and sensitive

7. Sufficient parental involvement so that the child's emotional needs are fulfilled

8. Parents who are suitable models for identification

9. Parents who *want* the child

10. Parents who will exercise the proper amount of control over their children, neither too much nor too little

11. Parents who demand responsible, independent behavior but who also explain, listen, and provide emotional support

12. Parents who consistently enforce their rules and demands

13. Vigilant parents who notice whether their children have complied with demands

14. Parents who are responsive to their children

15. Parents who can differentiate the child's needs and feelings from their own and who acknowledge and support the child as a separate person

16. Parents who can teach the child that anxiety can be tolerated, in part based on the parent's own ability to handle stress and anxiety

17. Parental understanding of the child's feelings and pleasurable responsiveness to his or her achievements

18. Parental efforts to guide the child toward an increasingly realistic sense of him- or herself and the world

19. Successful reciprocity between parent and child

20. Reasonable freedom from parental hostility, criticism, mixed messages, blurred boundaries, rigidity, lack of conflict resolution, inconsistency, coercion, demandingness, affective inhibition, enmeshment, and disengagement.

The parent who has no diagnosable mental disorder is likely to adequately address the above needs. So is the parent who has a short-lived mental disorder that is primarily or exclusively stress-related, including the person who has a single, stress-induced acute psychotic episode but had no diagnosable disorder prior to that episode and who receives good treatment during the episode.

§ 14.3   Nature of Mental Illness: Psychosis

When most people refer to *mental illness*, they are referring to an individual who is *psychotic*—that is, one who has a

> severe mental disorder characterized by gross impairment in reality testing, typically shown by delusions, hallucinations, disorganized speech, or disorganized or catatonic behavior. Persons with these disorders are termed psychotic. Among these illnesses are schizophrenia, delusional disorders, some secondary or symptomatic disorders ("organic psychoses"), and some mood disorders.[24]

---

[24] American Psychiatric Glossary 175 (Jane E. Edgerton & Robert J. Campbell III eds., 1994) [hereinafter American Psychiatric Glossary].

The *Psychiatric Dictionary* adds that

> in general . . . the disorders labeled psychoses differ from the other groups of psychiatric disorders in one or more of the following: (1) Severity—the psychoses are "major" disorders that are more severe, intense, and disruptive; they tend to affect all areas of the patient's life. . . . (2) Degree of withdrawal—the psychotic patient is less able to maintain effective object relationships; external, objective reality has less meaning for the patient or is perceived in a distorted way. (3) Affectivity—the emotions are often qualitatively different from the normal, at other times are so exaggerated quantitatively that they constitute the whole existence of the patient. (4) Intellect—intellectual functions may be directly involved by the psychotic process so that language and thinking are disturbed; judgment often fails; hallucinations and delusions may appear. (5) Regression—there may be generalized failure of functioning and a falling back to very early behavioral levels; such regression is more than a temporary lapse in maturity and may include a return to early and even primitive patterns.[25]

This is a particularly important group to study, since research indicates that women who have serious mental illnesses tend to both marry and have children at about the same rate as other women, but their rates of separation and divorce are higher.[26]

§ 14.4   Nature of Other Mental Disorders

A further distinction needs to be made among types of mental disorders. The most serious and severe disorders are the psychoses, as defined above. When the mental disorder is less serious and severe, but still significant, it may be classified by the type of dysfunction ("depression," "anxiety," and so forth) or as a "personality" or "character" disorder.

Nonpsychotic Disorders

Most disorders that do not involve psychosis or personality dysfunction fall within the category of "neuroses," though that term is not often used any longer. The term implies that the individual has a significant psychological disturbance, feels emotional pain, and is functioning significantly less well as a result. The disorder may be very disabling. Without treatment, it may last for many years. Symptoms may be controlled by antidepressant, antianxiety, or other medication, but full resolution often requires psychotherapy.

Personality or Character Disorders

Personality disorders are

> [e]nduring patterns of perceiving, relating to, and thinking about the environment and oneself that begin by early adulthood and are exhibited in a wide range of important social and

---

[25] Psychiatric Dictionary 510 (R. Campbell ed., 6th ed. 1989).

[26] Barry J. Ackerson, *Parents with Serious and Persistent Mental Illness: Issues in Assessment and Services*, 48 Soc. Work 187–94 (2003).

personal contexts. These patterns are inflexible and maladaptive, causing either significant functional impairment or subjective distress.[27]

DSM-IV groups the personality disorders into three clusters on the basis of similarities in their presentation:

> Cluster A includes the Paranoid, Schizoid, and Schizotypal Personality Disorders. Individuals with these disorders often appear odd or eccentric.
>
> Cluster B includes the Antisocial, Borderline, Histrionic, and Narcissistic Personality Disorders. Individuals with these disorders often appear dramatic, emotional, or erratic.
>
> Cluster C includes the Avoidant, Dependent, and Obsessive-Compulsive Personality Disorders. Individuals with these disorders often appear anxious or fearful.
>
> It should be noted that this clustering system . . . has serious limitations and has not been consistently validated. Moreover, individuals frequently present with co-occurring Personality Disorders from different clusters.[28]

Similarly, a *character disorder* is

> [a] personality disorder manifested by a chronic, habitual, maladaptive pattern of reaction that is relatively inflexible, limits the optimal use of potentialities, and often provokes the responses from the environment that the person wants to avoid. In contrast to the symptoms of neurosis, character traits are typically ego-syntonic.[29]

There is also a residual category, "Personality Disorder Not Otherwise Specified," to be used when diagnostic criteria for one of the listed specific disorders do not apply, or there is a mixed disorder in which many criteria apply.

For all practical purposes, the terms "personality disorder" and "character disorder" can be used interchangeably.

W.M. Meissner adds that

> a particular character pattern or type becomes pathological when its manifestations are exaggerated to the point that behavior destructive to the individual or to others is the result or when the functioning of the person becomes so disturbed or restricted that it becomes a source of distress to the person or to others. Characterological traits tend to be nearly lifelong and are usually deeply embedded in the organization of the individual's personality.[30]

According to DSM-IV (see **Chapter 17**),

> Only when personality traits are inflexible and maladaptive and cause significant functional impairment or subjective distress do they constitute *Personality* Disorders. . . . This enduring

---

[27] American Psychiatric Glossary at 153–54.

[28] Diagnostic and Statistical Manual of Mental Disorders 629–30 (4th ed. 1994) [hereinafter DSM-IV].

[29] American Psychiatric Glossary at 37.

[30] W.M. Meissner, *Theories of Personality and Psychopathology, in* Comprehensive Textbook of Psychiatry/IV 402 (H. Kaplan & B. Saddock eds., 1985).

pattern is inflexible and pervasive . . . and leads to clinically significant distress or impairment in social, occupational, or other important areas of functioning.[31]

Personality or character disorders are generally not treatable with psychotropic medications. Therefore, a parent with a personality or character disorder will require psychotherapy rather than medication if there is to be improvement in the condition.

EFFECTS OF PARENTAL MENTAL DISORDERS

§ 14.5   Competency and Parenting

An individual's ability to make knowing and voluntary decisions is obviously related to his or her capacity to parent. Individuals who are psychotic are not automatically incompetent by virtue of their disorders. The relevant issue is the functional ability of the individual, not whether he or she is mentally ill.[32] It is essential to specifically identify "what the caretaker understands, believes, knows, does and is capable of doing by way of parenting."[33]

For the most part, courts have held that parenting may be adequate in spite of even a serious mental disorder and that a specific finding must be made in each case based upon an evaluation by a psychologist or psychiatrist. See the case law summaries at the end of this chapter for court decisions regarding the relevance of mental disorders to parenting, child custody, and termination of parental rights.

§ 14.6   Effect of Major Parental Mental Disorders on Children

There is relatively little research on the direct effect of parental mental illnesses on children, so most conclusions have to be drawn from the nature of the disorders and the expected consequences for the children. Oliver Williams and Patrick Corrigan summarize the professional literature by indicating that

> [G]rowing up in a home in which parents are mentally ill . . . or alcoholic causes severe problems for the children. Specifically, children of alcoholic parents have shown greater rates of hyperactivity and conduct disorder . . . , substance abuse, delinquency, and truancy . . . , cognitive dysfunctioning . . . , social inadequacy . . . , and anxiety and depression. . . . Children of severely mentally ill parents show similar problems.[34]

---

[31] DSM-IV at 630.

[32] Grisso, *Clinical Assessments for Legal Decision Making: Research Recommendations, in* Law & Mental Health: Major Developments and Research Needs 49, 70 (S. Shah & B. Sales eds., 1991) [hereinafter Grisso].

[33] Otto & Edens at 250.

[34] Oliver Williams & Patrick Corrigan, *The Differential Effects of Parental Alcoholism and Mental Illness on Their Adult Children*, 48 J. Clinical Psychol. 406, 406 (1992).

To assess the impact of growing up with either type of dysfunctional parent, Williams and Corrigan studied 139 college students, who were divided into groups of children of alcoholics (20 students), children of severely mental ill parents (21 students), children of both (22 students), or normal control subjects (76 students). They found that students from either type of dysfunctional family had lower self-esteem, greater depression, and more social anxiety than did "normal" students. Importantly, Williams and Corrigan also found that students who had large and satisfactory support networks showed fewer negative effects of their upbringing than did students without such support groups.[35] Despite the psychological trauma of living with a mentally ill parent, "no empirical research or related type of evidence indicates that children of parents who are mentally ill or mentally retarded are at any greater risk [of parental abuse or neglect] than children in general, although the nature of risks in these populations may be different than in the general population."[36]

Effect of Acute Psychotic Episodes and Chronic Psychoses

During an acute psychotic episode, by definition, reality testing is grossly impaired. Many perceptions and thoughts are incorrectly evaluated, leading to a variety of incorrect actions. There is likely to be withdrawal from what most of us know as "reality." Emotions may be exaggerated and may be labile. The quality of judgment and insight may be minimal. Behavior may be regressed. Thus, during any period when a parent is acutely psychotic, parenting ability is likely to be minimal, the parent focusing on his or her own needs much more than those of others, dealing with his or her own reality rather than external reality, and using all available psychic energy to maintain personal control, with little or none left over for the child.

Between acute psychotic episodes, the parent will do better—with a psychological or psychiatric evaluation being necessary to assess how much better. Particularly with ongoing psychotherapy or counseling, many people can be much more than adequate parents in spite of a history of psychoses. As indicated above, people do not automatically become incompetent as a result of having a mental disorder. Nor do they automatically become inadequate parents, though during the period of acute psychosis parenting ability will likely be at a minimum.

Social worker Bonnie Dunn interviewed nine adults (four men, five women) who had lived with a psychotic mother as children. The interviewees reported five common themes: abuse and neglect, isolation, guilt and loyalty conflicts, grievances regarding mental health services, and lack of social supports. Most of them had feared physical harm as children. Some of them thought their perceived social isolation and alienation was due to something they had done themselves. Some of the isolation was self-imposed due to unwillingness to talk about what occurred at home, either out of loyalty to their mothers or out of a feeling of humiliation or shame regarding their families. They also reported confusion regarding the marked differences between their worlds at home and the outside world. Statements regarding guilt and loyalty conflicts were pervasive in the comments these children of psychotic mothers made.[37]

---

[35] *Id.* at 412.

[36] Grisso at 72.

[37] Bonnie Dunn, *Growing Up with a Psychotic Mother: A Retrospective Study*, 63 Am. J. Orthopsychiatry 177–89 (1993).

Psychiatrists Laura Miller and Molly Finnerty studied the child rearing of 46 women who were diagnosed with Schizophrenia or Schizoaffective Disorder, who were compared with a matched control group. They found that the women with Schizophrenia-spectrum disorders had far more difficulty with parenting than did the controls, and that these women were significantly less likely to have someone helping them with child care. They were also more likely to have experienced loss of their children through either a formal transfer of custody or an informal arrangement. "A majority of the women with Schizophrenia-spectrum disorders reported having been unable to meet their children's basic needs."[38]

Social workers Carol Mowbray, Daphna Oyserman, Judith Zemencuk, and Scott Ross reviewed published research on mothers with a "serious mental illness"—that is, a chronic psychosis. They found that research indicates that the severity of a psychosis correlates strongly with difficulty in parenting, and that depression in new mothers is higher when they have fewer resources and less assistance with child care. Resource problems include having few social supports, being at a low socioeconomic status, being vulnerable to discrimination in jobs and housing, being sexually victimized, and having to deal with the stigma of mental illness. While many of the mothers were in treatment, the treatment seldom focused on issues related to parenting.[39] In a later article, Oyserman, Mowbray, Meares, and Firminger indicated that the likelihood that children of parents with Schizophrenia or an affective disorder will themselves have a diagnosable disorder is 32 to 56 percent, with the understanding that some is passed on genetically and some via the environment within which they are raised. For individual disorders, they indicated that the likelihood of Bipolar Disorder in the child of a parent with the disorder is 80 percent, for Schizophrenia is 75 percent, and for depression is 34 to 48 percent. Clearly, genetics plays a significant factor.[40] Oyserman *et al.* also indicate that there is a complex interaction among the developmental status of the child, the type, severity, and frequency of the parent's disorder, and the context in which the parenting takes place (economic, social, family, and so forth). Women who are highly motivated to be good parents tend to remain in treatment, and to parent their children better overall. On the other hand, children of mothers with Schizophrenia, on average, did not parent well. The key factors include chronicity (for example, time the mother spent in the hospital) and the quality of the interaction between maternal and child behavior. Mothers who were highly motivated who did not spend much time hospitalized, and who had children who behaved relatively well, did a relatively good job of parenting, especially if supported by a husband and/or other adults. "Because separations from children may be particularly damaging, community-based treatment should be used to mediate the effects of stressors on mothers with" serious mental illness.[41] The greater the stress, the worse the parenting, on average, with social support helping to reduce negative effects.

---

[38] Laura J. Miller & Molly Finnerty, *Sexuality, Pregnancy, and Childrearing among Women with Schizophrenia-Spectrum Disorders*, 47 Psychiatric Serv. 502, 504 (1996).

[39] Carol T. Mowbray et al., *Motherhood for Women with Serious Mental Illness: Pregnancy, Childbirth, and the Postpartum Period*, 65 Am. J. Orthopsychiatry 21, 31–33 (1995).

[40] Daphna Oyserman, Carol T. Mowbray, Paula Allen Meares, & Kirsten B. Firminger, *Parenting among Mothers with a Serious Mental Illness*, 70 Am. J. Orthopsychiatry 296–315 (2000) [hereinafter Oyserman (2000)].

[41] *Id.* at 309.

In a 2003 study, some of the same researchers found that current symptoms of mental illness were the largest factor, but that the actual parenting ability was also significantly mediated by financial factors, social support, and involvement in mental health services. Diagnosis and history of substance abuse had relatively little relevance once the above factors were accounted for. It was also found that women who had been mentally ill for at least five years tended to function better, having come to terms with their disorders and having support mechanisms in place in needed areas. Women with Schizoaffective Disorders tended to be more impaired than mothers with Schizophrenia or a Bipolar Disorder.[42]

Barry Ackerson also reports that attachment research indicates that the severity and chronicity of the mother's disorder is more important than is her diagnosis. In particular, frequency of relapse had a significant negative affect on attitude toward parenting.[43]

In one of the few longitudinal studies of children of schizophrenic mothers ever done, 50 children of schizophrenic mothers were studied over a period of 25 years. Half of the children were raised by their mothers and half were raised by foster parents with no psychiatric history. The researchers found a slightly higher incidence of psychopathology in the children not raised by their own mothers, while children raised by their schizophrenic mothers evidence a slightly higher level of psychosocial functioning. Twelve of the children raised by their own mothers had no evident psychopathology, while only seven of the children who were adopted have no evident psychopathology. The greater prevalence of children with psychopathology in the non-mother-raised group may have been due to a greater genetic predisposition. Although this was a small study, it clearly demonstrated that being raised by a mother who is chronically mentally ill does not necessarily lead to psychopathology in the child.[44]

Teresa Jacobsen, Laura Miller, and Kathleen Kirkwood indicate that methodological problems in assessing parenting skills of parents with "severe mental illnesses" include the fact that some evaluations focus on optimal parenting skills rather than simply adequate skills, that most instruments for evaluating parenting were not validated on parents with severe mental disorders (and, therefore, did not take into consideration the influence of major tranquilizers on affective expression, among other problems), and that a person with a mental disorder may do very well in one context but very poorly in another—while the assessment typically involves an observation in only a single context.

To remedy these problems, Jacobsen and her colleagues recommend that, when one or both parents have a serious mental illness, the evaluation contain at least the following elements:

(1) Observation of parent and child(ren) in more than one setting, including assessment of parenting knowledge, skills, and attitudes in the home setting, rather than inferring that information from tests or other indirect sources.

(2) Screening the child(ren) for developmental delays.

---

[42] Deborah Bybee, Carol T. Mowbray, Daphna Oyserman, & Lisa Lewandowski, *Variability in Community Functioning of Mothers with Serious Mental Illness*, 14 J. Behav. Health Services & Res. 269–89 (2003).

[43] Barry J. Ackerson, *Parents with Serious and Persistent Mental Illness: Issues in Assessment and Services*, 48 Soc. Work 187–94 (2003).

[44] J. Higgins, R. Gore, & D. Gutkind, *Effects of Child-rearing by Schizophrenic Mothers: A 25-Year Follow-up*, 96 Acta Psychiatrica Scandinavica 402–04 (1997).

(3) Multiple sources of information should be used, including tests, medical records, hospital records (if any), criminal records (if any), information from the child(ren)'s school, records from therapists, interviews of neighbors, and so forth.

(4) If possible, the evaluation should be conducted by a multidisciplinary team, e.g., psychologist, psychiatrist, and social worker.

(5) The evaluator(s) should have extensive knowledge regarding serious mental illness as well as knowledge regarding healthy and unhealthy development of children.

(6) The criterion should be "adequate parenting," not "optimal parenting."[45]

Further, they indicate that specific risk factors that must be taken into consideration include

(1) Active psychiatric problems, particularly serious psychotic symptoms or mood disorders.

(2) Violent outbursts, denial of need for treatment, threats to harm oneself or a child, and/or denial of problems with parenting.

(3) Alcohol or other drug dependence or abuse.

(4) Whether the parent was abused as a child.

(5) Whether the parent is socially isolated.

(6) Grossly inappropriate notions of child development, particularly if this leads to markedly inappropriate expectations of the child(ren) at any age.

(7) Whether the parent is able to understand the child(ren)'s cues and needs, how secure the parent-child attachment appears to be, whether the child(ren) appear to be taking care of the parent rather than vice versa, and whether the child is scapegoated.

(8) How much stress the parent is under, and whether the parent perceives the child to be a significant cause of stress.

(9) Whether there are significant hazards in the home, e.g., open windows without screens, dangerous items within children's reach (knives, poisons, etc.).

(10) Whether the person has a history of successful treatment with psychotherapy and/or medication, reducing risk from the other factors.[46]

Supportive Services

There are ways to facilitate the ability of mentally ill parents to care for their children. According to a report in the *American Psychological Association Monitor*, a program in California has permitted "mentally handicapped" mothers to live in the community with their children, while receiving various supportive services. Participants in the program are single mothers with disorders such as Schizophrenia, Depression, or Mental Retardation. The women and children live in either a five-bedroom house or a three-bedroom apartment. Staff members and volunteers advise the mothers regarding child development,

---

[45] Teresa Jacobsen et al., *Assessing Parenting Competency in Individuals with Severe Mental Disorders: A Comprehensive Service*, 24 J. Mental Health Admin. 189, 192–94 (1997).

[46] *Id.* at 192.

caring for sick children, medications, and other topics. Both individual psychotherapy and case management are provided, and there is a weekly group problem-solving session. The goal is to move the women and children into individual apartments in the community. In its first two years, the program appeared to be successful at addressing the needs of both the mothers and the children.[47]

§ 14.7 Extent of Neurotic Conditions at Various Points in Time

With regard to nonpsychotic conditions, one must look at the extent of the disorder at any point in time to draw a conclusion about parenting ability. People who are neurotic do not lose touch with reality, so they will generally be at least adequate in dealing with their own real-world needs and those of their children. Under stress, however, these individuals will also demonstrate some loss of parenting ability, though generally not nearly to the degree of someone who has a history of psychotic episodes. It is the task of the psychologist or psychiatrist to assess the individual's functional ability at periods of both high and low stress, and to make recommendations to the court that address that range of parenting ability. As part of this process, the evaluator must determine whether the problems were a function of stress induced by the dysfunctional relationship with the spouse, or a long-standing underlying neurotic process. Many parents have presented themselves as quite psychologically unstable when in a dysfunctional relationship and per-ceiving no solution, only to become substantially more stable when out of the destructive relationship. In others, the symptoms did not disappear at termination of the relationship. It may not be possible for the evaluator to determine which of these is occurring through the usual time-limited evaluation process. As a result, a reasonable approach when there is a significant question about the stability of a parent might be to hold the matter open for six months, to see whether the parent or parents become more stable with time. Even though a six-month wait would add to the stress of the entire divorce matter, this is outweighed by the importance of making sure that the correct decision is made in choosing a custodial parent.

§ 14.8 Personality or Character Disorders

As indicated above, the neurotic individual feels distressed by his or her symptoms and feels such symptoms are alien to the individual's personality. This motivates the neurotic individual to seek treatment. In contrast, the individual with a *personality* or *character dis-order* may or may not feel distress from the symptoms, and finds those symptoms to be *ego-syntonic*—that is, acceptable to and consistent with the total personality.[48] The individual is relatively unlikely, therefore, to seek treatment voluntarily. Because the individual does not find the disorder to be unacceptable or inconsistent with his or her personality, he or she has no feelings of significant distress. People with personality or

---

[47] Bazar, *Mentally Ill Moms Aided in Keeping Their Children*, 21 APA Monitor 32 (Dec. 1990).

[48] American Psychiatric Glossary at 32, 59.

character disorders tend to be highly resistant to treatment. Even if these people are required to attend therapy as part of a court order, they are likely to manipulate the process, terminate early, and, in any event, derive little long-term benefit from the therapeutic process.

EFFECTS OF SPECIFIC NONPSYCHOTIC DISORDERS

§ 14.9   Bipolar Disorders

Bipolar Disorders may present with or without evidence of psychosis. If evidence of psychosis is present, the diagnosis has "with psychotic features" added to it. Bipolar Disorders are a

> group of mood disorders that includes Bipolar Disorder, Single Episode; Bipolar Disorder, Recurrent; and Cyclothymic Disorder. A Bipolar Disorder includes a manic episode at some time during its course. In any particular patient, the Bipolar Disorder may take the form of a single manic episode (rare) or it may consist of recurrent episodes that are either manic or depressive in nature (but at least one must have been predominantly manic). Bipolar II Disorder is used in . . . DSM-IV . . . to denote a mood disorder characterized by episodes of Major Depressive Disorder and hypomania (rather than full mania).[49]

During the manic episode, which typically lasts at least a week and/or requires hospitalization, the person may become grandiose, believing that he or she has special powers and is of special importance. There is generally a marked reduction in need for sleep, the person may become extremely talkative, thoughts may jump from one topic to another very quickly, the person may become highly distractible, may appear agitated, and/or may focus on pleasurable activities with a significant potential for causing problems—for example, buying sprees or hypersexuality.[50]

Gail Inoff-Germain, Edith D. Nottelmann, and Marian Radke-Yarrow found that mothers with Bipolar Disorder had the most extreme anger scores, mothers with unipolar depression were second, and control mothers had the least. The extreme anger scores were from only 30 percent of the Bipolar Disorder mothers, however; 70 percent showed no significant anger.[51]

Oyserman *et al.* report that mothers with unipolar depression (major depression) had a much more negative impact on their children than did mothers with bipolar disorders.[52]

---

[49] American Psychiatric Glossary at 29.

[50] DSM-IV at 332.

[51] Gail Inoff-Germain, Edith D. Nottelmann, & Marian Radke-Yarrow, *Relation of Parental Affective Illness to Family, Dyadic, and Individual Functioning: An Observational Study of Family Interaction*, 67 Am. J. Orthopsychiatry 433–48 (1997).

[52] Oyserman (2000) at 311.

§ 14.10   Depression

Depression may range from a brief Adjustment Disorder with Depressed Mood (which rarely lasts more than six months) to Dysthymic Disorder (which has lasted at least two years during which the person felt depressed more days than not) to Major Depression (where the depression is generally more severe and is present nearly every day for a period of at least two weeks). People who are depressed have difficulty functioning and may exhibit "feelings of inadequacy, generalized loss of interest or pleasure, social withdrawal, feelings of guilt or brooding about the past, subjective feelings of irritability or excessive anger, and decreased activity, effectiveness or productivity."[53] They may also have difficulty falling asleep, staying asleep, getting a restful night's sleep, and/or getting out of bed in the morning. Their typical difficulty with concentration, slowed thinking, and difficulty making decisions about even minor matters make functioning difficult. They may actively or passively withdraw from the outside world.[54] Most research indicates that children of depressed parents (with most research done on mothers) are generally more at risk than children of any other diagnostic group.

Researchers Jean Dumas and colleagues assessed the relationship between depression in mothers and the behavior of their children, utilizing 51 mother-child dyads. In all cases, the primary reason the children were referred for help was their oppositional, noncompliant, or aggressive behavior at home and the reported difficulty of the mothers in controlling this behavior. In the study, there were 36 male and 15 female children, ranging in age from 2 to 12 years. The researchers found that children diagnosed with conduct disorders whose mothers were depressed were more maladjusted than were children of nondepressed mothers. In addition, they found that these children were *less* deviant toward their mothers when those mothers were depressed, while being as deviant or more deviant toward other people at the same time. They also found that depressed mothers had difficulty paying appropriate attention to their children and difficulty in consistently and appropriately applying rewards and punishments.[55]

Geraldine Downey and James Coyne reviewed the professional literature on the subject of the effect of parental depression on children. First, Downey and Coyne note that there could be a genetic basis for the problem, but its effect is relatively small according to studies of twins and adoptions. They found substantial evidence that

> depression in parents is associated with problems of adjustment and diagnosable disorders, particularly depressive disorders, in their children. . . . The evidence at this point supports the tentative conclusion that an increase in diagnosable depression is specific to the children of depressed parents, but that more general problems in adjustment are shared with children of mothers with a physical illness or a psychiatric condition other than depression and of mothers who are otherwise under stress. In particular, marital discord is a

---

[53] DSM-IV at 346.

[54] Angus S. McDonald & Graham C.L. Davey, *Psychiatric Disorders and Accidental Injury*, 16 Clinical Psychol. Rev. 105, 119–20 (1996).

[55] Jean Dumas et al., *Behavioral Correlates of Maternal Depressive Symptomatology in Conduct-Disorder Children*, 57 J. Consulting & Clinical Psychol. 516 (1989).

viable alternative explanation for the general adjustment difficulties of children with a depressed parent.[56]

The problem with depressed mothers, they indicate, is that "depressed mothers emit lower rates of behavior and show constricted affect; they adopt less-effortful control strategies; and they show considerable hostility and negativity."[57] The result, the research indicates, is that children with depressed mothers tend to have greater levels of treatment for psychological problems, greater levels of functional impairment, deficits in social and academic competence that are not a result of lower intelligence, and poorer physical health than children of control-group parents.[58]

Constance Hammen, Dorli Burge, and Cheri Adrian did a three-year longitudinal study of diagnoses of mothers and children. Their sample included 90 children, including 22 who were children of depressed mothers and 15 who were children of bipolar mothers. Eighteen were the children of mothers with chronic medical illnesses, and 35 were children of "normal" mothers. The researchers found that "both for children's diagnoses overall, and specifically for diagnoses of major depression, the majority occurred in proximity to maternal episodes."[59] Only one of 11 children diagnosed to have a major depression did not become depressed about the time his or her mother was similarly diagnosed. "There [also] clearly appeared to be instances where the mother's episode followed that of the child (or both diagnoses might be associated with stressful events experienced by both)."[60] Part of the cause for the temporal relationship between children's and mother's diagnoses of depression, Hammen and her colleagues suggest, is that the mother may be psychologically unavailable to the child while the child is undergoing significant stress and especially in need of parental support. This factor may trigger a depression in the child, who urgently needs the parent to buffer the stress.[61] Finally, the researchers found that "children were more depressed when they experienced the combination of stressful events and maternal disorders. Youngsters who had high levels of stressors but whose mothers were not symptomatic did not become especially depressed, consistent with a stress-buffering effect of support."[62]

Laura Mufson and her colleagues studied the transmission of major depression and anxiety disorders between parents and children. Subjects were 214 children from 89 families, ages 6 to 23. The researchers found that

> children of parents with major depression with and without panic disorder are more impaired, receive more psychiatric treatment, and have more psychiatric diagnoses than children of parents with other psychiatric disorders or no psychiatric disorders. These results cannot be

---

[56] Geraldine Downey & James Coyne, *Children of Depressed Parents: An Integrative Review*, 108 Psychol. Bull. 50, 68 (1990).

[57] *Id.* at 68.

[58] *Id.* at 56.

[59] Constance Hammen et al., *Timing of Mother and Child Depression in a Longitudinal Study of Children at Risk*, 59 J. Consulting & Clinical Psychol. 341–45 (1991).

[60] *Id.* at 344.

[61] *Id.*

[62] *Id.* at 345.

explained by differences in IQ, school problems, age and sex or the child, or number of diagnoses.[63]

Paige Ouimette and her colleagues studied adolescent children of parents with unipolar affective disorder (depression).

> The results indicate that the adolescent offspring of parents with unipolar affective illness, chronic medical conditions, and normal controls are similar on a range of measures assessing neuroticism, introversion, dependency, self-criticism, constraint, obsessionality, emotional expressiveness, affective intensity, and attributional style. . . . These findings fail to support the role of personality traits as potential vulnerability markers in the offspring of depressed patients.[64]

Vicky Phares and Bruce Compas, in a review article addressing the role of fathers, concluded that "overall, there does not appear to be a strong link between paternal factors and childhood depression. Instead, there appears to be a somewhat stronger association between maternal characteristics and childhood depression than between paternal characteristics and childhood depression."[65] It has also been found that fathers of suicidal children tend to be more depressed and less happy with time spent with the family and spouse than is the case for fathers of normal children. Compared with fathers of nonsuicidal psychiatrically disturbed children, fathers of suicidal children tend to have a greater incidence of physically abusive behavior toward both children and spouses.[66]

Mary Chiariello and Helen Orvaschel reviewed research reports on the relationship between depression in parents and depression and other problems in children. They found that

> both depressed parents and parents of depressed children tend to communicate in a negative, critical, and hostile manner with their offspring. This type of parenting style impairs the development of healthy self-esteem in children and affects the way that children learn to communicate with others. . . . Even after the depression remits, chronic maladaptive patterns of relating persist, thereby potentiating recurrent episodes of depression.[67]

Gale Inoff-Germain, Editha Nottelmann, and Marian Radke-Yarrow studied 41 families in which the mother had an affective disorder, including 26 that had a father with a psychiatric history. They indicate that "[p]arental affective illness is known to place children at risk for maladaptive behavior and the presence of a diagnosable disorder."[68] Mothers in

---

[63] Laura Mufson et al., *Depression and Anxiety in Parents and Children: A Direct Interview Study*, 6 J. Anxiety Disorders 1, 1–2 (1992).

[64] Paige Ouimette et al., *Personality Traits in Offspring of Parents with Unipolar Affective Disorder: An Exploratory Study*, 6 J. Personality Disorders 91, 95–96 (1992).

[65] Vicky Phares & Bruce Compas, *The Role of Fathers in Child and Adolescent Psychopathology: Make Room for Daddy*, 111 Psychol. Bull. 387, 392 (1992) [hereinafter Phares & Compas].

[66] *Id.* at 393.

[67] Mary A. Chiariello & Helen Orvaschel, *Patterns of Parent-Child Communication: Relationship to Depression*, 15 Clinical Psychol. Rev. 395, 405 (1995).

[68] Gale Inoff-Germain et al., *Relation of Parental Affective Illness to Family, Dyadic, and Individual Functioning: An Observational Study of Family Interaction*, 67 Am. J. Orthopsychiatry 433, 443 (1997).

all three groups were able to be supportive to their children. However, for the mothers with unipolar depression this appeared to be in response to their own neediness rather than suggesting a positive parent-child relationship. The younger children of unipolar depressed mothers showed the most sadness and excess of anger. Despite the problems exhibited by mothers with both types of depression, many depressed mothers were able to function adequately and to provide competent parenting.

A study by Tytti Solantaus-Simula, Raija-Leena Punamaki, and William R. Beardsley found that 60 percent of the 990 children of depressed parents studied tended to attempt to cheer up their parents and felt empathy for their parents. Girls were more likely than boys to cheer up their parents. About 15 percent of depressed mothers and 10 percent of depressed fathers felt guilty. Boys were less likely to worry about their parents than were girls. A question was raised regarding whether, rather than parental depression *per se*, it was the parental irritability and excess criticism that led to negative effects for the children.[69]

A book entitled *Children of Depressed Parents*, edited by Sherryl H. Goodman and Ian H. Gotlib, adds to the database of information relevant to child custody evaluations. Among the findings of the chapter authors' research are the following:

1. A study by Karlen Lyone-Ruth, Amy Lyubchik, Rebecca Wolfe, and Elisa Bronfman indicated that there is mixed evidence regarding the effect of parental depression on the security of a young child's (infant to preschool) attachment to that parent. They identified two independent patterns of parenting by depressed parents that produced different results. In the first, the parents tended to be "negative, intrusive, and role-reversing." These parents displayed overt negativity, were demanding, and did relatively little caretaking of their children, while accepting caretaking from their children. In the second, parents evidenced a reduction in the rate of positive behavior toward the child, but without increased negative interactions. These parents were also relatively withdrawn. Young children of both types of parents tended to evidence disorganized attachments, but boys tended to reflect the type of parental behavior (confrontative or withdrawing), while girls tended to withdraw in both situations.

Two other important conclusions came from these researchers. The first was that parent-child interactions were more strongly influenced by the type of parenting the parent received than by the current psychiatric diagnosis. The second is that the problematic interactions between parent and child did not end with remission of the depressive episodes. Both of these conclusions strongly endorse the need for parents with depression to learn better parenting techniques.[70]

2. Constance Hammen addressed the role of stress in families with depressed parents. Regardless of how it is displayed, parental depression is a form of stress both directly and through its impact on marital, occupational and financial aspects of the family. Children old enough to provide some caretaking of the depressed parent tend to do so. There is a

---

[69] Tytti Solantaus-Simula, Raija-Leena Punamaki, & William R. Beardsley, *Children's Responses to Low Parental Mood. I. Balancing between Active Empathy, Overinvolvement, Indifference, and Avoidance*, 41 J. Am. Acad. Child & Adolescent Psychiatry 278–86 (2002).

[70] Karlen Lyone-Ruth, Amy Lyubchik, Rebecca Wolfe, & Elisa Bronfman, *Parental Depression and Child Attachment: Hostile and Helpless Profiles of Parent and Child Behavior among Families at Risk, in* Sherryl H. Goodman & Ian H. Gotlib eds., Children of Depressed Parents 89–120 (American Psychological Ass'n 2002).

positive correlation between the chronicity of parental depression and the negative affect of the depression on the child. There is some evidence that the negative affect of depression on children may be due to marital discord as much as to the depression itself. Research indicates that depressed women tend to marry men who have psychiatric disorders, complicating the attempt to isolate the effect of depression on children. Further, acute stress affects both parents and children, and in families with one or both parents having a psychiatric disorder stress is relatively likely to be common. These parents may also have difficulty modeling appropriate ways of coping with stress.[71]

3. Following up on her earlier research on fathers, Vicky Phares and colleagues Amy Duhig and Monica Watkins found that depression in fathers is generally less negative for a child than depression in mothers, but it does have an identifiable negative effect. Further, families with either parent having a psychiatric disorder are likely to be less stable, adaptable, cohesive, and caretaking, increasing the potential for a breakup of the marriage. As would be expected, older children are less affected by parental depression and discord, on average, as are children who have an easy temperament and relatively high intelligence, and children with good social skills. Boys tend to be less affected than are girls. Protective factors for children include having at least one sibling who is functioning well, having a warm, close relationship with one parent or parent-substitute, one or both parents exhibiting an authoritative (rather than authoritarian or permissive) parenting style, and being part of a supportive family network. They also note that even when the father is depressed, he is often not involved in therapy received by the child, though the child's need for therapy may involve the relationship with the father.[72]

4. Supporting findings of Lyone-Ruth *et al.*, above, Bruce Compas, Adela Langrock, Garry Keller, Mary Jane Merchant, and Mary Ellen Copeland found that parental intrusiveness and parental withdrawal are the two major patterns among depressed parents. A given parent will often exhibit both patterns, withdrawing while acutely depressed and becoming intrusive in a "worried and hostile manner" when less depressed. Children of these parents have difficulty predicting what the depressed parent will be like on a given day, have increased stress from the uncertainties of family life, and are relatively likely to exhibit anxiety and/or depression. Particularly younger children adapt to the vicissitudes of family life, finding that they are unable to change the aversive aspects of the home life.[73]

5. Tracy Gladstone and William Beardslee addressed the interaction of parental depression and children's developmental stages. They concluded that

> [p]arental depression affects children differently at each developmental stage. During infancy, maternal depression has been found to interfere with children's internal and social goals and

---

[71] Constance Hammen, *Context of Stress in Families of Children with Depressed Parents, in* Sherryl H. Goodman & Ian H. Gotlib eds., Children of Depressed Parents 175–99 (American Psychological Ass'n 2002).

[72] Vicky Phares, Amy M. Duhig, & M. Monica Watkins, *Family Context: Fathers and Other Supports, in* Sherryl H. Goodman & Ian H. Gotlib eds., Children of Depressed Parents 203–25 (American Psychological Ass'n 2002).

[73] Bruce Compas, Adela Langrock, Garry Keller, Mary Jane Merchant, & Mary Ellen Copeland, *Children Coping with Parental Depression: Processes of Adaptation to Family Stress, in* Sherryl H. Goodman & Ian H. Gotlib eds., Children of Depressed Parents 227–52 (American Psychological Ass'n 2002).

with their regulation of emotion and attention. During toddlerhood, maternal depression has been associated with insecure attachment and with deficits in socioemotional development. During adolescence, maternal depression has been associated with negative self-concept and the use of poor interpersonal strategies.[74]

In summary, parents—and particularly mothers—who are depressed are not very available to the child, physically or psychologically, during the depressive episode, and the child is likely to feel significant stress as a result. The younger the child, the more significant this effect is likely to be. The attorney and the evaluator should consider the affect of the parent's divorce-caused depression on the child(ren) when evaluating the case, and try to separate that precipitant of depression from the depression otherwise evidenced by the parent.

§ 14.11   Anxiety Disorders

Anxiety is

> apprehension, tension, or uneasiness from anticipation of danger, the source of which is largely unknown or unrecognized. Primarily of intrapsychic origin, in distinction to fear, which is the emotional response to a consciously recognized and usually external threat or danger. May be regarded as pathologic when it interferes with effectiveness in living, achievement of desired goals or satisfaction, or reasonable emotional comfort.[75]

Types of anxiety include Panic Disorder, Agoraphobia, Specific Phobia, Social Phobia, Obsessive-Compulsive Disorder, Post-traumatic Stress Disorder, Acute Stress Disorder, Generalized Anxiety Disorder, Anxiety Disorder Due to a General Medical Condition, and Substance-Induced Anxiety Disorder. It is also not extraordinary for anxiety and depression to be diagnosed in the same individual.

Research has indicated that people with high anxiety levels have less working memory and less attentional capacity. This appears to be due to their inclination to worry a great deal and/or their vigilance for potential danger.[76] Both the decrease in working memory and the limited attentional capacity would be expected to have an adverse impact upon the children of such individuals.

Researchers Samuel Turner and colleagues compared children of parents with anxiety disorders (16 subjects), children of parents with dysthymic (depressed) disorders (14 subjects), children of parents with no identifiable psychiatric disorders (13 subjects), and 16 children directly assessed to have no psychiatric disorders. Compared with normal children, the researchers found that the children of parents with anxiety disorders had the

---

[74] Tracy Gladstone & William Beardslee, *Treatment, Intervention, and Prevention with Children of Depressed Parents: A Developmental Perspective, in* Sherryl H. Goodman & Ian H. Gotlib, eds., Children of Depressed Parents 277–305, at 299 (American Psychological Ass'n 2002).

[75] American Psychiatric Glossary at 18.

[76] Angus S. McDonald & Graham C.L. Davey, *Psychiatric Disorders and Accidental Injury*, 16 Clinical Psychol. Rev. 105, 119 (1996).

greatest psychopathology, including more difficulty at school, fewer friendships, more time spent in solitary activities, more specific fears, more worries about family members and themselves, more depressed and anxious moods, more bodily complaints, and more episodes of confused thinking. They compared slightly more positively with the children of normal parents. Compared with the children of dysthymic parents, they reported more difficulties at school and more time in solitary activities as the only two significant differences.[77]

§ 14.12   Eating Disorders

"Eating disorders" primarily refers to two specific diagnoses, Anorexia Nervosa and Bulimia Nervosa. The former involves the person's refusal to maintain even minimally-normal nutrition and body weight, and extreme fear of gaining weight. The latter involves eating binges coupled with inappropriate means of losing weight such as self-induced vomiting and/or use of laxatives, diuretics, and enemas.[78]

A small study (five mothers, six children) by researchers Christopher Fairburn and Alan Stein of women with severe Bulimia Nervosa found that, in each instance, the mother's unhealthy eating habits and attitudes interfered with parenting. The disorder involves repeated cycles of binge eating, followed by vomiting, laxative abuse, or severe dieting. Three of the women admitted to ignoring their children for lengthy periods during binge/vomit cycles of up to seven times daily. Some kept so little food in the house, or had eaten so much of the children's food, that they had difficulty feeding the children. All of the mothers had trouble breast-feeding. Three of the six children had serious feeding problems.[79]

In their 1992 review article, Phares and Compas indicate that parents of children with eating disorders tend to be less supportive and nurturing than are parents of normal children.[80]

Tessa Leverton reports in an article that some women who have Anorexia Nervosa underfeed their children. It is therefore important to assess whether this is occurring if a parent in a child custody evaluation has this disorder.[81]

§ 14.13   Borderline Personality Disorder

According to DSM-IV, *Borderline Personality Disorder* (BPD) is "a pervasive pattern of instability of mood, interpersonal relationships, self-image, and affects, and

---

[77] Samuel Turner et al., *Psychopathology in the Offspring of Anxiety Disorder Patients*, 55 J. Consulting & Clinical Psychol. 229, 232 (1987).

[78] DSM-IV at 539–46.

[79] Christopher Fairburn & Alan Stein, *Bulimia Nervosa May Interfere with Parenting*, 18 Clinical Psychiatry News 12 (Feb. 1990).

[80] Phares & Compas at 394.

[81] Tessa J. Leverton, *Parental Psychiatric Illness: The Implications for Children*, 16 Current Opinion in Psychiatry 395–402 (2003).

marked impulsivity that begins by early adulthood," as indicated by five or more of the following criteria:[82]

(1)   frantic efforts to avoid real or imagined abandonment . . .

(2)   a pattern of unstable and intense interpersonal relationships characterized by alternating between extremes of idealization and devaluation

(3)   identity disturbance: markedly and persistently unstable self-image or sense of self

(4)   impulsivity in at least two areas that are potentially self-damaging (e.g., spending, sex, substance abuse, reckless driving, binge eating) . . .

(5)   recurrent suicidal behavior, gestures, or threats, or self-mutilating behavior

(6)   affective instability due to a marked reactivity of mood (e.g., intense episodic dysphoria, irritability, or anxiety usually lasting a few hours and only rarely more than a few days)

(7)   chronic feelings of emptiness

(8)   inappropriate, intense anger or difficulty controlling anger . . .

(9)   transient, stress-related paranoid ideation or severe dissociative symptoms.

According to John Gunderson:

> When the borderline person feels himself or herself to be in a supportive relationship to another person . . . , he or she is likely to experience sustained dysphoria and a lack of self-satisfaction, and to display an engaging, but clinging, dependent personal style. When such a relationship is disrupted by the threat of separation or the withdrawal of reassuring nurturance, an angry, hostile affect takes over, accompanied by highly characteristic manipulative, self-destructive acts. . . . Borderline patients can also develop psychotic ideation. . . . It is by far the most common form of personality disorder. Approximately two-thirds . . . of patients with BPD are female.[83]

The most accepted conceptualization of the genesis of BPD involves the infant or small child trying to form a consistent relationship with a parent, usually the mother, whose behavior is highly erratic, sometimes clinging, sometimes withdrawing and rejecting. The child is very confused, desperately needing the parent and at the same time being extremely angry at the rejection. The child learns to perceive the world as unpredictable and frightening. To give some order to the world, the child divides it into "good" and "bad," a process known as "splitting," with no shades of gray. One result is that these individuals generally lack an ability to empathize or to enter into close relationships. Functioning in the child's family is likely to be characterized by discord, confusion, and conflict.[84] "The result of such parental deprivation is that the child fails to develop a

---

[82] DSM-IV at 650.

[83] John Gunderson, *Borderline Personality Disorder, in* Comprehensive Textbook of Psychiatry/V 1387, 1387–88 (H. Kaplan & B. Sadock eds., 1989) [hereinafter Gunderson].

[84] Everett & Volgy, *Family Assessment and Treatment of Borderline Disorders, in* 10 Innovations in Clinical Prac.: A Source Book 59, 60–61 (P. Keller & S. Heyman eds., 1991); Perry & Vaillant, *Personality Disorders, in* Comprehensive Textbook of Psychiatry/V 1377–78 (H. Kaplan & B. Saddock eds., 1989) [hereinafter Perry & Vaillant].

positive and stable sense of self and becomes unable to feel comfortable in the absence of external supports."[85]

People diagnosed as having a BPD are very likely to have a history of physical or sexual abuse. Among adult women with BPD, studies have reported that between 67 percent and 86 percent have a history of child sexual abuse. Estimates of physical abuse in mixed-gender groups of BPD patients range from 46 percent to 71 percent.[86]

Research has established several characteristics of people with BPD. They are, in order of importance: "intense, unstable interpersonal relationships . . . , repetitive, self-destructive behaviors . . . , chronic abandonment fears . . . , chronic dysphoric affects . . . , cognitive distortions . . . , impulsivity . . . , [and] poor social adaptation."[87]

> When seen in a state of crisis, borderline patients may manifest overwhelming anger, dissociative states, or psychotic and psychotic-like symptoms. Patients are argumentative and demanding and try to make others feel responsible for their troubles. . . . The behavior of borderline patients is highly unpredictable. . . . [They] can express enormous anger at their intimate friends when frustrated. . . . [They] tolerate being alone very poorly and often prefer a frantic search for companionship, no matter how unsatisfactory, to sitting with feelings of loneliness and emptiness.[88]

> The short-term prognosis is poor. Follow-up studies that reassessed BPD individuals more than a decade later found that "considerable numbers of borderline patients move on into stable employment with reduced symptom problems and less need for psychiatric care. . . . A reasonably high percentage of borderline patients marry and establish their own families (roughly 20 to 40 percent). . . . Although interpersonal relations and employment often remain unstable for long periods of time during the young adult years, a substantial number of borderline patients manage to move out of these patterns into more stable, productive, and satisfying work and family lives. . . . A coexisting pattern of alcohol or substance abuse appears to worsen the prognosis.[89]

The attorney who accepts as a client an individual with BPD must be prepared for a difficult attorney-client relationship. Specifically, the attorney should

1. Carefully maintain boundaries—in other words, keep the relationship strictly professional and reasonably structured. Be specific about when it is all right to call the attorney and when it is not. Discourage calls to the attorney at home. Have all meetings at the attorney's office (no lunch or dinner meetings at restaurants; no meetings at the client's home or office).

2. Be prepared for the client to berate the attorney for real or imagined wrongs, personal or professional. People with BPD generally have great difficulty with trust and react strongly to perceived breaches of trust.

3. Expect a client with BPD to accuse the attorney of abandoning the client or the case at any point at which things are not going extremely well or even if the

---

[85] Gunderson at 1389.

[86] Shearer et al., *Frequency Correlates of Childhood Sexual and Physical Abuse Histories in Adult Female Borderline Inpatients*, 147 Am. J. Psychiatry 214, 214 (1990).

[87] Gunderson at 1390–91.

[88] Perry & Vaillant at 1378.

[89] Gunderson at 1393–94.

attorney is unable to return a phone call within minutes, due to the client's fear of abandonment.

4. Expect to be called "the best lawyer ever" one day but called the worst lawyer in history the next. Individuals with BPD tend to see the people involved in their lives as either wonderful or terrible.

5. Expect suicide threats and possibly gestures, since people with BPD tend to see suicide as a way to end their psychological pain.

6. Expect to have the client show a wide range of strong emotions, from great happiness to rage—sometimes within the same hour.

7. Expect the client to be very suspicious of the attorney's motives and behavior.

The final task for the attorney (and staff of the attorney's office) is to keep from being "sucked in." In other words, they should not take it personally when the client either gets angry and yells at them or tells them how fantastic they are. If the client tries to make the relationship personal rather than strictly professional, maintain professional boundaries. Do not overreact to suicide threats. And do not lose your cool just because the client has temporarily lost his or hers.

If the attorney has reason to believe that a client has a Borderline Personality Disorder, it would be a very good idea to have an evaluation by a psychologist or psychiatrist to establish this diagnosis. If it is established, the attorney will need that professional to help identify which of the client's characteristics are probably due to the preexisting personality disorder and which are the result of events leading up to the divorce or caused by the stress of the divorce process. Attorneys may also want to require that such a client be in psychotherapy during the entire lawsuit to try to ensure that a psychologist or psychiatrist is helping the person deal with issues related to the personality disorder—and helping the attorney deal with the difficult task of having someone with a Borderline Personality Disorder as a client.

§ 14.14   Antisocial Personality Disorder

Referred to as "psychopathy," "sociopathy," or "dyssocial" in the past, Antisocial Personality Disorder is characterized by

> a pervasive pattern of disregard for, and violation of, the rights of others. . . . Deceit and manipulation are central features. . . . [Individuals with the disorder may] fail to conform to social norms with respect to lawful behavior . . . , disregard the wishes, rights or feelings of others . . . , [may show a] pattern of impulsivity . . . manifested by a failure to plan ahead . . . [and] without consideration for the consequences to self or others. . . . [They] tend to be irritable and aggressive and may repeatedly get into physical fights or commit acts of physical assault (including spouse beating or child beating). . . . [They may] display a reckless disregard for the safety of themselves or others . . . , [and] may neglect or fail to care for a child in a way that puts the child in danger. . . . [They] tend to be consistently and extremely irresponsible . . . [and] show little remorse for the consequences of their acts. . . . They generally fail to compensate or make amends for their behavior.[90]

---

[90] DSM-IV at 645–46.

In addition, they have difficulty learning from experience, causing them to be involved in a disproportionate number of accidents of many types. It is possible that they have difficulty being able to foresee the potential results of their behavior.[91] Their potential to harm their children includes both the increased potential for accidental injuries or neglect and the potential for child abuse of many types. Most criminals are considered to have Antisocial Personality Disorders. See **Chapter 16** for a discussion regarding people with criminal histories.

People with Antisocial Personality Disorders will tend to try to manipulate the attorney and the case. They may lie in order to try to ensure that they win custody, primary placement, and a disproportionate share of the marital property. They may place the child or children in jeopardy of physical and/or emotional damage as a result of their impulsiveness and recklessness as well as their lack of remorse. They are also poor role models. As a result, they may hurt their own cases. It is strongly recommended that an attorney who suspects that a client has an Antisocial Personality Disorder have a psychologist do psychological testing in an effort to identify whether the diagnosis applies and whether there is in fact reason for concern. Having one of these individuals as a client is a case of "lawyer beware."

A study of 1,116 five-year-old twin pairs and their parents by Sara Jaffee, Terrie Moffitt, Avshalom Caspi, and Alan Taylor found that the more time that children lived with fathers who engaged in antisocial behavior the more likely the children were to have conduct problems, while the more time spent living with fathers with little or no antisocial behavior the fewer conduct problems the children had.[92]

§ 14.15   Chronic Fatigue Syndrome and Fibromyalgia

The disorder that is now known as Chronic Fatigue Syndrome (CFS) was once known as neurasthenia, a "lack of nerve strength." The term lost favor by the early 20th century, but interest was revived by the early 1980s by a number of reports about "immunologic disturbances, coupled with the clinical observation that many of these patients developed the syndrome following an episode of acute infectious mononucleosis, [which] led to the specific hypothesis that the illness was a manifestation of chronic Epstein-Barr virus infection."[93] Additional evidence indicated that there are too many cases with no evidence of the Epstein-Barr virus, however.

In 1988, the federal Centers for Disease Control and Prevention (CDC) published a set of diagnostic criteria for a disorder entitled "Chronic Fatigue Syndrome." There were a

---

[91] Angus S. McDonald & Graham C.L. Davey, *Psychiatric Disorders and Accidental Injury*, 16 Clinical Psychol. Rev. 105, 117 (1996).

[92] Sara R. Jaffee, Terrie E. Moffitt, Avshalom Caspi, & Alan Taylor, *Life with (or without) Father: The Benefits of Living with Two Biological Parents Depend on the Father's Antisocial Behavior*, 74 Child Dev. 109–26 (2003) [hereinafter Jaffee et al. (2003)].

[93] Mark A. Demitrack & Susan E. Abbey, *Historical Overview and Evolution of Contemporary Definitions of Chronic Fatigue States, in* Chronic Fatigue Syndrome: An Integrative Approach to Evaluation and Treatment 3, 21 (Mark A. Demitrack & Susan E. Abbey eds., 1996) [hereinafter Demitrack & Abbey].

number of problems with the criteria, and revised criteria were issued in 1994. The criteria include

> [c]linically evaluated, unexplained, persistent or relapsing chronic fatigue ([of at least] 6 months' duration) that is of new or definite onset (has not been lifelong); is not the result of ongoing exertion; is not substantially alleviated by rest; and results in substantial reduction in previous levels of occupational, educational, social, or personal activities.[94]

In addition, "four or more of the following symptoms are concurrently present" for at least six months:

1. Impaired memory or concentration
2. Sore throat
3. Tender cervical or axillary lymph nodes
4. Muscle pain
5. Multijoint pain
6. New headaches
7. Unrefreshing sleep
8. Post-exertion malaise.[95]

This was differentiated from "Idiopathic Chronic Fatigue," which was defined as "clinically evaluated, unexplained chronic fatigue ([of at least] 6 months' duration) that fails to meet the definition for Chronic Fatigue Syndrome."[96]

Exclusionary clinical diagnoses included "any active medical condition that could explain the chronic fatigue"; "any previously diagnosed medical condition whose resolution has not been documented beyond reasonable clinical doubt and whose continued activity may explain the chronic fatiguing illness"; "Psychotic Major Depression; Bipolar Affective Disorder; Schizophrenia; Delusional Disorders; Dementias; Anorexia Nervosa; Bulimia Nervosa"; "Alcohol or other substance abuse within 2 years prior to the onset of the chronic fatigue and at any time afterward."[97]

By 1990, it was evident that Chronic Fatigue Syndrome shared some characteristics with other "chronic, idiopathic illnesses," particularly fibromyalgia, "a debilitating clinical condition characterized by widespread musculoskeletal pain," with common symptoms including "fatigue, sleep disturbance, headache, depression, anxiety, and paresthesias" ["abnormal tactile sensation, often described as burning, pricking, tickling, tingling, or creeping"].[98] "Further complicating the clinical picture is the observation that

---

[94] Demitrack & Abbey at 26 (quoting from Centers for Disease Control & Prevention, Chronic Fatigue Syndrome (1994)).

[95] Id.

[96] Id.

[97] Demitrack & Abbey at 26.

[98] www.mayoclinic.com, accessed Aug. 25, 2004.

Fibromyalgia, like Chronic Fatigue Syndrome, often develops in the aftermath of an acute stressor, either physical (e.g., accidents or infections) or emotional."[99]

The American College of Rheumatology defined the criteria for fibromyalgia in 1990, which include pain in response to pressure at 11 or more of 18 specific parts of the body, as well as requiring that widespread pain have been present for at least three months. Previous names for fibromyalgia include fibrositis, chronic muscle pain syndrome, psychogenic rheumatism, and tension myalgia. While symptoms wax and wane, fibromyalgia is not progressive or crippling, and is not life-threatening.[100]

Common symptoms and signs of fibromyalgia include pain in a number of areas of the body, significant fatigue and disturbance of sleep, constipation and/or diarrhea, chronic headaches, facial pain, depression, numbness or tingling in feet and/or hands, and difficulty concentrating. Most victims are women, and most are between 20 and 60 years old.[101]

An estimated 50 to 85 percent of CFS patients complain of impaired cognitive functioning. Neuropsychologist Jordan Grafman reviewed the published research. He found that most CFS patients complain of deficits such as impaired memory, attention, concentration, and problem solving as well as complaints of emotional distress. Neuropsychological research has identified some deficits in memory, attention, and response speed, but most deficits are relatively mild, while CFS patients typically describe their degree of impairment as severe.[102]

Anthony Komaroff and Laura Fagioli indicate that the most frequent question regarding CFS is whether it is primarily an organic or a psychiatric disorder. They note that it shares symptoms with Depression, Generalized Anxiety Disorder, and Somatization Disorder but also indicate that it can be differentiated from psychiatric disorders in that it has a "sudden onset with an 'infectious-like' syndrome, recurrent fevers, adenopathy, arthralgias, and photophobias."[103] Most studies, they indicate, find that most CFS patients become depressed and anxious after the onset of the disorder. Research also indicates that between 25 and 60 percent of CFS patients evidence no active psychiatric disorder, while 20 to 50 percent of CFS patients had a pre-CFS psychiatric history, and 41 percent of CFS patients have neither a premorbid nor a current psychiatric diagnosis.[104]

In a presentation at the 1997 Convention of the American Psychological Association, Martin Arron indicated that research on prevalence of the disorder has ranged from 2/100,000 to 2,800/100,000, with more recent research tending toward higher prevalence rates. The risk factors for CFS include female gender, stressful life events (both physical and psychological), having a severe infection, vigorous exercise, and having a current or past psychological disorder. Medical studies have found minor abnormalities in muscle

[99] *Id.*

[100] www.rheumatology.org/publications_classification_fibromyalgia/fibro.asp, accessed Aug. 1, 2004.

[101] Demitrack & Abbey at 29.

[102] Jordan Grafman, *Neuropsychological Assessment of Patients with Chronic Fatigue Syndrome, in* Chronic Fatigue Syndrome: An Integrative Approach to Evaluation and Treatment 113–29 (Mark A. Demitrack & Susan E. Abbey eds., 1996).

[103] Anthony L. Komaroff & Laura Fagioli, *Medical Assessment of Fatigue and Chronic Fatigue Syndrome, in* Chronic Fatigue Syndrome: An Integrative Approach to Evaluation and Treatment 154, 161 (Mark A. Demitrack & Susan E. Abbey eds., 1996).

[104] *Id.* at 161–62.

tissue, that patients overestimate their degree of exertion, and that muscular capacity is reduced through inactivity and consequent muscle atrophy. No impairment of global intellectual functioning has been found. Memory is essentially normal but is increasingly vulnerable to interference from environmental events. CFS patients appear to have a slowed rate of information processing. At present, no consistent, all-inclusive biological marker has been identified. MRI and SPECT brain scans have not identified consistent evidence of brain abnormalities. The primary available treatments are exercise therapy and cognitive-behavioral therapy.[105]

A 1997 study by Alicia Deale, Trudie Chalder, Isaac Marks, and Simon Wessely found that 13 sessions of cognitive-behavioral therapy had a significant positive effect for people diagnosed with CFS, compared with a control group taught progressive muscle relaxation, visualization, and rapid relaxation techniques. Seventy percent of the CFS patients improved significantly, while only 19 percent of the control group improved. The improvement remained significant at a six-month follow-up.[106]

A 1997 report indicated that epidemiologists at the CDC placed the prevalence of CFS-like disorders at between 76 and 233 per 100,000 population, a rate far higher than even a few years before that.[107] The authors indicate that

> [p]atients with CFS differ from those with depression by more frequently having severe, debilitating fatigue (100% vs. 28%, respectively); acute onset of the illness (84% vs. 0%, respectively); postexertional malaise (79–87% vs. 19%, respectively); alcohol intolerance (60% vs. 21%, respectively); nausea (58% vs. 16%, respectively); and flu-like symptoms (43–65% vs. 10–22%, respectively). . . . CFS and generalized anxiety disorder share many symptoms (e.g., fatigue, difficulty concentrating, sleep disturbances, etc.), however, the most prominent symptom of generalized anxiety disorder is excessive, persistent worry, whereas the most prominent symptom of CFS is severe, debilitating fatigue. Finally, whereas those with somatization disorder also have multiple somatic complaints, for CFS the primary feature of the illness is fatigue, whereas this is not the case with somatization. . . . [T]here are probably different types of illnesses now contained within the CFS construct.[108]

Treatment for both CFS and fibromyalgia involves anti-inflammatory and pain-reducing medications, antidepressants, muscle relaxants and tranquilizers, and sleeping pills if needed. Psychotherapy frequently helps the individual deal with stress, learning to relax, and addressing the impact of the disorder in everyday life.[109]

While research on the effect of parental Chronic Fatigue Syndrome on children is not yet available, we would expect that it would resemble that of parents with a substantial

---

[105] Martin J. Arron, Chronic Fatigue Syndrome: The Role of Other Psychiatric and Medical Diseases, Paper presented at the 105th Annual Convention of the American Psychological Association, Chicago (Aug. 1997).

[106] Alicia Deale et al., *Cognitive Behavior Therapy for Chronic Fatigue Syndrome: A Randomized Controlled Trial*, 154 Am. J. Psychiatry 408–14 (1997).

[107] Leonard A. Jason et al., *Politics, Science, and the Emergence of a New Disease: The Case of Chronic Fatigue Syndrome*, 52 Am. Psychologist 973, 976 (1997).

[108] *Id.* at 980–81.

[109] www.mayoclinic.com, accessed Aug. 25, 2004.

degree of depression: the parent is not very available to the child, physically or psychologically, and the child is likely to feel significant stress as a result, from the lack of meaningful availability of the parent. The younger the child, the more significant this effect is likely to be. The child is likely to be overburdened by having to care for the parent.

§ 14.16   Munchausen Syndrome by Proxy

See **Chapter 12.**

§ 14.17   Alcohol and Other Drug Abuse

Alcohol and other drug abuse is mentioned at various places in this chapter, noting that alcohol abuse in particular is associated with family disruption. For a further discussion of alcohol and other drug abuse, see **Chapter 15.**

IMPACT OF OTHER FACTORS

§ 14.18   Marital Instability, Depression, and Inconsistent Parenting

It is often difficult to separate such factors as marital instability, depression, inconsistent parenting, and other factors, prompting some research addressing these factors together. In addition to the research discussed under "depression," above, researchers have found the following.

Psychologist Ian Goodyer, in a lengthy review article, focuses on the fact that each of us experiences a multitude of positive and negative interactions with the environment, human and otherwise, from birth on. He indicates that there is evidence that the quality of the relationship with the infant's caretaker in the first year or two of life largely predicts the quality of relationships for at least the next several years, particularly in terms of how secure or insecure the infant is in the relationship with the caretaker(s). Because infant care is still primarily the task of the mother, she can have a profound impact—positive or negative—on how the child functions socially.[110]

Lack of Emotional Support

There is evidence that mothers who lack emotional support (from friends and family) themselves may have diminished ability to care for their children competently. Among

---

[110] Ian Goodyer, *Family Relationships, Life Events and Childhood Psychopathology*, 31 J. Child Psychol. & Psychiatry 161, 168 (1990) [hereinafter Goodyer].

other problems, these women are also relatively likely to suffer from depression. Research is cited indicating that mother-child interactions tend to include more negative transactions (for example, physical smacking and negative verbal criticisms) and fewer positive transactions (for example, smiling and embracing) when the mother is depressed. When the depression is short-term, there may not be impairment of the child's continuity of care. When the depression is long-term, or is accompanied by a personality disorder, the likelihood of impairment is substantially greater.[111] At this point, Goodyer indicates, we do not know whether social, emotional, and cognitive deficits prior to the age of two can be substantially altered by later positive experiences. If maternal depression *does* exert a lasting influence, he indicates, it is likely through alteration of family relations and persistent disruption of parenting competence.[112]

Chronic Family Adversity

Goodyer cites research indicating that "chronic family adversity" is associated with conduct disorders, citing six specific stressors: "(i) father having an unskilled or semi-skilled job; (ii) large family size; . . . (iii) child having been in care; . . . (iv) maternal psychiatric disorders; (v) criminal history in fathers; and (vi) ongoing marital discord."[113] A single one of these factors does not have a significant effect, Goodyer indicates, but two or more together increases the risk by a factor of two to four.

Furthermore, Goodyer indicates that two factors associated with depression and anxiety in children of school age, including adolescents, are mothers who lack intimate relationships with other adults and mothers who report significant emotional problems in themselves. These provide chronic sources of stress for both mother and child. Whether acute or chronic, Goodyer notes, family adversities potentiate one another.[114]

Parenting Styles

In a review article, Coby Gerlsma, Paul Emmelkamp, and Willem Arrindell analyzed the effect of various parenting styles on children's mental disorders. They found that children with phobias tended to have parents who were especially low in showing affection toward their children, while being high in exercising control over these same children.[115]

A report of the work of Ariel Stravynski indicates that patients with avoidant personality disorders were relatively likely to see their parents as shaming, guilt-engendering, and intolerant. These patients also saw their parents as relatively low in showing affection; however, there was no difference from normals in perception of parental overcontrol.[116]

---

[111] *Id.*

[112] *Id.* at 169.

[113] *Id.* at 171.

[114] *Id.* at 172.

[115] Coby Gerlsma et al., *Anxiety, Depression, and Perception of Early Parenting: A Meta-Analysis,* 10 Clinical Psychol. Rev. 251–77 (1990).

[116] *Parenting Style May Help Foster Avoidant Personality in Child,* 18 Clinical Psychiatry News 15 (1990) (no author indicated).

Separation of Child and Parent

Although brief separations generally have no long-term effect on children, long-term or frequent separation of child and parents may have. Particularly for small children, absence of the primary caretaking parent may have a major, long-term impact. If, for example, the parent spends a lengthy period or several shorter periods in a psychiatric facility, this may compound problems engendered by the diminished parenting that likely preceded the hospitalization.

The diminished access of a child to the primary caretaking parent when a sibling is born may also have a significant effect, even in otherwise normal families. The birth of a child is a stressful event for every family member and may precipitate long-term negative consequences. There is evidence, however, that this effect is minimized when the child(ren) have a close, intense relationship with the other parent as well.[117]

Divorce

Divorce, of course, has a negative effect on nearly all family members during its acute phases, and often on a chronic basis as well. See **Chapter 4** for a complete discussion of the effect of divorce on families.

Child's Movement out of the Home

A period with a great potential to positively or negatively impact the child is at the point when the child moves out of the home. In a normal household, the child receives emotional and possibly other support from the parents, in an attempt to make this major transition as smooth as possible. When a parent is dependent on the child, or the child overly dependent on a parent, problems are likely to arise. The parent may not be willing to let go, trying to foster continued dependence. On the other hand, the child may be constantly homesick, unable to break the ties that bind him or her to the home and establish an independent life.[118] For many parents and children, this is the point at which a personality, depressive, or anxiety disorder will first fully bloom.

Other Factors

Sara Gable, Jay Belsky, and Keith Crnic reviewed research on factors that affected the adjustment of children in families. Among the factors they identified were the following:

1. [M]aternal accounts of power imbalance and limited intimacy in the marriage were associated with high levels of anxiety and/or aggression among preschool boys and girls;
2. [D]isagreement between spouses on issues related to parenting was linked with lower levels of ego-control and ego-resilience in the case of preschool boys;

---

[117] Goodyer at 175.

[118] *Id.* at 186–87.

3. [P]atterns of communication observed between spouses-to-be forecasted the attachment security of their preschoolers many years later.

4. Even though not all children exposed to marital discord develop serious behavior problems, the evidence is sufficient to conclude that exposure to marital distress is a stressor that poses risks for children apparently of all ages;

5. [T]he more often toddlers observe episodes of interparental anger, the more insecure and disturbed they behave when exposed to such conflicts;

6. When the topic of the inter-adult conflict is child-related, children are even more likely to respond with bad feelings about the self, helplessness, fear, and dysphoria;

7. [D]isagreements about parenting predicted child behavior problems more strongly than did general indices of marital satisfaction and interspousal conflict;

8. [U]nresolved anger evokes the most negative response and resolved anger elicits the least negative response. Additionally, apology elicits more child involvement in the conflict than does compromise, whereas continued fighting leaves children angrier than does "silent treatment."[119]

PARENTS OF CHILDREN WITH MENTAL DISORDERS

§ 14.19 Parents of Children with Avoidant Personality Disorders

A small study (15 subjects) by researchers Ariel Stravynski, R. Elie, and R.L. Franche found that patients who had an avoidant personality disorder (that is, who actively avoid social contacts and relationships despite a desire for them) perceived their parents as shaming, intolerant, and guilt-engendering. These tactics appear to have been the parents' means of exerting control over their children.[120]

§ 14.20 Parents of Children with Dependent Personality Disorders

Psychologist Robert Bornstein reviewed research on the etiology and other characteristics of people who are highly dependent—that is, those who look to others for help, guidance, and approval. At its extreme, such an individual has a *Dependent Personality Disorder*, "characterized by a lack of self-confidence, a tendency to have others assume responsibility

---

[119] Sara Gable et al., *Marriage, Parenting, and Child Development: Progress and Prospects*, 5 J. Fam. Psychol. 276, 279–80 (1992).

[120] Ariel Stravynski et al., *Parenting Style May Help Foster Avoidant Personality in Child*, 18 Clinical Psychiatry News 15 (Mar. 1990).

for one's life, and subordination of one's needs and wishes to the person(s) on whom one is dependent."[121] Bornstein found that

> [r]esults from studies of infant-parent interactions, investigations of parenting style, and studies of parental perceptions in adult subjects suggest that parental overprotectiveness and authoritarianism may play a significant role in determining level of dependency. Highly consistent results in this area were obtained in independent samples of American . . . , Indian . . . , and British subjects . . . , [attesting] to the robustness and generalizability of these findings. . . . Parental overprotectiveness and authoritarianism may serve simultaneously to reinforce dependent behaviors in children of both sexes and to prevent the child from developing independent, autonomous behaviors (because the parents do not permit the child to engage in the kinds of trial-and-error learning that is involved in developing a sense of independence and mastery during childhood). The results of studies . . . support this hypothesis. . . . It is [also] important to note that dependent behaviors exhibited by the child may also serve to encourage and reinforce overprotective, dependency-fostering behavior in the parents.[122]

§ 14.21   Parents of Children Who Have Conduct Disorders

Conduct Disorders involve a "repetitive and persistent pattern of behavior in which the basic rights of others or major age-appropriate societal norms or rules are violated, as manifested by" such behavior as "aggression to people and animals . . . , destruction of property . . . , deceitfulness or theft . . . , [or] serious violations of rules."[123] Onset may be in childhood or adolescence, and it may lead to an adult diagnosis of Antisocial Personality Disorder, though most children with diagnosed Conduct Disorders do not get so diagnosed.

Researchers Benjamin Lahey and colleagues gave the MMPI to the mothers of 100 outpatient children ages 6 to 13 years, of whom 13 had diagnoses of Conduct Disorder, 22 had diagnoses of Attention Deficit Disorder with Hyperactivity, and 27 had diagnoses of both Conduct Disorder and Attention Deficit Disorder with Hyperactivity. The remaining 38 children had other diagnoses or no diagnosis.

The researchers found that the mothers of children with Conduct Disorders had a significant likelihood of having higher scores than the other mothers on Scales 1 (Hs, mean score = 58.3), 3 (Hy, mean score = 63.5), 4 (Pd, mean score = 66.8), 8 (Sc, mean score = 60.2), and 9 (Ma, mean score = 62.2) of the MMPI. There was no MMPI scale profile that identified mothers of children with Attention Deficit Disorders. Although none of the mean scale scores is above the official cutoff score for psychopathology of 70, Lahey and his colleagues indicate that there is evidence that subtle disturbances in the personalities of mothers of conduct-disordered children are relatively common. The authors also suggest that antisocial behavior by children may relate to the personality makeup of both parents.[124]

---

[121] American Psychiatric Glossary 58 (1994).

[122] Robert Bornstein, *The Dependent Personality: Developmental, Social, and Clinical Perspectives*, 112 Psychol. Bull. 3, 7 (1992).

[123] DSM-IV at 90–91.

[124] Benjamin Lahey et al., *Personality Characteristics of the Mothers of Children with Disruptive Behavior Disorders*, 57 J. Consulting & Clinical Psychol. 512 (1989).

Psychologist John Reid indicates that the strongest predictors of Conduct Disorder are early parenting practices, together with stresses that impinge on the individual and the family. Examples of the latter include marital strife, divorce, number and spacing of children, socioeconomic problems, parental psychopathology, criminal behavior, and drug use. Parenting practices that are problematic include those that involve too little supervision and inappropriate discipline. Reid states, "A number of recent studies indicate that systematic parent training in child management, discipline, and supervision have at least short-term significant effect on child and adolescent conduct problems."[125]

Similarly, Rolf Loeber reports that poor parental child-rearing practices were among the best predictors of antisocial behavior. These practices included poor supervision, parental uninvolvement, and poor modeling via parental criminality and aggressiveness.[126]

Furthermore, there is evidence of a critical period during the first five years of life in which bonding must occur or it may never occur, with the consequence that socialization may never be complete. In addition, children who experienced several forms of deprivation during early childhood (for example, parental divorce or illness, poor physical care, overcrowding, or poor-quality mothering) were relatively likely to be convicted of crimes as adolescents and adults.[127]

Phares and Compas report in their 1992 review article that fathers of children with Conduct Disorder were relatively likely to be alcoholics or to have an Antisocial Personality Disorder, or both. Mothers tended to show higher rates of Antisocial Personality Disorder and depression. Fathers of aggressive children, particularly boys, also tended to be aggressive themselves.[128]

As indicated above under "Antisocial Personality Disorder" parents, children of fathers with Antisocial Personality Disorders are relatively likely to be diagnosed with conduct problems.[129]

OTHER ISSUES

§ 14.22   Role of the Father

Relatively few studies have paid much attention to the role of the father in influencing children's moods and disorders.

Amanda Thomas and Rex Forehand report one of the few research studies to address the effect of the father's mood state on children. Their research involved 115 adolescents (58 female, 57 male), their parents, and their social studies teachers. Neither the adolescents

---

[125] John Reid, *Involving Parents in the Prevention of Conduct Disorder: Rationale, Problems, and Tactics*, 24 Community Psychologist 28, 28 (1991).

[126] Rolf Loeber, *Development and Risk Factors of Juvenile Antisocial Behavior and Delinquency*, 10 Clinical Psychol. Rev. 1, 15–17 (1990).

[127] *Id.* at 27.

[128] Phares & Compas at 390.

[129] Jaffee et al. (2003).

nor the parents were from clinical populations (that is, they were not diagnosed with a depressive or other disorder, nor were they in treatment for any mental disorder). It was found that a strong relationship exists between the depressed mood of the father and adolescent functioning, and that the size of the effect is similar to that resulting when it is the mother who is depressed. It was also found that girls tended to internalize problems when their mothers were depressed, and boys tended to do so when their fathers were depressed. Cognitive performance in school tended to decrease as the father's depression increased for boys, while the opposite occurred for girls. It appears to be important for studies of parental depression to address separately the effect of each parent on children of each gender.[130]

Thomas and Forehand, in another study, explored the influence of married fathers' moods on their adolescent children. It was found that "as fathers' depressed mood was rated higher, adolescents' conduct and anxiety problems were rated higher."[131] Significant additional variance was accounted for when parental conflict was taken into account. The fathers' influence on their adolescents was less for divorced than for still-married fathers.

Psychologist Vicky Phares reports that most children have some contact during their lives with their biological fathers or stepfathers. She notes estimates that

> 67% of U.S. children under 18 years old live with both biological parents . . . , 7% live in stepfamilies . . . , 23% live in single-parent families headed by the mother, and 3% live in single-parent families headed by the father. . . . [Furthermore,] of children who live with their biological mothers, 35% have no contact with their biological fathers, 42% have some contact . . . and 19% have at least weekly contact with their biological fathers. . . . Of children who live with their biological fathers, 19% have no contact with their biological mothers, 54% have some contact, and 22% have at least weekly contact with their biological mothers. . . .[132]

> [In addition, with 60 percent of women with children under 18 working outside the home,] it cannot be assumed that the mother is automatically the primary source of parental influence on children's psychological adjustment.[133]

> It is estimated that only 16% of families in the United States are currently operating within the traditional sex role differentiation in which the father performs solely executive tasks such as wage earning and the mother performs solely nurturing tasks such as homemaking and child rearing.[134]

Furthermore:

> Research has shown that fathers influence their children in ways that are very similar to the ways that mothers do. . . . There is evidence that, beginning in infancy, infants show very

---

[130] Amanda McComb Thomas & Rex Forehand, *The Relationship between Paternal Depressive Mood and Early Adolescent Functioning*, 4 J. Fam. Psychol. 260–71 (1991).

[131] Amanda McCombs Thomas & Rex Forehand, *The Role of Paternal Variables in Divorced and Married Families: Predictability of Adolescent Adjustment*, 63 Am. J. Orthopsychiatry 126, 131 (1993).

[132] Vicky Phares, *Where's Poppa? The Relative Lack of Attention to the Role of Fathers in Child and Adolescent Psychopathology*, 47 Am. Psychologist 656 (1992).

[133] *Id.* at 656–57.

[134] *Id.* at 661.

similar patterns of attachment to their mothers and fathers. . . . Paternal warmth has been found to be similar to maternal warmth in its advantageous effects on child psychosocial adjustment, achievement, and sex role development. . . . [T]he amount of time that fathers spend with their children is less important than how they spend that time and how children, fathers, and mothers evaluate the time spent between fathers and their children. . . . [Research also shows that] paternal personality characteristics, behaviors, and psychopathology are all significantly related to child and adolescent psychopathology. . . . [There are also] more similarities than differences in the fathers' and mothers' roles in child and adolescent psychopathology.[135]

Phares indicates that prevalence rates for child physical abuse are about equal for fathers and mothers, though most studies of child physical abuse have addressed abuse by mothers. She also notes that "children of depressed fathers appear to be at an increased risk for a variety of emotional and behavioral problems when compared with control children."[136] Fathers tend to be the primary subjects of studies of incest and child sexual abuse, she writes, but in virtually all other areas of study mothers are looked at much more closely than are fathers.

Although mothers' working outside the home has not been found to have a negative affect on children's development, there usually is a negative affect when the father is unemployed. Loss of the father's income "may lead to increased paternal negativity and pessimism, which leads to deterioration of the father-child relationship and results in children's socioemotional problems, somatic symptoms, and reduced personal expectations and aspirations."[137]

In a review article, Phares and Compas summarize research on the effect of fathers on children's psychopathology. They found that, of 577 articles on the effect of parents on children's psychopathology, only eight studied fathers alone, while 277 studied mothers alone. The balance studied both parents, sometimes identifying data for each parent and sometimes not.[138]

Research has found that fathers of Attention Deficit Hyperactivity Disorder (ADHD) children tended to have a "shorter attention span . . . , poor behavioral interactions . . . , and less favorable perceptions of parenting behavior and parenting self-esteem."[139] These fathers do not have a higher rate of psychopathology than fathers of normal children, however, and are not significantly different from mothers of ADHD children.[140]

Phares and Compas conclude:

Overall, fathers of children who have received a psychiatric diagnosis or who have been referred for psychological treatment show increased levels of psychopathology when compared with fathers of children who have not been diagnosed or referred for psychological treatment. . . . Paternal characteristics are more consistently related to externalizing problems

---

[135] *Id.* at 657.

[136] *Id.* at 659.

[137] *Id.* at 661.

[138] Phares & Compas at 388.

[139] *Id.* at 390.

[140] *Id.*

(ADHD, conduct disorder, delinquent behaviors) than internalizing problems (depression, anxiety disorders) in their children.[141]

§ 14.23   Resilience in Children

It has long been evident that not all children of parents with mental disorders develop serious, long-term problems. Although there may be some innate qualities in these children that insulate them from their parents' disorders, research increasingly indicates that it is the presence of a supportive environment that is the primary factor in these childrens' resilience. Psychologist Byron Egeland from the Institute of Child Development at the University of Minnesota indicates that "rather than being born with the 'right stuff,' " these children "are often found to have environments that are supportive in critical ways or that change in positive ways prior to the child's recovery."[142]

A study by Ellen Herrenkohl, Roy Herrenkohl, and Brenda Egolf found that

> the protective influences associated with maintenance of at least a minimum standard of success in school include stability of home situation, clear parental expectations of academic performance, a home atmosphere in which abuse is not a chronic and pervasive theme, and at least average intellectual ability of the child.[143]

In contrast, "physical conflict between adult heads of household, often associated with physical abuse of the child, seemed to set the stage for violent acting-out by the adolescent."[144] Resilience is seen to depend on a combination of a reasonably stable home situation, relative absence of physical abuse of one family member by another, and a supportive extended family and wider community.

§ 14.24   Summary

In summary, there are a number of ways in which a parent's mental/emotional problems can impact a child negatively. It is critical to remember, however, that the mental health expert is to evaluate parenting, not mental illness per se.[145] Some children do well in spite of parental mental illness, and some parents adequately compensate in various ways for their mental illnesses. Although the clues from research studies give the expert direction regarding what to look for and questions to ask, the bottom line remains the ability of a given individual to adequately parent a given child.

---

[141] *Id.* at 394.

[142] *Quoted in* Tori DeAngelis, *"The Right Stuff" of Resilience Is a Supportive Environment*, 23 Am. Psychol. Ass'n Monitor 26, 26 (1992).

[143] Ellen C. Herrenkohl et al., *Resilient Early School-Age Children from Maltreating Homes: Outcomes in Late Adolescence*, 64 Am. J. Orthopsychiatry 301, 305 (1994).

[144] *Id.* at 307.

[145] Herman, *Special Issues in Child Custody Evaluations*, 29 J. Am. Acad. Child & Adolescent Psychiatry 969, 969 (1990).

§ 14.25   Implications for Child Custody Evaluations

1. **Do not make any assumptions regarding the parenting ability of any individual based primarily or exclusively on diagnosis**. Parenting ability must be formally assessed, and parents with even the most severe diagnoses may be able to parent adequately during an acute exacerbation of a disorder if he or she has support from a spouse and/or immediate or extended family and/or a community-based program. (See **Chapter 17.**)

2. Does either parent appear to be unable, for any reason, to understand and respond to the needs of the child? Are there any specific needs in the list in § **14.2** to which either parent appears unable to respond?

3. Does either parent appear to have difficulty separating his or her needs and feelings from the needs and feelings of the child?

4. Does either parent show evidence of significant difficulty at handling his or her own anxiety, thereby being a poor role model for the child in this area?

5. Does it appear that either parent has failed to bond with the child?

6. Recognizing that no parent is entirely incompetent in his or her ability to parent, what parenting skills does each parent exhibit, and what parenting skills does each parent lack?

7. If the parent is evaluated during an episode of a mental disorder, particularly an acute psychotic episode or a major depressive episode, or during a period of exceptional emotional stress, what parenting skills does the parent exhibit in spite of the disorder or stress, and what parenting skills are clearly lacking during the acute episode?

8. If the parent was evaluated during the above acute exacerbation, is it possible to postpone completion of the evaluation until the acute episode is waning or, ideally, over, so that a measure of parenting skills during a more "normal" period of time may be obtained?

9. Did the parent seek treatment during the acute exacerbation of his or her disorder? Did he or she comply with treatment (taking medication, if prescribed; attending therapy sessions, if scheduled, and so forth)?

10. Does the parent have a history of stopping treatment against medical or psychological advice? If yes, how recently, and for what stated reason? All psychotropic medications have side effects, some serious, and a parent who stopped his or her medication due to serious side effects has not behaved egregiously, while a parent who stops for a variety of other reasons may be indicating a lack of commitment to remission of the disorder. Also keep in mind that new psychotropic medications come onto the market every year, and a parent who was at best marginally helped by medications available a year ago may have one prescribed this year that is a great deal more effective and has fewer side effects as well.

11. If the parent has been hospitalized, what is the parent's frequency and length of hospitalizations for his or her disorder? While past hospitalizations do not guarantee that there will be future hospitalizations, they provide information regarding periods of time when the parent was not available to the child, and offer a means of estimating the chronicity of the parent's disorder.

12. What social support does the parent have, especially at times of an acute exacerbation of his or her disorder? If there is a spouse who is supportive and who has good

parenting skills, the impact of any disorder on the child will be lessened. Are there other immediate or extended family members who can and will become a caretaker for the child for as long as needed? Good social support reduces the impact of an acute exacerbation of a disorder on the child.

13. Is there community-based treatment available to the parent who has a chronic disorder, and does the parent avail him- or herself of that treatment?

14. If a parent had an acute exacerbation due to emotional, financial, or other stress, is there a community resource that will help alleviate that stressor? If yes, the evaluation should be updated when the stressor is under control.

15. Follow the suggestions of Jacobsen *et al.* (see **§ 14.2**):

   a. Observe each parent and child in more than one setting, including the home setting, rather than inferring that information indirectly.

   b. Screen the children for developmental delays.

   c. As in any child custody evaluation, use multiple sources of information. For a parent who has been hospitalized for a mental disorder, ensure that records from that hospitalization are reviewed if the hospitalization was within the past few years.

   d. If the child custody evaluator does not have significant experience with and knowledge of psychoses, major depression, and other serious and persistent disorders, ensure that the evaluator consults with someone who is an expert in these areas.

   e. Assess for "adequate," not "optimal," parenting.

   f. Assess whether the parent has any markedly inaccurate ideas about child development, and whether the parent has substantially inaccurate expectations of his or her children.

   g. Does it appear that the children are taking care of the parent? Is the caretaking sufficient to be defined as parentification?

   h. Does the parent believe that the child is a serious source of stress?

16. Try to identify the effect on the children if the evaluation was done in segments over a period of several months, to potentially permit the parent to recover from the acute exacerbation of whatever disorder he or she was experiencing.

17. If the parent has a Bipolar Disorder, chart the history of the disorder over the past five or more years—when has the individual been depressed or manic (or hypomanic), and for how long? If the disorder appears to cycle, how frequent is that cycling? Has the parent done anything while depressed or manic that was a threat to his or her own or anyone else's life or safety?

18. What evidence is there that a parent who is experiencing a Major Depression or another serious disorder is withdrawing from the children? Does the parent continue to be withdrawn when not severely depressed?

19. What contribution does a parent's psychological disorder make to the discord in the marriage?

20. Per the research by Lyone-Ruth *et al.*, what type of parenting did each parent receive while growing up, and does it appear—as the researchers found—that the parenting received back then has a greater influence on the current parenting than does the psychiatric diagnosis?

21. Per the recent research of Phares *et al.*, to what degree do the age, temperament, level of intelligence, social skills, having at least one sibling who is functioning well, having a close relationship with a parent or parent-substitute, the parents' authoritative (rather than authoritarian or permissive) parenting style, and being part of a supportive family network provide protection for the child from the parent's mental disorder?

22. If the child is in therapy, are both parents involved in the therapy?

23. How consistent are the parents in their behavior toward the child and in general? Are they consistent enough that the child can reasonably predict what the parents will be like from day to day, or is either parent sufficiently labile that the child cannot predict what a parent will be like (for example, hostile versus supportive)?

24. To what extent is the degree of depression assessed in the evaluation attributable to the divorce process, and to what degree is it the parent's "normal" degree of depression?

25. What impact does the shortened attention span and difficulty concentrating of the parent with an anxiety disorder impact on the child?

26. What specific type(s) of anxiety disorder does the parent evidence, and what impact on the child would one expect from the type of anxiety disorder? For example, a parent with Agoraphobia would have difficulty taking the child out of the house or far from home, while the parent with Social Phobia would have difficulty going places where he or she anticipates feeling embarrassed, and a parent with Post-traumatic Stress Disorder may have an increased startle response, flashbacks, emotional numbing, and so forth. To the degree it is measurable, does the parent's disorder have an adverse impact on the child?

27. Does a parent have an eating disorder? If yes, what impact does that disorder have on the child? Does the parent tend to ignore the child during bulimic cycles, keep an inadequate amount of food in the house, or underfeed the child?

28. Does a parent have a Borderline Personality Disorder? For each of the following possible/likely symptoms, what is the impact on the child of that parent's fear of abandonment, tendency to idealize or devalue other people, unstable self-image, impulsivity, suicidal gestures, affective instability, chronic feelings of emptiness, periodic rage, and/or paranoid ideation?

29. If either parent has an Antisocial Personality Disorder, what impact is there on the child of the possible/likely inadequate conscience development of that parent, the parent's being manipulative, the parent's failure to conform to social/legal norms, impulsivity, aggressiveness, poor caretaking, irresponsibility, lack of remorse, and difficulty learning from experience?

30. If the child has a Conduct Disorder, it there any evidence that a parent has an Antisocial Personality Disorder (see the research by Jaffee *et al.* in **§ 14.14**)?

31. If a parent has Chronic Fatigue Syndrome or fibromyalgia, what impact does it have on the child that the parent may evidence impaired memory or concentration, chronic pain, difficulty getting restful sleep, depression, and/or anxiety?

32. Is there evidence of Munchausen Syndrome by Proxy?

33. Is there evidence of alcohol or other drug abuse? (See **Chapter 15.**)

CHAPTER QUESTIONS AND CASES

§ 14.25   Questions for Chapter 14

Caution.   Attorneys should not expect to be able to go into court and ask all the following questions. Preparation is necessary, referring to the content of the chapter to determine whether a particular question applies to the case. The section number at the end of certain questions refers to the place in the chapter where the reader can find an explanation of why a particular question may be important.

1. If a parent is mentally ill, have adequate steps been taken to provide supportive services? See **§ 14.6.**

2. Does the parent demonstrate an overprotective or authoritarian parenting style? See **§ 14.20.**

3. Does the parent exhibit a parenting style that would promote a conduct disorder in his or her child(ren)? See **§ 14.21.**

4. Has the psychologist carefully evaluated the effect of a BPD on the child(ren)/family? See **§ 14.13.**

5. If the parent demonstrates mental illness, has the expert appropriately focused on evaluating parenting skills and not the mental illness per se? See **§ 14.24.**

6. Can the psychologist demonstrate that the parent has the qualities of good-enough mothering, separateness, anxiety mastery, mirroring of affect and achievement, and promotion of growth and maturation described in this chapter? See **§ 14.2.**

7. Does the parent have a history of mental illness?

8. If the parent has been hospitalized, have hospital records been reviewed?

9. If the parent has carried a psychiatric diagnosis, is that diagnosis still current? If not, why not?

10. If the parent is psychotic or was psychotic, what evidence can the psychologist provide that similar episodes will not occur in the future?

11. How will the type of mental disorder that the parent has experienced affect typical development of children in general and the children specifically involved in a custody matter? Ask the psychologist to make this determination. See **§§ 14.5** through **14.18.**

12. If the individual has taken psychiatric medication, how cooperative was the individual in taking the medication?

13. If the individual is currently on medication, is the individual likely to be taken off the medication? What effect will that have on the individual's overall stability?

14. If the individual has been treated by a number of inpatient or outpatient facilities, why have so many changes taken place in treatment, and what are the implications of a large number of changes on the patient's continued emotional stability?

15. Is there any evidence of diminished capacity (discussed in **Chapter 4**) that would affect the patient's availability to address the needs of the children? See **§ 14.18.**

16. Has the child been overburdened by being required to take on too much responsibility for growing up, maintaining the psychological functioning of the parent, or being caught in the middle of the parents' fights, or by the parents' distorting the perception of the child's abilities? See **Chapter 4.**

17. If the patient is currently in treatment, has the psychologist contacted the current treating therapist? If the patient has invoked privilege, how would this be interpreted?

18. If the patient carries a diagnosis of a character or personality disorder, what is the likelihood that therapy will be successful? Ask the psychologist to make this determination. See §§ **14.4, 14.8, 14.13,** and **14.14.**

19. If the individual has previously been diagnosed as psychotic, has the individual ever been found incompetent or has a guardian ever been appointed for the individual? See § **14.5.**

20. If the patient has a history of mental illness, is the parent currently able to address the needs described in this chapter?

21. If the psychologist has not felt it necessary to emphasize the mental illness of the individual, did the illness occur long enough ago so as not to be relevant?

22. If the individual has experienced recent hospitalizations or extensive psychotherapy, was it the result of the distress and trauma within a relationship or the result of events leading up to the divorce, as opposed to underlying emotional instability?

§ 14.26   Case Digest

The source of information for many of the following cases is the *Mental and Physical Disability Law Reporter* (MPDLR), a publication of the American Bar Association. Information for any other sources appears in the relevant references below. The following are direct quotations from the identified source. Quotations from the *Mental and Physical Disability Law Reporter*: Excerpted from *Mental and Physical Disability Law Reporter*. Copyright © 1989–2003 American Bar Association. Reprinted by permission. If no source is cited, it is a case summary based on the court decision.

Alabama

D.W. v. Alabama Department of Human Resources, 595 So. 2d 502 (Ala. Civ. App. 1992). An Alabama appeals court held that a lower court did not have to order rehabilitative measures for a father's mental illness before it could terminate his rights. The trial court found that the father had not carried out his parental duties due to his severe mood and behavioral disturbances and frequent hospitalizations for paranoid schizophrenia, which was aggravated by drug and alcohol abuse. The father already had been violent with a stepchild, and it was highly probable that he would experience a psychotic relapse and again become violent.

Because the father's inability to care for his child was not likely to improve, and could worsen, the lower court did not have to give the father an opportunity to obtain rehabilitation before terminating his rights. An attempt to rehabilitate the father would take a great deal of time and effort, at the expense of the child's chances for adoption. 16 *Mental & Physical Disability Law Reporter* 410 (1992).

Alaska

R.J.M. v. State of Alaska, Department of Health & Social Services, 973 P.2d 79, 1999 WL 35765 (Alaska 1999). While Alaska Statute Section 47.10.010(a)(2)(F) regarding children in need of aid (CINA) refers only to physical abuse, the Alaska Supreme Court expanded CINA jurisdiction by indicating that the statute includes situations in which no one is "caring or willing to provide care" for a child. Because the mother refused to get treatment for her mental illness, and the mental illness was found to interfere with her ability to care for her child, the state supreme court found that the mother was unwilling to care for her son.

California

In re Elizabeth R., 42 Cal. Rptr. 2d 200 (Cal. Ct. App. 1995). Rebecca, the mother, was diagnosed with bipolar disorder during her mid-teens and hospitalized frequently thereafter. During an unstable relationship, she had three daughters, and after their births she had numerous psychotic episodes. The children were placed in foster homes. While Rebecca was hospitalized, a reunification plan was prepared that required that she visit her children on a weekly basis, attend parenting class, learn nurturing skills, demonstrate parenting skills, and take her medications. Rebecca complied with nearly all of the terms of the reunification plan but continued to go in and out of hospitals. Her parental rights were terminated.

The court of appeals held . . . [f]amily preservation, with the attendant reunification plan and reunification services, is the first priority in child dependency proceedings. . . . Nonetheless, the legislature determined that a child's need for stability and security within a given time frame is paramount. . . . In its in-depth review of the facts, the court found that there was both mistreatment and misunderstanding of special needs parents such as Rebecca. The court held that if mental illness is involved, the reunification plan should accommodate the family's unique hardship. The plan's objective must be to provide services to facilitate the return of normal family relationships. . . . Absent physical or emotional abuse, family reunification efforts must be tailored to fit the unique challenges of individual families unless a § 361.5 disability is proven by clear and convincing evidence. 19 *Mental & Physical Disability Law Reporter* 605 (1995).

In re Jennilee T., 4 Cal. Rptr. 2d 101 (Cal. Ct. App. 1992). A California appeals court ruled that a statute specifying that reunification services need not be provided to parents with a mental disability before their child is put up for adoption did not violate the due process rights of a father with schizophrenia. . . . The father argued that the statute was overbroad because instead of exempting only those parents who have no chance of being united with their child, the statute also exempts those parents who are merely unlikely to benefit from reunification services. The appeals court found that the law created a permissible legislative classification, so it was not unconstitutional on its face. It was also constitutional as applied in this instance, because two clinical psychologists testified that the father's mental disorder made him incapable of utilizing any reunification services. 16 *Mental & Physical Disability Law Reporter* 290 (1992).

In re Cory M., 3 Cal. Rptr. 2d 627 (Cal. Ct. App. 1992). A California appeals court ruled that once the state proved that a mother's refusal to follow a course of treatment for her mental illness was harmful to her son, she had the burden of showing that she was emotionally and mentally fit to care for him. The appeals court found that the mother's failure to participate in court-ordered treatment programs constituted prima facie evidence that reunification with her child would be detrimental. . . . The appeals court noted that the mother's decision not to waive her psychotherapist-patient privilege and present expert evidence about her fitness denied the court crucial evidence about whether her treatment was successful, but that the decision rested with her. 16 *Mental & Physical Disability Law Reporter* 291 (1992).

San Diego Department of Social Services v. Nita M., 268 Cal. Rptr. 214 (Cal. Ct. App. 1990). A California appeals court affirmed a trial court's termination of the parental rights of a mother with schizophrenia. The child had been removed from the mother's care shortly after birth, due to the mother's inappropriate behavior in the hospital. The mother had visited her infant regularly, negating a finding of neglect, and allegations concerning the mother's sexual molestation of the child were inconclusive. The court nevertheless found clear and convincing evidence to support the trial court's finding that the mother, due to her mental disorder, was and would remain unable to care for her child. 14 *Mental & Physical Disability Law Reporter* 327 (1990).

Silva v. Lori S1, 270 Cal. Rptr. 411 (Cal. Ct. App. 1990). A California appeals court upheld the placement with his father of a nine-year-old boy with psychiatric disorders. The testimony indicated the boy's mother had "schizotypo" tendencies. A clinical psychologist testified that the mother demonstrated "a tendency toward isolation, difficulty establishing rapport with other people and peculiarities in thought process or in communication." Additional testimony indicated the boy functioned better with his father, there was no evidence that the father physically or sexually abused his son, and the risk of physical abuse was greater with the mother than the father. Moreover, the evidence established that reasonable efforts to rehabilitate the mother had failed. The court focused on evidence that the mother had induced her son to testify falsely against his father and had not heeded a court order to receive counseling as a condition of probation on a misdemeanor battery conviction. 14 *Mental & Physical Disability Law Reporter* 419 (1990).

Department of Public Social Services v. Diana G., 270 Cal. Rptr. 534 (Cal. Ct. App. 1990). A California appeals court upheld a child's placement with her maternal aunt when the child's mother was diagnosed with a schizotypal personality and evidence suggested the mother physically abused her daughter. The mother claimed that mental illness alone was an insufficient basis for a child's removal, but the appeals court found abundant evidence that the mother's schizotypal personality prevented her from adequately caring for her daughter. The daughter reported that her mother had tried to draw blood from her with a hypodermic needle and encouraged her to eat frozen vomit. 14 *Mental & Physical Disability Law Reporter* 420 (1990).

Colorado

Colorado ex rel. S.J.C., 776 P.2d 1103 (Colo. 1989). The Colorado Supreme Court upheld a parental rights termination statute as applied to a father with an emotional illness. The trial court terminated the father's rights under a statute that permitted the severance of the parent-child relationship if the parent was unfit because of *emotional illness*. Colo. Rev. Stat. § 19-3-604(1)(b)(I). The state supreme court found that although *emotional illness* was a lay term encompassing a broad range of emotional impairments, the term was not too vague as applied to the father. Additional statutory language indicated that the alleged illness must render the parent incapable of caring for the child, and a psychologist and a social worker testified that the father was unable to care for his children. The psychologist described this illness as a "*mixed personality disorder* related to feelings of narcissism, inadequacy, and passivity . . . exacerbated by episodic alcohol usage," but added that alcohol treatment alone would not improve the father's ability to care for the children, and the father's condition was not likely to change. 13 *Mental & Physical Disability Law Reporter* 520 (1989).

In re C.S.M., 805 P.2d 1129 (Colo. Ct. App. 1990). State law allows the termination of parental rights if the court finds "no appropriate treatment plan can be devised to address the unfitness of the parent." The trial court held that because no institution was willing to accept the mother due to the nature of her mental illness [Borderline Personality Disorder], it was impossible to devise an appropriate treatment plan. The appeals court rejected the mother's argument that treatment had to be offered before the court could determine treatment would be unsuccessful. The code provision was designed to avoid the futility of proceeding with treatment plans that were doomed to fail. 15 *Mental & Physical Disability Law Reporter* 373 (1991).

Connecticut

In re Alexander V., 223 Conn. 557, 613 A.2d 780 (1992). The Connecticut Supreme Court ruled that due process may require that a hearing be held to determine whether a parent in a termination of parental rights case is legally competent. The court indicated that an important interest of the parent is in jeopardy, and that interest must be protected. The court specified that a competency hearing is not required in all cases, however. It is required only if requested by the parent's attorney, or if the judge witnesses behavior that raises doubts in his or her mind about the competency of the parent. The standard for the judge to apply in such hearings is whether there are "specific factual allegations that, if true, would constitute substantial evidence of mental impairment." Evidence is "substantial" if it raises a reasonable doubt about the competency of the parent, the court indicated.

In re Kelly S., 616 A.2d 1161 (Conn. App. Ct. 1992). A Connecticut appeals court held that a trial court had erred in relying on a mother's long history of mental illness and aggression as the basis for removing her special needs child from her custody. The law required proof of parental harm to the child or the absence of an ongoing parent-child relationship. Baby Kelly was placed in temporary foster care immediately after birth based on the finding that she was in immediate physical danger. . . . She denied having a mental illness despite having two different personalities; hallucinations; angry, aggressive behavior; and poor hygiene. She was unemployed and lived in homeless shelters or one-room apartments without separate hygiene facilities. . . . When Kelly was a year old, a trial court simultaneously terminated her mother's parental rights and granted custody to the children's services agency on the ground that she was a neglected and uncared-for child. The appeals court affirmed the custody order, but reversed the termination of the mother's parental rights. . . . The mother's mental condition made her barely able to care for herself, let alone to provide constant medical care and therapy to Kelly. Although she regularly visited Kelly in supervised settings, she did not understand Kelly's needs or condition and showed little interest in bonding with Kelly. . . . The evidence did not support termination of the mother's parental rights, however. Termination requires evidence of parental acts or omissions that deny a child necessary care . . . and that cause serious harm to the child. . . . There was no proof that her mother's specific conduct had injured her. Any potential harm from her mother was only speculation. . . . Termination also requires lack of an ongoing parent-child relationship. . . . Where lack of an ongoing parent-child relationship is the direct result of a custody determination, termination of parental rights cannot be sustained. 17 *Mental & Physical Disability Law Reporter* 166–67 (1993).

In re Joshua Z., 597 A.2d 842 (Conn. App. Ct. 1991). A Connecticut appeals court found that clear and convincing evidence supported the termination of parental rights of a mother who made no sustained effort to address her psychological problems. At the time of her son's birth, the mother was diagnosed with a borderline personality disorder as well as other possible forms of mental illness. Three months later, she placed her son in foster care because she was having suicidal ideations as well as homicidal thoughts toward her son. While the child was not in any immediate physical danger, the appeals court found no statutory requirement of imminent physical harm, and refused to impose one. The appeals court found that termination was proper . . . because the mother's refusal to participate in treatment showed that she was unable to rehabilitate herself in order to properly care for her son. 16 *Mental & Physical Disability Law Reporter* 165 (1992).

District of Columbia

In re M.D., 602 A.2d 109 (D.C. 1992). The D.C. court of appeals held that a trial court abused its discretion by denying a father visitation rights without reading a psychiatric evaluation rebutting concerns that visitation would not be in the child's best interests. The trial court did not base its decision to deny visitation on factual findings made in an independent hearing. Instead, the judge had relied on a prior civil protection order, even though there was evidence that the father's mental health condition and his alcoholism no longer existed. Even if the father had a mental illness, this by itself would be insufficient to deny visitation. The appeals court reversed because it was impossible to know whether, after reading the psychiatric evaluation, the trial court still would deny the father visitation rights. 16 *Mental & Physical Disability Law Reporter* 428 (1992).

E.C. v. District of Columbia, 589 A.2d 1245 (D.C. 1991). A District of Columbia appeals court affirmed a decision to terminate the parental rights of a father whose mental illness made him unable to relate meaningfully with his children. While mental illness by itself is not a basis for termination, the lower court could consider the effects the father's condition had on his children's welfare. In doing so, the court found the father was emotionally unstable and showed no improvement during the nearly four-year period in which the children were in his custody. Moreover, an expert testified that the father had a personality disorder that was likely to have a destructive influence on his children. 15 *Mental & Physical Disability Law Reporter* 481 (1991).

Florida

S.Q. v. Department of Health & Rehabilitative Services, 687 So. 2d 319 (Fla. Dist. Ct. App. 1997). A Florida appeals court reversed a lower court's termination of parental rights of a mother with schizophrenia finding that her failure to substantially comply with her placement plan requirements, which mandated she acknowledge her mental health problem, did not establish by clear and convincing evidence prospective abuse or neglect. . . . Several psychiatric evaluations variously indicated that she had no severe psychiatric illness, that she had "schizophrenic disorder, paranoid type" and that she had psychothia, a mild form of depressive illness. 21 *Mental & Physical Disability Law Reporter* 328 (1997).

Georgia

In re M.A.V., 425 S.E.2d 377 (Ga. Ct. App. 1992). A Georgia appeals court held that a juvenile court improperly terminated the parental rights of a mother with Munchausen Syndrome by Proxy (MSP) by placing too much reliance on evidence from a proceeding involving her other child. In a prior proceeding, the juvenile court terminated the mother's parental rights to her younger son, finding that he was a victim of the mother's MSP—a condition in which a child's caretaker either induced the appearance of an illness in the child or actually inflicts harm on the child and then seeks medical care. A child psychiatrist had testified that younger, non-verbal children are more frequently the victims, but that an older child can be at risk if the younger child is removed from the home. The appeals court found that the mother's rights to her older son were terminated solely because he might become her next victim. The state had not presented clear and convincing evidence of the compelling circumstances necessary to terminate the mother's rights to her older child. . . . There was no evidence that the older child had been or currently was a victim of the mother's MSP. 17 *Mental & Physical Disability Law Reporter* 255–56 (1993).

In re J.R., 414 S.E.2d 540 (Ga. Ct. App. 1992). A Georgia appeals court affirmed a termination of parental rights, finding clear and convincing evidence that a mother's mental illness prevented her from adequately caring for her son, and also that the father was unwilling to care for their son or to secure psychological help for his wife. The mother was diagnosed with bipolar disorder, manic with psychotic features and, without treatment, could not adequately parent her three-and-a-half-year-old son. Both parents neglected to visit their son for periods exceeding one year. . . . The boy was a "deprived child" and termination of parental rights was in his best interests. Also, he had formed substantial bonds with his aunt's family and it was likely they would adopt him. 16 *Mental & Physical Disability Law Reporter* 409 (1992).

Illinois

In re K.S.T., 578 N.E.2d 306 (Ill. App. Ct. 1991). An Illinois appeals court affirmed the termination of a mother's parental rights based on clear and convincing evidence that her mental illness prevented her from properly caring for her child. The mother had a history of psychiatric hospitalizations for schizophrenia, and her psychiatrist testified that the illness was chronic and that even with parenting classes, the mother could not care for herself or her child during a psychotic episode. 16 *Mental & Physical Disability Law Reporter* 45 (1992).

In re I.D., 563 N.E.2d 1200 (Ill. App. Ct. 1990). An Illinois appeals court upheld the constitutionality of the state statute that allows the state to terminate the rights of parents whose mental impairment, illness, or retardation, makes them unable to discharge their parental responsibilities. A rational basis exists between the state's duty to ensure stability and an appropriate family life for minors, and the need to terminate the rights of parents whose mental disabilities would extend beyond a reasonable time, making them unable to discharge their parental responsibilities. If the parent has a continuing disability, the state can make a rational finding that it is less detrimental to the child to terminate the parental rights and encourage permanent adoption, than to place the child in long-term foster care. The court also upheld the termination of the rights of a mother with the mental age of a five- or six-year-old, who made some progress in learning routine tasks but would be unable to provide a sufficiently enriching environment for her child who was developmentally delayed. The court also noted the child's progress during temporary placement out of the home and concern the child would regress if returned to the mother. 15 *Mental & Physical Disability Law Reporter* 257 (1991).

Indiana

Tucker v. Shelby County Department of Public Welfare, 578 N.E.2d 774 (Ind. Ct. App. 1991). An Indiana statute that authorizes courts to consider a parent's mental illness in deciding whether to terminate the parent's rights does not deny federal equal protection. . . . Mental illness is only one factor to be considered, and the law does not permit termination based solely on a parent's mental illness or classify all parents with mental illness as unfit. The court upheld the termination of Tucker's parental rights based on evidence, including her mental illness, that she was incapable of providing adequate care for her child. Tucker had schizophrenic symptoms with strong paranoia, and her therapist testified that she was unable to develop parental bonds with her child. 16 *Mental & Physical Disability Law Reporter* 45 (1992).

R.M. v. Tippecanoe County Department of Public Welfare, 582 N.E.2d 417 (Ind. Ct. App. 1991). An Indiana appeals court found that clear and convincing evidence supported the termination of parental rights of a mother with " 'atypical psychosis and adjustment disorder with depressed mood,' " a history of drug and alcohol abuse, and an I.Q. of 75. In addition to these conditions, there was evidence of the child's unnatural and erratic behavior in the mother's presence, indicating problems involving mother-child bonding. The mother's inability or unwillingness to follow psychological advice and her refusal to participate in counseling programs presented clear and convincing evidence that no reasonable probability existed that she would be able to provide her child with the necessary care. Walker, "Family Law in the Fifty States: An Overview," 25 *Family Law Quarterly* 475 (1992).

Iowa

In re T.O., 470 N.W.2d 8 (Iowa 1991). The Iowa Supreme Court affirmed a decision not to terminate the parental rights of a mother with mental illness where the lower court ruled it would be in the children's best interest for them to be with their mother. While the mother's mental illness is one factor to be considered, standing alone it is insufficient to require termination. There also must be evidence that the mental illness contributes to an inability to perform parental duties. Here, despite evidence of child abuse by the mother's boyfriend and the mother's past problems, experts testified she now could care for her children. 15 *Mental & Physical Disability Law Reporter* 481 (1991).

Louisiana

Louisiana ex rel. Townzen, 527 So. 2d 579 (La. Ct. App. 1988). A Louisiana court of appeals upheld the termination of a mother's parental rights where the state showed by clear and convincing evidence that her mental illness rendered her incapable of caring for her child. In this case, two psychologists testified that the mother had a mixed personality disorder including passive/aggressive, passive/dependent and antisocial personality disorders. Both witnesses stated that these disorders made the mother incapable of properly caring for her son who had inherited some of his mother's personality disorders and would need counseling for an indefinite period. One of the psychologists stated that professional counseling would not improve the mother's parenting abilities, and a continued relationship between the son and his mother would be very destructive and greatly exacerbate his problems. 12 *Mental & Physical Disability Law Reporter* 512 (1988).

Maine

In re Misty Lee H., 529 A.2d 331 (Me. 1987). A divided Maine Supreme Judicial Court affirmed a decision terminating a mother's parental rights based on expert testimony that she had severe emotional problems, was prone to violent behavior, and lacked basic parenting skills. The mother had a diagnosis of borderline personality disorder and was informed that psychotherapy was crucial to her effective parenting. Yet she consistently resisted mental health counseling. The children suffered both physical neglect and emotional harm as a result of the mother's instability. 12 *Mental & Physical Disability Law Reporter* 44 (1988).

Montana

In re D.F.D., 261 Mont. 186 (1993). The Montana Supreme Court ruled that the fact a father cross-dressed was not a sufficient basis for denying his request for joint custody of his two-year-old son and for having restricted visitation imposed on him. The court indicated that there is a rebuttable presumption that joint custody is in the child's best interest. In the instant case, the supreme court indicated that there was evidence that the father's urge to wear women's clothes was under control, and that there would be a negative impact on the child if his father did not have custody and adequate visitation.

In re Marriage of Cook, 819 P.2d 180 (Mont. 1991). The Montana Supreme Court upheld a trial court's decision to grant a father sole custody of his son and to order supervised visitation with the child's mother because she needed treatment for what was described as either mixed personality or bipolar affective disorder. Both parties in a marriage dissolution proceeding presented testimony from mental health professionals who had treated the mother. While their diagnoses differed, they all agreed that she needed treatment. The supreme court noted that . . . none of the experts testified that placement with her would be in her son's best interests. Further, the trial court did not commit clear error in granting the mother only supervised visitation without finding that unsupervised visitation would seriously endanger her son's physical, mental, moral, or emotional health. Two expert witnesses had recommended supervised visitation until the mother received treatment for her mental conditions. 16 *Mental & Physical Disability Law Reporter* 193 (1992).

Nebraska

In re J.H., B.H., & J.H., Nos. A-92-588, A-92-936 (Neb. Ct. App. 1993). A Nebraska appeals court upheld an order giving the Department of Social Services (DSS) temporary legal custody of children whose mother had a multiple personality disorder (MPD).

   The juvenile court adopted a DSS plan providing that M.H. would retain physical custody of her children, but that DSS would retain temporary legal custody. The plan required M.H. to undertake therapy to address her MPD, to ensure that her children participated in family therapy and in a day care program, and to see a family support worker. . . . M.H. claimed the court improperly issued its order and challenged the plan. The appeals court affirmed the ruling, noting that the state sought . . . to ensure that M.H. followed through with obtaining necessary support services for her and the children. Furthermore, evidence showed that M.H. could not control which personality was present with the children or caring for them, and that not all of her different personalities were capable of caring for the children. Expert testimony also established that M.H. and her children needed close supervision, and that in the past M.H. failed to follow through with offered services. A preponderance of evidence established that— through no fault of her own—M.H. could not give her children proper parental support, which placed them within the juvenile court's jurisdiction. . . . Therefore, the DSS plan was in the best interest of the children. 18 *Mental & Physical Disability Law Reporter* 41 (1994).

In re B.M., 475 N.W.2d 909 (Neb. 1991). The Nebraska Supreme Court affirmed the termination of a mother's parental rights, finding clear and convincing evidence that her borderline personality disorder prevented her from performing her parental responsibilities. The court found that the mother's disorder would continue indefinitely and she had failed to comply with a court-ordered rehabilitation plan. 16 *Mental & Physical Disability Law Reporter* 44 (1992).

Nebraska v. D.S., 461 N.W.2d 415 (Neb. 1990). The Nebraska Supreme Court upheld the termination of parental rights of a mother who abused drugs and had a long history of depression and suicide attempts. The court found competent testimony to support the conclusion that the mother's mental condition rendered her incapable of being even a part-time parent to her seven-year-old son and her six-year-old daughter. The court doubted she would benefit from treatment before her children reached the age of majority. 15 *Mental & Physical Disability Law Reporter* 149 (1990).

Nebraska v. C.M., 452 N.W.2d 753 (Neb. 1990). The Nebraska Supreme Court affirmed the termination of parental rights of a mother with bipolar disorder. The high court held that the mother's mental illness would prevent her from adequately caring for her three children in the foreseeable future. The mother's psychiatrist testified that the mother had not complied with her treatment program. The children's baby sitters and foster parents testified about the mother's inappropriate care of her children and how her interactions with her children had an adverse affect on them. 14 *Mental & Physical Disability Law Reporter* 328 (1990).

New Jersey

In re Guardianship of J.C., 129 N.J. 1 (1992). According to the New Jersey Supreme Court, the harm that a child may suffer if separated from foster parents with whom the child has forged a strong parental relationship may be considered when deciding on the termination of parental rights, even if the biological parent is not deemed unfit. The context must include the quality of the relationship with both the natural and foster parents, the court indicated. The state must "prove by clear and convincing evidence that separating the child from his or her foster parents would cause serious and enduring emotional or psychological harm." The proof should include testimony from a qualified expert who has done a comprehensive, objective evaluation of the child and his or her relationships.

New York

In re Sheila S., 580 N.Y.S.2d 67 (N.Y. App. Div. 1992). A New York appeals court found that substantial evidence of a mother's mental incapacity supported an order terminating her parental rights. A court-appointed psychiatrist gave unequivocal testimony that the mother had a "chronic schizo-affective disorder" which would endanger the child's welfare. The mother's treating psychiatrist had testified only that the mother might improve if she took her medication and continued therapy, and this testimony did not contradict the court-appointed psychiatrist's testimony. 16 *Mental & Physical Disability Law Reporter* 409 (1992).

In re Omar B., 573 N.Y.S.2d 301 (N.Y. App. Div. 1991). A New York appeals court upheld the termination of the parental rights of a mother whose schizophrenia made her unable to provide proper care to her children. The court found clear and convincing evidence to support termination, noting that the mother had been hospitalized four times for treatment of chronic schizophrenia, and that her psychiatrist testified that her condition would not improve. 16 *Mental & Physical Disability Law Reporter* 45 (1992).

In re Stephen B., 576 N.Y.S.2d 701 (N.Y. App. Div. 1991). A New York appeals court found that the state law allowing for the termination of parental rights was not unconstitutional as applied to a mother with mental illness. . . . The state's compelling interest in protecting children justifies terminating parental rights when a parent's mental illness makes her incapable of caring for a child, both now and in the foreseeable future. The appeals court found that by presenting unequivocal evidence from an examining psychiatrist about the mother's inability to care for her son, the department of social services met its burden of proving that the mother was so disturbed in her behavior, feeling, thinking, and judgment that her son faced a danger of becoming a neglected child. 16 *Mental & Physical Disability Law Reporter* 166 (1992).

Penders v. Penders, 527 N.Y.S.2d 935 (N.Y. App. Div. 1988). A New York appeals court reversed the termination of a mother's parental rights that had been based on evidence of her previous episodes of schizophrenia. In the absence of evidence that the mother's past schizophrenic episodes resulted in neglect, the trial court had no basis for depriving the mother of custody and terminating her parental rights. 12 *Mental & Physical Disability Law Reporter* 432 (1988).

North Carolina

In re Guynn, 437 S.E.2d 532 (N.C. Ct. App. 1993). A North Carolina appeals court found sufficient evidence to terminate a couple's parental rights on the basis of the mother's mental illness and held that the Department of Social Services (DSS) did not have to diligently seek to remedy the mother's deficiencies before initiating termination proceedings. . . . The appeals court found clear and convincing evidence that Tammy's mental illness prevented her from properly caring for and supervising her daughter. Tammy was diagnosed as having adjustment problems, depression, suicidal tendencies, and borderline personality disorder. . . . Her personality disorder was demonstrated by drastic mood shifts, inappropriate intense anger, lack of anger control, suicidal threats, and self-mutilation. Expert witnesses opined that even with help she could not provide a stable home or care for a child. 18 *Mental & Physical Disability Law Reporter* 157 (1994).

North Dakota

Jensen v. Director, Cass County Social Services, 463 N.W.2d 918 (N.D. 1990). The North Dakota Supreme Court found that the trial record clearly established that a mother had chronic and debilitating schizophrenia that made her incapable of caring for her children. Although mental illness alone was an insufficient basis to terminate parental rights, the record showed the children would suffer serious harm if left in their mother's care.

Repeated trial placements with the mother showed she was unable to take care of her own needs and was overwhelmed in trying to care for her children. The child's development was already delayed, and the law did not require the 24-hour per day supervision the mother would need to take care of her own basic needs and those of her children. 15 *Mental & Physical Disability Law Reporter* 258 (1991).

In re Adoption of K.S.H., 442 N.W.2d 417 (N.D. 1989). The North Dakota Supreme Court upheld a trial court's refusal to terminate the parental rights of a father with schizophrenia. The father's parents had sought the severance of the father's parental rights to his 14-year-old son, as a statutory prerequisite to their adoption of the boy. The teen, who had lived with his grandparents for most of his life, had requested the adoption because of his feelings of insecurity. The trial court refused to terminate the father's rights, finding no compelling reason to do so. The state supreme court agreed. . . . [T]he grandparents had provided clear and convincing evidence that the father had been and would remain unable to care for the boy. However, the grandparents had not presented any objective evidence of harm to the child to justify terminating the father's rights, and denying the adoption would not change the child's situation. 13 *Mental & Physical Disability Law Reporter* 520 (1989).

Oregon

Oregon ex rel. Juvenile Department of Benton County v. Pennington, 799 P.2d 694 (Or. Ct. App. 1990). An Oregon appeals court found insufficient evidence to terminate the parental rights of a mother with mild mental retardation and a dependent and schizoid personality disorder. The appeals court relied on the testimony of the mother's psychologist and her mental retardation counselor that the mother had progressed in learning how to care for her children, and there was a probability they could rejoin her in the near future. The court rejected the state's argument that the children, who were angry, defensive, and withdrawn with their mother, but made remarkable progress with their foster parents, should remain in foster care. The court would not uphold the termination of parental rights simply because another environment might better allow the children to maximize their potential. 15 *Mental & Physical Disability Law Reporter* 150 (1991).

Pennsylvania

In re T.R. (Appeal of A.W.), 445 Pa. Super. 553 (1995). The Pennsylvania Superior Court found that a trial court had the power to order a mother to undergo a psychological evaluation to facilitate the court's ability to provide for the welfare of children and preserve family unity under the Juvenile Act. It also ruled that the trial court may release the results of the evaluation to "legitimately interested parties" without violating the constitutional right to privacy of the mother.

> In order for the trial court to enter a correct and proper disposition that is best suited to the protection and physical, mental and moral welfare of the child, the trial court must have the appropriate information before it, specifically, information that will help determine if A.W. is able to care for and protect her child, T.R. Instantly, the trial court's ordering of a psychological evaluation for A.W. was the most efficacious way to determine whether she understands her "high duty" to her child. . . . A.W. argues . . . that compelling her to submit involuntarily to a psychological evaluation to reveal her "innermost thoughts" violates all of these privacy rights and may impugn her reputation. . . . Absent the psychological evaluation, the only information about A.W.'s ability to care for T.R. that the trial court would have before it would be the testimony of two social services workers, both of whom testified as to A.W.'s lack of parenting ability. . . . Furthermore, the psychological evaluation was the least restrictive means to obtain information about A.W.'s caretaking ability. . . . The final issue we must address is whether the trial court erred in ruling that . . . the court has the authority to release the testing, evaluation, and psychological report of A.W. to the interested parties or whether this release violates A.W.'s constitutional right to privacy under Art. 1, § 1 of the Pennsylvania Constitution. . . . The two compelling state interests that justify disclosure of A.W.'s mental state of health are to provide for the protection of T.R. and to increase the likelihood of familial reunification. . . . Both of these state interests must be weighed against A.W.'s constitutional right to privacy in her reputation. However, such right is not being impinged upon because the information was placed under seal and is restricted to interested parties. . . . Finally, there was no alternative reasonable method of lesser intrusion than the release of A.W.'s evaluation to the parties because the information obtained from the parenting and disciplinary strategy sessions was inadequate. . . . We affirm the order of the trial court.

Schwarcz v. Schwarcz, 548 A.2d 556 (Pa. Super. Ct. 1988). A Pennsylvania appeals court held that a trial court had the authority to require that a father involved in a child custody case undergo psychotherapy. A psychologist mutually selected by the parties diagnosed the father as having a paranoid personality disorder and expressed concern regarding his stability. He recommended that the mother receive custody and advised against granting the father overnight visitation. The trial court awarded custody to the mother, and the father appealed. Affirming the trial court's decision, the appeals court rejected the father's argument that the trial court had no authority to require him to undergo psychotherapy. The father contended that the act limited the trial court's authority to ordering a parent to undergo "counseling" which was distinct from "psychotherapy." He asserted that "[c]ounseling suggests a conversational give and take as well as the receiving of advice," whereas "[p]sychotherapy indicates in depth treatment for a psychological problem." The stated purpose of the trial court's order was consistent with the legislative policy of encouraging contact between parent and child. 13 *Mental & Physical Disability Law Reporter* 130 (1989).

Rhode Island

In re Rene B., 544 A.2d 137 (R.I. 1988). The Rhode Island Supreme Court upheld the termination of parental rights based on the mother's mental illness and the likelihood she would not take her medication. The mother's case manager testified that the mother was admitted to a hospital because she was in a manic state. A mental health center's staff psychiatrist testified that the mother's psychiatric disorder was characterized by major mood swings. While her condition was stabilized on medication, he predicted, to a reasonable degree of medical certainty, that she periodically would discontinue her medication. While the child had not been harmed physically, his unstable home environment harmed him emotionally. 12 *Mental & Physical Disability Law Reporter* 511 (1988).

Texas

Lewelling v. Lewelling, 796 S.W.2d 164 (Tex 1990). Evidence that a parent is the victim of spousal abuse is not, standing alone, sufficient to overcome the statutory presumption that the best interest of a child is served by awarding custody to a natural parent, the Texas Supreme Court decided. The court noted that the state legislature has made clear the paramount importance of the parental presumption by providing that a parent shall be awarded custody unless "the appointment could significantly impair the child's physical health or emotional development." The court went on to overrule a lower court's grant of custody to a child's paternal grandparents based on evidence that the child's mother (who also sought custody) had suffered continual abuse by the child's father during the marriage. "As the abuser cannot take advantage of his acts of abuse in a custody battle with the abused, so the abuser's parents also may not benefit from that abuse," the court asserted. The lower court erred in accepting the abuse evidence as proof that awarding custody to the mother would result in significant impairment to the child, the court ruled. 16 *Mental & Physical Disability Law Reporter* 1566 (1990).

In re Carroll, 819 S.W.2d 591 (Tex. Ct. App. 1991). A Texas appeals court ruled that a state statute governing the termination of parental rights did not deny equal protection to parents with mental illness because it did not single out this group for harsh treatment. . . . While the statute treats parents with mental illness differently from parents who do not have a mental illness, the statute actually provides them with more protection against arbitrary state action than is provided to other parents in termination actions. The court also determined that the statute was not vague merely because it does not contain a definition of mental illness. 16 *Mental & Physical Disability Law Reporter* 166–67 (1992).

Vermont

In re S.R., 599 A.2d 364 (Vt. 1991). The Vermont Supreme Court found that a mother's Munchausen Syndrome by Proxy, and her seizure disorder, and a father's drinking problem, presented a significant risk to their child and supported the termination of their parental rights. A psychologist determined that the mother had Munchausen Syndrome by

Proxy, a rare psychological disorder that causes a parent, usually the mother, to report or cause a serious illness or injury in her child, in order to gain the attention and sympathy of the medical community. The psychologist testified that the child had a 10–20% chance of dying because her parents denied the existence of the mother's disorder. The appeals court also found that the mother's seizure disorder, the potential risk of injury and developmental harm to the child because of inadequate supervision, and the father's drinking problem all supported termination. 16 *Mental & Physical Disability Law Reporter* 166 (1992).

Washington

In re Dependency of Chubb, 773 P.2d 851 (Wash. 1989). The Washington Supreme Court affirmed the termination of a mother's parental rights based on her paranoid schizophrenia and delusions. Contrary to her argument that she had an absolute right to express her beliefs and opinions to her children and that the state may not judge the content of her delusions, the state sought to remove the children from their mother because of her mental illness, not her speech. Her mental illness, characterized by vocalized delusions, placed the children in "danger of substantial damage to . . . psychological . . . development." Moreover, the state's interest in protecting the children from psychological damage through continued exposure to those delusions at a critical state of their development overcame the mother's right to express her paranoid delusions to her children. 13 *Mental & Physical Disability Law Reporter* 359 (1989).

West Virginia

Snyder v. Scheerer, 436 S.E.2d 299 (W. Va. 1993). The West Virginia Supreme Court found insufficient evidence to prove that a woman who had bipolar disorder episodes was medically unfit to regain custody of her child. Gretchen Smith Snyder had a bipolar disorder for about fifteen years. With therapy and lithium medication, she kept the disorder under control for several years. . . . Shortly after her baby was born, Snyder again became mentally ill and was hospitalized. A month after her release she attempted suicide and was hospitalized for several months. Snyder signed an agreement granting temporary custody of her child to her sister and brother-in-law, but retained weekly visitation rights. Six months after her release Snyder found work and attempted to retain custody of her child, but her sister and brother-in-law were uncooperative, so Snyder filed a custody petition. The trial court expanded Snyder's visitation rights, but denied her custody, finding that her sister and brother-in-law were the child's psychological parents and that Snyder lacked medical fitness to regain custody.

   The state supreme court reversed the decision. Snyder had made substantial efforts to manage her illness and to maintain regular contact with her child. The trial court had found that if she were healthy, Snyder would make an excellent parent. Furthermore, no current evidence of mental incapacity or detrimental effects of Snyder's disorder on her parenting skills was presented at trial. Little more than speculation supported the conclusion that the potential for future harm to the child justified denying custody to the natural parent. Therefore, the court remanded for a gradual transition plan to minimize disturbance to the child as Snyder regained custody. 18 *Mental & Physical Disability Law Reporter* 156 (1994).

West Virginia Department of Human Services v. Peggy F., 399 S.E.2d 460 (W. Va. 1990). The West Virginia Supreme Court found that the department of social services had proven the need to terminate a mother's parental rights, by showing she had not improved her attitude and parenting skills despite her compliance with some aspects of a family case plan. The mother [was] diagnosed with an antisocial personality and an inability to conform to social norms. The department gave the mother an opportunity to demonstrate her ability to remedy family problems, and worked with her to develop a plan for solving them. Even with minimal compliance with the plan, however, the evidence clearly showed no likelihood the mother could correct the conditions of abuse and neglect in the near future. 15 *Mental & Physical Disability Law Reporter* 258 (1991).

David M. v. Margaret H., 182 W. Va. 57 (1989). The West Virginia Supreme Court of Appeals held that a lower court should not have treated the adulterous conduct of the mother as a reason for awarding custody of a child to the father. Custody of young children should be granted to the primary caretaker, in this case the mother, the [state supreme court] said. Although there is a parental-unfitness exception, the court noted, and one criterion is "refraining from immoral behavior under circumstances that would affect the child," the mother's marital misconduct did not warrant a finding of unfitness. The primary caretaker rule "inevitably involves some injustice to fathers who, as a group, are usually not primary caretakers," the court commented. 5 *Speaking Out for Children* 13 (Spring 1990).

CHAPTER 15

SPECIAL CONCERNS: ALCOHOL AND OTHER DRUG ABUSE

§ 15.1   Introduction

Although alcohol and other psychoactive drugs[1] are widely used in our culture for social, recreational, and medical purposes, there is a point at which use becomes abuse because of "a maladaptive pattern of substance use leading to clinically significant impairment or distress."[2] Because alcohol and other drug abuse (AODA) can have both an immediate and

---

[1] Although many books on the market are alleged to be accurate presentations of information regarding abusable drugs, most also present information slanted toward "legal drugs are okay and illegal ones are not," rather than simply offering objective information. Most publications from the U.S. government are good regarding most drugs but marginally accurate regarding psychedelic drugs. The best single book the authors of this text have seen is From Chocolate to Morphine, by Andrew Weil, M.D., and Winifred Rosen (1993).

[2] American Psychiatric Ass'n, Diagnostic and Statistical Manual of Mental Disorders 182 (4th ed. 1994).

a long-term deleterious effect on children, assessment of problems in this area is therefore a necessary part of a custody evaluation.

§ 15.2   Clinical Diagnosis

The *Diagnostic and Statistical Manual of Mental Disorders, Fourth Edition* (DSM-IV)[3] (discussed in **Chapter 17**), indicates the following diagnostic criteria for Substance Dependence:

Criteria for Substance Dependence

A maladaptive pattern of substance use, leading to clinically significant impairment or distress, as manifested by three (or more) of the following, occurring at any time in the same 12-month period:

(1) tolerance, as defined by either of the following:
    (a) a need for markedly increased amounts of the substance to achieve intoxication or desired effect
    (b) markedly diminished effect with continued use of the same amount of the substance

(2) withdrawal, as manifested by either of the following:
    (a) the characteristic withdrawal syndrome for the substance (refer to Criteria A and B of the criteria sets for Withdrawal from the specific substances)
    (b) the same (or a closely related) substance is taken to relieve or avoid withdrawal symptoms

(3) the substance is often taken in larger amounts or over a longer period than was intended

(4) there is a persistent desire or unsuccessful efforts to cut down or control substance use

(5) a great deal of time is spent in activities necessary to obtain the substance (e.g., visiting multiple doctors or driving long distances), use the substance (e.g., chain-smoking), or recover from its effects

(6) important social, occupational, or recreational activities are given up or reduced because of substance use

(7) the substance use is continued despite knowledge of having a persistent or recurrent physical or psychological problem that is likely to have been caused or exacerbated by the substance (e.g., current cocaine use despite recognition of cocaine-induced depression, or continued drinking despite recognition that an ulcer was made worse by alcohol consumption)

Specify if:

With Physiological Dependence: evidence of tolerance or withdrawal (i.e., either Item 1 or 2 is present)

---

[3] American Psychiatric Ass'n, Diagnostic and Statistical Manual of Mental Disorders 182 (4th ed. 1994).

Without Physiological Dependence: no evidence of tolerance or withdrawal (i.e., neither Item 1 nor 2 is present).[4]

If symptoms of an individual's alcohol or other drug abuse do not include tolerance, a withdrawal syndrome, or evidence of compulsive use, but continued use has harmful consequences, then the diagnosis would be Substance Abuse:

Criteria for Substance Abuse

A. A maladaptive pattern of substance use leading to clinically significant impairment or distress, as manifested by one (or more) of the following, occurring within a 12-month period:

(1) recurrent substance use resulting in a failure to fulfill major role obligations at work, school, or home (e.g., repeated absences or poor work performance related to substance use; substance-related absences, suspensions, or expulsions from school; neglect of children or household)

(2) recurrent substance use in situations in which it is physically hazardous (e.g., driving an automobile or operating a machine when impaired by substance use)

(3) recurrent substance-related legal problems (e.g., arrests for substance-related disorderly conduct)

(4) continued substance use despite having persistent or recurrent social or interpersonal problems caused or exacerbated by the effects of the substance (e.g., arguments with spouse about consequences of intoxication, physical fights)

B. The symptoms have never met the criteria for Substance Dependence for this class of substance.[5]

§ 15.3   Psychological Testing

Several psychological tests can be used to identify substance abuse problems. The Minnesota Multiphasic Personality Inventory (MMPI)/MMPI-2, including the MacAndrew Alcoholism Scale (MAC/MAC-R), provides a valid and reliable measure of alcohol and other drug abuse that is usable with nearly all populations. Unlike the Michigan Alcoholism Screening Test (MAST) and the Alcohol Use Inventory (AUI), the items on the MMPI by and large do not have face validity—that is, one cannot tell just by looking at most of the items that they could be used to diagnose alcohol or other drug abuse. This makes the MMPI/MMPI-2 (and the MAC/MAC-R) the test of choice in custody evaluations, where people are likely to at least "put their best foot forward," if not outright lie, in order to influence the outcome.[6] Each of these tests is discussed below.

---

[4] *Id.* at 181. Used with permission. Copyright 1994 American Psychiatric Association.

[5] *Id.* at 182–83.

[6] Readers interested in the psychopharmacology of drugs of abuse should consult Goodman and Gilman's The Pharmacological Basis of Therapeutics, 10th ed. (G. Goodman et al. eds., 2001).

§ 15.4   Minnesota Multiphasic Personality Inventory/Minnesota Multiphasic Personality Inventory–Second Edition

The MAC, part of the MMPI, and the MAC-R, which is contained in the MMPI-2, were developed to differentiate alcoholic from nonalcoholic psychiatric patients.[7] The test has high reliability according to a number of studies, even over a span of 13 years.[8] C. MacAndrew reported that a cutoff score of 24 correctly classified 82 percent of the alcoholics and nonalcoholics in his research. "Most subsequent research has indicated that the MAC effectively differentiates alcoholic from nonalcoholic patients in a variety of settings. . . . There also are data suggesting that drug addicts score higher than other psychiatric patients but not differently from alcoholics on the MAC."[9] "Research has indicated that the scale is a very useful one for identifying substance abuse problems of various kinds for men and women in a variety of settings."[10] Caution should be used when giving the MAC to black individuals, according to several studies, because nonalcoholic black psychiatric patients also tend to score high on the MAC.[11] George Jacobson, Ph.D., psychologist and researcher, indicates that the MAC appears to be "the best test of its kind."[12]

Researcher John Allen identified personality correlates of the MAC by reviewing 10 research studies. He found that male patients who had high MAC scores tended to have more characterological features than did low MAC males, and were more likely to act out. High MAC males also tended to have high scores on Scales 4 and 9 of the MMPI. High MAC female patients, in contrast, differed from low MAC females in having lower scores on Scales 2 and 0—in other words, women who had low MAC scores tended to be more depressed and introverted.[13]

Alcoholics who nonetheless scored low (below 24) on the MAC appeared to be Type I alcoholics, whose alcoholism was late-onset and less severe. Those with high scores on the MAC were largely Type II alcoholics, with early onset of alcohol abuse, family history of alcoholism, and psychopathic characteristics.[14]

A 1992 research study found similar results. High MAC patients tended to be gregarious drinkers, to have alcohol-related legal problems, to have a tendency to drink primarily in social situations, to be drunk three or more times a week, and to use other drugs as well. They also tended to have a 4-9 pattern on the MMPI and to be Type II alcoholics. Low MAC patients tended to have a 4-2 pattern on the MMPI—that is, they were more

---

[7] John Graham, The MMPI: A Practical Guide 170 (2d ed. 1987); J. Graham, MMPI-2 141 (1993).

[8] *Id.* at 170.

[9] *Id.* at 170–71.

[10] *Id.* at 89.

[11] *Id.* at 171; John Graham & V. Strenger, *MMPI Characteristics of Alcoholics: A Review*, 56 J. Consulting & Clinical Psychol. 201 (1988) [hereinafter *MMPI Characteristics of Alcoholics: A Review*].

[12] George Jacobson, The Alcoholisms: Detection, Assessment, and Diagnosis 237 (1976) [hereinafter The Alcoholisms].

[13] John P. Allen, *Personality Correlates of the MacAndrew Alcoholism Scale: A Review of the Literature*, 5 Psychol. Addictive Behav. 59–65 (1991).

[14] *Id.*

depressed and acted out less. Although low MAC patients had a similar degree of problems with alcohol, the problems were less likely to involve legal difficulties. It is suggested that low MAC scores not be used to rule out alcoholism, because these alcoholics got low scores but did not have fewer problems.[15]

However, psychologist John Graham, Ph.D., one of the foremost MMPI researchers, indicates that when the MAC score is less than 24, one may be confident that the individual is *not* a substance abuser, because there are few false negatives with this instrument. When the MAC is 28 or greater, he indicates, one may be confident that the individual *is* a substance abuser.[16]

> When MMPI scores of alcoholics were examined and/or compared with scores of nonalcoholics, the most consistent finding was that alcoholics scored relatively high on Scale 4. . . . Scale 4 elevations have been found for both male and female alcoholics. . . . Both younger and older alcoholics tend to produce elevated Scale 4 scores. . . . Scale 4 elevations of alcoholics tend to be quite stable over time.[17]

However, for psychiatric patients, Scale 4 does *not* consistently differentiate between alcoholic and nonalcoholic individuals.[18] Graham indicates that Scale 4 will be high for nearly all substance abusers.[19]

"Very consistent data have suggested that the mean profile for groups of alcoholics is characterized" by elevations of the fourth and second scales together.[20] However, Graham cautions, only one-quarter of alcoholics have this profile, and many people with elevations on Scales 2 and 4 are *not* alcoholics.[21]

Graham reports that S.G. Goldstein and J.D. Linden have identified four basic types of alcoholics in their 1969 cluster analysis.[22] Since that time, D.M. Eshbaugh, D.J. Tosi, and C. Hoyt identified a Type V alcoholic,[23] and K.L. Bean and G.O. Karasievich have identified a Type VI alcoholic.[24]

Type I alcoholics.   Type I alcoholics typically have a primary elevation on Scale 4 of the MMPI, secondary on Scale 2, and no other scales significantly elevated. They generally have some type of personality disorder diagnosis. They are not likely to have a previous

---

[15] Svanum & Ehrmann, *Alcoholic Subtypes and the MacAndrew Alcoholism Scale*, 58 J. Personality Assessment 411–22 (1992).

[16] John Graham, MMPI Workshop, Minneapolis, Minn. (June 1987).

[17] MMPI Characteristics of Alcoholics: A Review at 197.

[18] *Id.* at 198.

[19] John Graham, MMPI Workshop, Minneapolis, Minn. (June 1987).

[20] *MMPI Characteristics of Alcoholics: A Review* at 198.

[21] John Graham, MMPI Workshop, Minneapolis, Minn. (June 1987).

[22] S.G. Goldstein & J.O. Linden, *Multivariate Classification of Alcoholics by Means of the MMPI*, 6 J. Abnormal Psychol. 661 (1969).

[23] O.M. Eshbaugh et al., *Some Personality Patterns and Dimensions of Male Alcoholics: A Multivariate Description*, 42 J. Personality Assessment 409 (1978).

[24] K.L. Bean & G.O. Karasievich, *Psychological Test Results at Three Stages of Inpatient Alcoholism Treatment*, 36 J. Stud. on Alcohol 838 (1975).

psychiatric history, although they may have prior alcoholism treatment. Their problems are not as severe as other types, even though they may be long-standing. Frequency and quantity of alcohol consumed are not as severe as is the case with other types of alcoholics. Anger and acting out, along with poor marital and vocational adjustment, are followed by guilt and remorse. These individuals generally have a negative response to treatment, since they are generally denying their disorders. However, they will usually agree to treatment to avoid unpleasant consequences such as jail or divorce.[25]

Type II alcoholics.   Type II alcoholics also have an elevated Scale 4. However, Scales 2, 7, and 8 are generally higher than Scale 4. These individuals often fall in a "dual diagnosis" category, which includes alcoholism plus a separate diagnosis of a non-AODA psychological problem. They have a wide variety of symptoms, including depression, despondency, social withdrawal, feelings of inadequacy, eating disorders, and job instability. They tend to get angry when drinking and are more likely to get in trouble when they have been drinking. These individuals tend to drink to self-medicate and do respond well to treatment. They show a greater likelihood of staying in treatment, although progress is slow. Alcoholics in this group demonstrate a very high alcohol use.[26]

Type III alcoholics.   Type III alcoholics have a primary elevation on Scale 4 and secondary elevations on Scales 2 and/or 9. Their validity scales do not show a defensive pattern. Generally, the elevations on Scales 2 and 4 are within normal limits.[27] More than any other groups, these individuals receive a diagnosis of alcoholism. The next more frequent diagnosis for this group would be a personality disorder, an anxiety disorder, and/or a depressive disorder. They tend to have long histories of alcohol abuse, with periodic acute episodes. Many of them have had brief hospitalizations for alcoholism. They are seen as being impulsive and narcissistic. They tend to act insensitively toward others, then feel guilt and remorse. These individuals tend to respond poorly to treatment, because they do not see themselves as needing treatment. As a result, they tend to be uncooperative and terminate treatment prematurely.[28]

Type IV alcoholics.   Type IV alcoholics have an elevation on Scales 4 and 9 and no other significant elevations. The most frequent diagnoses are "alcohol abuse" or "alcohol dependence," coexisting with an Antisocial Personality Disorder. Type IV alcoholics are often in trouble with the authorities, and are narcissistic and impulsive. Their relationships tend to be shallow and superficial. They typically have low frustration tolerance and frequent emotional outbursts. These individuals tend not to have had previous psychological treatment and can achieve long periods of abstinence followed by periods of abuse. Since they do not perceive themselves as having problems, they are not likely to respond well to treatment.[29]

---

[25] *MMPI Characteristics of Alcoholics: A Review* at 198.

[26] *Id.* at 199.

[27] John Graham, MMPI Workshop, Oconomowoc, Wis. (Apr. 1988).

[28] *MMPI Characteristics of Alcoholics: A Review* at 199.

[29] *Id.* at 198–99.

Type V alcoholics. Type V alcoholics have elevations on Scales 1, 2, and 3, and some-times on Scale 4 as well. They are likely to have had previous outpatient treatment, and they use alcohol as self-treatment for symptoms of anxiety and depression. Gastrointestinal symptoms are the most common presenting complaint for these individu-als. They tend to see their problems as being more medical than psychological and do not perceive themselves as being alcoholics.[30]

Type VI alcoholics. Type VI alcoholics have significant elevations on Scales 8 and F, and several other scales may be elevated as well. A typical dual-diagnosis for this group is "schizophrenia" together with alcoholism. The psychological history of Type VI alcoholics is likely to include inpatient treatment for a psychosis, and often major tranquilizers are prescribed. This group of alcoholics have poor judgment, inappropriate affect, and diffi-culty coping with everyday life. They often become belligerent. They are likely to require inpatient treatment and do not do well in psychotherapy.[31]

Graham points out that alcoholics whose Scale 4 is elevated in conjunction with other scales are more likely to be "characterological alcoholics," while those with the Scale 1, 2, or 3 elevations (with or without other scale elevations) are more likely to be "neurotic alco-holics." The characterological alcoholics are much less likely to be able to benefit from treatment than are the neurotic alcoholics.[32]

> Psychologists Leslie Morey, William Roberts, and Walter Penk found that a large proportion of cluster analysis studies have identified an MMPI profile that is characteristic of this alco-hol dependence syndrome, namely, a profile characterized by a 2-8-7-4 configuration. Furthermore, the absolute elevation of this profile may be a useful estimate of the degree of alcohol dependence manifest in a particular individual.[33]

These people are "characterized by depression, alienation, anxiety, and impulsiveness."[34] Graham indicates that Scale 8 is rarely high for alcoholics, while it is often high for heroin addicts.[35]

The MMPI-2 has two new scales for assessing alcohol or other drug abuse: the 39-item Addiction Potential Scale (APS) and the 13-item Addiction Acknowledgement Scale (AAS). Both were found to discriminate well between samples who did and did not abuse alcohol or other drugs, and to do so better than the MAC-Revised (MAC-R) Scale. Test-retest reliability scores were .77 for females and .69 for males on the APS and .84 for females and .89 for males on the AAS. The former two scores are low but adequate; the latter two are quite acceptable. The authors of the study call for further research on these scales though, before they are fully accepted, due to several methodological questions.[36]

---

[30] *Id.* at 200.

[31] *Id.*

[32] John Graham, MMPI Workshop, Oconomowoc, Wis. (Apr. 1988).

[33] Leslie Morey et al., *MMPI Alcoholic Subtypes: Replicability and Validity of the 2-7-8-4 Subtype,* 96 J. Abnormal Psychol. 164, 166 (1987) [hereinafter *MMPI Alcoholic Subtypes*].

[34] *Id.*

[35] John Graham, MMPI Workshop, Minneapolis, Minn. (June 1987).

[36] Nathan C. Weed et al., *New Measures for Assessing Alcohol and Drug Abuse with the MMPI-2: The APS and AAS,* 58 J. Personality Assessment 389–404 (1992).

Another study evaluated whether the APS and AAS would work equally well in a different setting from that in which they were initially validated, using a private hospital and a state psychiatric hospital. It was found that the APS and AAS both discriminated well between the substance-abusing and psychiatric samples and, again, did so better than did the MAC-R. There was also evidence that the APS may be more resistant than the other scales to distortion caused by high F-Scale (F and FB) responses.[37]

See **Chapter 9** for further discussion regarding the MMPI/MMPI-2 and the above scales.

§ 15.5   Michigan Alcoholism Screening Test

Quoting M.L. Selzer, the author of the Michigan Alcoholism Screening Test (MAST), in a review article, James Hedlund and Bruce Vieweg indicate that the test was designed "to provide a consistent, quantifiable, structured interview instrument for the detection of alcoholism that could be rapidly administered by non-professional as well as professional personnel."[38]

The MAST consists of 25 "face valid" questions about the individual's drinking behavior and any problems that may have been associated with it. Each item requires only a yes or no answer, and administration takes only about 15 minutes. Individual items are scored 0, 1, 2, or 5 points, and the total score is the sum of the individual item scores. A score of 3 or less is considered an indication of the absence of alcoholism, a score of 4 represents a suspicion or suggestion of possible alcoholism, and a score of 5 or more is presumptive evidence of alcoholism.[39]

Reliability coefficients regarding internal consistency for the MAST range from .83 to .95 in six studies cited by Hedlund and Vieweg.[40] Most of the test-retest reliability coefficients were in the .80 to .96 range. Although the items on the test have face validity (that is, one can tell what the test is getting at by looking at what it asks), there is evidence that most alcoholics will admit enough about themselves to achieve a significant score on the test, as did 92 percent in the normative sample.[41] Twenty of 21 studies of the test's accuracy in identifying diagnosed alcoholics found success rates of 79 percent to 100 percent. One study was lower (57 percent). In 15 studies of the accuracy of diagnosis of *non*alcoholics, rates ranged from 36 percent to 95 percent, with a median in the upper 80s.[42] There is some indication that the MAST produces as many as 13 percent false-positives (nonalcoholics identified as alcoholics) among psychiatric patients,[43] so caution must be used when using the MAST to diagnose psychiatric patients.

---

[37] Greene et al., *A Cross-Validation of MMPI-2 Substance Abuse Scales*, 58 J. Personality Assessment 405–10 (1992).

[38] James Hedlund & Bruce Vieweg, *The Michigan Alcoholism Screening Test (MAST): A Comprehensive Review*, 15 J. Operational Psychiatry 55 (1984) [hereinafter *The Michigan Alcoholism Screening Test (MAST)*].

[39] The Alcoholisms at 264–65.

[40] *The Michigan Alcoholism Screening Test (MAST)* at 57.

[41] *Id.* at 58.

[42] *Id.*

[43] The Alcoholisms at 277–78.

Validity coefficients for the original alcoholic versus the control group study were from .79 to .90. It should be noted that the MAST does not distinguish between current substance abuse problems and past problems that have been resolved, so follow-up questioning must address this issue.[44]

A study by psychologists Randy Otto and James Hall found that the MAST is relatively easy to fake when the individual is so motivated. When alcoholics answered honestly, all of them were correctly identified by the test. When instructed to answer as if they wanted to make a good impression, however, only two of the 20 alcoholics in the study were identified by the test. Otto and Hall therefore caution against using the MAST in situations where people may be motivated to "fake good," which would certainly include nearly all forensic situations including custody evaluations.[45]

In their review of the MAST, Hedlund and Vieweg conclude by indicating that "its internal consistency and test-retest reliability appear to be satisfactory, it is significantly related to a number of other measures of alcoholism, and it has been demonstrated to be moderately effective in identifying alcoholics from among a variety of other clinical and non-clinical groups."[46]

In another study, the MAST was administered to college students under two conditions: the traditional self-administered questionnaire and the questionnaire plus an interview to assess why specific questions had been answered in an "alcoholic" direction. It was found that a number of answers were scored incorrectly because of idiosyncratic interpretations of the questions by the students. It was also found that 10 of the 24 MAST items had false-positive rates of 60 percent or more, and seven items had false-positive rates of 100 percent. The false-positive rate across all subjects was 25.6 percent. Finally, men from families with a history of alcoholism scored higher than did men without such a family history. It is suggested that interviews be conducted in actual assessments, to ensure that valid diagnoses are made.[47]

A 1997 survey of 100 alcohol treatment programs that offer services for people arrested for driving while intoxicated found that the MAST was the most-used assessment instrument, with 58 percent of the programs using it.[48]

§ 15.6   Alcohol Use Inventory

The Alcohol Use Inventory (AUI) was initially developed by Kenneth W. Wanberg, John L. Horn, and F. Mark Foster as the "Alcohol Use Questionnaire" but renamed when it was revised slightly. The current revision contains 228 questions that can be answered objectively by checking one or more specified alternative responses. It is appropriate for

---

[44] *The Michigan Alcoholism Screening Test (MAST)* at 59–61.

[45] Randy Otto & James Hall, *The Utility of the Michigan Alcoholism Screening Test in Detection of Alcoholics and Problem Drinkers*, 52 J. Personality Assessment 499–505 (1988).

[46] *The Michigan Alcoholism Screening Test (MAST)* at 62.

[47] Svikis et al., *Effect of Item Correction on Michigan Alcoholism Screening Test Scores in College Men with and without a Family History of Alcoholism*, 3 Psychol. Assessment 654–59 (1991).

[48] Linda E. Myerholtz & Harold Rosenberg, *Screening DUI Offenders for Alcohol Problems: Psychometric Assessment of the Substance Abuse Subtle Screening Inventory*, 11 Psychol. Addictive Behav. 155, 155 (1997).

individuals age 16 and older. It is not appropriate for people who do not drink. The test can be administered individually or in groups and takes about 30 to 60 minutes to complete.[49] The test authors' major premise is that alcoholism is probably not a unitary entity; rather, there are a number of *alcoholisms*.[50]

Most of the variables on the AUI have a high degree of face validity.[51] When individuals are willing to be open and honest, this is no problem. However, it may be a problem with people who are trying to hide or deny negative behavior—as one would expect of people in a custody dispute.

Carl Isenhart used the AUI to differentiate between alcoholics whose fathers abused alcohol and alcoholics whose fathers did not, on the basis of evidence that sons of alcoholic parents are likely to drink at an earlier age and to have more personal and social problems. It was found that the AUI was successful at differentiating between these groups, an indication that the test has criterion validity.[52]

The Supplement to the Eleventh Mental Measurements Yearbook includes two reviews of the AUI. The first, by professor Robert J. Drummond, notes that the AUI's newest revision added three new scales, bringing the number to 24, all derived by factor analysis. Reliability coefficients generally range from .65 to .80. There is inadequate data on use of the test with non-whites. Drummond considers the test to be valid and useful.[53]

The second review is by professor Sharon McNeely. She indicates concern that the AUI is labeled as a test on the cover and title pages, potentially leading respondents to believe that there is a correct answer to each question. The instrument has both content and criterion validity, she indicates. A drawback is that the test has primarily been evaluated with Caucasians, leading to questions regarding its validity with other ethnic groups.[54]

In custody evaluations, the AUI is likely to produce many false-negatives, as people try to present themselves in a positive light. Nevertheless, when it does indicate that alcoholism is present, that result may be taken in context as an indication of unusual openness and honesty.

§ 15.7   Effect of Alcohol and Other Drug Use/Abuse on Children

Alcohol

The above MMPI factor analytic and cluster analysis studies describe the alcoholic (and most other drug abusers) as being depressed, anxious, alienated, and impulsive,[55] as well

---

[49] Robert J. Drummond, *Alcohol Use Inventory, in* The Supplement to the Eleventh Mental Measurements Yearbook 9 (Jane Close Conoley & James C. Impara eds., 1994) [hereinafter Robert J. Drummond, *Alcohol Use Inventory.*

[50] The Alcoholisms at 80.

[51] *Id.* at 98–99.

[52] Carl Isenhart, *Further Support for the Criterion Validity of the Alcohol Use Inventory*, 4 Psychol. Addictive Behav. 77–81 (1990).

[53] Robert J. Drummond, *Alcohol Use Inventory*, at 9–10.

[54] Sharon McNeely, *Alcohol Use Inventory, in* The Supplement to the Eleventh Mental Measurements Yearbook 10–11 (Jane Close Conoley & James C. Impara eds., 1994).

[55] *MMPI Alcoholic Subtypes* at 166.

as having "a tendency to . . . resent authority, to have low frustration tolerance, and to have poorly controlled anger."[56] In addition, the fact that they are not meaningfully available to their families during periods of acute intoxication, during hangovers and other consequences of intoxication, and during time spent obtaining drugs worsens the picture.

It should be emphasized that it is not the drinking, per se, that is the problem. Drinking "becomes a 'problem' when it interferes with functioning in significant areas of life, e.g., work, family relationships, social relationships, etc."[57]

Alan Berkowitz and H. Wesley Perkins, of Hobart and William Smith Colleges, Geneva, New York, note that

> in a comprehensive review of the literature on children of alcoholics (COAs), Russell, Henderson and Blume (1985) concluded that such children are at a particularly high risk for alcoholism and other emotional and behavioral problems, including difficult social adjustment and substance abuse. They also cited studies in which COAs were found to possess distinctive personality characteristics, including lower self-esteem.[58]

Berkowitz and Perkins used eight personality measures with a group of self-identified COAs who were not in treatment. They found that the late-adolescent/young adult COAs in their study reported significantly greater self-depreciation than did non-COAs, and that the difference was greater for women than men. They also noted a greater propensity for depression among the women.[59] In addition, they found that some COAs showed little or no difference from their peers, indicating that some COAs are resilient enough to cope with the situation successfully.

Similarly, Janet G. Woititz identifies 13 problems that COAs are likely to experience to some degree and that can pose life-long struggles. Children of alcoholics

> guess what normal behavior is; have difficulty following a project through from beginning to end; lie when it would be just as easy to tell the truth; judge themselves without mercy; have difficulty having fun; take themselves very seriously; have difficulty with intimate relationships; overreact to changes over which they have no control; constantly seek approval and affirmation; feel that they are different from other people; are super-responsible or super-irresponsible; are extremely loyal, even in the face of evidence that the loyalty is undeserved; tend to lock themselves into a course of action without giving consideration to consequences.[60]

Laurie Chassin, Fred Rogosch, and Manuel Barrera studied the effect of parental alcoholism on adolescents, utilizing large experimental and control groups. They found that COAs have a significantly greater risk of either externalizing problems through development of conduct disorders, or internalizing problems through development of anxiety or depression. The COA adolescents also had a greater likelihood of using alcohol or other drugs themselves. There was some evidence that the risk for conduct disorders

---

[56] *MMPI Characteristics of Alcoholics: A Review* at 202.

[57] R. Gardner, Family Evaluation in Child Custody Litigation 257 (1982).

[58] Alan Berkowitz & H. Wesley Perkins, *Personality Characteristics of Children of Alcoholics*, 56 J. Consulting & Clinical Psychol. 206, 206 (1988).

[59] *Id.* at 209.

[60] Janet Geringer Woititz, *Adult Children of Alcoholics, quoted in* 5 Med. Psychotherapist 9 (1989).

was not unique to parental alcoholism but rather was related to co-occurring psychopathology in these parents and also to the stress and disruption that is associated with parental alcoholism. However, when the adolescent's alcohol or [other] drug use was the outcome variable, parent [and especially father's] alcoholism was a unique predictor even after the effects of co-occurring parental psychopathology and environmental stress were considered.[61]

Chassin, Rogosch, and Barrera concluded that

> parental alcoholism is associated with general parental impairment and poor role functioning that impairs the quality of the family environment and the stability of the child's life. Such increased stress and disruption raises the risk for negative outcomes in a rather non-specific way, so that all negative outcomes were more likely."[62]

Kenneth Sher, Kimberly Walitzer, Philip Wood, and Edward Brent studied a large sample of college freshmen who were children of alcoholics. They found that these children "evidenced greater alcohol involvement, greater negative consequences associated with drug use, greater behavioral undercontrol [more hyperactivity, impulsivity, extraversion, aggressiveness, antisociality, and sensation seeking], and greater psychiatric distress. In addition, they evidenced lower verbal abilities and academic achievement."[63] Freshmen who had an alcoholic father reported significantly greater rates of alcohol use during the past year—but not the past month—than did freshmen from nonalcoholic families.[64]

J. David Hawkins, Richard Catalano, and Janet Miller reviewed many research studies in an attempt to identify risk factors for alcohol or other drug abuse. They found that "poor parenting practices, high levels of conflict in the family, and a low degree of bonding between children and parents appear to increase risk for adolescent problem behaviors generally, including the abuse of alcohol and other drugs."[65] In addition, both parental and sibling alcoholism were found to increase the risk of alcohol or other drug abuse in children. Drug use by parents was associated with adolescents' starting to use alcohol and other drugs. Parental attitudes toward alcohol and other drugs were also found to be significant factors. When parents' attitudes were permissive toward these substances, both alcohol use and other drug use were higher.

Finally, Hawkins, Catalano, and Miller indicated that "the risk of drug abuse appears to be increased by family management practices characterized by unclear expectations for behavior, poor monitoring of behavior, few and inconsistent rewards for positive behavior, and excessively severe and inconsistent punishment for unwanted behavior."[66] The

---

[61] Laurie Chassin et al., *Substance Use and Symptomatology among Adolescent Children of Alcoholics*, 100 J. Abnormal Psychol. 449, 460 (1991).

[62] *Id.*

[63] Kenneth Sher et al., *Characteristics of Children of Alcoholics: Putative Risk Factors, Substance Use and Abuse, and Psychopathology*, 100 J. Abnormal Psychol. 427, 437 (1991).

[64] *Id.*

[65] J. David Hawkins et al., *Risk and Protective Factors for Alcohol and Other Drug Problems in Adolescence and Early Adulthood: Implications for Substance Abuse Prevention*, 112 Psychol. Bull. 64, 82 (1992).

[66] *Id.* at 83.

researchers also concluded that "children raised in families high in conflict appear at risk for both delinquency and illegal drug use."[67]

Carl Isenhart found that sons of fathers who had significant alcohol-related problems had "higher levels of alcohol-related loss of behavioral control, greater social role maladaptation, and more severe hangovers" than did the sons of fathers who did not have alcohol-related problems. "Overall, the [sons of alcoholic fathers] had more alcohol-related deterioration and more indicators of problematic drinking. . . . [This group] was also significantly younger . . . [suggesting] that [they] may become involved with an inpatient program at an earlier age.[68]

Diane Meyer and Walter Phillips indicate that estimates of the number of children living with an alcoholic parent range from 7 million to more than 28 million. They also report that an estimated 67 percent of children who have alcoholic mothers develop a diagnosable emotional disorder. Finally, they indicate that more than 5,000 young people between the ages of 15 and 22 have committed suicide each year since 1977. They investigated whether there may be a connection between the statistics on alcoholism and those on suicide. They note that children of an alcoholic or severely codependent mother may experience emotional deprivation from early in life. If the mother is unpredictable, belligerent, anxious, or preoccupied, this will also have an adverse effect on children, who may fear abandonment or feel shame. Such children may not develop a sense of confidence and power; the world may seem unpredictable. They may lack an adequate ability to experience themselves and relate to others. They may come to believe that no one will ever be available to address their needs. This feeling being intolerable for most people, such children develop defenses before they are teenagers to deal with the pain they feel.[69]

Unfortunately, these defense mechanisms are seldom effective during adolescence. The adolescent feels rage associated with the perceived abandonment in childhood, yet guilty over having such strong negative feelings toward parents, Meyer and Phillips continue. With time, adolescents begin to hate themselves and others. They find little psychological comfort alone, with peers, or with family, and often feel hopeless and helpless. The more demanding and sadistic the alcoholic parent(s), the worse the child is likely to feel. If the child feels responsible for the parent's behavior, the feelings of self-worth decline further. "Suicide provides the promise of a safe place without pain or pressure, a place where there is peace and serenity. . . . The act of suicide negates the pain of past helplessness and present hopelessness; it allows for distorted feelings of 'I am capable' and 'I am effective.' "[70]

Richard Velleman and Jim Orford compared 164 16- to 35-year-old children of parents with problem drinking and 80 control subjects. They found that the COAs "reported significantly worse childhood environments, substantially more traumatic child experiences, and substantially less happy, cohesive and stable childhood relationships, describing

---

[67] *Id.*

[68] Carl Isenhart, *Further Support for the Criterion Validity of the Alcohol Use Inventory*, 4 Psychol. Addictive Behav. 77, 80 (1990).

[69] Diane Meyer & Walter Phillips, *No Safe Place: Parental Alcoholism and Adolescent Suicide*, 44 Am. J. Psychotherapy 552, 556 (1990).

[70] *Id.*

negative and often violent parental and family relationships and a high degree of separateness between their home environments and their outside social activities."[71] Importantly, they found that the relevant problem was not the drinking per se; rather disharmony between the parents and within the family was the primary predictor of dysfunction among the children. For the relatively few children of alcoholics who reported no significant disharmony growing up, there was no significant difference from the control subjects. The researchers also found that a majority of the children of alcoholics coped with the problems at home by avoiding the alcoholic parent as much as possible.[72]

In a report based upon the National Institute of Mental Health Epidemiologic Catchment Area Project, 408 children of alcoholics were compared with 1,477 matched subjects without alcoholic parents. The COAs had significantly more psychiatric disorders (particularly anxiety disorders and depression) and antisocial symptoms than did the control subjects. Male COAs had significantly more diagnoses of alcohol or other drug abuse than had the male control subjects.[73] Similar results were also reported for another, larger (2,936) sample from the Epidemiologic Catchment Area Project. The authors of the latter study controlled for other sources of stress and found that both psychiatric problems and marital instability were more common among children of alcoholics. COAs were more likely to walk out on their spouses, and there was some evidence they may also have a greater probability of repeated separations and divorces.[74]

A small study of 32 children (ages 5 to 16) and their parents (one or both of whom had alcohol problems) was conducted to try to ascertain ways of preventing problems for the children as they grew up. The parents consistently believed that the children knew nothing of their problems with alcohol—on the contrary, the children consistently knew of the alcohol abuse for up to several years. Some of the younger children tried to stop their parent(s) from drinking, often utilizing magical thinking. The children voiced fear of abandonment, fear of parental death, fear they were not loved, and fear that they would be branded "losers" themselves if people found out about the parental alcohol abuse. Many of the children would cry, emotionally shut down, or hide when a parent was drinking—hoping the parent would notice and make a change. Some sought contact with children outside the home, but none sought contact with other adults. The children's primary need was for the parent(s) to stop drinking, followed by a need to have a break from living in the stressful family situation—for example, by going to camp or on a trip. The author of the study recommended that children of parents in treatment for alcohol abuse automatically receive help as well, to facilitate their current and future coping.[75]

---

[71] Richard Velleman & Jim Orford, *The Importance of Family Discord in Explaining Childhood Problems in the Children of Problem Drinkers*, 1 Addiction Res. 39, 51 (1993).

[72] *Id.* at 52–53.

[73] Roy J. Mathew et al., *Psychiatric Disorders in Adult Children of Alcoholics: Data from the Epidemiologic Catchment Area Project*, 150 Am. J. Psychiatry 793–800 (1993).

[74] Shelly F. Greenfield et al., *Long-Term Psychosocial Effects of Childhood Exposure to Parental Problem Drinking*, 150 Am. J. Psychiatry 608–13 (1993).

[75] Else Christensen, *Aspects of a Preventive Approach to Support Children of Alcoholics*, 6 Child Abuse Rev. 24–34 (1997).

Other Research Results

Not all research on children of alcoholics is negative, however. As noted by Theodore Jacob, while there is a lengthy list of problems experienced by these children,

> empirical substantiation of these characterizations has been marked by a lack of consistent findings, sound research methods, and comprehensive conceptualizations. Most important, this literature points to considerable variability among children of alcoholics. . . . Close examination of this literature, however, reveals few efforts that . . . distinguish patterns that are unique to alcoholic family interactions versus general stress factors associated with various types of psychopathology.[76]

Deborah Wright and P. Paul Heppner studied two groups of 40 college-age students, one with and one without a family history of alcoholism. Most were first-semester freshmen. The researchers found no differences between the groups on any of the studied variables: problem-solving appraisal, social support, shame, suicidal ideation, and substance use. The children of alcoholics seemed as well-adjusted as the children from nonalcoholic homes. Like Jacob, Wright and Heppner concluded that children of alcoholics may be a heterogeneous group—so it is not extraordinary to find that people in a research sample do not have the problems attributed to these children by a number of other studies.[77]

V.E. Pollock, John Briere, Lon Schneider, Joachim Knop, Sarnoff Mednick, and Donald Goodwin studied 131 sons of alcoholic fathers, comparing them with 70 sons from non-pathological families. The sons of alcoholics group included 32 subjects who indicated that they had been beaten by a parent—either many violent physical attacks or at least one so severe it required hospital treatment. The authors of the study found that the sons of alcoholic fathers did not have a history of antisocial behavior more extreme than that of the control subjects. Men who had been victims of child abuse did report significant anti-social behavior, however. Furthermore, the probability of antisocial behavior was greater among men who both had alcoholic fathers and were victims of physical abuse. The results suggest that being the child of an alcoholic, by itself, may not necessarily lead to an increase in psychopathology or behavioral pathology. The combination of alcoholic fathers and physical child abuse did lead to increased pathology in the children.[78]

Theodore Jacob, Gloria Krahn, and Kenneth Leonard studied parent-adolescent interactions in families with alcoholic fathers, comparing them with families in which the father was depressed and with families in which the father showed no significant psychopathology. They found that there are few parent-child interactions that are unique to families with an alcoholic parent. Both the "alcoholic father" and "depressed father" families evidenced communication and other problems among family members, and both had significantly more problems than did the nonpathological families. The study concluded that a father's

---

[76] Theodore Jacob, *Family Studies of Alcoholism*, 5 J. Fam. Psychol. 319, 321 (1992).

[77] Deborah Wright & P. Paul Heppner, *Coping among Nonclinical College-Age Children of Alcoholics*, 38 J. Counseling Psychol. 465–72 (1991).

[78] V.E. Pollock et al., *Childhood Antecedents of Antisocial Behavior*, 147 Am. J. Psychiatry 1290–93 (1990).

alcoholism, by itself, does not lead to adverse outcomes for the children of the family, though it may contribute to negative outcomes that involve other factors as well.[79]

Sedative-Hypnotics

Sedative-hypnotics are central nervous system depressants that, for all practical purposes in the context of this chapter, are like "solid alcohol." That is, drugs such as barbiturates (for example, Seconal, Luminal, Nembutal), non-barbiturate hypnotics (sleep-inducers) (for example, Doriden, Noludar, Quaalude), and antianxiety medications (for example, Librium, Valium, Xanax, Tranxene, Ativan, Halcion) will each have characteristics like those described above for alcohol at equivalent dosages. That is why the drugs of this type come with warnings not to operate heavy machinery (including cars) or otherwise do anything that requires one's full attention and the ability to respond quickly in an emergency.

Drugs of this type tend to be used or abused by people who feel overstimulated by life and, as a result, have difficulty relaxing, concentrating, sleeping, and so forth. None are dangerous for a healthy individual at low, physician-prescribed dosages. All can sufficiently alter attention, awareness, and responsiveness to make them dangerous when used abusively. In addition, most of them are *potentiated* by alcohol—that is, they have an additive effect, so that one "unit" of alcohol and one "unit" of the sedative-hypnotic-type drug approximately equal two "units" of psychomotor depression and other central nervous system effects. Some combinations are also *synergistic* with alcohol, whereby one plus one may equal more than two.

All of the cautions that apply to alcohol apply to this class of drugs as well. Like alcohol, these drugs may also cause physical dependence, and abrupt cessation of use of many of them may cause potentially life-threatening seizures. When prescribed by a physician for temporary use, it is not necessarily a negative in any sense for a parent to use these drugs. When abused, of course, they may make a parent less psychologically and physically available to the child, with deleterious consequences.

Stimulants

Stimulants are drugs that increase central nervous system activity, leading to generally good feelings at low doses—energetic, happier, better attention, and so forth. At high doses, however, they may cause nervousness, agitation, and even hallucinations. Examples of stimulants include caffeine, nicotine, amphetamines, and cocaine, each of which has legal uses as well as a potential for abuse.

People who use these drugs abusively may overestimate their ability to do various tasks, including driving, and may therefore take chances with their own lives and the lives of others. At high doses over an extended period of time, most of these drugs can cause an acute psychotic break due to a combination of the pharmacological effect of the drug, the lack of sleep, and inadequate nutrition (because these drugs are generally appetite suppressants) that accompany abusive use. Given these potentials, use of stimulants by a parent in any but the

---

[79] Theodore Jacob et al., *Parent-Child Interactions in Families with Alcoholic Fathers*, 59 J. Consulting & Clinical Psychol. 176–81 (1991).

lowest doses needs to be evaluated by the psychologist or psychiatrist assessing the family.

Narcotic Analgesics

Narcotic analgesics include the natural and synthetic opiates (for example, opium, heroin, morphine, codeine, Dilaudid, Percodan, Demerol). They tend to impart a feeling of well-being in the individual as well as reducing pain. As central nervous system depressants, the same sorts of cautionary statements accompany them as accompany the sedative-hypnotics. As with alcohol and the sedative-hypnotics, people may become physically dependent on these drugs, but such drugs tend to be safer to quit "cold turkey" than are alcohol and the sedative-hypnotics.

Like the sedative-hypnotics, these drugs may be appropriately used as prescribed by a physician. When abused, however, they are likely to make the parent less psychologically and physically available to the child, thereby having a deleterious effect on the child.

Psychedelics and Cannabis

Psychedelics and cannabis tend to be *illusionogenic*—that is, they tend to produce illusions regarding particularly what is seen, and sometimes what is heard, felt, tasted, or smelled. Examples include lysergic acid diethylamide (LSD), mescaline, psilocybin, phencyclidine, marijuana, and hashish. Although the term "hallucinogen" has been used for many years to describe this class of drugs, it is an error to do so except when they are used at toxic dosages—and at toxic dosages many of the above classes of drugs, particularly stimulants, may produce true hallucinations (seeing or otherwise experiencing something that is objectively not present).

At low doses, these drugs have been used to facilitate psychotherapy, used in religious ceremonies by American Indians, and used for a variety of medical purposes. Marijuana has been demonstrated to reduce the violent nausea that often accompanies chemotherapy or radiotherapy for cancer, to reduce the pressure inside the eye (reducing the effects of glaucoma), and as an appetite stimulant (especially for AIDS patients).

At high doses these drugs will tend to foster misperception of one's surroundings and may have a euphoriant effect similar to that accompanying the use of stimulants. It is therefore possible for an individual who is acutely intoxicated to make errors based on these misperceptions, potentially causing accidents of various kinds.

Because most drugs in this class are illegal, it complicates matters when a parent uses them. In theory, such drugs could be used in ways and at times that would not have a deleterious influence upon the children. In practice, merely possessing them could lead to legal difficulty for the parent, with consequent problems generated for the child. The psychologist or psychiatrist doing the evaluation needs to carefully consider the precise circumstances in a given case in order to determine the potential negative influence on the children.

Urine Screening

If an individual is found to be an abuser of alcohol or other drugs, or there is a strong suspicion that the individual is an abuser even if proof is lacking, it would be appropriate to require the individual to undergo random urine screening (at least weekly) for a period of up to six months. If the individual has one "dirty urine," the authors of this text would not recommend suspension of placement nor require supervised visits solely on that basis. However, if a second dirty urine is found, decisionmakers should not hesitate to take one of these actions to ensure the safety of the child(ren). Also, if a dirty urine is found, the six-month period should start over again. Urine screening may be suspended after 6 to 12 months of clean screens, depending upon the severity of the previous history.

§ 15.8   Summary

Living with an alcoholic or other drug-abusing parent is not healthy for children and is likely to have a deleterious effect on most children in most families. Although most of the hard data concerns families of alcoholics, the conclusions given for them should apply also to nonalcoholic substance abusers. All things being equal, it would usually be better for the child to live with a single parent who is not a substance abuser than in a home with two parents, one of whom is a substance abuser.

§ 15.9   Questions for Chapter 15

Caution.   An attorney should not expect to be able to go into court and ask all the questions listed below. Preparation is necessary, referring to the content of this chapter to determine whether the question applies to a particular case. The cross-references in some of the questions refer to the place in the chapter that contains an explanation of why the particular question may be important.

1. If the individual carries a diagnosis of alcoholism, what type of treatment has the individual undergone for the alcoholism? Make a detailed determination.

2. Is the individual still involved in any outpatient programming?

3. If the substance abused is other than alcohol, have urine screens been used as a method of determining compliance with programming?

4. Has the psychologist discriminated between whether the alcoholism is more a characterological defect, as evidenced by Type I to Type IV alcoholics, or less characterological, as evidenced by Type V or VI alcoholism? See **§ 15.4.**

5. If the individual carries a diagnosis of alcoholism, what special alcoholism tests were administered either by the examiner or a specialized alcoholism diagnostician? See **§§ 15.3** through **15.6.**

6. Was the MMPI/MMPI-2 used in addition to other alcoholism tests in an effort to make sure that faking was not the cause of the results? See **§ 15.4.** See also "Validity Scales" in **Chapter 9.**

7. If the individual is an ACOA, has he or she undergone treatment?

8. What role do psychoactive drugs other than alcohol play in the family, and what negative influence do these drugs have on the children, if any?

§ 15.10   Case Digest

The source of information for most of the following cases is the *Mental and Physical Disability Law Reporter* (MPDLR), a publication of the American Bar Association. Quotations from the *Mental and Physical Disability Law Reporter*: Excerpted from *Mental and Physical Disability Law Reporter*. Copyright © 1988–1997 by the American Bar Association. Reprinted by permission. Complete information for any other sources appears in the relevant references below. The following are direct quotations from the identified source. If no source is identified, it is a summary from the court ruling. See also **Chapter 14** for cases involving both mental disorders and alcohol or other drug abuse.

Alabama

D.G v. Alabama Department of Human Resources, 569 So. 2d 400 (Ala. Civ. App. 1990). An Alabama appeals court found sufficient evidence to terminate the parental rights of a mother with alcoholism. The court noted that the department of human resources made repeated efforts to assist the mother in obtaining treatment for her alcoholism and in attempting to return her children to her custody. The mother ignored some of these efforts and others were unsuccessful. Thus, the appeals court agreed it was time to terminate the mother's rights and seek a permanent placement for her children. 15 *Mental & Physical Disability Law Reporter* 150 (1990).

Arizona

In re Maricopa County Juvenile Action No. JS-6520, 756 P.2d 335 (Ariz. Ct. App. 1988). An Arizona court of appeals reversed the termination of a father's parental rights in the absence of evidence that his children would be endangered by continuing the parental relationship or would benefit from its termination. In this case, David and Teresa were made wards of the court and placed in foster care. Between 1982 and 1985 the Department of Economic Security (DES) offered the father services to facilitate the family's reintegration. . . . The father declined these services, claiming that he was able to control his admitted life-long drinking problem. The appeals court stated that the termination of parental rights on the basis of mental illness/alcoholism was not justified merely because the children might be better off in another environment. Rather, a parent's inability to care for a child must present a danger to the child. Here, a psychiatrist stated that the father's alcoholism was in remission. While he believed that the father's personality would make it extremely difficult for him to adequately parent his children, he stated that the children had to be evaluated before he could state whether they would benefit from termination. In addition, there was no evidence that they would be harmed or endangered by allowing the parent-child relationship to continue, or that they would benefit from the relationship's termination. Consequently, the court reversed the termination and remanded the matter to the juvenile court. 12 *Mental & Physical Disability Law Reporter* 512–13 (1988).

California

San Francisco Department of Social Services v. Joan R., 276 Cal. Rptr. 183 (Ct. App. 1990). A California appeals court found it would not be detrimental to return a child to the custody of his father, a recovering alcoholic. . . . Although the father had abused alcohol when the child first was removed from the family, there was no substantial evidence of further abuse. The appeals court overturned the trial court's order terminating the father's parental rights and awarded him custody because the lower court based its finding of detriment to the child on past, not present, circumstances. 15 *Mental & Physical Disability Law Reporter* 257 (1991).

Connecticut

In re Romance M., 622 A.2d 1047 (Conn. App. Ct. 1993). A state appeals court affirmed a decision terminating the parental rights of a woman addicted to alcohol to her three oldest children but not to her youngest child who was born in 1988. The mother's severe addiction, her poor prognosis for rehabilitation, and her failure to recognize her problem properly supported the lower court's determination as to the three older children. The petition to terminate the mother's parental rights as to the youngest child was properly denied because the grounds for termination had lasted less than one year. The appeals court also ruled that it was proper to disclose privileged communications between the mother and the psychiatrist treating her for alcoholism because it was disclosed in a parental termination case in which the mother's mental health was an issue. The patient-psychiatric privilege must give way once it is shown that the communications and records at issue are relevant to the termination proceedings. 17 *Mental & Physical Disability Law Reporter* 382 (1993).

Indiana

S.E.S. v. Grant County Department of Welfare, 582 N.E.2d 886 (Ind. Ct. App. 1991). An Indiana appeals court affirmed the termination of a mother's rights, where the evidence showed she was not likely to recover from her alcoholism. The mother claimed that her alcoholism was the root of the problems that led to her losing custody of her children, and that she had conquered this by remaining sober for six months. The appeals court stated that the trial court was entitled to find that the mother was likely to regress after she left a structured environment, as she had done in the past. The appeals court also rejected the mother's contention that the county department of public welfare was statutorily required to provide her with pre-termination services aimed at treating her alcoholism. 16 *Mental & Physical Disability Law Reporter* 167 (1992).

Iowa

In re M.Z., 481 N.W.2d 532 (Iowa Ct. App. 1991). An Iowa appeals court affirmed the termination of a mother's parental rights, finding clear and convincing evidence that her alcoholism made her incapable of adequately caring for her baby. The mother had not complied with a social services case plan's requirements that she undergo a psychological evaluation and obtain treatment for her serious alcohol and drug abuse problems. Also, despite a social service agency's efforts, she showed little improvement in her efforts to visit her baby or in her parenting skills. Because the mother remained unable to care for her child after the statutory time period, and because the court determined that the baby would again become a "child in need of assistance" if returned to the mother, terminating the mother's rights was in the child's best interests. 16 *Mental & Physical Disability Law Reporter* 410 (1992).

Kentucky

Thomas (Glick) v. Thomas, No. 89-CA-2543-MR (Ky. Ct. App. Oct. 19, 1990). The fact that guests have occasionally used marijuana in the custodial mother's home does not constitute "serious endangerment" of her child warranting a change of custody, according to the Kentucky Court of Appeals. . . . While condemning the use of illegal substances, the court indicated that "the fact that [the mother] occasionally allowed a friend to smoke marijuana in her home is not sufficient misconduct to meet the 'serious endangerment' test set out in the statute."

Maine

In re Elijah R., 620 A.2d 282 (Me. 1993). Maine's highest court affirmed the involuntary termination of a mother's parental rights because her substance abuse and mental illness prevented her from meeting her child's need for prompt medical attention. The district court found that the mother had a long history of mental illness and substance abuse. Her substance abuse precluded her treatment of her mental illness because of the danger of mixing medications with alcohol. . . . She was hospitalized a number of times, failed to regularly attend Alcoholics Anonymous and refused to enter a long-term rehabilitation program. . . . The supreme court found clear and convincing evidence supported the finding that she was able to protect her son from harm, that she failed to make a good faith to rehabilitate herself or reunify herself and her son, and that termination was in her son's best interest. . . . [A] district court may order the termination of parental rights if it finds by clear and convincing evidence that the termination is in the best interests of the child, and one of the following

> (i) "The parent is unwilling or unable to protect the child from jeopardy and these circumstances are unlikely to change; (ii) The parent has been unwilling or unable to take responsibility for the child; (iii) The child has been abandoned; [or] (iv) The parent has failed to make a good faith effort to rehabilitate and reunify with the child."

The mother's continued drinking precluded effective treatment of her mental illness, and her repeated hospitalizations resulted in her periodic inability to care for herself or her son. 17 *Mental & Physical Disability Law Reporter* 380–81 (1993).

Wisconsin

In re K.D.J., 470 N.W.2d 914 (Wis. 1991). The Wisconsin Supreme Court affirmed a decision terminating the parental rights of a mother who abused alcohol, even though the lower court never explicitly found her unfit. It was enough that the evidence implicitly supported parental unfitness by establishing that the mother had not come to grips with her alcohol problem, leaving her child in an untenable foster care situation. 15 *Mental & Physical Disability Law Reporter* 481 (1991).

CHAPTER 16

CRIMINAL HISTORY

§ 16.1   Analysis of the Record

If one or both of the parents have a criminal record, the nature of that record and the reasons behind it need to be analyzed carefully. Relevant factors to consider include the following:

1. Seriousness of the offense(s)
2. Contributing factors from the environment
3. Personality of the offender
4. Mental state of the offender
5. Recency of the offense(s)
6. Frequency of the offense(s)
7. Evidence of rehabilitation.

§ 16.2   Seriousness of the Offense

In determining the degree of severity of an offense, the following questions are helpful:

1. Was the offense a felony or a misdemeanor?
2. Was the offense a crime against person or property?
3. Was the offense a single occurrence of criminal behavior? Or have there been multiple offenses?

Obviously, the more serious the offense committed by a parent, the more concerns there are about the parent's having custody.

§ 16.3   Contributing Factors from the Environment

Although extraneous factors do not excuse criminal behavior, they may make it possible to understand the cause for the behavior and to better weigh the relevance of the criminal act to the custody decision. Was the person caught shoplifting food because he or she was hungry? Was money embezzled because of urgent personal or family needs—for example, for food or medical treatment? Was there pressure from the spouse to come up with money or goods "no matter what"? How responsible was the individual for the altercation that led to a disorderly conduct charge? Police and court documents may shed significant light on these factors, as may interviews with family members and other significant people. These reasons for an offense may evoke sympathy, but the offense is still a criminal offense and should be addressed as such.

§ 16.4   Contributing Factors from the Family, Including Child Abuse and Neglect

The section of **Chapter 14** on parents of children who have conduct disorders should be reviewed in the context of this chapter because a significant percentage of children with Conduct Disorder diagnoses grow up to be adult criminals, particularly children who have been abused or neglected or both.[1] The reader is also urged to review **Chapter 12** and **Chapter 13** for a more complete discussion of the influence of abuse on children.

Abused children tend to respond in one of two ways. Some become "excessively aggressive and provocative, disorganized in their behavior and their thoughts [and] often become school dropouts, teenage parents, delinquents and criminals, and . . . often become abusive parents themselves."[2] Others become "excessively shy and inhibited, fearful and anxious, and suspicious toward adults. . . . The common characteristics of adults with a history of abuse in childhood are low self-esteem and a history of incompetence and failure in such

---

[1] Raczek, *Child Abuse and Personality Disorders*, 6 J. Personality Disorders 109, 109 (1992).

[2] *Id.*

areas as school, work, and marriage."[3] Most adults with Borderline Personality Disorders were victims of child abuse.[4]

Stewart Gabel and Richard Shindledecker studied 37 children who were in treatment in a children's day hospital program, with a mean age of 8.7 years and a range from 5.5 to 12.5 years. One or both parents of 16 of the children had been imprisoned at some point. All 16 had parents who were substance abusers. The boys whose fathers had been incarcerated were rated as being significantly more delinquent. All 16 families were considered dysfunctional and more dysfunctional than the average family in the day hospital program, families in which no parent was incarcerated.[5]

Children and families in the Newcastle Thousand Family Study were followed beginning with the birth of the children in 1947. Families were divided into three groups: those in which there was no evidence of deprivation (57 percent), those in which there was at least one area of deprivation (43 percent), and those in which there were at least three areas of deprivation (14 percent). Areas of deprivation included marital instability, parental illness, poor care of children and household, social dependency, overcrowding, and/or poor mothering ability.[6] It was found that

1. Offenders were more likely to come from the two lowest social classes.

2. "Male offenders more often had parents who were characterized as 'ineffective,' i.e., who did not cope with family matters, and they were also slightly more likely to have aggressive fathers, and less likely to have parents who were 'effective and kind'."[7]

3. "The proportions of convictions for men ranged from one in six of men from families who were not deprived, to more than six in ten of men from families who were much deprived during their childhood. . . . The risks were about five in ten in families where there was marital breakdown, parental illness, overcrowding, or social dependency; and about six in ten in families with defective cleanliness and poor quality of mothering all suggesting that quality of parental care is of fundamental importance. . . . Some 60% of males coming from high-risk, much-deprived family backgrounds eventually end up with a criminal record. For females, the rates are very much lower, but the ratio of offenses in the much deprived, as compared with criminality in the non-deprived, is much higher—four times higher in males but seven times higher in females."[8]

4. "The mean number of convictions is closely tied to the severity of deprivation in childhood—the more severe the childhood deprivation, the earlier the offenses are committed, and the higher the mean number of subsequent convictions, with a peak in late adolescence."[9]

---

[3] *Id.*

[4] *Id.* at 109–10.

[5] Stewart Gabel & Richard Shindledecker, *Characteristics of Children Whose Parents Have Been Incarcerated*, 44 Hosp. & Community Psychiatry 656–60 (1993).

[6] Kolvin et al., *Social and Parenting Factors Affecting Criminal-Offense Rates: Findings from the Newcastle Thousand Family Study (1947–1980)*, 152 Brit. J. Psychiatry 80, 81 (1988) [hereinafter Kolvin et al.].

[7] *Id.* at 85.

[8] *Id.* at 87.

[9] *Id.*

5. "All types of deprivation we studied had significant correlations with criminality. First, there was a strong relationship between delinquency and severity of deprivation in the case of males. Second, there was a strong relationship between delinquency and the mother's poor care of the home and the child during the early years of life, [implying] poor appreciation of the need for good-quality parenting in the early formative years, or the ability to organize, plan, or make wise provision for the future. In such circumstances, these mothers fail to provide guidance, direction, and supervision, and are poor models for imitation."[10]

6. "The association with criminality proved stronger for deprivation than for occupational status of the parents."[11]

7. "Children of ineffective parents are at high risk of delinquency. . . . The findings again emphasize the importance of poor supervision, direction, and guidance of children in the genesis of delinquency."[12]

Psychiatrist Stewart Gabel reviewed the research on children of incarcerated, criminal parents. He found that there are very few studies published, and no longitudinal research. The major variable, he suggests, is the home and family environment—including the quality of child care by the parent who remains home. Some children would be better off with the incarcerated parent absent, in cases where there was child abuse, substance abuse, or other major negative influences on the children and the household. Separation, per se, does not appear to be a major factor. It is essential to look at the situation and needs of each specific child, and to provide treatment for those children who are adversely affected by the absence of a parent. In many cases, the focus will be on helping the remaining parent develop better parenting skills.[13]

Javad Kashani and co-researchers note that no specific response can be assumed for a given child. There are, however, tendencies for abused children to have impaired social interactions, low self-esteem, depression, symptoms of Post-traumatic Stress Disorder, nightmares, anxiety, emotional constriction, and regressive behavior. They also report on a two-year research project that found abused and neglected children were significantly more likely to have violent criminal behavior later in life.[14]

§ 16.5 Family Violence

Psychologist Honore Hughes indicates that the prevalence of spouse abuse is estimated at 10 to 30 percent of families in the United States. Surveys of battered women indicate that, during the battering episode, the children are in the same room or the next room about 90 percent of the time. Children of battered women tend to exhibit depression, anxiety,

---

[10] *Id.* at 88.

[11] *Id.* at 89.

[12] Kolvin et al. at 89.

[13] Stewart Gabel, *Children of Incarcerated and Criminal Parents: Adjustment, Behavior, and Prognosis*, 20 Bull. Am. Acad. Psychiatry & L. 33–45 (1992).

[14] Javad Kashani et al., *Family Violence: Impact on Children*, 31 J. Acad. Child & Adolescent Psychiatry 181–89 (1992).

aggression, and disobedience. It has also been suggested that such children are four times as likely to evidence psychopathology as are children from nonviolent homes.[15]

Jerome Kolbo, Eleanor Blakely, and David Engleman conducted a review of 29 empirical studies published during the previous decade regarding the impact on children of being witnesses to domestic violence. They found that the research strongly indicates "that children who witness domestic violence are at risk for maladaptation in one or more of the following domains of functioning: (a) behavioral, (b) emotional, (c) social, (d) cognitive, and (e) physical."[16]

Kym Kilpatrick and Leanne Williams studied a group of 35 children, ages 6 to 12, 20 of whom had witnessed domestic violence and 15 of whom had not. They found that none of the non-witnesses showed evidence of Post-traumatic Stress Disorder, while 19 of the 20 witnesses did qualify for that diagnosis. Kilpatrick and Williams concluded that witnessing domestic violence is "comparable as a stressor to that of child physical and sexual abuse."[17]

Sandra Graham-Berman and Alytia Levendosky compared the emotional adjustment and social interactions of 21 preschool children whose mothers had been battered with those of 25 age-matched children who were not exposed to violence at home. They found that the children of battered mothers had significantly

> higher rates of sadness, depression, worry and frustration than their peers. They had less appropriate emotional responses to events. . . . Of particular interest here is the higher rate of emotional abuse of peers found for children exposed to the physical and emotional abuse of their mothers. These children had higher rates of insulting, name calling, and putting down other children. . . . The coping strategies employed by the children of battered women included avoidance and withdrawal from others. However, one crucial task for the preschool-age child is the development of appropriate and successful social relationships. The greater use of avoidance and withdrawal sets the child apart and reduces the possibility of learning to resolve problems with others.[18]

Bonnie Carlson assessed the responses of adolescents to violence between their parents. She found that "boys exposed to domestic violence were more likely to run away from home and report suicidal thoughts; there was also a tendency for them to be more likely to hit their mothers, compared to boys from more peaceful homes. [There was] elevated depression among boys exposed to frequent wife abuse."[19] No consistent effect of witnessing marital violence was found for girls.[20]

---

[15] Honore M. Hughes, *Research Concerning Children of Battered Women: Clinical Implications*, 1 J. Aggression Maltreatment & Trauma 225–44 (1997).

[16] Jerome R. Kolbo et al., *Children Who Witness Domestic Violence: A Review of Empirical Literature*, 11 J. Interpersonal Violence 281, 282 (1997).

[17] Kym L. Kilpatrick & Leanne M. Williams, *Post-traumatic Stress Disorder in Child Witnesses to Domestic Violence*, 67 Am. J. Orthopsychiatry 639, 643 (1997).

[18] Sandra A. Graham-Berman & Alytia A. Levendosky, *The Social Functioning of Preschool-Age Children Whose Mothers Are Emotionally and Physically Abused*, 1 J. Emotional Abuse 59, 75–76 (1998).

[19] Bonnie Carlson, *Adolescent Observers of Marital Violence*, 5 J. Fam. Violence 285, 295 (1990).

[20] *Id.*

Mildred Pagelow's analysis of the research literature paints a bleaker picture. She indicates that most research has shown that 75 percent or more of children in violent homes witnessed the violence. In addition, some of the children were victims of physical abuse themselves. In one study, more than 80 percent of the children who observed violence between parents were also physically abused by one or both parents. Based on case histories and observations, children in violent families tend to suffer both physical and psychological symptoms, Pagelow indicates. Small children have nightmares, insomnia, bed-wetting, headaches, stomachaches, asthma, and enuresis. Older children often feel guilty that they cannot prevent the violence. Boys may tend to act out, showing aggression and disruptive behavior, while girls are more likely to become clinging, withdrawn, passive, and anxious.[21] There are few long-term studies, Pagelow indicates, but the few there are find that children who observe marital violence tend to have more social and behavioral problems than do children from nonviolent homes, with children who are also abused themselves having the greatest incidence of problems.[22]

John Fantuzzo and his co-researchers found that, among preschool children, parental arguing led to some behavioral and emotional problems, but these were relatively mild compared with the responses of children from homes in which the children observed physical violence. The effect of witnessing the aggression was further magnified if the mother sought help by moving to a shelter with her children. Preschool children evidenced the most severely problematic behavior.[23]

Javad Kashani and colleagues, in their review of the professional literature, found that children who witness aggression between their parents are likely to experience anxiety, depression, or other internalizing symptoms. As has been shown by other studies, children who were also abused themselves showed the greatest psychopathology and behavioral problems. In addition, latency-aged children who saw their mothers beaten have been found to be more willing to use violence themselves. They also tend to feel responsible for the violence against their mothers and often feel responsible for their mothers' safety.[24]

The reader should also see **Chapter 12** regarding the influence of physical abuse on children.

§ 16.6   Contributing Factors from the Personality

Not all antisocial *behavior* is due to an antisocial *personality*. The former may range from something many people do on occasion, for example, speeding, accepting too much change from a clerk, or not reporting all one's income on tax forms—to serious crimes involving major loss of money or goods, physical harm to others, and so forth. Thus, many

[21] Mildred Pagelow, *Effects of Domestic Violence on Children and Their Consequences for Custody and Visitation Agreements*, 7 Mediation Q. 347, 350–51 (1990).

[22] *Id.* at 351.

[23] John Fantuzzo et al., *Effects of Interparental Violence on the Psychological Adjustment and Competencies of Young Children*, 59 J. Consulting & Clinical Psychol. 258–65 (1991).

[24] Javad Kashani et al., *Family Violence: Impact on Children*, 31 J. Acad. Child & Adolescent Psychiatry 181–89 (1992).

people display antisocial behavior at some time, while relatively few would be diagnosed as having an Antisocial Personality Disorder.[25]

The fourth edition of the *Diagnostic and Statistical Manual of Mental Disorders* (DSM-IV) indicates that

> the essential feature of Antisocial Personality Disorder is a pervasive pattern of disregard for, and violation of, the rights of others that begins in childhood or early adolescence and continues into adulthood.
>
> This pattern has also been referred to as psychopathy, sociopathy, or dyssocial personality disorder. . . .
>
> For this diagnosis to be given, the individual must be at least 18 years of age . . . and must have had a history of some symptoms of Conduct Disorder before age 15 years. . . . Conduct Disorder involves a repetitive and persistent pattern of behavior in which the basic rights of others or major age-appropriate societal norms or rules are violated. . . .
>
> Individuals with Antisocial Personality Disorder fail to conform to social norms with respect to lawful behavior. . . . Persons with this disorder disregard the wishes, rights, or feelings of others. They are frequently deceitful and manipulative in order to gain personal profit or pleasure. . . . A pattern of impulsivity may be manifested by a failure to plan ahead. . . . Individuals with Antisocial Personality Disorder tend to be irritable and aggressive and may repeatedly get into physical fights or commit acts of physical assault (including spouse beating or child beating). . . . These individuals also display a reckless disregard for the safety of themselves or others. . . . Individuals with Antisocial Personality Disorder also tend to be consistently and extremely irresponsible. . . . [They] show little remorse for the consequences of their acts. . . .[26]
>
> They may be irresponsible as parents, as evidenced by malnutrition of a child, an illness in the child resulting from a lack of minimal hygiene, a child's dependence on neighbors or non-resident relatives for food or shelter, a failure to arrange for a caretaker for a young child when the individual is away from home, or repeated squandering of money required for household necessities. . . .
>
> The likelihood of developing Antisocial Personality Disorder in adult life is increased if the individual experienced an early onset of Conduct Disorder (before age 10 years) and accompanying Attention-Deficit/Hyperactivity Disorder. Child abuse or neglect, unstable or erratic parenting, or inconsistent parental discipline may increase the likelihood that Conduct Disorder will evolve into Antisocial Personality Disorder.[27]

In addition to the criteria in the DSM-IV, diagnosis may be facilitated by the MMPI/MMPI-2. A large body of research has shown that individuals with high scores on Scales 4 and 9 evidence

> a marked disregard for social standards and values. They frequently get into trouble with the authorities because of antisocial behavior. They have a poorly developed conscience, easy morals, and fluctuating ethical values. . . . [They] are narcissistic, selfish, and self-indulgent.

---

[25] Lewis, *Adult Antisocial Behavior and Criminality*, *in* Comprehensive Textbook of Psychiatry/IV 1865–70 (Kaplan & Saddock eds., 1985) [hereinafter *Adult Antisocial Behavior and Criminality*.]

[26] American Psychiatric Association, Diagnostic and Statistical Manual of Mental Disorders, Fourth Edition (DSM-IV) 645–46 (1994). Reprinted with permission. Copyright 1994 American Psychiatric Association.

[27] *Id.* at 647.

They are quite impulsive and are unable to delay gratification of their impulses. They show poor judgment, often acting without considering the consequences of their acts, and they fail to learn from experience. . . . They seem to be incapable of forming deep emotional ties and keep others at an emotional distance. . . . A diagnosis of Antisocial Personality Disorder is usually associated with the 49/94 code type.[28]

There are five subscales for Scale 4 of the MMPI, developed by R.E. Harris and J.C. Lingoes.[29] Those subscales, entitled *Familial Discord, Authority Problems, Social Imperturbability, Social Alienation,* and *Self-alienation,*[30] can be a valuable adjunct to the major scale information in determining why an individual has a high score on Scale 4. Someone in a divorce or custody matter will obviously have familial discord, which can contribute substantially to the overall score for Scale 4. It is therefore important to look at these subscales prior to drawing conclusions about the meaning of a "high 4."

Numerous studies have shown that, in mean profiles of groups of prisoners in correctional institutions, Scale 4 usually is the most elevated scale.

The 4-2 and 4-9 codetypes have been identified as the most frequently occurring ones for prisoners. . . . A comprehensive and useful system of classifying criminal offenders based on the MMPI was developed by Megargee and his associates. . . . These investigators used hier-archical profile analysis to identify clusters among the MMPIs of offenders . . . [yielding] ten types of offender MMPIs and explicit rules for classifying offenders into the type to which they were most similar.[31]

A detailed discussion of the Megargee offender types is offered in § **16.7.**

Another useful instrument is the *Carlson Psychological Survey.*[32] The test assesses the Antisocial Tendencies, Thought Disturbance, Chemical Abuse, and Self-Depreciation Scales. There is also a brief validity scale. Reliability and validity data are adequate. The test was standardized on an older and more criminal population than the MMPI's criterion group, with all of Kenneth Carlson's subjects being adult male offenders serving prison sentences.[33] Carlson includes 18 offender profiles with which an individual's scores can be compared.

An individual who is diagnosable as having an Antisocial Personality Disorder would rarely be a good candidate for a custodial parent. This individual would likely be self-centered, would fail to honor commitments or to plan ahead, would be unable to sustain consistent work behavior, would fail to conform to social norms, and would be irritable and aggressive—all qualities that virtually preclude successfully addressing a child's needs. G.R. Patterson, Barbara DeBaryshe, and Elizabeth Ramsey, of the Oregon Social Learning Center, Eugene, Oregon, report that

as a predictor of adult antisocial personality, having an antisocial parent places the child at sig-nificant risk for antisocial behavior; having two antisocial parents puts the child at even higher

---

[28] John Graham, The MMPI-2: Assessing Personality and Psychopathology 95 (2d ed. 1993).

[29] R.E. Harris & J.C. Lingoes, Subscales for the MMPI: An Aid to Profile Interpretation (1955) (unpublished manuscript, University of California).

[30] John Graham, The MMPI-2: Assessing Personality and Psychopathology 113–14 (2d ed. 1993).

[31] *Id.* at 211.

[32] K. Carlson, Carlson Psychological Survey (1982).

[33] *Id.* at 7.

risk. . . . There is considerable evidence that parental discipline practices may be an important mediating mechanism in this transmission. Our set of findings shows that antisocial parents are at significant risk for ineffective discipline practices. Ineffective discipline is significantly related to risk of having an antisocial child.[34]

Similarly, in their 1992 review article, Vicky Phares and Bruce Compas conclude, "Paternal criminality and antisocial behavior have been identified as significant risk factors for delinquent behavior in offspring in a number of studies."[35] These same qualities, plus the poor superego (conscience) development, make psychotherapy with these individuals very difficult. When an individual's criminal history is in question, use of the DSM-IV criteria, the MMPI data, and the Carlson data should yield a good estimate of the likelihood that an individual has an Antisocial Personality Disorder.

§ 16.7   Criminal Offender Profile

MMPI/MMPI-2

To try to develop a valid, reliable, brief taxonomy for classifying criminals, psychologist Edwin Megargee headed a 10-year research effort at the Federal Correctional Institution in Tallahassee, Florida. One part of that effort included the development of MMPI profiles that differentiated between 1,164 youthful male offenders, based on their behavior, social histories, lifestyles, and personality patterns.[36]

As with any classification system, the researchers caution that "these descriptions will be *modal characterizations of the hypothetical average member of each group*. Individual members of these groups can be expected to vary considerably from these stereotypes."[37] Furthermore, the authors indicate that "it is expected that an individual's group membership will change to reflect developments in his personality over the course of time."[38] It is also noted that more than half of the men in each group were convicted for some kind of property offense. The classifications, however, emphasize the *differences* among the men in the 10 groups: Able, Baker, Charlie, Delta, Easy, Foxtrot, George, How, Item, and Jupiter.[39]

Megargee ranked the following descriptions in order, from those with the most benign MMPI profiles to those with the most deviant profiles.

Group Item. This group was distinguished by the *lack* of any marked MMPI elevation, that is, it was an essentially normal population. This is the largest single group, made

---

[34] G.R. Patterson et al., *A Developmental Perspective on Antisocial Behavior*, 44 Am. Psychologist 329, 332 (1989).

[35] Vicky Phares & Bruce Compas, *The Role of Fathers in Child and Adolescent Psychopathology: Make Room for Daddy*, 111 Psychol. Bull. 394 (1992).

[36] Edwin Megargee & Martin J. Bohn Jr., *Empirically Determined Characteristics of the Ten Types*, 4 Crim. Just. & Behav. 149, 152 (1977) [hereinafter Megargee & Bohn].

[37] *Id.* at 167.

[38] *Id.* at 168.

[39] *Id.* at 168–69.

up of 19 percent of the original sample. "This group of offenders is a relatively normal and well-adjusted group whose offenses do not stem from serious problems in interpersonal adjustment or from internal conflicts or psychopathology."[40] Convictions related most often to alcohol and other drug law violations. Impulsive crimes were uncommon. Most members of Group Item were from middle-class homes, with well-socialized family members and a positive attitude toward achievement. They were viewed as outgoing, friendly, and nonaggressive. This was the most mature group and the most treatable. After release, they have a better than 50 percent chance of avoiding rearrest and a 75 percent chance of avoiding re-incarceration.

Group Easy. This is the next most benign group, constituting 7 percent of the original sample. Their modal MMPI profile was 432. There was a significant "fake good" tendency, suggesting that objective sources should be used to confirm self-report data. Their interpersonal relations and adjustment tended to be very good. This was the least violent of the 10 groups. They were not found to be especially impulsive. Their intellectual and academic abilities make them good candidates for insight-oriented psychotherapy. However, they were seen as difficult to motivate. Upon release, less than 40 percent of these offenders are rearrested, and less than 15 percent are re-incarcerated.

Group Baker. This group was made up of only 4 percent of the original sample. Its modal MMPI profile was 42. The absence of an elevation of Scale 3 indicates that they did not tend to use repression as a defense mechanism. Overall, the group was characterized as underachievers. They were found to be below average in interpersonal relations and adjustment. Their adult criminal record was the second most serious. They tended to use alcohol excessively but avoid other drugs. They evidenced much conflict with authority. They are "a withdrawn, anxious, socially isolated group, many of whom depend on alcohol to cope with the demands of everyday living. They internalize their problems."[41] They were not considered to be in urgent need of treatment. Supportive psychotherapy is seen as essential if these people are to stay out of trouble.

Group Able. This group constituted 17 percent of the sample. Its MMPI profile was 49—the classic profile of the individual with an antisocial personality disorder. These men had relatively few academic or vocational problems and ranked high in achievement motivation. Group members were found to form good interpersonal relationships and were consistently evaluated as being among the better-adjusted groups. Although the 49 code type indicates impulsiveness, they were at the median for a history of violence. Although not especially aggressive, they tended to react strongly if confronted. They had relatively good relationships with authority and showed the least anxiety of the 10 groups. "What emerges . . . is . . . a clever, opportunistic, daring, and amoral person who will risk taking illegal shortcuts to gratify his wants as soon as possible."[42] They have little desire to change. Treatment, if any, would not work well in a community or other loosely structured situation. They would not benefit from insight-oriented psychotherapy. A direct, confrontative approach would be better. They have one of the highest rates of recidivism and re-incarceration.

---

[40] *Id.* at 169.

[41] *Id.* at 182.

[42] Megargee & Bohn at 186.

Group George. This group was made up of 7 percent of the original sample and was characterized by a 42 MMPI profile that was similar to, but more elevated than, Group Baker's. However, this group is the better adjusted of the two. Although this group had the highest rate of alcohol and other drug abuse offenses, group members were not heavy users of drugs. Rather, they tended to be lower-level dealers. Group members were among the brightest and best-educated. Achievement motivation was relatively high. Group members had the fewest authority conflicts, and the least extensive prior criminal record, of the 10 groups. Social and personal relationships and aggressiveness were average. Their overall adjustment and ability to form lasting relationships were relatively good, with no predominant treatment issues. Assertiveness training would benefit many group members. While they got along well with others, it was most often as followers rather than as leaders. They generally have a high rate of recidivism.

Group Delta. With this group, MMPI profiles move from "moderately elevated" to "clearly deviant" and highly elevated. This group's profile has a very high score on Scale 4, with other scales much lower. These men were "'all id with no lid'—hedonistic, amoral people with little ability to postpone gratification or control their impulses . . . [but] charming, intelligent, and manipulative, who has little anxiety or guilt."[43] This group constituted 10 percent of the sample. Their families of origin tended to evidence serious family tension, rejection, and poor disciplinary practices. Members of this group reported more criminal behavior than any other group. Although they did not tend to seek violence, they showed few inhibitions against reacting with violence when provoked or when someone stood in the way of something they wanted. Strengths included being relatively intelligent and having ambition and assertiveness. Because they do not feel anxiety or distress, they do not seek treatment on their own, nor do they willingly stay in treatment. They have the highest recidivism rate among the 10 groups.

Group Jupiter. This group constituted 3 percent of the sample, with a modal MMPI profile of 89. The group contained a relatively high proportion of property offenders, and members of the sample had no crimes against persons. They were intellectually and academically average. Personality test data made them appear worse than did other sources of information. Group members tended to have good interpersonal relations. They had relatively benign criminal records, including being among the least violent groups. They had a low rate of alcohol abuse but were heavily involved with other drug abuse. The impulsivity suggested by Scale 9 was evident. They tended to have little achievement motivation. Treatment would generally best take place in a structured setting. Overall, Megargee and Bohn saw this group as among the most deviant.

Group Foxtrot. This group, which was made up of 8 percent of the sample, was characterized by a 948 MMPI profile, with a very high score on Scale 9. This group, the authors indicate, "exhibits deficits in almost every area of functioning. Foxtrot's family was characterized by coldness, rejection, instability, a frequently absent father, and inadequate parental discipline."[44] Further, the authors found indications that the men were getting worse as they aged. They tended to have extensive criminal records. Furthermore, they tended to be abrasive and bossy. They evidenced little guilt or

---

[43] *Id.* at 191.

[44] *Id.* at 198.

anxiety, providing little motivation to change their behavior. They were impulsive, even reckless. They ascribed to a criminal code of conduct. "Dishonest, deceitful, and supremely self-centered, they have minimal compunctions against moving against those who get in their way."[45] They have few strengths and little desire to change. They showed a propensity for violence. Treatment would need to include a great deal of structure as well as swift and certain responses to both positive and negative behavior. Considered the least socialized and most antisocial of the 10 groups, they need help with nearly all areas of functioning in society—help they were not likely to seek nor readily accept. They have a high rate of recidivism.

Group Charlie. This group constituted 12 percent of the sample. It was characterized by an 864 MMPI profile, with Scales 8 and 6 both over 80, and the means of all clinical scales exceeding T scores of 60. This, say the authors, "suggests an antisocial, misanthropic individual, bitter, hostile, sensitive to perceived insults, who readily lashes out at others."[46] This group had the highest proportion of crimes against persons (7.2 percent). They never learned to trust and evidenced major deficits in every area of functioning. They had among the most extensive criminal records, were the most likely to resort to violence, and had the greatest amount of substance abuse. They had the greatest authority conflict. They have minimal empathy for others. Treatment programs must have a great deal of structure. The area of greatest need is seen as that of interpersonal relations that, because of this group's paranoid thinking, is generally based on mistrust and misinterpretation of feelings and intentions, leading to inappropriate and often violent interactions. They have an average rate of re-incarceration.

Group How. This group, made up of 13 percent of the sample population, was characterized more by having a number of high MMPI scales than by code type. This suggests that there will be more individual variability from the modal description of the members of the group. They had the lowest achievement motivation and serious problems with school and employment. There were serious problems in all areas of interpersonal relations. Illicit drug use was the third highest of the 10 groups. Their adjustment to institutional life was also poor. They were one of the most aggressive groups and particularly prone to conflicts with authority. They were agitated and unstable, with an inability to cope with everyday life in or out of an institution. Treatment should take place in a mental health facility, where the irrational and confused thinking of these men could be addressed, in part with pharmacotherapy. Their psychopathology was seen as underlying and preceding their criminal behavior. They have a high rate of recidivism and reincarceration.

According to John Graham, 85 to 95 percent of offender profiles could be classified utilizing Megargee's criteria. Graham also suggests that "[s]ubsequent data indicated that the classification system also worked well in other settings (e.g., state prisons) . . . and with other kinds of offenders (e.g., women)."[47] Additional research has established the

---

[45] *Id.* at 199.

[46] *Id.* at 201.

[47] John Graham, MMPI-2: Assessing Personality and Psychopathology 211–12 (1993).

classification system to be valid for samples in "military prisons, halfway houses, community restitution centers, and local jails."[48]

Megargee has researched whether the MMPI classification rules could be used with the MMPI-2 without changing the resulting categorization of the 10 types of criminals. He found that it could *not*. As a result, he has empirically derived a new, very complex set of rules for classification of the groups. The new rules led to the same classification as the old for 82 percent of the cases and an ability to classify 91 percent of the cases in the offender samples. Research on application of the new classification rules for women is under way; until it is published, the rules should not be used for women.[49]

Citing his correspondence with A.F. Scheckenbach, psychologist Thomas Kennedy indicates that "from the practitioner's standpoint, accuracy of the typology groupings plummets with older (over 30) and more sophisticated inmates." Kennedy also emphasizes that group membership is somewhat likely to change over time, so that an assessment done at one point may not be fully applicable some distance into the future.[50]

It is still possible for the original MMPI to be used to classify criminal offenders, both males and females—but, as discussed in **Chapter 9,** for all other purposes the MMPI-2 is likely to be the preferred test.

Psychopathology Checklist-Revised (PCL-R)

Another reliable and valid instrument for assessing psychopathy in male criminals is the Psychopathy Checklist–Revised (PCL-R). Based on a meta-analysis of 18 studies, Randall Salekin, Richard Rogers, and Kenneth Sewell reported that the PCL (1985, with 22 items) and PCL-R (1991, with 20 items) are able to predict both recidivism and future violence among populations of white male offenders. There is also a Psychopathy Checklist-Screening Version (1994) (PCL-SV), a 12-item screening form of the PCL. Each item is scored on the basis of whether the clinician judges it to be absent, possibly present, or definitely present. On the PCL-R, the authors of the test suggest a cutoff score of 30, while Salekin and his co-researchers suggest a more conservative cutoff of at least 33 to minimize false-positives (though that increases the possibility of false negatives). They indicate that "the PCL-R appears to be unparalleled as a measure for making risk assessments with white male inmates."[51]

Gary Melton, John Petrila, Norman Poythress, and Christopher Slobogin note that the PCL (all three versions) does not measure psychopathy according to the criteria for the diagnosis of an Antisocial Personality Disorder (found in the fourth edition of the

---

[48] Edwin I. Megargee & Joyce L. Carbonell, *Use of the MMPI-2 in Correctional Settings, in* Forensic Applications of the MMPI-2. 150 (Yossef S. Ben-Porath et al. eds., 1995).

[49] Edwin I. Megargee, *Using the Megargee MMPI-Based Classification System with MMPI-2s of Male Prison Inmates*, 6 Psychol. Assessment 337–44 (1994).

[50] Thomas Kennedy, *Trends in Inmate Classification: A Status Report of Two Computerized Psychometric Approaches*, 13 Crim. Just. & Behav. 165, 170 (1986).

[51] Randall T. Salekin et al., *A Review and Meta-Analysis of the Psychopathy Checklist and Psychopathy Checklist-Revised: Predictive Validity and Dangerousness*, 3 Clinical Psychol.: Sci. & Prac. 203, 211 (1996).

Diagnostic and Statistical Manual of Mental Disorders (DSM-IV)), and that the DSM-IV criteria are not useful predictors of recidivism or violence.[52]

The PCL-SV is designed to take under 90 minutes to administer, compared with two to three hours for the full PCL-R. Norms are available for criminal and civil psychiatric and nonpsychiatric individuals.

§ 16.8   Mental State of the Offender

The mental state of the offender does not excuse an offense but may provide important data for the present custody evaluation. The following questions can be used to ascertain the mental state of the offender:

1.   What kind of stress was the individual experiencing at the time of the offense?
2.   How well does the individual handle stress when it is experienced?
3.   Was there any evidence of a major mental illness (psychosis) at the time of the offense?
4.   Was "not guilty by reason of insanity" (or "by reason of mental disease or defect") part of the defense?
5.   If so, was the individual found not guilty on that basis?
6.   Did the individual spend any time in a psychiatric hospital after the offense? After the trial?

§ 16.9   Recency of the Offense

Whether the offense was committed last year or 10 or more years ago could make a great deal of difference. Given the maxim that "the best predictor of the future is the past," the longer it has been since the offense and the better the individual's behavior since the offense, the less likely the offense is to have a significant bearing on the present custody decision.

§ 16.10   Evidence of Rehabilitation

Evidence of the likelihood that an individual can be rehabilitated successfully can take several forms. Does the individual appear to be honestly remorseful? Was there any attempt to make restitution in any meaningful sense, and how voluntary was that attempt? Although no specific form of treatment has been shown to be especially effective, nearly every form of treatment will be effective for some people.[53] Whether the individual was in psychotherapy at any time since the offense and how that therapy has contributed to his or

---

[52] Gary B. Melton et al., Psychological Evaluations for the Courts 289 (2d ed. 1997).

[53] *Adult Antisocial Behavior and Criminality* at 1869.

her understanding of the causes of the offense and the likelihood that there will not be another offense are both relevant determinations. Has the individual gone out of his or her way to make a contribution to society since the offense (such as volunteering for charities, becoming a civic leader, or helping other offenders)? Although it does not speak directly to the question of reha-bilitation, it should be noted that criminal behavior naturally seems to decrease at about age 40, so that is one more factor to take into consideration.[54] Is there any other evidence that the individual has been rehabilitated and will not commit another offense?

Psychological testing may be of some limited assistance here. The MMPI/MMPI-2, the Carlson Psychological Survey, and the PCL-R or PCL-SV will give some insight into the present status of antisocial beliefs and actions, as described above. The tests must be read with the awareness that one cannot erase the past experiences and behavior that will lead to substantial scores on the relevant scales; however, changes in subsequent beliefs and actions can lower the scores to some degree. The validity scales on the MMPI/MMPI-2 also provide a direct assessment of the individual's attitude—is the individual being hon-est and forthright in his or her approach to the test, or is the individual trying to present an image that is markedly different from reality? As indicated in **Chapter 9**, the MMPI/MMPI-2 provides the only well-researched, valid information about an individual's openness, honesty, and forthrightness.

The type of criminal behavior involved also gives some indication of how likely it is that an individual can be rehabilitated successfully. For example, W.L. Marshall and colleagues found that, among sex offenders, some treatment programs have been effective with child molesters and exhibitionists, but not, in general, with rapists.[55]

Although no mental health professional or jurist can be omniscient, consideration of the above data will maximize the likelihood that past criminality is seen in its proper context, permitting it to be weighed with other evidence in the process of investigation and decisionmaking.

§ 16.11   Questions for Chapter 16

Caution.   Attorneys should not expect to be able to go into court and ask all the follow-ing questions. Preparation is necessary, and referring to the particular topics in the chapter will help determine whether a particular question applies to a case. Some of the questions contain cross-references to sections in this chapter that include an explanation of why a question may be of importance.

1. How do the frequency, severity, and recency of the offenses affect the psychologist's opinion?

2. If the individual has been convicted of a felony crime, how does the type of person-ality component that would contribute to the crime affect the parent's child-rearing capabilities? Ask the psychologist to make this determination. See § **16.6.**

---

[54] Robert D. Hare et al., *Male Psychopaths and Their Criminal Careers*, 56 J. Consulting & Clinical Psychol. 710, 710 (1988).

[55] W.L. Marshall et al., *Treatment Outcome with Sex Offenders*, 11 Clinical Psychol. Rev. 465–85 (1991).

3. If a conviction took place, what were the original charges? Did plea bargaining lead to a lesser charge? If so, to what degree?

4. Was the crime a crime against a person or a crime against property? Ask the psychologist what the difference between these types of crimes means with regard to child-rearing capabilities of the offender.

5. What evidence is there of rehabilitation? See § **16.10.**

6. Has the psychologist identified whether the individual has demonstrated antisocial behavior or has an underlying antisocial personality? See § **16.6.**

7. Into which of the Megargee classifications does the subject fit? See § **16.7.**

§ 16.12   Case Digest

The source of information for most of the following cases is the *Mental and Physical Disability Law Reporter* (MPDLR), a publication of the American Bar Association. Quotations from the *Mental and Physical Disability Law Reporter:* Excerpted from *Mental and Physical Disability Law Reporter*. Copyright © 1989–1997. American Bar Association. Reprinted by permission. Complete information for any other sources appears in the relevant references below. The following are direct quotations from the identified source. Other than this book's authors' introductions, if no source is identified, it is a summary from the court ruling.

Illinois

In re B.C. v. Cheryl C., 617 N.E.2d 1207 (Ill. App. Ct. 1993). An Illinois appeals court ruled that a lower court had properly declared a woman to be an unfit parent based on her history of criminal convictions and drug use, but reversed the termination of her parental rights because clear and convincing evidence showed this would not be in her children's best interests. The evidence indicated Cheryl C.'s son loved her and did not want to be adopted by anyone else. His foster mother testified that she thought he would experience emotional problems if he could not see his mother, and a Department of Child and Family Services case worker corroborated this testimony. Furthermore, Cheryl C. had taken advantage of various programs to rehabilitate herself after her release from prison— including drug rehabilitation, vocational/educational classes, group therapy, and a religious program—and stated that she understood that she had to improve herself and her circumstances before the court would return custody of her children to her. 18 *Mental & Physical Disability Law Reporter* 43–44 (1994).

Naylor v. Kindred, 250 Ill. A 997 (1993). The Illinois Appellate Court for the Fourth District ruled that a non-custodial parent need not wait two years after a prior custody order to request a modification of custody, even without a showing of serious endangerment to the child, when the custodial parent is incarcerated. The appellate court noted that state courts have recognized an exception when a custodial parent dies within two years after a custody ruling, and it drew an analogy with incarceration, as an incarcerated parent cannot be the physical custodian for the child. Further, because the child was then in the physical custody of a third party, the parent's superior right to custody was being violated.

Illinois v. Smith (In re K.S.), 203 Ill. App. 586 (1990) (Ill. App. Ct. 4th Dist. Sept. 25, 1990). According to the Illinois Appellate Court for the Fourth District, a father who failed to attempt to make significant progress toward regaining his children during his incarceration is an *unfit person* as defined in the Illinois Adoption Act. The court indicated that the father could have done things while on work release to facilitate the return of his children, but did not do so. The parental rights of both parents were terminated.

Iowa

In re R.L.P.R., No. 2-205/91-1994 (Iowa Ct. App. 1992). The Iowa Court of Appeals ruled that a juvenile court erred when it terminated the parental rights of an incarcerated father, because the trial court did not determine whether the child would benefit from the termination and legal counsel was not provided for the boy. The father was imprisoned for sexual abuse of one of the boy's half-sisters. The appellate court found that the statutory requirements for termination had not been met, because the child was in a relative's legal custody, the boy was more than 10 years of age, the boy objected to the termination, and evidence showed that the termination would be detrimental to the child because of the close parent-child relationship. It also indicated that state law requires the appointment of counsel for a child in a termination proceeding.

Kansas

In re Marriage of Brewer, 13 Kan. App. 2d 44, 760 P.2d 1225 (1988). The court upheld a denial of visitation, stating that an incarcerated parent is not entitled to visitation as a matter of right. The question is whether the visitation is in the child's best interests. Doris Jonas Freed & Timothy B. Walker, "Family Law in the Fifty States: An Overview," 23 *Family Law Quarterly* 583 (1990).

Kentucky

Smith v. Smith, 869 S.W.2d 55 (Ky. Ct. App. 1994). The Kentucky Court of Appeals ruled that visitation may not be denied solely on the basis of the incarceration of the non-custodial parent. The court indicated that state law holds that visitation may be denied only when there has been a finding that the child will be placed in serious danger by the visitation. While the father was serving a life sentence for murder, robbery, and kidnapping, there was no showing that visitation would endanger the 13-year-old girl.

New Jersey

In re Adoption by L.A.S., 258 N.J. Super. 614 (1992). The New Jersey Supreme Court ruled that a parent's lengthy incarceration is only one factor to be considered in determining whether parental rights should be terminated. Incarceration may be considered as a factor in addressing questions of abandonment or unfitness of the parent, but not as the sole factor. The supreme court noted that the child may get "needed nuture" from the incarcerated parent, and it may harm the child to be denied that relationship. The nature of the crime committed by the parent also must be considered. The trial court must base its decision on a review of all relevant factors, and must weigh those factors against the criteria for abandonment or parental unfitness. The supreme court indicated that, in the instant case, the fact that the father was imprisoned for 30 years for first-degree murder made it unlikely that he was a fit parent, but said that the trial court must still review all the relevant factors before making its decision.

North Carolina

In re Murphy, 105 N.C. App. 651, 414 S.E.2d 396 (1992). Where father has been incarcerated for first degree sexual assault and indecent liberties with one of his daughters, he does not have an absolute right to attend a subsequent hearing of a motion to terminate his parental rights. The court must use the balancing test outlined in *Matthews v. Eldridge*, 424 U.S. 319 (1979), which weighs the private interests, the risk of error, and the state's interest in the procedure. T. Walker & L. Elrod, "Family Law in the Fifty States: An Overview," 26 *Family Law Quarterly* 414 (1993).

CHAPTER 17

CLASSIFICATION SYSTEMS

§ 17.1   Definition of Mental Disorder

According to the authors of the fourth edition of the *Diagnostic and Statistical Manual of Mental Disorders* (DSM-IV),

> the term *mental disorder* unfortunately implies a distinction between "mental" disorders and "physical" disorders that is a reductionistic anachronism of mind/body dualism. A compelling literature documents that there is much "physical" in "mental" disorders and much "mental" in "physical" disorders. . . . The concept of mental disorder, like many other concepts in medicine and science, lacks a consistent operational definition that covers all situations. . . .
>
> In DSM-IV, each of the mental disorders is conceptualized as a clinically significant behavioral or psychological syndrome or pattern that occurs in an individual and that is associated with

745

present distress (e.g., a painful symptom) or disability (i.e., impairment in one or more important areas of functioning) or with a significantly increased risk of suffering death, pain, disability, or an important loss of freedom. In addition, this syndrome or pattern must not be merely an expectable and culturally sanctioned response to a particular event, for example, the death of a loved one. Whatever its original cause, it must currently be considered a manifestation of a behavioral, psychological, or biological dysfunction in the individual. Neither deviant behavior (e.g., political, religious, or sexual) nor conflicts that are primarily between the individual and society are mental disorders unless the deviance or conflict is a symptom of a dysfunction in the individual.[1]

§ 17.2 Medical and Psychiatric Diagnoses of Mental Disorders

The "medical model" is used for diagnosing mental disorders both in the United States and by the World Health Organization. The *medical model* indicates that

(1) [t]here are disease entities, which have etiology, course, and outcome; (2) These diseases are of organic origin; (3) Even if conceived as psychological diseases, they are viewed in analogy with physical ailments. There is an underlying state which is manifested in surface symptoms. Disease is to be inferred from symptoms; changing symptoms will not cure the disease; (4) People get these diseases through no fault of their own; (5) Cure depends on professional intervention, preferably by people with medical training; and (6) The diseases are in the person and, although they may have culturally distinct manifestations, the essential disease process is universal and not culturally specific.[2]

Unlike most other medical diagnoses, however, psychiatric diagnoses carry a social stigma. There have been direct legal consequences of the development of a psychiatric diagnostic system, complicated by different classification systems and different terminology at the interface of law and psychiatry; for example, "insanity" has no unequivocal translation into any diagnostic classification.[3]

Diagnostic techniques in psychiatry and psychology depend, to a large extent, on the patient's self-reports or complaints, called symptoms, and to a lesser extent on observable abnormalities detected by the examiner, called signs. For this reason, diagnoses of mental disorders may be complicated by distortions, omissions, or outright falsifications of crucial information by the patient for either conscious or unconscious reasons, especially when the patient is involved in the legal system. The relative contribution of the role of symptoms and signs in the diagnosis of mental disorders depends on the specific disorder. For instance, a severe psychosis might be diagnosed quite reliably on the basis of observing acute symptoms while a personality disorder could rarely be diagnosed without the information acquired from a history and interview with the patient and supplementation with collateral sources.[4]

---

[1] Diagnostic and Statistical Manual of Mental Disorders at xxi–xxii (4th ed. 1994) [hereinafter DSM-IV].

[2] S. Korchin, Modern Clinical Psychology: Principles of Intervention in the Clinic and Community 90 (1976).

[3] D. Shuman, Psychiatric and Psychological Evidence 2-1 to 2-2 (2d ed. 1994) [hereinafter Shuman].

[4] *Id.* at 2-19.

Furthermore,

> [i]n science, the classification of phenomena is essential for systematic study to occur; within the mental health field this classification occurs when diagnoses are employed. Diagnoses begin as descriptions of signs and symptoms of illness; over time, as experience and empirical studies grow, clinicians' ability to predict the course of a mental disorder also grows; prognostic capabilities develop. Once this level of expertise has evolved, interventions can be tested; the course of treated patients can be compared with untreated ones and effective treatment developed. Eventually enough may be learned to understand why the disorder occurs and develops (etiology and pathogenesis).[5]

There are presently two diagnostic classification systems widely used in the United States: The fourth edition of the *Diagnostic and Statistical Manual of Mental Disorders*,[6] and the *International Classification of Diseases–9th Revision–Clinical Modification* (ICD-9-CM).[7] Both suffer from a significant shortcoming: they use broad criteria for the diagnosis of mental disorders rather than any specific tests, and the reliability and validity of diagnoses are relatively open to criticism on this basis. Furthermore, diagnoses in both manuals were formulated by learned individuals discussing diagnoses and the criteria for the diagnoses and then coming to a consensus about what those diagnoses and criteria would be. As a result, the diagnostic manuals contain thousands of diagnostic criteria with limited research support for most of them. Although ICD-10 was published in 1992, and has been the official diagnostic manual in every area of health other than mental health since January 1, 1999, ICD-9-CM remains the official diagnostic manual in the United States. Its revision, ICD-10-CM, is available in "pre-release" form, for purposes of soliciting comments from the professional community. No date has been set for finalizing it and adopting it as of November 2004, however. There will also be a two-year phase-in period once it becomes the official "mental health" system in the United States (National Center for Health Statistics, accessed Nov. 8, 2004, at www.cdc.gov/nchs/about/major/dvs/icd10des.htm).

§ 17.3   History and Development of the Diagnostic and Statistical Manuals

The first edition of the *Diagnostic and Statistical Manual of Mental Disorders* (DSM-I) of the American Psychiatric Association was published in 1952. Its purpose was to replace the separate—and therefore confusing—diagnostic systems utilized by the Army, the Navy, and the Veterans Administration.[8]

---

[5] S. Hoge & T. Grisso, *Accuracy and Expert Testimony*, 20 Bull. Am. Acad. Psychiatry & L. 67, 72 (1992).

[6] Published by the American Psychiatric Association in 1994.

[7] Commission on Professional and Hospital Activities (1979). *See also* Manual of the International Statistical Classification of Diseases, Injuries, and Causes of Death (World Health Organization 9th rev. 1977).

[8] R. Blashfield, Comments made at Symposium: DSM-IV Field Trials—Part One, Annual Convention of the American Psychological Association, Washington D.C. (Aug. 17, 1992).

The second edition, DSM-II, was published in 1968 and, unlike DSM-I, was based on the mental disorders section of the eighth *International Classification of Diseases* (ICD-8), published the same year. The third edition, DSM-III, was published in 1980. Although originally planned to go into effect along with ICD-9, which was published in 1975 and implemented in 1978, there was a substantial feeling that ICD-9 was not specific enough for clinical or research use in the United States. The major classifications were kept the same as those in ICD-9 for all practical purposes, but publication of DSM-III was postponed until 1980 so that greater specificity could be added.[9] In addition, because of dissatisfaction with the lack of specificity in ICD-9, "a decision was made to modify it for use in the United States, resulting in ICD-9-CM (for Clinical Modification)."[10]

Revision of DSM-III began in 1983, based on a need to address inconsistencies in the diagnostic system and to clarify many of the criteria. The result was DSM-III-R, published in 1987.[11]

§ 17.4   DSM-IV

Work on DSM-IV began in 1988. There were 13 work groups, each with five to seven members. This was a change from the work on DSM-III-R, for which each work group consisted of 15 to 30 members, making consensus difficult to achieve. In addition, there were 50 to 100 advisors for each work group on DSM-IV, as well as representatives of each of the major mental health professional organizations. These people were sent drafts of literature reviews, proposals generated by the work groups, and minutes of all meetings. About twice a year, periodic updates were sent to about 1,000 people, providing a summary of the major issues and information on the progress of each work group.[12]

An "options" text was published in 1991, identifying alternatives being considered and requesting input from the professionals regarding which directions to pursue, as well as requesting input from researchers working on various projects. Finally, a five-volume *Sourcebook* was compiled, providing the rationale and documentation for all of the major decisions.[13]

The process used to develop DSM-IV is an extraordinary change from the process involved in formulating DSM-III and DSM-III-R, where the diagnoses and criteria were largely the result of committee discussion of various diagnoses and criteria, which continued until something of a consensus could be reached. Psychologist William Doverspike indicates that the official policy was that "changes will be made only when they facilitate compatibility with ICD-10, increase the clarity of current criteria, or when empirical data indicate a need for revising criteria."[14] Something that will not change is the classification of most disorders "on the basis of similarities in phenomenology (rather than etiology)."[15]

---

[9] DSM-III-R at xviii–xix.

[10] DSM-IV at xviii.

[11] *Id.*

[12] Thomas A. Widiger, DSM-IV: Process and Progress, Paper presented at the 98th Annual Convention of the American Psychological Association, Boston (Aug. 1990) [hereinafter Widiger, DSM-IV].

[13] DSM-IV at xx.

[14] William Doverspike, *Development of the DSM-IV: An Overview*, 8 Med. Psychotherapist 1 (1992).

[15] *Id.*

Psychiatrist Allen Frances chaired the DSM-IV revision process. He and three of his colleagues write that "the major emphasis in the development of DSM-IV was to maximize the impact of empirical data on decision making and to provide explicit documentation for any changes that were made."[16] Problems they ran into included significant limits on the availability of research on a number of questions; data in response to other questions that could be interpreted as providing different answers, all plausible; and the requirement to make some decisions based on values rather than (or in addition to) empirical data (for example, the political meaning of considering a diagnosis of Premenstrual Dysphoric Disorder). They conclude by stating that "DSM-IV . . . is not a 'bible' based on any gold standard of psychiatric diagnosis. Rather, it is a document reflecting the current progress in knowledge of psychiatric disorders."[17]

Field Trials

Three types of field trials were conducted for DSM-IV. One was a survey, the second was a videotaped reliability study, and the third involved 12 focused validity studies. Surveys, used for all of the DSMs, were downplayed for DSM-IV, because of the highly equivocal nature of any results obtained. "Majority rules" is hardly a basis for a scientific nomenclature.

According to psychologist Thomas Widiger and his colleagues:

> The major emphasis in the development of DSM-IV is to maximize the impact of research on the deliberations of the work groups and to document the empirical support for any revisions that are implemented. . . . [Unlike DSM-III and III-R,] the development of DSM-IV need not rely so exclusively on the consensus of a committee of experts and can instead be more comprehensively informed by and explicitly based on empirical data.[18]

With DSM-III and DSM-III-R, any objective data were largely published and cited after the decisions regarding the manual's content had already been made. In contrast, with DSM-IV any major decision was required to be preceded by a systematic, comprehensive literature review. An attempt was made to keep the summary of the literature both comprehensive and unbiased. Because reviewers are likely to have some biases and opinions, however, each review was sent to a number of advisors, including those most likely to criticize the reviewer's perspective. Publication of the reviews as early as possible, in juried publications, was also encouraged to get input from professionals not among the formal consultants.[19]

Field trials were utilized to assess the criteria sets'

1. Acceptability (face validity)
2. Feasibility (understandability and ease of application)

---

[16] Allen Frances et al., *DSM-IV: Issues in Development*, 25 Psychiatric Annals 15, 17–18 (1995).

[17] *Id.*

[18] Thomas A. Widiger et al., *Toward an Empirical Classification for the DSM-IV*, 100 J. Abnormal Psychol. 280, 282 (1991) [hereinafter Widiger et al.].

[19] Thomas A. Widiger, Revisions of an Official Diagnostic Nomenclature: Scientific and Political Issues, Paper presented at the 100th Annual Convention of the American Psychological Association, Washington, D.C. (Aug. 1992) [hereinafter Widiger, 1992].

3. Coverage (breadth of coverage in normal clinical practice)
4. Generalizability (usefulness in various clinical settings)
5. Construct validity (descriptive, postdictive, concurrent, and predictive validity).

The field trials utilized surveys (the major source of data in DSM-III and DSM-III-R field studies), videotape reliability studies, and focused field trials. The latter two types of field trials were added because of the substantial bias that can be generated by surveys due to sampling methods, differential response rates, or the wording of questions.[20]

Role of Psychologists

Although most of the research establishing empirical bases for various diagnoses over the years has been done by psychologists, members of this profession were not permitted to have a significant decisionmaking role in DSM-I through DSM-III-R. This changed to some degree for DSM-IV. Some psychologists were appointed to the DSM-IV work groups, and they were among the advisors to whom drafts were sent. In fact, the research coordinator for the DSM-IV task force, Thomas Widiger, Ph.D., is a psychologist. Widiger indicates that he and the three other psychologists attended task force meetings, but they remained nonmembers of the task force. Still, he says, they were able to have an influence, in large part by making the decisionmakers accountable and forcing them to justify their decisions in the context of the literature reviews, data analyses, and field trials.[21] This process did not apply to all diagnoses, however, as "diagnoses already included in ICD-10 were given somewhat more consideration than those that were being proposed fresh for DSM-IV."[22]

Consistency with ICD

"The United States is under a treaty obligation with the World Health Organization to maintain a coding and terminological consistency with the ICD."[23] The diagnostic codes and terminology of DSM-IV are highly compatible with both ICD-9-CM and ICD-10.[24] Unfortunately,

> [t]he DSM and ICD have different constituencies and purposes. For example, the DSM need not be quite as concerned as is the ICD with the applicability of criteria sets across all cultures around the world. To meet this latter need, the ICD-10 requires the use of separate diagnostic criteria for clinicians and for researchers, whereas the DSM-IV will continue using the same system of diagnosis for both purposes.[25]

---

[20] Widiger et al. at 284.

[21] Widiger, 1992.

[22] DSM-IV at xx.

[23] A.J. Frances et al., *The Development of DSM-IV*, 46 Archives Gen. Psychiatry 373 (1989) [hereinafter Frances et al.].

[24] DSM-IV at xxi.

[25] Frances et al. at 374.

Concerns regarding Categorization of Diagnoses

Objections to the validity of the categorization of diagnoses and the specific diagnostic criteria did not cease with the publication of DSM-IV and ICD-10.

> There are objections to the use of categorical taxa. For example, they contribute to the fallacious belief that psychopathological processes constitute discrete entities, even medical diseases, when in fact they are merely concepts that help focus and coordinate our observations. Moreover, categories often fail to identify or include significant aspects of behavior because of the decision to narrow their list to a set of predetermined characteristics. . . . Not only are there problems in assigning many patients to the limited categories available, but clinicians often claim that the more they know patients, the greater the difficulty they have fitting them into a category.[26]

There is also concern that the categorization utilized in the DSMs continues to be used primarily because of

> its sponsorship by the medical community, chiefly psychiatry, which may have much to lose by conceding that disorders of behavior, with rare exception, bear very little relation to diseases, as that term is generally understood. . . . [T]he common retort that true medical diseases also have idiosyncratic features is somewhat disingenuous; they typically have in addition a specifically definable core pathophysiology and an associated array of signs and symptoms that . . . make sense in relation to that core, despite individual variations in the pattern.[27]

Other Concerns

A number of authors questioned publication of DSM-IV so soon after DSM-III-R, in part because "the rush may make a proper empirical basis, psychometric or otherwise, very difficult to establish."[28] In a *New York Times* article, Social Work Professors Stuart Kirk and Herb Kutchins questioned not only the frequency of publication but also the expansion from 106 mental disorders in DSM-I to more than 300 in DSM-IV. While acknowledging the higher standards of DSM-IV, they still called the book a "travesty," in part because nearly all the diagnoses from past editions were retained, though some do not meet the new requirements for inclusion.[29]

---

[26] Theodore Millon, *Classification in Psychopathology: Rationale, Alternatives, and Standards*, 100 J. Abnormal Psychol. 245, 255 (1991).

[27] R. Carson, *Dilemmas in the Pathway of the DSM-IV*, 100 J. Abnormal Psychol. 302–03 (1991).

[28] R. Nelson-Gray, *DSM-IV: Empirical Guidelines from Psychometrics*, 100 J. Abnormal Psychol. 314 (1991). *See also* M. Zimmerman, *Why Are We Rushing to Publish DSM-IV?*, 45 Archives Gen. Psychiatry 1135–38 (1988); R. Kendell, *Relationship between the DSM-IV and the ICD-10*, 100 J. Abnormal Psychol. 297–301 (1991) [hereinafter Kendell].

[29] Stuart A. Kirk & Herb Kutchins, *Standards Higher, Success Assured, But DSM-IV Book "A Travesty,"* reprinted in 3 Nat'l Psychologist 12–13 (1994).

Diagnosis: Improved But Still Imperfect

DSM-IV and ICD-10 are improvements over their predecessors, permitting greater reliability of diagnosis on the basis of more valid criteria. Even so, there is a great deal of room for further improvement. Diagnoses are likely to remain largely "explanatory fictions," terms used to permit meaningful discussion about the problems of a given individual or classes of individuals, but without the specificity or accuracy one would hope to have.

The good news is for the clinician, who has a workable diagnostic manual because it takes into consideration the limited ability presently available to make discrete diagnoses. The bad news is that, in spite of great research effort, it is rarely possible to make a highly specific, highly reliable, highly valid diagnosis using the manual. Instead, clinicians have labels that may be applied to mental conditions of individuals to facilitate understanding of and communication about those disorders among clinicians. The side benefit is that insurance companies will pay for services to people who have certain diagnoses. One consequence of the lack of precision is that mental health professionals who are comparing diagnostic conclusions, whether in court or any other arena, may come to different conclusions.

A social-psychological advance in DSM-III, carried forward into DSM-III-R and DSM-IV, is the affirmation that

> a common misconception is that a classification of mental disorders classifies people, when actually what are being classified are disorders that people have. For this reason, the text . . . avoids the use of such expressions as "a schizophrenic" or "an alcoholic," and instead uses the more accurate, but admittedly more cumbersome, "a person with Schizophrenia" or "a person with Alcohol Dependence."[30]

Unfortunately, mental health professionals seldom observe these verbal niceties and use the shorthand form in virtually all discussions.

§ 17.5   Changes from DSM-III-R

Appendix D of DSM-IV, pages 773 through 791, contains an annotated list of changes from DSM-III-R. Among the most significant in the context of this book are

1. The elimination of the term "organic mental disorders," on the basis that it was inappropriate to imply that some categories had a physical component while others did not. Now, diagnoses that used to include the term "organic" generally indicate "(condition) due to a general medical condition (to be specified)." Thus, "Organic Personality Disorder" became "Personality Change Due to a General Medical Condition," with specification of, for example, closed head trauma. Similarly, "Organic Mood Disorder" became "Mood Disorder Due to a General Medical Condition."

---

[30] DSM-IV at xxiii.

2.   The DSM-III-R criterion for Post-traumatic Stress Disorder that the trauma must be "outside the range of normal human experience" has been eliminated, and a requirement that the individual's response to the trauma involve "intense fear, helplessness, or horror" was added. By referring to "event or events" in Criterion A1, DSM-IV clarified that PTSD may result from a sequence of traumatic events, for example, periodic mental and physical abuse in domestic violence. It is anticipated that these changes will increase the frequency of diagnosis of PTSD.

3.   A diagnosis of Acute Stress Disorder was added. It covers the period from the trauma to four weeks post-trauma, and it may last from two days to four weeks. If it has not resolved within four weeks, the diagnosis changes to Post-traumatic Stress Disorder. It contains more dissociative symptoms than does PTSD.

4.   The criteria for Somatization Disorder and Conversion Disorder have been narrowed.

5.   The diagnosis of "Multiple Personality Disorder" has been changed to "Dissociative Identity Disorder."

6.   Most diagnoses now include a statement to the effect that the disorder "causes clinically significant distress or impairment in social, occupational, or other important areas of functioning."

7.   The diagnosis of Adjustment Disorder may be maintained for up to six months after termination of a chronic source of stress or the consequences of that stressor.[31]

8.   DSM-IV gives a higher profile to ethnic and cultural considerations than did its predecessors. In the text, it discusses cultural variations in the ways disorders may appear. There is also a description of syndromes that are largely limited to a single culture (for example, *amok*) and an outline designed to help the clinician evaluate and report on the relative importance of cultural factors. The intent is to help clinicians identify relevant cultural issues and properly address them in diagnosis and treatment. Most of the additions resulted from a three-year project of the NIMH Group on Culture and Diagnosis.[32]

9.   Mental retardation criteria have been changed to make them more compatible with those of the American Association of Mental Retardation.

10.   A Hypomanic Episode in a Bipolar Disorder is differentiated from Mania on the basis that it is not so severe as to cause gross impairment or to require hospitalization.

11.   Bipolar Disorder has been divided into Bipolar I and Bipolar II. The latter indicates that there is no history of Manic Episodes.

12.   Generalized Anxiety Disorder now requires only excessive anxiety and worry, not that the worries be unrealistic. A requirement that the individual must have difficulty controlling the worrying was added.

13.   The criteria for a Conversion Disorder have been changed to require that there be an effect upon voluntary motor or sensory functioning.

---

[31] DSM-IV at 773–91; Jerry von Talge, *Overcoming Courtroom Challenges to the New DSM-IV, Part I: The Major Changes in DSM-IV,* 13 Am. J. Forensic Psychol. 5, 12–24 (1995) [hereinafter Jerry von Talge, *Part I*].

[32] Tori DeAngelis, *Ethnic-Minority Issues Recognized in DSM-IV,* 25 Am. Psychol. Ass'n Monitor 36 (1994).

§ 17.6   Limitations of the DSM-IV Use of Categories

Although diagnosis should ideally be based upon discrete criteria, so that each set of criteria defines and describes a single, unique disorder,

> [i]n DSM-IV there is no assumption that each category of mental disorder is a completely dis-
> crete entity with absolute boundaries dividing it from other mental disorders or from no men-
> tal disorder. There is also no assumption that all individuals described as having the same
> mental disorder are alike in all important ways. The clinician using DSM-IV should therefore
> consider that individuals sharing a diagnosis are likely to be heterogeneous even in regard to
> the defining features of the diagnosis and that boundary cases will be difficult to diagnose in
> any but a probabilistic fashion. . . . DSM-IV often includes polythetic criteria sets, in which
> the individual need only present with a subset of items from a longer list (e.g., the diagnosis
> of Borderline Personality Disorder requires only five out of nine items).[33]

Similarly, it is noted, mental disorders are grouped into diagnostic classes on the basis of shared clinical features—for example, disturbances of mood rather than degree of dysfunction ("neurosis" versus "psychosis," for example). The psychotic/neurotic split was a useful dichotomy until the 1960s, when research clearly indicated that the presumed eti-ology of psychotic conditions (constitutional and biological forces) and of neurotic conditions (developmental, psychosocial, or personality factors) was not supported by the data available.[34]

> A major innovation in DSM-III[, retained in DSM-IV,] is the separation of the personality dis-
> orders into an independent axis. *Personality* refers to relatively enduring patterns of relating to,
> perceiving, and thinking about the self, significant others, and the environment. All individuals
> have such patterns. Personality *disorder* occurs only when the patterns become inflexible and
> maladaptive and/or significantly impair the individual's social or occupational functioning.
> Patients with personality disorder often do not experience subjective distress, but their behavior
> may generate distress and discomfort in others, particularly the immediate family.[35]

To enhance reliability, DSM-IV provides fairly specific diagnostic criteria, though many diagnoses are made by choosing from a list of symptoms those that apply in a given case, with a certain number required in order for the diagnosis to be made. Unfortunately, despite the marked improvement in research-based criteria, it is still clinical judgment that ultimately determines whether a diagnosis is used.

The fact that diagnoses are based on votes taken by committees of clinicians who are using their "clinical judgments" has led to the problem that

> it is a temptation for a task force or a work group member to argue for the inclusion of changes
> that express his or her theoretical or empirical perspective. We have noticed many such
> instances in the past and present effort. Revisions made in this way are less reflective of the

---

[33] DSM-IV at xxii.

[34] G. Klerman, *Classification and DSM-III-R, in* A. Nicholi Jr., The New Harvard Guide to Psychiatry 77 (1988).

[35] *Id.* at 79.

totality of the research evidence in the field than of the forces determining membership and influence on a particular committee.[36]

§ 17.7   Multiaxial System

DSM-IV uses a *multiaxial system* to provide a complete description:

1. Axis I is used to report all of the disorders except for Personality Disorders and Mental Retardation, both of which go on Axis II. Also on Axis I are "Other Conditions That May Be a Focus of Clinical Attention"—for example, "Psychological Factors Affecting Medical Condition," and "Medication-Induced Movement Disorders." These "other conditions" are found in a separate section of DSM-IV, starting on page 675 in the manual.
2. Axis II is "Personality Disorders" and "Mental Retardation."
3. Axis III is "General Medical Conditions."
4. Axis IV is "Psychosocial and Environmental Problems."
5. Axis V is the "Global Assessment of Functioning."[37]

Axis I and Axis II Disorders

An individual may have more than one Axis I disorder. Each disorder should be listed, with the most prominent or serious disorder listed first.[38] Similarly, all relevant Axis II disorders should be listed, as should "prominent maladaptive personality features that do not meet the threshold for a Personality Disorder. . . . The habitual use of maladaptive defense mechanisms may also be indicated on Axis II."[39]

A partial listing of the disorders that fall on first two axes includes

Axis I Clinical Disorders [and] Other Conditions That May Be a Focus of Clinical Attention

Disorders Usually First Diagnosed in Infancy, Childhood, or Adolescence (excluding Mental Retardation, which is diagnosed on Axis II)

Disruptive Behavior Disorders
Anxiety Disorders of Childhood or Adolescence
Eating Disorders
Gender Identity Disorders
Tic Disorders
Elimination Disorders

---

[36] Frances et al. at 374.

[37] DSM-IV at 25.

[38] *Id.* at 25–26.

[39] *Id.* at 26–27.

Speech Disorders Not Elsewhere Classified
Other Disorders of Infancy, Childhood, or Adolescence

Delirium, Dementia, and Amnestic and Other Cognitive Disorders

Dementias Arising in the Senium and Presenium
Psychoactive Substance-Induced Organic Mental Disorders
Organic Mental Disorders associated with Axis III physical disorders or conditions, or whose etiology is unknown

Mental Disorders Due to a General Medical Condition

Substance-Related Disorders

Schizophrenia and Other Psychotic Disorders

Schizophrenia
Schizophreniform Disorder
Schizoaffective Disorder
Delusional Disorder
Brief Psychotic Disorder
Shared Psychotic Disorder
Psychotic Disorder Due to [specify a General Medical Condition]
Substance-Induced Psychotic Disorder
Psychotic Disorder NOS [Not Otherwise Specified]

Mood Disorders

Depressive Disorders
Bipolar Disorders

Anxiety Disorders

Panic Disorder [with or without Agoraphobia]
Agoraphobia Without History of Panic Disorder
Specific Phobia
Social Phobia
Obsessive-Compulsive Disorder
Posttraumatic Stress Disorder
Acute Stress Disorder
Generalized Anxiety Disorder
Anxiety Disorder Due to [specify a General Medical Condition]
Anxiety Disorder NOS

Somatoform Disorders

Somatization Disorder
Undifferentiated Somatoform Disorder
Conversion Disorder
Pain Disorder
Hypochondriasis
Body Dysmorphic Disorder
Somatoform Disorder NOS

Factitious Disorders

Dissociative Disorders

Dissociative Amnesia
Dissociative Fugue
Dissociative Identity Disorder

    Depersonalization Disorder
    Dissociative Disorder NOS

Sexual and Gender Identity Disorders

Eating Disorders

    Anorexia Nervosa
    Bulimia Nervosa
    Eating Disorder NOS

Sleep Disorders

Impulse-Control Disorders Not Elsewhere Classified

Adjustment Disorders

Other Conditions That May Be a Focus of Clinical Attention

Axis II Disorders

Mental Retardation

    Mental Retardation

Personality Disorders

    Paranoid Personality Disorder
    Schizoid Personality Disorder
    Schizotypal Personality Disorder
    Antisocial Personality Disorder
    Borderline Personality Disorder
    Histrionic Personality Disorder
    Narcissistic Personality Disorder
    Avoidant Personality Disorder
    Dependent Personality Disorder
    Obsessive-Compulsive Personality Disorder
    Personality Disorder Not Otherwise Specified[40]

DSM-IV groups the Personality Disorders into three clusters on the basis of descriptive similarities. Cluster A consists of the "odd" or "eccentric" disorders: Paranoid, Schizoid, and Schizotypal Personality Disorders. Cluster B consists of "dramatic," "emotional," "erratic," or "acting-out" disorders: Antisocial, Borderline, Histrionic, and Narcissistic Personality Disorders. Cluster C consists of the "anxious" or "fearful" disorders: Avoidant, Dependent, and Obsessive-Compulsive Personality Disorders.[41] Although these are not considered official diagnostic categories, and it is acknowledged that an individual may have personality characteristics from any of the clusters, some psychologists and psychiatrists describe individuals as having, for example, "Cluster B" characteristics, rather than identifying a single Personality Disorder. These people tend to be emotionally unstable,

---

[40] *Id.* at 13–24. American Psychiatric Association, Diagnostic and Statistical Manual of Mental Disorders, Fourth Edition. Washington, D.C., American Psychiatric Association, 1994. Used with permission.

[41] DSM-IV at 629–30; Anthony L. LaBruzza, Using DSM-IV 392–93 (1994).

very self-centered, and somewhat impulsive, and to have trouble with interpersonal relationships. People with Antisocial Personality Disorders tend to be consciously deceitful and to take advantage of others; people with the other three personality disorders are more likely to exaggerate as part of the nature of the disorder than in a conscious attempt to deceive.[42]

Axis III and Axis IV Disorders

Axis III is used to report any medical conditions that are currently significant and potentially relevant to the person's mental disorder.[43]

Axis IV is new, and is used

> for reporting psychosocial and environmental problems that may affect the diagnosis, treatment, and prognosis of mental disorders (Axes I and II). A psychosocial or environmental problem may be a negative life event, an environmental difficulty or deficiency, a familial or other interpersonal stress, an inadequacy of social support or personal resources, or other problem related to the context in which a person's difficulties have developed. So-called positive stressors such as job promotion, should be listed only if they constitute or lead to a problem, as when a person has difficulty adapting to the new situation.[44]

The clinician may indicate as many psychosocial and environmental stressors as are relevant. The following is the list of categories and examples in DSM-IV:

Psychosocial and Environmental Problems

Problems with primary support group—e.g., death of a family member, health problems in family; disruption of family by separation, divorce, or estrangement; removal from the home; remarriage of parent; sexual or physical abuse; parental overprotection; neglect of child; inadequate discipline; discord with siblings; birth of a sibling

Problems related to the social environment—e.g., death or loss of friend; inadequate social support; living alone; difficulty with acculturation; discrimination; adjustment to life-cycle transition (such as retirement)

Educational problems—e.g., illiteracy; academic problems; discord with teachers or classmates; inadequate school environment

Occupational problems—e.g., unemployment; threat of job loss; stressful work schedule; difficult work conditions; job dissatisfaction; job change; discord with boss or co-workers

Housing problems—e.g., homelessness; inadequate housing; unsafe neighborhood; discord with neighbors or landlord

Economic problems—e.g., extreme poverty; inadequate finances; insufficient welfare support

---

[42] DSM-IV at 645–61; C.B. Scrignar, Post-Traumatic Stress Disorder: Diagnosis, Treatment, and Legal Issues 241–42 (3d ed. 1996).

[43] DSM-IV at 27.

[44] Id. at 29.

Problems with access to health care services—e.g., inadequate health care services; transportation to health care facilities unavailable; inadequate health insurance

Problems related to interaction with the legal system/crime—e.g., arrest; incarceration; litigation; victim of crime

Other psychosocial and environmental problems—e.g., exposure to disasters, war, other hostilities; discord with nonfamily caregivers such as counselor, social worker, or physician; unavailability of social service agencies.[45]

Axis V Disorders

Axis V uses the Global Assessment of Functioning (GAF) Scale, which ranges from 100 ("Superior functioning in a wide range of activities . . .") to 1 ("persistent danger of severely hurting self or others . . .").[46] The Global Assessment of Functioning Scale is reproduced below:

Global Assessment of Functioning Scale (GAF Scale)*

Consider psychological, social, and occupational functioning on a hypothetical continuum of mental health-illness. Do not include impairment in functioning due to physical (or environmental) limitations.

Code   (**Note:** Use intermediate codes when appropriate, e.g., 45, 68, 72.)

Code	
100 | 91	**Superior functioning in a wide range of activities, life's problems never seem to get out of hand, is sought out by others because of his or her many positive qualities.** **No symptoms.**
90 | 81	**Absent or minimal symptoms** (e.g., mild anxiety before an exam), **good functioning in all areas, interested and involved in a wide range of activities, socially effective, generally satisfied with life, no more than everyday problems or concerns** (e.g., an occasional argument with family members).
80 | 71	**If symptoms are present, they are transient and expectable reactions to psychosocial stressors** (e.g., difficulty concentrating after family argument); **no more than slight impairment in social, occupational, or school functioning** (e.g., temporarily falling behind in schoolwork).
70 | 61	**Some mild symptoms** (e.g., depressed mood and mild insomnia) **OR some difficulty in social, occupational, or school functioning** (e.g., occasional truancy, or theft within the household), **but generally functioning pretty well, has some meaningful interpersonal relationships.**
60 | 51	**Moderate symptoms** (e.g., flat affect and circumstantial speech, occasional panic attacks) **OR moderate difficulty in social, occupational, or school functioning** (e.g., few friends, conflicts with peers or co-workers).
50 | 41	**Serious symptoms** (e.g., suicidal ideation, severe obsessional rituals, frequent shoplifting) **OR any serious impairment in social, occupational, or school functioning** (e.g., no friends, unable to keep a job).

(continued)

---

[45] *Id.* at 29–30.

[46] *Id.* at 32.

Code	**(Note:** Use intermediate codes when appropriate, e.g., 45, 68, 72.)

| 40 | **Some impairment in reality testing or communication** (e.g., speech is at times illogical, obscure, or irrelevant) **OR major impairment in several areas, such as work or school, family relations, judgment, thinking, or mood** (e.g., depressed man avoids friends, neglects family, and is unable to work; child frequently beats up younger |
| 31 | children, is defiant at home, and is failing at school). |

| 30 | **Behavior is considerably influenced by delusions or hallucinations OR serious impairment in communication or judgment** (e.g., sometimes incoherent, acts grossly inappropriately, suicidal preoccupation) **OR inability to function in almost all areas** |
| 21 | (e.g., stays in bed all day; no job, home, or friends). |

| 20 | **Some danger of hurting self or others** (e.g., suicide attempts without clear expectation of death; frequently violent; manic excitement) **OR occasionally fails to maintain minimal personal hygiene** (e.g., smears feces) **OR gross impairment in communica-** |
| 11 | **tion** (e.g., largely incoherent or mute). |

| 10 | **Persistent danger of severely hurting self or others** (e.g., recurrent violence) **OR persistent inability to maintain minimal personal hygiene OR serious suicidal act with** |
| 1 | **clear expectation of death.** |

| 0 | **Inadequate information.** |

*American Psychiatric Association, *Diagnostic and Statistical Manual of Mental Disorders, Fourth Edition*, Washington, D.C., American Psychiatric Association, 1994, at 32. Used with permission.

§ 17.8   Social, Occupational, and Relational Functioning

With the increased emphasis on "clinically significant distress or impairment" in DSM-IV, it is important to formally assess quality of functioning in order to make a valid diagnosis. Quality of functioning is also an essential area for analysis in any forensic evaluation. DSM-IV offers three scales to assist in this assessment. The major assessment is done with the **Global Assessment of Functioning (GAF) Scale**, reprinted and discussed above. Two others are the **Global Assessment of Relational Functioning (GARF) Scale** and the **Social and Occupational Functioning Assessment Scale (SOFAS)**. While these scales are largely subjective, they offer a way of conceptualizing and roughly quantifying the range from functional to dysfunctional behavior.

§ 17.9   DSM-IV-TR

In 2000 the American Psychiatric Association published the *Diagnostic and Statistical Manual of Mental Disorders, Fourth Edition, Text Revision* (DSM-IV-TR). All of the revisions are in the text sections, the narrative portion of the manual that describes the disorders and offers comments on such things as the associated features and disorders, cultural and age factors, prevalence, course, and differential diagnosis. No changes have been made in the diagnostic criteria for any disorder. The intent of the revision is to correct factual errors and to add information not available at the time of the 1994 publication of DSM-IV. Since the diagnostic criteria are the part of DSM-IV essential to the forensic process, it is not necessary for an evaluator to have the "text revision" edition in order to be fully up to date.

§ 17.10   Criticisms of DSM-IV

Several valid criticisms have been leveled against DSM-IV (and some leveled against DSM-III or III-R remain valid). In his book, *Psychiatric and Psychological Evidence, Second Edition*, Professor of Law Daniel Shuman claims that

1. It emphasizes reliability at the expense of validity (in other words, it emphasizes having raters reach the same conclusion but does not emphasize the accuracy of that conclusion).[47]

2. "The more severe the disorder, the greater the reliability of the diagnosis." That is, it "is not equally reliable across the diagnostic spectrum, and this must be recognized when presenting or challenging psychiatric or psychological testimony."[48]

   [Note: The greatest reliability was shown in the DSM-III field trials for affective disorders, followed by schizophrenia, then by substance use disorders, then personality disorders, and, ultimately, showing dissociative disorders' reliability to be very low. Overall, interrater reliability for Axis I was .78 when two psychiatrists interviewed jointly and .66 after separate interviews. For Axis II (Personality Disorders), the ratings were .61 for joint assessment and .54 for separate interviews.[49]]

3. Two people with nearly identical symptoms may receive different diagnoses yet the same treatment.[50]

4. It makes it appear diagnostic classifications are discrete, "ignoring the reality of continua in psychological phenomena."[51]

5. "There is little explanation of the development or significance of symptoms. . . . When presenting an individual's story in litigating a case, a . . . diagnosis is not likely to communicate much in the way of understandable human pathos. It does not help to explain *why* the individual is suffering, only *from what* the individual is suffering."[52]

6. "[I]t is a politicized document. Physicists do not vote on whether some phenomenon should be included in the body of physical fact, but psychiatrists did vote to include tobacco and caffeine abuse as mental disorders and to exclude egosyntonic homosexuality."[53]

---

[47] Shuman at 2–8.

[48] *Id.*

[49] R. Spitzer & J. Williams, *Classification of Mental Disorders, in* H. Kaplan & B. Sadock, Comprehensive Textbook of Psychiatry/IV 611 (4th ed. 1985) [hereinafter Spitzer & Williams].

[50] Shuman at 2–9.

[51] *Id.*

[52] *Id.*

[53] *Id.*

Other criticisms:

1. Psychologist William Follette indicates that research is severely hampered by the lack of a coherent theory underlying the *Diagnostic and Statistical Manual of Mental Disorders*. Further, the division into categories on the basis of diagnosis rather than, for example, etiology, further serves to limit research.[54]

2. Psychologists William Follette and Arthur Houts indicate that the proliferation of diagnoses from DSM-III to III-R to IV demonstrates that the classification system used is "inadequate" and is unlikely to facilitate scientific progress. What is needed, they write, is a means of reducing the number of categories by identifying the underlying principles for the disorders.[55]

3. Psychiatrist Sheldon H. Preskorn criticizes DSM-IV for (1) its lack of validation; (2) its lack of thresholds for severity (no dividing lines between "normal" and "pathological"); (3) its implying that if one can identify a psychosocial stressor, one may conclude that the stressor caused the mental disorder; (4) its basing its diagnoses on cross-sectional rather than longitudinal data; and (5) its maintaining many separate diagnoses and discussing "comorbidity" rather than trying to identify syndromes that would encompass all of the symptoms.[56]

4. Psychologist Theodore Sarbin indicates that "unreliability of diagnosis is still a major problem and, more important, little attention has been paid to validity. . . . [Furthermore,] the *Manual* contributes to the increasing medicalization of distress and directs clinicians to search for causes of unwanted behavior in biochemical anomalies."[57]

5. Psychiatrist John Oldham and colleagues criticize the overlap between diagnoses, including the fact that many Axis I and Axis II disorders have overlapping symptoms. For example, nearly all personality disorders include some mood, anxiety, psychotic, and/or eating disorder. A diagnostic system with so much overlap leads to many arbitrary decisions regarding diagnoses used, and treatment planning is difficult.[58]

6. Psychologist Jerry von Talge notes that (1) there is no good definition for the term "mental disorders" (see § **17.1**); (2) the attempt at eliminating the implied distinction between "functional" and "organic" disorders was not highly successful; (3) despite improvement, the research base for many diagnoses remains inadequate; and (4) too many decisions were based upon committee votes rather than scientific data.[59]

---

[54] William C. Follette, *Introduction to the Special Section on the Development of Theoretically Coherent Alternatives to the DSM System*, 64 J. Consulting & Clinical Psychol. 1117–19 (1996).

[55] William C. Follette & Arthur C. Houts, *Models of Scientific Progress and the Role of Theory in Taxonomy Development: A Case Study of the DSM*, 64 J. Consulting & Clinical Psychol. 1120–32 (1996).

[56] Sheldon H. Preskorn, *Beyond DSM-IV: What Is the Cart and What Is the Horse?*, 25 Psychiatric Annals 53–62 (1995).

[57] Theodore R. Sarbin, *On the Futility of Psychiatric Diagnostic Manuals (DSMs) and the Return of Personal Agency*, 6 Applied & Preventive Psychol. 233, 233 (1997).

[58] John M. Oldham et al., *Comorbidity of Axis I and Axis II Disorders*, 152 Am. J. Psychiatry 571–78 (1995).

[59] Jerry von Talge, *Part I*, at 27–28.

In a second article, von Talge added that (1) DSM-IV's categories are neither discrete nor homogeneous; (2) not all relevant or important mental conditions are included; (3) DSM-IV has significant problems with validity and reliability; (4) DSM-IV may not be applicable to people from non-Western cultures; (5) DSM-IV is a clinical and not a forensic tool, and many of the diagnoses and criteria do not easily meld with legal criteria or requirements; and (6) because DSM-IV does not discuss the causes of most mental conditions, it is of limited use in civil litigation.[60]

7. ICD-10 contains a diagnosis that should be in DSM-IV: "Enduring Personality Change After Catastrophic Experience." The term is to be applied when an individual has a potentially permanent personality change in response to one of the most severe stressors—for example, being in a concentration camp, being tortured, experiencing a major disaster, or being a hostage. The change is not in response to a preexisting vulnerability—so motor vehicle accidents are not among the possible stressors, since research indicates that long-term changes after these accidents may depend on preexisting vulnerability. The symptoms must have previously been absent and include "(a) a hostile or mistrustful attitude towards the world; (b) social withdrawal; (c) feelings of emptiness or hopelessness; (d) a chronic feeling of being 'on edge,' as if constantly threatened; [and] (e) estrangement." The condition must have existed for at least two years, "should not be attributable to a pre-existing personality disorder or to a mental disorder other than post-traumatic stress disorder."[61]

8. There is little in DSM-IV regarding the long-term prognosis for most disorders; instead, emphasis is almost exclusively on current symptoms.

9. A single set of symptoms may lead to different diagnoses solely as a function of elapsed time. A person could enter treatment with a "Brief Psychotic Disorder," be re-diagnosed to have a "Schizophreniform Disorder" after one month, and then be re-diagnosed with Schizophrenia after six months.

10. Diagnosis in psychiatry substantially relies on the openness and honesty of the patient, and only secondarily on observable signs and symptoms except in the most major disorders—for example, Major Depression or an acute psychosis. Whether conscious or unconscious, distortions, omissions, and lies may preclude accurate diagnosis. Psychological testing will improve the accuracy of diagnosis somewhat, but its use is far from universal. (See **Chapters 8** through **11** for specific discussion regarding psychological testing.)

11. Psychologist Thomas Widiger, research coordinator for the task force on DSM-IV, notes that there is a significant degree to which the exact content of many diagnoses listed in DSM-III and III-R is a product of the makeup of the committees that worked on the criteria for each diagnosis. Each researcher on the committees tended to argue for the results of his or her own research. Thus, Theodore Millon successfully argued

---

[60] Jerry von Talge, *Overcoming Courtroom Challenges to the DSM-IV, Part II: Preparing for and Overcoming Courtroom Challenges to DSM-IV,* 13 Am. J. Forensic Psychol. 49, 49–54 (1995) [hereinafter Jerry von Talge, *Part II*].

[61] J. David Kinzie & Rupert Goetz, *A Century of Controversy Surrounding Posttraumatic Stress-Spectrum Syndromes: The Impact on DSM-III and DSM-IV,* 9 J. Traumatic Stress 159, 173 (1996); The ICD-10 Classification of Mental and Behavioural Disorders: Clinical Descriptions and Diagnostic Guidelines 209 (World Health Org. 1992).

for inclusion of an Avoidant Personality Disorder diagnosis, and Robert Spitzer and Lee Robins argued successfully for inclusion of their criteria, rather than the criteria of other researchers, for Antisocial Personality Disorder.[62] The same criticism applies to DSM-IV.

12. Finally, it has long struck the authors of this text that, while the name of the book is the *Diagnostic and Statistical Manual of Mental Disorders*, there is a virtually complete absence of statistics. DSM-IV does not identify base rates for disorders, does not identify etiology to any significant degree, and generally provides little data for the clinician or researcher. While the five-volume *Source Book* provides some of this information, very few people purchase that text. DSM-IV is simply a diagnostic manual.

The Bottom Line

These criticisms may be accurate, but for all practical purposes DSM-IV is the only show in town. It is necessary for any mental health practitioner to be familiar with it and to make the best of what is sometimes a bad situation. Diagnoses are "explanatory fictions"—intangible, inexact, but necessary for dialogue regarding psychological states.

§ 17.11 DSM-IV and the Law

DSM-IV Cautionary Statements regarding Forensic Use

DSM-IV offers a "cautionary statement" immediately prior to the major text. That statement indicates that the diagnostic criteria "are offered as guidelines for making diagnoses," to improve reliability, and that "proper use of these criteria requires specialized clinical training that provides both a body of knowledge and clinical skills." In addition, it notes, not all "conditions for which people may be treated or that may be appropriate topics for research efforts" are included. Finally,

> the purpose of DSM-IV is to provide clear descriptions of diagnostic categories in order to enable clinicians and investigators to diagnose, communicate about, study, and treat people with various mental disorders. It is to be understood that inclusion here . . . of a diagnostic category such as Pathological Gambling or Pedophilia does not imply that the condition meets legal or other nonmedical criteria for what constitutes mental disease, mental disorder, or mental disability. The clinical and scientific considerations involved in categorization of these conditions as mental disorders may not be wholly relevant to legal judgments, for example, that take into account such issues as individual responsibility, disability determination, and competency.[63]

---

[62] Widiger, 1992.

[63] DSM-IV at xxvii.

Separately, DSM-IV also states that

> [i]t is important that DSM-IV not be applied mechanically by untrained individuals. The specific diagnostic criteria included in DSM-IV are meant to serve as guidelines to be informed by clinical judgment and are not meant to be used in a cookbook fashion. For example, the exercise of clinical judgment may justify giving a certain diagnosis to an individual even though the clinical presentation falls just short of meeting the full criteria for the diagnosis as long as the symptoms that are present are persistent and severe. On the other hand, lack of familiarity with DSM-IV or excessively flexible and idiosyncratic application of DSM-IV criteria or conventions substantially reduces its utility as a common language for communication.[64]

Furthermore,

> [w]hen DSM-IV categories, criteria, and textual descriptions are employed for forensic purposes, there are significant risks that diagnostic information will be misused or misunderstood. These dangers arise because of the imperfect fit between the questions of ultimate concern to the law and the information contained in a clinical diagnosis. In most situations, the clinical diagnosis of a DSM-IV mental disorder is not sufficient to establish the existence for legal purposes of a "mental disorder," "mental disability," "mental disease," or "mental defect." In determining whether an individual meets a specified legal standard . . . , additional information is usually required beyond that contained in the DSM-IV diagnosis. This might include information about the individual's functional impairments and how these impairments affect the particular abilities in question. It is precisely because impairments, abilities, and disabilities vary widely within each diagnostic category that assignment of a particular diagnosis does not imply a specific level of impairment or disability.
>
> Nonclinical decision makers should also be cautioned that a diagnosis does not carry any necessary implications regarding the causes of the individual's mental disorder or its associated impairments.[65]

Having thus disclaimed any use of DSM-IV in legal contexts, it goes on to invite just such use:

> When used appropriately, diagnoses and diagnostic information can assist decision makers in their determinations. For example, when the presence of a mental disorder is the predicate for a subsequent legal determination (e.g., involuntary civil commitment), the use of an established system of diagnosis enhances the value and reliability of the determination. By providing a compendium based on a review of the pertinent clinical and research literature, DSM-IV may facilitate the legal decision makers' understanding of the relevant characteristics of mental disorders.[66]

---

[64] *Id.* at xxiii.

[65] *Id.*

[66] *Id.* at xxiv.

DSM-IV and Forensic Practice

The forensic expert will need to consider several factors as a result of the changes in DSM-IV:

1. With the increased emphasis on dysfunction ("clinically significant distress or impairment . . ."), it will be necessary for the clinician to specify the functional disability caused by or correlated with the diagnosis, and it may be necessary for the clinician to have external validation of disability (e.g., family members, co-workers, psychological testing, medical reports).

2. PTSD will be easier to diagnose, since the requirement for a trauma/stressor that is "outside the range of normal human experience" has been eliminated.

3. The forensic expert must be certain that DSM-IV criteria are addressed when making a diagnosis, since numerous changes were made from the criteria in DSM-III-R.

4. As the "diagnostic standard" in the United States, DSM-IV is generally accepted in the mental health community and will therefore meet the requirements of *Frye* and *Daubert* for general acceptance. (See **Chapter 1.**)[67]

§ 17.12   International Classification of Diseases, Injuries, and Causes of Death

The International Classification of Diseases, Injuries, and Causes of Death (ICD) was begun by the World Health Organization toward the end of the last century as the International List of Causes of Death, adding the ICD name only with the sixth revision in 1948.[68] It was not until the fifth revision, in 1938, that a separate section for mental disorders was included, a single category with four subcategories: mental deficiency, schizophrenia, manic depressive psychosis, and "all other mental disorders."[69] The sixth revision, in 1948, contained the first section on mental disorders, which was included in ICD-7 (1955) without major revisions. It was not until ICD-8, however, adopted in 1965, that the mental disorders classification was sufficiently broad and inclusive to be useful to most psychiatrists. Part of its usefulness was due to the development of a "Glossary of Mental Disorders and Guide to Their Classification," for use in conjunction with ICD-8.[70]

ICD-9 was adopted in 1975, with the glossary as an integral part of the mental disorders section, the only section of ICD-9 that includes such a glossary. The reason for its inclusion, according to the World Health Organization, is that "diagnosis of many of the most important mental disorders still relies largely upon descriptions of abnormal experience and behavior, and without some guidance in the form of a glossary that can serve as a

---

[67] Jerry von Talge, *Part II*, at 56–57.

[68] Spitzer & Williams at 598.

[69] DSM-III-R at 435.

[70] *Id.*

common frame of reference, psychiatric communications easily became unsatisfactory at both clinical and statistical levels."[71]

The ICD is a statistical classification of diseases and many other sources of morbidity and mortality. It has also been adapted as a nomenclature of diseases for indexing medical records. As a statistical classification system, designed to indicate the relationship between diagnostic categories but not to facilitate the description and recording of clinical and pathological observations, it is relatively static and not well suited to daily use by clinicians.[72]

The ICD-9 is organized into 17 major sections, the fifth of which is Mental Disorders. All mental disorders must be assigned a three-digit code, from 290 to 319. A fourth digit, from .0 to .9, may be used for greater specificity within a given code.[73] Even so, when clinicians in the United States sought greater specificity, ICD-9-CM—the *Clinical Modification of the World Health Organization's International Classification of Diseases, 9th Revision*—was developed. Although highly similar to ICD-9, it contains a fifth digit for many categories and a small number of four-digit codes not in ICD-9. The largest disparity between ICD-9 and ICD-9-CM is in the classification of affective psychoses (code 296). In some instances, the two sources use the same four-digit code to refer to different conditions: for example, code 296.2 in ICD-9 is "Manic-Depressive Psychosis, circular type but currently manic," and in ICD-9-CM, it is "Major Depressive Disorder, Single Episode."[74]

Most DSM-III three-digit codes were the same as ICD-9-CM codes, but some were different. However, all DSM-III-R and DSM-IV codes are legitimate ICD-9-CM/ICD-10 codes.[75]

Consistency with DSM-IV

In general, then, ICD-9-CM and DSM-IV are comparable texts but with sufficient differences that it should not be assumed that a given category is identical in both. At the least, DSM-IV is likely to be more detailed than ICD-9-CM or ICD-10 for any given category, and the content may in fact be substantially different.

Criticisms of ICD

The criticisms of DSM-III, DSM-III-R, and DSM-IV apply as well to ICD-9-CM, only more so. The ICD's lack of specificity is much greater than that of the DSMs, and it is much less in touch with current research. There are problems with DSM-IV in clinical use and in the courtroom, but those problems multiply with the ICD-9-CM and ICD-10.

---

[71] *Id.* at 437.

[72] *Id.* at 433–34.

[73] *Id.* at 434.

[74] *Id.* at 440–41.

[75] DSM-IV at xxi.

§ 17.13   ICD-10

The 1992 publication date for ICD-10 was determined by a timetable set many years prior to that date. Its contents were decided by consultation among the governments of more than 140 nations, and the final text is produced in at least eight languages. The preliminary formal meetings to plan ICD-10 took place in Geneva and Beijing in 1983, with the initial formal discussions of the mental disorders section held the following year.

> By 1986, a first draft of the whole of this section, including details of all its categories, complete with titles, code numbers, diagnostic guidelines, and precise diagnostic criteria for research, had been written, and by June 1987, a comprehensive text (the *Blue Book*) was being circulated by WHO's Division of Mental Health for field trials in 194 different centers in 55 different countries. . . . [I]n 1990, the World Health Assembly formally approved its introduction in member states from January 1, 1993.[76]

The final version of the *Blue Book*, entitled *The ICD-10 Classification of Mental and Behavioural Disorders*, was also published in 1992. The delay of the official introduction until 1993 was to permit the English text to be translated into the other seven official languages of the World Health Organization.[77]

Because the Task Force on DSM-IV had been established several years earlier—in 1988—"it was no longer feasible to change anything other than the subdivisions of the main categories of mental disorder and the details of some of the clinical descriptions and definitions" if DSM-IV and ICD-10 were in fact to be highly compatible. It would have been very beneficial to the development of ICD-10 to have had the DSM-IV literature surveys and data analyses several years earlier. "As it [was], by the time the blueprint [was] ready, the ship [was] already . . . built."[78] Even so, DSM-IV and ICD-10 have much more in common than DSM-III and ICD-9.[79] Both use an atheoretical approach to classification and use sets of diagnostic criteria.[80] The number of major diagnostic classes are different, however. DSM-IV has 17 diagnostic classes, but ICD-10 allotted only 10 two-digit categories for its section on mental disorders.[81] Thus, ICD-10 becomes a diagnostic version of the Procrustean bed.

Much of the problem involving inconsistencies between DSM-IV and ICD-10 stems from the decision to revise DSM-III (1980) early and publish DSM-III-R in 1987, rather than beginning work on DSM-IV in the mid-1980s.

> It was widely suspected that financial considerations had a major influence on this decision. . . . The DSM-III generated a huge and unexpected profit for the American Psychiatric Association, [because] any American psychiatrist or clinical psychologist who wished to

---

[76] Kendell at 297.

[77] *Id.* at 298.

[78] *Id.*

[79] *Id.* at 299.

[80] R. Spitzer, *An Outsider-Insider's Views about Revising the DSMs*, 100 J. Abnormal Psychol. 295 (1991).

[81] *Id.* at 296.

obtain reimbursement from major funding bodies, anyone involved in clinical research, and any pharmaceutical company that wished to obtain a product license from the U.S. Food and Drug Administration would have to buy any new DSM the American Psychiatric Association produced. . . . [Thus] the American Psychiatric Association has committed itself to producing successive revisions of its DSM at intervals first of 16 years, then of 12, then 7, and now after only 5 years.[82]

Field Trials

Field trials for ICD-10 were conducted in 55 countries, but lack of funding and a tight timetable limited data collection to the acceptability, feasibility, coverage, generalizability, and interrater reliability of the contents of the text. The critical aspect of construct validity was largely ignored.[83] Thus, it was reasonably assured that the diagnostic criteria were workable and that clinicians were likely to label similar disorders similarly, without also reasonably assuring that the diagnoses given were addressing a single theoretical entity.

The World Health Organization has decided that it will not continue to revise the ICD every 10 years, as it has for four decades. The precise year for the next ICD has not been selected, but ICD-10 will have to remain in use for more than the 10 years of each of its immediate predecessors.[84]

Adoption of ICD-10

The *Tenth Edition of the International Classification of Diseases*, originally scheduled for introduction worldwide in 1992, had been anticipated to be officially accepted in the United States by the year 2000, though the rest of the world was already using it. The psychiatric section of ICD-10, the *Blue Book*, was published in 1992. According to DSM-IV, however, ICD-9-CM will remain the official ICD in the United States until the U.S. Department of Health and Human Services begins to require the use of ICD-10 for purposes of reporting relevant statistics.[85]

An additional problem will arise when the United States officially adopts the ICD-10. ICD-10 uses an alphanumeric system, with a single letter followed by two numbers. Additional specificity is possible by adding a fourth and sometimes a fifth digit. The United States is required by treaty to adopt ICD-10 to report health statistics—and, when it does, to utilize the alphanumeric system in reimbursement of medical claims.[86] Clinicians will have to learn the ICD-10 coding system in order to get payment for provision of services.

---

[82] Kendell at 298.

[83] *Id.*

[84] *Id.* at 300.

[85] DSM-IV at 829.

[86] Rajani Thangavelu & Ronald L. Martin, *ICD-10 and DSM-IV: Depiction of the Diagnostic Elephant*, 25 Psychiatric Annals 20, 21–23 (1995).

§ 17.14   ICIDH-2

The World Health Organization has completed a final draft of a functionally based classification system, the *International Classification of Functioning, Disability and Health*.[87] It is a revision of the *International Classification of Impairments, Disabilities and Handicaps* (ICIDH), so its acronym is ICIDH-2, even though that is not consistent with the revised title. The document is available on the Internet at *www.who.int/icidh*.

While the International Classification of Diseases, Tenth Revision (ICD-10) focuses on health conditions, the ICIDH-2 focuses on functioning and disability that are associated with health conditions. Because the new document focuses on an individual's level of functioning, it is of potentially great benefit in identifying factors that go beyond medical diagnosis that cause an individual to have a less-than-optimal level of functioning. The ICIDH-2 has been field-tested in 40 countries and 22 sites in the United States. It is designed to be used along with ICD-10, since the medical diagnosis tells little about the level of functioning of a given individual. It may also be used alone to describe the functional level of an individual.

The ICIDH-2 consists of two sections. The first, Functioning and Disability, consists of two components: classification of body systems and body structures, and descriptions of the range of functional abilities from both individual and societal perspectives. The second section, Contextual Factors, consists of the components of Environmental Factors and Personal Factors. The former addresses everything from the individual's most immediate environment to the most general social environment. The latter addresses the fact that individual, unique factors must be taken into consideration, but does not go into detail because of the huge number of possibilities this implies. Thus, the ICIDH-2 classifies situations, not people, and does so within the context of the environmental and personal factors that have an impact on everyone.

Although the ICIDH-2 has been published, it is still in the process of formal adoption by the governing bodies of the World Health Organization. That process may take a number of months; however, the ICIDH-2 is already in use in the United States and elsewhere.

§ 17.15   Physicians' Current Procedural Terminology

The *Physicians' Current Procedural Terminology* (CPT) is published by the American Medical Association, usually on an annual basis. It is a list of categories of professional services, each with an identifying code, for reporting "medical" services and procedures performed by physicians and mental health professionals. It was designed to permit uniform designation of professional procedures, in large part for billing purposes.

The present revision is the 1998 version of a work that first appeared in 1966. It is known as CPT-98.

Each procedure in CPT has a unique five-digit code. The physician is to select the code that most closely describes his or her professional activity and use it (and the terminology accompanying it) to identify services he or she performs. The codes are certified by the federal Health Care Financing Administration, which periodically alters or adds codes as deemed necessary. The codes are nearly universally used for billing of psychological and psychiatric mental health services to insurance companies, Medicaid, and Medicare.

---

[87] World Health Organization, Geneva, Switzerland (2001).

Most codes are an indication of both the procedure (service) and the time involved. A number of commonly used psychiatric codes were revised or deleted as of January 1, 1998:

Old Code	New Code	Procedure
90801	same	Psychiatric diagnostic interview, 60–90 minutes
90841	deleted	Individual psychotherapy, time unspecified
90842	90808	Individual psychotherapy, approximately 75–80 minutes
90843	90804	Individual psychotherapy, approximately 20–30 minutes
90844	90806	Individual psychotherapy, approximately 45–50 minutes
90846	same	Family psychotherapy (without patient present), approximately 45–50 minutes
90847	same	Family psychotherapy (conjoint psychotherapy) (with patient), approximately 45–50 minutes
90830	96100	Psychological testing, 60 minutes

It is rare that an insurance company or other third party would pay for legal services of any kind, including evaluations conducted solely for legal purposes. If an evaluation were completed that included providing an individual's psychotherapist with a copy of all relevant parts of the evaluation, some insurance companies would pay for at least part of that evaluation. The provider is ethically required to indicate that it was, for example, a "court-ordered evaluation that was also furnished to the patient's psychotherapist for use in psychotherapeutic case management" or words to that effect.

§ 17.16   Examining Mental Health Professionals

The fact that neither DSM-IV nor ICD-9-CM (nor ICD-10) is a precise document raises significant questions about both their validity and their reliability. For example, with Brief Reactive Psychosis, Schizophreniform Disorder, and Schizophrenia, identical clinical features lead to different diagnoses over time. It becomes important to determine what criteria the expert used to make a diagnosis and what criteria permitted a differential diagnosis between two similar disorders. Because no mental disorder automatically renders an individual incompetent, it is also necessary to question the expert about competence and other issues directly related to the issues in the case. It is normally necessary for the attorney to retain a psychologist or psychiatrist to assist with this part of the examination of the expert.

For example, if the expert in a child custody case indicates that a parent has a diagnosis of Bipolar Disorder, the attorney may want to ask the following questions:

1. Which of the criteria in DSM-IV for Manic Episode, Major Depressive Episode, and Bipolar Disorder are met and which are not? What specific behavior or symptoms meet the required criteria for the diagnosis?

2. If the parent's mood does cycle into manic and depressed stages at times, is the reality testing so poor that the parent clearly qualifies for the psychotic label of Bipolar Disorder, or is Cyclothymia—a nonpsychotic disorder—more accurate? It is

obviously a more positive indicator of one's ability to function if psychosis has not been present.

3. If the parent has been only depressed (no manic periods) in recent years, are Major Depression or Dysthymia more likely than Bipolar Disorder at this time? Parents with a Bipolar Disorder are relatively more likely to be a problem for the children, particularly during manic periods when they feel exceptionally competent and powerful and may directly inflict harm, than would be parents who are depressed. With the depressed parent, the primary concern would be neglect of the children rather than direct infliction of harm, with that neglect being much more significant, on the average, for the person with a Major Depression than for one with Dysthymia.

Most diagnoses are open to some degree of questioning, and it is not uncommon for small changes in data (for example, how long a disorder has been present) to lead to a substantial change in diagnosis. When some question arises, it may be helpful for the attorney to present a photocopy of relevant sections of DSM-IV to the psychologist who is testifying, so that he or she may be questioned regarding precisely which diagnostic indicators are present and why one diagnosis was preferred over another similar one.

Finally, it is worth repeating the statement of psychiatrist Allen Frances and colleagues in § 17.4: "DSM-IV . . . is not a 'bible' based on any gold standard of psychiatric diagnosis. Rather, it is a document reflecting the current progress in knowledge of psychiatric disorders."[88]

§ 17.17   Example of Diagnostic Criteria from DSM-IV

Please see **Chapter 15** for the diagnoses of Substance Abuse and Substance Dependence.

§ 17.18   DSM-V

The American Psychiatric Association has published a timetable for the fifth edition of the *Diagnostic and Statistical Manual of Mental Disorders*:

2004–2005	Publication of "pre-planning white papers."
2004–2007	Review of data from ten conferences sponsored by the American Psychiatric Association and the National Institutes on Health on "the future of psychiatric diagnoses."
2007	Appointment of DSM-V Work Groups
2011	Publication of DSM-V

The web site for the DSM-V Prelude Project is *www.dsm5.org*. One may also sign up there for a free newsletter that will periodically update the planning process and planned content.

---

[88] Allen Frances et al., *DSM-IV: Issues in Development*, 25 Psychiatric Annals 15, 17–18 (1995).

§ 17.19   Questions for Chapter 17

Caution.   Attorneys should not expect to be able to go into court and ask all of the following questions. Preparation is necessary, reviewing material in the book to determine whether the question applies to a particular case. Section numbers at the end of some of the questions indicate where to find an explanation of why the question is important.

1. Is the expert using the DSM-IV classification system? See **§§ 17.4** and **17.10.**

2. If the psychologist has used a DSM-IV diagnosis, has he or she taken into account the criticisms leveled against the DSM-IV? See **§ 17.10.**

3. Has the expert assessed functional impairment? See **§ 17.11.**

4. What diagnoses did the expert consider in the process of arriving at a final diagnostic conclusion? Why were the other diagnoses rejected when the expert arrived at the final diagnosis?

PROFESSIONAL ORGANIZATIONS

Academy of Certified Social Workers. *See* National Association of Social Workers.

Academy of Family Mediators, 5 Militia Drive, Lexington, MA 02421. Phone: 781-674-2663.

American Academy of Forensic Psychiatry, c/o ABPP, 2100 E. Broadway, Suite 313, Columbia, MO 65201-6082. Phone: 314-875-1267.

American Academy of Forensic Psychology. *See* American Board of Forensic Psychology.

American Academy of Forensic Sciences, 410 North 21st Street, Suite 203, P.O. Box 669, Colorado Springs, CO 80904-2798. Phone: 719-636-1100.

American Academy of Psychiatry and the Law, One Regency Drive, P.O. Box 30, Bloomfield, CT 06002. Phone: 860-242-5450.

American Association for Marriage and Family Therapy (AAMFT), 112 S. Alfred Street, Alexandria, VA 22314-3061. Phone: 703-838-9808.

American Association of Sex Educators, Counselors and Therapists (AASECT), P.O. Box 5488, Richmond, VA 23220-0488. Note: they indicate they do not publish their phone number, preferring communication by e-mail or U.S. mail.

American Association of Suicidology, 4201 Connecticut Avenue NW, Suite 408, Washington, DC 20008. Phone: 202-237-2280.

American Board of Assessment Psychology, 1401 Brickell Avenue, Suite 320, Miami, FL 33131-3504. Phone: 305-372-0010.

American Board of Forensic Examiners, 3301 Dundak Avenue, Baltimore, MD 21222. Phone: 410-282-3376.

American Board of Forensic Psychiatry, 3301 Dundak Avenue, Baltimore, MD 21222. Phone: 410-282-3376.

American Board of Forensic Psychology, 2100 E. Broadway, Suite 313, Columbia, MO 65201. Phone: 314-875-1267.

American Board of Medical Psychotherapists and Psychodiagnosticians, Park Plaza Medical Building, 345 24th Avenue North, Suite 201, Nashville, TN 37203-1520.

American Board of Professional Psychology, 2100 E. Broadway, Suite 313, Columbia, MO 65201. Phone: 573-875-1267.

American Board of Psychiatry and Neurology, 500 Lake Cook Road, Suite 335, Deerfield, IL 60015. Phone: 847-945-7900.

American College of Forensic Psychiatry, 224 Grand Canal, P.O. Box 5870, Balboa Island, CA 92662. Phone: 949-673-7773.

American College of Forensic Psychology, 224 Grand Canal, P.O. Box 5870, Balboa Island, CA 92662. Phone: 714-831-0236.

American Medical Association, 515 N. State Street, Chicago, IL 60610. Phone: 312-464-5000.

American Orthopsychiatric Association, 2001 N. Beauregard, 12th Floor Alexandria, VA 22311. Phone: 703-797-2584

American Professional Society on the Abuse of Children, P.O. Box 26901, CHO 3B3406, Oklahoma City, OK 73190. Phone: 405-271-8202.

American Psychiatric Association, 1000 Wilson Boulevard, Suite 1825, Arlington, VA 22209-3901. Phone: 703-907-7300.

American Psychoanalytic Association, 309 E. 49th Street, New York, NY 10017. Phone: 212-752-0450.

American Psychological Association, 750 First Street NE, Washington, DC 20002. Phone: 800-374-2721; 202-336-5510.

American Psychology-Law Society, c/o American Psychological Association.

Association of Social Work Boards, 400 S. Ridge Parkway, Suite B, Culpepper, VA 22701. Phone: 800-225-6880, 540-829-6880.

Association of State and Provincial Psychology Boards, P.O. Box 241245, Montgomery, AL 36124-1245. Phone: 334-832-4580.

Canadian Psychiatric Association, 260-441 MacLaren Street, Ottawa, ON, Canada K2P-2H3. Phone: 613-234-2815.

Canadian Psychological Association, Suite 205, 151 Rue Slater, Ottawa, ON K1P 5H3. Phone: 613-237-2144; 888-472-0657.

Clinical Social Work Federation, P.O. Box 3740, Arlington, VA 22203. Phone: 703-522-3866.

National Association of Counsel for Children (NACC), 1825 Marion Street, Suite 340, Denver, CO 80218. Phone: 888-828-NACC, e-mail *advocate@NACCchildlaw.org.*

National Association of Social Workers, 750 First Street N.E., Suite 700, Washington, DC 20002-4241. Phone: 202-408-8600.

National Council of Juvenile and Family Court Judges: P.O. Box 8970 Reno, NV 89507. Phone: 775-784-6012. Fax: 775-784-6628. E-mail: *admin@ncjfcj.unr.edu.*

National Organization of Forensic Social Work, new address: 5784 E. Silo Ridge Drive, Ann Arbor, MI 48108. Phone: 734-944-2820.

National Register of Health Service Providers in Psychology, 1120 G Street NW, Suite 330, Washington, DC 20005. Phone: 202-783-7663.

Youth Law Center: 417 Montgomery Street, Suite 900, San Francisco, CA, 94104-1121. Phone: 415-543-3379, fax 415-956-9022, e-mail *info@youthlawcenter.com.*

Youth Law Center, 1010 Vermont Avenue NW, Suite 310, Washington, DC 20005-4902. Phone: 202-637-0377. Fax: 202-379-1600. E-mail: *info@youthlawcenter.com.*

For more information on other organizations, consult the *Encyclopedia of Associations.*

Web sites:

Academy of Family Mediators: *www.mediators.org* (*see also* Association for Conflict Resolution: *www.acresolution.org*)

American Academy of Forensic Psychiatry: *www.quincy.ca/forpsych.htm*

American Academy of Forensic Psychology: *www.abfp.com*

American Academy of Forensic Sciences: *www.aafs.org*

American Academy of Psychiatry and the Law: *www.emory.edu/aapl*

American Association of Sex Educators, Counselors, and Therapists: *www.aasect.org*

American Association of Suicidology: *www.suicidology.org*

American Association for Marriage and Family Therapy: *www.aamft.org*

American Board of Assessment Psychology: *www.assessmentpsychology.org*

American Board of Professional Neuropsychology: *www.abpn.net*

American Board of Professional Psychology: *www.abpp.org*

American Board/College of Forensic Examiners: *www.acfe.com*

American Board of Forensic Psychiatry: *www.forensicpsychiatry.cc*

American Board of Forensic Psychology: *www.abfp.com*

American Board of Psychiatry and Neurology: *www.abpn.com*

American College of Forensic Psychiatry: *www.forensicpsychonline.com*

American College of Forensic Psychology: *www.forensicpsychology.org*

American Medical Association: *www.ama-assn.org*

American Orthopsychiatric Association: *www.amerortho.org*

American Professional Society on the Abuse of Children: *www.apsac.org*

American Psychiatric Association: *www.psych.org*

American Psychoanalytic Association: *www.apsa.org*

American Psychological Association: *www.apa.org*

APA Divisions: *apa.org/about/division.html*

American Psychology-Law Society: *www.unl.edu/ap-ls*

Association of Social Work Boards: *www.aswb.org*

Association of State and Provincial Psychology Boards: *www.asppb.org*

Canadian Psychiatric Association: *www.cpa-apc.org*

Canadian Psychological Association: *www.cpa.ca*

Clinical Social Work Federation: *www.cswf.org*

National Association of Counsel for Children: *http://naccchildlaw.org/*

National Association of Social Workers: *www.naswdc.org*

National Council of Juvenile and Family Court Judges: *http://www.ncjfcj.org/*

National Organization of Forensic Social Work: *www.nofsw.org*

National Register of Health Service Providers in Psychology: *www.nationalregister.com*

Youth Law Center: *www.ylc.org*

ETHICAL PRINCIPLES OF PSYCHOLOGISTS AND CODE OF CONDUCT

Ethical Principles of Psychologists and Code of Conduct, 57 American Psychologist 1060–1073 (2002). © 2002 the American Psychological Association. Reprinted by permission.

Ethical Principles of Psychologists and Code of Conduct

CONTENTS

INTRODUCTION AND APPLICABILITY

The American Psychological Association's (APA's) Ethical Principles of Psychologists and Code of Conduct (hereinafter referred to as the Ethics Code) consists of an Introduction, a Preamble, five General Principles (A–E), and specific Ethical Standards. The Introduction discusses the intent, organization, procedural considerations, and scope of application of the Ethics Code. The Preamble and General Principles are aspirational goals to guide psychologists toward the highest ideals of psychology. Although the Preamble and General Principles are not themselves enforceable rules, they should be considered by psychologists in arriving at an ethical course of action. The Ethical Standards set forth enforceable rules for conduct as psychologists. Most of the Ethical Standards are written broadly, in order to apply to psychologists in varied roles, although the application of an Ethical Standard may vary depending on the context. The Ethical Standards are not exhaustive. The fact that a given conduct is not specifically addressed by an Ethical Standard does not mean that it is necessarily either ethical or unethical.

This Ethics Code applies only to psychologists' activities that are part of their scientific, educational, or professional roles as psychologists. Areas covered include but are not limited to the clinical, counseling, and school practice of psychology; research; teaching; supervision of trainees; public service; policy development; social intervention; development of assessment instruments; conducting assessments; educational counseling; organizational consulting; forensic activities; program design and evaluation; and administration. This Ethics Code applies to these activities across a variety of contexts, such as in person, postal, telephone, Internet, and other electronic transmissions. These activities shall be distinguished from the purely private conduct of psychologists, which is not within the purview of the Ethics Code.

Membership in the APA commits members and student affiliates to comply with the standards of the APA Ethics Code and to the rules and procedures used to enforce them. Lack of awareness or misunderstanding of an Ethical Standard is not itself a defense to a charge of unethical conduct.

The procedures for filing, investigating, and resolving complaints of unethical conduct are described in the current Rules and Procedures of the APA Ethics Committee. APA may impose sanctions on its members for violations of the standards of the Ethics Code, including termination of APA membership, and may notify other bodies and individuals of its actions. Actions that violate the standards of the Ethics Code may also lead to the imposition of sanctions on psychologists or students whether or not they are APA members by bodies other than APA, including state psychological associations, other professional groups, psychology boards, other state or federal agencies, and payors for health services. In addition, APA may take action against a member after his or her conviction of a felony, expulsion or suspension from an affiliated state psychological association, or suspension or loss of licensure. When the sanction to be imposed by APA is less than expulsion, the 2001 Rules and Procedures do not guarantee an opportunity for an in-person hearing, but generally provide that complaints will be resolved only on the basis of a submitted record.

The Ethics Code is intended to provide guidance for psychologists and standards of professional conduct that can be applied by the APA and by other bodies that choose to adopt them. The Ethics Code is not intended to be a basis of civil liability. Whether a psychologist has violated the Ethics Code standards does not by itself determine whether the psychologist is legally liable in a court action, whether a contract is enforceable, or whether other legal consequences occur.

The modifiers used in some of the standards of this Ethics Code (e.g., *reasonably*, *appropriate*, *potentially*) are included in the standards when they would (1) allow professional judgment on the part of psychologists, (2) eliminate injustice or inequality that would occur without the modifier, (3) ensure applicability across the broad range of activities conducted by psychologists, or (4) guard against a set of rigid rules that might be quickly outdated. As used in this Ethics Code, the term *reasonable* means the prevailing professional judgment of psychologists engaged in similar activities in similar circumstances, given the knowledge the psychologist had or should have had at the time.

This version of the APA Ethics Code was adopted by the American Psychological Association's Council of Representatives during its meeting, August 21, 2002, and is effective beginning June 1, 2003. Inquiries concerning the substance or interpretation of the APA Ethics Code should be addressed to the Director, Office of Ethics, American Psychological Association, 750 First Street, NE, Washington, DC 20002-4242. The Ethics Code and information regarding the Code can be found on the APA Web site, http://www.apa.org/ethics. The standards in this Ethics Code will be used to adjudicate complaints brought concerning alleged conduct occurring on or after the effective date. Complaints regarding conduct occurring prior to the effective date will be adjudicated on the basis of the version of the Ethics Code that was in effect at the time the conduct occurred.

The APA has previously published its Ethics Code as follows:

American Psychological Association. (1953). *Ethical standards of psychologists*. Washington, DC: Author.

American Psychological Association. (1959). Ethical standards of psychologists. *American Psychologist, 14*, 279–282.

American Psychological Association. (1963). Ethical standards of psychologists. *American Psychologist, 18*, 56–60.

American Psychological Association. (1968). Ethical standards of psychologists. *American Psychologist, 23*, 357–361.

American Psychological Association. (1977, March). Ethical standards of psychologists. *APA Monitor*, 22–23.

American Psychological Association. (1979). *Ethical standards of psychologists*. Washington, DC: Author.

American Psychological Association. (1981). Ethical principles of psychologists. *American Psychologist, 36*, 633–638.

American Psychological Association. (1990). Ethical principles of psychologists (Amended June 2, 1989). *American Psychologist, 45*, 390–395.

American Psychological Association. (1992). Ethical principles of psychologists and code of conduct. *American Psychologist, 47*, 1597–1611.

Request copies of the APA's Ethical Principles of Psychologists and Code of Conduct from the APA Order Department, 750 First Street, NE, Washington, DC 20002-4242, or phone (202) 336-5510.

In the process of making decisions regarding their professional behavior, psychologists must consider this Ethics Code in addition to applicable laws and psychology board regulations. In applying the Ethics Code to their professional work, psychologists may consider other materials and guidelines that have been adopted or endorsed by scientific and professional psychological organizations and the dictates of their own conscience, as well as consult with others within the field. If this Ethics Code establishes a higher standard of conduct than is required by law, psychologists must meet the higher ethical standard. If psychologists' ethical responsibilities conflict with law, regulations, or other governing legal authority, psychologists make known their commitment to this Ethics Code and take steps to resolve the conflict in a responsible manner. If the conflict is unresolvable via such means, psychologists may adhere to the requirements of the law, regulations, or other governing authority in keeping with basic principles of human rights.

PREAMBLE

Psychologists are committed to increasing scientific and professional knowledge of behavior and people's understanding of themselves and others and to the use of such knowledge to improve the condition of individuals, organizations, and society. Psychologists respect and protect civil and human rights and the central importance of freedom of inquiry and expression in research, teaching, and publication. They strive to help the public in developing informed judgments and choices concerning human behavior. In doing so, they perform many roles, such as researcher, educator, diagnostician, therapist, supervisor, consultant, administrator, social interventionist, and expert witness. This Ethics Code provides a common set of principles and standards upon which psychologists build their professional and scientific work.

This Ethics Code is intended to provide specific standards to cover most situations encountered by psychologists. It has as its goals the welfare and protection of the individuals and groups with whom psychologists work and the education of members, students, and the public regarding ethical standards of the discipline.

The development of a dynamic set of ethical standards for psychologists' work-related conduct requires a personal commitment and lifelong effort to act ethically; to encourage ethical behavior by students, supervisees, employees, and colleagues; and to consult with others concerning ethical problems.

GENERAL PRINCIPLES

This section consists of General Principles. General Principles, as opposed to Ethical Standards, are aspirational in nature. Their intent is to guide and inspire psychologists toward the very highest ethical ideals of the profession. General Principles, in contrast to Ethical Standards, do not represent obligations and should not form the basis for imposing sanctions. Relying upon General Principles for

either of these reasons distorts both their meaning and purpose.

Principle A: Beneficence and Nonmaleficence

Psychologists strive to benefit those with whom they work and take care to do no harm. In their professional actions, psychologists seek to safeguard the welfare and rights of those with whom they interact professionally and other affected persons, and the welfare of animal subjects of research. When conflicts occur among psychologists' obligations or concerns, they attempt to resolve these conflicts in a responsible fashion that avoids or minimizes harm. Because psychologists' scientific and professional judgments and actions may affect the lives of others, they are alert to and guard against personal, financial, social, organizational, or political factors that might lead to misuse of their influence. Psychologists strive to be aware of the possible effect of their own physical and mental health on their ability to help those with whom they work.

Principle B: Fidelity and Responsibility

Psychologists establish relationships of trust with those with whom they work. They are aware of their professional and scientific responsibilities to society and to the specific communities in which they work. Psychologists uphold professional standards of conduct, clarify their professional roles and obligations, accept appropriate responsibility for their behavior, and seek to manage conflicts of interest that could lead to exploitation or harm. Psychologists consult with, refer to, or cooperate with other professionals and institutions to the extent needed to serve the best interests of those with whom they work. They are concerned about the ethical compliance of their colleagues' scientific and professional conduct. Psychologists strive to contribute a portion of their professional time for little or no compensation or personal advantage.

Principle C: Integrity

Psychologists seek to promote accuracy, honesty, and truthfulness in the science, teaching, and practice of psychology. In these activities psychologists do not steal, cheat, or engage in fraud, subterfuge, or intentional misrepresentation of fact. Psychologists strive to keep their promises and to avoid unwise or unclear commitments. In situations in which deception may be ethically justifiable to maximize benefits and minimize harm, psychologists have a serious obligation to consider the need for, the possible consequences of, and their responsibility to correct any resulting mistrust or other harmful effects that arise from the use of such techniques.

Principle D: Justice

Psychologists recognize that fairness and justice entitle all persons to access to and benefit from the contributions of psychology and to equal quality in the processes, procedures, and services being conducted by psychologists. Psychologists exercise reasonable judgment and take precautions to ensure that their potential biases, the boundaries of their competence, and the limitations of their expertise do not lead to or condone unjust practices.

Principle E: Respect for People's Rights and Dignity

Psychologists respect the dignity and worth of all people, and the rights of individuals to privacy, confidentiality, and self-determination. Psychologists are aware that special safeguards may be necessary to protect the rights and welfare of persons or communities whose vulnerabilities impair autonomous decision making. Psychologists are aware of and respect cultural, individual, and role differences, including those based on age, gender, gender identity, race, ethnicity, culture, national origin, religion, sexual orientation, disability, language, and socioeconomic status, and consider these factors when working with members of such groups. Psychologists try to eliminate the effect on their work of biases based on those factors, and they do not knowingly participate in or condone activities of others based upon such prejudices.

ETHICAL STANDARDS

1.   Resolving Ethical Issues

1.01 Misuse of Psychologists' Work

If psychologists learn of misuse or misrepresentation of their work, they take reasonable steps to correct or minimize the misuse or misrepresentation.

1.02 Conflicts Between Ethics and Law, Regulations, or Other Governing Legal Authority

If psychologists' ethical responsibilities conflict with law, regulations, or other governing legal authority, psychologists make known their commitment to the Ethics Code and take steps to resolve the conflict. If the conflict is unresolvable via such means, psychologists may adhere to the requirements of the law, regulations, or other governing legal authority.

1.03 Conflicts Between Ethics and Organizational Demands

If the demands of an organization with which psychologists are affiliated or for whom they are working conflict with this Ethics Code, psychologists clarify the nature of the conflict, make known their commitment to the Ethics Code, and to the extent feasible, resolve the conflict in a way that permits adherence to the Ethics Code.

1.04 Informal Resolution of Ethical Violations

When psychologists believe that there may have been an ethical violation by another psychologist, they attempt to resolve the issue by bringing it to the attention of that individual, if an informal resolution appears appropri-

ate and the intervention does not violate any confidentiality rights that may be involved. (See also Standards 1.02, Conflicts Between Ethics and Law, Regulations, or Other Governing Legal Authority, and 1.03, Conflicts Between Ethics and Organizational Demands.)

1.05 Reporting Ethical Violations

If an apparent ethical violation has substantially harmed or is likely to substantially harm a person or organization and is not appropriate for informal resolution under Standard 1.04, Informal Resolution of Ethical Violations, or is not resolved properly in that fashion, psychologists take further action appropriate to the situation. Such action might include referral to state or national committees on professional ethics, to state licensing boards, or to the appropriate institutional authorities. This standard does not apply when an intervention would violate confidentiality rights or when psychologists have been retained to review the work of another psychologist whose professional conduct is in question. (See also Standard 1.02, Conflicts Between Ethics and Law, Regulations, or Other Governing Legal Authority.)

1.06 Cooperating With Ethics Committees

Psychologists cooperate in ethics investigations, proceedings, and resulting requirements of the APA or any affiliated state psychological association to which they belong. In doing so, they address any confidentiality issues. Failure to cooperate is itself an ethics violation. However, making a request for deferment of adjudication of an ethics complaint pending the outcome of litigation does not alone constitute noncooperation.

1.07 Improper Complaints

Psychologists do not file or encourage the filing of ethics complaints that are made with reckless disregard for or willful ignorance of facts that would disprove the allegation.

1.08 Unfair Discrimination Against Complainants and Respondents

Psychologists do not deny persons employment, advancement, admissions to academic or other programs, tenure, or promotion, based solely upon their having made or their being the subject of an ethics complaint. This does not preclude taking action based upon the outcome of such proceedings or considering other appropriate information.

2.   Competence

2.01 Boundaries of Competence

(a) Psychologists provide services, teach, and conduct research with populations and in areas only within the boundaries of their competence, based on their education, training, supervised experience, consultation, study, or professional experience.

(b) Where scientific or professional knowledge in the discipline of psychology establishes that an understanding of factors associated with age, gender, gender identity, race, ethnicity, culture, national origin, religion, sexual orientation, disability, language, or socioeconomic status is essential for effective implementation of their services or research, psychologists have or obtain the training, experience, consultation, or supervision necessary to ensure the competence of their services, or they make appropriate referrals, except as provided in Standard 2.02, Providing Services in Emergencies.

(c) Psychologists planning to provide services, teach, or conduct research involving populations, areas, techniques, or technologies new to them undertake relevant education, training, supervised experience, consultation, or study.

(d) When psychologists are asked to provide services to individuals for whom appropriate mental health services are not available and for which psychologists have not obtained the competence necessary, psychologists with closely related prior training or experience may provide such services in order to ensure that services are not denied if they make a reasonable effort to obtain the competence required by using relevant research, training, consultation, or study.

(e) In those emerging areas in which generally recognized standards for preparatory training do not yet exist, psychologists nevertheless take reasonable steps to ensure the competence of their work and to protect clients/patients, students, supervisees, research participants, organizational clients, and others from harm.

(f) When assuming forensic roles, psychologists are or become reasonably familiar with the judicial or administrative rules governing their roles.

2.02 Providing Services in Emergencies

In emergencies, when psychologists provide services to individuals for whom other mental health services are not available and for which psychologists have not obtained the necessary training, psychologists may provide such services in order to ensure that services are not denied. The services are discontinued as soon as the emergency has ended or appropriate services are available.

2.03 Maintaining Competence

Psychologists undertake ongoing efforts to develop and maintain their competence.

2.04 Bases for Scientific and Professional Judgments

Psychologists' work is based upon established scientific and professional knowledge of the discipline. (See also Standards 2.01e, Boundaries of Competence, and 10.01b, Informed Consent to Therapy.)

2.05 Delegation of Work to Others

Psychologists who delegate work to employees, supervisees, or research or teaching assistants or who use the services of others, such as interpreters, take reasonable steps to (1) avoid delegating such work to persons who have a multiple relationship with those being served that would likely lead to exploitation or loss of objectivity; (2) authorize only those responsibilities that such persons can be expected to perform competently on the basis of their education, training, or experience, either independently or with the level of supervision being provided; and (3) see that such persons perform these services competently. (See also Standards 2.02, Providing Services in Emergencies; 3.05, Multiple Relationships; 4.01, Maintaining Confidentiality; 9.01, Bases for Assessments; 9.02, Use of Assessments; 9.03, Informed Consent in Assessments; and 9.07, Assessment by Unqualified Persons.)

2.06 Personal Problems and Conflicts

(a) Psychologists refrain from initiating an activity when they know or should know that there is a substantial likelihood that their personal problems will prevent them from performing their work-related activities in a competent manner.

(b) When psychologists become aware of personal problems that may interfere with their performing work-related duties adequately, they take appropriate measures, such as obtaining professional consultation or assistance, and determine whether they should limit, suspend, or terminate their work-related duties. (See also Standard 10.10, Terminating Therapy.)

3. Human Relations

3.01 Unfair Discrimination

In their work-related activities, psychologists do not engage in unfair discrimination based on age, gender, gender identity, race, ethnicity, culture, national origin, religion, sexual orientation, disability, socioeconomic status, or any basis proscribed by law.

3.02 Sexual Harassment

Psychologists do not engage in sexual harassment. Sexual harassment is sexual solicitation, physical advances, or verbal or nonverbal conduct that is sexual in nature, that occurs in connection with the psychologist's activities or roles as a psychologist, and that either (1) is unwelcome, is offensive, or creates a hostile workplace or educational environment, and the psychologist knows or is told this or (2) is sufficiently severe or intense to be abusive to a reasonable person in the context. Sexual harassment can consist of a single intense or severe act or of multiple persistent or pervasive acts. (See also Standard 1.08, Unfair Discrimination Against Complainants and Respondents.)

3.03 Other Harassment

Psychologists do not knowingly engage in behavior that is harassing or demeaning to persons with whom they interact in their work based on factors such as those persons' age, gender, gender identity, race, ethnicity, culture, national origin, religion, sexual orientation, disability, language, or socioeconomic status.

3.04 Avoiding Harm

Psychologists take reasonable steps to avoid harming their clients/patients, students, supervisees, research participants, organizational clients, and others with whom they work, and to minimize harm where it is foreseeable and unavoidable.

3.05 Multiple Relationships

(a) A multiple relationship occurs when a psychologist is in a professional role with a person and (1) at the same time is in another role with the same person, (2) at the same time is in a relationship with a person closely associated with or related to the person with whom the psychologist has the professional relationship, or (3) promises to enter into another relationship in the future with the person or a person closely associated with or related to the person.

A psychologist refrains from entering into a multiple relationship if the multiple relationship could reasonably be expected to impair the psychologist's objectivity, competence, or effectiveness in performing his or her functions as a psychologist, or otherwise risks exploitation or harm to the person with whom the professional relationship exists.

Multiple relationships that would not reasonably be expected to cause impairment or risk exploitation or harm are not unethical.

(b) If a psychologist finds that, due to unforeseen factors, a potentially harmful multiple relationship has arisen, the psychologist takes reasonable steps to resolve it with due regard for the best interests of the affected person and maximal compliance with the Ethics Code.

(c) When psychologists are required by law, institutional policy, or extraordinary circumstances to serve in more than one role in judicial or administrative proceedings, at the outset they clarify role expectations and the extent of confidentiality and thereafter as changes occur. (See also Standards 3.04, Avoiding Harm, and 3.07, Third-Party Requests for Services.)

3.06 Conflict of Interest

Psychologists refrain from taking on a professional role when personal, scientific, professional, legal, financial, or other interests or relationships could reasonably be expected to (1) impair their objectivity, competence, or effectiveness in performing their functions as psychologists or (2) expose the person or organization with whom the professional relationship exists to harm or exploitation.

3.07 Third-Party Requests for Services

When psychologists agree to provide services to a person or entity at the request of a third party, psychologists attempt to clarify at the outset of the service the nature of the relationship with all individuals or organizations involved. This clarification includes the role of the psychologist (e.g., therapist, consultant, diagnostician, or expert witness), an identification of who is the client, the probable uses of the services provided or the information obtained, and the fact that there may be limits to confidentiality. (See also Standards 3.05, Multiple Relationships, and 4.02, Discussing the Limits of Confidentiality.)

3.08 Exploitative Relationships

Psychologists do not exploit persons over whom they have supervisory, evaluative, or other authority such as clients/patients, students, supervisees, research participants, and employees. (See also Standards 3.05, Multiple Relationships; 6.04, Fees and Financial Arrangements; 6.05, Barter With Clients/Patients; 7.07, Sexual Relationships With Students and Supervisees; 10.05, Sexual Intimacies With Current Therapy Clients/Patients; 10.06, Sexual Intimacies With Relatives or Significant Others of Current Therapy Clients/Patients; 10.07, Therapy With Former Sexual Partners; and 10.08, Sexual Intimacies With Former Therapy Clients/Patients.)

3.09 Cooperation With Other Professionals

When indicated and professionally appropriate, psychologists cooperate with other professionals in order to serve their clients/patients effectively and appropriately. (See also Standard 4.05, Disclosures.)

3.10 Informed Consent

(a) When psychologists conduct research or provide assessment, therapy, counseling, or consulting services in person or via electronic transmission or other forms of communication, they obtain the informed consent of the individual or individuals using language that is reasonably understandable to that person or persons except when conducting such activities without consent is mandated by law or governmental regulation or as otherwise provided in this Ethics Code. (See also Standards 8.02, Informed Consent to Research; 9.03, Informed Consent in Assessments; and 10.01, Informed Consent to Therapy.)

(b) For persons who are legally incapable of giving informed consent, psychologists nevertheless (1) provide an appropriate explanation, (2) seek the individual's assent, (3) consider such persons' preferences and best interests, and (4) obtain appropriate permission from a legally authorized person, if such substitute consent is permitted or required by law. When consent by a legally authorized person is not permitted or required by law, psychologists take reasonable steps to protect the individual's rights and welfare.

(c) When psychological services are court ordered or otherwise mandated, psychologists inform the individual of the nature of the anticipated services, including whether the services are court ordered or mandated and any limits of confidentiality, before proceeding.

(d) Psychologists appropriately document written or oral consent, permission, and assent. (See also Standards 8.02, Informed Consent to Research; 9.03, Informed Consent in Assessments; and 10.01, Informed Consent to Therapy.)

3.11 Psychological Services Delivered to or Through Organizations

(a) Psychologists delivering services to or through organizations provide information beforehand to clients and when appropriate those directly affected by the services about (1) the nature and objectives of the services, (2) the intended recipients, (3) which of the individuals are clients, (4) the relationship the psychologist will have with each person and the organization, (5) the probable uses of services provided and information obtained, (6) who will have access to the information, and (7) limits of confidentiality. As soon as feasible, they provide information about the results and conclusions of such services to appropriate persons.

(b) If psychologists will be precluded by law or by organizational roles from providing such information to particular individuals or groups, they so inform those individuals or groups at the outset of the service.

3.12 Interruption of Psychological Services

Unless otherwise covered by contract, psychologists make reasonable efforts to plan for facilitating services in the event that psychological services are interrupted by factors such as the psychologist's illness, death, unavailability, relocation, or retirement or by the client's/patient's relocation or financial limitations. (See also Standard 6.02c, Maintenance, Dissemination, and Disposal of Confidential Records of Professional and Scientific Work.)

4.   Privacy and Confidentiality

4.01 Maintaining Confidentiality

Psychologists have a primary obligation and take reasonable precautions to protect confidential information obtained through or stored in any medium, recognizing that the extent and limits of confidentiality may be regulated by law or established by institutional rules or professional or scientific relationship. (See also Standard 2.05, Delegation of Work to Others.)

4.02 Discussing the Limits of Confidentiality

(a) Psychologists discuss with persons (including, to the extent feasible, persons who are legally incapable of giving informed consent and their legal representatives) and organizations with whom they establish a scientific or professional relationship (1) the relevant limits of confidentiality and (2) the foreseeable uses of the information generated through their psychological activities. (See also Standard 3.10, Informed Consent.)

(b) Unless it is not feasible or is contraindicated, the discussion of confidentiality occurs at the outset of the relationship and thereafter as new circumstances may warrant.

(c) Psychologists who offer services, products, or information via electronic transmission inform clients/patients of the risks to privacy and limits of confidentiality.

4.03 Recording

Before recording the voices or images of individuals to whom they provide services, psychologists obtain permission from all such persons or their legal representatives. (See also Standards 8.03, Informed Consent for Recording Voices and Images in Research; 8.05, Dispensing With Informed Consent for Research; and 8.07, Deception in Research.)

4.04 Minimizing Intrusions on Privacy

(a) Psychologists include in written and oral reports and consultations, only information germane to the purpose for which the communication is made.

(b) Psychologists discuss confidential information obtained in their work only for appropriate scientific or professional purposes and only with persons clearly concerned with such matters.

4.05 Disclosures

(a) Psychologists may disclose confidential information with the appropriate consent of the organizational client, the individual client/patient, or another legally authorized person on behalf of the client/patient unless prohibited by law.

(b) Psychologists disclose confidential information without the consent of the individual only as mandated by law, or where permitted by law for a valid purpose such as to (1) provide needed professional services; (2) obtain appropriate professional consultations; (3) protect the client/patient, psychologist, or others from harm; or (4) obtain payment for services from a client/patient, in which instance disclosure is limited to the minimum that is necessary to achieve the purpose. (See also Standard 6.04e, Fees and Financial Arrangements.)

4.06 Consultations

When consulting with colleagues, (1) psychologists do not disclose confidential information that reasonably could lead to the identification of a client/patient, research participant, or other person or organization with whom they have a confidential relationship unless they have obtained the prior consent of the person or organization or the disclosure cannot be avoided, and (2) they disclose information only to the extent necessary to achieve the purposes of the consultation. (See also Standard 4.01, Maintaining Confidentiality.)

4.07 Use of Confidential Information for Didactic or Other Purposes

Psychologists do not disclose in their writings, lectures, or other public media, confidential, personally identifiable information concerning their clients/patients, students, research participants, organizational clients, or other recipients of their services that they obtained during the course of their work, unless (1) they take reasonable steps to disguise the person or organization, (2) the person or organization has consented in writing, or (3) there is legal authorization for doing so.

5. Advertising and Other Public Statements

5.01 Avoidance of False or Deceptive Statements

(a) Public statements include but are not limited to paid or unpaid advertising, product endorsements, grant applications, licensing applications, other credentialing applications, brochures, printed matter, directory listings, personal resumes or curricula vitae, or comments for use in media such as print or electronic transmission, statements in legal proceedings, lectures and public oral presentations, and published materials. Psychologists do not knowingly make public statements that are false, deceptive, or fraudulent concerning their research, practice, or other work activities or those of persons or organizations with which they are affiliated.

(b) Psychologists do not make false, deceptive, or fraudulent statements concerning (1) their training, experience, or competence; (2) their academic degrees; (3) their credentials; (4) their institutional or association affiliations; (5) their services; (6) the scientific or clinical basis for, or results or degree of success of, their services; (7) their fees; or (8) their publications or research findings.

(c) Psychologists claim degrees as credentials for their health services only if those degrees (1) were earned from a regionally accredited educational institution or (2) were the basis for psychology licensure by the state in which they practice.

5.02 Statements by Others

(a) Psychologists who engage others to create or place public statements that promote their professional practice, products, or activities retain professional responsibility for such statements.

(b) Psychologists do not compensate employees of press, radio, television, or other communication media in return for publicity in a news item. (See also Standard 1.01, Misuse of Psychologists' Work.)

(c) A paid advertisement relating to psychologists' activities must be identified or clearly recognizable as such.

5.03 Descriptions of Workshops and Non-Degree-Granting Educational Programs

To the degree to which they exercise control, psychologists responsible for announcements, catalogs, brochures, or advertisements describing workshops, seminars, or other non-degree-granting educational programs ensure that they accurately describe the audience for which the program is intended, the educational objectives, the presenters, and the fees involved.

5.04 Media Presentations

When psychologists provide public advice or comment via print, Internet, or other electronic transmission, they take precautions to ensure that statements (1) are based on their professional knowledge, training, or experience in accord with appropriate psychological literature and practice; (2) are otherwise consistent with this Ethics Code; and (3) do not indicate that a professional relationship has been established with the recipient. (See also Standard 2.04, Bases for Scientific and Professional Judgments.)

5.05 Testimonials

Psychologists do not solicit testimonials from current therapy clients/patients or other persons who because of their particular circumstances are vulnerable to undue influence.

5.06 In-Person Solicitation

Psychologists do not engage, directly or through agents, in uninvited in-person solicitation of business from actual or potential therapy clients/patients or other persons who because of their particular circumstances are vulnerable to undue influence. However, this prohibition does not preclude (1) attempting to implement appropriate collateral contacts for the purpose of benefiting an already engaged therapy client/patient or (2) providing disaster or community outreach services.

6. Record Keeping and Fees

6.01 Documentation of Professional and Scientific Work and Maintenance of Records

Psychologists create, and to the extent the records are under their control, maintain, disseminate, store, retain, and dispose of records and data relating to their professional and scientific work in order to (1) facilitate provision of services later by them or by other professionals, (2) allow for replication of research design and analyses, (3) meet institutional requirements, (4) ensure accuracy of billing and payments, and (5) ensure compliance with law. (See also Standard 4.01, Maintaining Confidentiality.)

6.02 Maintenance, Dissemination, and Disposal of Confidential Records of Professional and Scientific Work

(a) Psychologists maintain confidentiality in creating, storing, accessing, transferring, and disposing of records under their control, whether these are written, automated, or in any other medium. (See also Standards 4.01, Maintaining Confidentiality, and 6.01, Documentation of Professional and Scientific Work and Maintenance of Records.)

(b) If confidential information concerning recipients of psychological services is entered into databases or systems of records available to persons whose access has not been consented to by the recipient, psychologists use coding or other techniques to avoid the inclusion of personal identifiers.

(c) Psychologists make plans in advance to facilitate the appropriate transfer and to protect the confidentiality of records and data in the event of psychologists' withdrawal from positions or practice. (See also Standards 3.12, Interruption of Psychological Services, and 10.09, Interruption of Therapy.)

6.03 Withholding Records for Nonpayment

Psychologists may not withhold records under their control that are requested and needed for a client's/patient's emergency treatment solely because payment has not been received.

6.04 Fees and Financial Arrangements

(a) As early as is feasible in a professional or scientific relationship, psychologists and recipients of psychological services reach an agreement specifying compensation and billing arrangements.

(b) Psychologists' fee practices are consistent with law.

(c) Psychologists do not misrepresent their fees.

(d) If limitations to services can be anticipated because of limitations in financing, this is discussed with the recipient of services as early as is feasible. (See also Standards 10.09, Interruption of Therapy, and 10.10, Terminating Therapy.)

(e) If the recipient of services does not pay for services as agreed, and if psychologists intend to use collection agencies or legal measures to collect the fees, psychologists first inform the person that such measures will be taken and provide that person an opportunity to make prompt payment. (See also Standards 4.05, Disclosures; 6.03, Withholding Records for Nonpayment; and 10.01, Informed Consent to Therapy.)

6.05 Barter With Clients/Patients

Barter is the acceptance of goods, services, or other nonmonetary remuneration from clients/patients in return for psychological services. Psychologists may barter only if (1) it is not clinically contraindicated, and (2) the resulting arrangement is not exploitative. (See also Standards 3.05, Multiple Relationships, and 6.04, Fees and Financial Arrangements.)

6.06 Accuracy in Reports to Payors and Funding Sources

In their reports to payors for services or sources of research funding, psychologists take reasonable steps to ensure the accurate reporting of the nature of the service provided or research conducted, the fees, charges, or payments, and where applicable, the identity of the provider, the findings, and the diagnosis. (See also Standards 4.01, Maintaining Confidentiality; 4.04, Minimizing Intrusions on Privacy; and 4.05, Disclosures.)

6.07 Referrals and Fees

When psychologists pay, receive payment from, or divide fees with another professional, other than in an employer–employee relationship, the payment to each is based on the services provided (clinical, consultative, administrative, or other) and is not based on the referral itself. (See also Standard 3.09, Cooperation With Other Professionals.)

7.   Education and Training

7.01 Design of Education and Training Programs

Psychologists responsible for education and training programs take reasonable steps to ensure that the programs are designed to provide the appropriate knowledge and proper experiences, and to meet the requirements for licensure, certification, or other goals for which claims are made by the program. (See also Standard 5.03, Descriptions of Workshops and Non-Degree-Granting Educational Programs.)

7.02 Descriptions of Education and Training Programs

Psychologists responsible for education and training programs take reasonable steps to ensure that there is a current and accurate description of the program content (including participation in required course- or program-related counseling, psychotherapy, experiential groups, consulting projects, or community service), training goals and objectives, stipends and benefits, and requirements that must be met for satisfactory completion of the program. This information must be made readily available to all interested parties.

7.03 Accuracy in Teaching

(a) Psychologists take reasonable steps to ensure that course syllabi are accurate regarding the subject matter to be covered, bases for evaluating progress, and the nature of course experiences. This standard does not preclude an instructor from modifying course content or requirements when the instructor considers it pedagogically necessary or desirable, so long as students are made aware of these modifications in a manner that enables them to fulfill course requirements. (See also Standard 5.01, Avoidance of False or Deceptive Statements.)

(b) When engaged in teaching or training, psychologists present psychological information accurately. (See also Standard 2.03, Maintaining Competence.)

7.04 Student Disclosure of Personal Information

Psychologists do not require students or supervisees to disclose personal information in course- or program-related activities, either orally or in writing, regarding sexual history, history of abuse and neglect, psychological treatment, and relationships with parents, peers, and spouses or significant others except if (1) the program or training facility has clearly identified this requirement in its admissions and program materials or (2) the information is necessary to evaluate or obtain assistance for students whose personal problems could reasonably be judged to be preventing them from performing their training- or professionally related activities in a competent manner or posing a threat to the students or others.

7.05 Mandatory Individual or Group Therapy

(a) When individual or group therapy is a program or course requirement, psychologists responsible for that program allow students in undergraduate and graduate programs the option of selecting such therapy from practitioners unaffiliated with the program. (See also Standard 7.02, Descriptions of Education and Training Programs.)

(b) Faculty who are or are likely to be responsible for evaluating students' academic performance do not themselves provide that therapy. (See also Standard 3.05, Multiple Relationships.)

7.06 Assessing Student and Supervisee Performance

(a) In academic and supervisory relationships, psychologists establish a timely and specific process for providing feedback to students and supervisees. Information regarding the process is provided to the student at the beginning of supervision.

(b) Psychologists evaluate students and supervisees on the basis of their actual performance on relevant and established program requirements.

7.07 Sexual Relationships With Students and Supervisees

Psychologists do not engage in sexual relationships with students or supervisees who are in their department, agency, or training center or over whom psychologists have or are likely to have evaluative authority. (See also Standard 3.05, Multiple Relationships.)

8. Research and Publication

8.01 Institutional Approval

When institutional approval is required, psychologists provide accurate information about their research proposals and obtain approval prior to conducting the research. They conduct the research in accordance with the approved research protocol.

8.02 Informed Consent to Research

(a) When obtaining informed consent as required in Standard 3.10, Informed Consent, psychologists inform participants about (1) the purpose of the research, expected duration, and procedures; (2) their right to decline to participate and to withdraw from the research once participation has begun; (3) the foreseeable consequences of declining or withdrawing; (4) reasonably foreseeable factors that may be expected to influence their willingness to participate such as potential risks, discomfort, or adverse effects;

(5) any prospective research benefits; (6) limits of confidentiality; (7) incentives for participation; and (8) whom to contact for questions about the research and research participants' rights. They provide opportunity for the prospective participants to ask questions and receive answers. (See also Standards 8.03, Informed Consent for Recording Voices and Images in Research; 8.05, Dispensing With Informed Consent for Research; and 8.07, Deception in Research.)

(b) Psychologists conducting intervention research involving the use of experimental treatments clarify to participants at the outset of the research (1) the experimental nature of the treatment; (2) the services that will or will not be available to the control group(s) if appropriate; (3) the means by which assignment to treatment and control groups will be made; (4) available treatment alternatives if an individual does not wish to participate in the research or wishes to withdraw once a study has begun; and (5) compensation for or monetary costs of participating including, if appropriate, whether reimbursement from the participant or a third-party payor will be sought. (See also Standard 8.02a, Informed Consent to Research.)

8.03 Informed Consent for Recording Voices and Images in Research

Psychologists obtain informed consent from research participants prior to recording their voices or images for data collection unless (1) the research consists solely of naturalistic observations in public places, and it is not anticipated that the recording will be used in a manner that could cause personal identification or harm, or (2) the research design includes deception, and consent for the use of the recording is obtained during debriefing. (See also Standard 8.07, Deception in Research.)

8.04 Client/Patient, Student, and Subordinate Research Participants

(a) When psychologists conduct research with clients/patients, students, or subordinates as participants, psychologists take steps to protect the prospective participants from adverse consequences of declining or withdrawing from participation.

(b) When research participation is a course requirement or an opportunity for extra credit, the prospective participant is given the choice of equitable alternative activities.

8.05 Dispensing With Informed Consent for Research

Psychologists may dispense with informed consent only (1) where research would not reasonably be assumed to create distress or harm and involves (a) the study of normal educational practices, curricula, or classroom management methods conducted in educational settings; (b) only anonymous questionnaires, naturalistic observations, or archival research for which disclosure of responses would not place participants at risk of criminal or civil liability or damage their financial standing, employability, or reputation, and confidentiality is protected; or (c) the study of factors related to job or organization effectiveness conducted in organizational settings for which there is no risk to participants' employability, and confidentiality is protected or (2) where otherwise permitted by law or federal or institutional regulations.

8.06 Offering Inducements for Research Participation

(a) Psychologists make reasonable efforts to avoid offering excessive or inappropriate financial or other inducements for research participation when such inducements are likely to coerce participation.

(b) When offering professional services as an inducement for research participation, psychologists clarify the nature of the services, as well as the risks, obligations, and limitations. (See also Standard 6.05, Barter With Clients/Patients.)

8.07 Deception in Research

(a) Psychologists do not conduct a study involving deception unless they have determined that the use of deceptive techniques is justified by the study's significant prospective scientific, educational, or applied value and that effective nondeceptive alternative procedures are not feasible.

(b) Psychologists do not deceive prospective participants about research that is reasonably expected to cause physical pain or severe emotional distress.

(c) Psychologists explain any deception that is an integral feature of the design and conduct of an experiment to participants as early as is feasible, preferably at the conclusion of their participation, but no later than at the conclusion of the data collection, and permit participants to withdraw their data. (See also Standard 8.08, Debriefing.)

8.08 Debriefing

(a) Psychologists provide a prompt opportunity for participants to obtain appropriate information about the nature, results, and conclusions of the research, and they take reasonable steps to correct any misconceptions that participants may have of which the psychologists are aware.

(b) If scientific or humane values justify delaying or withholding this information, psychologists take reasonable measures to reduce the risk of harm.

(c) When psychologists become aware that research procedures have harmed a participant, they take reasonable steps to minimize the harm.

8.09 Humane Care and Use of Animals in Research

(a) Psychologists acquire, care for, use, and dispose of animals in compliance with current federal, state, and local laws and regulations, and with professional standards.

(b) Psychologists trained in research methods and experienced in the care of laboratory animals supervise all procedures involving animals and are responsible for ensuring appropriate consideration of their comfort, health, and humane treatment.

(c) Psychologists ensure that all individuals under their supervision who are using animals have received instruction in research methods and in the care, maintenance, and handling of the species being used, to the extent appropriate to their role. (See also Standard 2.05, Delegation of Work to Others.)

(d) Psychologists make reasonable efforts to minimize the discomfort, infection, illness, and pain of animal subjects.

(e) Psychologists use a procedure subjecting animals to pain, stress, or privation only when an alternative procedure is unavailable and the goal is justified by its prospective scientific, educational, or applied value.

(f) Psychologists perform surgical procedures under appropriate anesthesia and follow techniques to avoid infection and minimize pain during and after surgery.

(g) When it is appropriate that an animal's life be terminated, psychologists proceed rapidly, with an effort to minimize pain and in accordance with accepted procedures.

8.10 Reporting Research Results

(a) Psychologists do not fabricate data. (See also Standard 5.01a, Avoidance of False or Deceptive Statements.)

(b) If psychologists discover significant errors in their published data, they take reasonable steps to correct such errors in a correction, retraction, erratum, or other appropriate publication means.

8.11 Plagiarism

Psychologists do not present portions of another's work or data as their own, even if the other work or data source is cited occasionally.

8.12 Publication Credit

(a) Psychologists take responsibility and credit, including authorship credit, only for work they have actually performed or to which they have substantially contributed. (See also Standard 8.12b, Publication Credit.)

(b) Principal authorship and other publication credits accurately reflect the relative scientific or professional contributions of the individuals involved, regardless of their relative status. Mere possession of an institutional position, such as department chair, does not justify authorship credit. Minor contributions to the research or to the writing for publications are acknowledged appropriately, such as in footnotes or in an introductory statement.

(c) Except under exceptional circumstances, a student is listed as principal author on any multiple-authored article that is substantially based on the student's doctoral dissertation. Faculty advisors discuss publication credit with students as early as feasible and throughout the research and publication process as appropriate. (See also Standard 8.12b, Publication Credit.)

8.13 Duplicate Publication of Data

Psychologists do not publish, as original data, data that have been previously published. This does not preclude republishing data when they are accompanied by proper acknowledgment.

8.14 Sharing Research Data for Verification

(a) After research results are published, psychologists do not withhold the data on which their conclusions are based from other competent professionals who seek to verify the substantive claims through reanalysis and who intend to use such data only for that purpose, provided that the confidentiality of the participants can be protected and unless legal rights concerning proprietary data preclude their release. This does not preclude psychologists from requiring that such individuals or groups be responsible for costs associated with the provision of such information.

(b) Psychologists who request data from other psychologists to verify the substantive claims through reanalysis may use shared data only for the declared purpose. Requesting psychologists obtain prior written agreement for all other uses of the data.

8.15 Reviewers

Psychologists who review material submitted for presentation, publication, grant, or research proposal review respect the confidentiality of and the proprietary rights in such information of those who submitted it.

9.   Assessment

9.01 Bases for Assessments

(a) Psychologists base the opinions contained in their recommendations, reports, and diagnostic or evaluative statements, including forensic testimony, on information and techniques sufficient to substantiate their findings. (See also Standard 2.04, Bases for Scientific and Professional Judgments.)

(b) Except as noted in 9.01c, psychologists provide opinions of the psychological characteristics of individuals only after they have conducted an examination of the individuals adequate to support their statements or conclusions. When, despite reasonable efforts, such an examination is not practical, psychologists document the efforts they made and the result of those efforts, clarify the probable impact of their limited information on the reliability and validity of their opinions, and appropriately limit the nature and extent of their conclusions or recommendations. (See also Standards 2.01, Boundaries of Competence, and 9.06, Interpreting Assessment Results.)

(c) When psychologists conduct a record review or provide consultation or supervision and an individual examination is not warranted or necessary for the opinion, psychologists explain this and the sources of information on which they based their conclusions and recommendations.

9.02 Use of Assessments

(a) Psychologists administer, adapt, score, interpret, or use assessment techniques, interviews, tests, or instruments in a manner and for purposes that are appropriate in light of the research on or evidence of the usefulness and proper application of the techniques.

(b) Psychologists use assessment instruments whose validity and reliability have been established for use with members of the population tested. When such validity or reliability has not been established, psychologists describe the strengths and limitations of test results and interpretation.

(c) Psychologists use assessment methods that are appropriate to an individual's language preference and competence, unless the use of an alternative language is relevant to the assessment issues.

9.03 Informed Consent in Assessments

(a) Psychologists obtain informed consent for assessments, evaluations, or diagnostic services, as described in Standard 3.10, Informed Consent, except when (1) testing is mandated by law or governmental regulations; (2) informed consent is implied because testing is conducted as a routine educational, institutional, or organizational activity (e.g., when participants voluntarily agree to assessment when applying for a job); or (3) one purpose of the testing is to evaluate decisional capacity. Informed consent includes an explanation of the nature and purpose of the assessment, fees, involvement of third parties, and limits of confidentiality and sufficient opportunity for the client/patient to ask questions and receive answers.

(b) Psychologists inform persons with questionable capacity to consent or for whom testing is mandated by law or governmental regulations about the nature and purpose of the proposed assessment services, using language that is reasonably understandable to the person being assessed.

(c) Psychologists using the services of an interpreter obtain informed consent from the client/patient to use that interpreter, ensure that confidentiality of test results and test security are maintained, and include in their recommendations, reports, and diagnostic or evaluative statements, including forensic testimony, discussion of any limitations on the data obtained. (See also Standards 2.05, Delegation of Work to Others; 4.01, Maintaining Confidentiality; 9.01, Bases for Assessments; 9.06, Interpreting Assessment Results; and 9.07, Assessment by Unqualified Persons.)

9.04 Release of Test Data

(a) The term *test data* refers to raw and scaled scores, client/patient responses to test questions or stimuli, and psychologists' notes and recordings concerning client/patient statements and behavior during an examination. Those portions of test materials that include client/patient responses are included in the definition of *test data*. Pursuant to a client/patient release, psychologists provide test data to the client/patient or other persons identified in the release. Psychologists may refrain from releasing test data to protect a client/patient or others from substantial harm or misuse or misrepresentation of the data or the test, recognizing that in many instances release of confidential information under these circumstances is regulated by law. (See also Standard 9.11, Maintaining Test Security.)

(b) In the absence of a client/patient release, psychologists provide test data only as required by law or court order.

9.05 Test Construction

Psychologists who develop tests and other assessment techniques use appropriate psychometric procedures and current scientific or professional knowledge for test design, standardization, validation, reduction or elimination of bias, and recommendations for use.

9.06 Interpreting Assessment Results

When interpreting assessment results, including automated interpretations, psychologists take into account the purpose of the assessment as well as the various test factors, test-taking abilities, and other characteristics of the person being assessed, such as situational, personal, linguistic, and cultural differences, that might affect psychologists' judgments or reduce the accuracy of their interpretations. They indicate any significant limitations of their interpretations. (See also Standards 2.01b and c, Boundaries of Competence, and 3.01, Unfair Discrimination.)

9.07 Assessment by Unqualified Persons

Psychologists do not promote the use of psychological assessment techniques by unqualified persons, except when such use is conducted for training purposes with appropriate supervision. (See also Standard 2.05, Delegation of Work to Others.)

9.08 Obsolete Tests and Outdated Test Results

(a) Psychologists do not base their assessment or intervention decisions or recommendations on data or test results that are outdated for the current purpose.

(b) Psychologists do not base such decisions or recommendations on tests and measures that are obsolete and not useful for the current purpose.

9.09 Test Scoring and Interpretation Services

(a) Psychologists who offer assessment or scoring services to other professionals accurately describe the purpose, norms, validity, reliability, and applications of the procedures and any special qualifications applicable to their use.

(b) Psychologists select scoring and interpretation services (including automated services) on the basis of evidence of the validity of the program and procedures as well as on other appropriate considerations. (See also Standard 2.01b and c, Boundaries of Competence.)

(c) Psychologists retain responsibility for the appropriate application, interpretation, and use of assessment instruments, whether they score and interpret such tests themselves or use automated or other services.

9.10 Explaining Assessment Results

Regardless of whether the scoring and interpretation are done by psychologists, by employees or assistants, or by automated or other outside services, psychologists take reasonable steps to ensure that explanations of results are given to the individual or designated representative unless the nature of the relationship precludes provision of an explanation of results (such as in some organizational consulting, preemployment or security screenings, and forensic evaluations), and this fact has been clearly explained to the person being assessed in advance.

9.11 Maintaining Test Security

The term *test materials* refers to manuals, instruments, protocols, and test questions or stimuli and does not include *test data* as defined in Standard 9.04, Release of Test Data. Psychologists make reasonable efforts to maintain the integrity and security of test materials and other assessment techniques consistent with law and contractual obligations, and in a manner that permits adherence to this Ethics Code.

10.   Therapy

10.01 Informed Consent to Therapy

(a) When obtaining informed consent to therapy as required in Standard 3.10, Informed Consent, psychologists inform clients/patients as early as is feasible in the therapeutic relationship about the nature and anticipated course of therapy, fees, involvement of third parties, and limits of confidentiality and provide sufficient opportunity for the client/patient to ask questions and receive answers. (See also Standards 4.02, Discussing the Limits of Confidentiality, and 6.04, Fees and Financial Arrangements.)

(b) When obtaining informed consent for treatment for which generally recognized techniques and procedures have not been established, psychologists inform their clients/patients of the developing nature of the treatment, the potential risks involved, alternative treatments that may be available, and the voluntary nature of their participation. (See also Standards 2.01e, Boundaries of Competence, and 3.10, Informed Consent.)

(c) When the therapist is a trainee and the legal responsibility for the treatment provided resides with the supervisor, the client/patient, as part of the informed consent procedure, is informed that the therapist is in training and is being supervised and is given the name of the supervisor.

10.02 Therapy Involving Couples or Families

(a) When psychologists agree to provide services to several persons who have a relationship (such as spouses, significant others, or parents and children), they take reasonable steps to clarify at the outset (1) which of the individuals are clients/patients and (2) the relationship the psychologist will have with each person. This clarification includes the psychologist's role and the probable uses of the services provided or the information obtained. (See also Standard 4.02, Discussing the Limits of Confidentiality.)

(b) If it becomes apparent that psychologists may be called on to perform potentially conflicting roles (such as family therapist and then witness for one party in divorce proceedings), psychologists take reasonable steps to clarify and modify, or withdraw from, roles appropriately. (See also Standard 3.05c, Multiple Relationships.)

10.03 Group Therapy

When psychologists provide services to several persons in a group setting, they describe at the outset the roles and responsibilities of all parties and the limits of confidentiality.

10.04 Providing Therapy to Those Served by Others

In deciding whether to offer or provide services to those already receiving mental health services elsewhere, psychologists carefully consider the treatment issues and the potential client's/patient's welfare. Psychologists discuss these issues with the client/patient or another legally authorized person on behalf of the client/patient in order to minimize the risk of confusion and conflict, consult with the other service providers when appropriate, and proceed with caution and sensitivity to the therapeutic issues.

10.05 Sexual Intimacies With Current Therapy Clients/Patients

Psychologists do not engage in sexual intimacies with current therapy clients/patients.

10.06 Sexual Intimacies With Relatives or Significant Others of Current Therapy Clients/Patients

Psychologists do not engage in sexual intimacies with individuals they know to be close relatives, guardians, or significant others of current clients/patients. Psychologists do not terminate therapy to circumvent this standard.

10.07 Therapy With Former Sexual Partners

Psychologists do not accept as therapy clients/patients persons with whom they have engaged in sexual intimacies.

10.08 Sexual Intimacies With Former Therapy Clients/Patients

(a) Psychologists do not engage in sexual intimacies with former clients/patients for at least two years after cessation or termination of therapy.

(b) Psychologists do not engage in sexual intimacies with former clients/patients even after a two-year interval except in the most unusual circumstances. Psychologists who engage in such activity after the two years following cessation or termination of therapy and of having no sexual contact with the former client/patient bear the burden of demonstrating that there has been no exploitation, in light of all relevant factors, including (1) the amount of time that has passed since therapy terminated; (2) the nature, duration, and intensity of the therapy; (3) the circumstances of termination; (4) the client's/patient's personal history; (5) the client's/patient's current mental status; (6) the likelihood of adverse impact on the client/patient; and (7) any statements or actions made by the therapist during the course of therapy suggesting or inviting the possibility of a posttermination sexual or romantic relationship with the client/patient. (See also Standard 3.05, Multiple Relationships.)

10.09 Interruption of Therapy

When entering into employment or contractual relationships, psychologists make reasonable efforts to provide for orderly and appropriate resolution of responsibility for client/patient care in the event that the employment or contractual relationship ends, with paramount consideration given to the welfare of the client/patient. (See also Standard 3.12, Interruption of Psychological Services.)

10.10 Terminating Therapy

(a) Psychologists terminate therapy when it becomes reasonably clear that the client/patient no longer needs the service, is not likely to benefit, or is being harmed by continued service.

(b) Psychologists may terminate therapy when threatened or otherwise endangered by the client/patient or another person with whom the client/patient has a relationship.

(c) Except where precluded by the actions of clients/patients or third-party payors, prior to termination psychologists provide pretermination counseling and suggest alternative service providers as appropriate.

APPENDIX C

SPECIALTY GUIDELINES FOR FORENSIC PSYCHOLOGISTS[1]

Committee on Ethical Guidelines for Forensic Psychologists[2]

The Specialty Guidelines for Forensic Psychologists, while informed by the *Ethical Principles of Psychologists* (APA, 1990) and meant to be consistent with them, are designed to provide more specific guidance to forensic psychologists in monitoring their professional conduct when acting in assistance to courts, parties to legal proceedings, correctional and forensic mental health facilities, and legislative agencies. The primary goal of the Guidelines is to improve the quality of forensic psychological services offered to individual clients and the legal system and thereby to enhance forensic psychology as a discipline and profession. The *Specialty Guidelines for Forensic Psychologists* represent a joint statement of the American Psychology-Law Society and Division 41 of the American Psycholog-

[1] The *Specialty Guidelines for Forensic Psychologists were* adopted by majority vote of the members of Division *41* and the American Psychology-Law Society. They have also been endorsed by majority vote by the American Academy of Forensic Psychology. The Executive Committee of Division *41* and the American Psychology Law Society formally approved these *Guidelines on March 9, 1991.* The Executive Committee also voted to continue the Committee on Ethical Guidelines in order to disseminate the *Guidelines* and to monitor their implementation and suggestions for revision. Individuats wishing to reprint these *Guidelines* or who have queries about them should contact either Stephen L. Golding, Ph.D., Department of Psychology, University of Utah, Salt Lake City, UT *84*112,*80* l-58 1-8028 (voice) or 80 1-581-5841 (FAX) or other members of the Committee listed below. Reprint requests should be sent to Cathy Oslzly, Department of Psychology, University of Nebraska-Lincoln, Lincoln, NE 68588-0308.

[2] These Guidelines were prepared and principally authored by a joint Committee on Ethical Guidelines of Division *41* and the American Academy of Forensic-Psychology (Stephen L. Golding, [Chair], Thomas Grisso, David Shapiro, and Herbert Weissman [Co-chairs]). Other members of the Committee included Robert Fein, Kirk Heiibrun, Judith McKenna, Norman Poythress, and Daniel Schuman. Their hard work and willingness to tackle difficult conceptual and pragmatic issues is gratefully acknowledged. The Committee would also like to acknowledge specifically the assistance and guidance provided by Dort Bigg, Larry Cowan, Eric Harris, Arthur Lemer, Michael Miller, Russell Newman, Melvin Rudov, and Ray Fowler. Many other individuals also contributed by their thoughtful critique and suggestions for improvement of earlier drafts which were widely circulated.

Reprinted with permission from American Psychology—Law Society, *Specialty Guidelines for Forensic Psychologists,* Law & Human Behavior (1991).

ical Association and are endorsed by the American Academy of Forensic Psychology. The *Guidelines* do not represent an official statement of the American Psychological Association.

The Guidelines provide an aspirational model of desirable professional practice by psychologists, within any subdiscipline of psychology (e.g., clinical, developmental, social, experimental), when they are engaged regularly as experts and represent themselves as such, in an activity primarily intended to provide professional psychological expertise to the judicial system. This would include, for example, clinical forensic examiners; psychologists employed by correctional or forensic mental health systems; researchers who offer direct testimony about the relevance of scientific data to a psycholegal issue; trial behavior consultants; psychologists engaged in preparation of *amicus* briefs; or psychologists, appearing as forensic experts, who consult with, or testify before, judicial, legislative, or administrative agencies acting in an adjudicative capacity. Individuals who provide only occasional service to the legal system and who do so without representing themselves as *forensic experts* may find these *Guidelines* helpful, particularly in conjunction with consultation with colleagues who are forensic experts.

While the *Guidelines* are concerned with a model of desirable professional practice, to the extent that they may be construed as being applicable to the advertisement of services or the solicitation of clients, they are intended to prevent false or deceptive advertisement or solicitation, and should be construed in a manner consistent with that intent.

I.   PURPOSE AND SCOPE

A. Purpose

1. While the professional standards for the ethical practice of psychology, as a general discipline, are addressed in the American Psychological Association's *Ethical Principles of Psychologists,* these ethical principles do not relate, in sufficient detail, to current aspirations of desirable professional conduct for forensic psychologists. By design, none of the *Guidelines* contradicts any of the *Ethical Principles* of *Psychologists;* rather, they amplify those *Principles* in the context of the practice of forensic psychology, as herein defined.

2. The *Guidelines* have been designed to be national in scope and are intended to conform with state and Federal law. In situations where the forensic psychologist believes that the requirements of law are in conflict with the *Guidelines,* attempts to resolve the conflict should be made in accordance with the procedures set forth in these *Guidelines* [IV(G)] and in the *Ethical Principles of Psychologists.*

B. Scope

1. The *Guidelines* specify the nature of desirable professional practice by forensic psychologists, within any subdiscipline of psychology

(**e.g.**, clinical, developmental, social, experimental), **when engaged regularly** as forensic psychologists.

  a. "Psychologist" means any individual whose professional activities are defined by the American Psychological Association or by regulation of title by state registration or licensure, as the practice of psychology.

  b. "Forensic psychology" means all forms of professional psychological conduct when acting, with definable foreknowledge, as a psychological expert on explicitly psycholegal **issues, in direct** assistance to courts, parties to legal proceedings, correctional and forensic mental health facilities, and administrative, judicial, and legislative agencies acting in an adjudicative capacity.

  c. "Forensic psychologist" means psychologists who regularly engage in the practice of forensic psychology as defined in I(B)(l)(b).

2. The *Guidelines* do not apply to a psychologist who is asked to provide professional psychological services when the psychologist was not informed at the time of delivery of the services that they were to be used as forensic psychological services as defined above. The *Guidelines* may be helpful, however, in preparing the psychologist for the experience of communicating psychological data in a forensic context.

3. Psychologists who are not forensic psychologists as defined in I(B)(l)(c), but occasionally provide limited forensic psychological services, may find the Guidelines useful in the preparation and presentation of their professional services.

C. Related Standards

1. Forensic psychologists also conduct, their professional activites in accord with the *Ethical Principles of Psychologists* and the various other statements of the American Psychological Association that may apply to particular subdisciplines or areas of practice that are relevant to their professional activities.

2. The standards of practice and ethical guidelines of other relevant "expert professional organizations" contain useful guidance and should be consulted even though the present *Guidelines* take precedence for forensic psychologists.

II. RESPONSIBILITY

A. Forensic psychologists have an obligation to provide services in a manner consistent with the highest standards of their profession. They are responsible for their own conduct and the conduct of those individuals under their direct supervision.

B. Forensic psychologists make a reasonable effort to ensure that their services and the products of their services are used in a forthright and responsible manner.

III. COMPETENCE

A. Forensic psychologists provide services only in areas of psychology in which they have specialized knowledge, skill, experience, and education.

B. Forensic psychologists have an obligation to present to the court, regarding the specific matters to which they will testify, the boundaries of their competence, the factual bases (knowledge, skill, experience, training, and education) for their qualification as an expert, and the relevance of those factual bases to their qualification as an expert on the specific matters at issue.

C. Forensic psychologists are responsible for a fundamental and reasonable level of knowledge and understanding of the legal and professional standards that govern their participation as experts in legal proceedings.

D. Forensic psychologists have an obligation to understand the civil rights of parties in legal proceedings in which they participate, and manage their professional conduct in a manner that does not diminish or threaten those rights.

E. Forensic psychologists recognize that their own personal values, moral beliefs, or personal and professional relationships with parties to a legal proceeding may interfere with their ability to practice competently. Under such circumstances, forensic psychologists are obligated to decline participation or to limit their assistance in a manner consistent with professional obligations.

IV. RELATIONSHIPS

A. During initial consultation with the legal representative of the party seeking services, forensic psychologists have an obligation to inform the party of factors that might reasonably affect the decision to contract with the forensic psychologist. These factors include, but are not limited to

1. the fee structure for anticipated professional services;
2. prior and current personal or professional activities, obligations, and relationships that might produce a conflict of interests;
3. their areas of competence and the limits of their competence; and
4. the known scientific bases and limitations of the methods and procedures that they employ and their qualifications to employ such methods and procedures.

B. Forensic psychologists do not provide professional services to parties to a legal proceeding on the basis of "contingent fees," when those services involve the offering of expert testimony to a court or administrative body, or when they call upon the psychologist to make affirmations or representations intended to be relied upon by third parties.

C. Forensic psychologists who derive a substantial portion of their income from fee-for-service arrangements should offer some portion of their professional services on a pro bono or reduced fee basis where the public interest or the welfare of clients may be inhibited by insufficient financial resources.

D. Forensic psychologists recognize potential conflicts of interest in dual relationships with parties to a legal proceeding, and they seek to minimize their effects.

   1. Forensic psychologists avoid providing professional services to parties in a legal proceeding with whom they have personal or professional relationships that are inconsistent with the anticipated relationship.

   2. When it is necessary to provide both evaluation and treatment services to a party in a legal proceeding (as may be the case in small forensic hospital settings or small communities), the forensic psychologist takes reasonable steps to minimize the potential negative effects of these circumstances on the rights of the party, confidentiality, and the process of treatment and evaluation.

E. Forensic psychologists have an obligation to ensure that prospective clients are informed of their legal rights with respect to the anticipated forensic service, of the purposes of any evaluation, of the nature of procedures to be employed, of the intended uses of any product of their services, and of the party who has employed the forensic psychologist.

   1. Unless court ordered, forensic psychologists obtain the informed consent of the client or party, or their legal representative, before proceeding with such evaluations and procedures. If the client appears unwilling to proceed after receiving a thorough notification of the purposes, methods, and intended uses of the forensic evaluation, the evaluation should be postponed and the psychologist should take steps to place the client in contact with his/her attorney for the purpose of legal advice on the issue of participation.

   2. In situations where   the client or party may not have the capacity to provide informed consent to services or the evaluation is pursuant to court order, the forensic psychologist provides reasonable notice to the client's legal representative of the nature of the anticipated forensic service before proceeding. If the client's legal representative objects to the evaluation, the forensic psychologist notifies the court issuing the order and responds as directed.

   3. After a psychologist has advised the subject of a clinical forensic evaluation of the intended uses of the evaluation and its work product, the psychologist may not use the evaluation work product for

other purposes without explicit waiver to do so by the client or the client's legal representative.

F. When forensic psychologists engage in research or scholarly activities that are compensated financially by a client or party to a legal proceeding, or when the psychologist provides those services on a pro *bono* basis, the psychologist clarifies any anticipated further use of such research or scholarly product, discloses the psychologist's role in the resulting research or scholarly products, and obtains whatever consent or agreement is required by law or professional standards.

G. When conflicts arise between the forensic psychologist's professional standards and the requirements of legal standards, a particular court, or a directive by an officer of the court or legal authorities, the forensic psychologist has an obligation to make those legal authorities aware of the source of the conflict and to take reasonable steps to resolve it. Such steps may include, but are not limited to, obtaining the consultation of fellow forensic professionals, obtaining the advice of independent counsel, and conferring directly with the legal representatives involved.

V. CONFIDENTIALITY AND PRIVILEGE

A. Forensic psychologists have an obligation to be aware of the legal standards that may affect or limit the confidentiality or privilege that may attach to their services or their products, and they conduct their professional activities in a manner that respects those known rights and privileges.

1. Forensic psychologists establish and maintain a system of record keeping and professional communication that safeguards a client's privilege.

2. Forensic psychologists maintain active control over records and information. They only release information pursuant to statutory requirements, court order, or the consent of the client.

B. Forensic psychologists inform their clients of the limitations to the confidentiality of their services and their products (see also Guideline IV E) by providing them with an understandable statement of their rights, privileges, and the limitations of confidentiality,

C In situations where the right of the client or party to cofidentiality is limited, the forensic psychologist makes every effort to maintain confidentiality with regard to any information that does not bear directly upon the legal purpose of the evaluation.

D Forensic psychologists provide clients or their authorized legal representatives with access to the information in their records and a meaningful explanation of that information, consistent with existing Federal and state statutes, the *Ethical Principles of Psychologists,* the *Standards for Educational and Psychological Testing,* and institutional rules and regulations.

VI. METHODS AND PROCEDURES

A. Because of their special status as persons qualified as experts to the court, forensic psychologists have an obligation to maintain current knowledge of scientific, professional and legal developments within their area of claimed competence. They are obligated also to use that knowledge, consistent with accepted clinical and scientific standards, in selecting data collection methods and procedures for an evaluation, treatment, consultation or scholarly/empirical investigation.

B Forensic psychologists have an obligation to document and be prepared to make available, subject to court order or the rules of evidence, all data that form the basis for their evidence or services. The standard to be applied to such documentation or recording *anticipates* that the detail and quality of such documentation will be subject to reasonable judicial scrutiny; this standard is higher than the normative standard for general clinical practice. When forensic psychologists conduct an examination or engage in the treatment of a party to a legal proceeding, with fore-knowledge that their professional services will be used in an adjudicative forum, they incur a special responsibility to provide the best documentation possible under the circumstances.

   1. Documentation of the data upon which one's evidence is based is subject to the normal rules of discovery, disclosure, confidentiality, and privilege that operate in the jurisdiction in which the data were obtained. Forensic psychologists have an obligation to be aware of those rules and to regulate their conduct in accordance with them.

   2. The duties and obligations of forensic psychologists with respect to documentation of data that form the basis for their evidence apply from the moment they know or have a reasonable basis for knowing that their data and evidence derived from it are likely to enter into legally relevant decisions.

C. In providing forensic psychological services, forensic psychologists take special care to avoid undue influence upon their methods, procedures, and products, such as might emanate from the party to a legal proceeding by financial compensation or other gains. As an expert conducting an evaluation, treatment, consultation, or scholarly/empirical investigation, the forensic psychologist maintains professional integrity by examining the issue at hand from all reasonable perspectives, actively seeking information that will differentially test plausible rival hypotheses.

D Forensic psychologists do not provide professional forensic services to a defendant or to any party in, or in contemplation of, a legal proceeding prior to that individual's representation by counsel, except for persons judicially determined, where appropriate, to be handling their representation *pro se*. When the forensic services are pursuant to court order and the client is not represented by counsel, the forensic psychologist makes reasonable efforts to inform the court prior to providing the services.

   1. A forensic psychologist may provide emergency mental health ser-

vices to a pretrial defendant prior to court order or the appointment of counsel where there are reasonable grounds to believe that such emergency services are needed for the protection and improvement of the defendant's mental health and where failure to provide such mental health services would constitute a substantial risk of imminent harm to the defendant or to others. In providing such services the forensic psychologist nevertheless seeks to inform the defendant's counsel in a manner consistent with the requirements of the emergency situation.

2. Forensic psychologists who provide such emergency mental health services should attempt to avoid providing further professional forensic services to that defendant unless that relationship is reasonably unavoidable [see IV(D)(2)].

E. When forensic psychologists seek data from third parties, prior records, or other sources, they do so only with the prior approval of the relevant legal party or as a consequence of an order of a court to conduct the forensic evaluation.

F. Forensic psychologists are aware that hearsay exceptions and other rules governing expert testimony place a special ethical burden upon them. When hearsay or otherwise inadmissible evidence forms the basis of their opinion, evidence, or professional product, they seek to minimize sole reliance upon such evidence. Where circumstances reasonably permit, forensic psychologists seek to obtain independent and personal verification of data relied upon as part of their professional services to the court or to a party to a legal proceeding.

1. While many forms of data used by forensic psychologists are hearsay, forensic psychologists attempt to corroborate critical data that form the basis for their professional product. When using hearsay data that have not been corroborated, but are nevertheless utilized, forensic psychologists have an affirmative responsibility to acknowledge the uncorroborated status of those data and the reasons for relying upon such data.

2. With respect to evidence of any type, forensic psychologists avoid offering information from their investigations or evaluations that does not bear directly upon the legal purpose of their professional services and that is not critical as support for their product, evidence or testimony, except where such disclosure is required by law.

3. When a forensic psychologist relies upon data or information gathered by others, the origins of those data are clarified in any professional product. In addition, the forensic psychologist bears a special responsibility to ensure that such data, if relied upon, were gathered in a manner standard for the profession.

G. Unless otherwise stipulated by the parties, forensic psychologists are aware that no statements made by a defendant, in the course of any (forensic) examination, no testimony by the expert based upon such statements, nor any other fruits of the statements can be admitted into evidence against the defendant in any criminal proceeding, except on an issue respecting mental condition on which the defendant has introduced testimony. Forensic psychologists have an affirmative duty to ensure that their written products and oral testimony conform to this Federal Rule of Procedure (12.2[c]), or its state equivalent.

1. Because forensic psychologists are often not in a position to know what evidence, documentation, or element of a written product may be or may lend to a "fruit of the statement," they exercise extreme caution in preparing reports or offering testimony prior to the defendant's assertion of a mental state claim or the defendant's introduction of testimony regarding a mental condition. Consistent with the reporting requirements of state or federal law, forensic psychologists avoid including statements from the defendant relating to the time period of the alleged offense,

2. Once a defendant has proceeded to the trial stage, and all pretrial mental health issues such as competency have been resolved, forensic psychologists may include in their reports or testimony any statements made by the defendant that are directly relevant to supporting their expert evidence, providing that the defendant has "introduced" mental state evidence or testimony within the meaning of Federal Rule of Procedure 12.2(c), or its state equivalent.

H Forensic psychologists avoid giving written or oral evidence about the psychological characteristics of particular individuals when they have not had an opportunity to conduct an examination of the individual adequate to the scope of the statements, opinions, or conclusions to be issued. Forensic psychologists make every reasonable effort to conduct such examinations. When it is not possible or feasible to do so, they make clear the impact of such limitations on the reliability and validity of their professional products, evidence, or testimony.

VII. PUBLIC AND PROFESSIONAL COMMUNICATIONS

A, Forensic psychologists make reasonable efforts to ensure that the products of their services, as well as their own public statements and professional testimony, are communicated in ways that will promote understanding and avoid deception, given the particular characteristics, roles, and abilities of various recipients of the communications.

1. Forensic psychologists take reasonable steps to correct misuse or misrepresentation of their professional products, evidence, and testimony .

2. Forensic psychologists provide information about professional work to clients in a manner consistent with professional and legal standards

fur the disclosure of test results, interpretations of data, and the factual bases for conclusions. A full explanation of the results of tests and the bases for conclusions should be given in language that the client can understand.

    a. When disclosing information about a client to third parties who are not qualified to interpret test results and data, the forensic psychologist complies with Principle 16 of the ***Standards for Educational and Psychological Testing.*** When required to disclose results to a nonpsychologist, every attempt is made to ensure that test security is maintained and access to information is restricted to individuals with a legitimate and professional interest in the data. Other qualified mental health professionals who make a request for information pursuant to a lawful order are, by definition, "individuals with a legitimate and professional interest."

    b. In providing records and raw data, the forensic psychologist takes reasonable steps to ensure that the receiving party is informed that raw scores must be interpreted by a qualified professional in order to provide reliable and valid information.

B. Forensic psychologists realize that their public role as "expert to the court" or as "expert representing the profession" confers upon them a special responsibility for fairness and accuracy in their public statements. When evaluating or commenting upon the professional work product or qualifications of another expert or party to a legal proceeding, forensic psychologists represent their professional disagreements with reference to a fair and accurate evaluation of the data, theories, standards, and opinions of the other expert or party.

C. Ordinarily, forensic psychologists avoid making detailed public (out-of-court) statements about particular legal proceedings in which they have been involved. When there is a strong justification to do so, such public statements are designed to assure accurate representation of their role or their evidence, not to advocate the positions of parties in the legal proceeding. Forensic psychologists address particular legal proceedings in publications or communications only to the extent that the information relied upon is part of a public record, or consent for that use has been properly obtained from the party holding any privilege.

D. When testifying, forensic psychologists have an obligation to all parties to a legal proceeding to present their findings, conclusions, evidence, or other professional products in a fair manner. This principle does not preclude forceful representation of the data and reasoning upon which a conclusion or professional product is based. It does, however, preclude an attempt, whether active or passive, to engage in partisan distortion or misrepresentation. Forensic psychologists do not, by either commission or omission, participate in a misrepresentation of their evidence, nor do they participate in partisan attempts to avoid, deny, or subvert the presentation of evidence contrary to their own position.

E. Forensic psychologists, by virtue of their competence and rules of discovery, actively disclose all sources of information obtained in the course of their professional services; they actively disclose which information from which source was used in formulating a particular written product or oral testimony.

F. Forensic psychologists are aware that their essential role as expert to the court is to assist the trier of fact to understand the evidence or to determine a fact in issue. In offering expert evidence, they are aware that their own professional observations, inferences, and conclusions must be distinguished from legal facts, opinions, and conclusions. Forensic psychologists are prepared to explain the relationship between their expert testimony and the legal issues and facts of an instant case.

GENERAL GUIDELINES FOR PROVIDERS OF PSYCHOLOGICAL SERVICES

General Guidelines for Providers of Psychological Services, 42(7) American Psychologist (July 1987). © 1987 the American Psychological Association. Reprinted by permission.

General Guidelines for Providers of Psychological Services

Board of Professional Affairs, Committee on Professional Standards

Preamble

A set of practices and implicitly recognized principles of conduct evolves over the history of every profession. Such principles guide the relationships of the members of the profession to their users, to each other, and to the community of which both professionals and users are members. Making such guiding principles and practices explicit is a sign of the profession's maturity and serves the best interests of the profession, its users, and the community at large.

Because psychology is a continually evolving science and profession, guidelines for practice are living documents that require periodic review and revision. The *General Guidelines for Providers of Psychological Services*[1,2] represents an important milestone in the evolutionary development of professional psychology.

These General Guidelines are a set of aspirational statements for psychologists that encourage continual improvement in the quality of practice and service. Some of these General Guidelines have been derived from specific APA Ethical Principles (APA, 1981a).[3] Providers of psychological services have the same responsibility to uphold these specific General Guidelines as they would the corresponding Ethical Principles. The language of the other General Guidelines must at all times be interpreted in light of their aspirational intent.

These General Guidelines are general in nature and, as such, are intended for use by all providers of psychological services; they are supplemented by the *Specialty Guidelines for the Delivery of Services by Clinical (Counseling, Industrial/Organizational, and School) Psychologists* (APA, 1981b).

Introduction

This version of the *General Guidelines* is the second revision of the principles originally adopted by the American Psychological Association on September 4, 1974, and first revised in 1977.[4] The *General Guidelines* are intended to improve the quality, effectiveness, and accessibility of psychological services.

Since 1970, the American Psychological Association has worked to develop and codify a uniform set of guidelines for psychological practice that would serve the respective needs of users, providers, third-party purchasers, and other sanctioners of psychological services. In addition, the APA has established a Committee on Professional Standards, which is charged with keeping the General Guidelines responsive to the needs of these groups and with upgrading and extending them as the profession and science of psychology continue to develop knowledge, improved methods, and additional modes of psychological service. These General Guidelines have been established by organized psychology as a means of self-regulation in the public interest.

When providing any of the covered psychological service functions at any time and in any setting, whether public or private, profit or nonprofit, any persons representing themselves as psychologists are expected, where feasible, to observe these General Guidelines of practice to promote the best interests and welfare of the users of such services. Functions and activities related to the teaching of psychology, the writing or editing of scholarly or scientific manuscripts, and the conduct of scientific research do not fall within the purview of the present *General Guidelines.*[5]

Underlying Principles

Six basic principles have guided the development of these General Guidelines:

1. These General Guidelines apply to psychological service functions offered by psychologists, regardless of their specialty, of the setting, or of the form of remuneration given to them. Professional psychology has a uniform set of guidelines just as it has a common code of ethics (APA, 1981a). These General Guidelines apply equally to individual practitioners and to those who work in a group practice, an institutional agency, or another organizational setting.

2. Guidelines describe levels of quality for covered psychological services that providers strive to attain, regardless of the nature of the users, purchasers, or sanctioners of such covered services.

3. Those people who provide psychological services

These General Guidelines were revised by the Committee on Professional Standards (COPS) in consultation with the Board of Professional Affairs (BPA) and providers of psychological services from throughout the American Psychological Association (APA). The assistance of APA staff is gratefully acknowledged. The names of members and staff who supported this effort are included in Footnote 4. This document was approved by the APA Council of Representatives in February 1987.

Comments or questions on these General Guidelines should be addressed to the Committee on Professional Standards, American Psychological Association, 1200 Seventeenth Street, NW, Washington, DC 20036.

meet acceptable levels of education, training, and experience that are consistent and appropriate to the functions they perform. The final responsibility and accountability for defining qualifications and supervision requirements for service rest with a professional psychologist[6] (see Definitions).

4. Guidelines do not constrain psychologists from employing new methods (see Guideline 1.8) or from making flexible use of support personnel in staffing the delivery of services. The General Guidelines illuminate potential weaknesses in the delivery of psychological services and point to their correction. Some settings may require additional guidelines for specific areas of service delivery than those herein proposed. There is no intent to diminish the scope or quality of psychological services that exceed these General Guidelines. Systematically applied, these General Guidelines serve to establish desirable levels of psychological service. They serve to establish a more effective and consistent basis for evaluating the performance of individual service providers, and they serve to guide the organizing of psychological service units in human service settings.

5. It is recognized that there are significant differences among the established fields of professional psychology in regard to education and training, technical methodology, user populations served, and methods and settings of service delivery. The *Specialty Guidelines for the Delivery of Services* (APA, 1981b) provides acknowledgment of these differences while conforming to the guiding principles delineated by the General Guidelines.

6. These General Guidelines have been developed with the understanding that psychological services must be planned and implemented so that they are sensitive to factors related to life in a pluralistic society such as age, gender, affectional orientation, culture, and ethnicity.

Implications of Guidelines

The General Guidelines presented here have broad implications both for members of the public who use psychological services and for providers of such services.

1. The Guidelines furnish a basis for a mutual understanding between providers and users. Further, they facilitate improved quality of services and more effective evaluation of these services and their outcomes.

2. The Guidelines are an important step toward greater uniformity in legislative and regulatory actions involving providers of psychological services, and provide a model for the development of accreditation procedures for service facilities.

3. The Guidelines give specific content to the profession's concept of ethical practice as reflected in the APA *Ethical Principles of Psychologists* (1981a).

4. The Guidelines have significant impact on training models for both professional and support personnel in psychology.

5. Guidelines for the provision of psychological services influence what is considered desirable organizational structure, budgeting, and staffing patterns in these facilities.

Definitions

Providers of Psychological Services

This term subsumes two categories of providers of psychological services. The two categories are as follows:

A. Professional psychologists. Psychologists have a doctoral degree in psychology from an organized, sequential program in a regionally accredited university or professional school.[6,7,8] Specific definitions of professional psychologists by each of the recognized specialties are provided in the *Specialty Guidelines for the Delivery of Services* (APA, 1981b).

B. Other persons who provide psychological services. Qualifications and supervision for these persons are commensurate with their responsibilities and are further delineated in these policies[9] and in the *Specialty Guidelines for the Delivery of Services.*

Psychological Services

This term refers to one or more of the following:[10]

A. Evaluation, diagnosis,[11] and assessment of the functioning of individuals, groups, and organizations.

B. Interventions, preventive and ameliorative, that facilitate the functioning of individuals, groups, and organizations.[12]

C. Consultation relating to A and B.

D. Program development services in the areas of A, B, and C.[13]

E. Administration and supervision of psychological services.[14]

F. Evaluation of all psychological services.

Psychological Service Unit

This is the functional unit through which psychological services are provided:

A. A psychological service unit is a unit that provides predominantly psychological services and is composed of one or more professional psychologists and support staff.

B. A psychological service unit may operate as a functional or geographic component of a larger governmental, educational, correctional, health, training, industrial, or commercial organizational unit, or as an independent professional service unit.[15]

C. A psychological service unit may take the form of one or more psychologists providing professional services in a multidisciplinary setting.

D. A psychological service unit also may be an individual or group of individuals in a private practice or a psychological consulting firm.

Users

Users include the following:

A. Direct users or recipients of psychological services.

B. Public and private institutions, facilities, or organizations receiving psychological services.

Sanctioners

Sanctioners include the following:

A. Direct users or recipients of psychological services.

B. Public and private institutions, facilities, or organizations receiving psychological services.

C. Any other individual, group, organization, institution, or governing body having legitimate interaction with a psychologist functioning in a professional capacity.

General Guideline 1: Providers

1.1 Each psychological service unit offering psychological services has available at least one professional psychologist and as many more professional psychologists as are necessary to assure the quality of services offered.[16]

ILLUSTRATIVE STATEMENT:[17] The intent of this General Guideline is that one or more providers of psychological services in any psychological service unit meet the levels of training and experience of professional psychologists as specified in the preceding definitions.[18] When a professional psychologist is not available on a full-time basis, the facility retains the services of one or more professional psychologists on a regular part-time basis to supervise the psychological services provided. The psychologist who is so retained has authority and participates sufficiently to enable him or her to assess the needs for services, to review the content of services provided, and to assume professional responsibility and accountability for them.

1.2 Providers of psychological services who do not meet the requirements for professional psychologists are supervised, directed, and evaluated by a professional psychologist to the extent required by the tasks assigned (see Definitions and the *Specialty Guidelines for the Delivery of Services,* APA, 1981b). Tasks assigned to these providers are in keeping with their demonstrated areas of competence. The level and extent of supervision may vary from task to task, as long as the professional psychologist retains a close relationship that is sufficient to meet this General Guideline. In situations in which those providers work in a fair, autonomous fashion, they maintain an appropriate level of consultation and supervisory support from a professional psychologist. (See Ethical Principles 2, 7c, and 8f.)

ILLUSTRATIVE STATEMENT: For example, in health care settings, support personnel may be assigned varying levels of responsibility for providing designated functions within their demonstrated areas of competence. Support personnel are considered to be responsible for their functions and behavior when assisting in the provision of psychological services and are accountable to a professional psychologist. Ultimate professional responsibility and accountability for the services provided require that the supervisor review reports and test protocols and review and discuss intervention plans, strategies, and outcomes. In these settings, the nature and extent of supervision is determined by the professional psychologist to assure the adequacy of psychological services provided.

To facilitate the effectiveness of the psychological service unit, the nature of the supervisory relationship is

clearly and explicitly communicated to support personnel, preferably in writing. Such communications describe and delineate the duties of the employees, such as the range and type of services to be provided. The limits of independent action and decision making are defined. Descriptions of responsibilities specify the means by which employees will contact the professional psychologist in the event of emergency or crisis situations.

1.3 Wherever a psychological service unit exists, a professional psychologist is responsible for planning, directing, and reviewing the provision of psychological services.

ILLUSTRATIVE STATEMENT: The psychologist who directs or coordinates the unit maintains an ongoing or periodic review of the adequacy of services and plans in accordance with the results of such evaluation. This psychologist coordinates the activities of the psychological service unit with other professional, administrative, and technical groups, both within and outside the facility. This psychologist, who may be the director, chief, or coordinator of the psychological service unit, has related responsibilities including, but not limited to, recruiting qualified staff, directing training and research activities of the service, maintaining a high level of professional and ethical practice, and assuring that staff members function only within the areas of their competence.

To facilitate the effectiveness of services by increasing the level of staff sensitivity and professional skills, the psychologist who is designated as director participates in the selection of professional and support personnel whose qualifications include sensitivity and consideration for the language, cultural and experiential background, affectional orientation, ethnic identification, age, and gender of the users, and whose professional skills are directly relevant to the needs and characteristics of these users. Additionally, the director ensures that professional and support personnel do not provide services in any manner that is discriminatory or exploitative to users.

In other institutional and organizational settings, psychologists may be administratively responsible to individuals from disciplines other than psychology. In these instances, the psychologist should seek to sensitize the administrator to the need to allow participation of the psychologist in planning, directing, and reviewing the provision of psychological services.

1.4 When functioning within an organizational setting, professional psychologists seek, whenever appropriate and feasible, to bring their education, training, experience, and skills to bear upon the goals of the organization by participating in the planning and development of overall operations. (See Ethical Principle 1d.)

ILLUSTRATIVE STATEMENT: One way psychologists maintain high professional standards is by being active representatives on boards and committees concerned with service delivery and overall operation of their facility. These activities may include but are not limited to active participation as voting and as office-holding members, on the governance staff as well as on executive, planning, and evaluation boards and committees.

1.5 All providers of psychological services attempt to maintain and apply current knowledge of scientific and professional developments that are directly related to the services they render. This includes knowledge relating to special populations (such as ethnic or other minorities) that may compose a part of their practice. (See Ethical Principles 2, 2c, and 2d.)

ILLUSTRATIVE STATEMENT: Methods through which knowledge of scientific and professional developments may be gained include, but are not limited to, continuing education, attendance at workshops, participation in staff development programs, formal and informal on-the-job training, and reading scientific and professional publications. All providers have access to reference material related to the provision of psychological services. All providers are prepared to show evidence periodically that they are staying abreast of and utilizing current knowledge and practices.

1.6 Professional psychologists limit their practice, including supervision, to their demonstrated areas of professional competence. Special proficiency supervision of psychologists may be provided by professionals from other disciplines whose competence in the given area has been demonstrated by previous education, training, and experience. (See Ethical Principles 2 and 2d.)

ILLUSTRATIVE STATEMENT: Psychological services are offered in accordance with the providers' areas of competence as defined by verifiable education, training, and experience. Before offering professional services beyond the range of their experience and usual practice (e.g., providing services to culturally/linguistically diverse populations), psychologists strive to obtain pertinent knowledge through such means as education, training, reading, and appropriate professional consultation.

1.7 Psychologists who change or add a specialty meet the same requirements with respect to subject matter and professional skills that apply to doctoral education, training, and experience in the new specialty.[19]

ILLUSTRATIVE STATEMENT: Retraining psychologists to qualify them for a change in specialty must be under the auspices of a program in a regionally accredited university or professional school that offers the doctoral degree in that specialty. Such education and training are individualized, due credit being given for relevant coursework or requirements that have previously been satisfied. Merely taking an internship or acquiring experience in a practicum setting or in an employment setting is not considered adequate preparation for becoming a clinical, counseling, industrial/organizational, or school psychologist. Fulfillment of such an individualized training program is attested to by official certification by the supervising department or professional school indicating the successful completion of educational preparation in the

particular specialty. Specific requirements for retraining in each of the recognized specialties are detailed in the *Specialty Guidelines for the Delivery of Services* (APA, 1981b).

1.8 Psychologists are encouraged to develop and/or apply and evaluate innovative theories and procedures, to provide appropriate theoretical or empirical support for their innovations, and to disseminate their results to others. (See Ethical Principles 2 and 2c.)

ILLUSTRATIVE STATEMENT: A profession rooted in a science continually explores, studies, conducts, and evaluates applications of theories and procedures with a view toward developing, verifying, and documenting new and improved ways of serving users.

General Guideline 2: Programs

2.1 Composition and organization of a psychological service unit

2.1.1 The composition and programs of a psychological service unit strive to be responsive to the needs of the people and settings served.

ILLUSTRATIVE STATEMENT: A psychological service unit is structured to facilitate effective and economical delivery of services. For example, a psychological service unit serving a predominantly low-income or ethnic minority group has a staffing pattern and service program adapted to the linguistic, experiential, attitudinal, and financial characteristics of the user population.

2.1.2 A psychological service unit strives to include sufficient numbers of professional psychologists and support personnel to achieve its goals, objectives, and purposes.

ILLUSTRATIVE STATEMENT: The workload, diversity of the psychological services required, and the specific goals and objectives of the setting determine the numbers and qualifications of professional psychologists and support personnel in the psychological service unit. Where shortages in personnel exist, so that psychological services cannot be rendered in a professional manner, the director of the psychological service unit initiates action to modify appropriately the specific goals, objectives, and timetables of the service. If necessary, the director appropriately modifies the scope or workload of the unit to maintain the quality of the services and, at the same time, makes continued efforts to devise alternative systems for delivery of services.

2.2 Policies

2.2.1 A written description of roles, objectives, and scope of services is developed by multi-provider psychological service units as well as by psychological service units that are a component of an organization, unless the unit has a specific alternative approach. The written description or alternative approach is reviewed annually and is available to the staff of the unit and to users and sanctioners upon request.

ILLUSTRATIVE STATEMENT: The psychological service unit reviews its objectives and scope of services annually and makes revisions as necessary to ensure that the psychological services offered are consistent with staff competencies and current psychological knowledge and practice. This statement is discussed with staff, reviewed by the appropriate administrator, and distributed to users and sanctioners upon request and whenever appropriate. Psychologists strive to be aware of management theories and practices that will aid in the delivery of psychological services.

2.2.2 Providers of psychological services avoid any action that will violate or diminish the legal and civil rights of users or of others who may be affected by their actions.[20] (See Ethical Principles 3b, 3c, 5, 6, and 9.)

ILLUSTRATIVE STATEMENT: Providers of psychological services are continually sensitive to the issue of confidentiality of information; they strive to be sensitive to the potential impact of their decisions and recommendations, and to other matters pertaining to individual, legal, and civil rights. Providers of psychological services strive to be aware of issues such as self-incrimination in judicial proceedings, involuntary commitment to hospitals, protection of minors, protection of legal incompetents, discriminatory practices in employment selection procedures, recommendations for special education provisions, information relative to adverse personnel actions in the armed services, and adjudication of domestic relations disputes in divorce and custodial proceedings. Providers of psychological services are encouraged to make themselves available to local committees, review boards, and similar advisory groups established to safeguard the human, civil, and legal rights of service users.

2.2.3 Providers of psychological services are familiar with and abide by the American Psychological Association's *Ethical Principles of Psychologists* (1981a), *Specialty Guidelines for the Delivery of Services* (1981b), *Standards for Educational and Psychological Testing* (1985), *Ethical Principles in the Conduct of Research with Human Participants* (1982), *Guidelines for Computer-Based Tests and Interpretations* (1986), "Guidelines for Psychologists Conducting Growth Groups" (1973), and other APA policy statements relevant to guidelines for professional services issued by the Association.[21] (See Ethical Principle 3d.)

ILLUSTRATIVE STATEMENT: Psychological service units have available a copy of each of these documents, and providers maintain current knowledge of relevant APA guidelines and principles.

2.2.4 Providers of psychological services seek to conform to relevant statutes established by federal, state, and local governments. At times psychologists may seek to challenge legal constraints that they reasonably and honestly believe unduly infringe on the rights of their users or on the right of psychologists to practice their profession; however, any such challenges should conform to appropriate legal procedures. (See Ethical Principle 3d.)

ILLUSTRATIVE STATEMENT: All providers of psychological services seek to be familiar with and practice in conformity with relevant statutes that relate directly to the practice of psychology. They also endeavor to be informed about governmental agency regulations that have the force of law and that relate to the delivery of psychological services (e.g., evaluation for disability retirement or for special education placements). In addition, all providers seek to be aware that federal agencies such as the Veterans Administration, the Department of Education, and the Department of Health and Human Services have policy statements regarding psychological services. Providers of psychological services attempt to be familiar with other statutes and regulations, including those addressed to the civil and legal rights of users (e.g., those promulgated by the federal Equal Employment Opportunity Commission) that are pertinent to their scope of practice.

2.2.5 In recognizing the matrix of personal and societal problems, providers make available, when appropriate, information regarding additional human services, such as specialized psychological services, legal aid societies, social services, employment agencies, health resources, and educational and recreational facilities. (See Ethical Principle 7a.)

ILLUSTRATIVE STATEMENT: Psychologists and support personnel are sensitive to the broader context of human needs. They refer to such resources and are encouraged, when appropriate, to intervene actively on behalf of the users. Providers make appropriate use of other professional, research, technical, and administrative resources whenever these serve the best interests of the users, and they establish and maintain cooperative or collaborative arrangements with such other resources as are required to meet the needs of users.

2.2.6 In the best interest of the users, providers of psychological services endeavor to consult and collaborate with professional colleagues in the planning and delivery of services when such consultation is deemed appropriate. (See Ethical Principles 7 and 7a.)

ILLUSTRATIVE STATEMENT: Psychologists recognize the areas of special competence of other psychologists and of other professionals for consultation and referral purposes.

2.3 Procedures

2.3.1 Each psychological service unit is guided by a set of procedural guidelines for the delivery of psychological services.

ILLUSTRATIVE STATEMENT: Depending on the nature of the setting, and whenever feasible, providers are prepared to provide a statement of procedural guidelines in oral and/or written form that can be understood by users as well as sanctioners. This statement may describe the current methods, forms, procedures, and techniques being used to achieve the objectives and goals for psychological services.

This statement is communicated to staff and, when appropriate, to users and sanctioners. The psychological service unit provides for the annual review of its procedures for the delivery of psychological services.

2.3.2 Psychologists develop plans for psychological services appropriate to the problems presented by the users.

ILLUSTRATIVE STATEMENT: Ideally, a plan for intervention or consultation is in written form and serves as a basis for accountability. Regardless of the type of setting or users involved, a plan that describes the psychological services indicated and the manner in which they will be provided is developed and agreed upon by the providers and users.[22] A psychologist who provides services as one member of a collaborative effort participates in the development and implementation of the overall service plan and provides for its periodic review.

2.3.3 There is a mutually acceptable understanding between a provider and a user or that user's responsible agent regarding the delivery of service. (See Ethical Principles 6 and 6b.)

ILLUSTRATIVE STATEMENT: A psychologist discusses the plan for the provision of psychological services with the user, noting procedures that will be used and respective responsibilities of provider and user. This interaction is repeated whenever major changes occur in the plan for service. This understanding may be oral or written, but in any event, the psychologist documents the nature of the understanding.[23]

2.3.4 Professional psychologists clarify early on to users and sanctioners the exact fee structure or financial arrangements and payment schedule when providing services for a fee. (See Ethical Principle 6d.)

ILLUSTRATIVE STATEMENT: Psychologists inform users of their payment policies and of their willingness to assist users in obtaining reimbursement. Those who accept reimbursement from a third party are acquainted with the appropriate statutes and regulations, instruct their users on proper procedures for submitting claims, and inform them of limits on confidentiality of claims information, in accordance with pertinent statutes.

2.3.5 Accurate, current, and pertinent records of essential psychological services are maintained.

ILLUSTRATIVE STATEMENT: At a minimum, records kept of psychological services should include identifying data, dates of services, and types of services, and where appropriate, may include a record of significant actions taken.[24] Providers make all reasonable efforts to record essential information concerning psychological services within a reasonable time of their completion.

2.3.6 Each psychological service unit follows an established policy for the retention and disposition of records.[25] (See Ethical Principle 5c.)

ILLUSTRATIVE STATEMENT: Such a policy conforms to government statutes and regulations, or to organizational or institutional regulations, policies, or practices where such are applicable.

2.3.7 Psychologists establish and maintain a system that protects the confidentiality of their users' records. (See Ethical Principles 5, 5a, 5c, and 5d.)[26]

ILLUSTRATIVE STATEMENT: Psychologists establish and maintain the confidentiality of information about the users of services, whether obtained by themselves or by those they supervise. If directed otherwise by statute, by regulations with the force of law, or by court order, psychologists seek a resolution that is both ethically and legally feasible and appropriate; for example, psychologists might request in camera (judge's chambers) hearings when they are required by the court to produce records. All people who are supervised by psychologists, including nonprofessional personnel and students, and who have access to records of psychological services are also expected to maintain this confidentiality of information. Psychologists do not release confidential information, except with the written consent of the user involved, or of his or her legal representative, guardian, or other holder of the privilege on behalf of the user, and only after being assured by whatever means may be required that the user has been assisted in understanding the implications of the release. Even after the consent has been obtained for release, psychologists clearly identify such information as confidential for the recipient of the information.

Users are informed in advance of any limits in the setting for maintaining the confidentiality of psychological information. For instance, psychologists in hospital settings inform their patients that psychological information in a patient's clinical record may be available to other hospital personnel without the patient's written consent. Similar limitations on confidentiality of psychological information may be present in certain school, industrial, business, government, or military settings or in instances where the user has waived confidentiality for purposes of third-party payment. When the user's intention to waive confidentiality is judged by a professional psychologist to be contrary to the user's best interest or to be in conflict with that person's legal or civil rights, it is the responsibility of the psychologist to discuss the implications of releasing the psychological information and to assist the user in limiting disclosure by specifying the nature of the information, the recipients, and the time period during which the release is in effect, recognizing, however, that the ultimate decision concerning release of information is that of the user. Providers of psychological services are sensitive to both the benefits and the possible misuse of information regarding individuals that is stored in computerized data banks. Providers take necessary measures to ensure that such information is used in a socially responsible manner.

Users have the right to information in their agency

records and to be informed as to any regulations that govern the release of such information. However, the records are the property of the psychologist or of the facility in which the psychologist works and are, therefore, under the control of the psychologist or of the facility. Users have the right to examine such psychological records. Preferably such examination should be in the presence of a psychologist who judges how best to explain the material in a meaningful and useful manner.

In school settings, parents have the legal right to examine such psychological records, preferably in the presence of a psychologist. In the event that a family moves to another school system, the parents have the legal right to examine a copy of such records from the former school in the new school setting. In either circumstance, the rationale for allowing parents to examine such records is to assure that parents are not in a disadvantaged position if they choose to challenge a school's decision regarding the child. Disclosure of such psychological information in the records from a former school is conducted under secure conditions; such records have been transmitted to the new school to a psychologist under whose supervision the records may be examined. Psychologists and the institutions in which they work have written policy regarding the storage and access of pupils' records. Parents are informed of the results of a psychological assessment of their child in a form most meaningful and useful to the parents.

Raw psychological data (e.g., test protocols, therapy or interview notes, or questionnaire returns) in which a user is identified are ordinarily released only with the written consent of the user or of the user's legal representative, and are released only to a person recognized by the psychologist as competent to interpret the data. Any use made of psychological reports, records, or data for research or training purposes is consistent with this General Guideline. Additionally, providers of psychological services comply with statutory confidentiality requirements and with those embodied in the *Ethical Principles of Psychologists* (APA, 1981a).

2.3.8 Providers of psychological services do not use privileged information received in the course of their work for competitive advantage or personal gain. (See Ethical Principle 5.)

ILLUSTRATIVE STATEMENT: Providers of psychological services often obtain privileged information through their work with users, or while reviewing the proposals of competing practitioners or agencies. Such information may include but not be limited to users' or user associates' business interests, or the interests of competing colleagues or practitioners. When providers acquire such information and it is protected by applicable law or through agreement, it is held confidential and shall not be used for competitive advantage. Further, information that is potentially harmful to users or their associates, or to professional colleagues, should not be used for personal advantage.

2.4 Environment

2.4.1 Providers of psychological services promote the development of a physical, organizational, and social environment in the service setting that facilitates optimal human functioning.

ILLUSTRATIVE STATEMENT: As providers of services, professional psychologists are concerned with the environment of their service unit, especially as it affects the quality of service, but also as it impinges on human functioning in the larger unit of an organization when the service unit is included in such a larger context. Attention is given to the comfort and, where relevant, to the privacy of providers and users. Federal, state, and local requirements for safety, health, and sanitation are observed. Physical arrangements and organizational policies and procedures are conducive to the human dignity, self-respect, and optimal functioning of users and to the effective delivery of service. The atmosphere in which psychological services are rendered is appropriate to the service and to the users, whether in an office, clinic, school, college, university, industrial setting, or other organizational or institutional setting.

General Guideline 3: Accountability

3.1 The promotion of human welfare is the primary principle guiding the professional activities of all members of the psychological service unit. (See Preamble of Ethical Principles.)

ILLUSTRATIVE STATEMENT: Providers of psychological services are expected to interact with users in a manner that is considerate, effective, economical, and humane; to be mindful of their accountability to the sanctioners of psychological services and to the general public; and to see that appropriate steps are taken to protect the confidentiality of the service relationship.

The psychological service unit does not withhold services to a potential user on the basis of that user's national or ethnic origin, religion, gender, affectional orientation, or age; nor does it provide services in a discriminatory or exploitative fashion. However, this does not preclude psychologists from serving agencies whose publicly declared policy restricts users to membership of a particular religious, ethnic, or other specified group, as long as that policy does not constitute unlawful discrimination.[27] Professional psychologists who find that psychological services are being provided in a manner that is discriminatory or exploitative of users or that is contrary to these General Guidelines or to government statutes or regulations take appropriate corrective actions, which may include the refusal to provide services. When conflicts of interest arise, psychologists are guided in the resolution of differences by the principles set forth in the *Ethical Principles of Psychologists* (APA, 1981a).

Recognition is given to the following considerations in regard to the withholding of services: (1) the professional right of psychologists to limit their practice to a specific category of users with whom they have achieved demonstrated competence (e.g., individuals, families, groups, ethnic minorities, or organizations); (2) the right and responsibility of psychologists to withhold an assessment procedure when not validly applicable; (3) the right and responsibility of psychologists to withhold services in specific instances in which their own limitations or user characteristics might impair the quality of the services; (4) the obligation of psychologists to seek to ameliorate through peer review, consultation, therapeutic procedures, or other procedures those factors that inhibit the provision of services to particular individuals, families, groups, ethnic minorities, or organizations; and (5) the obligation of psychologists who withhold services to assist the users in obtaining services from another source.

3.2 Psychologists pursue their activities as members of the independent, autonomous profession of psychology.

ILLUSTRATIVE STATEMENT: Psychologists, as members of an independent profession, are responsible both to the public and to their peers through established review mechanisms. Psychologists are aware of the implications of their activities for the profession as a whole. They seek to eliminate discriminatory practices instituted for self-serving purposes that are not in the interest of the users (e.g., arbitrary requirements for referral and supervision or sign-off by another profession). They are cognizant of their responsibilities for the development of the profession. They participate where possible in the training and career development of students and other providers, participate as appropriate in the training of support personnel or other professionals, and integrate their contributions within the structure established for delivering psychological services. They facilitate the development of and participate in professional standards review mechanisms and seek to work with other professionals in a cooperative manner for the good of the users and for the benefit of the general public.

Psychologists recognize that it is their responsibility to keep supervisors, administrators, and other agency personnel informed of APA guidelines, principles, standards, policies, and other criteria related to their professional functioning. This information is imparted at times that are appropriate in the individual setting. This may include statements of policy procedures, disclaimers, and so forth. Psychologists are responsible for defining and developing their profession, consistent with the general canons of science and with the public welfare.[28]

3.3 There are periodic, systematic, and effective evaluations of psychological services.

ILLUSTRATIVE STATEMENT: When the psychological service unit is a component of a larger organization, regular assessment of progress in achieving goals is provided in the service delivery plan. Such evaluation could include consideration of the effectiveness of psychological services relative to costs in terms of time, money, and the availability of professional and support personnel. Evaluation of the psychological service delivery system could be conducted both internally and, when possible, under independent auspices. Descriptions of therapeutic procedures and other services as well as outcome measures should be as detailed as possible. This evaluation might include an assessment of effectiveness (to determine what the service accomplished), costs, continuity (to ensure that the services are appropriately linked to other human services), availability (to determine appropriate levels and distribution of services and personnel), accessibility (to ensure that the services are barrier-free to users), and adequacy (to determine whether the services meet the identified needs of users). In such evaluations, care is taken to maintain confidentiality of records and privacy of users. It is highly desirable that there be a periodic reexamination of review mechanisms to ensure that these attempts at public safeguards are effective and cost-efficient and do not place unnecessary encumbrances on providers or unnecessary additional expenses on users or sanctioners for services rendered.

3.4 Professional psychologists are accountable for all aspects of the services they provide and are appropriately responsive to those people who are concerned with these services.

ILLUSTRATIVE STATEMENT: Depending upon the settings, accurate and full information is made available to prospective individual or organizational users regarding the qualifications of providers, the nature and extent of services offered, and, where appropriate, financial costs and potential risks. In recognizing their responsibilities to users, sanctioners, third-party purchasers, and other providers, wherever appropriate and consistent with the users' legal rights and privileged communications, professional psychologists make available information about initiation, continuation, modification, termination, and evaluation of psychological services and provide counsel to users regarding their decisions about such issues.

3.5 In the public interest, professional psychologists may wish to provide some services to individuals or organizations for little or no financial return. (See Ethical Principle 6d.)

ILLUSTRATIVE STATEMENT: Professional psychologists are encouraged to contribute a portion of their services and work for which they receive little or no financial return, according to the *Ethical Principles of Psychologists* (APA, 1981a), and to encourage those they supervise to perform services on a similar basis.

FOOTNOTES

[1] The footnotes to these General Guidelines represent an attempt to provide a coherent context of other policy statements of the APA regarding professional practice. The General Guidelines extend these previous policy statements where necessary to reflect current concerns of the public and of the profession.

[2] Note that the title and emphasis of these General Guidelines have been changed from the 1977 version of the *Standards for Providers of Psychological Services.* This has been done to reflect the development and adoption of the *Specialty Guidelines for the Delivery of Services* by the APA in 1980. The profession continues to grow in a variety of areas

in which specific guidelines are not yet necessary. These General Guidelines are intended to support practitioners in these areas.

As stated later in the Preamble, the General Guidelines are aspirational in nature. The change in title is meant to signify that the professional practice of psychology is constantly changing. No collection of principles can adequately direct these changes, and there is no intent to limit future development even though this collection represents the consensus of the profession at this time.

[3] The Ethical Principles from which the General Guidelines have been derived are noted in parentheses at the end of the corresponding General Guidelines.

[4] Early in 1970, acting at the direction of the APA's Council of Representatives, the Board of Professional Affairs (BPA) appointed a task force composed of practicing psychologists with specialized knowledge in at least one of every major class of human service facility and with experience relevant to the setting of standards. The task force's charge was to develop a set of standards for psychological practice. Soon thereafter, partial support for this activity was obtained through a grant from the National Institute of Mental Health (NIMH Grant MH 21696).

The task force promptly established liaison with national groups already active in setting and accrediting standards. It was therefore able to influence two groups of the Joint Commission on Accreditation of Hospitals (JCAH), the Accreditation Council for Facilities for the Mentally Retarded (JCAH, 1971) and the Accreditation Council for Psychiatric Facilities (JCAH, 1972), in their adoption of certain basic principles and in their wording of their standards for psychological services. It also contributed substantially to the "constitutionally required minimum standards for adequate treatment of the mentally ill" ordered by the U.S. District Court in Alabama in the case of *Wyatt v. Stickney* (1972). In concert with other APA committees, the task force also represented the APA in national-level deliberations with government groups and insurance carriers that defined the qualifications necessary for psychologists involved in providing health services.

These interim outcomes involved influence by the APA on actions by groups of nonpsychologists that directly affected the manner in which psychological services were employed, particularly in health and rehabilitation settings. However, these measures did not relieve the Association from exercising its responsibility to speak out directly and authoritatively on what standards for psychological practice should be throughout a broad range of human service settings.

In September 1974, after more than four years of study and broad consultations, the task force completed the APA's first edition of the *Standards for Providers of Psychological Services* (1974). The task of collecting, analyzing, and synthesizing reactions to the original Standards fell to two successive committees. They were charged similarly to review and revise the Standards and to suggest means to implement them, including their acceptance by relevant government and private accreditation groups. The dedicated work of the psychologists who served on both of those committees is gratefully acknowledged. Also recognized with thanks are the several hundred comments received from scores of interested persons representing professional, academic, and scientific psychology; from consumer groups; from administrators of facilities; and from others.

Members of the Task Force on Standards for Service Facilities, which submitted the original Standards in September 1974, were Milton L. Blum, Jacqueline C. Bouhoutsos, Jerry H. Clark, Harold A. Edgerton, Marian D. Hall, Durand F. Jacobs (1972–1974 Chair), Floyd H. Martinez, John E. Muthard, Asher R. Pacht, William D. Pierce, Sue A. Warren, and Alfred M. Wellner (1970–1971 Chair). Staff liaisons from the APA Office of Professional Affairs were John J. McMillan (1970–1971), Gottlieb Simon (1971–1973), and Arthur Centor (1973–1974).

In January 1975, the APA Council of Representatives created the original Committee on Standards for Providers of Psychological Services. The Committee was charged with updating and revising the Standards adopted in September 1974. Members of the Committee were Jacqueline C. Bouhoutsos, Leon Hall, Marian D. Hall, Mary Henle, Durand F. Jacobs (Chair), Abel Ossorio, and Wayne Sorenson. The task force liaison was Jerry H. Clark, and the APA Central Office liaison was Arthur Centor.

In January 1976, the Council modified its charge to the Committee to review the Standards and to recommend revisions needed to reflect the varying needs of only those psychologists engaged in the activities of clinical psychology, counseling psychology, industrial/organizational psychology, and school psychology. The Committee was reconstituted with one member representing each of the four applied activities, plus one member representing institutional practice and one representing the public interest. Members were Jules Barron (later replaced by Morris Goodman), clinical; Barbara A. Kirk (later replaced by Milton Schwebel), counseling; Virginia Schein (later replaced by Frank Friedlander), industrial/organizational; Durand F. Jacobs (Chair), institutional practice; M. Brewster Smith (later replaced by Pearl Mayo Dansby), public interest; Marian D. Hall (later replaced by Jack I. Bardon and Nadine M. Lambert), school. Arthur Centor and Richard Kilburg were the APA Central Office liaisons. The revised *Standards for Providers of Psychological Services* was approved by the APA Council of Representatives in January 1977 (APA, 1977).

In January 1980, the APA Council of Representatives instructed the Board of Professional Affairs to amend the 1977 Standards in keeping with the principles enunciated by the Council in connection with its action approving the four sets of *Specialty Guidelines for the Delivery of Services* (APA, 1981b). The BPA referred the task of revising the 1977 Standards to the newly created Committee on Professional Standards, composed of Juanita Braddock, public member; Judy E. Hall, experimental/mental retardation; Nadine M. Lambert, school; David Mills (Chair, January–April 1981), clinical/counseling; Milton Schwebel, counseling; Gilfred Tanabe (1980 Chair), clinical; and Murphy Thomas (Chair, May–December 1981), clinical. Subsequent members of the Committee on Professional Standards included William Chestnut, counseling; Lorraine D. Eyde, industrial/ organizational; Morris Goodman (1982–1983 Chair), clinical; John H. Jackson, school; Caroline Miller, public member; William Schofield (1984 Chair), clinical; and Barbara Wand, social. These past members of the Committee on Professional Standards were responsible for completing the 1984 revision of the Standards. Central Office staff assistance was provided by Richard Kilburg and Joy Burke (1980), Sharon Shueman and Pam Juhl (1980–1982), Jutta N. Hagner (1982–1984), and Patricia J. Aletky (1982–1985).

The 1985 draft revision was prepared by Committee on Professional Standards members Susan Robbins Berger, school; LaMaurice Gardner, clinical; Jo-Ida Hansen, counseling; Marlene Muse, public member; Lyle Schoenfeldt, industrial/organizational; William Schofield (1985 Chair), clinical; and Barbara Wand (1985 Vice-Chair), social. Central Office staff assistance was provided by Patricia J. Aletky, Patricia Brown, and Rizalina Mendiola. Between March 1985 and June 1985, a BPA work group on the Standards (composed of John H. Jackson, Chair; Morris Goodman; and William Schofield) reviewed and modified the 1985 draft revision. Central Office staff assistance was provided by Patricia J. Aletky, Patricia Brown, and Rizalina Mendiola.

In November 1985, BPA approved a revised effort that involved Committee on Professional Standards members and work groups representing each of the recognized specialties. The Committee on Professional Standards members participating were Lyle Schoenfeldt (1986 Chair), industrial/organizational; Susan Robbins Berger (1986 Vice-Chair), school; LaMaurice Gardner, clinical; Jo-Ida Hansen, counseling; Richard Kilburg, clinical; and Alan Malyon, clinical. Work group participants, by specialty area and Division, were as follows: Clinical: Robert Weitz (Division 12); Patricia Hannigan and Gerald Koocher (Division 29); Donna Copeland, Marlene Eisen, and Billie S. Strauss (Division 30); Arthur Bodin (Divisions 31, 38, 39, 42, 43); Ronald Kurz (Division 38); and Florence Kaslow (Divisions 41 and 43); Counseling: Ricki Bander, John Corrigan, Thomas Dowd, David Fago, and Milton Schwebel (Division 17); Industrial/Organizational: Hannah R. Hirsh and Manuel London (Division 14); School: Judith Alpert, John H. Jackson, and Ralph D. Wenger (Division 16); and Milton Shore (Division 37). Central Office assistance was provided by Pam Juhl, Sheila Lane Forsyth, Russell Newman, and Mary Lisa Debraggio.

[5] These General Guidelines are designed to be consistent with existing APA policies. One APA policy governing this issue is the 1987 Model Act for State Licensure of Psychologists, prepared by a subcommittee of APA's Committee on Professional Practice and adopted by the APA Council of Representatives in February 1987.

[6] People who met the following criteria on or before the date of adoption of the original Standards on September 4, 1974, shall also be considered professional psychologists: (a) a master's degree in a program

primarily psychological in content from a regionally accredited university or professional school; (b) appropriate education, training, and experience in the area of service offered; (c) a license or certificate in the state in which they practice, conferred by a state board of psychological examiners; or, in the absence of statutory regulation, the endorsement of the state psychological association through voluntary certification; or, for practice in primary and secondary schools, a state department of education certificate as a school psychologist provided that the certificate required at least two graduate years. Wherever the term *psychologist* is used in these General Guidelines, it refers to *professional psychologist.*

Within the specialty of school psychology, those persons who met the following criteria on or before, but not beyond, January 31, 1985, are also recognized as professional school psychologists: (a) a master's or higher degree, requiring at least two years of full-time graduate study in school psychology, from a regionally accredited university or professional school; (b) at least three additional years of training and experience in school psychological services, including a minimum of 1,200 hours in school settings; and (c) a license or certificate conferred by a state board of psychological examiners or a state educational agency for practice in elementary or secondary schools.

[7] Some federal and state legislation uses the term *clinical psychologist* to identify a set of service providers that is not limited to clinical psychologists as defined by the APA in the *Specialty Guidelines for the Delivery of Services by Clinical Psychologists* (APA, 1981b). APA defines the term *clinical psychologist* in health service delivery legislation in a generic sense to include all qualified professional psychologists who provide relevant services. Intraprofessionally, as represented by its *Specialty Guidelines*, APA currently supports specific and meaningful differentiation in the education, training, and practices of the specialties of clinical psychology, counseling psychology, industrial/organizational psychology, and school psychology.

[8] This definition is similar to the recommended statutory language in the "Requirements for Licensure" section of the 1987 APA Model Act for State Licensure of Psychologists (APA, 1987b), a policy statement setting forth model state legislation affecting the practice of psychology and recognizing the doctorate as the minimum educational requirement for entry into professional practice as a psychologist:

Applicants for licensure shall possess a doctoral degree in psychology from an institution of higher education. The degree shall be obtained from a recognized program of graduate study in psychology as defined by the rules and regulations of the Board.

By 1995 applicants for licensure shall have completed a doctoral program in psychology that is accredited by the American Psychological Association (APA). In areas where no accreditation exists, applicants for licensure shall have completed a doctoral program in psychology that meets recognized acceptable professional standards as determined by the Board. When a new specialty of professional psychology is recognized as being within the accreditation scope of the APA, doctoral programs within that specialty will be afforded a transition period of eight years from their first class of students to the time of their accreditation. During that transition period, graduates of such programs may sit for licensure examination whether or not the program has been accredited. The same principle applies as well to new doctoral programs of specialties previously recognized within the scope of APA accreditation.

Applicants trained in institutions outside the United States shall meet requirements established by the Board. (APA, 1987b, p. 698)

In addition to the above educational requirements, the following experience requirements also appear in the 1987 APA Model Act for State Licensure of Psychologists:

For admission to the licensure examination, applicants shall demonstrate that they have completed two years of supervised professional experience, one year of which shall be postdoctoral. The criteria for appropriate supervision shall be in accordance with regulations to be promulgated by the Board. Postdoctoral experience shall be compatible with the knowledge and skills acquired during formal doctoral or postdoctoral education in accordance with professional requirements and relevant to the intended area of practice. Applicants shall be required to show evidence of good character, that is, that they have not been convicted of a criminal offense that bears directly on the fitness of the individual to be licensed. (APA, 1987b, p. 698)

[9] With regard to the roles, responsibilities, and supervision process for other persons who provide psychological services, a professional psychologist should consider the following issues and suggestions:

(a) A professional psychologist is identified as the ethically responsible agent in all advertising, public announcements, and billings for supervised psychological services.

(b) A supervising psychologist reviews and is responsible for all reports prepared by the assistant.

(c) Professional psychologists set a reasonable limit on the number of assistants who are employed and supervised by a single supervisor.

(d) Professional psychologists must be sufficiently available to ensure adequate evaluation or assessment, intervention planning, direction, and consultation.

(e) Assistants provide services or carry out activities at the direction of the psychologist employer/supervisor who is responsible for those services or activities.

(f) Assistants work in reasonably close physical proximity to the supervising psychologist so as to have available regular and continuing supervision.

[10] As was noted in the opening section of the General Guidelines, functions and activities of psychologists relating to the teaching of psychology, the writing or editing of scholarly or scientific manuscripts, the conduct of scientific research, and the activities of members of other professions do not fall within the purview of the General Guidelines.

[11] For the purposes of these General Guidelines and consistent with the 1987 APA Model Act for State Licensure of Psychologists, the term *diagnosis* may include the diagnosis of mental, emotional, nervous, or behavioral disorders or conditions of individuals and groups by professionals trained to do so, such as clinical, counseling, school, rehabilitation, and health psychologists (see Footnote 13).

[12] Consistent with the 1987 APA Model Act for State Licensure of Psychologists, such interventions include, but are not limited to, psychotherapy and counseling (see Footnote 13), and other interventions may include vocational development, cognitive rehabilitation, process consultation, psychological skills training, techniques of health psychology, selection and placement of personnel, and organizational development.

Specific definitions of interventions by each of the recognized specialties are provided in the *Specialty Guidelines for the Delivery of Services* (APA, 1981b).

[13] These definitions should be compared to the 1987 APA Model Act for State Licensure of Psychologists (APA, 1987b, p. 697), which includes definitions of *psychologist* and *practice of psychology* as follows:

Psychologist: A person represents himself or herself to be a psychologist if that person uses any title or description of services incorporating the words *psychology, psychological,* or *psychologist,* or if he or she possesses expert qualification in any area of psychology or if that person offers to the public or renders to individuals or to groups of individuals services defined as the practice of psychology in this Act.

Practice of Psychology is defined as the observation, description, evaluation, interpretation, and modification of human behavior by the application of psychological principles, methods, and procedures, for the purpose of preventing or eliminating symptomatic, maladaptive, or undesired behavior and of enhancing interpersonal relationships, work and life adjustment, personal effectiveness, behavioral health, and mental health. The practice of psychology includes, but is not limited to, psychological testing and the evaluation or assessment of personal characteristics such as intelligence, personality, abilities, interests, aptitudes, and neuropsychological functioning; counseling, psychoanalysis, psychotherapy, hypnosis, biofeedback, and behavior analysis and therapy; diagnosis and treatment of mental and emotional disorder or disability, alcoholism and substance abuse, disorders of habit or conduct, as well as of the psychological aspects of physical illness, accident, injury or disability; and psychoeducational evaluation, therapy, remediation and consultation. Psychological services may be rendered to individuals, families, groups, and the public. The practice of psychology shall be construed within the meaning of this definition without regard to whether payment is received for services rendered. (See Section J for exemptions.)

[14] As indicated in the *Ethical Principles of Psychologists* (APA, 1981a), especially Principle 1 (Responsibility) and Principle 3 (Moral and Legal Guidelines), when functioning as an administrator or manager in an organization or unit that is not a psychological services unit, psychologists apply their knowledge, skills, and abilities in furtherance of the objectives of that organization while remaining aware of the requirements of their profession's ethics and guidelines.

[15] The relation of a psychological service unit to a larger facility or institution is also addressed indirectly in the APA *Guidelines for Conditions of Employment of Psychologists* (APA, 1987a), which emphasizes the roles, responsibilities, and prerogatives of the psychologist when he or she is employed by or provides services for another agency, institution, or business.

[16] At the time of the adoption of these General Guidelines, there were four state statutes that did not require a doctoral degree for unsupervised provision of psychological services. Therefore, the goal of having the highest level of training for psychological practitioners is not, at the current time, fully achievable. (See Footnote 18 and Guideline 2.2.4.)

In addition to the small minority of states that recognize nondoctoral psychologists as independent providers of psychological services, almost all states recognize nondoctoral school psychologists who meet the requisite education, training, and experience prescribed by state departments of education as independent practitioners within local, regional, and state school systems.

[17] These illustrative statements have been selected to clarify how these General Guidelines might be implemented or apply in particular situations, and/or the importance of particular implications of the General Guidelines. The APA recognizes that there may be a variety of implications of and methods for implementing a specific General Guideline depending on the situation in a given setting.

[18] This General Guideline reflects changes in the 1987 revision of the Model Act for State Licensure of Psychologists adopted by the APA Council of Representatives in February 1987 (APA, 1987b). Guideline 1.1 expresses the goal of the APA that psychological service units in all organizations have at least one professional psychologist available to assure the quality of services offered.

[19] This General Guideline follows closely the statement regarding "Policy on Training for Psychologists Wishing to Change Their Specialty" adopted by the APA Council of Representatives in January 1976 and revised by the Council in January 1982. Included therein is the implementing provision that "this policy statement shall be incorporated in the guidelines of the Committee on Accreditation so that appropriate sanctions can be brought to bear on university and internship training programs which violate [it]" (Conger, 1976, p. 424).

[20] See also *Ethical Principles in the Conduct of Research with Human Participants* (APA, 1982) and *Principles Concerning the Counseling and Therapy of Women* (APA, 1978).

[21] These documents are available from the American Psychological Association, 1200 Seventeenth Street, NW, Washington, DC 20036.

[22] Another example of a specific application of this principle is found in Guideline 2 in "Guidelines for Psychologists Conducting Growth Groups" (APA, 1973):

2. The following information should be made available in writing to all prospective participants:
(a) An explicit statement of the purpose of the group;
(b) Types of techniques that may be employed;
(c) The education, training, and experience of the leader or leaders;
(d) The fee and any additional expense that may be incurred;
(e) A statement as to whether or not a follow-up service is included in the fee;
(f) Goals of the group experience and techniques to be used;
(g) Amounts and kinds of responsibility to be assumed by the leader and by the participants. For example, (i) the degree to which a participant is free not to follow suggestions and prescriptions of the group leader

and other group members; (ii) any restrictions on a participant's freedom to leave the group at any time; and
(h) Issues of confidentiality. (p. 933)

[23] When the user of the service is a child, it is desirable that both parent (or legal guardian) and child, to the extent possible, be involved in this understanding.

[24] Health care providers hold widely varying views about the wisdom of written records relating to the content of the psychotherapeutic relationship.

[25] In the absence of such, the policy is as follows:

1. Retain the full record intact for a specified period of time, if not in perpetuity. Some records need to be retained during the lifetime of an individual, either by the provider or by some other agency through arrangement by the provider. These records are necessary in special circumstances, such as in the case of handicapped individuals who need to comply with requests from the Social Security Administration for information on documented disabilities during their childhood years.

2. If a full record is not retained following completion of service delivery, a summary of the record is maintained for a specified period of time.

3. A record or the summary of a record may be disposed of only after a specified period of time following completion of planned services or the date of last contact, whichever comes later. (See the relevant sections of the *Specialty Guidelines for the Delivery of Services*, APA, 1981b, for specific retention and disposition guidelines. These are Guidelines 2.3.4 for clinical, counseling, and school psychologists.)

In the event of the death of or the incapacity of a psychologist in independent practice, special procedures are necessary to assure the continuity of active service to the user and the safeguarding of records in accordance with this Guideline. For this reason, with the approval of the affected user, it is appropriate for another psychologist, acting under the auspices of the Professional Standards Review Committee (PSRC) or the Ethics Committee of the state, where such a committee is available, to review the record with that user and recommend a course of action for continuing professional service, if needed. Depending on local circumstances, appropriate arrangements for record retention and disposal are also recommended by the reviewing psychologist. This General Guideline has been developed to address a variety of circumstances that may arise, often years after a set of psychological services has been completed. Increasingly, records are being utilized in forensic matters, for peer review, for investigation of ethical complaints, and in response to requests from users, other professionals, or other legitimate parties requiring accurate information about the exact dates, nature, course, and outcome of a set of psychological services.

[26] Support for the principle of privileged communication is found in the Model Act for State Licensure of Psychologists (APA, 1987b):

In judicial proceedings, whether civil, criminal, or juvenile; in legislative and administrative proceedings; and in proceedings preliminary and ancillary thereto, a patient or client, or his or her guardian or personal representative, may refuse to disclose or prevent the disclosure of confidential information, including information contained in administrative records, communicated to a psychologist licensed or otherwise authorized to practice psychology under the laws of this jurisdiction, or to persons reasonably believed by the patient or client to be so licensed, and their agents, for the purpose of diagnosis, evaluation, or treatment of any mental or emotional condition or disorder. In the absence of evidence to the contrary, the psychologist is presumed authorized to claim the privilege on the patient's or client's behalf.

This privilege may not be claimed by the patient or client, or on his or her behalf by authorized persons, in the following circumstances:
1. where abuse or harmful neglect of children, the elderly, or disabled or incompetent individuals is known or reasonably suspected;
2. where the validity of a will of a former patient or client is contested;
3. where such information is necessary for the psychologist to defend against a malpractice action brought by the patient or client;
4. where an immediate threat of physical violence against a readily identifiable victim is disclosed to the psychologist;
5. in the context of civil commitment proceedings, where an immediate threat of self-inflicted damage is disclosed to the psychologist;

6. where the patient or client, by alleging mental or emotional damages in litigation, puts his or her mental state at issue;

7. where the patient or client is examined pursuant to court order; or

8. in the context of investigations and hearings brought by the patient or client and conducted by the Board, where violations of this Act are at issue. (pp. 702–703)

Specific provisions for the maintenance of confidentiality are spelled out in each of the *Specialty Guidelines for the Delivery of Services* (APA, 1981b).

[27] Examples of such agencies are clinics for battered women, clinics for Spanish-speaking users, and clinics for members of a specific religious faith or church.

[28] The APA is prepared to provide appropriate assistance to responsible members who are subjected to unreasonable limitations upon their opportunities to function as practitioners, administrators, or consultants. The APA is prepared to cooperate with any responsible professional psychological organization in opposing any unreasonable limitations on the professional functions of the members of that organization. This insistence upon professional autonomy has been upheld over the years by the affirmative actions of the courts and of other public and private bodies in support of the right of psychologists to pursue those functions that they are trained and qualified to perform. Psychologists recognize that other professions and other groups will, from time to time, seek to define the roles and responsibilities of psychologists. The APA opposes such attempts.

REFERENCES

American Psychological Association. (1973). Guidelines for psychologists conducting growth groups. *American Psychologist, 28,* 933.

American Psychological Association. (1974). *Standards for providers of psychological services.* Washington, DC: Author.

American Psychological Association. (1977). Standards for providers of psychological services. *American Psychologist, 32.* 495–505.

American Psychological Association. (1978). Principles concerning the counseling and therapy of women. *Counseling Psychologist, 7*(4), 74–76.

American Psychological Association. (1981a). Ethical principles of psychologists. *American Psychologist, 36,* 633–638.

American Psychological Association. (1981b). Specialty guidelines for the delivery of services by clinical (counseling, industrial/organizational, and school) psychologists. *American Psychologist, 36.* 639–681.

American Psychological Association. (1982). *Ethical principles in the conduct of research with human participants.* Washington, DC: Author.

American Psychological Association. (1986). *Guidelines for computer-based tests and interpretations.* Washington, DC: Author.

American Psychological Association. (1987a). Guidelines for conditions of employment of psychologists. *American Psychologist, 42,* 724–729.

American Psychological Association. (1987b). Model act for state licensure of psychologists. *American Psychologist, 42.* 696–703.

Conger, J. J. (1976). Proceedings of the American Psychological Association, Incorporated, for the year 1975: Minutes of the annual meeting of the Council of Representatives. *American Psychologist, 31.* 406–434.

Joint Commission on Accreditation of Hospitals, Accreditation Council for Psychiatric Facilities. (1972). *Accreditation manual for psychiatric facilities: 1972.* Chicago, IL: Author.

Joint Commission on Accreditation of Hospitals, Accreditation Council for Facilities for the Mentally Retarded. (1971). *Standards for residential facilities for the mentally retarded.* Chicago, IL: Author.

Standards for educational and psychological testing. (1985). Washington, DC: American Psychological Association.

Wyatt v. Stickney, 325 F. Supp. (M.D. Ala. 1971), 334 F. Supp. 1341 (M.D. Ala.), 344 F. Supp. 373 (M.D. Ala. 1972), *aff'd sub nom.* Wyatt v. Aderholt, 503 F.2d 1305 (5th Cir. 1974).

APPENDIX E

SPECIALTY GUIDELINES FOR THE DELIVERY OF SERVICES

Clinical Psychologists
Counseling Psychologists
Industrial/Organizational Psychologists
School Psychologists

Committee on Professional Standards,
American Psychological Association,
Washington, D.C.

Specialty Guidelines for the Delivery of Services, 36(6) American Psychologist 640-81 (1981).
© 1981 the American Psychological Association. Reprinted by permission.

Introduction

In September 1976, the APA Council of Representatives reviewed and commented on the draft revisions of the *Standards for Providers of Psychological Services* prepared by the Committee on Standards for Providers of Psychological Services. During that discussion, the Council acknowledged the need for standards in certain specialty areas in addition to the generic Standards covered by the draft revision. The Council authorized the committee to hold additional meetings to develop multiple standards in all specialty areas of psychology.

Following the adoption of the revised generic *Standards* in January 1977, the committee, working with psychologists in the four recognized specialty areas of psychology, spent the next three years modifying the generic *Standards* to meet the needs of clinical, counseling, industrial/organizational, and school psychologists. The four documents produced by the committee went through extensive revisions. Convention programs discussing these developments were held every year. Comments were solicited from all major constituencies in psychology and from thousands of individuals. The comments received and reviewed by the committee were varied and numerous.

In January 1980, following this extensive process and after making several additional modifications, the Council of Representatives adopted as APA policy the *Specialty Guidelines for the Delivery of Services by Clinical (Counseling, Industrial/Organizational, School) Psychologists.* As stated in the introductions of these four documents, the intent of the *Specialty Guidelines* is "to educate the public, the profession, and other interested parties regarding specialty professional practices . . . and to facilitate the continued systematic development of the profession."

At the same meeting, the Council also approved a reorganization of the Board of Professional Affairs' committee structure, which included the establishment of the Committee on Professional Standards to succeed the Committee on Standards for Providers of Psychological Services. The Committee on Professional Standards has been directed to review all comments on the *Specialty Guidelines* when considering its revisions. APA members and other interested individuals or groups with comments or suggestions are requested to send them to the American Psychological Association, Committee on Professional Standards, 1200 Seventeenth Street, N.W., Washington, D.C. 20036.

The members of the Committee on Standards for Providers of Psychological Services (1977–1980) who developed the *Specialty Guidelines* were Jack I. Bardon, school; Jules Barron, clinical; Frank Friedlander, industrial/organizational; Morris Goodman, clinical; Durand F. Jacobs (Chair), institutional practice; Barbara A. Kirk, counseling; Nadine M. Lambert, school; Virginia Ellen Schein, industrial! organizational; and Milton Schwebel, counseling. Arthur Centor and Richard Kilburg were the Central Office liaisons.

The members of the Committee on Professional Standards (1980–1981) who made the final changes to the *Specialty Guidelines* and were charged with future revisions were Juanita Braddock, public member; Lorraine Eyde, industrial! organizational; Morris Goodman, clinical; Judy Hall, experimental/mental retardation; John H. Jackson, school; Nadine M. Lambert, school; Dave Mills (1981 Chair, partial), clinical/counseling; Milton Schwebel, counseling; Gilfred Tanabe (1980 Chair), clinical; and Murphy Thomas (1981 Chair, partial), clinical. The Central Office liaisons were Joy Burke, Sharon A. Shueman, and Pam Arnold.

Specialty Guidelines for the Delivery of Services
by Clinical Psychologists

These Specialty Guidelines were prepared through the cooperative efforts of the APA Committee on Standards for Providers of Psychological Services (COSPOPS) and many professional clinical psychologists from the divisions of APA, including those involved in education and training programs and in public and private practice. Jules Barron, succeeded by Morris Goodman, served as the clinical psychology representative on COSPOPS. The commtttee was chaired by Durand F. Jacobs. The Central Office liaisons were Arthur Centor and Richard Kilburg.

The Specialty Guidelines that follow are based on the generic *Standards for Providers of Psychological Services* originally adopted by the American Psychological Association (APA) in September 1974 and revised in January 1977 (APA, 1974b, 1977b). Together with the generic Standards, these Specialty Guidelines state the official policy of the Association regarding delivery of services by clinical psychologists. Admission to the practice of psychology is regulated by state statute. It is the position of the Association that licensing be based on generic, and not on specialty, qualifications. Specialty guidelines serve the additional purpose of providing potential users and other interested groups with essential information about particular services available from the several specialties in professional psychology.

Professional psychology specialties have evolved from generic practice in psychology and are supported by university training programs. There are now at least four recognized professional specialties—clinical, counseling, school, and industrial/organizational psychology.

The knowledge base in each of these specialty areas lass increased, refining the state of the art to the point that a set of uniform specialty guidelines is now possible and desirable. The present Guidelines are intended to educate the public, the profession, and other interested parties regarding specialty professional practices. They are also intended to facilitate the continued systematic development of the profession.

The content of each Specialty Guideline reflects a consensus of university faculty and public and private practitioners regarding the knowledge base, services provided, problems addressed, and clients served.

Traditionally, all learned disciplines have treated the designation of specialty practice as a reflection of preparation in greater depth in a particular subject matter, together with a voluntary limiting of focus to a more restricted area of practice by the professional. Lack of specialty designation does not preclude general providers of psychological services from using the methods or dealing with the populations of any specialty, except insofar as psychologists voluntarily refrain from providing services they are not trained to render. it is the intent of these Guidelines, however, that after the grandparenting period, psychologists not put themselves forward as specialists in a given area of practice unless they meet the qualifications noted in the Guidelines (see Definitions). Therefore, these Guidelines are meant to apply only to those psychologists who voluntarily wish to be designated as *clinical psychologists*. They do not apply to other psychologists.

These Guidelines represent the professions best judgment of the conditions, credentials, and experience that contribute to competent professional practice. The APA strongly encourages, and plans to participate its, efforts to identify professional practitioner behaviors and job functions and to validate the relation between these and desired client outcomes. Thus, future revisions of these Guidelines will increasingly reflect the results of such efforts.

These Guidelines follow the format and, wherever applicable, the wording of the generic *Standards*.[1] (Note Footnotes appear at the end of the Specialty Guidelines. See pp. 648–651.) The intent of these Guidelines is to improve the quality, effectiveness, and accessibility of psychological services. They are meant to provide guidance to providers, users, and sanctioners regarding the best judgment of the profession on these matters. Although the Specialty Guidelines have been derived from and are consistent with the generic *Standards*, they may be used as separate documents. However, *Standards for Providers of Psychological Services* (APA, 1977b) shall remain the basic policy statement and shall take precedence where there are questions of interpretation.

Professional psychology in general and clinical psychology as a specialty have labored long and diligently to codify a uniform set of guidelines for the delivery of services by clinical psychologists that would serve the respective needs of users, providers, third-party purchasers, and sanctioners of psychological services.

The Committee on Professional Standards, established by the APA in January 1980, is charged with keeping the generic *Standards* and the Specialty Guidelines responsive to the needs of the public and the profession. It is also charged with continually reviewing, modifying, and extending them progressively as the profession and the science of psychology develop new knowledge, improved methods, and additional modes of psychological services.

The Specialty Guidelines for the Delivery of Services by Clinical Psychologists that follow have been established by the APA as a means of self-regulation to protect the public interest. They guide the specialty practice of clinical psychology by specifying important areas of quality assurance and performance that contribute to the goal of facilitating more effective human functioning.

Principles and Implications of the Specialty Guidelines

These Specialty Guidelines have emerged from and reaffirm the same basic principles that guided the development of the generic *Standards for Providers of Psychological Services* (APA, 1977b):

1. These Guidelines recognize that admission to the practice of psychology is regulated by state statute.

2. It is the intention of the APA that the generic *Standards* provide appropriate guidelines for statutory licensing of psychologists. In addition, although it is the position of the APA that licensing be generic and not in specialty areas, these Specialty Guidelines in clinical psychology provide an authoritative reference for use in credentialing specialty providers of clinical psychological services by such groups as divisions of the APA and state associations and by boards and agencies that find such criteria useful for quality assurance.

3. A uniform set of Specialty Guidelines governs the quality of services to all users of clinical psychological services in both the private and the public sectors. Those receiving clinical psychological services are protected by the same kinds of safeguards,

irrespective of sector; these include constitutional guarantees, statutory regulation, peer review, consultation, record review, and supervision.

4. A uniform set of Specialty Guidelines governs clinical psychological service functions offered by clinical psychologists, regardless of setting or form of remuneration. All clinical psychologists in professional practice recognize and are responsive to a uniform set of Specialty Guidelines, just as they are guided by a common code of ethics.

5. Clinical psychology Guidelines establish clearly articulated levels of quality for covered clinical psychological service functions, regardless of the nature of the users, purchasers, or sanctioners of such covered services.

6. All persons providing clinical psychological services meet specified levels of training and experience that are consistent with, and appropriate to, the functions they perform. Clinical psychological services provided by persons who do not meet the APA qualifications for a professional clinical psychologist (see Definitions) are supervised by a professional clinical psychologist. Final responsibility and accountability for services provided rest with professional clinical psychologists.

7. When providing any of the covered clinical psychological service functions at any time and in any setting, whether public or private, profit or nonprofit, clinical psychologists observe these Guidelines in order to promote the best interests and welfare of the users of such services. The extent to which clinical psychologists observe these Guidelines is judged by peers.

8. These Guidelines, while assuring the user of the clinical psychologists accountability for the nature and quality of services specified in this document, do not preclude the clinical psychologist from using new methods or developing innovative procedures in the delivery of clinical services.

These Specialty Guidelines have broad implications both for users of clinical psychological services and for providers of such services:

1. Guidelines for clinical psychological services provide a foundation for mutual understanding between provider and user and facilitate more effective evaluation of services provided and outcomes achieved.

2. Guidelines for clinical psychologists are essential for uniformity in specialty credentialing of clinical psychologists.

3. Guidelines give specific content to the professions concept of ethical practice as it applies to the functions of clinical psychologists

4. Guidelines for clinical psychological services may have significant impact on tomorrows education and training models for both professional and support personnel in clinical psychology.

5. Guidelines for the provision of clinical psychological services in human service facilities influence the determination of acceptable structure, budgeting, and staffing patterns in these facilities.

6. Guidelines for clinical psychological services require continual review and revision.

The Specialty Guidelines here presented are intended to improve the quality and delivery of clinical psychological services by specifying criteria for key aspects of the practice setting. Some settings may require additional and/or more stringent criteria for specific areas of service delivery.

Systematically applied, these Guidelines serve to establish a more effective and consistent basis for evaluating the performance of individual service providers as well as to guide the organization of clinical psychological service units in human service settings.

Definitions

Providers of clinical psychological services refers to two categories of persons who provide clinical psychological services:

A. Professional clinical psychologists.[2] Professionalclinical psychologists have a doctoral degree from a regionally accredited university or professional school providing an organized, sequential clinical psychology program in a department of psychology in a university or college, or in an appropriate department or unit of a professional school. Clinical psychology programs that are accredited by the American Psychological Association are recognized as meeting the definition of a clinical psychology program. Clinical psychology programs that are not accredited by the American Psychological Association meet the definition of a clinical psychology program if they satisfy the following criteria.

1. The program is primarily psychological in nature and stands as a recognizable, coherent organizational entity within the institution.
2. The program provides an integrated, organized sequence of study.
3. The program has an identifiable body of students who are matriculated in that program for a degree.
4. There is a clear authority with primary responsibility for the core and specialty areas, whether or not the program cuts across administrative lines.
5. There is an identifiable psychology faculty, and a psychologist responsible for the program. In addition to a doctoral education, clinical psychologists acquire doctoral and postdoctoral training. Patterns of education and training in clinical psychology[3] are consistent with the functions to be performed and the services to be provided, in accordance with the ages, populations, and problems encountered in various settings.

B. All other persons who are not professional clinical psychologists and who participate in the delivery of clinical psychological services under the supervision of a professional clinical psychologist. Although there may be variations in the titles of such persons, they are not referred to as clinical psychologists. Their functions may be indicated by use of the adjective *psychological* preceding the noun, for example, *psychological associate, psychological assistant, psychological technician*, or *psychological aide*. Their services are rendered under the supervision of a professional clinical psychologist, who is responsible for the designation given them and for quality control. To be assigned such a designation, a person has the background, training, or experience that is appropriate to the functions performed.

Clinical psychological services refers to the application of principles, methods, and procedures for understanding, predicting, and alleviating intellectual, emotional, psychological, and behavioral disability and discomfort. Direct services are provided in a variety of health settings, and direct and supportive services are provided in the entire range of social, organizational, and academic institutions and agencies.[4] Clinical psychologicalservices include the following:[5]

A. Assessment directed toward diagnosing the nature and causes, and predicting the effects, of subjective distress; of personal, social, and work dysfunction; and of the psychological and emotional factors involved in, and consequent to, physical disease and disability. Procedures may include, but are not limited to, interviewing, and administering and interpreting tests of intellectual abilities, attitudes, emotions, motivations, personality characteristics, psychoneurological status, and other aspects of human experience and behavior relevant to the disturbance.

B. Interventions directed at identifying and correcting the emotional conflicts, personality disturbances. and skill deficits underlying a person's distress and/or dysfunction. Interventions may reflect a variety of theoretical orientations, techniques, and modalities. These may include, but are not limited to, psychotherapy, psychoanalysis, behavior therapy, marital and family therapy. group psychotherapy, hypnotherapy, social-learning approaches, biofeedback techniques, and environmental consultation and design.

C. Professional consultation in relation to A and B above.

D. Program development services in the areas of A. B, and C above.

E. Supervision of clinical psychological services.

F. Evaluation of all services noted in A through E above.

A *clinical psychological service* unit is the functional unit through which clinical psychological services are provided; such a unit may be part of a larger psychological service organization comprising psychologists of more than one specialty and headed by a professional psychologist:

A. A clinical psychological service unit provides predominantly clinical psychological services and is composed of one or more professional clinical psychologists and supporting staff.

B. A clinical psychological service unit may operate as a professional service or as a functional or geographic component of a larger multipsychological service unit or of a governmental, educational, correctional, health, training, industrial, or commercial organizational unit.[6]

C. One or more clinical psychologists providing professional services in a multidisciplinary setting constitute a clinical psychological service unit.

D. A clinical psychological service unit may also be one or more clinical psychologists in a private practice or a psychological consulting firm.

Users of clinical psychological services include:

A. Direct users or recipients of clinical psychological services.

B. Public and private institutions, facilities, or organizations receiving clinical psychological services.

C. Third-party purchasers—those who pay for the delivery of services but who are not the recipients of services.

D. Sanctioners—those who have a legitimate concern with the accessibility, timeliness, efficacy, and standards of quality attending the provision of clinical psychological services. Sanctioners may include members of the users family, the court, the probation officer, the school administrator, the employer, the union representative, the facility director, and so on. Sanctioners may also include various governmental, peer review, and accreditation bodies concerned with the assurance of quality.

Guideline 1
PROVIDERS

1.1 *Each clinical psychological service unit offering psychological services has available at least one professional clinical psychologist and as many more professional clinical psychologists as are necessary to assure the adequacy and quality of services offered.*

INTERPRETATION: The intent of this Guideline is that one or more providers of psychological services in any clinical psychological service unit meet the levels of training and experience of the professional clinical psychologist as specified in the preceding definitions.[7]

When a facility offering clinical psychological services does not have a full-time professional clinical psychologist available, the facility retains the services of one or more professional clinical psychologists on a regular part-time basis. The clinical psychologist so retained directs and supervises the psychological services provided, participates sufficiently to bet able to assess the need for services, reviews the content of services provided, and has the authority to assume professional responsibility and accountability for them.

The psychologist directing the service unit is responsible for determining and justifying appropriate ratios of psychologists to users and psychologists to support staff, in order to ensure proper scope, accessibility, and quality of services provided in that setting.

1.2 P*roviders of clinical psychological services who do not meet the requirements for the professional clinical psychologist are supervised directly by a professional clinical psychologist who assumes professional responsibility and accountability for the services provided. The level and extent of supervision may vary from task to task so long as the supervising psychologist retains a sufficiently close supervisory relationship to meet this guideline. Special proficiency training or supervision maybe provided by a professional psychologist of another specialty or by a professional from another discipline whose competence in the given area has been demonstrated by previous training and experience.*

INTERPRETATION: In each clinical psychological service unit there may be varying levels of responsibility with respect to the nature and quality of services provided. Support personnel are considered to be responsible for their functions and behavior when assisting in the provision of clinical psychological services and are accountable to the professional clinical psychologist. Ultimate professional responsibility and accountability for the services provided require that the supervisor review and approve reports and test protocols, review and approve intervention plans and strategies, and review outcomes. Therefore, the supervision of all clinical psychological services is provided directly by a professional clinical psychologist in individual and/or group face-to-face meetings.

In order to meet this Guideline, an appropriate number of hours per week are devoted to direct face-to-face supervision of each clinical psychological service unit staff member. In no event is such supervision less than 1 hour per week. The more comprehensive the psychological services are, the more supervision is needed. A plan or formula for relating increasing amounts of supervisory time to the complexity of professional responsibilities is to be developed. The amount and nature of supervision is made known to all parties concerned.

Such communications are in writing and describe and delineate the duties of the employee with respect to range and type of services to be provided. The limits of independent action and decision making are defined. The description of responsibility also specifies the means by which the employee will contact the professional clinical psychologist in the event of emergency or crisis situations.

1.3 *Wherever a clinical psychological service unit exists, a professional clinical psychologist I. responsible for planning, directing, and reviewing the provision of clinical psychological services. Whenever the clinical psychological service unit is part of a larger professional psychological service encompassing various psychological specialties, a professional psychologist is the administrative head of the service.*

INTERPRETATION: The clinical psychologist coordinates the activities of the clinical psychological service unit with other professional, administrative, and technical groups, both within and outside the facility. This clinical psychologist, who may be the director, chief, or coordinator of the clinical psychological service unit, has related responsibilities including, but not limited to, recruiting qualified staff, directing training and research activities of the service, maintaining a high level of professional and ethical practice, and ensuring that staff members function only within the areas of their competency.

To facilitate the effectiveness of clinical services by raising the level of staff sensitivity and professional skills, the clinical psychologist designated as director is responsible for participating in the selection of staff and support personnel whose qualifications and skills (e.g., language, cultural and experiential background, race, sex, and age) are directly relevant to the needs and characteristics of the users served.

1.4 *When functioning as part of an organizational setting, professional clinical psychologists bring their backgrounds and skills to bear on the goals of the organization, whenever appropriate, by participation in the planning and development of overall services.*[8]

INTERPRETATION: Professional clinical psychologists participate in the maintenance of high professional standards by representation on committees concerned with service delivery.

As appropriate to the setting, their activities may include active participation, as voting and as office-holding members, on the professional staffs of hospitals and other facilities and on other executive, planning, and evaluation boards and committees.

1.5 *Clinical psychologists maintain current knowledge of scientific and professional developments to preserve and enhance their professional competence.*[9]

INTERPRETATION: Methods through which knowledge of scientific and professional developments may be gained include, but are not limited to, reading scientific and professional publications, attendance at workshops, participation in staff development programs, and other forms of continuing education. The clinical psychologist has ready access to reference material related to the provision of psychological services. Clinical psychologists are prepared to show evidence periodically that they are staying abreast of current knowledge and practices in the field of clinical psychology through continuing education.

1.6 *Clinical psychologists limit their practice to their demonstrated areas of professional competence.*

INTERPRETATION: Clinical psychological services are offered in accordance with the providers areas of competence as defined by verifiable training and experience. When extending services beyond the range of their usual practice, psychologists obtain pertinent training or appropriate professional supervision. Such training or supervision is consistent with the extension of functions performed and services provided. An extension of services may involve a change in the theoretical orientation of the clinical psychologist, a change in modality or technique, or a change in the type of client and/or the kinds of problems or disorders for which services are to be provided (e.g., children, elderly persons, mental retardation, neurological impairment).

1.7 *Professional psychologists who wish to qualify as clinical psychologists meet the same requirements with respect to subject matter and professional skills that apply to doctoral and postdoctoral education and training in clinical psychology.*[10]

INTERPRETATION: Education of doctoral-level psychologists to qualify them for specialty practice in clinical psychology is under the auspices of a department in a regionally accredited university or of a professional school that offers the doctoral degree in clinical psychology. Such education is individualized, with due credit being given for relevant course work and other requirements that have previously been satisfied. In addition, doctoral-level training plus 1 year of postdoctoral experience supervised by a clinical psychologist is required. Merely taking an internship in clinical psychology or acquiring experience in a practicum setting is not adequate preparation for becoming a clinical psychologist when prior education has not been in that area. Fulfillment of such an individualized educational program is attested to by the awarding of a certificate by the supervising department or professional school that indicates the successful completion of preparation in clinical psychology.

1.8 *Professional clinical psychologists are encouraged to develop innovative theories and procedures and to provide appropriate theoretical and/or empirical support for their innovations.*

INTERPRETATION: A specialty of a profession rooted in a science intends continually to explore and experiment with a view to developing and verifying new and improved methods of serving the public in ways that can be documented.

Guideline 2
PROGRAMS

2.1 *Composition and organization of a clinical psychological service unit:*

2.1.1 *The composition and programs of a clinical psychological service unit are responsive to the needs of the persons or settings served.*

INTERPRETATION: A clinical psychological service unit is structured so as to facilitate effective and economical delivery of services. For example, a clinical psychological service unit serving predominantly a low-income, ethnic, or racial minority group has a staffing pattern and service programs that are adapted to the linguistic, experiential, and attitudinal characteristics of the users.

2.1.2 *A description of the organization of the clinical psychological service unit and its lines of responsibility and accountability for the delivery of psychological services is available in written form to staff of the unit and to users and sanctioners upon request.*

INTERPRETATION: The description includes lines of responsibility, supervisory relationships, and the level and extent of accountability for each person who provides psychological services.

2.1.3 *A clinical psychological service unit includes sufficient numbers of professional and support personnel to achieve its goals, objectives, and purposes.*

INTERPRETATION: The work load and diversity of psychological services required and the specific goals and objectives of the setting determine the numbers and qualifications of professional and support personnel in the clinical psychological service unit. Where shortages in personnel exist, so that psychological services cannot be rendered in a professional manner, the director of the clinical psychological service unit initiates action to remedy such shortages. When this fails, the director appropriately modifies the scope or work load of the unit to maintain the quality of the services rendered.

2.2 *Policies:*

2.2.1 *When the clinical psychological service unit is composed of more than one person or is a component of a larger organization, a written statement of its objectives and scope of services is developed, maintained, and reviewed.*

INTERPRETATION: The clinical psychological service unit reviews its objectives and scope of services annually and revises them as necessary to ensure that the psychological services offered are consistent with staff competencies and current psychological knowledge and practice. This statement is discussed with staff, reviewed with the appropriate administrator, and distributed to users and sanctioners upon request, whenever appropriate.

> 2.2.2 *All providers within a clinical psychological service unit support the legal and civil rights of the users.*[11]

INTERPRETATION: Providers of clinical psychological services safeguard the interests of the users with regard to personal, legal, and civil rights. They are continually sensitive to the issue of confidentiality of information, the short-term and long-term impacts of their decisions and recommendations, and other matters pertaining to individual, legal, and civil rights. Concerns regarding the safeguarding of individual rights of users include, but are not limited to, problems of self-incrimination in judicial proceedings, involuntary commitment to hospitals, protection of minors or legal incompetents, discriminatory practices in employment selection procedures, recommendation for special education provisions, information relative to adverse personnel actions in the armed services, and adjudication of domestic relations disputes in divorce and custodial proceedings. Providers of clinical psychological services take affirmative action by making themselves available to local committees, review boards, and similar advisory groups established to safeguard the human, civil, and legal rights of service users.

> 2.2.3 *All providers within a clinical psychological service unit are familiar with and adhere to the American Psychological Associations Standards for Providers of Psychological Services, Ethical Principles of Psychologists, Standards for Educational and Psychological Tests, Ethical Principles in the Conduct of Research With Human Participants, and other official policy statements relevant to standards for professional services issued by the Association.*

INTERPRETATION: Providers of clinical psychological services maintain up-to-date knowledge of the relevant standards of the American Psychological Association.

> 2.2.4 *All providers within a clinical psychological service unit conform to relevant statutes established by federal, state, and local governments.*

INTERPRETATION: All providers of clinical psychological services are familiar with appropriate statutes regulating the practice of psychology. They observe agency regulations that have the force of law and that relate to the delivery of psychological services (e.g., evaluation for disability retirement and special education placements). In addition, all providers are cognizant that federal agencies such as the Veterans Administration, the Department of Education, and the Department of Health and Human Services have policy statements regarding psychological services, and where relevant, providers conform to them. Providers of clinical psychological services are also familiar with other statutes and regulations, including those addressed to the civil and legal rights of users (e.g., those promulgated by the federal Equal Employment Opportunity Commission), that are pertinent to their scope of practice.

It is the responsibility of the American Psychological Association to maintain current files of those federal policies, statutes, and regulations relating to this section and to assist its members in obtaining them. The state psychological associations and the state licensing boards periodically publish and distribute appropriate state statutes and regulations.

> 2.2.5 *All providers within a clinical psychological service unit inform themselves about and use the network of human services in their communities in order to link users with relevant services and resources.*

INTERPRETATION: Clinical psychologists and support staff are sensitive to the broader context of human needs. In recognizing the matrix of personal and societal problems, providers make available to users information regarding human services such as legal aid societies, social services, employment agencies, health resources, and educational and recreational facilities. Providers of clinical psychological services refer to such community resources and, when indicated, actively intervene on behalf of the users.

Community resources include the private as well as the public sectors. Private resources include private agencies and centers and psychologists in independent private practice. Consultation is sought or referral made within the public or private network of services whenever required in the best interest of the users. Clinical psychologists, in either the private or the public setting, utilize other resources in the community whenever indicated because of limitations within the psychological service unit providing the services. Professional clinical psychologists in private practice are familiar with the types of services offered through local community mental health clinical and centers, including alternatives to hospitalization, and know the costs and eligibility requirements for those services.

> 2.2.6 *In the delivery of clinical psychological services, the providers maintain a cooperative relationship with colleagues and co-workers in the best interest of the users.*[12]

INTERPRETATION: Clinical psychologists recognize the areas of special competence of other professional psychologists and of professionals in other fields for either consultation or referral purposes. Providers of clinical psychological services make appropriate use of other professional, research, technical, and administrative resources to serve the best interests of users and establish and maintain cooperative arrangements with such other resources as required to meet the needs of users.

2.3 *Procedures:*

> 2.3.1 *Each clinical psychological service unit follows a set of procedural guidelines for the delivery of psychological services.*

INTERPRETATION: Providers are prepared to provide a statement of procedural guidelines, in either oral or written form, in terms that can be understood by users, including sanctioners and local administrators. This statement describes the current methods, forms, procedures and techniques being used to achieve the objectives and goals for psychological services.

2.3.2 *Providers of clinical psychological services develop plans appropriate to the providers professional practices and to the problems presented by the users.*

INTERPRETATION: A clinical psychologist develops a plan that describes the psychological services, their objectives, and the manner in which they will be provided.[13,14] This plan is in written form; it serves as a basis for obtaining understanding and concurrence from the user and provides a mechanism for subsequent peer review. This plan is, of course, modified as new needs or information develops.

A clinical psychologist who provides services as one member of a collaborative effort participates in the development and implementation of the overall service plan and provides for its periodic review.

2.3.3 *Accurate, current, and pertinent documentation of essential clinical psychological services provided is maintained.*

INTERPRETATION: Records kept of clinical psychological services may include, but are not limited to, identifying data, dates of services, types of services, significant actions taken, and outcome at termination. Providers of clinical psychological services ensure that essential information concerning services rendered is recorded within a reasonable time following their completion

2.3.4 *Each clinical psychological service unit follows an established record retention and disposition policy.*

INTERPRETATION: The policy on record retention and disposition conforms to federal or state statutes or administrative regulations where such are applicable. In the absence of such regulations, the policy is (a) that the full record be retained intact for 3 years after the completion of planned services or after the date of last contact with the user, whichever is later; (b) that a full record or summary of the record be maintained for an additional 12 years; and (c) that the record may be disposed of no sooner than 15 years after the completion of planned services or after the date of the last contact, whichever is later. These temporal guides are consistent with procedures currently in use by federal record centers.

In the event of the death or incapacity of a clinical psychologist in independent practice, special procedures are necessary to ensure the continuity of active services to users and the proper safeguarding of inactive records being retained to meet this Guideline. Following approval by the affected user, it is appropriate for another clinical psychologist, acting under the auspices of the local professional standards review committee (PSRC), to review the records with the user and recommend a course of action for continuing professional service, if needed. Depending on local circumstances, the reviewing psychologist may also recommend appropriate arrangements for the balance of the record retention and disposition period.

This Guideline has been designed to meet a variety of circumstances that may arise, often years after a set of psychological services has been completed. More and more records are being used in forensic matters, for peer review, and in response to requests from users, other professionals, or other legitimate parties requiring accurate information about the exact dates, nature, course, and outcome of a set of psychological services. These record retention procedures also provide valuable baseline data for the original psychologist—provider when a previous user returns for additional services.

    2.3.5 *Providers of clinical psychological services maintain a system to protect confidentiality of their records.*[15]

INTERPRETATION: Clinical psychologists are responsible for maintaining the confidentiality of information about users of services, from whatever source derived. All persons supervised by clinical psychologists, including nonprofessional personnel and students, who have access to records of psychological services are required to maintain this confidentiality as a condition of employment.

    The clinical psychologist does not release confidential information, except with the written consent of the user directly involved or his or her legal representative. Even after consent for release has been obtained, the clinical psychologist clearly identifies such information as confidential to the recipient of the information.[16] If directed otherwise by statute or regulations with the force of law or by court order, the psychologist may seek a resolution to the conflict that is both ethically and legally feasible and appropriate.

    Users are informed in advance of any limits in the setting for maintenance of confidentiality of psychological information. For instance, clinical psychologists in hospital, clinic, or agency settings inform their patients that psychological information in a patient's clinical record may be available without the patient's written consent to other members of the professional staff associated with the patients treatment or rehabilitation. Similar limitations on confidentiality of psychological information may be present in certain school, industrial, military, or other institutional settings, or in instances in which the user has waived confidentiality for purposes of third-party payment.

    Users have the right to obtain information from their psychological records. However, the records are the property of the psychologist or the facility in which the psychologist works and are, therefore, the responsibility of the psychologist and subject to his or her control.

    When the user's intention to waive confidentiality is judged by the professional clinical psychologist to be contrary to the user's best interests or to be in conflict with the user's civil and legal rights, it is the responsibility of the clinical psychologist to discuss the implications of releasing psychological information and to assist the user in limiting disclosure only to information required by the present circumstance.

    Raw psychological data (e.g., questionnaire returns or test protocols) in which a user is identified are released only with the written consent of the user or his or her legal representative and released only to a person recognized by the clinical psychologist as qualified and competent to use the data.

    Any use made of psychological reports, records, or data for research or training purposes is consistent with this Guideline. Additionally, providers of clinical psychological services comply with statutory confidentiality requirements and those embodied in the American Psychological Association's Ethical Principles of Psychologists (APA, 1981b).

    Providers of clinical psychological services remain sensitive to both the benefits and the possible misuse of information regarding individuals that is stored in large computerized data banks. Providers use their influence to ensure that such information is used in a socially responsible manner.

Guideline 3
ACCOUNTABILITY

3.1 *The clinical psychologist's professional activity is guided primarily by the principle of promoting human welfare.*

INTERPRETATION: Clinical psychologists provide services to users in a manner that is considerate, effective, economical, and humane. Clinical psychologists make their services readily accessible to users in a manner that facilitates the users' freedom of choice.

Clinical psychologists are mindful of their accountability to the sanctioners of clinical psychological services and to the general public, provided that appropriate steps are taken to protect the confidentiality of the service relationship. In the pursuit of their professional activities, they aid in the conservation of human, material, and financial resources.

The clinical psychological service unit does not withhold services to a potential client on the basis of that user's race, color, religion, gender, sexual orientation, age, or national origin. Recognition is given, however, to the following considerations: the professional right of clinical psychologists to limit their practice to a specific category of users (e.g.. children, adolescents, women); the right and responsibility of clinical psychologists to withhold an assessment procedure when not validly applicable; and the right and responsibility of clinical psychologists to withhold evaluative, psychotherapeutic, counseling, or other services in specific instances in which their own limitations or client characteristics might impair the effectiveness of the relationship.[17,18] Clinical psychologists seek to ameliorate through peer review, consultation, or other personal therapeutic procedures those factors that inhibit the provision of services to particular users. When indicated services are not available, clinical psychologists take whatever action is appropriate to inform responsible persons and agencies of the lack of such services.

Clinical psychologists who find that psychological services are being provided in a manner that is discriminatory or exploitative to users and/or contrary to these Guidelines or to state or federal statutes take appropriate corrective action, which may include the refusal to provide services. When conflicts of interest arise, the clinical psychologist is guided in the resolution of differences by the principles set forth in the American Psychological Association's *Ethical Principles of Psychologists* (APA, 1981b) and "Guidelines for Conditions of Employment of Psychologists" (APA, 1972).

3.2 *Clinical psychologists pursue their activities as members of the independent, autonomous profession of psychology.*[19]

INTERPRETATION: Clinical psychologists, as members of an independent profession, are responsible both to the public and to their peers through established review mechanisms. Clinical psychologists are aware of the implications of their activities for the profession as a whole. They seek to eliminate discriminatory practices instituted for self-serving purposes that are not in the interest of the users (e.g., arbitrary requirements for referral and supervision by another profession). They are cognizant of their responsibilities for the development of the profession. They participate where possible in the training and career development of students and other providers, participate as appropriate in the training of paraprofessionals or other professionals, and integrate and supervise the implementation of their contributions within the structure established for delivering psychological services. Clinical psychologists facilitate the development of, and participate in, professional standards review mechanisms.[20]

Clinical psychologists seek to work with other professionals in a cooperative manner for the good of the users and the benefit of the general public. Clinical psychologists associated with multidisciplinary settings support the principle that members of each participating profession have equal rights and opportunities to share all privileges and responsibilities of full membership in hospital facilities or other human service facilities and to administer service programs in their respective areas of competence.

3.3 *There are periodic, systematic, and effective evaluations of clinical psychological services.*[21]

INTERPRETATION: When the clinical psychological service unit is a component of a larger organization, regular evaluation of progress in achieving goals is provided for in the service delivery plan, including consideration of the effectiveness of clinical psychological services relative to costs in terms of use of time and money and the availability of professional and support personnel.

Evaluation of the clinical psychological service delivery system is conducted internally and, when possible, under independent auspices as well. This evaluation includes an assessment of effectiveness (to determine what the service unit accomplished), efficiency (to determine the total costs of providing the services), continuity (to ensure that the services are appropriately linked to other human services), availability (to determine appropriate levels and distribution of services and personnel), accessibility (to ensure that the services are barrier free to users), and adequacy (to determine whether the services meet the identified needs for such services).

There is a periodic reexamination of review mechanisms to ensure that these attempts at public safeguards are effective and cost efficient and do not place unnecessary encumbrances on the providers or impose unnecessary additional expenses on users or sanctioners for services rendered.

3.4 *Clinical psychologists are accountable for all aspects of the services they provide and are responsive to those concerned with these services.*[22]

INTERPRETATION: In recognizing their responsibilities to users, and where appropriate and consistent with the users' legal rights and privileged communications, clinical psychologists make available information about, and provide opportunity to participate in, decisions concerning such issues as initiation, termination, continuation, modification, and evaluation of clinical psychological services.

Depending on the settings, accurate and full information is made available to prospective individual or organizational users regarding the qualifications of providers, the nature and extent of services offered, and where appropriate, financial and social costs.

Where appropriate, clinical psychologists inform users of their payment policies and their willingness to assist in obtaining reimbursement. Those who accept reimbursement from a third party are acquainted with the appropriate statutes and regulations and assist their users in understanding procedures for submitting claims and limits on confidentiality of claims information, in accordance with pertinent statutes.

Guideline 4
ENVIRONMENT

4.1 *Providers of clinical psychological services promote the development in the service setting of a physical, organizational, and social environment that facilitates optimal human functioning.*

INTERPRETATION: Federal, state, and local requirements for safety, health, and sanitation are observed.

As providers of services, clinical psychologists are concerned with the environment of their service unit, especially as it affects the quality of service, but also as it impinges on human functioning when the service unit is included in a larger context. Physical arrangements and organizational policies and procedures are conducive to the human dignity, self-respect, and optimal functioning of users and to the effective delivery of service. Attention is given to the comfort and the privacy of users. The atmosphere in which clinical psychological services are rendered is appropriate to the service and to the users, whether in an office, clinic, school, industrial organization, or other institutional setting.

FOOTNOTES

[1] The footnotes appended to these Specialty Guidelines represent an attempt to provide a coherent context of other policy statements of the Association regarding professional practice. The Guidelines extend these previous policy statements where necessary to reflect current concerns of the public and the profession.

[2] The following two categories of professional psychologists who met the criteria indicated below on or before the adoption of these Specialty Guidelines on January 31, 1980. are also considered clinical psychologists: Category 1—persons who completed (a) a doctoral degree program primarily psychological in content at a regionally accredited university or professional school and (b) 3 postdoctoral years of appropriate education, training, and experience in providing clinical psychological services as defined herein, including a minimum of 1 year in a clinical setting; Category 2—persons who on or before September 4, 1974. (a) completed a master's degree from a program primarily psychological in content at a regionally accredited university or professional school and (b) held a license or certificate in the state in which they practiced, conferred by a state board of psychological examiners, or the endorsement of the state psychological association through voluntary certification and who, in addition, prior to January 31, 1980. (c) obtained 5 post-master's years of appropriate education, training, and experience in providing clinical psychological services as defined herein, including a minimum of 2 years in a clinical setting.

After January 31, 1980, professional psychologists who wish to be recognized as professional clinical psychologists are referred to Guideline 1.7.

The definition of the professional clinical psychologist in these Guidelines does not contradict or supersede in any way the broader definition accorded the term *clinical psychologist* in the Federal Employees Health Benefits Program (see *Access to Psychologists and Optometrists Under Federal Health Benefits Program*, U.S. Senate Report No. 93-961, June 25, 1974.

[3] The areas of knowledge and training that are a part of the educational program for all professional psychologists have been presented in two APA documents. *Education and Credentialing in Psychology II* (APA. 1977a) and *Criteria for Accreditation of Doctoral Training Programs and Internships in Professional Psychology* (APA, 1979). There is consistency in the presentation of

core areas in the education and training of all professional psychologists. The description of education and training in these Guidelines is based primarily on the document *Education and Credentialing In Psychology II*. It is intended to indicate broad areas of required curriculum, with the expectation that training programs will undoubtedly want to interpret the specific content of these areas in different ways depending on the nature, philosophy, and intent of the programs.

[4] Functions and activities of psychologists relating to the teaching of psychology, the writing or editing of scholarly or scientific manuscripts, and the conduct of scientific research do not fall within the purview of these Guidelines.

[5] The definitions should be compared with the APA (1967) guidelines for state legislation (hereinafter referred to as state guidelines), which define psychologist and the practice of psychology as follows:

A person represents himself [or herself] to be a psychologist when he [or she] holds himself [or herself] out to the public by any title or description of services incorporating the words "psychology," "psychological." "psychologist," and/or offers to render or renders services as defined below to individuals, groups, organizations, or the public for a fee, monetary or otherwise.

The practice of psychology within the meaning of this act is defined as rendering to individuals, groups, organizations, or the public any psychological service involving the application of principles, methods, and procedures of understanding, predicting, and influencing behavior, such as the principles pertaining to learning, perception, motivation, thinking, emotions and interpersonal relationships; the methods and procedures of interviewing, counseling, and psychotherapy; of constructing, administering, and interpreting tests of mental abilities, aptitudes, interests, attitudes, personality characteristics, emotion, and motivation, and of assessing public opinion.

The application of said principles and methods includes, but is not restricted to: diagnosis, prevention, and amelioration of adjustment problems and emotional and mental disorders of individuals and groups; hypnosis, educational and vocational counseling; personnel selection and management; the evaluation and planning for effective work and learning situations; advertising and market research; and the resolution of interpersonal and social conflicts.

Psychotherapy within the meaning of this act means the use of learning, conditioning methods, and emotional reactions, in a professional relationship, to assist a person or persons to modify feelings, attitudes, and behavior which are intellectually, socially or emotionally maladjustive or ineffectual.

The practice of psychology shall be as defined above, any existing statute in the state of—to the contrary notwithstanding (APA, 1967, pp. 1098–1099)

[6] The relation of a psychological service unit to a larger facility or institution is also addressed indirectly in the APA (1972) "Guidelines for Conditions of Employment of Psychologists" (hereinafter referred to as CEP Guidelines), which emphasizes the roles, responsibilities, and prerogatives of the psychologist when he or the is employed by or provides services for another agency, institution, or business.

[7] This Guideline replaces earlier recommendations in the 1967 state guidelines concerning exemption of psychologists from licensure. Recommendations 8 and 9 of those guidelines read as follows:

Persons employed as psychologists by accredited academic institutions, governmental agencies, research laboratories, and business corporations should be exempted, provided such employees are performing those duties for which they are employed by such organizations, said within the confines of such organizations.

Persons employed as psychologists by accredited academic institutions, governmental agencies, research laboratories, and business corporations consulting or offering their research findings or providing scientific information to like organizations for a fee should be exempted. (APA, 1967, p. 1100)

On the other hand, the 1967 state guidelines specifically denied exemptions under certain conditions, as nosed in Recommendations 10 and 11:

Persons employed as psychologists who offer or provide psychological services to the public for a fee, over and above the salary that they receive for the performance of their regular duties, should not be exempted.

Persons employed as psychologists by organizations that sell psychological services to the public should not be exempted. (APA, 1967, pp. 1100–1101)

The present APA policy, as reflected in this Guideline, establishes a single code of practice for psychologists providing covered services to users in any setting. The present position is that a psychologist providing any covered service meets local statutory requirements for licensure or certification. See the section entitled Principles and Implications of the Specialty Guidelines for an elaboration of this position.

[8] A closely related principle is found in the APA (1972) CEP Guidelines.

It is the policy of APA that psychology as an independent profession is entitled to parity with other health and human service professions in institutional practices and before the law. Psychologists in interdisciplinary settings such as colleges and universities, medical schools, clinics, private practice groups, and other agencies expect parity with other professions in such matters as academic rank, board status, salaries, fringe benefits, fees. participation in administrative decisions, and all other conditions of employment, private contractual arrangements, and status before the law said legal institutions. (APA, 1972, p. 333)

[9] See CEP Guidelines (section entitled Career Development) for a closely related statement:

Psychologists are expected to encourage institutions and agencies which employ them to sponsor or conduct career development programs. The purpose to these programs would be to enable psychologists to engage in study for professional advancement and to keep abreast of developments in their held (APA, 1972. p. 332)

[10] This Guideline follows closely the statement regarding "Policy on Training for Psychologists Wishing to Change Their Specialty" adopted by the APA Council of Representatives in January 1976. Included therein was the implementing provision that "this policy statement shall be incorporated in the guidelines of the Committee on Accreditation so that appropriate sanctions can be brought to bear on university and internship training programs that violate [it]" (Conger, 1976, p 424).

[11] See also APA's (1981b) *Ethical Principles of Psychologists.* especially Principles 5 (Confidentiality), 6 (Welfare of the Consumer), and 9 (Research with Human Participants); and see *Ethical Principles in the Conduct of Research With Human Participants* (APA, 1973a). Also, in 1978 Division 17 approved in principle a statement on "Principles for Counseling and Psychotherapy With Women," which was designed to protect the interests of female users of clinical psychological services.

[12] Support for this position is found in *Psychology as a Profession* in the section on relations with other professions:

Professional persons have an obligation to know and take into account the traditions and practices of other professional groups with whom they work and to cooperate fully with members of such groups with whom research, service, and other functions are shared. (APA, 1968, p. 5)

[13] One example of a specific application of this principle is found in Guideline 2 in APA's (1973b) "Guidelines for Psychologists Conducting Growth Groups":

The following information should be made available in writing [italics added] to all prospective participants:

(a)   An explicit statement of the purpose of the group;

(b)   Types of techniques that may be employed;

(c)   The education, training, and experience of the leader or leaders;

(d)   The fee and any additional expense that may be incurred;

(e)   A statement as to whether or not a follow-up service is included in the fee;

(f)   Goals of the group experience and techniques to be used;

(g)   Amounts and kinds of responsibility to be assumed by the leader and by the participants. For example, (i) the degree to which a participant is free not to follow suggestions and prescriptions of the group leader and other group members, (ii) any restrictions on a participant's freedom to leave the group at any time; and

(h)   Issues of confidentiality. (p. 933)

[14] See APA's (1981a) *APA/CHAMPUS Outpatient Psychological Provider Manual.*

[15] See Principle 5 (Confidentiality) in *Ethical Principles of Psychologists* (APA, 1981b).

[16] Support for the principle of privileged communication is found in at least two policy statements of the Association.

In the interest of both the public and the client and in accordance with the requirements of good professional practice, the profession of psychology seeks recognition of the privileged nature of confidential communications with clients. preferably through statutory enactment or by administrative policy where more appropriate. (APA, 1968, p. 8)

Wherever possible, a clause protecting the privileged nature of the psychologist-client relationship be included.

When appropriate, psychologists assist in obtaining general across the board legislation for such privileged communications (APA, 1967,. p 1103)

[17] This paragraph is directly adapted from the CEP Guidelines (APA, 1972, p. 333).

[18] The CEP Guidelines also include the following:

It is recognized that under certain circumstances, the interests and goals of a particular community or segment of interest in the population, may be in conflict with the general welfare. Under such circumstances, the psychologists professional activity must be primarily guided by the principle of "promoting human welfare." (APA, 1972, p. 334)

[19] Support for the principle of the independence of psychology as a profession is found in the following.

As a member of an autonomous profession, a psychologist rejects limitations upon his [or her] freedom of thought and action other than those imposed by his [or her] moral, legal, and social responsibilities. The Association is always prepared to provide appropriate assistance to any responsible member who becomes subjected to unreasonable limitations upon his [or her] opportunity to function as a practitioner, teacher, researcher, administrator, or consultant. The Association is always prepared to cooperate with any responsible professional organization in opposing any unreasonable limitations on the professional functions of the members of that organization.

This insistence upon professional autonomy has been upheld over the years by the affirmative actions of the courts and other public and private bodies in support of the right of the psychologist—and other professionals—to pursue those functions for which he [or she] is trained and qualified to perform. (APA, 1968, p. 9)

Organized psychology has the responsibility to define and develop its own profession, consistent with the general canons of science and with the public welfare.

Psychologists recognize that other professions and other groups will, from time to time, seek to define the roles and responsibilities of psychologists. The APA opposes such developments on the same principle that it is opposed to the psychological profession taking positions which would define the work and scope of responsibility of other duly recognized professions. (APA, 1972, p. 333)

[20] APA support for peer review is detailed in the following excerpt from the APA (1971) statement entitled "Psychology and National Health Care":

All professions participating in a national health plan should be directed to establish review mechanisms (or performance evaluations) that include not only peer review but active participation by persons representing the consumer. In situations where there are fiscal agents, they should also have representation when appropriate. (p. 1026)

[21] This Guideline on program evaluation is based directly on the following excerpts from two APA position papers:

The quality and availability of health services should be evaluated continuously by both consumers and health professionals. Research into the efficiency and effectiveness of the system should be conducted both internally and under in dependent auspices. (APA.1971, p. 1025)

The comprehensive community mental health center should devote an explicit portion of its budget to program evaluation. All centers should inculcate is their staff attention to and respect for research findings; the larger centers have an obligation to set a high priority on basic research and to give formal recognition to research as a legitimate part of the duties of staff members.

. . . Only through explicit appraisal of program effects can worthy approaches be retained and refined, ineffective ones dropped. Evaluative monitoring of program achievements may vary, of course, from the relatively informal to the systematic and quantitative, depending on the importance of the issue, the availability of resources, and the willingness of those responsible to take risks of substituting informed judgment for evidence. (Smith & Hobbs, 1966, pp. 21–22)

[22] See also the CEP Guidelines for the following statement: "A psychologist recognizes that . . . he [or she] alone is accountable for the consequences and effects of his [or her] services whether as teacher, researcher, or practitioner. This responsibility cannot be shared, delegated, or reduced" (APA, 1972. p. 334).

REFERENCES

American Psychological Association, Committee on Legislation. A model for state legislation affecting the practice of psychology. *American Psychologist*, 1967, 22, 1095–1103.

American Psychological Association. *Psychology as a profession.* Washington, DC: Author, 1968.

American Psychological Association, Psychology and national health care. *American Psychologist*, 1971, 26, 1025–1096.

American Psychological Association. Guidelines for conditions of employment of psychologists. *American Psychologist.* 1972, 27, 331–434.

American Psychological Association. *Ethical principles in the conduct of research with human participants.* Washington, DC: Author, 1973(a).

American Psychological Association. Guidelines for psychologists conducting growth groups. *American Psychologist*, 1973, 26, 933(b).

American Psychological Association. *Standards for educational and psychological tests.* Washington, DC: Author, 1974(a).

American Psychological Association. *Standards for providers of psychological services.* Washington, DC: Author, 1974(b).

American Psychological Association. *Education and credentialing in psychology II.* Report of a meeting, June 4–5 1977. Washington, DC: Author, 1977(a).

American Psychological Association. *Standards for providers of psychological services* (Rev. ed.). Washington, DC: Author, 1977(b).

American Psychological Association. *Criteria for accreditation of doctoral training programs and internships in professional psychology.* Washington, DC: Author, 1979 (amended 1980).

American Psychological Association. *APA/CHAMPUS outpatient psychological provider manual* (Rev. ed.). Washington, DC: Author, 1961(a).

American Psychological Association. *Ethical principles of psychologists* (Rev. ed.) Washington, DC: Author, 1981(b).

Conger, J. J. Proceedings of the American Psychological Association, Incorporated, for the year 1975: Minutes of the annual meeting of the Council of Representatives. *American Psychologist*, 1976, 31, 406–434.

Smith, M. B. & Hobbs N. *The community and the community mental health center.* Washington, DC: American Psychological Association, 1966.

Specialty Guidelines for the Delivery of Services
by Counseling Psychologists

These Specialty Guidelines were prepared by the APA Committee on Standards for Providers of Psychological Services (COSPOPS), chaired by Durand F. Jacobs, with the advice of the officers and committee chairpersons of the Division of Counseling Psychology (Division 17). Barbara A. Kirk and Milton Schwebel served successively as the counseling psychology representative of COSPOPS and Arthur Cantor and Richard Kuburg were the Central Office liaisons to the committee. Norman Kagan, Samuel H. Osipow, Carl E. Thoresen, and Allen E. Ivey served successively as Division 17 presidents.

The Specialty Guidelines that follow are based on the generic Standards for *Providers of Psychological Services* originally adopted by the American Psychological Association (APA) in September 1974 and revised in January 1977 (APA, 1974b, 1977b). Together with the generic *Standards*, these Specialty Guidelines state the official policy of the Association regarding delivery of services by counseling psychologists. Admission to the practice of psychology is regulated by state statute. It is the position of the Association that licensing be based on generic, and not on specialty, qualifications. Specialty guidelines serve the additional purpose of providing potential users and other interested groups with essential information about particular services available from the several specialties in professional psychology.

Professional psychology specialties have evolved [roan generic practice in psychology and are supported by university training programs. There are now at least four recognized professional specialties—clinical, counseling, school, and industrial/organizational psychology.

The knowledge base in each of these specialty areas has increased, refining the state of the art to the point that a set of uniform specialty guidelines is now possible and desirable. The present Guidelines are intended to educate the public, the profession, and other interested parties regarding specialty professional practices. They are also intended to facilitate the continued systematic development of the profession.

The content of each Specialty Guideline reflects a consensus of university faculty and public and private practitioners regarding the knowledge bass, services provided. problems addressed, and clients served.

Traditionally, all learned disciplines have treated the designation of specialty practice as a reflection of preparation in greater depth in a particular subject matter, together with a voluntary limiting of focus to a more restricted area of practice by the professional. Lack of specialty designation does not preclude general providers of psychological services from using the methods or dealing with the populations of any specialty, except insofar as psychologists voluntarily refrain from providing services they are not trained to render. It is the intent of these guidelines, however, that after the grandparenting period. Psychologists not put themselves forward as *specialists* in a given area of practice unless they meet the qualifications noted in the Guidelines (see Definitions). Therefore, these Guidelines are meant to apply only to those psychologists who voluntarily wish to be designated as *counseling psychologists*. They do not apply to other psychologists.

These Guidelines represent the professions best judgment of the conditions, credentials, and experience that contribute to competent professional practice. The APA strongly encourages, and plans to participate in, efforts to identify professional practitioner behaviors and job functions and to validate the relation between these and desired client outcomes. Thus, future revisions of these Guidelines will increasingly reflect the results of such efforts.

These Guidelines follow the format and, wherever applicable, the wording of the generic *Standards*.[1] (Note:Footnotes appear at the end of the Specialty Guidelines. See pp. 661–663.) The intent of these Guidelines is to improve the quality, effectiveness, and accessibility of psychological services. They are meant to provide guidance to providers, users, and sanctioners regarding the best judgment of the profession on these matters. Although the Specialty Guidelines have been derived from and are consistent with the generic *Standards*, they may be used as separate documents. However, *Standards for Providers of Psychological Services* (APA, 1977b) shall remain the basic policy statement and shall take precedence where there are questions of interpretation.

Professional psychology in general and counseling psychology as a specialty have labored long and diligently to codify a uniform set of guidelines for the delivery of services by counseling psychologists that would serve the respective needs of users, providers, third-party purchasers, and sanctioners of psychological services.

The Committee on Professional Standards, established by the APA in January 1980, is charged with keeping the generic *Standards* and the Specialty Guidelines responsive to the needs of the public and the profession. It is also charged with continually reviewing, modifying, and extending them progressively as the profession and the science of psychology develop new knowledge, improved methods, and additional modes of psychological services.

The Specialty Guidelines for the Delivery of Services by Counseling Psychologists that follow have been established by the APA as a means of self-regulation to protect the public interest. They guide the specialty practice of counseling psychology by specifying important areas of quality assurance and performance that contribute to the goal of facilitating more effective human functioning.

Principles and Implications of the Specialty Guidelines

These Specialty Guidelines emerged from and reaffirm the same basic principles that guided the development of the generic *Standards forProviders of Psychological Services* (APA, 1977b):

1. These Guidelines recognize that admission to the practice of psychology is regulated by state statute.

2. It is the intention of the APA that the generic *Standards* provide appropriate guidelines for statutory licensing of psychologists. In addition, although it is the position of the APA that licensing be generic and not in specialty areas, these Specialty Guidelines in counseling psychology provide an authoritative reference for use in credentialing specialty providers of counseling psychological services by such groups as divisions of the APA and state associations and by boards and agencies that find such criteria useful for quality assurance.

3. A uniform set of Specialty Guidelines governs the quality of services to all users of counseling psychological services in both the private and the public sectors. Those receiving counseling psychological services are protected by the same kinds of safeguards, irrespective of sector; these include constitutional guarantees, statutory regulation, peer review, consultation, record review, and supervision.

4. A uniform set of Specialty Guidelines governs counseling psychological service functions offered by counseling psychologists, regardless of setting or form of remuneration. All counseling psychologists in professional practice recognize and are responsive to a uniform set of Specialty Guidelines, just as they are guided by a common code of ethics.

5. Counseling psychology Guidelines establish clear, minimally acceptable levels of quality for covered counseling psychological service functions, regardless of the nature of the users, purchasers, or sanctioners of such covered services.

6. All persons providing counseling psychological services meet specified levels of training and experience that are consistent with, and appropriate to, the functions they perform. Counseling psychological services provided by persons who do not meet the APA qualifications for a professional counseling psychologist (see Definitions) are supervised by a professional counseling psychologist. Final responsibility and accountability for services provided rest with professional counseling psychologists.

7. When providing any of the covered counseling psychological service functions at any time and in any setting, whether public or private, profit or nonprofit, counseling psychologists observe these Guidelines in order to promote the best interests and welfare of the users of such services. The extent to which counseling psychologists observe these Guidelines is judged by peers.

8. These Guidelines, while assuring the user of the counseling psychologists accountability for the nature and quality of services specified in this document, do not preclude the counseling psychologist from using new methods or developing innovative procedures in the delivery of counseling services.

These Specialty Guidelines have broad implications bosh for users of counseling psychological services and or providers of such services:

1. Guidelines for counseling psychological services provide a foundation for mutual understanding between provider and user and facilitate more effective evaluation of services provided and outcomes achieved.

2. Guidelines for counseling psychologists are essential or uniformity in specialty credentialing of counseling psychologists.

3. Guidelines give specific content to the profession's concept of ethical practice as it applies to the functions of counseling psychologists.

4. Guidelines for counseling psychological services may have significant impact on tomorrow's education and training models for both professional and support personnel in counseling psychology.

5. Guidelines for the provision of counseling psychological services in human service facilities influence the determination of acceptable structure, budgeting, and staffing patterns in these facilities.

6. Guidelines for counseling psychological services require continual review and revision.

The Specialty Guidelines here presented are intended to improve the quality and delivery of counseling psychological services by specifying criteria for key aspects of the practice setting. Some settings may require additional and/or more stringent criteria for specific areas of service delivery.

Systematically applied. these Guidelines serve to establish a more effective and consistent basis for evaluating the performance of individual service providers as well as to guide the organization of counseling psychological service units in human service settings.

Definitions

Providers of counseling psychological services refers to two categories of persons who provide counseling psychological services:

A. Professional counseling psychologists.[2] Professional counseling psychologists have a doctoral degree from a regionally accredited university or professional school providing an organized, sequential counseling psychology program in an appropriate academic department in a university or college, or in an appropriate department or unit of a professional school. Counseling psychology programs that are accredited by the American Psychological Association are recognized as meeting the definition of a counseling psychology program. Counseling psychology programs that are not accredited by the American Psychological Association meet the definition of a counseling psychology program if they satisfy the following criteria:

1. The program is primarily psychological in nature and stands as a recognizable, coherent organizational entity within the institution.
2. The program providers an integrated, organized sequence of study.
3. The program has an identifiable body of students who are matriculated in that program for a degree.
4. There is a clear authority with primary responsibility for the core and specialty areas, whether or not the program cuts across administrative lines.
5. There is an identifiable psychology faculty, and a psychologist is responsible for the program.

The professional counseling psychologist's doctoral education and training experience[3] is defined by the institution offering the program. Only counseling psychologists, that is, those who meet the appropriate education and training requirements, have the minimum professional qualifications to provide unsupervised counseling psychological services. A professional counseling psychologist and others providing counseling psychological services under supervision (described below) form an integral part of a multilevel counseling psychological service delivery system.

B. All other persons who provide counseling psychological services under the supervision of a professional counseling psychologist. Although there may be variations in the titles of such persons, they are not referred to as counseling psychologists. Their functions may be indicated by use of the adjective *psychological* preceding the noun, for example, *psychological associate, psychological assistant, psychological technician*, or *psychological aide*.

Counseling psychological services refers to services provided by counseling psychologists that apply principles, methods, and procedures for facilitating effective functioning during the life-span developmental process.[4,5] In providing such services, counseling psychologists approach practice with a significant emphasis on positive aspects of growth and adjustment and with a developmental orientation. These services are intended—to help persons acquire or alter personal—social skills, improve adaptability to changing life demands, enhance environmental coping skills, and develop a variety of problem-solving and decision-making capabilities. Counseling psychological services are used by individuals, couples, and families of all age groups to cope with problems connected with education, career choice, work, sex, marriage, family, other social relations, health, aging, and handicaps of a social or physical nature. The services are offered in such organizations as educational, rehabilitation, and health institutions and in a variety of other public and private agencies committed to service in one or more of the problem areas cited above. Counseling psychological services include the following:

A. Assessment, evaluation, and diagnosis. Procedures may include, but are not limited to: behavioral observation, interviewing, and administering and interpreting instruments for the assessment of educational achievement, academic skills, aptitudes, interests, cognitive abilities, attitudes, emotions, motivations, psychoneurological status, personality characteristics, or any other aspect of human experience and behavior that may contribute to understanding and helping the user.

B. Interventions with individuals and groups Procedures include individual and group psychological counseling (e.g., education, career, couples, and family counseling) and may use a therapeutic, group process, or social-learning approach, or any other deemed to be appropriate. Interventions are used for purposes of prevention, remediation, and rehabilitation; they may incorporate a variety of psychological modalities, such as psychotherapy, behavior therapy, marital and family therapy, biofeedback techniques, and environmental design.

C. Professional consultation relating to A and B above, for example, in connection with developing in-service training for staff or assisting an educational institution or organization to design a plan to cope with persistent problems of its students.

D. Program development services in the areas of A, B, and C above, such as assisting a rehabilitation center to design a career-counseling program.

E. Supervision of all counseling psychological services, such as the review of assessment and intervention activities of staff.

F. Evaluation of all services noted in A through E above and research for the purpose of their improvement.

A *counseling psychological service unit* is the functional unit through which counseling psychological services are provided; such a unit may be part of a larger psychological service organization comprising psychologists of more than one specialty and headed by a professional psychologist:

A. A counseling psychological service unit provides predominantly counseling psychological services and is composed of one or more professional counseling psychologists and supporting staff.

B. A counseling psychological service unit may operate as a functional or geographic component of a larger multipsychological service unit or of a governmental, educational, correctional, health, training, industrial, or commercial organizational unit, or it may operate as an independent professional service.[6]

C. A counseling psychological service unit may take the form of one or more counseling psychologists providing professional services in a multidisciplinary setting

D. A counseling psychological service unit ma also sake the form of a private practice, composed of one or more counseling psychologists serving individuals or groups, or the form of a psychological consulting firm serving organizations and institutions.

Users of counseling psychological services include

A. Direct users or recipients of counseling psychological services.

B. Public and private institutions, facilities, or organizations receiving counseling psychological services.

C. Third-party purchasers—those who pay for the delivery of services but who are not the recipients of services.

D. Sanctioners—those who have a legitimate concern with the accessibility, timeliness, efficacy, and standards of quality attending the provision of counseling psychological services. Sanctioners may include members of the user's family, the court, the probation officer, the school administrator, the employer, the union representative, the facility director, and so on. Sanctioners may also include various governmental, peer review, and accreditation bodies concerned with the assurance of quality.

Guideline 1
PROVIDERS

1.1 *Each counseling psychological service unit offering psychological services has available at least one professional counseling psychologist and as many more professional counseling psychologists as are necessary to assists the adequacy and quality of services offered.*

INTERPRETATION: The Intent of this Guideline is that one or more providers of psychological services in any counseling psychological service unit meet the levels of training and experience of the professional counseling psychologist as specified in the preceding definitions.[7]

When a professional counseling psychologist is not available on a full-time basis, the facility retains the services of one or more professional counseling psychologists on a regular part-time basis. The counseling psychologist so retained directs the psychological services, including supervision of the support staff, has the authority and participates sufficiently to assess the need for services, reviews the content of services provided, and assumes professional responsibility and accountability for them.

The psychologist directing the service unit is responsible for determining and justifying appropriate ratios of psychologists to users and psychologists to support staff, in order to ensure proper scope, accessibility, and quality of services provided in that setting.

1.2 *Providers of counseling psychological services who do not meet the requirements for the professional counseling psychologist are supervised directly by a professional counseling psychologist who assumes professional responsibility and accountability for the services provided. The level and extent of supervision may vary from task to task so long as the supervising psychologist retains a sufficiently close supervisory relationship to meet this Guideline. Special proficiency training or supervision may be provided by a professional psychologist of another specialty or by a professional from another discipline whose competence in the given area has been demonstrated by previous training and experience.*

INTERPRETATION: In each counseling psychological service unit there may be varying levels of responsibility with respect to the nature and quality of services provided. Support personnel are considered to be responsible for their functions and behavior when assisting in the provision of counseling psychological services and are accountable to the professional counseling psychologist. Ultimate professional responsibility and accountability for the services provided require that the supervisor review reports and test protocols, and review and discuss intervention plans, strategies, and outcomes. Therefore, the supervision of all counseling psychological services is provided directly by a professional counseling psychologist in a face-to-face arrangement involving individual and/or group supervision. The extent of supervision is determined by the needs of the providers, but in no event is it less than 1 hour per week for each support staff member providing counseling psychological services.

To facilitate the effectiveness of the psychological service unit, the nature of the supervisory relationship is communicated to support personnel in writing. Such communications delineate the duties of the employees, describing the range and type of services to be provided. The limits of independent action and decision making are defined. The description of responsibility specifies the means by which the employee will contact the professional counseling psychologist in the event of emergency or crisis situations.

1.3 *Wherever a counseling psychological service unit exists, a professional counseling psychologist is responsible for planning, directing, and reviewing the provision of counseling psychological services. Whenever the counseling psychological service unit is part of a larger professional psychological service encompassing various psychological specialties, a professional psychologist shall be the administrative head of the service.*

INTERPRETATION: The counseling psychologist who directs or coordinates the unit is expected to maintain an ongoing or periodic review of the adequacy of services and to formulate plans in accordance with the results of such evaluation. He or the coordinates the activities of the counseling psychology unit with other professional, administrative, and technical groups, both within and outside the institution or agency. The counseling psychologist has related responsibilities including, but not limited to, directing the training and research activities of the service, maintaining a high level of professional and ethical practice, and ensuring that staff members function only within the areas of their competency.

To facilitate the effectiveness of counseling services by raising the level of staff sensitivity and professional skills, the counseling psychologist designated as director is responsible for participating in the selection of staff and support personnel whose qualifications and skills (e.g., language, cultural and experiential background, race, sex, and age) are relevant to the steeds and characteristics of the users served.

1.4 *When functioning as part of an organizational setting, professional counseling psychologists bring their back grounds and skills to bear on the goals of the organization, whenever appropriate, by participation in the planning and development of overall services.*[8]

INTERPRETATION: Professional counseling psychologists participate in the maintenance of high professional standards by representation on committees concerned with service delivery.

As appropriate to the setting, their activities may include active participation, as voting and as office-holding members, on the facility's professional staff and on other executive, planning, and evaluation boards and committees.

1.5 *Counseling psychologists maintain current knowledge of scientific and professional developments to preserve and enhance their professional competence.*

INTERPRETATION: Methods through which knowledge of scientific and professional developments may be gained include, but are not limited to, reading scientific and professional publications, attendance at professional workshops and meetings, participation in staff development programs, and other forms of continuing education.[9] The counseling psychologist has ready access to reference material related to the provision of psychological services. Counseling psychologists are prepared to show evidence periodically that they are staying abreast of current knowledge and practices in the field of counseling psychology through continuing education.

1.6 *Counseling Psychologists limit their practice to their demonstrated areas of professional competence.*

INTERPRETATION: Counseling psychological services are offered in accordance with the providers' areas of competence as defined by verifiable training and experience. When extending services beyond the range of their usual practice, counseling psychologists obtain pertinent training or appropriate professional supervision. Such training or supervision is consistent with the extension of functions performed and services provided. An extension of services may involve a change in the theoretical orientation of the counseling psychologist, in the modality or techniques used, in the type of client, or in the kinds of problems or disorders for which services are to be provided.

1.7 *Professional psychologists who wish to qualify as counseling psychologists meet the same requirements with respect to subject matter and professional skills that apply to doctoral education and training in counseling psychology.*[10]

INTERPRETATION: Education of doctoral-level psychologists to qualify them for specialty practice in counseling psychology is under the auspices of a department in a regionally accredited university or of a professional school that offers the doctoral degree in counseling psychology. Such education is individualized, with due credit being given for relevant course work and other requirements that have previously been satisfied, in addition, doctoral-level training supervised by a counseling psychologist is required. Merely taking an internship in counseling psychology or acquiring experience in a practicum setting is not adequate preparation for becoming a counseling psychologist when prior education has not been in that area. Fulfillment of such an individualized educational program is attested to by the awarding of a certificate by the supervising department or professional school that indicates the successful completion of preparation in counseling psychology.

1.8 *Professional counseling psychologists are encouraged to develop innovative theories and procedures and to provide appropriate theoretical and/or empirical support for their innovations.*

INTERPRETATION: A specialty of a profession rooted in a science intends continually to explore and experiment with a view to developing and verifying new and improved ways of serving the public and documents the innovations.

Guideline 2
PROGRAMS

2.1 *Composition and organization of a counseling psychological service unit.*

>   2.1.1 *The composition and programs of a counseling psychological service unit are responsive to the needs of the persons or settings served.*

INTERPRETATION: A counseling psychological service unit is structured so as to facilitate effective and economical delivery of services. For example, a counseling psychological service unit serving predominantly a low-income, ethnic, or racial minority group has a staffing pattern and service programs that are adapted to the linguistic, experiential, and attitudinal characteristics of the users.

>   2.1.2 *A description of the organization of the counseling psychological service unit and its lines of responsibility and accountability for the delivery of psychological services is available in written form to staff of the unit and to users and sanctioners upon request.*

INTERPRETATION: The description includes lines of responsibility, supervisory relationships, and the level and extent of accountability for each person who provides psychological services.

2.1.3 A counseling psychological service unit includes sufficient numbers of professional and support personnel to achieve its goals, objectives, and purposes.

INTERPRETATION: The work load and diversity of psychological services required and the specific goals and objectives of the setting determine the numbers and qualifications of professional and support personnel in the counseling psychological service unit. Where shortages in personnel exist, so that psychological services cannot be rendered in a professional manner, the director of the counseling psychological service unit initiates action to remedy such shortages. When this fails, the director appropriately modifies the scope or work load of the unit to maintain the quality of the services rendered and, at the same time, makes continued efforts to devise alternative systems for delivery of services.

2.2 Policies:

2.2.1 When the counseling psychological service unit is composed of more than one person or is a component of a larger organization, a written statement of its objectives and scope of services is developed, maintained, and reviewed.

INTERPRETATION: The counseling psychological service unit reviews its objectives and scope of services annually and revises them as necessary to ensure that the psychological services offered are consistent with staff competencies and current psychological knowledge and practice. This statement is discussed with staff, reviewed with the appropriate administrator, and distributed to users and sanctioners upon request, whenever appropriate.

2.2.2 All providers within a counseling psychological service unit support the legal and civil rights of the users.[11]

INTERPRETATION: Providers of counseling psychological services safeguard the interests of the users with regard to personal, legal, and civil rights. They are continually sensitive to the issue of confidentiality of information, the short-term and long-term impacts of their decisions and recommendations, and other matters pertaining to individual, legal, and civil rights. Concerns regarding the safeguarding of individual rights of users include, bus are not limited to, problems of access to professional records in educational institutions, self-incrimination in judicial proceedings, involuntary commitment to hospitals, protection of minors or legal incompetents discriminatory practices in employment selection procedures, recommendation for special education provisions, information relative to adverse personnel actions in the armed services, and adjudication of domestic relations disputes in divorce and custodial proceedings. Providers of counseling psychological services take affirmative action by making themselves available to local committees, review boards, and similar advisory groups established to safeguard the human, civil, and legal rights of service users.

2.2.3 All providers within a counseling psychological service unit are familiar with and adhere to the American Psychological Associations Standards for Providers of Psychological Services, Ethical Principles of Psychologists, Standards for

APPENDIXES

Educational and Psychological Tests, Ethical Principles in the Conduct of Research With Human Participants, and other official policy statements relevant to standards for professional services issued by the Association.

INTERPRETATION: Providers of counseling psychological services maintain current knowledge of relevant standards of the American Psychological Association.

2.2.4 *All providers within a counseling psychological service unit conform to relevant statutes established by federal, state, and local governments.*

INTERPRETATION: All providers of counseling psychological services are familiar with and conform to appropriate statutes regulating the practice of psychology. They also observe agency regulations that have the force of law and that relate to the delivery of psychological services (e.g., evaluation for disability retirement and special education placements). In addition, all providers are cognizant that federal agencies such as the Veterans Administration, the Department of Education, and the Department of Health and Human Services have policy statements regarding psychological services. Providers are familiar as well with other statutes and regulations, including those addressed to the civil and legal rights of users (e.g., those promulgated by the federal Equal Employment Opportunity Commission), that are pertinent to their scope of practice.

It is the responsibility of the American Psychological Association to maintain current files of those federal policies, statutes, and regulations relating to this section and to assist its members in obtaining them. The state psychological associations and the state licensing boards periodically publish and distribute appropriate state statutes and regulations, and these are on file in the counseling psychological service unit or the larger multipsychological service unit of which it is a part.

2.2.5 *All providers within a counseling psychological service unit inform themselves about and use the network of human services in their communities is order to link users with relevant services and resources.*

INTERPRETATION: Counseling psychologists and support staff are sensitive to the broader contest of human seeds in recognizing the matrix of personal and social problems, providers make available to clients information regarding human services such as legal aid societies, social services, employment agencies, health resources, and educational and recreational facilities. Providers of counselling psychological services refer to such community resources and when indicated, actively intervene on behalf of the users. Community resources include the private as well as the public sectors.

Consultation is sought or referral made within the public or private network of services whenever required in the best interest of the users. Counseling psychologists, in either the private or the public setting, utilize other resources in the community whenever indicated because of limitations within the psychological service unit providing the services. Professional counseling psychologists in private practice know the types of services offered through local community mental health clinics and centers, through family-service, career, and placement agencies. and through reading and other educational improvement centers and know the coats and the eligibility requirements for those services.

2.2.6 *In the delivery of counseling psychological services, the providers maintain a cooperative relationship with colleagues and co-workers in the best interest of the users.*[12]

INTERPRETATION: Counseling psychologists recognize the areas of special competence of other professional psychologists and of professionals in other fields for either consultation or referral purposes. Providers of counseling psychological services make appropriate use of other professional, research, technical, and administrative resources to serve the best interests of users and establish and maintain cooperative arrangements with such other resources as required to meet the needs of users.

2.3 *Procedures:*

2.3.1 *Each counseling psychological service unit is guided by a set of procedural guidelines for the delivery of psychological services.*

INTERPRETATION: Providers are prepared to provide a statement of procedural guidelines, in either oral or written form, in terms that can be understood by users, including sanctioners and local administrators. This statement describes the current methods, forms, procedures, and techniques being used to achieve the objectives and goals for psychological services.

2.3.2 *Providers of counseling psychological services develop plans appropriate to the providers professional practices and to the problems presented by the users.*

INTERPRETATION: A counseling psychologist, after initial assessment, develops a plan describing the objectives of the psychological services and the manner in which this will be provided.[13] To illustrate: The agreement spells out the objective (e.g., a career decision), the method (e.g., short-term counseling), the roles (e.g., active participation by the user as well as the provider), and the cost. This plan is in written form. It serves as a basis for obtaining understanding and concurrence from the user and for establishing accountability and provides a mechanism for subsequent peer review. This plan is, of course, modified as changing needs dictate.

A counseling psychologist who provides services as one member of a collaborative effort participates in the development, modification (if needed), and implementation of the overall service plan and provides for its periodic review

2.3.3 *Accurate, current, and pertinent documentation of essential counseling psychological services provided is maintained.*

INTERPRETATION: Records kept of counseling psychological services include, bus are not limited to, identifying data, dates of services, types of services, significant actions taken, and outcome at termination. Providers of counseling psychological services ensure that essential information concerning services rendered is recorded within a reasonable time following their completion.

2.3.4 *Each counseling psychological service unit follows an established record retention and disposition policy.*

INTERPRETATION: The policy on record retention and disposition conforms to state statutes or federal regulations where such are applicable. In the absence of such regulations, the policy is (a) that the full record be maintained intact for at least 4 years after the completion of planned services or after the date of last contact with the user, whichever is later; (b) that if a full record is not retained, a summary of the record be maintained for an additional 3 years; and (c) that the record may be disposed of no sooner than 7 years after the completion of planned services or after the date of last contact, whichever is later.

In the event of the death or incapacity of a counseling psychologist in independent practice, special procedures are necessary to ensure the continuity of active service to users and the proper safeguarding of records in accordance with this Guideline. Following approval by the affected user, it is appropriate for another counseling psychologist, acting under the auspices of the professional standards review committee (PSRC) of the state, to review the record with the user and recommend a course of action for continuing professional service, if needed. Depending on local circumstances, appropriate arrangements for record retention and disposition may also be recommended by the reviewing psychologist.

This Guideline has been designed to meet a variety of circumstances that may arise, often years after a set of psychological services has been completed. Increasingly, psychological records are being used in forensic matters, for peer review, and in response to requests from users, other professionals, and other legitimate parties requiring accurate information about the exact dates, nature, course, and outcome of a set of psychological services. The 4-year period for retention of the full record covers the period of either undergraduate or graduate study of most students in postsecondary educational institutions, and the 7-year period for retention of as least a summary of the record covers the period during which a previous user is most likely to return for counseling psychological services in an educational institution or other organization or agency.

> 2.3.5 *Providers of counseling psychological services maintain a system to protect confidentiality of their records.*[14]

INTERPRETATION: Counseling psychologists are responsible for maintaining the confidentiality of information about users of services, from whatever source derived. All persons supervised by counseling psychologists, including nonprofessional personnel and students, who have access to records of psychological services maintain this confidentiality as a condition of employment and/or supervision.

The counseling psychologist does not release confidential information, except with the written consent of the user directly involved or his or her legal representative. The only deviation from this rule is in the event of clear and imminent danger to, or involving, the user. Even after consent for release has been obtained, the counseling psychologist clearly identifies such information as confidential to the recipient of the information.[15] If directed otherwise by statute or regulations with the force of law or by court order, the psychologist seeks a resolution to the conflict that is both ethically and legally feasible and appropriate.

Users are informed in advance of any limits in the setting for maintenance of confidentiality of psychological information. For instance, counseling psychologists in agency, clinic, or hospital settings inform their clients that psychological information in a client's record may be available without the clients written consent to other members of the professional staff associated with service to the client. Similar limitations on confidentiality of psychological information may be present in certain educational, industrial, military, or other institutional settings, or in instances in which the user has waived confidentiality for purposes of third-party payment.

Users have the right to obtain information from their psychological records. However, the records are the property of the psychologist or the facility in which the psychologist works and are, therefore, the responsibility of the psychologist and subject to his or her control.

When the users intention to waive confidentiality is judged by the professional counseling psychologist to be contrary to the user's best interests or to be in conflict with the users civil and legal rights, it is the responsibility of the counseling psychologist to discuss the implications of releasing psychological information and to assist the user in limiting disclosure only to information required by the present circumstance.

Raw psychological data (e.g., questionnaire returns or test protocols) in which a user is identified are released only with the written consent of the user or his or her legal representative and released only to a person recognized by the counseling psychologist as qualified and competent to use the data.

Any use made of psychological reports, records, or data for research or training purposes is consistent with this Guideline. Additionally, providers of counseling psychological services comply with statutory confidentiality requirements and those embodied in the American Psychological Associations *Ethical Principles of Psychologists* (APA, 1981b).

Providers of counseling psychological services who use information about individuals that is stored in large computerized data banks are aware of the possible misuse of such data as well as the benefits and take necessary measures to ensure that such information is used in a socially responsible manner.

Guideline 3
ACCOUNTABILITY

3.1 *The promotion of human welfare is the primary principle guiding the professional activity of the counseling psychologist and the counseling psychological service unit.*

INTERPRETATION: Counseling psychologists provide services to users in a manner that is considerate, effective, economical, and humane. Counseling psychologists are responsible for making their services readily accessible to users in a manner that facilitates the users' freedom of choice.

Counseling psychologists are mindful of their accountability to the sanctioners of counseling psychological services and to the general public, provided that appropriate steps are taken to protect the confidentiality of the service relationship. In the pursuit of their professional activities, they aid in the conservation of human, material, and financial resources.

The counseling psychological service unit does not withhold services to a potential client on the basis of that user's race, color, religion, gender, sexual orientation, age, or national origin; nor does it provide services in a discriminatory or exploitative fashion. Counseling psychologists who find that psychological services are being provided in a manner that is discriminatory or exploit. alive to users and/or contrary to these Guidelines or to state or federal statutes take appropriate corrective action, which may include the refusal to provide services When conflicts of interest arise, the counseling psychologist is guided in the resolution of differences by the principles set forth in the American Psychological Association's *Ethical Principles of Psychologists* (APA, l981b) and "Guidelines for Conditions of Employment of Psychologists" (APA, 1972).[16]

Recognition is given to the following considerations in regard to the withholding of service: (a) the professional right of counseling psychologists to limit their practice to a specific category of users with whom they have achieved demonstrated competence (e.g., adolescents or families); (b) the right and responsibility of counseling psychologists to withhold an assessment procedure when not validly applicable; (c) the right and responsibility of counseling psychologists to withhold services in specific instances in which their own limitations or client characteristics might impair the quality of the services, (d) the obligation of counseling psychologists to seek to ameliorate through peer review, consultation, or other personal therapeutic procedures those factors that inhibit the provision of services to particular individuals; and (e) the obligation of counseling psychologists who withhold services to assist clients in obtaining services from other sources.[17]

3.2 *Counseling psychologists pursue their activities as members of the independent, autonomous profession of psychology.*[18]

INTERPRETATION: Counseling psychologists, as members of an independent profession, are responsible bosh to the public and to their peers through established review mechanisms. Counseling psychologists are aware of the implications of their activities for the profession as a whole. They seek to eliminate discriminatory practices instituted for self-serving purposes that are not in the interest of the users (e.g., arbitrary requirements for referral and supervision by another profession). They are cognizant of their responsibilities for the development of the profession, participate where possible in the training and career development of students and other providers, participate as appropriate in the training of paraprofessionals or other professionals, and integrate and supervise the implementation of their contributions within the structure established for delivering psychological services. Counseling psychologists facilitate the development of, and participate in, professional standards review mechanisms.[19]

Counseling psychologists seek to work with other professionals is a cooperative manner for the good of the users and the benefit of the general public. Counseling psychologists associated with multidisciplinary settings support the principle that members of each participating profession have equal rights and opportunities to share all privileges and responsibilities of full membership in human service facilities and to administer service programs in their respective areas of competence.

3.3 *There are periodic, systematic, and effective evaluations of counseling psychological services.*[20]

INTERPRETATION: When the counseling psychological service unit is a component of a larger organization, regular evaluation of progress in achieving goals is provided for in the service delivery plan, including consideration of the effectiveness of counseling psychological services relative to costs in terms of use of time and money and the availability of professional and support personnel.

Evaluation of the counseling psychological service delivery system is conducted internally and, when possible, under independent auspices as well. This evaluation includes an assessment of effectiveness (to determine what the service unit accomplished), efficiency (to determine the total costs of providing the services), continuity (to ensure that the services are appropriately linked to other human services), availability (to determine appropriate levels and distribution of services and personnel), accessibility (to ensure that the services are barrier free to users), and adequacy (to determine whether the services meet the identified needs for such services).

There is a periodic reexamination of review mechanisms to ensure that these attempts as public safeguards are effective and cost efficient and do not place unnecessary encumbrances on the providers or impose unnecessary additional expenses on users or sanctioners for services rendered.

3.4 *Counseling psychologists are accountable for all aspects of the services they provide and are responsive to those concerned with these services.*[21]

INTERPRETATION: In recognizing their responsibilities to users, sanctioners, third-party purchasers, and other providers, and where appropriate and consistent with the users legal rights and privileged communications, counseling psychologists make available information about, and provide opportunity to participate in, decisions concerning such issues as initiation, termination, continuation, modification, and evaluation of counseling psychological services.

Depending on the settings, accurate and full information is made available to prospective individual or organizational users regarding the qualifications of providers, the nature and extent of services offered, and where appropriate, financial and social costs.

Where appropriate, counseling psychologists inform users of their payment policies and their willingness to assist in obtaining reimbursement. To assist their users, those who accept reimbursement from a third party are acquainted with the appropriate statutes and regulations, the procedures for submitting claims, and the limits on confidentiality of claims information, in accordance with pertinent statutes.

Guideline 4
ENVIRONMENT

4.1 *Providers of counseling psychological services promote the development in the service setting of a physical, organizational, and social environment that facilitates optimal human functioning.*

INTERPRETATION: Federal, state, and local requirements for safety, health, and sanitation are observed.

As providers of services, counseling psychologists are concerned with the environment of their service unit, especially as it affects the quality of service, bus also as it impinges on human functioning in the larger context. Physical arrangements and organizational policies and procedures are conducive to the human dignity, self-respect, and optimal functioning of users and to the effective delivery of service. Attention is given to the comfort and the privacy of providers and users. The atmosphere in which counseling psychological services are rendered is appropriate to the service and to the users, whether in an office, clinic, school, college, university, hospital, industrial organization, or other institutional setting.

FOOTNOTES

[1] The footnotes appended to these Specialty Guidelines represent an attempt to provide a coherent contest of other policy statements of the Association regarding professional practice The Guidelines extend these previous policy statements where necessary to reflect current concerns of the public and the profession.

[2] The following two categories of professional psychologists who met the criteria indicated below on or before the adoption of these Specialty Guidelines on January 31, 1980, are also considered counseling psychologists: Category 1—persons who completed (a) a doctoral degree program primarily psychological in content as a regionally accredited university or professional school and (b) 3 postdoctoral years of appropriate education, training, and experience in providing counseling psychological services as defined herein, including a minimum of 5 year in a counseling setting; Category 2—persons who or or before September 4, 1974: (a) completed a masters degree from a program primarily psychological is consent at a regionally accredited university or professional school and (b) held a license or certificate in the state in which they practiced conferred by a state board of psychological examiners, or the endorsement of the state psychological association through voluntary certification, and who, in addition prior to January 31 1980, (c) obtained 5 post-master's years of appropriate education, training, and experience in providing counseling psychological services as defined herein, secluding a minimum of 2 years in a counseling setting.

After January 31, 1980. professional psychologists who with to be recognized as professional counseling psychologists are referred to Guideline 1.7.

[3] The areas of knowledge and training that are a part of the educational program for all professional psychologists have been presented in two APA documents, *Education and Credentialing in Psychology II (APA, 1977a) and Criteria for Accreditation of Doctoral Training Programs and Internships in Professional Psychology* (APA, 1979). There is consistency in the presentation of core areas in the education and training of all professional psychologists. The description of education and training in these Guidelines is based primarily on the document *Education and Credentialing in Psychology II*. It is intended to indicate broad areas of required curriculum, with the expectation that training programs will undoubtedly want to interpret the specific content of these areas in different ways depending on the nature, philosophy, and intent of the programs.

[4] Functions and activities of counseling psychologists relating to the teaching of psychology, the writing or editing of scholarly or scientific manuscripts, and the conduct of scientific research do not fall within the purview of these Guidelines.

[5] These definitions should be compared with the APA (1967) guidelines for state legislation (hereinafter referred to as state guidelines), which define *psychologist* (i.e. the generic professional psychologist, not the specialist counseling psychologist) and the *practice of psychology* as follows.

A person represents himself [or herself] to be a psychologist when he [or she] holds himself [or herself] I out to the public by any title or description of services incorporating the words "psychology", "psychological," "psychologist," and/or offers to render or renders services as defined below to individuals, groups, organizations, or the public for a fee, monetary or otherwise.

The practice of psychology within the meaning of this act is defined as rendering to individuals, groups, organizations, or the public any psychological service involving the application of principles, methods, and procedures of understanding, predicting, and influencing behavior, such as the principles pertaining to learning perception, motivation thinking, emotions, and interpersonal relationships, the methods and procedures of interviewing, counseling, and psychotherapy, of constructing, administering, and interpreting tests of mental abilities, aptitudes, interests, attitudes, personality characteristics, emotion, and motivation; and of assessing public opinion.

The application of said principles and methods includes, but is not restricted to: diagnosis, prevention, and amelioration of adjustment problems and emotional and mental disorders of individuals and groups; hypnosis; educational and vocational counseling; personnel selection and management; the evaluation and planning for effective work and learning situations, advertising and market research, and the resolution of interpersonal and social conflicts.

Psychotherapy within the meaning of this act means the use of learning, conditioning methods, and emotional reactions, in a professional relationship, to assist a person or persons to modify feelings, attitudes, and behavior which are intellectually, socially, or emotionally maladjustive or ineffectual.

The practice of psychology shall be as defined above, any existing statute in the state of _____ to the contrary notwithstanding (APA, 1967, pp. 1098–1099)

[6] The relation of a psychological service unit to a larger facility or institution is also addressed indirectly in the APA (1972) "Guidelines for Conditions of Employment of Psychologists" (hereinafter referred to as CEP Guidelines), which emphasize the roles responsibilities and prerogatives of the psychologist when he or the is employed by or provides services for another agency, institution, or business.

[7] This Guideline replaces earlier recommendations in the 1967 state guidelines concerning exemption of psychologists from licensure. Recommendations 8 and 9 of those guidelines read as follows:

Persons employed as psychologists by accredited academic institutions, governmental agencies, research laboratories, and business corporations should bet exempted, provided such employees are performing those duties for which they are employed by such organizations, and within the confines of such organizations.

Persons employed as psychologists by accredited academic institutions, governmental agencies, research laboratories, and business corporations consulting or offering their research findings or providing scientific information to *like organizations* for a fee should be exempted. (APA, 1967, p. 1100)

On the other hand, the 1967 state guidelines specifically denied exemptions under certain conditions as noted in Recommendations 10 and 11:

Persons employed as psychologists who offer or provide psychological services to the public for a fee, over and above the salary that they receive for the performance of their regular duties, should not be exempted.

Persons employed as psychologists by organizations that sell psychological services to the public should not be exempted. (APA, 1967, pp. 1100–1101)

The present APA policy, as reflected in this Guideline, establishes a single code of practice for psychologists providing covered services to users in any setting. The present position is that a psychologist providing any covered service meets local statutory requirements for licensure or certification. See the section entitled Principles and Implications of the Specialty Guidelines for further elaboration of this point.

[8] A closely related principle is found in the APA (1972) CEP Guidelines:

It is the policy of APA that psychology as an independent profession is entitled to parity with other health and human service professions in institutional practices and before the law.

Psychologists in interdisciplinary settings such as colleges and universities, medical schools, clinics, private practice groups, and other agencies expect parity with other professions in such matters as academic rank, board status, salaries, fringe benefits, fees, participation in administrative decisions, and all other conditions of employment, private contractual arrangements, and status before the law and legal institutions. (APA, 1972, p. 333).

[9] See CEP Guidelines (section entitled Career Development) for a closely related statement:

Psychologists are expected to encourage institutions and agencies which employ them to sponsor or conduct career development programs. The purpose of these programs would be to enable psychologists to engage in study for professional advancement and to keep abreast of developments in their field. (APA, 1972, p. 332)

[10] This Guideline follows closely the statement regarding "Policy on Training for Psychologists Wishing to Change Their Specialty" adopted by the APA Council of Representatives in January 1976. Included therein was the implementing provision that "this policy statement shall be incorporated in the guidelines of the Committee on Accreditation so that appropriate sanctions can be brought to bear on university and internship training programs that violate [it]" (Conger, 1976, p. 424).

[11] See also APAs (1981b) *Ethical Principles of Psychologists,* especially Principles 5 (Confidentiality), 6 (Welfare of the (Consumer), and 9 (Research With Human Participants), and *see Ethical Principles in the Conduct of Research With Human Participants* (APA, 1973a). Also, in 1978 Division 17 approved in principle a statement on "Principles for Counseling and Psychotherapy With Women," which was designed to protect the interests of female users of counseling psychological services.

[12] Support for this position is found in the section on relations with other professions in *Psychology as a Profession*:

Professional persons have an obligation to know and take into account the traditions and practices of other professional groups with whom they work and to cooperate fully with members of such groups with whom research, service, and other functions are shared. (APA, 1968, p. 5)

[13] One example of a specific application of this principle is found in APA's (1981a) revised *APA/CHAMPUS Outpatient Psychological Provider Manual*. Another example, quoted below, is found in Guideline 2 in APA's (1973b) "Guidelines for Psychologists Conducting Growth Groups":

The following information should be made available in writing (italics added) to all prospective participants.

(a) An explicit statement of the purpose of the group;

(b) Types of techniques that may be employed;

(c) The education, training, and experience of the leader or leaders;

(d) The fee and any additional expense that may be incurred;

(e) A statement as to whether or not a follow-up service is included in the fee,

(f) Goals of the group experience and techniques to be used;

(g) Amounts and kinds of responsibility to be assumed by the leader and by the participants. For example, (i) the degree to which a participant is free not to follow suggestions and prescriptions of the group leader and other group members (ii) any restrictions on a participant's freedom to leave the group at any time; and

(h) issues of confidentiality. (p. 933)

[14] See Principle 5 (Confidentiality) in *Ethical Principles of Psychologists* (APA, 1981b).

[15] Support for the principles of privileged communication is found in as least two policy statements of the Association:

In the interest of both the public and the client and in accordance with the requirements of good professional practice, the profession of psychology seeks recognition of the privileged nature of confidential communications with clients, preferably through statutory enactment or by administrative policy where more appropriate. (APA, 1968, p. 8)

Wherever possible, a clause protecting the privileged nature of the psychologist-client relationship be included.

When appropriate, psychologists assist in obtaining general "across the board" legislation for such privileged communications. (APA, 1967, p. 1103)

[16] The GEP Guidelines include the following:

It is recognized that under certain circumstances, the interests and goals of a particular community or segment of interest in the population may be in conflict with the general welfare. Under such circumstances, the psychologist's professional activity must be primarily guided by the principle of promoting human welfare." (APA, 1972, p. 334)

[17] This paragraph is adapted in pert from the CEP Guidelines (APA, 1972, p. 333)

[18] Support for the principle of the independence of psychology as a profession is found in the following

As a member of an autonomous profession, a psychologist rejects limitations upon his [or her] freedom of thought and action other than those imposed by his for heel moral, legal, and social responsibilities. The Association is always prepared to provide appropriate assistance to any responsible member who becomes subjected to unreasonable limitations upon his [or her] opportunity to function as a practitioner teacher, researcher, administrator, or consultant. The Association is always prepared to cooperate with any responsible professional organization in opposing any unreasonable limitations on the professional functions of the members of that organization.

This insistence upon professional autonomy has been upheld over the years by the affirmative actions of the courts and other public and private bodies in support of the right of the psychologist—and other professionals—to pursue those functions for which he [or she] is trained and qualified to perform. (APA, 1968, p. 9)

Organized psychology has the responsibility to define and develop its own profession, consistent with the general canons of science and with the public welfare.

Psychologists recognize that other professions and other groups will, from time to time, seek to define the roles and responsibilities of psychologists. The APA opposes such developments on the same principle that it is opposed to the psychological profession taking positions which would define the work and scope of responsibility of other duly recognized professions. (APA, 1972, p. 333)

[19] APA support for peer review is detailed in the following excerpt from the APA (1971) statement entitled "Psychology and National Health Care":

All professions participating in a national health plan should be directed to establish review mechanisms (or performance evaluations) that include not only peer review but active participation by persons representing the consumer. In situations where there are fiscal agents, they should also have representation when appropriate. (p. 1026)

[20] This Guideline on program evaluation is based directly on the following excerpts from two APA position papers:

The quality and availability of health services should be evaluated continuously by both consumers and health professionals. Research into the efficiency and effectiveness of the system should be conducted both internally and under independent auspices (APA, 1971, p. 1025)

The comprehensive community mental health center should devote an explicit portion of its budget to program evaluation. All centers should inculcate in their staff attention to and respect for research findings; the larger centers have an obligation to set a high priority on basic research and to give formal recognition to research as a legitimate part of the duties of staff members

. . . Only through explicit appraisal of program effects can worthy approaches be retained and refined, ineffective ones dropped. Evaluative monitoring of program achievements may vary, of course, from the relatively informal to the systematic and quantitative, depending on the importance of the issue, the availability of resources, and the willingness of those responsible to take risks of substituting informed judgment for evidence. (Smith & Hobbs, 1966, pp. 21–22)

[21] See also the CEP Guidelines for the following statement: "A psychologist recognizes that . . . he [or she] alone is accountable for the consequences and effects of his [or her] services, whether as teacher, researcher, or practitioner. This responsibility cannot be shared, delegated, or reduced" (APA, 1972, p. 334)

REFERENCES

American Psychological Association, Committee on Legislation. A model for state legislation affecting the practice of psychology. *American Psychologist*, 1967, 22, 1095–1103.

American Psychological Association. *Psychology as a profession*. Washington, D.C.: Author, 1968.

American Psychological Association. Psychology and national health care. *American Psychologist*, 1971, 26, 1025–1026.

American Psychological Association. Guidelines for conditions of employment of psychologists. *American Psychologist*, 1972, 27, 331–334.

American Psychological Association. *Ethical principles in the conduct of research with human participants*. Washington, D.C.: Author, 1973(a).

American Psychological Association. Guidelines for psychologists conducting growth groups. *American Psychologist,* 1973, 28, 963(b).

American Psychological Association. *Standards for educational and psychological tests*. Washington, D.C.: Author, 1974(a).

American Psychological Association. *Standards for providers of psychological services*. Washington, D.C.: Author, 1974(b).

American Psychological Association *Education and credentialing in psychology II*. Report of a meeting, June 4–5, 1977. Washington, D.C.: Author, 1977(a).

American Psychological Association. *Standards for providers of psychological services* (Rev. ed.). Washington, D.C.: Author, 1977(b).

American Psychological Association. *Criteria for accreditation of doctoral training programs and internships in professional psychology*. Washington, D.C.: Author, 1979 (amended 1980).

American Psychological Association. *APA/CHAMPUS outpatient psychological provider manual* (Rev. ed.). Washington, D.C.: Author, 1981(a).

American Psychological Association. *Ethical principles of psychologists* (Rev. ed). Washington, D.C.: Author, 1981(b).

Conger, J. J. Proceedings of the American Psychological Association. Incorporated, for the year 1975: Minutes of the annual meeting of the Council of Representatives. *American Psychologist*, 1976, 31, 406-434.

Smith, M. B., & Hobbs, N. *The community and the community mental health center* Washington, D.C.: American Psychological Association. 1966.

Specialty Guidelines for the Delivery of Services
by Industrial/Organizational Psychologists

These Specialty Guidelines were prepared through the cooperative efforts of the APA Committee on Standards for Providers of Psychological Services (COSPOPS), chaired by Durand F. Jacobs, and the APA Division of Industrial and Organizational Psychology (Division 14). Virginia Ellen Schein and Frank Friedlander served as the I/O representatives on COSPOPS and Arthur Centor and Richard Kilburg served as the Central Office liaisons to the committee Thomas E. Tice and C. Bartlett were the key liaison persons from the Division 14 Professional Affairs Committee Drafts of these Guidelines were reviewed and commented on by members of the Division 14 Executive Committee.

The Specialty Guidelines that follow are supplements to the generic *Standards for Providers of Psychological Services*, originally adopted by the American Psychological Association (APA) in September 1974 and revised in January 1977 (APA, 1974b, 1977). Admission to the practice of psychology is regulated by state statute. Isis the position of the Association that licensing be based on generic and not on specialty, qualifications. Specialty guidelines serve the additional purpose of providing potential users and other interested groups with essential information about particular services available from the several specialties in professional psychology. Although the original APA *Standards* were designed to fill the needs of several classes of psychological practitioners and a wide variety of users, the diversity of professional practice and the use of psychological services require specialty guidelines to clarify the special nature of bosh practitioners and users. These Specialty Guidelines for the Delivery of Services by Industrial/Organizational (I/O) Psychologists are designed to define the roles of I/O psychologists and the particular needs of users of I/O psychological services.

Professional psychology specialties have evolved from generic practice in psychology and are supported by university training programs. There are now at least four recognized professional specialties—clinical, counseling, school, and industrial/organizational psychology,

The knowledge base in each of these specialty areas has increased, refining the state of the art to the point that a set of uniform specialty guidelines is now possible and desirable. The present Guidelines are intended to educate the public, the profession, and other interested parties regarding specialty professional practices. They are also intended to facilitate the continued systematic development of the profession.

The content of each specialty guideline reflects a consensus of university faculty and public and private practitioners regarding the knowledge base, services provided, problems addressed, and clients served.

Traditionally, all learned disciplines have treated the designation of specialty practice as a reflection of preparation in greater depth in a particular subject matter, together with a voluntary limiting of focus to a more restricted area of practice by the professional. Lack of specialty designation does not preclude general providers of psychological services from using the methods on dealing with the populations of any specialty, except insofar as psychologists voluntarily refrain from providing services they are not trained to render. Isis the intent of these Guidelines, however, that after the grandparenting period, psychologists not put themselves forward as specialists in a given area of practice unless they meet the qualifications noted in the Guidelines (see Definitions). Therefore, these Guidelines are meant to apply only to those psychologists who voluntarily wish to be designated as *industrial/organizational psychologists*. They do not apply to other psychologists.

These Guidelines represent the profession's best judgment of the conditions, credentials, and experience that contribute to competent professional practice. The APA strongly encourages, and plans to participate in, efforts to identify professional practitioner behaviors and job functions and to validate the relation between these and desired client outcomes. Thus, future revisions of these Guidelines will increasingly reflect the results of such efforts.

Like the APA generic *Standards*, the I/O Specialty Guidelines are concerned with improving the quality, effectiveness, and accessibility of psychological services for all who require benefit from them. These Specialty Guidelines are intended to clarify questions of interpretation of the APA generic *Standards* as they are applied to I/O psychology.

This document presents the APA's position on I/O practice. Ethical standards applicable to I/O psychologists are already in effect[1] as are other documents thatprovide guidance to I/O practitioners in specific applications of I/O psychology[2] (Note: Footnotes appear at the end of the Specialty Guidelines. See p. 669.)

The Committee on Professional Standards established by the APA in January 1980 is charged with keeping the generic *Standards* and the Specialty Guidelines responsive to the needs of the public and the profession—Isis also charged with continually reviewing, modifying, and extending them progressively as the profession and the science of psychology develop new knowledge, improved methods, and additional modes of psychological services.

The Specialty Guidelines for the Delivery of Services by Industrial/Organizational Psychologists that follow have been established by the APA as a means of self-regulation to protect the public interest. They guide the specialty practice of I/O psychology by specifying important areas of quality assurance and performance that contribute to the goal of facilitating more effective human functioning.

Principles and Implications of the Specialty Guidelines

These Specialty Guidelines have emerged from and reaffirm the same basic principles that guided the development of the generic *Standards for Providers of Psychological Services* (APA, 1977):

1. These Guidelines recognize that where the practice of I/O psychology is regulated by federal, state, or local statuses, all providers of I/O psychological services conform to such statuses.

2. A uniform set of Specialty Guidelines governs I/O psychological service functions offered by I/O psychologists, regardless of setting or form of remuneration. All I/O psychologists in professional practice recognize and are responsive to a uniform set of Specialty Guidelines, just as they are guided by a common code of ethics.

3. The I/O Specialty Guidelines establish clearly articulated levels of quality for covered I/O psychological service functions, regardless of the nature of the users, purchasers, or sanctioners of such covered services

4. All persons providing I/O psychological services meet specified levels of training and experience that are consistent with, and appropriate to, the functions they perform. Persons providing such services who do not meet the APA qualifications for a professional I/O psychologist (see Definitions) are supervised by a psychologist with the requisite training. This level of qualification is necessary to ensure that the public receives services of high quality. Final responsibility and accountability for services provided rest with professional I/O psychologists.

5. These Specialty Guidelines for I/O psychologists are intended to present the APA's position on levels for training and professional practice and to provide clarification of the APA generic Standards.

6. A uniform set of Specialty Guidelines governs the quality of I/O psychological services in bosh the private and the public sectors. Those receiving I/O psychological services are protected by the same kinds of safeguards, irrespective of sector.

7. All persons representing themselves as I/O psychologists as any time and in any setting, whether public or private, profit or nonprofit, observe these Guidelines in order to promote the interests and welfare of the users of I/O psychological services. Judgment of the degree to which these Guidelines are observed take into consideration the capabilities for evaluation and the stances that prevail in the setting at the time the program or service is evaluated.

8. These Guidelines, while assuring the user of the I/O psychologist's accountability for the nature and quality of services rendered, do not preclude the providers of I/O psychological services from using new methods or developing innovative procedures in the delivery of such services.

These Specialty Guidelines have broad implications bosh for users of I/O psychological services and for providers of such services:

1. Guidelines for I/O psychological services provide a basis for a mutual understanding between provider and user and facilitate effective evaluation of services provided and outcomes achieved.

2. Guidelines for I/O psychological services make an important contribution toward greaser uniformity in legislative and regulatory actions involving I/O psychologists. Guidelines for providers of I/O psychological services may be useful for uniformity in specialty credentialing of I/O psychologists, if such specialty credentialing is required.

3. Although guidelines for I/O psychological services may have an impact on tomorrow's training models for bosh professional and support personnel in f/O psychology, they are not intended to interfere with innovations in the training of I/O psychologists,

4. Guidelines for I/O psychological services require continual review and revision.

The Specialty Guidelines here presented are intended to improve the quality and delivery of I/O psychological services by specifying criteria for key aspects of the practice setting. Some settings may require additional and/or more stringent criteria for specific areas of service delivery.

Definitions

A fully qualified I/O *psychologist* has a doctoral degree earned in a program primarily psychological in nature. This degree may be from a department of psychology or from a school of business, management, or administrative science in a regionally accredited university. Consistent with the commitment of I/O psychology to the scientist—professional model I/O psychologists are thoroughly prepared in basic scientific methods as well as in psychological science; therefore, programs that do not include training in basic scientific methods and research are not considered appropriate educational and training models for

I/O psychologists. The I/O psychology doctoral program provides training in (a) scientific and professional ethics, (b) general psychological science, (c) research design and methodology, (d) quantitative and qualitative methodology, and (e) psychological measurement, as well as (f) a supervised practicum or laboratory experience in an area of I/O psychology, (g) a field experience in the application and delivery of I/O services, (h) practice in the conduct of applied research, (i) training in other areas of psychology, in business, and in the social and behavioral sciences, as appropriate, and (j) preparation of a doctoral research dissertation.[3]

Although persons who do not meet all of the above qualifications may provide I/O psychological services, such services are performed under the supervision of a fully qualified I/O psychologist. The supervising I/O psychologist may be a full-time member of the same organization or may be retained on a part-time basis. Psychologists so retained have the authority and participate sufficiently to assess the need for services, to review the services provided, and to ensure professional responsibility and accountability for them. Special proficiency training or supervision may be provided by professional psychologists of other specialties or by professionals of other disciplines whose competencies in the given area have been demonstrated by previous training and experience.

Industrial/organizational psychological services involve the development and application of psychological theory and methodology to problems of organizations and problems of individuals and groups in organizational settings. The purpose of such applications to the assessment, development, or evaluation of individuals, groups, or organizations is to enhance the effectiveness of these individuals, groups, or organizations. The following areas represent some examples of such applications:

A. Selection and placement of employees. Services include development of selection programs, optimal placement of key personnel, and early identification of management potential.

B. Organization development. Services include analyzing organizational structure, formulating corporate personnel strategies, maximizing the effectiveness and satisfaction of individuals and work groups, effecting organizational change, and counseling employees for purposes of improving employee relations, personal and career development, and superior-subordinate relations.

C. Training and development of employees. Services include identifying training and development needs; formulating and implementing programs for technical training, management training, and organizational development; and evaluating the effectiveness of training and development programs in relation to productivity and satisfaction criteria,

D. Personnel research. Services include continuing development of assessment tools for selection, placement, classification, and promotion of employees; validating test instruments; and measuring the effect of cultural factors on test performance.

E. Improving employee motivation. Services include enhancing the productive output of employees, identifying and improving factors associated with job satisfaction, and redesigning jobs to make them more meaningful.

F. Design and optimization of work environments. Services include designing work environments and optimizing person-machine effectiveness.

Guideline 1
PROVIDERS

Staffing and Qualifications of Staff

1.1 *Professional I/O psychologists maintain current knowledge of scientific and professional developments shot are related to the services they render.*

INTERPRETATION: Methods through which knowledge of scientific and professional development may be gained include, but are not limited to, continuing education, attendance at workshops, participation in staff development, and reading scientific publications.

The I/O psychologist has ready access to reference material related to the provision of psychological services.

1.2 *Professional I/O psychologists limit their practice to their demonstrated areas of professional competence.*

INTERPRETATION: I/O psychological services are offered in accordance with the providers' areas of competence as defined by verifiable training and experience.

When extending services beyond the range of their usual practice, professional I/O psychologists obtain pertinent training or appropriate professional supervision.

1.3 *Professional psychologists who wish to change their specialty to I/O areas meet the same requirements with respect to subject matter and professional skills shot apply to doctoral training in the new specialty.*

INTERPRETATION: Education and training of doctoral-level psychologists, when prior preparation has not been in the I/O areas, includes education and training in the content, methodology, and practice of I/O psychology. Such preparation is individualized and may be acquired in a number of ways. Formal education in I/O psychology under the auspices of university departments that offer the doctoral degree in I/O psychology, with certification by the supervising department indicating competency in I/O psychology, is recommended. However, continuing education courses and workshops in I/O psychology, combined with supervised experience as an I/O psychologist, may also be acceptable.

1.4 *Professional I/O psychologists are encouraged to develop innovative procedures and theory.*

INTERPRETATION: Although these Guidelines give examples of I/O psychologist activities, such activities are not limited to those provided I/O psychologists are encouraged to develop innovative ways of approaching problems.

Guideline 2
PROFESSIONAL CONSIDERATIONS

Protecting the User

2.1 *I/O psychological practice supports the legal and civil rights of the user.*

INTERPRETATION: Providers of I/O psychological services safeguard the interests of the user with regard to legal and civil rights—I/O psychologists are especially sensitive to issues of confidentiality of information. In the case of dual users (e.g., individuals and organizations), I/O psychologists, insofar as possible, anticipate possible conflicts of interest and clarify with both users how such conflicts might be resolved. In addition, I/O service providers make every effort to safeguard documents and files containing confidential information.

2.2 *All providers of I/O psychological services abide by policies of the American Psychological Association that are relevant to I/O psychologists.*

INTERPRETATION: While many official APA policies are relevant to I/O psychology, such as those embodied in the *Ethical Principles of Psychologists* (APA, 1981) and the *Standards of Educational and Psychological Tests* (APA, 1974a). It is recognized that some specific policies which apply only to certain subspecialties (e.g., health care providers) may not be applicable to I/O psychologists.

2.3 *All providers within an I/O psychological service unit are familiar with relevant statutes, regulations, and legal precedents established by federal, state, and local governmental groups.*

INTERPRETATION: Insofar as statutes exist relevant to the practice of the I/O psychological service provider, the provider is familiar with them and conforms to the law. In addition, the provider is familiar with statutes that may govern activities of the user as they relate to services provided. For example, an I/O psychologist who establishes selection systems for a user is aware of and conforms to the statutes governing selection systems for that user. This guideline does not imply that inappropriate statuses, regulations, and legal precedents cannot be opposed through legal processes.

Although I/O psychologists may be required by law to be licensed or certified, moss I/O psychological services can be provided by persons who are not licensed or certified. Examples of such services are the administration of standardized group tests of mental abilities, aptitudes, personality characteristics, and so on for instructional or personnel screening uses; interviews, such as employment or curriculum advisory interviews, that do not involve the assessment of individual personality characteristics; the design, administration, and interpretation of opinion surveys; the design and evaluation of person—machine systems, the conduct of employee development programs; the counseling of employees by supervisors regarding job performance and working relationships; and the teaching of psychological principles or techniques that do not involve ameliorative services to individuals or groups.

Planning Organizational Goals

2.4 *Providers of I/O psychological services state explicitly what can and cannot reasonably be expected from the services.*

INTERPRETATION: In marketing psychological services, the I/O psychologist realistically appraises the chances of meeting the client's goal(s) and informs the client of the degree of success that can be anticipated. Since the user may or may not possess sophistication in psychological methods and applications, the limitations are stated in terms that are comprehensible to the user.

In presenting statements of reasonable anticipation, the I/O psychologist attempts to be accurate in all regards. This guideline also applies to statements of personal competency and of the competency and experience of the psychological service unit that the I/O psychologist represents. Statements and materials do not make claims or suggest benefits that are not supportable by scientifically acceptable evidence. Since the I/O psychologist may stand to gain financially through the recommendation of a given product or service, particular sensitivity to such issues is essential to avoid compromise of professional responsibilities and objectives.

2.5 *Providers of I/O psychological services do not seek to gain competitive advantage through the use of privileged information.*

INTERPRETATION: In the course of work with a user, I/O practitioners may become aware of the management practices, organizational structure, personnel policies, or financial structure of competing units. Since such information is usually revealed in a privileged context, it is not employed for competitive advantage. Similarly, practitioners may be called on to review the proposal of a competing unit. Information so gained is not used to gain competitive advantage.

2.6 *Providers of I/O psychological services who purchase the services of another psychologist provide a clear statement of the role of the purchaser.*

INTERPRETATION: When an I/O psychological service unit purchases the services of another such unit, the purchasing unit states in advance whether is perceives its role as that of a collaborator, a technical advisor, a scientific monitor, or an informed layperson. The purchaser clearly defines its anticipated role specifies the extent to which it wishes to be involved in various aspects of program planning and work definition, and describes how differences of opinion on technical and scientific masters are to be resolved. Members of the staff of bosh the unit purchasing services and the unit providing services are made fully aware of the various role definitions. Deferring all major project decisions to the purchaser is not necessarily considered appropriate in scientific development.

2.7 *Providers of I/O psychological services establish a system to protect confidentiality of their records.*

INTERPRETATION: I/O psychologists are responsible for maintaining the confidentiality of information about users of services, whether obtained by themselves or by those they supervise. All persons supervised by I/O psychologists, including nonprofessional person-nel and students, who have access to records of psychological services are required to maintain this confidentiality as a condition of employment.

The I/O psychologist does not release confidential information, except with the written consent of the user directly involved or the users' legal representative. Even after the con-sent for release has been obtained, the I/O psychologist clearly identifies such information as confidential to the recipient of the information, if directed otherwise by statute or regu-lations with the force of law or by court order, the psychologist seeks a resolution to the conflict that is both ethically and legally feasible and appropriate.

Users are informed in advance of any limits in the setting for maintenance of confidentiality of psychological information. When the user intends to waive confidential-ity, the psychologist discusses the implications of releasing psychological information and assists the user in limiting disclosure only to information required by the present circumstances.

Raw psychological data (e.g., test protocols, interview notes, or questionnaire returns) in which a user is identified are released only with the written consent of the user or the users legal representative and released only to a person recognized by the I/O psychologist as qualified and competent to use the data. (Note: The user may be an individual receiving career counseling, in which case individual confidentiality must be maintained, or the user may be an organization, in which case individual data may be shared with others within the organization. When individual information is to be shared with others, e.g., managers, the individual supplying the information is made aware of how this information is to be used.)

Any use made of psychological reports, records, or data for research or training purposes is consistent with this Guideline. Additionally, providers of I/O psycho-logical services comply with statutory confidentiality requirements and those embodied in the American Psychological Association's *Ethical Principles of Psychologists* (APA, 1981).

Providers of I/O psychological services remain sensitive to both the benefits and the possible misuse of information regarding individuals that is stored in computerized data banks. Providers use their influence to ensure that such information is used in a socially responsible manner.

Guideline 3
ACCOUNTABILITY

Evaluating I/O Psychological Services

3.1 *The professional activities of providers of I/O psychological services are guided primarily by the principle of promoting human welfare.*

INTERPRETATION: I/O psychologists do not withhold services to a potential client on the basis of race, color, religion, sex, age, handicap, or national origin. Recognition is given, however, to the following considerations: the professional right of I/O psychologists to limit their practice to avoid potential conflict of interest (e.g., as between union and management, plaintiff and defendant, or business competitors); the right and responsibility of psychologists to withhold a procedure when it is not validly applicable; the right and responsibility of I/O psychologists to withhold evaluative, diagnostic, or change procedures or other services where they might be ineffective or detrimental to the achievement of goals and fulfillment of needs of individuals or organizations.

I/O psychologists who find that psychological services are being provided in a manner that is discriminatory or exploitative to users and/or contrary to these Guidelines or to state or federal statutes take appropriate corrective action, which may include the refusal to provide services. When conflicts of interest arise, the I/O psychologist is guided in the resolution of differences by the principles set forth by the American Psychological Association in the *Ethical Principles of Psychologists* (APA, 1981) and the "Guidelines for Conditions of Employment of Psychologists" (APA, 1972).

3.2 *There are periodic, systematic, and effective evaluations of psychological services.*

INTERPRETATION: Regular assessment of progress in achieving goals and meeting needs is provided in all I/O psychological service units. Such assessment includes both the validation of psychological services designed to predict outcomes and the evaluation of psychological services designed to induce organizational or individual change. This evaluation includes consideration of the effectiveness of I/O psychological services relative to costs in terms of use of time and money and the availability of professional and support personnel.

Evaluation of the efficiency and effectiveness of the I/O psychological service delivery system is conducted internally and, when possible, under independent auspices as well.

It is clearly explained to the user that evaluation of services is a necessary part of providing I/O psychological services and that the cost of such evaluation is justified as part of the cost of services.

FOOTNOTES

[1] See *Ethical Principles of Psychologists* (APA, 1981).

[2] See *Principles for the Validation and Use of Personnel Selection Procedures* (APA Division of Industrial and Organizational Psychology, 1980).

[3] The following two categories of persons who met the criteria indicated below on or before the adoption of these Specialty Guidelines on January 31, 1980, shall also be considered professional I/O psychologists: Category I—persons who on or before September 4, 1974, (a) completed a masters degree from a program primarily psychological in content as a regionally accredited university, (b) completed 5 post-master's years of appropriate education, training, and experience in providing I/O psychological services as defined herein in the Definitions section, including a minimum of 2 years in an organizational setting, and (c) received a license or certificate in the state in which they practiced, conferred by a state board of psychological examiners, Category 2—persons who completed (a) a doctoral degree f mm a program primarily psychological in content as a regionally accredited university and (b) 3 postdoctoral years of appropriate education, training, and experience in providing 1/O services as defined herein in the Definitions section, including a minimum of 1 year in an organizational setting.

REFERENCES

American Psychological Association. Guidelines for conditions of employment of psychologists. *American Psychologist,* 1972, 27, 331–334.

American Psychological Association. *Standards for educational and psychological tests.* Washington, D.C.: Author, 1974(a).

American Psychological Association. *Standards for providers of psychological services.* Washington, D.C.: Author. 1974(b).

American Psychological Association. *Standards for providers of psychological services* (Rev. ed.). Washington, D.C.: Author, 1977.

American Psychological Association, Division of Industrial and Organizational Psychology. *Principles for the validation and use of personnel selection procedures* (2nd ed.). Berkeley, Calif.: Author, ( ) (Copies may be ordered from Lewis E Albright, Kaiser Aluminum & Chemical Corporation, 300 Lakeside Drive—Room KB 2140, Oakland, California 94643)

American Psychological Association. *Ethical principles of psychologists* (Rev. ed.). Washington, D.C.: Author, 1981.

Specialty Guidelines for the Delivery of Services
by School Psychologists

These Specialty Guidelines were prepared through the cooperative efforts of the APA Committee on Standards for Providers of Psychological Services (COSPOPS) and the APA Professional Affairs Committee of the Division of School Psychology (Division 16). Jack I. Bardon and Nadine M. Lambert served as the school psychology representatives of COSPOPS and Arthur Centor and Richard Kilburg were the Central Office liaisons to the committee Durand F. Jacobs served as chair of COSPOPS, and Walter B. Pryzwansky chaired the Division 16 committee. Drafts of the school psychology Guidelines were reviewed and commented on by members of the Executive Committee of Division 16, representatives of the National Association of School Psychologists, state departments of education, consultants in school psychology, and many professional school psychologists in training programs and in practice in the schools.

The Specialty Guidelines that follow are based on the generic *Standards for Providers of Psychological Services* originally adopted by the American Psychological Association (APA) in September 1974 and revised in January 1977 (APA, 1974b, 1977b). Together with the generic Standards, these Specialty Guidelines state the official policy of the Association regarding delivery of services by school psychologists. Admission to the practice of psychology is regulated by state statute. Is in the position of the Association that licensing be based on generic, and not on specialty, qualifications Specialty guidelines serve the additional purpose of providing potential users and other interested groups with essential information about particular services available from the several specialties in professional psychology.

Professional psychology specialties have evolved from generic practice in psychology and are supported by university training programs. There are now at least four recognized professional specialties—clinical, counseling, school, and industrial/organizational psychology.

The knowledge base in each of these specialty areas has increased, refining the state of the art to the point that a set of uniform specialty guidelines is now possible and desirable. The present Guidelines are intended to educate the public, the profession, and other interested pasties regarding specialty professional practices. They are also intended to facilitate the continued systematic development of the profession.

The content of each Specialty Guideline reflects a consensus of university faculty and public and private practitioners regarding the knowledge base, services provided, problems addressed, and clients served.

Traditionally, all learned disciplines have treated the designation of specialty practice as a reflection of preparation in greater depth in a particular subject matter, together with a voluntary limiting of focus to a more restricted area of practice by the professional. Lack of specialty designation does not preclude general providers of psychological services from using the methods or dealing with the populations of any specialty, except insofar as psychologists voluntarily refrain from providing services they are not trained to render. It is the intent of these Guidelines, however, that after the grandparenting period, psychologists not put themselves forward as specialists in a given area of practice unless they meet the qualifications noted in the Guidelines (see Definitions). Therefore, these Guidelines are meant to apply only to those psychologists who wish to be designated as school psychologists. They do not apply to other psychologists.

These Guidelines represent the profession's best judgment of the conditions, credentials, and experience that contribute to competent professional practice. The APA strongly encourages, and plans to participate in efforts to identify professional practitioner behaviors and job functions and to validate the relation between these and desired client outcomes. Thus, future revisions of these Guidelines will increasingly reflect the results of such efforts.

These Guidelines follow the format and, wherever applicable, the wording of the generic *Standards*.[1] (Note: Footnotes appear at the end of the Specialty Guidelines. See pp. 679–681.) The intent of these Guidelines is to improve the quality, effectiveness, and accessibility of psychological services. They are meant to provide guidance to providers, users and sanctioners regarding the best judgment of the profession on these matters. Although the Specialty Guidelines have been derived from and are consistent with the generic *Standards*, they may be used as a separate document. *Standards for Providers of Psychological Services* (APA, 1977b), however, shall remain the basic policy statement and shall take precedence where there are questions of interpretation.

Professional psychology in general and school psychology in particular have had a long and difficult history of attempts to establish criteria for determining guidelines for the delivery of services. In school psychology, state departments of education have traditionally had a strong influence on the content of programs required for certification and on minimum competency levels for practice, leading to wide variations in requirements among the many states. These national Guidelines will reduce confusion, clarify important dimensions of specialty practice, and provide a common basis for peer review of school psychologists' performance.

The Committee on Professional Standards established by the APA in January 1980 is charged with keeping the generic *Standards* and the Specialty Guidelines responsive to the needs of the public and the profession. It is also charged with continually reviewing, modifying, and extending them progressively as the profession and the science of psychology develop new knowledge, improved methods, and additional modes of psychological services

The Specialty Guidelines for the Delivery of Services by School Psychologists have been established by the APA as a means of self-regulation to protect the public interest. They guide the specialty practice of school psychology by specifying important areas of quality assurance and performance that contribute to the goal of facilitating more effective human functioning.

Principles and Implications of the Specialty Guidelines

These Specialty Guidelines have emerged from and reaffirm the same basic principles that guided the development of the generic *Standards for Providers of Psychological Services* (APA, 1977b):

1. These Guidelines recognize that admission to the practice of school psychology is regulated by state statute.

2. It is the intention of the APA that the generic Standards provide appropriate guidelines for statutory licensing of psychologists. In addition, although it is the position of the APA that licensing be generic and not in specialty areas, these Specialty Guidelines in school psychology should provide an authoritative reference for use in

credentialing specialty providers of school psychological services by such groups as divisions of the APA and state associations and by boards and agencies that find such criteria useful for quality assurance.

3. A uniform set of Specialty Guidelines governs school psychological service functions offered by school psychologists, regardless of setting or source of remuneration. All school psychologists in professional practice recognize and are responsive to a uniform set of Specialty Guidelines, just as they are guided by a common code of ethics.

4. School psychology Guidelines establish clearly articulated levels of training and experience that are consistent with, and appropriate to, the functions performed. School psychological services provided by persons who do not meet the APA qualifications for a professional school psychologist (see Definitions) are to be supervised by a professional school psychologist, Final responsibility and accountability for services provided rest with professional school psychologists.

5. A uniform set of Specialty Guidelines governs the quality of services to all users of school psychological services in both the private and the public sectors. Those receiving school psychological services are protected by the same kinds of safeguards, irrespective of sector; these include constitutional guarantees, statutory regulation, peer review, consultation, record review, and staff supervision.

6. These Guidelines, while assuring the user of the school psychologist's accountability for the nature and quality of services specified in this document, do not preclude the school psychologist from using new methods or developing innovative procedures for the delivery of school psychological services.

These Specialty Guidelines for school psychology have broad implications both for users of school psychological services and for providers of such services:

1. Guidelines for school psychological services provide a foundation for mutual understanding between provider and user and facilitate more effective evaluation of services provided and outcomes achieved.

2. Guidelines for school psychological services are essentials for uniformity of regulation by state departments of education and other regulatory or legislative agencies concerned with the provision of school psychological services. In addition, they provide the basis for state approval of training programs and for the development of accreditation procedures for schools and other facilities providing school psychological services.

3. Guidelines give specific content to the profession's concept of ethical practice as is applies to the functions of school psychologists.

4. Guidelines for school psychological services have significant impact on tomorrow's education and training models for both professional and support personnel in school psychology

5. Guidelines for the provision of school psychological services influence the determination of acceptable structure, budgeting, and staffing patterns in schools and other facilities using these services.

6. Guidelines for school psychological services require continual review and revision

The Specialty Guidelines presented here are intended to improve the quality and the delivery of school psychological services by specifying criteria for key aspects of the service setting. Some school settings may require additional and/or more stringent criteria for specific areas of service delivery.

Systematically applied, these Guidelines serve to establish a more effective and consistent basis for evaluating the performance of individual service providers as well as to guide the organization of school psychological service units.

Definitions

Providers of school psychological services refers to two categories of persons who provide school psychological services:

A. Professional school psychologists.[2,3] Professional school psychologists have a doctoral degree from a regionally accredited university or professional school providing an organized, sequential school psychology program in a department of psychology in a university or college, in an appropriate department of a school of education or other similar administrative organization, or in a unit of a professional school. School psychology programs that are accredited by the American Psychological Association are recognized as meeting the definition of a school psychology program. School psychology programs that are not accredited by the American Psychological Association meet the definition of a school psychology program if they satisfy the following criteria:

1. The program is primarily psychological in nature and stands as a recognizable, coherent organizational entity within the institution.
2. The program provides an integrated, organized sequence of study.
3. The program has an identifiable body of students who are matriculated in that program for a degree.
4. There is a clear authority with primary responsibility for the core and specialty areas, whether or not the program cuts across administrative lines.
5. There is an identifiable psychology faculty, and a psychologist is responsible for the program. Patterns of education and training in school psychology[4] are consistent with the functions to be performed and the services to be provided, in accordance with the ages, populations, and problems found in the various schools and other settings in which school psychologists are employed. The program of study includes a core of academic experience, both didactic and experiential, in basic areas of psychology, includes education related to the practice of the specialty, and provides training in assessment, intervention, consultation, research, program development, and supervision, with special emphasis on school-related problems or school settings.[5]

Professional school psychologists who wish to represent themselves as proficient in specific applications of school psychology that are not already part of their training are required to have further academic training and supervised experience in those areas of practice.

B. All other persons who offer school psychological services under the supervision of a school psychologist. Although there may be variations in the titles and job descriptions of such persons, they are not called school psychologists. Their functions may be indicated by use of the adjective psychological preceding the noun.

1. A *specialist in school psychology* has successfully completed as least 2 years of graduate education in school psychology and a training program that includes as least 1,000 hours of experience supervised by a professional school psychologist, of which at least 500 hours must be in school settings. A specialist in school psychology provides psychological services under the supervision of a professional school psychologist.[6]

2. Titles for others who provide school psychological services under the supervision of a professional school psychologist may include *school psychological examiner, school psychological technician, school psychological assistant, school psychometrist, or school psychometric assistant.*

School psychological services refers to one or more of the following services offered to clients involved in educational settings, from preschool through higher education, for the protection and promotion of mental health and the facilitation of learning.[7]

A. Psychological and psychoeducational evaluation and assessment of the school functioning of children and young persons. Procedures include screening, psychological and educational tests (particularly individual psychological tests of intellectual functioning, cognitive development, affective behavior, and neuropsychological status), interviews, observation, and behavioral evaluations, with explicit regard for the context and setting in which the professional judgments based on assessment, diagnosis, and evaluation will be used.

B. Interventions to facilitate the functioning of individuals or groups, with concern for how schooling influences and is influenced by their cognitive, conative, affective, and social development. Such interventions may include, bus are not limited to, recommending, planning, and evaluating special education services; psychoeducational therapy; counseling; affective educational programs; and training programs to improve coping skills.[8]

C. Interventions to facilitate the educational services and child care functions of school personnel, parents, and community agencies. Such interventions may include, bus are not limited to, in-service school-personnel education programs, parent education programs, and parent counseling.

D. Consultation and collaboration with school personnel and/or parents concerning specific school-related problems of students and the professional problems of staff. Such services may include, but are not limited to, assistance with the planning of educational programs from a psychological perspective; consultation with teachers and other school personnel to enhance their understanding of the needs of particular pupils; modification of classroom instructional programs to facilitate children's learning; promotion of a positive climate for learning and teaching; assistance to parents to enable them to contribute to their children's development and school adjustment; and other staff development activities.

E. Program development services to individual schools, to school administrative systems, and to community agencies in such areas as needs assessment and evaluation of regular and special education programs; liaison with community, state, and federal agencies concerning the mental health and educational needs of children; coordination, administration, and planning of specialized educational programs; the generation, collection, organization, and dissemination of information from psychological research and theory to educate staff and parents.

F. Supervision of school psychological services (see Guideline 1.2, Interpretation).

A *school psychological service unit* is the functional unit through which school psychological services are provided; any such unit has as least one professional school psychologist associated with it:

A. Such a unit provides school psychological services to individuals, a school system, a district, a community agency, or a corporation, or to a consortium of school systems, districts, community agencies, or corporations that contract together to employ providers of school psychological services. A school psychological service unit is composed of one or more professional school psychologists and, in most instances, supporting psychological services staff.

B. A school psychological service unit may operate as an independent professional service to schools or as a functional component of an administrative organizational unit, such as a state department of education, a public or private school system, or a community mental health agency.

C. One or more professional school psychologists providing school psychological services in an interdisciplinary or a multidisciplinary setting constitute a school psychological service unit.

D. A school psychological service unit may also be one or more professional psychologists offering services in private practice, in a school psychological consulting firm, or in a college or university-based facility or program that contracts to offer school psychological services to individuals, groups, school systems, districts, or corporations.

Users of school psychological services include:

A. Direct users or recipients of school psychological services, such as pupils, instructional and administrative school staff members, and parents.

B. Public and private institutions, facilities, or organizations receiving school psychological services, such as boards of education of public or private schools, mental health facilities, and other community agencies and educational institutions for handicapped or exceptional children.

C. Third-party purchasers—those who pay for the delivery of services but who are not the recipients of services.

D. Sanctioners—such as those who have a legitimate concern with the accessibility, time-liness, efficacy, and standards of quality attending the provision of school psychological services. Sanctioners may include members of the users' family, the court, the probation officer, the school administrator, the employer, the facility director, and so on. Sanctioners may include various governmental, peer review, and accreditation bodies concerned with the assurance of quality.

Guideline 1
PROVIDERS

1.1 *Each school psychological service unit offering school psychological services and as accessible at least one professional school psychologist and as many additional profes-sional school psychologists and support personnel as are necessary to assure the adequacy and quality of services offered.*

INTERPRETATION: The intent of this Guideline is that one or more providers of psy-chological services in any school psychological service unit meet the levels of training and experience of the professional school psychologist specified in the preceding definitions.

When a professional school psychologist is not available on a full-time basis to provide school psychological services, the school district obtains the services of a professional school psychologist on a regular part-time basis. Yearly contracts are desirable to ensure continuity of services during a school year. The school psychologist so retained directs the psychological services, supervises the psychological services provided by support person-nel, and participates sufficiently to be able to assess the need for services, review the con-tent of services provided, and assume professional responsibility and accountability for them. A professional school psychologist supervises no more than the equivalent of 15 full-time specialists in school psychology and/or other school psychological personnel.

Districts that do not have easy access to professional school psychologists because of geographic considerations, or because professional school psychologists do not live or work in the area employ as least one full-time specialist in school psychology and as many more support personnel as are necessary to assure the adequacy and quality of services. The following strategies may be considered to acquire the necessary supervisory services from a professional school psychologist:

A. Employment by a county, region, consortium of schools, or state department of educa-tion of full-time supervisory personnel in school psychology who meet appropriate levels of training and experience, as specified in the definitions, to visit school districts regularly for supervision of psychological services staff.

B. Employment of professional school psychologists who engage in independent practice for the purpose of providing supervision to school district psychological services staff.

C. Arrangements with nearby school districts that employ professional school psycholo-gists for part-time employment of such personnel on a contract basis specifically for the purpose of supervision as described in Guideline 1.

The school psychologist directing the school psychological service unit, whether on a full- or part-time basis, is responsible for determining and justifying appropriate ratios of school psychologists to users, to specialists in school psychology, and to support personnel, in order to ensure proper scope, accessibility, and quality of services provided in that setting. The school psychologist reports to the appropriate school district representatives any findings regarding the need to modify psychological services or staffing pasterns to assure the adequacy and quality of services offered.

1.2 *Providers of school psychological services who do not meet the requirements for the professional school psychologist are supervised directly by a professional school psychologist who assumes professional responsibility and accountability for the services provided. The level and extent of supervision may vary from task to task to long as the supervising psychologist retains a sufficiently close supervisory relationship to meet this Guideline. Special proficiency training or supervision may be provided by a professional psychologist of another specialty or by a professional from another discipline whose competency in the given area has been demonstrated.*[9]

INTERPRETATION: Professional responsibility and accountability for the services provided require that the supervisor review reports and test protocols; review and discuss intervention strategies, plans, and outcomes; maintain a comprehensive view of the schools procedures and special concerns; and have sufficient opportunity to discuss discrepancies among the views of the supervisor, the supervised, and other school personnel on any problem or issue. In order to meet this Guideline, an appropriate number of hours per week are devoted to direct face-to-face supervision of each full-time school psychological service staff member. In no event is this supervision less than one hour per week for each staff member. The more comprehensive the psychological services are, the more supervision is needed. A plan or formula for relating increasing amounts of supervisory time to the complexity of professional responsibilities is to be developed. The amount and nature of supervision is specified in writing to all parties concerned.

1.3 *Wherever a school psychological service unit exists, a professional school psychologist is responsible for planning, directing, and reviewing the provision of school psychological services.*

INTERPRETATION: A school psychologist coordinates the activities of the school psychological service unit with other professionals, administrators, and community groups, bosh within and outside the school. This school psychologist, who may be the director, coordinator, or supervisor of the school psychological service unit, has related responsibilities including, but not limited to: recruiting qualified staff, directing training and research activities of the service, maintaining a high level of professional and ethical practice, and ensuring that staff members function only within the areas of their competency.

To facilitate the effectiveness of services by raising the level of staff sensitivity and professional skills, the psychologist designated as director is responsible for participating in the selection of staff and support personnel whose qualifications are directly relevant to the needs and characteristics of the users served.

In the event that a professional school psychologist is employed by the school psychological service unit on a basis that affords him or her insufficient time to carry out full responsibility for coordinating or directing the unit, a specialist in school psychology is designated as director or coordinator of the school psychological services and is supervised by a professional school psychologist employed on a part-time basis, for a minimum of 2 hours per week.

1.4 *When functioning as part of an organizational setting, professional school psychologists bring their backgrounds and skills to bear on the goals of the organization, whenever appropriate, by participating in the planning and development of overall services.*

INTERPRETATION: Professional school psychologists participate in the maintenance of high professional standards by serving as representatives on, or consultants to, committees and boards concerned with service delivery, especially when such committees deal with special education, pupil personnel services, mental health aspects of schooling, or other services that use or involve school psychological knowledge and skills.

As appropriate to the setting, school psychologists' activities may include active participation, as voting and as office-holding members, on the facility's executive planning, and evaluation boards and committees.

1.5 *School psychologists maintain current knowledge of scientific and professional developments to preserve and enhance their professional competence.*

INTERPRETATION: Methods through which knowledge of scientific and professional developments may be gained include, but are not limited to, (a) the reading or preparation of scientific and professional publications and other materials, (b) attendance as workshops and presentations at meetings and conventions, (c) participation in on-the-job staff development programs, and (d) other forms of continuing education. The school psychologist and staff have available reference material and journals related to the provision of school psychological services. School psychologists are prepared to show evidence periodically that they are staying abreast of current knowledge in the field of school psychology and are also keeping their certification and licensing credentials up-to-date.

1.6 *School psychologists limit their practice to their demonstrated areas of professional competence.*

INTERPRETATION: School psychological services are offered in accordance with the providers areas of competence as defined by verifiable training and experience. When extending services beyond the range of their usual practice, school psychologists obtain pertinent training or appropriate professional supervision. Such training or supervision is consistent with the extension of functions performed and services provided. An extension of services may involve a change in the theoretical orientation of the practitioner, in the techniques used, in the client age group (e.g., children, adolescents, or parents), or in the kinds of problems addressed (e.g., mental retardation, neurological impairment, learning disabilities, family relationships).

1.7 *Psychologists who wish to qualify as school psychologists meet the same requirements with respect to subject matter and professional skills that apply to doctoral training in school psychology.*[10]

INTERPRETATION: Education of psychologists to qualify them for specialty practice in school psychology is under the auspices of a department in a regionally accredited university or of a professional school that offers the doctoral degree in school psychology through campus- and/or field-based arrangements. Such education is individualized, with due credit being given for relevant course work and other requirements that have previously been satisfied. In addition to the doctoral-level education specified above, appropriate doctoral-level training is required. An internship or experience in a school setting is not adequate preparation for becoming a school psychologist when prior education has not been in that area. Fulfillment of such an individualized training program is attested to by the awarding of a certificate by the supervising department or professional school that indicates the successful completion of preparation in school psychology.

1.8 *Professional school psychologists are encouraged to develop innovative theories and procedures and to provide appropriate theoretical and/or empirical support for their innovations.*

INTERPRETATION: A specialty of a profession rooted in science intends continually to explore study, and conduct research with a view to developing and verifying new and improved methods of serving the school population in ways that can be documented.

Guideline 2
PROGRAMS

2.1 *Composition and organization of a school psychological service unit:*

 2.1.1 *The composition and programs of a school psychological service unit are responsive to the needs of the school population that is served.*

INTERPRETATION: A school psychological service unit is structured so as to facilitate effective and economical delivery of services, for example, a school psychological service unit serving predominantly low-income, ethnic, or racial minority children has a staffing pastern and service programs that are adapted to the linguistic, experiential, and attitudinal characteristics of the users. Appropriate types of assessment materials and norm reference groups are utilized in the practice of school psychology.

 2.1.2 *A description of the organization of the school psychological service unit and its lines of responsibility and accountability for the delivery of school psychological services is available in written form to instructional and administrative staff of the unit and to parents, students, and members of the community.*

INTERPRETATION: The description includes lines of responsibility, supervisory relationships, and the level and extent of accountability for each person who provides school psychological services.

 2.1.3 *A school psychological service unit includes sufficient numbers of professional and support personnel to achieve its goals, objectives, and purposes.*

INTERPRETATION: A school psychological service unit includes one or more professional school psychologists, specialists in school psychology, and other psychological services support personnel. When a professional school psychologist is not available to provide services on a full-or part-time basis, the school psychological services are conducted by a specialist in school psychology, supervised by a professional school psychologist (see Guideline 1.2).

The work load and diversity of school psychological services required and the specific goals and objectives of the setting determine the numbers and qualifications of professional and support personnel in the school psychological service unit. For example, the extent to which services involve case study, direct intervention, and/or consultation will be significant in any service plan. Case study frequently involves teacher and/or parent conferences, observations of pupils, and a multi-assessment review, including student interviews, Similarly, the target populations for services affect the range of services that can be offered. One school psychologist, or one specialist in school psychology under supervision, for every 2,000 pupils is considered appropriate.[11]

Where shortages in personnel exist, so that school psychological services cannot be rendered in a professional manner, the director of the school psychological service unit informs the supervisor/administrator of the service about the implications of the shortage and initiates action to remedy the situation, When this fails, the director appropriately modifies the scope or work load of the unit to maintain the quality of services rendered.

2.2 *Policies:*

> 2.2.1 *When the school psychological service unit is composed of more than one person or is a component of a larger organization, a written statement of its objectives and scope of services is developed, maintained, and reviewed.*

INTERPRETATION: The school psychological service unit reviews its objectives and scope of services annually and revises them as necessary to ensure that the school psychological services offered are consistent with staff competencies and current psychological knowledge and practice. This statement is discussed with staff, reviewed by the appropriate administrators, distributed to instructional and administrative staff and school board members, and when appropriate, made available to parents, students and members of the community upon request.

> 2.2.2 *All providers within a school psychological service unit support the legal and civil rights of the users.*[12]

INTERPRETATION: Providers of school psychological services safeguard the interests of school personnel, students, and parents with regard to personal, legal, and civil rights. They are continually sensitive to the issue of confidentiality of information, the short-term and long-term inspects of their decisions and recommendations, and other matters pertaining to individual, legal, and civil rights. Concerns regarding the safeguarding of individual rights of school personnel, students, and parents include, but are not limited to, due-process rights of parents and children, problems of self-incrimination in judicial proceedings, involuntary commitment to hospitals, child abuse, freedom of choice, protection of minors or legal incompetents, discriminatory practices in identification and placement, recommendations for special education provisions and adjudication of domestic relations disputes in divorce and custodial proceedings. Providers of school psychological services take affirmative action by making themselves available to local committees, review boards, and similar advisory groups established to safeguard the human, civil, and legal rights of children and parents.

> 2.2.3 *All providers within a school psychological service unit are familiar with and adhere to the American Psychological Association's Standards for Providers of Psychological Services, Ethical Principles of Psychologists, Standards for Educational and Psychological Tests, Ethical Principles in the Conduct of Research With Human Participants, and other official policy statements relevant to standards for professional services issued by the Association.*

INTERPRETATION: A copy of each of these documents is maintained by providers of school psychological services and is available upon request to all school personnel and officials, parents, members of the community, and where applicable, students and other sanctioners.

> 2.2.4 *All providers within a school psychological service unit conform to relevant statutes established by federal, state, and local governments.*

INTERPRETATION: All providers of school psychological services are familiar with and conform to appropriate statutes regulating the practice of psychology. They also are informed about state department of education requirements and other agency regulations that have the force of law and that relate to the delivery of school psychological services (e.g., certification of eligibility for, and placement in, special education programs). In addition, all providers are cognizant that federal agencies such as the Department of Education and the Department of Health and Human Services have policy statements regarding psychological services. Providers of school psychological services are familiar as well with other statutes and regulations, including those addressed to the civil and legal rights of users (e.g., Public Law 94-142. The Education for All Handicapped Children Act of 1975), that are pertinent to their scope of practice.

It is the responsibility of the American Psychological Association to maintain files of those federal policies, statutes, and regulations relating to this section and to assist its members in obtaining them. The state psychological associations, school psychological associations, and state licensing boards periodically publish and distribute appropriate state statutes and regulations.

> 2.2.5 *All providers within a school psychological service unit inform themselves about and use the network of human services in their communities in order to link users with relevant services and resources.*

INTERPRETATION: School psychologists and support staff are sensitive to the broader contest of human needs. In recognizing the matrix of personal and societal problems, providers make available to clients information regarding human services such as legal aid societies, social services, health resources like mental health centers, private practitioners, and educational and recreational facilities. School psychological staff formulates and maintains a file of such resources for reference. The specific information provided is such that users can easily make contact with the services and freedom of choice can be honored. Providers of school psychological services refer to such community resources and, when indicated, actively intervene on behalf of the users. School psychologists seek opportunities to serve on boards of community agencies in order to represent the needs of the school population in the community.

> 2.2.6 *In the delivery of school psychological services, providers maintain a cooperative relationship with colleagues and co-workers in the best interest of the users.*

INTERPRETATION: School psychologists recognize the areas of special competence of other psychologists and of other professionals in the school and in the community for either consultation or referral purposes (e.g., school social workers, speech therapists, remedial reading teachers, special education teachers, pediatricians, neurologists, and public health nurses). Providers of school psychological services make appropriate use of other professional, research, technical, and administrative resources whenever these serve the best interests of the school staff, children, and parents and establish and maintain cooperative and/or collaborative arrangements with such other resources as required to meet the needs of users.

2.3 *Procedures:*

> 2.3.1 *A school psychological service unit follows a set of procedural guidelines for the delivery of school psychological services.*

INTERPRETATION: The school psychological service staff is prepared to provide a statement of procedural guidelines in written form in terms that can be understood by school staff, parents, school board members, interested members of the community, and when appropriate, students and other sanctioners. The statement describes the current methods, forms, case study and assessment procedures, estimated time lines, interventions, and evaluation techniques being used to achieve the objectives and goals for school psychological services.

This statement is communicated to school staff and personnel, school board members, parents, and when appropriate, students or other sanctioners through whatever means are feasible, including in-service activities, conferences, oral presentations, and dissemination of written materials.

The school psychological service unit provides for the annual review of its procedures for the delivery of school psychological services

> 2.3.2 *Providers of school psychological services develop plans appropriate to the providers professional practices and to the problems presented by the users. There is a mutually acceptable understanding between providers and school staff, parents, and students or responsible agents regarding the goals and the delivery of services.*

INTERPRETATION: The school psychological service unit notifies the school unit in writing of the plan that is adopted for use and resolves any points of difference. The plan includes written consent of guardians of students and, when appropriate, consent of students for the services provided. Similarly, the nature of the assessment tools that are to be used and the reasons for their inclusion are spelled out. The objectives of intervention(s) of a psychological nature as well as the procedures for implementing the intervention(s) are specified. An estimate of time is noted where appropriate. Parents and/or students are made aware of the various decisions that can be made as a result of the service(s), participate in accounting for decisions that are made, and are informed of how appeals may be instituted.

2.3.3 *Accurate, current, and pertinent documentation of essential school psychological services provided is maintained.*

INTERPRETATION Records kept of psychological services may include, bus are not limited to, identifying data, dates of services, names of providers of services, types of services, and significant actions taken. These records are maintained separately from the child's cumulative record folder. Once a case study is completed and/or an intervention begun, records are reviewed and updated as least monthly.

2.3.4 *Each school psychological services unit follows an established record retention and disposition policy.*

INTERPRETATION: The policy on maintenance and review of psychological records (including the length of time that records not already part of school records are to be kept) is developed by the local school psychological service unit. This policy is consistent with existing federal and state statutes and regulations.

2.3.5 *Providers of school psychological services maintain a system to protect confidentiality of their records.*

INTERPRETATION: School psychologists are responsible for maintaining the confidentiality of information about users of services, from whatever source derived. All persons supervised by school psychologists, including nonprofessional personnel and students, who have access to records of psychological services maintain this confidentiality as a condition of employment. All appropriate staff receive training regarding the confidentiality of records.

Users are informed in advance of any limits for maintenance of confidentiality of psychological information. Procedures for obtaining informed consent are developed by the school psychological service unit. Written informed consent is obtained to conduct assessment or to carry out psychological intervention services. Informing users of the manner in which requests for information will be handled and of the school personnel who will share the results is pars of the process of obtaining consent.

The school psychologist conforms to current laws and regulations with respect to the release of confidential information. As a general rule, however, the school psychologist does not release confidential information, except with the written consent of the parent or, where appropriate, the student directly involved or his or her legal representative. Even after consent for release has been obtained, the school psychologist clearly identifies such information as confidential to the recipient of the information. When there is a conflict with a statute, with regulations with the force of law, or with a court order, the school psychologist seeks a resolution to the conflict that is both ethically and legally feasible and appropriate.

Providers of school psychological services ensure that psychological reports which will become part of the school records are reviewed carefully so that confidentiality of pupils and parents is protected. When the guardian or student intends to waive confidentiality, the school psychologist discusses the implications of releasing psychological information and assists the user in limiting disclosure to only that information required by the present circumstance.

Raw psychological data (e.g., test protocols, counseling or interview notes, or questionnaires) in which a user is identified are released only with the written consent of the user or his or her legal representative, or by court order when such material is not covered by legal confidentiality, and are released only to a person recognized by the school psychologist as competent to use the data.

Any use made of psychological reports, records, or data for research or training purposes is consistent with this Guideline. Additionally, providers of school psychological services comply with statutory confidentiality requirements and those embodied in the American Psychological Association's *Ethical Principles of Psychologists* (APA, 1981).

Providers of school psychological services remain sensitive to both the benefits and the possible misuse of information regarding individuals that is stored in large computerized databanks, Providers use their influence to ensure that such information is managed in a socially responsible manner.

Guideline 3
ACCOUNTABILITY

3.1 *The promotion of human welfare is the primary principle guiding the professional activity of the school psychologist and the school psychological service unit.*

INTERPRETATION: School psychological services staff provide services to school staff members, students, and parents in a manner that is considerate and effective.

School psychologists make their services readily accessible to users in a manner that facilitates the users' freedom of choice. Parents, students, and other users are made aware that psychological services may be available through other public or private sources, and relevant information for exercising such options is provided upon request.

School psychologists are mindful of their accountability to the administration, to the school board, and to the general public, provided that appropriate steps are taken to protect the confidentiality of the service relationship. In the pursuit of their professional activities, they aid in the conservation of human, material, and financial resources.

The school psychological service unit does not withhold services to children or parents on the basis of the users' race, color, religion, gender, sexual orientation, age, or national origin. Recognition is given, however, to the following considerations: (a) the professional right of school psychologists, as the time of their employment, to state that they with to limit their services to a specific category of users (e.g., elementary school children, exceptional children, adolescents), nosing their reasons so that employers can make decisions regarding their employment, assignment of their duties, and so on, (b) the right and responsibility of school psychologists to withhold an assessment procedure when not validly applicable; (c) the right and responsibility of school psychologists to withhold evaluative, psychotherapeutic, counseling, or other services in specific instances in which their own limitations or client characteristics might impair the effectiveness of the relationship; and (d) the obligation of school psychologists to seek to ameliorate through peer review, consultation, or other personal therapeutic procedures those factors that inhibit the provision of services to particular users. In such instances, it is incumbent on school psychologists to advise clients about appropriate alternative services. When appropriate services are not available, school psychologists inform the school district administration and/or other sanctioners of the unmet needs of clients. In all instances, school psychologists make available information, and provide opportunity to participate in decisions, concerning such issues as initiation, termination, continuation, modification, and evaluation of psychological services. These Guidelines are also made available upon request.

Accurate and full information is made available to prospective individual or organizational users regarding the qualifications of providers, the nature and extent of services offered, and where appropriate, the financial costs as well as the benefits and possible risks of the proposed services.

Professional school psychologists offering services for a fee inform users of their payment policies, if applicable, and of their willingness to assist in obtaining reimbursement when such services have been contracted for as an external resource.

3.2 *School psychologists pursue their activities as members of the independent, autonomous profession of psychology.*[13]

INTERPRETATION: School psychologists are aware of the implications of their activities for the profession of psychology as a whole. They seek to eliminate discriminatory practices instituted for self-serving purposes that are not in the interest of the users (e.g., arbitrary requirements for referral and supervision by another profession) and to discourage misuse of psychological concepts and tools (e.g., use of psychological instruments for special education placement by school personnel or others who lack relevant and adequate education and training). School psychologists are cognizant of their responsibilities for the development of the profession and for the improvement of schools. They participate where possible in the training and career development of students and other providers; they participate as appropriate in the training of school administrators, teachers, and paraprofessionals; and they integrate, and supervise the implementation of their contributions within the structure established for delivering school psychological services. Where appropriate, they facilitate the development of, and participate in professional standards review mechanisms

School psychologists seek to work with other professionals in a cooperative manner for the good of the users and the benefit of the general public. School psychologists associated with special education or mental health seams or with multidisciplinary settings support the principle that members of each participating profession have equal rights and opportunities to share all privileges and responsibilities of full membership in the educational or human service activities or facilities and to administer service programs in their respective areas of competence. (Refer also to Guideline 2.2.5, Interpretation.)

3.3 *There are periodic, systematic, and effective evaluations of school psychological services.*

INTERPRETATION: When the psychological service unit representing school psychology is a component of a larger organization (e.g., school system, county or state regional district, state department of education), regular evaluation of progress in achieving goals is provided for in the service delivery plan, including consideration of the effectiveness of school psychological services relative to costs in terms of use of time and money and the availability of professional and support personnel.

Evaluation of the school psychological service delivery system is conducted internally and, when possible, under independent auspices as well. This evaluation includes an assessment of effectiveness (to determine what the service unit accomplished), efficiency (to determine the costs of providing the services), continuity (to ensure that the services are appropriately linked to other educational services), availability (to determine the appropriateness of staffing ratios), accessibility (to ensure that the services are readily available to members of the school population), and adequacy (to determine whether the services meet the identified needs of the school population).

It is highly desirable that there be a periodic reexamination of review mechanisms to ensure that these attempts as public safeguards are effective and cost efficient and do not place unnecessary encumbrances on the providers or impose unnecessary expenses on users or sanctioners for services rendered

3.4 *School psychologists are accountable for all aspects of the services they provide and are responsive to those concerned with these services.*

INTERPRETATION: In recognizing their responsibilities to users sanctioners, and other providers, and where appropriate and consistent with the users legal rights and privileged communications, school psychologists make available information about, and provide opportunity to participate in, decisions concerning such issues as initiation, termination, continuation, modification, and evaluation of school psychological services.

Guideline 4
ENVIRONMENT

4.1 *Providers of psychological services promote development in the school setting of a physical, organizational, and social environment that facilitates optimal human functioning.*

INTERPRETATION: Federal, state, and local requirements for safety, health, and sanitation are observed.

As providers of services, school psychologists are concerned with the environment of their service units, especially as it affects the quality of service, but also as it impinges on human functioning in the school. Attention is given to the privacy and comfort of school staff, students, and parents. Parent and staff interviews are conducted in a professional atmosphere, with the option for private conferences available. Students are seen under conditions that maximize their privacy and enhance the possibility for meaningful intervention; for example, they should have the opportunity to leave their classroom inconspicuously and should be free from interruptions when meeting with the psychologist. Physical arrangements and organizational policies and procedures are conducive to the human dignity, self-respect, and optimal functioning of school staff, students, and parents and to the effective delivery of service.

FOOTNOTES

[1] The footnotes appended to these Specialty Guidelines represent an attempt to provide a coherent contest of earlier APA policy statements and other documents regarding professional practice. The Guidelines extend these previous policy statements where necessary to reflect current concerns of the public and the profession.

[2] There are three categories of individuals who do not meet the definition of *professional school psychologist* but who can be considered professional school psychologists if they meet certain criteria.

The following two categories of professional psychologists who met the criteria indicated below on or before the adoption of these Specialty Guidelines on January 31, 1980, are considered professional school psychologists. Category 1—those who completed (a) a doctoral degree program primarily psychological is content, but not in school psychology, at a regionally accredited university or professional school and (b) 3 postdoctoral years of appropriate education, training, and experience in providing school psychological services as defined herein, including a minimum of 1,200 hours in school settings; Category 2—those who on or before September 4, 1974, (a) completed a masters degree from a program primarily psychological in content as a regionally accredited university or professional school and (b) held a license or certificate in the state in which they practiced, conferred by a state board of psychological examiners, or the endorsement of a state psychological association through voluntary certification, and who, in addition, prior to January 31, 1980, (c) obtained 5 post-masters years of appropriate education, training, and experience in providing school psychological services as defined herein, including a minimum of 2,400 hours in school settings.

After January 31, 1980, professional psychologists who wish to be recognized as professional school psychologists are referred to Guideline 1.7.

The APA Council of Representatives passed a "Resolution on the Master's-Level Issue" in January 1977 containing the following statement, which influenced the development of a third category of professional school psychologists:

> The title "Professional Psychologist" has been used so widely and by persons with such a wide variety of training and experience that it does not provide the information the public deserves.

> As a consequence, the APA takes the position and makes it a part of its policy that the use of the title "Professional Psychologist," and its variations such as "Clinical Psychologist," "Counseling Psychologist," "School Psychologist," and "Industrial Psychologist" are reserved for those who have completed a Doctoral Training Program in Psychology is a university college, or professional school of psychology that is APA or regionally accredited. In order to meet this standard a transition period will be acknowledged for the use of the title "School Psychologist." so that ways may be sought to increase opportunities for doctoral training and to improve the level of educational codes pertaining to the title. (Conger, 1977, p. 426)

> For the purpose of transition, then, there is still another category of persons who can be considered professional school psychologists for practice in elementary and secondary schools. Category 3 consists of persons who meet the following criteria on or before, but not beyond, January 31, 1985: (a) a master's or higher degree, requiring at least 2 years of full-time graduate study in school psychology, from a regionally accredited university or professional school; (b) at least 3 additional years of training and experience in school psychological services, including a minimum of 1,200 hours in school settings; and (c) a license or certificate conferred by a state board of psychological examiners or a state educational agency for practice in elementary or secondary schools.

> Preparation equivalent to that described in Category 3 entitles an individual to use the title professional school psychologist in school practice, bus is does not exempt the individual from meeting the requirements of licensure or other requirements for which a doctoral degree is prerequisite.

[3] A professional school psychologist who is licensed by a state or District of Columbia board of examiners of psychology for the independent practice of psychology and who has 2 years of

supervised (or equivalent) experience in health services, of which as least 1 year is postdoctoral may be listed as a "Health Service Provider in Psychology" is the *National Register of Health Service Providers in Psychology:*

> A Health Service Provider in Psychology is defined as a psychologist, certified/licensed at the independent practice level in his/her state, who is duly trained and experienced is the delivery of direct, preventive, assessment and therapeutic intervention services to individuals whose growth, adjustment, or functioning is actually impaired or is demonstrably as high risk of impairment. (Council for the National Register of Health Service Providers in Psychology,) 1980, p. xi)

[4] The areas of knowledge and training that are a part of the educational program for all professional psychologists have bees presented in two APA documents, *Education and Credentialing in Psychology II* (APA, 1977a) and *Criteria for Accreditation of Doctoral Training Programs and Internships in Professional Psychology* (APA, 1979). There is consistency is the presentation of core areas in the education and training of all professional psychologists. The description of education and training in these Guidelines is based primarily on the document *Education and Credentialing in Psychology II.* It is intended to indicate broad areas of required curriculum, with the expectation that training programs will undoubtedly want to interpret the specific content of these areas in different ways depending on the nature, philosophy, and intent of the programs.

[5] Although specialty education and training guidelines have not yet been developed and approved by APA, the following descriptions of education and training components of school psychology programs represents a consensus regarding specialty training in school psychology at this time.

The *education* of school psychologists encompasses the equivalent of as least 3 years of full-time graduate academic study. While instructional formats and course titles may vary from program to program, each program has didactic and experiential instruction (a) in scientific and professional areas common to all professional psychology programs, such as ethics and standards, research design and methodology, statistics, and psychometric methods, and (b) in such substantive areas as the biological bases of behavior, the cognitive and affective bases of behavior, the social, cultural, ethnic, and sex role bases of behavior, and individual differences. Course work includes social and philosophical bases of education, curriculum theory and practice, etiology of learning and behavior disorders, exceptional children, and special education. Organization theory and administrative practice should also be included in the program. This list is not intended to dictate specific courses or a sequence of instruction. It is the responsibility of programs to determine how these areas are organized and presented to students. Variations in educational format are to be expected.

The *training* of school psychologists includes practicum and field experience in conjunction with the educational program. In addition, the program includes a supervised internship experience beyond practicum and field work, equivalent to at least I academic school year, but in no event fewer than 1,200 hours, in schools or in a combination of schools and community agencies and centers, with as least 600 hours of the internship in the school setting. An appropriate number of hours per week should be devoted to direct face-to-face supervision of each intern. In no event is there less than 1 hour per week of direct supervision. Overall professional supervision is provided by a professional school psychologist. However, supervision in specific procedures and techniques may be provided by others, with the agreement of the supervising professional psychologist and the supervisee. The training experiences provided and the competencies developed occur in settings in which there are opportunities to work with children, teachers, and parents and to supervise others providing psychological services to children.

[6] In order to implement these Specialty Guidelines, it will be necessary to determine in each state which non-doctoral-level school psychologists certified by the state department of education are eligible to be considered professional school psychologists for practice in elementary and secondary schools. A national register of all professional school psychologists and specialists in school

psychology would be a useful and efficient means by which to inform the public of the available school psychological services personnel.

[7] Functions and activities of school psychologists relating to the teaching of psychology, the writing or editing of scholarly or scientific manuscripts, and the conduct of scientific research do not fall within the purview of these Guidelines.

[8] Nothing in these Guidelines precludes the school psychologist from being trained beyond the areas described herein (e.g., in psychotherapy for children, adolescents, and their families in relation to school-related functioning and problems) and, therefore, from providing services on the basis of this training to clients as appropriate.

[9] In some states, a supervisor's certificate is required in order to use the title supervisor in the public schools. Supervision of providers of psychological services by a professional school psychologist does not mean that the school psychologist is thereby authorized or entitled to offer supervision to other school personnel Supervision by the school psychologist is confined to those areas appropriate to his or her training and educational background and is viewed as part of the school psychologist's professional responsibilities and duties.

The following guideline for supervision has been written by the Executive Committee of the Division of School Psychology.

In addition to being a professional school psychologist, the person who supervises school psychological services and/or school psychological personnel shall have the following qualifications: broad understanding of diagnostic assessment, consultation, programming, and other intervention strategies; skills in supervision; the ability to empathize with supervisees; and commitment to continuing education. The supervising school psychologist also shall have had the equivalent of as least 2 years of satisfactory full-time, on-the-job experience as a school psychologist practicing directly in the school or dealing with school-related problems in independent practice.

[10] This Guideline follows closely the statement regarding "Policy on Training for Psychologists Wishing to Change Their Specialty" adopted by the APA Council of Representatives in January 1976. Included therein was the implementing provision that "this policy statement shall be incorporated in the guidelines of the Committee on Accreditation so that appropriate sanctions can be brought to bear on university and internship training programs that violate [it]" (Conger, 1976, p. 424).

[11] Two surveys of school psychological practice provide a rationale for the specification of this Guideline (Farling & Hoedt, 1971; Kicklighter, 1976). The median ratios of psychologists to pupils were 1 to 9000 in 1966 and 1 to 4,000 in 1974. Those responding to Kicklighter's survey projected that the ratio of psychologists to pupils would be 1 to 2,500 in 1980. These data were collected before the passage of Public Law 94-142, the Education for All Handicapped Children Act of 1975. The regulations for implementing this act require extensive identification, assessment, and evaluation services to children, and it is reasonable in 1981 to set an acceptable ratio of psychologists to pupils at 1 to 2,000.

[12] See also *Ethical Principles of Psychologists* (APA, 1981) especially Principles 5 (Confidentiality), 6 (Welfare of the Consumer), and 9 (Research With Human Participants), and *Ethical Principles in the Conduct of Research With Human Participants* (APA, 1973). Also, in 1978 Division 17 approved in principle a statement on "Principles for Counseling and Psychotherapy With Women," which was designed to protect the interests of female users of counseling psychological services.

[13] Support for the principle of the independence of psychology as a profession is found in the following:

As a member of an autonomous profession, a psychologist rejects limitations upon his [or her] freedom of thought and action other than those imposed by his [or bed moral, legal, and social responsibilities. The Association is always prepared to provide appropriate assistance to any responsible member who becomes subjected to unreasonable limitations upon his [or her] opportunity to function as a practitioner, teacher, researcher, administrator, or consultant. The Association is always prepared to cooperate with any responsible professional organization in opposing any unreasonable limitations on the professional functions of the members of that organization.

This insistence upon professional autonomy has been upheld over the years by the affirmative actions of the courts and other public and private bodies in support of the right of the psychologist—and other professionals—to pursue those functions for which he [or she] is trained and qualified to perform. (APA, 1968 p. 9)

Organized psychology has the responsibility to define and develop its own profession, consistent with the general canons of science and with the public welfare.

Psychologists recognize that other professions and other groups will, from time to time, seek to define the roles and responsibilities of psychologists. The APA opposes such developments on the same principle that it is opposed is the psychological profession taking positions which would define the work and scope of responsibility of other duly recognized professions (APA, 1972, p. 333)

REFERENCES

American Psychological Association, *Psychology as a profession.* Washington, D.C.: Author, 1968.

American Psychological Association, Guidelines for conditions of employment of psychologists. *American Psychologist,* 1972, 27, 331–334.

American Psychological Association. *Ethical principles in the conduct of research with human participants.* Washington, D.C.: Author, 1973.

American Psychological Association, *Standards for educational and psychological tests.* Washington, D.C.: Author, 1974(a).

American Psychological Association, *Standards for providers of psychological services.* Washington, D.C.: Author. 1974(b).

American Psychological Association, *Education and credentialing in psychology II.* Report of a meeting, June 4-5, 1977. Washington, D.C.: Author, 1977(a).

American Psychological Association. *Standards for providers of psychological services* (Rev. ed.). Washington, D.C.: Author, 1977(b).

American Psychological Association. *Criteria for accreditation of doctoral training programs and internships in professional psychology.* Washington, D.C.: Author, 1979 (amended 1980).

American Psychological Association. *Ethical principles of psychologists* (Rev. ed.). Washington, D.C.: Author, 1981.

Conger, J. J. Proceedings of the American Psychological Association, Incorporated, for the year 1975: Minutes of the annual meeting of the Council of Representatives. *American Psychologist,* 1976, 31, 406–434.

Conger, J. J. Proceedings of the American Psychological Association, Incorporated, for the year 1976: Minutes of the annual meeting of the Council of Representatives. *American Psychologist,* 1977, 32, 408–438.

Council for the National Register of Health Service Providers in Psychology. *National register of health service providers in psychology*. Washington, D.C.: Author, 1980.

Farling, W. H., & Hoedt, K. C. *National survey of school psychologists*. Washington, D.C.: Department of Health, Education, and Welfare, 1971.

Kicklighter, R. H. School psychology in the U.S.: A quantitative survey. *Journal of School Psychology*, 1976, 14, 151–156.

APA RECORD KEEPING GUIDELINES

Record Keeping Guidelines

Drafted by the Committee on Professional Practice & Standards,

A committee of the Board of Professional Affairs

Adopted by the Council of Representatives,

February 1993

Introduction[1]

The guidelines that follow are based on the General Guidelines, adopted by the American Psychological Association (APA) in July 1987 (APA, 1987). The guidelines receive their inspirational guidance from specific APA *Ethical Principles of Psychologists and Code of Conduct* (APA, 1992).

These guidelines are aspirational and professional judgment must be used in specific applications. They are intended for use by providers of health care services.[2,3] The language of these guidelines must be interpreted in light of their aspirational intent, advancements in psychology and the technology of record keeping, and the professional judgment of the individual psychologist. It is important to highlight that professional judgment is not preempted by these guidelines; rather, the intent is to enhance it.

Underlying Principles and Purpose

Psychologists maintain records for a variety of reasons, the most important of which is the benefit of the client. Records allow a psychologist to document and review the delivery of psychological services. The nature and extent of the record will vary depending upon the type and purpose of psychological services. Records can provide a history and current status in the event that a user seeks psychological services from another psychologist or mental health professional.

Conscientious record keeping may also benefit psychologists themselves, by guiding them to plan and implement an appropriate course of psychological services, to review work as a whole, and to self-monitor more precisely.

Maintenance of appropriate records may also be relevant for a variety of other institutional, financial, and legal purposes. State and federal laws in many cases require maintenance of appropriate records of certain kinds of psychological services. Adequate records may be a re-

---

[1] In 1988 the Board of Professional Affairs (BPA) directed the Committee on Professional Practice and Standards (COPPS) to determine whether record keeping guidelines would be appropriate. COPPS was informed that these guidelines would supplement the provisions contained in the *General Guidelines for Providers of Psychological Services*, which had been amended two years earlier. The Council of Representatives approved the General Guidelines records provisions after extended debate on the minimum recordation concerning the nature and contents of psychological services. The General Guidelines reflect a compromise position that psychologists hold widely varying views on the wisdom of recording the content of the psychotherapeutic relationship. In light of the Council debate on the content of psychological records and the absence of an integrated document, BPA instructed COPPS to assess the need for such guidelines, and, if necessary, the likely content.

COPPS undertook a series of interviews with psychologists experienced in this area. The consensus of the respondents indicated that practicing psychologists could benefit from guidance in this area. In addition, an APA legal intern undertook a 50-state review of laws governing psychologists with respect to record keeping provisions. The survey demonstrated that while some states have relatively clear provisions governing certain types of records, many questions are often left unclear. In addition, there is a great deal of variability among the states, so that consistent treatment of records as people move from state to state, or as records are sought from other states, may not be easy to achieve.

Based on COPPS' survey and legal research, BPA in 1989 directed COPPS to prepare an initial set of record keeping guidelines. This document resulted.

[2] These guidelines apply to Industrial/Organizational psychologists providing health care services but generally not to those providing non-health care I/O services. For instance, in I/O psychology, written records may constitute the primary work product, such as a test instrument or a job analysis, while psychologists providing health care services may principally use records to document non-written services and to maintain continuity.

[3] Rather than keeping their own record system, psychologists practicing in institutional settings comply with the institution's policies on record keeping, so long as they are consistent with legal and ethical standards.

---

quirement for receipt of third party payment for psychological services.

In addition, well documented records may help protect psychologists from professional liability, if they become the subject of legal or ethical proceedings. In these circumstances, the principal issue will be the professional action of the psychologist, as reflected in part by the records.

At times, there may be conflicts between the federal, state or local laws governing record keeping, the requirements of institutional rules, and these guidelines. In these circumstances, psychologists bear in mind their obligations to conform to applicable law. When laws or institutional rules appear to conflict with the principles of these guidelines, psychologists use their education, skills and training to identify the relevant issues, and to attempt to resolve it in a way that, to the maximum extent feasible, conforms both to law and to professional practice, as required by ethical principles.

Psychologists are justifiably concerned that, at times, record keeping information will be required to be disclosed against the wishes of the psychologist or client, and may be released to persons unqualified to interpret such records. These guidelines assume that no record is free from disclosure all of the time, regardless of the wishes of the client or the psychologist.

1. Content of Records

a. Records include any information (including information stored in a computer) that may be used to document the nature, delivery, progress, or results of psychological services. Records can be reviewed and duplicated.

b. Records of psychological services minimally include (a) identifying data, (b) dates of services, (c) types of services, (d) fees, (e) any assessment, plan for intervention, consultation, summary reports, and/or testing reports and supporting data as may be appropriate, and (f) any release of information obtained.

c. As may be required by their jurisdiction and circumstances, psychologists maintain to a reasonable degree accurate, current, and pertinent records of psychological services. The detail is sufficient to permit planning for continuity in the event that another psychologist takes over delivery of services, including, in the event of death, disability, and retirement. In addition, psychologists maintain records in sufficient detail for regulatory and administrative review of psychological service delivery.

d. Records kept beyond the minimum requirements are a matter of professional judgment for the psychologist. The psychologist takes into account the nature of the psychological services, the source of the information recorded, the intended use of the records, and his or her professional obligation.

e. Psychologists make reasonable efforts to protect against the misuse of records. They take into account the anticipated use by the intended or anticipated recipients when preparing records. Psychologists adequately identify impressions and tentative conclusions as such.

2. Construction and Control of Records

a. Psychologists maintain a system that protects the confidentiality of records. They must take reasonable steps to establish and maintain the confidentiality of information arising from their own delivery of psychological services, or the services provided by others working under their supervision.

b. Psychologists have ultimate responsibility for the content of their records and the records of those under their supervision. Where appropriate, this requires that the psychologist oversee the design and implementation of record keeping procedures, and monitor their observance.

c. Psychologists maintain control over their clients' records, taking into account the policies of the institutions in which they practice. In situations where psychologists have control over their clients' records and where circumstances change such that it is no longer feasible to maintain control over such records, psychologists seek to make appropriate arrangements for transfer.

d. Records are organized in a manner that facilitates their use by the psychologist and other authorized persons. Psychologists strive to assure that record entries are legible. Records are to be completed in a timely manner.

e. Records may be maintained in a variety of media, so long as their utility, confidentiality and durability are assured.

3. Retention of Records

a. The psychologist is aware of relevant federal, state and local laws and regulations governing record retention. Such laws and regulations supersede the requirements of these guidelines. In the absence of such laws and regulations, complete records are maintained for a minimum of 3 years after the last contact with the client. Records, or a summary, are then maintained for an additional 12 years before disposal.[4] If the client is a minor, the record period is extended until 3 years after the age of majority.

b. All records, active and inactive, are maintained safely, with properly limited access, and from which timely retrieval is possible.

4. Outdated Records

a. Psychologists are attentive to situations in which record information has become outdated, and may therefore be invalid, particularly in circumstances where disclosure might cause adverse effects. Psychologists ensure that when disclosing such information that its outdated nature and limited utility are noted using professional judgment and complying with applicable law.

---

[4] These time limits follow the APA's specialty guidelines. If the specialty guidelines should be revised, a simple 7 year requirement for the retention of the complete record is preferred, which would be a more stringent requirement than any existing state statute.

b. When records are to be disposed of, this is done in an appropriate manner that ensures nondisclosure (or preserves confidentiality) (see Section 3a).

5. Disclosure of Record Keeping Procedures

a. When appropriate, psychologists may inform their clients of the nature and extent of their record keeping procedures. This information includes a statement on the limitations of the confidentiality of the records.

b. Psychologists may charge a reasonable fee for review and reproduction of records. Psychologists do not withhold records that are needed for valid healthcare purposes solely because the client has not paid for prior services.

REFERENCES

American Psychological Association. (1987). General guidelines for providers of psychological services. *American Psychologist, 42,* 712–723.

American Psychological Association. (1992). Ethical principles of psychologists and code of conduct. *American Psychologist, 47,* 1597–1611.

Manuscript Checklist

You can help your manuscript for the *American Psychologist* move smoothly through review and production by taking care of the items below before you send it to the editorial office. For further information, please refer to the Instructions to Authors, in the back of each issue of the *American Psychologist,* and the *Publication Manual of the American Psychological Association* (3rd ed.).

❑ Leave a margin of at least one inch on all sides of the paper.

❑ Double-space everything, including references, footnotes, tables, and figure captions. Double-space within each reference and within each footnote.

❑ Type the title of the work, corresponding author's name, complete address (with a street address), phone numbers, fax numbers, and electronic mail address on a separate page after the title page of the manuscript. Note any address change during the next six months.

❑ Write an abstract of no more than 960 characters and spaces (120 words maximum).

❑ Put all footnotes at the end of the article. Do not print a footnote at the bottom of the page on which it is mentioned.

❑ Send permission letters for tables, figures, or long quotations adapted or reprinted from another source. See the *Publication Manual of the American Psychological Association* (3rd ed., p. 93) for proper citation formats.

❑ If your manuscript has been accepted or conditionally accepted, submit glossies or photostats for all figures.

❑ If your manuscript has been accepted or conditionally accepted, sign and return the Copyright Transfer Form.

❑ If your manuscript has been accepted or conditionally accepted, include a diskette containing a word-processing file of the final version of your manuscript and sign and return the Author's Diskette Description Form.

GUIDELINES FOR CHILD CUSTODY EVALUATIONS IN DIVORCE PROCEEDINGS

Introduction

Decisions regarding child custody and other parenting arrangements occur within several different legal contexts, including parental divorce, guardianship, neglect or abuse proceedings, and termination of parental rights. The following guidelines were developed for psychologists conducting child custody evaluations, specifically within the context of parental divorce. These guidelines build upon the American Psychological Association's *Ethical Principles of Psychologists and Code of Conduct* (APA, 1992) and are aspirational in intent. *As guidelines, they are not intended to be either mandatory or exhaustive. The goal of the guidelines is to promote proficiency in using psychological expertise in conducting child custody evaluations.*

Parental divorce requires a restructuring of parental rights and responsibilities in relation to children. If the parents can agree to a restructuring arrangement, which they do in the overwhelming proportion (90%) of divorce custody cases (Melton, Petrila, Poythress, & Slobogin, 1987), there is no dispute for the court to decide. However, if the parents are unable to reach such an agreement, the court must help to determine the relative allocation of decision making authority and physical contact each parent will have with the child. The courts typically apply a "best interest of the child" standard in determining this restructuring of rights and responsibilities.

Psychologists provide an important service to children and the courts by providing competent, objective, impartial information in assessing the best interests of the child; by demonstrating a clear sense of direction and purpose in conducting a child custody evaluation; by performing their roles ethically; and by clarifying to all involved the nature and scope of the evaluation. The Ethics Committee of the American Psychological Association has noted that psychologists' involvement in custody disputes has at times raised questions in regard to the misuse of psychologists' influence, sometimes resulting in complaints against psychologists being brought to the attention of the APA Ethics Committee

Guidelines for Child Custody Evaluations in Divorce Proceedings, 49(7) American Psychologist 677–80 (1994). © 1994 the American Psychological Association. Reprinted by permission.

(APA Ethics Committee, 1985; Hall & Hare-Mustin, 1983; Keith-Spiegel & Koocher, 1985; Mills, 1984) and raising questions in the legal and forensic literature (Grisso, 1986; Melton et al., 1987; Mnookin, 1975; Ochroch, 1982; Okpaku, 1976; Weithorn, 1987).

Particular competencies and knowledge are required for child custody evaluations to provide adequate and appropriate psychological services to the court. Child custody evaluation in the context of parental divorce can be an extremely demanding task. For competing parents the stakes are high as they participate in a process fraught with tension and anxiety. The stress on the psychologist/evaluator can become great. Tension surrounding child custody evaluation can become further heightened when there are accusations of child abuse, neglect, and/or family violence.

Psychology is in a position to make significant contributions to child custody decisions. Psychological data and expertise, gained through a child custody evaluation, can provide an additional source of information and an additional perspective not otherwise readily available to the court on what appears to be in a child's best interest, and thus can increase the fairness of the determination the court must make.

Guidelines for Child Custody Evaluations in Divorce Proceedings

I. Orienting Guidelines: Purpose of a Child Custody Evaluation

1 The primary purpose of the evaluation is to assess the best psychological interests of the child.

The primary consideration in a child custody evaluation is to assess the individual and family factors that affect the best psychological interests of the child. More specific questions may be raised by the court.

2 The child's interests and well-being are paramount.

In a child custody evaluation, the child's interests and well-being are paramount. Parents competing for custody, as well as others, may have legitimate concerns, but the child's best interests must prevail.

3 The focus of the evaluation is on parenting capacity, the psychological and developmental needs of the child, and the resulting fit.

In considering psychological factors affecting the best interests of the child, the psychologist focuses on the parenting capacity of the prospective custodians in conjunction with the psychological and developmental needs of each involved child. This involves (a) an assessment of the adults' capacities for parenting, including whatever knowledge, attributes, skills, and abilities, or lack thereof, are present; (b) an assessment of the psychological functioning and developmental needs of each child and of the wishes of each child where appropriate; and (c) an assessment of the functional ability of each parent to meet these needs, including an evaluation of the interaction between each adult and child.

The values of the parents relevant to parenting, ability to plan for the child's future needs, capacity to provide a stable and loving home, and any potential for inappropriate behavior or misconduct that might negatively influence the child also are considered. Psychopathology may be relevant to such an assessment, insofar as it has impact on the child or the ability to parent, but it is not the primary focus.

II. General Guidelines: Preparing for a Child Custody Evaluation

4 The role of the psychologist is that of a professional expert who strives to maintain an objective, impartial stance.

The role of the psychologist is as a professional expert. The psychologist does not act as a judge, who makes the ultimate decision applying the law to all relevant evidence. Neither does the psychologist act as an advocating attorney, who strives to present his or her client's best possible case. The psychologist, in a balanced, impartial manner, informs and advises the court and the prospective custodians of the child of the relevant psychological factors pertaining to the custody issue. The psychologist should be impartial regardless of whether he or she is retained by the court or by a party to the proceedings. If either the psychologist or the client cannot accept this neutral role, the psychologist should consider withdrawing from the case. If not permitted to withdraw, in such circumstances, the psychologist acknowledges past roles and other factors that could affect impartiality.

5 The psychologist gains specialized competence.

A. A psychologist contemplating performing child custody evaluations is aware that special competencies and knowledge are required for the undertaking of such evaluations. Competence in performing psychological assessments of children, adults, and families is necessary but not sufficient. Education, training, experience, and/or supervision in the areas of child and family development, child and family psychopathology, and the impact of divorce on children help to prepare the psychologist to participate competently in child custody evaluations. The psychologist also strives to become familiar with applicable legal standards and procedures, including laws governing divorce and custody adjudications in his or her state or jurisdiction.

B. The psychologist uses current knowledge of scientific and professional developments, consistent with accepted clinical and scientific standards, in selecting data collection methods and procedures. The *Standards for Educational and Psychological Testing* (APA, 1985) are adhered to in the use of psychological tests and other assessment tools.

C. In the course of conducting child custody evaluations, allegations of child abuse, neglect, family violence, or other issues may occur that are not necessarily within the scope of a particular evaluator's expertise. If this is so, the psychologist seeks additional consultation, supervision, and/or specialized knowledge, training, or experience in child abuse, neglect, and family violence to address these complex issues. The psychologist is familiar with the laws of his or her state addressing child abuse, neglect, and family violence and acts accordingly.

6 The psychologist is aware of personal and societal biases and engages in nondiscriminatory practice.

The psychologist engaging in child custody evaluations is aware of how biases regarding age, gender, race, ethnicity, national origin, religion, sexual orientation, disability, language, culture, and socioeconomic status may interfere with an objective evaluation and recommendations. The psychologist recognizes and strives to overcome any such biases or withdraws from the evaluation.

7 The psychologist avoids multiple relationships.

Psychologists generally avoid conducting a child custody evaluation in a case in which the psychologist served in a therapeutic role for the child or his or her immediate family or has had other involvement that may compromise the psychologist's objectivity. This should not, however, preclude the psychologist from testifying in the case as a fact witness concerning treatment of the child. In addition, during the course of a child custody evaluation, a psychologist does not accept any of the involved participants in the evaluation as a therapy client. Therapeutic contact with the child or involved participants following a child custody evaluation is undertaken with caution.

A psychologist asked to testify regarding a therapy client who is involved in a child custody case is aware of the limitations and possible biases inherent in such a role and the possible impact on the ongoing therapeutic relationship. Although the court may require the psychologist to testify as a fact witness regarding factual information he or she became aware of in a professional relationship with a client, that psychologist should generally decline the role of an expert witness who gives a professinal opinion regarding custody and visitation issues (see Ethical Standard 7.03) unless so ordered by the court.

III. Procedural Guidelines: Conducting a Child Custody Evaluation

8 The scope of the evaluation is determined by the evaluator, based on the nature of the referral question.

The scope of the custody-related evaluation is determined by the nature of the question or issue raised by the referring person or the court, or is inherent in the situation. Although comprehensive child custody evaluations generally require an evaluation of all parents or guardians and children, as well as observations of interactions between them, the scope of the assessment in a particular case may be limited to evaluating the parental capacity of one parent without attempting to compare the parents or to make recommendations. Likewise, the scope may be limited to evaluating the child. Or a psychologist may be asked to critique the assumptions and methodology of the assessment of another mental health professional. A psychologist also might serve as an expert witness in the area of child development, providing expertise to the court without relating it specifically to the parties involved in a case.

9 The psychologist obtains informed consent from all adult participants and, as appropriate, informs child participants.

In undertaking child custody evaluations, the psychologist ensures that each adult participant is aware of (a) the purpose, nature, and method of the evaluation; (b) who has requested the psychologist's services; and (c) who will be paying the fees. The psychologist informs adult participants about the nature of the assessment instruments and techniques and informs those participants about the possible disposition of the data collected. The psychologist provides this information, as appropriate, to children, to the extent that they are able to understand.

10 The psychologist informs participants about the limits of confidentiality and the disclosure of information.

A psychologist conducting a child custody evaluation ensures that the participants, including children to the extent feasible, are aware of the limits of confidentiality characterizing the professional relationship with the psychologist. The psychologist informs participants that in consenting to the evaluation, they are consenting to disclosure of the evaluation's findings in the context of the forthcoming litigation and in any other proceedings deemed necessary by the courts. A psychologist obtains a waiver of confidentiality from all adult participants or from their authorized legal representatives.

11 The psychologist uses multiple methods of data gathering.

The psychologist strives to use the most appropriate methods available for addressing the questions raised in a specific child custody evaluation and generally uses multiple methods of data gathering, including, but not limited to, clinical interviews, observation, and/or psychological assessments. Important facts and opinions are documented from at least two sources whenever their reliability is questionable. The psychologist, for example, may review potentially relevant reports (e.g., from schools, health care providers, child care providers, agencies, and institutions). Psychologists may also interview extended family, friends, and other individuals on occasions when the information is likely to be useful. If information is gathered from third parties that is significant and may be used as a basis for conclusions, psychologists corroborate it by at least one other source wherever possible and appropriate and document this in the report.

12 The psychologist neither overinterprets nor inappropriately interprets clinical or assessment data.

The psychologist refrains from drawing conclusions not adequately supported by the data. The psychologist interprets any data from interviews or tests, as well as any questions of data reliability and validity, cautiously and conservatively, seeking convergent validity. The psychologist strives to acknowledge to the court any limitations in methods or data used.

13 The psychologist does not give any opinion regarding the psychological functioning of any individual who has not been personally evaluated.

This guideline, however, does not preclude the psychologist from reporting what an evaluated individual (such as the parent or child) has stated or from addressing theoretical issues or hypothetical questions, so long as the limited basis of the information is noted.

14 Recommendations, if any, are based on what is in the best psychological interests of the child.

Although the profession has not reached consensus about whether psychologists ought to make recommendations about the final custody determination to the courts, psychologists are obligated to be aware of the arguments on both sides of this issue and to be able to explain the logic of their position concerning their own practice.

If the psychologist does choose to make custody recommendations, these recommendations should be derived from sound psychological data and must be based on the best interests of the child in the particular case. Recommendations are based on articulated assumptions, data, interpretations, and inferences based upon established professional and scientific standards. Psychologists guard against relying on their own biases or unsupported beliefs in rendering opinions in particular cases.

15 The psychologist clarifies financial arrangements.

Financial arrangements are clarified and agreed upon prior to commencing a child custody evaluation. When billing for a child custody evaluation, the psychologist does not misrepresent his or her services for reimbursement purposes.

16 The psychologist maintains written records.

All records obtained in the process of conducting a child custody evaluation are properly maintained and filed in accord with the APA *Record Keeping Guidelines* (APA, 1993) and relevant statutory guidelines.

All raw data and interview information are recorded with an eye toward their possible review by other psychologists or the court, where legally permitted. Upon request, appropriate reports are made available to the court.

REFERENCES

American Psychological Association. (1985). Standards for educational and psychological testing. (Washington, DC: Author.)

American Psychological Association. (1992). Ethical principles of psychologists and code of conduct. *American Psychologist, 47,* 1597–1611.

American Psychological Association. (1993). Record keeping guidelines. (Washington, DC: Author.)

American Psychological Association, Ethics Committee. (1985). Annual report of the American Psychological Association Ethics Committee. (Washington, DC: Author.)

Grisso, T. (1986). Evaluating competencies: Forensic assessments and instruments. (New York: Plenum.)

Hall, J. E., & Hare-Mustin, R. T. (1983). Sanctions and the diversity of ethical complaints against psychologists. *American Psychologist, 38,* 714–729.

Keith-Spiegel, P., & Koocher, G. P. (1985). Ethics in psychology. (New York: Random House.)

Melton, G. B., Petrila, J., Poythress, N. G., & Slobogin, C. (1987). Psychological evaluations for the courts: A handbook for mental health professionals and lawyers. (New York: Guilford Press.)

Mills, D. H. (1984). Ethics education and adjudication within psychology. *American Psychologist, 39,* 669–675.

Mnookin, R. H. (1975). Child-custody adjudication: Judicial functions in the face of indeterminacy. *Law and Contemporary Problems, 39,* 226–293.

Ochroch, R. (1982, August). Ethical pitfalls in child custody evaluations. (Paper presented at the 90th Annual Convention of the American Psychological Association, Washington, DC.)

Okpaku, S. (1976). Psychology: Impediment or aid in child custody cases? *Rugers Law Review, 29,* 1117–1153.

Weithorn, L. A. (1987). Psychology and child custody determinations: Knowledge, roles, and expertise. (Lincoln: University of Nebraska Press.)

Georgia Psychological Association. (1990). Recommendations for psychologists' involvement in child custody cases. (Atlanta, GA: Author.)

Metropolitan Denver Interdisciplinary Committee on Child Custody. (1989). Guidelines for child custody evaluations. (Denver, CO: Author.)

Nebraska Psychological Association. (1986). Guidelines for child custody evaluations. (Lincoln, NE: Author.)

New Jersey State Board of Psychological Examiners. (1993). Specialty guidelines for psychologists in custody/visitation evaluations. (Newark, NJ: Author.)

North Carolina Psychological Association. (1993). Child custody guidelines. (Unpublished manuscript.)

Oklahoma Psychological Association. (1988). Ethical guidelines for child custody evaluations. (Oklahoma City, OK: Author.)

Committee on Ethical Guidelines for Forensic Psychologists. (1991). Specialty guidelines for forensic psychologists. *Law and Human Behavior, 6,* 655–665.

Committee on Ethical Guidelines for Forensic Psychologists. (1991). Specialty guidelines for forensic psychologists. *Law and Human Behavior, 6,* 655–665.

Ackerman, M. J., & Kane, A. W. (1993). Psychological experts in divorce, personal injury and other civil actions. (New York: Wiley.)

American Psychological Association, Board of Ethnic Minority Affairs. (1991). Guidelines for providers of psychological services to ethnic, linguistic, and culturally diverse populations. (Washington, DC: American Psychological Association.)

American Psychological Association, Committee on Women in Psychology and Committee on Lesbian and Gay Concerns. (1988). Lesbian parents and their children: A resource paper for psychologists. (Washington, DC: American Psychological Association.)

Beaber, R. J. (1982, Fall). Custody quagmire: Some psycholegal dilemmas. *Journal of Psychiatry & Law,* 309–326.

Beaber, R. J. (1982, Fall). Custody quagmire: Some psycholegal dilemmas. *Journal of Psychiatry & Law,* 309–326.

Bennett, B. E., Bryant, B. K., VandenBos, G. R., & Greenwood, A. (1990). Professional liability and risk management. (Washington, DC: American Psychological Association.)

Bolocofsky, D. N. (1989). Use and abuse of mental health experts in child custody determinations. *Behavioral Sciences and the Law, 7,* 197–213.

Bolocofsky, D. N. (1989). Use and abuse of mental health experts in child custody determinations. *Behavioral Sciences and the Law, 7,* 197–213.

Bozett, F. (1987). Gay and lesbian parents. (New York: Praeger.)

Bray, J. H. (1993). What's the best interest of the child?: Children's adjustment issues in divorce. *The Independent Practitioner, 13,* 42–45.

Bray, J. H. (1993). What's the best interest of the child?: Children's adjustment issues in divorce. *The Independent Practitioner, 13,* 42–45.

Bricklin, B. (1992). Data-based tests in custody evaluations. *American Journal of Family Therapy, 20,* 254–265.

Bricklin, B. (1992). Data-based tests in custody evaluations. *American Journal of Family Therapy, 20,* 254–265.

Cantor, D. W., & Drake, E. A. (1982). Divorced parents and their children: A guide for mental health professionals. (New York: Springer.)

Chesler, P. (1991). Mothers on trial: The battle for children and custody. (New York: Harcourt Brace Jovanovich.)

Deed, M. L. (1991). Court-ordered child custody evaluations: Helping or victimizing vulnerable families. *Psychotherapy, 28,* 76–84.

Deed, M. L. (1991). Court-ordered child custody evaluations: Helping or victimizing vulnerable families. *Psychotherapy, 28,* 76–84.

Falk, P. J. (1989). Lesbian mothers: Psychosocial assumptions in family law. *American Psychologist, 44,* 941–947.

Falk, P. J. (1989). Lesbian mothers: Psychosocial assumptions in family law. *American Psychologist, 44,* 941–947.

Gardner, R. A. (1989). Family evaluation in child custody mediation, arbitration, and litigation. (Cresskill, NJ: Creative Therapeutics.)

Gardner, R. A. (1992). The parental alienation syndrome: A guide for mental health and legal professionals. (Cresskill, NJ: Creative Therapeutics.)

Gardner, R. A. (1992). True and false accusations of child abuse. (Cresskill, NJ: Creative Therapeutics.)

Goldstein, J., Freud, A., & Solnit, A. J. (1980). Before the best interests of the child. (New York: Free Press.)

Goldstein, J., Freud, A., & Solnit, A. J. (1980). Beyond the best interests of the child. (New York: Free Press.)

Goldstein, J., Freud, A., Solnit, A. J., & Goldstein, S. (1986). In the best interests of the child. (New York: Free Press.)

Grisso, T. (1990). Evolving guidelines for divorce/custody evaluations. *Family and Conciliation Courts Review, 28,* 35–41.

Grisso, T. (1990). Evolving guidelines for divorce/custody evaluations. *Family and Conciliation Courts Review, 28,* 35–41.

Halon, R. L. (1990). The comprehensive child custody evaluation. *American Journal of Forensic Psychology, 8,* 19–46.

Halon, R. L. (1990). The comprehensive child custody evaluation. *American Journal of Forensic Psychology, 8,* 19–46.

Hetherington, E. M. (1990). Coping with family transitions: Winners, losers, and survivors. *Child Development, 60,* 1–14.

Hetherington, E. M. (1990). Coping with family transitions: Winners, losers, and survivors. *Child Development, 60,* 1–14.

Hetherington, E. M., Stanley-Hagen, M., & Anderson, E. R. (1988). Marital transitions: A child's perspective. *American Psychologist, 44,* 303–312.

Hetherington, E. M., Stanley-Hagen, M., & Anderson, E. R. (1988). Marital transitions: A child's perspective. *American Psychologist, 44,* 303–312.

Johnston, J., Kline, M., & Tschann, J. (1989). Ongoing postdivorce conflict: Effects on children of joint custody and frequent access. *Journal of Orthopsychiatry, 59,* 576-592.

Johnston, J., Kline, M., & Tschann, J. (1989). Ongoing postdivorce conflict: Effects on children of joint custody and frequent access. *Journal of Orthopsychiatry, 59,* 576–592.

Koocher, G. P., & Keith-Spiegel, P. C. (1990). Children, ethics, and the law: Professional issues and cases. (Lincoln: University of Nebraska Press.)

Kreindler, S. (1986). The role of mental health professions in custody and access disputes. (In R. S. Parry, E. A. Broder, E. A. G. Schmitt, E. B. Saunders, & E. Hood (Eds.), Custody disputes: Evaluation and intervention. New York:Free Press.)

Martindale, D. A., Martindale, J. L., & Broderick, J. E. (1991). Providing expert testimony in child custody litigation. (In P. A. Keller & S. R. Heyman (Eds.), Innovations in clinical practice: A source book (Vol. 10, pp. 481–497). Sarasota, FL: Professional Resource Exchange.)

Patterson, C. J. (in press). Children of lesbian and gay parents. *Child Development,* Pennsylvania Psychological Association, Clinical Division Task Force on Child Custody Evaluation. (1991). Roles for psychologists in child custody disputes. (Unpublished manuscript.)

Saunders, T. R. (1991). An overview of some psycholegal issues in child physical and sexual abuse. *Psychotherapy in Private Practice, 9,* 61–78.

Saunders, T. R. (1991). An overview of some psycholegal issues in child physical and sexual abuse. *Psychotherapy in Private Practice, 9,* 61–78.

Schutz, B. M., Dixon, E. B., Lindenberger, J. C., & Ruther, N. J. (1989). Solomon's sword: A practical guide to conducting child custody evaluations. (San Francisco: Jossey-Bass.)

Stahly, G. B. (1989, August 9). Testimony on child abuse policy to APA Board. (Paper presented at the meeting of the American Psychological Association Board of Directors, New Orleans, LA.)

Thoennes, N., & Tjaden, P. G. (1991). The extent, nature, and validity of sexual abuse allegations in custody/visitation disputes. *Child Abuse & Neglect, 14,* 151–163.

Thoennes, N., & Tjaden, P. G. (1991). The extent, nature, and validity of sexual abuse allegations in custody/visitation disputes. *Child Abuse & Neglect, 14,* 151–163.

Wallerstein, J. S., & Blakeslee, S. (1989). Second chances: Men, women, and children a decade after divorce. (New York: Ticknor & Fields.)

Wallerstein, J. S., & Kelly, J. B. (1980). Surviving the breakup. (New York: Basic Books.)

Weissman, H. N. (1991). Child custody evaluations: Fair and unfair professional practices. *Behavioral Sciences and the Law, 9,* 469–476.

Weissman, H. N. (1991). Child custody evaluations: Fair and unfair professional practices. *Behavioral Sciences and the Law, 9,* 469–476.

Weithorn, L. A., & Grisso, T. (1987). Psychological evaluations in divorce custody: Problems, principles, and procedures. (In L. A. Weithorn (Ed.), Psychology and child custody determinations (pp. 157–158). Lincoln: University of Nebraska Press.)

White, S. (1990). The contamination of children's interviews. *Child Youth and Family Services Quarterly, 13,* (6, 17–18.)

Wyer, M. M., Gaylord, S. J., & Grove, E. T.. The legal context of child custody evaluations. (In L. A. Weithorn (Ed.), Psychology and child custody determinations (pp. 3–23). Lincoln: University of Nebraska Press.)

These guidelines were drafted by the Committee on Professional Practice and Standards (COPPS), a committee of the Board of Professional Affairs (BPA), with input from the Committee on Children, Youth, and Families (CYF). They were adopted by the Council of Representatives of the American Psychological Association in February 1994.

COPPS members in 1991–1993 were Richard Cohen, Alex Carballo Dieguez, Kathleen Dockett, Sam Friedman, Colette Ingraham, John Northman, John Robinson, Deborah Tharinger, Susana Urbina, Phil Witt, and James Wulach; BPA liaisons in 1991–1993 were Richard Cohen, Joseph Kobos, and Rodney Lowman; CYF members were Don Routh and Carolyn Swift.

Correspondence concerning this article should be addressed to, Practice Directorate, American Psychological Association, 750 First Street NE, Washington, DC 20002-4242.

APPENDIX H

CANADIAN CODE OF ETHICS FOR PSYCHOLOGISTS

ADVANCING PSYCHOLOGY FOR ALL

L'AVANCEMENT DE LA PSYCHOLOGIE POUR LA COLLECTIVITÉ

Revised, 2000

Third Edition

Introduction

Every discipline that has relatively autonomous control over its entry requirements, training, development of knowledge, standards, methods, and practices does so only within the context of a contract with the society in which it functions. This social contract is based on attitudes of mutual respect and trust, with society granting support for the autonomy of a discipline in exchange for a commitment by the discipline to do everything it can to assure that its members act ethically in conducting the affairs of the discipline within society; in particular, a commitment to try to assure that each member will place the welfare of the society and individual members of that society above the welfare of the discipline and its own members. By virtue of this social contract, psychologists have a higher duty of care to members of society than the general duty of care that all members of society have to each other.

The Canadian Psychological Association recognizes its responsibility to help assure ethical behaviour and attitudes on the part of psychologists. Attempts to assure ethical behaviour and attitudes include articulating ethical principles, values, and standards; promoting those principles, values, and standards through education, peer modelling, and consultation; developing and implementing methods to help psychologists monitor the ethics of their behaviour and attitudes; adjudicating complaints of unethical behaviour; and, taking corrective action when warranted.

This *Code* articulates ethical principles, values, and standards to guide all members of the Canadian Psychological Association, whether scientists, practitioners, or scientist practitioners, or whether acting in a research, direct service, teaching, student, trainee, administrative, management, employer, employee, supervisory, consultative, peer review, editorial, expert witness, social policy, or any other role related to the discipline of psychology.

Structure and Derivation of *Code*

Structure. Four ethical principles, to be considered and balanced in ethical decision making, are presented. Each principle is followed by a statement of those values that are included in and give definition to the principle. Each values statement is followed by a list of ethical standards that illustrate the application of the specific principle and values to the activities of psychologists. The standards range from minimal behavioural expectations (e.g., Standards I.28, II.28, III.33, IV.27) to more idealized, but achievable, attitudinal and behavioural expectations (e.g., Standards I.12, II.12, III.10, IV.6). In the margin, to the left of the standards, key words are placed to guide the reader through the standards and to illustrate the relationship of the specific standards to the values statement.

Derivation. The four principles represent those ethical principles used most consistently by Canadian psychologists to resolve hypothetical ethical dilemmas sent to them by the CPA Committee on Ethics during the initial development of the *Code*. In addition to the responses provided by Canadian psychologists, the values statements and ethical standards have been derived from interdisciplinary and international ethics codes, provincial and specialty codes of conduct, and ethics literature.

When Principles Conflict

- **Principle I: Respect for the Dignity of Persons.** This principle, with its emphasis on moral rights, generally should be given the highest weight, except in circumstances in which there is a clear and imminent danger to the physical safety of any person.
- **Principle II: Responsible Caring.** This principle generally should be given the second highest weight. Responsible caring requires competence and should be carried out only in ways that respect the dignity of persons.
- **Principle III: Integrity in Relationships.** This principle generally should be given the third highest weight. Psychologists are expected to demonstrate the highest integrity in all of their relationships. However, in rare circumstances, values such as openness and straightforwardness might need to be subordinated to the values contained in the Principles of Respect for the Dignity of Persons and Responsible Caring.
- **Principle IV: Responsibility to Society.** This principle generally should be given the lowest weight of the four principles when it conflicts with one or more of them. Although it is necessary and important to consider responsibility to society in every ethical decision, adherence to this principle must be subject to and guided by Respect for the Dignity of Persons, Responsible Caring, and Integrity in Relationships. When a person's welfare appears to conflict with benefits to society, it is often possible to find ways of working for the benefit of society that do not violate respect and responsible caring for the person. However, if this is not possible, the dignity and well-being of a person should not be sacrificed to a vision of the greater good of society, and greater weight must be given to respect and responsible caring for the person.

Even with the above ordering of the principles, psychologists will be faced with ethical dilemmas that are difficult to resolve. In these circumstances, psychologists are expected to engage in an ethical decision-making process that is explicit enough to bear public scrutiny. In some cases, resolution might be a matter of personal conscience. However, decisions of personal conscience are also expected to be the result of a decision-making process that is based on a reasonably coherent set of ethical principles and that can bear public scrutiny. If the psychologist can demonstrate that every reasonable effort was made to apply the ethical principles of this *Code* and resolution of the conflict has had to depend on the personal conscience of the psychologist, such a psychologist would be deemed to have followed this *Code*.

The Ethical Decision-Making Process

The ethical decision-making process might occur very rapidly, leading to an easy resolution of an ethical issue. This is particularly true of issues for which clear-cut guidelines or standards exist and for which there is no conflict between principles. On the other hand, some ethical issues (particularly those in which ethical principles conflict) are not easily resolved, might be emotionally distressful, and might require time-consuming deliberation.

The following basic steps typify approaches to ethical decision making:

1. Identification of the individuals and groups potentially affected by the decision.
2. Identification of ethically relevant issues and practices, including the interests, rights, and any relevant characteristics of the individuals and groups involved and of the system or circumstances in which the ethical problem arose.
3. Consideration of how personal biases, stresses, or self-interest might influence the development of or choice between courses of action.
4. Development of alternative courses of action.
5. Analysis of likely short-term, ongoing, and long-term risks and benefits of each course of action on the individual(s)/group(s) involved or likely to be affected (e.g., client, client's family or employees, employing institution, students, research participants, colleagues, the discipline, society, self).
6. Choice of course of action after conscientious application of existing principles, values, and standards.
7. Action, with a commitment to assume responsibility for the consequences of the action.
8. Evaluation of the results of the course of action.
9. Assumption of responsibility for consequences of action, including correction of negative consequences, if any, or re-engaging in the decision-making process if the ethical issue is not resolved.
10. Appropriate action, as warranted and feasible, to prevent future occurrences of the dilemma (e.g., communication and problem solving with colleagues; changes in procedures and practices).

Psychologists engaged in time-consuming deliberation are encouraged and expected to consult with parties affected by the ethical problem, when appropriate, and with colleagues and/or advisory bodies when such persons can add knowledge or objectivity to the decision-making process. Although the decision for action remains with the individual psychologist, the seeking and consideration of such assistance reflects an ethical approach to ethical decision making.

Uses of the *Code*

This *Code* is intended to guide psychologists in their everyday conduct, thinking, and planning, and in the resolution of ethical dilemmas; that is, it advocates the practice of both proactive and reactive ethics.

The *Code* also is intended to serve as an umbrella document for the development of codes of conduct or other more specific codes. For example, the *Code* could be used as an ethical framework for the identification of behaviours that would be considered enforceable in a jurisdiction, the violation of which would constitute misconduct; or, jurisdictions could identify those standards in the *Code* that would be considered of a more serious nature and, therefore, reportable and subject to possible discipline. In addition, the principles and values could be used to help specialty areas develop standards that are specific to those areas. Some work in this direction has already occurred within CPA (e.g., *Guidelines for the Use of Animals in Research and Instruction in Psychology, Guidelines for Non-Discriminatory Practice, Guidelines for Psychologists in Addressing Recovered Memories*). The principles and values incorporated into this *Code*, insofar as they come to be reflected in other documents guiding the behaviour of psychologists, will reduce inconsistency and conflict between documents.

A third use of the *Code* is to assist in the adjudication of complaints against psychologists. A body charged with this responsibility is required to investigate allegations, judge whether unacceptable behaviour has occurred, and determine what corrective action should be taken. In judging whether unacceptable conduct has occurred, many jurisdictions refer to a code of conduct. Some complaints, however, are about conduct that is not addressed directly in a code of conduct. The *Code* provides an ethical framework for determining whether the complaint is of enough concern, either at the level of the individual psychologist or at the level of the profession as a whole, to warrant corrective action (e.g., discipline of the individual psychologist, general educational activities for members, or incorporation into the code of conduct). In determining corrective action for an individual psychologist, one of the judgments the adjudicating body needs to make is whether an individual conscientiously engaged in an ethical decision-making process and acted in good faith, or whether there was a negligent or willful disregard of ethical principles. The articulation of the ethical decision-making process contained in this *Code* provides guidance for making such judgements.

Responsibility of the Individual Psychologist

The discipline's contract with society commits the discipline and its members to act as a moral community that develops its ethical awareness and sensitivity, educates new members in the ethics of the discipline, manages its affairs and its members in an ethical manner, is as self-correcting as possible, and is accountable both internally and externally.

However, responsibility for ethical action depends foremost on the integrity of each individual psychologist; that is, on each psychologist's commitment to behave as ethically as possible in every situation. Acceptance to membership in the Canadian Psychological Association, a scientific and professional association of psychologists, commits members:

1. To adhere to the Association's *Code* in all current activities as a psychologist.
2. To apply conscientiously the ethical principles and values of the *Code* to new and emerging areas of activity.
3. To assess and discuss ethical issues and practices with colleagues on a regular basis.
4. To bring to the attention of the Association ethical issues that require clarification or the development of new guidelines or standards.
5. To bring concerns about possible unethical actions by a psychologist directly to the psychologist when the action appears to be primarily a lack of sensitivity, knowledge, or experience, and attempt to reach an agreement on the issue and, if needed, on the appropriate action to be taken.

6. To bring concerns about possible unethical actions of a more serious nature (e.g., actions that have caused or could cause serious harm, or actions that are considered misconduct in the jurisdiction) to the person(s) or body(ies) best suited to investigating the situation and to stopping or offsetting the harm.

7. To consider seriously others' concerns about one's own possibly unethical actions and attempt to reach an agreement on the issue and, if needed, take appropriate action.

8. In bringing or in responding to concerns about possible unethical actions, not to be vexatious or malicious.

9. To cooperate with duly constituted committees of the Association that are concerned with ethics and ethical conduct.

Relationship of *Code* to Personal Behaviour

This *Code* is intended to guide and regulate only those activities a psychologist engages in by virtue of being a psychologist. There is no intention to guide or regulate a psychologist's activities outside of this context. Personal behaviour becomes a concern of the discipline only if it is of such a nature that it undermines public trust in the discipline as a whole or if it raises questions about the psychologist's ability to carry out appropriately his/her responsibilities as a psychologist.

Relationship of *Code* to Provincial Regulatory Bodies

In exercising its responsibility to articulate ethical principles, values, and standards for those who wish to become and remain members in good standing, the Canadian Psychological Association recognizes the multiple memberships that some psychologists have (both regulatory and voluntary). The *Code* has attempted to encompass and incorporate those ethical principles most prevalent in the discipline as a whole, thereby minimizing the possibility of variance with provincial/territorial regulations and guidelines. Psychologists are expected to respect the requirements of their provincial/territorial regulatory bodies. Such requirements might define particular behaviours that constitute misconduct, are reportable to the regulatory body, and/or are subject to discipline.

Definition of Terms

For the purposes of this *Code:*

a. **"Psychologist"** means any person who is a Fellow, Member, Student Affiliate or Foreign Affiliate of the Canadian Psychological Association, or a member of any psychology voluntary association or regulatory body adopting this *Code*. (Readers are reminded that provincial/territorial jurisdictions might restrict the legal use of the term psychologist in their jurisdiction and that such restrictions are to be honoured.)

b. **"Client"** means an individual, family, or group (including an organization or community) receiving service from a psychologist.

c. Clients, research participants, students, and any other persons with whom psychologists come in contact in the course of their work, are **"independent"** if they can independently contract or give informed consent. Such persons are **"partially dependent"** if the decision to contract or give informed consent is shared between two or more parties (e.g., parents and school boards, workers and Workers' Compensation Boards, adult members of a family). Such persons are considered to be **"fully dependent"** if they have little or no choice about whether or not to receive service or participate in an activity (e.g., patients who have been involuntarily committed to a psychiatric facility, or very young children involved in a research project).

d. **"Others"** means any persons with whom psychologists come in contact in the course of their work. This may include, but is not limited to: clients seeking help with individual, family, organizational, industrial, or community issues; research participants; employees; students; trainees; supervisees; colleagues; employers; third party payers; and, members of the general public.

e. **"Legal or civil rights"** means those rights protected under laws and statutes recognized by the province or territory in which the psychologist is working.

f. **"Moral rights"** means fundamental and inalienable human rights that might or might not be fully protected by existing laws and statutes. Of particular significance to psychologists, for example, are rights to: distributive justice; fairness and due process; and, developmentally appropriate privacy, self-determination, and personal liberty. Protection of some aspects of these rights might involve practices that are not contained or controlled within current laws and statutes. Moral rights are not limited to those mentioned in this definition.

g. **"Unjust discrimination"** or **"unjustly discriminatory"** means activities that are prejudicial or promote prejudice to persons because of their culture, nationality, ethnicity, colour, race, religion, sex, gender, marital status, sexual orientation, physical or mental abilities, age, socio-economic status, or any other preference or personal characteristic, condition, or status.

h. **"Sexual harassment"** includes either or both of the following: (i) The use of power or authority in an attempt to coerce another person to engage in or tolerate sexual activity. Such uses include explicit or implicit threats of reprisal for noncompliance, or promises of reward for compliance. (ii) Engaging in deliberate and/or repeated unsolicited sexually oriented comments, anecdotes, gestures, or touching, if such behaviours: are offensive and unwelcome; create an offensive, hostile, or intimidating working, learning, or service environment; or, can be expected to be harmful to the recipient.[1]

i. The **"discipline of psychology"** refers to the scientific and applied methods and knowledge of psychology, and to the structures and procedures used by its members for conducting their work in relationship to society, to members of the public, to students or trainees, and to each other.

Review Schedule

To maintain the relevance and responsiveness of this *Code*, it will be reviewed regularly by the CPA Board of Directors, and revised as needed. You are invited to forward comments and suggestions, at any time, to the CPA office. In addition to psychologists, this invitation is extended to all readers, including members of the public and other disciplines.

Principle I: Respect for the Dignity of Persons

Values Statement

In the course of their work as scientists, practitioners, or scientist-practitioners, psychologists come into contact with many different individuals and groups, including: research participants; clients seeking help with individual, family, organizational, industrial, or community issues; students; trainees; supervisees; employees; business partners; business competitors; colleagues; employers; third party payers; and, the general public.

In these contacts, psychologists accept as fundamental the principle of respect for the dignity of persons; that is, the belief that each person should be treated primarily as a person or an end in him/herself, not as an object or a means to an end. In so doing, psychologists acknowledge that all persons have a right to have their innate worth as human beings appreciated and that this worth is not dependent upon their culture, nationality, ethnicity, colour, race, religion, sex, gender, marital status, sexual orientation, physical or mental abilities, age, socio-economic status, or any other preference or personal characteristic, condition, or status.

Although psychologists have a responsibility to respect the dignity of all persons with whom they come in contact in their role as psychologists, the nature of their contract with society demands that their greatest responsibility be to those persons in the most vulnerable position. Normally, persons directly receiving or involved in the psychologist's activities are in such a position (e.g., research participants, clients, students). This responsibility is almost always greater than their responsibility to those indirectly involved (e.g., employers, third party payers, the general public).

Adherence to the concept of moral rights is an essential component of respect for the dignity of persons. Rights to privacy, self-determination, personal liberty, and natural justice are of particular importance to psychologists, and they have a responsibility to protect and promote these rights in all of their activities. As such, psychologists have a responsibility to develop and follow procedures for informed consent, confidentiality, fair treatment, and due process that are consistent with those rights.

As individual rights exist within the context of the rights of others and of responsible caring (see Principle II), there might be circumstances in which the possibility of serious detrimental consequences to themselves or others, a diminished capacity to be autonomous, or a court order, would disallow some aspects of the rights to privacy, self-determination, and personal liberty. Indeed, such circumstances might be serious enough to create a duty to warn or protect others (see Standards I.45 and II.39). However, psychologists still have a responsibility to respect the rights of the person(s) involved to the greatest extent possible under the circumstances, and to do what is necessary and reasonable to reduce the need for future disallowances.

Psychologists recognize that, although all persons possess moral rights, the manner in which such rights are promoted, protected, and exercised varies across communities and cultures. For instance, definitions of what is considered private vary, as does the role of families and other community members in personal decision making. In their work, psychologists acknowledge and respect such differences, while guarding against clear violations of moral rights.

In addition, psychologists recognize that as individual, family, group, or community vulnerabilities increase, or as the power of persons to control their environment or their lives decreases, psychologists have an increasing responsibility to seek ethical advice and to establish safeguards to protect the rights of the persons involved. For this reason, psychologists consider it their responsibility to increase safeguards to protect and promote the rights of persons involved in their activities proportionate to the degree of dependency and the lack of voluntary initiation. For example, this would mean that there would be more safeguards to protect and promote the rights of fully dependent persons than partially dependent persons, and more safeguards for partially dependent than independent persons.

Respect for the dignity of persons also includes the concept of distributive justice. With respect to psychologists, this concept implies that all persons are entitled to benefit equally from the contributions of psychology and to equal quality in the processes, procedures, and services being conducted by psychologists, regardless of the person's characteristics, condition, or status. Although individual psychologists might specialize and direct their activities to particular populations, or might decline to engage in activities based on the limits of their competence or acknowledgment of problems in some relationships, psychologists must not exclude persons on a capricious or unjustly discriminatory basis.

By virtue of the social contract that the discipline has with society, psychologists have a higher duty of care to members of society than the general duty of care all members of society have to each other. However, psychologists are entitled to protect themselves from serious violations of their own moral rights (e.g., privacy, personal liberty) in carrying out their work as psychologists.

Ethical Standards

In adhering to the Principle of Respect for the Dignity of Persons, psychologists would:

General respect

> I.1 Demonstrate appropriate respect for the knowledge, insight, experience, and areas of expertise of others.

> I.2 Not engage publicly (e.g., in public statements, presentations, research reports, or with clients) in degrading comments about others, including demeaning jokes based on such characteristics as culture, nationality, ethnicity, colour, race, religion, sex, gender, or sexual orientation.

> I.3 Strive to use language that conveys respect for the dignity of persons as much as possible in all written or oral communication.

> I.4 Abstain from all forms of harassment, including sexual harassment.

General rights

I.5 Avoid or refuse to participate in practices disrespectful of the legal, civil, or moral rights of others.

I.6 Refuse to advise, train, or supply information to anyone who, in the psychologist's judgement, will use the knowledge or skills to infringe on human rights.

I.7 Make every reasonable effort to ensure that psychological knowledge is not misused, intentionally or unintentionally, to infringe on human rights.

I.8 Respect the right of research participants, clients, employees, supervisees, students, trainees, and others to safeguard their own dignity.

Non-discrimination

I.9 Not practice, condone, facilitate, or collaborate with any form of unjust discrimination.

I.10 Act to correct practices that are unjustly discriminatory.

I.11 Seek to design research, teaching, practice, and business activities in such a way that they contribute to the fair distribution of benefits to individuals and groups, and that they do not unfairly exclude those who are vulnerable or might be disadvantaged.

Fair treatment/due process

I.12 Work and act in a spirit of fair treatment to others.

I.13 Help to establish and abide by due process or other natural justice procedures for employment, evaluation, adjudication, editorial, and peer review activities.

I.14 Compensate others fairly for the use of their time, energy, and knowledge, unless such compensation is refused in advance.

I.15 Establish fees that are fair in light of the time, energy, and knowledge of the psychologist and any associates or employees, and in light of the market value of the product or service. (Also see Standard IV.12.)

Informed consent

I.16 Seek as full and active participation as possible from others in decisions that affect them, respecting and integrating as much as possible their opinions and wishes.

I.17 Recognize that informed consent is the result of a process of reaching an agreement to work collaboratively, rather than of simply having a consent form signed.

I.18 Respect the expressed wishes of persons to involve others (e.g., family members, community members) in their decision making regarding informed consent. This would include respect for written and clearly expressed unwritten advance directives.

I.19 Obtain informed consent from all independent and partially dependent persons for any psychological services provided to them except in circumstances of urgent need (e.g., disaster or other crisis). In urgent circumstances, psychologists would proceed with the assent of such persons, but fully informed consent would be obtained as soon as possible. (Also see Standard I.29.)

I.20 Obtain informed consent for all research activities that involve obtrusive measures, invasion of privacy, more than minimal risk of harm, or any attempt to change the behaviour of research participants.

I.21 Establish and use signed consent forms that specify the dimensions of informed consent or that acknowledge that such dimensions have been explained and are understood, if such forms are required by law or if such forms are desired by the psychologist, the person(s) giving consent, or the organization for whom the psychologist works.

I.22 Accept and document oral consent, in situations in which signed consent forms are not acceptable culturally or in which there are other good reasons for not using them.

I.23 Provide, in obtaining informed consent, as much information as reasonable or prudent persons would want to know before making a decision or consenting to the activity. The psychologist would relay this information in language that the persons understand (including providing translation into another language, if necessary) and would take whatever reasonable steps are needed to ensure that the information was, in fact, understood.

I.24 Ensure, in the process of obtaining informed consent, that at least the following points are understood: purpose and nature of the activity; mutual responsibilities; confidentiality protections and limitations; likely benefits and risks; alternatives; the likely consequences of non-action; the option to refuse or withdraw at any time, without prejudice; over what period of time the consent applies; and, how to rescind consent if desired. (Also see Standards III.23-30.)

I.25 Provide new information in a timely manner, whenever such information becomes available and is significant enough that it reasonably could be seen as relevant to the original or ongoing informed consent.

I.26 Clarify the nature of multiple relationships to all concerned parties before obtaining consent, if providing services to or conducting research at the request or for the use of third parties. This would include, but not be limited to: the purpose of the service or research; the reasonably anticipated use that will be made of information collected; and, the limits on confidentiality. Third parties may include schools, courts, government agencies, insurance companies, police, and special funding bodies.

Freedom of consent

I.27 Take all reasonable steps to ensure that consent is not given under conditions of coercion, undue pressure, or undue reward. (Also see Standard III.32.)

I.28 Not proceed with any research activity, if consent is given under any condition of coercion, undue pressure, or undue reward. (Also see Standard III.32.)

I.29 Take all reasonable steps to confirm or re-establish freedom of consent, if consent for service is given under conditions of duress or conditions of extreme need.

I.30 Respect the right of persons to discontinue participation or service at any time, and be responsive to non-verbal indications of a desire to discontinue if a person has difficulty with verbally communicating such a desire (e.g., young children, verbally disabled persons) or, due to culture, is unlikely to communicate such a desire orally.

Protections for vulnerable persons

I.31 Seek an independent and adequate ethical review of human rights issues and protections for any research involving members of vulnerable groups, including persons of diminished capacity to give informed consent, before making a decision to proceed.

I.32 Not use persons of diminished capacity to give informed consent in research studies, if the research involved may be carried out equally well with persons who have a fuller capacity to give informed consent.

I.33 Seek to use methods that maximize the understanding and ability to consent of persons of diminished capacity to give informed consent, and that reduce the need for a substitute decision maker.

I.34 Carry out informed consent processes with those persons who are legally responsible or appointed to give informed consent on behalf of persons not competent to consent on their own behalf, seeking to ensure respect for any previously expressed preferences of persons not competent to consent.

I.35 Seek willing and adequately informed participation from any person of diminished capacity to give informed consent, and proceed without this assent only if the service or research activity is considered to be of direct benefit to that person.

I.36 Be particularly cautious in establishing the freedom of consent of any person who is in a dependent relationship to the psychologist (e.g., student, employee). This may include, but is not limited to, offering that person an alternative activity to fulfill their educational or employment goals, or offering a range of research studies or experience opportunities from which the person can select, none of which is so onerous as to be coercive.

Privacy

I.37 Seek and collect only information that is germane to the purpose(s) for which consent has been obtained.

I.38 Take care not to infringe, in research, teaching, or service activities, on the personally, developmentally, or culturally defined private space of individuals or groups, unless clear permission is granted to do so.

I.39 Record only that private information necessary for the provision of continuous, coordinated service, or for the goals of the particular research study being conducted, or that is required or justified by law. (Also see Standards IV.17 and IV.18.)

I.40 Respect the right of research participants, employees, supervisees, students, and trainees to reasonable personal privacy.

I.41 Collect, store, handle, and transfer all private information, whether written or unwritten (e.g., communication during service provision, written records, e-mail or fax communication, computer files, video-tapes), in a way that attends to the needs for privacy and security. This would include having adequate plans for records in circumstances of one's own serious illness, termination of employment, or death.

I.42 Take all reasonable steps to ensure that records over which they have control remain personally identifiable only as long as necessary in the interests of those to whom they refer and/or to the research project for which they were collected, or as required or justified by law (e.g., the possible need to defend oneself against future allegations), and render anonymous or destroy any records under their control that no longer need to be personally identifiable. (Also see Standards IV.17 and IV.18.)

Confidentiality

I.43 Be careful not to relay information about colleagues, colleagues' clients, research participants, employees, supervisees, students, trainees, and members of organizations, gained in the process of their activities as psychologists, that the psychologist has reason to believe is considered confidential by those persons, except as required or justified by law. (Also see Standards IV.17 and IV.18.)

I.44 Clarify what measures will be taken to protect confidentiality, and what responsibilities family, group, and community members have for the protection of each other's confidentiality, when engaged in services to or research with individuals, families, groups, or communities.

I.45 Share confidential information with others only with the informed consent of those involved, or in a manner that the persons involved cannot be identified, except as required or justified by law, or in circumstances of actual or possible serious physical harm or death. (Also see Standards II.39, IV.17, and IV.18.)

Extended responsibility

I.46 Encourage others, in a manner consistent with this *Code*, to respect the dignity of persons and to expect respect for their own dignity.

I.47 Assume overall responsibility for the scientific and professional activities of their assistants, employees, students, supervisees, and trainees with regard to Respect for the Dignity of Persons, all of whom, however, incur similar obligations.

Principle II: Responsible Caring

Values Statement

A basic ethical expectation of any discipline is that its activities will benefit members of society or, at least, do no harm. Therefore, psychologists demonstrate an active concern for the welfare of any individual, family, group, or community with whom they relate in their role as psychologists. This concern includes both those directly involved and those indirectly involved in their activities. However, as with Principle I, psychologists' greatest responsibility is to protect the welfare of those in the most vulnerable position. Normally, persons directly involved in their activities (e.g., research participants, clients, students) are in such a position. Psychologists' responsibility to those indirectly involved (e.g., employers, third party payers, the general public) normally is secondary.

As persons usually consider their own welfare in their personal decision making, obtaining informed consent (see Principle I) is one of the best methods for ensuring that their welfare will be protected. However, it is only when such consent is combined with the responsible caring of the psychologist that there is considerable ethical protection of the welfare of the person(s) involved.

Responsible caring leads psychologists to take care to discern the potential harm and benefits involved, to predict the likelihood of their occurrence, to proceed only if the potential benefits outweigh the potential harms, to develop and use methods that will minimize harms and maximize benefits, and to take responsibility for correcting clearly harmful effects that have occurred as a direct result of their research, teaching, practice, or business activities.

In order to carry out these steps, psychologists recognize the need for competence and self-knowledge. They consider incompetent action to be unethical per se, as it is unlikely to be of benefit and likely to be harmful. They engage only in those activities in which they have competence or for which they are receiving supervision, and they perform their activities as competently as possible. They acquire, contribute to, and use the existing knowledge most relevant to the best interests of those concerned. They also engage in self-reflection regarding how their own values, attitudes, experiences, and social context (e.g., culture, ethnicity, colour, religion, sex, gender, sexual orientation, physical and mental abilities, age, and socio-economic status) influence their actions, interpretations, choices, and recommendations. This is done with the intent of increasing the probability that their activities will benefit and not harm the individuals, families, groups, and communities to whom they relate in their role as psychologists. Psychologists define harm and benefit in terms of both physical and psychological dimensions. They are concerned about such factors as: social, family, and community relationships; personal and cultural identity; feelings of self-worth, fear, humiliation, interpersonal trust, and cynicism; self-knowledge and general knowledge; and, such factors as physical safety, comfort, pain, and injury. They are concerned about immediate, short-term, and long-term effects.

Responsible caring recognizes and respects (e.g., through obtaining informed consent) the ability of individuals, families, groups, and communities to make decisions for themselves and to care for themselves and each other. It does not replace or undermine such ability, nor does it substitute one person's opinion about what is in the best interests of another person for that other person's competent decision making. However, psychologists recognize that, as vulnerabilities increase or as power to control one's own life decreases, psychologists have an increasing responsibility to protect the well-being of the individual, family, group, or community involved. For this reason, as in Principle I, psychologists consider it their responsibility to increase safeguards proportionate to the degree of dependency and the lack of voluntary initiation on the part of the persons involved. However, for Principle II, the safeguards are for the well-being of persons rather than for the rights of persons.

Psychologists' treatment and use of animals in their research and teaching activities are also a component of responsible caring. Although animals do not have the same moral rights as persons (e.g., privacy), they do have the right to be treated humanely and not to be exposed to unnecessary discomfort, pain, or disruption.

By virtue of the social contract that the discipline has with society, psychologists have a higher duty of care to members of society than the general duty of care all members of society have to each other. However, psychologists are entitled to protect their own basic well-being (e.g., physical safety, family relationships) in their work as psychologists.

Ethical Standards

In adhering to the Principle of Responsible Caring, psychologists would:

General caring

> II.1 Protect and promote the welfare of clients, research participants, employees, supervisees, students, trainees, colleagues, and others.

> II.2 Avoid doing harm to clients, research participants, employees, supervisees, students, trainees, colleagues, and others.

> II.3 Accept responsibility for the consequences of their actions.

II.4 Refuse to advise, train, or supply information to anyone who, in the psychologist's judgment, will use the knowledge or skills to harm others.

II.5 Make every reasonable effort to ensure that psychological knowledge is not misused, intentionally or unintentionally, to harm others.

Competence and self-knowledge

II.6 Offer or carry out (without supervision) only those activities for which they have established their competence to carry them out to the benefit of others.

II.7 Not delegate activities to persons not competent to carry them out to the benefit of others.

II.8 Take immediate steps to obtain consultation or to refer a client to a colleague or other appropriate professional, whichever is more likely to result in providing the client with competent service, if it becomes apparent that a client's problems are beyond their competence.

II.9 Keep themselves up to date with a broad range of relevant knowledge, research methods, and techniques, and their impact on persons and society, through the reading of relevant literature, peer consultation, and continuing education activities, in order that their service or research activities and conclusions will benefit and not harm others.

II.10 Evaluate how their own experiences, attitudes, culture, beliefs, values, social context, individual differences, specific training, and stresses influence their interactions with others, and integrate this awareness into all efforts to benefit and not harm others.

II.11 Seek appropriate help and/or discontinue scientific or professional activity for an appropriate period of time, if a physical or psychological condition reduces their ability to benefit and not harm others.

II.12 Engage in self-care activities that help to avoid conditions (e.g., burnout, addictions) that could result in impaired judgment and interfere with their ability to benefit and not harm others.

Risk/benefit analysis

II.13 Assess the individuals, families, groups, and communities involved in their activities adequately enough to ensure that they will be able to discern what will benefit and not harm the persons involved.

II.14 Be sufficiently sensitive to and knowledgeable about individual, group, community, and cultural differences and vulnerabilities to discern what will benefit and not harm persons involved in their activities.

II.15 Carry out pilot studies to determine the effects of all new procedures and techniques that might carry more than minimal risk, before considering their use on a broader scale.

II.16 Seek an independent and adequate ethical review of the balance of risks and potential benefits of all research and new interventions that involve procedures of unknown consequence, or where pain, discomfort, or harm are possible, before making a decision to proceed.

II.17 Not carry out any scientific or professional activity unless the probable benefit is proportionately greater than the risk involved.

Maximize benefit

II.18 Provide services that are coordinated over time and with other service providers, in order to avoid duplication or working at cross purposes.

II.19 Create and maintain records relating to their activities that are sufficient to support continuity and appropriate coordination of their activities with the activities of others.

II.20 Make themselves aware of the knowledge and skills of other disciplines (e.g., law, medicine, business administration) and advise the use of such knowledge and skills, where relevant to the benefit of others.

II.21 Strive to provide and/or obtain the best possible service for those needing and seeking psychological service. This may include, but is not limited to: selecting interventions that are relevant to the needs and characteristics of the client and that have reasonable theoretical or empirically-supported efficacy in light of those needs and characteristics; consulting with, or including in service delivery, persons relevant to the culture or belief systems of those served; advocating on behalf of the client; and, recommending professionals other than psychologists when appropriate.

II.22 Monitor and evaluate the effect of their activities, record their findings, and communicate new knowledge to relevant others.

II.23 Debrief research participants in such a way that the participants' knowledge is enhanced and the participants have a sense of contribution to knowledge. (Also see Standards III.26 and III.27.)

II.24 Perform their teaching duties on the basis of careful preparation, so that their instruction is current and scholarly.

II.25 Facilitate the professional and scientific development of their employees, supervisees, students, and trainees by ensuring that these persons understand the values and ethical prescriptions of the discipline, and by providing or arranging for adequate working conditions, timely evaluations, and constructive consultation and experience opportunities.

II.26 Encourage and assist students in publication of worthy student papers.

Minimize harm

II.27 Be acutely aware of the power relationship in therapy and, therefore, not encourage or engage in sexual intimacy with therapy clients, neither during therapy, nor for that period of time following therapy during which the power relationship reasonably could be expected to influence the client's personal decision making. (Also see Standard III.31.)

II.28 Not encourage or engage in sexual intimacy with students or trainees with whom the psychologist has an evaluative or other relationship of direct authority. (Also see Standard III.31.)

II.29 Be careful not to engage in activities in a way that could place incidentally involved persons at risk.

II.30 Be acutely aware of the need for discretion in the recording and communication of information, in order that the information not be misinterpreted or misused to the detriment of others. This includes, but is not limited to: not recording information that could lead to misinterpretation and misuse; avoiding conjecture; clearly labelling opinion; and, communicating information in language that can be understood clearly by the recipient of the information.

II.31 Give reasonable assistance to secure needed psychological services or activities, if personally unable to meet requests for needed psychological services or activities.

II.32 Provide a client, if appropriate and if desired by the client, with reasonable assistance to find a way to receive needed services in the event that third party payments are exhausted and the client cannot afford the fees involved.

II.33 Maintain appropriate contact, support, and responsibility for caring until a colleague or other professional begins service, if referring a client to a colleague or other professional.

II.34 Give reasonable notice and be reasonably assured that discontinuation will cause no harm to the client, before discontinuing services.

II.35 Screen appropriate research participants and select those least likely to be harmed, if more than minimal risk of harm to some research participants is possible.

II.36 Act to minimize the impact of their research activities on research participants' personalities, or on their physical or mental integrity.

Offset/correct harm

II.37 Terminate an activity when it is clear that the activity carries more than minimal risk of harm and is found to be more harmful than beneficial, or when the activity is no longer needed.

II.38 Refuse to help individuals, families, groups, or communities to carry out or submit to activities that, according to current knowledge, or legal or professional guidelines, would cause serious physical or psychological harm to themselves or others.

II.39 Do everything reasonably possible to stop or offset the consequences of actions by others when these actions are likely to cause serious physical harm or death. This may include reporting to appropriate authorities (e.g., the police), an intended victim, or a family member or other support person who can intervene, and would be done even when a confidential relationship is involved. (Also see Standard I.45.)

II.40 Act to stop or offset the consequences of seriously harmful activities being carried out by another psychologist or member of another discipline, when there is objective information about the activities and the harm, and when these activities have come to their attention outside of a confidential client relationship between themselves and the psychologist or member of another discipline. This may include reporting to the appropriate regulatory body, authority, or committee for action, depending on the psychologist's judgment about the person(s) or body(ies) best suited to stop or offset the harm, and depending upon regulatory requirements and definitions of misconduct.

II.41 Act also to stop or offset the consequences of harmful activities carried out by another psychologist or member of another discipline, when the harm is not serious or the activities appear to be primarily a lack of sensitivity, knowledge, or experience, and when the activities have come to their attention outside of a confidential client relationship between themselves and the psychologist or member of another discipline. This may include talking informally with the psychologist or member of the other discipline, obtaining objective information and, if possible and relevant, the assurance that the harm will discontinue and be corrected. If in a vulnerable position (e.g., employee, trainee) with respect to the other psychologist or member of the other discipline, it may include asking persons in less vulnerable positions to participate in the meeting(s).

II.42 Be open to the concerns of others about perceptions of harm that they as a psychologist might be causing, stop activities that are causing harm, and not punish or seek punishment for those who raise such concerns in good faith.

II.43 Not place an individual, group, family, or community needing service at a serious disadvantage by offering them no service in order to fulfill the conditions of a research design, when a standard service is available.

II.44 Debrief research participants in such a way that any harm caused can be discerned, and act to correct any resultant harm. (Also see Standards III.26 and III.27.)

Care of animals

II.45 Not use animals in their research unless there is a reasonable expectation that the research will increase understanding of the structures and processes underlying behaviour, or increase understanding of the particular animal species used in the study, or result eventually in benefits to the health and welfare of humans or other animals.

II.46 Use a procedure subjecting animals to pain, stress, or privation only if an alternative procedure is unavailable and the goal is justified by its prospective scientific, educational, or applied value.

II.47 Make every effort to minimize the discomfort, illness, and pain of animals. This would include performing surgical procedures only under appropriate anaesthesia, using techniques to avoid infection and minimize pain during and after surgery and, if disposing of experimental animals is carried out at the termination of the study, doing so in a humane way.

II.48 Use animals in classroom demonstrations only if the instructional objectives cannot be achieved through the use of video-tapes, films, or other methods, and if the type of demonstration is warranted by the anticipated instructional gain.

Extended responsibility

II.49 Encourage others, in a manner consistent with this *Code*, to care responsibly.

II.50 Assume overall responsibility for the scientific and professional activities of their assistants, employees, supervisees, students, and trainees with regard to the Principle of Responsible Caring, all of whom, however, incur similar obligations.

Principle III: Integrity in Relationships

Values Statement

The relationships formed by psychologists in the course of their work embody explicit and implicit mutual expectations of integrity that are vital to the advancement of scientific knowledge and to the maintenance of public confidence in the discipline of psychology. These expectations include: accuracy and honesty; straightforwardness and openness; the maximization of objectivity and minimization of bias; and, avoidance of conflicts of interest. Psychologists have a responsibility to meet these expectations and to encourage reciprocity.

In addition to accuracy, honesty, and the obvious prohibitions of fraud or misrepresentation, meeting expectations of integrity is enhanced by self-knowledge and the use of critical analysis. Although it can be argued that science is value-free and impartial, scientists are not. Personal values and self-interest can affect the questions psychologists ask, how they ask those questions, what assumptions they make, their selection of methods, what they observe and what they fail to observe, and how they interpret their data.

Psychologists are not expected to be value-free or totally without self-interest in conducting their activities. However, they are expected to understand how their backgrounds, personal needs, and values interact with their activities, to be open and honest about the influence of such factors, and to be as objective and unbiased as possible under the circumstances.

The values of openness and straightforwardness exist within the context of Respect for the Dignity of Persons (Principle I) and Responsible Caring (Principle II). As such, there will be circumstances in which openness and straightforwardness will need to be tempered. Fully open and straightforward disclosure might not be needed or desired by others and, in some circumstances, might be a risk to their dignity or well-being, or considered culturally inappropriate. In such circumstances, however, psychologists have a responsibility to ensure that their decision not to be fully open or straightforward is justified by higher-order values and does not invalidate any informed consent procedures.

Of special concern to psychologists is the provision of incomplete disclosure when obtaining informed consent for research participation, or temporarily leading research participants to believe that a research project has a purpose other than its actual purpose. These actions sometimes occur in research where full disclosure would be likely to influence the responses of the research participants and thus invalidate the results. Although research that uses such techniques can lead to knowledge that is beneficial, such benefits must be weighed against the research participant's right to self-determination and the importance of public and individual trust in psychology. Psychologists have a serious obligation to avoid as much as possible the use of such research procedures. They also have a serious obligation to consider the need for, the possible consequences of, and their responsibility to correct any resulting mistrust or other harmful effects from their use.

As public trust in the discipline of psychology includes trusting that psychologists will act in the best interests of members of the public, situations that present real or potential conflicts of interest are of concern to psychologists. Conflict-of-interest situations are those that can lead to distorted judgment and can motivate psychologists to act in ways that meet their own personal, political, financial, or business interests at the expense of the best interests of members of the public. Although avoidance of all conflicts of interest and potential exploitation of others is not possible, some are of such a high risk to protecting the interests of members of the public and to maintaining the trust of the public, that they are considered never acceptable (see Standard III.31). The risk level of other conflicts of interest (e.g., dual or multiple relationships) might be partially dependent on cultural factors and the specific type of professional relationship (e.g., long-term psychotherapy vs. community development activities). It is the responsibility of psychologists to avoid dual or multiple relationships and other conflicts of interest when appropriate and possible. When such situations cannot be avoided or are inappropriate to avoid, psychologists have a responsibility to declare that they have a conflict of interest, to seek advice, and to establish safeguards to ensure that the best interests of members of the public are protected.

Integrity in relationships implies that psychologists, as a matter of honesty, have a responsibility to maintain competence in any specialty area for which they declare competence, whether or not they are currently practising in that area. It also requires that psychologists, in as much as they present themselves as members and representatives of a specific discipline, have a responsibility to actively rely on and be guided by that discipline and its guidelines and requirements.

Ethical Standards

In adhering to the Principle of Integrity in Relationships, psychologists would:

Accuracy/honesty

> III.1 Not knowingly participate in, condone, or be associated with dishonesty, fraud, or misrepresentation.
>
> III.2 Accurately represent their own and their colleagues' credentials, qualifications, education, experience, competence, and affiliations, in all spoken, written, or printed communications, being careful not to use descriptions or information that could be misinterpreted (e.g., citing membership in a voluntary association of psychologists as a testament of competence).
>
> III.3 Carefully protect their own and their colleagues' credentials from being misrepresented by others, and act quickly to correct any such misrepresentation.
>
> III.4 Maintain competence in their declared area(s) of psychological competence, as well as in their current area(s) of activity. (Also see Standard II.9.)
>
> III.5 Accurately represent their own and their colleagues' activities, functions, contributions, and likely or actual outcomes of their activities (including research results) in all spoken, written, or printed communication. This includes, but is not limited to: advertisements of services or products; course and workshop descriptions; academic grading requirements; and, research reports.
>
> III.6 Ensure that their own and their colleagues' activities, functions, contributions, and likely or actual outcomes of their activities (including research results) are not misrepresented by others, and act quickly to correct any such misrepresentation.
>
> III.7 Take credit only for the work and ideas that they have actually done or generated, and give credit for work done or ideas contributed by others (including students), in proportion to their contribution.
>
> III.8 Acknowledge the limitations of their own and their colleagues' knowledge, methods, findings, interventions, and views.
>
> III 9. Not suppress disconfirming evidence of their own and their colleagues' findings and views, acknowledging alternative hypotheses and explanations.

Objectivity/lack of bias

III.10 Evaluate how their personal experiences, attitudes, values, social context, individual differences, stresses, and specific training influence their activities and thinking, integrating this awareness into all attempts to be objective and unbiased in their research, service, and other activities.

III.11 Take care to communicate as completely and objectively as possible, and to clearly differentiate facts, opinions, theories, hypotheses, and ideas, when communicating knowledge, findings, and views.

III.12 Present instructional information accurately, avoiding bias in the selection and presentation of information, and publicly acknowledge any personal values or bias that influence the selection and presentation of information.

III.13 Act quickly to clarify any distortion by a sponsor, client, agency (e.g., news media), or other persons, of the findings of their research.

Straightforwardness/openness

III.14 Be clear and straightforward about all information needed to establish informed consent or any other valid written or unwritten agreement (for example: fees, including any limitations imposed by third-party payers; relevant business policies and practices; mutual concerns; mutual responsibilities; ethical responsibilities of psychologists; purpose and nature of the relationship, including research participation; alternatives; likely experiences; possible conflicts; possible outcomes; and, expectations for processing, using, and sharing any information generated).

III.15 Provide suitable information about the results of assessments, evaluations, or research findings to the persons involved, if appropriate and if asked. This information would be communicated in understandable language.

III.16 Fully explain reasons for their actions to persons who have been affected by their actions, if appropriate and if asked.

III.17 Honour all promises and commitments included in any written or verbal agreement, unless serious and unexpected circumstances (e.g., illness) intervene. If such circumstances occur, then the psychologist would make a full and honest explanation to other parties involved.

III.18 Make clear whether they are acting as private citizens, as members of specific organizations or groups, or as representatives of the discipline of psychology, when making statements or when involved in public activities.

III.19 Carry out, present, and discuss research in a way that is consistent with a commitment to honest, open inquiry, and to clear communication of any research aims, sponsorship, social context, personal values, or financial interests that might affect or appear to affect the research.

III.20 Submit their research, in some accurate form and within the limits of confidentiality, to persons with expertise in the research area, for their comments and evaluations, prior to publication or the preparation of any final report.

III.21 Encourage and not interfere with the free and open exchange of psychological knowledge and theory between themselves, their students, colleagues, and the public.

III.22 Make no attempt to conceal the status of a trainee and, if a trainee is providing direct client service, ensure that the client is informed of that fact.

Avoidance of incomplete disclosure

III.23 Not engage in incomplete disclosure, or in temporarily leading research participants to believe that a research project or some aspect of it has a different purpose, if there are alternative procedures available or if the negative effects cannot be predicted or offset.

III.24 Not engage in incomplete disclosure, or in temporarily leading research participants to believe that a research project or some aspect of it has a different purpose, if it would interfere with the person's understanding of facts that clearly might influence a decision to give adequately informed consent (e.g., withholding information about the level of risk, discomfort, or inconvenience).

III.25 Use the minimum necessary incomplete disclosure or temporary leading of research participants to believe that a research project or some aspect of it has a different purpose, when such research procedures are used.

III.26 Debrief research participants as soon as possible after the participants' involvement, if there has been incomplete disclosure or temporary leading of research participants to believe that a research project or some aspect of it has a different purpose.

III.27 Provide research participants, during such debriefing, with a clarification of the nature of the study, seek to remove any misconceptions that might have arisen, and seek to re-establish any trust that might have been lost, assuring the participants that the research procedures were neither arbitrary nor capricious, but necessary for scientifically valid findings. (Also see Standards II.23 and II.44.)

III.28 Act to re-establish with research participants any trust that might have been lost due to the use of incomplete disclosure or temporarily leading research participants to believe that the research project or some aspect of it had a different purpose.

III.29 Give a research participant the option of removing his or her data, if the research participant expresses concern during the debriefing about the incomplete disclosure or the temporary leading of the research participant to believe that the research project or some aspect of it had a different purpose, and if removal of the data will not compromise the validity of the research design and hence diminish the ethical value of the participation of the other research participants.

III.30 Seek an independent and adequate ethical review of the risks to public or individual trust and of safeguards to protect such trust for any research that plans to provide incomplete disclosure or temporarily lead research participants to believe that the research project or some aspect of it has a different purpose, before making a decision to proceed.

Avoidance of conflict of interest

III.31 Not exploit any relationship established as a psychologist to further personal, political, or business interests at the expense of the best interests of their clients, research participants, students, employers, or others. This includes, but is not limited to: soliciting clients of one's employing agency for private practice; taking advantage of trust or dependency to encourage or engage in sexual intimacies (e.g., with clients not included in Standard II.27, with clients' partners or relatives, with students or trainees not included in Standard II.28, or with research participants); taking advantage of trust or dependency to frighten clients into receiving services; misappropriating students' ideas, research or work; using the resources of one's employing institution for purposes not agreed to; giving or receiving kickbacks or bonuses for referrals; seeking or accepting loans or investments from clients; and, prejudicing others against a colleague for reasons of personal gain.

III.32 Not offer rewards sufficient to motivate an individual or group to participate in an activity that has possible or known risks to themselves or others. (Also see Standards I.27, I.28, II.2, and II.49.)

III.33 Avoid dual or multiple relationships (e.g.. with clients, research participants, employees, supervisees, students, or trainees) and other situations that might present a conflict of interest or that might reduce their ability to be objective and unbiased in their determinations of what might be in the best interests of others.

III.34 Manage dual or multiple relationships that are unavoidable due to cultural norms or other circumstances in such a manner that bias, lack of objectivity, and risk of exploitation are minimized. This might include obtaining ongoing supervision or consultation for the duration of the dual or multiple relationship, or involving a third party in obtaining consent (e.g., approaching a client or employee about becoming a research participant).

III.35 Inform all parties, if a real or potential conflict of interest arises, of the need to resolve the situation in a manner that is consistent with Respect for the Dignity of Persons (Principle I) and Responsible Caring (Principle II), and take all reasonable steps to resolve the issue in such a manner.

Reliance on the discipline

III.36 Familiarize themselves with their discipline's rules and regulations, and abide by them, unless abiding by them would be seriously detrimental to the rights or welfare of others as demonstrated in the Principles of Respect for the Dignity of Persons or Responsible Caring. (See Standards IV.17 and IV.18 for guidelines regarding the resolution of such conflicts.)

III.37 Familiarize themselves with and demonstrate a commitment to maintaining the standards of their discipline.

III.38 Seek consultation from colleagues and/or appropriate groups and committees, and give due regard to their advice in arriving at a responsible decision, if faced with difficult situations.

Extended responsibility

III.39 Encourage others, in a manner consistent with this *Code*, to relate with integrity.

III.40 Assume overall responsibility for the scientific and professional activities of their assistants, employees, supervisees, students, and trainees with regard to the Principle of Integrity in Relationships, all of whom, however, incur similar obligations.

Principle IV: Responsibility to Society

Values Statement

Psychology functions as a discipline within the context of human society[2]. Psychologists, both in their work and as private citizens, have responsibilities to the societies in which they live and work, such as the neighbourhood or city, and to the welfare of all human beings in those societies.

Two of the legitimate expectations of psychology as a science and a profession are that it will increase knowledge and that it will conduct its affairs in such ways that it will promote the welfare of all human beings.

Freedom of enquiry and debate (including scientific and academic freedom) is a foundation of psychological education, science, and practice. In the context of society, the above expectations imply that psychologists will exercise this freedom through the use of activities and methods that are consistent with ethical requirements.

The above expectations also imply that psychologists will do whatever they can to ensure that psychological knowledge, when used in the development of social structures and policies, will be used for beneficial purposes, and that the discipline's own structures and policies will support those beneficial purposes. Within the context of this document, social structures and policies that have beneficial purposes are defined as those that more readily support and reflect respect for the dignity of persons, responsible caring, integrity in relationships, and responsibility to society. If psychological knowledge or structures are used against these purposes, psychologists have an ethical responsibility to try to draw attention to and correct the misuse. Although this is a collective responsibility, those psychologists having direct involvement in the structures of the discipline, in social development, or in the theoretical or research data base that is being used (e.g., through research, expert testimony, or policy advice) have the greatest responsibility to act. Other psychologists must decide for themselves the most appropriate and beneficial use of their time and talents to help meet this collective responsibility.

In carrying out their work, psychologists acknowledge that many social structures have evolved slowly over time in response to human need and are valued by the societies that have developed them. In such circumstances, psychologists convey respect for such social structures and avoid unwarranted or unnecessary disruption. Suggestions for and action toward changes or enhancement of such structures are carried out through processes that seek to achieve a consensus within those societies and/or through democratic means.

On the other hand, if structures or policies seriously ignore or oppose the principles of respect for the dignity of persons, responsible caring, integrity in relationships, or responsibility to society, psychologists involved have a responsibility to speak out in a manner consistent with the principles of this *Code*, and advocate for appropriate change to occur as quickly as possible.

In order to be responsible and accountable to society, and to contribute constructively to its ongoing development, psychologists need to be willing to work in partnership with others, be self-reflective, and be open to external suggestions and criticisms about the place of the discipline of psychology in society. They need to engage in even-tempered observation and interpretation of the effects of societal structures and policies, and their process of change, developing the ability of psychologists to increase the beneficial use of psychological knowledge and structures, and avoid their misuse. The discipline needs to be willing to set high standards for its members, to do what it can to assure that such standards are met, and to support its members in their attempts to maintain the standards. Once again, individual psychologists must decide for themselves the most appropriate and beneficial use of their time and talents in helping to meet these collective responsibilities.

Ethical Standards

In adhering to the Principle of Responsibility to Society, psychologists would:

Development of knowledge

> IV.1 Contribute to the discipline of psychology and of society's understanding of itself and human beings generally, through free enquiry and the acquisition, transmission, and expression of knowledge and ideas, unless such activities conflict with other basic ethical requirements.

> IV.2 Not interfere with, or condone interference with, free enquiry and the acquisition, transmission, and expression of knowledge and ideas that do not conflict with other basic ethical requirements.

IV.3 Keep informed of progress in their area(s) of psychological activity, take this progress into account in their work, and try to make their own contributions to this progress.

Beneficial activities

IV.4 Participate in and contribute to continuing education and the professional and scientific growth of self and colleagues.

IV.5 Assist in the development of those who enter the discipline of psychology by helping them to acquire a full understanding of their ethical responsibilities, and the needed competencies of their chosen area(s), including an understanding of critical analysis and of the variations, uses, and possible misuses of the scientific paradigm.

IV.6 Participate in the process of critical self-evaluation of the discipline's place in society, and in the development and implementation of structures and procedures that help the discipline to contribute to beneficial societal functioning and changes.

IV.7 Provide and/or contribute to a work environment that supports the respectful expression of ethical concern or dissent, and the constructive resolution of such concern or dissent.

IV.8 Engage in regular monitoring, assessment, and reporting (e.g., through peer review, and in programme reviews, case management reviews, and reports of one's own research) of their ethical practices and safeguards.

IV.9 Help develop, promote, and participate in accountability processes and procedures related to their work.

IV.10 Uphold the discipline's responsibility to society by promoting and maintaining the highest standards of the discipline.

IV.11 Protect the skills, knowledge, and interpretations of psychology from being misused, used incompetently, or made useless (e.g., loss of security of assessment techniques) by others.

IV.12 Contribute to the general welfare of society (e.g., improving accessibility of services, regardless of ability to pay) and/or to the general welfare of their discipline, by offering a portion of their time to work for which they receive little or no financial return.

IV.13 Uphold the discipline's responsibility to society by bringing incompetent or unethical behaviour, including misuses of psychological knowledge and techniques, to the attention of appropriate authorities, committees, or regulatory bodies, in a manner consistent with the ethical principles of this *Code*, if informal resolution or correction of the situation is not appropriate or possible.

IV.14 Enter only into agreements or contracts that allow them to act in accordance with the ethical principles and standards of this *Code*.

Respect for society

IV.15 Acquire an adequate knowledge of the culture, social structure, and customs of a community before beginning any major work there.

IV.16 Convey respect for and abide by prevailing community mores, social customs, and cultural expectations in their scientific and professional activities, provided that this does not contravene any of the ethical principles of this *Code*.

IV.17 Familiarize themselves with the laws and regulations of the societies in which they work, especially those that are related to their activities as psychologists, and abide by them. If those laws or regulations seriously conflict with the ethical principles contained herein, psychologists would do whatever they could to uphold the ethical principles. If upholding the ethical principles could result in serious personal consequences (e.g., jail or physical harm), decision for final action would be considered a matter of personal conscience.

IV.18 Consult with colleagues, if faced with an apparent conflict between abiding by a law or regulation and following an ethical principle, unless in an emergency, and seek consensus as to the most ethical course of action and the most responsible, knowledgeable, effective, and respectful way to carry it out.

Development of society

IV.19 Act to change those aspects of the discipline of psychology that detract from beneficial societal changes, where appropriate and possible.

IV.20 Be sensitive to the needs, current issues, and problems of society, when determining research questions to be asked, services to be developed, content to be taught, information to be collected, or appropriate interpretation of results or findings.

IV.21 Be especially careful to keep well informed of social issues through relevant reading, peer consultation, and continuing education, if their work is related to societal issues.

IV.22 Speak out, in a manner consistent with the four principles of this *Code*, if they possess expert knowledge that bears on important societal issues being studied or discussed.

IV.23 Provide thorough discussion of the limits of their data with respect to social policy, if their work touches on social policy and structure.

IV.24 Consult, if feasible and appropriate, with groups, organizations, or communities being studied, in order to increase the accuracy of interpretation of results and to minimize risk of misinterpretation or misuse.

IV.25 Make themselves aware of the current social and political climate and of previous and possible future societal misuses of psychological knowledge, and exercise due discretion in communicating psychological information (e.g., research results, theoretical knowledge), in order to discourage any further misuse.

IV.26 Exercise particular care when reporting the results of any work regarding vulnerable groups, ensuring that results are not likely to be misinterpreted or misused in the development of social policy, attitudes, and practices (e.g., encouraging manipulation of vulnerable persons or reinforcing discrimination against any specific population).

IV.27 Not contribute to nor engage in research or any other activity that contravenes international humanitarian law, such as the development of methods intended for use in the torture of persons, the development of prohibited weapons, or destruction of the environment.

IV.28 Provide the public with any psychological knowledge relevant to the public's informed participation in the shaping of social policies and structures, if they possess expert knowledge that bears on the social policies and structures.

IV.29 Speak out and/or act, in a manner consistent with the four principles of this *Code*, if the policies, practices, laws, or regulations of the social structure within which they work seriously ignore or contradict any of the principles of this *Code*.

Extended responsibility

IV.30 Encourage others, in a manner consistent with this *Code*, to exercise responsibility to society.

IV.31 Assume overall responsibility for the scientific and professional activities of their assistants, employees, supervisees, students, and trainees with regard to the Principle of Responsibility to Society, all of whom, however, incur similar obligations.

Footnotes

[1] Adapted from: Canadian Psychological Association. (1985). *Guidelines for the elimination of sexual harassment.* Ottawa, Author.

[2] Society is used here in the broad sense of a group of persons living as members of one or more human communities, rather than in the limited sense of state or government.

ASSOCIATION OF STATE AND PROVINCIAL PSYCHOLOGY BOARDS' CODE OF CONDUCT

FOREWORD

Enclosed is the ASPPB Code of Conduct, which was approved by the Delegates to the Annual Meeting in October 1990. Since that meeting, several suggestions for minor revisions were incorporated by the Model Licensure Committee, which was responsible for the previous draft versions.

It is important to note that this version of the Code of Conduct began with the review and distillation of similar codes from fourteen (14) U.S. and Canadian jurisdictions. These fourteen were selected as representative from twenty-seven (27) U.S./Canadian regulatory codes. The rules contained in the Code reflect suggestions of many jurisdictions and many concerned individuals following the review of former drafts of the Code. The rules contained in the Code also reflect much debate and scrutiny by the Model Licensure Committee which spent approximately two years in the drafting stage.

The committee that prepared the various drafts, as well as the approved version of the Code, represented considerable geographic and professional diversity, yet was able to reach an essentially enthusiastic consensus on nearly all of the rules contained in the Code. Generally favorable reaction by many boards and board members, as well as the vote of the delegates, supports the impression that a consensus Code of Conduct is possible.

Certain concepts should be kept in mind while reviewing and applying the rules contained in the Code. Regulatory rules of conduct protect the public welfare by assuring that the client of a licensed psychologist can have a reasonable, legally protected, understanding of the rules that will govern the professional's behavior in the professional relationship. Effective rules of conduct, in the opinion of the committee, have several characteristics of note:

1. They pertain to the process or "mechanics" of the professional relationship, not to the content of the professional judgment itself. They set the boundaries within which the professional relationship functions and are not intended to determine or dictate professional judgment as such.

2. They primarily protect the public interest. They secondarily protect the interests of the profession only as they assure public confidence and trust in the predictability of the professional relationship.

3. They are as nonintrusive as possible, interfering as little as possible with professional work while still accomplishing their necessary function of protecting the public from exploitation secondary to particular characteristics of the professional relationship.

4. They are essentially unambiguous concerning what behavior is acceptable and what is not.

5. Among other functions, they assure the creation/ existence/retention of appropriate information with which the regulatory board can judge compliance with or deviation from its requirements.

6. They are sufficient unto themselves, without dependence for interpretation on additional explanatory materials, since they will be applied in a judicial/legal context interpreting the regulatory code which they are a part, and the explanatory materials would not be an incorporated part of the regulatory code.

7. They are not optional and always pertain. They are coercive, not advisory or aspirational. They are nontrivial, to the extent that any violation is basis for formal disciplinary action, including loss of licensure.

Rules of conduct differ in function in critical ways from a professional association ethics code, with which they are sometimes confused. The professional association ethics code is the profession's own standards and guidelines to its own professionals about how to handle the professional-client relationship. Its ultimate purpose is to protect the welfare and integrity of the profession, although it accomplishes these functions partially by structuring professional behavior such as to build confidence in the profession, by much the same process as do the rules of conduct. It may, and usually does, incorporate the basic concepts or structure of regulatory rules of conduct as those are herein conceptualized. Rules of conduct in a professional association ethics code may be dealt with in less detail or specificity, however, than is desirable for a regulatory code. They also often address aspirational or advisory issues as well as coercive ones, and professional matters as well as regulatory matters.

At least one recent court ruling, White v. N.C. State Bd. of Examiners, 388 S.E.2nd 148 (N.C. App. 1990) highlights distinctions between aspirational ethics code language and enforceable regulatory code of conduct language. In this case, which involved the utilization of the American Psychological Association's "Ethical Principles of Psychologists", a reviewing court held that the preambles to the various ethical principles could not be used as the basis for disciplinary action against a psychologist. At the same time, this court upheld the use of certain specific principles in such disciplinary proceedings. The questionable use of principles adopted by a professional association, was one of the reasons that the ASPPB Executive Committee directed the development of this Code of Conduct. Board members and attorneys involved in disciplinary proceedings based on codes of conduct or ethical principles should review White v. N.C. State Bd. of Examiners, supra for its most instructive language.

The primary work in drafting the Code was done by the ASPPB Model Licensure Committee consisting of David Rodgers, OH (Chair); Stephen DeMers, KY; Terez Retfalvi, NB; Norma Simon, NY; Robert Tipton, VA; Randolph P. Reaves, AL.

ASPPB views this code as one that may change over time.* We trust that it will be a useful and productive document for boards, board members, staff and board attorneys. As always we welcome your comments and suggestions.

Gerald T. Jorgensen, Ph.D.
President 1990–1991

*This edition of the ASPPB Code of Conduct was amended and adopted during the month of June 2001.

ASPPB CODE OF CONDUCT

I. INTRODUCTION

A. Purpose. The rules within this Code of Conduct constitute the standards against which the required professional conduct of a psychologist is measured.

B. Scope. The psychologist shall be governed by this Code of Conduct whenever providing psychological services in any context. This Code shall not supersede state, federal, or provincial statutes. This Code shall apply to the conduct of all licensees and applicants, including the applicant's conduct during the period of education, training, and employment which is required for licensure. The term "psychologist," as used within this Code, shall be interpreted accordingly.

C. Responsibility for own actions. The psychologist shall be fully responsible for his/her own professional decisions and professional actions.

D. Violations. A violation of this Code of Conduct constitutes unprofessional conduct and is sufficient reason for disciplinary action or denial of either original licensure or reinstatement of licensure.

E. Aids to interpretation. Ethics codes and standards for providers promulgated by the American Psychological Association, the Canadian Psychological Association, and other relevant professional groups shall be used as an aid in resolving ambiguities which may arise in the interpretation of this Code of Conduct, except that this Code of Conduct shall prevail whenever any conflict exists between this Code and any professional association standard.

II. DEFINITIONS

A. Client. "Client" means a receiver of psychological services. A corporate entity or other organization can be a client when the professional contract is to provide services of benefit primarily to the organization rather than to individuals. In the case of individuals with legal guardians, including minors and legally incompetent adults, the legal guardian shall be the client for decision making purposes, except that the individual receiving services shall be the client for:

1. Issues directly affecting the physical or emotional safety of the individual, such as sexual or other exploitative dual relationships, and

2. Issues specifically reserved to the individual, and agreed to by the guardian prior to rendering of services, such as confidential communication in a therapy relationship.

B. Confidential information. "Confidential information" means information revealed by a client or clients or otherwise obtained by a psychologist, where there is reasonable expectation that because of the relationship between the client(s) and the psychologist, or the circumstances under which the information was revealed or obtained, the information shall not be disclosed by the psychologist without the informed written consent of the client(s). When a corporation or other organization is the client, rules of confidentiality apply to information pertaining to the organization, including personal information about individuals when obtained in the proper course of that contract. Such information about individuals is subject to confidential control of the organization, not of the individual, and can be made available to the organization, unless there is reasonable expectation by such individual that such information was obtained in a separate professional relationship with that individual and is therefore subject to confidentiality requirements in itself.

C. Court order. "Court order" means the written or oral communication of a member of the judiciary, or other court magistrate or administrator, if such authority has been lawfully delegated to such magistrate or administrator.

D. Licensed. "Licensed" means licensed, certified, registered, or any other term when such term identifies a person whose professional behavior is subject to regulation by the Board.

E. Professional relationship. "Professional relationship" means a mutually agreed upon relationship between a psychologist and a client(s) for the purpose of the client(s) obtaining the psychologist's professional expertise.

F. Professional service. "Professional service" means all actions of the psychologist in the context of a professional relationship with a client.

G. Supervisee. "Supervisee" means any person who functions under the extended authority of the psychologist to provide, or while in training to provide, psychological services.

III. RULES OF CONDUCT

A. COMPETENCE

1. Limits on practice. The psychologist shall limit practice and supervision to the areas of competence in which proficiency has been gained through education, training, and experience.

2. Maintaining competency. The psychologist shall maintain current competency in the areas in which he/she practices, through continuing education, consultation, and/or other procedures, in conformance with current standards of scientific and professional knowledge.

3. Accurate representation. A licensee shall accurately represent his or her areas of competence, education, training, experience, and professional affiliations to the boards, the public, and colleagues.

4. Adding new services and techniques. The psychologist, when developing competency in a service or technique that is either new to the psychologist or new to the profession, shall engage in ongoing consultation with other psychologists or relevant professionals and shall seek appropriate education and training in the new area. The psychologist shall inform clients of the innovative nature and the known risks associated with the services, so that the client can exercise freedom of choice concerning such services.

5. Referral. The psychologist shall make or recommend referral to other professional, technical, or administrative resources when such referral is clearly in the best interests of the client.

6. Sufficient professional information. A psychologist rendering a formal professional opinion about a person, for example about the fitness of a parent in a custody hearing, shall not do so without direct and substantial professional contact with or a formal assessment of that person.

7. Maintenance and retention of records.

a. The psychologist rendering professional services to an individual client (or a dependent), or services billed to a third party payer, shall maintain professional records that include:

1) the name of the client and other identifying information

2) the presenting problem(s) or purpose or diagnosis,

3) the fee arrangement,

4) the date and substance of each billed or service-count contact or service,

5) any test results or other evaluative results obtained and any basic test data from which they were derived,

6) notation and results of formal consults with other providers,

7) a copy of all test or other evaluative reports prepared as part of the professional relationship.

8) any releases executed by the client.

b. To meet the requirements of this rule, so as to provide a formal record for review, but not necessarily for other legal purposes, the psychologist shall assure that all data entries in the professional records are maintained for a period of not less than five years after the last date that service was rendered. The psychologist shall also abide by other legal requirements for record retention, even if longer periods of retention are required for other purposes.

c. The psychologist shall store and dispose of written, electronic and other records in such a manner as to ensure their confidentiality. The psychologist shall maintain the confidentiality of all psychological records in the psychologist's possession or under the psychologist's control except as otherwise provided by law or pursuant to written or signed authorization of a client specifically requesting or authorizing release or disclosure of the client's psychological records.

d. For each person professionally supervised, the psychologist shall maintain, for a period of not less than five years after the last date of supervision, a record of the supervisory session that shall include, among other information, the type, place, and general content of the session.

8. Continuity of care. The psychologist shall make arrangements for another appropriate professional or professionals to deal with emergency needs of his/her clients, as appropriate, during periods of his/her foreseeable absences from professional availability.

B. IMPAIRED OBJECTIVITY AND DUAL RELATIONSHIPS

1. Impaired psychologist. The psychologist shall not undertake or continue a professional relationship with a client when the psychologist is, or could reasonably be expected by the Board to be, impaired due to mental, emotional, physiologic, pharmacologic, or substance abuse conditions. If such a condition develops after a professional relationship has been initiated, the psychologist shall terminate the relationship in an appropriate manner, shall notify the client in writing of the termination, and shall assist the client in obtaining services from another professional.

2. Prohibited Dual Relationships.

a. The psychologist shall not undertake or continue a professional relationship with a client when the objectivity or competency of the psychologist is, or could reasonably be expected by the Board to be, impaired because of the psychologist's present or previous familial, social, sexual, emotional, financial, supervisory, political, administrative, or legal relationship with the client or a relevant person associated with or related to the client.

b. The psychologist, in interacting with a client or former client to whom the psychologist has at anytime within the previous 24 months rendered counseling, psychotherapeutic, or other professional psychological services for the treatment or amelioration of emotional distress or behavioral inadequacy, shall not:

1) engage in any verbal or physical behavior toward him/ her which is sexually seductive, demeaning, or harassing; or

2) engage in sexual intercourse or other physical intimacies with him/her; or

3) enter into a financial or other potentially exploitative relationship to him/her.

c. The prohibitions set out in (b.) above shall not be limited to the 24-month period but and shall extend indefinitely if the client is proven to be clearly vulnerable, by reason of emotional or cognitive disorder, to exploitative influence by the psychologist.

C. CLIENT WELFARE

1. Providing explanation of procedures. The psychologist shall give a truthful, understandable, and appropriate account of the client's condition to the client or to those responsible for the care of the client. The psychologist shall keep the client fully informed as to the purpose and nature of any evaluation, treatment, or other procedures, and of the client's right to freedom of choice regarding services provided.

2. Termination of services. Whenever professional services are terminated, the psychologist shall offer to help locate alternative sources of professional services or assistance if indicated. The psychologist shall terminate a professional relationship when it is reasonably clear that the client is not benefitting from the relationship, and shall prepare the client appropriately for such termination.

3. Stereotyping. The psychologist shall not impose on the client any stereotypes of behavior, values, or roles related to age, gender, religion, race, disability, nationality, sexual preference, or diagnosis which would interfere with the objective provision of psychological services to the client.

4. Sexual or other dual relationship with a client. The psychologist shall not enter into a sexual or other dual relationship with a client, as specified in Section III, B. of this Code of Conduct.

5. Solicitation of business by clients. The psychologist providing services to an individual client shall not induce that client(s) to solicit business on behalf of the psychologist.

6. Referrals on request. The psychologist providing services to a client shall make an appropriate referral of the client to another professional when requested to do so by the client.

D. WELFARE OF SUPERVISEES AND RESEARCH SUBJECTS

1. Welfare of supervisees. The psychologist shall not exploit a supervisee in any way—sexually, financially, or otherwise.

2. Welfare of research subjects. The psychologist shall respect the dignity and protect the welfare of his/her research subjects, and shall comply with all relevant statutes and administrative rules concerning treatment of research subjects.

E. PROTECTING CONFIDENTIALITY OF CLIENTS

1. In general. The psychologist shall safeguard the confidential information obtained in the course of practice, teaching, research, or other professional services. With the exceptions set forth below, the psychologist shall disclose confidential information to others only with the informed written consent of the client.

2. Disclosure without informed written consent. The psychologist may disclose confidential information without the informed written consent of the client when the psychologist judges that disclosure is necessary to protect against a clear and substantial risk of imminent serious harm being inflicted by the client on the client or another person. In such case, the psychologist shall limit disclosure of the otherwise confidential information to only those persons and only that content which would be consistent with the standards of the profession in addressing such problems. When the client is an organization, disclosure shall be made only after the psychologist has made a reasonable and unsuccessful attempt to have the problems corrected within the organization.

3. Services involving more than one interested party. In a situation in which more than one party has an appropriate interest in the professional services rendered by the psychologist to a client or clients, the psychologist shall, to the extent possible, clarify to all parties prior to rendering the services the dimensions of confidentiality and professional responsibility that shall pertain in the rendering of services. Such clarification is specifically indicated, among other circumstances, when the client is an organization.

4. Multiple clients. When service is rendered to more than one client during a joint session, for example to a family or a couple or a parent and child or a group, the psychologist shall, at the beginning of the professional relationship, clarify to all parties the manner in which confidentiality will be handled. All parties shall be given opportunity to discuss and to accept whatever limitations to confidentiality adhere in the situation.

5. Legally dependent clients. At the beginning of a professional relationship, to the extent that the client can understand, the psychologist shall inform a client who is below the age of majority or who has a legal guardian, of the limit the law imposes on the right of confidentiality with respect to his/her communications with the psychologist.

6. Limited access to client records. The psychologist shall limit access to client records to preserve their confidentiality and shall assure that all persons working under the psychologist's authority comply with the requirements for confidentiality of client material.

7. Release of confidential information. The psychologist may release confidential information upon court order, as defined in Section II of this Code, or to conform with state, federal or provincial law, rule, or regulation.

8. Reporting of abuse of children and vulnerable adults. The psychologist shall be familiar with any relevant law concerning the reporting of abuse of children and vulnerable adults, and shall comply with such laws.

9. Discussion of client information among professionals. When rendering professional services as part of a team or when interacting with other appropriate professionals concerning the welfare of the client, the psychologist may share confidential information about the client provided the psychologist takes reasonable steps to assure that all persons receiving the information are informed about the confidential nature of the information and abide by the rules of confidentiality.

10. Disguising confidential information. When case reports or other confidential information is used as the basis of teaching, research, or other published reports, the psychologist shall exercise reasonable care to insure that the reported material is appropriately disguised to prevent client identification.

11. Observation and electronic recording. The psychologist shall ensure that diagnostic interviews or therapeutic sessions with a client are observed or electronically recorded only with the informed written consent of the client.

12. Confidentiality after termination of professional relationship. The psychologist shall continue to treat as confidential information regarding a client after the professional relationship between the psychologist and the client has ceased.

F. REPRESENTATION OF SERVICES

1. Display of license. The psychologist shall display his/her current (name of jurisdiction) license to practice psychology, on the premises of his/her professional office.

2. Misrepresentation of qualifications. The psychologist shall not misrepresent directly or by implication his/her professional qualifications such as education, experience, or areas of competence.

3. Misrepresentation of affiliations. The psychologist shall not misrepresent directly or by implication his/her affiliations, or the purposes or characteristics of institutions and organizations with which the psychologist is associated.

4. False or misleading information. The psychologist shall not include false or misleading information in public statements concerning professional services offered.

5. Misrepresentation of services or products. The psychologist shall not associate with or permit his/her name to be used in connection with any services or products in such a way as to misrepresent (a) the services or products, (b) the degree of his/her responsibility for the services or products, or (c) the nature of his/her association with the services or products.

6. Correction of misrepresentation by others. The psychologist shall correct others who misrepresent the psychologist's professional qualifications or affiliations.

G. FEES AND STATEMENTS

1. Disclosure of cost of services. The psychologist shall not mislead or withhold from the client, a prospective client, or third party payer, information about the cost of his/her professional services.

2. Reasonableness of fee. The psychologist shall not exploit the client or responsible payer by charging a fee that is excessive for the services performed or by entering into an exploitative bartering arrangement in lieu of a fee.

H. Assessment Procedures

1. Confidential information. The psychologist shall treat an assessment result or interpretation regarding an individual as confidential information.

2. Communication of results. The psychologist shall accompany communication of results of assessment procedures to the client, parents, legal guardians, or other agents of the client by adequate interpretive aids or explanations.

3. Reservations concerning results. The psychologist shall include in his/her report of the results of a formal assessment procedure for which norms are available, any deficiencies of the assessment norms for the individual assessed and any relevant reservations or qualifications which affect the validity, reliability, or other interpretation of results.

4. Protection of integrity of assessment procedures. The psychologist shall not reproduce or describe in popular publications, lectures, or public presentations psychological tests or other assessment devices in ways that might invalidate them.

5. Information for professional users. The psychologist offering an assessment procedure or automated interpretation service to other professionals shall accompany this offering by a manual or other printed materials which fully describes the development of the assessment procedure or service, the rationale, evidence of validity and reliability, and characteristics of the normative population. The psychologist shall explicitly state the purpose and application for which the procedure is recommended and identify special qualifications required to administer and interpret it properly. The psychologist shall ensure that the advertisements for the assessment procedure or interpretive service are factual and descriptive.

I. VIOLATIONS OF LAW

1. Violation of applicable statutes. The psychologist shall not violate any applicable statute or administrative rule regulating the practice of psychology.

2. Use of fraud, misrepresentation, or deception. The psychologist shall not use fraud, misrepresentation, or deception in obtaining a psychology license, in passing a psychology licensing examination, in assisting another to obtain a psychology license or to pass a psychology licensing examination, in billing clients or third party payers, in providing

psychological service, in reporting the results of psychological evaluations or services, or in conducting any other activity related to the practice of psychology.

J. AIDING ILLEGAL PRACTICE

1. Aiding unauthorized practice. The psychologist shall not aid or abet another person in misrepresenting his/her professional credentials or in illegally engaging in the practice of psychology.

2. Delegating professional responsibility. The psychologist shall not delegate professional responsibilities to a person not appropriately credentialed or otherwise appropriately qualified to provide such services.

3. Providing supervision. The psychologist shall exercise appropriate supervision over supervisees, as set forth in the rules and regulations of the Board.

4. Reporting of violations to Board. The psychologist who has substantial reason to believe that there has been a violation of the statutes or rules of the Board shall so inform the Board in writing, except that when the information regarding such violation is obtained in a professional relationship with a client, the psychologist shall report it only with the written permission of the client. Nothing in this Code shall relieve a psychologist of the duty to file any report required by applicable statutes.

AMERICAN PROFESSIONAL SOCIETY ON THE ABUSE OF CHILDREN GUIDELINES FOR PSYCHOSOCIAL EVALUATION OF SUSPECTED SEXUAL ABUSE IN YOUNG CHILDREN

Statement of Purpose

These Guidelines for mental health professionals reflect current knowledge and consensus about the psychosocial evaluation of suspected sexual abuse in young children. They are not intended as a standard of practice to which practitioners are expected to adhere in all cases. Evaluators must have the flexibility to exercise clinical judgment in individual cases. Laws and local customs may also influence the accepted method in a given community. Practitioners should be knowledgeable about various constraints on practice/and prepared to justify their decisions about particular practices in specific cases. As experience and scientific knowledge expand, further refinement and revision of these Guidelines are expected.

These Guidelines are specific to psychosocial assessments. Sexual abuse is known to produce both acute and long-term negative psychological effects requiring therapeutic intervention. Psychosocial assessments are a systematic process of gathering information and forming professional opinions about the source of statements, behavior, and other evidence that form the basis of concern about possible sexual abuse. Psychosocial evaluations are broadly concerned with understanding developmental, familial, and historical factors and events that may be associated with psychological adjustment. The results of

Reprinted with permission from American Professional Society on the Abuse of Children, Guidelines for Psychosocial Evaluation of Suspected Sexual Abuse in Young Children, 1990.

such evaluations may be used to assist in legal decision making and in directing treatment planning.

Interviews of children for possible sexual abuse are conducted by other professionals as well, including child protective service workers, law enforcement investigators, special "child interviewers," and medical practitioners. Such interviews are most often limited to a single, focused session which concentrates on eliciting reliable statements about possible sexual abuse; they are not designed to assess the child's general adjustment and functioning. Principles about interviewing contained in the Guidelines may be applied to investigatory or history-taking interviews. Some of the preferred practices, however (e.g., number of interviews), will not apply.

Psychosocial evaluators should first establish their role in the evaluation process. Evaluations performed at the request of a court may require a different stance and include additional components than those conducted for purely clinical reasons. The difference between the evaluation phase and a clinical phase must be clearly articulated if the same professional is to be involved. In all cases, evaluators should be aware that any interview with a child regarding possible sexual abuse may be subject to scrutiny and have significant implications for legal decision making and the child's safety and well-being.

Guidelines

I. The Evaluator

A. Characteristics

1. The evaluator should possess an advanced mental health degree in a recognized discipline (e.g., MD, or Masters or Ph.D. in psychology, social work, counseling, or psychiatric nursing).

2. The evaluator should have experience evaluating and treating children and families. A minimum of two years of professional experience with children is expected, three to five years is preferred. The evaluator should also possess at least two years of professional experience with sexually abused children. If the evaluator does not possess such experience, supervision is essential.

3. It is essential that the evaluator have specialized training in child development and child sexual abuse. This should be documented in terms of formal course work, supervision, or attendance at conferences, seminars, and workshops.

4. The evaluator should be familiar with current professional literature on sexual abuse and be knowledgeable about the dynamics and the emotional and behavioral consequences of abuse experiences.

5. The evaluator should have experience in conducting forensic evaluations and providing court testimony. If the evaluator does not possess such experience, supervision is essential.

6. The evaluator should approach the evaluation with an open mind to all possible responses from the child and all possible explanations for the concern about possible sexual abuse.

II. Components of the Evaluation

A. Protocol

1. A written protocol is not necessary; however evaluations should routinely involve reviewing all pertinent materials; conducting collateral interviews when necessary; establishing rapport; assessing the child's general functioning, developmental status; and memory capacity; and thoroughly evaluating the possibility of abuse. The evaluator may use discretion in the order of presentation and method of assessment.

B. Employer of the Evaluator

1. Evaluation of the child may be conducted at the request of a legal guardian prior to court involvement.

2. If a court proceeding is involved, the preferred practice is a court-appointed or mutually agreed upon evaluation of the child.

3. Discretion should be used in agreeing to conduct an evaluation of a child when the child has already been evaluated or when there is current court involvement. Minimizing the number of evaluations should be a consideration; additional evaluations should be conducted only if they clearly further the best interests of the child. When a second opinion is required, a review of the records may eliminate the need for reinterviewing the child.

C. Number of Evaluators

1. It is acceptable to have a single evaluator. However, when the evaluation will include the accused or suspected individual, a team approach is the preferred practice, with information concerning the progress of the evaluation readily available among team members. Consent should be obtained from all participants prior to releasing information.

D. Collateral Information Gathered as Part of the Evaluation

1. Review of all relevant background material as part of the evaluation is the preferred practice.

2. The evaluation report should document all the materials used and demonstrate their objective review in the evaluation process.

E. Interviewing the Accused or Suspected Individual

1. It is not necessary to interview the accused or suspected individual in order to form an opinion about possible sexual abuse of the child.

2. An interview with or review of the statements from a suspected or accused individual (when available) may provide additional relevant information (e.g., alternative explanations, admissions, insight into relationship between child and accused individual).

3. If the accused or suspected individual is a parent, preferred practice is for the child evaluator to contact or interview that parent. If a full assessment of the accused or suspected parent is indicated, a team approach is the preferred practice.

F. Releasing Information

1. Suspected abuse should always be reported to authorities as dictated by state law.

2. Permission should be obtained from legal guardians for receipt of collateral materials and for release of information about the examination to relevant medical or mental health professionals, other professionals (e.g., schoolteachers), and involved legal systems (e.g., CPS, law enforcement). Discretion should be used in releasing sensitive individual and family history which does not directly relate to the purpose of the assessment.

3. When an evaluation is requested by the court, information should be released to all parties to the action after consent is obtained.

III. Interviewing

A. Recording of Interviews

1. Audio or video recording may be preferred practice in some communities. Professional preference, logistics, or clinical consideration may contraindicate recording of interviews. Professional discretion is permitted in recording policies and practices.

2. Detailed written documentation is the minimum requirement, with specific attention to questions and responses (verbal and nonverbal) regarding possible sexual abuse. Verbatim quotes of significant questions and answers are desirable.

3. When audio and video recording are used, the child must be informed. It is desirable to obtain written agreement from the child and legal guardian(s).

B. Observation of the Interview

1. Observation of interviews by involved professionals (CPS, law enforcement, etc.) may be indicated if it reduces the need for additional interviews.

2. Observation by non-accused and non-suspected primary caregiver(s) may be indicated for particular clinical reasons; however, great care should be taken that the observation is clinically appropriate, does not unduly distress the child, and does not affect the validity of the evaluation process.

3. If interviews are observed, the child must be informed and it is desirable to obtain written agreement from the child and legal guardian(s).

C. Number of Interviews

1. Preferred practice is two to six sessions for directed assessment. This does not imply that all sessions must include specific questioning about possible sexual abuse. The evaluator may decide based on the individual case circumstances to adopt a less direct approach and reserve questioning. Repeated direct questioning of the child regarding sexual abuse when the child is not reporting or is denying abuse is contraindicated.

2. If the child does not report abuse within the two to six sessions of directed evaluation, but the evaluator has continuing concerns about the possibility of abuse, the child should be referred for extended evaluation or therapy which is less directive but diagnostically focused, and the child's protection from possible abuse should be recommended.

D. Format of Interview

1. Preferred practice is whenever possible, to interview first the primary caretaker to gather background information.

2. The child should be seen individually for initial interviews, except when the child refuses to separate. Discussion of possible abuse in the presence of the caretaker during initial interviews should be avoided except when necessary to elicit information from the child. In such cases, the interview setting should be structured to reduce the possibility of improper influence by the caretaker upon the child's behavior.

3. Joint sessions with the child and the non-accused caretaker or accused or suspected individual may be helpful to obtain information regarding the overall quality of the relationships. The sessions should not be conducted for the purpose of determining whether abuse occurred based on the child's reactions to the accused or suspected individual. Nor should joint sessions be conducted if they may cause significant additional trauma to the child. A child should never be asked to confirm the abuse statements in front of an accused individual.

IV. Child interview

A. General Principles

1. The evaluator should create an atmosphere that enables the child to talk freely, including providing physical surroundings and a climate that facilitates the child's comfort and communication.

2. Language and interviewing approach should be developmentally appropriate.

3. The evaluator should take the time necessary to perform a complete evaluation and should avoid any coercive quality to the interview.

4. Interview procedures may be modified in cases involving very young, pre-verbal, or minimally verbal children or children with special problems (e.g., developmentally delayed, electively mute).

B. Questioning

1. The child should be questioned directly about possible sexual abuse at some point in the evaluation.

2. Initial questioning should be as non-directive as possible to elicit spontaneous responses. If open-ended questions are not productive, more directive questioning should follow.

3. The evaluator may use the form of questioning deemed necessary to elicit information on which to base an opinion. Highly specific questioning should only be used when other methods of questioning have failed, when previous information warrants substantial concern, or when the child's developmental level precludes more non-directive approaches. However, responses to these questions should be carefully evaluated and weighed accordingly.

C. Use of Dolls and Other Devices

1. A variety of non-verbal tools should be available to assist the child in communication, including drawings, toys, doll-houses, dolls, puppets, etc.

2. Anatomically detailed dolls should be used with care and discretion. Preferred practice is to have them available for identification of body parts, clarification of previous statements, or demonstration by non- or low-verbal children after there is indication of abuse activity.

3. The anatomically detailed dolls should not be considered a diagnostic test. Unusual behavior with the dolls may suggest further lines of inquiry and should be noted in the evaluation report, but is not generally considered conclusive of a history of sexual abuse.

D. Psychological Testing

1. Formal psychological testing of the child is not indicated for the purpose of proving or disproving a history of sexual abuse.

2. Testing is useful when the clinician is concerned about the child's intellectual or developmental level, or about the possible presence of a thought disorder. Psychological tests can also provide helpful information regarding a child's emotional status.

3. Evaluation of non-accused and accused individuals often involves complete psychological testing to assess for significant psychopathology or sexual deviance.

V. Conclusions/Report

A. General Principles

1. The evaluator should take care to communicate that mental health professionals have no special ability to detect whether an individual is telling the truth.

2. The evaluator may directly state that abuse did or did not occur, or may say that a child's behavior and words are consistent or inconsistent with abuse, or with a history or absence of history of abuse.

3. Opinions about whether abuse occurred or did not occur should include supporting information (e.g., the child's and/or the accused individual's statements, behavior, psychological symptoms). Possible alternative explanations should be addressed and ruled out.

4. The evaluation may be inconclusive. If so, the evaluator should cite the information that causes continuing concern but does not enable confirmation or disconfirmation of abuse. If inconclusiveness is due to such problems as missing information or an untimely or poorly-conducted investigation, these obstacles should be clearly noted in the report.

5. Recommendations should be made regarding therapeutic or environmental interventions to address the child's emotional and behavioral functioning and to ensure the child's safety.

Acknowledgments

These Guidelines are the product of APSAC's Task Force on the Psychosocial Evaluation of Suspected Sexual Abuse in Young Children, chaired by Lucy Berliner, MSW.

A group of experts who responded to a lengthy, open-ended, mailed survey provided the content for the first draft. That draft was revised based on comments from a large number of practitioners who responded to mailed requests for input and who participated in the open Task Force meeting held at the Fourth Annual Health Science Response to Child Maltreatment conference, held in San Diego, California, in January, 1990.

The next draft was published for comment in APSAC's newsletter, The Advisor, in Spring, 1990. Revised according to suggestions made by APSAC members and Board, this is the final result.

Appreciation goes to all the practitioner/experts who contributed much of their time and expertise to make these Guidelines valuable. Special thanks goes to Richard Stille, Ph.D., who helped synthesize the first draft. The Guidelines will be updated periodically. Any comments or suggestions about them should be directed to Lucy Berliner through APSAC, 332 So. Michigan Avenue, Suite 1600, Chicago, Illinois, 60604, (312) 554-0166.

GLOSSARY

abnormality   In psychological terms, any mental, emotional, or behavioral activity that deviates from culturally or scientifically accepted norms.

abstinence   Forgoing some kind of gratification; in the area of alcohol or drug dependence, being without the substance on which the subject had been dependent.

acting out   Expressions of *unconscious* emotional conflicts or feelings in actions rather than words. The person is not consciously aware of the meaning of such acts (see *conscious*). Acting out may be harmful or, in controlled situations, therapeutic (e.g., children's play therapy).

addiction   Dependence on a chemical substance to the extent that a physiological and/or psychological need is established. This may be manifested by any combination of the following symptoms: tolerance, preoccupation with obtaining and using the substance, use of the substance despite anticipation of probable adverse consequences, repeated efforts to cut down or control substance use, and *withdrawal symptoms* when the substance is unavailable or not used.

affect   Behavior that expresses a subjectively experienced feeling state (*emotion*); affect is responsive to changing emotional states, whereas mood refers to a pervasive and sustained emotion. Common affects are euphoria, anger, and sadness. Some types of affect disturbance are:

   blunted   Severe reduction in the intensity of affective expression.

   flat   Absence or near absence of any signs of affective expression, such as a monotonous voice and an immobile face.

   inappropriate   Discordance of voice and movements with the content of the person's speech or ideation.

   labile   Abnormal variability, with repeated, rapid, and abrupt shifts in affective expression.

   restricted or constricted   Reduction in the expressive range and intensity of affects.

affective disorder   A disorder in which mood change or disturbance is the primary manifestation. Now referred to as *mood disorder*. See *depression*.

Selected terms reprinted with permission from American Psychiatric Association, *American Psychiatric Glossary*, 7th ed. J. Edgerton & R. Campbell, eds. Copyright 1994, American Psychiatric Press.

agitated depression   A severe major depressive disorder in which *psychomotor agitation* is prominent; formerly known as *involutional melancholia*. See *depression*.

analysis of variance (ANOVA)   A widely used statistical procedure for determining the significance of differences obtained on an experimental variable studied under two or more conditions. Differences are commonly assigned to three aspects: the individual differences among the subjects or patients studied; group differences, however classified (e.g., by sex); and differences according to the various treatments to which the subjects have been assigned. The method can assess both the main effects of a variable and its interaction with other variables that have been studied simultaneously.

anhedonia   Inability to experience pleasure from activities that usually produce pleasurable feelings. Contrast with *hedonism*.

anorexia nervosa   An *eating disorder* characterized by refusal or inability to maintain minimum normal weight for age and height combined with intense fear of gaining weight, denial of the seriousness of current low weight, undue influence of body weight or shape on self-evaluation, and, in females, amenorrhea or failure to menstruate. Weight is typically 15% or more below normal, and it may decrease to life-threatening extremes. In the restricting subtype, the person does not engage regularly in binge eating. In the binge eating/purging, or bulimic, subtype, the person engages in recurrent episodes of *binge eating* or purging during the episode of anorexia nervosa. See also *bulimia nervosa*.

anxiety   Apprehension, tension, or uneasiness from anticipation of danger, the source of which is largely unknown or unrecognized. Primarily of *intrapsychic* origin, in distinction to *fear*, which is the emotional response to a consciously recognized and usually external threat or danger. May be regarded as pathologic when it interferes with effectiveness in living, achievement of desired goals or satisfaction, or reasonable emotional comfort.

apperception   Perception as modified and enhanced by one's own *emotions*, memories, and biases.

attention-deficit/hyperactivity disorder (ADHD)   A child whose inattention and hyperactivity-impulsivity cause problems may have this disorder. *Symptoms* appear before the age of 7 years and are inconsistent with the subject's developmental level and severe enough to impair social or academic functioning.

In the predominantly inattentive type, characteristic symptoms include distractibility, difficulty in sustaining attention or following through on instructions in the absence of close supervision, avoidance of tasks that require sustained mental effort, failure to pay close attention to details in schoolwork or other activities, difficulty in organizing activities, not listening to what is being said to him or her, loss of things that are necessary for assignments, and forgetfulness in daily activities.

In the predominantly hyperactive-impulsive type, characteristic symptoms are that the person inappropriately leaves his or her seat in the classroom or runs about, fidgets or squirms, has difficulty in engaging in leisure activities quietly, has difficulty in awaiting his or her turn in games, and blurts out answers to questions before they are completed.

The two types may be combined.

attributable risk   The rate of the disorder in exposed subjects that can be attributed to the exposure; derived from subtracting the rate (usually incidence or mortality) of the disorder of the nonexposed population from the corresponding rate of the exposed population.

autism   A form of thinking or a style of object relationships and life approach in which the subjective predominates and the "me" is favored, sometimes resulting in the exclusion of the "not-me." The subject is unable to turn his or her energies to outside reality. *Introversion* may be marked, with an avoidance of contact with life and satisfying relationships with peers.

behavior therapy   A mode of treatment that focuses on modifying observable and, at least in principle, quantifiable behavior by means of systematic manipulation of the environment and variables thought to be functionally related to the behavior. Some behavior therapy techniques are *operant conditioning, shaping, token economy, systematic desensitization, aversion therapy,* and *flooding (implosion).*

bipolar disorders   In DSM-IV, a group of *mood disorders* that includes bipolar disorder, single episode; bipolar disorder, recurrent; and *cyclothymic disorder.*

A bipolar disorder includes a *manic* episode at some time during its course. In any particular patient, the bipolar disorder may take the form of a single manic episode (rare), or it may consist of recurrent episodes that are either manic or depressive in nature (but at least one must have been predominantly manic).

Bipolar II disorder is used in some classifications (including DSM-IV) to denote a mood disorder characterized by episodes of major depressive disorder and *hypomania* (rather than full mania). Other authorities prefer to call such a mood disorder "major depressive disorder with hypomanic episodes."

bulimia nervosa   An *eating disorder* characterized by recurrent episodes of *binge eating* followed by compensatory behavior such as purging (i.e., self-induced vomiting or the use of diuretics and laxatives) or other methods to control weight (e.g., strict dieting, fasting, or vigorous exercise).

circumstantiality   Pattern of speech that is indirect and delayed in reaching its goal because of excessive or irrelevant detail or parenthetical remarks. The speaker does not lose the point, as is characteristic of *loosening of associations*, and clauses remain logically connected, but to the listener it seems that the end will never be reached. Compare with *tangentiality*.

cognition   A general term encompassing all the various modes of knowing and reasoning.

concrete thinking   Thinking characterized by immediate experience, rather than abstractions. It may occur as a primary, developmental defect, or it may develop secondary to organic brain disease or *schizophrenia.*

concordance   In genetic studies, the similarity in a twin pair with respect to the presence or absence of a disease or trait.

control   The term is used in three contexts: (1) keeping the relevant conditions of an experiment constant, (2) causing an *independent variable* to vary in a specified and known manner, and (3) using a spontaneously occurring and discoverable fact as a check or standard of comparison to evaluate the facts obtained after the manipulation of the independent variable.

control group   In the ideal case, a group of subjects matched as closely as possible to an experimental group of subjects on all relevant aspects and exposed to the same treatments except the independent variable under investigation.

conversion disorder   One of the *somatoform disorders* (but in some classifications called a *dissociative disorder*), characterized by a *symptom* suggestive of a neurologic disorder that affects sensation or voluntary motor function. The symptom is not consciously or intentionally produced, it cannot be explained fully by any known *general medical condition*, and it is severe enough to impair functioning or require medical attention. Commonly seen symptoms are blindness, double vision, deafness, impaired coordination, paralysis, and seizures.

correlation   The extent to which two measures vary together, or a measure of the strength of the relationship between two variables. It is usually expressed by a coefficient that varies between $+1.0$ (perfect agreement) and -1.0 (a perfect inverse relationship). A correlation coefficient of 0.0 would mean a perfectly random relationship. The correlation coefficient signifies the degree to which knowledge of one score or variable can predict the score on the other variable. A high correlation between two variables does not necessarily indicate a causal relationship between them; the correlation may follow because each of the variables is highly related to a third, as yet unmeasured, factor.

criterion variable   Something to be predicted.

decompensation   The deterioration of existing defenses (see *defense mechanism*), leading to an exacerbation of pathological behavior.

defense mechanism   *Unconscious* intrapsychic processes serving to provide relief from emotional *conflict* and *anxiety. Conscious* efforts are frequently made for the same reasons, but true defense mechanisms are unconscious. Some of the common defense mechanisms defined in this glossary are *compensation, conversion, denial, displacement, dissociation, idealization, identification, incorporation, introjection, projection, rationalization, reaction formation, regression, sublimation, substitution, symbolization,* and *undoing.*

delusion   A false belief based on an incorrect inference about external reality and firmly sustained despite clear evidence to the contrary. The belief is not part of a cultural tradition such as an article of religious faith. Among the more frequently reported delusions are the following:

> **delusion of control**   The belief that one's feelings, impulses, thoughts, or actions are not one's own but have been imposed by some external force.

> **delusion of poverty**   The conviction that one is, or will be, bereft of all material possessions.

> **delusion of reference**   The conviction that events, objects, or other people in the immediate environment have a particular and unusual significance (usually negative).

> **delusional jealousy**   The false belief that one's sexual partner is unfaithful; also called the Othello delusion.

> **grandiose delusion**   An exaggerated belief of one's importance, power, knowledge, or identity.

> **nihilistic delusion**   A conviction of nonexistence of the self, part of the self, or others, or of the world. "I no longer have a brain" is an example.

> **persecutory delusion**   The conviction that one (or a group or institution close to one) is being harassed, attacked, persecuted, or conspired against.

> **somatic delusion**   A false belief involving the functioning of one's body, such as the conviction of a postmenopausal woman that she is pregnant, or a person's conviction that his nose is misshapen and ugly when there is nothing wrong with it.

> **systematized delusion**   A single false belief with multiple elaborations or a group of false beliefs that the person relates to a single event or theme. This event is believed to have caused every problem in life that the person experiences.

demand characteristics   The sum total of cues that communicates the purpose of the experiment and the nature of the behavior expected of the subject. (The cues are derived from the manner in which the subject is solicited, the manner in which he or she is treated by the experimenter, the scuttlebutt about the experiment, the experimental instructions, and, most important, the experimental procedure itself.) Subjects may confirm the investigator's hypothesis in an effort to behave appropriately rather than respond directly to the independent variables under investigation. By extension, as applied to nonexperimental settings, the tendency of individuals to live up to what is implicitly expected of them, a factor that may play a major role in the outcome of treatment.

denial   A *defense mechanism*, operating unconsciously, used to resolve emotional *conflict* and allay *anxiety* by disavowing thoughts, feelings, wishes, needs, or external reality factors that are consciously intolerable.

discordance   In genetic studies, dissimilarity in a twin pair with respect to the presence or absence of a disease or trait.

disorientation   Loss of awareness of the position of the self in relation to space, time, or other persons; confusion.

dissociation   The splitting off of clusters of mental contents from *conscious* awareness, a mechanism central to hysterical conversion and *dissociative disorders*; the separation of an idea from its emotional significance and affect as seen in the inappropriate *affect* of schizophrenic patients.

double-blind   Referring to a study design in which a number of treatments, usually one or more drugs and a placebo, are compared in such a way that neither the patient nor the persons directly involved in the treatment know which preparation is being administered.

drug dependence   Habituation to, abuse of, and/or *addiction* to a chemical substance. Largely because of psychological craving, the life of the drug-dependent person revolves around the need for the specific effect of one or more chemical agents on *mood* or state of consciousness. The term thus includes not only the addiction (which emphasizes the physiological dependence) but also drug abuse (in which the pathological craving for drugs seem unrelated to physical dependence). Examples include alcohol, *opiates*, synthetic analgesics with morphine-like effects, *barbiturates*, other hypnotics, sedatives, some antianxiety agents, *cocaine*, psychostimulants, marijuana, and *psychotomimetic* drugs.

ecological validity   The extent to which controlled experimental results can be generalized beyond the confines of the particular experimental context [to] a variety of contexts in the real world.

executive functioning   Cognitive abilities such as planning, organizing, sequencing, and abstracting; loss or deterioration may be seen in *dementia*.

experimental design   The logical framework of an experiment that maximizes the probability of obtaining or detecting real effects and minimizes the likelihood of ambiguities regarding the significance of the experimentally observed differences. Experimental study designs include:

   case control   An investigation in which groups of individuals are selected in terms of whether they do (cases) or do not (controls) have the disorder the etiology of which is being studied.

   cohort   An important form of epidemiological investigation to test hypotheses regarding the causation of disease. The distinguishing factors are that (1) the group or groups of persons to be studied (the cohorts) are defined in terms of characteristics evident prior to appearance of the disorder being investigated; and (2) the study groups so defined are observed over a period of time to determine the frequency of the disorder among them.

   cross-sectional   Study in which measurements are made in different samples at the same point in time.

independent group Study in which different treatments are given to different groups; for example, comparing an untreated group with a treated group. Methodologically very sound, but often requires large samples if there is much variability between individuals.

longitudinal Study in which observations on the same individuals are made at two or more different points in time. Most cohort and case-control studies are longitudinal.

prospective Study based on data or events that occur subsequent in time relative to the initiation of the investigation. This type of predictive study usually requires many years in order to develop a large enough study population.

retrospective Study based on data or events that occurred prior in time relative to the investigation.

subjects as their own control The same individual is compared with herself or himself before and after a given treatment. This has the advantage of decreasing error variance and the likelihood of showing significant differences with relatively small groups, though it has the disadvantage of practice effects that may occur with repeated measurements.

experimenter bias Experimenter expectations that are inadvertently communicated to patients or subjects. Such expectations may influence experimental findings.

external validity The applicability of the generalizations that may be made from the experimental findings beyond the occasion with those specific subjects, experimental conditions, experimenters, or measurements.

factitious disorders A group of disorders characterized by intentional production or feigning of physical or psychological *symptoms* or signs related to a need to assume the sick role rather than for obvious *secondary gains* such as economic support or obtaining better care. The symptoms produced may be predominantly psychological, predominantly physical, or a combination of both. An example is *Munchausen syndrome*.

falsifiable hypothesis A hypothesis stated in sufficiently precise fashion that it can be tested by acceptable rules of logic and empirical and statistical evidence, and thereby found to be either confirmed or disconfirmed. An unfalsifiable hypothesis is one that is so general and/or ambiguous that all conceivable evidence can be "explained" by it.

flight of ideas A nearly continuous flow of accelerated speech with abrupt changes from one topic to another, usually based on understandable associations, distracting stimuli, or playing on words. When severe, however, this may lead to disorganized and incoherent speech. Flight of ideas is characteristic of *manic episodes*, but it may occur also in *organic mental disorders, schizophrenia*, other *psychoses*, and, rarely, acute reactions to stress.

hallucination   A sensory perception in the absence of an actual external stimulus; to be distinguished from an *illusion*, which is a misperception or misinterpretation of an external stimulus. Hallucinations may involve any of the senses.

heuristic   Serving to encourage discovery of problem solutions.

hyperactivity   Excessive motor activity that may be purposeful or aimless; movements and utterances are usually more rapid than normal. Hyperactivity is a prominent feature of attention-deficit disorder, so much so that in DSM-IV the latter is called *attention deficit/hyperactivity disorder (ADHD)*.

hypomania   A psychopathological state and abnormality of *mood* falling somewhere between normal *euphoria* and *mania*. It is characterized by unrealistic optimism, pressure of speech and activity, and a decreased need for *sleep*. Some people show increased creativity during hypomanic states, whereas others show poor judgment, irritability, and irascibility. See *bipolar disorders*.

inappropriate affect   A display of *emotion* that is out of harmony with reality or with the verbal or intellectual content that it accompanies. See *affect*.

incidence   The number of cases of disease that come into being during a specific period of time.

intervening variable   Something intervening between an antecedent circumstance and its consequence, modifying the relation between the two. For example, appetite can be an intervening variable determining whether or not a given food will be eaten. The intervening variable may be inferred rather than empirically detected.

learning disability   A *syndrome* affecting school-age children of normal or above-normal intelligence, characterized by specific difficulties in learning to read (*dyslexia*, word-blindness), write (dysgraphia), and/or calculate (dyscalculia). The disorder is believed to be related to slow developmental progress of perceptual motor skills. See *minimal brain dysfunction*.

loosening of associations   A disturbance of thinking shown by speech in which ideas shift from one subject to another that is unrelated or minimally related to the first. Statements that lack a meaningful relationship may be juxtaposed, or speech may shift suddenly from one frame of reference to another. The speaker gives no indication of being aware of the disconnectedness, contradictions, or illogicality of speech. See also *incoherence*.

magical thinking   A conviction that thinking equals doing. Occurs in dreams, in children, in primitive peoples, and in patients under a variety of conditions. Characterized by lack of realistic relationship between cause and effect.

mean The arithmetic average of a set of observations; the sum of scores divided by the number of scores.

median The middle value in a set of values that have been arranged in order from highest to lowest.

mode The most frequently occurring observation in a set of observations.

narcissism Self-love as opposed to object-love (love of another person). In classical psychoanalytic theory (see *psychoanalysis*), *cathexis* (investment) of the psychic representation of the self with *libido* (sexual interest and energy). An excess of narcissism interferes with relations with others. To be distinguished from egotism, which carries the connotation of self-centeredness, selfishness, and conceit. Egotism is but one expression of narcissism. Recent revisions in psychoanalytic theory (*self psychology*) have viewed the concept of narcissism in less pathological terms.

nonparametric tests of significance Specialized statistical procedures that do not require assumptions of normality when data do not satisfy certain statistical assumptions, such as being normally distributed. These procedures are often based on an analysis of ranks rather than on the distribution of the actual scores themselves. Widely used examples are the chi-square, Spearman rank order correlation, median, and Mann-Whitney U tests.

null hypothesis Predicting that an experiment will show no difference between conditions or no relationship between variables. Statistical tests are then applied to the results of the experiment to try to disprove the null hypothesis. Testing requires a computation to determine the limits within which two groups may differ in their results (e.g., an experimental and a control group) even though if the experiment were often repeated or the groups were larger no difference would be found. The probability of the obtained difference being found if no true difference existed is commonly expressed as a P value (e.g., P less than .05 that the null hypothesis is true).

operational definition The meaning of a concept when it is translated to terms amenable to systematic observation and measurement (e.g., temperature defined by a thermometer reading under standard conditions).

parameter Any quantitative value that a variable can take.

parametric study One that examines the effects on a dependent variable of variations, usually across a broad range, in the base values of the independent variable.

parametric tests of significance Tests based on the assumption that the form of the distribution of the observations is known, usually a so-called normal distribution. Widely used tests based on such an assumption include analysis of variance, t tests, and Pearson coefficient of correlation.

period prevalence   A measure that expresses the total number of cases of a disease known to have existed at some time during a specified period. It is the sum of point prevalence and incidence.

phobia   *Fear* cued by the presence or anticipation of a specific object or situation, exposure to which almost invariably provokes an immediate *anxiety* response or *panic attack* even though the subject recognizes that the fear is excessive or unreasonable. The phobic stimulus is avoided or endured with marked distress. In earlier psychoanalytic literature, phobia was called *anxiety hysteria.*

Two types of phobia have been differentiated: specific phobia (simple phobia) and social phobia. Specific phobia is subtyped on the basis of the object feared. The natural environment (animals, insects, storms, water, etc.); blood, injection, or injury; situations (cars, airplanes, heights, tunnels, etc.); and other situations that may lead to choking, vomiting, or contracting an illness are all specific phobias.

In social phobia (social anxiety disorder), the persistent fear is of social situations that might expose one to scrutiny by others and induce one to act in a way or show anxiety symptoms that will be humiliating or embarrassing. Avoidance may be limited to one or only a few situations, or it may occur in most social situations. Performing in front of others or social interactions may be the focus of concern. It is sometimes difficult to distinguish between social phobia and *agoraphobia* when social avoidance accompanies panic attacks. *Avoidant disorder* has been used to refer to social phobia occurring in childhood and adolescence.

Some of the common phobias are abnormal fear of:

acrophobia   Heights.

agoraphobia   Open spaces or leaving the familiar setting of the home.

algophobia   Pain.

androphobia   Men.

autophobia   Being alone or solitude.

claustrophobia   Closed spaces.

demophobia   Crowds.

gynophobia   Women.

mysophobia   Dirt and germs.

pedophobia   Children.

xenophobia   Strangers.

placebo   In psychopharmacology, a pill that contains no pharmacologically active ingredient.

active placebo   A placebo that may mimic the side effects but does not have the specific and assumed therapeutic pharmacological action of the drug under investigation.

placebo effect   Either therapeutic effects or side effects following the ingestion of a placebo. By extension, one may speak of a placebo effect as comprising the nonspecific aspects of any treatment procedure, usually mediated by the patient's expectations of improvement, such as the placebo effect of psychotherapy.

point prevalence   The frequency of a disease at a designated point in time.

population   A statistical concept that refers to all individuals or instances that theoretically could be available for study or measurement. Statistical inference involves generalizing from the observation of some specified sample to the population.

practice effects   The modification in task performances as a result of repeated trials or training in the task.

predictor variable   The test or other form of performance that is used to predict the person's status on a criterion variable. For example, scores on the Scholastic Aptitude Test might be used to predict the criterion "finishing college within the top 33% of graduating class." Scores on the SAT would be predictor scores.

projection   A *defense mechanism*, operating unconsciously (see *unconscious*), in which what is emotionally unacceptable in the self is unconsciously rejected and attributed (projected) to others.

Q-sort   A personality assessment technique in which the subject (or some observer) indicates the degree to which a standardized set of descriptive statements actually describes him or her (the subject). The term reflects the "sorting" procedures occasionally used with this technique.

quantitative variable   An object of observation that varies in manner or degree in such a way that it may be measured.

random sample   A group of subjects selected in such a way that each member of the population from which the sample is derived has an equal or known chance (i.e., probability) of being chosen for the sample.

reality testing   The ability to evaluate the external world objectively and to differentiate adequately between it and the internal world. Falsification of reality, as with massive *denial* or *projection*, indicates a severe disturbance of *ego* functioning and/or of the perceptual and memory processes upon which it is partly based.

regression   Partial or symbolic return to earlier patterns of reacting or thinking. Manifested in a wide variety of circumstances such as normal *sleep*, play, physical illness, and many *mental disorders*.

relative risk   The ratio of a disorder (usually incidence of mortality) of those exposed to the disorder to the rate of those not exposed.

reliability   The extent to which the same test or procedure will yield the same result either over time or with different observers. The most commonly reported reliabilities are:

> **interrater reliability**   The agreement between different individuals scoring the same procedure or observations.

> **split-half reliability**   The correlation within a single test of two similar parts of the test.

> **test-retest reliability**   The correlation between the first and second test of a number of subjects.

repression   A *defense mechanism*, operating unconsciously, that banishes unacceptable ideas, fantasies, *affects*, or impulses from consciousness or that keeps out of consciousness what has never been *conscious*. Although not subject to voluntary recall, the repressed material may emerge in disguised form. Often confused with the conscious mechanism of *suppression*.

secondary gain   The external gain derived from any illness, such as personal attention and service, monetary gains, disability benefits, and release from unpleasant responsibilities.

selection bias   The inadvertent selection of a nonrepresentative sample of subjects or observations. A classic example is a 1936 *Literary Digest* poll that predicted Landon's election over Roosevelt in which telephone directories were used as the basis for selecting respondents.

separation anxiety   The normal *fear* and apprehension noted in infants when they are removed from the mother (or surrogate mother) or when approached by strangers. Most marked from age 6 to 10 months. In later life, similar reactions may be caused by separation from significant persons or familiar surroundings.

sign   Objective evidence of disease or disorder. See also *symptom*.

significant differences   Statistical tests showing that a given difference is not likely to have occurred by chance. In many behavioral studies, the likelihood of an event occurring less frequently than 1 in 20 times (P 0.05) is considered the minimal acceptable significance level. The determination that a given difference between two groups is significant can merely serve to identify the likelihood that it was not a chance event. In no way does this prove that the demonstrated systematic difference is necessarily due to the reasons hypothesized by an investigator. Systematic factors not considered by the investigator can sometimes be responsible for significant differences.

significant level   The arbitrarily selected probability level for rejecting the null hypothesis, commonly 0.05 or 0.01.

standard deviation (SD)   A mathematical measure of the dispersion or spread of scores clustered about the mean. In any distribution that approximates the normal curve in form, about 65% of the measurements will lie within one SD of the mean, and about 95% will lie within two SDs of the mean.

statistical inference   The process of using a limited sample of data to infer something about a larger population of potentially obtainable data that have not been observed.

symptom   A specific manifestation of a patient's condition indicative of an abnormal physical or mental state; a subjective perception of illness.

syndrome   A configuration of *symptoms* that occur together and constitute a recognizable condition.

tangentiality   Replying to a question in an oblique or irrelevant way. Compare with *circumstantiality*.

test of significance   A comparison of the observed probability of an event with the predicted probability based on calculations deduced from statistical chance distributions of such events.

theory   A general statement predicting, explaining, or describing the relationships among a number of constructs.

thought disorder   A disturbance of speech, communication, or content of thought, such as *delusions, ideas of reference*, poverty of thought, *flight of ideas, perseveration, loosening of associations*, and so forth. A thought disorder can be caused by a functional emotional disorder or an organic condition. A formal thought disorder is a disturbance in the form of thought rather than in the content of thought (e.g., loosening of associations).

type I error   The error that is made when the null hypothesis is true but, as the result of the test of significance, is rejected or declared false. Also called false negative.

type II error   The error that is made when the null hypothesis is false but, as a result of the test of significance, is not rejected or declared false. Also called false positive.

unconscious   That part of the mind or mental functioning that is only rarely subject to awareness. It is a repository for data that have never been *conscious* (primary *repression)* or that may have been conscious and are later repressed (secondary repression).

variable   Any characteristic in an experiment that may assume different values.

> **independent variable**   The variable under the experimenter's control.

> **dependent variable**   That aspect of the subject that is measured after the manipulation of the independent variable and that is assumed to vary as a function of the independent variable.

variance   The square of the standard deviation.

volunteer bias   Bias that may occur when individuals who volunteer for some procedures are not generally representative of the total population. Self-selected patients who seek out treatment based on newspaper publicity, for example, are likely to do significantly better than random patients who are simply offered the treatment.

zygosity   (1) Dizygotic: fraternal twins, the product of two fertilized ova. They have the genetic relationship of any two siblings. (2) Monozygotic: identical twins, the product of a single fertilized ovum.

REFERENCES

Abidin, R.A. *Parenting Stress Index.* 3rd ed. Psychological Assessment Resources, Lutz, Fla., 1995.

Ackerman, Marc J. *The Essentials of Forensic Psychological Assessment.* John Wiley & Sons, Inc. New York, New York, 1999.

Ackerman, Marc J. *Clinicians Guide to Child Custody Evaluations*—Second Edition, John Wiley & Sons, Inc. New York, New York, 2001.

Ackerman, Marc J. & Melissa Ackerman. "Child Custody Evaluation Practices: A 1996 Survey of Psychologists." *Family Law Quarterly* 30 (1996): 565-86.

Ackerman, Marc J. & Melissa Ackerman. "Child Custody Evaluation Practices: A Survey of Experienced Professionals (Revisited). *Professional Psychology: Research and Practice* 28 (1997): 137-45.

Ackerman, Marc J. & Scott Ackerman. "Comparison of Different Subgroups on MMPI of Parents Involved in Custody Litigation." 1992 (unpublished).

Ackerman, Marc J. & Andrew Kane. *Psychological Experts in Divorce Actions—Third Edition.* Aspen Publishers, New York, New York, 1998.

Ackerman, Marc J. & Una O'Leary. "Comparison of Different Subgroups on the MMPI-2 of Parents Involved in Custody Litigation." Paper presented at the 103rd Annual Convention of the American Psychological Association, New York (1995).

Ackerman, Marc J. & Linda Steffen. "Child Custody Evaluation Practices: A Survey of Family Law Judges." *American Journal of Family Law* 15 (2001): 12-16.

Ackerman, Marc J., Melissa C. Ackerman, Linda Steffen & Shannon Kelly-Poulos. "Psychologists' Practices Compared to the Expectations of Family Law Judges and Attorneys in Child Custody Cases." *Journal of Child Custody* 1 (2004): 41-60.

Ackerman, Robert J. *Children of Alcoholics: A Guidebook for Educators, Therapists, and Parent.* 2nd ed. Holmes Beach, Fla., Learning Publications, 1983.

Ackerson, Barry J. "Parents with Serious and Persistent Mental Illness: Issues in Assessment and Services." *Social Work* 48 (2003): 187-94.

Ahrons, Constance & Richard Miller. "The Effect of the Post-Divorce Relationship on Parental Involvement: A Longitudinal Study." *American Journal of Orthopsychiatry* 60 (1993): 441-50.

Aldridge, Jan, Michael E. Lamb, Kathleen J. Steinberg, Yael Orbach, Phillip W. Esplin & Lynn Bowler." Using a Human Figure Drawing to Elicit Information From Alleged Victims of Child Sexual Abuse." *Journal of Consulting and Clinical Psychology* 72 (2004): 304-316.

Alexander, Pamela & Cindy Schaeffer. "A Typology of Incestuous Families Based on Cluster Analysis." *Journal of Family Psychology* 4 (1994): 458.

Allen, John P. "Personality Correlates of the MacAndrew Alcoholism Scale: A Review of the Literature." *Psychol. Addictive Behav.* 5 (1991): 59-65.

Amato, Paul R. & Joan L. Gibreth. "Non Resident Fathers and Children's Well-Being: A Meta Analysis." *Journal of Marriage and Family* 61 (1999): 557-73.

Amato, Paul R. & Bruce Keith. "Parental Divorce and the Well-Being of Children: a Meta-Analysis." *Psychological Bulletin* 10 (1991): 24-26.

American Academy of Forensic Sciences, retrieved July 4, 2004 from www.aafs.org/.

American Association of Child Abuse Prevention. "Practice Parameters for the Forensic Evaluation of Children and Adolescents Who May Have Been Physically or Sexually Abused." *Journal of the American Academy of Child and Adolescent Psychology* 36 (1997): 37(s)-56(s).

American Academy of Psychiatry and the Law, web site, http://www.aapl.org/index.html, accessed July 3, 2004.

American Academy of Psychiatry & the Law. "Ethics Guidelines for the Practice of Forensic Psychiatry." *Bulletin of the American Academy of Psychiatry and the Law* (1995). Retrieved July 3, 2004, www.aapl.org/index/html.

American Bar Association, Family Law Section, and The Johnson Foundation Wingspread Conference Center, "High-Conflict Custody Cases: Reforming the System for Children, Conference Report and Action Plan." Racine, Wisconsin, September 8-10, 2000. Retrieved from www.abanet.org/child/wingspread.html on July 9, 2004.

American Bar Association Commission on Mental and Physical Disability Law. *National Benchbook on Psychiatric and Psychological Evidence and Testimony*. Washington, D.C.: American Bar Association, 1998.

American Bar Association Model Rules of Professional Conduct, Rule 1.6. See Melton et al., 1997, at 659.

American Board of Assessment Psychology, http://www.assessmentpsychologyboard.org/, retrieved July 1, 2004.

American Board of Forensic Psychology: www.abfp.com/diplomate_search_results.asp, retrieved 7/1/04.

American Board of Psychiatry and Neurology *Update* 9 Winter, 2004 at 4.

American Board of Psychiatry and Neurology web site, www.abpn.com, retrieved July 5, 2004.

American Law Institute. Conference-Workshop on the American Law Institute's *Principles of the Law of Family Dissolution: Analysis and Recommendations*, a discussion for Judges and Practioners, Woodrow Wilson International Center for Scholars, May 20, 2003, http://wwics.si.edu/index.cfm?fuseaction=events.event_summary&event_id=39231, retrieved July 9, 2004.

American Orthopsychiatric Association web site, retrieved July 4, 2004, www.amerortho.org/.

American Professional Society on the Abuse of Children (APSAC) Task Force, 2002: 106.

American Psychiatric Association. *Diagnostic and Statistical Manual of Mental Disorders*, 4th ed. (DSM-IV) (1994), Washington, D.C.: Author.

American Psychiatric Association. DSM-V Prelude Project, www.dsm5.org, retrieved August 18, 2004.

American Psychiatric Association. *Principles of Medical Ethics With Annotations Especially Applicable to Psychiatry*, 2001 edition (including November, 2003 amendments). American Psychiatric Association (2001, 2003). The *Principles* . . . may be accessed at http://www.psych.org/psych_pract/ethics/ethics.cfm.

American Psychiatric Association web site, www.psych.org/, retrieved June 30, 2004.

American Psychological Association. "Ethical Principles of Psychologists and Code of Conduct." 57 *American Psychologist* (2002): 1060-73 (2002).

American Psychological Association Statement on the Use of Anatomically Detailed Dolls in Forensic Evaluations, American Psychological Association Council of Representatives (Feb. 8, 1991).

American Psychological Association Committee on Professional Practice. "American Psychological Association Record Keeping Guidelines." 48 *American Psychologist* (1993): 640-41.

American Psychological Association. "Guidelines for Child Custody and Divorce Proceedings." *American Psychologist* 49 (1994): 677-80.

American Psychological Association, "Twenty Four Questions (and Answers) about Professional Practice in the Area of Child Abuse." *Professional Psychology: Research and Practice* 26 (1995): 377-85.

American Psychological Association. "Casebook for Providers of Psychological Services." in *American Psychologist* 39 (1984): 663-68.

American Psychological Association web site, www.apa.org, retrieved June 30 and July 1, 2004.

American Psychological Association, Division of Counseling Psychology, "What is a Counseling Psychologist." August, 1999: Author.

American Psychological Association, Division of Counseling Psychology web site, http://www.div17.org/Students/difference.htm, accessed August 27, 2004.

American Psychological Association, *General Guidelines for Providers of Psychological Services* (1987).

APA Office of Ethnic Minority Affairs, "Guidelines for Providers of Psychological Services to Ethnic, Linguistic, and Culturally Diverse Populations." 48 *Am. Psychologist* (1993): 45-48.

American Psychology-Law Society, "Graduate Programs in Psychology and Law—Related Programs." http://www.unl.edu/ap-ls/graduateprograms.htm, accessed August 27, 2004.

Anastasi, Anne. *Psychological Testing.* 5th ed. New York, MacMillan, 1982.

Anastasi, Anne. *Psychological Testing.* 6th ed. New York, MacMillan, 1988.

Anstasi, Anne. *Psychological Testing.* 7th ed. New York, McMillan, 1997.

Anderson, T.W. & Stanley L Sclove. *An Introduction to DTE Statistical Analysis of Data.* Boston: Houghton Mifflin, 1978.

Anthony, N.C. "Comparison of Client Standard, Exaggerated and Matching MMPI Profiles." *Psychological Assessment: A Journal of Consulting and Clinical Psychology* 36 (1971): 100-03.

Appelbaum, Paul S. "Ethics in Evolution: The Incompatibility of Clinical and Forensic Functions." *American Journal of Psychiatry* 154 (1997): 445-46.

Arata, C.M. "Child Sexual Abuse and Sexual Re-victimization." *Clinical Psychology: Science and Practice* 9 (2002): 135-164.

Archer, Robert. "Development of the Immaturity Scale and Gender Community Scales for the MMPI-A." Paper presented at the American Psychological Association Convention (Aug. 1991).

Archer, Robert. "Are Critical Items 'Critical' for the MMPI-A?" Paper presented at the 100th Annual Convention of the American Psychological Association, Washington, D.C. (1992).

Archer, Robert. "MMPI-Rorschach Interrelationship: Proposed Criteria for Evaluating Explanatory Models." *Journal of Personality Assessment* 67 (1996): 504-15.

Archer, Robert. *MMPI-A: Assessing Adolescent Psychopathology.* 2nd ed. Lawrence Erlbaum Associates, New Jersey, 1997.

Archer, Robert. "Future Directions of the MMPI-A: Research In Clinical Issues." *Journal of Personality Assessment* 68 (1997): 95-109.

Archer, Robert P., Richard W. Handel, Kathleen D. Lynch & David E. Elkins. "MMPI Validity Scale Uses and Limitations in Detecting Varying Levels of Random Responding." *Journal of Personality Assessment* 78 (2002): 417-31.

Archer, Robert, Mark Maruish, Eric Imhof & Christopher Piotrowski, "Psychological Test Usage with Adolescent Clients: 1990 Survey Findings." *Professional Psychology: Research & Practice* 22 (1991): 248-50.

Arditti, Joyce. "Differences Between Fathers with Joint Custody and Non-Custodial Fathers." *American Journal of Orthopsychiatry* 62 (1992): 187-95.

Arditti, Joyce. "Ackerman-Schoendorf Scales for Parent Evaluation of Custody." Eleventh Mental Measurement Yearbook. Jack Kramer & Jane Close Conoley, eds., University of Nebraska Press, Lincoln, Nebraska, 1997.

Aronow, Edward, C.S. Norms, "Psychometrics, and Possibilities for the Rorschach Technique," *Clinical Psychology: Science and Practice* 8 (2001): 383-85.

Aronow, Edward. "Children's Apperceptive Storytelling Test (CAST)." *in Twelfth Mental Measurements Yearbook* 181 (1995).

Arron, Martin J. "Chronic Fatigue Syndrome: The Role of Other Psychiatric and Medical Diseases." Paper presented at the 105th Annual Convention of the American Psychological Association, Chicago (Aug. 1997).

Association of State and Provincial Psychology Boards, web site www.asppb.org, retrieved June 30, 2004.

Austin, William G. "Guidelines for Utilizing Collateral Sources of Information in Child Custody Evaluations." *Family Court Review* 40 (2000): 177-84.

Austin, William G. "Assessing Credibility in Allegations of Marital Violence in the High-Conflict Child Custody Case." *Family and Conciliation Courts Review* 38 (2000): 462-77.

Austin, William G. "Partner Violence & Risk Assessment in Child Custody Evaluations." *Family Court Review* 39 (2001): 483-96.

Axelrod, B.N. "Validity of the Wechsler Abbreviated Scales of Intelligence and Other Very Short Forms of Estimating Intellectual Functioning." *Assessment* 9 (2002): 17-23.

Azar, Beth. "Changes Will Improve Quality of Tests." 30 *APA Monitor* (1999): 30.

Azar, Beth. "The Bond Between Mother and Child." *American Psychological Association Monitor* 26 (1995): 28.

Baer, Ruth, Martha Wetter & David Berry. "Effects of Information About Validity Scales on Understanding of Symptoms on the MMPI-2: An Analogue Investigation." *Assessment: A Journal of Consulting and Clinical Psychology* 2 (1995): 189-200.

Baer, Ruth, Martha Wetter, Roger Greene, David Nichols & David Berry. "Sensitivity of MMPI-2 Validity Scales to Underreporting of Symptoms." *Psychological Assessment: A Journal of Consulting and Clinical Psychology* 5 (1995): 419-23.

Baer, Ruth, James Ballenger, David Berry & Martha Wetter. "Detection of Random Responding on the MMPI-A." *Journal of Personality Assessment* 68 (1997): 139-51.

Bagley, R. Michael, Tom Buis & Robert Nicholson. "Relative Effectiveness of the Standard Validity Scales in Detecting Fake-Bad and Fake-Good Responding: Replication and Extension." *Psychological Assessment: A Journal of Consulting and Clinical Psychology* 7 (1995): 84-92.

Bagby, R. Michael, J. Roy Gillis & Richard Rogers. "Effectiveness of the Millon Clinical Multiaxial Inventory Validity in the Detection of Random Responding." *Psychological Assessment: A Journal of Consulting and Clinical Psychology* 3 (1991): 285-87.

Bagby, R. Michael, J. Roy Gillis, Brenda Toner & Joel Goldberg. "Detecting Fake-Good and Fake-Bad Responding on the Millon Clinical Multiaxial Inventory-II." *Psychological Assessment: A Journal of Consulting and Clinical Psychology* 3 (1991): 496-98.

Bales, J. "APA Rebuts Criticism of Clinician Witnesses." *APA Monitor* 19 (1988): 17.

Banks, Steve. "An Open Letter to Division 41 Members Interested in the American Board of Forensic Psychology." *American Psychology-Law Society News* 14 (1994): 3.

Banyard, Victoria L., Linda M. Williams, & Jane A. Siegel. "The long-term mental health consequences of child sexual abuse: An exploratory study of the impact of multiple traumas in a sample of women." *Journal of Traumatic Stress* 14(4) (2001): 697-715.

Barber, Bonnie L. & Jacquelynne S. Eccles. "Long-Term Influence of Divorce in Single Parenting and Adolescent Families and Work-Related Values, Behaviors, and Aspirations." *Psychological Bulletin* 111 (1992): 108-26.

Barnard, C.P., & G. Jenson. "Child Custody Evaluations: A Rationale Process for an Emotion-laden Event." *The American Journal of Family Therapy* 12 (1984): 61-67.

Barnett, D., J. Ganiban & D. Cicchetti. "Maltreatment, Negative Expressivity, and the Development of Type D Attachments From 12 to 24 months of Age." *Monographs of the Society for Research in Child Development* 64 (1991): 97-118.

Bass, Ellen & Laura Davis. "*The Courage to Heal.*" (1988).

Bass, Larry J., Stephen T. DeMers, James R.P. Ogloff, Christa Peterson, Jean L. Pettifor, Randolph P. Reaves, Terez Retfalvi, Norma P. Simon, Carole Sinclair, Robert M. Tipton. *Professional Conduct and Discipline in Psychology. American Psychological Association.* Washington, D.C., 1996.

Bartoi, M.G., & B.N. Kinder. "Effects of Child and Adult Sexual Abuse on the Adult Sexuality." *Journal of Sex and Marital Therapy* 24 (1998): 75-90.

Bathurst, Kay, Allen Gottfried & Adelle Gottfried. "Normative Data on the MMPI-2 in Child Custody Litigation." *Psychological Assessment* 9 (1997): 205-11.

Baum, Nehami. "The Male Way of Mourning Divorce: When, What, and How." *Clinical Social Work Journal* 31 (2003): 37-50.

Bauserman Robert. "Child Adjustment and Joint-Custody Verses Sole-Custody Arrangements: A Meta-Analytic Review." *Journal of Family Psychology* 16 (2002): 91-102.

Bazar, Joan. "Mentally Ill Moms Aided in Keeping Their Children." *APA Monitor* 21 (December 1990): 32.

Bazelon, D. "Veils, Values and Social Responsibility." *American Psychologist* 37 (1982): 115-21.

Beaber, R.J. "Custody Quagmire: Some Psychological Dilemmas." *Journal of Psychiatry* 10 (1982): 309-26.

Beal, Carole R., Kelly L. Schmitt & Dawn J. Dekle. "Eye Witness Identification of Children: Effects of Absolute Judgments, Non-Verbal Response Options and Event Encoding." *Law & Human Behavior* 19 (1995): 197-216.

Bean, Kenneth L. & George O. Karasievich. "Psychological Test Results at Three Stages of Inpatient Alcoholism Treatment." *Journal of Studies on Alcohol* 36 (1975): 838-52.

Beardslee, William R., Jules Bemporad, Martin Keller & Gerald L. Klerman. "Children of Parents with Major Affective Disorder: A Review." *American Journal of Psychiatry* 140 (1983): 825-32.

Beck, Aaron, Robert A. Steer, Roberta Ball & William F. Ranieri. "Comparison of Beck Depression Inventories-IA and -II in Psychiatric Outpatients." *Journal of Personality Assessment* 67 (1996): 588-97.

Beck, Aaron T., Robert A. Steer & Margery G. Garbin. "Psychometric Properties of the Beck Depression Inventory: Twenty-Five Years of Evaluation." *Clinical Psychology Review* 8 (1988): 77-100.

Beck, S.J., A.G. Beck, Eugene E. Levitt & Herman B. Molish. *Rorschach's Test.* 3rd ed. New York, Grune & Stratton, 1961.

Beck, Connie & Bruce D. Sales. "A Critical Re-Appraisal of Divorce Mediation Research and Policy." *Psychology, Public Policy and Law* 6 (2000): 989-56.

Becker, Judith, Judith Alpert, Delores Bigfoot, Barbara Bonner, Lane Geddi, Scott Henggeler, Keith Kaufman & Eugene Walker. "Empirical Research on Child Abuse Treatment: Report by the Child Abuse and Neglect Treatment Working Group." *Journal of Clinical Psychology* 24 (1995): 23-46.

Behnke, Stephen. "Release of Test Data and APA's New Ethics Code." *Monitor on Psychology* 34 (2003): 70-72.

Bellak, Leopold. "Projective Techniques in the Computer Age." *Journal of Personality Assessment* 58 (1992): 445-53.

Bellak, L. *The TAT, CAT and SAT in Clinical Use*, 5th ed., 1993.

Bellak, Leopold. *T.A.T., C.A.T. and S.A.T. in Clinical Use*. 4th ed. Orlando, Fla., Grune & Stratton, 1986.

Bellak, Leopold & Sonya Bellak. *Children's Apperception Test*. Larchmont, N.Y., C.P.S., Inc., 1949.

Belsky J., J. Robbins & W. Gamble. "*The Determinants of Parental Competence*: *Toward a Theory*, in M. Lewis (ed.), Beyond the Dyad. New York, Plenum Press (1984).

Ben-Porath, Yossef. "New Subscales for the MMPI-2 Social Introversions (Si) Scale." *Psychological Assessment: Journal of Consulting and Clinical Psychology* (1989): 172.

Ben-Porath, Yossef. "Standardization and Interpretation of Scores on the MMPI-A." *Psychological Assessment: A Journal of Consulting and Clinical Psychology* (1989): 169-74.

Ben-Porath, Yossef, J.N. Butcher & J.R. Graham. "Contributions of the MMPI-2 Content Scales to the Differential Diagnosis of Schizophrenia and Major Depression." *Psychological Assessment, Journal of Consulting and Clinical Psychology* 3 (1991): 634-40.

Benjamin, G. Andrew & Gollan, Jackie K. *Family Evaluations in Custody Litigation*. American Psychological Association, Washington, D.C., 2003.

Benjet, Corina, Sandra T. Azar, & Regina Kuersten-Hogan. "Evaluating the Parental Fitness of Psychiatrically Diagnosed Individuals: Advocating a Functional-Contextual Analysis of Parenting." *Journal of Family Psychology* 17 (2003): 238-51.

Bennett, Bruce, Brenda Bryant, Gary VandenBos & Addison Greenwood. *Professional Liability and Risk Assessment*. American Psychological Association, Washington, D.C., 1990.

Bent, Russell, Robert Goldberg & Ralph Packard. "A Very Brief History of ABPP: 1947-1997." *The ABPP Specialist* 21 (2002): 4, 19-20.

Berkman, C.F. "Psychodynamic and Family Issues in Post-Divorce Child Custody Litigation." *Journal of the American Academy of Child Psychiatry* 23 (1984): 708-12.

Berkowitz, Alan & H. Wesley Perkins. "Personality Characteristics of Children of Alcoholics." *Journal of Consulting and Clinical Psychology* 56 (1988): 206-09.

Berliner, I. & Saunders, B.E. "Treating Fear and Anxiety in Sexually Abused Children: Results of a Controlled Two Year Follow-up Study." *Child Maltreatment* 1 (1996): 294-309.

Berman, A. "The Expert at Trial: Personality Persuades." *Family Advocate* 9 (1986): 11-12.

Bernstein, D.E. & J.D. Jackson. (2004) "The *Daubert* trilogy in the states." *Jurimetrics* (2004): 44, in press. Accessed April 6, 2004, Social Science Research Network Electronic Paper collection, http://ssrn.com/abstract=498786.

Bernstein, Lewis, Ph.D. "Psychological Testing: II. The Rorschach Test." Reprinted from the *Journal of Children's Asthma Research Institute and Hospital* 1 (1961).

Berry, David, Jennifer Adams, Gregory Smith, Roger Greene, Gerlinde Serkinjak, Gordon Wielnad & Bryon Tharpe. "MMPI-2 Clinical Scales in 2-Code Types: Impact of Varying Levels of Omitted Items." *Psychological Assessment: A Journal of Consulting and Clinical Psychology* 9 (1997): 158-60.

Bersoff, Donald. "Judicial Deference to Nonlegal Decisionmakers: Imposing Simplistic Solutions on Problems of Cognitive Complexity in Mental Disability Law." *Southern Methodist University Law Review 46* (1992): 327.

Bisbing, Steven B., Linda M. Jorgenson & Pamela K. Sutherland. *Sexual Abuse by Professionals: A Legal Guide*. Charlottesville, Va., Michie, 1995.

Bischoff, Lisa. "Parent Awareness Skills Survey." In *The Eleventh Mental Measurement Yearbook*. Jack Kramer & Jane Close Conoley, Lincoln, Neb., University of Nebraska Press, 1992.

Bisnair, Liese, Philip Firestone & David Rynard. "Factors Associated with Academic Achievement in Children Following Parental Separation." *American Journal of Orthopsychiatry* 60 (1990): 67-76.

Blanchard, R., M.S. Watson, A. Choy, R. Dickey, P. Klassen & D.J. Ferren. "Pedophiles: Mental Retardation, Maternal Age, and Sexual Orientation." *Archives of Sexual Behavior* 28 (1999): 111-27.

Blashfield, Roger. "Symposium: DSM-IV Field Trials—Part One." Comments at the 100th Annual Convention of the American Psychological Association, Washington D.C., Aug. 1992.

Blatt, Sidney J. "The Rorschach: A Test of Perception or an Evaluation of Representation." *Journal of Personality Assessment* 55 (1990): 394-416.

Blau, Theodore. *The Psychologist as Expert Witness*. New York, John Wiley & Sons, Inc., 1984.

Blau, Theodore. *The Psychologist as Expert Witness*. 2nd ed., New York, John Wiley & Sons, Inc., 1998.

Block, A.P. "Rape Trauma Syndrome as Scientific Expert Testimony." *Archives of Sexual Behavior* 19 (1990): 309-323.

Board of Registration in Medicine, 662 N.E.2d 1020 (Mass. 1996), *reported in* Howard V. Zonana, "AAPL Ethical Guidelines in Appellate Decision," 22 *Am. Ass'n Psychiatry & L. Newsl.* 3 (1997).

Boat, Barbara W., Mark D. Everson & Lisa Amaya-Jackson. "Consistency of Children's Sexualized or Avoidant Reactions to Anatomical Dolls: A Pilot Study." *Journal of Child Sexual Abuse* 36 (1997): 89-105.

Bolton, F.G. & S.R. Bolton. *A Guide for Clinical and Legal Practitioners, Working with the Violent Family.* Sage Publishers, Troy, N.Y., 1987.

Bolton, Brian. Review of the California Psychological Inventory (CPI) in *The Eleventh Mental Measurements Yearbook.* Jack Kramer & Jane Close Conoley, eds. University of Nebraska Press, Lincoln, Neb, 1992.

Boney-McCoy, S., & Finkelhor, D. "Psychosocial Sequelae of Violent Victimization in a National Youth Sample." *Journal of Consulting and Clinical Psychology* 63 (1995): 726-36.

Bongar, Bruce. "Risk Management and the Suicidal Patient." *The Psychotherapy Bulletin* 27 (1992): 27-29.

Bongar, Bruce. *The Suicidal Patient: Clinical and Legal Standards of Care.* American Psychological Association, Washington, D.C., 1991.

Bonkowski, Sara E. "Lingering Sadness: Young Adult's Response to Parental Divorce." *Journal of Contemporary Social Work* (1989): 219-23.

Bornstein, Robert F. "The Dependent Personality: Developmental, Social, and Clinical Perspectives." *Psychological Bulletin* 112 (1992): 3-23.

Borum, Randy, Randy Otto & Stephen Golding. "Improving Clinical Judgment and Decision Making in Forensic Assessment." *Journal of Psychiatry & Law* 21 (1993): 35-76.

Bottoms, Bette. "Attitudinal Determinations of Child Sexual Assault Victims: Perceived Credibility." Paper presented at the 100th Annual Convention of the American Psychological Association, Washington, D.C., 1992.

Bottoms, Bette L., Gayle S. Goodman, Beth M. Schwartz-Kenney & Sherilyn N. Thomas. "Understanding Children's Use of Secrecy in the Context of Eye Witness Reports." *Law & Human Behavior* 26 (2002): 285-313.

Bow, James N. & Francella A. Quinnell, "Critique of Child Custody Evaluations by the Legal Profession." *Family Court Review* 42 (2004): 115-27.

Bow, James N. & Francella A. Quinnell. "A Critical Review of Child Custody Evaluation Reports." *Family Court Review* 40 (2002): 164-76.

Bow, James N. & Francella Quinnell. "Psychologists' Current Practices and Procedures in Child Custody Evaluations: Five Years After: American Psychological Association Guidelines." *Professional Psychology: Research and Practice* 32 (2001): 261-68.

Bow, James N., Francella A. Quinnell, Mark Zaroff & Amy Assemany. "Assessment of Sexual Abuse Allegations in Child Custody Cases and Practice." *Professional Psychology: Research and Practice* 33 (2001): 566-75.

Bowman, M.L. "Problems Inherent to the Diagnosis of Posttraumatic Stress Disorder," in *Psychological Injuries at Trial* 820-849, I. Z. Schulze & D.O. Brady (eds.), Chicago, Ill., American Bar Association, 2003.

Boyer, Jenny. "Assuming Risk in Child Custody Evaluations." *Register Report* 16 (1990): 8-9.

Boyle, Gregory. "Rotter Incomplete Sentences Blank—2nd Edition," in *The Twelfth Mental Measurements Yearbook*, The Buros Institute of Mental Measurements, Jane Close Conoley & James C. Impara (eds.), Lincoln, Neb., 1995.

Bradway, K.P., C.W. Thompson & R.B. Cravens. "Preschool I.Q.'s after 25 Years." *Journal of Educational Psychology* 49 (1958): 278-81.

Brassard, M.B. Germsin & S. Hart (eds.). *Psychological Maltreatment of Children and Youth*. Elmsford, NY, Pergamon, 1987.

Braver, M., J. Bumberry, K. Green & R. Rawson. "Childhood Abuse and Current Psychological Functioning in a University Counseling Center Population." *Journal of Counseling Psychology* 39 (1992): 252-57.

Braver, Sanford L., Ira M. Ellman & William V. Fabucius. "Relocation of Children After Divorce and Children's Best Interests: New Evidence and Legal Considerations." *Journal of Family Psychology* 17 (2003): 206-19.

Braver, Sanford, Sharlene Wolchik, Irwin Sandler, Virgil Sheets, Bruce Fogas & R. Curtis Bay. "A Longitudinal Study of Non-custodial Parents: Parents Without Children." *Journal of Family Psychology* 7 (1993): 9-23.

Bravor-Rosewater, Lynn W. "The Problems with Computerized Test Interpretations in a Forensic Arena." A paper presented at the 107th Annual Convention of the American Psychological Association, Boston, MA, Aug. 1999.

Bray, James H. & Mavis Hetherington. "Families in Transition: Introduction and Overview." 7 *Journal of Psychology* 1 (1993): 3-8.

Bremner, J. Douglas, John Krystal, Dennis Charney & Steven Southwick. "Neural Mechanisms in Dissociative Amnesia Childhood Abuse: Relevance to the Current Controversy Surrounding the "False Memory Syndrome." *American Journal of Psychiatry* 153 (1996): 71-82.

Brems, Christiane & Pamela Lloyd. "Validation of the MMPI-2 Low Self-esteem Content Scale." *Journal of Personality Assessment* 65 (1995): 550-56.

Bresee, Patricia, Jeffrey Stearns, Bruce Bess & Leslie Pecker. "Allegations of Child Sexual Abuse in Child Custody Disputes: A Therapeutic Assessment Model." *American Journal of Orthopsychiatry* 56 (1986): 550-59.

Bricklin, Barry. *Custody Newsletter* (Dec. 1993): 1.

Bricklin, Barry. *Perception of Relationships Test (PORT)*. Village Publishing, Doylestown, Pa., 1990.

Bricklin, Barry. *PORT Handbook: Perception of Relationships Test*. Village Publishing, Furlong, Pa., 1990.

Bricklin Perceptual Scales Test Manual Supplement No. 6, June 30, 1988.

Bricklin Perceptual Scales Test Manual Supplement No. 3, Mar. 28, 1986.

Bricklin Perceptual Scales Test Manual Supplement No. 5, Feb. 15, 1988.

Bricklin, Barry. *Bricklin Perceptual Scales*. Village Publishing, Furlong, Pa., 1984.

Briere, John. "Repressed Memories and False Memory Syndrome—Memory: True or False?" Paper presented at the Wisconsin Psychological Association Spring Meeting (April 6, 1994).

Briere, John & John R. Conte. "Self-Reported Amnesia for Abuse in Adults Molested as Children." *Journal of Traumatic Stress* 6 (1993): 21-31.

Briere, John & E. Gil. "Self-Mutilation in Clinical and General Population Samples: Prevalence, Correlates, and Function." *American Journal of Orthopsychiatry* 68 (1998): 609-20.

Briere, John & M. Runtz. "Differential Adult Symptomotology Associated with Three Types of Child Abuse Histories." *Child Abuse & Neglect* 14 (1990): 357-64.

Briere, John & M. Runtz, "Post-Sexual Abuse Trauma: Data and Implications for Clinical Practice." *Journal of Interpersonal Violence* 2 (1993): 367-79.

Briere, John, & M. Runtz, "Child Sexual Abuse, Long-Term Sequelae and Implications for Psychological Assessment." *Journal of Interpersonal Violence* 3 (1993): 312-30.

Brigham, John C. & Stacy A. Spier. "Opinions Held by Professionals Who Work with Child Witnesses," in Helen Dent & Rhonda Flin, *Children As Witnesses.* Chichester, England, John Wiley & Sons, Inc., 1992.

Brodsky, Stanley. *Testifying in Court: Guidelines and Maxims for the Expert Witness.* American Psychological Association, Washington, D.C., 1991.

Brodzinsky, David. "The Use and Misuse of Psychological Testing in Child Custody Evaluation." *Professional Psychology: Research and Practice* 24 (1993): 213-18.

Bronfenbrenner, U. *The Ecology of Human Development: Experiments by Nature and Design.* Cambridge, Mass., Harvard University Press, 1979.

Brown, Douglas T. "Millon Adolescent Personality Inventory," in O. Buros, *The Ninth Mental Measurements Yearbook,* 978-79. Lincoln, Neb., University of Nebraska, 1985.

Brown, Laura. "Pseudomemories: The Standard of Silence and the Standard of Care in Trauma Treatment." *American Journal of Clinical Hypnosis* 3 (1995): 1-15.

Bruch, Carol S. "Parental Alienation Syndrome and Alienated Children—Getting it Wrong in Child Custody Cases." *Child and Family Law Quarterly* 14 (2002): 381-400.

Bruck, Maggie, Stephen J. Ceci & Helene Hembrooke. "Reliability and Credibility of Young Children's Reports: From Research to Policies and Practice." *American Psychologist* 53 (1998): 136-51.

Bruck, Maggie. "Suggestibility and Credibility of Child Witnesses: Research Findings." Annual Meeting of the Wisconsin Judicial Conference, Lake Geneva, Wisc., (Sept. 1995).

Bruck, Maggie, Steven Ceci, Emmett Francouer & Ashley Renik. "Anatomically Detailed Dolls Do Not Facilitate Pre-Schoolers' Reports of a Pediatric Examination Involving Genital Touching." *Journal of Experimental Psychology: Applied* 1 (1995): 95-109.

Bryer, Jeffrey B., Kristine A. Martines & Melissa A. Dignan. "Millon Clinical Multiaxial Inventory Alcohol Abuse and Drug Abuse Scales and the Identification of Substance-Abuse Patients." *Psychological Assessment: A Journal of Consulting and Clinical Psychology* 2 (1990): 438-41.

Buchanan, Christy. "Patterns of Children's Responses to Parent's Marital Conflict." Paper presented at Children and Marital Conflict: Process of Effects Symposium. Annual Meeting of the Midwestern Psychological Association, Chicago (May 1994).

Buck, J., & E.F. Hammer. *Advances in the House-Tree-Person Technique: Variations in Applications.* Los Angeles, Western Psychological Services, 1969.

Budwin v. American Psychological Assoc., 24 Cal. App. 4th 875, 29 Cal. Rptr. 2d 453 (Cal. App. 3d Dist. 1994).

Buist, Anne & Helen Janson. "Childhood Sexual Abuse, Parenting and Postpartum Depression—3-Year Follow-up Study." *Child Abuse and Neglect* 25 (2001): 909-21.

"Bulimia Nervosa May Interfere with Parenting." *Clinical Psychiatry News* 18 (Feb. 1990): 12.

Bumby, K.M., & D.J. Hudson. "Intimacy Deficits, Fear of Intimacy and Loneliness Among Sexual Offenders." *Criminal Justice and Behaviors* 24 (1997): 315-31.

Burgess, A.W. & L.L. Holmstrom. "Rape trauma syndrome and post-traumatic stress response." *Research Handbook on Rape and Sexual Assault* (1985): 46-61.

Burgess, A.W. & L.L. Holmstrom. "Rape Trauma Syndrome." *American Journal of Psychiatry* 131 (1974): 981-99.

Burns, R.C., & S.H. Kaufman. *Kinetic Family Drawings (KFD): An Introduction to Understanding Children Through Kinetic Drawings*. Brunner-Mazel, New York, 1970.

Buros, O., ed. *Eighth Mental Measurements Yearbook*. Gryphon Press/Highland Press, Highland Park, N.J., 1978.

Butcher, James. "Assessment with the MMPI-2: Decisions in Diverse Applications." Presented at the 109th Annual Convention of the American Psychological Association, San Francisco, Cal. (Aug. 2001).

Butcher, James & John Graham, eds. *MMPI Workshops and Symposia, Topics in MMPI-2 Interpretation.* University of Minnesota Press, 1989.

Butcher, James N., Julia N. Perry & Mira M. Atlics. "Validity and Utility of Computer-Based Test Interpretation." *Psychological Assessment* 12 (2000): 6-18.

Butcher, James N. & Kenneth S. Pope, "Seven Issues in Conducting Forensic Assessments: Ethical Responsibilities in Light of New Standards and New Tests." 3 *Ethics & Behav.* (1993): 267-271.

Butcher, James N., John R. Graham, W. Grant Dahlstrom & Eric Bowman. "The MMPI-2 With College Students." *Journal of Personality Assessment* 54 (1990): 1-15.

Butcher, James N., Timothy Jeffrey, Tommie G. Kayton, Susan Colligan, Jerry R. DeVore & Rahn Minegawa. "A Study of Active Military Personnel with the MMPI-2." *Military Psychology* 2 (1990): 47-61.

Butcher, James N., Carolyn Aldwin, Michael Levenson, Yossef S. Ben-Porath, Avron Spiro & Raymond Bosse. "Personality and Aging: A Study of the MMPI-2 Among Older Men." Paper presented at the 98th Annual Convention of the American Psychological Association, Boston (Aug. 1990).

Buxton, A. "The Best Interests of the Child of Gay and Lesbian Parents," in R. Galatzer-Levy, L. Kraus & B. Leventhal (eds), *The Scientific Basis of Custody Decisions in Divorce,* 319-56, John Wiley & Sons, Inc., New York, New York, 1999.

Bybee, Deborah, Carol T. Mowbray, Daphna Oyserman, & Lisa Lewandowski, "Variability in Community Functioning of Mothers With Serious Mental Illness." The *Journal of Behavioral Health Services and Research* 14 (2003): 269-89.

Cain, Barbara S. "Parental Divorce During the College Years." *Psychiatry* 52 (May 1989): 135-46.

Caldwell, Alexander. "Families of MMPI Code Types." Paper presented at the 12th Annual Symposium on the MMPI, Tampa, Fla. (1982).

Caldwell, Alexander. "MMPI-2 Content Scales: What You Say Is What You Get?" *Contemporary Psychology* 7 (1991): 560.

Caldwell, Alexander. "The MMPI: An Advanced Level Workshop." Paper presented at the Fall Conference of the Society of Consulting and Clinical Psychologists, Brookfield, Wisc. (Oct. 25, 26, 1996).

Caldwell, Alexander. "*Forensic Questions and Answers on the MMPI/MMPI-2*." Caldwell Report. Los Angeles, Cal., 1997.

Caldwell, Alexander, & Christopher O'Hare. *A Handbook for MMPI Personality Types*. (1986) (referring to Daniel Newberger, Reid & Kotelchuck).

Callnuf, Bradford, Greenburg & Currey, 1996.

Calsyn, Donald A., Andrew J. Saxon & Fransing Daisy. "Validity of the MCMI Drug Abuse Scale with Drug Abusing and Psychiatric Samples." *Journal of Clinical Psychology* 46 (1990): 244-46.

Cambias, Ron D., Grant Aram Killian & Jan Faust. "Robert's Apperception Test for Children: Supplementary Test Pictures for Black Children," in Daniel J. Keyser & Richard C. Sweetland, eds., *Test Critiques* 9. Austin, Tex.: Pro-Ed., 1992.

Campbell, Robert Jean. *Psychiatric Dictionary*. 6th ed. Oxford University Press, New York, 1989.

Cameron, Paul & Kirk Cameron. "Children of Homosexual Parents Report Childhood Difficulties." *Psychological Reports* 90 (2000): 71-82.

Cameron, P. & K. Cameron. "Did the APA Misrepresent the Scientific Literature to Courts in Support of Homosexual Custody?" *The Journal of Psychology* 13 (1997): 313-32.

Campbell, Keith A, Diane J. Rohlman, Daniel Storzbach, Lawrence M. Binder, W. Kent Anger, Craig A. Covera, Kelly L. Davis & Sandra S. Grossman. "Test-Re-Test Reliability of Psychological and Neurobehavioral Tests Self-Administered by Computer." *Assessment* 6 (1999): 21-32.

Canadian Academy of Psychiatry and Law web site, www.caplnet.org/, retrieved July 3, 2004.

Canadian Psychiatric Association web site, www.cap-apc.org/, retrieved July 1, 2004.

Canadian Psychological Association web site, www.cpa.ca/, accessed July 1, 2004.

Canadian Psychological Association. *Canadian Code of Ethics for Psychologist, Revised*. Ottawa, Ont., Canadian Psychological Association, 2000.

Canadian Register of Health Service Providers in Psychology. "Criteria for Listing in the Canadian Register of Health Service Providers in Psychology." Ottawa, Ont., Canadian Register of Health Service Providers in Psychology. http://www.crhspp.ca/eligible.htm, accessed August 26, 2004.

Carkhauff, R.R., L. Barnette & J.N. McCall. *The Counselor's Handbook: Scale and Profile Interpretations of the MMPI*. Urban, Ill., R.W. Parkinson, 1965.

Carlson, Bonnie E. "Adolescent Observers of Marital Violence." *Journal of Family Violence* 5 (1990): 285-99.

Carlson, Bonnie E. "Children's Beliefs About Punishment." *American Journal of Orthopsychiatry* 56 (1996): 308-12.

Carlson, Janet. "Perception-of-Relationships-Test," in *The Eleventh Mental Measurement Yearbook*. Jack Kramer & Jane Close Conoley, eds., University of Nebraska Press, Lincoln, Nebraska, 1992.

Carlson, Kenneth A. *Carlson Psychological Survey*. Port Huron, Mich., Research Psychologists Press, 1982.

Carr, A.C. "Psychological Testing of Personality," in H. Kaplan & B. Sadock, *Comprehensive Textbook of Psychiatry/IV*, 514-35. Baltimore, Md., Williams & Wilkins, 1985.

Carson, R. "Interpretive Manual to the MMPI," in *MMPI: Research Developments and Clinical Applications*, New York, McGraw Hill, 1969.

Carson, R. "MMPI Profile Interpretation." Paper presented at the 7th Annual Symposium on the MMPI, Mexico City, 1972.

Carstensen, Peter C. "The Evolving Duty of Mental Health Professionals to Third Parties: A Doctrinal and Institutional Examination." *International Journal of Law and Psychiatry* 17 (1994): 8-9.

Carter, Kathleen, Bette Bottoms & Murray Levine. "Linguistic and Socioemotional Influences on the Accuracy of Children's Reports." *Law and Human Behavior* 20 (1996): 335-58.

Cashmore, Judy & Kay Bussey. "Judicial Perceptions of Child Witness Competence." *Law & Human Behavior* 20 (1996): 313-33.

Castlebury, Frank, Mark Hilsenroth, Leonard Handler, Thomas Durham. "The Use of the MMPI-2 Personality Disorder Scales in the Assessment of the DSM-IV Antisocial, Borderline, and Narcissistic Personality Disorders. *Assessment* 4 (1997): 155-68.

Ceci, Steven & Maggie Bruck. "Social Policy Report for the Society for Research and Child Development in 1993." *Child Witnesses: Translating Research into Policy* 7 (1993): 1-30.

Ceci, Steven, Elizabeth Loftus, Leichtman & Maggie Bruck. "The Possible Role of Source Misattributions in the Creation of False Beliefs among Pre-Schoolers." *International Journal of Clinical and Experimental Hypnosis* 52 (1994): 304-20.

Cecil, Heather & Steven C. Matson. "Psychological Function and Family Discord Among African American Adolescent Families With and Without a History of Childhood Sexual Abuse." *Child Abuse and Neglect* 25 (2001): 973-88.

Cecil, Joe S. & Thomas E. Willging. "Court-Appointed Experts: Defining the Role of Experts Appointed Under Federal Rule of Evidence 706." Federal Judicial Center, Washington, D.C., 1993.

Chasen, R. & Greenbaum, H. "A Model for Evaluation in Custody Disputes." *The American Journal of Family Therapy* 9 (1981): 43-47.

Chassin, Laurie, Fred Rogosch & Manuel Barrera. "Substance Use and Symptomatology among Adolescent Children of Alcoholics." *Journal of Abnormal Psychology* 100 (1991): 449-63.

Chester, B, R.W. Robin, M.P. Koss, T. Lopez & D. Goldman. "Grandmother Dishonored: Violence Against Women by Male Partners in American Indian Communities." *Violence & Victims* 9 (1994): 248-58.

Chiariello, Mary A. and Helen Orvaschel. "Patterns of Parent-Child Communication: Relationship to Depression." *Clinical Psychology Review* 15 (1995): 395-407.

Christensen, Else. "Aspects of a Preventive Approach to Support Children of Alcoholics." *Child Abuse Review* 6 (1997): 24-34.

Clark, Beth. "Acting in the Best Interest of the Child: Essential Components of a Child Custody Evaluation." *Family Law Quarterly* 29 (1995): 19-38.

Clark, Charles R. "Agreeing to Be an Expert Witness: Considerations of Competence and Role Integrity." *Register Report* 16 (1990): 4-5.

Chu, J.A., & Dill, D.L. "Dissociative Symptoms in Relation to Childhood Physical and Sexual Abuse." *American Journal of Psychiatry* 147 (1990): 887-92.

Ciccherri, D., S.L. Toth. "Child Maltreatment and Attachment Organization: Implications for Intervention," in S. Goldberg, R. Muir, & J. Kerr, eds., *Attachment Theory,* Hillsdale, N.J., Analytic Press, 1995.

Clark-Stewart, K.A., D.L. Vandell, D.L. McCarthy, M.T. Owens & C. Booth. "Effects of Parental Separation and Divorce on Very Young Children." *Journal of Family Psychology* 14 (2000): 304-26.

Clements, Richard & Joann M. Heintz. "Diagnostic Accuracy and Factor Structure pf the AAS and the APS Scales of the MMPI-2." *Journal of Personality Assessment* 79 (2002): 564-82.

Clute, Sylvia. "Adult Survivor Litigation as an Integral part of the Therapeutic Process." *Journal of Sexual Abuse* (1993): 121-27.

Cohn, Jay B. "On the Practicalities of Being an Expert Witness." *American Journal of Forensic Psychiatry* 11 (1990): 11-20.

Cohen, Elizabeth J. "Don't Take Experts from Strangers." Originally published in the ABA Journal, 2000. Retrieved July 8, 2004 from http://expertpages.com/news/don't_take_experts.htm.

Colavito, Valerie & George F. Ronan. "The TAT as a Measure of Personal Problem-Solving." Paper presented at the 98th Annual Convention of the American Psychological Association, Boston, Aug. 1990.

Cole, Debra. "Parent Awareness Skills Survey," in *Eleventh Mental Measurement Yearbook*, Jack Kramer & Jane Close Conoley, eds., University of Nebraska Press, Lincoln, Neb., 1992.

Colligan, Robert, "Relationships Between MMPI/MMPI-2 Content Scales: A Preliminary Study." Paper presented at the 99th Annual Convention of the American Psychological Association Convention, San Francisco, Aug. 1991.

Colligan, R.C. "Subtitles of MMPI/MMPI-2 Interpretation: Use and Misuse of Critical Items." Symposium presented at the 100th Annual Convention of the American Psychological Association, Washington, D.C., Aug. 1992.

Colligan, R.C., D. Osborn, W.M. Swenson & K.P. Offord. "Development of Contemporary Norms." *Journal of Clinical Psychology* 40 (1984): 100-07.

Colorado Bar Association, Interprofessional Committee. "Expert Compensation and Expert Witness Fees." Retrieved from www.cobar.org/group/display.cfm? GenID=1354, July 9, 2004.

Colorado Mental Health Statute § 12-43-215(7), 1998.

Committee on Legal Issues, American Psychological Association. *Strategies for Private Practitioners Coping with Subpoenas or Compelled Testimony for Client Records and/or Test Data.* Professional Psychology: Research and Practice 27 (1996): 245-51.

Committee on Psychiatry and the Law of the Group for the Advancement of Psychiatry. *The Mental Health Professional and the Legal System.* New York, N.Y., Brunner/Mazel, 1991.

Compas, Bruce, Adela Langrock, Garry Keller, Mary Jane Merchant & Mary Ellen Copeland, "Children Coping With Parental Depression: Processes of Adaptation to Family Stress," in Sherryl H. Goodman & Ian H. Gotlib, eds., *Children of Depressed Parents.* American Psychological Association, Washington, D.C., 2002: 227-252.

Conger, Judith. "Perception-of-Relationship-Test," in *Eleventh Mental Measurement Yearbook.* Jack Kramer & Jane Close Conoley, eds. University of Nebraska Press, Lincoln, Neb., 1992.

Connell, Mary A. "Expert Opinion: Are Forensic Evaluations Eligible to be Reimbursed by Health Care Providers?" *American Psychology-Law News* 20 (2000): 16-17.

Connell, Mary & Gerald P. Koocher. "Expert Opinion: HIPAA and Forensic Practice." *American Psychology-Law Society News* 23 (2003): 18-19.

Conoley, Collie. "Review of the Beck Depression Inventory (BDI) in *The Eleventh Mental Measurements Yearbook*, Jack Kramer & Jane Close Conoley, eds., University of Nebraska Press, Lincoln, Neb., 1992: 72-81.

Conoley, Jane Close & James Impara, eds., *The Supplement to the Eleventh Mental Measurements Yearbook.* University of Nebraska Press, Lincoln, Neb., 1994.

Conoley, Jane Close & James Impara. *The Twelfth Mental Measurements Yearbook.* The Buros Institute of Mental Measurements. Lincoln, Neb., 1995.

Constantinou, M. & R.J. McCaffrey. "The effects of 3rd party observation: When the observer is a video camera." *Archives of Clinical Neuropsychology* 18 (2003): 788-89.

Constantinou, M., L. Ashendorf, & R. J. McCaffrey. "When the 3rd party observer of a neuropsychological evaluation is an audio-recorder." *The Clinical Neuropsychologist,* 16 (2002): 407-12.

Cooperstein, Eric T. "Using Trial Consultants on a Contingent-Fee Basis." Retrieved from **www.courts.state.mn.us/lprb/fc00/fc032700.html** on July 9, 2004.

Corrigan, Patrick W. & Daniel M. Storzbach. "Behavioral Interventions for Alleviating Psychotic Symptoms." *Hospital and Community Psychiatry* 44 (1993): 341-47.

Cosden, Merith. "Rotter Incomplete Sentences Blank, Julian B. Rotter," in D. Keyser & R. Sweetland, *Test Critiques*. Kansas City, Mo.: Test Corporation of America 2 (1984): 653-60.

Cottle, W.C. *The MMPI: A Review*. University of Kansas Press, Lawrence, Kan., 1953.

Craig, R. "A Comparison of MMPI Profiles of Heroin Addicts Based on Multiple Methods of Classification." *Journal of Personality Assessment* 48 (1984): 115-29.

Craig, Robert J. "Testimony Based on the Millon Clinical Multiaxial Inventory: Review, Commentary, and Guidelines." *Journal of Personality Assessment* 73 (1999): 290-304.

Criteria for Listing in the Canadian Register of Health Service Providers in Psychology, Canadian Register of Health Service Providers in Psychology (Ottawa, Ont., 1994).

Crites, C. & Coker. "What Therapists See That Judges Miss." *The Judges Journal* 27 (1988): 9-41.

Crittenden, P., A. Claussen & D. Sugarman. "Physical and Psychological Maltreatment in Middle Childhood and Adolescence." *Development and Psychopathology* 6 (1994): 145-64.

Crum v. Sullivan, 921 F.2d 642 (6th Cir. 1990).

Cummings, E. Mark, Patrick T. Davis & Kelly S. Simpson. "Marital Conflict, Gender, and Children's Appraisals Coping Efficiency as Mediators of Child Adjustment." *Journal of Family Psychology* 8 (1994): 141-49.

Dahlstrom, Grant W. & Robert Archer. "A Shortened Version of the MMPI-2." *Assessment* 7 (2000): 131-37.

Dahlstrom, W. Grant, George Schlager Welsh & Leona E. Dahlstrom. *An MMPI Handbook, Vol. 1, Clinical Interpretation (A Revised Ed.) & Vol. 11. Research Applications*. University of Minnesota Press, Minneapolis, Minn., 1982.

Dana, R.H. "Rorschach," in O. Buros, *The Eighth Mental Measurements Yearbook*, Gryphon Press, Highland Park, N.J., 1978: 1040-42.

Dana, Richard H. "Culturally Competent Assessment Practice in the United States." *Journal of Personality Assessment* 66 (1996): 472-76.

Daubert v. Merrill Dow Pharmaceuticals, Inc., 509 U.S. 579 (1993).

Davis, J., P. Petretic-Jackson, L. Pitman, J. Waitzman, L. Clark, M. Justice, & V. Simpson. "Impact of Abuse Indicators and Reporting Criteria on Mandated Reporting." Paper Presented at the 104th Annual Convention of the American Psychological Association, Toronto, Canada, Aug. 1996.

Davis, Joseph A. "Establishing a Successful Litigation Consulting Practice: What You Need to Know to Be a Credible Witness." *The Forensic Examiner* (1997): 36-37.

Davis, William E., Richard L. Greenblatt & Jonathan M. Pochyly. "Test of MCMI Black Norms for Five Scales." *Journal of Clinical Psychology* 46 (1990): 175-78.

Dawson-McClure, Spring R., Irwin N. Sandler, Sharlene A. Wolchik & Roger E. Mellsap. "Risk as a Moderator of the Effects of Prevention Programs for Children from Divorced Families: A Six-year Longitudinal Study." *Journal of Abnormal Child Psychology* 32 (2004): 175-90.

Dawson, Brenda, Allyson R. Vaughn & William G. Wagner. "Normal Responses to Sexually Anatomically Detailed Dolls." *Journal of Family Violence* 7 (1992): 135-52.

Day, Deborah. "Personality Evaluation of the Perpetrator, Spouse, Sibling, and Victims of Munchausen by Proxy Syndrome." Paper presented at the 103rd Annual Convention of the American Psychological Association, New York, Aug. 1995.

Deale, Alicia, Trudie Chalder, Isaac Marks & Simon Wessely. "Cognitive Behavior Therapy for Chronic Fatigue Syndrome: A Randomized Controlled Trial." *American Journal of Psychiatry*. 154 (1997): 408-14.

DeAngelis, Tori. "Ethnic-Minority Issues Recognized in DSM-IV." *American Psychological Association Monitor* 25 (1994): 36.

DeAngelis, Tori. "The Right Stuff of Resilience is a Supportive Environment." *American Psychological Association Monitor* 23 (1992): 26.

Deaton, William, "The Shipley Institute of Living Scale," in *Eleventh Mental Measurements Yearbook*. Jack Kramer & Jane Close Conoley, eds., University of Nebraska Press, Lincoln, Neb. (1992): 821-23.

DeBruyn, Lemyra, Michelle Chino, Patricia Serna & Lynn Fullerton-Gleason. "Child Maltreatment in American Indian and Alaska Native Communities: Integrating Culture, History, and Public Health for Intervention and Prevention." *Child Maltreatment* 6 (2001): 89-201.

Deed, M. "Court-ordered Child Custody Evaluations: Helping or Victimizing Vulnerable Families." *Psychotherapy* 28 (1991): 76-80.

De la Cruz, Arnold. "Replication and Unique Considerations in a Student Counseling Center Population." Paper presented at the 100th Annual Convention of the American Psychological Association, Washington, D.C., Aug. 1992.

Demitrack, Mark A. & Susan E. Abbey. "Historical Overview and Evolution of Contemporary Definitions of Chronic Fatigue States," in *Chronic Fatigue Syndrome: An Integrative Approach to Evaluation and Treatment*. M. Demitrack & S. Abbey, eds., Guilford, New York, 1996: 3-35.

Demo, David & Alan Acock. "The Impact of Divorce on Children." *Journal of Marriage and Family* 50 (1988): 619-48.

Denham, Susanne. "Maternal Affect and Toddlers' Social-Emotional Competence." *American Journal of Orthopsychiatry* 59 (1989): 368-76.

Dent, Helen & Rhonda Flin, eds. *Children As Witnesses.* John Wiley & Sons, Inc., Chichester, England, 1992.

DePanfiles, Diane & Susan Zuravin. "Predicting Child Maltreatment Recurrences During Treatment. *Child Abuse and Neglect* 23 (1999): 729-43.

DePanfilis, Diane, & Susan J. Zuravin. "The Effect of Services on the Recurrence of Child Maltreatment." *Child Abuse and Neglect* 26 (2002): 187-205.

Dezwirek-Sas, Louise. "Empowering Child Witness for Sexual Abuse Prosecution," in H. Dent and R. Flin, eds., *Children As Witnesses,* John Wiley & Sons, Inc., Chichester, England, 1992: 181-200.

Dhaliwal, G, L. Guasas, D. Antonwicz & R. Ross. "Adult Male Survivors of Child Abuse: Prevalence, Sexual Abuse Characteristics, and Long-Term Effects." *Clinical Psychology Review* 16 (1996): 619-39.

Diagnostic and Statistical Manual of Mental Disorders 4th ed. (DSM-IV). American Psychiatric Association, Washington, D.C., 1994.

Dickson, Donald T. *Law in the Health and Human Services.* Free Press, New York, N.Y., 1995.

Diehl, Amy S., & Maurice F. Prout. "Effects of Posttraumatic Stress Disorder and Child Sexual Abuse on Self-Efficacy Development." *American Journal of Orthopsychiatry* 72 (2002): 262-65.

Dierdre, Rand C. "The Spectrum of Parental Alienation Syndrome (Part 1)." *American Journal of Forensic Psychology* 15 (1997): 53-92.

DiLeo, J. *Children's Drawings as Diagnostic Aids.* Brunner-Mazel, New York, 1973.

Dillon, Kathleen. "False Sexual Abuse Allegations: Causes and Concerns." *Social Work* 32 (1987): 540-41.

Dillon, Peter & Robert E. Emery. "Divorce, Mediation, and Solution of Child Custody Disputes: Long Term Effects." *American Journal of Orthopsychiatry* 66 (1996): 131-41.

Dion, M. Robbin, Sanford Braver, Sharlene Wolchik & Irwin Sandler. "Alcohol Abuse and Psychopathic Deviance in Non-Custodial Parents Are Predictors of Child-support Payment and Visitation." *American Journal of Orthopsychiatry.* 67 (1997): 70-79.

Doverspike, William. "Development of the DSM-IV: An Overview." *The Medical Psychotherapist* 8 (1992): 1-4.

Downey, Geraldine & James C. Coyne. "Children of Depressed Parents: An Integrative Review." *Psychological Bulletin* 108 (1990): 50-76.

Downs, William, N. Smyth, & B. Miller. "The Relationship Between Childhood Violence and Alcohol Problems Among Men Who Batter: An Empirical Review and Synthesis." *Aggression and Violent Behavior* 1 (Winter 1996): 327-44.

Drake, L.E., & E.R. Oetting. *An MMPI Codebook for Counselors.* University of Minneapolis Press, Minneapolis, Minn., 1959.

Drauker, Clair. "Family-Of-Origin, Variables and Adult Female Survivors of Childhood Sexual Abuse. A Review of Research." *Child Sexual Abuse* 5 (1996): 335-63.

Drogin, Eric Y. "Prophets in Another Land: Utilizing Psychological Expertise from Foreign Jurisdictions." *Mental and Physical Disability Law Reporter* 23 (1999): 767-71.

Drummond, Robert J. "Alcohol Use Inventory," in *The Supplement to The Eleventh Mental Measurements Yearbook.* Jane Close Conoley & James C. Impara. eds., University of Nebraska Press, Lincoln, Neb. 1994: 9.

Dube, Shanta R., Robert F. Anda, Vincent J. Felitti, Janet B. Croft, Valerie J. Edwards, & Wayne H. Giles. "Growing Up With Parental Alcohol Abuse: Exposure to Childhood Abuse, Neglect, and Household Dysfunction, *Child Abuse and Neglect* 25 (2001): 1627-40.

Dubner, A.E., & R.W. Motta. "Sexually and Physically Abused Foster Care Children and Post-Traumatic Stress Disorder." *Journal of Consulting and Clinical Psychology* 67 (1999): 367-73.

Duckworth, Jane C. & Wayne P. Anderson. *MMPI & MMPI-2 Interpretation Manual for Counselors and Clinicians,* 4th ed., Accelerated Development, Bristol, Penn., 1995.

Dumas, Jean E., Julie A. Gibson & Jack B. Albin. "Behavioral Correlates of Maternal Depressive Symptomatology in Conduct-Disorder Children." *A Journal of Consulting and Clinical Psychology* 57 (1989): 516-21.

Dunn, Bonnie. "Growing Up with a Psychotic Mother: A Retrospective Study." *American Journal of Orthopsychiatry* 63 (1993): 177-89.

Dyer, Frank J. & Joseph T. McCann. "The Millon Clinical Inventories, Research Critical of Their Forensic Application, and Daubert Criteria." *Law and Human Behavior* 24 (2000): 487-97.

Dyer, Frank J. "Millon Adolescent Personality Inventory," in D. Keyser & R. Sweetland, *Test Critiques,* Kansas City, Mo., Test Corporation of America 4, (1985): 425-33.

Eckenrode, J., J. Powers, J. Doris, J. Munsch, & N. Bolger. "Substantiation of Child Abuse and Neglect Reports." *Journal of Consulting and Clinical Psychology* 6 (1988): 9-16.

Eddelson, J.L. "Problems with Children's Witnessing of Domestic Violence." National Resource Center on Domestic Violence. Available at http://www.vaw.umn.edu.

Edgerton, Jane E. & Robert J. Campbell, III, eds. *American Psychiatric, Seventh Edition.* American Psychiatric Association, Washington, D.C., 1994.

Edwards, Daniel W. & Ronald Allen. "Replication and Unique Considerations in a V.A. Outpatient Population." Paper presented at the 100th Annual Meeting of the American Psychological Association, Washington, D.C., Aug. 1992.

Egami, Yuriko, D. Ford, S. Greenfield, & R. Crum. "Psychiatric Profiles and Sociodemographic Characteristics of Adults Who Report Physically Abusing or Neglecting Children." *American Journal of Psychiatry* 7 (1996): 921-28.

Egeland, B., & M.F. Erickson. "Psychologically Unavailable Caregiving," in M. Brassard, B. Germsin, & S. Hart, eds., *Psychological Maltreatment of Children and Youth.* Pergamon, Elmsford, N.Y., 1987: 110-120.

Egeland, Byron, Martha Erickson, James N. Butcher & Yossef Ben-Porath "MMPI-2 Profiles of Women at Risk for Child Abuse." *Journal of Personality Assessment* 57 (1991): 254-63.

Egley, Lance C. "Defining the Tarasoff Duty." *Journal of Psychiatry and Law* 19 (1991): 99-133.

Eisenstein, Norman & Charles Engelhart. "Comparison of the K-BIT with Short Forms of the WAIS-R in a Neuropsychological Population." *Psychological Assessment: A Journal of Consulting and Clinical Psychology* 9 (1997): 57-62.

Elliott, D.M. "Impaired Object Relations in Professional Women Molested as Children." *Psychotherapy* 21 (1994): 79-86.

Elliott, D.M., & Briere, J. "Sexual Abuse Trauma Among Professional Women. Validating the Trauma Symptom Checklist-40 (TSG-40). *Child Abuse and Neglect* 16 (1992): 391-98.

Elliott, Robert W. & Arthur M. Horton, Jr., "The American Board of Professional Neuropsychology." *The Independent Practitioner* 5 (1995): 175-77.

Ellison, Edythe. "Issues Concerning Parental Harmony and Children's Psychosocial Adjustment." *American Journal of Orthopsychiatry* 53 (1983): 73-79.

Emery, R.E. *Marriage, Divorce and Children's Adjustment.* Sage, Newberry Park, Cal., 1988.

Engels, M., & D. Mosian. "The Psychological Maltreatment Inventory: Development of a Measure of Psychological Maltreatment in Childhood for Use in Adult Clinical Settings." *Psychological Reports* 74 (1994): 595-604.

Engelhard, George, Jr. "The Second Review of the California Psychological Inventory (CPI)," in *Eleventh Mental Measurements Yearbook*, Jack Kramer & Jane Close Conoley, eds., University of Nebraska Press, Lincoln, Neb., 1992: 139-41.

Erdberg, Philip. "Rorschach Assessment," in Gerald Goldstein & Michael Hersen, eds., *Handbook of Psychological Assessment,* 2nd ed., Pergamon, New York, 1990: 387-99.

Erikson, E. *Childhood and Society.* W.W. Norton, New York, N.Y., 1963.

Esbaugh. "Some Personality Patterns and Dimensions of Male Alcoholics: A Multivariate Description." *Journal of Personality Assessment*, 42 (1978): 409.

Estelle v. Smith, 451 U.S. 454.

Everett, Craig & Sandra Volgy. "Family Assessment and Treatment of Borderline Disorders," in Peter Keller & Steven Heyman, *Innovations in Clinical Practice: A Source Book, Vol. 10,* Professional Resource Exchange, Sarasota, Fla., 1991: 59-68.

Everson, Mark D. "Understanding Bizarre, Improbable and Fantastic Elements in Children's Accounts of Abuse." *Child Maltreatment* 2 (1997): 134-49.

Everson, Mark, Barbara Boat, Sherrie Bourg & Kevin Robertson. "Beliefs Among Professionals About Rates of False Allegations of Child Sexual Abuse." *Journal of Interpersonal Violence* 1 (1996): 541-53.

Exner, John E., Jr. "A New Nonpatient Sample for the Rorschach Comprehensive System: A Progress Report." *Journal of Personality Assessment* 78 (2002): 391-404.

Exner, John E., Jr. "A Comment on 'The Misperception of Psychopathology: Problems With the Norms of the Comprehensive System for the Rorschach.'" *Clinical Psychology: Science and Practice* 8 (2001): 386-88.

Exner, John E., Jr. "The Rorschach in the '90's." Paper presented at the 100th Annual Convention of the American Psychological Association, Washington, D.C., Aug. 1992.

Exner, John E., Jr. *A Rorschach Workbook for the Comprehensive System,* 3rd ed., Rorschach Workshops, Asheville, N.C., 1990.

Exner, John E., Jr. "Searching for Projection in the Rorschach."*Journal of Personality Assessment* 53 (1989): 520-36.

Exner, John E., Jr. "Problems with Brief Rorschach Protocols." *Journal of Personality Assessment* 52 (1988): 640-47.

Exner, John E., Jr. & D.E. Exner. "How Clinicians Use the Rorschach." *Journal of Personality Assessment* 36 (1972): 403-08.

Exner, John E., Jr., Eugene A. Thomas & Barbara Mason. "Children's Rorschachs: Description and Prediction." *Journal of Personality Assessment* 49 (1985): 13-20.

Exner, John E., Jr. & Beth Clark. "The Rorschach," in B. Wolman, ed., *Clinical Diagnosis of Mental Disorders,* Plenum Press, New York, N.Y., 1978.

Eyde, Lorraine. "Identifying and Preventing the Misuse of Psychological Testing." Paper presented at the 101st Annual Convention of the American Psychological Association, Toronto, Canada, Aug. 1993.

Facchino, Dennis & Arthur Aron. "Divorced Fathers with Custody: Method of Obtaining Custody in Divorce Adjustment." *Journal of Divorce* 13 (1990): 45-56.

Faigman, D.L. The Gatekeepers: Scientific Expert Testimony in the Trial Process. *The Trial Lawyer* 23 (1999): 335-46.

Fairburn, Christopher & Alan Stein. "Bulimia Nervosa May Interfere with Parenting. *Clinical Psychiatry News* 18 (1990): 12.

Falk, Patricia. "Lesbian Mothers: Psychosocial Assumptions in Family Law." *American Psychologist* 44 (1989): 941-47.

Faller, Kathleen. *Understanding Child Sexual Maltreatment*. Sage Publications, Newbury Park, Cal., 1990.

Faller, Kathleen. "A Clinical Sample of Women Who Have Sexually Abused Children." *Child Sexual Abuse* 3 (1995): 13-30.

Faller, Kathleen C. "The Parental Alienation Syndrome: What Is It and What Data Support It?" *Child Maltreatment* 3 (1998): 100-15.

Faller, Kathleen, Mary Froning & Julie Lipovsky. "The Parent-Child Interview: Use in Evaluating Child Allegations of Sexual Abuse by the Parent." *American Journal of Orthopsychiatry* 61 (1991): 552-57.

Famulario, R., T. Fenton, M. Augustyn, & B. Zukerman. "Persistence of Pediatric Post Traumatic Stress Disorder After 2 Years." *Child Abuse & Neglect* 20 (1996): 1245-48.

Famulario, R., R. Kinschereff & T. Fenton. "Posttraumatic Stress Disorder Among Children Clinically Diagnosed as Borderline Personality Disorder." *Journal of Nervous and Mental Disorders* 179 (1991): 428-31.

Fantoni-Salvador, Patricia & Richard Rogers. "Spanish Version of the MMPI-2 and PAI: An Investigation of Concurrent Validity with Hispanic Patients." *Assessment* 4 (1997): 29-39.

Fantuzzo, John, W. DelGaudio, M. Atkins, R. Meyers & M. Noone. "A Contextually Relevant Assessment of the Impact of Child Maltreatment on the Social Competencies of Low-Income Urban Children." *Journal of American Academy of Child and Adolescent Psychiatry* 37 (1998): 1201-08.

Fantuzzo, John & W. Mohr. "Prevalence and Effects of Child Exposure to Domestic Violence: The Future of Children." *Domestic Violence and Children* 9 (1999): 21-32.

"Federal Definitions of Serious Mental Illness Established by CMHS." *Hospital and Community Psychiatry* 44 (1993): 801.

Federal Rules of Civil Procedure, Rule 26(a)(2)(b).

Federal Rules of Evidence, http://www.house.gov/judiciary/evid00.pdf.

Feldman-Somers, Shirley & Kenneth Pope. "The Experience of 'Forgetting' Childhood Abuse: A National Survey of Psychologists." *Journal of Consulting and Clinical Psychology* 62 (1994): 636-39.

Finch, A.J., Jr., Pamela S. Imm & Ronald W. Belter. "Brief Rorschach Records with Children and Adolescents." *Journal of Personality Assessment* 55 (1990): 640-46.

Fine, Eric W. *Alcohol Intoxication: Psychiatric, Psychological, Forensic Issues.* American College of Forensic Psychology, Balboa Island, Cal., 1996.

Finger, Michael S. & Deniz J. Ones. "Psychometric Equivalence of the Computer and Booklet Forms of the MMPI-2: A Meta-Analysis." *Psychological Assessment* 11 (1999): 58-66.

Finkelhor, David, *The Dark Side of Families: Current Family Violence Research.* Sage Publications, Beverly Hills, Cal., 1983.

Finkelhor, David. "The Sexual Abuse of Children: Current Research Reviewed." *Psychiatric Annals* 17 (1987): 233-41.

Finkelhor, David. "Anger, Hostility and Depression in Domestically Violent verses Generally Assaultive Men and Nonviolent Control Subjects." *Journal of Consulting and Clinical Psychology* 17 (1988).

Fisher, Celia B. *Decoding the Ethics Code: A Practical Guide for Psychologists.* Sage Publications, Thousand Oaks, Cal., 2003.

Flynn, Patrick & Joseph McCann. "Issues and Dilemmas in Clinical Diagnosis Using the MCMI-II." Paper presented at the 98th Annual Convention of the American Psychological Association, Boston, Aug. 1990.

Follette, William, Amy Naugle & Victoria Follette. "MMPI-2 Profiles of Adult Women with Child Sexual Abuse Histories: Cluster Analytic Findings." *Journal of Consulting and Clinical Psychology* 5 (1997): 585.

Follette, William, Amy Naugle & Victoria Follette. "MMPI-2 Profiles of Adult Women with Child Sexual Abuse Histories: Cluster—Analytic findings." *A Journal of Consulting and Clinical Psychology* 65 (1997): 858-66.

Follette, William C. "Introduction to the Special Section on the Development of Theoretically Coherent Alternatives to the DSM System."*A Journal of Consulting and Clinical Psychology* 64 (1996): 1117-19.

Follette, William & Arthur C. Houts. "Models of Scientific Progress and the Role of Theory in Taxonomy Development: A Case Study of the DSM." *A Journal of Consulting and Clinical Psychology* 64 (1996):1120-32.

Fontaine, Jennifer Lee, Robert P. Archer, David E. Elkins & John Johansen. "The Effects of MMPI-A T-Score Elevation on Classification Accuracy for Normal and Clinical Adolescent Samples." *Journal of Personality Assessment* 76 (2001): 264-81.

Fontes, Lisa A., Mario Cruz & Joan Tabachnick. "Views of Child Sexual Abuse in Two Cultural Communities: An Exploratory Study Among African Americans and Latinos." *Child Maltreatment* 6 (2001): 103-17.

Foote, William E., "Practical Advice to Practitioners on Privileged Communications." Paper presented at the 104th Annual Convention of the American Psychological Association, Toronto, Canada, Aug. 1996.

Forehand, Rex. "Parental Divorce and Adolescent Maladjustment: Scientific Inquiry Versus Public Information." *Behavior Research and Therapy* 4 (1992): 319-27.

Forman, B. "Psychotherapy with Rape Victims." *Psychotherapy: Theory, Research and Practice* 17 (1980): 304-11.

Fowler, Raymond & Joseph Matarazzo. "APA Rebuts Criticism of Clinician Witnesses." *APA Monitor* 19 (1988): 17.

Frances, A.J., T.A. Widiger & H.A. Pincus. "The Development of DSM-IV." *Archives of General Psychiatry* 46 (1989): 373-75.

Frances, Allen, Avram Mack, Michael B. First, & Cindy Jones. "DSM-IV: Issues in Development." *Psychiatric Annals* 25 (1995):15-19.

Frank, E., & B.D. Stewart. "Depressive Symptoms in Rape Victims: A Revisit." *Journal of Affective Disorders* 7 (1984): 77-85.

Frank, George. "The Response of African Americans to the Rorschach: A Review of the Research." *Journal of Personality Assessment* 59 (1992): 317-25.

Franke, Linda B. *Growing Up Divorced.* Linden Press/Simon & Schuster, New York, N.Y., 1983.

Franklin, Katherine M., Ronnie Janoff-Bulman & John E. Roberts. "Long-Term Impact of Parental Divorce on Optimism and Trust: Changes in General Assumptions of Narrow Beliefs?" *Journal of Personality and Social Psychology* 59 (1990): 743-55.

Friedrich, William N., Jennifer Fisher, Daniel Broughton, Margaret Houston & Constance R. Shafran. "Normative Sexual Behavior in Children: A Contemporary Sample." *Pediatrics* 101 (1998): 1-8.

Frosch, William A. "Toward a Definition of Psychiatry." *Psychiatric News* 26 (April 19, 1991).

Frost, Abbie K. & Bilge Pakiz. "The Effects of Marital Disruption on Adolescence: Time as a Dynamic." *American Journal of Orthopsychiatry* 60 (1990): 544-50.

Gabel, Stewart. "Children of Incarcerated and Criminal Parents: Adjustment, Behavior, and Prognosis." *Bulletin of the American Academy of Psychiatry and Law* 20 (1992) 33-45.

Gabel, Stewart & Richard Shindledecker. "Characteristics of Children Whose Parents Have Been Incarcerated." *Hospital & Community Psychiatry* 44 (1993): 656-60.

Gable, Sara, Jay Belsky & Keith Crnic. "Marriage, Parenting, and Child Development: Progress and Prospects." *Journal of Family Psychology* 5 (1992): 276-94.

Gallen, Robert & David Berry. "Detection of Random Responding in MMPI-2 Protocols." *Assessment* 3 (1996): 171-78.

Gallen, Robert & David Berry. "Partially Random MMPI-2 Protocols: When Are They Interpretable?" *Assessment* 4 (1997): 61-68.

Galucci, Nicholas. "Correlates of MMPI-A Substance Abuse Scales." *Assessment* 4 (1997): 87-94.

Ganellen, Ronald. "Exploring MMPI-Rorschach Relationships." *Journal of Personality Assessment* 67 (1996): 529-42.

Ganellen, Ronald J., "Weighing Evidence for the Rorschach's Validity: A Response to Wood et al." *Journal of Personality Assessment* 77 (2001): 1-15.

Garb, Howard. "The *Trained* Psychologist as Expert Witness." *Clinical Psychology Review* 12 (1992): 451-67.

Garb, Howard N., James M. Wood, M. Teresa Nezworski, William M. Grove & William J. Stejskal, "Toward a Resolution of the Rorschach Controversy." *Psychological Assessment* 13 (2001): 433-48.

Garb, Howard N., James M. Wood, Scott O. Lilienfeld & M. Teresa Nezworski. "Effective Use of Projective Techniques in Clinical Practice: Let the Data Help With Selection and Interpretation" *Professional Psychology: Research and Practice* 33 (2002): 454-463.

Garb, Howard N. "Validity of Projective Techniques and Self-Report Tests." Paper presented at the 110th Annual Convention of the American Psychological Association, Chicago, Aug. 25, 2002.

Garbarino, James, Edna Guttmann & Janice Seeley. *The Psychologically Battered Child.* Jossey-Bass, San Francisco, Cal., 1987.

Gardner, Richard. "Issues in Child and Adolescent Therapy in Divorce." Workshop at the 5th Annual Intervention for the Child and Family at Risk Workshop, Milwaukee, Wisc., April 1986.

Gardner, Richard. *Family Evaluations and Child Custody, Mediation, Arbitration, and Litigation.* Creative Therapeutics, Cresskill, N.J., 1989.

Gardner, Richard. "Recommendations for Dealing with Parents Who Induce Parent Alienation Syndrome in Their Children." *Journal of Divorce and Remarriage* (1998): 1-23.

Gardner, Richard A. "Parental Alienation Syndrome Verses Parental Alienation: Which Diagnosis Should Evaluators use in Child-Custody Disputes." *The American Journal of Family Therapy* 30 (2002): 93-115.

Garrison, Arthur H. "Child Sexual Abuse Accommodation Syndrome: Issues of Admissibility in Criminal Trials." *IPTG Journal* 10 (1998): 1-19.

Gartrell, Nanette, Jean Hamilton, Amy Banks, Dee Mosbacher, Nancy Reed, Caroline Sparks & Holly Bishop. "The National Lesbian Family Study: Interviews with Prospective Mothers." *American Journal of Orthopsychiatry* 6 (1996): 272-81.

Gass, Carlton S. & Cheryl A. Luis. "MMPI-2 Short Form: Psychometric Characteristics in a Neuropsychological Setting." *Assessment* 8 (2000): 213-19.

Geddie, Lane, Brenda Swanson & Kare Weinsch. "Socioeconomic Status and Ethnic Differences in Pre-Schoolers' Interactions with Anatomically Correct Dolls." *Child Maltreatment* 3 (1998): 43.

Geffner, Robert. "Characteristics of Victims of Sexual Abuse: Relevance for Child Witnesses." Paper presented at the 98th Annual Meeting of the American Psychological Association, Boston, 1990.

Gelles, Richard & M. Strauss. *Intimate Violence: The Cause and Consequences of Abuse in the American Family.* Simon & Schuster, New York, N.Y., 1988.

Gerlsma, Coby, Paul M.G. Emmelkamp & Willem A. Arrindell. "Anxiety, Depression, and Perception of Early Parenting: A Meta-Analysis." *Clinical Psychology Review* 10 (1990): 251-77.

Gibson, Laura E. & Harold Leitenberg. "The Impact of Child Sexual Abuse and Stigma on Methods of Coping with Sexual Assault among Undergraduate Women." *Child Abuse and Neglect* 25 (2001): 1343-61.

Giddie, Brenda Dawson & Karl Weunsch. "Socioeconomic Status and Ethnic Differences in Preschoolers' Interactions with Anatomically Detailed Dolls." *Child Maltreatment* 3 (1998): 43-52.

Gindes, Marion. "Guidelines for Child Custody Evaluations for Psychologists: An Overview and Commentary." *Family Law Quarterly* 29 (1995): 39-62.

Gindes, Marion. "Child Custody Evaluations-competence in Training." Paper presented at the 102nd Annual Convention of the American Psychological Association, Los Angeles, Cal., Aug. 1994.

Gindes, Marion. "Competence and Training in Child Custody Evaluation." *The American Journal of Family Therapy* (1995): 273-80.

Givelber, F. "The Parent-Child Relationship and the Development of Self-Esteem," in J. Mack & S. Ablon, eds., *The Development and Sustenance of Self-Esteem in Children,* International Universities Press, New York, N.Y., 1983: 163-67.

Gladstone, Tracy & William Beardslee. "Treatment, Intervention, and Prevention with Children of Depressed Parents: A Developmental Perspective," in Sherryl H. Goodman & Ian H. Gotlib, eds., *Children of Depressed Parents.* American Psychological Association, Washington, D.C., 2002: 277-305.

Glenn, Norval D. & Katherine B. Kramer. "The Marriages and Children of Children of Divorce." *Journal of Marriage and Family* 49 (1987): 811-25.

Goddard, Elizabeth, Traci Edwardson & Shane Lopez. "Belief in Repressed Memories and Therapists' Suggestion: A Survey of Counseling Psychology Doctoral Students." Paper presented at the 104th Annual Convention of the American Psychological Association, Toronto, Ont., Aug. 1996.

Goldberg, L.R. "Diagnosticians vs. Diagnostic Signs: The Diagnosis of Psychosis vs. Neurosis for the MMPI." *Psychological Monographs* 79 (1965): Whole Number 602.

Goldberg, R., W. Pachas, & D. Keith. "Relationship Between Traumatic Events in Childhood and Chronic Pain." *Disability and Rehabilitation: An International Multidisciplinary Journal* 21 (1999): 23-30.

Golding, Steven. "Expert Opinion." *American Psychology Law Society News.* 14 (1994): 5.

Goldman, Howard, Andrew Skodol & Tamara Lave. "Revising Axis V for DSM-IV: A Review of Measures of Social Functioning." *American Journal of Psychiatry* 149 (1992): 1148-56.

Goldman, Vinston, Arlene Cooke & W. Grant Dahlstrom. "Black-White Differences Among College Students: A Comparison on the MMPI and the MMPI-2 Norms." *Assessment* 2 (1995): 293-99.

Goldstein, Joseph. "In Whose Best Interest?" in Jay Folberg, *Joint Custody and Shared Parenting,* The Guilford Press, New York, N.Y., 1991.

Goldstein, Robert Lloyd. "Consequences of Surveillance of the Forensic Psychiatric Examination: An Overview." *American Journal of Psychiatry* 145 (1988): 1243-47.

Goldstein, Joseph A., Anna Freud & A.J. Solnit. *Beyond the Best Interests of the Child.* Free Press, New York, N.Y., 1973.

Goldstein, Michael J. "Psychosocial (Nonpharmacologic) Treatments for Schizophrenia," in Allan Tasman & Stephen Goldfinder, eds., *10 American Psychiatric Press Review of Psychiatry,* American Psychiatric Press, Washington, D.C., 1991: 116-35.

Goldstein, Robert L. "Consequences of Surveillance of the Forensic Psychiatric Examination: An Overview." *American Journal of Psychiatry* 145 (1988): 1243-47.

Goldstein, Steven G. & James D. Linden. "Multivariate Classification of Alcoholics by Means of the MMPI." *Journal of Abnormal Psychology* 74 (1969): 661-69.

Good, P. & J. Brantner. *A Practical Guide to the MMPI.* University of Minnesota, Minneapolis, Minn., 1974.

Goodman, Gayle S., Rosenberg, M. "The Child Witness to Family Violence: Clinical and Legal Considerations," in *Domestic Violence on Trial*, Daniel J. Sonkin, ed., Springer Publishing, New York, N.Y., 1991: 97-125.

Goodman, Gayle S. & Beth M. Schwartz-Kenney. "Why Knowing a Child's Age Is Not Enough: Influences of Cognitive, Social and Emotional Factors on Children's Testimony," in Helen Dent & Rhonda Flin, eds., *Children As Witnesses,* John Wiley & Sons, Inc., Chichester, England, 1992.

Goodman, Gayle S., Bette L. Bottoms, Leslie Rudy, Suzanne L. Davis, & Beth M. Schwartz-Kenney. "Affects of Past Abuse Experiences on Children's Eye Witness Memory. *Law and Human Behavior* 25 (2001): 269-98.

Goodman, Gayle S., Murray Levine, Gary Melton & David Ogden. "Child Witnesses and the Confrontation Clause." *The American Psychological Association Brief in Maryland v. Craig. Law and Human Behavior* 15 (1991): 13-29.

Goodman, Gayle S., Toby Batterman, Jennifer Faunce, Ann E. Tobey, Sherry Thomas, Holly Orcutt & Beth M. Schwartz-Kenney. "Impact of Innovative Court Procedures on Children's Testimony." Paper presented at the 100th Annual Convention of the American Psychological Association, Washington, D.C., 1992.

Goodman, Gayle S. "Understanding Children's Testimony." Paper presented at the 99th Annual Convention of the American Psychological Association, San Francisco, 1991.

Goodman, Louis, Alfred Gilman, Joel G. Hardman & Lee E. Limbird. *Goodman and Gilman's The Pharmacological Basis of Therapeutics.* McGraw Hill, New York, N.Y., 2001.

Goodman-Delahunty, Jane. "Forensic Psychological Expertise in the Wake of Daubert." *Law and Human Behavior* 21 (1997): 121-40.

Goodman-Brown, Tina, Robin S. Edelstein, Gail S. Goodman, David P.H. Jones, & David S. Gordon. "Why Children Tell: A Model of Children's Disclosure of Sexual Abuse." *Child Abuse and Neglect* 27 (2003): 525, 540.

Goodyer, Ian M. "Family Relationships, Life Events and Childhood Psychopathology." *Journal of Child Psychology and Psychiatry* 31 (1990): 161-92.

Gordon, Betty, Carolyn S. Schroeder & J. Michael Abrams. "Age and Social Class Differences in Children." *American Journal of Orthopsychiatry* 3 (1990). 250-55.

Gordon, Betty, Carolyn Schroeder & Michael Abrams. "Children's Knowledge of Sexuality: A Comparison of Sexually Abused and Nonabused Children." *American Journal of Orthopsychiatry* 60 (1990): 250-57.

Gordon, Michael. "Males and Females as Victims of Childhood Abuse: An Examination of Gender Effect." *Journal of Family Violence* 5 (1990): 321-22.

Gottman, John M. & Lynn Fainsilber Katz. "Effects of Marital Discord on Young Children's Peer Interaction and Health." *Developmental Psychology* 25 (1989): 378-81.

Gould, Jonathan W. "Evaluating the Probative Value of Child Custody Evaluations: A Guide for Forensic Mental Health Professionals." *Journal of Child Custody* 1 (2004): 77-96.

Grafman, Jordan. "Neuropsychological Assessment of Patients with Chronic Fatigue Syndrome," in *Chronic Fatigue Syndrome: An Integrative Approach to Evaluation and Treatment*, Mark A. Demitrack & Susan E. Abbey, eds., Guilford, New York, 1996: 113-29.

Graham, John R. *The MMPI: A Practical Guide.* 2nd ed., Oxford University Press, New York, N.Y., 1987.

Graham, John. "Development and Validation of MMPI-A Content Scales." Paper presented at the 99th Annual Convention of the American Psychological Association Convention, Aug. 1991.

Graham, John R. *MMPI-2 Assessing Personality and Psychopathology*, 3rd ed. Oxford University Press, New York, N.Y., 2000.

Graham, John. MMPI Workshop, Minneapolis, Minn. (June 1987).

Graham, John R. & Reis Lilly, *Psychological Testing.* Prentice Hall, Engelwood Cliffs, N.J., 1984.

Graham, John R. & Virginia E. Strenger. "MMPI Characteristics of Alcoholics: A Review." *Journal of Consulting and Clinical Psychology* 56 (1988): 197-205.

Graham, Kathy T. "How the ALI Child Custody Principles Help Eliminate Gender and Sexual Orientation Bias from Child Custody Determinations." Accessed July 9, 2004 at www.law.duke.edu/journals/djglp/articles/gen8p323.htm.

Graham-Berman, Sandra A. "Family Worries: The Assessment of Interpersonal Anxiety in Children from Violent and Nonviolent Families." *Journal of Clinical Child Psychology* 25 (1996): 280-87.

Graham-Berman, Sandra, & Alytia Levendosky, "The Social Functioning of Pre-School-Aged Children Whose Mothers are Emotionally and Physically Abused." *Journal of Emotional Abuse* 1 (1998): 59-84.

Graham-Bermann, S.A. "Family Worries: The Assessment of Interpersonal Anxiety in Children from Violent and Nonviolent Families." *Journal of Clinical Child Psychology* 25(3) (1996): 280-87.

Green, Bert. "Validity Arguments in the Standards for Educational and Psychological Testing (Revised)." Paper presented at the 105th Annual Convention of the American Psychological Association, Chicago, Ill., Aug. 1997.

Greenberg, Lyn R., David A. Martindale, Jonathan W. Gould, & Dianna J. Gould-Saltman, "Ethical Issues in Child Custody and Dependency Cases: Enduring Principles and Emerging Challenges." *Journal of Child Custody* (2004): 7-30.

Greenberg, S. "Liability and Immunity of the Expert Witness." Symposium presented at the Annual Convention of the American Psychological Association, San Francisco, Cal., Aug. 2001.

Greenberg, Stuart & Daniel Shuman. "Irreconcilable Conflict Between Therapeutic and Forensic Roles." *Professional Psychology: Research and Practice* 28 (1997): 50-7.

Greene, Robert & Leigh Leslie. "Mother's Behavior and Son's Adjustment Following Divorce." *Journal of Divorce* (1989): 235-51.

Greene, Roger. *MMPI-2/MMPI An Interpretive Manual.* Allyn & Bacon, Needham, Mass., 1991.

Greene, Roger. "Critical Issues in the Integration of the MMPI-2 and Rorschach." Paper presented as part a symposium at the 95th Annual Convention of the American Psychological Association, Chicago, Ill., Aug. 1997.

Greene, Roger L., Rudy Arredondo & Ann Mann. "MMPI-2 Critical Items: How Critical Are They?" Paper presented at the 100th Annual Convention of the American Psychological Association, Washington, D.C., Aug. 1992.

Greene, Roger L., Nathan C. Weed, James N. Butcher, Rudy Arredondo & Harry G. Davis, "A Cross Validation of MMPI-2 Substance Abuse Scales." *Journal of Personality Assessment* 58 (1992): 405-10.

Greene, Roger, Roy Gwyn, Mark Staal. "The Current Status of MMPI-2 Research: A Methodologic Overview." *Journal of Personality Assessment* 68 (1997): 20-36.

Greene, Roger L. *The MMPI-2 An Interpretation Manual*, 2nd ed. Allyn & Bacon, Needham Heights, Mass., 2000.

Greene, Roger L., Stuart A. Greenberg, Jeffrey Davis, Marc J. Ackerman, & Richard I. Fredrick. "MMPI-2 Stability Within and Across Forensic Settings." A paper presented at the 109th Annual Meeting of the American Psychological Association, San Francisco, Cal., 2001.

Greenfield, Shelly F. "Long-term Psychosocial Effects of Childhood Exposure to Parental Problem Drinking." *American Journal of Psychiatry* 150 (1993): 608-13.

Greenwald, Michael. "American Law Institute Publishes *Principles of the Law of Family Dissolution*." Press release dated May 15, 2002. Retrieved July 9, 2004 at www.ali.org/ali/pro051502.htm.

Greif, Geoffrey & Alfred DeMaris. "Single Fathers with Custody." *Journal of Contemporary Human Services* (1990): 259-66.

Greif, Geoffrey. "Mothers Without Custody." *Social Work* (1987): 11-16.

Greif, Geoffrey & Alfred DeMaris. "Single Fathers with Custody." *The Journal of Contemporary Human Services* (1990): 259-66.

Gries, Leonard, David Goh & Jeanne Cavanah. "Factors Associated with Disclosure During Child Sexual Abuse Assessment." *Journal of Sexual Abuse* 5 (1996): 1-19.

Grinspoon, L. & J. Bakalar. "Substance Use Disorders," in A. Nicholi, Jr., ed., *The New Harvard Guide to Psychiatry*. Harvard University Press, Boston:, 1988.

Grisso, Thomas. "Advances in Assessments for Legal Competencies," in Thomas Grisso, ed., *Evaluating Competencies*, 2nd ed., Kluwer/Plenum, New York, N.Y., 2003: 1-20.

Grisso, Thomas. "Clinical Assessments for Legal Decisionmaking: Research Recommendations," in Saleem Shah & Bruce Sales, eds., *Law & Mental Health: Major Developments and Research Needs,* National Institute of Mental Health, Rockville, Md., 1991: 49-80.

Grisso, Thomas. "Evolving Guidelines for Divorce/Custody Evaluations." *Family & Conciliation Courts* 28 (1990): 35-40.

Gronnerod, Cato. "Temporal Stability in the Rorschach Method: A MetaAnalytic Review." *Journal of Personality Assessment* 80 (2003): 287.

Gross, A.B., & H.R. Keller. "Long-term Consequences of Childhood Physical and Psychological Maltreatment." *Aggressive Behavior* 18 (1992): 171-185.

Gross, Julian & Harlene Hayne. "Eye Witness Identification By 5-to-6-Year-Old Children." *Law & Human Behavior* 20 (1996): 359-73.

Grosz, Candace, Ruth S. Kempe, & Michele Kelly. "Extrafamilial Sexual Abuse: Treatment for Child Victims and Their Families." *Child Abuse and Neglect* 24 (1999): 9-23.

Groth-Marnat, Gary. *Handbook of Psychological Assessment,* 3rd ed. John Wiley & Sons, Inc., New York, N.Y., 1997.

Groth-Marnat, Gary. *Handbook of Psychological Assessment,* 4th ed. John Wiley & Sons, Inc., New York, N.Y., 2003.

Guarnaccia, Vincent, Charles A. Dill, Susan Sabatino, & Sarah Southwick, "Scoring Accuracy Using the Comprehensive System for the Rorschach." *Journal of Personality Assessment* 77 (2001): 464-74.

Guidubaldi, J.H., J. Cleminshaw, Perry B. Nastasi & B. Adams. "Longitudinal Effects of Divorce on Children: A Report from the NASPKSU Nationwide Study." Paper presented at the 92nd Annual Convention of the American Psychological Association, Toronto, Canada, Aug. 1984.

Guigan, William, Aphra R. Katzev, & Clara C. Pratt. "Multi-levels Determinants of Retention in a Home-Visiting Child Abuse Prevention Program." *Child Abuse and Neglect* 27 (2003): 363-80.

Gunderson, John. "Borderline Personality Disorder," in H. Kaplan & B. Sadock, *Comprehensive Textbook of Psychiatry/V,.* Williams & Wilkins, Baltimore, Md, 1989: 1387-95.

Gynther, M., "White Norms and Black MMPI's: A Prescription for Discrimination?" *Psychological Bulletin* 78 (1972): 386-402.

Hagen, Margaret A. & Nicole Castagna. "The Real Numbers: Psychological Testing in Custody Evaluations." *Professional Psychology: Research and Practice* 32 (2001): 269-71.

Hagin, Rosa. "Bricklin Perceptual Scales," in *The Eleventh Mental Measurement Yearbook*. Jack Kramer and Jane Close Conoley, eds., University of Nebraska Press, Lincoln, Neb., 1992.

Haladyna, Thomas. "Review of the Millon Clinical Multiaxial Inventory-II (MCMI-II)," in *The Eleventh Mental Measurements Yearbook*. Jack Kramer & Jane Close Conoley, eds., University of Nebraska Press. Lincoln, Neb., 1992: 530-35.

Hall, Gordon et al. "The Utility of the MMPI with Men Who Have Sexually Assaulted Children." *Journal of Consulting and Clinical Psychology* 54 (1986): 493-96.

Hall, Marian. "The Role of Psychologists as Experts in Cases Involving Allegations of Child Sexual Abuse." *Family Law Quarterly* 23 (1989): 451-64.

Halon, Robert L. The Millon Clinical Multiaxial Inventory-III, The Normal Quartet in Child Custody Cases. *American Journal of Forensic Psychology* 19 (2001): 57-75.

Hamberger, L. Kevin & James E. Hastings. "Racial Differences on the MCMI in an Outpatient Clinical Sample." Paper presented at the 98th Annual Convention of the American Psychological Association, Boston, Aug. 1990.

Hamel, Mel, Thomas W. Shaffer & Philip Erdberg. "A Study of Nonpatient Adolescent Rorschach Protocols." *Journal of Personality Assessment* 75 (2000): 280-94.

Hammen, Constance. "Context of Stress in Families of Children with Depressed Parents," in Sherryl H. Goodman & Ian H. Gotlib, eds., *Children of Depressed Parents.* American Psychological Association, Washington, D.C., 2002: 175-99.

Hammen, Constance, Dorli Burge & Cheri Adrian. "Timing of Mother and Child Depression in a Longitudinal Study of Children at Risk." *Journal of Consulting and Clinical Psychology* 59 (1991): 341-45.

Hammer, E.F. *The Clinical Application of Projective Drawings*. C.C. Thomas, Springfield, Ill., 1958.

Hampton, R.L. & R.J. Gelles. "Violence Toward Black Women in a Nationally Representative Sample of Black Families." *Journal of Comparative Family Studies* 25 (1994): 105-19.

Hansen, Jo-Ida. "Practitioner Concerns Regarding the Standards for Educational and Psychological Testing." Paper presented at the 105th Annual Convention of the American Psychological Association, Chicago, Ill., Aug. 1997.

Hanson, R.K., R.A. Steffy & R. Gauthier. "Long Term Recidivism of Child Molesters." *Journal of Consulting and Clinical Psychology* 64 (1993): 646-52.

Hare, Robert D., Leslie M. McPherson & Adelle E. Forth. "Male Psychopaths and Their Criminal Careers." *Journal of Consulting and Clinical Psychology* 56 (1988): 710-14.

Hargrave, George, Deidre Hiatt, Earnest Ogard & Chad Karr. "Replication and Unique Considerations for a Sample of Peace Officers." Paper presented at the 100th Annual Convention of the American Psychological Association, Washington, D.C., Aug. 1992.

Harpur, Timothy J., A. Ralph Hakstian & Robert D. Hare. "Factor Structure of the Psychopathy Checklist." *Journal of Consulting and Clinical Psychology* 56 (1988) 741-47.

Harris, D. *Children's Drawings As Measures of Intellectual Maturity*. Harcourt, Brace and World, New York, N.Y., 1963.

Harris, R.E. & J.C. Lingoes. "Subscales for the MMPI: An Aid to Profile Interpretation." Unpublished manuscript, University of California, 1995.

Hart, Stuart, Nelson Binggeli & Marla Brassard. "Evidence of the Effects of Psychological Maltreatment." *Journal of Emotional Abuse* 1 (1998): 27-58.

Haskett, Mary, Kathleen Weiland, James Hutcheson & Tiersa Tavana. "Substantiation of Sexual Abuse Allegations: Factors Involved in the Decision-making Process." *Journal of Child Sexual Abuse* 4 (1995): 19-47.

Hatt, Clifford V. "Children's Apperception Test," in *Ninth Mental Measurements Yearbook,* J. Mitchell Jr. ed., 1985: 315.

Hatton, Mary Jane. "Assessments: A Judge's Perspective." Symposium presented at the 104th Annual Convention of the American Psychological Association, Toronto, Canada, 1996.

Haugaard, Jeffrey J., N. Dickon Repucci, Jennifer Laird & Tara Nauful. "Children's Definitions of the Truth and their Competency as Witnesses in Legal Proceedings." *Law and Human Behavior* 15 (1991): 253-71.

Hawkins, J. David, Richard F. Catalano, & Janet Y. Miller. "Risk and Protective Factors for Alcohol and Other Drug Problems in Adolescence and Early Adulthood: Implications for Substance Abuse Prevention." *Psychological Bulletin* 112 (1992): 64-105.

Hawkins, J. David, Joseph M. Healy & C. Smith. "Batterer Programs: What Criminal Justice Agencies Need to Know." Research in Action, July, (1988), National Institute of Justice. Washington, D.C. (NCJ171683).

Healy, Joseph, Janet Malley & Abigail Stewart. "Children and Their Fathers After Parental Separation." *American Journal of Orthopsychiatry* 60 (1990): 531-43.

Heather, Cecil & Steven C. Matson. "Psychological Function and Family Discord among African American Adolescent Females With and Without a History of Childhood Sexual Abuse." *Child Abuse and Neglect* 25 (2001): 973-88.

Hedlund, James L. & Bruce W. Vieweg. "The Michigan Alcoholism Screening Test (MAST): A Comprehensive Review." *Journal of Operational Psychiatry* 15 (1984): 55-64.

Heilbrun, Kirk. "Substance and Style of Expert Testimony: Ethics and Effectiveness." Paper presented at the 112th Annual Convention of the American Psychological Association, Honolulu, HI, July 28, 2004.

Heilbrun, Kirk. *Principles of Forensic Mental Health Assessment.* Kluwer/Plenum, New York, N.Y., 2001.

Heilbrun, Kirk. "The Role of Psychological Testing in Forensic Assessment." *Law & Human Behavior* 16 (1992): 257-72.

Heilbrun, Kirk, Geoffrey R. Marczyk, & David DeMatteo, *Forensic Mental Health Assessment: A Casebook.* Oxford University Press, Oxford, Eng., 2002.

Herman, Stephen P. "Special Issues in Child Custody Evaluations." *Journal of the American Academy of Child and Adolescent Psychiatry* 29 (1990): 969-74.

Herrenkohl, Roy, B. Egolf, E. Herrenkohl. "Preschool Antecedents of Adolescent Assaultive Behavior: A Longitudinal Study." *American Journal of Orthopsychiatry* 67 (1997): 422-32.

Herrenkohl, Roy C. & E.C. Herrenkohl. "Circumstances Surrounding the Occurrence of Child Maltreatment." *Journal of Consulting and Clinical Psychology* 51 (1983): 424-31.

Hertz, Marguerite R. "Rorschachbound: A 50-year Memoir." *Professional Psychology: Research and Practice* 23 (1992): 168-71.

Hess, Allen. "Millon Clinical Multiaxial Inventory-III," in James C. Impara & Barbara S. Plake, eds., *The Thirteenth Mental Measurements Yearbook.* University of Nebraska, Lincoln, Neb., 1998: 665-67.

Hetherington, Mavis. "Lessons Learned and Unlearned in 35 years of Studying Martial Transitions." Paper presented at the 112th Annual Convention of the American Psychological Association, Honolulu, July, 30, 2004.

Hetherington, Mavis. "An Overview of the Virginia Longitudinal Study of Divorce and Remarriage with a Focus Early Adolescents." *Journal of Family Psychology* 7 (1993): 39-59.

Hetherington, Mavis, M. Bridges & G.M. Insabella. "What Matters? What Does Not? Five Perspectives on the Association Between Transitions and Children's Adjustment." *American Psychologist* 53 (1998): 167-84.

Hetherington, Mavis E., M. Cox & R. Cox. "The Aftermath of Divorce," in J. Stevens & M. Matthews, eds., *Mother-Child, Father-Child Relations,* National Association for the Education of Young Children, Washington, D.C., 1978.

Hetherington, Mavis E. "Divorce: A Child's Perspective." *American Psychologist* 34 (1979): 851-58.

Hibbard, Stephen. "A Critique of Lilienfeld et al.'s 'The Scientific Status of Projective Techniques.' " *Journal of Personal Assessment* 80 (2003): 260-71.

Hibbard, Stephen. "Personality and Object Relational Pathology in Young Adult Children of Alcoholics." *Psychotherapy* 26 (1989): 504-09.

Hibbs, B.L., J.C. Kobas & J. Gonzales. "Effects of Ethnicity, Sex and Age on MMPI Profiles." *Psychological Reports* 45 (1979): 591-97.

Higgins, J., R. Gore & D. Gutkind. "Effects of Child-rearing by Schizophrenic Mothers: A 25-Year Follow-up." *Acta Psychiatrica Scandinavica* 96 (1997): 402-04.

Hiltonsmith, Robert. "Parent Perception of Child Profile," in *The Eleventh Mental Measurement Yearbook*, Jack Kramer & Jane Close Conoley, eds., University of Nebraska Press, Lincoln, Neb., 1992.

Ho, M.K. *Minority Children and Adolescents in The*rapy. Sage, Newbury Park, Cal., 1992.

Ho, C.K. "An Analysis of Domestic Violence in Asian American Communities: A Multicultural Approach to Counseling," in K.P. Monterio, ed., *Ethnicity and Psychology* Kendall-Hunt, Dubuque, Ia., 1996: 138-51.

Hodges, William F. *Interventions for Children of Divorce: Custody, Access, and Psychotherapy*, 2nd ed. John Wiley & Sons, Inc., New York, N.Y., 1991.

Hoeffer, Beverly. "Children's Acquisition of Sex-Role Behavior in Lesbian-Mother Families." *American Journal of Orthopsychiatry* 51 (1981): 536-43.

Hoge, Steve K. & Thomas Grisso. "Accuracy and Expert Testimony." *Bulletin of the American Academy of Psychiatry and Law* 20 (1992): 67-76.

Hokanson, J.E. & G. Calden. "Negro-White Differences on the MMPI." *Journal of Clinical Psychology* 16 (1960): 32-33.

Holden, E. Wayne, Diane J. Willis & Linda Foltz. "Child Abuse Potential and Parenting Stress: Relationships in Maltreating Parents." *Psychological Assessment: A Journal of Consulting and Clinical Psychology* 1 (1989): 64-67.

Holmes, G., L. Offen & G. Waller. "See No Evil, Hear No Evil, Speak No Evil: Why Do Relatively Few Male Victims of Childhood Sexual Abuse Receive Help for Abuse-Related Issues in Adulthood?" Paper presented at the 104th Annual Convention of the American Psychological Association, Toronto, Canada, Aug. 1996.

Hoppe, Carl & Lynn Kenney. "Integrating MMPI, Rorschach and Other Test Data in Custody Evaluations." Paper presented at the 103rd Annual Convention of the American Psychological Association, New York, 1995.

Hoppe, Carl. "Rorschach and MMPI in Custody Cases." Paper presented at the American Psychological Association Convention, Toronto, Canada, 1993.

Howard v. Drapkin, 271 Cal. Rptr. 893 (Ct. App. 1990).

Howell, Robert J. "Duty to Warn: A Case Study in Child Custody." *Psychotherapy in Private Practice*. 6 (1988): 37-44.

Hughes, Honore M. "Impact of Spouse Abuse on Children of Battered Women." *Violence Update* 2 (1992): 8-11.

Hughes, Honore M., S.A. Graham-Berman. "Children of Battered Women: Impact or Emotional Abuse on Adjustment and Development." *Journal of Emotional Abuse* 1 (1998): 23-50.

Hunsley, John & J. Michael Bailey. "Whither the Rorschach? An Analysis of the Evidence," *Psychological Assessment* 13 (2001): 472-85.

Hunsley, John & Gina Di Giulio. "Norms, Norming, and Clinical Assessment." 8 *Clinical Psychology: Science and Practice* 8 (2001): 378-82.

Hynan, Daniel J. "Unsupported General Differences on Some Personality Disorder Scales of the Millon Clinical Multiaxial Inventory-III." *Professional Psychology: Research and Practice* 35 (2004): 105-10.

Idaho v. Wright, 497 U.S. 805, 112 L. Ed. 2d 638, 110 S. Ct. 736 (1990).

Imwinkelried, E.J. "Evaluating the reliability of nonscientific expert testimony: a partial answer to the questions left unresolved by *Kumho Tire Co. v. Carmichael.*" 52 *Maine Law Review* (2000): 20-41.

Inoff-Germain, Gale, Edith D. Nottelmann, & Marian Radke-Yarrow. "Relation of Parental Affective Illness to Family, Dyadic, and Individual Functioning: An Observational Study of Family Interaction." *American Journal of Orthopsychiatry* 67 (1997): 433-48.

International Classification of Diseases. See *Manual of the International Statistical Classification of Diseases, Injuries, and Causes of Death, Clinical Modification, ICD-9-CM. International Classification of Diseases.* See *Manual of the International Statistical Classification of Diseases, Injuries, and Causes of Death, Clinical Modification, ICD-10-CM.*

International Classification of Diseases and Related Health Problems. Tenth Revision. Vol. 1, Tabular list. Vol. 2, Instruction Manual. Vol. 3, Geneva, World Health Organization, 1992.

Isenhart, Carl E. "Further Support for the Criterion Validity of the Alcohol Use Inventory." *Psychology of Addictive Behavior* 4 (1990): 77-81.

Iverson, Grant L. "Dual Relationships in Psycholegal Evaluations: Treating Psychologists Serving as Expert Witnesses." *American Journal of Forensic Psychology* 18 (2000): 79-87.

Jackson, A.M., N.S. Warner, R. Hornbein, N. Nelson & E. Fortescue. "Beyond the Best Interests of the Child Revisited: An Approach to Custody Evaluations." *Journal of Divorce* 3 (1980): 207-22.

Jackson, Douglas, Maryann Fraboni & Edward Helms. "MMPI-2 Content Scales: How Much Content Do They Measure?" *Assessment* 4 (1994): 112-17.

Jacob, Theodore. "Family Studies of Alcoholism." *Journal of Family Psychology* 5 (1992): 319-38.

Jacob, Theodore, Gloria Krahn & Kenneth Leonard. "Parent-Child Interactions in Families with Alcoholic Fathers." *Journal of Consulting and Clinical Psychology* 59 (1991): 176-81.

Jacobsen, Teresa, Laura J. Miller & Kathleen Pesek-Kirkwood. "Assessing Parenting Competency in Individuals with Severe Mental Illness: A Comprehensive Service." *Journal of Mental Health Administration* 24 (1997): 189-99.

Jacobson, George R. *The Alcoholisms: Detection, Assessment, and Diagnosis.* Human Sciences Press, New York, N.Y., 1976.

Jaffe v. Redmond, 116 S. Ct. 1923, 64 U.S.L.W. 4490 (1996).

Jaffee, Sara R., Terrie E. Moffitt, Avshalom Caspi, & Alan Taylor, "Life With (or Without) Father: The Benefits of Living with Two Biological Parents Depend on the Father's Antisocial Behavior." *Child Development* 74 (2003): 109-26.

Jason, Leonard A., Judith A. Richman, Fred Friedberg, Lynne Wagner, Renee Taylor & Karen M. Jordan. "Politics, Science, and the Emergency of a New Disease: The Case of Chronic Fatigue Syndrome." *American Psychologist* 52 (1997): 973-83.

Johnson, Jeanne J. & Jeffrey L. Helms. "Test Security in the Twenty-First Century." *American Journal of Forensic Psychology* 21 (2003): 24 & 27-28.

Johnson-Rein, Melissa, Brett Drake, Sulki Chung & Inecke Way. "Cross-Type Recidivism among Child Maltreatment Victims and Perpetrators." *Child Abuse and Neglect* 27 (2003): 899-917.

Joint Committee on Standards for Educational and Psychological Testing of the American Education Research Association, the American Psychological Association, and the National Council on Measurement in Education. *Standards for Educational and Psychological Testing*. Washington, D.C.: American Educational Research Association, 1999.

Joint Committee on Testing Practices. *Rights and Responsibilities of Test Takers: Guidelines and Expectations*. JCTP Publications, Washington D.C., 2000.

Jones, Linda M. & Christopher M. Gordon. "The Influence of Detail in Child Witness Testimony. Paper presented at the 100th Annual Convention of the American Psychological Association," Washington, D.C., Aug. 1992.

Jones, A. *Next Time She'll be Dead: Battering and How To Stop It*. Boston Beacon Press, 1994.

Johnson, E. Kay, & Robert Howell. "Memory Processes in Children: Implications for Investigation of Alleged Child Sexual Abuse." *Bulletin of American Academy of Psychiatry and Law* 21 (1993): 213-26.

Johnson-Reid, M.B. Drake, S. Chung & I. Way. "Cross-type Recidivism among Child Maltreatment Victims and Perpetrators." *Child Abuse and Neglect* 27 (2003): 899-917.

Jouriles, E.N. & W.D. Norwood. "Physical Aggression Toward Boys and Girls in Families Characterized by the Battering of Women." *Journal of Family Psychology* 9 (1995): 69-78.

Jurjevick, R.M. "Short Interval Test/Retest of the MMPI, CPI, Cornell, Index and Symptoms Checklist." *Journal of General Psychology* 74 (1966): 201-06.

Kalter, Neil, Amy Kloner, Shelly Schreier & Katherine Okla. "Predictors of Children's Post-Divorce Adjustment." *American Journal of Orthopsychiatry* 59 (Oct. 1989): 605-18.

Kandel, Randy Frances. "Family Law: Essential Terms and Concepts." Aspen Law & Business, New York, 2000; www.naswdc.org, accessed July 1, 2004.

Kantor, G.K., J.L. Jasinski, & E. Aldarondo. "Predictors of Children's Post-Divorce Adjustment." *Journal of Orthopsychiatry* 59 (1989): 605-18.

Kantor, Glenda, Jana L. Jasinski & Etiony Aldarondo. "Socioeconomic Status and Incidents of Marital Violence in Hispanic Families." *Violence & Victims* 9 (1994): 207-22.

Kaplan, Arline. " 'Serious Mental Illness' Definitions Elicit Mixed Reviews from Experts." *Psychiatric Times* 10 (1993): 1, 14.

Kaplan, Harold I. & Benjamin J. Saddock, eds. *Comprehensive Textbook of Psychiatry/IV*. Williams & Wilkins, Baltimore, Md., 1985.

Kaplan, Harold I. & Benjamin J. Saddock, eds. *Comprehensive Textbook of Psychiatry/V.* Williams & Wilkins, Baltimore, Md., 1989.

Karon, Bertram. "Psychotherapy: The Appropriate Treatment of Schizophrenia." Paper presented at the 102nd Annual Convention of the American Psychological Association, Los Angeles, Cal., Aug. 1994.

Kashani, Javed, et al. "Family Violence: Impact on Children." 31 *J. Acad. Child & Adolescent Psychiatry* (1992): 181-89.

Karras, D., & K. Berry. "Custody Evaluations: A Critical Review." *Professional Psychology: Research and Practice* 16 (1985): 76-85.

Katz, Steven. "Hospitalization and the Mental Health Service System," in *Comprehensive Textbook of Psychiatry,* H. Kaplan & B. Saddock, eds., Williams & Wilkins, Baltimore, Md., 1989: 2083-90.

Kaufman, Allen S. *Intelligence Testing with the WISC-R.* John Wiley & Sons, Inc., New York, N.Y., 1979.

Kaufman, Allen S., & Nadeen L. Kaufman. *Administration and Scoring Manual for the Kaufman Brief Intelligence Test.* American Guidance Services Publishing, Circle Pines, Minn., 1990.

Kaufman, Allen S., & Nadeem Kaufman. *Manual-Kaufman Assessment Battery for Children* 2nd ed. American Guidance Services Publishing, Circle Pines, Minn., 2004.

Kay, Steven. "The Impact of Divorce on Children's Academic Performance," in *Children of Divorce: Developmental and Clinical Issues,* Hayworth Press, 1989.

Keary, Kay & Carol Fitzpatrick. "Children's Disclosure of Sexual Abuse During Formal Investigations." *Child Abuse & Neglect* 18 (1994): 543-48.

Keeney, Kathryn, Ethel Amacher Sisterman & Julie Kastankis. "The Court Prep Group: A Vital Part of the Corut Process," in Helen Dent & Rhona Flin, eds., *Children As Witnesses,* John Wiley & Sons, Inc., Chichester, Eng., 1992: 201-10.

Kehrer, C.A., P.N. Sanchez, U. Habif, J.G. Rosenbaum, & B.D. Townes. "Effects of a Significant-Other Observer on Neuropsychological Test Performance." *The Clinical Neuropsychologist* 14 (2000): 67-71.

Keilin, W.G. & L.J. Bloom. "Child Custody Evaluation Practices: A Survey of Experienced Professionals." *Professional Psychology: Research and Practice* 17 (1986): 338-46.

Keilitz, S., P. Hannaford, & H. Efkman. "The Effectiveness of Civil Protection Orders," in *Legal Interventions in Family Violence: Research Findings and Policy Implications: A Project of the American Bar Association's Criminal Justice Section, Commission on Domestic Violence, Center on Children and the Law and Commission on Legal Problems of the Elderly Presented to the National Institute of Justice.* (July 1998). Available at www.ncjrs.org/txtfiles/171666.txt.

Keiller, Scott & John Graham. "The Meaning of Low Scores on the MMPI-2, Clinical Scales of Normal Persons." *MMPI-2 News and Profiles* 3 (1992): 2-3.

Keiser, Ross E. & Ellen N. Prather. "What is the TAT? A Review of Ten Years of Research." *Journal of Personality Assessment* 55 (1990): 800-03.

Keith-Spiegel, Patricia & Gerald P. Koocher. *Ethics in Psychology: Professional Standards and Cases*. Random House, New York, N.Y., 1998.

Kelly, Joan B. "Children's Adjustment to Conflicted Marriage and Divorce: A Decade Review of Research." *Journal of the American Academy of Children and Adolescents* 39 (2000): 963-73.

Kelly, Joan B., & Michael E. Lamb. "Using Child Development Research to Make Appropriate Custody and Access Decisions for Young Children." *Family and Conciliation Courts Review* 38 (2000): 297-311.

Kelly, Joan B. & Michael E. Lamb. "Developmental Issues in Relocation Cases Involving Young Children: When, Whether and How?" *Journal of Family Psychology* 17 (2003): 193-205.

Kelly, Mary. "Parent Perception of Child Profile," in *The Eleventh Mental Measurement Yearbook*. Jack Kramer & Jane Close Conoley, eds., University of Nebraska Press, Lincoln, Neb., 1992.

Kelley, Noble H. "ABPP: The Early Years." *The ABPP Specialist* 22 (2003): 11.

Kendell-Tackett, Kathleen A., L.M. Williams & D. Finkelhor. "Impact of Sexual Abuse on Children. A Review and Synthesis of Recent Empirical Studies." *Psychology Bulletin* 113 (1993): 164-80.

Kendell-Tackett, Kathleen & Malcolm Watson. "Factors That Influence Professionals' Perceptions of Behavioral Indicators in Child Sexual Abuse." *Journal of Interpersonal Violence* 6 (1991): 385-95.

Kennedy, Thomas. "Trends in Inmate Classification: A Status Report of Two Computerized Psychometric Approaches." *Criminal Justice & Behavior* 13 (1986): 165-70.

Kenney, K. et al. "The Court Prep Group: A Vital Part of the Court Process." in Dent (1992): 207.

Kendell, R.E. "Relationship Between the DSM-IV and the ICD-10." *Journal of Abnormal Psychology* 100 (1991): 297-301.

Kennedy, Thomas D. "Trends in Inmate Classification: A Status Report of Two Computerized Psychometric Approaches." *Criminal Justice and Behavior* 13 (1986): 165-84.

Keyser, Daniel & Richard Sweetland, eds., *Test Critiques*. Vol. 1-10, Pro. Ed., Austin, Tex., 1994.

Kilpatrick, D.G., P. Resnick & L. Veronen. "Effects of a Rape Experience: A Longitudinal Study." *Journal of Social Issues* 37 (1981): 105-12.

Kilpatrick, Kym L. & Leanne M. Williams. "Post-traumatic Stress Disorder in Child Witnesses to Domestic Violence." *American Journal of Orthopsychiatry* 67 (1997): 639-43.

Kirk, Stuart A. & Herb Kutchins. "Standards Higher, Success Assured, but DSM-IV Book A 'Travesty'." Reprinted in *The National Psychologist* 3 (1994): 12-13.

Kirkland, Karl & Kristen L. Kirkland. "Frequency of Child Custody Evaluation Complaints and Related Disciplinary Action: A Survey of the Association of State and Provincial Psychology Boards." *Professional Psychology: Research and Practice* 32 (2001): 171-74.

Kirkpatrick, H.D. "A Floor, Not a Ceiling: Beyond Guidelines—An Argument of Minimum Standards of Practice in Conducting Child Custody and Visitation Evaluations." *Journal of Child Custody* 1 (2004): 61-75.

Kirkpatrick, Laird C. & Christopher B. Mueller. *Evidence: Practice Under the Rules.* Aspen Law & Business, New York, N.Y., 2003.

Kirkpatrick, Martha, Catherine Smith & Ron Roy. "Lesbian Mothers and Their Children: A Comparative Study." *American Journal of Orthopsychiatry* 51 (1981): 545-51.

Kitsmann, Katherine & Robert E. Emery. "Child and Family Coping One Year After Mediated and Litigated Custody Disputes." *Journal of Family Psychology* 8 (1994): 150-59.

Kleber, David J., Robert J. Howell & Alta Lura Tibbits-Kleber. "The Impact of Parental Homosexuality on Child Custody Cases: A Review of the Literature." *Bulletin of the American Academy of Psychiatry & Law* 14 (1986): 81-87.

Klein, Andrew R. "Re-Abuse in a Population of Court Restrained Male Batterers: Why Restraining Orders Don't Work In Legal Interventions in Family Violence: Research Findings and Policy Implications." A Project of the American Bar Association's Criminal Justice Section, Commission on Domestic Violence, Center on Children and the Law, and Commission on Legal Problems of the Elderly, Presented to the National Institute of Justice (1998).

Klerman, Gerald L. "Classification and DSM-III-R," in Armand M. Nicholi, Jr., *The New Harvard Guide to Psychiatry*, Harvard University Press, Cambridge, Mass., 1988.

Kline, Marsha, Jeanne M. Tschann, R. Johnston & Judith Wallerstein. "Children's Adjustment in Joint and Sole Physical Custody Families." *Developmental Psychology* 25 (1989): 430-38.

Kline-Pruett, Marsha, Rachel Ebling & Glendessa Insabella. "Critical Aspects of Parenting Plans for Young Children: Interjecting Data into the Debate About Overnights." *Family Court Review* 42 (2004): 39-59.

Klopfer, B. & D.M. Kelley. *The Rorschach Technique*. World Book, Yonkers, N.Y., 1942.

Klopfer, Bruno, Mary Ainsworth, Walter Klopfer & Robert Holt. *Developments in the Rorschach Technique. Vol. 1*. Harcourt, Brace and World, New York, 1954.

Kluft, Richard. *Incest and Adult Psychopathology: An Overview and Study of the Sitting Duck Syndrome*. The Institute of the Pennsylvania Hospital, Philadelphia, Pa., 1988.

Knapp, Samuel & Leon VandeCreek, *A Guide to the 2002 Revision of the American Psychological Association's Ethics Code*. Professional Resources Press, Sarasota, Fla., 2003.

Kolbo, Jerome, Eleanor Blakely & David Engelman. "Children Who Witness Domestic Violence. A Review of Empirical Literature." *Journal of Interpersonal Violence* 11 (1996): 281-93.

Kolvin, I., F.J.W. Miller, M. Fleeting & P.A. Kolvin. "Social and Parenting Factors Affecting Criminal-Offence Rates: Findings from the Newcastle Thousand-Family Study (1947-1980)." *British Journal of Psychiatry* 152 (1988): 80-90.

Komaroff, Anthony L. & Laura Fagioli. "Medical Assessment of Fatigue and Chronic Fatigue Syndrome," in *Chronic Fatigue Syndrome: An Integrative Approach to Evaluation and Treatment*, M. Demitrack & S. Abbey, eds. Guilford, New York, 1996: 154-81.

Koppitz, E. *The Psychological Evaluation of Children's Human Figure Drawings* (1968).

Koppitz, E. "Emotional Indicators in Human Figure Drawings of Shy and Aggressive Children." *Journal of Clinical Psychology* 22 (1966): 466-69.

Koss, M.P., & M.R. Harvey. *The Rape Victim: Clinical and Community Interventions* 2nd ed. Sage, Thousand Oaks, Cal., 1991.

Kozuch, Patrick & Theresa M. Cooney. "Young Adult's Marital and Family Attitudes: The Role of Recent Parental Divorce, and Family and Parental Conflict." *Journal of Divorce and Remarriage* 23 (1995): 45-62.

Kramer, Jack & Jane Close Conoley. eds. *The Eleventh Mental Measurements Yearbook.* University of Nebraska Press, Lincoln, Neb., 1992.

Krauss, Daniel A. & Bruce D. Sales. "Legal Standards, Expertise, and Experts in the Resolution of Contested Child Custody Cases." *Psychology, Public Policy and Law* 4 (1998).

Krishnamurthy, Radhika, Robert Archer & Joseph House. "The MMPI-A and Rorschach: A Failure to Establish Convergent Validity." A*ssessment* 3 (1996): 179-91.

Krugman, R.D. & M.K. Krugman. "Emotional Abuse in the Classroom." *American Journal of Diseases of Children* 138 (1984): 284-86.

Kuehnle, Kathryn, Lyn Greenberg & Michael Gottlieb. "Incorporating the Principles of Scientifically Based Child Interviews Into Family Law Cases." *Journal of Child Custody* 1 (2004): 97-114.

Kunce, J. & W. Anderson, "Normalizing the MMPI." *Journal of Clinical Psychology* 32 (1976): 776-80.

Kunce, J. & W. Anderson. "Perspectives on Uses of the MMPI and Non-Psychiatric Settings," in P. McReynolds & G. Chelune, eds. *Advances in Psychological Assessment,* Jossey-Bass, San Francisco, Cal., 1984.

Kunz, Jenifer. "Parental Divorce and Children's Interpersonal Relationships: A meta-Analysis." *Journal of Divorce and Re-Marriage* 34 (2001): 19-47.

Kurdek, L.A., & B. Berg. "Correlates of Children's Adjustment to Their Parents' Divorces," in L. Kurdek, ed., *Children and Divorce, New Decisions for Child Development.* Jossey-Bass, San Francisco, Cal., 1983.

LaBruzza, Anthony L. *Using DSM-IV.* Aronson, Northvale, N.J., 1994.

LaFortune, K. & B. Carpenter. "Child Custody Evaluation Practices: A Survey of Mental Health Professionals." *Behavioral Sciences and the Law* 16 (1998): 207-24.

Lahey, Benjamin B., Mary F. Russo, Jason L. Walker & John C. Piacentini. "Personality Characteristics of the Mothers of Children with Disruptive Behavior Disorders." *Journal of Consulting and Clinical Psychology* 57 (1989): 512-15.

Lachar, David. *The MMPI: Clinical Assessment and Automative Interpretation.* Western Psychological Services, Los Angeles, 1974.

LaFortune, K. & B. Carpenter. "Child Custody Evaluation Practices: A Survey of Mental Health Professionals." *Behavioral Sciences and the Law* 16 (1998): 207-24.

Lahey, Benjamin B., Mary F. Russo, Jason L. Walker & John C. Piacentini. "Personality Characteristics of the Mothers of Children with Disruptive Behavior Disorders." *Journal of Consulting and Clinical Psychology* 57 (1989): 512-15.

Lamb, Michael & Joan B. Kelly. "Using the Empirical Literature to Guide the Development of Parenting Plans for Young Children: A Rejoinder to Solomon & Birgenger." *Family Court Review* 39 (2001): 365-71.

Lamb, Sharon & Mary Cullinan. "Normal Childhood Sexual Play and Games. A Survey of Female Undergraduates' Memories." Paper presented at the 99th Annual Convention of the American Psychological Association, San Francisco, Aug. 1991.

Lampel, Anita. "Use of the Millon Clinical Multiaxial Inventory-III in Evaluating Child Custody Litigants." *American Journal of Forensic Psychology* 17 (1999): 19-31.

LaVoie, Allan L. "Millon Clinical Multiaxial Inventory II," in Daniel J. Keyser & Richard C. Sweetland, *Test Critiques, Vol. 8,* Pro-Ed, Austin, Tex., 1991: 457-69.

Lee, Catherine M. & Ian H. Gotlib. "Clinical Status and Emotional Adjustment of Children of Depressed Mothers." *American Journal of Psychiatry* 146 (1989): 478-83.

Lee, M.Y. & P. Au. "Chinese Battered Women in North America: Their Experiences and Treatment," in A.R. Roberts, ed., *Battered Women and Their Families,* 2nd ed., Springer, New York, 1998: 448-92.

Lees-Haley, Paul. "Effects of MMPI-2 Validity Scales and MCMI-II Modifier Scales Detecting Spurious PTSD Claims: F, F-K, Fake-Bade Scale, Ego Strength, Subtle-Obvious Subscales, DIS and DEB," *Journal of Clinical Psychology* 48 (1992): 681-88.

Lees-Haley, Paul R. "Psychodiagnostic Test Usage By Forensic Psychologists." *American Journal of Forensic Psychology* 25 (1992): 25-30.

Lees-Haley, Paul R. "Innocent Lies, Tragic Consequences: The Manipulation of Child's Testimony." *Trial Diplomacy Journal* 10 (1987): 23-26.

Leifer, Myra, Jeremy P. Shapiro, Mary W. Martone & Layla Kassem. "Rorschach Assessment of Psychological Functioning in Sexually Abused Girls." *Journal of Personality Assessment* 56 (1991): 14-28.

Lenihan, Genie. "Childhood Sexual Abuse: Gender Differences in Prevalence, Experience, and Outcomes." Paper presented at the Annual Convention of the American Psychological Association. Toronto, Aug. 1996.

Leonard, Sean, William Dorfman, Joseph Burns & Edward Simco. "Assessing Sexual and Physical Abuse in Adolescents Using the MMPI-A." Paper presented at the 104th Annual Convention of the American Psychological Association, Toronto, Aug. 1996.

Lerner, Howard & Paul M. Lerner. "Rorschach Inkblot Test," in D. Keyser & R. Sweetland, *Test Critiques,* Test Corporation of America, Kansas City, 1984: 523-52.

Lesserman, J., Z. Li, D. Drossman, T.C. Toomey, G. Nachman, & L. Glogau. "Impact of Sexual and Physical Abuse Dimensions on Health Status: Development of an Abuse Severity Measure." *Psychomatic Medicine* 59 (1997): 152-60.

Leverton, Tessa J. "Parental Psychiatric Illness: The Implications for Children." *Current Opinion in Psychiatry* 16 (2003): 395-402.

Levitan, R.D., S.V. Parikh, A.D. Lesage, K.M. Hegaforen, M. Adams, S.H. Kennedy, & P.N. Goering. "Major Depression in Individuals with a History of Childhood Physical or Sexual Abuse: Relationship to Neurovegatative Features, Mania, and Gender." *American Journal of Psychiatry* 155 (1998): 1746-52.

Lewin, Linda & Christie Bergin. "Attachment Behaviors, Depression, and Anxiety in Non-Offending Mothers of Child Sexual Abuse Victims." *Child Maltreatment* 6 (2001): 365-75.

Lewis, Dorothy Otnow. "Adult Antisocial Behavior and Criminality," in H. Kaplan & B. Sadock, *Comprehensive Textbook of Psychiatry/IV,* Williams & Wilkins, Baltimore, Md., 1985: 1865-70.

Lezak, Muriel D. *Neuropsychological Assessment, Third Edition.* Oxford University Press, New York, N.Y., 1995.

Libb, J. Wesley, Srdjan Stankovic, Arthur Freeman, Roberta Sokol, Paul Switzer & Carl Houck. "Personality Disorders Among Depressed Outpatients as Identified by the MCMI." *Journal of Clinical Psychology* 46 (1990): 277-84.

Libb, J. Wesley, Srdjan Stankovic, Roberta Sokol, Arthur Freeman, Carl Houck & Paul Switzer. "Stability of the MCMI Among Depressed Psychiatric Outpatients." *Journal of Personality Assessment* 55 (1990): 209-18.

Lilienfeld, Scott. "The MMPI-2 Antisocial Practices Content Scale: Construct Validity and Comparison with the Psychopathic Deviate Scale." *Psychological Assessment: A Journal of Consulting and Clinical Psychology* 8 (1996): 281-93.

Lilienfeld, Scott O., James M. Wood & Howard N. Garb. "The Scientific Status of Projective Techniques." *Psychological Science in the Public Interest* 1 (2000): 27-66.

Lim, Jeeyoung & James Butcher. "Detection of Faking on the MMPI-2: Differentiation Among Faking-bad, Denial and Claiming Extreme Virtue." *Journal of Personality Assessment* 67 (1996): 1-25.

Lindsay, Stephen & J. Don Read. "Psychotherapy and Memories of Childhood Sexual Abuse: A Cognitive Perspective." *Applied Cognitive Psychology* (1994).

Linihan, Genie. "Childhood Sexual Abuse: Gender Differences in Prevalence Experience and Outcomes." Paper presented at the 104th Annual Convention of the American Psychological Association, Toronto, Canada, 1996.

Lipovsky, Julie A., Ritchie P. Todwell, Dean G. Kilpatrick, Benjamin E. Saunders, Jayne Crisp & Vicky L. Dawson. "Children As Witnesses in Criminal Court: Examination of Current Practice." Paper presented as the 99th Annual Convention of the American Psychological Association, San Francisco, Aug. 1991.

Loeber, Rolf. "Development and Risk Factors of Juvenile Antisocial Behavior and Delinquency." *Clinical Psychology Review* 10 (1990): 1-41.

Loftus, Elizabeth. "Memory Distortion and False Memory Creations." *Bulletin of American Academy of Psychiatry Law* 24 (1996): 281-95.

Loftus, Elizabeth. "False Memories in a Court." Paper presented at the 99th Annual Convention of the American Psychological Association, San Francisco, Aug. 1991.

Loftus, Elizabeth & Laura Rosenwald. "Recovered Memories: Unearthing the Past in Court." *Journal of Psychiatry and Law* 3 (1996): 281-93.

Loftus, Elizabeth, Maryannne Garry & Julie Feldman. "Forgetting Sexual Trauma: What Does It Mean When 38 Percent Forgot?" *Journal of Consulting and Clinical Psychology* 62 (1994): 1177-81.

Lohr, Jeffrey M., Katherine A. Fowler & Scott O. Lilienfeld. "The Dissemination and Promotion of Pseudoscience in Clinical Psychology: The Challenge to Legitimate Clinical Science." *The Clinical Psychologist* 55 (2002): 5.

Lombardo, S., & R. Pohl. "Sexual Abuse History of Women Treated in Psychiatric Outpatient Clinic." *Psychiatric Services* 48 (1997): 534-36.

Long, Kathleen & John R. Graham. "The Masculinity-Femininity Scale of the MMPI-2: Is It Useful with Normal Men?" *Journal of Personality Assessment* 57 (1991): 46-51.

Lopez, Frederick G., Vicki L. Campbell & C. Edward Wadkins, Jr. "The Relation of Parental Divorce to College Student Development." *Journal of Divorce* 1 (1988): 83-98.

Lowenstein, L.F. "Parental Alienation Syndrome: A Two-Step Approach Toward a Solution." *Contemporary Family* 3 (1998): 505-20.

Lowery, C.R. "Parents and Divorce: Identifying the Support Network for Decisions About Custody." *The American Journal of Family Therapy* 12 (1984): 26-32.

Lubin, Bernard, Reed M. Larsen & Joseph D. Matarazzo. "Patterns of Psychological Test Usage in the United States: 1935-1982." *American Psychologist* 39 (1984): 451-54.

Lundy, Allen. "Instructional Set and Thematic Apperception Test Validity." *Journal of Personality Assessment* 52 (1988): 309-20.

Lundy, Allan. "The Reliability of the Thematic Apperception Test." *Journal of Personality Assessment* 49 (1985): 141-45.

Lundy, Allan. "Testing Conditions and TAT Validity: Meta-analysis of the Literature Through 1983." Paper presented at the 92nd Annual Convention of the American Psychological Association, Toronto, Aug. 1984.

Luus, Elizabeth & Gary Wells. "The Perceived Credibility of Child Eye Witnesses," in Helen Dent & Rhonda Flins, eds., *Children As Witnesses,* John Wiley & Sons, Inc., Chichester, England, 1992.

Lyons-Ruth, Karlen, Amy Lyubchik, Rebecca Wolfe & Elisa Bronfman. "Parental Depression and Child Attachment: Hostile and Helpless Profiles of Parent and Child Behavior Among Families at Risk," in Sherryl H. Goodman & Ian H. Gotlib, eds., *Children of Depressed Parents*, American Psychological Association, Washington, D.C., 2002: 89-120.

MacAndrew, C. "The Differentiation of Male Alcoholic Outpatients from Non-alcoholic Psychiatric Outpatients by Using the MMPI." *Quarterly Journal of Studies in Alcohol* 26 (1965): 238-46.

Macfie, Jenny, Dante Cicchetti, & Sheree L. Toth. "Dissociation in Maltreated Versus Nonmaltreated Pre High School-Age Children." *Child Abuse and Neglect* 25 (2001): 1253-67.

Maccoby, Eleanor, Charlene Depner & Robert Mookin. "Co-Parenting in the Second Year after Divorce." *Journal of Divorce and the Family* 52 (1990): 141-55.

Maccoby, Eleanor E. *Social Development: Psychological Growth and the Parent-Child Relationship*. Harcourt Brace Jovanovich, New York, N.Y., 1980.

Maguire, Edward. "The Professionalism of Police in Child Sexual Abuse Cases." *Journal of Sexual Abuse* 2 (1993): 107-16.

Major, A. Jayne. "Parents Who Have Successfully Fought Parent Alienation Syndrome. *www.livingmedia2000.com*, (2000), 1-9.

Malinosky-Rummell, Robin J. Hansen. "Long-Term Consequences of Childhood Physical Abuse." *Psychological Bulletin* 114 (1993): 68-79.

Mannarino, A.P., & Cohen, J.A., "Abuse-Related Attributions and Perceptions, General Attributions, and Locus of Control in Sexually Abused Girls." *Journal of Interpersonal Violence* 11 (1996): 162-80.

Mantel, David. "Clarifying Erroneous Child Sexual Abuse Allegations." *American Journal of Orthopsychiatry* 58 (1998): 618-21.

Manual of the International Statistical Classification of Diseases, Injuries, and Causes of Death. 9th revision. Geneva: World Health Organization, 1977. *Manual of the International Statistical Classification of Diseases, Injuries, and Causes of Death, Clinical Modification, ICD-9-CM*. 9th ed., Commission on Professional and Hospital Activities, Ann Arbor, Mich., 1979.

Manual of the International Statistical Classification of Diseases, Injuries, and Causes of Death. 10th revision. World Health Organization, Geneva, 1992.

Manual of the International Statistical Classification of Diseases, Injuries, and Causes of Death, Clinical Modification ICD-10-CM, 10th ed. In preparation.

Mara, Barbara. "Child Sexual Abuse." A Workshop presented at the Southeastern Psychological Association Convention, Orlando, Fla., March 1986.

Marshall, W.L., D. Anderson, F. Champagne. "The Importance of Self-esteem in Sexual Offenders." *Psychology, Crime and Laws* 3 (1996): 81-106.

Marshall, W.L., F. Champagne, C. Brown, & S. Miller. "Empathy, Intimacy, Loneliness, and Self-esteem in Non-Familial Child Molesters: A Brief Report." *Journal of Child Sexual Abuse* 6 (1997): 87-98.

Marshall, W.L., S.M. Hudson, R. Jones, & Y.M. Fernandez. "Empathy in Sex Offenders." *Clinical Psychology Review* 15 (1995): 99-113.

Martindale, David, Judith Martindale & Joan Broderick. "Providing Expert Testimony in Child Custody Litigation," in Peter Keller & Steven Heyman, *Innovations in Clinical Practice: A Source Book, 10,* Professional Resource Exchange, Sarasota, Fla. 1991: 481-97.

Martindale, David A. & Jonathan W. Gould. "The Forensic Model: Ethics and Scientific Methodology Applied to Custody Evaluations." *Journal of Child Custody: Research, Issues, and Practices* 1 (2004): 1-22.

Maryland v. Craig, 110 S. Ct. 3157 (1990).

Masheter, Carol. "Post-Divorce Relationships Between Ex-Spouses: A Literature Review." *Journal of Divorce and Remarriage* 14 (1990): 97-122.

Masheter, Carol. "Post-Divorce Relationships Between Ex-Spouses: The Roles of Attachment and Interpersonal Conflict." *Journal of Marriage and Family* 53 (1991): 103-10.

Mason, Mary Ann. "Social Workers as Expert Witnesses in Child Sexual Abuse Cases." *Social Work, the Journal of the National Association of Social Workers* 37 (1992): 30-34.

Matarazzo, Joseph. "Psychological Assessment versus Psychological Testing: Validation from Binet to the School, Clinic, Courtroom." *American Psychologist* 45 (1990): 999-1017.

Mathew, Roy J. "Psychiatric Disorders in Adult Children of Alcoholics: Data from the Epidemiologic Catchment Area Project." *Am. J. Psychiatry* 150 (1993): 793-800.

Mathew, Roy J. "Psychiatric Disorders in Adult Children of Alcoholics: Data from the Epidemiologic Catchment Area Project." *American Journal of Psychiatry* 150 (1993): 793-800.

Mayers, Kathleen. "Non-Leading Techniques in the Assessment of the Alleged Child Molest Victim." *Journal of Forensic Psychology* 9 (1991): 37-39.

Maynes, L.C., & Feinauer, L.L. "Acute and Chronic Dissociation and Somatized Anxiety as Related to Childhood Sexual Abuse." *American Journal of Family Therapy* 22 (1994): 165-75.

Mayo Clinic web site, www.mayoclinic.com, retrieved August 25, 2004.

McCann, Joseph T. "Guidelines for Forensic Application of the MCMI-III." *Journal of Forensic Psychology Practice* 2 (2002): 55-69.

McCann, Joseph T. "Convergent and Discriminant Validity of the MCMI-II and MMPI Personality Disorder Scales." *Psychological Assessment: A Journal of Consulting and Clinical Psychology* 3 (1991): 9-18.

McCann, Joseph T. "A Multitrait-Multimethod Analysis of the MCMI-II Clinical Syndrome Scales." *Journal of Personality Assessment* 55 (1990): 465-76.

McCann, Joseph T., Jay R. Flens, Vicky Campagna, P. Collman, T. Lazzaro & E. Connor. "The MCMI-III in Child Custody Evaluations: A Normative Study." *Journal of Forensic Psychology Practice* 1 (2001): 27-44.

McCann, Joseph T., Patrick M. Flynn & David M. Gersh. "MCMI-II Diagnosis of Borderline Personality: Base Rates vs. Prototypic Items." Paper presented at the 98th Annual Convention of the American Psychological Association Conference, Boston, Aug. 1990.

McCann, Joseph T. & Frank J. Dyer. *Forensic Assessment with the Millon Inventories.* (1996).

McCombs, Amanda Thomas & Rex Forehand. "The Relationship Between Paternal Depressive Mood and Early Adolescent Functioning." *Journal of Family Psychology* 4 (1991): 260-71.

McDonald, Angus S. & Graham C.L. Davey, "Psychiatric Disorders and Accidential Injury." 16 *Clinical Psychol. Rev.* 105 (1996): 119-20.

McGaughey, Bernalyn D. & John D. Walker, "The Scientific Expert's Approaches to Litigation Testimony," in James J. Brown, *Scientific Evidence and Experts Handbook*. Aspen Law & Business, New York, 1999 (2002 Cumulative Supplement), 43-67.

McGuigan, William M., Aphra R. Katzev, & Clara C. Pratt. "Multi-level Determinants of Retention in a Home-Visiting Child Abuse Prevention Program" *Child Abuse and Neglect* 27 (2003): 363-80.

McHale, Michael J., Leonard L. Cavise & William G. Mulligan. "Expert Witnesses: Direct and Cross-Examination." John Wiley & Sons, New York, 1997.

McIver, William II, Hollida Wakefield, & Ralph Underwager. "Behavior of Abused and Non-Abused Children in Interviews with Anatomically Correct Dolls." Paper presented at the 98th Annual Convention of the American Psychological Association, Boston, 1990.

McKinney, Barbara, & Rolf A. Peterson. "Parenting Stress Index," in D. Keyser and R. Sweetland, *Test Critiques,* Test Corporation of America, Kansas City, 1984: 504-05.

McKinzie, R.K. & Campagna, Victoria, *The Rorschach, Exner's Comprehensive System, Interscorer Agreement, and Death*, WebPsychEmpiricist Apr. 27, 2002. Retrieved Aug. 14, 2002 from www.wpe.info/papers table.

McMellan, Mary J. "Rotter Incomplete Sentences Blank—2nd Edition." *In The Twelfth Mental Measurements Yearbook* (1995): 883.

McMillen, C., S. Zuravin, G. & Rideout. "Perceived Benefit from Child Sexual Abuse." *Journal of Consulting Psychology* 63 (1995): 1037-43.

McMinn, Mark R., Brent M. Ellis & Joref Erez. "Ethical Descriptions and Practice Behaviors Involving Computer-Based Test Interpretation." *Assessment* 6 (1999): 71-77.

McNaulty, J.L., J.R. Graham, Y.S. Ben-Porath & L.A.R. Stein. "Comparative Validity of MMPI-2 Scores of African American and Caucasian Mental Health Center Clients." *Psychological Assessment* 9 (1997): 464-70.

McNeely, Sharon. "Alcohol Use Inventory." In *The Supplement to the Eleventh Mental Measurements Yearbook*, Jane Close Conoley & James C. Impara, eds. University of Nebraska Press, Lincoln, Neb., 1994: 10-11.

McPhearson, Dan. "Gay Parenting Couples: Parenting Arrangements, Arrangement Satisfaction, and Relationship Satisfaction." Symposium presented at the 102nd Annual Convention of the American Psychological Association, Los Angeles, Cal., Aug. 1994.

Medhoff, David. "MMPI-2 Validity Scales in Child Custody Evaluations: Clinical Versus Statistical Significance." *Behavioral Sciences and the Law* 17 (1999): 410-11.

Megargee, Edwin. "Using the Magargee MMPI-based Classification System with MMPI's of Male Prison Inmates." *Psychological Assessment: A Journal of Consulting and Clinical Psychology* 6 (1994): 337-44.

Megargee, E.I., P.E. Cook & G.A. Mendelsohn. "Development and Validation of an MMPI Scale of Assaultiveness and Over-Controlled Individuals." *Journal of Abnormal Psychology* 72 (1967): 519-28.

Megargee, Edwin I. & Joyce L. Carbonell, "Use of the MMPI-2 in Correctional Settings," in Yossef S. Ben-Porath, John R. Graham, Gordon C.N. Hall, Richard D. Hirschman & Maria S. Zaragoza, eds., *Forensic Applications of the MMPI-2*. (1995): 127-59.

Megargee, Edwin I. & Martin J. Bohn, Jr. "Empirically Determined Characteristics of the Ten Types." *Criminal Justice and Behavior* 4 (1977): 149-210.

Meissner, W.M. "Theories of Personality and Psychopathology," in *Comprehensive Textbook of Psychiatry/IV*, H. Kaplan & B. Saddock, eds., 1985: 402

Melendez & Marcus (1990) Mental Distress Claims: Testing the Psychological Tests, 11 *American Journal of Forensic Psychiatry* 11 (1990): 19-22.

Meloy, J. Reid, Trayce L. Hansen & Irving B. Weiner. "Authority of the Rorschach: Legal Citations During the Past 50 Years." *Journal of Personality Assessment* 69 (1997): 53-62.

Melton, Gary B., John Petrila, Norman G. Poythress & Christopher Slobogin. *Psychological Evaluations for the Courts*. 2nd ed. Guilford Press, New York, N.Y., 1997.

Melton, Gary. "Can Caring and Coercion Coexist? Child Protection and the Law." Paper Presented at the 100th Annual meeting of the American Psychological Association, Washington, D.C., 1992.

Melton, Gary. "Ackerman-Schoendorf Scales for Parent Evaluation for Custody." *Eleventh Mental Measurement Yearbook*, Jack Kramer & Jane Close Conoley, eds., University of Nebraska Press, Lincoln, Neb., 1992.

Melton, Gary. "The Improbability of Prevention of Sexual Abuse," in D. Willis, E.J. Holden, & M. Rosenberg, eds., *Child Abuse Prevention* 1992: 168-92.

Melton, Gary. B. & Susan Limber. "Psychologists' Involvement in Cases of Child Maltreatment: Limits of Role and Expertise, *American Psychologist* 44 (1989): 1225-31.

Melton, Gary, Gail Goodman, Seth Kalichman, Murray Levine, Karen Saywitz, Gerald Koocher. "Empirical Research on Child Maltreatment and the Law." *Journal of Clinical Child Psychology* 24 (1995): 47-77.

Menendez v. Superior Court, 3 Cal. 4th 435, 834 P.2d 786, 11 Cal. Rptr. 2d 92 (1992).

"Mental Patients Are Able to Give Informed Consent." *ADAMHA News 11* (1985): 11.

Meyer, Diane C. & Walter M. Phillips. "No Safe Place: Parental Alcoholism and Adolescent Suicide." *American Journal of Psychotherapy* 44 (1990): 552-62.

Meyer, Gregory J., Mark J. Hilsenroth, Dirk Baxter, John E. Exner, Jr., J. Christopher Fowler, Craig C. Piers & Justin Resnick. "An Examination of Interrater Reliability for Scoring the Rorschach Comprehensive System in Eight Data Sets." 78 *Journal of Personality Assessment* (2002): 219-74.

Meyer, Gregory J. "Overview of Evidence on the Rorschach and TAT." Paper presented at the 110th Annual Convention of the American Psychological Association, Chicago, Aug. 25, 2002.

Meyer, Gregory J., Stephen E. Finn, Lorraine D. Eyde, Gary G. Kay, Kevin L. Moreland, Robert R. Dies, Elena J. Eisman, Tom W. Kubisyn & Geoffrey M. Reed.

"Psychological Testing and Psychological Assessment: A Review of Evidence and Issues." *American Psychologist* 56 (2001): 128-65.

Meyer, Gregory J. & Robert P. Archer. "The Hard Science of Rorschach Research: What Do We Know and Where Do We Go?" *Psychological Assessment* 13 (2001): 486-502.

Meyer, Gregory J. "Evidence to Correct Misperceptions About Rorschach Norms." 8 *Clinical Psychology: Science and Practice* (2001): 389-96.

Meyer, Gregory. "On the Integration of Personality Assessment Methods: The Rorschach and MMPI." *Journal of Personality Assessment* 68 (1997): 297-330.

Meyer, Gregory. "The Rorschach and MMPI: Toward A More Scientifically Differentiated Understanding of Cross-method Assessment." *Journal of Personality Assessment.* 67 (1996): 558-78.

Meyer, Gregory. "On the Integration of Personality Assessment Methods: The Rorschach and MMPI." *Journal of Personality Assessment* 68 (1997): 297-330.

Meyer, Linda Williams. "Recall of Childhood Trauma: A Prospective Study of Women's Memories of Child Sexual Abuse." *Journal of Consulting and Clinical Psychology* 62 (1995): 1167-75.

Meyers, Charles J. "Where the Protective Privilege Ends: California Changes the Rules for Dangerous Psychotherapy Patients." *Journal of Psychiatry and Law* 19 (1991): 5.

Michelson, Edwin A., Thomas Gutheil & Margaret Emens. "False Sexual-Abuse Allegations by Children and Adolescents: Contextual Factors and Clinical Subtypes." *American Journal of Psychotherapy* 46 (1992): 557-63.

Michaelson, Robin. "New Mental Illness Definitions Should Help States Plan Care." *American Psychological Association Monitor* 24 (1993): 7.

Miller v. Gentry (*In re*), No 93-4221-SAC (D. Kan. June 3, 1994).

Miller, David. "Review of the Kaufman Brief Intelligence Test," in *Twelfth Mental Measurements Yearbook,* Jane Close Conoley & James C. Impara, eds., The Buros Institute of Mental Measurements, Lincoln, Neb., 1995.

Miller, Laura J. and Molly Finnerty. "Sexuality, Pregnancy, and Childrearing Among Women with Schizophrenia-Spectrum Disorder." *Psychiatric Services* 47 (1996): 502-06.

Miller, R.D. "Professional versus Personal Ethics: Methods for System Reform" *Bull. Am. Acad. Psychiatry & L.* 20 (1992): 163.

Millon Adolescent Personality Inventory. Minneapolis, Minn.: National Computer Systems, 1989.

Millon Clinical Multiaxial Inventory-II. Minneapolis, Minn.: National Computer Systems, 1987.

Millon, C. & R. Davis. "MCMI-III Manual: Millon Clinical Multiaxial Inventory-III." Minneapolis, Minnesota, National Computer Systems (1994).

Millon, Theodore. "Classification in Psychopathology: Rationale, Alternative, and Standards." *Journal of Abnormal Psychology* 100 (1991): 245-61.

Millon, Theodore & Roger Davis. *Disorders of Personality: DSM-IV and Beyond*. Wiley, New York, 1996.

Millon T., R. Davis & C. Millon. "The Millon Clinical Multiaxial Inventory-III Manual." 2nd ed. Minneapolis, Minn., National Computer Systems (1997).

Milner, Joel & Chinni Chilamkurti. "Physical Child Abuse Perpetrator Characteristics. A Review of the Literature." *Journal of Interpersonal Violence* 6 (1991): 345-66.

"MIPS: Millon Index of Personality Styles." Brochure from The Psychological Corporation, 1994.

"MIPS-Revised," accessed at publisher's web site, www.personassessments.com/tests/mips.htm on Aug. 23, 2004.

Miryam R. Mitchell. "*Daubert*, Its Progeny, and Their Effect on Family Law Litigation in State Courts." Paper presented to the American Academy of Matrimonial Lawyers, Kohala Coast, Hawaii, March 3, 2000.

Mitler, C., C. Wertz & S. Counts. "Racial Differences on the MMPI." *Journal of Clinical Psychology* 17 (1961): 140-59.

Moenssens, Andre A., ed. www.forensic-evidence.com. University of Missouri-Kansas City School of Law.

Mok, D., & Elliott, D. "Gender Comparison of Child Sexual Abuse." Paper presented at the 104th Annual Convention of the American Psychological Association, Toronto, Canada, Aug. 1996.

Monahan, John. "Mental Disorder and Violent Behavior: Perceptions and Evidence." *American Psychologist 47* (1992): 511-21.

Moon, Gary., William A. Blakey, Richard Gorsuch & John W. Fantuzzo. "Frequent WAIS-R Administration Errors: An Ignored Source of Inaccurate Measurement." *Professional Psychology: Research and Practice* 22 (1991): 256-58.

Morey, L., W. Roberts & W. Penk. "MMPI Alcoholic Subtypes: Replication and Validity of the 2-7-8-4 Subtype." *Journal of Abnormal Psychology* 96 (1987): 164-66.

Morgan, C.D. & H.A. Murray. "A Method for Investigating Fantasies: The Thematic Apperception Test." *Archives of Neurology and Psychiatry* 34 (1935): 289-306.

Mowbray, Carol T., Daphna Oyserman, Judith K. Zemencuk & Scott R. Ross. "Motherhood for Women with Serious Mental Illness: Pregnancy, Childbirth, and Postpartum Period." *American Journal of Orthopsychiatry* 65 (1995): 21-38.

Mufson, Lauran, Myrna Weissman & Virginia Warner. "Depression and Anxiety in Parents and Children: A Direct Interview Study." *Journal of Anxiety Disorders* 6 (1992): 1-13.

Mulholland, Debra Japzon, Norman F. Watt, Anne Philpot & Neil Sarlin. "Academic Performance of Children of Divorce: Psychological Resilience and Vulnerability." *Psychiatry* 54 (1991): 268-80.

Mullen, P., J. Martin, S. Romans, & G. Herbison. "The Long-Term Impact of the Physical, Emotional and Sexual Abuse of Children: A Community Study." *Child Abuse & Neglect* 17 (1996): 623-40.

Mulligan, William G., *Expert Witnesses: Direct and Cross Examination*. Wiley, New York, N.Y. (1994 and 1997 supplement).

Mullins v. Mullins, 490 N.E.2d 1375 (Ill. App. Ct. 1986).

Munley, Patricia H. "Comparability of MMPI-2 Scales and Profiles Over Time." *Journal of Personality Assessment* 58 (2002): 145-60.

Murray, H.A. & Staff of the Harvard Psychology Clinic. *Explorations in Personality*. Oxford University Press, New York, 1938.

Murray, H.A. & Staff of the Harvard Psychology Clinic. *Thematic Apperception Test Manual*. Harvard University Press, Cambridge, Mass., 1943.

Myerholtz, Linda E. & Harold Rosenberg. "Screening DUI Offenders for Alcohol Problems: Psychometric Assessment of the Substance Abuse Subtle Screening Inventory." *Psychology of Addictive Behaviors* 11 (1997): 155-65.

Myers, Charles J. "Where the Protective Privilege Ends: California Changes the Rules for Dangerous Psychotherapy Patients." *Journal of Psychiatry & Law* 19 (1991): 5-31.

Myers, John. *Evidence of Child Sexual Abuse and Neglect Cases*. 2nd ed. Vol. 1. John Wiley & Sons, 1992.

Nagy, Thomas, "Guidelines and Directions When Treating Clients with Repressed Memories." *Nat'l Psychologist,* July-Aug. 1994: 8-9.

Nathan, Peter E. "DSM-IV: Getting Better." *Register Report* 20 (1994): 10-11.

National Academy of Sciences (2002). *The age of expert testimony: Science in the courtroom, report of a workshop*. Washington, D.C. (Feb. 22, 2004). http://www.nap.edu/openbook/0309083109/html/.

National Association of Social Workers (NASW) web site, http://naswdc.org/, retrieved July 3, 2004.

National Center for Health Statistics, retrieved Nov. 8, 2004, at www.cdc.gov/nchs/about/major/dvs/icd10des.htm.

National Register of Health Service Providers in Psychology, 2004 ed. Council for the National Register of Health Service Providers in Psychology, Washington, D.C., 2004.

National Register of Health Service Providers in Psychology web site, www.nationalregister.com/, retrieved June 30, 2004.

Naugle, Richard J. "Validity of the Kaufman Brief Intelligence Test." *Psychological Assessment: A Journal of Consulting and Clinical Psychology* 5 (1993): 182-86.

Neal, J.H. "Children's Understanding of Their Parent's Divorces," in L. Kurdek, ed., *Children and Divorce, New Directions for Child Development*. Jossey-Bass, San Francisco, 1983.

Neff, J.A., B. Holamon, & T.D. Schluter. "Spousal Violence among Anglos, Blacks, and Mexican Americans: The Role of Demographic Variables." *Journal of Family Violence* 10 (1995): 1-21.

Nelson-Gray, Rosemary. "DSM-IV: Empirical Guidelines from Psychometrics." *Journal of Abnormal Psychology* 100 (1991): 308-15.

Neska, Marc. "Seeking a Middle Ground on the Recovered Memories Controversy." *American Journal of Forensic Psychology* 12 (1997): 3.

Nichols, David. "The MMPI-2 Content Scales: In Interim Clinical Assessment." Paper presented at the 99th Annual Convention of the American Psychological Association Convention, San Francisco, Aug. 1991.

Nichols, David. "Remarks on Methods for MMPI-Rorschach Studies." *Journal of Personality Assessment* 67 (1996): 516-28.

Nichols, David S. & Roger L. Greene. "Dimensions of Deception in Personality Assessment: The Example of the MMPI-2." *Journal of Personality Assessment* 68 (1997): 251-66.

"N.J. Starts Issuing Domestic Partnerships to Same-Sex Couples." *The Milwaukee Journal Sentinel*, July 11, 2004.

Norton, I.M. & S.M. Manson. "A Silent Minority: Battered American Indian Women, *Journal of Family Violence* 10 (1995): 307-17.

Oberlander, Lois. "Ethical Responsibilities in Child Custody Evaluations: Implications for Evaluation Methodology." *Ethics and Behavior* 5 (1995): 311-32.

Oberlander, Lois. "The Utility of Ethical Standards in Specialty Guidelines in Child Custody Evaluations." Paper presented at the 102nd Annual Convention of the American Psychological Association, Los Angeles, Cal., Aug. 1994.

Oberholser, James C. "Retest Reliability of the Millon Clinical Multiaxial Inventory." *Journal of Personality Assessment* 55 (1990): 202-08.

Ofshe, Richard. "Making Monsters: The Mistake That Is Fracturing Psychology-Memory: True or False?" Presentation at the Wisconsin Association Spring Meeting, Milwaukee, Wisc., April 16, 1994.

Okami, Paul, Thomas Weisner & Richard Olmstead. "Outcome Correlates of Parent-Child Bedsharing: An Eighteen-Year Longitudinal Study." *Developmental and Behavioral Pediatrics* 23 (2002): 244-53.

Oldham, John M. Andrew E. Skodol, H. David Kellman, Steven E. Hyler, Norman Doidge, Lyle Rosnick & Peggy E. Gallaher. "Comorbidity of Axis I and Axis II Disorders." *American Journal of Psychiatry* 152 (1995): 571-78.

Ollendick, Duane G. & Brenda J. Otto. "MMPI Characteristics of Parents Referred for Child Custody Studies." *Journal of Psychology* 117 (1984): 227-32.

Ondrovik, Joann & David Hamilton. "Forensic Challenge: Expert Testimony." *American Journal of Forensic Psychology* 10 (1992): 15-24.

Orcutt, Holly K., Gayle S. Goodman, Ann E. Tobey, Jennifer M. Batterman-Faunce & Shelly Thomas. "Detecting Deception in Children's Testimony: Fact Finders' Abilities to Reach the Truth in Open Court and Closed-Circuit Trials." *Law & Human Behavior* 25 (2001): 339-72.

Otto, Randy F. & John F. Edens. *Parenting Capacity. In Thomas Grisso, ed., Evaluating Competencies,* 2nd ed.: Kluwer/Plenum, New York, N.Y., 2003.

Otto, Randy K Jacqueline K. Buffington-Vollum, & John F. Edens. "Child Custody Evaluation," in Alan M. Goldstein & Irving B. Weiner, *Handbook of Psychology*, Vol. 11. Wiley, Hoboken, New Jersey, 2003.

Otto, Randy & J. Hall. "The Utility of the Michigan Alcoholism Screening Test in the Detection of Alcoholics and Problem Drinkers." *Journal of Personality Assessment* 52 (1988): 499-505.

Ouimette, Paige Crosby, Daniel N. Klein, David C. Clark & Eliezer T. Margolis. "Personality Traits in Offspring of Parents with Unipolar Affective Disorder: An Exploratory Study." *Journal of Personality Disorders* 6 (1992): 91-98.

Oyserman, Daphna, Carol T. Mowbray, Paula Allen Meares & Kirsten B. Firminger. "Parenting Among Mothers with a Serious Mental Illness." *American Journal of Orthopsychiatry* 70 (2000): 296-315.

Pagelow, Mildred. "Effects of Domestic Violence on Children and Their Consequences for Custody and Visitation Agreements." *Mediation Quarterly* 7 (1990): 347-63.

Pagelow, Mildred. *Family Violence*, Praeger, New York, 1984.

Panish, Jacqueline B. & George Stricker. "Parental Marital Conflict in Childhood and Influence on Adult Sibling Relationships." *Journal of Psychotherapy in Independent Practice* 2 (2001): 3-16.

Pantle, Mark, Jill Evert & Max Trenerry. "The Utility of the MAPI in the Assessment of Depression." *Journal of Personality Assessment* 55 (1990): 673-82.

Paola, Anthony et al. "Reading Difficulty of MMPI-2 Subscales." *Journal of Clinical Psychology* 47 (1991): 532.

"Parenting Style May Help Foster Avoidant Personality in Child." *Clinical Psychiatry News* 18 (Mar. 1990): 15.

Paris, Joel. "A Critical Review of Recovered Memories in Psychotherapy: Part 1—Trauma and Memory." *Canadian Journal of Psychiatry* 41 (1996): 210-05.

Parker, J.G. & Herrera, C. "Interpersonal Processes in Friendships: A Comparison of Abused and NonAbused Children's Experiences." *Developmental Psychology* 32 (1996): 1025-38.

Parry, John W. "Expert Evidence and Testimony: *Daubert* Versus *Frye*." *Mental and Physical Disability Law Reporter* 28 (2004): 136-40.

Parry, John W. "Admissibility of Expert Evidence." *Mental and Physical Disability Law Reporter* 24 (2000): 10.

Patelis, Thanos "What's New." *The Score* 24 (2002): 8-9.

Patterson, Charlotte J. & Richard E. Redding. "Lesbian and Gay Families with Children: Implications of Social Science Research for Policy." *Social Issues* 52 (1990): 29-50.

Patterson, G., B. DeBaryshe & E. Ramsey. "Developmental Perspective on Antisocial Behavior." *American Psychologist* 44 (1989): 329-35.

Pearson Assessments: "MACI: Millon Adolescent Clinical Inventory." 2004 Catalog.

Pearson, Jessica & Nancy Thoennes. "Custody after Divorce: Demographic and Attitudinal Patterns." *American Journal of Orthopsychiatry* 60 (1990): 223-49.

Pelcovitz, D., S. Kaplan, B.Goldenberg, F. Mandel, J. Lehane & G. Guarrera. "Posttraumatic Stress Disorder in Physically Abused Adolescents." *Journal of the American Academy of Child and Adolescent Psychiatry* 33(3) (1996): 305-12.

Pedez, Kathy & Danelle Hodge. "Planting False Childhood Memories in Children: The Role of Event Plausibility Child Development." *Child Development* 4 (1999): 887-95.

Pena, Liana, Edwin Magargee & Erica Brody. "MMPI-A Patterns of Male Juvenile Delinquents." *Psychological Assessment: A Journal of Consulting and Clinical Psychology* 8 (1996): 388-97.

People v. Clark, 50 Cal. 3d 583, 789 P.2d 127, 268 Cal. Rptr. 399 (1990).

People v. Wharton, 53 Cal. 3d 522, 809 P.2d 290, 280 Cal. Rptr. 631 (1991).

Perlin, Michael. *Law and Mental Disability*. Michie, Charlottesville, Va., 1994.

Perr, Irwin N. "Psychiatric Confidentiality and the Work Product Rule: *State v. Pawlyk.*" *Newsletter* 17 (American Academy of Psychiatry and the Law 1992): 10-13.

Perry, Glenn G. & Bill N. Kinder. "The Susceptibility of the Rorschach to Malingering: A Critical Review." *Journal of Personality Assessment* 54 (1990): 47-57.

Perry, J. Christopher & George Vaillant. "Personality Disorders," in H. Kaplan & B. Sadock, *Comprehensive Textbook of Psychiatry/V.* Williams & Wilkins, Baltimore, Md., 1989. 1377-88.

Perry, Nancy, Bradley McCauliff, Paulette Tam, Linda Claycomb, Colleen Dostal & Cameron Flanagan. "When Lawyers Question Children, Is Justice Served?" *Law and Human Behavior* 19 (1995): 609-29.

Peters, Debra & Lillian Range. "Self-Blame and Self-Destruction in Sexually Abused Children." *Journal of Child Sexual Abuse* (1996): 19-33.

Peterson, Christopher, Steven F. Maier and Martin E.P. Seligman. *Learned Helplessness: A Theory for the Age of Personal Control.* Oxford University Press, New York, 1993.

Peterson, Rolf A. "Rorschach" in O.K. Buros, *The Eighth Mental Measurements Yearbook,* Gryphon Press, Highland Park, N.J., 1978: 1042-45.

Pezdek, Kathy & Danelle Hodge. "Planting False Childhood Memories in Children: The Role of Event Plausibility." *Child Development* 70 (1990): 887-95.

Phares, Vicky. "Where's Poppa? The Relative Lack of Attention to the Role of Fathers in Child and Adolescent Psychopathology." *American Psychologist* 47 (1992): 656-64.

Phares, Vicky & Bruce Compas. "The Role of Fathers in Child and Adolescent Psychopathology: Make Room for Daddy." *Psychological Bulletin* 111 (1992): 387-412.

Phares, Vicky, Amy M. Duhig, & M. Monica Watkins. "Family Context: Fathers and Other Supports," in Sherryl H. Goodman & Ian H. Gotlib, eds., *Children of Depressed Parents.* American Psychological Association, Washington, D.C., 2002: 203-225.

Philo, H. "Rules to Follow RE: Expert Witnesses," quoted in J. Romano & R. Romano, "How to Avoid the Traps of Expert Witness: The Seven Deadly Sins." *Trial Diplomacy Journal* 16 (1993): iv-viii.

Phillips, Leslie & Joseph G. Smith. *Rorschach Interpretation: Advanced Technique.* Grune & Stratton, New York, 1953.

Piersma, Harry L. "The MCMI-II Depression Scales: Do They Assist in the Differential Prediction of Depressive Disorders?" *Journal of Personality Assessment* 56 (1991): 478-86.

Pincus, Harold, Allen Frances, Wendy Davis, Michael First & Thomas Widiger. "DSM-IV and New Diagnostic Categories: Holding the Line on Proliferation." *American Journal of Psychiatry* 149 (1992): 112-17.

Piotrowski, Chris & John Keller. "Psychological Testing in Outpatient Mental Health Facilities: A National Study." *Professional Psychology: Research and Practice* 20 (1989): 423-25.

Piran, N., P. Lerner, P.E. Garfinkel, S.H. Kennedy, & C. Brouillette. "Personality Disorders in Anorectic Patients." *International Journal of Eating Disorders* 7 (1998): 589-59.

Plake, Barbara S., James C. Impara & Robert A. Spies, eds. *Fifteenth Mental Measurements Yearbook.* University of Nebraska Press, Lincoln, Neb., 2003.

Podboy, John & Albert Kastle. "The Intentional Misuse of Standard Psychological Tests in Complex Trials." Paper presented at the American College of Forensic Psychology's 80th Annual Symposium in Forensic Psychology, San Francisco, April 1992.

Pollack, Daniel & Susan Mason. "Mandatory Visitation in the Best Interest of the Child." *Family Court Review* 42 (2004): 74-84.

Pollock, V.E., John Briere, Lon Schneider, Joachim Knop, Sarnoff Mednick & Donald Goodwin. "Childhood Antecedents of Antisocial Behavior." *American Journal of Psychiatry* 147 (1990): 1290-93.

Polusny, Melissa, & Victoria Follette. "Long-Term Correlates of Child Sexual Abuse: The Theory and Review of the Empirical Literature." *Applied and Preventive Psychology* 4 (1995): 143-66.

Poole, Debra, Stephen Lindsay, Amina Memon, & Ray Bull. "Psychotherapy and the Recovery of Memories of Childhood Sexual Abuse: U.S. British Practitioners' Opinions, Practices and Experiences." *Journal of Consulting and Clinical Psychology* 62 (1995): 426-37.

Pope, Kenneth & Laura Brown. *Recovered Memories of Abuse, Assessment, Therapy, Forensics.* American Psychological Association, Washington, D.C., 1996.

Pope, Kenneth, James Butcher & Joyce Seelen. *The MMPI, MMPI-2 and MMPI-A in Court: A Practical Guide for Expert Witnesses and Attorneys,* American Psychological Association, Washington, D.C., 1993.

Pope, Kenneth, James Butcher & Joyce Seelen. "MMPI, MMPI-2 and MMPI-A" in Court, *A Practical Guide for Expert Witnesses and Attorneys*, 2nd ed. American Psychological Association, Washington, D.C., 2000.

Pope, Kenneth & Barbara Tabachnik. "Recovered Memories of Abuse among Therapy Patients: A National Survey." *Ethics and Behavior* 5 (1995): 237-48.

Pope, Kenneth S. & Melba J.T. Vasquez. *Ethics in Psychotherapy and Counseling*, 2nd ed. Jossey-Bass, San Francisco, 1998.

Porter, Stephen, John C. Yuille & Darrin R. Lehman. "The Nature of Real, Implanted, and Fabricated Memories for Emotional Childhood Events: Implications for the Recovered Memory Debate." *Law & Human Behavior* 23 (1999): 517-37.

"Position Statement: Adult Recovered Memories of Childhood Sexual Abuse." 41 *Canadian Journal of Psychiatry* 5 (1996): 305-06.

Preng, Kathryn W. & James R. Clopton. "Application of the MacAndrews Alcoholism Scale to Alcoholics with Psychiatric Diagnosis." *Journal of Personality Assessment* 50 (1986): 113-22.

Preskorn, Sheldon H. "Beyond DSM-IV: What is the Cart and What is the Horse?" *Psychiatric Annals.* 25 (1995): 53-62.

Pruett, M. & K. Pruett. "Fathers, Divorce and Their Children." *Child and Adolescent Psychiatric Clinics of North America* 7 (1998): 389-407.

Psychological Corporation (WPPSI-III) Technical and Interpretive Manual, 2002, San Antonio, TX.

Public Law, Keeping Children and Families Safe Act. Public Law 108-36, June 25, 2003.

Putnam, Frank. "Ten-Year Research Update Review: Child Sexual Abuse." *American Academy of Child and Adolescent Psychiatry* 42 (2003): 269-78.

Quincy, V.L., M.E. Rice & G.T. Harris. "Actuarial Prediction of Sexual Recidivism." *Journal of Interpersonal Violence* 10 (1995): 85-105.

Quinnell, Francella & James Bow. "Psychological Tests Used in Child Custody Evaluations." *Behavioral Science and Law* 19 (2001): 491-501.

Raczek, "Child Abuse and Personality Disorders." 6 *J. Personality Disorders* (1992): 109.

Rae-Grant, Q. & G. Award. "The Effects of Marital Breakdown," in P.D. Steinhauer & Q. Rae-Grant, eds., *Psychological Problems of the Child in the Family,* 1977: 565-91.

Rafael, Alan Jay. President's Column. *The Newsletter of the American Board of Assessment Psychology* 1 (1995): 1.

Rapee, Ronald M. "Potential Role of Childrearing Practices in the Development of Anxiety and Depression. *Clinical Psychology Review* 17 (1997): 47-67.

Rappeport, Jonas R. "Reasonable Medical Certainty." *Bulletin of the American Academy of Psychiatry and Law* 13 (1985): 5-15.

Raymond, N.C., E. Coleman, E. Ohlerking, F. Christenson & M. Minor. "Psychiatric Co-Morbidity in Pedophilic Sex Offenders." *American Journal of Psychiatry* 156 (1999): 786-88.

Read, Don & D. Stephen Lindsay. "Moving Toward a Middle Ground in the 'False Memory' Debate: Reply to Commentaries on Lindsey and Read." *Applied Cognitive Psychology* 8 (1994): 407.

Reed, Deborah B. "Therapist's Duty to Protect Third Parties: Balancing Public Safety and Patient Confidentiality." *Community Mental Health Report* 1 (2001): 1-3.

Reed, L. Dennison. "Findings From Research on Children's Suggestibility and Implications for Conducting Child Interviews." *Child Maltreatment* 1 (1996): 105-20.

Reid, John B. "Involving Parents in the Prevention of Conduct Disorder: Rationale, Problems, and Tactics." *The Community Psychologist* 24 (1991): 28-30.

Reidy, Thomas & Christopher Carstens. "Stability of the Millon Adolescent Personality Inventory in an Incarcerated Delinquent Population." *Journal of Personality Assessment* 55 (1990): 692-97.

Reidy, Thomas, Richard Silver & Alan Carlson. "Child Custody Decisions: A Survey of Judges." *Family Law Quarterly* 23 (1989): 75-87.

Retzlaff, Paul. "MCMI-III Diagnostic Validity: Bad Test or Bad Validity Study." *Journal of Personality Assessment*, 66 (1996): 431-37.

Retzlaff, Paul. "Millon Adolescent Clinical Inventory." in *The Twelfth Mental Measurements Yearbook*. Jane Close Conoloy & James C. Impara, eds. The Buros Institute of Mental Measurements, Lincoln, Neb., 1995, 621-22.

Retzlaff, Paul, Eugene Sheehan & Alan Fiel. "MCMI-II Report Style and Bias: Profile and Validity Scales Analyses." *Journal of Personality Assessment* 56 (1991): 466-77.

Retzlaff, Paul D. "Comment on the Validity of the MCMI-III." *Law and Human Behavior* 24 (2000): 499-500.

Retzlaff, Paul. "Millon Clinical Multiaxial Inventory-III," in James C. Impara and Barbara S. Plake, *The Thirteenth Mental Measurements Yearbook*. University of Nebraska Press, Lincoln, Neb., 1998: 667-68.

Reynolds, Cecil. "Second Review of the Millon Clinical Multiaxial Inventory-II (MCMI-II)." in *The Eleventh Mental Measurements Yearbook*, Jack Kramer & Jane Close Conoley, eds., University of Nebraska Press, Lincoln, Neb., 1992: 533-35.

Reynolds, Matthew W., Joanna Wallace, Tyra F. Hill, Mark D. Weist & Laura A. Nebors. "The Relationship Between Gender, Depression, and Self-Esteem in Children Who Have Witnessed Domestic Violence." *Child Abuse and Neglect* 25 (2001): 1201-06.

Ricci, Christine, Carole Beal & Dawn Deckle. "The Effect of Parent Versus Unfamiliar Interviewers on Children's Eyewitness Memory and Identification Accuracy." *Law and Human Behavior* 20 (1996): 483-500.

Richters, J. & Pellegrini, D. "Depressed Mothers' Judgment About Their Children: An Examination of the Depression-Distortion Hypothesis." *Child Development* 60 (1989): 1068-75.

Risen, Leslie & Regis MacNamara. "Validation of Child Sexual Abuse: The Psychologist's Role." *Journal of Clinical Psychiatry* 45 (1989): 175-284.

Risinger, D.M., Michael J. Saks, W. C. Thompson, & R. Rosenthal, "The *Daubert/Kumho* implications of observer effects in forensic science: Hidden problems of expectation and suggestion." *California Law Review* 90 (2002): 1-56.

Roberts, A.R. *Battered Women and Their Families,* 2nd ed. Springer, 1998.

Robins, Lee. Comments at "Symposium: DSM-IV Field Trials—Part Two," at the 100th Annual Convention of the American Psychological Association, Washington, D.C., Aug. 1992.

Rogers, Richard. "Diagnostic Explanatory, Detection Models of Munchausen by Proxy: Extrapolations from Malingering and Deception." *Child Abuse and Neglect* 28 (2004): 225-39.

Rogers, Richard & Charles Patrick Ewing, "The Prohibition of Ultimate Opinions: A Misguided Enterprise." *Journal of Forensic Psychology Practice* 3 (2003): 65-75.

Rogers, Richard, Randall Salekin & Kenneth Sewell. "Convergent and Discriminant Validity of the Millon Clinical Multiaxial Inventory for Axis II Disorders: Time for a Moratorium?" Paper presented at the 105th Annual Convention of the American Psychological Association. Chicago, Ill., Aug. 1997.

Rogers, Richard, Randall T. Salekin, & Kenneth W. Sewell. "The MCMI-III and the *Daubert* Standard: Separating Rhetoric from Reality." *Law and Human Behavior* 24 (2000): 501-06.

Rogers, Richard, Randall T. Salekin, and Kenneth W. Sewell. "Validation of the Millon Clinical Multiaxial Inventory for Axis II Disorders: Does It Meet the *Daubert* Standard?" *Law and Human Behavior* 23 (1999): 425-33.

Rogers, Richard, Kenneth Sewell & Karen Ustad. "Feigning Among Chronic Outpatients on the MMPI-2: A Systematic Examination of Fake Bad Indicators." *Assessment* 2 (1995): 81-89.

Romano, John & Rodney Romano. "How to Avoid the Traps of Expert Witness: The Seven Deadly Sins." *Trial Diplomacy Journal* 16 (1993): iv-viii.

Rorty, M., J. Yager, & E. Rossotto. "Childhood Sexual, Physical, and Psychological Abuse in Bulimia Nervosa." *American Journal of Psychiatry* 151 (1994): 1122-26.

Roseby, Vivian. "A Custody Evaluation Model for Pre-School Children." Paper presented at the 92nd Annual Convention of the American Psychological Association, Toronto, Aug. 1984.

Rosenthal, Robert, Hiller, Jordan B., Bornstein, Robert F., Berry, David T.R. & Brunell-Neuleib, Sherrie, "Meta-Analytic Methods, the Rorschach, and the MMPI." *Psychological Assessment* 13 (2001): 449-51.

Rosman, BB. Robbie, Honore M. Hughes, Mindy S. Rosenberg. *Children and Interparental Violence, The Impact of Exposure*. Brunner/Mazel, Philadelphia, 2000.

Rotgers, Frederick & Deirdre Barrett, "*Daubert v. Merrell Dow* and Expert Testimony by Clinical Psychologists: Implications and Recommendations for Practice." *Professional Psychology: Research and Practice* 27 (1996): 467-74.

Rotter, J. & J. Rafferty. *Manual, The Rotter Incomplete Sentences Blank*. The Psychological Corp., Cleveland, Oh., 1950.

Rowan, Edward L., Judith B. Rowan & Pamela Langelier. "Women Who Molest Children." *Bulletin of the American Academy of Psychiatry & Law* 18 (1990): 79-83.

Roys, D. & R. Timms. "Personality Profile of Adult Males Sexually Molested by Their Maternal Caregivers: Preliminary Findings." *Journal of Child Sexual Abuse* (1995): 63-77.

Rubin, Linda. "Childhood Sexual Abuse: False Accusations of: 'False Memory'." *Professional Psychology: Research and Practice* 27 (1996): 447-51.

Runyon, Melissa K. & Maureen C. Kenney. "Relationship of Attributional Style, Depression, Post-Trauma Distress Among Children Who Suffer Physical or Sexual Abuse, *Child Maltreatment* 7 (2002): 254-64.

Rutledge-Newsom, Kathleen, Robert P. Archer, Susan Trumbetta & Irving I. Gottesman. "Changes in Adolescents' Response Patterns on the MMPI/MMPI-A." *Personality Assessment* 81 (2003): 74-84.

Ryan, R. "Thematic Apperception Test." in D. Keyser & R. Sweetland, *Test Critiques,* Test Corporation of America, Kansas City, 1984: 799-814.

Sageman, M. "Three Types of Skills for Effective Forensic Psychological Assessments." *Assessment* 10 (2003): 321-28.

Saks, Michael J. The Aftermath of *Daubert*: An Evolving Jurisprudence of Expert Evidence. 40 *Jurimetrics* (2000): 229-41.

Saks, Michael J. "Expert Witnesses, Nonexpert Witnesses, and Nonwitness Experts." *Law and Human Behavior* 148 (1990): 291-313.

Salekin, Randall, T., Richard Rogers & Kenneth W. Sewell. "A Review and Meta-Analysis of the Psychopathy Checklist and Psychopathy Checklist-Revised: Predictive Validity and Dangerousness." 3 *Clinical Psychology: Science and Practice* 3 (1996): 302-15.

Salmon, P., & Calderbank, S. "The Relationship of Childhood Physical and Sexual Abuse to Adult Illness Behavior." *Journal of Psychosomatic Research* 40 (1996): 329-36.

Samek, William. "Forensic Assessment of Incest Families." Paper presented at the 99th Annual Convention of the American Psychological Association. San Francisco, Cal.

Sanders, Mary J. & Brenda Bursch. "Forensic Assessment of Illness Falsification, Munchausen by Proxy, and Factitious Disorders, NOS." *Child Maltreatment* 17 (2002): 112-24.

Sandler, Irwin, Sharlene Wolchik, Sanford Braver & Bruce Fogas. "Stability and Quality of Life Events and Psychological Symptomotology in Children of Divorce." *American Journal of Community Psychology* 19 (1991): 501-20.

Sarbin, Theodore R. "On the Futility of Psychiatric Diagnostic Manuals (DSMs) and the Return of Personal Agency." *Applied and Preventive Psychology* 6 (1997): 233.

Sass, Louis & David Wolfe. "Preparing Sexually Abused Children for the Stress of Court." Paper presented at the 99th Annual Convention of the American Psychological Association, San Francisco, Cal., 1991.

Sattler, Jerome M. *Assessment of Children.* 3rd ed. Jerome Sattler, San Diego 1988.

Sattler, Jerome. *Clinical and Forensic Interviewing of Children and Families.* Jerome M. Sattler Publishing, Inc., San Diego, 1998.

Sattler, Jerome M. "Vineland Adaptive Behavior Scales." in *Tenth Mental Measurements Yearbook,* Jane Close Conoley & Jack J. Kramer, eds., 1989: 881.

Saunders, B.E., D.G. Kilpatrick, R.F. Hanson, H.S. Resnick, & M.E. Walker. "Prevalence, Case Characteristics, and Long-Term Psychological Correlates of Child Rape among Women: A National Survey." *Child Maltreatment: Journal of the American Professional Society on the Abuse of Children* 4 (1999): 187-200.

Saywitz, Karen. "Developmental Sensitivity in the Assessment of Child Sexual Abuse," Paper presented at the 99th Annual Meeting of the American Psychological Association, San Francisco, Cal., 1991.

Saywitz, Karen, "Preparing Children for the Investigative and Judicial Process: Improving Communication, Memory and Emotional Resiliency." Final report to the National Center on Child Abuse and Neglect, 1993.

Saywitz, Karen. "Improving the Reliability of Children's Reports: A Symposium presented at the 105th Convention of the American Psychological Association, Chicago, Ill., 1997.

Saywitz, Karen & Rebecca Nathanson, "Effects of Environment on Children's Testimony and Perceived Stress." Paper presented at the 100th Annual Convention of the American Psychological Association, Washington, D.C., 1992.

Saywitz, Karen & Lynn Snyder. "Narrative Elaboration: Test of a New Procedure for Interviewing Children." *Journal of Consulting and Clinical Psychology* 64 (1996): 1347-57.

Saywitz, Karen, Lynn Snyder & Vivian Lamphear. "Helping Children Tell What Happened: A Follow-up Study of the Narrative Elaboration Procedure." *Child Maltreatment* 1 (1996): 200-12.

Scarr, Sandra. "How People Make Their Own Environments: Implications for Parents and Policy Makers." *Psychology Public Policy and Law* 2 (1996): 204-28.

Schachere, Karen. "Attachment Between Working Mothers and Their Infants: The Influence of Family Processes." *American Journal of Orthopsychiatry* 60 (1990): 19-34.

Schacter, Daniel, Jerome Kagan & Michelle Leictman. "True and False Memories in Children and Adults: A Cognitive Neuroscience Perspective." *Psychology, Public Policy and Law* 1 (1995): 411-28.

Schaefer, Milton & Melvin Guyer. "Allegations of Sexual Abuse and Custody and Visitation Disputes: A Level and Clinical Challenge." Paper presented at the 96th Annual Convention of the American Psychological Association Convention, Aug. 1988.

Schenk, Paul. "MMPI-2 Norms and Child Custody Litigants," in *The Custody Newsletter,* Village publishing, Jan. 1997, No. 15.

Schenkenberg, T., D. Gottsfredson & P. Christensen. "Age Differences in the MMPI Scale Scores from 1189 Psychiatric Patients." *Journal of Clinical Psychology* 40 (1984): 1420-26.

Schetky, Diane H. "Ethical Issues in Forensic Child and Adolescent Psychiatry." *Journal of the American Academy of Child & Adolescent Psychiatry* 31 (1992): 403-07.

Schever v. Rhodes, 416 U.S. 232 (1974).

Schiller, V. "Joint Versus Maternal Custody for Families with Latency Age Boys: Parent Characteristics and Child Adjustment." *Journal of Orthopsychiatry* 56 (1986): 486.

Schinnar, Arie P., Aileen Rothbard, Rebekah Kanter & Yoon Soo Jung. "An Empirical Literature Review of Definitions of Severe and Persistent Mental Illness." *American Journal of Psychiatry* 147 (1990): 1602-08.

Schneider, Jeffrey. "Legal Issues Involving 'Repressed Memory' of a Childhood Sexual Abuse," in the *Psychologist's Legal Update*, National Register of Health Service Providers in Psychology, Aug. 1994.

Schneidman, Edwin S. "Overview: A Multidimensional Approach to Suicide," in Douglas Jacobs & Herbert N. Brown, eds., *Suicide: Understanding and Responding,* 1-30, International Universities Press, Madison, Conn., 1989.

Schondrick, Denise et al. "Forensic Applications of the MMPI-2." *MMPI News and Profiles,* 3 (Oct. 1992): 6-7.

Schreier, Herbert & Judith Libow. "Munchausen Syndrome by Proxy: Diagnosis and Prevalence." *American Journal of Orthopsychiatry* 63 (1993): 318-29.

Schuck,Wiat M. & Kathy Spatz, "Childhood Victimization and Alcohol Symptoms in Females: Causal Inferences and Hypothesized Mediators." *Child Abuse and Neglect* 25 (2001): 1069-92.

Schuckit, Marc. "DSM-IV What Is It Going to Do to Us?" *Drug Abuse & Alcoholism Newsletter* 21 (1992): 1-3.

Schudson, Charles B. "Escape from Wonderland: The United States Supreme Court Decision in *White v. IL.*" *Family Violence and Sexual Assault Bulletin* 8 (1992).

Schutte, James W. "Using the MCMI-III in Forensic Evaluations." *American Journal of Forensic Psychology* 19 (2000): 5-20.

Schwartz-Kenney, Beth M., Bette L. Bottoms, Gail S. Goodman & Mary Elizabeth Wilson. "Improving Children's Accuracy for Person Identification." Paper presented at the 100th Annual Convention of the American Psychological Association, Washington, D.C., 1992.

Scott, Ronald & David Stone. "MMPI Measures of Psychological Disturbances in Adolescent and Adult Victims of Father-Daughter Incest." *Journal of Clinical Psychology* 42 (1986): 257.

Sears v. Rutishauser, 466 N.E.2d 210 (Ill. 1984).

Segal, Jeffrey. "Traditional MMPI-2 Validity Indicators and Initial Presentation of Custody Evaluations." *American Journal of Forensic Psychology* 14 (1996): 55-63.

Seltzer, Judith A. "Relationships Between Fathers and Children Who Live Apart: The Father's Role after Separation." *Journal of Marriage and Family* 53 (1991): 79-101.

Sexton, M.C., C.D. Grant & M.R. Nash. "Sexual Abuse and Body Image: A Comparison of Abused and Non-Abused Women." Paper Presented at the 98th Annual Convention of the American Psychological Association, Boston, Aug. 1990.

Shaevel, Bradley & Robert Archer. "Effects of MMPI-2 and MMPI-A Norms on T-score Elevations for 18 Year Olds." *Journal of Personality Assessment* 67 (1996): 72-78.

Shaffer, Marsha. "Bricklin Perceptual Scales," in *The Eleventh Mental Measurements Yearbook*. Jack Kramer & Jane Close Conoley, eds., University of Nebraska Press, Lincoln, Neb., 1992.

Shaffer, Marcie B. "Children's Apperception Test." in *Ninth Mental Measurements Yearbook,* J. Mitchell Jr. ed., 1985: 316-17.

Shaffer, Thomas W., Philip Erdberg & John Haroian. "Current Nonpatient Data For the Rorschach, WAIS-R, and MMPI-2." *Journal of Psychological Assessment* 73 (1999): 305-16.

Shapiro, David L. "Problems Encountered in the Preparation and Presentation of Expert Testimony," in *The Encyclopedic Handbook of Private Practice*, Eric Margenau, ed., Gardner Press, New York, 1990: 739-58.

Shapiro, David L. "Standard of Care in Forensic Assessments." Paper presented at the 103rd Annual Convention of the American Psychologist Association. New York, N.Y., Aug. 1995.

Shaw, Jon A., John E. Lewis, Andrea Loeb, James Rosado & Rosemarie A. Rodriguez. "A Comparison of Hispanic African American Sexually Abused Girls and Their Families." *Child Abuse and Neglect* 25 (2001): 1363-79.

Shaw, Rizwan et al. "Familial Influences on the Occurrences of Childhood Sexual Abuse." *Journal of Child Sexual Abuse* 4 (1995): 45-61.

Shealy, Craig N. "From Boys Town to Oliver Twist: Separating Fact from Fiction in Welfare Reform and Out-of-Home Placement of Children and Youth." *American Psychologist* 50 (1995): 565-80.

Shear L.E. "Children's Lawyers in California Family Law Courts: Balancing Competing Policies and Values Regarding Questions of Ethics." *Family Court Review* 34(2) (1996): 256-302.

Shear, Leslie Ellen "When Form Fails to Follow Function: Benjamin & Gollan's Family Evaluation in Custody Litigation." *Journal of Child Custody* 1 (2003): 129.

Sher, Kenneth, Kimberly Walitzer, Phillip Wood & Edward Brent. "Characteristics of Children of Alcoholics: Putative Risk Factors, Substance Use and Abuse, and Psychopathology." *Journal of Abnormal Psychology* 100 (1991): 427-48.

Shearer, Steven L., Charles P. Peters, Miles S. Quaytman & Richard L. Ogden. "Frequency Correlates of Childhood Sexual and Physical Abuse Histories in Adult Female Borderline Inpatients." *Am. J. Psychiatry* 147 (1990): 214-16.

Sheridan, Mary S. "The Deceit Continues: An Updated Literature Review of Munchausen Syndrome by Proxy." *Child Abuse and Neglect* 27 (2003): 431-51.

Sherman, Judith. "I've Always Wondered If Something Would Happen to Me: Assessment of Child Sexual Abuse Survivors with Amnesia." *Journal of Child Sexual Abuse* 1 (1993): 13-21.

Shondrick, Denise D., Yossef S. Ben-Porath & Kathleen P. Stafford. "Forensic Applications of the MMPI-2." *MMPI News and Profiles* 3 (1992).

Shontz, Franklin & Patricia Green. "Trends in Research on the Rorschach: Review and Recommendations." *Applied & Preventive Psychology* 1 (1992): 149-56.

Shui, Doris, Yink Mok & Diana Elliott. "Gender Comparison of Child Sexual Abuse." Paper presented at the 104th Annual Meeting of the American Psychological Association, Toronto, Can., 1996.

Shuman, Daniel W. *Psychiatric and Psychological Evidence*. Shepard's/McGraw-Hill, Colorado Springs, 1986.

Shuman, Daniel W. *Psychiatric and Psychological Evidence.* 2nd ed. West, Eagen, Minn. (1994, annual supplements).

Shuman, Daniel. "The Use of Empathy in Forensic Examinations." *Ethics & Behav.* 3 (1993): 289-302.

Shuman, Daniel. "Reporting of Child Abuse During Forensic Evaluations." *American Psychology-Law Society News* 15 (1995): 3.

Shuman, Daniel W. & Sales, Bruce D. "*Daubert*'s wager." *Journal of Forensic Psychology Practice* 1 (2001): 69-77.

Shybunko, Daniel E. "Effects of Post-Divorce Relationships on Child Adjustment," in *Children of Divorce: Developmental and Clinical Issues,* Haworth Press, Inc., 1989: 299-313.

Siegel, M. "Cognitive and Projective Test Assessment," in C. Kestenbaum & D. Williams, eds., *Handbook of Clinical Assessment of Children and Adolescents,* New York University Press, New York, 1988: 59-84.

Sigmon, S., M. Greene, K. Rohan & J. Nichols. "Coping and Adjustment in Male and Female Survivors of Childhood Sexual Abuse." *Child Sexual Abuse* 5 (1996): 57-75.

Simon, L. "A Therapeutic Jurisprudence Approach to the Legal Processing of Domestic Violence Cases." *Psychology, Public Policy and Law* 1 (1995): 43-79.

Simon, Robert I. *Clinical Psychiatry and the Law,* 2nd ed. American Psychiatric Press, Washington, D.C., 1992.

Simon, Robert I. *Concise Guide to Psychiatry and Law for Clinicians.* American Psychiatric Press, Washington, D.C., 1992.

Simon, Robert I. "Three's a Crowd: The Presence of Third Parties During the Forensic Psychiatric Examination." *Journal of Psychiatry and Law* 24 (1996): 3-25.

Simon, Robert I. & Daniel W. Shuman. "Conducting Forensic Examinations on the Road: Are You Practicing Your Profession Without a License?" *Journal of the American Academy of Psychiatry & Law* 27 (1999): 75-82.

Simon, Robert I. & Robert M. Wettstein. "Toward the Development of Guidelines for the Conduct of Forensic Psychiatric Examinations." *Journal of the American Academy of Psychiatry and Law* 25 (1997): 17-30.

Simons, Roland, Richard Goddard & Wendy Patton. "Hand-Scoring Error Rates in Psychological Testing." *Assessment* 9 (2002): 292-300.

16 PF: Fifth Edition, Pamphlet from IPAT, the publisher, undated.

"Skeletons in the Closet Haunt Experts." *Testifying Expert* 2 (1994): 1.

Skinner, Linda & Kenneth K. Berry. "Anatomically Detailed Dolls and the Evaluation of Child Sexual Abuse Allegations: Psychometric Considerations." *Law & Human Behavior* 17 (1993): 399-421.

Slovenko, Ralph. "Blaming a Book." *The Journal of Psychiatry and Law* 22 (1994): 437-51.

Smith, Joseph. *Medical Malpractice Psychiatric Care.* Wiley, New York, 1995.

Smith, Steven R. "Politics, Disability, Sexual Predators and More: Recent Decisions of the U.S. Supreme Court." *Bulletin of the American Academy of Forensic Psychology* 22 (2001): 1, 6-18.

Smith, Thomas Ewin. "What a Difference A Measure Makes: Parental Separation Effect on School Grades, Not School Achievement." *Journal of Divorce and Remarriage* 23 (1995): 151-65.

Solantaus-Simula, Tytti, Raija-Leena Punamaki & William R. Beardsley. "Children's Responses to Low Parental Mood. I. Balancing Between Active Empathy, Overinvolvement, Indifference, and Avoidance." *Journal of the American Academy of Child and Adolescent Psychiatry* 41 (2002): 278-86.

Solomon, Judith & Zeynep Beringen. "Another Look at the Developmental Research. Commentary on Kelly & Lamb's 'Using Child Development Research to Make Appropriate Custody and Access Decisions for Young Children.'" *Family Court Review* 39 (2001): 355-64.

Somer, Eli, & Sharona Szwarcberg. "Variables in Delayed Disclosure of Childhood Sexual Abuse." *American Journal of Orthopsychiatry* 71 (2001): 332-41.

Sorensen, Eric & Jacqueline Goldman. "Judicial Perceptions in Determining Primary Physical Residence." *Journal of Divorce* 12 (1989): 69-87.

Sorenson, S.B., D.M. Upchurch, & H. Shen. "Violence and Injury in Marital Arguments: Risk Patterns and Gender Differences." *American Journal of Public Health* 86 (1996): 35-40.

Spatz, Cathy W. & Suzanne Morris. "Accuracy of Adult Recollections of Childhood Victimization: Part 2, Child Sexual Abuse." 9 *Psychological Assessment* 1 (1997): 34-46.

Spatz, Cathy W. & Robin Shepart. "Academy of Adult Recollections of Childhood Victimization: Part 1, Child Physical Abuse." *Assessment* 4 (1996): 412-21.

Spence, Janet T., John W. Cotton, Benton J. Underwood & Carl P. Duncan. *Elementary Statistics,* 4th ed. Prentice-Hall, Englewood Cliffs, N.J., 1983.

Speth, Eric B. "Test-Retest Reliability of Bricklin Perceptual Scales." Unpublished doctoral dissertation, Hahnemann University, May 1992.

Spitzer, R. & J. Williams. "Classification of Mental Disorders," in H. Kaplan & B. Sadock, *Comprehensive Textbook of Psychiatry/IV,* 4th ed., Williams & Wilkins, Baltimore, 1985: 591-613.

Spitzer, Robert L. "An Outsider-Insider's Views About Revising the DSM's." *Journal of Abnormal Psychology* 100 (1991): 294-96.

Spohn, Cassie. "A Comparison of Sexual Assault Cases with Child and Adult Victims." *Journal of Child Sexual Abuse* 4 (1994): 59-78.

Sprinthall, Richard C. *Basic Statistical Analysis.* 2nd ed. Prentice-Hall, Englewood Cliffs, N.J., 1987.

Stahl, Phillip. "Second Opinions: An Ethical and Professional Process for Reviewing Child Custody Evaluations." *Family and Conciliation Courts Review* 34 (1996): 386-95.

Stahl, Phillip. *Conducting Child Custody Evaluations: A Comprehensive Guide.* Sage Publishing, Inc., 1994.

State v. Pawlyk, 115 Wn. 2d 457, 800 P.2d 338 (1990).

Stein, L.A.R., John R. Graham & Carolyn Williams. "Detecting Fake-bad and Fake-good MMPI-A Profiles." *Journal of Personality Assessment* 65 (1995): 415-27.

Stein, M.I. "Thematic Apperception Test and Related Methods." In B. Wolman, ed., *Clinical Diagnosis of Mental Disorders,* Plenum Press, NewYork, 1978: 179-235.

Steven Stein & Rita Chadda, "Revised Ethics Code—Release of Test Information to Nonpsychologists." Paper presented at the 112th Annual Convention of the American Psychological Association, Honolulu, Hawaii, Aug. 1, 2004.

Steinman, Susan. "The Experience of Children in a Joint Custody Arrangement: A Report of a Study." *American Journal of Orthopsychiatry* 51 (1981): 403-14.

Steller, Max & G. Koehnken. "Criteria-Based Statement Analysis," in *Psychological Methods in Criminal Investigation and Evidence,* D.C. Raskin, ed., 1989: 138.

Stern, Tina, Judy Marx & Royalty Georgia. "Study of Self-help Books on Recovering Memories of Childhood Sexual Abuse: Preliminary Findings." Paper presented at the 104th Annual Convention of the American Psychological Association, Toronto, Can., Aug. 1996.

Stieger, H. & M. Zanko. "Sexual Trauma Among Eating Disordered, Psychiatric and Normal Female Groups: Comparison of Prevalences and Defense Styles." *Journal of Interpersonal Violence* 5 (1990): 74-86.

Stolberg, A.L. & J.M Anker. "Cognitive and Behavioral Changes in Children Resulting from Parental Divorce and Consequent Environmental Changes." *Journal of Divorce* 7 (1984): 23-40.

Stoneman, Zolinda, Gene H. Brody & Michelle Burke. "Marital Quality, Depression, and Inconsistent Parenting: Relationship with Observed Mother-Child Conflict." *American Journal of Orthopsychiatry* 59 (1989): 105-17.

Strasburger, Larry, Thomas Gutheil, & Archie Brodsky. "On Wearing Two Hats: Role Conflict in Service as Both Psychotherapist and Expert Witness." *American Journal of Psychiatry* 154 (1997): 448-50.

Stravynski, Ariel, R. Elie & R.L. Franche "Parenting Style May Help Foster Avoidant Personality in Child." *Clinical Psychiatry News* 18 (1990): 15.

Strodel, Robert C. "Basics in Handling Treating and Expert Medical Witnesses." *Trial Diplomacy Journal* 20 (1997): 157-63.

Stromberg, Clifford D., D.J. Haggarty, R.F. Leibenluft, M.H. McMillian, B. Mishkin, B.L. Robin & H.R. Trilling. *The Psychologist's Legal Handbook.* Council for the National Register of Health Service Providers in Psychology, Washington, D.C., 1988.

Stuart, Richard. "Millon Adolescent Clinical Inventory," in *The Twelfth Mental Measurements Yearbook.* Jane Close Conoley & James C. Impara, eds. The Buros Institute of Mental Measurements. Lincoln, Neb., 1995: 622-23.

Sugarman v. Board of Registration in Medicine, 662 N.E.2d 1020 (Mass. 1996).

Sundberg, Norman. "Second Review of the Beck Depression Inventory (BDI)", in *Eleventh Mental Measurements Yearbook,* Jack Kramer & Jane Close Conoley, eds., University of Nebraska Press, Lincoln, Neb., 1992: 79-81.

Susan A. v. County of Sonoma, 3 Cal. Rptr. 2d 27 (Ct. App. 1991).

Svanum, Soren & Lisa C. Ehrmann. "Alcoholic Subtypes and the MacAndrew Alcoholism Scale." *Journal of Personality Assessment* 58 (1992): 411-22.

Svikis, Dace S., Mary E. McCaul, Jaylan S. Turkkan & George Bigelow. "Effect of Item Correction on Michigan Alcoholism Screening Test Scores in College Men with and Without a Family History of Alcoholism." *Psychological Assessment: A Journal of Consulting and Clinical Psychology* 3 (1991): 654-59.

Swanson, Lisa & Mark K. Biaggio. "Therapeutic Perspectives on Father-Daughter Incest." *American Journal of Psychiatry* 142 (1995): 673.

Swartz, Jon D. "Thematic Apperception Test," in O. Buros, *The Eighth Mental Measurements Yearbook,* Gryphon Press/Highland Press, Highland Park, N.J., 1978: 1127-30.

Swim, Janet, Eugene Borgida & Kathy McCoy. "Videotape Versus In-Court Witness Testimony: Is Protecting the Child Witness Jeopardizing Due Process?" Paper presented at the 99th Annual Convention of the American Psychological Association, San Francisco, 1991.

Talwar, Victoria, Kang Lee, Nicholas Bala & R.C.L. Lindsay. "Children's Conceptual Knowledge of Lying and Its Relation to Their Actual Behavior: Implications for Court Competence Examinations." *Law & Human Behavior* 26 (2002): 395-415.

Tarasoff v. Regents of the University of California, 529 P.2d 553 (Cal. 1974).

Tarasoff v. Regents of the University of California, 551 P.2d 334 (Cal.1976).

Taussig, Heather N. & Ayelet Talmi. "Ethnic Differences in Risk Behaviors and Related Psychosocial Variables Among a Cohort of Maltreated Adolescents in Foster Care." *Child Maltreatment* 6 (2001): 180-192.

Terr, Lenore, Danile Bloch, Beat Michael, Hong Shi, John Reinhardt & SuzAnne Metayer. "Children's Memories in the Wake of Challenger." *American Journal of Psychology* 153 (1996): 618-25.

"Test Security: Protecting the Integrity of Tests." Editorial in 54 *American Psychologist* 1078 (1999).

Thangavelu, Rajani & Ronald L. Martin. "ICD-10 and DSM-IV: Depiction of the Diagnostic Elephant." *Psychiatric Annals* 25 (1995): 21-3.

Tharinger, D. "Impact of Child Sexual Abuse on Development Sexuality." *Professional Psychology: Research and Practice* 21 (1990): 331-37.

Thomas, Amanda McCombs & Rex Forehand. "The Relationship Between Paternal Depressive Mood and Early Adolescent Functioning." *Journal of Family Psychology* 4 (1991): 260-71.

Thomas, Amanda McCombs & Rex Forehand. "The Role of Paternal Variables in Divorced and Married Families: Predictability of Adolescent Adjustment." *American Journal of Orthopsychiatry* 63 (1993): 126-35.

Thompson, William, et al. "Children's Susceptibility in Suggestive Interrogation." Paper presented at the 99th Annual Convention of the American Psychological Association, San Francisco, 1991.

Thompson, William K., Allison Clarke-Stewart & Stephen Lepore. "What Did the Janitor Do? Suggestive Interviewing and the Accuracy of Children's Accounts." *Law and Human Behavior* 21 (1997): 405-26.

Thornberry, T. "Violent Families and Youth Violence." *Office of Juvenile Justice and Delinquency Prevention.* Fact Sheet #21, Dec. 1994.

Tillbrook, Chad, Denise Mumley & Thomas Grisso. "Avoiding Expert Opinions on the Ultimate Legal Question: The Case for Integrity." 3 *Journal of Forensic Psychology Practice* 3 (2003): 77-78.

Timbrook, R.E. & J.R.Graham. "Ethnic Differences on the MMPI-2?" *Psychological Assessment* 6 (1994): 212-17.

Tindall, Gerald & Michelle Nutter. "Wechsler Individual Achievement Test—Second Edition," in Buros, *The Fifteenth Mental Measurements Yearbook,* The University of Nebraska Press, 2003: 1001.

Tischler, G. "Evaluation of DSM-III," in H. Kaplan & B. Sadock, *Comprehensive Textbook of Psychiatry/IV,* 4th ed. Williams & Wilkins, Baltimore, 1985: 617-21.

Tranel, Daniel. "The Release of Psychological Data to Nonexperts: Ethical and Legal Considerations." *Professional Psychology: Research and Practice* 25 (1994): 33-38.

Tromboli, R. & R. Kilgore. "A Psychodynamic Approach to MMPI Interpretation." *Journal of Personality Assessment* 47 (1983): 614-26.

Tucillo, Jill A., Nick A. DeFilippis, Robert L. Denney & John Dsurney. "Licensure Requirements for Interjurisdictional Forensic Evaluations." *Professional Psychology Research and Practice* 3 (2002): 377-83.

Turner, S.M., D.C. Beidel & A. Costello. "Psychopathology in the Offspring of Anxiety Disorder Patients." *Journal of Consulting and Clinical Psychology* 55 (1987): 229-35.

Twaite, James A. & Anya K. Luchow. "Custodial Arrangements and Parental Conflict Following Divorce: The Impact of Children's Adjustment." *Journal of Psychiatry and Law* 24 (1996): 53-75.

Underwood, Richard H., KBA E-394 (ethics opinion on contingency fees for experts by the Chair of the Kentucky Bar Association Ethics Committee), retrieved from www.uky.edu/Law/Library/kba/kba394.htm on July 9, 2004.

U.S. Department of Health and Human Services. *Family Violence: An Overview.* Jan. 1991.

U.S. Department of Health and Human Services. *Child Abuse and Neglect: A Shared Community Concern.* National Center on Abuse and Neglect, Washington, D.C, March 1991.

Van der Kolk, B.A., J.C. Perry & J.L. Herman. "Childhood Origins of Self-Destructive Behavior." *American Journal of Psychiatry* 148 (1991): 1665-71.

Van Horne, Barbara. *8 Wisconsin Regulatory Digest,* Dec. 1995.

Velleman, Richard & Jim Orford, "The Importance of Family Discord in Explaining Childhood Problems in the Children of Problem Drinkers." 1 *Addiction Res.* 39 (1993): 51.

Veltcamp, Lane & Thomas Miller. "Clinical Strategies in Recognizing Spouse Abuse." *Psychiatric Quarterly* 61 (1990): 179-87.

Veltcamp, Lane & Thomas Miller. *Clinical Handbook of Child Abuse and Neglect.* International Universities Press, Madison, Conn., 1995.

Veronen, L.J., D.G. Kilpatrick & P.A. Resnick. "Treatment of Fear and Anxiety in Rape Victims: Implications for the Criminal Justice System," in W.H. Parsonage, ed., *Perspectives on Victimology Thousand Oaks,* Cal., 1979: 148-59.

Viglione, Donald J. & Hilsenroth, Mark J. "The Rorschach: Facts, Fictions, and Future." 13 *Psychological Assessment* 452-471: 120.

Vincent, Ken R. & Marsha J. Harman. "The Exner Rorschach: An Analysis of Its Clinical Validity." *Journal of Clinical Psychology* 47 (1991): 596-99.

Vissing, Y.M., M.A. Straus, R.J. Gelles & J.W. Harrop. "Verbal Aggression by Parents and Psychosocial Problems of Children." *Child Abuse & Neglect* 15 (1991): 223-38.

Von Talge, Jerry. "Overcoming Courtroom Challenges to the DSM-IV, Part I: The Major Changes in DSM-IV." *American Journal of Forensic Psychology* 13 (1995): 12-24.

Von Talge, Jerry. "Overcoming Courtroom Callenges to the DSM-IV, Part II: Preparing for and Overcoming Courtroom Challenges to the DSM-IV." *Journal of Forensic Psychology* 13 (1995): 49-54.

Vrondra, Joan, Anne Kolar, & Barbara Radigan. "Psychological Maltreatment of Children," in Ammerman & Michael Hersen, *Assessment of Family Violence. A Clinical and Legal Source Book.* John Wiley & Sons, New York, 1992.

WAIS-III, WMS-III Technical Manual, Psychological Corporation, 1997.

Wagner, Edwin E., Ralph A. Alexander, Gary Roos & Holiday Adair. "Optimum Split-Half Reliabilities for the Rorschach: Projective Techniques Are More Reliable Than We Think." *Journal of Personality Assessment* 50 (1986): 107-12.

Wakefield, Hollida & Ralph Underwager. "Misuse of Psychological Tests in Forensic Settings: Some Horrible Examples." 11 *American Journal of Forensic Psychology* 11 (1993): 55-75.

Wakefield, Hollida & Robert Underwager. "Female Child Sexual Abusers: A Critical Review of the Literature." *American Journal of Forensic Psychology* 9 (1991): 43-70.

Walker, Anne. "Questioning Young Children in Court. A Linguistic Case-Study." *Law and Human Behavior* 17 (1993): 59-81.

Walker, Lenore L. *The Battered Woman Syndrome*, 2nd ed. Springer Publishing, New York, 2000.

Wallerstein, Judith S. "Children of Divorce: The Psychological Tasks of the Child." *American Journal of Orthopsychiatry* 53 (1983): 230-43.

Wallerstein, Judith. "Children of Divorce: Preliminary Report of a Ten-Year Follow-up of Older Children and Adolescents." *Journal of the American Academy of Child Psychiatry* 24 (1985): 545-53.

Wallerstein, Judith. *Cape Cod Institute.* Institute for Psychological Study, Greenwich, Conn., 1986.

Wallerstein, Judith. "The Long-Term Effects of Divorce on Children: A Review." *Journal of the American Academy of Child and Adolescent Psychiatry* 30 (1991): 349-60.

Wallerstein, Judith S. & Joan B. Kelly. *"Surviving the Break-up: How Children and Parents Cope with Divorce.* Basic Books, New York, 1980.

Wallerstein, Judith & Tony J. Tanke. "To Move or Not to Move: Psychological and Legal Considerations in the Relocation Following Divorce." *Journal of Family Law,* (1996): 305-32.

Walsh, Bill. "The Law Enforcement Response to Child Sexual Abuse Cases." *Journal of Sexual Abuse* 2 (1993): 117-21.

Walsh, Bill W., & P.M. Rosen. *Self-Mutilation: Theory, Research and Treatment.* Guilford, New York, (1998).

Ward, A., S.M. Hudson & W.L. Marshall. "Attachment Style in Sex Offenders: A Preliminary Study." *Journal of Sex Research* 33 (1996): 17-26.

Ware, Ciji. *Sharing Parenthood after Divorce.* Viking Press, New York, 1982.

Warren, Amye R., Katherine Hulse-Trotter & Ernest C. Tubs. "Inducing Resistance to Suggestibility in Children." *Law and Human Behavior* 15 (1991): 273-85.

Warren, Amye, Cara Woodall, Jennifer Hunt & Nancy Perry. "It Sounds Good in Theory, but … Do Investigators Follow Guidelines Based on Memory Research?" *Child Maltreatment* 1 (1996): 231-45.

Warren, John F., III. "Roles and Dilemmas of Mental Health Professionals in Child Custody Evaluations." *American Journal of Family Law* 4 (1990): 251-56.

Warshak, Richard A. "Who Will Be There When I Cry in the Night? Revisiting Overnights—A Rejoinder to Beringen et al." *Family Court Review* 40 (2002): 208-19.

Watkins, C. Edward, Jr. "Contemporary Practice of Psychological Assessment by Clinical Psychologists." *Professional Psychological: Research and Practice* 26 (1995): 54-57.

Watkins, C. Edward, Vicki Campbell, Ron Nieberding & Rebecca Hallmark. "Contemporary Practice of Psychological Assessment by Clinical Psychologists." *Professional Psychology: Research and Practice* 26 (1995): 54-60.

Watkins, John. "Dealing with the Problem of 'False Memory' in Clinic and Court." *Journal of Psychiatry and Law* 21 (1993): 297-303.

Watson, Robert I., Jr. "The Sentence Completion Method," in B. Wolman, ed., *Clinical Diagnosis of Mental Disorders: A Handbook,* Plenum Press, New York, 1978: 255-79.

Way, I., S. Chung, M. Johnson-Reid & B. Drake. "Maltreatment Perpetrators: A 54-Month Analysis of Recidivism." *Child Abuse and Neglect* 25 (2001): 1093-1108.

Wayte, T., J. Samra, J. K. Robbennolt, L. Heuer & W. J. Koch, "Psychological Issues in Civil Law," in J.R.P. Ogloff, ed., *Taking Psychology and Law into the Twenty-First Century.* Kluwer/Plenum, New York, 2003: 323-69.

Wechsler, David. *The Measurement and Appraisal of Adult Intelligence.* 4th ed. William & Wilkins, Baltimore, 1958.

Weed, Nathan C., James N. Butcher, Thomas McKenna & Yossef S. Ben-Porath. "New Measures for Assessing Alcohol and Drug Abuse with the MMPI-2: The APS and AAS." *Journal of Personality Assessment* 58 (1992): 389-404.

Weil, Andrew & Winifred Rosen. *From Chocolate to Morphine.* Houghton Mifflin, Boston, 1993.

Weill, Robin, Brenda L. Dawson & Lillian M. Range. "Behavioral and Verbal Responses to Unabused Externalizing Children to Anatomically Detailed Doll Interviews." *Journal of Family Violence* 14 (1999): 61-69.

Weiner, Irving. *Principles of Rorschach Interpretation*, 2nd ed. Erlbaum, Mahwah, N.J., 2003: 65-66.

Weiner, Irving B. "Advancing the Science of Psychological Assessment: The Rorschach Inkblot Method as Exemplar." *Psychological Assessment* 13 (2001): 423-32.

Weiner, Irving B. "Current Status of the Rorschach Inkblot Method." *Journal of Personality Assessment* 68 (1997): 5-19.

Weiner, Irving B. "On Competence and Ethicality in Psychodiagnostic Assessment." *Journal of Personality Assessment* 53 (1989): 827-31.

Weiner, Irving B., Charles D. Spielberger & Norman Abeles. "Scientific Psychology and the Rorschach Inkblot Method." *The Clinical Psychologist* 55(4) (2002): 7-12.

Weiner, Irving B., John E. Exner, Jr. & Anthony Sciara. "Is the Rorschach Welcome in the Courtroom?" *Journal of Personality Assessment* 67 (1996): 422-24.

Weiner, Jennifer, Lisa Harlow, Jerome Adams & Lawrence Grebstein. "Psychological Adjustment of College Students from Families of Divorce." *Journal of Divorce and Remarriage* 23 (1995): 75-95.

Weinstock, Robert & Thomas Garrick. "Is Liability Possible for Forensic Psychiatrists?" *Bulletin of the American Academy of Psychiatry and Law* 23 (1995): 183-93.

Weinstock, Robert, Gregory Leong & Arturo Silva. "Ethics and Forensic Psychiatry." *American Psychiatric Press Review of Psychiatry* 13 (1994): 379.

Weise, Martin. "Children's Apperceptive Storytelling Test (CAST)," in *Twelfth Mental Measurements Yearbook*, 1995: 182-83.

Weissman, Herbert N., & Thomas L. Morrison. "Implications of Differences (Coded-types, T-Scores) for Clinical and Forensic Practice." Paper presented at the 100th Annual Convention of the American Psychological Association, Washington, D.C., Aug. 1992.

Welch, Kathleen. "Gender Differences and the Impact of Parental Divorce on Parent-Child Relationships and Future Plans." Paper presented at the 99th Annual Convention of the American Psychological Association, San Francisco, 1991.

Wellman, Mary. "Ackerman-Schoendorf Scales for Parent Evaluation of Custody." *Test Critiques* 10 (1994): 13-19.

Wenar, Charles & Kent M. Curtis. "The Validity of the Rorschach for Assessing Cognitive and Affective Changes." *Journal of Personality Assessment* 57 (1991): 291-308.

Wetzler, Scott. "The Millon Clinical Multiaxial Inventory (MCMI): A Review." *Journal of Personality Assessment* 55 (1990): 445-64.

Wetzler, Scott & Alan Dubro. "Diagnosis of Personality Disorders by the Millon Clinical Multiaxial Inventory." *Journal of Nervous and Mental Disease* 178 (1990): 261-63.

Whitcomb, Debra. "Legal Reforms on Behalf of Child Witnesses: Recent Developments in the American Courts," in H. Dent and R. Flin, eds., *Children As Witnesses,* John Wiley & Sons, Inc., Chichester, England, 1992.

Whiteside, Mary. "Custody for Children Age Five and Younger." *Family Court Review"* 36 (1998): 479-502.

Whiteside, Mary F., Betsy Jane Becker. "Parental Factors and the Young Child's Post-Divorce Adjustment: A Meta-Analysis with Implications for Parenting Arrangements." *Journal of Family Psychology* (2000) 5-26.

Widiger, Thomas A., *"Training Implications of Empirically Supported Assessments."* Paper presented at the 110th Annual Convention of the American Psychological Association, Chicago, Aug. 25, 2002.

Widiger, Thomas A., "The Best and Worst of Us?" 8 *Clinical Psychology: Science and Practice* (2001): 375.

Widiger, Thomas A. "DSM-IV Reviews of the Personality Disorders: Introduction to Special Series." *Journal of Personality Disorders* 5 (1991): 122-34.

Widiger, Thomas A. "DSM-IV: Process and Progress." Paper presented at the 98th Annual Convention of the American Psychological Association, Boston, Aug. 1990.

Widiger, Thomas A. "Millon Adolescent Personality Inventory," in O. Buros, *The Ninth Mental Measurements Yearbook,* University of Nebraska, Lincoln, Neb., 1985: 979-81.

Widiger, Thomas A. "Revisions of an Official Diagnostic Nomenclature: Scientific and Political Issues." Paper presented at the 100th Annual Convention of the American Psychological Association, Washington, D.C., Aug. 1992.

Widiger, Thomas A., Allen J. Frances, Harold A. Pincus, Wendy W.Davis & Michael B. First. "Toward an Empirical Classification for the DSM-IV." *Journal of Abnormal Psychology* 100 (1991): 280-88.

Wiehe, V.R. "Empathy and Narcissism in a Sample of Child Abuse Perpetrators and a Comparison Sample of Foster Parents." *Child Abuse and Neglect* 27 (2003): 541-55.

Wiener, Richard. "Extending Daubert Beyond Scientific Expert Testimony," *APA Monitor* 30 (1999): 47.

Wilkox, Kathryn L., Sharlene A. Wolchik & Sanford Braver. "Predictors of Maternal Preference of Joint or Sole Custody. *Family Relations* 47 (1998): 93-101.

Will, Thomas. "The MCMI-III and Personality Disorders." Paper presented at the 1994 Fall Conference of the Wisconsin Psychologist Association, Madison, Wis., Nov. 18, 1994.

Williams, Arthur, D. "Bias and Debiasing Techniques in Forensic Psychology." *American Journal of Forensic Psychology* 10 (1992): 19-26.

Williams, Carolyn. "An Examination of the Changes in the Descriptors of the MMPI-A Validity and Standard Scales." Paper presented at the 99th Annual Convention of the American Psychological Association. San Francisco, 1991.

Williams, Carolyn. "Introducing the New MMPI-2 Content Scales," in J. Butcher & J. Graham, eds., *Topics in MMPI-2 Interpretations, (1990).* National Computer Scoring, Minneapolis, Minn.

Williams, Linda M. "Recall of Childhood Memory Trauma: A Prospective Study of Women's Memories of Child Sexual Abuse." *Journal of Consulting and Clinical Psychology* 62 (1994): 1167-76.

Williams, Oliver B. & Patrick W. Corrigan. "The Differential Effects of Parental Alcoholism and Mental Illness on Their Adult Children." *Journal of Clinical Psychology* 48 (1992): 406-13.

Willock, Brent. "Projection, Transitional Phenomena, and the Rorschach." *Journal of Personality Assessment* 59 (1992): 99-116.

Wisconsin statute § 48.981(2).

Woititz, J. "Adult Children of Alcoholics." *The Medical Psychotherapist* 5 (1989): 9.

Wolfe, David A. "Child-Abusive Parents: An Empirical Review and Analysis," in D. Keyser & R.Sweetwater, eds., *Test Critiques,* (1994): Vol. 10., Test Corporation of America, Austin, Texas, 1994.

Wolf, David A. & P.G. Jaffe. "Prevention of Domestic Violence: Emerging Initiatives." Paper Presented at the Asilomar Conference on Children and Intimate Violence, Pacific Grove, Cal.

Wolfe, David, Betty Edwards, Ian Manion & Catherine Koverola. "Early Intervention for Parents at Risk of Child Abuse and Neglect: A Preliminary Investigation." *Journal of Consulting and Clinical Psychology* 6 (1988): 4-47.

Wolfe, David, Claire V. Crocks, Vivien Lee, Alexandra McIntyre-Smith & Peter G. Jaffe. "The Affects of Children's Exposure to Domestic Violence: A Meta-Analysis and Critique." *Child and Family Psychology Review* 6 (2003): 171-87.

Wood, James M., Theresa M. Nezworski, Howard N. Garb & Scott O. Lilienfeld. "The Misperception of Psychopathology: Problems With the Norms of the Comprehensive System for the Rorschach." *Clinical Psychology: Science and Practice* 8 (2001): 350-73.

Wood, James M., Nezworski, M. Teresa, Stejskal, William & McKinzey, R.K., *Problems of the Comprehensive System for the Rorschach inForensic Settings: Recent Developments,* 1 Journal of Forensic Psychology Practice 89-103 (2001).

World Health Organization. *International Classification of Diseases and Related Health Problems, 10th Revision.* Clinical Description and Diagnostic Guidelines. World Health Organization, Geneva, 1992.

Wright, Deborah M. & P. Paul Heppner. "Coping Among Nonclinical College-Age Children of Alcoholics." *Journal of Counseling Psychology* 38 (1991): 465-72.

Wright, David, Wendy L. Woo, Robert T. Muller, Cheryl B. Fernandes & Erin R. Craftcheck. "An Investigation of Trauma Center Inpatient Treatment for Adult Survivors of Abuse." *Child Abuse and Neglect* 27 (2003): 393-406.

Wyatt, G.E., D. Guthrie & C.M. Notgrass. "Differential Effects of Women's Child Sexual Abuse and Subsequent Sexual Revictimization." *Journal of Consulting and Clinical Psychology* 60 (1992): 167-73.

Wynkoop, Timothy, Steven Capps & Bobby Priest. "Incidence and Prevalence of Child Sexual Abuse: A Critical Review of Data Collection Procedures." *Journal of Child Abuse* 4 (1995): 49-66.

Yanagida, Evelyn & June Chin. "MMPI Profiles of Child Abusers." *Journal of Consulting and Clinical Psychology* 49 (1993): 569-76.

Yanez, Tami Y., & William Fremouw. "The Application of the *Daubert* Standard to Parental Capacity Measures." *American Journal of Forensic Psychology* 22 (2004): 5-28.

Yates, Elaine & Tim Musty. "Preschool Children's Erroneous Allegations of Sexual Molestation: Causes and Concerns." *American Journal of Psychiatry* 145 (1988): 989-92.

Yoshihama, M. & S.B. Sorenson. "Physical, Sexual and Emotional Abuse by Male Inmates: Experiences of Women in Japan." *Violence & Victims* 9 (1994): 63-77.

Youngstrom, Eric A. & Christine P. Busch. "Expert Testimony in Psychology: Ramifications of Supreme Court Decision in *Kumho Tire Co., Ltd. v. Carmichael.*" *Ethics & Behavior* 10 (2000): 185-93.

Zamstein v. Marvasti, 692 A.2d 781 (Conn. 1997).

Zaslow, Martha J. "Sex Differences in Children's Responses to Parental Divorce: 2. Samples, Variables, Ages, and Sources." *American Journal of Orthopsychiatry* 59 (1989): 118-41.

Zill, Nicholas, Donna Ruane Morrison & Mary Jo Cioro. "Long-term Effects of Parental Divorce and Parent/Child Relationships, Adjustment and Achievement in Young Adulthood." *Journal of Family Psychology* 7 (1993): 91-103.

Zinberg, Norman E. "The Private Versus the Public Psychiatric Interview." American Journal of Psychiatry 142 (1985): 889-94.

Ziskin, Jay. *Coping with Psychiatric and Psychological Testimony*, 4th ed. Law & Psychology Press, Venice, Cal., 1988.

Zlotnick, Caron, Jill Mattia, & Mark Zimmerman. "Clinical Features of Survivors of Sexual Abuse with Major Depression." *Child Abuse and Neglect* 25 (2001): 357-67.

Zonana, Howard. "AMA Adopts New Ethics Principles." *American Academy of Psychiatry and the Law Newsletter* 26 (2001).

Zonana, H.V. "The Final Nail in the Coffin—*Daubert v. Merrell Dow Pharmaceuticals, Inc.*" *American Academy of Psychiatry and the Law Newsletter* 20 (1995): 42.

Zonona, H.V. "AAPL Ethical Guidelines in Appellate Decision." *American Association of Psychiatry and Law Newsletter* 22 (1997): 3.

Zuravin, Susan J. "Severity of Maternal Depression and Three Types of Mother-to-Child Aggression." *American Journal of Orthopsychiatry* 59 (1989): 377-89.

Zuravin, Susan, Curtis McMillen, Diane DePaniflis & Christine Risley-Curtiss. "The Intergenerational Cycle of Maltreatment Continuity Versus Discontinuity." *Journal of Interpersonal Violence* 11 (1996): 315-34.

INDEX